U.S. GAAP
Financial Statements

Best Practices in Presentation and Disclosure

D1501393

19632-360

AICPA

SEVENTIETH EDITION

1 2 3 4 5 6 7 8 9 0 AAP 1 9 8 7 6

ISSN 1531-4340

ISBN 978-1-94354-698-5

Notice to readers: This book does not represent an official position of the American Institute of Certified Public Accountants, and it is distributed with the understanding that the authors and publisher are not rendering legal, accounting, or other professional services via this publication.

Director, Content Development: Linda Cohen
Senior Technical Manager: Doug Bowman
Technical Manager: Liese Faircloth
Senior Developmental Editor: David Cohen
Project Manager: Charlotte Ingles

Recognition

The 2016 edition of *U.S. GAAP Financial Statements—Best Practices in Presentation and Disclosure* was developed by

RAYMOND J. PETRINO, CPA
CONTENT MATTER EXPERT

DAVID J. COHEN
*SENIOR DEVELOPMENTAL EDITOR
AICPA CONTENT
DEVELOPMENT*

LIESE FAIRCLOTH, CPA
*TECHNICAL MANAGER
AICPA ACCOUNTING AND AUDITING CONTENT
DEVELOPMENT*

About This Edition of *U.S. GAAP Financial Statements—Best Practices in Presentation and Disclosure*

This book remains the best source for reporting and disclosure examples from real world financial statements, providing accounting professionals with an invaluable resource for incorporating new and existing accounting and reporting guidance into financial statements using presentation techniques adopted by companies across numerous industries, all of which are headquartered in the United States.

Organization and Content

This 2016 edition surveyed annual reports of 350 entities of various sizes representing over 100 industries with fiscal periods ending between January and December 2015. The industry classifications of survey entities (as shown in the "Appendix of Survey Entity Industries") were obtained from Morningstar, Inc.

To provide you with the most useful and comprehensive look at current financial reporting presentation and disclosure, this book is topically organized and offers the following:
- Examples taken from the surveyed annual reports illustrating financial statement presentation and virtually every required U.S. GAAP disclosure.
- Descriptive guidance that includes current reporting requirements under U.S. generally accepted accounting principles (GAAP). U.S. GAAP is generally considered to be the requirements of the FASB *Accounting Standards Codification®* (ASC). Select SEC guidance is also included.
- Detailed indexes.

ILLUSTRATIVE REPORTING EXAMPLES

AICPA leverages its decades of experience as the CPA national membership organization to select the most useful, comprehensive presentation and disclosure examples, which comprise the majority of this book. Every edition of *Best Practices in Presentation and Disclosure* includes all new annual report excerpts that were chosen to be particularly relevant and useful to financial statement preparers in illustrating current reporting practices.

Because survey entities may present disclosures on specific topics within different footnotes in their annual filings, including those ostensibly about a separate accounting topic, the excerpts presented herein to illustrate a given topic may have been taken from footnotes about other topics. The full text of the financial statements from which the excerpts in this publication have been obtained can be found on the SEC's web site at www.sec.gov/edgar/searchedgar/companysearch.html.

GUIDANCE

Discerning, plain English guidance covers the significant U.S. GAAP accounting and financial statement reporting requirements in narrative form. These narratives use common headings (recognition and measurement, presentation, and disclosure) to achieve a consistent presentation throughout all the sections. Although not a substitute for the authoritative accounting and reporting standards, the reporting guidance herein encapsulates the complex requirements to facilitate your understanding of the content. The related authoritative sources for each requirement are cited within the narratives (for example, FASB ASC 310, *Receivables*, or Regulation S-K).

SEC rules and interpretative releases may expand, modify, or decrease accounting and disclosure requirements for foreign private issuers, regardless of whether they file their annual financial statements with the SEC in Forms 10-K, 20-F, or 40-F (Canadian issuers). Therefore, it is critical to consider SEC requirements, as well as those of FASB ASC, when reviewing the financial statements of SEC registrants. A general reference to FASB ASC in this publication does not include the SEC materials. When requirements are taken from an SEC rule or regulation, that rule or regulation will be cited directly.

INDEXES

Indexes in this edition include the "Appendix of 350 Entities," which alphabetically lists each of the 350 survey entities included in the current edition and notes where in the text excerpts from their annual reports can be found; the "Appendix of Survey Entity Industries," which lists the industries represented by the 350 survey entities and lists the entities within each industry classification; the "Index of Authoritative Accounting & Auditing Guidance," which provides for easy cross-referencing of pronouncements to the applicable descriptive narratives; and a detailed "Subject Index," which is fully cross-referenced to all significant topics included throughout the narratives.

FASB ASC

Because FASB ASC is the source of authoritative U.S. GAAP for nongovernmental entities, in addition to guidance issued by the SEC, the guidance herein refers only to the appropriate FASB ASC reference for all standards.

Note that the effective dates of recently released guidance affect the timing of its inclusion in the financial statements of the survey entities, thereby affecting the availability of illustrative excerpts for potential inclusion in each edition of *Best Practices in Presentation and Disclosure*. This 2016 edition includes survey entities having fiscal years ending within calendar year 2015. Technical guidance for which this edition supplies illustrative annual report excerpts includes the following, among other recently issued guidance:
- ASU No. 2014-08, *Presentation of Financial Statements (Topic 205) and Property, Plant, and Equipment (Topic 360): Reporting Discontinued Operations and Disclosures of Disposals of Components of an Entity*
- ASU No. 2014-11, *Transfers and Servicing (Topic 860): Repurchase-to-Maturity Transaction. Repurchase Financings, and Disclosures*
- ASU No. 2014-17, *Business Combinations (Topic 805): Pushdown Accounting (a Consensus of the FASB Emerging Issues Task Force)*

Related Products

U.S. GAAP Financial Statements—Best Practices in Presentation and Disclosure is the flagship product in the AICPA's *Best Practices in Presentation and Disclosure* series; it is also available in an interactive, online format. Other titles in the *Best Practices in Presentation and Disclosure* series include
- *Employee Benefit Plans Financial Statements—Best Practices in Presentation and Disclosure*
- *Not-for-Profit Entities Financial Statements—Best Practices in Presentation and Disclosure*

Notice

This book is a nonauthoritative practice aid and is not designed to provide a comprehensive understanding of all the requirements contained in U.S. GAAP. The guidance provided herein may not discuss all relevant accounting guidance on a given topic and should not be relied upon for its completeness. Users are encouraged to consult FASB ASC for complete, authoritative discussion of U.S. GAAP. Users are also encouraged to consult the complete body of SEC rules and regulations for regulatory requirements. In addition, this book does not include reporting requirements relating to other matters such as internal control or agreed-upon procedures.

Authoritative guidance on accounting treatments in accordance with U.S. GAAP can be made only by reference to the FASB ASC, which is copyright of the FAF and can be acquired directly from FASB.

This book has not been reviewed, approved, disapproved, or otherwise acted on by any senior technical committee of the AICPA and does not represent official positions or pronouncements of the AICPA.

The use of this publication requires the exercise of individual professional judgment. It is not a substitute for the original authoritative accounting and auditing guidance. Users are urged to refer directly to applicable authoritative pronouncements, when appropriate. As an additional resource, users may call the AICPA Technical Hotline at 1.877.242.7212.

Feedback

We hope that you find this edition to be informative and useful. Please let us know! What features do you like? What do you think can be improved or added? We encourage you to submit your comments and questions to Liese Faircloth, using the following contact information. All feedback is greatly appreciated and kept strictly confidential.

Liese Faircloth— Accounting and Auditing Content Development

AMERICAN INSTITUTE OF CERTIFIED PUBLIC ACCOUNTANTS

220 Leigh Farm Road

Durham, NC 27707-8110

Telephone: 919.402.4819

E-mail: lfaircloth@aicpa.org

You can also contact the Accounting and Auditing Content Development team of the AICPA directly via e-mail at A&Apublications@aicpa.org.

TABLE OF CONTENTS

Section		Paragraph

Survey Entities

1.01 All 350 entities included in the survey are registered with the SEC. All of the survey entities have securities traded on one of the major stock exchanges: 83 percent on the New York Stock Exchange and 17 percent on the NASDAQ.

1.02 Each year, entities are selected across various industry classifications with the purpose of highlighting those entities that exhibit best practices.

General Financial Statement Considerations

RECOGNITION AND MEASUREMENT

1.03 FASB *Accounting Standards Codification*® (ASC) 105-10-05-2 explains that if the necessary guidance for a transaction or event is not specified within a source of authoritative generally accepted accounting principles (GAAP), an entity should first consider accounting principles for similar transactions or events within a source of authoritative GAAP for that entity and then consider nonauthoritative guidance from other sources. When those accounting principles either prohibit the application of the accounting treatment to the particular transaction or event or indicate that the accounting treatment should not be applied by analogy, an entity should not follow those accounting principles.

1.04 FASB ASC 105-10-05-3 explains that accounting and financial reporting practices not included in FASB ASC are nonauthoritative. FASB Concepts Statements are not considered authoritative sources of GAAP, and no preference is given to the FASB Concepts Statements over other nonauthoritative sources. FASB ASC does not state that consistency with the FASB Concept Statements in connection with an entity's application of an accounting treatment is necessary. Sources of nonauthoritative accounting guidance include the following:
- Practices that are widely recognized and prevalent, either generally or in the industry
- FASB Concepts Statements
- AICPA Issues Papers
- International Financial Reporting Standards (IFRSs) of the International Accounting Standards Board (IASB)
- Pronouncements of professional associations or regulatory agencies
- Technical Questions and Answers included in AICPA *Technical Questions and Answers*
- Accounting textbooks, handbooks, and articles

The appropriateness of other sources of accounting guidance depends on its relevance to particular circumstances, the specificity of the guidance, the general recognition of the issuer or author as an authority, and the extent of its use in practice.

1.05 As discussed in FASB ASC 105-10-05-1, GAAP, as codified in FASB ASC, includes the rules and interpretive releases of the SEC as sources of authoritative GAAP as a convenience only to SEC registrants. In addition to the SEC's rules and interpretive releases, the SEC staff issues Staff Accounting Bulletins that represent practices that the staff follows when administering SEC disclosure requirements. SEC staff announcements and observer comments made at meetings of the Emerging Issues Task Force announce the staff's views on certain accounting issues for SEC registrants.

1.06 In June 2009, FASB issued the last FASB statement referenced in that form: FASB Statement No. 168, *The FASB* Accounting Standards Codification® *and the Hierarchy of Generally Accepted Accounting Principles—a replacement of FASB Statement No. 162*. This standard established FASB ASC as the source of authoritative U.S. accounting and reporting standards for nongovernmental companies, in addition to guidance issued by the SEC, and was effective for financial statements issued for interim and annual periods ending after September 15, 2009.

1.07 In FASB ASC's Notice to Constituents (NTC), FASB suggests the use of plain English references to describe broad FASB ASC topics going forward in financial statements and related footnote disclosures. FASB provides the following example of plain English references in the NTC when referring to the requirements of FASB ASC 815, *Derivatives and Hedging*: "as required by the Derivatives and Hedging Topic of the FASB Accounting Standards Codification."

1.08 A natural business year is the period of 12 consecutive months that ends when the business activities of an entity have reached the lowest point in their annual cycle. In many instances, the natural business year of an entity ends December 31.

PRESENTATION

1.09 Rule 14 a-3 of the Securities Exchange Act of 1934 states that annual reports furnished to stockholders in connection with the annual meetings of stockholders should include audited financial statements: balance sheets as of the end of the two most recent fiscal years and statements of income and cash flows for each of the three most recent fiscal years. Rule 14 a-3 also states that the following information, as specified in SEC Regulation S-K should be included in the annual report to stockholders:
- Selected quarterly financial data
- Changes in, and disagreements with, accountants on accounting and financial disclosure
- Summary of selected financial data for the last five years
- Description of business activities
- Segment information
- Listing of company directors and executive officers
- Market price of, and dividends on, the company's common stock for each quarterly period within the two most recent fiscal years
- Management's discussion and analysis (MD&A) of financial condition and results of operations
- Quantitative and qualitative disclosures about market risk

1.10 FASB ASC 205-10-45-2 states that it is ordinarily desirable for an entity to present the statement of financial position; the income statement; and the statement of changes in equity for one or more preceding years, in addition to those of the current year.

1.11 Paragraphs 3–4 of FASB ASC 205-10-45 require these statements to be comparable, and any exceptions to comparability should be described as required by FASB ASC 250, *Accounting Changes and Error Corrections*. An entity is required to repeat, or at least refer to, any notes to financial statements, other explanations, or accountants' reports that contain qualifications for prior years that appeared in the comparative statements when originally issued, to the extent this information remains significant. Multiple rules set forth in SEC Regulation S-X provide guidance to SEC registrants on the form and ordering of financial statements, the presentation of amounts, the omission of certain items, and requirements for supplemental schedules. Rule 14 a-3 requires that annual reports to stockholders should include comparative balance sheets and statements of income and cash flows for each of the three most recent fiscal years. All the survey entities are SEC registrants and conformed to the aforementioned requirements of Rule 14 a-3.

1.12 FASB ASC permits an entity to offset a liability with an asset only when the following certain conditions discussed in FASB ASC 210-20-45-1 are met:
- Each of two parties owes the other determinable amounts
- The reporting party has the right to set off the amount owed with the amount owed by the other party
- The reporting party intends to set off
- The right of setoff is enforceable at law

1.13 FASB ASC 210-20-50 requires an entity to disclose in tabular format the following:
- a. The gross amounts of those recognized assets and those recognized liabilities
- b. The amounts offset in accordance with the guidance in FASB ASC 210-20-45 and 815-10-45 to determine the net amounts presented in the statement of financial position
- c. The net amounts presented in the statement of financial position
- d. The amounts subject to an enforceable master netting arrangement or similar agreement not otherwise included in (b):
  - 1. The amounts related to recognized financial instruments and other derivative instruments that either:
    - i. Management makes an accounting policy election not to offset
    - ii. Do not meet some or all of the guidance in either FASB ASC 210-20-45 or 815-10-45
  - 2. The amounts related to financial collateral (including cash collateral).
- e. The net amount after deducting the amounts in (d) from the amounts in (c).

DISCLOSURE

1.14 FASB ASC 205-20-50 explains the disclosures required for all types of discontinued operations. These include the following:

  a. A description of:
      1. The fact and circumstances leading to the disposal or expected disposal
      2. The expected manner and timing of that disposal.
  b. If not separately presented on the face of the statement where net income is reported as part of discontinued operations, the gain or loss recognized in accordance with FASB ASC 205-20-45-3 C
  c. If applicable, the segment(s) in which the discontinued operation is reported under FASB ASC 280, Segment Reporting.

1.15 SEC Regulations S-X and S-K and paragraphs .19–.20 and .A22–.A23 of AU-C section 705, *Modifications to the Opinion in the Independent Auditor's Report* (AICPA, *Professional Standards*), state the need for adequate disclosure in financial statements. Normally, the financial statements alone cannot present all information necessary for adequate disclosure without considering appended notes that disclose information. All surveyed entities provided footnote disclosures to their financial statements.

1.16 FASB ASC 235, *Notes to Financial Statements*, sets forth guidelines about the content and format of disclosures of accounting policies. FASB ASC 235-10-50-1 requires that the significant accounting policies of an entity be presented as an integral part of the financial statements of the entity. FASB ASC 235-10-50-6 states that the preferable format is to present a summary of significant accounting policies preceding notes to financial statements, or as the initial note, under the same or a similar title.

1.17 FASB ASC 205-10-50-1 requires an entity to provide information explaining changes due to reclassifications or other reasons that affect the manner of, or basis for, presenting corresponding items for two or more periods. FASB ASC 250-10 does not require an entity to present an opening balance sheet of the earliest period presented when an entity retrospectively applies a change in accounting policy or restates to correct an error.

1.18 FASB ASC 275, *Risks and Uncertainties*, requires reporting entities to disclose information about the risks and uncertainties resulting from the nature of their operations, the use of estimates in preparing financial statements, and significant concentrations in certain aspects of the entity's operations.

1.19 FASB ASC 205-30-50-2 identifies the disclosures required when a company determines that the liquidation basis of accounting is required. The requirements include disclosing the facts and circumstances surrounding the adoption of the liquidation basis of accounting and the entity's determination that liquidation is imminent. Also required is a description of the entity's plan for liquidation, including how the entity will dispose of its assets, how liabilities will be settled, and an expected date for the completion of the liquidation. Entities should also disclose the methods and significant assumptions used to measure the assets and liabilities and the type and amount of costs and income accrued in the statement of net assets in liquidation and the period over which those costs are expected to be paid or income earned.

PRESENTATION AND DISCLOSURE EXCERPTS

QUARTERLY FINANCIAL DATA

1.20 SPX CORPORATION (DEC)
NOTES TO CONSOLIDATED FINANCIAL STATEMENTS (in part)

(All currency and share amounts are in millions, except per share and par value data)

(17) Quarterly Results (Unaudited)

	First[3]		Second		Third		Fourth[3]	
	2015	2014	2015	2014	2015	2014	2015	2014
Operating revenues	$376.3	$418.4	$459.4	$489.1	$374.1	$489.6	$509.5	$555.6
Gross profit	74.5	93.6	96.0	108.2	2.9	112.5	119.0	111.9
Income (loss) from continuing operations, net of tax[1][4]	(41.0)	248.9	(11.9)	(19.2)	(130.7)	(12.2)	(7.6)	(101.4)
Income (loss) from discontinued operations, net of tax[2]	31.0	66.4	48.2	69.0	0.1	75.8	(5.1)	56.6
Net income (loss)[4]	(10.0)	315.3	36.3	49.8	(130.6)	63.6	(12.7)	(44.8)
Less: Net income (loss) attributable to noncontrolling interests[1]	(2.9)	(0.4)	(2.6)	(1.2)	(25.6)	0.3	(3.2)	(8.2)
Net income (loss) attributable to SPX Corporation common shareholders[4]	$ (7.1)	$315.7	$ 38.9	$ 51.0	$(105.0)	$ 63.3	$ (9.5)	$ (36.6)
Basic income (loss) per share of common stock:								
Continuing operations, net of tax[4]	$ (0.95)	$ 5.63	$ (0.24)	$ (0.40)	$ (2.58)	$ (0.28)	$ (0.11)	$ (2.27)
Discontinued operations, net of tax	0.77	1.51	1.20	1.58	—	1.79	(0.12)	1.37
Net income (loss)[4]	$ (0.18)	$ 7.14	$ 0.96	$ 1.18	$ (2.58)	$ 1.51	$ (0.23)	$ (0.90)
Diluted income (loss) per share of common stock:								
Continuing operations, net of tax[4]	$ (0.95)	$ 5.52	$ (0.24)	$ (0.40)	$ (2.58)	$ (0.28)	$ (0.11)	$ (2.27)
Discontinued operations, net of tax	0.77	1.48	1.20	1.58	—	1.79	(0.12)	1.37
Net income (loss)[4]	$ (0.18)	$ 7.00	$ 0.96	$ 1.18	$ (2.58)	$ 1.51	$ (0.23)	$ (0.90)

Note: The sum of the quarters' income per share may not equal the full year per share amounts.

[1] As discussed in Note 9, during the first quarter of 2014, we completed the sale of our 44.5% interest in EGS to Emerson Electric Co. for cash proceeds of $574.1, which resulted in a pre-tax gain of $491.2.

We completed the redemption of all our 7.625% senior notes during the first quarter of 2014. As a result of the redemption, we recorded a pre-tax charge of $32.5 during the quarter.

During the first quarter of 2014, we recognized a pre-tax loss of $15.3 related to settlement losses and actuarial losses, which resulted primarily from the lump-sum payment action associated with the U.S. Plan that took place during the quarter (see Note 10 for further details).

During the third quarter of 2015, we revised our estimates of expected revenues and profits associated with our large power projects in South Africa. As a result of these revisions, we reduced revenue and pre-tax income from continuing operations by $ 57.2 and $ 95.0, respectively. In addition, the revision resulted in an increase to "Net loss attributable to noncontrolling interests" of $23.8. See Notes 5 and 14 for additional details.

During the fourth quarter of 2014, we revised our estimates of revenues and profits associated with our large power projects in South Africa. As a result of these revisions, revenues and pre-tax income from continuing operations for the fourth quarter of 2014 were reduced by $25.0. In addition, the revision resulted in an increase to "Net loss attributable to noncontrolling interests" of $6.3. See Note 5 for additional details.

During the fourth quarter of 2015 and 2014, we recognized pre-tax actuarial losses of $12.0 and $80.6, respectively, associated with our pension and postretirement benefit plans (see Note 10 for further details).

During the fourth quarter of 2015 and 2014, we recognized impairment charges of $13.7 and $28.9, respectively, associated with goodwill and other long-term assets of certain businesses within our Power segment (see Note 8 for further details).

[2] As discussed in Note 4, we sold TPS for cash consideration of $42.5 during the first quarter of 2014. The sale resulted in a gain, net of taxes, of $21.5 during that quarter.

[3] We establish actual interim closing dates using a fiscal calendar, which requires our businesses to close their books on the Saturday closest to the end of the first calendar quarter, with the second and third quarters being 91 days in length. Our fourth quarter ends on December 31. The interim closing dates for the first, second and third quarters of 2015 are March 28, June 27 and September 26, compared to the respective March 29, June 28 and September 27, 2014 dates. This practice only affects the quarterly reporting periods and not the annual reporting period. We had one less day in the first quarter of 2015 and we had one more day in the fourth quarter of 2015 than in the respective 2014 periods.

[4] As discussed in Note 1, certain corrections were made to previously reported amounts. Within the quarterly results presented above, we have decreased income from continuing operations, net of tax, net income, and net income attributable to SPX Corporation common shareholders for the quarters ended March 29, 2014, June 28, 2014, September 27, 2014, and December 31, 2014 by $2.5, $0.2, $0.2 and $1.6, respectively. The earnings per share impact of the above mentioned items for the same periods was a decrease of $0.06, $0.01, $0.01, and $0.04, respectively, for both basic and diluted earnings per share from continuing operations, as well as both total basic and diluted earnings per share.

SELECTED INFORMATION FOR FIVE YEARS

1.21 THE SCOTTS MIRACLE-GRO COMPANY (SEP)
SELECTED FINANCIAL DATA

Five-Year Summary[1]

	Year Ended September 30,				
(In millions, except per share amounts)	2015	2014	2013	2012	2011
Operating Results:					
Net sales	$3,016.5	$2,841.3	$2,773.7	$2,770.5	$2,718.1
Gross profit	1,064.9	1,031.4	978.2	956.6	1,013.8

| | Year Ended September 30, | | | | |
(In millions, except per share amounts)	2015	2014	2013	2012	2011
Income from operations	294.6	314.6	310.5	241.2	301.8
Income from continuing operations	158.7	165.4	159.4	111.6	157.5
Income (loss) from discontinued operations, net of tax	—	0.8	1.7	(5.1)	10.4
Net income	158.7	166.2	161.1	106.5	167.9
Net income attributable to controlling interest	159.8	166.5	161.1	106.5	167.9
Adjusted Operating Results[2]:					
Adjusted income from operations	$ 386.1	$ 365.6	$ 330.8	$ 256.5	$ 346.2
Adjusted income from continuing operations	218.2	206.0	172.6	123.3	187.4
Adjusted income attributable to controlling interest from continuing operations	219.3	206.3	172.6	123.3	187.4
Financial Position:					
Working capital[3]	$ 335.5	$ 390.3	$ 371.2	$ 566.4	$ 523.9
Current ratio[3]	1.5	1.7	1.7	2.3	2.1
Property, plant and equipment, net	$ 453.7	$ 437.0	$ 422.3	$ 427.4	$ 394.7
Total assets	2,527.2	2,058.3	1,937.2	2,074.4	2,052.2
Total debt to total book capitalization[4]	65.2%	58.6%	44.5%	56.6%	58.7%
Total debt	$1,163.3	$ 784.3	$ 570.5	$ 782.6	$ 795.0
Total shareholders' equity—controlling interest	620.7	553.7	710.5	601.9	559.8
Cash Flows:					
Cash flows from operating activities	$ 246.9	$ 240.9	$ 342.0	$ 153.4	$ 122.1
Investments in property, plant and equipment	61.7	87.6	60.1	69.4	72.7
Investment in marketing and license agreement	300.0	—	—	—	—
Investments in acquired businesses, net of cash acquired and payments on sellers notes	181.7	114.8	4.0	7.0	7.9
Total cash dividends paid	111.3	230.8	87.8	75.4	67.9
Total purchases of Common Shares	14.8	120.0	—	17.5	358.7
Per Share Data:					
Earnings per common share from continuing operations:					
Basic	$ 2.62	$ 2.69	$ 2.58	$ 1.83	$ 2.43
Diluted	2.57	2.64	2.55	1.80	2.38
Adjusted diluted[2]	3.53	3.29	2.76	1.99	2.84
Dividends per common share[5]	1.820	3.763	1.413	1.225	1.050
Stock price at year-end	60.82	55.00	55.03	43.47	44.60
Stock price range—High	68.99	60.30	55.99	55.95	60.62
Stock price range—Low	54.71	50.51	39.64	35.49	39.99
Other:					
Adjusted EBITDA[6]	$ 471.8	$ 412.4	$ 390.5	$ 302.9	$ 393.0
Leverage ratio[6]	2.63	2.18	2.05	2.93	1.98
Interest coverage ratio[6]	9.34	9.41	6.59	4.90	7.47
Weighted average Common Shares outstanding	61.1	61.6	61.7	61.0	64.7
Common shares and dilutive potential common shares used in diluted EPS calculation	62.2	62.7	62.6	62.1	66.2

[1] On July 8, 2009, we announced a plan to close our Smith & Hawken business. During our first quarter of the fiscal year ended September 30, 2010 ("fiscal 2010"), all Smith & Hawken stores were closed and substantially all operational activities of Smith & Hawken were discontinued. As a result, effective in our first quarter of fiscal 2010, we classified Smith & Hawken as discontinued operations in accordance with accounting principles generally accepted in the United States of America ("GAAP"). Smith & Hawken® is a registered trademark of Target Brands, Inc. We sold the Smith & Hawken brand and certain intellectual property rights related thereto to Target Brands, Inc. on December 30, 2009, and subsequently changed the name of the subsidiary entity formerly known as Smith & Hawken, Ltd. to Teak 2, Ltd. References in this Annual Report on Form 10-K to Smith & Hawken refer to the subsidiary entity, not the brand itself.

On February 28, 2011, we completed the sale of Global Pro to ICL. In conjunction with the transaction, Scotts LLC and ICL entered into several product supply agreements which are generally up to five years in duration, as well as various trademark and technology licensing agreements with varying durations. Our continuing cash inflows and outflows related to these agreements are not considered to be significant in relation to the overall cash flows of Global Pro. Furthermore, none of these agreements permit us to influence the operating or financial policies of Global Pro under the ownership of ICL. Therefore, Global Pro met the criteria for presentation as discontinued operations. As such, effective in the first quarter of fiscal 2011, we classified Global Pro as discontinued operations in accordance with GAAP.

In the fourth quarter of fiscal 2012, the Company completed the wind down of our professional seed business ("Pro Seed"). As a result, effective in our fourth quarter of fiscal 2012, we classified Pro Seed as discontinued operations in accordance with GAAP.

In the second quarter of fiscal 2014, we completed the sale of our wild bird food business. As a result, effective in our second quarter of fiscal 2014, we classified the wild bird food business as discontinued operations in accordance with GAAP.

The Selected Financial Data has been retrospectively updated to recast Smith & Hawken, Global Pro, Pro Seed, and the wild bird food business as discontinued operations for each period presented.

[2] The Five-Year Summary includes non-GAAP financial measures, as defined in Item 10(e) of SEC Regulation S-K, of adjusted income from operations, adjusted income from continuing operations, adjusted income attributable to controlling interest from continuing operations and adjusted diluted earnings per share from continuing operations, which exclude costs or gains related to discrete projects or transactions. Items excluded during the five-year period ended September 30, 2015 consisted of charges or credits relating to refinancings, impairments, restructurings, product registration and recall matters, discontinued operations, and other unusual items such as costs or gains related to discrete projects or transactions that are apart from and not indicative of the results of the operations of the business. The comparable GAAP measures are reported income from operations, reported income from continuing operations and reported diluted earnings per share from continuing operations. Our management believes that these non-GAAP measures are the most indicative of our earnings capabilities and that disclosure of these non-GAAP financial measures therefore provides useful information to investors or other users of the financial statements, such as lenders. Non-GAAP financial measures should be viewed in addition to, and not as an alternative for, the Company's reported results prepared in accordance with GAAP. A reconciliation of the non-GAAP measures to the most directly comparable GAAP measures is presented in the following tables:

(continued)

(Table footnote continued)

(In millions, except per share data)	**2015**	**2014**	**2013**	**2012**	**2011**
	Year Ended September 30,				
Income from operations	$294.6	$314.6	$310.5	$241.2	$301.8
Impairment, restructuring and other	91.5	51.0	20.3	7.1	29.8
Product registration and recall matters	—	—	—	8.2	14.6
Adjusted income from operations	$386.1	$365.6	$330.8	$256.5	$346.2
Income from continuing operations	$158.7	$165.4	$159.4	$111.6	$157.5
Impairment, restructuring and other, net of tax	59.5	33.6	13.2	4.3	17.9
Costs related to refinancing, net of tax	—	7.0	—	—	—
Product registration and recall matters, net of tax	—	—	—	7.4	12.0
Adjusted income from continuing operations	$218.2	$206.0	$172.6	$123.3	$187.4
Loss attributable to noncontrolling interest [7]	1.1	0.3			
Adjusted income attributable to controlling interest from continuing operations	$219.3	$206.3	$172.6	$123.3	$187.4
Diluted earnings per share from continuing operations	$ 2.57	$ 2.64	$ 2.55	$ 1.80	$ 2.38
Impairment, restructuring and other, net of tax	0.96	0.54	0.21	0.07	0.27
Costs related to refinancing, net of tax		0.11			
Product registration and recall matters, net of tax	—	—	—	0.12	0.19
Adjusted diluted earnings per share from continuing operations	$ 3.53	$ 3.29	$ 2.76	$ 1.99	$ 2.84

[3] Working capital is calculated as current assets minus current liabilities. Current ratio is calculated as current assets divided by current liabilities.

[4] The total debt to total book capitalization percentage is calculated by dividing total debt by total debt plus total shareholders' equity—controlling interest.

[5] Scotts Miracle-Gro pays a quarterly dividend to the holders of its Common Shares. On August 8, 2011, Scotts Miracle-Gro announced that its Board of Directors had increased the quarterly cash dividend to $0.30 per Common Share, which was first paid in the fourth quarter of fiscal 2011. On August 9, 2012, Scotts Miracle-Gro announced that its Board of Directors had increased the quarterly cash dividend to $0.325 per Common Share, which was first paid in the fourth quarter of fiscal 2012. On August 6, 2013, Scotts Miracle-Gro announced that its Board of Directors had increased the quarterly cash dividend to $0.4375 per Common Share, which was first paid in the fourth quarter of fiscal 2013. On August 11, 2014, Scotts Miracle-Gro announced that its Board of Directors had (i) further increased the quarterly cash dividend to $0.45 per Common Share, which was paid in the fourth quarter of fiscal 2014 and (ii) a special one-time cash dividend of $2.00 per Common Share, which was paid on September 17, 2014. On August 3, 2015, Scotts Miracle-Gro announced that its Board of Directors had further increased the quarterly cash dividend to $0.47 per Common Share, which was paid in the fourth quarter of fiscal 2015.

[6] We view our credit facility as material to our ability to fund operations, particularly in light of our seasonality. Please refer to "ITEM 1A. RISK FACTORS—Our indebtedness could limit our flexibility and adversely affect our financial condition" of this Annual Report on Form 10-K for a more complete discussion of the risks associated with our debt and our credit facility and the restrictive covenants therein. Our ability to generate cash flows sufficient to cover our debt service costs is essential to our ability to maintain our borrowing capacity. We believe that Adjusted EBITDA provides additional information for determining our ability to meet debt service requirements. The presentation of Adjusted EBITDA herein is intended to be consistent with the calculation of that measure as required by our borrowing agreements, and used to calculate a leverage ratio (maximum of 4.50 at September 30, 2015) and an interest coverage ratio (minimum of 3.00 for the twelve months ended September 30, 2015). Leverage ratio is calculated as average total indebtedness, as described in our credit facility, divided by Adjusted EBITDA. Interest coverage ratio is calculated as Adjusted EBITDA divided by interest expense, as described in our credit facility, and excludes costs related to refinancings. Our leverage ratio was 2.63 at September 30, 2015 and our interest coverage ratio was 9.34 for the twelve months ended September 30, 2015. Please refer to "ITEM 7. MANAGEMENT'S DISCUSSION AND ANALYSIS OF FINANCIAL CONDITION AND RESULTS OF OPERATIONS—Liquidity and Capital Resources—Borrowing Agreements" of this Annual Report on Form 10-K for a discussion of our credit facility.

In accordance with the terms of our credit facility, Adjusted EBITDA is calculated as net income (loss) before interest, taxes, depreciation and amortization as well as certain other items such as the impact of the cumulative effect of changes in accounting, costs associated with debt refinancing and other non-recurring or non-cash items affecting net income. For the fourth quarter of fiscal 2015, the Company changed its calculation of Adjusted EBITDA to reflect the measure as defined in our fourth amended credit agreement. Prior periods have not been adjusted as they reflect the presentation consistent with the calculation as required by our borrowing agreements in place at that time. The revised calculation adds adjustments for share-based compensation expense, expense on certain leases, and impairment, restructuring and other charges (including cash and non-cash charges) and no longer includes an adjustment for mark-to-market adjustments on derivatives. Our calculation of Adjusted EBITDA does not represent and should not be considered as an alternative to net income or cash flows from operating activities as determined by GAAP. We make no representation or assertion that Adjusted EBITDA is indicative of our cash flows from operating activities or results of operations. We have provided a reconciliation of Adjusted EBITDA to income from continuing operations solely for the purpose of complying with SEC regulations and not as an indication that Adjusted EBITDA is a substitute measure for income from continuing operations.

A numeric reconciliation of Adjusted EBITDA to income from continuing operations is as follows:

(In millions, except per share data)	**2015**	**2014**	**2013**	**2012**	**2011**
	Year Ended September 30,				
Income from continuing operations	$158.7	$165.4	$159.4	$111.6	$157.5
Income tax expense from continuing operations	85.4	91.2	91.9	67.8	92.1
Income (loss) from discontinued operations, net of tax (excluding Global Pro sale)	—	0.8	1.7	(3.4)	(29.1)
Income tax expense (benefit) from discontinued operations	—	0.9	0.7	(1.2)	(16.6)
Costs related to refinancings	—	10.7	—	—	1.2
Interest expense	50.5	47.3	59.2	61.8	51.0
Interest expense from discontinued operations	—	—	—	—	1.7
Depreciation	51.4	50.6	54.9	51.5	50.3
Amortization	17.6	13.8	11.2	10.9	11.4
Gain on investment of unconsolidated affiliate [8]	—	(3.3)	—	—	—
Loss on impairment and other charges	91.5	33.7	11.2	4.7	64.3
Product registration and recall matters, non-cash portion	—	—	—	0.2	8.7
Mark-to-market adjustments on derivatives	—	1.3	0.3	(1.0)	0.5
Expense on certain leases	3.5	—	—	—	—
Share-based compensation expense	13.2	—	—	—	—
Adjusted EBITDA	$471.8	$412.4	$390.5	$302.9	$393.0

[7] Amount represents the earnings attributable to the noncontrolling interest of AeroGrow which was consolidated in the fourth quarter of fiscal 2014.

[8] Amount represents a gain on our investment in AeroGrow recognized during the fourth quarter of 2014 as a result of our consolidation of the business. Excluded from this amount is $2.4 million of earnings on AeroGrow's unconsolidated results for fiscal year 2014 recorded within "Other income, net" in the Consolidated Statements of Operations.

FORWARD-LOOKING INFORMATION

1.22 KB HOME (NOV)

MANAGEMENT'S DISCUSSION AND ANALYSIS OF FINANCIAL CONDITION AND RESULTS OF OPERATIONS (in part)

Forward-Looking Statements

Investors are cautioned that certain statements contained in this report, as well as some statements by us in periodic press releases and other public disclosures and some oral statements by us to securities analysts, stockholders and others during presentations, are "forward-looking statements" within the meaning of the Private Securities Litigation Reform Act of 1995 (the "Act"). Statements that are predictive in nature, that depend upon or refer to future events or conditions, or that include words such as "expects," "anticipates," "intends," "plans," "believes," "estimates," "hopes," and similar expressions constitute forward-looking statements. In addition, any statements that we may make or provide concerning future financial or operating performance (including, without limitation, future revenues, community count, homes delivered, net orders, selling prices, sales pace per new community, expenses, expense ratios, housing gross profits, housing gross profit margins, earnings or earnings per share, or growth or growth rates), future market conditions, future interest rates, and other economic conditions, ongoing business strategies or prospects, future dividends and changes in dividend levels, the value of our backlog (including amounts that we expect to realize upon delivery of homes included in our backlog and the timing of those deliveries), the value of our net orders, potential future asset acquisitions and the impact of completed acquisitions, future share issuances or repurchases, future debt issuances, repurchases or redemptions and other possible future actions are also forward-looking statements as defined by the Act. Forward-looking statements are based on our current expectations and projections about future events and are subject to risks, uncertainties, and assumptions about our operations, economic and market factors, and the homebuilding industry, among other things. These statements are not guarantees of future performance, and we have no specific policy or intention to update these statements. In addition, forward-looking and other statements in this report and in other public or oral disclosures that express or contain opinions, views or assumptions about market or economic conditions; the success, performance, effectiveness and/or relative positioning of our strategies, initiatives or operational activities; and other matters, may be based in whole or in part on general observations of our management, limited or anecdotal evidence and/or business or industry experience without in-depth or any particular empirical investigation, inquiry or analysis.

Actual events and results may differ materially from those expressed or forecasted in forward-looking statements due to a number of factors. The most important risk factors that could cause our actual performance and future events and actions to differ materially from such forward-looking statements include, but are not limited to the following:

- general economic, employment and business conditions;
- population growth, household formations and demographic trends;
- adverse market conditions, including an increased supply of unsold homes, declining home prices and greater foreclosure and short sale activity, among other things, that could negatively affect our consolidated financial statements, including due to additional inventory impairment or land option contract abandonment charges, lower revenues and operating and other losses;
- conditions in the capital, credit and financial markets (including mortgage lending standards, the availability of mortgage financing and mortgage foreclosure rates);
- material prices and availability;
- trade costs and availability;
- changes in interest rates;
- inflation;
- our debt level, including our ratio of debt to capital, and our ability to adjust our debt level, maturity schedule and structure and to access the equity, credit, capital or other financial markets or other external financing sources, including raising capital through the public or private issuance of common stock, debt or other securities, and/or project financing, on favorable terms;
- our compliance with the terms and covenants of the Credit Facility;
- weak or declining consumer confidence, either generally or specifically with respect to purchasing homes;
- competition for home sales from other sellers of new and resale homes, including lenders and other sellers of homes obtained through foreclosures or short sales;
- the impact of weather events, significant natural disasters and other climate and environmental factors, including the severe prolonged drought and related water-constrained conditions in the southwest United States and California;
- government actions, policies, programs and regulations directed at or affecting the housing market (including the Dodd-Frank Act, tax credits, tax incentives and/or subsidies for home purchases, tax deductions for mortgage interest payments and property taxes, tax exemptions for profits on home sales, programs intended to modify existing mortgage loans and to prevent mortgage foreclosures and the standards, fees and size limits applicable to the purchase or insuring of mortgage loans by government-sponsored enterprises and government agencies), the homebuilding industry, or construction activities;
- decisions regarding federal fiscal and monetary policies, including those relating to taxation, government spending, interest rates and economic stimulus measures;

- the availability and cost of land in desirable areas;
- our warranty claims experience with respect to homes previously delivered and actual warranty costs incurred, including our warranty claims and costs experience at certain of our communities in Florida;
- costs and/or charges arising from regulatory compliance requirements or from legal, arbitral or regulatory proceedings, investigations, claims or settlements, including unfavorable outcomes in any such matters resulting in actual or potential monetary damage awards, penalties, fines or other direct or indirect payments, or injunctions, consent decrees or other voluntary or involuntary restrictions or adjustments to our business operations or practices that are beyond our current expectations and/or accruals;
- our ability to use/realize the net deferred tax assets we have generated;
- our ability to successfully implement our current and planned strategies and initiatives with respect to product, geographic and market positioning (including our efforts to expand our inventory base/pipeline with desirable land positions or interests at reasonable cost and to expand our community count, open additional communities for sales, sell higher-priced homes and more design options, increase the size and value of our backlog, and our operational and investment concentration in markets in California), revenue growth, asset optimization (including by effectively balancing home sales prices and sales pace in our communities), asset activation and/or monetization, local field management and talent investment, containing and leveraging overhead costs, gaining share and scale in our served markets and increasing our housing gross profit margins and profitability;
- consumer traffic to our communities and consumer interest in our product designs and offerings, particularly higher-income consumers;
- cancellations and our ability to realize our backlog by converting net orders to home deliveries and revenues;
- our home sales and delivery performance, particularly in key markets in California;
- our ability to generate cash from our operations, enhance our asset efficiency, increase our operating income margin and/or improve our return on invested capital;
- the manner in which our homebuyers are offered and whether they are able to obtain mortgage loans and mortgage banking services, including from HCM;
- the performance of HCM;
- information technology failures and data security breaches; and
- other events outside of our control.

LIQUIDITY AND CAPITAL RESOURCES

1.23 CISCO SYSTEMS, INC. (JUL)
MANAGEMENT'S DISCUSSION AND ANALYSIS OF FINANCIAL CONDITION AND RESULTS OF OPERATIONS (in part)

Liquidity and Capital Resources

The following sections discuss the effects of changes in our balance sheet, our capital allocation strategy including stock repurchase program and dividends, our contractual obligations, and certain other commitments and activities on our liquidity and capital resources.

Balance Sheet and Cash Flows

Cash and Cash Equivalents and Investments The following table summarizes our cash and cash equivalents and investments (in millions):

	July 25, 2015	July 26, 2014	Increase (Decrease)
Cash and cash equivalents	$ 6,877	$ 6,726	$ 151
Fixed income securities	51,974	43,396	8,578
Publicly traded equity securities	1,565	1,952	(387)
Total	$60,416	$52,074	$8,342

The net increase in cash and cash equivalents and investments from fiscal 2014 to fiscal 2015 was primarily the result of cash provided by operating activities of $12.6 billion, a net increase in debt of $4.5 billion and the net issuance of common stock of $1.5 billion pursuant to employee stock incentive and purchase plans. These sources of cash were partially offset by the repurchase of common stock of $4.3 billion under the stock repurchase program, cash dividends paid of $4.1 billion, capital expenditures of $1.2 billion and net cash paid for acquisitions of $0.3 billion.

Our total in cash and cash equivalents and investments held by various foreign subsidiaries was $53.4 billion and $47.4 billion as of July 25, 2015 and July 26, 2014, respectively. Under current tax laws and regulations, if these assets were to be distributed from the foreign subsidiaries to the United States in the form of dividends or otherwise, we would be subject to additional U.S. income taxes (subject to an adjustment for foreign tax credits) and foreign withholding taxes. The balance of cash and cash equivalents and investments available in the United States as of July 25, 2015 and July 26, 2014 was $7.0 billion and $4.7 billion, respectively.

We maintain an investment portfolio of various holdings, types, and maturities. We classify our investments as short-term investments based on their nature and their availability for use in current operations. We believe the overall credit quality of our portfolio is strong, with our cash equivalents and our fixed income investment portfolio consisting primarily of high quality investment-grade securities. We believe that our strong cash and cash equivalents and investments position allows us to use our cash resources for strategic investments to gain access to new technologies, for acquisitions, for customer financing activities, for working capital needs, and for the repurchase of shares of common stock and payment of dividends as discussed below.

Free Cash Flow and Capital Allocation   As part of our capital allocation strategy, we intend to return a minimum of 50% of our free cash flow annually to our shareholders through cash dividends and repurchases of common stock.

We define free cash flow as net cash provided by operating activities less cash used to acquire property and equipment. The following table reconciles our net cash provided by operating activities to free cash flow (in millions):

Years Ended	July 25, 2015	July 26, 2014	July 27, 2013
Net cash provided by operating activities	$12,552	$12,332	$12,894
Acquisition of property and equipment	(1,227)	(1,275)	(1,160)
Free cash flow	$11,325	$11,057	$11,734

We expect that cash provided by operating activities may fluctuate in future periods as a result of a number of factors, including fluctuations in our operating results, the rate at which products are shipped during the quarter (which we refer to as shipment linearity), the timing and collection of accounts receivable and financing receivables, inventory and supply chain management, deferred revenue, excess tax benefits resulting from share-based compensation, and the timing and amount of tax and other payments. For additional discussion, see "Part I, Item 1A. Risk Factors" in this report.

We consider free cash flow to be a liquidity measure that provides useful information to management and investors because of our intent to return a stated percentage of free cash flow to shareholders in the form of dividends and stock repurchases. We further regard free cash flow as a useful measure because it reflects cash that can be used to, among other things, invest in our business, make strategic acquisitions, repurchase common stock, and pay dividends on our common stock, after deducting capital investments. A limitation of the utility of free cash flow as a measure of financial performance and liquidity is that the free cash flow does not represent the total increase or decrease in our cash balance for the period. In addition, we have other required uses of cash, including repaying the principal of our outstanding indebtedness. Free cash flow is not a measure calculated in accordance with U.S. generally accepted accounting principles and should not be regarded in isolation or as an alternative for net income provided by operating activities or any other measure calculated in accordance with such principles, and other companies may calculate free cash flow in a different manner than we do.

The following table summarizes the dividends paid and stock repurchases (in millions, except per-share amounts):

	Dividends		Stock Repurchase Program			Total
Years Ended	Per Share	Amount	Shares	Weighted-Average Price per Share	Amount	Amount
July 25, 2015	$0.80	$4,086	155	$27.22	$4,234	$ 8,320
July 26, 2014	$0.72	$3,758	420	$22.71	$9,539	$13,297
July 27, 2013	$0.62	$3,310	128	$21.63	$2,773	$ 6,083

Any future dividends will be subject to the approval of our Board of Directors.

Accounts Receivable, Net   The following table summarizes our accounts receivable, net (in millions), and DSO:

	July 25, 2015	July 26, 2014	Increase (Decrease)
Accounts receivable, net	$5,344	$5,157	$187
DSO	38	38	—

Our accounts receivable net, as of July 25, 2015 increased by approximately 4% compared with the end of fiscal 2014. Our DSO as of July 25, 2015 was flat compared with the end of fiscal 2014, as factors that drive DSO such as shipment linearity and collections were similar for the periods presented.

Inventory Supply Chain   The following table summarizes our inventories and purchase commitments with contract manufacturers and suppliers (in millions, except annualized inventory turns):

	July 25, 2015	July 26, 2014	Increase (Decrease)
Inventories	$1,627	$1,591	$ 36
Annualized inventory turns	12.1	12.7	(0.6)
Purchase commitments with contract manufacturers and suppliers	$4,078	$4,169	$ (91)

Inventory as of July 25, 2015 increased by 2% from our inventory balance at the end of fiscal 2014, and for the same period purchase commitments with contract manufacturers and suppliers decreased by approximately 2%. On a combined basis, inventories and purchase commitments with contract manufacturers and suppliers decreased by 1% compared with the end of fiscal 2014. We believe our inventory and purchase commitments levels are in line with our current demand forecasts.

Our finished goods consist of distributor inventory and deferred cost of sales and manufactured finished goods. Distributor inventory and deferred cost of sales are related to unrecognized revenue on shipments to distributors and retail partners as well as shipments to customers. Manufactured finished goods consist primarily of build-to-order and build-to-stock products.

We purchase components from a variety of suppliers and use several contract manufacturers to provide manufacturing services for our products. During the normal course of business, in order to manage manufacturing lead times and help ensure adequate component supply, we enter into agreements with contract manufacturers and suppliers that allow them to procure inventory based upon criteria as defined by us or that establish the parameters defining our requirements and our commitment to securing manufacturing capacity. A significant portion of our reported purchase commitments arising from these agreements are firm, noncancelable, and unconditional commitments. In certain instances, these agreements allow us the option to cancel, reschedule, and adjust our requirements based on our business needs prior to firm orders being placed. Our purchase commitments are for short-term product manufacturing requirements as well as for commitments to suppliers to secure manufacturing capacity.

Inventory and supply chain management remain areas of focus as we balance the need to maintain supply chain flexibility to help ensure competitive lead times with the risk of inventory obsolescence because of rapidly changing technology and customer requirements. We believe the amount of our inventory and purchase commitments is appropriate for our revenue levels.

Financing Receivables and Guarantees   We measure our net balance sheet exposure position related to our financing receivables and financing guarantees by reducing the total of gross financing receivables and financing guarantees by the associated allowances for credit loss and deferred revenue. As of July 25, 2015, our net balance sheet exposure position related to financing receivables and financing guarantees was as follows (in millions):

July 25, 2015	Financing Receivables				Financing Guarantees			
	Lease Receivables	Loan Receivables	Financed Service Contracts and Other	Total	Channel Partner	End-User Customers	Total	Total
Financing receivables and guarantees	$3,395	$1,763	$ 3,573	$ 8,731	$ 288	$ 129	$ 417	$ 9,148
Allowance for credit loss	(259)	(87)	(36)	(382)	—	—	—	(382)
Deferred revenue	(5)	(13)	(1,853)	(1,871)	(127)	(107)	(234)	(2,105)
Net balance sheet exposure	$3,131	$1,663	$ 1,684	$ 6,478	$ 161	$ 22	$ 183	$ 6,661

Financing Receivables   Financing receivables less unearned income increased by 4% compared with the end of fiscal 2014. The change was primarily due to an 11% increase in financed service contracts and other, and a 5% increase in loan receivables, partially offset by a 4% decrease in lease receivables. We provide financing to certain end-user customers and channel partners to enable sales of our products, services, and networking solutions. These financing arrangements include leases, financed service contracts, and loans. Arrangements related to leases are generally collateralized by a security interest in the underlying assets. Lease receivables include sales-type and direct-financing leases. We also provide certain qualified customers financing for long-term service contracts, which primarily relate to technical support services. Our loan financing arrangements may include not only financing the acquisition of our products and services but also providing additional funds for other costs associated with network installation and integration of our products and services. We expect to continue to expand the use of our financing programs in the near term.

Financing Guarantees   In the normal course of business, third parties may provide financing arrangements to our customers and channel partners under financing programs. The financing arrangements to customers provided by third parties are related to leases and loans and typically have terms of up to three years. In some cases, we provide guarantees to third parties for these lease and loan arrangements. The financing arrangements to channel partners consist of revolving short-term financing provided by third parties, generally with payment terms ranging from 60 to 90 days. In certain instances, these financing arrangements result in a transfer of our receivables to the third party. The receivables are derecognized upon transfer, as these transfers qualify as true sales, and we receive payments for the receivables from the third party based on our standard payment terms. The volume of channel partner financing was $25.9 billion, $24.6 billion, and $23.8 billion in fiscal 2015, 2014, and 2013, respectively. These financing arrangements facilitate the working capital requirements of the channel partners, and in some cases, we guarantee a portion of these arrangements. The balance of the channel partner financing subject to guarantees was $1.2 billion as of each of July 25, 2015 and July 26, 2014. We could be called upon to make payments under these guarantees in the event of nonpayment by the channel partners or end-user customers. Historically, our payments under these arrangements have been immaterial. Where we provide a guarantee, we defer the revenue associated with the channel partner and end-user financing arrangement in accordance with revenue recognition policies, or we record a liability for the fair value of the guarantees. In either case, the deferred revenue is recognized as revenue when the guarantee is removed.

Deferred Revenue Related to Financing Receivables and Guarantees   The majority of the deferred revenue in the preceding table is related to financed service contracts. The majority of the revenue related to financed service contracts, which primarily relates to technical support services, is deferred as the revenue related to financed service contracts is recognized ratably over the period during which the related services are to be performed. A portion of the revenue related to lease and loan receivables is also deferred and included in deferred product revenue based on revenue recognition criteria not currently having been met.

Borrowings

Senior Notes   The following table summarizes the principal amount of our senior notes (in millions):

	Maturity Date	July 25, 2015	July 26, 2014
Senior notes:			
Floating-rate notes:			
Three-month LIBOR plus 0.05%	September 3, 2015	$ 850	$ 850
Three-month LIBOR plus 0.28%	March 3, 2017	1,000	1,000
Three-month LIBOR plus 0.31%	June 15, 2018[1]	900	—
Three-month LIBOR plus 0.50%	March 1, 2019	500	500
Fixed-rate notes:			
2.90%	November 17, 2014	—	500
5.50%	February 22, 2016	3,000	3,000
1.10%	March 3, 2017	2,400	2,400
3.15%	March 14, 2017	750	750
1.65%	June 15, 2018[1]	1,600	—
4.95%	February 15, 2019	2,000	2,000
2.125%	March 1, 2019	1,750	1,750
4.45%	January 15, 2020	2,500	2,500
2.45%	June 15, 2020[1]	1,500	—
2.90%	March 4, 2021	500	500
3.00%	June 15, 2022[1]	500	—
3.625%	March 4, 2024	1,000	1,000
3.50%	June 15, 2025[1]	500	—
5.90%	February 15, 2039	2,000	2,000
5.50%	January 15, 2040	2,000	2,000
Total		$25,250	$20,750

[1]   In June 2015, we issued senior notes with an aggregate principal amount of $5.0 billion.

Interest is payable semiannually on each class of the senior fixed-rate notes, each of which is redeemable by us at any time, subject to a make-whole premium. Interest is payable quarterly on the floating-rate notes. We were in compliance with all debt covenants as of July 25, 2015.

We repaid the fixed-rate notes (2.90%) due on November 17, 2014, for an aggregate principal amount of $500 million upon maturity.

We repaid the floating-rate notes due on September 3, 2015 for an aggregate principal amount of $850 million upon maturity.

Other Debt   Other debt as of July 25, 2015 and July 26, 2014 includes secured borrowings associated with customer financing arrangements. The amount of borrowings outstanding under these arrangements was $4 million and $12 million as of July 25, 2015 and July 26, 2014, respectively.

Commercial Paper   In fiscal 2011, we established a short-term debt financing program of up to $3.0 billion through the issuance of commercial paper notes. We use the proceeds from the issuance of commercial paper notes for general corporate purposes. We had no commercial paper notes outstanding as of each of July 25, 2015 and July 26, 2014.

Credit Facility   On May 15, 2015, we entered into a credit agreement with certain institutional lenders that provides for a $3.0 billion unsecured revolving credit facility that is scheduled to expire on May 15, 2020. Any advances under the credit agreement will accrue interest at rates that are equal to, based on certain conditions, either (i) the highest of (a) the Federal Funds rate plus 0.50%, (b) Bank of America's "prime rate" as announced from time to time, or (c) LIBOR, or a comparable or successor rate that is approved by the Administrative Agent ("Eurocurrency Rate"), for an interest period of one month plus 1.00%, or (ii) the Eurocurrency Rate, plus a margin that is based on our senior debt credit ratings as published by Standard & Poor's Financial Services, LLC and Moody's Investors Service, Inc., provided that in no event will the Eurocurrency Rate be less than zero. The credit agreement requires that we comply with certain covenants, including that it maintains an interest coverage ratio as defined in the agreement.

We may also, upon the agreement of either the then-existing lenders or additional lenders not currently parties to the agreement, increase the commitments under the credit facility by up to an additional $2.0 billion and/or extend the expiration date of the credit facility up to May 15, 2022. We were in compliance with the required interest coverage ratio and the other covenants, and we had not borrowed any funds under the credit facility.

This credit facility replaces our prior credit facility that was entered into on February 17, 2012, which was terminated in connection with its entering into the new credit facility.

Deferred Revenue   The following table presents the breakdown of deferred revenue (in millions):

	July 25, 2015	July 26, 2014	Increase (Decrease)
Service	$ 9,757	$ 9,640	$ 117
Product	5,426	4,502	924
Total	$15,183	$14,142	$1,041
Reported as:			
Current	$ 9,824	$ 9,478	$ 346
Noncurrent	5,359	4,664	695
Total	$15,183	$14,142	$1,041

Deferred product revenue increased 21% primarily due to increased deferrals related to subscription and software revenue arrangements and also, to a lesser extent, to an increase in shipments not having met revenue recognition criteria as of July 25, 2015. The product categories of Collaboration, Security, and Wireless were the key contributors to the increase. The increase in deferred service revenue in fiscal 2015 was driven by the timing of multiyear arrangements, an increase in customers paying technical support service contracts over time and the impact of ongoing amortization of deferred service revenue.

Contractual Obligations

The impact of contractual obligations on our liquidity and capital resources in future periods should be analyzed in conjunction with the factors that impact our cash flows from operations discussed previously. In addition, we plan for and measure our liquidity and capital resources through an annual budgeting process. The following table summarizes our contractual obligations at July 25, 2015 (in millions):

		Payments Due By Period			
July 25, 2015	Total	Less than 1 Year	1 to 3 Years	3 to 5 Years	More than 5 Years
Operating leases	$ 1,142	$ 346	$ 435	$ 178	$ 183
Purchase commitments with contract manufacturers and suppliers	4,078	4,078	—	—	—
Other purchase obligations	2,012	604	815	536	57
Long-term debt including the current portion	25,251	3,850	6,651	8,250	6,500
Other long-term liabilities	1,213	—	350	72	791
Total by period	$33,696	$8,878	$8,251	$9,036	$7,531
Other long-term liabilities (uncertainty in the timing of future payments)	2,122				
Total	$35,818				

Operating Leases   For more information on our operating leases, see Note 12 to the Consolidated Financial Statements.

Purchase Commitments with Contract Manufacturers and Suppliers   We purchase components from a variety of suppliers and use several contract manufacturers to provide manufacturing services for our products. A significant portion of our reported estimated purchase commitments arising from these agreements are firm, noncancelable, and unconditional commitments. We record a liability for firm, noncancelable, and unconditional purchase commitments for quantities in excess of our future demand forecasts consistent with the valuation of our excess and obsolete inventory. See further discussion in "Inventory Supply Chain." As of July 25, 2015, the liability for these purchase commitments was $156 million and is recorded in other current liabilities and is not included in the preceding table.

Other Purchase Obligations Other purchase obligations represent an estimate of all contractual obligations in the ordinary course of business, other than operating leases and commitments with contract manufacturers and suppliers, for which we have not received the goods or services. Purchase orders are not included in the preceding table as they typically represent our authorization to purchase rather than binding contractual purchase obligations.

Long-Term Debt The amount of long-term debt in the preceding table represents the principal amount of the respective debt instruments. See Note 10 to the Consolidated Financial Statements.

Other Long-Term Liabilities Other long-term liabilities primarily include noncurrent income taxes payable, accrued liabilities for deferred compensation, noncurrent deferred tax liabilities, and certain other long-term liabilities. Due to the uncertainty in the timing of future payments, our noncurrent income taxes payable of approximately $1,876 million and noncurrent deferred tax liabilities of $246 million were presented as one aggregated amount in the total column on a separate line in the preceding table. Noncurrent income taxes payable include uncertain tax positions (see Note 16 to the Consolidated Financial Statements).

Other Commitments

In connection with our business combinations and asset purchases, we have agreed to pay certain additional amounts contingent upon the achievement of certain agreed-upon technology, development, product, or other milestones or the continued employment with us of certain employees of the acquired entities. See Note 12 to the Consolidated Financial Statements.

Insieme Networks, Inc. In the third quarter of fiscal 2012, we made an investment in Insieme, an early stage company focused on research and development in the data center market. As set forth in the agreement between Cisco and Insieme, this investment included $100 million of funding and a license to certain of our technology. Immediately prior to the call option exercise and acquisition described below, we owned approximately 83% of Insieme as a result of these investments and have consolidated the results of Insieme in our Consolidated Financial Statements. In connection with this investment, we entered into a put/call option agreement that provided us with the right to purchase the remaining interests in Insieme. In addition, the noncontrolling interest holders could require us to purchase their shares upon the occurrence of certain events.

During the first quarter of fiscal 2014, we exercised our call option and entered into an agreement to purchase the remaining interests in Insieme. The acquisition closed in the second quarter of fiscal 2014, at which time the former noncontrolling interest holders became eligible to receive up to two milestone payments, which will be determined using agreed-upon formulas based primarily on revenue for certain of Insieme's products. During fiscal 2015 and 2014, we recorded compensation expense of $207 million and $416 million, respectively, related to the fair value of the vested portion of amounts that were earned or expected to be earned by the former noncontrolling interest holders. Continued vesting and changes to the fair value of the amounts probable of being earned will result in adjustments to the recorded compensation expense in future periods. Based on the terms of the agreement, we have determined that the maximum amount that could be recorded as compensation expense by us is approximately $843 million (which includes the $623 million that has been expensed to date), net of forfeitures. The milestone payments, to the extent earned, are expected to be paid primarily during the first half of each of fiscal 2016 and fiscal 2017.

Other Funding Commitments We also have certain funding commitments primarily related to our investments in privately held companies and venture funds, some of which are based on the achievement of certain agreed-upon milestones, and some of which are required to be funded on demand. The funding commitments were $205 million as of July 25, 2015, compared with $255 million as of July 26, 2014.

Off-Balance Sheet Arrangements

We consider our investments in unconsolidated variable interest entities to be off-balance sheet arrangements. In the ordinary course of business, we have investments in privately held companies and provide financing to certain customers. These privately held companies and customers may be considered to be variable interest entities. We evaluate on an ongoing basis our investments in these privately held companies and customer financings, and we have determined that as of July 25, 2015 there were no material unconsolidated variable interest entities.

On an ongoing basis, we reassess our investments in privately held companies and customer financings to determine if they are variable interest entities and if we would be regarded as the primary beneficiary pursuant to the applicable accounting guidance. As a result of this ongoing assessment, we may be required to make additional disclosures or consolidate these entities. Because we may not control these entities, we may not have the ability to influence these events.

We provide financing guarantees, which are generally for various third-party financing arrangements extended to our channel partners and end-user customers. We could be called upon to make payments under these guarantees in the event of nonpayment by the channel partners or end-user customers. See the previous discussion of these financing guarantees under "Financing Receivables and Guarantees."

Securities Lending

We periodically engage in securities lending activities with certain of our available-for-sale investments. These transactions are accounted for as a secured lending of the securities, and the securities are typically loaned only on an overnight basis. The average daily balance of securities lending for fiscal 2015 and 2014 was $0.4 billion and $1.5 billion, respectively. We require collateral equal to at least 102% of the fair market value of the loaned security and that the collateral be in the form of cash or liquid, high-quality assets. We engage in these secured lending transactions only with highly creditworthy counterparties, and the associated portfolio custodian has agreed to indemnify us against collateral losses. As of July 25, 2015 and July 26, 2014, we had no outstanding securities lending transactions. We believe these arrangements do not present a material risk or impact to our liquidity requirements.

Liquidity and Capital Resource Requirements

Based on past performance and current expectations, we believe our cash and cash equivalents, investments, cash generated from operations, and ability to access capital markets and committed credit lines will satisfy, through at least the next 12 months, our liquidity requirements, both in total and domestically, including the following: working capital needs, capital expenditures, investment requirements, stock repurchases, cash dividends, contractual obligations, commitments, principal and interest payments on debt, future customer financings, and other liquidity requirements associated with our operations. There are no other transactions, arrangements, or relationships with unconsolidated entities or other persons that are reasonably likely to materially affect the liquidity and the availability of, as well as our requirements for, capital resources.

NEW ACCOUNTING STANDARDS

1.24 THE DUN & BRADSTREET CORPORATION (DEC)
NOTES TO CONSOLIDATED FINANCIAL STATEMENTS (in part)

(Tabular dollar amounts in millions, except per share data)

Note 2. Recent Accounting Pronouncements

We consider the applicability and impact of all Accounting Standards Updates ("ASUs"). The ASUs not listed below were assessed and determined to be either not applicable or are expected to have minimal impact on our consolidated financial position and/or results of operations.

In February 2016, the Financial Accounting Standards Board ("FASB") issued ASU 2016-02 "Leases (Topic 842)." This standard requires entities that lease assets to recognize on the balance sheet the assets and liabilities for the rights and obligations created by those leases. The standard is effective for fiscal years and the interim periods within those fiscal years beginning after December 15, 2018. The guidance is required to be applied by the modified retrospective transition approach. Early adoption is permitted. We are currently assessing the impact of the adoption of this authoritative guidance on our consolidated financial statements.

In November 2015, the FASB issued ASU 2015-17 "Income Taxes (Topic 740): Balance Sheet Classification of Deferred Taxes." This standard requires entities to present deferred tax assets and deferred tax liabilities to be classified as noncurrent in the balance sheet. The standard is effective for fiscal years and the interim periods within those fiscal years beginning after December 15, 2016. The guidance can be applied either prospectively or retrospectively. In the period that the ASU is adopted, an entity will need to disclose the nature of and the reason for the change in accounting principle. If the new guidance is applied prospectively, the entity should disclose that prior balance sheets were not retrospectively adjusted. If the new guidance is applied retrospectively, the entity will need to disclose the quantitative effects of the change on the prior balance sheets presented. Early adoption is permitted. We do not expect that the adoption of this authoritative guidance will have a material impact on our consolidated financial statements.

In September 2015, the FASB issued ASU 2015-16 "Business Combinations (Topic 805): Simplifying the Accounting for Measurement-Period Adjustments." This standard eliminates the requirement for an acquirer in a business combination to account for measurement-period adjustments retrospectively. The new standard requires an acquirer to recognize a measurement-period adjustment during the period in which it determines the amount of the adjustment. In addition, it requires the acquirer to record in the same period's financial statements, the effect on earnings of changes in depreciation, amortization, or other income effects, if any, as a result of the change to the provisional amounts as if the accounting had been completed at the acquisition date. This standard was effective prospectively for fiscal years beginning after December 15, 2015, and interim periods within those fiscal years. Early application is permitted. We have adopted the guidance of this standard prospectively during the quarter ended September 30, 2015 in connection with the accounting for measurement-period adjustments related to our acquisitions of Dun & Bradstreet Credibility Corp. ("DBCC") and NetProspex. The adoption of this authoritative guidance did not have a material impact on our consolidated financial statements. See Note 18 to the consolidated financial statements included in this Annual Report for further details on the acquisitions.

In August 2015, the FASB issued ASU 2015-15 "Interest-Imputation (Subtopic 835-30): Presentation and Subsequent Measurement of Debt Issuance Costs Associated with Line-of-Credit Arrangements." This standard incorporates into the Accounting Standards Codification ("ASC") the Securities and Exchange Commission's ("SEC") view on the presentation and subsequent measurement of debt issuance costs related to line-of-credit arrangements. The SEC staff announced that it would not object to an entity presenting the cost of securing a revolving line-of-credit as an asset, regardless of whether a balance is outstanding. The guidance in this ASU provides an alternative for presentation of these costs. This guidance retains the requirement to subsequently amortize the deferred debt issuance costs ratably over the term of the line-of-credit arrangement. We do not expect that the adoption of this authoritative guidance will have a material impact on our consolidated financial statements.

In July 2015, the FASB issued ASU 2015-12 "Plan Accounting: Defined Benefit Pension Plans (Topic 960), Defined Contribution Pension Plans (Topic 962) and Health and Welfare Benefit Plans (Topic 965): I. Fully Benefit-Responsive Investment Contracts; II. Plan Investment Disclosures; III. Measurement Date Practical Expedient." This three-part ASU simplifies current benefit plan accounting and requires (i) fully benefit-responsive investment contracts ("FBRICs") to be measured, presented, and disclosed only at contract value and accordingly removes the requirement to reconcile their contract value to fair value; (ii) benefit plans to disaggregate their investments measured using fair value by general type, either on the face of the financial statements or in the notes to the financial statements; (iii) the net appreciation or depreciation in investments for the period to be presented in the aggregate rather than by general type, and removes certain disclosure requirements relevant to individual investments that represent five percent or more of net assets available for benefits. Further, the amendments in this ASU eliminate the requirement to disclose the investment strategy for certain investments that are measured using Net Asset Value ("NAV") per share using the practical expedient in the FASB ASC Topic 820. Part III of the ASU provides a practical expedient to permit employee benefit plans to measure investments and investment-related accounts as of the month-end that is closest to the plan's fiscal year-end, when the fiscal period does not coincide with a month-end, while requiring certain additional disclosures. The amendments in Parts I and II of this standard were effective retrospectively for fiscal years beginning after December 15, 2015. The amendments in Part III of this standard were effective prospectively for fiscal years beginning after December 15, 2015. Early application for all amendments is permitted. We do not expect that the adoption of this authoritative guidance will have a material impact on our consolidated financial statements.

In May 2015, the FASB issued ASU 2015-08 "Business Combinations (Topic 805): Pushdown Accounting—Amendments to SEC Paragraphs Pursuant to Staff Accounting Bulletin No. 115." This standard removes the Securities and Exchange Commission's guidance on pushdown accounting from the FASB ASC, and conforms it with ASU 2014-17 "Business Combinations (Topic 805): Pushdown Accounting (a Consensus of the FASB Emerging Issues Task Force)." This standard became effective upon issuance as it relates to new change-in-control events or to the most recent change-in-control events consistent with ASU 2014-17. The adoption of the amendments in this guidance did not have a material impact on our consolidated financial statements.

In May 2015, the FASB issued ASU 2015-07 "Fair Value Measurement (Topic 820): Disclosures for Investments in Certain Entities that Calculate Net Asset Value per Share (or its Equivalent)." This standard removes the requirement to categorize within the fair value hierarchy all investments for which fair value is measured using the NAV per share practical expedient. In addition, this standard eliminates the requirement to make certain disclosures for all investments that are eligible to be measured at fair value using the NAV per share practical expedient, and instead limits the disclosure to those investments for which the entity has elected to measure fair value using the NAV practical expedient. The new standard retains the existing requirement to disclose information related to the nature and risks of investments for which fair value is measured using the NAV per share practical expedient and requires expanded disclosures. The standard was effective for fiscal years and the interim periods within those fiscal years beginning on or after December 15, 2015. The guidance should be applied retrospectively to all periods presented. Early adoption is permitted. We have adopted the guidance of this standard retrospectively during the second quarter ended June 30, 2015. The adoption of this authoritative guidance did not have a material impact on our consolidated financial statements.

In April 2015, the FASB issued ASU 2015-05 "Intangibles—Goodwill and Other—Internal-Use Software (Subtopic 350-40): Customer's Accounting for Fees Paid in a Cloud Computing Arrangement." This standard provides guidance to assist an entity in evaluating the accounting for fees paid by a customer in a cloud computing arrangement. Specifically, the amendments in this update provide guidance to customers related to whether a cloud computing arrangement includes a software license. If the cloud computing arrangement includes a software license, the guidance requires that the customer account for the software license element of the arrangement in a manner consistent with the acquisition of other software licenses. Where the arrangement does not include a software license, the guidance requires the customer to account for the arrangement as a service contract. The amendments in this update apply only to internal-use software that a customer obtains access to in a hosting arrangement if certain criteria are met. The new standard supersedes certain guidance in ASC

350-40 "Internal-Use Software" which will require the accounting for all software licenses within the scope of such guidance to be consistent with the accounting for other licenses of intangible assets. The standard was effective for fiscal years and the interim periods within those fiscal years beginning on or after December 15, 2015. The guidance may be applied (i) prospectively to all arrangements entered into or materially modified after the effective date, or (ii) retrospectively. The standard requires additional disclosures under each method of adoption. Early adoption is permitted. We do not expect that the adoption of this authoritative guidance will have a material impact on our consolidated financial statements.

In April 2015, the FASB issued ASU 2015-03 "Interest—Imputation of Interest (Subtopic 835-30): Simplifying the Presentation of Debt Issuance Costs." The new standard requires debt issuance costs related to a recognized debt liability to be presented in the balance sheet as a direct deduction from the carrying amount of that debt liability in a manner consistent with the treatment for debt discounts. The amendments in this update do not affect the recognition and measurement guidance for debt issuance costs. In addition, the ASU requires that the amortization of debt issuance costs be reported as interest expense. The standard was effective for fiscal years and the interim periods within those fiscal years beginning on or after December 15, 2015. The guidance should be applied retrospectively to all prior periods presented in the financial statements, subject to the disclosure requirements for a change in an accounting principle. Early adoption is permitted for financial statements that have not been previously issued. We do not expect that the adoption of this authoritative guidance will have a material impact on our consolidated financial statements.

In January 2015, the FASB issued ASU 2015-01 "Income Statement Extraordinary and Unusual Items (Subtopic 225-20): Simplifying Income Statement Presentation by Eliminating the Concept of Extraordinary Items." This standard eliminates such concept from existing GAAP. Under the new guidance an entity is no longer required to: (i) segregate an extraordinary item from the results of ordinary operations; (ii) separately present an extraordinary item on its income statement, net of tax, after income from continuing operations; and (iii) disclose income taxes and earnings-per share data applicable to an extraordinary item. The new standard retains the existing requirement to separately present on a pre-tax basis within income from continuing operations items that are of an unusual nature or occur infrequently. Additionally, the new standard requires similar separate presentation of items that are both unusual and infrequent in nature. The standard was effective for fiscal years and the interim periods within those fiscal years beginning on or after December 15, 2015. The guidance may be applied prospectively or retrospectively to all prior periods presented in the financial statements, with additional disclosures for entities electing prospective application. Early application is permitted as of the beginning of the fiscal year of adoption. We do not expect that the adoption of this authoritative guidance will have a material impact on our consolidated financial statements.

In November 2014, the FASB issued ASU 2014-17 "Business Combinations (Topic 805): Pushdown Accounting (a Consensus of the FASB Emerging Issues Task Force)." This standard provides an acquired business the option to apply pushdown accounting in its separate financial statements upon a change-in-control event. Concurrently, the SEC eliminated its guidance under SAB Topic 5 .J. "New Basis of Accounting Required in Certain Circumstances" which had required or precluded pushdown accounting based on the percentage of ownership. The standard became effective upon issuance for new change-in-control events or to the most recent change-in-control event. An acquiree may elect to apply pushdown accounting retrospectively, as a change in accounting principle, for its most recent change-in-control event for which it did not previously apply pushdown accounting. The new standard requires the acquiree to provide certain disclosures upon election of pushdown accounting consistent with those required under the guidance for business combinations. The adoption of this authoritative guidance did not have a material impact on our consolidated financial statements.

In May 2014, the FASB issued ASU No. 2014-09, "Revenue from Contracts with Customers (Topic 606)," which outlines a single comprehensive model to use in accounting for revenue arising from contracts with customers and supersedes and replaces nearly all existing GAAP revenue recognition guidance, including industry-specific guidance. The authoritative guidance provides a five-step analysis of transactions to determine when and how revenue is recognized. The five steps are: (i) identify the contract with the customer; (ii) identify the performance obligations in the contract; (iii) determine the transaction price; (iv) allocate the transaction price to the performance obligations; and (v) recognize revenue when or as each performance obligation is satisfied. The authoritative guidance applies to all contracts with customers except those that are within the scope of other topics in the FASB ASC. The authoritative guidance requires significantly expanded disclosures about revenue recognition and was initially effective for fiscal years and the interim periods within these fiscal years beginning on or after December 15, 2016. In August 2015, the FASB issued ASU 2015-14 "Revenue from Contracts with Customers (Topic 606): Deferral of the Effective Date." This standard defers for one year the effective date of ASU 2014-09. The deferral will result in this standard being effective for fiscal years and interim periods within those fiscal years beginning after December 15, 2017. Earlier application is permitted only as of annual reporting periods beginning after December 15, 2016 including interim reporting periods within that reporting period. We are currently assessing the impact of the adoption of this authoritative guidance on our consolidated financial statements.

In April 2014, the FASB issued ASU No. 2014-08, "Presentation of Financial Statements (Topic 205) and Property, Plant, and Equipment (Topic 360): Reporting Discontinued Operations and Disclosures of Disposals of Components of an Entity," which changes the requirements for reporting discontinued operations by limiting it to disposals representing a strategic shift that has or will have a major effect on the entity's operations and financial results. An entity is now required to: (i) present the assets and liabilities of a disposal group that includes a discontinued operation separately in the statement of financial position; and (ii) expand disclosures about the discontinued operations. The authoritative guidance was effective for fiscal years and the interim periods within those fiscal years beginning on or after December 15, 2014 and should be applied on a prospective basis. We adopted the provisions of this guidance in connection with the reporting and disclosure requirements related to the divestiture of our business in Australia and New Zealand. See Note 17 to the consolidated financial statements included in this Annual Report for further details on the divestiture.

MARKET RISK INFORMATION

1.25 PRUDENTIAL FINANCIAL, INC. (DEC)
QUANTITATIVE AND QUALITATIVE DISCLOSURES ABOUT MARKET RISK

Market Risk

Market risk is defined as the risk of loss from changes in interest rates, equity prices and foreign currency exchange rates resulting from asset/liability mismatches where the change in the value of our liabilities is not offset by the change in value of our assets.

For additional information regarding the potential impacts of interest rate and other market fluctuations, as well as general economic and market conditions on our businesses and profitability, see Item 1A. "Risk Factors" above. For additional information regarding the overall management of our general account investments and our asset mix strategies, see "Management's Discussion and Analysis of Financial Condition and Results of Operations—General Account Investments—Management of Investments" above. For additional information regarding our liquidity and capital resources, which may be impacted by changing market risks, see "Management's Discussion and Analysis of Financial Condition and Results of Operations—Liquidity and Capital Resources" above.

Market Risk Management

Management of market risk, which we consider to be a combination of both investment risk and market risk exposures as described in "Management's Discussion and Analysis of Financial Condition and Results of Operations—Risk Management" above, includes the identification and measurement of various forms of risk, the establishment of risk thresholds and the creation of processes intended to maintain risks within these thresholds while optimizing returns on the underlying assets or liabilities. Risk range limits are established for each type of market risk and are approved by the Investment Committee of the Board of Directors and subject to ongoing review.

Our risk management process utilizes a variety of tools and techniques, including:
- Measures of price sensitivity to market changes (e.g., interest rates, equity index prices, foreign exchange);
- Asset/liability mismatch analytics;
- Stress scenario testing;
- Hedging programs; and
- Risk management governance, including policies, limits, and a committee that oversees investment and market risk. For additional information regarding our overall risk management framework and governance structure, see "Management's Discussion and Analysis of Financial Condition and Results of Operations—Risk Management" above.

Market Risk Mitigation

Risk mitigation takes three primary forms:
- Asset/Liability Management: Managing assets to liability-based measures. For example, investment policies identify target durations for assets based on liability characteristics and asset portfolios are managed to within ranges around them. This mitigates potential unanticipated economic losses from interest rate movements.
- Hedging non-strategic exposures. For example, our investment policies for our general account portfolios generally require hedging currency risk for cash flows not offset by similarly denominated liabilities.
- Management of portfolio concentration risk. For example, ongoing monitoring and management at the enterprise level of key rate, currency and other concentration risks support diversification efforts to mitigate exposure to individual markets and sources of risk.

Market Risk Related to Interest Rates

We perform liability-driven investing and engage in careful asset/liability management. Asset/liability mismatches create the risk that changes in liability values will differ from the changes in the value of the related assets. Additionally, changes in interest rates may impact other items including, but not limited to, the following:
- Net investment spread between the amounts that we are required to pay and the rate of return we are able to earn on investments for certain products supported by general account investments;

- Asset-based fees earned on assets under management or contractholder account values;
- Estimated total gross profits and the amortization of deferred policy acquisition and other costs;
- Net exposure to the guarantees provided under certain products; and
- Capital levels of our regulated entities.

We use duration and convexity analyses to measure price sensitivity to interest rate changes. Duration measures the relative sensitivity of the fair value of a financial instrument to changes in interest rates. Convexity measures the rate of change of duration with respect to changes in interest rates. We use asset/liability management and derivative strategies to manage our interest rate exposure by legal entity by matching the relative sensitivity of asset and liability values to interest rate changes, or controlling "duration mismatch" of assets and liabilities. We have duration mismatch constraints tailored to the rate sensitivity of products in each entity. In certain markets, primarily outside the U.S. and Japan, capital market limitations that hinder our ability to acquire assets that approximate the duration of some of our liabilities are considered in setting the limits. As of December 31, 2015 and 2014, the difference between the duration of assets and the target duration of liabilities in our duration-managed portfolios was within our policy limits. We consider risk-based capital and tax implications as well as current market conditions in our asset/liability management strategies.

We assess the impact of interest rate movements on the value of our financial assets, financial liabilities and derivatives using hypothetical test scenarios that assume either upward or downward 100 basis point parallel shifts in the yield curve from prevailing interest rates, reflecting changes in either credit spreads or the risk-free rate. The following table sets forth the net estimated potential loss in fair value on these financial instruments from a hypothetical 100 basis point upward shift as of December 31, 2015 and 2014. This table is presented on a gross basis and excludes offsetting impacts to insurance liabilities that are not considered financial liabilities under U.S. GAAP. This scenario results in the greatest net exposure to interest rate risk of the hypothetical scenarios tested at those dates. While the test scenario is for illustrative purposes only and does not reflect our expectations regarding future interest rates or the performance of fixed income markets, it is a near-term, reasonably possible hypothetical change that illustrates the potential impact of such events. These test scenarios do not measure the changes in value that could result from non-parallel shifts in the yield curve which we would expect to produce different changes in discount rates for different maturities. As a result, the actual loss in fair value from a 100 basis point change in interest rates could be different from that indicated by these calculations. The estimated changes in fair values do not include separate account assets.

	As of December 31, 2015			As of December 31, 2014		
(In millions)	Notional	Fair Value	Hypothetical Change in Fair Value	Notional	Fair Value	Hypothetical Change in Fair Value
Financial assets with interest rate risk:						
Fixed maturities[1]		$322,207	$(27,832)		$328,942	$(27,812)
Commercial mortgage and other loans		51,853	(2,369)		49,097	(2,176)
Derivatives with interest rate risk:						
Swaps	$219,511	8,423	(5,960)	$224,345	6,316	(5,690)
Futures	28,538	10	(131)	32,357	6	102
Options	89,107	232	(868)	85,354	952	(337)
Forwards	17,809	204	(5)	22,517	(165)	(27)
Synthetic GICs	72,585	7	0	74,707	6	0
Variable annuity and other living benefit feature embedded derivatives[2]		(8,434)	5,072		(8,182)	5,560
Financial liabilities with interest rate risk[3]:						
Short-term and long-term debt		(22,522)	3,214		(25,974)	3,039
Limited recourse notes issued by consolidated VIEs[4]		0	0		(18)	0
Policyholders' account balances—investment contracts		(94,271)	3,302		(96,375)	3,480
Net estimated potential loss			$(25,577)			$(23,861)

[1] Includes fixed maturities classified as "trading account assets supporting insurance liabilities" and other fixed maturities classified as trading securities under U.S. GAAP, but are held for "other than trading" activities in our segments that offer insurance, retirement and annuities products.

[2] Excludes any offsetting impact of derivative instruments purchased to hedge changes in the embedded derivatives. Amounts reported net of third-party reinsurance.

[3] Excludes approximately $267 billion and $259 billion as of December 31, 2015 and 2014, respectively, of insurance reserve and deposit liabilities which are not considered financial liabilities. We believe that the interest rate sensitivities of these insurance liabilities would serve as an offset to the net interest rate risk of the financial assets and liabilities, including investment contracts.

[4] See Note 5 to the Consolidated Financial Statements for additional information regarding consolidated VIEs.

Under U.S. GAAP, the fair value of the embedded derivatives for certain variable annuity and other living benefit features, reflected in the table above, includes the impact of the market's perception of our own NPR. The additional credit spread over LIBOR rates incorporated into the discount rate as of December 31, 2015, to reflect NPR in the valuation of these embedded derivatives, ranged from 6 to 176 basis points.

The following table provides a demonstration of the sensitivity of these embedded derivatives to our NPR credit spread by quantifying the adjustments that would be required assuming both a 50 basis point parallel increase and decrease in our NPR credit spreads. While the information below is for illustrative purposes only and does not reflect our expectations regarding our credit spreads, it is a near-term, reasonably possible change that illustrates the potential impact of such a change. This information considers only the direct effect of changes in our credit spread on operating results due to the change in these embedded derivatives, and not changes in any other assumptions such as persistency, utilization and mortality, or the effect of these changes on DAC or other balances.

	December 31, 2015	December 31, 2014
(In millions)	(Increase)/Decrease in Embedded Derivative Liability	(Increase)/Decrease in Embedded Derivative Liability
Increase in credit spread by 50 basis points	$ 1,714	$ 1,814
Decrease in credit spread by 50 basis points	$(2,047)	$(2,203)

For an additional discussion of our variable annuity optional living benefit guarantees accounted for as embedded derivatives and related derivatives used to hedge the changes in fair value of these embedded derivatives, see "Market Risk Related to Certain Variable Annuity Products" below. For additional information about the key estimates and assumptions used in our determination of fair value, see Note 20 to the Consolidated Financial Statements below. For information on the impacts of a sustained low interest rate environment, see "Management's Discussion and Analysis of Financial Condition and Results of Operations—Executive Summary—Impact of a Low Interest Rate Environment" above.

Market Risk Related to Equity Prices

We have exposure to equity risk through asset/liability mismatches, including our investments in equity securities held in our general account investment portfolio and unhedged exposure in our insurance liabilities, principally related to certain variable annuity living benefit feature embedded derivatives. Our equity-based derivatives primarily hedge the equity risk embedded in these living benefit feature embedded derivatives, and are also part of our capital hedging program. Changes in equity prices create risk that the resulting changes in asset values will differ from the changes in the value of the liabilities relating to the underlying or hedged products. Additionally, changes in equity prices may impact other items including, but not limited to, the following:
- Asset-based fees earned on assets under management or contractholder account value;
- Estimated total gross profits and the amortization of deferred policy acquisition and other costs; and
- Net exposure to the guarantees provided under certain products.

We manage equity risk against benchmarks in respective markets. We benchmark our return on equity holdings against a blend of market indices, mainly the S&P 500 and Russell 2000 for U.S. equities. We benchmark foreign equities against the Tokyo Price Index, and the MSCI EAFE, a market index of European, Australian, and Far Eastern equities. We target price sensitivities that approximate those of the benchmark indices.

We estimate our equity risk from a hypothetical 10% decline in equity benchmark market levels. The following table sets forth the net estimated potential loss in fair value from such a decline as of December 31, 2015 and 2014. While these scenarios are for illustrative purposes only and do not reflect our expectations regarding future performance of equity markets or of our equity portfolio, they represent near-term reasonably possible hypothetical changes that illustrate the potential impact of such events. These scenarios consider only the direct impact on fair value of declines in equity benchmark market levels and not changes in asset-based fees recognized as revenue, changes in our estimates of total gross profits used as a basis for amortizing deferred policy acquisition and other costs, or changes in any other assumptions such as market volatility or mortality, utilization or persistency rates in our variable annuity contracts that could also impact the fair value of our living benefit features. In addition, these scenarios do not reflect the impact of basis risk, such as potential differences in the performance of the investment funds underlying the variable annuity products relative to the market indices we use as a basis for developing our hedging strategy. The impact of basis risk could result in larger differences between the change in fair value of the equity-based derivatives and the related living benefit features in comparison to these scenarios. In calculating these amounts, we exclude separate account equity securities.

	As of December 31, 2015			As of December 31, 2014		
(In millions)	Notional	Fair Value	Hypothetical Change in Fair Value	Notional	Fair Value	Hypothetical Change in Fair Value
Equity securities[1]		$11,626	$(1,163)		$12,152	$(1,215)
Equity-based derivatives[2]	$68,011	(38)	1,917	$73,138	69	1,617
Variable annuity and other living benefit feature embedded derivatives[2][3]		(8,434)	(1,355)		(8,182)	(1,193)
Net estimated potential loss			$ (601)			$ (791)

[1] Includes equity securities classified as "trading account assets supporting insurance liabilities" and other equity securities classified as trading securities under U.S. GAAP, but are held for "other than trading" activities in our segments that offer insurance, retirement and annuities products.
[2] The notional and fair value of equity-based derivatives and the fair value of variable annuity and other living benefit feature embedded derivatives are also reflected in amounts under "Market Risk Related to Interest Rates" above, and are not cumulative.
[3] Excludes any offsetting impact of derivative instruments purchased to hedge changes in the embedded derivatives. Amounts reported net of third-party reinsurance.

Market Risk Related to Foreign Currency Exchange Rates

As a U.S.-based company with significant business operations outside of the U.S., particularly in Japan, we are exposed to foreign currency exchange rate risk related to these operations, as well as in our general account investment portfolio and other proprietary investment portfolios.

For our international insurance operations, changes in foreign currency exchange rates create risk that we may experience volatility in the U.S. dollar-equivalent earnings and equity of these operations. We actively manage this risk through various hedging strategies, including the use of foreign currency hedges and through holding U.S. dollar-denominated securities in the investment portfolios of certain of these operations. Additionally, our Japanese insurance operations offer a variety of non-yen denominated products which are supported by investments in corresponding currencies. While these non-yen denominated assets are economically matched, the accounting may differ for changes in the value of these assets and liabilities due to moves in foreign currency exchange rates, resulting in volatility in reported U.S. GAAP earnings. Beginning in 2015 we have mitigated this volatility through the implementation of a new structure in Gibraltar Life that disaggregated the U.S. and Australian dollar-denominated businesses into separate divisions, each with its own functional currency that aligns with the underlying products and investments. For certain of our international insurance operations outside of Japan, we elect to not hedge the risk of changes in our equity investments due to foreign exchange rate movements. For further information, see "Management's Discussion and Analysis of Financial Condition and Results of Operations—International Insurance Division—Impact of foreign currency exchange rate movements on earnings—U.S. GAAP earnings impact of products denominated in non-local currencies" above.

For our domestic general account investment portfolios supporting our U.S. insurance operations and other proprietary investment portfolios, our foreign currency exchange rate risk arises primarily from investments that are denominated in foreign currencies. We manage this risk by hedging substantially all domestic foreign currency denominated fixed income investments into U.S. dollars. We generally do not hedge all of the foreign currency risk of our investments in equity securities of unaffiliated foreign entities.

We manage our foreign currency exchange rate risks within specified policy limits, and estimate our exposure, excluding equity in our Japanese insurance operations, to a hypothetical 10% change in foreign currency exchange rates. The following table sets forth the net estimated potential loss in fair value from such a change as of December 31, 2015 and 2014. While these scenarios are for illustrative purposes only and do not reflect our expectations regarding future changes in foreign exchange markets, they represent reasonably possible near-term hypothetical changes that illustrate the potential impact of such events.

| | As of December 31, 2015 | | As of December 31, 2014 | |
| | Fair Value | Hypothetical Change in Fair Value | Fair Value | Hypothetical Change in Fair Value |
(In millions)				
Unhedged portion of equity investment in international subsidiaries and foreign currency denominated investments in domestic general account portfolio	$3,934	$(393)	$4,726	$(473)

For additional information, see "Management's Discussion and Analysis of Financial Condition and Results of Operations—General Account Investments—Portfolio Composition" and "Management's Discussion and Analysis of Financial Condition and Results of Operations—Results of Operations by Segment—International Insurance Division" above.

Derivatives

We use derivative financial instruments primarily to reduce market risk from changes in interest rates, equity prices and foreign currency exchange rates, including their use to alter interest rate or foreign currency exposures arising from mismatches between assets and liabilities. Our derivatives primarily include swaps, futures, options and forward contracts that are exchange-traded or contracted in the OTC market.

Our derivatives also include interest rate guarantees we provide on our synthetic Guaranteed Investment Contract ("GIC") products. Synthetic GICs simulate the performance of traditional insurance-related GICs but are accounted for as derivatives under U.S. GAAP due to the fact that the policyholders own the underlying assets, and we only provide a book value "wrap" on the customers' funds, which are held in a client-owned trust. Since these wraps provide payment of guaranteed principal and interest to the customer, changes in interest rates create risk that declines in the market value of customers' funds would increase our net exposure to these guarantees; however, our obligation is limited to payments that are in excess of the existing customers' fund value. Additionally, we have the ability to periodically reset crediting rates, subject to a 0% minimum floor, as well as the ability to increase prices. Further, our contract provisions provide that, although participants may withdraw funds at book value, contractholder withdrawals may only occur at market value immediately, or at book value over time. These factors, among others, result in these contracts experiencing minimal changes in fair value, despite a more significant notional value.

Our derivatives also include those that are embedded in certain financial instruments, and primarily relate to certain optional living benefit features associated with our variable annuity products, as discussed in more detail in "Market Risk Related to Certain Variable Annuity Products" below. For additional information on our derivative activities, see Note 21 to the Consolidated Financial Statements below.

Market Risk Related to Certain Variable Annuity Products

The primary risk exposures of our variable annuity contracts relate to actual deviations from, or changes to, the assumptions used in the original pricing of these products, including capital markets assumptions, such as equity market returns, interest rates and market volatility and actuarial assumptions. For our capital markets assumptions, we manage our exposure to the risk created by capital markets fluctuations through a combination of product design elements, such as an automatic rebalancing element and inclusion of certain optional living benefits in our living benefits hedging program. In addition, we consider external reinsurance a form of risk mitigation. Certain variable annuity optional living benefit features are accounted for as an embedded derivative and recorded at fair value. The market risk sensitivities associated with U.S. GAAP values of both the embedded derivatives and the related derivatives used to hedge the changes in fair value of these embedded derivatives are provided under "Market Risk Related to Interest Rates" and "Market Risk Related to Equity Prices" above.

For additional information regarding our risk management strategies, including our living benefit hedging program and other product design elements, see "Management's Discussion and Analysis of Financial Condition and Results of Operations—Results of Operations by Segment—Individual Annuities" above.

CRITICAL ACCOUNTING POLICIES AND ESTIMATES

1.26 CA, INC. (MAR)
MANAGEMENT'S DISCUSSION AND ANALYSIS OF FINANCIAL CONDITION AND RESULTS OF OPERATIONS (in part)

Critical Accounting Policies and Estimates

We review our financial reporting and disclosure practices and accounting policies quarterly to help ensure that they provide accurate and transparent information relative to the current economic and business environment. Note 1, "Significant Accounting Policies" in the Notes to the Consolidated Financial Statements contains a summary of the significant accounting policies that we use. Many of these accounting policies involve complex situations and require a high degree of judgment, either in the application and interpretation of existing accounting literature or in the development of estimates that affect our financial statements. On an ongoing basis, we evaluate our estimates and judgments based on historical experience as well as other factors that we believe to be reasonable under the circumstances. These estimates may change in the future if underlying assumptions or factors change.

We consider the following significant accounting policies to be critical because of their complexity and the high degree of judgment involved in implementing them.

Revenue Recognition

We generate revenue from the following primary sources: (1) licensing software products, including SaaS license agreements; (2) providing customer technical support (referred to as maintenance); and (3) providing professional services, such as product implementation, consulting, customer education and customer training.

Software license agreements under our subscription model include the right to receive and use unspecified future software products for no additional fee during the term of the agreement. We are required under generally accepted accounting principles (GAAP) to recognize revenue from these subscription licenses ratably over the term of the agreement. These amounts are recorded as subscription and maintenance revenue.

We also license our software products without the right to unspecified future software products. Revenue from these arrangements is either recognized at the inception of the license agreement (up-front basis) or ratably over the term of any maintenance agreement that is bundled with the license. Revenue is recognized up-front only when we have established VSOE for all of the undelivered elements of the agreement. We use the residual method to determine the amount of license revenue to be recognized up-front. The residual method allocates arrangement consideration to the undelivered elements based upon VSOE of the fair value of those elements, with the residual of the arrangement consideration allocated to the license. The portion allocated to the license is recognized "up-front" once all four of the revenue recognition criteria are met as described below. We establish VSOE of the fair value of maintenance from either contractually stated renewal rates or using the bell-shaped curve method. VSOE of the fair value of professional services is established using the bell-shaped curve method based on hourly rates when sold on a stand-alone basis. Up-front revenue is recorded as Software Fees and Other. Revenue recognized on an up-front model will result in higher total revenue in a reporting period than if that revenue was recognized ratably.

If VSOE does not exist for all undelivered elements of an arrangement, we recognize total revenue from the arrangement ratably over the term of the maintenance agreement. Revenue recognized ratably is recorded as "Subscription and maintenance revenue."

Revenue recognition does not commence until (1) we have evidence of an arrangement with a customer; (2) we deliver the specified products; (3) license agreement terms are fixed or determinable and free of contingencies or uncertainties that may alter the agreement such that it may not be complete and final; and (4) collection is probable. Revenue from sales to distributors and volume partners, value-added resellers and exclusive representatives commences, either on an up-front basis or ratably as described above, when these entities sell the software product to their customers. This is commonly referred to as the sell-through method.

Revenue from professional services arrangements is generally recognized as the services are performed. Revenue and costs from committed professional services that are sold as part of a software license agreement are deferred and recognized on a ratable basis over the life of the related software transaction.

In the event that agreements with our customers are executed in close proximity of other license agreements with the same customer, we evaluate whether the separate arrangements are linked, and, if so, they are considered a single multi-element arrangement for which revenue is recognized ratably as "Subscription and maintenance revenue" in the Consolidated Statements of Operations. In the case of a professional services arrangement that is linked to a subscription-based software license arrangement, revenue is recognized as "Professional services" for its respective portion, in the Consolidated Statements of Operations.

We have an established business practice of offering installment payment options to customers and a history of successfully collecting substantially all amounts due under those agreements. We assess collectability based on a number of factors, including past transaction history with the customer and the creditworthiness of the customer. If, in our judgment, collection of a fee is not probable, we will not recognize revenue until the uncertainty is removed through the receipt of cash payment. We do not typically offer installment payments for perpetual license agreements that are recognized up-front, within "Software fees and other."

See Note 1, "Significant Accounting Policies" for additional information on our revenue recognition policy.

Accounts Receivable

The allowance for doubtful accounts is a reserve for the impairment of accounts receivable on the Consolidated Balance Sheets. In developing the estimate for the allowance for doubtful accounts, we rely on several factors, including:
- Historical information, such as general collection history of multi-year software agreements;
- Current customer information and events, such as extended delinquency, requests for restructuring and filings for bankruptcy;
- Results of analyzing historical and current data; and
- The overall macroeconomic environment.

The allowance includes two components: (1) specifically identified receivables that are reviewed for impairment when, based on current information, we do not expect to collect the full amount due from the customer; and (2) an allowance for losses inherent in the remaining receivable portfolio based on historical activity.

Income Taxes

We account for income taxes under the asset and liability method. We recognize deferred tax assets and liabilities for the future tax consequences attributable to differences between the financial statement carrying amounts of existing assets and liabilities and their respective tax bases, along with net operating losses and tax credit carryforwards. We measure deferred tax assets and liabilities using enacted tax rates expected to apply to taxable income in the years in which those temporary differences are expected to be recovered or settled. We recognize the effect on deferred tax assets and liabilities of a change in tax rates on income in the period that includes the enactment date.

We recognize the effect of income tax positions only if those positions are more likely than not of being sustained. We reflect changes in recognition or measurement in a period in which the change in judgment occurs. We record interest and penalties related to uncertain tax positions in income tax expense.

Goodwill, Capitalized Software Products, and Other Intangible Assets

Goodwill represents the excess of the purchase price over the fair value of net assets acquired in connection with business combinations accounted for using the purchase method of accounting. Goodwill is not amortized, but instead goodwill is required to be tested for impairment annually and under certain circumstances. We review goodwill for impairment on an annual basis on the first day of the fourth quarter of each fiscal year, and on an interim basis whenever events or changes in circumstances indicate that the carrying value may not be recoverable, at the reporting unit level. Our reporting units are the same as our operating segments.

When evaluating goodwill for impairment, based upon our annual test or due to changes in circumstances described above, we first can opt to perform a qualitative assessment to determine if the fair value of a reporting unit is more likely than not (*i.e.*, a likelihood of more than 50 percent) less than the reporting unit's carrying amount, including goodwill, or we can directly perform the two-step impairment test. This qualitative assessment includes, among other things, consideration of: (i) identifying inputs and assumptions that most affect fair value; (ii) identifying relevant events and circumstances that may have an impact on those inputs and assumptions; (iii) weighing the events and circumstances; and (iv) concluding on the totality of events and circumstances. If this assessment indicates that the fair value of the reporting unit exceeds the carrying value of the net assets assigned to that unit, goodwill is not considered impaired and we are not required to perform further testing. However, if the fair value of a reporting unit is more likely than not to be less than its carrying amount, the two-step impairment test will be performed.

When performing the two-step impairment test, we first determine the estimated fair value of our reporting units based on use of the income and market approaches. Under the income approach, we calculate the estimated fair value of a reporting unit based on the present value of estimated future cash flows. If the carrying value of the reporting unit exceeds the estimated fair value, we then calculate the implied fair value of goodwill for the reporting unit and compare it to the carrying amount of goodwill for the reporting unit. If the carrying amount of goodwill exceeds the implied fair value, an impairment charge is recorded to our statement of operations to reduce the carrying value to implied value.

Significant judgments and estimates are required in determining the reporting units and assessing the fair value of the reporting units. These estimates and assumptions are complex and subject to a significant degree of judgment with respect to certain factors including, but not limited to, revenue growth rates and operating profit margins that are used to project future cash flows, discount rates, future economic and market conditions and determination of appropriate market comparables. We make certain judgments and assumptions in allocating shared costs among reporting units. We base our fair value estimates on assumptions that are consistent with information used by the business for planning purposes and that we believe to be reasonable; however, actual future results may differ from those estimates. Changes in judgments on any of these factors could materially affect the value of the reporting unit.

Based on our qualitative impairment analysis performed for fiscal 2015, we determined that it was more likely than not that there was no impairment of any of our reporting units and that the estimated fair value of each of our reporting units exceeded the carrying amount of the unit by more than 10% of the carrying amount.

The carrying values of purchased software, internally developed software and other intangible assets are reviewed for recoverability on a quarterly basis. The facts and circumstances considered include an assessment of the net realizable value for capitalized software products and the recoverability of the cost of other intangible assets from future cash flows to be derived from the use of the asset. It is not possible for us to predict the likelihood of any possible future impairments or, if such an impairment were to occur, the magnitude of any impairment.

Intangible assets with finite useful lives are subject to amortization over the expected period of economic benefit to us. We evaluate whether events or circumstances have occurred that warrant a revision to the remaining useful lives of intangible assets. In cases where a revision is deemed appropriate, the remaining carrying amounts of the intangible assets are amortized over the revised remaining useful life.

Accounting for Business Combinations

The allocation of the purchase price for acquisitions requires extensive use of accounting estimates and judgments to allocate the purchase price to the identifiable tangible and intangible assets acquired, including in-process research and development, and liabilities assumed based on their respective fair values.

Product Development and Enhancements

GAAP specifies that costs incurred internally in researching and developing a computer software product should be charged to expense until technological feasibility has been established for the product. Once technological feasibility is established, all software costs are capitalized until the product is available for general release to customers. Judgment is required in determining when technological feasibility of a product is established and assumptions are used that reflect our best estimates and is influenced by our product release strategies and software development methodologies. Annual amortization of capitalized software costs is the greater of the amount computed using the ratio that current gross revenues for a product bear to the total of current and anticipated future gross revenues for that product or the straight-line method over the remaining estimated economic life of the software product, generally estimated to be five years from the date the product became available for general release to customers. We amortize capitalized software costs using the straight-line method.

We expect that our product offerings and go-to-market strategy will continue to evolve in future periods to include solutions and product suites that may be delivered either on-premise or via SaaS or cloud platforms. We expect these product offerings will continue to become available to customers at more frequent intervals than our historical release cycles. We also expect a more extensive adoption of Agile development methodologies which are characterized by a more dynamic development process with more frequent revisions to a product release's features and functions as the software is being developed. These factors will result in our commencing capitalization much later in the development life cycle.

Accounting for Share-Based Compensation

We currently maintain several stock-based compensation plans. We use the Black-Scholes option-pricing model to compute the estimated fair value of certain share-based awards. The Black-Scholes model includes assumptions regarding dividend yields, expected volatility, expected lives, and risk-free interest rates. These assumptions reflect our best estimates, but these items involve uncertainties based on market and other conditions outside of our control. As a result, if other assumptions had been used, stock-based compensation expense could have been materially affected. Furthermore, if different assumptions are used in future periods, stock-based compensation expense could be materially affected in future years.

As described in Note 14, "Stock Plans," in the Notes to the Consolidated Financial Statements, performance share units (PSUs) are awards under the long-term incentive programs for senior executives where the number of shares or restricted shares, as applicable, ultimately received by the senior executives depends on our performance measured against specified targets and will be determined at the conclusion of the three-year or one-year period, as applicable. The fair value of each award is estimated on the date that the performance targets are established based on the fair value of our stock and our estimate of the level of achievement of our performance targets. We are required to recalculate the fair value of issued PSUs each reporting period until the underlying shares are granted. The adjustment is based on the quoted market price of our stock on the reporting period date. Each quarter, we compare the actual performance we expect to achieve with the performance targets.

Fair Value of Financial Instruments

The measurement of fair value for our financial instruments is based on the authoritative guidance which establishes a fair value hierarchy that is based on three levels of inputs and requires an entity to maximize the use of observable inputs and minimize the use of unobservable inputs when measuring fair value. See Note 10, "Fair Value Measurements," for additional information.

We are exposed to financial market risks arising from changes in interest rates and foreign exchange rates. Changes in interest rates could affect our monetary assets and liabilities, and foreign exchange rate changes could affect our foreign currency denominated monetary assets and liabilities and forecasted transactions. We enter into derivative contracts with the intent of mitigating a portion of these risks. See Note 9, "Derivatives," for additional information.

Legal Contingencies

We are currently involved in various legal proceedings and claims. Periodically, we review the status of each significant matter and assess our potential financial exposure. If the potential loss from any legal proceeding or claim is considered probable and the amount can be reasonably estimated, we accrue a liability for the estimated loss. Significant judgment is required in both the determination of the probability of a loss and the determination as to whether the amount of loss is reasonably estimable. Due to the uncertainties related to these matters, the decision to record an accrual and the amount of accruals recorded are based only on the information available at the time. As additional information becomes available, we reassess the potential liability related to our pending litigation and claims, and may revise our estimates. Any revisions could have a material effect on our results of operations. Refer to Note 11, "Commitments and Contingencies," in the Notes to the Consolidated Financial Statements for a description of our material legal proceedings.

SUMMARY OF SIGNIFICANT ACCOUNTING POLICIES

1.27 BARNES & NOBLE, INC. (APR)
NOTES TO CONSOLIDATED FINANCIAL STATEMENTS (in part)

(Thousands of dollars, except per share data)

1. Summary of Significant Accounting Policies

Business

Barnes & Noble, one of the nation's largest booksellers (based upon sales reported in trade publications and public filings), is a leading content, commerce and technology company providing customers easy and convenient access to trade books, textbooks, magazines, newspapers and other content across its multi-channel distribution platform. As of May 2, 2015, the Company operated 1,372 bookstores in 50 states, including 724 bookstores on college campuses, operates one of the Web's largest eCommerce sites, develops digital reading products and operates one of the largest digital bookstores. Given the dynamic nature of the book industry, the challenges faced by traditional booksellers, and the robust innovation pipeline fueling new opportunities in hardware, software and content creation and delivery, Barnes & Noble is utilizing the strength of its retail footprint to bolster its leadership in selling content to drive sales across its multiple channels.

Of the 1,372 bookstores, Barnes & Noble Retail (B&N Retail) operates 648 retail bookstores, primarily under the Barnes & Noble Booksellers® trade name, and includes the Company's eCommerce site. Barnes & Noble College Booksellers, LLC (B&N College) operates 724 college bookstores at colleges and universities across the United States, of which 154 stores are co-branded with the universities' names and Barnes & Noble name. B&N Retail also includes Sterling Publishing Co., Inc. (Sterling or Sterling Publishing), a leader in general trade book publishing. The NOOK segment represents the Company's digital business, offering digital books and magazines for sale and consumption online, NOOK® reading devices, co-branded NOOK® tablets and reading software for iOS, Android and Windows 8. (Any reference to NOOK® include the Company's Samsung Galaxy Tab® 4 NOOK® 7.0 and 10.1 devices and NOOK GlowLight TM, and each of which includes the trademark symbol [® or ™, as applicable] even if a trademark symbol is not included.)

The Company's principal business is the sale of trade books (generally hardcover and paperback consumer titles), mass market paperbacks (such as mystery, romance, science fiction and other popular fiction), children's books, eBooks and other digital content, textbooks and course-related materials, NOOK® and related accessories, bargain books, magazines, gifts, emblematic apparel and gifts, school and dorm supplies, café products and services, educational toys & games, music and movies direct to customers through its bookstores or on barnesandnoble.com. The Company also offers a textbook rental option to its customers, as well as digital textbooks and other course materials through a proprietary digital platform (Yuzu™). The Company offers its customers a full suite of textbook options—new, used, digital and rental.

The Company identifies its operating segments based on the way the business is managed (focusing on the financial information distributed) and the manner in which the chief operating decision maker interacts with other members of management. The Company has three operating segments: B&N Retail, B&N College and NOOK.

Separation of B&N Education, Inc.

On February 26, 2015, Barnes & Noble announced plans for the legal and structural separation of Barnes & Noble Education, Inc. (Barnes & Noble Education or B&N Education) (formerly known as NOOK Media Inc.) from Barnes & Noble into an independent public company (the Spin-Off).

This Spin-Off is expected to be executed by means of a pro-rata distribution of B&N Education's common stock to Barnes & Noble's existing shareholders and is expected to be a non-taxable event for Barnes & Noble and its shareholders.

The distribution of B&N Education's common stock to Barnes & Noble shareholders is conditioned on, among other things, final approval of the Spin-Off plan by the Barnes & Noble Board of Directors; the receipt of opinions from external legal counsel and KPMG LLP to Barnes & Noble, confirming the tax-free status of the Spin-Off for U.S. federal income tax purposes; and the United States Securities and Exchange Commission (SEC) declaring effective the Registration Statement, which was filed on a Registration Statement on Form S-1 with the SEC on February 26, 2015, which has been amended on April 29, 2015 and June 4, 2015.

History of B&N Education, Inc.

On September 30, 2009, Barnes & Noble acquired Barnes & Noble College Booksellers, LLC (B&N College) from Leonard and Louise Riggio. From that date until October 4, 2012, B&N College was wholly owned by Barnes & Noble Booksellers, Inc. B&N Education was initially incorporated under the name NOOK Media Inc. in July 2012 to hold Barnes & Noble's B&N College and NOOK digital businesses. On October 4, 2012, Microsoft Corporation (Microsoft) acquired a 17.6% non-controlling preferred membership interest in B&N Education's subsidiary B&N Education, LLC (formerly NOOK Media LLC) (the LLC), and through B&N Education, Barnes & Noble maintained an 82.4% controlling interest of the B&N College and NOOK digital businesses.

On January 22, 2013, Pearson Education, Inc. (Pearson) acquired a 5% non-controlling preferred membership interest in the LLC, entered into a commercial agreement with the LLC relating to the B&N College business and received warrants to purchase an additional preferred membership interest in the LLC.

On December 4, 2014, B&N Education re-acquired Microsoft's interest in the LLC in exchange for cash and common stock of Barnes & Noble and the Microsoft commercial agreement was terminated effective as of such date. On December 22, 2014, B&N Education also re-acquired Pearson's interest in the LLC and certain related warrants previously issued to Pearson. In connection with these transactions, Barnes & Noble entered into contingent payment agreements with Microsoft and Pearson providing for additional payments upon the occurrence of certain events, including upon a sale of the NOOK digital business. As a result of these transactions, Barnes & Noble owns, and will own prior to the Spin-Off, 100% of B&N Education.

On May 1, 2015, B&N Education distributed to Barnes & Noble all of the membership interests in B&N Education's NOOK digital business. As a result, B&N Education ceased to own any interest in the NOOK digital business, which will remain a wholly owned subsidiary of Barnes & Noble.

The Company expects that the completion of the potential separation of the Company's businesses could occur by the end of August 2015, although there can be no assurances regarding the timing of such potential separation or that such separation will be completed.

Consolidation

The consolidated financial statements include the accounts of Barnes & Noble, Inc. and its wholly and majority-owned subsidiaries. All significant intercompany accounts and transactions have been eliminated in consolidation.

Use of Estimates

In preparing financial statements in conformity with generally accepted accounting principles, the Company is required to make estimates and assumptions that affect the reported amounts of assets and liabilities and the disclosure of contingent assets and liabilities at the date of the financial statements and revenues and expenses during the reporting period. Actual results could differ from those estimates.

Cash and Cash Equivalents

The Company considers all short-term, highly liquid instruments purchased with an original maturity of three months or less to be cash equivalents.

Merchandise Inventories

Merchandise inventories, which primarily consist of finished goods, are stated at the lower of cost or market. Cost is determined primarily by the retail inventory method under both the first-in, first-out (FIFO) basis and the last-in, first-out (LIFO) basis. B&N College's textbook and trade book inventories are valued using the LIFO method, where the related reserve was not material to the recorded amount of the Company's inventories at May 2, 2015. There were no LIFO adjustments in fiscal 2015 compared to a favorable adjustment of $7,692 in fiscal 2014, respectively. NOOK merchandise inventories are recorded based on the average cost method.

Market is determined based on the estimated net realizable value, which is generally the selling price. Reserves for non-returnable inventory are based on the Company's history of liquidating non-returnable inventory.

The Company also estimates and accrues shortage for the period between the last physical count of inventory and the balance sheet date. Shortage rates are estimated and accrued based on historical rates and can be affected by changes in merchandise mix and changes in actual shortage trends.

Property and Equipment, and Other Long-Lived Assets

Property and equipment are carried at cost, less accumulated depreciation and amortization. For financial reporting purposes, depreciation is computed using the straight-line method over estimated useful lives. For tax purposes, different methods are used. Maintenance and repairs are expensed as incurred, while major maintenance and remodeling costs are capitalized if they extend the useful life of the asset. Leasehold improvements are capitalized and amortized over the shorter of their estimated useful lives or the terms of the respective leases. Fixtures and equipment are capitalized and amortized over the shorter of their estimated useful lives or 10 years. Capitalized lease acquisition costs are being amortized over the lease terms of the underlying leases. System costs are capitalized and included in property and equipment. These costs are depreciated over their estimated useful lives from the date the systems become operational. The Company had $449,292 and $490,713 of property and equipment, net of accumulated depreciation, at May 2, 2015 and May 3, 2014, respectively, and

$179,462, $198,972 and $205,708 of depreciation expense for fiscal 2015, fiscal 2014 and fiscal 2013, respectively. Capitalized software costs of $54,205 and $68,107 for fiscal 2015 and fiscal 2014, respectively, are included in property and equipment.

Other Long-Lived Assets

The Company's other long-lived assets include property and equipment and amortizable intangibles. The Company had $200,708 and $215,442 of amortizable intangible assets, net of amortization, at May 2, 2015 and May 3, 2014, respectively. The Company reviews its long-lived assets for impairment whenever events or changes in circumstances indicate that the carrying amount of an asset may not be recoverable and considers market participants in accordance with Accounting Standards Codification (ASC) 360-10, *Accounting for the Impairment or Disposal of Long-Lived Assets* (ASC 360-10). The Company evaluates long-lived assets for impairment at the individual Barnes & Noble store level, except for B&N College long-lived assets, which are evaluated for impairment at the school contract combined store level, which is the lowest level at which individual cash flows can be identified. When evaluating long-lived assets for potential impairment, the Company will first compare the carrying amount of the assets to the individual store's estimated future undiscounted cash flows. If the estimated future cash flows are less than the carrying amount of the assets, an impairment loss calculation is prepared. The impairment loss calculation compares the carrying amount of the assets to the individual store's fair value based on its estimated discounted future cash flows. If required, an impairment loss is recorded for that portion of the asset's carrying value in excess of fair value. Impairment losses included in selling and administrative expenses totaled $373, $32,390 and $4,168 during fiscal 2015, fiscal 2014 and fiscal 2013, respectively.

Goodwill and Unamortizable Intangible Assets

The costs in excess of net assets of businesses acquired are carried as goodwill in the accompanying consolidated balance sheets.

At May 2, 2015, the Company had $489,267 of goodwill and $313,134 of unamortizable intangible assets (those with an indefinite useful life), accounting for approximately 24.8% of the Company's total assets. ASC 350-30, *Goodwill and Other Intangible Assets*, requires that goodwill and other unamortizable intangible assets no longer be amortized, but instead be tested for impairment at least annually or earlier if there are impairment indicators. The Company performs a two-step process for impairment testing of goodwill as required by ASC 350-30. The first step of this test, used to identify potential impairment, compares the fair value of a reporting unit with its carrying amount. The second step (if necessary) measures the amount of the impairment. The Company completed its annual goodwill impairment test as of the first day of the third quarter of fiscal 2015. In performing the valuations, the Company used cash flows that reflected management's forecasts and discount rates that included risk adjustments consistent with the current market conditions. Based on the results of the Company's step one testing, the fair values of the B&N Retail, B&N College and NOOK reporting units as of that date exceeded their carrying values; therefore, the second step of the impairment test was not required to be performed and no goodwill impairment was recognized. Impairment losses included in selling and administrative expenses related to goodwill totaled $0, $0 and $20,278 during fiscal 2015, fiscal 2014 and fiscal 2013, respectively.

The Company tests unamortizable intangible assets by comparing the fair value and the carrying value of such assets. The Company also completed its annual impairment tests for its other unamortizable intangible assets by comparing the estimated fair value to the carrying value of such assets. Impairment losses included in selling and administrative expenses related to unamortizable intangible assets totaled $0, $1,602 and $0 during fiscal 2015, fiscal 2014 and fiscal 2013, respectively. Changes in market conditions, among other factors, could have a material impact on these estimates.

The impairments in fiscal 2014 related to certain publishing contracts. The publishing contracts include the value of long-standing relationships with authors, agents and publishers established upon the Company's acquisition of Sterling in 2003. Given Sterling's strong history of maintaining such relationships, the Company believes they produce value indefinitely without an identifiable remaining useful life. However, given the continued declines in the physical book business, certain of these contracts were impaired.

During the fourth quarter of 2013, the Company determined that goodwill impairment indicators arose in its NOOK reporting unit as recurring losses have led to revisions in its strategic plans. As a result, during the fourth quarter of fiscal 2013, the Company recorded a non-cash goodwill impairment charge of $18,332 in selling and administrative expenses, which represented all the goodwill in the NOOK reporting unit.

In fiscal 2013, the Company decided to shut down the operations of Tikatok. Tikatok was an online platform where parents and their children and others can write, illustrate and publish stories into hardcover and paperback books. This decision resulted in an impairment charge of $1,973, including the write-off of goodwill of $1,947 and intangible assets of $26 during the second quarter of fiscal 2013. The effect of Tikatok operations is not material to the overall results of the Company.

Deferred Charges

Costs incurred to obtain long-term financing are amortized over the terms of the respective debt agreements using the straight-line method, which approximates the interest method. Unamortized costs included in other noncurrent assets as of May 2, 2015 and May 3, 2014 were $5,371 and $10,897, respectively. Amortization expense included in interest and amortization of deferred financing fees was $5,477, $5,957 and $5,470 during fiscal 2015, fiscal 2014 and fiscal 2013, respectively.

Revenue Recognition

Revenue from sales of the Company's products is recognized at the time of sale or shipment, other than those with multiple elements and Free On Board (FOB) destination point shipping terms. Certain of the Company sales agreements with its distribution partners contain rights of inspection or acceptance provisions as is standard in the Company's industry. The Company accrues for estimated sales returns in the period in which the related revenue is recognized based on historical experience and industry standards. ECommerce revenue from sales of products ordered through the Company's websites is recognized upon delivery and receipt of the shipment by its customers. Sales taxes collected from retail customers are excluded from reported revenues. All of the Company's sales are recognized as revenue on a "net" basis, including sales in connection with any periodic promotions offered to customers. The Company does not treat any promotional offers as expenses.

In accordance with ASC No. 605-25, *Revenue Recognition, Multiple Element Arrangements* and Accounting Standards Updates (ASU) 2009-13 and 2009-14, for multiple-element arrangements that involve tangible products that contain software that is essential to the tangible product's functionality, undelivered software elements that relate to the tangible product's essential software and other separable elements, the Company allocates revenue to all deliverables using the relative selling-price method. Under this method, revenue is allocated at the time of sale to all deliverables based on their relative selling price using a specific hierarchy. The hierarchy is as follows: vendor-specific objective evidence, third-party evidence of selling price, or best estimate of selling price. NOOK® device revenue is recognized at the segment point of sale.

The Company includes post-service customer support (PCS) in the form of software updates and potential increased functionality on a when-and-if-available basis, as well as wireless access and wireless connectivity with the purchase of a NOOK® from the Company. Using the relative selling price described above, the Company allocates revenue based on the best estimate of selling price for the deliverables as no vendor-specific objective evidence or third-party evidence exists for any of the elements. Revenue allocated to NOOK® and the software essential to its functionality is recognized at the time of sale, provided all other conditions for revenue recognition are met. Revenue allocated to the PCS and the wireless access is deferred and recognized on a straight-line basis over the 2-year estimated life of a NOOK®.

The average percentage of a NOOK®'s sales price that is deferred for undelivered items and recognized over its 2-year estimated life ranges between 0% and 6%, depending on the type of device sold. The amount of NOOK®-related deferred revenue as of May 2, 2015 and May 3, 2014 was $2,406 and $9,934, respectively. These amounts are classified on the Company's balance sheet in accrued liabilities for the portion that is subject to deferral for one year or less and other long-term liabilities for the portion that is subject to deferral for more than one year.

The Company also pays certain vendors who distribute NOOK® a commission on the content sales sold through that device. The Company accounts for these transactions as a reduction in the sales price of the NOOK® based on historical trends of content sales and a liability is established for the estimated commission expected to be paid over the life of the product. The Company recognizes revenue of the content at the point of sale of the content. The Company records revenue from sales of digital content, sales of third-party extended warranties, service contracts and other products, for which the Company is not obligated to perform, and for which the Company does not meet the criteria for gross revenue recognition under ASC 605-45-45, *Reporting Revenue Gross as a Principal versus Net as an Agent*, on a net basis. All other revenue is recognized on a gross basis.

The Company rents both physical and digital textbooks. Revenue from the rental of physical textbooks is deferred and recognized over the rental period commencing at point of sale. Revenue from the rental of digital textbooks is recognized at time of sale. A software feature is imbedded within the content of our digital textbooks, such that upon expiration of the rental term the customer is no longer able to access the content. While the digital rental allows the customer to access digital content for a fixed period of time, once the digital content is delivered to the customer our obligation is complete. The Company offers a buyout option to allow the purchase of a rented book at the end of the semester. The Company records the buyout purchase when the customer exercises and pays the buyout option price. In these instances, the Company would accelerate any remaining deferred rental revenue at the point of sale.

NOOK acquires the rights to distribute digital content from publishers and distributes the content on barnesandnoble.com, NOOK® devices and other eBookstore platforms. Certain digital content is distributed under an agency pricing model in which the publishers set prices for eBooks and NOOK receives a commission on content sold through the eBookstore. The majority of the Company's eBook sales are sold under the agency model.

The Barnes & Noble Member Program offers members greater discounts and other benefits for products and services, as well as exclusive offers and promotions via e-mail or direct mail generally for an annual fee of $25.00, which is non-refundable after the first 30 days. Revenue is recognized over the twelve-month period based upon historical spending patterns for Barnes & Noble Members.

In May 2014, the Financial Accounting Standards Board (FASB) issued ASU No. 2014-09, *Revenue from Contracts with Customers* (ASU 2014-09). The standard provides companies with a single model for use in accounting for revenue arising from contracts with customers and supersedes current revenue recognition guidance, including industry-specific revenue guidance. The core principle of the model is to recognize revenue when control of the goods or services transfers to the customer, as opposed to recognizing revenue when the risks and rewards transfer to the customer under the existing revenue guidance. ASU 2014-09 is effective for annual reporting periods beginning after December 15, 2016. Early adoption is not permitted. The guidance permits companies to either apply the requirements retrospectively to all prior periods presented, or apply the requirements in the year of adoption, through a cumulative adjustment. The Company has not yet selected a transition method nor has it determined the impact of adoption on its consolidated financial statements.

Research and Development Costs for Software Products

The Company follows the guidance in ASC 985-20, *Cost of Software to Be Sold, Leased or Marketed,* regarding software development costs to be sold, leased, or otherwise marketed. Capitalization of software development costs begins upon the establishment of technological feasibility and is discontinued when the product is available for sale. A certain amount of judgment and estimation is required to assess when technological feasibility is established, as well as the ongoing assessment of the recoverability of capitalized costs. The Company's products reach technological feasibility shortly before the products are released and therefore research and development costs are generally expensed as incurred.

Internal-use Software and Website Development Costs

Direct costs incurred to develop software for internal-use and website development costs are capitalized and amortized over an estimated useful life of three to seven years. During fiscal 2015 and 2014, the Company capitalized costs, primarily related to labor, consulting, hardware and software of $42,699 and $50,565, respectively. Amortization of previously capitalized amounts was $27,568, $24,145 and $19,044 for fiscal 2015, 2014 and 2013, respectively. Costs related to the design or maintenance of internal-use software and website development are expensed as incurred.

Advertising Costs

The costs of advertising are expensed as incurred during the year pursuant to ASC 720-35, *Advertising Costs*. Advertising costs charged to selling and administrative expenses were $58,823, $61,527 and $110,878 during fiscal 2015, fiscal 2014 and fiscal 2013, respectively.

The Company receives payments and credits from vendors pursuant to co-operative advertising and other programs, including payments for product placement in stores, catalogs and online. In accordance with ASC 605-50-25-10, *Customer's Accounting for Certain Consideration Received from a Vendor*, the Company classifies certain co-op advertising received as a reduction in costs of sales and occupancy. Allowances received from vendors exceeded gross advertising costs in each of the fiscal years noted above.

Closed Store Expenses

When the Company closes or relocates a store, the Company charges unrecoverable costs to expense. Such costs include the net book value of abandoned fixtures and leasehold improvements and, when a store is closed prior to the expiration of the lease, a provision for future lease obligations, net of expected sublease recoveries. Costs associated with store closings of $1,201, $929 and $5,006 during fiscal 2015, fiscal 2014 and fiscal 2013, respectively, are included in selling and administrative expenses in the accompanying consolidated statements of operations.

Net Earnings (Loss) Per Common Share

Basic earnings per share represent net earnings (loss) attributable to common shareholders divided by the weighted-average number of common shares outstanding for the period. Diluted earnings per share reflect, in periods in which they have a dilutive effect, the impact of common shares issuable upon exercise of the Company's outstanding stock options. The Company's unvested restricted shares, unvested restricted stock units and common shares issuable under the Company's deferred compensation plan are deemed participating securities and are excluded from the dilutive impact of common equivalent shares outstanding under the two-class method since these shares are entitled to participate in dividends declared on common shares. Under the two-class method, earnings (loss) attributable to unvested restricted shares, unvested restricted stock units and common shares issuable under the Company's deferred compensation plan are excluded from net earnings (loss) attributable to common shareholders for purposes of calculating basic and diluted earnings (loss) per common share. See Note 7 for further information regarding the calculation of basic and diluted earnings (loss) per common share.

Income Taxes

The provision for income taxes includes federal, state and local income taxes currently payable and those deferred because of temporary differences between the financial statement and tax bases of assets and liabilities. The deferred tax assets and liabilities are measured using the enacted tax rates and laws that are expected to be in effect when the differences reverse. The Company regularly reviews its deferred tax assets for recoverability and establishes a valuation allowance, if determined to be necessary.

Stock-Based Compensation

The calculation of stock-based employee compensation expense involves estimates that require management's judgment. These estimates include the fair value of each of the stock option awards granted, which is estimated on the date of grant using a Black-Scholes option pricing model. There are two significant inputs into the Black-Scholes option pricing model: expected volatility and expected term. The Company estimates expected volatility based on traded option volatility of the Company's stock over a term equal to the expected term of the option granted. The expected term of stock option awards granted is derived from historical exercise experience under the Company's stock option plans and represents the period of time that stock option awards granted are expected to be outstanding. The assumptions used in calculating the fair value of stock-based payment awards represent management's best estimates, but these estimates involve inherent uncertainties and the application of management's judgment. As a result, if factors change and the Company uses different assumptions, stock-based compensation expense could be materially different in the future. In addition, the Company is required to estimate the expected forfeiture rate, and only recognize expense for those shares expected to vest. If the Company's actual forfeiture rate is materially different from its estimate, the stock-based compensation expense could be significantly different from what the Company has recorded in the current period. See Note 3 to the Consolidated Financial Statements for a further discussion on stock-based compensation.

Gift Cards

The Company sells gift cards, which can be used in its stores, on barnesandnoble.com and NOOK® devices. The Company does not charge administrative or dormancy fees on gift cards and gift cards have no expiration dates. Upon the purchase of a gift card, a liability is established for its cash value. Revenue associated with gift cards is deferred until redemption of the gift card. Over time, some portion of the gift cards issued is not redeemed. The Company estimates the portion of the gift card liability for which the likelihood of redemption is remote based upon the Company's historical redemption patterns. The Company records this amount in income on a straight-line basis over a 12-month period beginning in the 13th month after the month the gift card was originally sold. The Company does not believe there is a reasonable likelihood that there will be a material change in the estimates or assumptions used to recognize revenue associated with gift cards. However, additional breakage may be required if gift card redemptions continue to run lower than historical patterns. The Company recognized gift card breakage of $26,080, $23,221 and $23,929 during fiscal 2015, fiscal 2014 and fiscal 2013, respectively. The Company had gift card liabilities of $358,146 and $356,700 as of May 2, 2015 and May 3, 2014, respectively.

Accounts Receivable

Accounts receivable, as presented on the Company's Consolidated Balance Sheets, is net of allowances. An allowance for doubtful accounts is determined through an analysis of the aging of accounts receivable and assessments of collectibility based on historic trends, the financial condition of the Company's customers and an evaluation of economic conditions. The Company writes off uncollectible trade receivables once collection efforts have been exhausted. Costs associated with allowable customer markdowns and operational chargebacks, net of the expected recoveries, are part of the provision for allowances included in accounts receivable. These provisions result from seasonal negotiations, as well as historic deduction trends net of expected recoveries, and the evaluation of current market conditions.

Reclassifications

Certain prior-period amounts have been reclassified for comparative purposes to conform with the fiscal 2015 presentation.

Recent Accounting Pronouncements

In April 2015, the FASB issued ASU No. 2015-04, *Practical Expedient for the Measurement Date of an Employer's Defined Benefit Obligation and Plan Assets* (ASU 2015-04). For an entity with a fiscal year-end that does not coincide with a month-end, the amendments in this ASU provide a practical expedient that permits the entity to measure defined benefit plan assets and obligations using the month-end that is closest to the entity's fiscal year-end and apply that practical expedient consistently from year to year. The practical expedient should be applied consistently to all plans if an entity has more than one plan. ASU 2015-04 is effective for annual reporting periods beginning after December 15, 2016, and interim periods within fiscal years beginning after December 15, 2017. Earlier application is permitted. The amendments in this ASU should be applied prospectively. The Company has not yet selected a transition method nor has it determined the impact of adoption on its consolidated financial statements.

Reporting Period

The Company's fiscal year is comprised of 52 or 53 weeks, ending on the Saturday closest to the last day of April. The reporting periods ended May 2, 2015 contained 52 weeks, May 3, 2014 contained 53 weeks, and April 27, 2013 contained 52 weeks.

NATURE OF OPERATIONS

1.28 ARMSTRONG WORLD INDUSTRIES, INC. (DEC)
NOTES TO CONSOLIDATED FINANCIAL STATEMENTS (in part)

(dollar amounts in millions, except share data)

Note 3. Nature of Operations

Building Products—produces suspended mineral fiber, soft fiber and metal ceiling systems for use in commercial, institutional and residential settings. In addition, our Building Products segment sources complementary ceiling products. Our products, which are sold worldwide, are available in numerous colors, performance characteristics and designs, and offer attributes such as acoustical control, rated fire protection and aesthetic appeal. Commercial ceiling materials and accessories are sold to resale distributors and to ceiling systems contractors. Residential ceiling products are sold in North America primarily to wholesalers and retailers (including large home centers). Our Worthington Armstrong Venture ("WAVE") joint venture with Worthington Industries, Inc. manufactures suspension system (grid) products which are sold by both us and WAVE.

Resilient Flooring—designs, manufactures, sources and sells a broad range of floor coverings primarily for homes and commercial and institutional buildings. Manufactured products in this segment include vinyl sheet, vinyl tile, and luxury vinyl tile ("LVT") flooring. In addition, our Resilient Flooring segment sources and sells laminate flooring products, vinyl tile products, vinyl sheet products, LVT products, linoleum products, adhesives, and installation and maintenance materials and accessories. Resilient Flooring products are offered in a wide variety of types, designs, colors and installation options. We sell these products to independent wholesale flooring distributors, large home centers, retailers, contractors and to the manufactured homes industry, and secure specifications for these products through architects, designers and end users. When market conditions and available capacity warrant, we also provide product on an original equipment manufacturer ("OEM") basis to other flooring companies.

Wood Flooring—designs, manufactures, sources and sells hardwood flooring products for use in new residential construction and renovation, with some commercial applications in stores, restaurants and high-end offices. The product offering includes pre-finished solid and engineered wood floors in various wood species, and related accessories. Virtually all of our Wood Flooring sales are in North America. Our Wood Flooring products are generally sold to independent wholesale flooring distributors, large home centers, retailers and flooring contractors. When market conditions and available capacity warrant, we also provide product on an OEM basis to other flooring companies.

Unallocated Corporate—includes assets, liabilities, income and expenses that have not been allocated to the business units. Balance sheet items classified as Unallocated Corporate are primarily income tax related accounts, cash and cash equivalents, the Armstrong brand name, the U.S. pension and long-term debt. Expenses for our corporate departments and certain benefit plans are allocated to the reportable segments based on known metrics, such as specific activity or headcount. The remaining items, which cannot be attributed to the other reportable segments without a high degree of generalization, are reported in Unallocated Corporate.

	Building Products	Resilient Flooring	Wood Flooring	Unallocated Corporate	Total
For the Year Ended 2015					
Net sales to external customers	$1,231.3	$713.3	$475.4	—	$2,420.0
Equity (earnings) from joint venture	(66.1)	—	—	—	(66.1)
Segment operating income (loss)	264.8	42.2	19.2	($138.8)	187.4
Segment assets	1,068.9	510.2	337.4	775.4	2,691.9
Depreciation and amortization	67.6	26.1	12.0	12.6	118.3
Investment in joint venture	130.8	—	—	—	130.8
Purchases of property, plant and equipment	86.7	40.8	20.8	22.4	170.7
For the Year Ended 2014					
Net sales to external customers	$1,294.3	$712.9	$508.1	—	$2,515.3
Equity (earnings) from joint venture	(65.1)	—	—	—	(65.1)
Segment operating income (loss)	264.7	61.6	(14.9)	($ 72.3)	239.1
Segment assets	1,079.7	492.7	329.8	704.0	2,606.2
Depreciation and amortization[1]	66.0	29.6	16.5	11.3	123.4
Asset impairment[1]	0.4	—	15.4	—	15.8
Investment in joint venture	129.0	—	—	—	129.0
Purchases of property, plant and equipment[1]	128.1	51.6	26.0	11.4	217.1
For the Year Ended 2013					
Net sales to external customers	$1,264.6	$728.8	$534.0	—	$2,527.4
Equity (earnings) from joint venture	(59.4)	—	—	—	(59.4)
Segment operating income (loss)	263.1	69.8	6.0	($ 73.3)	265.6
Segment assets	1,071.9	462.9	335.2	852.0	2,722.0
Depreciation and amortization[1]	56.3	25.8	11.4	9.0	102.5
Investment in joint venture	132.0	—	—	—	132.0
Purchases of property, plant and equipment[1]	134.5	50.7	8.0	15.8	209.0

[1] Totals for 2014 and 2013 will differ from the totals on our Consolidated Statement of Cash Flow by the amounts that have been classified as discontinued operations.

Segment operating income (loss) is the measure of segment profit or loss reviewed by the chief operating decision maker. The sum of the segments' operating income (loss) equals the total consolidated operating income as reported on our income statement. The following reconciles our total consolidated operating income to earnings from continuing operations before income taxes. These items are only measured and managed on a consolidated basis:

	2015	2014	2013
Segment operating income	$187.4	$239.1	$265.6
Interest expense	45.3	46.0	68.7
Other non-operating expense	23.5	10.5	2.0
Other non-operating income	(5.3)	(2.6)	(3.8)
Earnings from continuing operations before income taxes	$123.9	$185.2	$198.7

Accounting policies of the segments are the same as those described in the summary of significant accounting policies.

The sales in the table below are allocated to geographic areas based upon the location of the customer.

Geographic Areas Net Trade Sales	2015	2014	2013
Americas:			
United States	$1,738.5	$1,728.3	$1,743.8
Canada	131.5	164.9	176.6
Other	31.8	33.5	33.9
Total Americas	1,901.8	1,926.7	1,954.3
Europe, Middle East & Africa:			
United Kingdom	85.8	80.1	82.3
France	43.6	55.9	55.6
Russia	37.9	64.9	68.0
Saudi Arabia	10.8	20.8	18.1
Other	109.8	125.0	127.3
Total Europe, Middle East & Africa	287.9	346.7	351.3
Pacific Rim:			
China	85.5	92.4	81.3
India	54.0	50.5	40.3
Australia	53.9	64.2	66.2
Other	36.9	34.8	34.0
Total Pacific Rim	230.3	241.9	221.8
Total net trade sales	$2,420.0	$2,515.3	$2,527.4

Property, Plant and Equipment, Net at December 31,	2015	2014
Americas:		
United States	$ 769.8	$ 715.8
Other	4.4	5.4
Total Americas	774.2	721.2
Europe, Middle East & Africa:		
Russia	48.3	62.7
Germany	28.5	29.9
France	27.6	18.8
United Kingdom	21.8	19.1
Other	18.8	16.2
Total Europe, Middle East & Africa	145.0	146.7
Pacific Rim:		
China	163.8	179.1
Other	13.3	15.4
Total Pacific Rim	177.1	194.5
Total property, plant and equipment, net	$1,096.3	$1,062.4

Impairment testing of our tangible assets occurs whenever events or changes in circumstances indicate that the carrying amount of the assets may not be recoverable. In 2014, we made the decision to dispose of certain idle equipment at five of our wood flooring manufacturing facilities and as a result we recorded a $4.4 million impairment charge in cost of goods sold.

During 2014, we decided to close our resilient flooring plant in Thomastown, Australia and our engineered wood flooring plant in Kunshan, China. We recorded $2.2 million in cost of goods sold for accelerated depreciation due to the closure of the resilient flooring plant in Australia. We sold this facility in January 2015 for a gain of approximately $2 million. We also recorded $4.0 million in cost of goods sold for accelerated depreciation and $0.8 million for the impairment of intangible assets due to the closure of the wood flooring plant in China in 2014.

USE OF ESTIMATES

1.29 SPX CORPORATION (DEC)
NOTES TO CONSOLIDATED FINANCIAL STATEMENTS (in part)

(All currency and share amounts are in millions, except per share and par value data)

(2) Use of Estimates

The preparation of our consolidated financial statements in conformity with GAAP requires us to make estimates and assumptions. These estimates and assumptions affect the reported amounts of assets and liabilities, the disclosure of contingent assets and liabilities at the date of the consolidated financial statements, and the reported amounts of revenues (e.g., our percentage-of-completion estimates described above) and expenses during the reporting period. We evaluate these estimates and judgments on an ongoing basis and base our estimates on experience, current and expected future conditions, third-party evaluations and various other assumptions that we believe are reasonable under the circumstances. The results of these estimates form the basis for making judgments about the carrying values of assets and liabilities as well as identifying and assessing the accounting treatment with respect to commitments and contingencies. Actual results may differ from the estimates and assumptions used in the consolidated financial statements and related notes.

Listed below are certain significant estimates and assumptions used in the preparation of our consolidated financial statements. Certain other estimates and assumptions are further explained in the related notes.

Accounts Receivable Allowances—We provide allowances for estimated losses on uncollectible accounts based on our historical experience and the evaluation of the likelihood of success in collecting specific customer receivables. In addition, we maintain allowances for customer returns, discounts and invoice pricing discrepancies, with such allowances primarily based on historical experience. Summarized below is the activity for these allowance accounts.

	Year Ended December 31,		
	2015	2014	2013
Balance at beginning of year	$ 14.8	$ 24.7	$ 26.9
Allowances provided	14.1	16.2	19.4
Write-offs, net of recoveries, credits issued and other	(18.7)	(26.1)	(21.6)
Balance at end of year	$ 10.2	$ 14.8	$ 24.7

Inventory—We estimate losses for excess and/or obsolete inventory and the net realizable value of inventory based on the aging and historical utilization of the inventory and the evaluation of the likelihood of recovering the inventory costs based on anticipated demand and selling price.

Long-Lived Assets and Intangible Assets Subject to Amortization—We continually review whether events and circumstances subsequent to the acquisition of any long-lived assets, or intangible assets subject to amortization, have occurred that indicate the remaining estimated useful lives of those assets may warrant revision or that the remaining balance of those assets may not be fully recoverable. If events and circumstances indicate that the long-lived assets should be reviewed for possible impairment, we use projections to assess whether future cash flows on an undiscounted basis related to the assets are likely to exceed the related carrying amount. We will record an impairment charge to the extent that the carrying value of the assets exceed their fair values as determined by valuation techniques appropriate in the circumstances, which could include the use of similar projections on a discounted basis.

In determining the estimated useful lives of definite-lived intangibles, we consider the nature, competitive position, life cycle position, and historical and expected future operating cash flows of each acquired asset, as well as our commitment to support these assets through continued investment and legal infringement protection.

Goodwill and Indefinite-Lived Intangible Assets—We test goodwill and indefinite-lived intangible assets for impairment annually during the fourth quarter and continually assess whether a triggering event has occurred to determine whether the carrying value exceeds the implied fair value. The fair value of reporting units is based generally on discounted projected cash flows, but we also consider factors such as comparable industry price multiples. We employ cash flow projections that we believe to be reasonable under current and forecasted circumstances, the results of which form the basis for making judgments about the carrying values of the reported net assets of our reporting units. Many of our businesses closely follow changes in the industries and end markets that they serve. Accordingly, we consider estimates and judgments that affect the future cash flow projections, including principal methods of competition, such as volume, price, service, product performance and technical innovations, as well as estimates associated with cost reduction initiatives, capacity utilization and assumptions for inflation and foreign currency changes. Actual results may differ from these estimates under different assumptions or conditions. See Note 8 for further information, including discussion of impairment charges recorded in 2015 and 2014.

Accrued Expenses—We make estimates and judgments in establishing accruals as required under GAAP. Summarized in the table below are the components of accrued expenses at December 31, 2015 and 2014.

	December 31,	
	2015	**2014**
Employee benefits	$ 83.8	$ 96.2
Unearned revenue[1]	193.3	170.9
Warranty	20.3	20.8
Other[2]	131.6	152.3
Total[3]	$429.0	$440.2

[1] Unearned revenue includes billings in excess of costs and estimated earnings on uncompleted contracts accounted for under the percentage-of-completion method of revenue recognition, customer deposits and unearned amounts on service contracts.

[2] Other consists of various items including, among other items, accrued legal costs, interest, restructuring costs and dividends payable, none of which is individually material.

[3] The balance at December 31, 2015 includes $25.3 related to our dry cooling business. As indicated in Note 1, on November 20, 2015, we entered into an agreement to sell the dry cooling business. As a result, the assets and liabilities of the dry cooling business have been classified as "held for sale" in the accompanying consolidated balance sheet as of December 31, 2015. See Note 4 for information on the assets and liabilities of the dry cooling business as of December 31, 2015.

Legal—It is our policy to accrue for estimated losses from legal actions or claims when events exist that make the realization of the losses probable and they can be reasonably estimated. We do not discount legal obligations or reduce them by anticipated insurance recoveries.

Environmental Remediation Costs—We expense costs incurred to investigate and remediate environmental issues unless they extend the economic useful lives of related assets. We record liabilities when it is probable that an obligation has been incurred and the amounts can be reasonably estimated. Our environmental accruals cover anticipated costs, including investigation, remediation and operation and maintenance of clean-up sites. Our estimates are based primarily on investigations and remediation plans established by independent consultants, regulatory agencies and potentially responsible third parties. We generally do not discount environmental obligations or reduce them by anticipated insurance recoveries.

Risk Management Matters—We are subject to claims associated with risk management matters (e.g., product liability, predominately associated with alleged exposure to asbestos-containing materials, general liability, automobile, and workers' compensation claims). The liabilities we record for these claims are based on a number of assumptions, including historical claims and payment experience and, with respect to asbestos claims, actuarial estimates of the future period during which additional claims are reasonably foreseeable. We also have recorded insurance recovery assets associated with the asbestos product liability matters. These assets represent amounts that we believe we are or will be entitled to recover under agreements we have with insurance companies. The assets we record for these insurance recoveries are based on a number of assumptions, including the continued solvency of the insurers, and are subject to a variety of uncertainties. In addition, we are self-insured for certain of our workers' compensation, automobile, product, general liability, disability and health costs, and we maintain adequate accruals to cover our retained liabilities. Our accruals for self-insurance liabilities are based on claims filed and an estimate of claims incurred but not yet reported, and generally are not discounted. We consider a number of factors, including third-party actuarial valuations, when making these determinations. We maintain third-party stop-loss insurance policies to cover certain liability costs in excess of predetermined retained amounts; however, this insurance may be insufficient or unavailable (e.g., because of insurer insolvency) to protect us against potential loss exposures. The key assumptions considered in estimating the ultimate cost to settle reported claims and the estimated costs associated with incurred but not yet reported claims include, among other things, our historical and industry claims experience, trends in health care and administrative costs, our current and future risk management programs, and historical lag studies with regard to the timing between when a claim is incurred and reported. See Note 14 for additional details.

Warranty—In the normal course of business, we issue product warranties for specific products and provide for the estimated future warranty cost in the period in which the sale is recorded. We provide for the estimate of warranty cost based on contract terms and historical warranty loss experience that is periodically adjusted for recent actual experience. Because warranty estimates are forecasts that are based on the best available information, claims costs may differ from amounts provided. In addition, due to the seasonal fluctuations at certain of our businesses, the timing of warranty provisions and the usage of warranty accruals can vary period to period. We make adjustments to initial obligations for warranties as changes in the obligations become reasonably estimable. The following is an analysis of our product warranty accrual for the periods presented:

	Year Ended December 31,		
	2015	2014	2013
Balance at beginning of year	$ 37.5	$ 34.7	$ 36.8
Provisions	18.8	21.4	17.8
Usage	(16.1)	(17.8)	(20.1)
Currency translation adjustment	(0.6)	(0.8)	0.2
Balance at end of year	39.6	37.5	34.7
Less: Current portion of warranty	20.3	20.8	22.2
Non-current portion of warranty	$ 19.3	$ 16.7	$ 12.5

Income Taxes—We perform reviews of our income tax positions on a continuous basis and accrue for potential uncertain tax positions in accordance with the Income Taxes Topic of the Codification. Accruals for these uncertain tax positions are classified as "Income taxes payable" and "Deferred and other income taxes" in the accompanying consolidated balance sheets based on an expectation as to the timing of when the matter will be resolved. As events change or resolutions occur, these accruals are adjusted, such as in the case of audit settlements with taxing authorities. For tax positions where it is more likely than not that a tax benefit will be sustained, we record the largest amount of tax benefit with a greater than 50% likelihood of being realized upon ultimate settlement with a taxing authority, assuming such authority has full knowledge of all relevant information. These reviews also entail analyzing the realization of deferred tax assets. When we believe that it is more likely than not that we will not realize a benefit for a deferred tax asset based on all available evidence, we establish a valuation allowance.

Employee Benefit Plans—Defined benefit plans cover a portion of our salaried and hourly employees, including certain employees in foreign countries. As discussed in Note 1, we recognize changes in the fair value of plan assets and actuarial gains and losses associated with our pension and postretirement benefit plans in earnings during the fourth quarter of each year, unless earlier remeasurement is required, as a component of net periodic benefit expense. The remaining components of pension/postretirement expense, primarily service and interest costs and expected return on plan assets, are recorded on a quarterly basis. See Note 10 for further discussion of our pension and postretirement benefits.

We derive pension expense from an actuarial calculation based on the defined benefit plans' provisions and our assumptions regarding discount rate and rate of increase in compensation levels. We determine the discount rate for our more significant U.S. plans by matching the expected projected benefit obligation cash flows of the plans to a yield curve that is representative of long-term, high-quality (rated AA or higher) fixed income debt instruments as of the measurement date. For our other plans, we determine the discount rate based on representative bond indices. The rate of increase in compensation levels is established based on our expectations of current and foreseeable future increases in compensation. We also consult with independent actuaries in determining these assumptions.

VULNERABILITY DUE TO CERTAIN CONCENTRATIONS

1.30 THE SCOTTS MIRACLE-GRO COMPANY (SEP)
NOTES TO CONSOLIDATED FINANCIAL STATEMENTS (in part)

Note 19. Concentrations of Credit Risk

The Company maintains cash depository accounts with major financial institutions around the world and invests in high quality, short-term liquid investments. Such investments are made only in investments issued by highly rated institutions. These investments mature within three months and have not historically incurred any losses.

Trade accounts receivable are exposed to a concentration of credit risk with retailers principally located in the United States. The Company's retail customers include home centers, mass merchandisers, warehouse clubs, large hardware chains, independent hardware stores, nurseries, garden centers, food and drug stores, and indoor gardening and hydroponic stores. Concentrations of net sales and accounts receivable by segment in the United States as a percentage of consolidated net sales and accounts receivable at September 30 were as follows:

	Percentage of Net Sales			Percentage of Net Accounts Receivable at September 30,	
	2015	2014	2013	2015	2014
Global Consumer segment	73%	72%	72%	63%	62%
Scotts LawnService® segment	9%	9%	9%	10%	9%
Total Concentration in United States	82%	81%	81%	73%	71%

The remainder of the Company's net sales and accounts receivable at September 30, 2015, 2014 and 2013 were generated from customers located outside of the United States, primarily retailers, distributors and nurseries in Europe, Canada and Australia. No concentrations of these customers or individual customers within this group accounted for more than 10% of the Company's net sales or accounts receivable for any period presented above.

The Company's three largest customers are reported within the Global Consumer segment and are the only customers that individually represent more than 10% of reported consolidated net sales and accounts receivable for each of the last three fiscal years. These three customers accounted for the following percentages of Global Consumer segment net sales for the fiscal years ended September 30:

	Percentage of Net Sales		
	2015	2014	2013
Home Depot	34%	36%	34%
Lowe's	17%	19%	18%
Walmart	12%	13%	13%

Accounts receivable for these three largest customers as a percentage of consolidated accounts receivable were 54% and 55% for September 30, 2015 and 2014, respectively.

1.31 VISHAY INTERTECHNOLOGY, INC. (DEC)
NOTES TO THE CONSOLIDATED FINANCIAL STATEMENTS (in part)

(dollars in thousands, except per share amounts)

Note 14—Current Vulnerability Due to Certain Concentrations

Market Concentrations

While no single customer comprises greater than 10% of consolidated net revenues, a material portion of the Company's revenues are derived from the worldwide industrial, automotive, telecommunications, and computing markets. These markets have historically experienced wide variations in demand for end products. If demand for these end products should decrease, the producers thereof could reduce their purchases of the Company's products, which could have an adverse effect on the Company's results of operations and financial position.

While no single customer comprises greater than 10% of consolidated net revenues, certain subsidiaries and product lines have customers which comprise greater than 10% of the subsidiary's or product line's net revenues. The loss of one of these customers could have a material effect on the results of operations of the subsidiary or product line and financial position of the subsidiary, which could result in an impairment charge which could be material to the Company's consolidated financial statements.

Credit Risk Concentrations

Financial instruments with potential credit risk consist principally of cash and cash equivalents, short-term investments, accounts receivable, and notes receivable. Concentrations of credit risk with respect to receivables are generally limited due to the Company's large number of customers and their dispersion across many countries and industries. As of December 31, 2015, one customer comprised 14.6% of the Company's accounts receivable balance. This customer comprised 14.7% of the Company's accounts receivable balance as of December 31, 2014. No other customer comprised greater than 10% of the Company's accounts receivable balance as of December 31, 2015 or December 31, 2014. The Company continually monitors the credit risks associated with its accounts receivable and adjusts the allowance for uncollectible accounts accordingly. The credit risk exposure associated with the accounts receivable is limited by the allowance and is not considered material to the financial statements.

The Company maintains cash and cash equivalents and short-term investments with various major financial institutions. The Company is exposed to credit risk related to the potential inability to access liquidity in financial institutions where its cash and cash equivalents and short-term investments are concentrated. As of December 31, 2015, the following financial institutions held over 10% of the Company's combined cash and cash equivalents and short-term investments balance:

Bank Hapoalim*	12.5%
Bank Leumi*	12.5%
Bank of Tokyo Mitsubishi*	11.5%
HSBC*	11.4%
Deutsche Bank	11.2%
UniCredit*	10.7%
* Participant in Credit Facility.	

Sources of Supplies

Many of the Company's products require the use of raw materials that are produced in only a limited number of regions around the world or are available from only a limited number of suppliers. The Company's consolidated results of operations may be materially and adversely affected if there are significant price increases for these raw materials, the Company has difficulty obtaining these raw materials, or the quality of available raw materials deteriorates. For periods in which the prices of these raw materials are rising, the Company may be unable to pass on the increased cost to the Company's customers, which would result in decreased margins for the products in which they are used. For periods in which the prices are declining, the Company may be required to write down its inventory carrying cost of these raw materials which, depending on the extent of the difference between market price and its carrying cost, could have a material adverse effect on the Company's net earnings.

Vishay is a major consumer of the world's annual production of tantalum. Tantalum, a metal purchased in powder or wire form, is the principal material used in the manufacture of tantalum capacitors. There are few suppliers that process tantalum ore into capacitor grade tantalum powder.

From time to time, there have been short-term market shortages of raw materials utilized by the Company. While these shortages have not historically adversely affected the Company's ability to increase production of products containing these raw materials, they have historically resulted in higher raw material costs for the Company. The Company cannot assure that any of these market shortages in the future would not adversely affect the Company's ability to increase production, particularly during periods of growing demand for the Company's products.

Certain raw materials used in the manufacture of the Company's products, such as gold, copper, palladium, and other metals, are traded on active markets and can be subject to significant price volatility. To ensure adequate supply and to provide cost certainty, the Company's policy is to enter into short-term commitments to purchase defined portions of annual consumption of the raw materials utilized by the Company if market prices decline below budget. If after entering into these commitments, the market prices for these raw materials decline, the Company must recognize losses on these adverse purchase commitments.

Recently enacted rules in the U.S. on conflict minerals, which include tantalum, tungsten, tin, and gold, all of which are used in the Company's products, could result in increased prices and decreased supply of conflict minerals, which could negatively affect the Company's consolidated results of operations.

Geographic Concentration

The Company has operations outside the United States, and approximately 74% of revenues earned during 2015 were derived from sales to customers outside the United States. Additionally, as of December 31, 2015, $1,080,858 of the Company's cash and cash equivalents and short-term investments were held in countries outside of the United States. Some of the Company's products are produced and cash and cash equivalents and short-term investments are held in countries which are subject to risks of political, economic, and military instability. This instability could result in wars, riots, nationalization of industry, currency fluctuations, and labor unrest. These conditions could have an adverse impact on the Company's ability to operate in these regions and, depending on the extent and severity of these conditions, could materially and adversely affect the Company's overall financial condition, operating results, and ability to access its liquidity when needed.

As of December 31, 2015 the Company's cash and cash equivalents and short-term investments were concentrated in the following countries:

Germany	43.5%
Israel	29.6%
People's Republic of China	8.5%
The Republic of China (Taiwan)	6.5%
Singapore	5.4%
United States	1.7%
Other Asia	2.5%
Other Europe	1.6%
Other	0.7%

Vishay has been in operation in Israel for 45 years. The Company has never experienced any material interruption in its operations attributable to these factors, in spite of several Middle East crises, including wars.

Segment Reporting

PRESENTATION

1.32 FASB ASC 280, *Segment Reporting*, requires that a public business enterprise report a measure of segment profit or loss, certain specific revenue and expense items, and segment assets. FASB ASC 280-10 requires that all public business enterprises report information about the revenues derived from the enterprise's products or services or groups of similar products and services; about the countries in which the enterprise earns revenues and holds assets; and about major customers, regardless of whether that information is used in making operating decisions. Even if a public company has only one operating segment, FASB ASC 280 requires that it report information about geographic areas and major customers. However, FASB ASC does not require an enterprise to report information that is impracticable to present because the necessary information is not available, and the cost to develop it would be excessive.

1.33 According to FASB ASC 280-10-50-1, an operating segment of a public entity has all of the following characteristics:
- It engages in business activities from which it may earn revenues and incur expenses, including revenues and expenses relating to transactions with other components of the same public entity
- Its operating results are regularly reviewed by the public entity's chief operating decision maker to make decisions about resources to be allocated to the segment and assess its performance
- Its discrete financial information is available

1.34 FASB ASC 280 uses the management approach to identify operating segments and measure the financial information disclosed based on information reported internally to the Chief Operating Decision Maker (CODM) to make resource allocation and performance assessment decisions. However, according to FASB ASC 280-10-50-9, entities that have a matrix organization should identify operating segments based on products and services when more than one type of component is reviewed by the CODM.

1.35 FASB ASC 280-10-50-30 requires reconciliations of total segment revenues, total segment profit or loss, total segment assets, and other amounts disclosed for segments to corresponding amounts in the enterprise's general purpose financial statements. FASB ASC 350-20-50-1 states that entities that report segment information should provide information about the changes in the carrying amount of goodwill during the period for each reportable segment.

PRESENTATION AND DISCLOSURE EXCERPTS

SEGMENT INFORMATION

1.36 HP INC. (OCT)
NOTES TO CONSOLIDATED FINANCIAL STATEMENTS (in part)

Note 2: Segment Information

HP is a leading global provider of products, technologies, software, solutions and services to individual consumers, small- and medium-sized businesses ("SMBs") and large enterprises, including customers in the government, health and education sectors. HP's offerings span the following:

- personal computing and other access devices;
- imaging- and printing-related products and services;
- enterprise information technology ("IT") infrastructure, including enterprise server and storage technology, networking products and solutions, and technology support and maintenance;
- multi-vendor customer services, including technology consulting, outsourcing and support services across infrastructure, applications and business process domains; and
- software products and solutions, including application testing and delivery, big data analytics, enterprise security, information governance and IT Operations Management.

HP's operations are organized into seven segments for financial reporting purposes: Personal Systems, Printing, the Enterprise Group ("EG"), Enterprise Services ("ES"), Software, HP Financial Services ("HPFS") and Corporate Investments. HP's organizational structure is based on a number of factors that management uses to evaluate, view and run its business operations, which include, but are not limited to, customer base and homogeneity of products and technology. The segments are based on this organizational structure and information reviewed by HP's management to evaluate segment results.

The Personal Systems segment and the Printing segment are structured beneath a broader Printing and Personal Systems Group ("PPS"). While PPS is not a reportable segment, HP may provide financial data aggregating the Personal Systems and the Printing segments in order to provide a supplementary view of its business.

As a result of the Separation, beginning November 1, 2015, HP will report three segments as part of continuing operations: Personal Systems, Printing and Corporate Investments.

A summary description of each segment follows.

The *Printing and Personal Systems Group's* mission is to leverage the respective strengths of the Personal Systems business and the Printing business by creating a unified organization that is customer-focused and poised to capitalize on rapidly shifting industry trends. Each of the segments within PPS is described below.

Personal Systems provides commercial personal computers ("PCs"), consumer PCs, workstations, thin clients, tablets, retail point-of-sale systems, calculators and other related accessories, software, support and services for the commercial and consumer markets. HP groups commercial notebooks, commercial desktops, commercial services, commercial tablets, workstations and thin clients into commercial clients and consumer notebooks, consumer desktops, consumer services and consumer tablets into consumer clients when describing performance in these markets. Described below are HP's global business capabilities within Personal Systems.

- *Commercial PCs* are optimized for enterprise and SMB customers, with a focus on robust designs, serviceability, connectivity, reliability and manageability in networked environments.
- *Consumer PCs* are notebooks, desktops, and hybrids that are optimized for consumer usage, focusing on multi-media consumption, online browsing, and light productivity.

Printing provides consumer and commercial printer hardware, supplies, media, software and services, as well as scanning devices. Printing is also focused on imaging solutions in the commercial markets. HP groups LaserJet, large format printers and commercial inkjet printers into Commercial Hardware and consumer inkjet printers into Consumer Hardware when describing performance in these markets. Described below are HP's global business capabilities within Printing.

- *LaserJet and Enterprise Solutions* deliver HP's LaserJet and enterprise products, services and solutions to SMBs and large enterprises. Managed Print Services provides printing equipment, supplies, support, workflow optimization and security services for SMBs and enterprise customers around the world, utilizing proprietary HP tools and fleet management solutions as well as third-party software.

- *Inkjet and Printing Solutions* deliver HP's consumer and SMB inkjet solutions (hardware, supplies, media, and web-connected hardware and services). Ongoing initiatives and programs such as Ink in the Office and Ink Advantage and newer initiatives such as Instant Ink provide innovative printing solutions to consumers and SMBs.
- *Graphics Solutions* deliver large format printers (Designjet, Large Format Production, and Scitex Industrial), specialty printing, digital press solutions (Indigo and Inkjet Webpress), supplies and services to print service providers and design and rendering customers.
- *Software and Web Services* delivers a suite of solutions and services, including photo storage and web-connected printing services.
- *Marketing Optimization* focuses on delivering solutions that help businesses engage audiences, reach new customer segments and markets and deliver compelling content across channels. The group provides solutions for augmented reality, contact center analytics, customer communications management and digital experience management.

The *Enterprise Group* provides servers, storage, networking and technology services that, when combined with HP's cloud solutions, enable customers to manage applications across public cloud, virtual private cloud, private cloud and traditional IT environments. Described below are HP's business units and capabilities within EG.
- *Industry Standard Servers* offers a range of products from entry-level servers through premium ProLiant servers, which run primarily *Windows*, Linux and virtualization platforms from software providers such as Microsoft Corporation ("Microsoft") and VMware, Inc. ("VMware") and open sourced software from other major vendors while leveraging x86 processors from Intel Corporation ("Intel") and Advanced Micro Devices, Inc. ("AMD").
- *Business Critical Systems* offers HP Integrity servers based on the Intel® Itanium® and x86 processors, HP Integrity NonStop solutions and mission-critical x86 ProLiant servers.
- *Storage* offers traditional storage and Converged Storage solutions. Traditional storage includes tape, storage networking and legacy external disk products such as EVA and XP. Converged Storage solutions include 3PAR StoreServ, StoreOnce and StoreVirtual products.
- *Networking* offers wireless local area network, mobility and security software, switches, routers and network management products that span data centers, campus and branch environments and deliver software-defined networking and unified communications capabilities.
- *Technology Services* provides support services and technology consulting to integrate and optimize EG's hardware platforms for the new style of IT. These services are available in the form of service contracts, pre-packaged offerings or on a customized basis.

Enterprise Services provides technology consulting, outsourcing and support services across infrastructure, applications and business process domains. ES is comprised of the Infrastructure Technology Outsourcing ("ITO") and the Application and Business Services ("ABS") business units.
- *Infrastructure Technology Outsourcing* delivers comprehensive services that encompass the management of data centers, IT security, cloud computing, workplace technology, networks, unified communications and enterprise service management.
- *Application and Business Services* helps clients develop, revitalize and manage their applications and information assets.

Software provides big data analytics and applications, enterprise security, application testing and delivery management and IT Operations Management solutions for businesses and other enterprises of all sizes. These software offerings include licenses, support, professional services and software-as-a-service.

HP Financial Services provides flexible investment solutions, such as leasing, financing, IT consumption and utility programs and asset management services, for customers to enable the creation of unique technology deployment models and acquire complete IT solutions, including hardware, software and services from HP and others. Providing flexible services and capabilities that support the entire IT lifecycle, HPFS partners with customers globally to help build investment strategies that enhance their business agility and support their business transformation. HPFS offers a wide selection of investment solution capabilities for large enterprise customers and channel partners, along with an array of financial options to SMBs and educational and governmental entities.

Corporate Investments includes HP Labs and certain enterprise-related business incubation projects and venture focused minority investments among others.

Segment Policy

HP derives the results of the business segments directly from its internal management reporting system. The accounting policies HP uses to derive segment results are substantially the same as those the consolidated company uses. Management measures the performance of each segment based on several metrics, including earnings from operations. Management uses these results, in part, to evaluate the performance of, and to allocate resources to, each of the segments.

Segment revenue includes revenues from sales to external customers and intersegment revenues that reflect transactions between the segments on an arm's-length basis. Intersegment revenues primarily consist of sales of hardware and software that are sourced internally and, in the majority of the cases, are financed as operating leases by HPFS. HP's consolidated net revenue is derived and reported after the elimination of intersegment revenues from such arrangements.

HP periodically engages in intercompany advanced royalty payment and licensing arrangements that may result in advance payments between subsidiaries. Revenues from these intercompany arrangements are deferred and recognized as earned over the term of the arrangement by the HP legal entities involved in such transactions; however, these advanced payments are eliminated from revenues as reported by HP and its business segments. As disclosed in Note 6, during fiscal 2015, HP executed an intercompany advanced royalty payment arrangement resulting in advanced payments of $8.8 billion, while during fiscal 2014 HP executed a multi-year intercompany licensing arrangement and intercompany advanced royalty payment arrangement which resulted in combined advanced payments of $11.5 billion. In these transactions, the payments were received in the U.S. from a foreign consolidated affiliate, with a deferral of intercompany revenues over the term of the arrangements, approximately 5 years and 15 years, respectively. The impact of these intercompany arrangements is eliminated from both HP consolidated and segment revenues.

Financing interest in the Consolidated Statements of Earnings reflects interest expense on debt attributable to HPFS. Debt attributable to HPFS consists of intercompany equity that is treated as debt for segment reporting purposes, intercompany debt, and borrowing- and funding-related activity associated with HPFS and its subsidiaries.

HP does not allocate to its segments certain operating expenses, which it manages at the corporate level. These unallocated costs include certain corporate governance costs, stock-based compensation expense, amortization of intangible assets, restructuring charges, acquisition and other related charges, separation costs, defined benefit plan settlement charges and impairment of data center assets.

Segment Realignment

Effective at the beginning of the first quarter of fiscal 2015, HP implemented an organizational change to align its segment financial reporting more closely with its current business structure. This organizational change resulted in the transfer of third-party multi-vendor support arrangements from the Technology Services ("TS") business unit within the EG segment to the ITO business unit within the ES segment. HP has reflected this change to its segment information retrospectively to the earliest period presented, which has resulted in the removal of intersegment revenue from the TS business unit within the EG segment and the related corporate intersegment revenue eliminations, and the transfer of operating profit from the TS business unit within the EG segment to the ITO business unit within the ES segment.

In connection with the Separation, effective at the beginning of the fourth quarter of fiscal 2015, HP implemented an organizational change which resulted in the transfer of marketing optimization solutions business from the Software segment to the Commercial Hardware business unit within the Printing segment. HP has reflected this change to its segment information in prior reporting periods on an as-if basis, which resulted in the transfer of net revenue from the Software segment to the Commercial Hardware business unit within the Printing segment. This change also resulted in the transfer of operating profit from the Software segment to the Commercial Hardware business unit within the Printing segment. In addition, this change resulted in the reclassification of $512 million of goodwill from the Software segment to the Printing segment.

These changes had no impact on HP's previously reported consolidated net revenue, earnings from operations, net earnings or net EPS.

Segment Operating Results

| In millions | Printing and Personal Systems | | Enterprise Group | Enterprise Services | Software | HP Financial Services | Corporate Investments | Total |
	Personal Systems	Printing						
2015								
Net revenue	$30,438	$20,938	$26,670	$19,009	$3,142	$3,131	$ 27	$103,355
Intersegment net revenue and other	1,031	294	1,237	797	316	85	—	3,760
Total segment net revenue	$31,469	$21,232	$27,907	$19,806	$3,458	$3,216	$ 27	$107,115
Earnings (loss) from operations	$ 1,064	$ 3,865	$ 3,981	$ 1,051	$ 760	$ 349	$(565)	$ 10,505
2014								
Net revenue	$33,304	$22,951	$26,809	$21,297	$3,375	$3,416	$ 302	$111,454
Intersegment net revenue and other	999	260	914	1,101	326	82	—	3,682
Total segment net revenue	$34,303	$23,211	$27,723	$22,398	$3,701	$3,498	$ 302	$115,136
Earnings (loss) from operations	$ 1,270	$ 4,229	$ 3,995	$ 816	$ 828	$ 389	$(199)	$ 11,328
2013								
Net revenue	$31,232	$23,917	$27,045	$23,041	$3,469	$3,570	$ 24	$112,298
Intersegment net revenue and other	947	211	958	1,020	320	59	—	3,515
Total segment net revenue	$32,179	$24,128	$28,003	$24,061	$3,789	$3,629	$ 24	$115,813
Earnings (loss) from operations	$ 980	$ 3,953	$ 4,245	$ 693	$ 848	$ 399	$(316)	$ 10,802

The reconciliation of segment operating results to HP consolidated results was as follows:

In millions	For the Fiscal Years Ended October 31		
	2015	2014	2013
Net Revenue:			
Total segments	$107,115	$115,136	$115,813
Elimination of intersegment net revenue and other	(3,760)	(3,682)	(3,515)
Total HP consolidated net revenue	$103,355	$111,454	$112,298
Earnings Before Taxes:			
Total segment earnings from operations	$ 10,505	$ 11,328	$ 10,802
Corporate and unallocated costs and eliminations	(724)	(953)	(786)
Stock-based compensation expense	(709)	(560)	(500)
Amortization of intangible assets	(931)	(1,000)	(1,373)
Restructuring charges	(1,017)	(1,619)	(990)
Acquisition and other related charges	(90)	(11)	(22)
Separation costs	(1,259)	—	—
Defined benefit plan settlement charges	(168)	—	—
Impairment of data center assets	(136)	—	—
Interest and other, net	(739)	(628)	(621)
Total HP consolidated earnings before taxes	$ 4,732	$ 6,557	$ 6,510

Segment Assets

HP allocates assets to its business segments based on the segments primarily benefiting from the assets. Total assets by segment and the reconciliation of segment assets to HP consolidated assets were as follows:

In millions	As of October 31	
	2015	2014
Personal Systems	$ 9,534	$ 12,104
Printing	8,994	10,666
Printing and Personal Systems Group	18,528	22,770
Enterprise Group[1]	33,499	27,236
Enterprise Services	14,354	13,472
Software	11,226	10,972
HP Financial Services	13,093	13,529
Corporate Investments	56	34
Corporate and unallocated assets	16,126	15,193
Total HP consolidated assets	$106,882	$103,206

[1] In connection with the acquisition of Aruba Networks, Inc. ("Aruba") in fiscal 2015, HP recorded approximately $1.8 billion of goodwill, $643 million of intangible assets and $153 million of IPR&D. HP reports the financial results of Aruba's business in the Networking business unit within the EG segment.

Major Customers

No single customer represented 10% or more of HP's total net revenue in any fiscal year presented.

Geographic Information

Net revenue by country is based upon the sales location that predominately represents the customer location. For each of the fiscal years of 2015, 2014 and 2013, other than the U.S., no country represented more than 10% of HP's net revenue.

Net revenue by country in which HP operates was as follows:

In millions	For the Fiscal Years Ended October 31		
	2015	2014	2013
U.S.	$ 37,679	$ 38,805	$ 40,284
Other countries	65,676	72,649	72,014
Total net revenue	$103,355	$111,454	$112,298

As of October 31, 2015, the U.S. and Netherlands each represented more than 10% of net assets. As of October 31, 2014, the U.S., Netherlands and Ireland each represented 10% or more of net assets.

Net property, plant and equipment by country in which HP operates was as follows:

	As of October 31	
In millions	2015	2014
U.S.	$ 5,501	$ 5,668
United Kingdom.	955	1,053
Other countries	4,634	4,619
Total net property, plant and equipment	$11,090	$11,340

Net revenue by segment and business unit was as follows:

	For the Fiscal Years Ended October 31		
In millions	2015	2014	2013
Notebooks	$ 17,271	$ 17,540	$ 16,029
Desktops	10,941	13,197	12,844
Workstations	2,018	2,218	2,147
Other	1,239	1,348	1,159
Personal Systems	31,469	34,303	32,179
Supplies	13,979	14,917	15,716
Commercial Hardware	5,378	5,949	5,976
Consumer Hardware	1,875	2,345	2,436
Printing	21,232	23,211	24,128
Total Printing and Personal Systems Group	52,701	57,514	56,307
Industry Standard Servers	13,412	12,474	12,102
Technology Services	7,662	8,375	8,710
Storage	3,180	3,316	3,475
Networking	2,846	2,629	2,526
Business Critical Systems	807	929	1,190
Enterprise Group	27,907	27,723	28,003
Infrastructure Technology Outsourcing	12,107	14,038	15,223
Application and Business Services	7,699	8,360	8,838
Enterprise Services	19,806	22,398	24,061
Software	3,458	3,701	3,789
HP Financial Services	3,216	3,498	3,629
Corporate Investments	27	302	24
Total segment net revenue	107,115	115,136	115,813
Eliminations of intersegment net revenue and other	(3,760)	(3,682)	(3,515)
Total net revenue	$103,355	$111,454	$112,298

1.37 UNIVERSAL CORPORATION (MAR)
NOTES TO CONSOLIDATED FINANCIAL STATEMENTS (in part)

(All dollar amounts are in thousands, except per share amounts or as otherwise noted.)

Note 15. Operating Segments

Universal's operations involve selecting, procuring, processing, packing, storing, shipping, and financing leaf tobacco for sale to, or for the account of, manufacturers of consumer tobacco products throughout the world. Through various operating subsidiaries located in tobacco-growing countries around the world and significant ownership interests in unconsolidated affiliates, the Company processes and/or sells flue-cured and burley tobaccos, dark air-cured tobaccos, and oriental tobaccos. Flue-cured, burley, and oriental tobaccos are used principally in the manufacture of cigarettes, and dark air-cured tobaccos are used mainly in the manufacture of cigars, pipe tobacco, and smokeless tobacco products. A substantial portion of the Company's revenues are derived from sales to a limited number of large, multinational cigarette manufacturers.

The principal approach used by management to evaluate the Company's performance is by geographic region, although the dark air-cured and oriental tobacco businesses are each evaluated on the basis of their worldwide operations. Oriental tobacco operations consist principally of a 49% interest in an affiliate, and the performance of those operations is evaluated based on the Company's equity in the pretax earnings of that affiliate. Under this structure, the Company has the following primary operating segments: North America, South America, Africa, Europe, Asia, Dark Air-Cured, Oriental, and Special Services. North America, South America, Africa, Europe, and Asia are primarily involved in flue-cured and/or burley leaf tobacco operations for supply to cigarette manufacturers. The Dark Air-Cured group supplies dark air-cured tobacco principally to manufacturers of cigars, pipe tobacco, and smokeless tobacco products, and the Oriental business supplies oriental tobacco to cigarette manufacturers. From time to time, the segments may trade in tobaccos that differ from their main varieties, but those activities are not significant to their overall results. Special Services includes the Company's laboratory services business, which provides physical and chemical product testing and smoke testing for customers, as well as its liquid nicotine joint venture and its food and vegetable ingredients business.

The five regional operating segments serving the Company's cigarette manufacturer customer base share similar characteristics in the nature of their products and services, production processes, class of customer, product distribution methods, and regulatory environment. Based on the applicable accounting guidance, four of the regions—South America, Africa, Europe, and Asia—are aggregated into a single reporting segment, "Other Regions", because they also have similar economic characteristics. North America is reported as an individual operating segment because its economic characteristics differ from the other regions, generally because its operations require lower working capital investments for crop financing and inventory. The Dark Air-Cured, Oriental and Special Services segments, which have dissimilar characteristics in some of the categories mentioned above, are reported together as "Other Tobacco Operations" because each is below the measurement threshold for separate reporting.

Universal incurs overhead expenses related to senior management, finance, legal, and other functions that are centralized at its corporate headquarters, as well as functions performed at several sales and administrative offices around the world. These overhead expenses are allocated to the various operating segments, generally on the basis of tobacco volumes planned to be purchased and/or processed. Management believes this method of allocation is representative of the value of the related services provided to the operating segments. The Company evaluates the performance of its segments based on operating income after allocated overhead expenses, plus equity in the pretax earnings of unconsolidated affiliates.

Reportable segment data as of, or for, the fiscal years ended March 31, 2015, 2014, and 2013, is as follows:

	Sales and Other Operating Revenues			Operating Income		
	Fiscal Year Ended March 31,			Fiscal Year Ended March 31,		
	2015	2014	2013	2015	2014	2013
Flue-Cured and Burley Leaf Tobacco Operations:						
North America	$ 305,028	$ 348,627	$ 334,676	$ 31,060	$ 23,217	$ 19,740
Other Regions[1]	1,739,781	1,932,228	1,871,880	125,839	133,447	192,556
Subtotal	2,044,809	2,280,855	2,206,556	156,899	156,664	212,296
Other Tobacco Operations[2]	226,992	261,260	255,143	10,326	18,511	20,461
Segment total	2,271,801	2,542,115	2,461,699	167,225	175,175	232,757
Deduct: Equity in pretax earnings of unconsolidated affiliates[3]				(7,137)	(3,897)	(5,635)
Restructuring costs[4]				(4,890)	(6,746)	(4,113)
Add: Other income[5]				12,676	81,619	—
Consolidated total	$2,271,801	$2,542,115	$2,461,699	$167,874	$246,151	$223,009

	Segment Assets			Goodwill		
	March 31,			March 31,		
	2015	2014	2013	2015	2014	2013
Flue-Cured and Burley Leaf Tobacco Operations:						
North America	$ 289,792	$ 277,028	$ 295,785	$ —	$ —	$ —
Other Regions[1]	1,611,083	1,677,654	1,682,581	97,372	97,367	96,667
Subtotal	1,900,875	1,954,682	1,978,366	97,372	97,367	96,667
Other Tobacco Operations[2]	297,598	316,225	327,789	1,713	1,713	1,713
Segment and consolidated totals	$2,198,473	$2,270,907	$2,306,155	$99,085	$99,080	$98,380

	Depreciation and Amortization			Capital Expenditures		
	Fiscal Year Ended March 31,			Fiscal Year Ended March 31,		
	2015	2014	2013	2015	2014	2013
Flue-Cured and Burley Leaf Tobacco Operations:						
North America	$ 4,284	$ 6,018	$11,017	$ 5,814	$ 2,676	$ 2,459
Other Regions[1]	28,827	29,044	30,118	39,303	37,584	24,886
Subtotal	33,111	35,062	41,135	45,117	40,260	27,345
Other Tobacco Operations[2]	4,213	3,837	3,981	13,268	5,589	3,438
Segment and consolidated totals	$37,324	$38,899	$45,116	$58,385	$45,849	$30,783

[1] Includes South America, Africa, Europe, and Asia regions, as well as inter-region eliminations.

[2] Includes Dark Air-Cured, Oriental, and Special Services, as well as inter-company eliminations. Sales and other operating revenues, goodwill, depreciation and amortization, and capital expenditures include limited amounts or no amounts for Oriental because the business is accounted for on the equity method and its financial results consist principally of equity in the pretax earnings of the unconsolidated affiliate. The investment in the unconsolidated affiliate is included in segment assets and was approximately $74.9 million, $93.3 million, and $91.8 million, at March 31, 2015, 2014, and 2013, respectively.

[3] Equity in pretax earnings of unconsolidated affiliates is included in segment operating income (Other Tobacco Operations segment), but is reported below consolidated operating income and excluded from that total in the consolidated statements of income.

[4] Restructuring costs are excluded from segment operating income, but are included in consolidated operating income in the consolidated statements of income (see Note 2).

[5] Other income represents the reversal of a valuation allowance on the remaining unused balance of IPI excise tax credits in Brazil in fiscal year 2015 and the gain on the favorable outcome of the IPI tax credit case in fiscal year 2014 (see Note 14).

Geographic data as of, or for, the fiscal years ended March 31, 2015, 2014, and 2013, is presented below. Sales and other operating revenues are attributed to individual countries based on the final destination of the shipment. Long-lived assets generally consist of net property, plant, and equipment, goodwill, and other intangibles.

| Geographic Data | Sales and Other Operating Revenues | | |
| | Fiscal Year Ended March 31, | | |
	2015	2014	2013
United States	$ 290,950	$ 304,527	$ 324,285
Belgium	226,562	218,550	203,539
China	174,872	210,956	229,112
Germany	170,338	173,872	128,144
Russia	126,652	123,114	130,906
Poland	114,765	106,443	126,826
Netherlands	113,297	208,031	174,481
All other countries	1,054,365	1,196,622	1,144,406
Consolidated total	$2,271,801	$2,542,115	$2,461,699

| | Long-Lived Assets | | |
| | March 31, | | |
	2015	2014	2013
United States	$ 70,929	$ 61,347	$ 64,235
Brazil	135,980	135,359	137,133
Mozambique	55,733	49,543	48,016
All other countries	141,893	149,750	137,132
Consolidated total	$404,535	$395,999	$386,516

Accounting Changes and Error Corrections

PRESENTATION

1.38 FASB ASC 250 defines various types of accounting changes, including changes in accounting principles and accounting estimates, and provides guidance on the accounting for and reporting of each type of change.

1.39 FASB ASC 250-10-45-1 includes the presumption that, once adopted, an entity should not change an accounting principle (policy) to account for events and transactions of a similar type. FASB ASC 250-10-45-2 permits an entity to change an accounting principle in certain circumstances, such as when required to do so by new authoritative accounting guidance that mandates the use of a new accounting principle, interprets an existing principle, expresses a preference for an accounting principle, or rejects a specific principle. This paragraph also permits an entity to change an accounting principle if it can justify the use of an allowable alternative accounting principle on the basis that it is preferable.

1.40 FASB ASC 250-10-45-1 does not consider the following to be changes in accounting principle:
- Initial adoption of an accounting principle for new events or transactions
- Initial adoption of an accounting principle for new events or transactions that previously were immaterial in their effect
- Adoption or modification of an accounting principle for substantively different transactions or events from those occurring previously

1.41 FASB ASC 250-10-45-5 requires an entity to apply a change in accounting principle retrospectively to all prior periods, unless it is impracticable to do so. Retrospective application requires cumulative adjustments to the carrying amounts of assets and liabilities at the beginning of the earliest period presented; an adjustment, if any, to the opening balance of retained earnings or other relevant equity account; and adjusted financial statements for each individual prior period presented to reflect the period-specific effects of applying the new accounting principle. FASB ASC 250-10-45-7 provides an exception if it is impracticable to determine the cumulative effect of applying a change in accounting principle to any prior period; the new accounting principle should be applied as if the change was made prospectively as of the earliest date practicable. FASB ASC 250-10-45-8 permits only direct effects of the change in accounting principle, including any related income tax effects, to be included in the retrospective adjustment and prohibits an entity from including indirect effects that would have been recognized if the newly adopted accounting principle had been followed in prior periods. If indirect effects are actually incurred and recognized, an entity should only report for those indirect effects in the period in which the accounting change is made.

1.42 FASB ASC 250-10-45-17 requires an entity to account for a change in accounting estimate prospectively in the period of change if the change affects that period only or in the period of change and future periods if the change affects both.

1.43 Paragraphs 18–19 of FASB ASC 250-10-45 recognize that it may be difficult to distinguish between a change in an accounting principle and a change in an accounting estimate. Additional guidance is provided for those circumstances when an entity's change in estimate is affected by a change in accounting principle, recognizing that the effect of a change in accounting principle or the method of applying it may be inseparable from the effect of the change in accounting estimate. An example of such change is a change in the method of depreciation, amortization, or depletion for long-lived nonfinancial assets. Although an entity is permitted to apply this change prospectively as a change in accounting estimate, an entity should only make a change in accounting estimate affected by a change in accounting principle if the entity can justify the new accounting principle on the basis that it is preferable.

1.44 Paragraphs 23–24 of FASB ASC 250-10-45 require an entity to correct any error in the financial statements of a prior period discovered after the financial statements are issued or are available to be issued by restating the prior-period financial statements. Such errors are required to be reported as an error correction by restating the prior-period financial statements retrospectively with adjustments to the financial statements.

DISCLOSURE

1.45 As discussed in FASB ASC 250-10-50, among the required disclosures for a change in accounting principle, the reason should be disclosed, including an explanation about why the new method is preferable. Specific disclosures are also required for a change in accounting estimate, a change in reporting entity, correction of an error in previously-issued financial statements, and error corrections related to prior interim periods of the current fiscal year.

PRESENTATION AND DISCLOSURE EXCERPTS

CHANGE IN ACCOUNTING PRINCIPLE—INVENTORY

1.46 CVS HEALTH CORPORATION (DEC)
NOTES TO CONSOLIDATED FINANCIAL STATEMENTS (in part)

1. Significant Accounting Policies (in part)

Inventories —All inventories are stated at the lower of cost or market. Prescription drug inventories in the RLS and PSS, as well as front store inventories in the RLS stores are accounted for using the weighted average cost method. See Note 2, "Changes in Accounting Principle." Physical inventory counts are taken on a regular basis in each retail store and long-term care pharmacy and a continuous cycle count process is the primary procedure used to validate the inventory balances on hand in each distribution center and mail facility to ensure that the amounts reflected in the accompanying consolidated financial statements are properly stated. During the interim period between physical inventory counts, the Company accrues for anticipated physical inventory losses on a location-by-location basis based on historical results and current trends.

2. Changes in Accounting Principle

Effective January 1, 2015, the Company changed its methods of accounting for "front store" inventories in the Retail/LTC Segment. Prior to 2015, the Company valued front store inventories at the lower of cost or market on a first-in, first-out ("FIFO") basis in retail stores using the retail inventory method and in distribution centers using the FIFO cost method. Effective January 1, 2015, all front store inventories in the Retail/LTC Segment have been valued at the lower of cost or market using the weighted average cost method. These changes affected approximately 36% of consolidated inventories.

These changes were made primarily to provide the Company with better information to manage its retail front store operations and to bring all of the Company's inventories to a common inventory valuation methodology. The Company believes the weighted average cost method is preferable to the retail inventory method and the FIFO cost method because it results in greater precision in the determination of cost of revenues and inventories at the stock keeping unit ("SKU") level and results in a consistent inventory valuation method for all of the Company's inventories as all of the Company's remaining inventories, which consist of prescription drugs, were already being valued using the weighted average cost method.

The Company recorded the cumulative effect of these changes in accounting principle as of January 1, 2015. The Company determined that retrospective application for periods prior to 2015 is impracticable, as the period-specific information necessary to value front store inventories in the Retail/LTC Segment under the weighted average cost method is unavailable. The Company implemented a new perpetual inventory system to manage front store inventory at the SKU level and valued front store inventory as of January 1, 2015 and calculated the cumulative impact. The effect of these changes in accounting principle as of January 1, 2015, was a decrease in inventories of $7 million, an increase in current deferred income tax assets of $3 million and a decrease in retained earnings of $4 million.

Had the Company not made these changes in accounting principle, for the year ended December 31, 2015, income from continuing operations would have been lower by $27 million. Basic and diluted earnings per share from continuing operations attributable to CVS Health would have been approximately $0.02 per share lower for the year ended December 31, 2015.

CHANGE IN ACCOUNTING PRINCIPLE—DEFINED BENEFIT AND OTHER POST-EMPLOYMENT BENEFIT PLANS

1.47 COMPUTER SCIENCES CORPORATION (MAR)
NOTES TO CONSOLIDATED FINANCIAL STATEMENTS (in part)

Note 1—Summary of Significant Accounting Policies (in part)

Basis of Presentation and Principles of Consolidation (in part)

During the first quarter of fiscal 2015, the Company changed its accounting policy for the recognition of actuarial gains and losses for its defined benefit pension and other post-employment benefit plans. These changes have been reported through retrospective application of the new accounting methods to all periods presented (see Note 3).

Pension and Other Benefit Plans

The Company and its subsidiaries offer a number of pension and postretirement benefits, life insurance benefits, deferred compensation, and other plans. Most of CSC's pension liabilities are frozen to new accruals. All plans are accounted for using the guidance of Accounting Standards Codification (ASC) 710 "Compensation—General" and ASC 715 "Compensation—Retirement Benefits" and are measured as of the end of the fiscal year.

Effective the first quarter of fiscal 2015, the Company changed its accounting policy for measuring and recognition of actuarial gains and losses for its defined benefit pension and other post-retirement benefit plans and the calculation of the expected return on pension plan assets. Historically, the Company recognized actuarial gains and losses in excess of 10% of the greater of the market-related value of plan assets or the plans' projected benefit obligations (the "corridor") as a component of accumulated other comprehensive loss and, depending on the benefit plan, the Company amortized these gains and losses to earnings either over the remaining average service period for the active participants or over the average remaining life expectancy of the inactive participants. Additionally, for the Company's U.S. plans and the Australian plan, the Company previously used a calculated value for the market-related valuation of pension plan assets, reflecting changes in the fair value of plan assets over a three-year and a one-year period, respectively. Under the Company's new accounting policy, the Company recognizes changes in actuarial gains and losses and the changes in fair value of plan assets in earnings at the time of plan remeasurement, typically annually during the fourth quarter of each year as a component of net periodic benefit expense, and the Company no longer applies a corridor and, therefore, no longer defers any gains or losses.

The new accounting policies result in the changes in actuarial gains and losses and the changes in fair value of plan assets being recognized in earnings in the year they occur, rather than amortized over time, and therefore recognized earlier than under the Company's previous methods of accounting. The Company believes the new pension accounting policies are preferable as they recognize the effects of plan investment performance, interest rate changes, changes in actuarial assumptions as a component of earnings in the year in which they occur rather than amortized over time, and additionally, conform all plans to a consistent policy for determining market-related value of plan assets.

The remaining components of pension/postretirement expense, primarily current period service and interest costs and expected return on plan assets, will continue to be recorded on a quarterly basis.

Inherent in the application of the actuarial methods are key assumptions, including, but not limited to, discount rates, expected long-term rates of return on plan assets, mortality rates, rates of compensation increases, and medical cost trend rates. Company management evaluates these assumptions annually and updates assumptions as necessary. The fair value of assets are determined based on the prevailing market prices or estimated fair value of investments when quoted prices are not available.

Note 3—Defined Benefit Pension Plan Accounting Policy Changes

During the first quarter of fiscal 2015, the Company changed its accounting policy for the recognition of actuarial gains and losses for its defined benefit pension and other post-retirement benefit plans and the calculation of expected return on pension plan assets. Historically, the Company recognized actuarial gains and losses in excess of 10% of the greater of the market-related value of plan assets or the plans' projected benefit obligations (the "corridor") as a component of accumulated other comprehensive loss in its Consolidated Balance Sheets and, depending on the benefit plan, the Company amortized these gains and losses to earnings either over the remaining average service period for the active participants or over the average remaining life expectancy of the inactive participants. Additionally, for the Company's U.S. plans and the Australian plan, the Company previously used a calculated value for the market-related valuation of pension plan assets, reflecting changes in the fair value of plan assets over a three-year and a one-year period, respectively.

Under the Company's new accounting policies, the Company recognizes changes in actuarial gains and losses and the changes in fair value of plan assets in earnings at the time of plan remeasurement, annually during the fourth quarter of each year, or if there is an interim remeasurement, as a component of net periodic (benefit)/cost (and the Company no longer applies a corridor and, therefore, no longer defers any gains or losses). The new accounting policies result in the changes in actuarial gains and losses and the changes in fair value of plan assets being recognized in earnings in the year they occur, rather than amortized over time, and therefore recognized earlier than under the Company's previous methods of accounting. The Company believes the new pension accounting policies are preferable as they recognize the effects of plan investment performance, interest rate changes, and changes in actuarial assumptions as a component of earnings in the year in which they occur rather than amortized over time, and additionally, conform all plans to a consistent policy for determining market-related value of plan assets. These changes have been reported through retrospective application of the new accounting methods to all periods presented. The remaining components of pension/post-retirement expense, primarily current period service and interest costs and expected return on plan assets, will continue to be recorded on a quarterly basis.

In addition to the above mentioned accounting policy changes, the Company also changed the way in which it allocates the elements of net periodic pension (benefit) cost to its reportable segments to be aligned with changes in how the Company's chief operating decision maker evaluates segment performance. Historically, total net periodic pension (benefit) cost, including the amortization of deferred actuarial losses/(gains) and changes in fair value of plan assets, were reported within operating income, as defined by the Company, and fully allocated to reportable segments. Under the new allocation approach, net actuarial gains and losses as well as settlement gain and losses components of the net periodic pension (benefit) cost are excluded entirely from the Company's definition of operating income and not allocated to the reportable segments. All of the other elements of net periodic pension (benefit)/cost, excluding actuarial gains and losses and settlement gains and losses, will continue to be included within operating income of the Company's reportable segments. The Company has applied the change in the allocation approach retrospectively, adjusting segment reporting for all prior periods presented (see Note 20).

The following tables present the effects of applying the change in the pension accounting policies, on select line items of the accompanying fiscal 2015 Consolidated Financial Statements:

Impact on Consolidated Statements of Operations

(Amounts in millions, except per-share amounts)	Twelve Months Ended April 3, 2015		
	Previous Accounting Methods	As Reported	Impact of Change in Accounting Method Increase/(Decrease)
Costs of services	$9,084	$9,534	$ 450
Selling, general and administrative expenses	1,271	1,340	69
Income (loss) from continuing operations, before taxes	243	(276)	(519)
Income tax benefit	(164)	(312)	(148)
Income from continuing operations	407	36	(371)
Net income	378	7	(371)
Net income attributable to noncontrolling interest, net of tax	13	15	2
Net income (loss) attributable to CSC common stockholders	365	(8)	(373)
Basic EPS—Continuing operations	$ 2.76	$ 0.15	$(2.61)
Diluted EPS—Continuing operations	$ 2.70	$ 0.15	$(2.55)

Impact on Consolidated Statements of Comprehensive (Loss) Income

(Amounts in millions)	Twelve Months Ended April 3, 2015		
	Previous Accounting Methods	As Reported	Impact of Change in Accounting Method Increase/(Decrease)
Net income (loss)	$ 378	$ 7	$(371)
Foreign currency translation adjustments	(207)	(310)	(103)
Net actuarial gain	(639)	—	639
Amortization of prior service (cost)	(18)	(16)	2
Amortization of net actuarial gain	159	—	(159)
Foreign currency exchange gain (loss)	8	—	(8)
Pension and other post-retirement benefit plans, net of taxes	(432)	42	474
Other comprehensive loss, net of taxes	(641)	(270)	371
Comprehensive income attributable to noncontrolling interest	13	15	2
Comprehensive income (loss) attributable to CSC common stockholders	(276)	(278)	(2)

Impact on Consolidated Balance Sheets

(Amounts in millions)	As of April 3, 2015		
	Previous Accounting Methods	As Reported	Impact of Change in Accounting Method Increase/(Decrease)
Earnings retained for use in business	$ 2,475	$912	$(1,563)
Accumulated other comprehensive (loss) income	(1,539)	21	1,560
Noncontrolling interest in subsidiaries	25	28	3

Impact on Consolidated Statements of Cash Flows

(Amounts in millions)	Twelve Months Ended April 3, 2015		
	Previous Accounting Methods	As Reported	Impact of Change in Accounting Method Increase/(Decrease)
Net income (loss)	$ 378	$ 7	$(371)
Pension & OPEB actuarial & settlement losses (gains)	—	782	782
Deferred taxes	(301)	(449)	(148)
Increase (decrease) in accounts payable and accrued expenses	(86)	(335)	(249)
Increase (decrease) in income taxes payable and income tax liability	(112)	(23)	89
Other operating activities, net	119	16	(103)

CHANGE IN ACCOUNTING PRINCIPLE—INCOME TAXES

1.48 ELECTRONIC ARTS INC. (MAR)
NOTES TO CONSOLIDATED FINANCIAL STATEMENTS (in part)

(1) Description of Business and Summary of Significant Accounting Policies (in part)

Recently Adopted Accounting Standards

On April 1, 2014, we adopted ASU 2013-11, *Presentation of an Unrecognized Tax Benefit When a Net Operating Loss Carryforward, a Similar Tax Loss, or a Tax Credit Carryforward Exists*. Under the new accounting standard, an unrecognized tax benefit is required to be presented as a reduction to a deferred tax asset if the disallowance of the uncertain tax position would reduce an available tax loss or tax credit carryforward instead of resulting in a cash tax liability. The ASU applies prospectively to all unrecognized tax benefits that exist as of the adoption date. As a result of the adoption, we reduced: (a) noncurrent income tax obligations by $96 million; (b) current deferred income tax assets by $18 million; and (c) noncurrent deferred income tax assets by $11 million. We increased noncurrent deferred income tax liabilities by $67 million. As the new accounting standard only impacted presentation, it did not have an impact on the Company's net financial position, results of operations, or cash flows.

(11) Income Taxes

The components of our income before provision for (benefit from) income taxes for the fiscal years ended March 31, 2015, 2014 and 2013 are as follows (in millions):

	Year Ended March 31,		
	2015	2014	2013
Domestic	$232	$(146)	$ (15)
Foreign	693	153	154
Income before provision for (benefit from) income taxes	$925	$ 7	$139

Provision for (benefit from) income taxes for the fiscal years ended March 31, 2015, 2014 and 2013 consisted of (in millions):

	Current	Deferred	Total
Year Ended March 31, 2015			
Federal	$ 10	$ 17	$ 27
State	—	—	—
Foreign	21	2	23
	$ 31	$ 19	$ 50
Year Ended March 31, 2014			
Federal	$ (2)	$ (9)	$(11)
State	1	(2)	(1)
Foreign	8	3	11
	$ 7	$ (8)	$ (1)
Year Ended March 31, 2013			
Federal	$—	$ 5	$ 5
State	—	1	1
Foreign	39	(4)	35
	$ 39	$ 2	$ 41

Excess tax benefits from stock-based compensation deductions are allocated to contributed capital before historical net operating losses are utilized to reduce tax expense. Deferred income tax provision includes tax benefits allocated directly to contributed capital of $21 million and $12 million for fiscal years 2015 and 2014, respectively, and none for fiscal year 2013.

The differences between the statutory tax expense rate and our effective tax expense (benefit) rate, expressed as a percentage of income before provision for (benefit from) income taxes, for the fiscal years ended March 31, 2015, 2014 and 2013 were as follows:

	Year Ended March 31,		
	2015	2014	2013
Statutory federal tax expense rate	35.0%	35.0%	35.0%
State taxes, net of federal benefit	0.1%	(242.9)%	(5.0)%
Differences between statutory rate and foreign effective tax rate	(22.3)%	(142.9)%	(15.2)%
Valuation allowance	(9.2)%	936.5%	35.0%
Research and development credits	(1.1)%	(128.6)%	(8.6)%
Differences between book and tax on sale of strategic investments	—	—	(15.2)%
Resolution of tax matters with authorities	(0.5)%	(657.1)%	—
Non-deductible stock-based compensation	3.5%	385.7%	21.5%
Acquisition-related contingent consideration	(0.2)%	(185.7)%	(16.5)%
Other	0.1%	(14.3)%	(1.5)%
Effective tax expense (benefit) rate	5.4%	(14.3)%	29.5%

During the fiscal year 2014, we made a one-time repatriation of $700 million from certain of our wholly-owned subsidiaries. This repatriation did not have a material impact on our effective tax rate for fiscal year 2014 due to the deferred tax valuation allowance.

Undistributed earnings of our foreign subsidiaries amounted to approximately $752 million as of March 31, 2015. Those earnings are considered to be indefinitely reinvested and, accordingly, no U.S. income taxes have been provided thereon. Upon distribution of those earnings in the form of dividends or otherwise, we would be subject to both U.S. income taxes (subject to an adjustment for foreign tax credits) and withholding taxes payable to various foreign countries. It is not practicable to determine the income tax liability that might be incurred if these earnings were to be distributed.

The components of net deferred tax assets, as of March 31, 2015 and 2014 consisted of (in millions):

	As of March 31,	
	2015	2014
Deferred tax assets:		
Accruals, reserves and other expenses	$ 193	$ 163
Tax credit carryforwards	358	462
Stock-based compensation	35	43
Net operating loss & capital loss carryforwards	53	199
Total	639	867
Valuation allowance	(555)	(675)
Deferred tax assets, net of valuation allowance	84	192
Deferred tax liabilities:		
Depreciation	(9)	(12)
State effect on federal taxes	(62)	(63)
Amortization	(23)	(28)
Prepaids and other liabilities	(8)	(9)
Total	(102)	(112)
Deferred tax assets, net of valuation allowance and deferred tax liabilities	$ (18)	$ 80

On April 1, 2014, we adopted ASU 2013-11, *Presentation of an Unrecognized Tax Benefit When a Net Operating Loss Carryforward, a Similar Tax Loss, or a Tax Credit Carryforward Exists.* Under the new accounting standard, an unrecognized tax benefit is required to be presented as a reduction to a deferred tax asset if the disallowance of the uncertain tax position would reduce an available tax loss or tax credit carryforward instead of resulting in a cash tax liability. The ASU applies prospectively to all unrecognized tax benefits that exist as of the adoption date. Prior to adoption, the deferred tax assets were presented without reduction for uncertain tax positions.

The valuation allowance decreased by $120 million in fiscal year 2015, primarily due to the current fiscal year utilization of U.S. deferred tax assets. We have not yet been able to establish a sustained level of profitability in the U.S. or other sufficient significant positive evidence to conclude that our U.S. deferred tax assets are more likely than not to be realized. Therefore, we continue to maintain a valuation allowance against most of our U.S. deferred tax assets. It is possible that a significant portion of the valuation allowance recorded against our U.S. deferred tax assets at March 31, 2015 could be reversed by the end of fiscal year 2016.

As of March 31, 2015, we have state net operating loss carry forwards of approximately $785 million of which approximately $114 million is attributable to various acquired companies. These carry forwards, if not fully realized, will begin to expire in 2016. We also have U.S. federal, California and Canada tax credit carry forwards of $320 million, $131 million and $7 million, respectively. The U.S. federal tax credit carry forwards will begin to expire in 2024. The California and Canada tax credit carry forwards can be carried forward indefinitely.

The total unrecognized tax benefits as of March 31, 2015 and 2014 were $254 million and $232 million, respectively. A reconciliation of the beginning and ending balance of unrecognized tax benefits is summarized as follows (in millions):

Balance as of March 31, 2013	$297
Increases in unrecognized tax benefits related to prior year tax positions	10
Decreases in unrecognized tax benefits related to prior year tax positions	(79)
Increases in unrecognized tax benefits related to current year tax positions	44
Decreases in unrecognized tax benefits related to settlements with taxing authorities	(29)
Reductions in unrecognized tax benefits due to lapse of applicable statute of limitations	(9)
Changes in unrecognized tax benefits due to foreign currency translation	(2)
Balance as of March 31, 2014	232
Increases in unrecognized tax benefits related to prior year tax positions	9
Decreases in unrecognized tax benefits related to prior year tax positions	(14)
Increases in unrecognized tax benefits related to current year tax positions	50
Decreases in unrecognized tax benefits related to settlements with taxing authorities	(6)
Reductions in unrecognized tax benefits due to lapse of applicable statute of limitations	(7)
Changes in unrecognized tax benefits due to foreign currency translation	(10)
Balance as of March 31, 2015	$254

A portion of our unrecognized tax benefits will affect our effective tax rate if they are recognized upon favorable resolution of the uncertain tax positions. As of March 31, 2015, approximately $58 million of the unrecognized tax benefits would affect our effective tax rate and approximately $195 million would result in adjustments to deferred tax valuation allowance. As of March 31, 2014, approximately $84 million of the unrecognized tax benefits would affect our effective tax rate and approximately $148 million would result in corresponding adjustments to the deferred tax valuation allowance.

Interest and penalties related to estimated obligations for tax positions taken in our tax returns are recognized in income tax expense in our Consolidated Statements of Operations. The combined amount of accrued interest and penalties related to tax positions taken on our tax returns and included in non-current other liabilities was approximately $16 million as of March 31, 2015 and 2014. There is no material change in accrued interest and penalties during fiscal year 2015.

We file income tax returns in the United States, including various state and local jurisdictions. Our subsidiaries file tax returns in various foreign jurisdictions, including Canada, France, Germany, Switzerland and the United Kingdom. The IRS is currently examining our returns for fiscal years 2009 through 2011, and we remain subject to income tax examination by the IRS for fiscal years after 2011.

We are also currently under income tax examination in the United Kingdom for fiscal years 2010 through 2013, and in Germany for fiscal years 2008 through 2012. We remain subject to income tax examination for several other jurisdictions including in France for fiscal years after 2011, in Germany for fiscal years after 2012, in the United Kingdom for fiscal years after 2013, and in Canada and Switzerland for fiscal years after 2007.

The timing of the resolution of income tax examinations is highly uncertain, and the amounts ultimately paid, if any, upon resolution of the issues raised by the taxing authorities may differ materially from the amounts accrued for each year. Although potential resolution of uncertain tax positions involve multiple tax periods and jurisdictions, it is reasonably possible that a reduction of up to $11 million of unrecognized tax benefits may occur within the next 12 months, some of which, depending on the nature of the settlement or expiration of statutes of limitations, may affect the Company's income tax provision and therefore benefit the resulting effective tax rate. The actual amount could vary significantly depending on the ultimate timing and nature of any settlements.

CHANGE IN ACCOUNTING PRINCIPLE—DISCONTINUED OPERATIONS

1.49 EBAY INC. (DEC)
NOTES TO CONSOLIDATED FINANCIAL STATEMENTS (in part)

Note 1—The Company and Summary of Significant Accounting Policies (in part)

The Company (in part)

eBay Inc. is a global commerce leader, including our Marketplace, StubHub and Classifieds platforms. Our Marketplace platforms include our online marketplace located at www.ebay.com, its localized counterparts and the eBay mobile apps. Our StubHub platforms include our online ticket platform located at www.stubhub.com and the StubHub mobile apps. Our Classifieds platforms include a collection of brands such as Mobile.de, Kijiji, Gumtree, Marktplaats, eBay Classifieds and others.

On July 17, 2015, we completed the distribution of 100% of the outstanding common stock of PayPal Holdings, Inc. ("PayPal") to our stockholders (the "Distribution"), pursuant to which PayPal became an independent company. Beginning in the third quarter of 2015, PayPal's financial results for periods prior to the Distribution have been reflected in our consolidated statement of income, retrospectively, as discontinued operations. Additionally, the related assets and liabilities associated with the discontinued operations in the prior year consolidated balance sheet are classified as discontinued operations. Pursuant to the terms of the separation and distribution agreement entered into between us and PayPal on June 26, 2015, upon Distribution, assets related to the PayPal business were transferred to, and liabilities related to the PayPal business were retained or assumed by, PayPal. See "Note 4—Discontinued Operations" for additional information.

During the second quarter of 2015, our Board of Directors ("Board") approved a plan to sell the businesses underlying our former Enterprise segment ("Enterprise"). As a result, the Enterprise financial results were reflected in our consolidated statement of income, retrospectively, as discontinued operations beginning in the second quarter of 2015. On July 16, 2015, we signed a definitive agreement to sell Enterprise and on November 2, 2015, the sale closed. As a result, the related assets and liabilities associated with the discontinued operations in the prior year consolidated balance sheet are classified as discontinued operations. See "Note 4—Discontinued Operations" for additional information.

Recent Accounting Pronouncements (in part)

In 2014, the FASB issued new guidance related to reporting discontinued operations. This new standard raises the threshold for a disposal to qualify as a discontinued operation and requires new disclosures of both discontinued operations and certain other disposals that do not meet the definition of a discontinued operation. The new standard is now effective. The standard impacted the presentation of Enterprise during the second quarter of 2015 and PayPal during the third quarter of 2015 related to the financial statement presentation of assets held for sale and discontinued operations and required additional disclosures as presented in "Note 4—Discontinued Operations."

Note 2—Net Income (loss) Per Share

Basic net income (loss) per share is computed by dividing net income (loss) for the period by the weighted average number of common shares outstanding during the period. Diluted net income (loss) per share is computed by dividing net income (loss) for the period by the weighted average number of shares of common stock and potentially dilutive common stock outstanding during the period. The dilutive effect of outstanding options and equity incentive awards is reflected in diluted net income (loss) per share by application of the treasury stock method. The calculation of diluted net income (loss) per share excludes all anti-dilutive common shares. The following table sets forth the computation of basic and diluted net income (loss) per share for the periods indicated:

(In millions, except per share amounts)	Year Ended December 31,		
	2015	2014	2013
Numerator:			
Income (loss) from continuing operations	$1,947	$ (865)	$2,067
Income (loss) from discontinued operations, net of income taxes	(222)	911	789
Net income	$1,725	$ 46	$2,856
Denominator:			
Weighted average shares of common stock—basic	1,208	1,251	1,295
Dilutive effect of equity incentive awards	12	—	18
Weighted average shares of common stock—diluted	1,220	1,251	1,313
Income (loss) per share—basic:			
Continuing operations	$ 1.61	$(0.69)	$ 1.60
Discontinued operations	(0.18)	0.73	0.60
Net income per share—basic	$ 1.43	$ 0.04	$ 2.20
Income (loss) per share—diluted:			
Continuing operations	$ 1.60	$(0.69)	$ 1.58
Discontinued operations	(0.18)	0.73	0.60
Net income per share—diluted	$ 1.42	$ 0.04	$ 2.18
Common stock equivalents excluded from income per diluted share because their effect would have been anti-dilutive	2	54	4

Note 4—Discontinued Operations

On June 26, 2015, our Board approved the separation of PayPal through the Distribution. To consummate the Distribution, our Board declared a pro rata dividend of PayPal Holdings, Inc. common stock to eBay's stockholders of record as of the close of business on July 8, 2015 (the "Record Date"). Each eBay stockholder received one (1) share of PayPal Holdings, Inc. common stock for every share of eBay common stock held at the close of business on the Record Date. The Distribution occurred on July 17, 2015. Immediately following the Distribution, PayPal became an independent, publicly traded company and is listed on The NASDAQ Stock Market under the ticker "PYPL." eBay continues to trade on The NASDAQ Stock Market under the ticker "EBAY." We have classified the results of PayPal as discontinued operations in our consolidated statement of income for all periods presented. Additionally, the related assets and liabilities associated with the discontinued operations in the prior year consolidated balance sheet are classified as discontinued operations. In connection with the Distribution, we reviewed our capital allocation strategy to ensure that each of PayPal and eBay would be well capitalized at Distribution. As part of this strategy, we contributed approximately $3.8 billion of cash to PayPal.

During the second quarter of 2015, our Board approved a plan to sell Enterprise. Based on the expected sales proceeds, we recorded a goodwill impairment of $786 million in the second quarter of 2015. On July 16, 2015, we signed a definitive agreement to sell Enterprise for $925 million and on November 2, 2015, the sale closed. We recorded a loss of $35 million upon closing included within income (loss) from discontinued operations, net of income taxes. We have classified the results of Enterprise as discontinued operations in our consolidated statement of income for all periods presented. Additionally, the related assets and liabilities associated with the discontinued operations in the prior year consolidated balance sheet are classified as discontinued operations.

The following table presents the aggregate carrying amounts of the classes of assets and liabilities of discontinued operations of PayPal and Enterprise:

(In millions)	December 31, 2014
PayPal current assets classified as discontinued operations	$16,795
Enterprise current assets classified as discontinued operations	253
Current assets of discontinued operations	$17,048
PayPal long-term assets classified as discontinued operations	$ 4,506
Enterprise long-term assets classified as discontinued operations	1,862
Long-term assets of discontinued operations	$ 6,368
PayPal current liabilities classified as discontinued operations	$12,137
Enterprise current liabilities classified as discontinued operations	374
Current liabilities of discontinued operations	$12,511
PayPal long-term liabilities classified as discontinued operations	$ 243
Enterprise long-term liabilities classified as discontinued operations	74
Long-term liabilities of discontinued operations	$ 317

The financial results of PayPal and Enterprise are presented as income (loss) from discontinued operations, net of income taxes in our consolidated statement of income. The following table presents financial results of PayPal and Enterprise:

	Year Ended December 31,		
	2015 [1]	2014	2013
PayPal income from discontinued operations, net of income taxes	$ 516	$1,024	$ 926
Enterprise loss from discontinued operations, net of income taxes	(738)	(113)	(137)
Income (loss) from discontinued operations, net of income taxes	$(222)	$ 911	$ 789

[1] Includes PayPal financial results from January 1, 2015 to July 17, 2015 and Enterprise financial results from January 1, 2015 to November 2, 2015.

The following table presents cash flows of PayPal and Enterprise:

	Year Ended December 31,		
	2015 [1]	2014	2013
PayPal net cash provided by discontinued operating activities	$ 1,252	$ 2,280	$ 1,913
Enterprise net cash provided by (used in) discontinued operating activities	(96)	169	150
Net cash provided by discontinued operating activities	$ 1,156	$ 2,449	$ 2,063
PayPal net cash used in discontinued investing activities	$(3,725)	$(1,218)	$(2,221)
Enterprise net cash provided by (used in) discontinued investing activities	787	(130)	(171)
Net cash used in discontinued investing activities	$(2,938)	$(1,348)	$(2,392)
PayPal net cash provided by (used in) discontinued financing activities[2]	$(1,594)	$ 40	$ 76
Enterprise net cash used in discontinued financing activities	—	(15)	1
Net cash provided by (used in) discontinued financing activities	$(1,594)	$ 25	$ 77

[1] Includes PayPal financial results from January 1, 2015 to July 17, 2015 and Enterprise financial results from January 1, 2015 to November 2, 2015.
[2] Includes $1.6 billion of PayPal cash and cash equivalents as of July 17, 2015.

PayPal

The financial results of PayPal through the Distribution are presented as income (loss) from discontinued operations, net of income taxes on our consolidated statement of income. The following table presents financial results of PayPal:

	Year Ended December 31,		
	2015 [1]	2014	2013
Net revenues	$4,793	$7,895	$6,640
Cost of net revenues	1,918	3,140	2,696
Gross profit	2,875	4,755	3,944
Operating expenses:			
Sales and marketing	534	1,027	794
Product development	527	879	712
General and administrative	741	892	724
Provision for transaction and loan losses	418	688	551
Amortization of acquired intangible assets	30	53	41
Total operating expenses	2,250	3,539	2,822
Income from operations of discontinued operations	625	1,216	1,122
Interest and other, net	1	(7)	(7)
Income from discontinued operations before income taxes	626	1,209	1,115
Provision for income taxes	(110)	(185)	(189)
Income from discontinued operations, net of income taxes	$ 516	$1,024	$ 926

[1] Includes PayPal financial results from January 1, 2015 to July 17, 2015.

The following table presents the aggregate carrying amounts of the classes of assets and liabilities of discontinued operations of PayPal:

(In millions)	December 31, 2014
Carrying amounts of assets included as part of discontinued operations:	
Cash and cash equivalents	$ 2,194
Short-term investments	39
Accounts receivable, net	51
Loans and interest receivable, net	3,600
Funds receivable and customer accounts	10,545
Other current assets	366
Current assets classified as discontinued operations	16,795
Long-term investments	31
Property and equipment, net	1,113
Goodwill	3,136
Intangible assets, net	172
Other assets	54
Long-term assets classified as discontinued operations	4,506
Total assets classified as discontinued operations in the consolidated balance sheet	$21,301
Carrying amounts of liabilities included as part of discontinued operations:	
Accounts payable	$115
Funds receivable and customer accounts	10,545
Accrued expenses and other current liabilities	1,448
Income taxes payable	29
Current liabilities classified as discontinued operations	12,137
Deferred and other tax liabilities, net	197
Other liabilities	46
Long-term liabilities classified as discontinued operations	243
Total liabilities classified as discontinued operations in the consolidated balance sheet	$12,380

Enterprise

The financial results of Enterprise are presented as income (loss) from discontinued operations, net of income taxes on our consolidated statement of income. The following table presents financial results of Enterprise:

	Year Ended December 31,		
	2015 [1]	2014	2013
Net revenues	$ 904	$1,217	$1,150
Cost of net revenues	654	929	848
Gross profit	250	288	302
Operating expenses:			
Sales and marketing	95	118	122
Product development	91	138	141
General and administrative	118	62	99
Provision for transaction losses	12	8	4
Amortization of acquired intangible assets	70	140	141
Goodwill impairment	786	—	—
Total operating expenses	1,172	466	507
Loss from operations of discontinued operations	(922)	(178)	(205)
Interest and other, net	1	(15)	(15)
Pretax loss on disposal of the discontinued operation	(35)	—	—
Loss from discontinued operations before income taxes	(956)	(193)	(220)
Income tax benefit	218	80	83
Loss from discontinued operations, net of income taxes	$ (738)	$ (113)	$ (137)

[1] Includes Enterprise financial results from January 1, 2015 to November 2, 2015.

The following table presents the aggregate carrying amounts of the classes of assets and liabilities of discontinued operations of Enterprise:

(In millions)	December 31, 2014
Carrying amounts of assets included as part of discontinued operations:	
Cash and cash equivalents	$ 29
Short-term investments	1
Accounts receivable, net	146
Other current assets	77
Current assets classified as discontinued operations	253
Long-term investments	10
Property and equipment, net	303
Goodwill	1,287
Intangible assets, net	259
Other assets	3
Long-term assets classified as discontinued operations	1,862
Total assets classified as discontinued operations in the consolidated balance sheet	$2,115
Carrying amounts of liabilities included as part of discontinued operations:	
Accounts payable	$ 179
Accrued expenses and other current liabilities	115
Deferred revenue	80
Current liabilities classified as discontinued operations	374
Deferred and other tax liabilities, net	73
Other liabilities	1
Long-term liabilities classified as discontinued operations	74
Total liabilities classified as discontinued operations in the consolidated balance sheet	$ 448

Note 6—Segments

We have one operating and reportable segment. Our chief operating decision maker reviews financial information presented on a consolidated basis for purposes of allocating resources and evaluating financial performance. During the second quarter of 2015, we classified the results of Enterprise, formerly our Enterprise segment, as discontinued operations in our consolidated statement of income for all periods presented. During the third quarter of 2015, we have classified the results of PayPal, formerly our Payments segment, as discontinued operations in our consolidated statement of income for all periods presented. See "Note 4—Discontinued Operations" for additional information.

The following table sets forth the breakdown of net revenues by type:

(In millions)	Year Ended December 31,		
	2015	2014	2013
Net Revenues by Type:			
Net transaction revenues:			
Marketplace	$6,103	$6,351	$5,900
StubHub	725	629	653
Total net transaction revenues	6,828	6,980	6,553
Marketing services and other revenues:			
Marketplace	1,078	1,103	1,090
Classifieds	703	716	621
Corporate and other	(17)	(9)	(7)
Total marketing services and other revenues	1,764	1,810	1,704
Total net revenues	$8,592	$8,790	$8,257

The following table summarizes the allocation of net revenues based on geography:

(In millions)	Year Ended December 31,		
	2015	2014	2013
Net Revenues by Geography:			
U.S.	$3,624	$3,525	$3,419
United Kingdom	1,403	1,464	1,290
Germany	1,310	1,511	1,466
Rest of world	2,255	2,290	2,082
Total net revenues	$8,592	$8,790	$8,257

The following table summarizes the allocation of long-lived tangible assets based on geography:

(In millions)	December 31, 2015	December 31, 2014
Long-Lived Tangible Assets by Geography:		
U.S.	$1,668	$1,578
International	116	132
Total long-lived tangible assets	$1,784	$1,710

Net revenues are attributed to U.S. and international geographies primarily based upon the country in which the seller, platform that displays advertising, other service provider, or customer, as the case may be, is located. Long-lived assets attributed to the U.S. and international geographies are based upon the country in which the asset is located or owned.

1.50 CLIFFS NATURAL RESOURCES INC. (DEC)
STATEMENTS OF CONSOLIDATED OPERATIONS

(In Millions, Except Per Share Amounts)	Year Ended December 31, 2015	Year Ended December 31, 2014	Year Ended December 31, 2013
Revenues From Product Sales And Services			
Product	$ 1,832.4	$ 3,095.2	$ 3,631.8
Freight and venture partners' cost reimbursements	180.9	278.0	259.0
	2,013.3	3,373.2	3,890.8
Cost Of Goods Sold And Operating Expenses	(1,776.8)	(2,487.5)	(2,406.4)
Sales Margin	236.5	885.7	1,484.4
Other Operating Income (Expense)			
Selling, general and administrative expenses	(110.0)	(154.7)	(163.8)
Impairment of goodwill and other long-lived assets	(3.3)	(635.5)	(14.3)
Miscellaneous—net	28.1	34.6	74.0
	(85.2)	(755.6)	(104.1)
Operating Income	151.3	130.1	1,380.3
Other Income (Expense)			
Interest expense, net	(228.5)	(176.7)	(186.4)
Gain on extinguishment of debt	392.9	16.2	—
Other non-operating income (expense)	(2.6)	10.7	(3.0)
	161.8	(149.8)	(189.4)
Income (Loss) From Continuing Operations Before Income Taxes And Equity Loss From Ventures	313.1	(19.7)	1,190.9
Income Tax Benefit (Expense)	(169.3)	86.0	(237.6)
Equity Loss From Ventures, Net Of Tax	(0.1)	(9.9)	(74.4)
Income From Continuing Operations	143.7	56.4	878.9
Loss From Discontinued Operations, Net Of Tax	(892.1)	(8,368.0)	(517.1)
Net Income (Loss)	(748.4)	(8,311.6)	361.8
Loss (Income) Attributable To Noncontrolling Interest	(0.9)	1,087.4	51.7
(Year Ended December 31, 2015—Loss of $7.7 million related to Discontinued Operations, Year Ended December 31, 2014—Loss of $1,113.3 million and Year Ended December 31, 2013—Loss of $66.5 million related to Discontinued Operations)			
Net Income (Loss) Attributable To Cliffs Shareholders	$ (749.3)	$(7,224.2)	$ 413.5
Preferred Stock Dividends	(38.4)	(51.2)	(48.7)
Net Income (Loss) Attributable To Cliffs Common Shareholders	$ (787.7)	$(7,275.4)	$ 364.8
Earnings (Loss) Per Common Share Attributable To Cliffs Shareholders—Basic			
Continuing operations	$ 0.63	$ (0.14)	$ 5.37
Discontinued operations	(5.77)	(47.38)	(2.97)
	$ (5.14)	$ (47.52)	$ 2.40
Earnings (Loss) Per Common Share Attributable To Cliffs Shareholders—Diluted			
Continuing operations	$ 0.63	$(0.14)	$ 4.95
Discontinued operations	(5.76)	(47.38)	(2.58)
	$ (5.13)	$ (47.52)	$ 2.37
Average Number Of Shares (In Thousands)			
Basic	153,230	153,098	151,726
Diluted	153,605	153,098	174,323
Cash Dividends Declared Per Depositary Share	$ 1.32	$ 1.76	$ 1.66
Cash Dividends Declared Per Common Share	$ —	$ 0.60	$ 0.60

The accompanying notes are an integral part of these consolidated financial statements .

NOTES TO CONSOLIDATED FINANCIAL STATEMENTS (in part)

Note 1—Basis of Presentation and Significant Accounting Policies (in part)

Business Summary

We are a leading mining and natural resources company in the United States. We are a major supplier of iron ore pellets to the North American steel industry from our five iron ore mines and pellet plants located in Michigan and Minnesota. Additionally, Cliffs operates an iron ore mining complex in Western Australia. Our continuing operations are organized according to geography: U.S. Iron Ore and Asia Pacific Iron Ore.

As more fully described in NOTE 14—DISCONTINUED OPERATIONS, in January 2015, we announced that the Bloom Lake Group commenced restructuring proceedings in Montreal, Quebec under the CCAA. At that time, we had suspended Bloom Lake operations and for several months had been exploring options to sell certain of our Canadian assets, among other initiatives. Effective January 27, 2015, following the CCAA filing of the Bloom Lake Group, we deconsolidated the Bloom Lake Group and certain other wholly-owned subsidiaries comprising substantially all of our Canadian operations. Additionally, on May 20, 2015, the Wabush Group commenced restructuring proceedings in Montreal, Quebec under the CCAA which resulted in the deconsolidation of the remaining Wabush Group entities that were not previously deconsolidated. The Wabush Group was no longer generating revenues and was not able to meet its obligations as they came due. As a result of this action, the CCAA protections granted to the Bloom Lake Group were extended to include the Wabush Group to facilitate the reorganization of each of their businesses and operations. Financial results prior to the respective deconsolidations of the Bloom Lake and Wabush Groups and subsequent expenses directly associated with the Canadian Entities are included in our financial statements and classified within discontinued operations.

Also, for the majority of 2015, we operated two metallurgical coal operations in Alabama and West Virginia. In December 2015, we completed the sale of these two metallurgical coal operations, which marked our exit from the coal business. As of March 31, 2015, management determined that our North American Coal operating segment met the criteria to be classified as held for sale under *ASC 205, Presentation of Financial Statements*. As such, all current year and historical North American Coal operating segment results are included in our financial statements and classified within discontinued operations. Refer to NOTE 14—DISCONTINUED OPERATIONS for further discussion of the North American Coal segment discontinued operations.

Discontinued Operations

In April 2014, the FASB issued ASU 2014-08, *Reporting Discontinued Operations and Disclosures of Disposals of Components of an Entity*, which changes the criteria for reporting discontinued operations and requires additional disclosures about discontinued operations. The standard requires that an entity report as a discontinued operation only a disposal that represents a strategic shift in operations that has a major effect on its operations and financial results. ASU 2014-08 is effective prospectively for new disposals that occur within annual periods beginning on or after December 15, 2014. Early adoption was permitted and we adopted ASU 2014-08 during the three months ended December 31, 2014.

North American Coal Operations

As we execute our strategy to focus on strengthening our U.S. Iron Ore operations, management determined as of March 31, 2015 that our North American Coal operating segment met the criteria to be classified as held for sale under *ASC 205, Presentation of Financial Statements* and continued to meet the criteria throughout 2015. In December 2015, we completed the sale of our remaining two metallurgical coal operations, Oak Grove and Pinnacle mines, which marked our exit from the coal business. Our plan to sell the Oak Grove and Pinnacle mine assets represented a strategic shift in our business. For this reason, our previously reported North American Coal operating segment results for all periods, prior to the March 31, 2015 held for sale determination, are classified as discontinued operations. Additionally, the results for the remainder of 2015 were reported as discontinued operations. This also includes our CLCC assets, which were sold during the fourth quarter of 2014. Refer to NOTE 14—DISCONTINUED OPERATIONS for further discussion of our discontinued operations.

Canadian Operations

As more fully described in NOTE 14—DISCONTINUED OPERATIONS, in January 2015, we announced that the Bloom Lake Group commenced restructuring proceedings in Montreal, Quebec under the CCAA. At that time, we had suspended Bloom Lake operations and for several months had been exploring options to sell certain of our Canadian assets, among other initiatives. Effective January 27, 2015, following the CCAA filing of the Bloom Lake Group, we deconsolidated the Bloom Lake Group and certain other wholly-owned subsidiaries comprising substantially all of our Canadian operations. Additionally, on May 20, 2015, the Wabush Group commenced restructuring proceedings in Montreal, Quebec under the CCAA which resulted in the deconsolidation of the remaining Wabush Group entities that were not previously deconsolidated. The Wabush Group was no longer generating revenues and was not able to meet its obligations as they came due. As a result of this action, the CCAA protections granted to the Bloom Lake Group were extended to include the Wabush Group to facilitate the reorganization of each of their businesses and operations. Our Canadian exit represents a strategic shift in our business. For this reason, our previously reported Eastern Canadian Iron Ore and Ferroalloys operating segment results for all periods prior to the respective deconsolidations as well as costs to exit are classified as discontinued operations.

Note 14—Discontinued Operations

The information below sets forth selected financial information related to operating results of our businesses classified as discontinued operations. While the reclassification of revenues and expenses related to discontinued operations from prior periods have no impact upon previously reported net income, the Statements of Consolidated Operations present the revenues and expenses that were reclassified from the specified line items to discontinued operations and the Statements of Consolidated Financial Position present the assets and liabilities that were reclassified from the specified line items to assets and liabilities of discontinued operations.

The chart below provides an asset group breakout for each financial statement line impacted by discontinued operations.

(In Millions)		North American Coal	Canadian Operations: Eastern Canadian Iron Ore	Canadian Operations: Other	Total Canadian Operations	Total of Discontinued Operations
Statements of Consolidated Operations						
Loss from Discontinued Operations, net of tax	YTD December 31, 2015	$ (152.4)	$ (638.7)	$(101.0)	$ (739.7)	$ (892.1)
Loss from Discontinued Operations, net of tax	YTD December 31, 2014	$(1,134.5)	$(6,952.9)	$(280.6)	$(7,233.5)	$(8,368.0)
Loss from Discontinued Operations, net of tax[1]	YTD December 31, 2013	$ (9.3)	$ (370.4)	$(139.4)	$ (509.8)	$ (519.1)
Statements of Consolidated Financial Position						
Short-term assets of discontinued operations	As of December 31, 2015	$ 14.9	$ —	$ —	$ —	$ 14.9
Long-term assets of discontinued operations	As of December 31, 2015	$ —	$ —	$ —	$ —	$ —
Short-term liabilities of discontinued operations	As of December 31, 2015	$ 6.9	$ —	$ —	$ —	$ 6.9
Long-term liabilities of discontinued operations	As of December 31, 2015	$ —	$ —	$ —	$ —	$ —
Short-term assets of discontinued operations	As of December 31, 2014	$ 140.1	$ 183.5	$ 3.3	$ 186.8	$ 326.9
Long-term assets of discontinued operations	As of December 31, 2014	$ 113.3	$ 256.0	$ 13.7	$ 269.7	$ 383.0
Short-term liabilities of discontinued operations	As of December 31, 2014	$ 80.1	$ 316.3	$ 3.0	$ 319.3	$ 399.4
Long-term liabilities of discontinued operations	As of December 31, 2014	$ 117.3	$ 304.6	$ 5.6	$ 310.2	$ 427.5
Non-Cash Operating and Investing Activities						
Depreciation, depletion and amortization:	YTD December 31, 2015	$ 3.2	$ —	$ —	$ —	$ 3.2
Purchase of property, plant and equipment	YTD December 31, 2015	$ 15.9	$ —	$ —	$ —	$ 15.9
Impairment of goodwill and other long-lived assets	YTD December 31, 2015	$ 73.4	$ —	$ —	$ —	$ 73.4
Depreciation, depletion and amortization:	YTD December 31, 2014	$ 106.9	$ 135.6	$ 0.5	$ 136.1	$ 243.0
Purchase of property, plant and equipment	YTD December 31, 2014	$ 29.9	$ 190.3	$ —	$ 190.3	$ 220.2
Impairment of goodwill and other long-lived assets	YTD December 31, 2014	$ 857.5	$ 7,269.2	$ 267.6	$ 7,536.8	$ 8,394.3
Depreciation, depletion and amortization:	YTD December 31, 2013	$ 128.9	$ 178.6	$ 1.0	$ 179.6	$ 308.5
Purchase of property, plant and equipment	YTD December 31, 2013	$ 64.1	$ 718.3	$ 1.0	$ 719.3	$ 783.4
Impairment of goodwill and other long-lived assets	YTD December 31, 2013	$ —	$ 154.6	$ 81.8	$ 236.4	$ 236.4

[1] Loss from Discontinued Operations, net of tax during the year end December 31, 2013 also includes an additional income tax benefit of $2.0 million resulting from the actual tax gain from the Sale of Sonoma as included in the 2012 tax return, which was filed during the year ended December 31, 2013. During the fourth quarter of 2012, we sold our 45 percent economic interest in Sonoma. The Sonoma operations previously were included in *Other* within our reportable segments.

North American Coal Operations

Background

As we continue to execute our strategy which focuses on strengthening our U.S. Iron Ore operations, management determined as of March 31, 2015 that our North American Coal operating segment met the criteria to be classified as held for sale under *ASC 205, Presentation of Financial Statements*. The North American Coal segment continued to meet the criteria throughout 2015 until we sold our held for sale North American Coal operations during the fourth quarter of 2015. As such, all current and historical North American Coal operating segment results are included in our financial statements and classified within discontinued operations.

In the first quarter of 2015, as part of the held for sale classification assigned to North American Coal, an impairment of $73.4 million was recorded. The impairment charge was to reduce the assets to their estimated fair value which was determined based on potential sales scenarios. No further impairment was recorded in 2015.

Consistent with our strategy to extract maximum value from our current assets, we sold all the remaining North American Coal operations during the fourth quarter of 2015. On December 22, 2015, we closed the sale of our remaining North American Coal business which included Pinnacle mine in West Virginia and Oak Grove mine in Alabama. Pinnacle mine and Oak Grove mine were sold to Seneca and the deal structure was a sale of equity interests of our remaining coal business. Additionally, Seneca may pay Cliffs an earn-out of up to $50 million contingent upon the terms of a revenue sharing agreement which extends through the year 2020. However, we have not recorded a gain contingency in relation to this earn-out. We recorded the results of this sale in our fourth quarter earnings within *Loss from Discontinued Operations, net of tax* as the transaction closed on December 22, 2015.

On December 31, 2014, we completed the sale of our CLCC assets in West Virginia to Coronado Coal II, LLC, an affiliate of Coronado Coal LLC, for $174.0 million in cash and the assumption of certain liabilities, of which $155.0 million was collected as of December 31, 2014. We recorded the results of this sale in our fourth quarter earnings within *Loss from Discontinued Operations, net of tax* as the transaction closed on December 31, 2014.

Loss on Discontinued Operations

Our planned sale of the Oak Grove and Pinnacle mine assets represented a strategic shift in our business. For that reason, our previously reported North American Coal operating segment results for all periods, prior to the March 31, 2015 held for sale determination, are classified as discontinued operations. On December 22, 2015, we completed the sale of the Oak Grove and Pinnacle mines, which marked our exit from the coal business. Historic results also include our CLCC assets, which were sold during the fourth quarter of 2014.

(In Millions)	Twelve Months Ended December 31,		
Loss from Discontinued Operations	2015	2014	2013
Revenues from product sales and services	$ 392.9	$ 687.1	$ 821.9
Cost of goods sold and operating expenses	(449.2)	(822.9)	(836.4)
Sales margin	(56.3)	(135.8)	(14.5)
Other operating (expense)/income	(30.4)	(20.8)	13.8
Gain (loss) on sale of coal mines	9.3	(419.6)	—
Other expense	(1.8)	(3.0)	(2.4)
Loss from discontinued operations before income taxes	(79.2)	(579.2)	(3.1)
Impairment of long-lived assets	(73.4)	(857.5)	—
Income tax benefit (expense)	0.2	302.2	(6.2)
Loss from discontinued operations, net of tax	$(152.4)	$(1,134.5)	$ (9.3)

Items Measured at Fair Value on a Non-Recurring Basis

The following table presents information about the impairment charge on non-financial assets that was measured on a fair value basis at March 31, 2015 for the North American Coal operations. There were no financial and non-financial assets and liabilities that were measured on a non-recurring fair value basis at December 31, 2015 for the North American Coal operations. The table also indicates the fair value hierarchy of the valuation techniques used to determine such fair value.

(In Millions)	March 31, 2015				
Description	Quoted Prices in Active Markets for Identical Assets/Liabilities (Level 1)	Significant Other Observable Inputs (Level 2)	Significant Unobservable Inputs (Level 3)	Total	Total Losses
Assets:					
Other long-lived assets—Property, plant and equipment and Mineral rights: North American Coal operating unit	$—	$—	$20.4	$20.4	$73.4
	$—	$—	$20.4	$20.4	$73.4

In the first quarter of 2015, as part of the held for sale classification assigned to North American Coal, an impairment charge of $73.4 million was recorded. The impairment charge was to reduce the assets to their estimated fair value which was determined based on potential sales scenarios. We determined the fair value and recoverability of our North American Coal operating segment by comparing the estimated fair value of the underlying assets and liabilities to the estimated sales price of the operating segment held for sale. No further impairment was recorded in 2015.

Recorded Assets and Liabilities

	(In Millions)	
Assets and Liabilities of Discontinued Operations[1]	**December 31, 2015**	**December 31, 2014**
Accounts receivable, net	$ —	$ 44.8
Inventories	—	50.3
Supplies and other inventories	—	28.2
Other current assets	14.9	16.8
Property, plant and equipment, net	—	94.7
Other non-current assets	—	18.6
Total assets of discontinued operations	$14.9	$253.4
Accounts payable	$ —	$ 22.4
Accrued liabilities	—	27.9
Other current liabilities	6.9	29.8
Pension and postemployment benefit liabilities	—	47.1
Environmental and mine closure obligations	—	33.9
Other liabilities	—	36.3
Total liabilities of discontinued operations	$ 6.9	$197.4

[1] At December 31, 2015, we also recorded $7.8 million of contingent liabilities associated with our exit from the coal business. These contingent liabilities are recorded on our parent company.

As part of the CLCC asset sale during the fourth quarter of 2014, there was an amount placed in escrow to cover decreases in working capital, indemnity obligations and regulatory liabilities. The amount held in escrow was $14.9 million and $17.5 million at December 31, 2015, and 2014, respectively and recorded within *Short-term assets of discontinued operations* and *Long-term assets of discontinued operations*, respectively, on the Statements of Consolidated Financial Position.

Income Taxes

We have recognized a tax benefit of $0.2 million and $302.2 million for the years ended December 31, 2015 and 2014, respectively, in *Loss from Discontinued Operations, net of tax*, related to a loss on our North American Coal investments. The benefit for the year ended December 31, 2014 is primarily the result of the impairment of long-lived assets in the third quarter of 2014. We recognized a tax expense of $6.2 million for the year ended December 31, 2013 in *Loss from Discontinued Operations, net of tax*, related to the impact of the North American Coal losses on the AMT credit and associated valuation allowance.

Canadian Operations

Background

On November 30, 2013, we suspended indefinitely our Chromite Project in Northern Ontario. The Chromite Project remained suspended throughout 2014 and until final sale in 2015. Our Wabush Scully iron ore mine in Newfoundland and Labrador was idled by the end of the first quarter of 2014 and subsequently began to commence permanent closure in the fourth quarter of 2014. During 2014, we also limited exploration spending on the Labrador Trough South property in Québec. In November 2014, we announced that we were pursuing exit options for our Eastern Canadian Iron Ore operations. In December 2014, iron ore production at the Bloom Lake mine was suspended and the Bloom Lake mine was placed in "care-and-maintenance" mode. Together, the suspension of exploration efforts, shutdown of the Wabush Scully mine and the cessation of operations at our Bloom Lake mine represent a complete curtailment of our Canadian operations.

On January 27, 2015, we announced the Bloom Filing under the CCAA with the Québec Court in Montreal. At that time, the Bloom Lake Group was no longer generating revenues and was not able to meet its obligations as they came due. The Bloom Filing addressed the Bloom Lake Group's immediate liquidity issues and permits the Bloom Lake Group to preserve and protect its assets for the benefit of all stakeholders while restructuring and sale options are explored. As part of the CCAA process, the Court approved the appointment of a Monitor and certain other financial advisors.

Additionally, on May 20, 2015, we announced the Wabush Filing in the Court under the CCAA. As a result of this action, the CCAA protections granted to the Bloom Lake Group were extended to include the Wabush Group to facilitate the reorganization of each of their businesses and operations. The Wabush Group was no longer generating revenues and was not able to meet its obligations as they came due. The inclusion of the Wabush Group in the existing Bloom Filing facilitates a more comprehensive restructuring and sale process of both the Bloom Lake Group and the Wabush Group which collectively include mine, port and rail assets and leads to a more effective and streamlined exit from Eastern Canada. The Wabush Filing also mitigates various legacy related long-term liabilities associated with the Wabush Group. As part of the Wabush Filing, the Court approved the appointment of a Monitor and certain other financial advisors. The Monitor of the Wabush Group is also the Monitor of the Bloom Lake Group.

As a result of the Bloom Filing on January 27, 2015, we no longer have a controlling interest in the Bloom Lake Group. For that reason, we deconsolidated the Bloom Lake Group and certain other wholly-owned subsidiaries effective January 27, 2015, which resulted in a pretax impairment loss on deconsolidation and other charges, totaling $818.7 million that was recorded in the first quarter of 2015. The pretax loss on deconsolidation includes the derecognition of the carrying amounts of the Bloom Lake Group and certain other wholly-owned subsidiaries assets, liabilities and accumulated other comprehensive loss and the recording of our remaining interests at fair value.

As a result of the Wabush Filing, we deconsolidated certain Wabush Group wholly-owned subsidiaries effective May 20, 2015. The certain wholly-owned subsidiaries that were deconsolidated effective May 20, 2015 are Wabush Group entities that were not deconsolidated as part of the deconsolidation effective January 27, 2015 as discussed previously in this section. This deconsolidation, effective May 20, 2015, resulted in a pretax gain on deconsolidation and other charges, totaling $134.7 million. The pretax gain on deconsolidation includes the derecognition of the carrying amounts of these certain deconsolidated Wabush Group wholly-owned subsidiaries' assets, liabilities and accumulated other comprehensive loss and the adjustment of our remaining interests in the Canadian Entities to fair value.

Subsequent to each of the deconsolidations discussed above, we utilized the cost method to account for our investment in the Canadian Entities, which has been reflected as zero in our Statements of Consolidated Financial Position as of December 31, 2015 based on the estimated fair value of the Canadian Entities' net assets. Loans to and accounts receivable from the Canadian Entities are recorded at an estimated fair value of $72.9 million classified as *Loans to and accounts receivables from the Canadian Entities* in the Statements of Consolidated Financial Position as of December 31, 2015 .

Loss on Discontinued Operations

Our Canadian exit represents a strategic shift in our business. For this reason, our previously reported Eastern Canadian Iron Ore and Ferroalloys operating segment results for all periods prior to the respective deconsolidations, as well as costs to exit, are classified as discontinued operations.

| (In Millions) | Twelve Months Ended December 31, | | |
Loss from Discontinued Operations	2015	2014	2013
Revenues from product sales and services	$ 11.3	$ 563.5	$ 978.7
Cost of goods sold and operating expenses	(11.1)	(808.4)	(1,082.0)
Eliminations with continuing operations	—	(53.6)	(217.3)
Sales margin	0.2	(298.5)	(320.6)
Other operating (expense)/income	(33.8)	(306.3)	(151.5)
Other expense	(1.0)	(5.6)	10.0
Loss from discontinued operations before income taxes	(34.6)	(610.4)	(462.1)
Loss from deconsolidation	(710.9)	—	—
Impairment of long-lived assets	—	(7,536.8)	(236.4)
Income tax benefit	5.8	913.7	188.7
Loss from discontinued operations, net of tax	$(739.7)	$(7,233.5)	$ (509.8)

Canadian Entities loss from deconsolidation totaled $710.9 million for the twelve months ended December 31, 2015 and included the following:

(In Millions)	Twelve Months Ended December 31, 2015
Investment impairment on deconsolidation[1]	$(507.8)
Guarantees and contingent liabilities	(203.1)
Total loss from deconsolidation	$(710.9)

[1] Includes the adjustment to fair value of our remaining interest in the Canadian Entities.

As a result of the deconsolidation, we recorded accrued expenses for the estimated probable loss related to claims that may be asserted against us, primarily under guarantees of certain debt arrangements and leases for a loss on deconsolidation of $203.1 million, for the twelve months ended December 31, 2015.

Investments in the Canadian Entities

Cliffs continues to indirectly own a majority of the interest in the Canadian Entities but has deconsolidated those entities because Cliffs no longer has a controlling interest as a result of the Bloom Filing and the Wabush Filing. At the respective dates of deconsolidation, January 27, 2015 or May 20, 2015 and subsequently at each reporting period, we adjusted our investment in the Canadian Entities to fair value with a corresponding charge to *Loss from Discontinued Operations, net of tax*. As the estimated amount of the Canadian Entities' liabilities exceeded the estimated fair value of the assets available for distribution to its creditors, the fair value of Cliffs' equity investment is approximately zero.

Amounts Receivable from the Canadian Entities

Prior to the deconsolidations, various Cliffs wholly-owned entities made loans to the Canadian Entities for the purpose of funding its operations and had accounts receivable generated in the ordinary course of business. The loans, corresponding interest and the accounts receivable were considered intercompany transactions and eliminated in our consolidated financial statements. Additionally, we procured funding subsequent to the deconsolidation through a debtor-in-possession credit facility (the "DIP financing"). Since the deconsolidations, the loans, associated interest and accounts receivable are considered related party transactions and have been recognized in our consolidated financial statements at their estimated fair value of $72.9 million classified as *Other current assets* in the Statements of Consolidated Financial Position at December 31, 2015.

Guarantees and Contingent Liabilities

Certain liabilities, consisting primarily of equipment loans and environmental obligations of the Canadian Entities, were secured through corporate guarantees and standby letters of credit. As of December 31, 2015, we have liabilities of $96.5 million and $35.9 million in our consolidated results, classified as *Guarantees* and *Other liabilities*, respectively, in the Statements of Consolidated Financial Position.

Contingencies

The recorded expenses include an accrual for the estimated probable loss related to claims that may be asserted against us, primarily under guarantees of certain debt arrangements and leases. The beneficiaries of those guarantees may seek damages or other related relief as a result of our exit from Canada. Our probable loss estimate is based on the expectation that claims will be asserted against us and negotiated settlements will be reached, and not on any determination that it is probable we would be found liable were these claims to be litigated. Our estimates involve significant judgment. Our estimates are based on currently available information, an assessment of the validity of certain claims and estimated payments by the Canadian Entities. We are not able to reasonably estimate a range of possible losses in excess of the accrual because there are significant factual and legal issues to be resolved. We believe that it is reasonably possible that future changes to our estimates of loss and the ultimate amount paid on these claims could be material to our results of operations in future periods. Any such losses would be reported in discontinued operations.

Items Measured at Fair Value on a Non-Recurring Basis

The following table presents information about the financial assets and liabilities that were measured on a fair value basis at December 31, 2015 for the Canadian Operations. The table also indicates the fair value hierarchy of the valuation techniques used to determine such fair value.

(In Millions)	December 31, 2015				
Description	Quoted Prices in Active Markets for Identical Assets/ Liabilities (Level 1)	Significant Other Observable Inputs (Level 2)	Significant Unobservable Inputs (Level 3)	Total	Total Losses
Assets:					
Loans to and accounts receivables from the Canadian Entities	$—	$—	$ 72.9	$ 72.9	$507.8
Liabilities:					
Guarantees and contingent liabilities	$—	$—	$132.4	$132.4	$203.1

We determined the fair value and recoverability of our Canadian investments by comparing the estimated fair value of the remaining underlying assets of the Canadian Entities to remaining estimated liabilities. We recorded the guarantees and contingent liabilities at book value which best approximated fair value.

Outstanding liabilities include accounts payable and other liabilities, forward commitments, unsubordinated related party payables, lease liabilities and other potential claims. Potential claims include an accrual for the estimated probable loss related to claims that may be asserted against the Bloom Lake Group and Wabush Group under certain contracts. Claimants may seek damages or other related relief as a result of the Canadian Entities' exit from Canada. Based on our estimates, the fair value of liabilities exceeds the fair value of assets.

To assess the fair value and recoverability of the amounts receivable from the Canadian Entities, we estimated the fair value of the underlying net assets of the Canadian Entities available for distribution to their creditors in relation to the estimated creditor claims and the priority of those claims.

Our estimates involve significant judgment and are based on currently available information, an assessment of the validity of certain claims and estimated payments made by the Canadian Entities. Our ultimate recovery is subject to the final liquidation value of the Canadian Entities. Further, the final liquidation value and ultimate recovery of the creditors of the Canadian Entities, including Cliffs Natural Resources and various subsidiaries, may impact our estimates of contingent liability exposure described previously.

Pre-Petition Financing

Prior to the Wabush Filing on May 20, 2015, a secured credit facility (the "Pre-Petition financing") was put into place to provide support to the Wabush Group for ongoing business activities until the DIP financing was in place. As of December 31, 2015, there was a total of $7.2 million drawn and outstanding under the Pre-Petition financing funded by Wabush Iron Co. Limited's parent company, Cliffs Mining Company. The Pre-Petition financing amount of $7.2 million is included within the *Loans to and accounts receivables from the Canadian Entities* of $72.9 million. The Pre-Petition financing is secured by certain equipment of the Wabush Group.

DIP Financing

In connection with the Wabush Filing on May 20, 2015, the Court approved the DIP financing to the Wabush Group, which provides for borrowings under the facility up to $10.0 million. As of December 31, 2015, there was $6.8 million drawn and outstanding under the DIP financing funded by Wabush Iron Co. Limited's parent company, Cliffs Mining Company. At December 31, 2015, the DIP financing is included within *Loans to and accounts receivables from the Canadian Entities* on the Statements of Consolidated Financial Position. The DIP financing is secured by a court order over the assets of the Wabush Group.

Recorded Assets and Liabilities

	(In Millions)
Assets and Liabilities of Discontinued Operations	**December 31, 2014**
Cash and cash equivalents	$ 19.7
Accounts receivable, net	37.9
Inventories	16.3
Supplies and other inventories	48.5
Income tax receivable	20.1
Other current assets	44.3
Property, plant and equipment, net	249.8
Other non-current assets	19.9
Total Assets	$456.5
Accounts payable	$83.6
Accrued expenses	200.0
Other current liabilities	35.7
Pension and postemployment benefit liabilities	79.8
Environmental and mine closure obligations	56.5
Other liabilities	173.9
Total Liabilities	$629.5

Income Taxes

We recognized a tax benefit of $5.8 million and $913.7 million for the years ended December 31, 2015 and 2014, respectively, in *Loss from Discontinued Operations, net of tax*. The benefit for the year ended December 31, 2014 was the result of the impairment of long-lived assets in the third quarter of 2014 offset by the placement of a valuation allowance against the Canadian operations net deferred tax assets. Canadian deferred tax assets relating to both historical and current year net operating losses were included in our equity investment in the Canadian Subsidiaries that has been reduced to zero. We recognized a tax benefit of $188.7 million for the year ended December 31, 2013 in *Loss from Discontinued Operations, net of tax* related to losses in our Canadian operations.

CHANGE IN ACCOUNTING PRINCIPLE—FAIR VALUE MEASUREMENT

1.51 THE BRINK'S COMPANY (DEC)
NOTES TO CONSOLIDATED FINANCIAL STATEMENTS (in part)

Note 1—Summary of Significant Accounting Policies (in part)

New Accounting Standards (in part)

In May 2015, the FASB issued ASU 2015-07, *Disclosures for Investments in Certain Entities That Calculate Net Asset Value per Share (or its Equivalent)*. This new standard eliminates the requirement to categorize investments in the fair value hierarchy if their fair values are measured at net asset value per share (or its equivalent) using the practical expedient in the FASB's fair value measurement guidance. This new standard impacted our fair value disclosures related to retirement benefit plan investments. We elected to early adopt this ASU as of December 31, 2015 using the retrospective transition method. As a result, the fair value hierarchy presentation as reported at December 31, 2014 has been updated to reflect this guidance.

Note 3—Retirement Benefits (in part)

Retirement Plan Assets

U.S. Plans

(In millions, except for percentages)	Fair Value Level	December 31, 2015 Total Fair Value	% Actual Allocation	% Target Allocation	December 31, 2014 Total Fair Value	% Actual Allocation	% Target Allocation
U.S. Pension Plans							
Cash, cash equivalents and receivables		$ 4.2	1	—	4.1	1	—
Equity securities:							
U.S. large-cap[a]	1	80.1	11	12	93.1	12	12
U.S. small/mid-cap[a]	1	30.0	4	5	40.2	5	5
International[a]	1	66.1	9	10	72.6	9	10
Emerging markets[b]	1	8.6	1	2	13.8	2	2
Dynamic asset allocation[c]	1	23.9	4	4	33.7	4	4
U.S. managed volatility equities[n]	1	—	—	5	—	—	—
Fixed-income securities:							
Long duration—mutual fund[d]	1	290.0	50	48	277.6	47	48
Long duration—Treasury strips[d]	2	71.7			95.7		
High yield[e]	1	9.0	1	2	15.3	2	2
Emerging markets[f]	1	9.0	1	2	14.5	2	2
Other types of investments:							
Hedge fund of funds[g] [m]		36.6	5	—	37.9	5	5
Core property[h] [m]		51.5	7	5	45.0	6	5
Structured credit[i] [m]		40.7	6	5	42.8	5	5
Total		$721.4	100	100	786.3	100	100
UMWA Plans							
Cash, cash equivalents and receivables		$ 1.6	1	—	—	—	—
Equity securities:							
U.S. large-cap[a]	1	47.5	21	22	58.5	21	21
U.S. small/mid-cap[a]	1	20.2	9	10	25.5	10	9
International[a]	1	40.5	18	19	49.3	19	18
Emerging markets[b]	1	9.0	4	4	10.7	4	4
Dynamic asset allocation[c]	1	15.9	7	7	20.0	8	7
Fixed-income securities:							
High yield[e]	1	6.9	3	2	10.9	4	4
Emerging markets[f]	1	9.0	4	4	10.4	4	4
Multi asset real return[j]	1	14.7	6	5	21.6	8	8

(continued)

(In millions, except for percentages)	Fair Value Level	December 31, 2015			December 31, 2014		
		Total Fair Value	% Actual Allocation	% Target Allocation	Total Fair Value	% Actual Allocation	% Target Allocation
Other types of investments:							
Hedge fund of funds[(g) (m)]		6.4	3	—	14.6	6	3
Core property[(h) (m)]		32.9	14	10	28.8	11	10
Structured credit[(i) (m)]		13.6	6	5	14.3	5	5
Global private equity[(k) (m)]		3.2	1	7	—	—	7
Energy debt[(l) (m)]		6.0	3	5	—	—	—
Total		$227.4	100	100	264.6	100	100

[(a)] These categories include passively managed U.S. large-cap mutual funds and actively managed U.S. small/mid-cap and international mutual funds that track various indices such as the S&P 500 Index, the Russell 2500 Index and the MSCI All Country World Ex-U.S. Index.

[(b)] This category represents an actively managed mutual fund that invests primarily in equity securities of emerging market issuers. Emerging market countries are those countries that are characterized as developing or emerging by any of the World Bank, the United Nations, the International Finance Corporation, or the European Bank for Reconstruction and Development or included in an emerging markets index by a recognized index provider.

[(c)] This category represents an actively managed mutual fund that seeks to generate total return over time by selecting investments from among a broad range of asset classes. The fund's allocations among asset classes may be adjusted over short periods and can vary from multiple to a single asset class.

[(d)] This category represents actively managed mutual funds that seek to duplicate the risk and return characteristics of a long-term fixed-income security portfolio with approximate duration of 10 years and longer by using a long duration bond portfolio. This category also includes Treasury future contracts and zero-coupon securities created by the U.S. Treasury.

[(e)] This category represents an actively managed mutual fund that invests primarily in fixed-income securities rated below investment grade, including corporate bonds and debentures, convertible and preferred securities and zero-coupon obligations. The fund's average weighted maturity may vary and will generally not exceed ten years.

[(f)] This category represents an actively managed mutual fund that invests primarily in U.S. dollar-denominated debt securities of government, government-related and corporate issuers in emerging market countries, as well as entities organized to restructure the outstanding debt of such issuers.

[(g)] This category represents an actively managed hedge fund of funds. The fund holds approximately 30 separate hedge-fund investments. Strategies included (1) long-short equity, (2) event-driven and distressed-debt, (3) global macro, (4) credit hedging, (5) multi-strategy, and (6) fixed-income arbitrage. Its investment objective is to seek to achieve an attractive risk-adjusted return with moderate volatility and moderate directional market exposure over a full market cycle.

[(h)] This category represents an actively managed real estate fund of funds that seeks both current income and long-term capital appreciation through investing in underlying funds that acquire, manage, and dispose of commercial real estate properties. These properties are high-quality, low-leveraged, income-generating office, industrial, retail, and multi-family properties, generally fully-leased to creditworthy companies and governmental entities.

[(i)] This category invests primarily in a diversified portfolio comprised primarily of collateralized loan obligations and other structured credit investments backed primarily by bank loans.

[(j)] This category represents an actively managed mutual fund that invests primarily in fixed income and equity securities and commodity linked instruments. The category seeks total returns that exceed the rate of inflation over a full market cycle regardless of market conditions.

[(k)] This category will offer exposure to a diversified pool of global private assets fund investments. Further, the category will seek to shorten the duration of the typical private assets fund of funds through a dedicated focus on secondary strategies (i.e. funds whose investment strategy is to purchase interests in other private market investments/funds as a way to provide the original investors liquidity prior to the end of those investments'/funds' contracted end date), income-producing investment strategies (e.g. debt, real estate, and to a lesser extent, real assets), and underlying funds whose stated life is five to seven years, as opposed to the more typical 10-year life of private assets funds.

[(l)] This category invests in credit securities of commodity oriented companies affected by the dislocation in the commodity markets with the investment objective of producing an equity like return with less downside risk than equity or commodity investments. The fund has a three year lock on each investment and semi-annual redemptions. 50% of the fund balance is redeemable in the first redemption period following the end of the lock up and then 25% of the fund balance in each of the next two redemptions periods.

[(m)] In accordance with Subtopic 820-10, certain investments that are measured at fair value using the net asset value per share (or its equivalent) practical expedient have not been classified in the fair value hierarchy. The fair value amounts presented in this table are intended to permit reconciliation of the fair value hierarchy to the amounts presented in the consolidated balance sheets.

[(n)] The U.S. managed volatility fund seeks capital appreciation with lower volatility than the broad U.S. equity market. The Fund will typically invest in equity securities of U.S. companies of all capitalization ranges that exhibit low relative volatility. Over the long term, the Fund is expected to achieve a return similar to that of the Russell 3000 Index with a lower level of volatility.

Assets of our U.S. plans are invested with an objective of maximizing the total return, taking into consideration the liabilities of the plan, and minimizing the risks that could create the need for excessive contributions. Plan assets are invested primarily using actively managed accounts with asset allocation targets listed in the tables above. Our policy does not permit the purchase of Brink's common stock if immediately after any such purchase the aggregate fair market value of the plan assets invested in Brink's common stock exceeds 10% of the aggregate fair market value of the assets of the plan, except as permitted by an exemption under ERISA. The plans rebalance their assets on a quarterly basis if actual allocations of assets are outside predetermined ranges. Among other factors, the performance of asset groups and investment managers will affect the long-term rate of return.

The pension plan acquired the structured-credit investment in 2013. The investment is subject to a two-year lockup provision, which expired in 2015.

The UMWA plans acquired the structured-credit investment in 2014. The investment is subject to a two-year lockup provision, which will expire in 2016. The UMWA plans also acquired the energy debt investment in 2015, which is subject to a three-year lockup provision, which will expire in 2018.

Most of the investments of our U.S. retirement plans can be redeemed daily. The core-property and structured-credit investments can be redeemed quarterly with 65 days' notice. The hedge fund of funds investment can be redeemed quarterly with 95 days' notice. The energy debt investment can be redeemed semi-annually with 95 days' notice.

The global private equity investment cannot be redeemed due to the nature of the underlying investments. As the global private equity investment matures and becomes fully invested, liquidating distributions will be provided back to investors. We expect to receive liquidating distributions over the stated life of the underlying investments. We have $18 million in unfunded commitments related to the global private equity investment. We believe all plans have sufficient liquidity to meet the needs of the plans' beneficiaries in all market scenarios.

Non-U.S. Plans

	December 31, 2015			December 31, 2014		
(In millions, except for percentages)	Total Fair Value	% Actual Allocation	% Target Allocation	Total Fair Value	% Actual Allocation	% Target Allocation
Non-U.S. Pension Plans						
Cash and cash equivalents	$ 0.8	—	—	1.1	—	—
Equity securities:						
U.S. equity funds[a]	24.5			31.6		
Canadian equity funds[a]	28.6			39.6		
European equity funds[a]	9.5			8.8		
Asia Pacific equity funds[a]	1.8			1.7		
Emerging markets[a]	4.5			3.5		
Other non-U.S. equity funds[a]	17.2			20.4		
Total equity securities	86.1	52	60	105.6	59	65
Fixed-income securities:						
Global credit[b]	0.4			0.3		
Canadian fixed-income funds[c]	—			25.7		
European fixed-income funds[d]	13.0			14.9		
High-yield[e]	1.2			1.0		
Emerging markets[f]	1.2			1.2		
Long-duration[g]	60.8			27.9		
Total fixed-income securities	76.6	47	38	71.0	40	35
Other types of investments:						
Other	1.3			1.6		
Total other types of investments	1.3	1	2	1.6	1	—
Total	$164.8	100	100	179.3	100	100

[a] These categories are comprised of equity index actively and passively managed funds that track various indices such as S&P 500 Composite Total Return Index, Russell 1000 and 2000 Indices, MSCI Europe Ex-UK Index, S&P/TSX Total Return Index, MSCI EAFE Index and others. Some of these funds use a dynamic asset allocation investment strategy seeking to generate total return over time by selecting investments from among a broad range of asset classes, investing primarily through the use of derivatives.

[b] This category represents investment-grade fixed income debt securities of European issuers from diverse industries.

[c] This category seeks to achieve a return that exceeds the Scotia Capital Markets Universe Bond Index.

[d] This category is designed to generate income and exhibit volatility similar to that of the Sterling denominated bond market. This category primarily invests in investment grade or better securities.

[e] This category consists of global high-yield bonds. This category invests in lower rated and unrated fixed income, floating rate and other debt securities issued by European and American companies.

[f] This category consists of a diversified portfolio of debt securities issued by governments, financial institutions, companies or other entities domiciled in emerging market countries.

[g] This category is designed to achieve a return consistent with holding longer term debt instruments. This category invests in interest rate and inflation derivatives, government-issued bonds, real-return bonds, and futures contracts.

Asset allocation strategies for our non-U.S. plans are designed to accumulate a diversified portfolio among markets and asset classes in order to reduce market risk and increase the likelihood that pension assets are available to pay benefits as they are due. Assets of non-U.S. pension plans are invested primarily using actively managed accounts. The weighted-average asset allocation targets are listed in the table above, and reflect limitations on types of investments held and allocations among assets classes, as required by local regulation or market practice of the country where the assets are invested. Most of the investments of our non-U.S. retirement plans can be redeemed at least monthly, except for a portion of "Other" in the above table, which can be redeemed quarterly.

Non-U.S. Plans—Fair Value Measurements

(In millions)	December 31, 2015	December 31, 2014
Quoted prices in active markets for identical assets (Level 1)	$149.1	177.9
Net asset value per share practical expedient[a]	15.7	1.4
Total fair value	$164.8	179.3

[a] In accordance with Subtopic 820-10, certain investments that are measured at fair value using the net asset value per share (or its equivalent) practical expedient have not been classified in the fair value hierarchy. The fair value amounts presented in this table are intended to permit reconciliation of the fair value hierarchy to the amounts presented in the consolidated balance sheets.

1.52 ASHLAND INC. (SEP)
CONSOLIDATED BALANCE SHEETS (in part)

(In millions)	2015	2014
Assets		
Current assets		
Cash and cash equivalents	$ 1,257	$ 1,393
Accounts receivable[a]	961	1,202
Inventories—Note A	706	765
Deferred income taxes—Note L	155	118
Other assets	169	83
Total current assets	3,248	3,561
Noncurrent assets		
Property, plant and equipment—Note G		
Cost	4,144	4,275
Accumulated depreciation	1,962	1,861
Net property, plant and equipment	2,182	2,414
Goodwill—Note H	2,486	2,643
Intangibles—Note H	1,142	1,309
Restricted investments—Note F	285	—
Asbestos insurance receivable—Note N	180	433
Equity and other unconsolidated investments—Note D	65	81
Other assets—Note J	476	479
Total noncurrent assets	6,816	7,359
Total assets	$10,064	$10,920
Liabilities and Stockholders' Equity (in part)		
Current liabilities		
Short-term debt—Note I	$ 326	$ 329
Current portion of long-term debt—Note I	55	9
Trade and other payables	573	674
Accrued expenses and other liabilities	494	675
Total current liabilities	1,448	1,687
Noncurrent liabilities		
Long-term debt—Note I	3,348	2,911
Employee benefit obligations—Note M	1,076	1,468
Asbestos litigation reserve—Note N	661	701
Deferred income taxes—Note L	89	110
Other liabilities—Note J	405	460
Total noncurrent liabilities	5,579	5,650

NOTES TO CONSOLIDATED FINANCIAL STATEMENTS (in part)

Note A—Significant Accounting Policies (in part)

Principles of consolidation and basis of presentation (in part)

The accompanying Consolidated Financial Statements have been prepared in accordance with accounting principles generally accepted in the United States of America (U.S. GAAP) and U.S. Securities and Exchange Commission regulations. All material intercompany transactions and balances have been eliminated. Additionally, certain prior period data has been reclassified in the Consolidated Financial Statements and accompanying notes to conform to the current period presentation, which includes the adoption of new accounting guidance during the current year related to debt issuance costs presented as a direct deduction from the carrying amount of debt. The Consolidated Financial Statements include the accounts of Ashland and its majority owned subsidiaries. Investments in joint ventures and 20% to 50% owned affiliates where Ashland has the ability to exert significant influence are accounted for under the equity method.

New Accounting Pronouncements (in part)

In April 2015 and August 2015, the FASB issued accounting guidance to simplify the presentation of debt issuance costs by requiring that debt issuance costs related to a recognized debt liability be presented in the balance sheet as a direct deduction from the carrying amount of that debt liability, consistent with debt discounts. The recognition and measurement guidance for debt issuance costs were not affected by this amendment. The adoption of the new guidance was on a retrospective basis. Ashland elected to early adopt this guidance for debt issuance costs during 2015. As a result, $28 million was presented as long-term debt as of September 30, 2015 and Ashland reclassified $31 million from other noncurrent assets to long-term debt as of September 30, 2014 within the Consolidated Balance Sheets.

Note I—Debt (in part)

The following table summarizes Ashland's current and long-term debt at September 30, 2015 and 2014.

(In millions)	2015	2014
4.750% notes, due 2022	$1,120	$1,120
Term Loan, due 2020	1,086	—
3.875% notes, due 2018	700	700
6.875% notes, due 2043	376	376
Accounts receivable securitization(a)	190	255
6.50% junior subordinated notes, due 2029	136	134
Revolving credit facility	110	45
Other international loans, interest at a weighted-average rate of 6.2% at September 30, 2015 (5.3% to 9.5%)	25	29
Medium-term notes, due 2019, interest of 9.4% at September 30, 2015	5	14
3.000% notes, due 2016	—	600
Other(b)	(19)	(24)
Total debt	3,729	3,249
Short-term debt	(326)	(329)
Current portion of long-term debt	(55)	(9)
Long-term debt (less current portion and debt issuance cost discounts)	$3,348	$2,911

(a) During 2015, the potential funding for qualified receivables was reduced from $275 million to $250 million.
(b) Other includes $28 million and $31 million of debt issuance cost discounts as of September 30, 2015 and 2014, respectively.

At September 30, 2015, Ashland's total debt had an outstanding principal balance of $3,907 million, discounts of $150 million and debt issuance costs of $28 million. The scheduled aggregate maturities of debt for the next five fiscal years are as follows: $381 million in 2016, $69 million in 2017, $810 million in 2018, $143 million in 2019 and $715 million in 2020.

1.53 TEXAS INSTRUMENTS INCORPORATED (DEC)
CONSOLIDATED BALANCE SHEETS (in part)

	December 31,	
(Millions of dollars, except share amounts)	2015	2014
Assets		
Current assets:		
Cash and cash equivalents	$ 1,000	$ 1,199
Short-term investments	2,218	2,342
Accounts receivable, net of allowances of ($7) and ($12)	1,165	1,246
Raw materials	109	101
Work in process	846	896
Finished goods	736	787
Inventories	1,691	1,784
Prepaid expenses and other current assets	1,000	850
Total current assets	7,074	7,421
Property, plant and equipment at cost	5,465	6,266
Accumulated depreciation	(2,869)	(3,426)
Property, plant and equipment, net	2,596	2,840
Long-term investments	221	224
Goodwill, net	4,362	4,362
Acquisition-related intangibles, net	1,583	1,902
Deferred income taxes	201	180
Capitalized software licenses, net	46	83
Overfunded retirement plans	85	127
Other assets	62	233
Total assets	$16,230	$17,372
Liabilities and Stockholders' Equity (in part)		
Current liabilities:		
Current portion of long-term debt	$ 1,000	$ 1,001
Accounts payable	386	437
Accrued compensation	664	651
Income taxes payable	95	71
Accrued expenses and other liabilities	410	498
Total current liabilities	2,555	2,658
Long-term debt	3,120	3,630
Underfunded retirement plans	196	225
Deferred income taxes	37	64
Deferred credits and other liabilities	376	405
Total liabilities	6,284	6,982

2. Basis of Presentation and Significant Accounting Policies and Practices (in part)

Basis of Presentation

The consolidated financial statements have been prepared in accordance with accounting principles generally accepted in the United States (GAAP). The basis of these financial statements is comparable for all periods presented herein.

The consolidated financial statements include the accounts of all subsidiaries. All intercompany balances and transactions have been eliminated in consolidation. All dollar amounts in the financial statements and tables in these notes, except per-share amounts, are stated in millions of U.S. dollars unless otherwise indicated. We have reclassified certain amounts in the prior periods' financial statements to conform to the 2015 presentation, including to apply retrospectively the following:
- A new standard on classifying deferred income taxes (see Changes in accounting standards below and Note 6), and
- A new standard on classifying debt issuance costs (see Changes in accounting standards below and Note 11).

The preparation of financial statements requires the use of estimates from which final results may vary.

Changes in Accounting Standards

Adopted Standards for Current Period

In April and August 2015, respectively, the Financial Accounting Standards Board (FASB) issued Accounting Standards Update (ASU) No. 2015-03, *Interest—Imputation of Interest (Subtopic 835-30): Simplifying the Presentation of Debt Issuance Costs*, and ASU 2015-15, *Presentation and Subsequent Measurement of Debt Issuance Costs Associated with Line-of-Credit Arrangements—Amendments to SEC Paragraphs Pursuant to Staff Announcement at June 18, 2015 EITF Meeting*. These standards require that costs associated with the issuance of debt, except for costs associated with line-of-credit arrangements, be reported as a direct reduction of the related debt balance. Previously, such costs were recorded as deferred assets. Costs associated with line-of-credit arrangements may continue to be recorded as deferred assets. We adopted these standards as of December 31, 2015, and retrospectively applied the standards to prior periods presented herein. The effect of the reclassification on our Consolidated Balance Sheets is quantified in Note 11. The reclassification we made to address these standards had no impact on our Consolidated Statements of Income.

In November 2015, the FASB issued ASU 2015-17, *Balance Sheet Classification of Deferred Taxes*. This standard requires that companies classify all deferred tax assets and liabilities within a taxing jurisdiction as noncurrent on their consolidated balance sheets. The effect of this new requirement is that deferred income taxes previously reported in either current assets or current liabilities shall be reclassified to noncurrent assets or liabilities. This standard can be applied either prospectively or retrospectively, and is effective for annual and interim periods beginning after December 15, 2016. Early adoption is allowed. We adopted this standard as of December 31, 2015, and retrospectively applied it to prior periods presented herein. The effect of the reclassifications on our Consolidated Balance Sheets is quantified in Note 6.

6. Income Taxes (in part)

Income before Income Taxes

	U.S.	Non-U.S.	Total
2015	$3,218	$ 998	$4,216
2014	2,684	1,190	3,874
2013	1,507	1,247	2,754

Provision (Benefit) for Income Taxes

	U.S. Federal	Non-U.S.	U.S. State	Total
2015				
Current	$1,110	$168	$ 7	$1,285
Deferred	(72)	14	3	(55)
Total	$1,038	$182	$10	$1,230
2014				
Current	$ 911	$194	$ 9	$1,114
Deferred	(73)	11	1	(61)
Total	$ 838	$205	$10	$1,053
2013				
Current	$ 291	$247	$ 4	$ 542
Deferred	17	33	—	50
Total	$ 308	$280	$ 4	$ 592

Principal reconciling items from income tax computed at the statutory federal rate follow:

	For Years Ended December 31,		
	2015	2014	2013
Computed tax at statutory rate	$1,476	$1,356	$ 964
Non-U.S. effective tax rates	(167)	(212)	(156)
U.S. tax benefit for manufacturing	(69)	(51)	(66)
U.S. R&D tax credit	(56)	(59)	(129)
Non-deductible expenses	13	6	13
Impact of changes to uncertain tax positions	8	3	(14)
Other	25	10	(20)
Total provision for income taxes	$1,230	$1,053	$ 592

The total provision for 2013 in the reconciliation above includes $79 million of discrete tax benefits primarily for the reinstatement of the U.S. R&D tax credit retroactive to 2012.

Our annual effective tax rate benefits from lower rates (compared to the U.S. statutory rate) applicable to our operations in many of the jurisdictions in which we operate and from U.S. tax benefits. These lower non-U.S. tax rates are generally statutory in nature, without expiration and available to companies that operate in those taxing jurisdictions. Also included in the non-U.S. effective tax rates reconciling item above are benefits from tax holidays of $60 million, $44 million and $40 million in 2015, 2014 and 2013, respectively. The tax benefits relate to our operations in Malaysia and the Philippines, and expire in 2018 and 2017, respectively. The terms of the Malaysia tax holiday are currently under governmental review as required for the end of the first five years of the holiday period. We do not expect any potential change in the holiday to have a material impact on the financial statements.

The primary components of deferred income tax assets and liabilities were as follows:

	December 31,	
	2015	2014
Deferred income tax assets:		
Stock-based compensation	$ 244	$ 229
Deferred loss and tax credit carryforwards	226	289
Accrued expenses	215	246
Inventories and related reserves	147	156
Retirement costs for defined benefit and retiree health care	87	80
Other	101	87
Total deferred income tax assets, before valuation allowance	1,020	1,087
Valuation allowance	(186)	(195)
Total deferred income tax assets, after valuation allowance	834	892
Deferred income tax liabilities:		
Acquisition-related intangibles and fair-value adjustments	(565)	(672)
International earnings	(105)	(104)
Total deferred income tax liabilities	(670)	(776)
Net deferred income tax asset	$ 164	$ 116

The deferred income tax assets and liabilities based on tax jurisdictions are presented on the Consolidated Balance Sheets as follows:

	December 31,	
	2015	2014
Noncurrent deferred income tax assets	$201	$180
Noncurrent deferred income tax liabilities	(37)	(64)
Net deferred income tax asset	$164	$116

As a result of our early adoption of ASU 2015-17, *Balance Sheet Classification of Deferred Taxes*, we have adjusted the presentation of deferred taxes on the Consolidated Balance Sheets. We have retrospectively adjusted the 2014 Consolidated Balance Sheets to conform to the 2015 presentation by reclassifying current deferred income tax assets and liabilities to noncurrent deferred income tax assets and liabilities. The effect of applying the new standard, as shown in the following table, is the result of netting Current deferred income tax assets with Noncurrent deferred income tax liabilities, by tax jurisdiction. See Note 2 for additional information.

	2014 As Reported	Effect of Applying New Standard	2014 As Adjusted
Current deferred income tax assets	$ 347	$(347)	$—
Noncurrent deferred income tax assets	172	8	180
Current deferred income tax liabilities	(4)	4	—
Noncurrent deferred income tax liabilities	(399)	335	(64)
Net deferred income tax asset	$ 116	$ —	$116

We make an ongoing assessment regarding the realization of U.S. and non-U.S. deferred tax assets. This assessment is based on our evaluation of relevant criteria, including the existence of deferred tax liabilities that can be used to absorb deferred tax assets, taxable income in prior carryback years and expectations for future taxable income. Changes in valuation allowance balances in the years 2015, 2014 and 2013 of $9 million, $24 million and $2 million, respectively, had no impact on Net income.

We have U.S. and non-U.S. tax loss carryforwards of approximately $35 million, none of which will expire before the year 2025.

A provision has been made for deferred taxes on undistributed earnings of non-U.S. subsidiaries to the extent that dividend payments from these subsidiaries are expected to result in additional tax liability. The remaining undistributed earnings of approximately $8.35 billion at December 31, 2015, have been indefinitely reinvested outside of the United States; therefore, no U.S. tax provision has been made for taxes due upon remittance of these earnings. The indefinitely reinvested earnings of our non-U.S. subsidiaries are primarily invested in working capital and property, plant and equipment. Determination of the amount of unrecognized deferred income tax liability is not practical because of the complexities associated with its hypothetical calculation.

Cash payments made for income taxes, net of refunds, were $1.167 billion, $1.104 billion and $569 million for the years ended December 31, 2015, 2014 and 2013, respectively.

11. Debt and Lines of Credit

Short-Term Borrowings

We maintain a line of credit to support commercial paper borrowings, if any, and to provide additional liquidity through bank loans. As of December 31, 2015, we had a variable-rate revolving credit facility from a consortium of investment-grade banks that allows us to borrow up to $2 billion until March 2020. The interest rate on borrowings under this credit facility, if drawn, is indexed to the applicable London Interbank Offered Rate (LIBOR). As of December 31, 2015, our credit facility was undrawn and we had no commercial paper outstanding.

Long-Term Debt

We retired $250 million of maturing debt in April 2015 and another $750 million in August 2015.

In May 2015, we issued a principal amount of $500 million of fixed-rate long-term debt due in 2020. We incurred $3 million of issuance and other related costs, which are amortized to Interest and debt expense over the term of the debt. The proceeds of the offering were $498 million, net of the original issuance discount, and were used toward the repayment of a portion of the debt that matured in August 2015.

In March 2014, we issued an aggregate principal amount of $500 million of fixed-rate long-term debt, with $250 million due in 2017 and $250 million due in 2021. We incurred $3 million of issuance and other related costs, which are amortized to Interest and debt expense over the term of the debt. The proceeds of the offering were $498 million, net of the original issuance discount and were used toward the repayment of the $1.0 billion of debt that matured in May 2014.

In May 2013, we issued an aggregate principal amount of $1.0 billion of fixed-rate long-term debt, with $500 million due in 2018 and $500 million due in 2023. We incurred $6 million of issuance and other related costs, which are amortized to Interest and debt expense over the term of the debt. The proceeds of the offering were $986 million, net of the original issuance discount and were used toward the repayment of $1.5 billion of maturing debt, including floating-rate notes. In connection with this repayment, we settled a floating-to-fixed interest rate swap associated with the maturing debt.

Long-term debt outstanding as of December 31, 2015 and 2014 is as follows:

	December 31,	
	2015	2014
Notes due 2015 at 3.95% (assumed with National acquisition)	$ —	$ 250
Notes due 2015 at 0.45%	—	750
Notes due 2016 at 2.375%	1,000	1,000
Notes due 2017 at 6.60% (assumed with National acquisition)	375	375
Notes due 2017 at 0.875%	250	250
Notes due 2018 at 1.00%	500	500
Notes due 2019 at 1.65%	750	750
Notes due 2020 at 1.75%	500	—
Notes due 2021 at 2.75%	250	250
Notes due 2023 at 2.25%	500	500
Total debt	4,125	4,625
Net unamortized (discount) premium and debt issuance costs	(5)	6
Total debt, including net unamortized (discount) premium and debt issuance costs	4,120	4,631
Current portion of long-term debt	(1,000)	(1,001)
Long-term debt	$3,120	$3,630

As of December 31, 2015, we retrospectively applied the provisions of ASU 2015-03 and ASU 2015-15 regarding the classification of debt issuance costs. See Note 2 for additional information. As a result, we reclassified $11 million of applicable debt issuance costs as of December 31, 2014, from Other assets to Long-term debt, as comprehended in Net unamortized (discount) premium and debt issuance costs, in the table above.

Interest and debt expense was $90 million in 2015, $94 million in 2014 and $95 million in 2013. This was net of the amortization of the debt (discount) premium and other debt issuance costs. Cash payments for interest on long-term debt were $99 million in 2015 and $102 million in both 2014 and 2013. Capitalized interest was not material.

CHANGE IN ACCOUNTING PRINCIPLE—SIMPLIFYING THE ACCOUNTING FOR MEASUREMENT-PERIOD ADJUSTMENTS

1.54 DANAHER CORPORATION (DEC)
NOTES TO CONSOLIDATED FINANCIAL STATEMENTS (in part)

Note 1. Business and Summary of Significant Accounting Policies (in part)

New Accounting Standards (in part)—

In September 2015, the FASB issued ASU No. 2015-16, *Simplifying the Accounting for Measurement-Period Adjustments (Topic 805)*, which eliminates the requirement for an acquirer in a business combination to account for measurement-period adjustments retrospectively. The new guidance requires that the cumulative impact of a measurement-period adjustment (including the impact on prior periods) be recognized in the reporting period in which the adjustment is identified which eliminates the requirement to restate prior period financial statements. The ASU requires disclosure of the nature and amount of measurement-period adjustments as well as information with respect to the portion of the adjustments recorded in current-period earnings that would have been recorded in previous reporting periods if the adjustments to provisional amounts had been recognized as of the acquisition date. The Company has chosen to early adopt this ASU and therefore, disclosures included within these consolidated financial statements have been updated to reflect the new disclosure requirements.

Note 2. Acquisitions

The Company continually evaluates potential acquisitions that either strategically fit with the Company's existing portfolio or expand the Company's portfolio into a new and attractive business area. The Company has completed a number of acquisitions that have been accounted for as purchases and have resulted in the recognition of goodwill in the Company's consolidated financial statements. This goodwill arises because the purchase prices for these businesses reflect a number of factors including the future earnings and cash flow potential of these businesses, the multiple to earnings, cash flow and other factors at which similar businesses have been purchased by other acquirers, the competitive nature of the processes by which the Company acquired the businesses, the avoidance of the time and costs which would be required (and the associated risks that would be encountered) to enhance the Company's existing product offerings to key target markets and enter into new and profitable businesses, and the complementary strategic fit and resulting synergies these businesses bring to existing operations.

The Company makes an initial allocation of the purchase price at the date of acquisition based upon its understanding of the fair value of the acquired assets and assumed liabilities. The Company obtains this information during due diligence and through other sources. In the months after closing, as the Company obtains additional information about these assets and liabilities, including through tangible and intangible asset appraisals, and learns more about the newly acquired business, it is able to refine the estimates of fair value and more accurately allocate the purchase price. Only items identified as of the acquisition date are considered for subsequent adjustment. The Company is continuing to evaluate certain pre-acquisition contingencies associated with certain of its 2015 acquisitions and is also in the process of obtaining valuations of certain property, plant and equipment, acquired intangible assets and certain acquisition related liabilities in connection with these acquisitions. The Company will make appropriate adjustments to the purchase price allocation prior to completion of the measurement period, as required.

The following briefly describes the Company's acquisition activity for the three years ended December 31, 2015.

On August 31, 2015, Pentagon Merger Sub, Inc., a New York corporation and an indirect, wholly-owned subsidiary of the Company, acquired all of the outstanding shares of common stock of Pall Corporation ("Pall"), a New York corporation, for $127.20 per share in cash, for a total purchase price of approximately $13.6 billion, net of assumed debt of $417 million and acquired cash of approximately $1.2 billion (the "Pall Acquisition"). Pall is a leading global provider of filtration, separation and purification solutions that remove contaminants or separate substances from a variety of solids, liquids and gases, and is now part of the Company's Life Sciences & Diagnostics segment. In its fiscal year ended July 31, 2015, Pall generated consolidated revenues of approximately $2.8 billion. Pall serves customers in the biopharmaceutical, food and beverage and medical markets as well as the process technologies, aerospace and microelectronics markets. The Company preliminarily recorded approximately $9.6 billion of goodwill related to the Pall Acquisition.

The Company financed the approximately $13.6 billion acquisition price of Pall with approximately $2.5 billion of available cash, approximately $8.1 billion of net proceeds from the issuance and sale of U.S. dollar and Euro-denominated commercial paper and €2.7 billion (approximately $3.0 billion based on currency exchange rates as of the date of issuance) of net proceeds from the issuance and sale of Euro-denominated senior unsecured notes. Subsequent to the Pall Acquisition, the Company used the approximately $2.0 billion of net proceeds from the issuance of U.S. dollar-denominated senior unsecured notes and the approximately CHF 755 million ($732 million based on currency exchange rates as of date of issuance) of net proceeds, including the related premium, from the issuance and sale of Swiss franc-denominated senior unsecured bonds to repay a portion of the commercial paper issued to finance the Pall Acquisition.

In addition to the Pall Acquisition, during 2015 the Company acquired 11 businesses for total consideration of approximately $727 million in cash, net of cash acquired. The businesses acquired complement existing units of each of the Company's five segments. The aggregate annual sales of these 11 businesses at the time of their respective acquisitions, in each case based on the company's revenues for its last completed fiscal year prior to the acquisition, were approximately $375 million. The Company preliminarily recorded an aggregate of $306 million of goodwill related to these acquisitions.

In December 2014, the Company successfully completed its tender offer for the outstanding shares of common stock of Nobel Biocare Holding AG ("Nobel Biocare") and acquired substantially all of the Nobel shares, with the remainder of the Nobel shares acquired in 2015 pursuant to a squeeze-out transaction, for an aggregate cash purchase price of approximately CHF 1.9 billion (approximately $1.9 billion based on exchange rates as of the date the shares of common stock were acquired) including debt assumed and net of cash acquired. Headquartered in Zurich, Switzerland, Nobel Biocare is a world leader in the field of innovative implant-based dental restorations with a portfolio of solutions that include dental implant systems, high-precision individualized prosthetics, biomaterials and digital diagnostics, treatment planning and guided surgery. Nobel Biocare had revenues of €567 million in 2013 (approximately $780 million based on exchange rates as of December 31, 2013), and is now part of the Company's Dental segment. The Company recorded approximately $1.0 billion of goodwill related to the acquisition of Nobel Biocare. The Company financed the acquisition of Nobel Biocare from available cash.

In addition to the acquisition of Nobel Biocare, during 2014 the Company acquired 16 businesses for total consideration of approximately $1.3 billion in cash, net of cash acquired. The businesses acquired complement existing units of the Test & Measurement, Environmental, Life Sciences & Diagnostics and Dental segments. The aggregate annual sales of these 16 businesses at the time of their respective acquisitions, in each case based on the company's revenues for its last completed fiscal year prior to the acquisition, were approximately $420 million. The Company preliminarily recorded an aggregate of $630 million of goodwill related to these acquisitions.

During 2013, the Company acquired 12 businesses for total consideration of $883 million in cash, net of cash acquired. The businesses acquired complement existing units of the Environmental, Life Sciences & Diagnostics and Industrial Technologies segments. The aggregate annual sales of these 12 businesses at the time of their respective acquisitions, in each case based on the company's revenues for its last completed fiscal year prior to the acquisition, were approximately $300 million. The Company recorded an aggregate of $518 million of goodwill related to these acquisitions.

The following summarizes the estimated fair values of the assets acquired and liabilities assumed at the date of acquisition ($ in millions):

	2015	2014	2013
Trade accounts receivable	$ 593.4	$ 196.4	$ 84.8
Inventories	524.9	174.0	10.4
Property, plant and equipment	740.9	91.0	45.7
Goodwill	9,862.2	1,643.6	517.5
Other intangible assets, primarily customer relationships, trade names and technology	5,058.3	1,658.2	334.3
In-process research and development	—	56.0	—
Trade accounts payable	(182.8)	(54.7)	(22.5)
Other assets and liabilities, net	(1,827.6)	(497.6)	(66.2)
Assumed debt	(417.0)	(138.5)	(21.2)
Attributable to noncontrolling interest	—	—	(0.3)
Net assets acquired	14,352.3	3,128.4	882.5
Less: noncash consideration	(47.3)	—	—
Net cash consideration	$14,305.0	$3,128.4	$882.5

The following summarizes the estimated fair values of the assets acquired and liabilities assumed at the date of acquisition for the individually significant acquisition in 2015 discussed above, and all of the other 2015 acquisitions as a group ($ in millions):

	Pall	Others	Total
Trade accounts receivable	$ 509.7	$ 83.7	$ 593.4
Inventories	475.5	49.4	524.9
Property, plant and equipment	713.4	27.5	740.9
Goodwill	9,556.2	306.0	9,862.2
Other intangible assets, primarily customer relationships, trade names and technology	4,798.0	260.3	5,058.3
Trade accounts payable	(155.8)	(27.0)	(182.8)
Other assets and liabilities, net	(1,855.2)	27.6	(1,827.6)
Assumed debt	(416.9)	(0.1)	(417.0)
Net assets acquired	13,624.9	727.4	14,352.3
Less: noncash consideration	(47.3)	—	(47.3)
Net cash consideration	$13,577.6	$727.4	$14,305.0

The following summarizes the estimated fair values of the assets acquired and liabilities assumed at the date of acquisition for the individually significant acquisition in 2014 discussed above, and all of the other 2014 acquisitions as a group ($ in millions):

	Nobel Biocare	Others	Total
Trade accounts receivable	$ 124.9	$ 71.5	$ 196.4
Inventories	69.0	105.0	174.0
Property, plant and equipment	59.4	31.6	91.0
Goodwill	1,013.6	630.0	1,643.6
Other intangible assets, primarily customer relationships, trade names and technology	1,049.3	608.9	1,658.2
In-process research and development	—	56.0	56.0
Trade accounts payable	(30.8)	(23.9)	(54.7)
Other assets and liabilities, net	(291.0)	(206.6)	(497.6)
Assumed debt	(132.7)	(5.8)	(138.5)
Net cash consideration	$1,861.7	$1,266.7	$3,128.4

During 2015, in connection with the Pall Acquisition, the Company incurred $47 million of pretax transaction-related costs, primarily banking fees, legal fees, amounts paid to other third party advisers and change in control costs. In addition, the Company's earnings for 2015 reflect the impact of additional pretax charges of $91 million associated with fair value adjustments to acquired inventory and deferred revenue related to the Pall Acquisition and $20 million associated with fair value adjustments to acquired inventory related to the acquisition of Nobel Biocare. During 2014, in connection with the Nobel Biocare acquisition, the Company incurred $12 million of pretax transaction related costs, primarily banking fees, legal fees, amounts paid to other third party advisers and change in control costs. In addition, the Company's earnings for 2014 reflect the impact of additional pretax charges of $5 million associated with fair value adjustments to acquired inventory related to the Nobel Biocare acquisition. Transaction-related costs and acquisition related fair value adjustments attributable to other acquisitions were not material to 2015, 2014, or 2013 earnings.

Pro Forma Financial Information (Unaudited)

The unaudited pro forma information for the periods set forth below gives effect to the 2015 and 2014 acquisitions as if they had occurred as of January 1, 2014. The pro forma information is presented for informational purposes only and is not necessarily indicative of the results of operations that actually would have been achieved had the acquisitions been consummated as of that time ($ in millions except per share amounts):

	2015	2014
Sales	$22,491.2	$23,310.3
Net earnings from continuing operations	2,741.6	2,571.3
Diluted net earnings per share from continuing operations	3.87	3.60

The 2015 unaudited pro forma revenue and earnings set forth above were adjusted to exclude the impact of nonrecurring acquisition date fair value adjustments to inventory and deferred revenue related to the Pall Acquisition of $91 million pretax and exclude the impact of the Nobel Biocare acquisition date fair value adjustments of $20 million pretax. The 2014 unaudited pro forma earnings set forth above were adjusted to include the impact of these nonrecurring acquisition date fair value adjustments to inventory and deferred revenue related to the Pall and Nobel Biocare acquisitions as noted above.

In addition, the acquisition-related transaction costs and change in control payments of approximately $47 million in 2015 associated with the Pall Acquisition and $12 million in 2014 related to the Nobel Biocare acquisition were excluded from pro forma earnings in those periods.

CHANGE IN ACCOUNTING ESTIMATES

1.55 VISTEON CORPORATION (DEC)
NOTES TO CONSOLIDATED FINANCIAL STATEMENTS (in part)

Note 14. Employee Benefit Plans (in part)

Defined Benefit Plans (in part)

2016 Discount Rate for Estimated Service and Interest Cost: Through December 31, 2015, the Company recognized service and interest cost components of pension expense using a single weighted average discount rate derived from the yield curve used to measure the benefit obligation at the beginning of the period. The single weighted average discount method represents the constant annual rate required to discount all future benefit payments related to past service from the date of expected future payment to the measurement date, such that the aggregate present value equals the obligation. The U.S. and certain non-U.S. frozen plans do not have a service component, as additional benefits are no longer accrued.

During the fourth quarter of 2015, the Company changed the method used to estimate the service and interest components of net periodic benefit cost for pension benefits for its U.S. and certain non-U.S. plans. The Company has elected to utilize an approach that discounts individual expected cash flows underlying interest and service costs using the applicable spot rates derived from the yield curve used to determine the benefit obligation to the relevant projected cash flows. The election and adoption of this method provides a more precise measurement of service and interest costs by improving the correlation between projected benefit cash flows and the corresponding spot yield curve rates. The use of disaggregated discount rates results in a different amount of interest cost compared to the traditional single weighted-average discount rate approach because of different weightings given to each subset of payments. The use of disaggregated discount rates affects the amount of service cost because the benefit payments associated with new service credits for active employees tend to be of longer duration than the overall benefit payments associated with the plan's benefit obligation. As a result, the payments would be associated with longer-term spot rates on the yield curve, resulting in lower present values than the calculations using the traditional single weighted-average discount rate.

This change does not affect the measurement of the total benefit obligation, but will result in a decrease in the service and interest components of benefit cost beginning in 2016. Based on current economic conditions, the Company estimates that the service cost and interest cost for the affected plans will be reduced by approximately $7 million in 2016 as a result of the change in method. The Company has accounted for this as a change in accounting estimate that is inseparable from a change in accounting principle, and accordingly has accounted for it on a prospective basis.

CORRECTION OF ERRORS

1.56 FIRST SOLAR, INC. (DEC)
SELECTED FINANCIAL DATA

The following tables set forth our selected consolidated financial data for the periods and at the dates indicated. The selected consolidated financial data from the consolidated statements of operations and consolidated statements of cash flows for the years ended December 31,

2015, 2014, and 2013 and the selected consolidated financial data from the consolidated balance sheets for the years ended December 31, 2015 and 2014 have been derived from the audited consolidated financial statements included in this Annual Report on Form 10-K. The selected consolidated financial data from the consolidated balance sheets for the years ended December 31, 2013, 2012, and 2011 and selected consolidated financial data from the consolidated statements of operations and consolidated statements of cash flows for the years ended December 31, 2012 and 2011 have been derived from audited consolidated financial statements not included in this Annual Report on Form 10-K. We have revised our previously issued financial statements from 2011 to 2014 to properly record a liability associated with an uncertain tax position related to income of a foreign subsidiary. Additional revisions have been made for previously identified errors that were corrected in a period subsequent to the period in which the error originated. All financial information presented herein was revised to reflect the correction of these errors. See "Note 1. First Solar and Its Business—Revision of Previously Issued Financial Statements" to our consolidated financial statements for the year ended December 31, 2015 included in this Annual Report on Form 10-K for additional information. The information presented below should also be read in conjunction with Item 7: "Management's Discussion and Analysis of Financial Condition and Results of Operations" and our consolidated financial statements and the related notes thereto.

| | Years Ended | | | | |
| | December 31, 2015 | December 31, 2014 | December 31, 2013 | December 31, 2012 [2] | December 31, 2011 [3] |
(In thousands, except per share amounts)					
Net sales	$3,578,995	$3,391,187	$3,309,616	$3,354,920	$2,779,832
Gross profit	919,267	824,941	864,632	847,820	976,966
Operating income (loss)	516,664	421,999	370,407	(42,933)	(63,008)
Net income (loss)	$ 546,421	$ 395,964	$ 350,718	$ (106,909)	$ (61,648)
Net income (loss) per share:					
Basic	$ 5.42	$ 3.96	$ 3.74	$ (1.23)	$ (0.72)
Diluted	$ 5.37	$ 3.90	$ 3.67	$ (1.23)	$ (0.72)
Cash dividends declared per common share	$ —	$ —	$ —	$ —	$ —
Net cash (used in) provided by operating activities	$ (360,919)	$ 680,989	$ 856,126	$ 762,209	$ (33,463)
Net cash used in investing activities	(112,140)	(511,879)	(537,106)	(383,732)	(676,457)
Net cash provided by (used in) financing activities	137,103	7,359	101,164	(89,109)	571,218

| | December 31, 2015 | December 31, 2014 | December 31, 2013 [1] | December 31, 2012 [2] | December 31, 2011 [3] |
(In thousands)					
Cash and cash equivalents	$1,126,826	$1,482,054	$1,325,072	$ 901,294	$ 605,619
Marketable securities, current and noncurrent	703,454	509,032	439,102	102,578	182,338
Total assets	7,316,331	6,720,991	6,876,586	6,356,975	5,782,339
Total long-term debt	289,415	213,473	223,323	562,572	663,648
Total liabilities	1,767,844	1,729,504	2,408,516	2,783,681	2,163,593
Total stockholders' equity	5,548,487	4,991,487	4,468,070	3,573,294	3,618,746

[1] Includes adjustments for the revisions described above, which decreased total assets by $6.9 million, increased total liabilities by $28.1 million, and decreased total stockholders' equity by $35.0 million.

[2] Includes adjustments for the revisions described above, which decreased net sales by $13.6 million, decreased gross profit by $4.9 million, increased operating loss by $5.4 million, increased net loss by $10.6 million, increased total assets by $8.3 million, increased total liabilities by $40.5 million, and decreased total stockholders' equity by $32.2 million.

[3] Includes adjustments for the revisions described above, which increased net sales by $13.6 million, increased gross profit by $5.2 million, decreased operating loss by $5.6 million, increased net loss by $22.2 million, increased total assets by $4.7 million, increased total liabilities by $29.8 million, and decreased total stockholders' equity by $25.1 million.

NOTES TO CONSOLIDATED FINANCIAL STATEMENTS (in part)

1. First Solar and Its Business (in part)

First Solar Holdings, LLC was formed as a Delaware limited liability company in May 2003 to act as the holding company for First Solar, LLC, which was formed in 1999 and renamed First Solar US Manufacturing, LLC in the second quarter of 2006, and other subsidiaries formed during 2003 and later. On February 22, 2006, First Solar Holdings, LLC was incorporated in Delaware as First Solar Holdings, Inc. and, also during the first quarter of 2006, was renamed First Solar, Inc.

Revision of Previously Issued Financial Statements

During the three months ended September 30, 2015, we revised our previously issued financial statements from 2011 to 2014 to properly record a liability associated with an uncertain tax position, including penalties, related to income of a foreign subsidiary along with corresponding adjustments in each successive period for the effect of changes in foreign currency exchange rates associated with the liability. The prior periods also include revisions for previously disclosed errors from 2012 primarily related to "cut-off" of our inventories and balance of systems ("BoS") parts and foreign tax credits. Additional revisions were made for previously identified errors related to sales taxes, use taxes, share-based compensation, and miscellaneous items that were corrected in a period subsequent to the period in which the error originated. As several of these errors affected the estimated costs for systems business sales arrangements accounted for under the percentage-of-completion method, we also recorded adjustments to revenue for the changes in the percentage completion of the affected projects.

We evaluated the aggregate effects of the errors to our previously issued financial statements in accordance with SEC Staff Accounting Bulletins No. 99 and No. 108 and, based upon quantitative and qualitative factors, determined that the errors were not material to our previously issued financial statements. As part of this evaluation, we considered a number of qualitative factors, including, among others, that the errors did not change a net loss into net income or vice versa, did not have an impact on our long-term debt covenant compliance, and did not mask a change in earnings or other trends when considering the overall competitive and economic environment within the industry during the periods. However, the cumulative effect of the errors, including the uncertain tax position matter identified during the three months ended September 30, 2015, was significant to our financial results for the year ended December 31, 2015. Accordingly, we revised our historical financial statements, which resulted in decreases to our accumulated earnings of $36.0 million, $35.0 million, and $32.7 million as of December 31, 2014, 2013, and 2012, respectively.

All financial information presented in the accompanying notes to these consolidated financial statements was revised to reflect the correction of these errors. Periods not presented herein will be revised, as applicable, as they are included in future filings.

The following table presents the effect of the aforementioned revisions on our consolidated balance sheet as of December 31, 2014 (in thousands):

| | December 31, 2014 | | |
	As Reported	Adjustment	As Revised
Other liabilities	$ 284,584	$ 36,000	$ 320,584
Total liabilities	1,693,504	36,000	1,729,504
Accumulated earnings	2,279,689	(36,000)	2,243,689
Total stockholders' equity	5,027,487	(36,000)	4,991,487

The following tables present the effect of the aforementioned revisions on our consolidated statements of operations for the years ended December 31, 2014 and 2013 (in thousands, except per share amounts):

| | Year Ended December 31, 2014 | | |
	As Reported	Adjustment	As Revised
Net sales	$3,391,814	$ (627)	$3,391,187
Cost of sales	2,564,709	1,537	2,566,246
Gross profit	827,105	(2,164)	824,941
Operating income	424,163	(2,164)	421,999
Foreign currency loss, net	(3,017)	1,556	(1,461)
Other expense, net	(5,203)	718	(4,485)
Income before taxes and equity in earnings of unconsolidated affiliates	431,991	110	432,101
Income tax expense	(30,124)	(1,064)	(31,188)
Net income	396,918	(954)	395,964
Comprehensive income	472,834	(954)	471,880
Basic net income per share	$ 3.97	$ (0.01)	$ 3.96
Diluted net income per share	$ 3.91	$ (0.01)	$ 3.90

| | Year Ended December 31, 2013 | | |
	As Reported	Adjustment	As Revised
Net sales	$3,308,989	$ 627	$3,309,616
Cost of sales	2,446,235	(1,251)	2,444,984
Gross profit	862,754	1,878	864,632
Operating income	368,529	1,878	370,407
Foreign currency (loss) gain, net	(259)	1,152	893
Other expense, net	(4,758)	(431)	(5,189)
Income before taxes and equity in earnings of unconsolidated affiliates	378,380	2,599	380,979
Income tax expense	(25,179)	(4,919)	(30,098)
Net income	353,038	(2,320)	350,718
Comprehensive income	317,083	(2,320)	314,763
Basic net income per share	$ 3.77	$ (0.03)	$ 3.74
Diluted net income per share	$ 3.70	$ (0.03)	$ 3.67

The following tables present the effect of the aforementioned revisions on our consolidated statements of cash flows for the years ended December 31, 2014 and 2013 (in thousands):

	Year Ended December 31, 2014		
	As Reported	Adjustment	As Revised
Net income	$396,918	$ (954)	$395,964
Adjustments to reconcile net income to cash provided by operating activities:			
Remeasurement of monetary assets and liabilities	8,772	(1,556)	7,216
Changes in operating assets and liabilities:			
Accounts receivable, trade, unbilled and retainage	453,826	8,804	462,630
Prepaid expenses and other current assets	(19,947)	(16,858)	(36,805)
Project assets and deferred project costs	141,908	1,139	143,047
Accounts payable	(52,339)	(718)	(53,057)
Income taxes payable	(989)	(142)	(1,131)
Accrued expenses and other liabilities	(452,438)	10,285	(442,153)
Net cash provided by operating activities	680,989	—	680,989

	Year Ended December 31, 2013		
	As Reported	Adjustment	As Revised
Net income	$353,038	$(2,320)	$350,718
Adjustments to reconcile net income to cash provided by operating activities:			
Share-based compensation	55,079	(494)	54,585
Remeasurement of monetary assets and liabilities	(15,109)	(1,152)	(16,261)
Changes in operating assets and liabilities:			
Accounts receivable, trade, unbilled and retainage	564,964	5,767	570,731
Prepaid expenses and other current assets	109,126	10,115	119,241
Project assets and deferred project costs	(316,022)	(683)	(316,705)
Accounts payable	(93,259)	431	(92,828)
Income taxes payable	36,307	85	36,392
Accrued expenses and other liabilities	(138,937)	(11,749)	(150,686)
Net cash provided by operating activities	856,126	—	856,126

1.57 NIKE, INC. (MAY)

NOTES TO CONSOLIDATED FINANCIAL STATEMENTS (in part)

Note 1—Summary of Significant Accounting Policies (in part)

Revisions

During the third quarter of fiscal 2015, management determined it had incorrectly reflected unrealized gains and losses from re-measurement of non-functional currency intercompany balances between certain of its foreign wholly-owned subsidiaries in its Consolidated Statements of Cash Flows. These unrealized gains and losses should have been classified as non-cash reconciling items from *Net income* to *Cash provided by operations*, but were instead reported on the *Effect of exchange rate changes on cash and equivalents* line of the Consolidated Statements of Cash Flows. This resulted in an understatement of *Cash provided by operations* reported on the Consolidated Statements of Cash Flows for certain prior periods; there was no impact for any period to *Net increase (decrease) in cash and equivalents* reported on the Consolidated Statements of Cash Flows, or *Cash and equivalents* reported on the Consolidated Statements of Cash Flows and Balance Sheets. The Company assessed the materiality of the misclassifications on prior periods' financial statements in accordance with SEC Staff Accounting Bulletin ("SAB") No. 99, Materiality, codified in Accounting Standards Codification ("ASC") 250, Presentation of Financial Statements, and concluded that these misstatements were not material to any prior annual or interim periods. Accordingly, in accordance with ASC 250 (SAB No. 108, Considering the Effects of Prior Year Misstatements when Quantifying Misstatements in Current Year Financial Statements), the amounts have been revised in the applicable Consolidated Statements of Cash Flows. For the three and six months ended August 31, 2014 and November 30, 2014 of fiscal 2015, the revisions increased *Cash provided by operations* and decreased *Effect of exchange rate changes on cash and equivalents* by $95 million and $312 million, respectively. For the fiscal years ended May 31, 2014 and 2013, the revisions increased *Cash provided by operations* and decreased *Effect of exchange rate changes on cash and equivalents* by $10 million and $64 million, respectively. These amounts have been reflected in the applicable tables below. As part of the revision to the Consolidated Statements of Cash Flows, the Company has updated its presentation to separately report *Net foreign currency adjustments*, which was previously included within *Amortization and other*.

The following are selected line items from the Company's Unaudited Condensed Consolidated Statements of Cash Flows illustrating the effect of these corrections:

(In millions)	NIKE, Inc. Unaudited Condensed Consolidated Statements of Cash Flows					
	Three Months Ended August 31, 2014			Six Months Ended November 30, 2014		
	As Reported	Adjustment	As Revised	As Reported	Adjustment	As Revised
Cash Provided by Operations:						
Net income	$ 962	$—	$ 962	$1,617	$ —	$1,617
Income charges (credits) not affecting cash:						
Amortization and other	(34)	42	8	(54)	69	15
Net foreign currency adjustments	—	53	53	—	243	243
Cash provided by operations	588	95	683	1,235	312	1,547
Effect of exchange rate changes on cash and equivalents	97	(95)	2	288	(312)	(24)
Net increase (decrease) in cash and equivalents	83	—	83	53	—	53
Cash and equivalents, beginning of period	2,220	—	2,220	2,220	—	2,220
Cash and Equivalents, End of Period	$2,303	$—	$2,303	$2,273	$ —	$2,273

The following are selected line items from the Company's Consolidated Statements of Cash Flows illustrating the effect of these corrections on the amounts previously reported in the Company's fiscal 2014 Annual Report on Form 10-K:

(In millions)	NIKE, Inc. Consolidated Statements of Cash Flows					
	Year Ended May 31, 2014			Year Ended May 31, 2013		
	As Reported	Adjustment	As Revised	As Reported	Adjustment	As Revised
Cash Provided by Operations:						
Net income	$2,693	$—	$2,693	$2,472	$—	$2,472
Income charges (credits) not affecting cash:						
Amortization and other	114	(46)	68	66	(2)	64
Net foreign currency adjustments	—	56	56	—	66	66
Cash provided by operations	3,003	10	3,013	2,968	64	3,032
Effect of exchange rate changes on cash and equivalents	1	(10)	(9)	100	(64)	36
Net increase (decrease) in cash and equivalents	(1,117)	—	(1,117)	1,083	—	1,083
Cash and equivalents, beginning of year	3,337	—	3,337	2,254	—	2,254
Cash and Equivalents, End of Period	$2,220	$—	$2,220	$3,337	$—	$3,337

Consolidation

Author's Note

In August 2014, FASB issued ASU No. 2014-13, *Consolidation (Topic 810): Measuring the Financial Assets and the Financial Liabilities of a Consolidated Collateralized Financing Entity (a consensus of the FASB Emerging Issues Task Force)*. The fair value of the financial assets of a collateralized financing entity, as determined under GAAP, may differ from the fair value of its financial liabilities even when the financial liabilities have recourse only to the financial assets. Before this ASU, there was no specific guidance in GAAP on how a reporting entity should account for that difference. The amendments in this ASU provide an alternative to FASB ASC 820, *Fair Value Measurement*, for measuring the financial assets and the financial liabilities of a consolidated collateralized financing entity to eliminate that difference. When the measurement alternative is not elected for a consolidated collateralized financing entity within the scope of this ASU, the amendments clarify that (1) the fair value of the financial assets and the fair value of the financial liabilities of the consolidated collateralized financing entity should be measured using the requirements of FASB ASC 820, and (2) any differences in the fair value of the financial assets and the fair value of the financial liabilities of that consolidated collateralized financing entity should be reflected in earnings and attributed to the reporting entity in the consolidated statement of income (loss). The amendments in this ASU are effective for public business entities for annual periods, and interim periods within those annual periods, beginning after December 15, 2015. For entities other than public business entities, the amendments in this ASU are effective for annual periods ending after December 15, 2016, and interim periods beginning after December 15, 2016. Early adoption is permitted as of the beginning of an annual period. None of the examples that follow contain an example of these disclosures due to the effective date.

RECOGNITION AND MEASUREMENT

1.58 FASB ASC 810-10-10 states that the purpose of consolidated financial statements is to present, primarily for the benefit of the owners and creditors of the parent, the results of operations and the financial position of a parent and all its subsidiaries as if the consolidated group were a single economic entity. It is presumed that consolidated financial statements are more meaningful than separate financial statements and are usually necessary for a fair presentation when one of the entities in the consolidated group directly or indirectly has a controlling financial interest in the other entities.

1.59 As noted in the "Pending Content" in FASB ASC 810-10-05-8,

> [t]he Variable Interest Entities Subsections clarify the application of the General Subsections to certain legal entities in which equity investors do not have sufficient equity at risk for the legal entity to finance its activities without additional subordinated financial support or, as a group, the holders of the equity investment at risk lack any one of the following three characteristics:
> a. The power, through voting rights or similar rights, to direct the activities of a legal entity that most significantly impact the entity's economic performance.
> b. The obligation to absorb the expected losses of the legal entity.
> c. The right to receive the expected residual returns of the legal entity.

Consolidated financial statements are usually necessary for a fair presentation if one of the entities in the consolidated group directly or indirectly has a controlling financial interest, typically a majority voting interest, in the other entities. Application of the majority voting interest requirement to certain types of entities may not identify the party with a controlling financial interest because that interest may be achieved through other arrangements. The "Pending Content" in FASB ASC 810-10-25-38A explains that a reporting entity with a variable interest in a variable interest entity (VIE) should assess whether the reporting entity has a controlling financial interest in the VIE and, thus, is the VIE's primary beneficiary. The reporting enterprise with a variable interest(s) that provides the reporting entity with a controlling financial interest in a VIE will have both the following characteristics: (*a*) the power to direct the activities of a VIE that most significantly affect the VIE's economic performance and (*b*) the obligation to absorb losses of the VIE that could potentially be significant to the VIE or the right to receive benefits from the VIE that could potentially be significant to the VIE. Only one reporting entity, if any, is expected to be identified as the primary beneficiary of a VIE. Although more than one reporting entity could have the obligation to absorb losses previously mentioned, only one reporting entity (if any) will have the power to direct the activities of a VIE that most significantly affect the VIE's economic performance. Further, the concept of a qualifying special-purpose entity no longer exists in FASB ASC.

1.60 FASB ASC 810 also establishes accounting and reporting standards for the noncontrolling interest in a subsidiary and the deconsolidation of a subsidiary. A *noncontrolling interest* is the portion of equity (net assets) in a subsidiary not directly or indirectly attributable to a parent. FASB ASC 810-10-45-16 requires the entity to present any noncontrolling interest within the "Equity" or "Net Assets" section of the consolidated statement of financial position separately from the parent's equity or net assets.

1.61 It is preferable under FASB ASC that the subsidiary's financial statements have the same or nearly the same fiscal period as the parent. However, FASB ASC 810-10-45-12 states that for consolidation purposes, it is usually acceptable to use the subsidiary's financial statements if the difference in fiscal period is not more than approximately three months. In addition, when a difference in the fiscal periods exists, FASB ASC does not require adjustments to be made for the effects of significant transactions that occurred between the parents' and subsidiaries' fiscal year-ends. FASB ASC 810-10-45-12 does require recognition by disclosure or otherwise of the effect of intervening events that materially affect the financial position or results of operations.

1.62 FASB ASC 810-10-45-11 recognizes that an entity may need to prepare parent-entity (separate) financial statements in addition to consolidated financial statements. This paragraph provides guidance on how an entity may choose to present these statements. For example, consolidating financial statements, in which one column is used for the parent and other columns for particular subsidiaries or groups of subsidiaries, is an effective means of presenting the pertinent information.

PRESENTATION

1.63 FASB ASC 810-10-45-23 requires that a change in a parent's ownership interest while the parent retains its controlling financial interest in its subsidiary should be accounted for as equity transactions (investments by owners and distributions to owners acting in their capacity as owners). Therefore, no gain or loss shall be recognized in consolidated net income or comprehensive income. The carrying amount of the noncontrolling interest should be adjusted to reflect the change in its ownership interest in the subsidiary. Any difference between the fair value of the consideration received or paid and the amount by which the noncontrolling interest is adjusted should be recognized in equity attributable to the parent.

1.64 "Pending Content" in FASB ASC 810-10-40-4 states that a parent should deconsolidate a subsidiary or derecognize a group of assets specified in FASB ASC 810-10-40-3A as of the date the parent ceases to have a controlling financial interest in that subsidiary or group of assets. FASB ASC 810-10-40-5 states that if a parent deconsolidates a subsidiary or derecognizes a group of assets through a nonreciprocal transfer to owners, such as a spinoff, the guidance in FASB ASC 845-10 applies. Otherwise, a parent should account for the deconsolidation of a subsidiary or derecognition of a group of assets by recognizing a gain or loss in net income attributable to the parent. This gain or loss is measured as the difference between (a) the aggregate of the fair value of any consideration received; the fair value of any retained noncontrolling interest in the former subsidiary or group of assets at the date the subsidiary is deconsolidated or the group of assets is derecognized, and the carrying amount of any noncontrolling interest in the former subsidiary, including any accumulated other comprehensive income attributable to the noncontrolling interest, at the date the subsidiary is deconsolidated and (b) the carrying amount of the former subsidiary's assets and liabilities or the carrying amount of the group of assets.

DISCLOSURE

1.65 FASB ASC 810-10-50-1 states in part that consolidated financial statements should disclose the consolidation policy that is being followed. In most cases, this can be made apparent by the headings or other information in the financial statements, but in other cases, a footnote is required.

1.66 FASB ASC 810-10-50-1A also requires disclosure on the face of the consolidated financial statements of the amounts of consolidated net income and consolidated comprehensive income attributable to the parent and noncontrolling interest. Disclosures in the consolidated financial statements should clearly identify and distinguish between the interests of the parent's owners and the interests of the noncontrolling owners of a subsidiary. Those disclosures include a reconciliation of the beginning and ending balances of the equity attributable to the parent and noncontrolling owners and a schedule showing the effects of changes in a parent's ownership interest in a subsidiary on the equity attributable to the parent.

1.67 FASB ASC 810-10-50-5 A requires a reporting entity that is a primary beneficiary of a VIE or a reporting entity that holds a variable interest in a VIE but is not the entity's primary beneficiary to disclose all qualitative and quantitative information about the reporting entity's involvement (giving consideration to both explicit arrangements and implicit variable interests) with the VIE, including, but not limited to, the nature, purpose, size, and activities of the VIE, including how the VIE is financed. Paragraphs 49–54 of FASB ASC 810-10-25 provide guidance on how to determine whether a reporting entity has an implicit variable interest in a VIE.

PRESENTATION AND DISCLOSURE EXCERPTS

CONSOLIDATION

1.68 THE DOW CHEMICAL COMPANY (DEC)
NOTES TO THE CONSOLIDATED FINANCIAL STATEMENTS (in part)

Note 1—Summary of Significant Accounting Policies (in part)

Principles of Consolidation and Basis of Presentation

The accompanying consolidated financial statements of The Dow Chemical Company and its subsidiaries ("Dow" or the "Company") were prepared in accordance with accounting principles generally accepted in the United States of America ("U.S. GAAP") and include the assets, liabilities, revenues and expenses of all majority-owned subsidiaries over which the Company exercises control and, when applicable, entities for which the Company has a controlling financial interest or is the primary beneficiary. Intercompany transactions and balances are eliminated in consolidation. Investments in nonconsolidated affiliates (20-50 percent owned companies, joint ventures and partnerships) are accounted for using the equity method.

Note 2—Recent Accounting Guidance (in part)

Accounting Guidance Issued But Not Adopted as of December 31, 2015 (in part)

In February 2015, the FASB issued ASU 2015-02, "Consolidation (Topic 810): Amendments to the Consolidation Analysis," which makes changes to both the variable interest model and voting interest model and eliminates the indefinite deferral of FASB Statement No. 167, included in ASU 2010-10, for certain investment funds. All reporting entities that hold a variable interest in other legal entities will need to re-evaluate their consolidation conclusions as well as disclosure requirements. This ASU is effective for annual periods beginning after December 15, 2015, and early adoption is permitted, including any interim period. The Company does not expect the adoption of this guidance to have an impact on the consolidated financial statements.

Note 4—Acquisitions (in part)

Step Acquisition of Univation Technologies, LLC

On May 5, 2015, Univation Technologies, LLC ("Univation"), previously a 50:50 joint venture between Dow and ExxonMobil Chemical Company ("ExxonMobil"), became a wholly owned subsidiary of Dow as a result of ExxonMobil redeeming its entire equity interest in Univation in exchange for certain assets and liabilities of Univation. The Company's equity interest in Univation of $159 million, previously classified as "Investment in nonconsolidated affiliates" in the consolidated balance sheets, was remeasured to fair value which resulted in a non-taxable gain of $361 million recognized in the second quarter of 2015, included in "Sundry income (expense)—net" and reflected in the Performance Plastics segment.

The following table summarizes the fair values of Univation's remaining assets and liabilities on May 5, 2015, which are fully consolidated by Dow:

Assets Acquired and Liabilities Assumed on May 5, 2015 In millions	
Fair Value of Previously Held Equity Investment	$520
Fair Value of Assets Acquired	
Current assets	$113
Property	56
Other intangible assets[(1)]	433
Total Assets Acquired	$602
Fair Value of Liabilities Assumed	
Current liabilities	$102
Long-term debt	9
Deferred income tax liabilities—noncurrent	126
Total Liabilities Assumed	$237
Goodwill[(2)]	$141

[(1)] Includes $340 million of licenses and intellectual property, $5 million of software, $12 million of trademarks and $76 million of customer-related intangibles. See Note 10 for additional information.
[(2)] Net of a $14 million settlement of an affiliate's pre-existing obligations and not deductible for tax purposes.

Beginning in May 2015, Univation's results of operations were fully consolidated in the Company's consolidated statements of income. Prior to May 2015, the Company's 50 percent share of Univation's results of operations was reported as "Equity in earnings of nonconsolidated affiliates" in the consolidated statements of income.

Note 9—Nonconsolidated Affiliates and Related Company Transactions

The Company's investments in companies accounted for using the equity method ("nonconsolidated affiliates") were $3,810 million at December 31, 2015, of which $3,958 million is classified as "Investment in nonconsolidated affiliates" and $148 million is classified as "Other noncurrent obligations" in the consolidated balance sheets, and $4,201 million at December 31, 2014, classified as "Investment in nonconsolidated affiliates." At December 31, 2015, the carrying amount of the Company's investments in nonconsolidated affiliates was $97 million more than its share of the investees' net assets, exclusive of additional differences for Dow Corning Corporation ("Dow Corning") and EQUATE Petrochemical Company K.S.C. ("EQUATE"), which are discussed separately below. At December 31, 2014, the carrying amount of the Company's investments in nonconsolidated affiliates was $56 million more than its share of the investees' net assets, exclusive of additional differences for Dow Corning and MEGlobal. Dividends received from the Company's nonconsolidated affiliates were $816 million in 2015, $961 million in 2014 (including accrued dividends of $5 million) and $905 million in 2013.

At December 31, 2015, the Company's investment in Dow Corning was $149 million less than the Company's proportionate share of Dow Corning's underlying net assets ($149 million less at December 31, 2014). This amount is considered a permanent difference related to the other-than-temporary decline in the Company's investment in Dow Corning, triggered by Dow Corning's May 15, 1995, bankruptcy filing, and Dow Corning's purchase of additional ownership interests in its Hemlock Semiconductor Group entities in 2013. Dow Corning emerged from bankruptcy in 2004.

On December 23, 2015, the Company sold its interest in MEGlobal to EQUATE. The Company eliminated 42.5 percent of the gain on the sale (equivalent to Dow's ownership interest in EQUATE), or $555 million, against the Company's investment in EQUATE, resulting in a negative investment of $148 million at December 31, 2015, which is classified as "Other noncurrent obligations" in the consolidated balance sheets. The Company's investment in EQUATE was $555 million less than the Company's proportionate share of EQUATE's underlying net assets, which represents the difference between the preliminary fair values of certain MEGlobal assets acquired and the Company's related valuation on a U.S. GAAP basis, of which approximately $250 million is being amortized over the remaining useful lives of the assets and approximately $305 million is considered a permanent difference. Final determination of the fair value of MEGlobal assets acquired by EQUATE may result in adjustments to the preliminary values assigned at the date of acquisition, and could impact the difference between the Company's investment in EQUATE and its proportionate share of EQUATE's assets and the amount of the difference assigned to goodwill and assets to be amortized.

At December 31, 2014, the Company's investment in MEGlobal was $177 million less than the Company's proportionate share of MEGlobal's underlying net assets. This amount represented the difference between the value of certain assets of the joint venture and the Company's related valuation on a U.S. GAAP basis, of which $41 million was being amortized over the remaining useful lives of the assets and $136 million was considered to be a permanent difference. In the fourth quarter of 2014, MEGlobal purchased the noncontrolling interest of a subsidiary, which resulted in a $3 million reduction in the permanent difference.

On July 31, 2015, the Company sold its AgroFresh business to AFSI. Proceeds received on the divestiture of AgroFresh included 17.5 million common shares of AFSI, which were valued at $210 million and represent an approximate 35 percent ownership interest in AFSI. The Company has accounted for its ownership interest in AFSI using the equity method of accounting with the Company's investment in AFSI classified as "Investment in nonconsolidated affiliates" in the consolidated balance sheets and the Company's share of AFSI's results of operations included in "Equity in earnings of nonconsolidated affiliates" in the consolidated statements of income, aligned with the Agricultural Sciences segment. If the Company valued its investment in AFSI based on the December 31, 2015, closing stock price of AFSI, the value of this investment would have been lower than the carrying value by $80 million. See Note 5 for further information on this transaction.

The Company and Saudi Arabian Oil Company formed Sadara Chemical Company ("Sadara") to build and operate a world-scale, fully integrated chemicals complex in Jubail Industrial City, Kingdom of Saudi Arabia. Sadara achieved its first polyethylene production in December 2015 and will follow a phased approach to start up the remaining manufacturing facilities. At December 31, 2014, the Company had a $193 million note receivable with Sadara, included in "Noncurrent receivables" in the consolidated balance sheets, that was converted to equity in the first quarter of 2015 and reclassified to "Investment in nonconsolidated affiliates" in the consolidated balance sheets. During 2015, the Company loaned an additional $753 million to Sadara, of which $280 million has been converted to equity. Approximately $460 million of the outstanding note receivable is expected to be converted to equity in the first quarter of 2016.

The nonconsolidated affiliates in which the Company has investments, excluding AFSI, are privately held companies; therefore, quoted market prices are not available.

Sales to and purchases from nonconsolidated affiliates were not material to the consolidated financial statements. Balances due to or due from nonconsolidated affiliates at December 31, 2015 and 2014 are as follows:

Balances Due To or Due From Nonconsolidated Affiliates at December 31		
In millions	2015	2014
Accounts and notes receivable—other	$389	$511
Noncurrent receivables[1]	473	212
Total assets	$862	$723
Notes payable	$171	$189
Accounts payable—other	230	274
Total current liabilities	$401	$463

[1] Included in "Noncurrent receivables" is a $473 million note receivable with Sadara at December 31, 2015, of which $460 million is expected to be converted to equity in the first quarter of 2016 ($193 million at December 31, 2014, which was converted to equity in the first quarter of 2015).

Principal Nonconsolidated Affiliates

Dow had an ownership interest in 55 nonconsolidated affiliates at December 31, 2015 (59 at December 31, 2014). The Company's principal nonconsolidated affiliates and its ownership interest (direct and indirect) for each at December 31, 2015, 2014 and 2013 are as follows:

Principal Nonconsolidated Affiliates at December 31	Ownership Interest		
	2015	2014	2013
Dow Corning Corporation[1]	50%	50%	50%
EQUATE Petrochemical Company K.S.C.	42.5%	42.5%	42.5%
The Kuwait Olefins Company K.S.C.	42.5%	42.5%	42.5%
The Kuwait Styrene Company K.S.C.[2]	42.5%	42.5%	N/A
Map Ta Phut Olefins Company Limited[3]	32.77%	32.77%	32.77%
MEGlobal[4]	N/A	50%	50%
Sadara Chemical Company	35%	35%	35%
The SCG-Dow Group:			
Siam Polyethylene Company Limited	50%	50%	50%
Siam Polystyrene Company Limited	50%	50%	50%
Siam Styrene Monomer Co., Ltd.	50%	50%	50%
Siam Synthetic Latex Company Limited	50%	50%	50%
Univation Technologies, LLC[5]	N/A	50%	50%

[1] On December 10, 2015, the Company entered into a definitive agreement to restructure the ownership of Dow Corning. Under the terms of the agreements, Dow will become the 100 percent owner of Dow Corning, currently a 50:50 joint venture between Dow and Corning Incorporated ("Corning"). Dow and Corning will maintain their current equity stake in the Hemlock Semiconductor Group. The transaction is expected to close in the first half of 2016.

[2] The Kuwait Styrene Company K.S.C. was added as a principal nonconsolidated affiliate in the fourth quarter of 2014.

[3] The Company's effective ownership of Map Ta Phut Olefins Company Limited is 32.77 percent, of which the Company directly owns 20.27 percent and indirectly owns 12.5 percent through its equity interest in Siam Polyethylene Company Limited and Siam Synthetic Latex Company Limited.

[4] On December 23, 2015, the Company sold its 50 percent ownership interest in MEGlobal to EQUATE. MEGlobal is treated as a separate principal nonconsolidated affiliate through the date of divestiture. See Note 5 for additional information.

[5] On May 5, 2015, Univation, previously a 50:50 joint venture between Dow and ExxonMobil, became a wholly owned subsidiary of Dow. See Note 4 for additional information on this transaction.

The Company's investment in its principal nonconsolidated affiliates was $2,972 million at December 31, 2015 and $3,487 million at December 31, 2014. Equity earnings from these companies were $704 million in 2015, $845 million in 2014 and $951 million in 2013. Equity earnings from principal nonconsolidated affiliates equity earnings decreased in 2015 as higher earnings at The SCG-Dow Group and Map Ta Phut Olefins Company Limited were more than offset by increased equity losses from Sadara, lower earnings from Univation resulting from the May 5, 2015, step acquisition, and lower earnings from EQUATE, TKOC and MEGlobal.

The summarized financial information that follows represents the combined accounts (at 100 percent) of the principal nonconsolidated affiliates.

Summarized Balance Sheet Information at December 31		
In millions	2015[1]	2014
Current assets	$ 8,794	$ 9,611
Noncurrent assets	31,723	27,025
Total assets	$40,517	$36,636
Current liabilities	$ 9,850	$ 6,321
Noncurrent liabilities	21,461	21,047
Total liabilities	$31,311	$27,368
Noncontrolling interests	$ 663	$ 666

[1] The summarized balance sheet information for 2015 does not include Univation; MEGlobal is included as part of EQUATE.

Summarized Income Statement Information			
In millions	2015[1]	2014	2013[2]
Sales	$15,468	$19,333	$18,257
Gross profit	$ 3,206	$ 3,526	$ 3,403
Net income	$ 1,343	$ 1,673	$ 1,906

[1] The summarized income statement information for 2015 includes the results of Univation through April 30, 2015 and MEGlobal through November 30, 2015.

[2] The summarized income statement information for 2013 does not include the results of The Kuwait Styrene Company K.S.C. as this entity became a principal nonconsolidated affiliate in 2014.

The Company has service agreements with some of these entities, including contracts to manage the operations of manufacturing sites and the construction of new facilities; licensing and technology agreements; and marketing, sales, purchase, lease and sublease agreements.

The Company sells excess ethylene glycol produced at Dow's manufacturing facilities in the United States and Europe to MEGlobal, an EQUATE subsidiary as of December 23, 2015. The Company also sells ethylene to MEGlobal as a raw material for its ethylene glycol plants in Canada. Sales of these products to MEGlobal represented 1 percent of total net sales in 2015 (1 percent of total net sales in 2014 and 1 percent of total net sales in 2013). Sales of ethylene glycol to MEGlobal are reflected in the Performance Materials & Chemicals segment and represented 2 percent of the segment's sales in 2015 (2 percent in 2014 and 2 percent in 2013). Sales of ethylene to MEGlobal are reflected in the Performance Plastics segment and represented 1 percent of the segment's sales in 2015 (1 percent in 2014 and 2 percent in 2013).

Note 20—Variable Interest Entities

Consolidated Variable Interest Entities

The Company holds a variable interest in six joint ventures for which the Company is the primary beneficiary.

Three joint ventures own and operate manufacturing and logistics facilities, which produce chemicals and provide services in Asia Pacific. The Company's variable interest in these joint ventures relates to arrangements between the joint ventures and the Company, involving the majority of the output on take-or-pay terms with pricing ensuring a guaranteed return to the joint ventures.

The fourth joint venture manufactures products in Japan for the semiconductor industry. Each joint venture partner holds several equivalent variable interests, with the exception of a royalty agreement held exclusively between the joint venture and the Company. In addition, the entire output of the joint venture is sold to the Company for resale to third-party customers.

The fifth joint venture provides ethylene storage in Alberta, Canada. The Company's variable interests relate to arrangements involving a majority of the joint venture's storage capacity on take-or-pay terms with pricing ensuring a guaranteed return to the joint venture; and favorably priced leases provided to the joint venture. The Company provides the joint venture with operation and maintenance services and utilities.

The sixth joint venture is located in Brazil and produces ethanol from sugarcane. The Company's variable interests in this joint venture relate to an equity option between the partners, a parental loan and guarantee related to debt financing, and contractual arrangements limiting the partner's initial participation in the economics of certain assets and liabilities. Since formation of the joint venture, the partners have amended the governing documents, including terms of the equity option. These amendments did not result in a change to the Company's accounting treatment of the joint venture. Terms of the equity option require the Company to purchase the partner's equity investment at a price based on a specified formula if the partner elects to exit the joint venture. In August 2015, the partner exercised its equity option which requires Dow to purchase their equity investment for approximately $200 million before July 12, 2016. As a result, in the third quarter of 2015, the Company reclassified the partner's equity investment from "Redeemable Noncontrolling Interest" to "Accrued and other current liabilities" in the consolidated balance sheets. The joint venture's ethanol mill commenced production in the second quarter of 2015. Original plans for the joint venture's expansion into downstream derivative products have been postponed. This joint venture also holds variable interests in an entity that owns a cogeneration facility. The joint venture's variable interests are the result of a tolling arrangement where it provides fuel to the entity and purchases a majority of the cogeneration facility's output on terms that ensure a return to the entity's equity holders.

The Company previously held an equity interest in a joint venture that owns and operates a membrane chlor-alkali manufacturing facility. The Company's variable interests in this joint venture related to equity options between the partners and a cost-plus off-take arrangement between the joint venture and the Company, involving proportional purchase commitments on take-or-pay terms and ensuring a guaranteed return to the joint venture. During the second quarter of 2015, Mitsui & Co. Texas Chlor-Alkali Inc. ("Mitsui"), a 50 percent equity owner in this joint venture, provided notice of its intention to transfer its equity interest to Dow as part of the Reverse Morris Trust transaction ("Transaction") with Olin. On October 5, 2015, the Company purchased Mitsui's equity interest in the membrane chlor-alkali joint venture for $133 million, which resulted in a loss of $25 million included in "Sundry income (expense)—net" in the consolidated statements of income and included as a component of the pretax gain on the Transaction. The loss is reflected in the Performance Materials & Chemicals segment. See Note 6 for additional information on this Transaction.

The Company held a 49 percent equity interest in a joint venture that managed the growth, harvest and conditioning of soybean seed and grain, corn and wheat in the United States. The Company's variable interest in this joint venture related to an equity option between the partners. Terms of the equity option required the Company to purchase the partner's equity investment at a price based on a specified formula, after a specified period of time, and satisfaction of certain conditions, if the partner elected to sell its equity investment. On August 10, 2015, the equity option was determined to be exercisable and the partner provided notice to the Company of its intent to exercise the equity option, which resulted in an after-tax loss of $22 million, included in "Net income attributable to noncontrolling interests" in the consolidated statements of income. The Company purchased the partner's equity investment on September 18, 2015, which resulted in the joint venture becoming a wholly owned subsidiary of Dow. Subsequent to the purchase of the partner's equity investment, the Company sold its entire ownership interest in the subsidiary to a third party and recognized a pretax gain of $44 million on the sale in the third quarter of 2015, included in "Sundry income (expense)—net" in the consolidated statements of income and reflected in the Agricultural Sciences segment.

The Company previously held a variable interest in an owner trust, for which the Company was the primary beneficiary. The owner trust leased an ethylene production facility in The Netherlands to the Company, whereby substantially all of the rights and obligations of ownership were transferred to the Company. The Company's variable interest in the owner trust related to a fixed purchase price option. On January 2, 2014, the Company purchased the ethylene production facility for $406 million. The Company classified $346 million as "Payments on long-term debt" and $60 million as "Purchases of noncontrolling interests" in the consolidated statements of cash flows.

The Company's consolidated financial statements include the assets, liabilities and results of operations of variable interest entities ("VIEs") for which the Company is the primary beneficiary. The other equity holders' interests are reflected in "Net income attributable to noncontrolling interests" in the consolidated statements of income and "Redeemable Noncontrolling Interest," "Non-redeemable noncontrolling interests" and "Accrued and other current liabilities" in the consolidated balance sheets. The following table summarizes the carrying amounts of these entities' assets and liabilities included in the Company's consolidated balance sheets at December 31, 2015 and 2014:

Assets and Liabilities of Consolidated VIEs at December 31		
In millions	2015	2014
Cash and cash equivalents[1]	$ 158	$ 190
Other current assets[2]	112	174
Property	1,717	2,726
Other noncurrent assets[2]	65	72
Total assets[2][3]	$2,052	$3,162
Current liabilities (nonrecourse 2015: $256; 2014: $389)[2]	$ 258	$ 392
Long-term debt (nonrecourse 2015: $487; 2014: $1,216)[2]	504	1,247
Other noncurrent obligations (nonrecourse 2015: $51; 2014: $62)	51	62
Total liabilities[2]	$ 813	$1,701

[1] Included $20 million at December 31, 2014 specifically restricted for the debt servicing and operational expenses of a manufacturing facility.

[2] Presented in accordance with newly implemented ASU 2015-03. See Note 2 for additional information.

[3] All assets were restricted at December 31, 2015 and December 31, 2014.

In addition, the Company holds a variable interest in an entity created to monetize accounts receivable of select European entities. The Company is the primary beneficiary of this entity as a result of holding subordinated notes while maintaining servicing responsibilities for the accounts receivable. The carrying amounts of assets and liabilities included in the Company's consolidated balance sheets pertaining to this entity were current assets of $103 million (zero restricted) at December 31, 2015 ($99 million, zero restricted, at December 31, 2014) and current liabilities were less than $1 million (zero nonrecourse) at December 31, 2015 (less than $1 million, zero nonrecourse, at December 31, 2014).

Amounts presented in the consolidated balance sheets and the table above as restricted assets or nonrecourse obligations relating to consolidated VIEs at December 31, 2015 and 2014 are adjusted for intercompany eliminations and parental guarantees.

Nonconsolidated Variable Interest Entities

The Company holds a variable interest in a joint venture that manufactures crude acrylic acid in the United States and Germany on behalf of the Company and the other joint venture partner. The variable interest relates to a cost-plus arrangement between the joint venture and each joint venture partner. The Company is not the primary beneficiary, as a majority of the joint venture's output is committed to the other joint venture partner; therefore, the entity is accounted for under the equity method of accounting. At December 31, 2015, the Company's investment in the joint venture was $160 million ($162 million at December 31, 2014), classified as "Investment in nonconsolidated affiliates" in the consolidated balance sheets, representing the Company's maximum exposure to loss.

The Company holds variable interests in AFSI, a company that produces and sells proprietary technologies for the horticultural and agronomic markets. The variable interests in AFSI relate to a sublease agreement between Dow and AFSI; a tax receivable agreement that entitles Dow to additional consideration in the form of tax savings, which is contingent on the operations and earnings of AFSI; and contingent consideration, which is subject to certain performance conditions. The Company is not the primary beneficiary, as Dow is a minority shareholder in AFSI and AFSI is governed by a board of directors, the composition of which is mandated by AFSI's corporate governance requirements that a majority of the directors be independent. At December 31, 2015, the Company's investment in AFSI was

$191 million (zero at December 31, 2014), and is classified as "Investment in nonconsolidated affiliates" in the consolidated balance sheets. In addition, the Company has a receivable with AFSI for six million warrants, which is currently valued at $6 million and classified as "Accounts and notes receivable—other" in the consolidated balance sheets. The Company's maximum exposure to loss was $197 million at December 31, 2015.

1.69 CONAGRA FOODS, INC. (MAY)
NOTES TO CONSOLIDATED FINANCIAL STATEMENTS (in part)

(columnar dollars in millions, except per share amounts)

1. Summary of Significant Accounting Policies (in part)

Fiscal Year —The fiscal year of ConAgra Foods, Inc. ("ConAgra Foods", "Company", "we", "us", or "our") ends the last Sunday in May. The fiscal years for the consolidated financial statements presented consist of a 53-week period for fiscal year 2015 and 52-week periods for fiscal years 2014 and 2013.

Basis of Consolidation —The consolidated financial statements include the accounts of ConAgra Foods, Inc. and all majority-owned subsidiaries. In addition, the accounts of all variable interest entities for which we have been determined to be the primary beneficiary are included in our consolidated financial statements from the date such determination is made. All significant intercompany investments, accounts, and transactions have been eliminated.

Investments in Unconsolidated Affiliates —The investments in, and the operating results of, 50%-or-less-owned entities not required to be consolidated are included in the consolidated financial statements on the basis of the equity method of accounting or the cost method of accounting, depending on specific facts and circumstances.

We review our investments in unconsolidated affiliates for impairment whenever events or changes in business circumstances indicate that the carrying amount of the investments may not be fully recoverable. Evidence of a loss in value that is other than temporary includes, but is not limited to, the absence of an ability to recover the carrying amount of the investment, the inability of the investee to sustain an earnings capacity which would justify the carrying amount of the investment, or, where applicable, estimated sales proceeds which are insufficient to recover the carrying amount of the investment. Management's assessment as to whether any decline in value is other than temporary is based on our ability and intent to hold the investment and whether evidence indicating the carrying value of the investment is recoverable within a reasonable period of time outweighs evidence to the contrary. Management generally considers our investments in equity method investees to be strategic long-term investments. Therefore, management completes its assessments with a long-term viewpoint. If the fair value of the investment is determined to be less than the carrying value and the decline in value is considered to be other than temporary, an appropriate write-down is recorded based on the excess of the carrying value over the best estimate of fair value of the investment.

8. Variable Interest Entities

Variable Interest Entities Consolidated

We own a 49.99% interest in Lamb Weston BSW, LLC ("Lamb Weston BSW"), a potato processing venture with Ochoa Ag Unlimited Foods, Inc. ("Ochoa"). We provide all sales and marketing services to Lamb Weston BSW. Under certain circumstances, we could be required to compensate Ochoa for lost profits resulting from significant production shortfalls ("production shortfalls"). Commencing on June 1, 2018, or on an earlier date under certain circumstances, we have a contractual right to purchase the remaining equity interest in Lamb Weston BSW from Ochoa (the "call option"). We are currently subject to a contractual obligation to purchase all of Ochoa's equity investment in Lamb Weston BSW at the option of Ochoa (the "put option"). The purchase prices under the call option and the put option (the "options") are based on the book value of Ochoa's equity interest at the date of exercise, as modified by an agreed-upon rate of return for the holding period of the investment balance. The agreed-upon rate of return varies depending on the circumstances under which any of the options are exercised. As of May 31, 2015, the price at which Ochoa had the right to put its equity interest to us was $41.6 million. This amount is presented within other noncurrent liabilities in our Consolidated Balance Sheets. We have determined that Lamb Weston BSW is a variable interest entity and that we are the primary beneficiary of the entity. Accordingly, we consolidate the financial statements of Lamb Weston BSW.

We hold a promissory note from Lamb Weston BSW, the balance of which was $36.1 million at May 31, 2015. The promissory note is due in December 2015. The promissory note is currently accruing interest at a rate of LIBOR plus 200 basis points with a floor of 3.25%. In addition, as of May 31, 2015, we provided lines of credit of up to $15.0 million to Lamb Weston BSW. Borrowings under the lines of credit bear interest at a rate of LIBOR plus 200 basis points with a floor of 3.25%. The amounts owed by Lamb Weston BSW to the Company are not reflected in our Consolidated Balance Sheets, as they are eliminated in consolidation.

Our variable interests in Lamb Weston BSW include an equity investment in the venture, the options, the promissory note, certain fees paid to us by Lamb Weston BSW for sales and marketing services, the contingent obligation related to production shortfalls, and the lines of credit advanced to Lamb Weston BSW. Our maximum exposure to loss as a result of our involvement with this venture is equal to our equity investment in the venture, the balance of the promissory note extended to the venture, the amount, if any, advanced under the lines of credit, and the amount, if any, by which the put option exercise price exceeds the fair value of the noncontrolling interest in Lamb Weston BSW upon its exercise. Also, in the event of a production shortfall, we could be required to compensate Ochoa for lost profits. It is not possible to determine the maximum exposure to losses from the potential exercise of the put option or from potential production shortfalls. However, we do not expect to incur material losses resulting from these potential exposures.

Due to the consolidation of these variable interest entities, we reflected the following in our Consolidated Balance Sheets:

	May 31, 2015	May 25, 2014
Cash and cash equivalents	$13.7	$17.7
Receivables, less allowance for doubtful accounts	0.2	—
Inventories	1.3	1.4
Prepaid expenses and other current assets	0.3	0.3
Property, plant and equipment, net	53.2	51.8
Goodwill	18.8	18.8
Brands, trademarks and other intangibles, net	6.0	6.7
Total assets	$93.5	$96.7
Accounts payable	$16.9	$12.2
Accrued payroll	0.7	0.5
Other accrued liabilities	0.6	0.6
Other noncurrent liabilities (minority interest)	31.3	33.3
Total liabilities	$49.5	$46.6

The liabilities recognized as a result of consolidating the Lamb Weston BSW entity do not represent additional claims on our general assets. The creditors of Lamb Weston BSW have claims only on the assets of Lamb Weston BSW. The assets recognized as a result of consolidating Lamb Weston BSW are the property of the venture and are not available to us for any other purpose, other than as a secured lender under the promissory note and lines of credit.

Variable Interest Entities Not Consolidated

We also have variable interests in certain other entities that we have determined to be variable interest entities, but for which we are not the primary beneficiary. We do not consolidate the financial statements of these entities.

We hold a 50% interest in Lamb Weston RDO, a potato processing venture (see Note 7). We provide all sales and marketing services to Lamb Weston RDO. We receive a fee for these services based on a percentage of the net sales of the venture. We reflect the value of our ownership interest in this venture in other assets in our Consolidated Balance Sheets, based upon the equity method of accounting. The balance of our investment was $14.6 million and $12.6 million at May 31, 2015 and May 25, 2014, respectively, representing our maximum exposure to loss as a result of our involvement with this venture. The capital structure of Lamb Weston RDO includes owners' equity of $29.2 million and term borrowings from banks of $41.6 million as of May 31, 2015. We have determined that we do not have the power to direct the activities that most significantly impact the economic performance of this venture.

We lease certain office buildings from entities that we have determined to be variable interest entities. The lease agreements with these entities include fixed-price purchase options for the assets being leased, representing our only variable interest in these lessor entities. These leases are accounted for as operating leases, and accordingly, there are no material assets or liabilities associated with these entities included in our Consolidated Balance Sheets. We have no material exposure to loss from our variable interests in these entities. We have determined that we do not have the power to direct the activities that most significantly impact the economic performance of these entities. In making this determination, we have considered, among other items, the terms of the lease agreements, the expected remaining useful lives of the assets leased, and the capital structure of the lessor entities.

Business Combinations

RECOGNITION AND MEASUREMENT

1.70 FASB ASC 805, *Business Combinations*, requires that the acquisition method be used for all business combinations. An acquirer is required to recognize the identifiable acquired assets, the liabilities assumed, and any noncontrolling interest in the acquiree at the acquisition date, measured at their fair values as of that date. Additionally, FASB ASC 805-10-25-23 requires acquisition-related costs to be recognized as expenses as incurred, rather than included in the cost allocated to the acquired assets and assumed liabilities. However, the costs to issue debt or equity securities should be recognized in accordance with other applicable GAAP. In a business combination achieved in stages, the "Pending Content" in FASB ASC 805-10-25-10 also requires the acquirer to remeasure its previously held equity interest in the acquiree at its acquisition date fair value and recognize the resulting gain or loss, if any, in earnings. For all business combinations, the guidance requires the acquirer to recognize goodwill as of the acquisition date, measured as the excess of (*a*) over (*b*):

a. The aggregate of the following:
   i. The transferred consideration measured in accordance with FASB ASC 805-30, which generally requires acquisition-date fair value
   ii. The fair value of any noncontrolling interest in the acquiree
   iii. In a business combination achieved in stages, the acquisition-date fair value of the acquirer's previously-held equity interest in the acquiree
b. The net of the acquisition-date amounts of the identifiable acquired assets and the assumed liabilities, measured in accordance with FASB ASC 805

If the amounts in (*b*) are in excess of those in (*a*), a bargain purchase has occurred. Before recognizing a gain on a bargain purchase, FASB ASC 805-30-30-5 requires the acquirer to reassess whether it has correctly identified all the acquired assets and assumed liabilities and to recognize any additional assets or liabilities identified in that review. If an excess still remains, the acquirer should recognize the resulting gain in earnings on the acquisition date.

DISCLOSURE

1.71 FASB ASC 805-10-50 requires the acquirer to disclose information that enables financial statement users to evaluate the nature and financial statement effect of a business combination that occurs during the current reporting period or after the reporting date but before the financial statements are issued or are available to be issued. To meet this objective, the following items should be disclosed:

- The name and a description of the acquiree
- The acquisition date
- The percentage of voting equity interests acquired
- The primary reasons for the business combination and a description of how control was obtained
- For public business entities:
  — The amounts of revenue and earnings of the acquiree since the acquisition date included in the consolidated income statement for the reporting period
  — Pro forma information that differs depending upon whether the entity presents comparative financial statements. If an entity presents comparative financial statements, it should provide pro forma disclosures for the comparative prior period for revenue and earnings of the combined entity
  — Nature and amount of any material, nonrecurring pro forma adjustments directly attributable to the business combination, that are included in the reported pro forma revenue and earnings
- For a business combination achieved in stages:
  — The acquisition-date fair value of the equity interest in the acquiree held by the acquirer immediately before the acquisition date
  — The amount of any gain or loss recognized as a result of remeasuring to fair value the equity interest in the acquiree that the acquirer held immediately before the business combination
  — The valuation technique(s) used to measure the acquisition-date fair value of the equity interest in the acquiree that the acquirer held immediately before the business combination
  — Other information helpful to users in assessing the inputs used to develop the fair value measurement of the equity interest in the acquiree held by the acquirer immediately before the business combination.

If any of the preceding disclosures for public business entities are impracticable, the acquirer should disclose that fact and explain why. Additional disclosures are required for transactions that are recognized separately from the acquisition of assets and assumptions of liabilities in the business combination.

1.72 FASB ASC 805-50-50-6 includes guidance on the information that may be helpful to users of the financial statements in order to evaluate the effect of pushdown accounting. Information to evaluate the effect of pushdown accounting may include the following:

   a. The name and a description of the acquirer and a description of how the acquirer obtained control of the acquiree.

   b. The acquisition date.

   c. The acquisition-date fair value of the total consideration transferred by the acquirer.

   d. The amounts recognized by the acquiree as of the acquisition date for each major class of assets and liabilities as a result of applying pushdown accounting. If the initial accounting for pushdown accounting is incomplete for any amounts recognized by the acquiree, the reasons why the initial accounting is incomplete.

   e. A qualitative description of the factors that make up the goodwill recognized, such as expected synergies from combining operations of the acquiree and the acquirer, or intangible assets that do not qualify for separate recognition, or other factors. In a bargain purchase (see paragraphs 2–4 of FASB ASC 805-30-25), the amount of the bargain purchase recognized in additional paid-in capital (or net assets of a not-for-profit acquiree) and a description of the reasons why the transaction resulted in a gain.

   f. Information to evaluate the financial effects of adjustments recognized in the current reporting period that relate to pushdown accounting that occurred in the current or previous reporting periods (including those adjustments made as a result of the initial accounting for pushdown accounting being incomplete [see paragraphs 13 and 14 of FASB ASC 805-10-25]).

PRESENTATION AND DISCLOSURE EXCERPTS

BUSINESS COMBINATIONS

1.73 NOBLE ENERGY, INC. (DEC)
CONSOLIDATED STATEMENTS OF SHAREHOLDERS' EQUITY

(Millions)

	Common Stock [1]	Additional Paid in Capital [1]	Accumulated Other Comprehensive Loss	Treasury Stock at Cost	Retained Earnings	Total Share-holders' Equity
December 31, 2012	$4	$3,302	$(113)	$(648)	$5,713	$ 8,258
Net Income	—	—	—	—	978	978
Stock-based Compensation	—	80	—	—	—	80
Exercise of Stock Options	—	51	—	—	—	51
Tax Benefits Related to Exercise of Stock Options	—	20	—	—	—	20
Dividends (55 cents per share)	—	—	—	—	(198)	(198)
Changes in Treasury Stock, Net	—	—	—	(14)	—	(14)
Rabbi Trust Shares Sold	—	10	—	3	—	13
Net Change in Pension and Other	—	—	(4)	—	—	(4)
December 31, 2013	$4	$3,463	$(117)	$(659)	$6,493	$ 9,184
Net Income	—	—	—	—	1,214	1,214
Stock-based Compensation	—	87	—	—	—	87
Exercise of Stock Options	—	48	—	—	—	48
Tax Benefits Related to Exercise of Stock Options	—	19	—	—	—	19
Dividends (68 cents per share)	—	—	—	—	(249)	(249)
Changes in Treasury Stock, Net	—	—	—	(16)	—	(16)
Rabbi Trust Shares Sold	—	7	—	4	—	11
Net Change in Pension and Other	—	—	27	—	—	27
December 31, 2014	$4	$3,624	$(90)	$(671)	$7,458	$10,325
Net Loss	—	—	—	—	(2,441)	(2,441)
Rosetta Merger	1	1,528	—	—	—	1,529
Stock-based Compensation	—	86	—	—	—	86
Exercise of Stock Options	—	8	—	—	—	8
Tax Benefits Related to Exercise of Stock Options	—	(1)	—	—	—	(1)
Dividends (72 cents per share)	—	—	—	—	(291)	(291)
Changes in Treasury Stock, Net	—	—	—	(21)	—	(21)
Rabbi Trust Shares Sold	—	3	—	4	—	7
Issuance of Shares of Common Stock to Public, Net of Offering Costs	—	1,112	—	—	—	1,112
Net Change in Pension and Other	—	—	57	—	—	57
December 31, 2015	$5	$6,360	$(33)	$(688)	$4,726	$10,370

[1] Amounts reflect impact of 2-for-1 stock split which occurred during second quarter 2013.

The accompanying notes are an integral part of these financial statements.

NOTES TO CONSOLIDATED FINANCIAL STATEMENTS (in part)

Note 1. Summary of Significant Accounting Policies (in part)

Unproved Property Impairment Our unproved properties consist of leasehold costs and allocated value to probable and possible reserves from acquisitions. We assess individually significant unproved properties for impairment on a quarterly basis and recognize a loss at the time of impairment by providing an impairment allowance. In determining whether a significant unproved property is impaired we consider numerous factors including, but not limited to, current exploration plans, favorable or unfavorable exploration activity on the property being evaluated and/or adjacent properties, our geologists' evaluation of the property, and the remaining months in the lease term for the property.

When we have allocated fair value to an unproved property as the result of a transaction accounted for as a business combination, we use a future cash flow analysis to assess the unproved property for impairment. Cash flows used in the impairment analysis are determined based on management's estimates of crude oil, natural gas and NGL reserves, future commodity prices and future costs to produce the reserves. Cash flow estimates related to probable and possible reserves are reduced by additional risk-weighting factors. Other individually insignificant unproved properties are amortized on a composite method based on our experience of successful drilling and average holding period. It is reasonably possible that unproved oil and gas properties could become impaired in the future if commodity prices decline. See Note 5. Asset Impairments.

Properties Acquired in Business Combinations When sufficient market data is not available, we determine the fair values of proved and unproved properties acquired in transactions accounted for as business combinations by preparing our own estimates of cash flows from the production of crude oil, natural gas and NGL reserves. We estimate future prices to apply to the estimated reserves quantities acquired, and estimate future operating and development costs, to arrive at estimates of future net cash flows. For the fair value assigned to proved reserves, future net cash flows are discounted using a market-based weighted average cost of capital rate determined appropriate at the time of the business combination. To compensate for the inherent risk of estimating and valuing unproved reserves, discounted future net cash flows of probable and possible reserves are reduced by additional risk-weighting factors.

Recently Issued Accounting Standards (in part)

Business Combinations In September 2015, the FASB issued Accounting Standards Update No. 2015-16 (ASU 2015-16): Business Combinations (Topic 805), effective for annual reporting periods beginning after December 15, 2015, including interim periods within that reporting period, to simplify the accounting for measurement-period adjustments for an acquirer in a business combination. ASU 2015-16 requires an acquirer to recognize adjustments to provisional amounts that are identified during the measurement period in the reporting period in which the adjustment amounts are determined. The acquirer is required to adjust its financial statements for the effect on earnings of changes in depreciation, amortization, or other income effects, if any, as a result of the change to the provisional amounts calculated as if the accounting had been completed at the acquisition date. We are currently evaluating the provisions of ASU 2015-16 and assessing the impact, if any, it may have on our financial position and results of operations.

Note 3. Merger, Acquisitions and Divestitures

Rosetta Merger On July 20, 2015, Noble Energy completed the merger of Rosetta into a subsidiary of Noble Energy (Rosetta Merger). The results of Rosetta's operations since the merger date are included in our consolidated statement of operations. The merger was effected through the issuance of approximately 41 million shares of Noble Energy common stock in exchange for all outstanding shares of Rosetta using a ratio of 0.542 of a share of Noble Energy common stock for each share of Rosetta common stock and the assumption of Rosetta's liabilities, including approximately $2 billion fair value of outstanding debt.

The merger adds two new onshore US shale positions to our portfolio including approximately 50,000 net acres in the Eagle Ford Shale and 54,000 net acres in the Permian Basin 45,000 acres in the Delaware Basin and 9,000 acres in the Midland Basin). In connection with the Rosetta Merger, we incurred merger-related costs of approximately $81 million to date, including (i) $66 million of severance, consulting, investment, advisory, legal and other merger-related fees, and (ii) $15 million of noncash share-based compensation expense, all of which were expensed and are included in Other Operating (Income) Expense, Net.

Allocation of Purchase Price The merger has been accounted for as a business combination, using the acquisition method. The following table represents the preliminary allocation of the total purchase price of Rosetta to the assets acquired and the liabilities assumed based on the fair value at the merger date, with any excess of the purchase price over the estimated fair value of the identifiable net assets acquired recorded as goodwill. Certain data necessary to complete the purchase price allocation is not yet available, and includes, but is not limited to, valuation of pre-merger contingencies, final tax returns that provide the underlying tax basis of Rosetta's assets and liabilities, and final appraisals of assets acquired and liabilities assumed. We expect to complete the purchase price allocation during the 12-month period following the merger date, in line with the acquisition method of accounting, during which time the value of the assets and liabilities may be revised as appropriate.

The following table sets forth our preliminary purchase price allocation which was based on fair values of assets acquired and liabilities assumed at the merger date, July 20, 2015, with the excess of the purchase price over the estimated fair value of the identifiable net assets acquired recorded as goodwill:

	(in millions, except stock price)
Shares of Noble Energy common stock issued to Rosetta shareholders	41
Noble Energy common stock price on July 20, 2015	$36.97
Fair value of common stock issued	$1,518
Plus: fair value of Rosetta's restricted stock awards and performance awards assumed	10
Plus: Rosetta stock options assumed	1
Total purchase price	1,529
Plus: liabilities assumed by Noble Energy	
Accounts Payable	100
Current Liabilities	37
Long-Term Deferred Tax Liability	8
Long-Term Debt	1,992
Other Long Term Liabilities	23
Asset Retirement Obligation	27
Total purchase price plus liabilities assumed	$3,716
Fair Value of Rosetta Assets	
Cash and Equivalents	$ 61
Other Current Assets	76
Derivative Instruments	209
Oil and Gas Properties:	
Proved Properties	1,613
Undeveloped Leaseholds	1,355
Gathering and Processing Assets	207
Asset Retirement Obligation	27
Other Property Plant and Equipment	5
Implied Goodwill[1]	163
Total Asset Value	$3,716

[1] Goodwill was fully impaired at December 31, 2015. See Note 4. Goodwill.

The fair value measurements of derivative instruments assumed were determined based on published forward commodity price curves as of the date of the merger and represent Level 2 inputs. Derivative instruments in an asset position include a measure of counterparty nonperformance risk, and the fair values of commodity derivative instruments in a liability position include a measure of our own nonperformance risk, each based on the current published credit default swap rates. The fair value measurements of long-term debt were estimated based on published market prices and represent Level 1 inputs. The long-term debt balance includes amounts outstanding under Rosetta's credit facility which was assumed by Noble and repaid subsequent to the merger in third quarter 2015.

The fair value measurements of oil and natural gas properties and asset retirement obligations are based on inputs that are not observable in the market and therefore represent Level 3 inputs. The fair values of oil and natural gas properties and asset retirement obligations were measured using valuation techniques that convert future cash flows to a single discounted amount. Significant inputs to the valuation of oil and natural gas properties included estimates of: (i) recoverable reserves; (ii) production rates; (iii) future operating and development costs; (iv) future commodity prices; and (v) a market-based weighted average cost of capital rate. These inputs required significant judgments and estimates by management at the time of the valuation and are the most sensitive and may be subject to change.

The results of operations attributable to Rosetta are included in our consolidated statement of operations beginning on July 21, 2015. Revenues of $181 million and pre-tax net loss of $120 million, inclusive of $163 million goodwill impairment, from Rosetta were generated from July 21, 2015 to December 31, 2015.

Proforma Financial Information The following pro forma condensed combined financial information was derived from the historical financial statements of Noble Energy and Rosetta and gives effect to the merger as if it had occurred on January 1, 2014. The below information reflects pro forma adjustments based on available information and certain assumptions that we believe are reasonable, including (i) Noble Energy's common stock and equity awards issued to convert Rosetta's outstanding shares of common stock and equity awards as of the closing date of the merger, (ii) adjustments to conform Rosetta's historical policy of accounting for its oil and natural gas properties from the full cost method to the successful efforts method of accounting, (iii) depletion of Rosetta's fair-valued proved oil and gas properties, and (iv) the estimated tax impacts of the pro forma adjustments. Additionally, pro forma earnings for the year ended December 31, 2015 were adjusted to exclude $81 million of merger-related costs incurred by Noble Energy and $37 million incurred by Rosetta. The pro forma results of operations do not include any cost savings or other synergies that may result from the Rosetta Merger or any estimated costs that have been or will be incurred by us to integrate the Rosetta assets.

The pro forma condensed combined financial information has been included for comparative purposes and is not necessarily indicative of the results that might have actually occurred had the Rosetta Merger taken place on January 1, 2014; furthermore, the financial information is not intended to be a projection of future results.

(In millions, except per share amounts)	Year Ended December 31,	
	2015	2014
Revenues	$ 3,428	$6,112
Net Income (Loss)	$(2,393)	$1,607
Earnings (Loss) Per Share		
Basic	$ (5.64)	$ 4.01
Diluted	$ (5.64)	$ 3.94

Sale of Non-Core Onshore US Properties During the past three years, we closed the sales of non-core onshore US crude oil and natural gas properties. The information regarding the assets sold is as follows:

(Millions)	Year Ended December 31,		
	2015	2014	2013
Cash Proceeds	$151	$135	$150
Less			
Net Book Value of Assets Sold	(156)	(150)	(117)
Goodwill Allocated to Assets Sold[1]	(4)	(7)	(8)
Asset Retirement Obligations Associated with Assets Sold	8	48	8
Other Closing Adjustments	1	10	3
Gain on Divestitures	$ —	$ 36	$ 36

[1] See Note 4. Goodwill.

China In June 2014, we sold our China assets. We determined the sale of our China assets did not meet the criteria for discontinued operations presentation under ASU 2014-08. The information regarding the China assets sold is as follows:

(Millions)	Year Ended December 31, 2014
Sales Proceeds	$186
Less	
Net Book Value of Assets Sold	(149)
Other Closing Adjustments	(2)
Gain on Divestiture	$ 35

Assets Held for Sale In November 2015, we executed an agreement to divest our 47% interest in the Alon A and Alon C offshore Israel licenses, which include the Karish and Tanin fields, for a total transaction value of $73 million ($67 million for asset consideration and $6 million from adjustment of costs). These assets were held for sale as of December 31, 2015, and the transaction closed in January 2016.

DJ Basin Acreage Exchange In October 2013, we closed an acreage exchange agreement with another operator related to our position in the DJ Basin. Each party exchanged approximately 50,000 net acres within the same field. The exchange consolidated our acreage into large contiguous blocks, which has provided the opportunity to optimize drilling, production, and gathering activities and add more extended-reach lateral wells to our development program. In accordance with guidance for oil and gas property conveyances, the transaction was accounted for at net book value, with no gain or loss recognized. We received $105 million in cash related to reimbursement of capital expenditures and other normal closing adjustments from the effective date of January 1, 2013 to closing date, which was recorded as a reduction in the net book value of the field.

North Sea Properties During 2013, we sold additional non-operated, North Sea properties. The 2013 sales resulted in a $65 million gain based on net sales proceeds of $56 million. During 2013, the North Sea geographical segment was presented as discontinued operations in our consolidated statements of operations. However, we were unable to locate purchasers for the remaining properties, and as of January 1, 2014, we no longer considered a sale probable. Therefore, the remaining assets were reclassified to assets held and used. See Note 5. Asset Impairments.

Summarized results of discontinued operations are as follows:

(Millions)	Year Ended December 31, 2013
Oil and Gas Sales	$37
Income Before Income Taxes	12
Income Tax Expense	6
Operating Income, Net of Tax	6
Gain on Sale, Net of Tax	65
Discontinued Operations, Net of Tax	$71

Note 17. Additional Shareholders' Equity Information

Equity Offerings On March 3, 2015, we closed an underwritten public offering of 21 million shares of common stock, par value $0.01 per share, at a price of $47.50 per share. In addition, on March 25, 2015, we completed the issuance of an additional 3.15 million shares of common stock, par value $0.01 per share, in connection with the exercise of the option of the underwriters to purchase additional shares of common stock. The aggregate net proceeds of the offerings were approximately $1.1 billion (after deducting underwriting discounts and commissions and offering expenses). We used approximately $150 million of the net proceeds to repay outstanding indebtedness under our revolving credit facility and the remainder was used for general corporate purposes, including the funding of our capital investment program.

Activity in shares of our common stock and treasury stock was as follows:

	Year Ended December 31,	
	2015	2014
Common Stock Shares Issued		
Shares, Beginning of Period	402,329,325	399,841,717
Exercise of Common Stock Options	343,145	1,459,490
Restricted Stock Awards, Net of Forfeitures	1,847,802	1,028,118
Public Equity Offering	24,150,000	—
Shares Exchanged in Rosetta Merger	41,048,240	—
Shares, End of Period	469,718,512	402,329,325
Treasury Stock		
Shares, Beginning of Period	37,635,890	37,600,051
Shares Received From Employees in Payment of Withholding Taxes Due on Vesting of Shares of Restricted Stock	490,744	254,888
Rabbi Trust Shares Distributed and/or Sold	(201,009)	(219,049)
Shares, End of Period	37,925,625	37,635,890

Accumulated other comprehensive loss in the shareholders' equity section of the balance sheet included:

	Accumulated Other Comprehensive Loss		
(Millions)	Interest Rate Cash Flow Hedges	Pension- Related and Other	Total
December 31, 2012	$(25)	$(88)	$(113)
Realized Amounts Reclassified Into Earnings	1	12	13
Unrealized Change in Fair Value	—	(17)	(17)
December 31, 2013	(24)	(93)	(117)
Realized Amounts Reclassified Into Earnings	1	11	12
Unrealized Change in Fair Value	—	15	15
December 31, 2014	(23)	(67)	(90)
Realized Amounts Reclassified Into Earnings	1	62	63
Unrealized Change in Fair Value	—	(6)	(6)
December 31, 2015	$(22)	$(11)	$ (33)

All amounts in the table above are reported net of tax, using an effective income tax rate of 35%.

AOCL at December 31, 2015 included deferred losses of $22 million, net of tax, related to interest rate derivative instruments. This amount will be reclassified to earnings as an adjustment to interest expense over the terms of our senior notes due March 2041.

1.74 BASSETT FURNITURE INDUSTRIES, INCORPORATED (NOV)

NOTES TO CONSOLIDATED FINANCIAL STATEMENTS (in part)

(In thousands, except share and per share data)

1. Description of Business (in part)

Zenith Acquisition

Prior to February 2, 2015 we held a 49% interest in Zenith Freight Lines, LLC ("Zenith") for which we used the equity method of accounting. On February 2, 2015 we acquired the remaining 51% ownership interest (see Note 3, Business Combinations). Zenith provides over-the-road transportation of furniture, operates regional freight terminal, warehouse and distribution facilities in eleven states, and manages various home delivery facilities that service Bassett Home Furnishings stores and other clients in local markets around the United States. With the acquisition of Zenith, we established our logistical services operating segment.

2. Significant Accounting Policies (in part)

Other Intangible Assets (in part)

Intangible assets acquired in a business combination and determined to have an indefinite useful life are not amortized but are tested for impairment annually or between annual tests when an impairment indicator exists. The recoverability of indefinite-lived intangible assets is assessed by comparison of the carrying value of the asset to its estimated fair value. If we determine that the carrying value of the asset exceeds its estimated fair value, an impairment loss equal to the excess would be recorded.

Recent Accounting Pronouncements (in part)

In July 2015, the FASB issued Accounting Standards Update No. 2015-16, Business Combinations (Topic 805): Simplifying the Accounting for Measurement Period Adjustments. ASU 2015-16 requires that an acquirer recognize adjustments to provisional amounts that are identified during the measurement period in the reporting period in which the adjustment amounts are determined. The amendments in this Update require that the acquirer record, in the same period's financial statements, the effect on earnings of changes in depreciation, amortization, or other income effects, if any, as a result of the change to the provisional amounts, calculated as if the accounting had been completed at the acquisition date. Any current period adjustments to provisional amounts that would have impacted a prior period's earnings had they been recognized at the acquisition date are required to be presented separately on the face of the income statement or disclosed in the notes. The amendments in this Update are effective for fiscal years beginning after December 15, 2015, including interim periods within those fiscal years. The amendments in this Update should be applied prospectively to adjustments to provisional amounts that occur after the effective date of this Update with earlier application permitted for financial statements that have not been issued. Therefore the amendments in ASU 2015-16 will become effective for us as of the beginning of our 2017 fiscal year. The adoption of this guidance is not expected to have a material impact upon our financial condition or results of operations.

3. Business Combination—Acquisition of Zenith

Prior to February 2, 2015 we held a 49% interest in Zenith for which we used the equity method of accounting. Zenith provides domestic transportation and warehousing services primarily to furniture manufacturers and distributors and also provides home delivery services to furniture retailers. We historically have contracted with Zenith to provide substantially all of our domestic freight, transportation and warehousing needs for the wholesale business. In addition, Zenith provides home delivery services for many of our Company-owned retail stores. On February 2, 2015, we acquired the remaining 51% of Zenith in exchange for cash, Bassett common stock and a note payable with a total fair value of $19,111. The value of the Bassett common stock was based on the closing market price of our shares on the acquisition date, discounted for lack of marketability due to restrictions on the seller's ability to transfer the shares. The restrictions on one half of the shares expire on the first anniversary of the acquisition, with the remainder expiring on the second anniversary. The note is payable in three annual installments of $3,000 each beginning February 2, 2016, and has been discounted to its fair value as of the date of the acquisition based on our estimated borrowing rate.

The carrying value of our 49% interest in Zenith prior to the acquisition was $9,480 (see Note 9, Unconsolidated Affiliated Company). In connection with the acquisition, this investment was remeasured to a fair value of $16,692 resulting in the recognition of a gain of $7,212 during the year ended November 28, 2015. The impact of this gain upon our basic and diluted earnings per share for the year ended

November 28, 2015 is approximately $0.41 net of the related tax expense. The remeasured fair value of our prior interest in Zenith was estimated based on the fair value of the consideration transferred to acquire the remaining 51% of Zenith less an estimated control premium.

Under the acquisition method of accounting, the fair value of the consideration transferred along with the fair value of our previous 49% interest in Zenith was allocated to the tangible and intangible assets acquired and the liabilities assumed based on their estimated fair values as of the acquisition date with the remaining unallocated amount recorded as goodwill.

The total fair value of the acquired business was determined as follows:

Fair value of consideration transferred in exchange for 51% of Zenith:	
Cash	$ 9,000
Bassett common stock, 89,485 shares, par value $5.00 per share, fair value at closing $18.72 per share	1,675
Note payable	8,436
Total fair value of consideration transferred to seller	19,111
Less effective settlement of previous amounts payable to Zenith at acquisition	(3,622)
Total fair value of consideration net of effective settlement	15,489
Fair value of Bassett's previous 49% interest in Zenith	16,692
Total fair value of acquired business	$32,181

The preliminary allocation of the fair value of the acquired business was based upon a preliminary valuation. Our estimates and assumptions are subject to change as we obtain additional information for our estimates during the measurement period (up to one year from the acquisition date). The primary areas of the preliminary allocation of the fair value of consideration transferred that are not yet finalized relate to the fair values of certain tangible and intangible assets acquired and the residual goodwill. The preliminary allocation of the fair value of the acquired business is as follows:

Identifiable assets acquired:	
Acquired cash and cash equivalents	$ 1,677
Accounts receivable, net	3,399
Prepaid expenses and other current assets	496
Property and equipment	18,110
Other long-term assets	646
Intangible assets	6,362
Total identifiable assets acquired	30,690
Liabilities assumed:	
Accounts payable and accrued liabilities	(4,038)
Notes payable	(4,329)
Total liabilities assumed	(8,367)
Net identifiable assets acquired	22,323
Goodwill	9,858
Total net assets acquired	$32,181

Goodwill was determined based on the residual difference between the fair value of the consideration transferred and the value assigned to tangible and intangible assets and liabilities. Approximately $6,982 of the acquired goodwill is deductible for tax purposes. Among the factors that contributed to a purchase price resulting in the recognition of goodwill were Zenith's reputation for best-in-class, fully integrated logistical services which are uniquely tailored to the needs of the furniture industry, as well as their ability to provide expedited delivery service which is increasingly in demand in the furniture industry.

A portion of the fair value of consideration transferred has been provisionally assigned to identifiable intangible assets as follows:

Description:	Useful Life In Years	Fair Value
Customer relationships	15	$3,038
Trade names	Indefinite	2,490
Technology—customized applications	7	834
Total acquired intangible assets		$6,362

The finite-lived intangible assets are being amortized on a straight-line basis over their useful lives. The indefinite-lived intangible asset and goodwill are not amortized but will be tested for impairment annually or between annual tests if an indicator of impairment exists.

The fair values of consideration transferred and net assets acquired were determined using a combination of Level 2 and Level 3 inputs as specified in the fair value hierarchy in ASC 820, *Fair Value Measurements and Disclosures*. See Note 4.

Acquisition costs related to the Zenith acquisition totaled $209 during the year ended November 28, 2015 and are included in selling, general and administrative expenses in the consolidated statements of income. The acquisition costs are primarily related to legal, accounting and valuation services.

Zenith's revenue since February 2, 2015 included in our consolidated statement of income for the year ended November 28, 2015 is $43,522 after the elimination of intercompany transactions. Net income of Zenith included in our consolidated statement of income for the year ended November 28, 2015 is $2,078. The pro forma results of operations for the acquisition of Zenith have not been presented because they are not material to our consolidated results of operations.

8. Goodwill and Other Intangible Assets

At November 28, 2015 goodwill and other intangible assets consisted of the following:

	Gross Carrying Amount	Accumulated Amortization	Intangible Assets, Net
Intangibles subject to amortization:			
Customer relationships	$ 3,038	$(169)	$ 2,869
Technology—customized applications	834	(99)	735
Total intangible assets subject to amortization	3,872	(268)	3,604
Intangibles not subject to amortization:			
Trade names	2,490	—	2,490
Goodwill	11,588	—	11,588
Total goodwill and other intangible assets	$17,950	$(268)	$17,682

At November 29, 2014 our only intangible asset was goodwill with a carrying value of $1,730.

Changes in the carrying amounts of goodwill by reportable segment were as follows:

	Wholesale	Retail	Logistics	Total
Balance as of November 29, 2014	$1,128	$ 602	$ —	$ 1,730
Goodwill arising from acquisition of Zenith	3,711	1,218	4,929	9,858
Balance as of November 28, 2015	$4,839	$1,820	$4,929	$11,588

The goodwill recognized in connection with our acquisition of Zenith remains subject to future adjustments before the close of the measurement period in the first quarter of fiscal 2016. Refer to Note 3, Business Combinations, for additional information regarding the Zenith acquisition. There were no changes in the carrying value of our goodwill during fiscal 2014, and there were no accumulated impairment losses on goodwill as of November 28, 2015 or November 29, 2014.

Amortization expense associated with intangible assets during the year ended November 28, 2015 was $268 and is included in selling, general and administrative expense in our consolidated statement of income. All expense arising from the amortization of intangible assets is associated with our logistical services segment. There was no amortization expense recognized during fiscal 2014 or 2013. Estimated future amortization expense for intangible assets that exist at November 28, 2015 is as follows:

Fiscal 2016	$ 322
Fiscal 2017	322
Fiscal 2018	322
Fiscal 2019	322
Fiscal 2020	322
Thereafter	1,994
Total	$3,604

Commitments

DISCLOSURE

1.75 FASB ASC 440, *Commitments*, requires the disclosure of commitments such as those for unused letters of credit; long-term leases; assets pledged as security for loans; pension plans; cumulative preferred stock dividends in arrears; plant acquisition, obligations to reduce debts, maintain working capital, and restrict dividends; and unconditional purchase obligations.

PRESENTATION AND DISCLOSURE EXCERPTS

RESTRICTIVE COVENANTS

1.76 ALLIANCE ONE INTERNATIONAL, INC. (MAR)
NOTES TO CONSOLIDATED FINANCIAL STATEMENTS (in part)

(in thousands)

Note 8—Long-Term Debt (in part)

Senior Secured Credit Facility

On August 1, 2013, the agreement governing the Company's senior secured credit facility was amended and restated to provide for a senior secured revolving credit facility with a syndicate of banks of approximately $303,900, that automatically reduced to approximately $210,300 on April 15, 2014, and will mature in April 15, 2017. The senior secured credit facility was subject to a springing maturity on April 15, 2014 if by that date the Company had not deposited in the Blocked Account (as defined below) sufficient amounts to fund the repayment at maturity of all then outstanding $5^1/_2$% Convertible Senior Subordinated Notes due 2014 of the Company (the "Convertible Notes"). The Company deposited the requisite amount in the Blocked Account prior to April 15, 2014. Borrowings under the amended and restated senior secured credit facility initially bear interest at an annual rate of LIBOR plus 3.75% and base rate plus 2.75%, as applicable, though the interest rate under the amended and restated senior secured credit facility is subject to increase or decrease according to the Company's consolidated interest coverage ratio.

The agreement governing the senior secured credit facility required the Company to deposit with the lenders, in a segregated account that the Company may not use other than for specified purposes (the "Blocked Account"), the net proceeds from the sale of $735,000 in aggregate principal amount of the Company's 9.875% Senior Secured Second Lien Notes due 2021 (the "Second Lien Notes") that were not immediately applied to redeem all of the Company's outstanding 10% Senior Notes due 2016 (the "Senior Notes"). Amounts held in the Blocked Account may be used solely to purchase any and all Convertible Notes tendered in the Company's cash tender offer to purchase up to $60,000 in aggregate principal amount of the Convertible Notes commenced on July 17, 2013 (the "Convertible Notes Tender Offer") and, subject to conditions, to retire any remaining Convertible Notes not purchased in the Convertible Notes Tender Offer, including repayment at maturity. All amounts deposited in the Blocked Account from the net proceeds of the sale of the Second Lien Notes were applied to the purchase of Convertible Notes in the Convertible Notes Tender Offer. Borrowings under the amended and restated senior secured credit facility are secured by a first priority lien on specified property of the Company, including the capital stock of specified subsidiaries, all U.S. accounts receivable, certain U.S. inventory, intercompany notes evidencing loans or advances, certain U.S. fixed assets and the Blocked Account.

First amendment. On May 30, 2014, the Company entered into the First Amendment to the Amended and Restated Credit Agreement (the "First Amendment"), which amended the credit agreement (the "Credit Agreement") governing the Company's senior secured credit facility. The First Amendment modified the definition of Consolidated EBIT to permit add backs in connection with dispositions of, and investments in, certain subsidiaries and permitted joint ventures and certain other accounting adjustments, modified the Minimum Consolidated Interest Coverage Ratio to 1.85 to 1.00 for the period ending March 31, 2014 and 1.70 to 1.00 for the periods ending June 30, 2014, September 30, 2014, December 31, 2014 and March 31, 2015, modified the Maximum Consolidated Leverage Ratio to 7.25 to 1.00 for the period ending June 30, 2014 and 7.50 to 1.00 for the period ending September 30, 2014 and increased the basket to $200,000 for permitted Guaranty Obligations that can be incurred by the Company and its subsidiaries with respect to indebtedness of China Brasil Tabacos Exportadora Ltda. (which is the joint venture entity with China Tobacco in Brazil) while striking the requirement that such Guaranty Obligations of the Company and its subsidiaries may not exceed the percentage of the Company's direct or indirect ownership of China Brasil Tabacos Exportadora Ltda. in relation to all Guaranty Obligations with respect to Indebtedness of China Brasil Tabacos Exportadora Ltda.

Second amendment. On February 6, 2015, the Company entered into the Second Amendment to Amended and Restated Credit Agreement (the "Second Amendment"), which amended the Credit Agreement. The Second Amendment modified the Minimum Consolidated Interest Coverage Ratio (as defined in the Credit Agreement) to 1.50 to 1.00 for the period ended December 31, 2014 and the period ended March 31, 2015 and modified the Maximum Consolidated Leverage Ratio (as defined in the Credit Agreement) to 7.90 to 1.00 for the period ended December 31, 2014.

Third Amendment. On June 2, 2015, the Company entered into the Third Amendment to the Amended and Restated Credit Agreement (the "Third Amendment"), which amended the Credit Agreement. The Third Amendment modified the definition of Consolidated EBIT to permit add backs for specified periods for reserves taken with respect to receivables, restructuring charges and adjustments for applying the rule of lower of cost or market to inventories, modified the Minimum Consolidated Interest Coverage Ratio to 1.60 to 1.00 for the periods ending June 30, 2015 and September 30, 2015, 1.65 to 1.00 for the period ending December 31, 2015 and 1.70 to 1.00 for the period ending March 31, 2016, modified the Maximum Consolidated Leverage Ratio to 7.60 to 1.00 for the periods ending June 30, 2015 and September 30, 2015 and 7.15 to 1.00 for the period ending December 31, 2015, modified the restricted payments covenant to permit repayment of the Company's Senior Secured Second Lien Notes by up to $50,000 in any fiscal year, with carry forward of any unused amount into the next fiscal year, modified a covenant to provide a 90-day cure period if Uncommitted Inventories (as defined in the Credit Agreement) exceed the threshold of $250,000, but only to the extent that they do not exceed $285,000, and provides for first-lien mortgages on the Company's facilities located in Farmville, King and Wilson, North Carolina.

Financial covenants. After giving effect to the First Amendment, the Second Amendment and the Third Amendment to the Amended and Restated Credit Agreement, the financial covenants and required financial ratios at March 31, 2015 are as follows:
- a minimum consolidated interest coverage ratio of not less than 1.50 to 1.00 for the fiscal quarter ended March 31, 2015 (1.60 to 1.00 for the fiscal quarters ending June 30, 2015 and September 30, 2015, 1.65 to 1.00 for the fiscal quarter ending December 31, 2015 and 1.70 to 1.00 for the fiscal quarter ending March 31, 2016);
- a maximum consolidated leverage ratio specified for each fiscal quarter, which ratio is 5.85 to 1.00 for the fiscal quarter ended March 31, 2015 (7.60 to 1.00 for the fiscal quarters ending June 30, 2015 and September 30, 2015, 7.15 to 1.00 for the fiscal quarter ending December 31, 2015, and 5.85 to 1.00 for the fiscal quarter ending March 31, 2016);
- a maximum consolidated total senior debt to working capital ratio of not more than 0.80 to 1.00 other than during periods in which the consolidated leverage ratio is less than 4.00 to 1.00 if the consolidated leverage ratio has been less than 4.00 to 1.00 for the prior two consecutive fiscal quarters; and
- a maximum amount of the Company's annual capital expenditures of $51,605 during the fiscal year ending March 31, 2015 and $40,000 during any fiscal year thereafter, in each case with a one-year carry-forward (not in excess of $40,000) for unused capital expenditures in any fiscal year below the maximum amount.

Certain of these financial covenants are calculated on a rolling twelve-month basis and certain of these financial covenants and required financial ratios adjust over time in accordance with schedules in the agreement governing the senior secured credit facility. The Company continuously monitors compliance with debt covenants. At March 31, 2015 and during the fiscal year, the Company was in compliance with the covenants under the senior secured credit facility agreement. While the Company anticipates it will be in compliance in fiscal 2016, significant changes in market conditions or other factors could adversely affect the Company's business and future debt covenant compliance thereunder. In such a circumstance, the Company may not be able to maintain compliance with the covenants, which would cause a default under the credit facility. A default, if not waived and/or amended, would prevent us from taking certain actions, such as incurring additional debt, paying dividends, or redeeming senior notes or subordinated debt. A default also could result in a default or acceleration of our other indebtedness with cross-default provisions.

If the Company were unable to maintain compliance with the covenants in the senior secured credit facility agreement, we would seek modification to the then existing agreement to further amend covenants and extend maturities, as necessary. If we were unable to obtain such modification, we could potentially decide to pay off the credit facility and terminate the agreement. In such case, the liquidity provided by the agreement would not be available in the future; however, we believe the Company has sufficient liquidity from operations and other available funding sources to meet future operating, debt service and capital expenditure requirements for the next twelve months.

Affirmative and restrictive covenants. The agreement governing the senior secured credit facility contains affirmative and negative covenants (subject, in each case, to exceptions and qualifications), including covenants that limit the Company's ability to, among other things, incur additional indebtedness, incur certain guarantees, merge, consolidate or dispose of substantially all of its assets, grant liens on its assets, pay dividends, redeem stock or make other distributions or restricted payments, create certain dividend and payment restrictions on its subsidiaries, repurchase or redeem capital stock or prepay subordinated debt, make certain investments, agree to restrictions on the payment of dividends to it by its subsidiaries, sell or otherwise dispose of assets, including equity interests of its subsidiaries, enter into transactions with its affiliates, and enter into certain sale and leaseback transactions.

Note 21—Subsequent Event (in part)

On June 2, 2015, the Company entered into the Third Amendment to the Amended and Restated Credit Agreement (the "Third Amendment"), which amended the credit agreement, as amended (the "Credit Agreement"), governing the Company's senior secured credit facility. The Third Amendment modified the definition of Consolidated EBIT to permit add backs for specified periods for reserves taken with respect to receivables, restructuring charges and adjustments for applying the rule of lower of cost or market to inventories, modified the Minimum Consolidated Interest Coverage Ratio to 1.60 to 1.00 for the periods ending June 30, 2015 and September 30, 2015, 1.65 to 1.00 for the period ending December 31, 2015 and 1.70 to 1.00 for the period ending March 31, 2016, modified the Maximum Consolidated Leverage Ratio to 7.60 to 1.00 for the periods ending June 30, 2015 and September 30, 2015 and 7.15 to 1.00 for the period ending December 31, 2015, modified the restricted payments covenant to permit repayment of the Company's Senior Secured Second Lien Notes by up to $50,000 in any fiscal year, with carry forward of any unused amount into the next fiscal year, modified a covenant to provide a 90-day cure period if Uncommitted Inventories (as defined in the Credit Agreement) exceed the threshold of $250,000, but only to the extent that they do not exceed $285,000, and provides for first-lien mortgages on the Company's facilities located in Farmville, King and Wilson, North Carolina. See Note 8 "Long-Term Debt-Senior Secured Credit Facility-Financial Covenants" to the "Notes to Consolidated Financial Statements" for further information.

1.77 FREEPORT-MCMORAN INC. (DEC)
NOTES TO CONSOLIDATED FINANCIAL STATEMENTS (in part)

Note 8. Debt (in part)

FCX's debt at December 31, 2015, included additions of $210 million for unamortized fair value adjustments (primarily from the 2013 oil and gas acquisitions), and is net of reductions of $129 million for unamortized net discounts and unamortized debt issuance costs; and at December 31, 2014, included additions of $240 million for unamortized fair value adjustments, and is net of reductions of $143 million for unamortized net discounts and unamortized debt issuance costs. The components of debt follow:

	December 31,	
	2015	2014
Bank term loan	$ 3,032	$ 3,036
Revolving credit facility	—	—
Lines of credit	442	474
Cerro Verde credit facility	1,781	402
Cerro Verde shareholder loans	259	—
Senior notes and debentures:		
Issued by FCX:		
2.15% Senior Notes due 2017	499	498
2.30% Senior Notes due 2017	747	745
2.375% Senior Notes due 2018	1,495	1,493
3.100% Senior Notes due 2020	995	993
4.00% Senior Notes due 2021	594	593
3.55% Senior Notes due 2022	1,987	1,985
3.875% Senior Notes due 2023	1,987	1,986
4.55% Senior Notes due 2024	843	842
5.40% Senior Notes due 2034	788	787
5.450% Senior Notes due 2043	1,973	1,972
Issued by Freeport-McMoRan Oil & Gas LLC (FM O&G LLC):		
6.125% Senior Notes due 2019	251	255
$6\frac{1}{2}$% Senior Notes due 2020	662	670
6.625% Senior Notes due 2021	281	284
6.75% Senior Notes due 2022	488	493
$6\frac{7}{8}$% Senior Notes due 2023	857	866
Issued by FMC:		
$7\frac{1}{8}$% Debentures due 2027	115	115
$9\frac{1}{2}$% Senior Notes due 2031	128	129
$6\frac{1}{8}$% Senior Notes due 2034	116	116
Other (including equipment capital leases and other short-term borrowings)	108	115
Total debt	20,428	18,849
Less current portion of debt	(649)	(478)
Long-term debt	$19,779	$18,371

Bank Term Loan. In February 2013, FCX entered into an agreement for a $4.0 billion unsecured bank term loan (Term Loan) in connection with the acquisitions of PXP and MMR. Upon closing the PXP acquisition, FCX borrowed $4.0 billion under the Term Loan, and FM O&G LLC (a wholly owned subsidiary of FM O&G and the successor entity of PXP) joined the Term Loan as a borrower. In February and December 2015, FCX's Term Loan was modified to amend the maximum total leverage ratio. In addition, in conjunction with the February 2015 amendment, the Term Loan amortization schedule was extended such that, as amended, the Term Loan's scheduled payments total $205 million in 2016, $272 million in 2017, $1.0 billion in 2018, $313 million in 2019 and $1.3 billion in 2020, compared with the previous amortization schedule of $650 million in 2016, $200 million in 2017 and $2.2 billion in 2018. At FCX's option, the Term Loan bears interest at either an adjusted London Interbank Offered Rate (LIBOR) or an alternate base rate (ABR) (as defined under the Term Loan agreement) plus a spread determined by reference to FCX's credit ratings (LIBOR plus 1.75 percent or ABR plus 0.75 percent at December 31, 2015; as of February 12, 2016, LIBOR plus 2.25 percent or ABR plus 1.25 percent). The interest rate on the Term Loan was 2.18 percent at December 31, 2015. In February 2016, the Term Loan was amended (refer to Note 18 for further discussion).

Revolving Credit Facility. In May 2014, FCX, PT-FI and FM O&G LLC amended the senior unsecured $3.0 billion revolving credit facility to extend the maturity date one year to May 31, 2019, and increase the aggregate facility amount from $3.0 billion to $4.0 billion, with $500 million available to PT-FI. FCX, PT-FI and FM O&G LLC had entered into the $3.0 billion revolving credit facility on May 31, 2013 (upon completion of the acquisition of PXP). In February and December 2015, FCX modified the revolving credit facility to amend the maximum total leverage ratio. At December 31, 2015, FCX had no borrowings outstanding and $36 million of letters of credit issued under the revolving credit facility, resulting in availability of approximately $4 billion, of which $1.5 billion could be used for additional letters of credit. In February 2016, the revolving credit facility was amended (refer to Note 18 for further discussion).

Cerro Verde Credit Facility. In March 2014, Cerro Verde entered into a five -year, $1.8 billion senior unsecured credit facility that is nonrecourse to FCX and the other shareholders of Cerro Verde. The credit facility allows for term loan borrowings up to the full amount of the facility, less any amounts issued and outstanding under a $500 million letter of credit sublimit. Interest on amounts drawn under the term loan is based on LIBOR plus a spread (2.40 percent at December 31, 2015) based on Cerro Verde's total net debt to EBITDA ratio as defined in the agreement. At December 31, 2015, term loan borrowings under the facility totaled $1.8 billion and were used to fund a portion of Cerro Verde's expansion project and for Cerro Verde's general corporate purposes. The credit facility amortizes in four installments in amounts necessary for the aggregate borrowings and outstanding letters of credit not to exceed 85 percent of the $1.8 billion commitment on September 30, 2017, 70 percent on March 31, 2018, and 35 percent on September 30, 2018, with the remaining balance due on the maturity date of March 10, 2019. At December 31, 2015, no letters of credit were issued under Cerro Verde's credit facility. The interest rate on Cerro Verde's credit facility was 2.82 percent at December 31, 2015.

Restrictive Covenants. FCX's Term Loan and revolving credit facility contain customary affirmative covenants and representations, and also contain a number of negative covenants that, among other things, restrict, subject to certain exceptions, the ability of FCX's subsidiaries that are not borrowers or guarantors to incur additional indebtedness (including guarantee obligations) and FCX's ability or the ability of FCX's subsidiaries to: create liens on assets; enter into sale and leaseback transactions; engage in mergers, liquidations and dissolutions; and sell all or substantially all of the assets of FCX and its subsidiaries, taken as a whole. FCX's Term Loan and revolving credit facility also contain financial ratios governing maximum total leverage and minimum interest coverage. Following the December 2015 amendment, FCX's leverage ratio (Net Debt/EBITDA, as defined in the credit agreement) cannot exceed 5.5 x at December 31, 2015, 5.9 x for the quarters ending March 31, 2016, and June 30, 2016, and declining to 5.0 x by the quarter ending December 31, 2016, 4.25 x in 2017 and 3.75 x thereafter. The December 2015 amendment also increases the interest rate spreads under specified conditions. Additionally, the Term Loan's December 2015 amendment requires prepayment of the Term Loan with 50 percent of the net proceeds of certain asset dispositions. In February 2016, the Term Loan and revolving credit facility were amended (refer to Note 18 for further discussion). FCX's senior notes contain limitations on liens. At December 31, 2015, FCX was in compliance with all of its covenants.

Note 18. Subsequent Events

As a result of the downgrade of the credit ratings of FCX debt below investment grade, FCX may be required to provide additional or alternative forms of financial assurance, such as letters of credit, surety bonds or collateral, related to its ARO and environmental obligations (refer to Note 12 for further discussion).

On February 15, 2016, FCX announced it had entered into a definitive agreement to sell a 13 percent undivided interest in its Morenci unincorporated joint venture to SMM for $1.0 billion in cash. The transaction is subject to customary closing conditions, including regulatory approvals, and is expected to close in mid-2016. FCX expects to record an approximate $550 million gain on the transaction and use losses to offset cash taxes on the transaction. Proceeds from the transaction will be used to repay borrowings under FCX's Term Loan and revolving credit facility.

The Morenci unincorporated joint venture is currently owned 85 percent by FCX and 15 percent by Sumitomo. Following completion of the transaction, the unincorporated joint venture will be owned 72 percent by FCX, 15 percent by Sumitomo and 13 percent by an affiliate that is wholly owned by SMM.

On February 26, 2016, FCX reached an agreement to further amend its revolving credit facility and Term Loan. The amendments to FCX's revolving credit facility and Term Loan include (i) modification of the maximum leverage ratio from 5.90 x to 8.00 x for the quarters ending March 31, 2016, and June 30, 2016, from 5.75 x to 8.00 x for the quarter ending September 30, 2016, and from 5.00 x to 6.00 x for the quarter ending December 31, 2016; and no changes to 2017 (remains 4.25 x) or thereafter (reverts to 3.75 x) and (ii) modification to the minimum interest expense coverage ratio (ratio of consolidated EBITDAX, as defined in the amended agreements, to consolidated cash interest expense) from 2.50 x to 2.25 x.

The commitment under FCX's revolving credit facility has been reduced from $4.0 billion to $3.5 billion.

A springing collateral and guarantee trigger was also added to the revolving credit facility and Term Loan. Under this provision, if FCX has not entered into definitive agreements for asset sales totaling $3.0 billion in aggregate by June 30, 2016, that are reasonably expected to close by December 31, 2016, FCX will be required to secure the revolving credit facility and Term Loan with a mutually acceptable collateral and guarantee package. The springing collateral and guarantee trigger will also go into effect if such asset sales totaling $3.0 billion in aggregate have not occurred by December 31, 2016.

In addition, the mandatory prepayment provision was modified to provide that 100 percent (rather than the 50 percent under the December 2015 amendment) of the net proceeds received on or prior to December 31, 2016, in excess of the first $1.0 billion from asset sales, subject to certain exceptions, must be applied to repay the Term Loan if the lenders are unsecured and the leverage ratio (as defined in the amended agreement) is equal to or greater than 6.00 x.

The Term Loan and revolving credit facility contain a number of negative covenants that, among other things, restrict, subject to certain exceptions, the ability of FCX's subsidiaries that are not borrowers or guarantors to incur additional indebtedness (including guarantee obligations) and FCX's ability or the ability of FCX's subsidiaries to: create liens on assets; enter into sale and leaseback transactions; engage in mergers, liquidations and dissolutions; or sell assets. Many of the exceptions to the subsidiary indebtedness restrictions and the lien restrictions have been narrowed significantly through March 31, 2017. In addition, on or prior to March 31, 2017, FCX is not permitted to pay dividends on its common stock or make other restricted payments. The pricing under the amended Term Loan and revolving credit facility also changed. If the total leverage ratio is greater than 6.00 x, then the existing interest rate will be increased by 0.50 percent, with an additional increase of 0.50 percent if the total leverage ratio is greater than 7.00 x.

FCX evaluated events after December 31, 2015, and through the date the financial statements were issued, and determined any events or transactions occurring during this period that would require recognition or disclosure are appropriately addressed in these financial statements.

1.78 RITE AID CORPORATION (FEB)
CONSOLIDATED BALANCE SHEETS (in part)

(In thousands, except per share amounts)

	February 28, 2015	March 1, 2014
Liabilities and Stockholders' Equity (Deficit) (in part)		
Current liabilities:		
Current maturities of long-term debt and lease financing obligations	$ 100,376	$ 49,174
Accounts payable	1,133,520	1,292,419
Accrued salaries, wages and other current liabilities	1,193,419	1,165,859
Deferred tax liabilities	57,685	—
Total current liabilities	2,485,000	2,507,452
Long-term debt, less current maturities	5,483,415	5,632,798
Lease financing obligations, less current maturities	61,152	75,171
Other noncurrent liabilities	776,629	843,152
Total liabilities	8,806,196	9,058,573

(In thousands, except per share amounts)

13. Indebtedness and Credit Agreement

Following is a summary of indebtedness and lease financing obligations at February 28, 2015 and March 1, 2014:

	2015	2014
Secured Debt:		
Senior secured revolving credit facility due February 2018	$ —	$ 400,000
Senior secured revolving credit facility due January 2020	1,725,000	—
Tranche 6 Term Loan due February 2020	—	1,152,293
8.00% senior secured notes (senior lien) due August 2020	650,000	650,000
Tranche 1 Term Loan (second lien) due August 2020	470,000	470,000
Tranche 2 Term Loan (second lien) due June 2021	500,000	500,000
10.25% senior secured notes (second lien) due October 2019 ($270,000 face value less unamortized discount of $1,160)	—	268,840
Other secured	5,367	5,324
	3,350,367	3,446,457
Guaranteed Unsecured Debt:		
6.75% senior notes due June 2021	810,000	810,000
9.25% senior notes due March 2020 ($902,000 face value plus unamortized premium of $3,415 and $4,087)	905,415	906,087
	1,715,415	1,716,087
Unguaranteed Unsecured Debt:		
8.5% convertible notes due May 2015	64,168	64,188
7.7% notes due February 2027	295,000	295,000
6.875% fixed-rate senior notes due December 2028	128,000	128,000
	487,168	487,188
Lease financing obligations	91,993	107,411
Total debt	5,644,943	5,757,143
Current maturities of long-term debt and lease financing obligations	(100,376)	(49,174)
Long-term debt and lease financing obligations, less current maturities	$5,544,567	$5,707,969

Credit Facility

On January 13, 2015, the Company amended and restated its senior secured credit facility ("Amended and Restated Senior Secured Credit Facility" or "revolver"), which, among other things, increased borrowing capacity from $1,795,000 to $3,000,000 (increasing to $3,700,000 upon the repayment of its 8.00% senior secured notes due August 2020 ("8.00% Notes")), and extended the maturity to January 2020 from February 2018. The Company used borrowings under the revolver to repay and retire all of the $1,143,650 outstanding under its Tranche 7 Senior Secured Term Loan due 2020, along with associated fees and expenses. Borrowings under the revolver bear interest at a rate per annum between LIBOR plus 1.50% and LIBOR plus 2.00% based upon the average revolver availability (as defined in the Amended and Restated Senior Secured Credit Facility). The Company is required to pay fees between 0.250% and 0.375% per annum on the daily unused amount of the revolver, depending on the Average Revolver Availability (as defined in the Amended and Restated Senior Secured Credit Facility). Amounts drawn under the revolver become due and payable on January 13, 2020.

On February 10, 2015, the Company amended the Amended and Restated Senior Secured Credit Facility to, among other things, increase the flexibility of Rite Aid to incur and/or issue unsecured indebtedness, including in connection with the arrangements contemplated by the merger agreement executed in connection with the pending acquisition of EnvisionRx, and made certain other modifications to the covenants applicable to Rite Aid and its subsidiaries.

The Company's ability to borrow under the revolver is based upon a specified borrowing base consisting of accounts receivable, inventory and prescription files. At February 28, 2015, the Company had $1,725,000 of borrowings outstanding under the revolver and had letters of credit outstanding against the revolver of $71,084, which resulted in additional borrowing capacity of $1,203,916.

The Amended and Restated Senior Secured Credit Facility restricts the Company and the subsidiary guarantors from accumulating cash on hand, and under certain circumstances, requires the funds in the Company's deposit accounts to be applied first to the repayment of outstanding revolving loans under the senior secured credit facility and then to be held as collateral for the senior obligations.

The Amended and Restated Senior Secured Credit Facility allows the Company to have outstanding, at any time, up to $1,500,000 (or $1,800,000 solely to the extent incurred in anticipation of the funding of the Pending Acquisition) in secured second priority debt, split-priority term loan debt, unsecured debt and disqualified preferred stock in addition to borrowings under the Amended and Restated Senior Secured Credit Facility and existing indebtedness, provided that not in excess of $750,000 of such secured second priority debt, split-priority term loan debt, unsecured debt and disqualified preferred stock shall mature or require scheduled payments of principal prior to 90 days after the latest of (a) the fifth anniversary of the effectiveness of the Amended and Restated Senior Secured Credit Facility and (b) the latest maturity date of any Term Loan or Other Revolving Loan (each as defined in the Amended and Restated Senior Secured Credit Facility) (excluding bridge facilities allowing extensions on customary terms to at least the date that is 90 days after such date and, with respect to any escrow notes issued by Rite Aid, excluding any special mandatory redemption of the type described in clause (iii) of the definition of "Escrow Notes" in the Amended and Restated Senior Secured Credit Facility). Subject to the limitations described in clauses (a) and (b) of the immediately preceding sentence, the Amended and Restated Senior Secured Credit Facility additionally allows the Company to issue or incur an unlimited amount of unsecured debt and disqualified preferred stock so long as a Financial Covenant Effectiveness Period (as defined in the Amended and Restated Senior Secured Credit Facility) is not in effect; provided, however, that certain of the Company's other outstanding indebtedness limits the amount of unsecured debt that can be incurred if certain interest coverage levels are not met at the time of incurrence or other exemptions are not available. The Amended and Restated Senior Secured Credit Facility also contains certain restrictions on the amount of secured first priority debt the Company is able to incur. The Amended and Restated Senior Secured Credit Facility also allows for the voluntary repurchase of any debt or the mandatory repurchase of the Company's 8.5% convertible notes due 2015 or other convertible debt, so long as the Amended and Restated Senior Secured Credit Facility is not in default and the Company maintains availability under its revolving credit facility of more than (i) prior to the repayment of our 8.00% Notes, $300,000 and (ii) on and after the repayment of the Company's 8.00% Notes, $365,000.

As of January 13, 2015, the Amended and Restated Senior Secured Credit Facility has a financial covenant that requires the Company to maintain a minimum fixed charge coverage ratio of 1.00 to 1.00 (a) on any date on which availability under the revolving credit facility is less than (i) in the case of dates prior to the repayment of our 8.00% Notes, $175,000 and (ii) in the case of dates on and after the repayment of the Company's 8.00% Notes, $200,000 or (b) on the third consecutive business day on which availability under the revolving credit facility is less than (i) in the case of dates prior to the repayment of the Company's 8.00% Notes, $225,000 and (ii) in the case of dates on or after the repayment of the Company's 8.00% Notes, $250,000 and, in each case, ending on and excluding the first day thereafter, if any, which is the 30th consecutive calendar day on which availability under the revolving credit facility is equal to or greater than (i) in the case of dates prior to the repayment of the Company's 8.00% Notes, $225,000 and (ii) in the case of dates on or after the repayment of the Company's 8.00% Notes, $250,000. As of February 28, 2015, the availability was at a level that did not did not trigger this covenant. The Amended and Restated Senior Secured Credit Facility also contains covenants which place restrictions on the incurrence of debt, the payments of dividends, sale of assets, mergers and acquisitions and the granting of liens.

The Amended and Restated Senior Secured Credit Facility also provides for customary events of default.

The Company also has two second priority secured term loan facilities. The first includes a $470,000 second priority secured term loan (the "Tranche 1 Term Loan"). The Tranche 1 Term Loan matures on August 21, 2020 and currently bears interest at a rate per annum equal to LIBOR plus 4.75% with a LIBOR floor of 1.00%, if the Company chooses to make LIBOR borrowings, or at Citibank's base rate plus 3.75%. The second includes a $500,000 second priority secured term loan (the "Tranche 2 Term Loan"). The Tranche 2 Term Loan matures on June 21, 2021 and currently bears interest at a rate per annum equal to LIBOR plus 3.875% with a LIBOR floor of 1.00%, if the Company chooses to make LIBOR borrowings, or at Citibank's base rate plus 2.875%.

Substantially all of Rite Aid Corporation's 100 percent owned subsidiaries guarantee the obligations under the Amended and Restated Senior Secured Credit Facility, second priority secured term loan facilities, secured guaranteed notes and unsecured guaranteed notes. The Amended and Restated Senior Secured Credit Facility, second priority secured term loan facilities and secured guaranteed notes are secured, on a senior or second priority basis, as applicable, by a lien on, among other things, accounts receivable, inventory and prescription files of the subsidiary guarantors. The subsidiary guarantees related to the Company's Amended and Restated Senior Secured Credit Facility, second priority secured term loan facilities and secured guaranteed notes and, on an unsecured basis, the unsecured guaranteed notes are full and unconditional and joint and several, and there are no restrictions on the ability of the Company to obtain funds from its subsidiaries. The Company has no independent assets or operations. Additionally, the subsidiaries, including joint ventures, that do not guaranty the credit facility, second priority secured term loan facilities and applicable notes, are minor. Accordingly, condensed consolidating financial information for the Company and subsidiaries is not presented.

1.79 REGAL ENTERTAINMENT GROUP (DEC)
CONSOLIDATED BALANCE SHEETS (in part)

(in millions, except share data)

Liabilities and Deficit (in part)	December 31, 2015	January 1, 2015
Current Liabilities:		
Current portion of debt obligations	$ 27.4	$ 26.6
Accounts payable	229.7	165.7
Accrued expenses	70.8	76.0
Deferred revenue	203.4	188.2
Interest payable	20.0	20.5
Total Current Liabilities	551.3	477.0
Long-Term Debt, Less Current Portion	2,228.3	2,238.8
Lease Financing Arrangements, Less Current Portion	77.8	83.8
Capital Lease Obligations, Less Current Portion	8.9	11.0
Non-Current Deferred Revenue	415.2	418.0
Other Non-Current Liabilities	228.4	208.2
Total Liabilities	3,509.9	3,436.8

NOTES TO CONSOLIDATED FINANCIAL STATEMENTS (in part)

2. Summary of Significant Accounting Policies (in part)

Leases

The majority of the Company's operations are conducted in premises occupied under non-cancelable lease agreements with initial base terms generally ranging from 15 to 20 years. The Company, at its option, can renew a substantial portion of the leases at defined or then fair rental rates for various periods. Certain leases for Company theatres provide for contingent rentals based on the revenue results of the underlying theatre and require the payment of taxes, insurance, and other costs applicable to the property. Also, certain leases contain escalating minimum rental provisions. There are no conditions imposed upon us by our lease agreements or by parties other than the lessor that legally obligate the Company to incur costs to retire assets as a result of a decision to vacate our leased properties. None of our lease agreements require us to return the leased property to the lessor in its original condition (allowing for normal wear and tear) or to remove leasehold improvements at our cost.

The Company accounts for leased properties under the provisions of ASC Topic 840, *Leases* and other authoritative accounting literature. ASC Subtopic 840-10, *Leases—Overview* requires that the Company evaluate each lease for classification as either a capital lease or an operating lease. The Company performs this evaluation at the inception of the lease and when a modification is made to a lease. As to those arrangements that are classified as capital leases, the Company records property under capital leases and a capital lease obligation in an amount equal to the lesser of the present value of the minimum lease payments to be made over the life of the lease at the beginning of the lease term, or the fair value of the leased property. The property under capital lease is amortized on a straight-line basis as a charge to expense over the lease term, as defined, or the economic life of the leased property, whichever is less. During the lease term, as defined, each minimum lease payment is allocated between a reduction of the lease obligation and interest expense so as to produce a constant periodic rate of interest on the remaining balance of the lease obligation. The Company does not believe that exercise of the renewal options in its leases are reasonably assured at the inception of the lease agreements because such leases: (i) provide for either (a) renewal rents based on market rates or (b) renewal rents that equal or exceed the initial rents, and (ii) do not impose economic penalties upon the determination whether or not to exercise the renewal option. As a result, there are not sufficient economic incentives at the inception of the leases to consider the lease renewal options to be reasonably assured of being exercised and therefore, the initial base term is generally considered as the lease term under ASC Subtopic 840-10.

The Company records rent expense for its operating leases with contractual rent increases in accordance with ASC Subtopic 840-20, *Leases—Operating Leases,* on a straight-line basis from the "lease commencement date" as specified in the lease agreement until the end of the base lease term.

The Company accounts for lease incentive payments received from a landlord in accordance with ASC Subtopic 840-20, *Leases—Lease Incentives*, and records the proceeds as a deferred lease incentive liability and amortizes the liability as a reduction in rent expense over the base term of the lease.

For leases in which the Company is involved with construction of the theatre, the Company accounts for the lease during the construction period under the provisions of ASC Subtopic 840-40, *Leases—Sale-Leaseback Transactions*. The landlord is typically responsible for constructing a theatre using guidelines and specifications agreed to by the Company and assumes substantially all of the risk of construction. In accordance with ASC Subtopic 840-40, if the Company concludes that it has substantially all of the construction period risks, it records a construction asset and related liability for the amount of total project costs incurred during the construction period. Once construction is completed, the Company considers the requirements under ASC Subtopic 840-40, for sale-leaseback treatment, and if the arrangement does not meet such requirements, it records the project's construction costs funded by the landlord as a financing obligation. The obligation is amortized over the financing term based on the payments designated in the contract.

In accordance with ASC Subtopic 840-20, we expense rental costs incurred during construction periods for operating leases as such costs are incurred. For rental costs incurred during construction periods for both operating and capital leases, the "lease commencement date" is the date at which we gain access to the leased asset. Historically, and for the years ended December 31, 2015, January 1, 2015 and December 26, 2013, these rental costs have not been significant to our consolidated financial statements.

Sale and Leaseback Transactions

The Company accounts for the sale and leaseback of real estate assets in accordance with ASC Subtopic 840-40. Losses on sale leaseback transactions are recognized at the time of sale if the fair value of the property sold is less than the undepreciated cost of the property. Gains on sale and leaseback transactions are deferred and amortized over the remaining lease term.

3. Acquisitions (in part)

Acquisition of Hollywood Theaters

On March 29, 2013, Regal completed the acquisition of Hollywood Theaters, whereby it acquired a total of 43 theatres with 513 screens for an aggregate net cash purchase price of $194.4 million. In addition, the Company assumed approximately $47.9 million of capital lease and lease financing obligations, and certain working capital. The cash portion of the purchase price included repayment of approximately $167.0 million of the sellers' debt. The acquisition of Hollywood Theaters enhanced the Company's presence in 16 states and 3 U.S. territories. The Company incurred approximately $3.0 million in transaction costs in connection with this transaction. The aggregate net cash purchase price was allocated to the identifiable assets acquired and liabilities assumed for each of the respective theatre locations based on their estimated fair values at the date of acquisition using the acquisition method of accounting. The allocation of the purchase price is based on management's judgment after evaluating several factors, including an independent third party valuation. The results of operations of the acquired theatres have been included in the Company's consolidated financial statements for periods subsequent to the acquisition date.

The following is a summary of the final allocation of the aggregate net cash purchase price to the estimated fair values of the identifiable assets acquired and liabilities assumed that have been recognized by the Company in its consolidated balance sheet as of the date of acquisition (in millions):

Current assets	$ 8.7
Property and equipment	143.2
Favorable leases and other intangible assets	35.6
Goodwill	46.4
Deferred income tax asset	35.8
Other assets	0.2
Current liabilities	(14.2)
Lease financing obligations	(40.4)
Capital lease obligations	(7.5)
Unfavorable leases	(10.7)
Other liabilities	(2.7)
Total purchase price	$194.4

The transaction included the assumption of lease financing obligations associated with 14 acquired theatres and various capital lease obligations, which are presented in the Company's consolidated balance sheets. Such obligations have a weighted average interest rate of approximately 10.7% and mature in various installments through December 2030. In addition, the transaction included the acquisition of favorable leases (approximately $34.4 million) and unfavorable leases (approximately $10.7 million), which are presented in the Company's consolidated balance sheet as a component of "Intangible Assets, net" and "Other Non-Current Liabilities," respectively. The weighted average amortization period for the favorable leases and the unfavorable leases are approximately 18 years and 15 years, respectively. Goodwill represents the excess purchase price over the amounts assigned to assets acquired, including intangible assets, and liabilities assumed and is not deductible for tax purposes.

4. Investments (in part)

Investment in Digital Cinema Implementation Partners

We maintain an investment in Digital Cinema Implementation Partners, LLC, a Delaware limited liability company ("DCIP"). DCIP is a joint venture company formed by Regal, AMC and Cinemark. Regal holds a 46.7% economic interest in DCIP as of December 31, 2015 and a one-third voting interest along with each of AMC and Cinemark. Since the Company does not have a controlling financial interest in DCIP or any of its subsidiaries, it accounts for its investment in DCIP under the equity method of accounting. The Company's investment in DCIP is included as a component of "Other Non-Current Assets" in the accompanying consolidated balance sheets. The changes in the carrying amount of our investment in DCIP for the years ended December 31, 2015, January 1, 2015, and December 26, 2013 are as follows (in millions):

Balance as of December 27, 2012	$ 72.8
Equity contributions	3.5
Equity in earnings of DCIP[1]	22.9
Change in fair value of equity method investee interest rate swap transactions	2.4
Balance as of December 26, 2013	101.6
Equity contributions	3.6
Equity in earnings of DCIP[1]	28.6
Receipt of cash distributions[2]	(6.3)
Change in fair value of equity method investee interest rate swap transactions	(1.2)
Balance as of January 1, 2015	126.3
Equity contributions	0.4
Equity in earnings of DCIP[1]	37.0
Receipt of cash distributions[2]	(2.0)
Change in fair value of equity method investee interest rate swap transactions	(1.0)
Balance as of December 31, 2015	$160.7

[1] Represents the Company's share of the net income of DCIP. Such amount is presented as a component of "Equity in income of non-consolidated entities and other, net" in the accompanying consolidated statements of income.
[2] Represents cash distributions from DCIP as a return on its investment.

DCIP funds the cost of digital projection principally through the collection of virtual print fees from motion picture studios and equipment lease payments from participating exhibitors, including us. In accordance with the master equipment lease agreement (the "Master Lease"), the digital projection systems are leased from a subsidiary of DCIP under a twelve-year term with ten one-year fair value renewal options. The Master Lease also contains a fair value purchase option. On March 31, 2014, the junior capital raised by DCIP in the initial financing transactions was paid in full by DCIP. In connection with this repayment, the Master Lease was amended to eliminate the incremental minimum rent payment provision of $2,000 per digital projection system. DCIP incurred a loss on debt extinguishment of approximately $6.0 million as a result of the debt repayment and Regal recorded its pro rata share of such loss (approximately $2.8 million) during the year ended January 1, 2015 as a reduction of equity in earnings of DCIP. As a result of the amendment to the Master Lease, the Company's deferred rent balance associated with the incremental minimum rental payment of $2,000 per digital projection system is being amortized on a straight-line basis as a reduction of rent expense from the effective date of the amendment (March 31, 2014) through the end of the remaining lease term. As of December 31, 2015, under the Master Lease, the Company continues to pay annual minimum rent of $1,000 per digital projection system from the effective date of the original agreement through the end of the lease term. The Company considers the $1,000 rent payment to be a minimum rental and accordingly records such rent on a straight-line basis in its consolidated financial statements. The Company is also subject to various types of other rent if such digital projection systems do not meet minimum performance requirements as outlined in the Master Lease. Certain of the other rent payments are subject to either a monthly or an annual maximum. The Company accounts for the Master Lease as an operating lease for accounting purposes. During the years ended December 31, 2015, January 1, 2015, and December 26, 2013, the Company incurred total rent expense of approximately $5.4 million, $7.7 million, and $14.5 million, respectively, associated with the leased digital projection systems. Such rent expense is presented as a component of "Other operating expenses" in the Company's consolidated statements of income.

Summarized consolidated statements of operations information for DCIP for the years ended December 31, 2015, December 31, 2014, and December 31, 2013 is as follows (in millions):

	Year Ended December 31, 2015	Year Ended December 31, 2014	Year Ended December 31, 2013
Net revenues	$172.3	$170.7	$182.7
Income from operations	103.4	102.0	116.2
Net income	79.3	61.3	49.0

Summarized consolidated balance sheet information for DCIP as of December 31, 2015 and 2014 is as follows (in millions):

	December 31, 2015	December 31, 2014
Current assets	$ 48.8	$ 53.2
Noncurrent assets	956.0	1,044.4
Total assets	1,004.8	1,097.6
Current liabilities	32.5	24.0
Noncurrent liabilities	642.7	821.3
Total liabilities	675.2	845.3
Members' equity	329.6	252.3
Liabilities and members' equity	1,004.8	1,097.6

5. Debt Obligations (in part)

Debt obligations at December 31, 2015 and January 1, 2015 consist of the following (in millions):

	December 31, 2015	January 1, 2015
Regal Cinemas Amended Senior Credit Facility, net of debt discount	$958.8	$965.8
Regal 5 $\frac{3}{4}$ % Senior Notes Due 2022	775.0	775.0
Regal 5 $\frac{3}{4}$ % Senior Notes Due 2025	250.0	250.0
Regal 5 $\frac{3}{4}$ % Senior Notes Due 2023	250.0	250.0
Lease financing arrangements, weighted average interest rate of 11.29% as of December 31, 2015 maturing in various installments through November 2028	89.4	94.5
Capital lease obligations, 8.5% to 10.7%, maturing in various installments through December 2030	11.1	13.1
Other	8.1	11.8
Total debt obligations	2,342.4	2,360.2
Less current portion	27.4	26.6
Total debt obligations, less current portion	$2,315.0	$2,333.6

Lease Financing Arrangements —These obligations primarily represent lease financing obligations resulting from the requirements of ASC Subtopic 840-40. In connection with the acquisition of Hollywood Theaters discussed further in Note 3—"Acquisitions," the Company assumed approximately $40.4 million of lease financing obligations associated with 14 acquired theatres. As of December 31, 2015, such obligations have a weighted average interest rate of approximately 10.9% and mature in various installments through November 2028.

As a result of certain lease extensions effected during the year ended December 31, 2015, the Company increased the carrying amount of its lease financing obligations by approximately $5.1 million (an amount equal to the present value of the revised lease payments at the date of the lease extensions).

Maturities of Debt Obligations —The Company's long-term debt and future minimum lease payments for its capital lease obligations and lease financing arrangements are scheduled to mature as follows:

(In millions)	Long-Term Debt and Other	Capital Leases	Lease Financing Arrangements	Total
2016	$ 13.6	$ 3.3	$ 21.0	$ 37.9
2017	11.1	3.0	21.2	35.3
2018	11.0	0.9	21.3	33.2
2019	11.0	0.9	19.5	31.4
2020	9.7	0.9	12.0	22.6
Thereafter	2,185.5	9.8	35.0	2,230.3
Less: interest on capital leases and lease financing arrangements	—	(7.7)	(40.6)	(48.3)
Totals	$2,241.9	$11.1	$ 89.4	$2,342.4

Covenant Compliance —As of December 31, 2015, we are in full compliance with all agreements, including all related covenants, governing our outstanding debt obligations.

6. Leases

The Company accounts for a majority of its leases as operating leases. Minimum rentals payable under all non-cancelable operating leases with terms in excess of one year as of December 31, 2015, are summarized for the following fiscal years (in millions):

2016	$ 428.5
2017	412.4
2018	386.4
2019	333.5
2020	276.1
Thereafter	1,176.0
Total	$3,012.9

Rent expense under such operating leases amounted to $421.5 million, $423.4 million and $413.6 million for the years ended December 31, 2015, January 1, 2015 and December 26, 2013, respectively. Contingent rent expense was $22.7 million, $23.7 million and $23.7 million for the years ended December 31, 2015, January 1, 2015 and December 26, 2013, respectively.

Sale-Leaseback Transactions

The Company has historically entered into sale and leaseback transactions whereby owned properties were sold and leased back under operating leases. The minimum rentals for these operating leases are included in the table above.

In December 1995, United Artists Theatre Circuit, Inc. ("UATC") entered into a sale and leaseback transaction whereby 31 owned properties were sold to and leased back from an unaffiliated third party under a Master Lease. In conjunction with the transaction, the buyer of the properties issued publicly traded pass-through certificates. In connection with this sale and leaseback transaction, UATC entered into a Participation Agreement that requires UATC to comply with various covenants, including limitations on indebtedness, restricted payments, transactions with affiliates, guarantees, issuance of preferred stock of subsidiaries and subsidiary distributions, transfer of assets and payment of dividends. As of January 1, 2015, nine properties were subject to the sale leaseback transaction and approximately $7.7 million in principal amount of pass-through certificates were outstanding.

On March 27, 2015, the nine operating properties were sold to a third party buyer and the Master Lease and related agreements associated with the December 1995 sale and leaseback transaction were terminated. Upon termination of the Master Lease, United Artists entered into new lease agreements for the nine operating properties. As part of the transaction, United Artists received a reimbursement of its January 2015 rent payment under the Master Lease totaling approximately $4.9 million and received approximately $3.2 million in landlord contributions for three properties that it expects to renovate as part of the transaction. In addition, United Artists is expected to receive an additional $3.2 million of landlord contributions at various milestones starting with commencement of renovation of the three properties. As of December 31, 2015, United Artists has received approximately $1.6 million of such landlord contributions. The new lease agreements associated with the three properties each carry an initial base rent term of 15 years beginning at the completion of renovation, and in the interim, provide for contingent rentals based on the revenue results of the underlying theatres. The new lease agreements associated with the six remaining properties each carry a maturity date of December 31, 2016, the same maturity date under the former Master Lease. All nine lease agreements provide for the payment of taxes, insurance, and other costs applicable to the properties and have been accounted for as operating leases for accounting purposes. The pass-through certificates fully matured on July 1, 2015.

Contingencies

RECOGNITION AND MEASUREMENT

1.80 The FASB ASC glossary defines a *contingency* as an existing condition, situation, or set of circumstances involving uncertainty about possible gain (gain contingency) or loss (loss contingency) to an entity that will ultimately be resolved when one or more future events occur or fail to occur. FASB ASC 450-20 sets forth guidance for the recognition and disclosure of loss contingencies. An estimated loss from a loss contingency should be accrued by a charge to income if both of the following conditions are met:
- Information available before the financial statements are issued or are available to be issued indicates that it is probable that an asset had been impaired or a liability had been incurred at the date of the financial statements. It is implicit in this condition that it must be probable that one or more future events will occur confirming the fact of the loss.
- The amount of loss can be reasonably estimated.

1.81 Disclosure is preferable to accrual when a reasonable estimate of loss cannot be made. Even losses that are reasonably estimable should not be accrued if it is not probable that an asset has been impaired or a liability has been incurred at the date of the entity's financial statements because those losses relate to a future period, rather than the current period. In accordance with FASB ASC 450-20-30-1, if some amount within a range of loss appears at the time to be a better estimate than any other amount within the range, that amount should be accrued. When no amount within the range is a better estimate than any other amount, however, the minimum amount in that range should be accrued. Select loss contingency disclosures do not apply to loss contingencies arising from an entity's recurring estimation of its allowance for credit losses. FASB ASC 450-30-25-1 usually does not permit recognition of gain contingencies because to do so might be to recognize revenue before its realization. When contingency disclosures exist, public companies generally present a balance sheet caption for contingencies, in accordance with Rule 5-02 of Regulation S-X.

1.82 FASB ASC 460-10-25-5 considers warranties to fall within the definition of a contingency. Therefore, an entity should meet the two conditions described in paragraph 1.80 before recognizing a loss and related liability. FASB ASC 460-10 contains additional guidance concerning the items that an entity should consider in order to meet the probability recognition criteria, including references to the entity's own and others' experience. FASB ASC also provides more specific guidance for extended warranties and product maintenance contracts.

PRESENTATION AND DISCLOSURE EXCERPTS

LEGAL MATTERS

1.83 OWENS-ILLINOIS, INC. (DEC)
CONSOLIDATED BALANCE SHEETS (continued)

Dollars in millions, except per share amounts

December 31,	2015	2014
Liabilities and Share Owners' Equity (in part)		
Current liabilities:		
Accounts payable	$1,212	$1,137
Salaries and wages	145	145
U.S. and foreign income taxes	36	43
Current portion of asbestos-related liabilities	130	143
Other accrued liabilities	371	372
Short-term loans	160	127
Long-term debt due within one year	68	361
Total current liabilities	2,122	2,328
Long-term debt	5,345	2,957
Deferred taxes	124	121
Pension benefits	504	465
Nonpension postretirement benefits	155	178
Other liabilities	205	227
Asbestos-related liabilities	392	292
Commitments and contingencies		

NOTES TO CONSOLIDATED FINANCIAL STATEMENTS (in part)

Tabular data dollars in millions, except per share amounts

12. Contingencies

Asbestos

The Company is a defendant in numerous lawsuits alleging bodily injury and death as a result of exposure to asbestos. From 1948 to 1958, one of the Company's former business units commercially produced and sold approximately $40 million of a high-temperature, calcium-silicate based pipe and block insulation material containing asbestos. The Company exited the insulation business in April 1958. The typical asbestos personal injury lawsuit alleges various theories of liability, including negligence, gross negligence and strict liability and seeks compensatory and, in some cases, punitive damages in various amounts (herein referred to as "asbestos claims").

The following table shows the approximate number of plaintiffs and claimants who had asbestos claims pending against the Company at the beginning of each listed year, the number of claims disposed of during that year, the year's filings and the claims pending at the end of each listed year (eliminating duplicate filings):

	2015	2014	2013
Pending at beginning of year	2,260	2,620	2,610
Disposed	1,460	1,830	1,700
Filed	1,280	1,470	1,710
Pending at end of year	2,080	2,260	2,620

Based on an analysis of the lawsuits pending as of December 31, 2015, approximately 82% of plaintiffs either do not specify the monetary damages sought, or in the case of court filings, claim an amount sufficient to invoke the jurisdictional minimum of the trial court. Approximately 11% of plaintiffs specifically plead damages above the jurisdictional minimum up to, and including, $15 million or less, and 7% of plaintiffs specifically plead damages greater than $15 million but less than or equal to $100 million.

As indicated by the foregoing summary, current pleading practice permits considerable variation in the assertion of monetary damages. The Company's experience resolving hundreds of thousands of asbestos claims and lawsuits over an extended period demonstrates that the monetary relief alleged in a complaint bears little relevance to a claim's merits or disposition value. Rather, the amount potentially recoverable is determined by such factors as the severity of the plaintiff's asbestos disease, the product identification evidence against the Company and other defendants, the defenses available to the Company and other defendants, the specific jurisdiction in which the claim is made, and the plaintiff's medical history and exposure to other disease-causing agents.

In addition to the pending claims set forth above, the Company has claims-handling agreements in place with many plaintiffs' counsel throughout the country. These agreements require evaluation and negotiation regarding whether particular claimants qualify under the criteria established by such agreements. The criteria for such claims include verification of a compensable illness and a reasonable probability of exposure to a product manufactured by the Company's former business unit during its manufacturing period ending in 1958.

The Company has also been a defendant in other asbestos-related lawsuits or claims involving maritime workers, medical monitoring claimants, co-defendants and property damage claimants. Based upon its past experience, the Company believes that these categories of lawsuits and claims will not involve any material liability and they are not included in the above description of pending matters or in the following description of disposed matters.

Since receiving its first asbestos claim, the Company as of December 31, 2015, has disposed of the asbestos claims of approximately 396,000 plaintiffs and claimants at an average indemnity payment per claim of approximately $9,200. Certain of these dispositions have resulted in deferred amounts payable. Deferred amounts payable totaled approximately $17 million at December 31, 2015 ($13 million at December 31, 2014) and are included in the foregoing average indemnity payment per claim. The Company's asbestos indemnity payments have varied on a per claim basis, and are expected to continue to vary considerably over time. Asbestos-related cash payments for 2015, 2014 and 2013 were $138 million, $148 million, and $158 million, respectively.

As discussed above, the Company's objective is to achieve, where possible, resolution of asbestos claims pursuant to claims-handling agreements. Failure of claimants to meet certain medical and product exposure criteria in the Company's administrative claims handling agreements has generally reduced the number of claims that would otherwise have been received by the Company in the tort system. In addition, certain court orders and legislative acts have reduced or eliminated the number of claims that the Company otherwise would have received by the Company in the tort system. These developments generally have had the effect of increasing the Company's per-claim average indemnity payment over time.

The Company believes that its ultimate asbestos-related liability (i.e., its indemnity payments or other claim disposition costs plus related legal fees) cannot reasonably be estimated. Beginning with the initial liability of $975 million established in 1993, the Company has accrued a total of approximately $4.6 billion through 2015, before insurance recoveries, for its asbestos-related liability. The Company's ability to reasonably estimate its liability has been significantly affected by, among other factors, the volatility of asbestos-related litigation in the United States, the significant number of co-defendants that have filed for bankruptcy, the inherent uncertainty of future disease incidence and claiming patterns against the Company, the significant expansion of the defendants that are now sued in this litigation, and the continuing changes in the extent to which these defendants participate in the resolution of cases in which the Company is also a defendant.

The Company continues to monitor trends that may affect its ultimate liability and analyze the developments and variables likely to affect the resolution of pending and future asbestos claims against the Company. The material components of the Company's accrued liability are determined by the Company in connection with its annual comprehensive legal review and consist of the following estimates, to the extent it is probable that such liabilities have been incurred and can be reasonably estimated: (i) the liability for asbestos claims already asserted against the Company; (ii) the liability for asbestos claims not yet asserted against the Company, but which the Company believes will be asserted in the next four years; and (iii) the legal defense costs estimated to be incurred in connection with the claims already asserted and those claims the Company believes will be asserted in the next four years.

As noted above, the Company conducts a comprehensive legal review of its asbestos-related liabilities and costs annually in connection with finalizing and reporting its annual results of operations, unless significant changes in trends or new developments warrant an earlier review. If the results of an annual comprehensive legal review indicate that the existing amount of the accrued liability is insufficient to cover its reasonably estimable asbestos-related costs, then the Company records an appropriate charge to increase the accrued liability. As part of the annual comprehensive legal review, the Company considers the factors that affect its estimated accrued liability, and reconsiders the timeframe used to estimate the liability for asbestos claims not yet asserted against the Company using primarily a qualitative assessment of the state of the asbestos litigation, as well as a quantitative hindsight review. The hindsight review includes an examination of the Company's prior estimates of the accrual for unasserted claims compared to the estimated value of claims actually received in those periods.

Based on its 2015 comprehensive legal review, the Company determined that it was able to reasonably estimate probable losses for asbestos claims not yet asserted against the Company for a period of four years. Therefore, the Company's charge for 2015 is for a period one year longer than the accrual period determined as reasonably estimable in the annual comprehensive legal reviews conducted since 2003. This is a change in estimate resulting from an assessment of the qualitative and quantitative factors in the Company's 2015 comprehensive legal review. The Company will continue to evaluate the qualitative factors relating to the litigation and also conduct its annual hindsight reviews to determine the appropriate period of time for which it can reasonably estimate probable losses for unasserted claims. Because part of the Company's asbestos liability at any year end is an estimate of the asbestos claims and legal defense costs that are expected to be incurred in the time horizon for which it is able to reasonably estimate probable losses, the Company usually expects to record an annual charge to account for the inclusion of one or more additional years in its time horizon.

The Company's reported results of operations for 2015 were materially affected by the $225 million fourth quarter charge for asbestos-related costs and asbestos-related payments continue to be substantial. Given the inherent volatility involved in the asbestos litigation, the Company is unable to provide an estimate of possible loss or range of loss beyond the $522 million recorded as of December 31, 2015. Any future additional charge would likewise materially affect the Company's results of operations for the period in which it is recorded.

Other Matters

The Company conducted an internal investigation into conduct in certain of its overseas operations that may have violated the anti-bribery provisions of the United States Foreign Corrupt Practices Act (the "FCPA"), the FCPA's books and records and internal controls provisions, the Company's own internal policies, and various local laws. In October 2012, the Company voluntarily disclosed these matters to the U.S. Department of Justice (the "DOJ") and the Securities and Exchange Commission (the "SEC").

On July 18, 2013, the Company received a letter from the DOJ indicating that it presently did not intend to take any enforcement action and is closing its inquiry into the matter.

As disclosed in previous periods, the Company is presently unable to predict the duration, scope or result of an investigation by the SEC, if any, or whether the SEC will commence any legal action. The SEC has a broad range of civil sanctions under the FCPA and other laws and regulations including, but not limited to, injunctive relief, disgorgement, penalties, and modifications to business practices. The Company could also be subject to investigation and sanctions outside the United States. While the Company is currently unable to quantify the impact of any potential sanctions or remedial measures, it does not expect such actions will have a material adverse effect on the Company's liquidity, results of operations or financial condition.

Other litigation is pending against the Company, in many cases involving ordinary and routine claims incidental to the business of the Company and in others presenting allegations that are non-routine and involve compensatory, punitive or treble damage claims as well as other types of relief. The Company records a liability for such matters when it is both probable that the liability has been incurred and the amount of the liability can be reasonably estimated. Recorded amounts are reviewed and adjusted to reflect changes in the factors upon which the estimates are based, including additional information, negotiations, settlements and other events.

TAX CONTINGENCIES

1.84 AMAZON.COM, INC. (DEC)
NOTES TO CONSOLIDATED FINANCIAL STATEMENTS (in part)

Note 1—Description of Business and Accounting Policies (in part)

Income Taxes

Income tax expense includes U.S. (federal and state) and foreign income taxes. Except as required under U.S. tax laws, we do not provide for U.S. taxes on our undistributed earnings of foreign subsidiaries that have not been previously taxed since we intend to invest such undistributed earnings indefinitely outside of the U.S. If our intent changes or if these funds are needed for our U.S. operations, we would be required to accrue or pay U.S. taxes on some or all of these undistributed earnings and our effective tax rate would be adversely affected. Undistributed earnings of foreign subsidiaries that are indefinitely invested outside of the U.S were $1.5 billion as of December 31, 2015. Determination of the unrecognized deferred tax liability that would be incurred if such amounts were repatriated is not practicable.

Deferred income tax balances reflect the effects of temporary differences between the carrying amounts of assets and liabilities and their tax bases and are stated at enacted tax rates expected to be in effect when taxes are actually paid or recovered.

Deferred tax assets are evaluated for future realization and reduced by a valuation allowance to the extent we believe they will not be realized. We consider many factors when assessing the likelihood of future realization of our deferred tax assets, including our recent cumulative earnings experience and expectations of future taxable income and capital gains by taxing jurisdiction, the carry-forward periods available to us for tax reporting purposes, and other relevant factors. We allocate our valuation allowance to current and long-term deferred tax assets on a pro-rata basis.

We utilize a two-step approach to recognizing and measuring uncertain income tax positions (tax contingencies). The first step is to evaluate the tax position for recognition by determining if the weight of available evidence indicates it is more likely than not that the position will be sustained on audit, including resolution of related appeals or litigation processes. The second step is to measure the tax benefit as the largest amount which is more than 50% likely of being realized upon ultimate settlement. We consider many factors when evaluating our tax positions and estimating our tax benefits, which may require periodic adjustments and which may not accurately forecast actual outcomes. We include interest and penalties related to our tax contingencies in income tax expense.

Note 6—Other Long-Term Liabilities (in part)

Our other long-term liabilities are summarized as follows (in millions):

	December 31,	
	2015	2014
Long-term capital lease obligations	$4,212	$3,026
Long-term finance lease obligations	1,736	1,198
Construction liabilities	378	467
Tax contingencies	932	510
Long-term deferred tax liabilities	1,084	1,021
Other	1,584	1,188
Total other long-term liabilities	$9,926	$7,410

	December 31, 2015
Gross finance lease obligations	$2,390
Less imputed interest	(555)
Present value of net minimum lease payments	1,835
Less current portion of finance lease obligations	(99)
Total long-term finance lease obligations	$1,736

Tax Contingencies

We have recorded tax reserves for tax contingencies, inclusive of accrued interest and penalties, for U.S. and foreign income taxes. These contingencies primarily relate to transfer pricing, state income taxes, and research and development credits. See "Note 10—Income Taxes" for discussion of tax contingencies.

Note 7—Commitments and Contingencies (in part)

Commitments

We have entered into non-cancellable operating, capital, and finance leases for equipment and office, fulfillment, sortation, delivery, data center, and renewable energy facilities. Rental expense under operating lease agreements was $1.1 billion, $961 million, and $759 million for 2015, 2014, and 2013.

The following summarizes our principal contractual commitments, excluding open orders for purchases that support normal operations, as of December 31, 2015 (in millions):

	Year Ended December 31,						
	2016	2017	2018	2019	2020	Thereafter	Total
Debt principal and interest	$ 526	$1,322	$ 310	$1,272	$ 246	$ 9,157	$12,833
Capital lease obligations, including interest	3,128	2,521	1,277	304	139	83	7,452
Finance lease obligations, including interest	166	168	172	176	178	1,530	2,390
Operating leases	1,181	897	800	698	616	2,325	6,517
Unconditional purchase obligations[1]	614	547	399	166	43	13	1,782
Other commitments[2] [3]	851	273	188	132	86	1,112	2,642
Total commitments	$6,466	$5,728	$3,146	$2,748	$1,308	$14,220	$33,616

[1] Includes unconditional purchase obligations related to long-term agreements to acquire and license digital media content that are not reflected on the consolidated balance sheets. For those agreements with variable terms, we do not estimate the total obligation beyond any minimum quantities and/or pricing as of the reporting date. Purchase obligations associated with renewal provisions solely at the option of the content provider are included to the extent such commitments are fixed or a minimum amount is specified.

[2] Includes the estimated timing and amounts of payments for rent and tenant improvements associated with build-to-suit lease arrangements that have not been placed in service and digital media content liabilities associated with long-term digital media content assets with initial terms greater than one year.

[3] Excludes $1.2 billion of tax contingencies for which we cannot make a reasonably reliable estimate of the amount and period of payment, if any.

Note 10—Income Taxes (in part)

Tax Contingencies

We are subject to income taxes in the U.S. (federal and state) and numerous foreign jurisdictions. Significant judgment is required in evaluating our tax positions and determining our provision for income taxes. During the ordinary course of business, there are many transactions and calculations for which the ultimate tax determination is uncertain. We establish reserves for tax-related uncertainties based on estimates of whether, and the extent to which, additional taxes will be due. These reserves are established when we believe that certain positions might be challenged despite our belief that our tax return positions are fully supportable. We adjust these reserves in light of changing facts and circumstances, such as the outcome of tax audits. The provision for income taxes includes the impact of reserve provisions and changes to reserves that are considered appropriate.

The reconciliation of our tax contingencies is as follows (in millions):

	December 31,		
	2015	2014	2013
Gross tax contingencies—January 1	$ 710	$407	$294
Gross increases to tax positions in prior periods	254	351	78
Gross decreases to tax positions in prior periods	(22)	(50)	(18)
Gross increases to current period tax positions	242	20	54
Audit settlements paid	—	(16)	(1)
Lapse of statute of limitations	(3)	(2)	—
Gross tax contingencies—December 31[1]	$1,181	$710	$407

[1] As of December 31, 2015, we had $1.2 billion of tax contingencies, of which $882 million, if fully recognized, would decrease our effective tax rate.

As of December 31, 2015 and 2014, we had accrued interest and penalties, net of federal income tax benefit, related to tax contingencies of $59 million and $41 million. Interest and penalties, net of federal income tax benefit, recognized for the years ended December 31, 2015, 2014, and 2013 was $18 million, $8 million, and $8 million.

We are under examination, or may be subject to examination, by the Internal Revenue Service ("IRS") for the calendar year 2005 and thereafter. These examinations may lead to ordinary course adjustments or proposed adjustments to our taxes or our net operating losses with respect to years under examination as well as subsequent periods. As previously disclosed, we have received Notices of Proposed Adjustment from the IRS for transactions undertaken in the 2005 and 2006 calendar years relating to transfer pricing with our foreign subsidiaries. The IRS is seeking to increase our U.S. taxable income by an amount that would result in additional federal tax of approximately

$1.5 billion, subject to interest. To date, we have not resolved this matter administratively and are currently contesting it in U.S. Tax Court. We continue to disagree with these IRS positions and intend to defend ourselves vigorously in this matter. In addition to the risk of additional tax for 2005 and 2006 transactions, if this litigation is adversely determined or if the IRS were to seek transfer pricing adjustments of a similar nature for transactions in subsequent years, we could be subject to significant additional tax liabilities.

Certain of our subsidiaries are under examination or investigation or may be subject to examination or investigation by the French Tax Administration ("FTA") for calendar year 2006 and thereafter. These examinations may lead to ordinary course adjustments or proposed adjustments to our taxes. In September 2012, we received proposed tax assessment notices for calendar years 2006 through 2010 relating to the allocation of income between foreign jurisdictions. In June 2015, we received final tax collection notices for these years assessing additional French tax of €196 million, including interest and penalties through September 2012. We disagree with the assessment and intend to contest it vigorously. We plan to pursue all available administrative remedies at the FTA, and if we are not able to resolve this matter with the FTA, we plan to pursue judicial remedies. In addition to the risk of additional tax for years 2006 through 2010, if this litigation is adversely determined or if the FTA were to seek adjustments of a similar nature for subsequent years, we could be subject to significant additional tax liabilities. In addition, in October 2014, the European Commission opened a formal investigation to examine whether decisions by the tax authorities in Luxembourg with regard to the corporate income tax paid by certain of our subsidiaries comply with European Union rules on state aid. If this matter is adversely resolved, Luxembourg may be required to assess, and we may be required to pay, additional amounts with respect to current and prior periods and our taxes in the future could increase. We are also subject to taxation in various states and other foreign jurisdictions including Canada, China, Germany, India, Japan, Luxembourg, and the United Kingdom. We are under, or may be subject to, audit or examination and additional assessments in respect of these particular jurisdictions for 2003 and thereafter.

We expect the total amount of tax contingencies will grow in 2016. In addition, changes in state, federal, and foreign tax laws may increase our tax contingencies. The timing of the resolution of income tax examinations is highly uncertain, and the amounts ultimately paid, if any, upon resolution of the issues raised by the taxing authorities may differ from the amounts accrued. It is reasonably possible that within the next 12 months we will receive additional assessments by various tax authorities or possibly reach resolution of income tax examinations in one or more jurisdictions. These assessments or settlements may or may not result in changes to our contingencies related to positions on tax filings in years through 2015. The actual amount of any change could vary significantly depending on the ultimate timing and nature of any settlements. We cannot currently provide an estimate of the range of possible outcomes.

ENVIRONMENTAL MATTERS

1.85 AXIALL CORPORATION (DEC)
NOTES TO CONSOLIDATED FINANCIAL STATEMENTS (in part)

1. Summary of Significant Accounting Policies and Nature of Business (in part)

Environmental Expenditures. Environmental expenditures related to current operations or future revenues are expensed or capitalized, consistent with our capitalization policy. Expenditures that relate to an existing condition caused by past operations and do not contribute to future revenues are expensed in the period incurred.

We monitor our estimate for reasonably possible environmental contingencies on a quarterly basis to determine if any of the reasonably possible environmental contingencies have become probable and estimable during the current quarter. It is our policy to accrue material expenses for environmental contingencies when management believes losses from the particular contingencies are probable and estimable. Reserves for environmental liabilities do not include any potential offsets related to claims against third parties.

12. Commitments and Contingencies (in part)

Legal Proceedings. We are involved in a number of contingencies incidental to the normal conduct of our business including lawsuits, claims and environmental contingencies. The outcome of these contingencies is inherently unpredictable. We believe that, in the aggregate, the outcome of all known contingencies including lawsuits, claims and environmental contingencies will not have a material adverse effect on our consolidated financial statements; however, specific outcomes with respect to such contingencies may be material to the consolidated financial statements of any particular period in which costs, if any, are recognized. Our assessment of the potential impact of environmental contingencies is subject to uncertainty due to the complex, ongoing and evolving process of investigation and remediation of such environmental contingencies, and the potential for technological and regulatory developments. In addition, the impact of evolving programs, such as natural resource damage claims, industrial site reuse initiatives and state remediation programs creates further uncertainty of the ultimate resolution of these environmental contingencies. We anticipate that the resolution of many contingencies, and in particular environmental contingencies, will occur over an extended period of time.

On December 20, 2013, a fire occurred at our PHH Monomers, LLC ("PHH") vinyl chloride monomer ("VCM") manufacturing plant in Lake Charles, Louisiana. As of December 31, 2015, approximately 2,607 individuals have lawsuits against the Company alleging personal injury or property damage related to the incident. We do not expect any other individuals to file lawsuits regarding this matter, as the prescribed deadline for doing so has expired. We have not recorded an accrual in connection with any of these lawsuits because, at this time, we are unable to reasonably determine whether any potential loss is probable or estimable. In addition, we currently are unable to provide a reasonable estimate of the potential loss or range of loss, if any, expected to result from this contingency. We are unable to make these determinations due to a number of variables, including without limitation, uncertainties related to: (i) the fact that no written or oral discovery has been conducted by the Company in any of these lawsuits; (ii) the parties' respective litigation strategies; (iii) the fact that none of the complaints have alleged specific injuries or a specific amount of damages; (iv) any symptoms experienced by any of the plaintiffs, and whether there will be any reliable information, documentation or other discovery related thereto; (v) the pre-and-post fire medical or physical condition of the plaintiffs, and whether there will be any reliable information, documentation or other discovery related thereto; and (vi) the location of any plaintiff at the time of the fire, and the duration of any exposure related thereto, and whether there will be any reliable information, documentation or other discovery related thereto.

Environmental Remediation. Our operations and assets are subject to extensive environmental, health and safety regulations, including laws and regulations related to air emissions, water discharges, waste disposal and remediation of contaminated sites, at both the national and local levels in the United States. We are also subject to similar laws and regulations in Canada and other jurisdictions in which we operate. The nature of the chemical and building products industries exposes us to risks of liability under these laws and regulations due to the production, storage, use, transportation and sale of materials that can cause contamination or personal injury, including, in the case of chemicals, potential releases into the environment. Environmental laws may have a significant effect on the costs of use, transportation and storage of raw materials and finished products, as well as the costs of the storage and disposal of wastes. We have incurred and will continue to incur substantial operating and capital costs to comply with environmental laws and regulations. In addition, we may incur substantial costs, including fines, damages, criminal or civil sanctions and remediation costs, or experience interruptions in our operations for violations arising under these laws and regulations.

As of December 31, 2015 and 2014, we had reserves for environmental contingencies totaling approximately $41 million and $54 million, respectively, of which approximately $1 million and $12 million, respectively, were classified as current liabilities. Our assessment of the potential impact of these environmental contingencies is subject to considerable uncertainty due to the complex, ongoing and evolving process of investigation and remediation, if necessary, of such environmental contingencies, and the potential for technological and regulatory developments.

Some of our significant environmental contingencies include the following matters:
- We have entered into a Cooperative Agreement with the Louisiana Department of Environmental Quality ("LDEQ") and various other parties for the environmental remediation of a portion of the Bayou d'Inde area of the Calcasieu River Estuary in Lake Charles, Louisiana. Remedy implementation began in the fourth quarter of 2014 and is expected to be completed during 2016 with a period of monitoring for remedy effectiveness to follow remediation. As of December 31, 2015 and 2014, we have reserved approximately $4 million and $18 million, respectively, for the costs associated with this matter. The decrease in the amount of this reserve is primarily due to spending against the reserve.
- As of December 31, 2015 and 2014 we had reserved approximately $12 million and $15 million, respectively, for environmental contingencies related to on-site remediation at the Lake Charles South Facility, principally for ongoing remediation of groundwater and soil in connection with our corrective action permit issued pursuant to the Hazardous and Solid Waste Amendments of the Resource Conservation and Recovery Act. The remedial activity is primarily related to the operation of a series of well water treatment systems across the Lake Charles South Facility. In addition, remediation of possible soil contamination will be conducted in certain areas. These remedial activities are expected to continue for an extended period of time. The reduction in the amount of this reserve is due to our assessment, during the year ended December 31, 2015, of the estimated costs to be incurred after December 31, 2015 to conduct this on-going remedial activity, and in particular, our assessment of the portion of the future operating costs of certain water treatment assets at our Lake Charles South Facility that should be allocated to this remediation project, as opposed to other non-remediation uses of those water treatment assets.
- As of December 31, 2015 and 2014, we had reserved approximately $18 million and $15 million, respectively, for environmental contingencies related to remediation activities at our Natrium, West Virginia facility (the "Natrium Facility"). The remedial actions address National Pollutant Discharge Elimination System permit requirements related primarily to hexachlorocyclohexane (commonly referred to as BHC) and mercury. We expect that these remedial actions will be in place for an extended period of time. The increase in the amount of this reserve is due to our assessment, during the year ended December 31, 2015, of the estimated costs that will be incurred after December 31, 2015 to conduct this on-going remedial activity, and in particular, due to an increase in the estimated duration of the remediation period.

Environmental Laws and Regulations. Due to the nature of environmental laws, regulations and liabilities, it is possible that we may not have identified all potentially adverse conditions. Such conditions may not currently exist or be detectable through reasonable methods, or may not be estimable. For example, our Natrium Facility and Lake Charles South Facility have both been in operation for over 65 years. There may be significant latent liabilities or future claims arising from the operation of facilities of this age, and we may be required to incur material future remediation or other costs in connection with future actions or developments at these or other facilities.

We expect to be continually subjected to increasingly stringent environmental and health and safety laws and regulations, and that continued compliance will require increased capital expenditures and increased operating costs or may impose restrictions on our present or future operations. It is difficult to predict the future interpretation and development of these laws and regulations or their impact on our future earnings and operations. Any increase in these costs, or any material restrictions on our ability to operate or the manner in which we operate, could materially adversely affect our liquidity, financial condition and results of operations. However, estimated costs for future environmental compliance and remediation may be materially lower than actual costs, or we may not be able to quantify potential costs in advance. Actual costs related to any environmental compliance in excess of estimated costs could have a material adverse effect on our financial condition in one or more future periods.

Heightened interest in environmental regulation, such as climate change issues, has the potential to materially impact our costs and present and future operations. We, and other chemical companies, are currently required to file certain governmental reports relating to greenhouse gas ("GHG") emissions. The U.S. Government has considered, and may in the future implement restrictions or other controls on GHG emissions, any of which could require us to incur significant capital expenditures or further restrict our present or future operations.

In addition to GHG regulations, the United States Environmental Protection Agency (the "EPA") has recently taken certain actions to limit or control certain pollutants created by companies such as ours. For example:
- In January 2013, the EPA issued Clean Air Act emission standards for boilers and incinerators (the "Boiler MACT regulations"), which are aimed at controlling emissions of toxic air contaminants at covered facilities. The coal fired power plant at our Natrium Facility is our source most significantly impacted by the Boiler MACT regulations. Pursuant to an extension granted by the West Virginia Department of Environmental Protection (WVDEP), we expect to comply with the requirements of the Boiler MACT regulations on or before December 2016.
- In April 2012, the EPA issued final regulations to update emissions limits for polyvinyl chloride ("PVC") and copolymer production (the "PVC MACT regulation"). The PVC MACT regulation sets standards for major sources of PVC production and establishes certain working practices, as well as monitoring, reporting and record-keeping requirements. Following the issuance of the PVC MACT regulation, a variety of legal challenges were filed by the vinyl industry's trade organization, several vinyl manufacturers and several environmental groups. Most of these challenges have been resolved; however, there are several petitions to reconsider certain provision in the rule that are still pending. We anticipate that some of these provisions will likely be changed as a result of these petitions, and there could be significant changes from the currently existing PVC MACT regulation after all legal challenges have been exhausted. These changes could require us to incur further capital expenditures, or increase our operating costs, to levels significantly higher than what we have previously estimated.
- In March 2011, the EPA proposed amendments to the emission standards for hazardous air pollutants for mercury emissions from mercury cell chlor-alkali plants. These proposed amendments would require improvements in work practices to reduce fugitive mercury emissions and would result in reduced levels of mercury emissions while still allowing the mercury cell facilities to continue to operate. We operate a mercury cell production unit at our Natrium Facility. No assurances as to the timing or content of the final regulation, or its ultimate cost to, or impact on us, can be provided.

The potential impact of these and/or unrelated future, legislative or regulatory actions on our current or future operations cannot be predicted at this time but could be significant. Such impacts could include the potential for significant compliance costs, including capital expenditures, which could result in operating restrictions or could require us to incur significant legal or other costs related to compliance or other activities. For example, a recent revision to ambient air quality standards for ozone may, in the future, result in significant operating costs, compliance costs, and capital expenditures at some of our facilities. Any increase in the costs related to these initiatives, or restrictions on our operations, could materially adversely affect our liquidity, financial condition or results of operations.

Environmental Remediation: Reasonably Possible Matters. Our assessment of the potential impact of environmental contingencies is subject to considerable uncertainty due to the complex, ongoing and evolving process of investigation and remediation, if necessary, of such environmental contingencies, and the potential for technological and regulatory developments. As such, in addition to the amounts currently reserved, we may be subject to reasonably possible loss contingencies related to environmental matters in the range of $40 million to $80 million.

1.86 COMMUNITY HEALTH SYSTEMS, INC. (DEC)
NOTES TO CONSOLIDATED FINANCIAL STATEMENTS (in part)

17. Commitments and Contingencies (in part)

Professional Liability Claims. As part of the Company's business of owning and operating hospitals, it is subject to legal actions alleging liability on its part. The Company accrues for losses resulting from such liability claims, as well as loss adjustment expenses that are out-of-pocket and directly related to such liability claims. These direct out-of-pocket expenses include fees of outside counsel and experts. The Company does not accrue for costs that are part of corporate overhead, such as the costs of in-house legal and risk management departments. The losses resulting from professional liability claims primarily consist of estimates for known claims, as well as estimates for incurred but not reported claims. The estimates are based on specific claim facts, historical claim reporting and payment patterns, the nature and level of hospital operations and actuarially determined projections. The actuarially determined projections are based on the Company's actual claim data, including historic reporting and payment patterns which have been gathered over an approximate 20-year period. As discussed below, since the Company purchases excess insurance on a claims-made basis that transfers risk to third-party insurers, the liability it accrues does include an amount for the losses covered by its excess insurance. The Company also records a receivable for the expected reimbursement of losses covered by excess insurance. Since the Company believes that the amount and timing of its future claims payments are reliably determinable, it discounts the amount accrued for losses resulting from professional liability claims using the risk-free interest rate corresponding to the timing of expected payments.

The net present value of the projected payments was discounted using a weighted-average risk-free rate of 1.6%, 1.7% and 1.6% in 2015, 2014 and 2013, respectively. This liability is adjusted for new claims information in the period such information becomes known. The Company's estimated liability for professional and general liability claims was $901 million and $924 million as of December 31, 2015 and 2014, respectively. The estimated undiscounted claims liability was $949 million and $964 million as of December 31, 2015 and 2014, respectively. The current portion of the liability for professional and general liability claims was $156 million and $164 million as of December 31, 2015 and 2014, respectively, and is included in other accrued liabilities in the accompanying consolidated balance sheets, with the long-term portion recorded in other long-term liabilities. Professional malpractice expense includes the losses resulting from professional liability claims and loss adjustment expense, as well as paid excess insurance premiums, and is presented within other operating expenses in the accompanying consolidated statements of income.

The Company's processes for obtaining and analyzing claims and incident data are standardized across all of its hospitals and have been consistent for many years. The Company monitors the outcomes of the medical care services that it provides and for each reported claim, the Company obtains various information concerning the facts and circumstances related to that claim. In addition, the Company routinely monitors current key statistics and volume indicators in its assessment of utilizing historical trends. The average lag period between claim occurrence and payment of a final settlement is between four and five years, although the facts and circumstances of individual claims could result in the timing of such payments being different from this average. Since claims are paid promptly after settlement with the claimant is reached, settled claims represent less than 1.0% of the total liability at the end of any period.

For purposes of estimating its individual claim accruals, the Company utilizes specific claim information, including the nature of the claim, the expected claim amount, the year in which the claim occurred and the laws of the jurisdiction in which the claim occurred. Once the case accruals for known claims are determined, information is stratified by loss layers and retentions, accident years, reported years, geography and claims relating to the acquired HMA hospitals versus claims relating to the Company's other hospitals. Several actuarial methods are used against this data to produce estimates of ultimate paid losses and reserves for incurred but not reported claims. Each of these methods uses company-specific historical claims data and other information. This company-specific data includes information regarding the Company's business, including historical paid losses and loss adjustment expenses, historical and current case loss reserves, actual and projected hospital statistical data, a variety of hospital census information, employed physician information, professional liability retentions for each policy year, geographic information and other data.

Based on these analyses the Company determines its estimate of the professional liability claims. The determination of management's estimate, including the preparation of the reserve analysis that supports such estimate, involves subjective judgment of the management. Changes in reserving data or the trends and factors that influence reserving data may signal fundamental shifts in the Company's future claim development patterns or may simply reflect single-period anomalies. Even if a change reflects a fundamental shift, the full extent of the change may not become evident until years later. Moreover, since the Company's methods and models use different types of data and the Company selects its liability from the results of all of these methods, it typically cannot quantify the precise impact of such factors on its estimates of the liability. Due to the Company's standardized and consistent processes for handling claims and the long history and depth of company-specific data, the Company's methodologies have produced reliably determinable estimates of ultimate paid losses.

The Company is primarily self-insured for professional liability claims; however, the Company obtains excess insurance that transfers the risk of loss to a third-party insurer for claims in excess of self-insured retentions. The Company's excess insurance is underwritten on a claims-made basis. For claims reported prior to June 1, 2002, substantially all of the Company's professional and general liability risks were subject to a less than $1 million per occurrence self-insured retention and for claims reported from June 1, 2002 through June 1, 2003, these self-insured retentions were $2 million per occurrence. Substantially all claims reported after June 1, 2003 and before June 1, 2005 are self-insured up to $4 million per claim. Substantially all claims reported on or after June 1, 2005 and before June 1, 2014 are self-insured up to $5 million per claim. Substantially all claims reported on or after June 1, 2014 are self-insured up to $10 million per claim. Management on occasion has selectively increased the insured risk at certain hospitals based upon insurance pricing and other factors and may continue that practice in the future. Excess insurance for all hospitals has been purchased through commercial insurance companies and generally covers the Company for liabilities in excess of the self-insured retentions. The excess coverage consists of multiple layers of insurance, the sum of which totals up to $95 million per occurrence and in the aggregate for claims reported on or after June 1, 2003, up to $145 million per occurrence and in the aggregate for claims reported on or after January 1, 2008, up to $195 million per occurrence and in the aggregate for claims reported on or after June 1, 2010, and up to $220 million per occurrence and in the aggregate for claims reported on or after June 1, 2015. In addition, for integrated occurrence malpractice claims, there is an additional $50 million of excess coverage for claims reported on or after June 1, 2014 and an additional $75 million of excess coverage for claims reported on or after June 1, 2015. For certain policy years prior to June 1, 2014, if the first aggregate layer of excess coverage becomes fully utilized, then the Company's self-insured retention will increase to $10 million per claim for any subsequent claims in that policy year until the Company's total aggregate coverage is met.

Effective June 1, 2014, the hospitals acquired from HMA were insured on a claims-made basis as described above and through commercial insurance companies as described above for substantially all claims reported on or after June 1, 2014 except for physician-related claims with an occurrence date prior to June 1, 2014. Prior to June 1, 2014, the former HMA hospitals obtained insurance coverage through a wholly-owned captive insurance subsidiary and a risk retention group subsidiary which are domiciled in the Cayman Islands and South Carolina, respectively. Those insurance subsidiaries, which are collectively referred to as the "Insurance Subsidiaries," provided (i) claims-made coverage to all of the former HMA hospitals and (ii) occurrence-basis coverage to most of the physicians employed by the former HMA hospitals. The employed physicians not covered by the Insurance Subsidiaries generally maintained claims-made policies with unrelated third party insurance companies. To mitigate the exposure of the program covering the former HMA hospitals and other healthcare facilities, the Insurance Subsidiaries bought claims-made reinsurance policies from unrelated third parties for claims above self-retention levels of $10 million or $15 million per claim, depending on the policy year.

Effective January 1, 2008, the hospitals acquired from Triad were insured on a claims-made basis as described above and through commercial insurance companies as described above for substantially all claims occurring on or after January 1, 2002 and reported on or after January 1, 2008. Substantially all losses for the former Triad hospitals in periods prior to May 1, 1999 were insured through a wholly-owned insurance subsidiary of HCA, Triad's owner prior to that time, and excess loss policies maintained by HCA. HCA has agreed to indemnify the former Triad hospitals in respect of claims covered by such insurance policies arising prior to May 1, 1999. After May 1, 1999 through December 31, 2006, the former Triad hospitals obtained insurance coverage on a claims incurred basis from HCA's wholly-owned insurance subsidiary, with excess coverage obtained from other carriers that is subject to certain deductibles. Effective for claims incurred after December 31, 2006, Triad began insuring its claims from $1 million to $5 million through its wholly-owned captive insurance company, replacing the coverage provided by HCA. Substantially all claims occurring during 2007 were self-insured up to $10 million per claim.

GOVERNMENT MATTERS

1.87 JOHNSON & JOHNSON (DEC)
NOTES TO CONSOLIDATED FINANCIAL STATEMENTS (in part)

21. Legal Proceedings (in part)

Johnson & Johnson and certain of its subsidiaries are involved in various lawsuits and claims regarding product liability, intellectual property, commercial and other matters; governmental investigations; and other legal proceedings that arise from time to time in the ordinary course of their business.

The Company records accruals for loss contingencies associated with these legal matters when it is probable that a liability will be incurred and the amount of the loss can be reasonably estimated. As of January 3, 2016, the Company has determined that the liabilities associated with certain litigation matters are probable and can be reasonably estimated. The Company has accrued for these matters and will continue to monitor each related legal issue and adjust accruals as might be warranted based on new information and further developments in accordance with ASC 450-20-25. For these and other litigation and regulatory matters discussed below for which a loss is probable or reasonably possible, the Company is unable to estimate the possible loss or range of loss beyond the amounts already accrued. Amounts accrued for legal contingencies often result from a complex series of judgments about future events and uncertainties that rely heavily on estimates and assumptions. The ability to make such estimates and judgments can be affected by various factors, including whether damages sought in the proceedings are unsubstantiated or indeterminate; scientific and legal discovery has not commenced or is not complete; proceedings are in early stages; matters present legal uncertainties; there are significant facts in dispute; or there are numerous parties involved.

In the Company's opinion, based on its examination of these matters, its experience to date and discussions with counsel, the ultimate outcome of legal proceedings, net of liabilities accrued in the Company's balance sheet, is not expected to have a material adverse effect on the Company's financial position. However, the resolution of, or increase in accruals for, one or more of these matters in any reporting period may have a material adverse effect on the Company's results of operations and cash flows for that period.

Government Proceedings

Like other companies in the pharmaceutical and medical devices industries, Johnson & Johnson and certain of its subsidiaries are subject to extensive regulation by national, state and local government agencies in the United States and other countries in which they operate. As a result, interaction with government agencies is ongoing. The most significant litigation brought by, and investigations conducted by, government agencies are listed below. It is possible that criminal charges and substantial fines and/or civil penalties or damages could result from government investigations or litigation.

Average Wholesale Price (AWP) Litigation

Johnson & Johnson and several of its pharmaceutical subsidiaries (the J&J AWP Defendants), along with numerous other pharmaceutical companies, are defendants in a series of lawsuits in state and federal courts involving allegations that the pricing and marketing of certain pharmaceutical products amounted to fraudulent and otherwise actionable conduct because, among other things, the companies allegedly reported an inflated Average Wholesale Price (AWP) for the drugs at issue. Payors alleged that they used those AWPs in calculating provider reimbursement levels. Many of these cases, both federal actions and state actions removed to federal court, were consolidated for pre-trial purposes in a Multi-District Litigation (MDL) in the United States District Court for the District of Massachusetts.

The plaintiffs in these cases included three classes of private persons or entities that paid for any portion of the purchase of the drugs at issue based on AWP, and state government entities that made Medicaid payments for the drugs at issue based on AWP. In June 2007, after a trial on the merits, the MDL Court dismissed the claims of two of the plaintiff classes against the J&J AWP Defendants. In March 2011, the Court dismissed the claims of the third class against the J&J AWP Defendants without prejudice.

AWP cases brought by various Attorneys General have proceeded to trial against other manufacturers. Several state cases against certain subsidiaries of Johnson & Johnson have been settled, including the case in Alaska, which settled in April 2014, and cases are still pending in Illinois, New Jersey, Wisconsin and Utah. The cases in Illinois, New Jersey and Wisconsin have not yet proceeded to trial. In Utah, the claims brought by the Attorney General were dismissed by the Court in 2013, but the State may appeal the dismissal after the conclusion of similar pending matters against other defendants. The AWP case against the J&J AWP Defendants brought by the Attorney General of the Commonwealth of Pennsylvania was tried in Commonwealth Court in 2010. The Court found in the Commonwealth's favor with regard to certain of its claims under the Pennsylvania Unfair Trade Practices and Consumer Protection Law ("UTPL"), entered an injunction, and awarded $45 million in restitution and $6.5 million in civil penalties. The Court found in the J&J AWP Defendants' favor on the Commonwealth's claims of unjust enrichment, misrepresentation/fraud, civil conspiracy, and on certain of the Commonwealth's claims under the UTPL. The J&J AWP Defendants appealed the Commonwealth Court's UTPL ruling, and in June 2014, the Pennsylvania Supreme Court vacated the judgment entered by the Commonwealth Court and remanded the case for further proceedings. On remand, in January 2015, the Commonwealth Court dismissed the monetary awards against the J&J AWP Defendants. In March 2015, the ruling was appealed back to the Pennsylvania Supreme Court. In December 2015, the Pennsylvania Supreme Court affirmed the Order of the Commonwealth Court dismissing the monetary awards against the J&J AWP Defendants.

RISPERDAL®

In November 2013, Johnson & Johnson and its subsidiary, Janssen Pharmaceuticals, Inc. (JPI), finalized previously disclosed settlement agreements with the United States Department of Justice and forty-five states resolving federal investigations and state Medicaid claims related to past promotional practices of RISPERDAL® from 1999 through 2005, and other matters. JPI had also settled alleged consumer fraud claims in connection with the sale and marketing of RISPERDAL® with thirty-six states and the District of Columbia in September 2012. In addition to these actions, the Attorneys General of several states brought actions against JPI, related to the sale and marketing of RISPERDAL®, seeking one or more of the following remedies: reimbursement of Medicaid or other public funds for RISPERDAL® prescriptions written for off-label use, compensation for treating their citizens for alleged adverse reactions to RISPERDAL®, civil fines or penalties for violations of state false claims acts or consumer fraud statutes, punitive damages, or other relief relating to alleged unfair business practices. Certain of these actions also sought injunctive relief relating to the promotion of RISPERDAL®. Many of the actions and claims brought by the state Attorneys General have been settled, either individually or as part of the settlements described above. The cases brought by the Attorneys General of Mississippi and Kentucky were settled in December 2015, without any admission of wrongdoing on the part of JPI. State cases that went to judgment after trial are discussed below.

In 2004, the Attorney General of West Virginia commenced a lawsuit against Janssen Pharmaceutica, Inc. (now JPI) based on claims of alleged consumer fraud as to DURAGESIC®, as well as RISPERDAL®. JPI was found liable and damages were assessed at $4.5 million. JPI filed an appeal, and in November 2010, the West Virginia Supreme Court of Appeals reversed the trial court's decision. In December 2010, the Attorney General of West Virginia dismissed the case as it related to RISPERDAL® without any payment. Thereafter, JPI settled the case insofar as it related to DURAGESIC®.

In 2004, the Attorney General of Louisiana filed a multi-count Complaint against Janssen Pharmaceutica, Inc. (now JPI). Johnson & Johnson was later added as a defendant. The case was tried in October 2010. The issue tried to the jury was whether Johnson & Johnson or JPI had violated the State's Medical Assistance Program Integrity Law (the Act) through misrepresentations allegedly made in the mailing of a November 2003 Dear Health Care Professional letter regarding RISPERDAL®. The jury returned a verdict that JPI and Johnson & Johnson had violated the Act and awarded $257.7 million in damages. The trial judge subsequently awarded the Attorney General counsel fees and expenses in the amount of $73 million. In January 2014, the Louisiana Supreme Court reversed the District Court's judgment in favor of the Attorney General, and rendered judgment in favor of Johnson & Johnson and JPI. In April 2014, the Louisiana Supreme Court denied the Attorney General's petition seeking a rehearing of the appellate arguments, resulting in final dismissal of the case.

In 2007, the Office of General Counsel of the Commonwealth of Pennsylvania filed a lawsuit against Janssen Pharmaceutica, Inc. (now JPI) on a multi-Count Complaint related to Janssen Pharmaceutica's sale of RISPERDAL® to the Commonwealth's Medicaid program. The trial occurred in June 2010. The trial judge dismissed the case after the close of the plaintiff's evidence. The Commonwealth filed an appeal and in July 2012, the Pennsylvania Appeals Court upheld the dismissal of the Commonwealth's case.

In 2007, the Attorney General of South Carolina filed a lawsuit against Johnson & Johnson and Janssen Pharmaceutica, Inc. (now JPI) on several counts. In March 2011, the matter was tried to a jury on liability only, at which time the lawsuit was limited to claims of violation of the South Carolina Unfair Trade Practices Act, including, among others, questions of whether Johnson & Johnson or JPI engaged in unfair or deceptive acts or practices in the conduct of any trade or commerce by distributing the November 2003 Dear Health Care Professional letter regarding RISPERDAL® or in their use of the product's FDA-approved label. The jury found in favor of Johnson & Johnson and against JPI. In June 2011, the Court awarded civil penalties of approximately $327.1 million against JPI. JPI appealed this judgment and in February 2015, the South Carolina Supreme Court affirmed the trial court's decision in part, reversed it in part and remanded the case back to the trial court. The net effect of the decision was to reduce the judgment to approximately $136 million, plus interest. In the first fiscal quarter of 2015, the Company accrued $136 million. In March 2015, JPI filed a Petition for Rehearing. In July 2015, the South Carolina Supreme Court granted the Petition and filed a substituted opinion. The new opinion reduced the judgment from approximately $136 million to approximately $124 million. In January 2016, the United States Supreme Court denied JPI's request for review, putting an end to this case.

In April 2012, in the lawsuit brought by the Attorney General of Arkansas, the jury found against both JPI and Johnson & Johnson, and the Court imposed penalties in the amount of approximately $1.2 billion. In January 2013, the trial court awarded attorney fees of approximately $181 million. JPI and Johnson & Johnson appealed both awards to the Arkansas Supreme Court, and in March 2014, the Arkansas Supreme Court dismissed the State's claim under the Arkansas Medicaid Fraud False Claims Act, as well as the approximately $1.2 billion in penalties, and reversed and remanded a claim under the Arkansas Deceptive Trade Practices Act. In April 2014, the Arkansas Supreme Court rejected a petition by the State for rehearing on the case. In May 2015, the matter settled for $7.75 million.

McNeil Consumer Healthcare

Starting in June 2010, McNeil Consumer Healthcare Division of McNEIL-PPC, Inc. (now Johnson & Johnson Consumer Inc., McNeil Consumer Healthcare Division) (McNeil Consumer Healthcare) and certain affiliates, including Johnson & Johnson (the Companies), received grand jury subpoenas from the United States Attorney's Office for the Eastern District of Pennsylvania requesting documents broadly relating to recalls of various products of McNeil Consumer Healthcare, and the FDA inspections of the Fort Washington, Pennsylvania and Lancaster, Pennsylvania manufacturing facilities, as well as certain documents relating to recalls of a small number of products of other subsidiaries. In addition, in February 2011, the government served McNEIL-PPC, Inc. (McNEIL-PPC) with a Civil Investigative Demand seeking records relevant to its investigation to determine if there was a violation of the Federal False Claims Act. In March 2015, McNEIL-PPC entered a guilty plea in the United States District Court for the Eastern District of Pennsylvania to a misdemeanor violation of the U.S. Food, Drug and Cosmetic Act. McNEIL- PPC agreed to pay a $20 million fine and a $5 million forfeiture to resolve the matter.

The Companies have also received Civil Investigative Demands from multiple State Attorneys General Offices broadly relating to the McNeil recall issues. The Companies continue to cooperate with these inquiries, which are being coordinated through a multi-state coalition. If a resolution cannot be reached with this multi-state coalition, it is possible that individual State Attorneys General Offices may file civil monetary claims against the Companies. In January 2011, the Oregon Attorney General filed a civil complaint against Johnson & Johnson, McNEIL-PPC and McNeil Healthcare LLC in state court alleging civil violations of the Oregon Unlawful Trade Practices Act relating to an earlier recall of a McNeil OTC product. In November 2012, the state court granted a motion by the Companies to dismiss Oregon's complaint in its entirety, with prejudice, and Oregon appealed that decision. In November 2015, the Court of Appeals of the State of Oregon reversed the trial court and reinstated Oregon's consumer protection claims. In December 2015, the Companies filed a petition for review with the Oregon Supreme Court.

Opioids Litigation

Along with other pharmaceutical companies, Johnson & Johnson (J&J) and Janssen Pharmaceuticals, Inc. (JPI) have been named in two lawsuits alleging claims related to marketing of opioids, including DURAGESIC®, NUCYNTA® and NUCYNTA® ER. In May 2014, Santa Clara and Orange Counties in California (the Counties) filed a complaint in state court in Orange County, California against numerous pharmaceutical manufacturers, including J&J and JPI, alleging claims related to opioid marketing practices, including false advertising, unfair competition, and public nuisance. The Counties seek injunctive and monetary relief. In February 2015, the defendants filed motions challenging the sufficiency of the complaint. In August 2015, the Court stayed the case until the FDA concludes its ongoing inquiry into the safety and effectiveness of long-term opioid treatment.

In June 2014, the City of Chicago filed a complaint in Cook County Circuit Court against the same group of pharmaceutical manufacturers, including J&J and JPI, alleging a number of claims related to opioid marketing practices, including consumer fraud violations and false claims, and seeking injunctive and monetary relief. The case was later removed to the United States District Court for the Northern District of Illinois, and in December 2014, J&J and JPI filed a motion to dismiss the City of Chicago's First Amended Complaint for failure to state a claim. In November 2015, J&J and JPI filed a motion to dismiss the City of Chicago's Second Amended Complaint for failure to state a claim.

In September 2014, the Tennessee Attorney General Division of Consumer Affairs issued a Request for Information to JPI and other pharmaceutical companies related to opioids marketing practices.

In August 2015, the New Hampshire Attorney General, Consumer Protection and Antitrust Bureau issued a subpoena to JPI and other pharmaceutical companies related to opioids marketing practices. JPI objected to private contingent fee counsel's participation in the investigation on the State's behalf, and in October 2015, the State moved to enforce the subpoena.

In December 2015, the State of Mississippi filed a complaint in the Chancery Court of the First Judicial District of Hinds County against the same group of pharmaceutical manufacturers, including J&J and JPI, alleging a number of claims related to opioid marketing practices. The State of Mississippi is seeking penalties and injunctive and monetary relief.

Other

In September 2011, Synthes, Inc. (Synthes) received a Civil Investigative Demand issued pursuant to the False Claims Act from the United States Attorney's Office for the Eastern District of Pennsylvania. The Demand sought information regarding allegations that fellowships had been offered to hospitals in exchange for agreements to purchase products. Synthes has produced documents and information in response to the Demand and is cooperating with the inquiry.

In May 2012, Acclarent, Inc. (Acclarent) received a subpoena from the United States Attorney's Office for the District of Massachusetts requesting documents broadly relating to the sales, marketing and alleged off-label promotion by Acclarent of the RELIEVA STRATUS® MicroFlow Spacer product (the STRATUS® Spacer). In April 2015, an Indictment was filed in the United States District Court for the District of Massachusetts charging the former President/CEO and Vice President of Sales of Acclarent (the former Acclarent officers). The Indictment charges the former Acclarent officers with various violations related to the off-label promotion of the STRATUS® Spacer. The allegations against the former Acclarent officers relate to the development, sale and marketing of the STRATUS® Spacer, as well as actions allegedly taken by the former Acclarent officers in connection with the acquisition of Acclarent by Ethicon, Inc. in 2010. There are no charges against Acclarent, Ethicon, Inc. or Johnson & Johnson.

In August 2012, DePuy Orthopaedics, Inc., DePuy, Inc. (now DePuy Synthes, Inc.), and Johnson & Johnson Services, Inc. (the Companies) received an informal request from the United States Attorney's Office for the District of Massachusetts and the Civil Division of the United States Department of Justice (the United States) for the production of materials relating to the ASR™ XL Hip device. In July 2014, the United States notified the United States District Court for the District of Massachusetts that it had declined to intervene in a *qui tam* case filed pursuant to the False Claims Act against the Companies. The District Court issued an order in August 2014 that publicly unsealed the United States' declination notice; however, the complaint in the matter remains under seal. In addition, in October 2013, a group of state Attorneys General issued Civil Investigative Demands relating to the development, sales and marketing of several of DePuy Orthopaedics, Inc.'s hip products. In July 2014, the Oregon Department of Justice, which was investigating these matters independently of the other states, announced a settlement of its ASR™ XL Hip device investigation for a total payment of $4 million to the State of Oregon.

In October 2012, Johnson & Johnson was contacted by the California Attorney General's office regarding a multi-state Attorney General investigation of the marketing of surgical mesh products for hernia and urogynecological purposes by Johnson & Johnson's subsidiary, Ethicon, Inc. (Ethicon). Johnson & Johnson and Ethicon have since entered into a series of tolling agreements with the 47 states and the District of Columbia participating in the multi-state investigation and have responded to Civil Investigative Demands served by certain of the participating states. The states are seeking monetary and injunctive relief.

In December 2012, Therakos, Inc. (Therakos), formerly a subsidiary of Johnson & Johnson and part of the Ortho-Clinical Diagnostics, Inc. (OCD) franchise, received a letter from the civil division of the United States Attorney's Office for the Eastern District of Pennsylvania informing Therakos that the United States Attorney's Office was investigating the sales and marketing of Uvadex® (methoxsalen) and the Uvar Xts® System during the period 2000 to the present. The United States Attorney's Office requested that OCD and Johnson & Johnson preserve documents that could relate to the investigation. Therakos was subsequently acquired by an affiliate of Gores Capital Partners III, L.P. in January 2013. OCD and Johnson & Johnson retain certain liabilities that may result from the investigation for activity that occurred prior to the sale of Therakos. In March 2014, the United States Attorney's Office requested that Johnson & Johnson produce certain documents, and Johnson & Johnson is cooperating with the request. Following the divestiture of OCD, Johnson & Johnson retains OCD's portion of any liability that may result from the investigation for activity that occurred prior to the sale of Therakos.

In recent years, Johnson & Johnson has received numerous requests from a variety of United States Congressional Committees to produce information relevant to ongoing congressional inquiries. It is the policy of Johnson & Johnson to cooperate with these inquiries by producing the requested information.

WARRANTY

1.88 KB HOME (NOV)
NOTES TO CONSOLIDATED FINANCIAL STATEMENTS (in part)

Note 1. Summary of Significant Accounting Policies (in part)

Warranty Costs. We provide a limited warranty on all of our homes. We estimate the costs that may be incurred under each limited warranty and record a liability in the amount of such costs at the time the revenue associated with the sale of each home is recognized. Our primary assumption in estimating the amounts we accrue for warranty costs is that historical claims experience is a strong indicator of future claims experience. Factors that affect our warranty liability include the number of homes delivered, historical and anticipated rates of warranty claims, and cost per claim. We periodically assess the adequacy of our accrued warranty liability and adjust the amount as necessary based on our assessment.

Note 11. Accrued Expenses and Other Liabilities

Accrued expenses and other liabilities consisted of the following (in thousands):

	November 30,	
	2015	2014
Inventory-related obligations[a]	$148,887	$ 52,009
Employee compensation and related benefits	114,456	113,875
Self-insurance and other litigation liabilities	96,496	89,606
Accrued interest payable	62,645	63,275
Warranty liability	49,085	45,196
Customer deposits	14,563	15,197
Real estate and business taxes	14,255	13,684
Other	13,027	17,040
Total	$513,414	$409,882

[a] Represents liabilities for inventory not owned associated with financing arrangements discussed in Note 8. Variable Interest Entities, as well as liabilities for fixed or determinable amounts associated with TIFE assessments. As homes are delivered, the obligation to pay the remaining TIFE assessments associated with each underlying lot is transferred to the homebuyer. As such, these assessment obligations will be paid by us only to the extent we do not deliver homes on applicable lots before the related TIFE obligations mature.

Note 15. Commitments and Contingencies (in part)

Commitments and contingencies include typical obligations of homebuilders for the completion of contracts and those incurred in the ordinary course of business.

Warranty. We provide a limited warranty on all of our homes. The specific terms and conditions of our limited warranty program vary depending upon the markets in which we do business. We generally provide a structural warranty of 10 years, a warranty on electrical, heating, cooling, plumbing and certain other building systems each varying from two to five years based on geographic market and state law, and a warranty of one year for other components of the home. Our limited warranty program is ordinarily how we respond to and account for homeowners' requests to local division offices seeking repairs, including claims where we could have liability under applicable state statutes or tort law for a defective condition in or damages to a home.

We estimate the costs that may be incurred under each limited warranty and record a liability in the amount of such costs at the time the revenue associated with the sale of each home is recognized. Our primary assumption in estimating the amounts we accrue for warranty costs is that historical claims experience is a strong indicator of future claims experience. Factors that affect our warranty liability include the number of homes delivered, historical and anticipated rates of warranty claims, and cost per claim. We periodically assess the adequacy of our accrued warranty liability, which is included in accrued expenses and other liabilities in our consolidated balance sheets, and adjust the amount as necessary based on our assessment. Our assessment includes the review of our actual warranty costs incurred to identify trends and changes in our warranty claims experience, and considers our home construction quality and customer service initiatives and outside events. While we believe the warranty liability currently reflected in our consolidated balance sheets to be adequate, unanticipated changes or developments in the legal environment, local weather, land or environmental conditions, quality of materials or methods used in the construction of homes or customer service practices and our warranty claims experience could have a significant impact on our actual warranty costs in future periods and such amounts could differ significantly from our current estimates.

The changes in our warranty liability are as follows (in thousands):

| | Years Ended November 30, | | |
	2015	2014	2013
Balance at beginning of year	$ 45,196	$ 48,704	$ 47,822
Warranties issued	23,018	18,479	14,261
Payments	(26,367)	(39,458)	(45,338)
Adjustments[a]	7,238	17,471	31,959
Balance at end of year	$ 49,085	$ 45,196	$ 48,704

[a] As discussed below, adjustments in 2015 and 2014 were primarily comprised of the reclassification of estimated minimum probable recoveries to receivables. Adjustments in 2014 also included a reclassification of estimated minimum probable recoveries to establish a separate accrual for a water intrusion-related inquiry. Adjustments in 2013 were comprised of charges associated with water intrusion-related issues in central and southwest Florida.

<u>Central and Southwest Florida Claims.</u> Since 2012, we have received warranty claims from homeowners in certain of our communities in central and southwest Florida primarily involving framing, stucco, roofing and/or sealant matters on homes we delivered between 2003 and 2009, with many concerning water intrusion-related issues. Based on the status of our ongoing investigation and repair efforts with respect to homes affected by these water intrusion-related issues, our overall warranty liability at November 30, 2015, 2014 and 2013 included $2.2 million, $9.4 million and $28.9 million, respectively, for estimated remaining repair costs associated with (a) 69, 324 and 710 identified affected homes, respectively, and (b) similarly affected homes that we believed at each respective date may be identified in the future. The $2.2 million at November 30, 2015 encompasses what we believe to be the probable overall cost of the repair effort remaining with respect to affected homes before insurance and other recoveries. However, our actual costs to fully resolve repairs on affected homes could differ from the overall costs we have estimated depending on the identification of additional affected homes in future periods, if any, and the nature of the work that is undertaken to complete repairs on identified affected homes. In 2015, we resolved repairs on 356 identified affected homes and identified 101 additional affected homes. During 2014, we resolved repairs on 536 identified affected homes and identified 150 additional affected homes, most of which were in one attached home community. During 2013, repairs were resolved on 754 identified affected homes. We consider repairs for identified affected homes to be resolved when all repairs are completed and all repair costs are fully paid. In 2015, 2014 and 2013, we paid $8.4 million, $26.6 million and $32.7 million, respectively, to repair identified affected homes. Since first identifying affected homes in 2012, we have identified a total of 1,715 affected homes requiring more than minor repairs and resolved repairs on 1,646 of those homes through November 30, 2015. As of November 30, 2015, we had paid $71.7 million of the probable total repair costs of $73.9 million that we have estimated for the overall repair effort.

We believe it is probable that we will recover a portion of our repair costs associated with affected homes from various sources, including our insurers and independent subcontractors involved with the original construction of the homes and their insurers. In 2015 and 2014, we collected $7.0 million and $.9 million, respectively, of such recoveries. Based on a review of our estimated potential recoveries in 2015, we increased our estimate of minimum probable recoveries. As of November 30, 2015, our estimated minimum probable recoveries, net of amounts collected, totaled $20.6 million, of which $2.2 million was included as an offset to our overall warranty liability and the remainder was included in receivables. During 2014, we recorded adjustments to increase our warranty liability mainly to reflect additional affected homes identified at one attached home community and our updated estimate of repair costs on identified affected homes. We also recorded adjustments to increase our estimated minimum probable recoveries during the period based on our updated estimate of repair costs. Together, these items did not have an impact on our consolidated statement of operations for 2014. As of November 30, 2014, our estimated minimum probable recoveries, net of amounts collected, totaled $26.6 million, of which $9.4 million was included as an offset to our overall warranty liability and the remainder was included in receivables. As of November 30, 2013, our estimated minimum probable recoveries, all of which were included as an offset to our overall warranty liability, totaled $19.4 million. The estimated minimum probable recoveries pertaining to affected homes are included in receivables to the extent they exceed the estimated remaining repair costs in our overall warranty liability associated with such homes. During 2015 and 2014, we reclassified $7.2 million and $18.1 million, respectively, of estimated minimum probable recoveries that were in excess of the estimated remaining repair costs to a receivable. Our assessment of the water intrusion-related issues in central and southwest Florida, including the process of determining potentially responsible parties and our efforts to obtain recoveries, is ongoing, and as a result, our estimate of minimum probable recoveries may change as additional information is obtained.

In 2013, based on our assessment of our overall warranty liability, we recorded adjustments to increase our warranty liability by $32.0 million with a corresponding charge to construction and land costs in our consolidated statement of operations. The adjustments reflected our then-current estimate of remaining repair costs associated with homes in central and southwest Florida that had been identified as having water intrusion-related issues and our estimate of repair costs associated with similarly affected homes in central and southwest Florida then-believed likely to be identified in the future, net of an increase in estimated minimum probable recoveries of such repair costs and other adjustments.

Overall Warranty Liability Assessment. In assessing our overall warranty liability at a reporting date, we evaluate the costs for warranty-related items on a combined basis for all of our previously delivered homes that are under our limited warranty program, which would include homes in central and southwest Florida that have been or may in the future be identified as affected by water intrusion-related issues. Based on this evaluation, we believe our overall warranty liability as of November 30, 2015 is adequate. Depending on the number of additional homes in central and southwest Florida that are identified as affected by water intrusion-related issues, if any, and the actual costs we incur in future periods to repair such affected homes and/or homes affected by other issues, we may revise the amount of our estimated liability, which could result in an increase or decrease in our overall warranty liability. Based on our assessment of the water intrusion-related issues in central and southwest Florida, and the substantial wind down of these issues in 2015, we believe that our overall warranty liability as of November 30, 2015 is adequate to cover the estimated probable total repair costs with respect to affected homes.

Florida Attorney General's Office Inquiry. In 2013, we were notified by the Florida Attorney General's Office that it was making a preliminary inquiry into the status of our communities in Florida affected by water intrusion-related issues. We established an accrual for the estimated minimum probable loss with respect to this inquiry during 2014 and increased the accrual during 2015. We anticipate that this inquiry will be resolved through an agreement with the Florida Attorney General's Office, requiring approval by a Florida circuit court in order to become effective. We believe that the amount accrued for this matter is adequate as of November 30, 2015.

Guarantees. In the normal course of our business, we issue certain representations, warranties and guarantees related to our home and land sales. Based on historical evidence, we do not believe any potential liability with respect to these representations, warranties or guarantees would be material to our consolidated financial statements.

FAVORABLE TAX OUTCOME

1.89 UNIVERSAL CORPORATION (MAR)
NOTES TO CONSOLIDATED FINANCIAL STATEMENTS (in part)

(All dollar amounts are in thousands, except per share amounts or as otherwise noted.)

Note 3. European Commission Fines and Other Legal and Tax Matters (in part)

Other Legal and Tax Matters

In addition to the above-mentioned matter, various subsidiaries of the Company are involved in other litigation and tax examinations incidental to their business activities, including the assessments disclosed in Note 14 related to inter-state value added taxes in Brazil. While the outcome of these matters cannot be predicted with certainty, management is vigorously defending the matters and does not currently expect that any of them will have a material adverse effect on the Company's business or financial position. However, should one or more of these matters be resolved in a manner adverse to management's current expectation, the effect on the Company's results of operations for a particular fiscal reporting period could be material.

Note 14. Commitments and Other Matters (in part)

Favorable Outcome of IPI Tax Credit Case in Brazil

During the quarter ended June 30, 2013, a longstanding lawsuit related to IPI tax credits filed by the Company's operating subsidiary in Brazil was concluded in the subsidiary's favor with a decision by the Brazilian Superior Court of Justice on the final appeal filed by the Brazilian federal government. Although additional appeals by the government were expected in the case, the time period to file those appeals expired before the end of the quarter, and the decision and overall outcome of the case were confirmed.

IPI tax credits were established under Brazilian tax laws to allow recovery of a portion of the excise taxes paid on manufactured products when those products are sold in export markets. In prior years, the subsidiary paid excise taxes on the component cost of unprocessed tobacco purchased from growers, as well as the cost of electricity, packing materials, and other inputs used in its manufacturing process. Under the law, the subsidiary believed it was entitled to use IPI tax credits to recover excise taxes on the processed tobacco it exported. However, specific regulations issued by the Brazilian tax authorities did not permit the subsidiary to claim those credits. The suit filed by the subsidiary challenged the denial of the tax credits based on the law. Several decisions in lower courts were decided in the subsidiary's favor for a portion of the tax credits claimed in the suit, but those decisions were appealed on various grounds by both the government and the subsidiary. The expiration of the appeal period ended the matter in the courts.

The final court decision entitled the subsidiary to approximately $104 million of IPI tax credits (based on the exchange rate at the date of the decision), which can be used to offset future payments of other Brazilian federal taxes for a period of up to five years. That amount includes the tax credits generated over the period granted by the courts, as well as interest calculated from the date those credits should have been available to the subsidiary. As noted, the ability to use the tax credits to offset other Brazilian federal tax payments expires five years after the subsidiary's right to claim the credits was confirmed. Utilization of the credits is also subject to audit by the tax authorities. Based on estimates of the tax credits that were probable of being realized at the time the case was decided, the subsidiary recorded an allowance, reducing the net book value of the credits to approximately $90 million. After deducting related legal fees and Brazilian social contribution taxes assessed on the interest portion of the total IPI tax credits received, the subsidiary recorded a net gain of $81.6 million ($53.1 million after tax, or $1.87 per diluted share) during the quarter ended June 30, 2013, as a result of the favorable outcome of the case. That gain is reported in Other Income for the fiscal year ended March 31, 2014 in the consolidated statement of income. The subsidiary began using the credits to offset tax payments during the quarter ended December 31, 2013. At March 31, 2015, the remaining unused tax credits totaled approximately $30 million at the current exchange rate. Actual realization of the tax credits to date, as well as updated tax payment projections prepared during the quarter ended March 31, 2015, indicate that all remaining IPI tax credits will be fully utilized prior to expiration. On that basis, the subsidiary reversed the full remaining valuation allowance on the credits of $12.7 million (based on the current exchange rate) during the quarter. Consistent with the reporting of the original gain in fiscal year 2014, the reversal of the valuation allowance is reported in Other Income for the fiscal year ended March 31, 2015 in the consolidated statement of income.

Financial Instruments

RECOGNITION AND MEASUREMENT

1.90 FASB ASC 815, *Derivatives and Hedging*, establishes accounting and reporting standards for derivative instruments, including certain derivative instruments embedded in other contracts (collectively referred to as derivatives), and hedging activities. FASB ASC 815 requires that an entity recognize all derivatives as either assets or liabilities in the statement of financial position and measure those instruments at fair value. In addition, paragraphs 4–6 of FASB ASC 815-15-25 simplify the accounting for certain hybrid financial instruments by permitting an entity to irrevocably elect to initially and subsequently measure that hybrid financial instrument in its entirety at fair value, with changes recognized in earnings. This election is also available when a previously recognized financial instrument is subject to a remeasurement (new basis) event and the separate recognition of an embedded derivative.

1.91 FASB ASC 825, *Financial Instruments*, permits entities to choose to measure at fair value many financial instruments and certain other items that are not currently required to be measured at fair value. Further, under FASB ASC 825, a business entity should report unrealized gains and losses on eligible items for which the fair value option has been elected in earnings at each subsequent reporting date. The irrevocable election of the fair value option is made on an instrument by instrument basis, with certain exceptions, and applied to the entire instrument, not only to specified risks, specific cash flows, or portions of that instrument.

DISCLOSURE

1.92 The disclosures required by FASB ASC 815 for entities with derivative instruments or nonderivative instruments that are designated and qualify as hedging instruments are intended to enable users of financial statements to understand
- How and why an entity uses derivative or such nonderivative instruments.
- How derivative instruments or such nonderivative instruments and related hedged items are accounted for under FASB ASC 815.
- How derivative instruments or such nonderivative instruments and related hedged items affect an entity's financial position, financial performance, and cash flows.

1.93 To meet those objectives, FASB ASC 815-10-50-1A requires qualitative disclosures about an entity's objectives and strategies for using derivatives and such nonderivative instruments. An entity that holds or issues derivative instruments or such nonderivative instruments should disclose all of the following for each interim and annual reporting period for which a statement of financial position and statement of financial performance are presented:
- Its objectives for holding or issuing those instruments.
- The context needed to understand those objectives. This should be disclosed in the context of each instrument's primary underlying risk exposure.
- Its strategies for achieving those objectives. This should be disclosed in the context of each instrument's primary underlying risk exposure.
- Information that would enable users of its financial statements to understand the volume of its activity in those instruments.

1.94 These instruments should be disclosed in the context of each instrument's primary underlying risk exposure and should be distinguished among those used for risk management purposes, those used as economic hedges and other purposes related to risk exposure, and those used for other purposes. Those used for risk management purposes should be distinguished between those designated as hedging instruments and, further, whether they are fair value hedges, cash flow hedges, or foreign currency hedges. An entity should select the format and specifics that are most relevant and practicable for individual facts and circumstances. For any derivatives not designated as hedging instruments under FASB ASC 815-20, the description should include the purpose of the derivative activity.

1.95 Paragraphs .4A–E of FASB ASC 815-10-50 explain the quantitative disclosures about derivatives and such nonderivative instruments. For every annual and interim reporting period for which a statement of financial position and statement of financial performance are presented, an entity that holds or issues derivative instruments is required to disclose the location and fair value amounts of derivative instruments and such nonderivative instruments reported in the statement of financial position. The fair value of those instruments should be presented on a gross basis, even when those instruments are subject to master netting arrangements and qualify for net presentation in the statement of financial position. Cash collateral payables and receivables associated with these instruments should not be added to, or netted against, the fair value amounts.

1.96 Fair value amounts should be presented as separate asset and liability values segregated between derivatives that are designated and qualifying as hedging instruments presented separately by type of contract and those that are not. The disclosure should also identify the line item(s) in the statement of financial position in which the fair value amounts for these categories of derivative instruments are included. Also, disclosure of the location and amount of the gains and losses on derivative instruments and such nonderivative instruments and related hedged items in the statement of financial performance or statement of financial position (for example, in other comprehensive income) is required. These gain and loss disclosures should be presented separately by type of contract. These quantitative disclosures are required to be presented in tabular format, except for disclosures regarding hedged items that can be presented in either tabular or nontabular format.

1.97 For derivative instruments not designated or qualifying as hedging instruments under FASB ASC 815-20, if the entity's policy is to include them in its trading activities, the entity can elect not to separately disclose gains and losses, provided that the entity discloses certain other information. Additionally, FASB ASC 815 requires specific disclosures for derivative instruments that contain credit-risk-related features and credit derivatives.

1.98 FASB ASC 825 requires certain reporting entities to disclose the fair value of financial instruments and disclosure requirements of credit risk concentrations of all financial instruments, and it provides guidance on the fair value option. FASB ASC 825 also establishes presentation and disclosure requirements designed to facilitate comparison between entities that choose different measurement attributes for similar types of assets and liabilities.

PRESENTATION AND DISCLOSURE EXCERPTS

LINE OF CREDIT

1.99 VULCAN MATERIALS COMPANY (DEC)
CONSOLIDATED BALANCE SHEETS (in part)

As of December 31 in thousands	2015	2014
Liabilities		
Current maturities of long-term debt	130	150,137
Trade payables and accruals	175,729	145,148
Accrued salaries, wages and management incentives	91,440	84,722
Accrued interest	9,752	8,212
Other accrued liabilities	76,428	63,139
Liabilities of assets held for sale	0	520
Total current liabilities	353,479	451,878
Long-term debt	1,980,334	1,834,642
Noncurrent deferred income taxes	681,096	691,137
Deferred management incentive and other compensation	15,980	22,421
Pension benefits	233,661	252,531
Other postretirement benefits	42,318	76,372
Asset retirement obligations	226,594	226,565
Deferred revenue	207,660	213,968
Other noncurrent liabilities	106,322	94,884
Total liabilities	$3,847,444	$3,864,398

NOTES TO CONSOLIDATED FINANCIAL STATEMENTS (in part)

Note 6: Debt (in part)

Debt at December 31 is detailed as follows:

(In thousands)	Effective Interest Rates	2015	2014
Short-term Debt			
Bank line of credit expires 2020[1,2,3]	n/a	$ 0	$ 0
Total short-term debt		$ 0	$ 0
Long-term Debt			
Bank line of credit expires 2020[1,2,3]	1.75%	$ 235,000	$ 0
10.125% notes due 2015	n/a	0	150,000
6.50% notes due 2016	n/a	0	125,001
6.40% notes due 2017	n/a	0	218,633
7.00% notes due 2018	7.87%	272,512	400,000

(continued)

(In thousands)	Effective Interest Rates	2015	2014
10.375% notes due 2018	10.63%	250,000	250,000
7.50% notes due 2021	7.75%	600,000	600,000
8.85% notes due 2021	8.88%	6,000	6,000
Industrial revenue bond due 2022	n/a	0	14,000
4.50% notes due 2025	4.65%	400,000	0
7.15% notes due 2037	8.05%	240,188	240,188
Other notes 2	6.25%	498	637
Unamortized discounts and debt issuance costs	n/a	(23,734)	(22,716)
Unamortized deferred interest rate swap gain[4]	n/a	0	3,036
Total long-term debt including current maturities[5]		$1,980,464	$1,984,779
Less current maturities		130	150,137
Total long-term debt		$1,980,334	$1,834,642
Total debt[6]		$1,980,464	$1,984,779
Estimated fair value of long-term debt		$2,204,816	$2,092,673

[1] Borrowings on the bank line of credit are classified as short-term debt if we intend to repay within twelve months and as long-term debt otherwise.

[2] Non-publicly traded debt.

[3] The effective interest rate is the spread over LIBOR as of the balance sheet dates.

[4] The unamortized deferred gain was realized upon the August 2011 settlement of interest rate swaps as discussed in Note 5.

[5] The debt balances as of December 31, 2014 have been adjusted to reflect our early adoption of ASU 2015-03 and related election as discussed in Note 1 under the caption New Accounting Standards.

[6] Face value of our debt is equal to total debt plus unamortized discounts and debt issuance costs, and unamortized deferred interest rate swap gain, as follows: December 31, 2015— $2,004,198 thousand and December 31, 2014—$2,004,459 thousand.

Line Of Credit

In June 2015, we cancelled our secured $500,000,000 line of credit and entered into an unsecured $750,000,000 line of credit (incurring $2,589,000 of transaction fees).

The line of credit agreement expires in June 2020 and contains affirmative, negative and financial covenants customary for an unsecured facility. The primary negative covenant limits our ability to incur secured debt. The financial covenants are: (1) a maximum ratio of debt to EBITDA of 3.5:1 through September 2016 and 3.25:1 thereafter, and (2) a minimum ratio of EBITDA to net cash interest expense of 3.0:1. As of December 31, 2015, we were in compliance with the line of credit covenants.

Borrowings on our line of credit are classified as short-term debt if we intend to repay within twelve months and as long-term debt if we have the intent and ability to extend repayment beyond twelve months. Borrowings bear interest, at our option, at either LIBOR plus a credit margin ranging from 1.00% to 2.00%, or SunTrust Bank's base rate (generally, its prime rate) plus a credit margin ranging from 0.00% to 1.00%. The credit margin for both LIBOR and base rate borrowings is determined by either our ratio of debt to EBITDA or our credit ratings, based on the metric that produces the lower credit margin. Standby letters of credit, which are issued under the line of credit and reduce availability, are charged a fee equal to the credit margin for LIBOR borrowings plus 0.175%. We also pay a commitment fee on the daily average unused amount of the line of credit that ranges from 0.10% to 0.35% based on either our ratio of debt to EBITDA or our credit ratings, based on the metric that produces the lower fee. As of December 31, 2015, the credit margin for LIBOR borrowings was 1.75%, the credit margin for base rate borrowings was 0.75%, and the commitment fee for the unused amount was 0.25%.

As of December 31, 2015, our available borrowing capacity was $476,136,000. Utilization of the borrowing capacity was as follows:
- $235,000,000 was borrowed
- $38,864,000 was used to provide support for outstanding standby letters of credit

Term Debt (in part)

In August 2015, we repaid our $14,000,000 industrial revenue bond due 2022 via borrowing on our line of credit. The repayment did not incur any prepayment penalties. Additionally, in December 2015, we repaid our $150,000,000 10.125% notes due 2015 via borrowing on our line of credit.

In March 2015, we issued $400,000,000 of 4.50% senior notes due 2025. Proceeds (net of underwriter fees and other transaction costs) of $395,207,000 were partially used to fund the March 30, 2015 purchase, via tender offer, of $127,303,000 principal amount (32%) of the 7.00% notes due 2018. The March 2015 debt purchase cost $145,899,000, including an $18,140,000 premium above the principal amount of the notes and transaction costs of $456,000. The premium primarily reflects the trading price of the notes relative to par prior to the tender offer commencement. Additionally, we recognized $3,138,000 of net noncash expense associated with the acceleration of a proportional amount of unamortized discounts, deferred debt issuance costs, and deferred interest rate derivative settlement gains and losses. The combined first quarter charge of $21,734,000 is presented in the accompanying Consolidated Statement of Comprehensive Income as a component of interest expense for the year ended December 31, 2015.

The remaining net proceeds from the March 2015 debt issuance, together with cash on hand and borrowings under our line of credit, funded: (1) the April 2015 redemption of $218,633,000 principal amount (100%) of the 6.40% notes due 2017, (2) the April 2015 redemption of $125,001,000 principal amount (100%) of the 6.50% notes due 2016 and (3) the April 2015 purchase, via the tender offer commenced in March 2015 of $185,000 principal amount (less than 1%) of the 7.00% notes due 2018. The April 2015 debt purchases cost $385,024,000, including a $41,153,000 premium above the principal amount of the notes and transaction costs of $52,000. The premium primarily reflects the make-whole value of the 2016 notes and the 2017 notes. Additionally, we recognized $4,136,000 of net noncash expense associated with the acceleration of unamortized discounts, deferred debt issuance costs, and deferred interest rate derivative settlement gains and losses. The combined second quarter charge of $45,341,000 is presented in the accompanying Consolidated Statement of Comprehensive Income as a component of interest expense for the year ended December 31, 2015.

Debt Payments

As described above, during the first and second quarters of 2015, we purchased/redeemed $471,122,000 principal amount of debt using the proceeds from the March 2015 debt issuance, cash on hand and borrowings on our line of credit. Additionally in 2015, we borrowed on our line of credit during August to repay our $14,000,000 industrial revenue bond due 2022 and during December to repay our $150,000,000 10.125% notes due 2015.

There were no material scheduled debt payments during 2014. However, as described above, we purchased $506,366,000 principal amount of debt through a tender offer in the first quarter of 2014.

The total scheduled (principal and interest) debt payments, excluding draws, if any, on the line of credit, for the five years subsequent to December 31, 2015 are as follows:

In thousands	Total	Principal	Interest
Debt Payments (excluding the line of credit)			
2016	$125,878	$ 130	$125,748
2017	125,878	138	125,740
2018	638,728	522,534	116,194
2019	80,740	23	80,717
2020	80,740	25	80,715

Standby Letters of Credit

We provide, in the normal course of business, certain third-party beneficiaries standby letters of credit to support our obligations to pay or perform according to the requirements of an underlying agreement. Such letters of credit typically have an initial term of one year, typically renew automatically, and can only be modified or cancelled with the approval of the beneficiary. All of our standby letters of credit are issued by banks that participate in our $750,000,000 line of credit, and reduce the borrowing capacity thereunder. Our standby letters of credit as of December 31, 2015 are summarized by purpose in the table below:

In thousands	
Standby Letters of Credit	
Risk management insurance	$33,111
Reclamation/restoration requirements	5,753
Total	$38,864

DERIVATIVE FINANCIAL INSTRUMENTS—INTEREST RATE SWAP AGREEMENTS

1.100 ANADARKO PETROLEUM CORPORATION (DEC)
NOTES TO CONSOLIDATED FINANCIAL STATEMENTS (in part)

1. Summary of Significant Accounting Policies (in part)

Fair Value (in part)

In arriving at fair-value estimates, the Company uses relevant observable inputs available for the valuation technique employed. If a fair-value measurement reflects inputs at multiple levels within the hierarchy, the fair-value measurement is characterized based on the lowest level of input that is significant to the fair-value measurement. For Anadarko, recurring fair-value measurements are performed for interest-rate derivatives, commodity derivatives, and investments in trading securities.

Derivative Instruments Anadarko uses derivative instruments to manage its exposure to cash-flow variability from commodity-price and interest-rate risks. Derivatives are carried on the balance sheet at fair value and are included in other current assets, other assets, accrued expenses, or other long-term liabilities, depending on the derivative position and the expected timing of settlement, unless they satisfy the normal purchases and sales exception criteria. Where the Company has the contractual right and intends to net settle, derivative assets and liabilities are reported on a net basis.

Gains and losses on derivative instruments are recognized currently in earnings. Net losses attributable to derivatives previously subject to hedge accounting reside in accumulated other comprehensive income (loss) and will be reclassified to earnings in future periods as the economic transactions to which the derivatives relate affect earnings. See *Note 9—Derivative Instruments*.

9. Derivative Instruments (in part)

Objective and Strategy The Company uses derivative instruments to manage its exposure to cash-flow variability from commodity-price and interest-rate risks. Futures, swaps, and options are used to manage exposure to commodity-price risk inherent in the Company's oil and natural-gas production and natural-gas processing operations (Oil and Natural-Gas Production/Processing Derivative Activities). Futures contracts and commodity-price swap agreements are used to fix the price of expected future oil and natural-gas sales at major industry trading locations such as Henry Hub, Louisiana for natural gas and Cushing, Oklahoma or Sullom Voe, Scotland for oil. Basis swaps are periodically used to fix or float the price differential between product prices at one market location versus another. Options are used to establish a floor price, a ceiling price, or a floor and a ceiling price (collar) for expected future oil and natural-gas sales. Derivative instruments are also used to manage commodity-price risk inherent in customer price requirements and to fix margins on the future sale of natural gas and NGLs from the Company's leased storage facilities (Marketing and Trading Derivative Activities).

Interest-rate swaps are used to fix or float interest rates on existing or anticipated indebtedness. The purpose of these instruments is to manage the Company's existing or anticipated exposure to interest-rate changes. The fair value of the Company's current interest-rate swap portfolio increases (decreases) when interest rates increase (decrease).

The Company does not apply hedge accounting to any of its derivative instruments. As a result, gains and losses associated with derivative instruments are recognized currently in earnings. Net derivative losses attributable to derivatives previously subject to hedge accounting reside in accumulated other comprehensive income (loss) and are reclassified to earnings as the transactions to which the derivatives relate are recognized in earnings. See *Note 18—Accumulated Other Comprehensive Income (Loss)*.

Interest-Rate Derivatives Anadarko has outstanding interest-rate swap contracts to manage interest-rate risk associated with anticipated debt issuances. The Company has locked in a fixed interest rate in exchange for a floating interest rate indexed to the three-month LIBOR.

In 2015, the Company extended the reference-period start dates on interest-rate swaps with an aggregate notional principal amount of $1.0 billion to align the portfolio with anticipated debt refinancing. The Company also amended the mandatory termination dates on interest-rate swaps with an aggregate notional principal amount of $1.8 billion so that, at the start of the reference period, Anadarko will receive quarterly payments based on the floating rate and make semi-annual payments based on the fixed interest rate. The interest-rate swaps are required to be settled in full at the mandatory termination date. As part of these interest-rate swap modifications, the fixed interest rates on the swaps were also adjusted, and the Company recognized a loss of $137 million, which is included in gains (losses) on derivatives, net in the Company's Consolidated Statement of Income, and increased the related derivative liability. In 2014, in anticipation of the July 2014 issuance of an aggregate $1.25 billion of Senior Notes, interest-rate swap agreements with an aggregate notional principal amount of $750 million were settled in 2014, resulting in a cash payment of $222 million.

Derivative settlements and collateralization are classified as cash flows from operating activities unless the derivatives contain an other-than-insignificant financing element, in which case the settlements and collateralization are classified as cash flows from financing activities. As a result of prior extensions of reference-period start dates without settlement of the related interest-rate derivative obligations, the interest-rate derivatives in the Company's portfolio contain an other-than-insignificant financing element, and therefore, any settlements or collateralization related to these extended interest-rate derivatives are classified as cash flows from financing activities.

The Company had the following outstanding interest-rate swaps at December 31, 2015:

Millions except percentages Notional Principal Amount	Reference Period	Mandatory Termination Date	Weighted-Average Interest Rate
$ 50	September 2016–2026	September 2016	5.910%
$ 50	September 2016–2046	September 2016	6.290%
$250	September 2016–2046	September 2018	6.310%
$300	September 2016–2046	September 2020	6.509%
$250	September 2016–2046	September 2021	6.724%
$200	September 2017–2047	September 2018	6.049%
$300	September 2017–2047	September 2020	6.569%
$500	September 2017–2047	September 2021	6.654%

Effect of Derivative Instruments—Balance Sheet The following summarizes the fair value of the Company's derivative instruments at December 31:

Millions	Gross Derivative Assets		Gross Derivative Liabilities	
Balance Sheet Classification	2015	2014	2015	2014
Commodity derivatives				
Other current assets	$462	$421	$ (177)	$ (118)
Other assets	8	1	—	—
Accrued expenses	—	71	(3)	(114)
Other liabilities	—	—	—	(6)
	470	493	(180)	(238)
Interest-rate derivatives				
Other current assets	2	—	—	—
Other assets	54	—	—	—
Accrued expenses	—	—	(54)	—
Other liabilities	—	—	(1,488)	(1,217)
	56	—	(1,542)	(1,217)
Total derivatives	$526	$493	$(1,722)	$(1,455)

Effect of Derivative Instruments—Statement of Income The following summarizes gains and losses related to derivative instruments:

Millions			
Classification of (Gain) Loss Recognized	2015	2014	2013
Commodity derivatives			
Gathering, processing, and marketing sales[1]	$ (1)	$ 10	$ 6
(Gains) losses on derivatives, net	(367)	(589)	141
Interest-rate derivatives			
(Gains) losses on derivatives, net	268	786	(539)
Total (gains) losses on derivatives, net	$(100)	$207	$(392)

[1] Represents the effect of Marketing and Trading Derivative Activities.

Fair Value Fair value of futures contracts is based on unadjusted quoted prices in active markets for identical assets or liabilities, which represent Level 1 inputs. Valuations of physical-delivery purchase and sale agreements, over-the-counter financial swaps, and commodity option collars are based on similar transactions observable in active markets and industry-standard models that primarily rely on market-observable inputs. Inputs used to estimate fair value in industry-standard models are categorized as Level 2 inputs because substantially all assumptions and inputs are observable in active markets throughout the full term of the instruments. Inputs used to estimate the fair value of swaps and options include market-price curves; contract terms and prices; credit-risk adjustments; and, for Black-Scholes option valuations, discount factors and implied market volatility.

The following summarizes the fair value of the Company's derivative assets and liabilities, by input level within the fair-value hierarchy:

Millions	Level 1	Level 2	Level 3	Netting[1]	Collateral	Total
December 31, 2015						
Assets						
Commodity derivatives	$ 10	$ 460	$—	$(178)	$ (8)	$ 284
Interest-rate derivatives	—	56	—	—	—	56
Total derivative assets	$ 10	$ 516	$—	$(178)	$ (8)	$ 340
Liabilities						
Commodity derivatives	$ (1)	$ (179)	$—	$ 178	$—	$ (2)
Interest-rate derivatives	—	(1,542)	—	—	58	(1,484)
Total derivative liabilities	$ (1)	$(1,721)	$—	$ 178	$ 58	$(1,486)
December 31, 2014						
Assets						
Commodity derivatives	$—	$ 493	$—	$(189)	$(13)	$ 291
Total derivative assets	$—	$ 493	$—	$(189)	$(13)	$ 291
Liabilities						
Commodity derivatives	$—	$ (238)	$—	$ 189	$—	$ (49)
Interest-rate derivatives	—	(1,217)	—	—	23	(1,194)
Total derivative liabilities	$—	$(1,455)	$—	$ 189	$ 23	$(1,243)

[1] Represents the impact of netting commodity derivative assets and liabilities with counterparties where the Company has the contractual right and intends to net settle.

1.101 NATIONAL OILWELL VARCO, INC. (DEC)
NOTES TO CONSOLIDATED FINANCIAL STATEMENTS (in part)

2. Summary of Significant Accounting Policies (in part)

Derivative Financial Instruments

Accounting Standards Codification ("ASC") Topic 815, "Derivatives and Hedging" ("ASC Topic 815") requires companies to recognize all derivative instruments as either assets or liabilities in the Consolidated Balance Sheet at fair value. The accounting for changes in the fair value (i.e., gains or losses) of a derivative instrument depends on whether it has been designated and qualifies as part of a hedging relationship and further, on the type of hedging relationship. For those derivative instruments that are designated and qualify as hedging instruments, a company must designate the hedging instrument, based upon the exposure being hedged, as a fair value hedge, cash flow hedge, or a hedge of a net investment in a foreign operation.

The Company records all derivative financial instruments at their fair value in its Consolidated Balance Sheet. Except for certain non-designated hedges discussed below, all derivative financial instruments that the Company holds are designated as cash flow hedges and are highly effective in offsetting movements in the underlying risks. Such arrangements typically have terms between two and 24 months, but may have longer terms depending on the underlying cash flows being hedged, typically related to the projects in our backlog.

3. Derivative Financial Instruments

The Company is exposed to certain risks relating to its ongoing business operations. The primary risk managed by using derivative instruments is foreign currency exchange rate risk. Forward contracts against various foreign currencies are entered into to manage the foreign currency exchange rate risk on forecasted revenues and expenses denominated in currencies other than the functional currency of the operating unit (cash flow hedge). Other forward exchange contracts against various foreign currencies are entered into to manage the foreign currency exchange rate risk associated with certain firm commitments denominated in currencies other than the functional currency of the operating unit (fair value hedge). In addition, the Company will enter into non-designated forward contracts against various foreign currencies to manage the foreign currency exchange rate risk on recognized nonfunctional currency monetary accounts (non-designated hedge).

At December 31, 2015, the Company has determined that the fair value of its derivative financial instruments representing assets of $26 million and liabilities of $286 million (primarily currency related derivatives) are determined using level 2 inputs (inputs other than quoted prices in active markets for identical assets and liabilities that are observable either directly or indirectly for substantially the full term of the asset or liability) in the fair value hierarchy as the fair value is based on publicly available foreign exchange and interest rates at each financial reporting date. At December 31, 2015, the net fair value of the Company's foreign currency forward contracts totaled a net liability of $260 million.

At December 31, 2015, the Company's financial instruments do not contain any credit-risk-related or other contingent features that could cause accelerated payments when the Company's financial instruments are in net liability positions. We do not use derivative financial instruments for trading or speculative purposes.

Cash Flow Hedging Strategy

To protect against the volatility of forecasted foreign currency cash flows resulting from forecasted revenues and expenses, the Company has instituted a cash flow hedging program. The Company hedges portions of its forecasted revenues and expenses denominated in nonfunctional currencies with forward contracts. When the U.S. dollar strengthens against the foreign currencies, the decrease in present value of future foreign currency revenues and expenses is offset by gains in the fair value of the forward contracts designated as hedges. Conversely, when the U.S. dollar weakens, the increase in the present value of future foreign currency cash flows is offset by losses in the fair value of the forward contracts.

For derivative instruments that are designated and qualify as a cash flow hedge (i.e., hedging the exposure to variability in expected future cash flows that is subject to a particular currency risk), the effective portion of the gain or loss on the derivative instrument is reported as a component of Other Comprehensive Income (Loss) and reclassified into earnings in the same line item associated with the forecasted transaction and in the same period or periods during which the hedged transaction affects earnings (e.g., in "revenues" when the hedged transactions are cash flows associated with forecasted revenues). The remaining gain or loss on the derivative instrument in excess of the cumulative change in the present value of future cash flows of the hedged item, if any (i.e., the ineffective portion), or hedge components excluded from the assessment of effectiveness, is recognized in the Consolidated Statements of Income (Loss) during the current period.

The Company had the following outstanding foreign currency forward contracts that were entered into to hedge nonfunctional currency cash flows from forecasted revenues and expenses (in millions):

	Currency Denomination			
Foreign Currency	December 31, 2015		December 31, 2014	
Norwegian Krone	NOK	9,655	NOK	10,781
U.S. Dollar	USD	321	USD	231
Euro	EUR	78	EUR	462
Danish Krone	DKK	57	DKK	227
Singapore Dollar	SGD	14	SGD	44
British Pound Sterling	GBP	4	GBP	80
Canadian Dollar	CAD	2	CAD	14

Non-designated Hedging Strategy

The Company enters into forward exchange contracts to hedge certain nonfunctional currency monetary accounts. The purpose of the Company's foreign currency hedging activities is to protect the Company from risk that the eventual U.S. dollar equivalent cash flows from the nonfunctional currency monetary accounts will be adversely affected by changes in the exchange rates.

For derivative instruments that are non-designated, the gain or loss on the derivative instrument subject to the hedged risk (i.e., nonfunctional currency monetary accounts) is recognized in other income (expense), net in current earnings.

The Company had the following outstanding foreign currency forward contracts that hedge the fair value of nonfunctional currency monetary accounts (in millions):

	Currency Denomination			
Foreign Currency	December 31, 2015		December 31, 2014	
Norwegian Krone	NOK	2,265	NOK	4,052
Russian Ruble	RUB	2,164	RUB	—
U.S. Dollar	USD	515	USD	1,092
Euro	EUR	371	EUR	401
Danish Krone	DKK	153	DKK	322
British Pound Sterling	GBP	11	GBP	19
Canadian Dollar	CAD	7	CAD	4
Singapore Dollar	SGD	5	SGD	4
Mexican Peso	MXN	—	MXN	118
Brazilian Real	BRL	—	BRL	57
Swedish Krone	SEK	—	SEK	3

The Company has the following fair values of its derivative instruments and their balance sheet classifications (in millions):

	Fair Values of Derivative Instruments (In millions)						
	Asset Derivatives			Liability Derivatives			
	Balance Sheet Location	Fair Value December 31,		Balance Sheet Location	Fair Value December 31,		
		2015	2014		2015	2014	
Derivatives designated as hedging instruments under ASC Topic 815							
Foreign exchange contracts	Prepaid and other current assets	$ 5	$18	Accrued liabilities	$212	$204	
Foreign exchange contracts	Other Assets	—	8	Other Liabilities	25	102	
Total derivatives designated as hedging instruments under ASC Topic 815		$ 5	$26		$237	$306	
Derivatives not designated as hedging instruments under ASC Topic 815							
Foreign exchange contracts	Prepaid and other current assets	$21	$27	Accrued liabilities	$ 49	$ 93	
Total derivatives not designated as hedging instruments under ASC Topic 815		$21	$27		$ 49	$ 93	
Total derivatives		$26	$53		$286	$399	

The Effect of Derivative Instruments on the Consolidated Statements of Income (Loss) ($ in millions)								
Derivatives Designated as Hedging Instruments under ASC Topic 815	Amount of Gain (Loss) Recognized in OCI on Derivatives (Effective Portion)(a)		Location of Gain (Loss) Reclassified from Accumulated OCI into Income (Effective Portion)	Amount of Gain (Loss) Reclassified from Accumulated OCI into Income (Effective Portion)		Location of Gain (Loss) Recognized in Income on Derivatives (Ineffective Portion and Amount Excluded from Effectiveness Testing)	Amount of Gain (Loss) Recognized in Income on Derivatives (Ineffective Portion and Amount Excluded from Effectiveness Testing)(b)	
	Years Ended December 31,			Years Ended December 31,			Years Ended December 31,	
	2015	2014		2015	2014		2015	2014
			Revenue	19	26	Cost of revenue	(33)	(1)
Foreign exchange contracts	(243)	(340)	Cost of revenue	(262)	(43)	Other income (expense), net	4	36
Total	(243)	(340)		(243)	(17)		(29)	35

Derivatives Not Designated as Hedging Instruments under ASC Topic 815	Location of Gain (Loss) Recognized in Income on Derivatives	Amount of Gain (Loss) Recognized in Income on Derivatives	
		Years Ended December 31,	
		2015	2014
Foreign exchange contracts	Other income (expense), net	(97)	(61)
Total		(97)	(61)

(a) The Company expects that $(223) million of the Accumulated Other Comprehensive Income (Loss) will be reclassified into earnings within the next twelve months with an offset by gains from the underlying transactions resulting in no impact to earnings or cash flow.

(b) The amount of gain (loss) recognized in income represents $(33) million and $(1) million related to the ineffective portion of the hedging relationships for the years ended December 31, 2015 and 2014, respectively, and $4 million and $36 million related to the amount excluded from the assessment of the hedge effectiveness for the years ended December 31, 2015 and 2014, respectively.

CREDIT FACILITY

1.102 HANESBRANDS INC. (DEC)
CONSOLIDATED BALANCE SHEETS (in part)

(in thousands, except share and per share amounts)

	January 2, 2016	January 3, 2015
Liabilities and Stockholders' Equity (in part)		
Accounts payable	$ 672,972	$ 621,220
Accrued liabilities and other:		
Payroll and employee benefits	142,154	143,335
Advertising and promotion	125,948	149,345
Other	192,231	198,759
Notes payable	117,785	144,438
Accounts Receivable Securitization Facility	195,163	210,963
Current portion of long-term debt	57,656	14,354
Total current liabilities	1,503,909	1,482,414
Long-term debt	2,254,162	1,613,997
Pension and postretirement benefits	362,266	472,003
Other noncurrent liabilities	222,812	253,007
Total liabilities	4,343,149	3,821,421

NOTES TO CONSOLIDATED FINANCIAL STATEMENTS (in part)

(amounts in thousands, except per share data)

(10) Debt (in part)

The Company had the following debt at January 2, 2016 and January 3, 2015:

	Interest Rate as of January 2, 2016	Principal Amount		Maturity Date
		January 2, 2016	January 3, 2015	
Senior Secured Credit Facility:				
Revolving Loan Facility	2.34%	$ 63,500	$ 176,500	April 2020
Euro Term Loan	3.50%	113,098	436,953	August 2021
Term Loan A	1.89%	705,313	—	April 2020
Term Loan B	3.25%	421,813	—	April 2022
6.375% Senior Notes	6.38%	1,000,000	1,000,000	December 2020
Accounts Receivable Securitization Facility	1.17%	195,163	210,963	March 2016
Other International Debt	Various	8,094	14,898	Various
		2,506,981	1,839,314	
Less current maturities		252,819	225,317	
		$2,254,162	$1,613,997	

The Company's primary financing arrangements are the senior secured credit facility (the "Senior Secured Credit Facility"), 6.375% senior notes (the " 6.375% Senior Notes"), the Term Loan a (the "Term Loan A"), the Term Loan b (the "Term Loan B"), the euro term loan (the "Euro Term Loan") and the Accounts Receivable Securitization Facility. The outstanding balances at January 2, 2016 are reported in the "Current portion of long-term debt", "Long-term debt" and "Accounts Receivable Securitization Facility" lines of the Consolidated Balance Sheets.

Total cash paid for interest related to debt in 2015, 2014 and 2013 was $106,231, $85,512 and $96,434, respectively.

Senior Secured Credit Facility

On April 29, 2015, the Company refinanced its senior secured credit facility (the "Senior Secured Credit Facility") to extend the maturity date of the revolving loan facility (the "Revolving Loan Facility") to April 2020 and reduce the maximum borrowing capacity from $1,100,000 to $1,000,000, re-price the Revolving Loan Facility at favorable rates, and add an additional $850,000 in term loan borrowings ($425,000 for a new Term Loan A and $425,000 for a new Term Loan B. The Company incurred $10,900 in fees related to this refinancing. The proceeds of the Term Loan A and the Term Loan B were used to refinance existing revolving borrowings under the prior senior secured credit facility, pay fees and expenses in connection with the closing of the Senior Secured Credit Facility and for general corporate purposes. Proceeds of the Revolving Loan Facility are used for general corporate purposes and working capital needs. On October 23, 2015, the Company amended the Senior Secured Credit Facility to increase the principal amount of the Term Loan A by an additional $300,000. The Company incurred $1,603 in fees related to this refinancing.

In July 2014, the Company amended and restated the Senior Secured Credit Facility to increase the committed aggregate facility size to $1,600,000 (from $1,100,000), consisting of (a) Revolving Loan Facility, and (b) the Euro Term Loan. The Euro Term Loan accrues interest utilizing the EURIBOR rate (as defined in the Senior Secured Credit Facility) plus 2.75%. The proceeds of the Euro Term Loan are denominated in Euros and were utilized in part to purchase Hanes Europe Innerwear. Proceeds of the Revolving Loan Facility are used for general corporate purposes and working capital needs. All borrowings under the Revolving Loan Facility must be repaid in full upon maturity. Outstanding borrowings under the Euro Term Loan are repayable in quarterly payments of 0.25% of the original borrowings, with the remainder of the outstanding principle due at maturity.

All borrowings under the Revolving Loan Facility must be repaid in full upon maturity.

Outstanding borrowings under the Term Loan A are repayable in equal quarterly installments in the following annual percentages, with the remainder of the outstanding principal to be repaid at maturity: year one, 5.0%; year two, 7.5%; years three and four, 10.0%; and year five, 15.0%.

Outstanding borrowings under the Term Loan B are repayable in 0.25% quarterly installments, with the remainder of the outstanding principal to be repaid at maturity. If the Term Loan B is repriced or refinanced on or prior to the twelve month anniversary of its funding and as a result of such repricing or refinancing the effective interest rate of the Term Loan B decreases, the Company shall be required to pay a prepayment fee equal to 1.0% of the aggregate principal amount of the Term Loan B subject to such repricing or refinancing.

A portion of the Revolving Loan Facility is available for the issuances of letters of credit and the making of swingline loans, and any such issuance of letters of credit or making of a swingline loan will reduce the amount available under the Revolving Loan Facility. At the Company's option, it may add one or more term loan facilities or increase the commitments under the Revolving Loan Facility so long as certain conditions are satisfied, including, among others, that no default or event of default is in existence, that the Company is in pro forma compliance with the financial covenants described below and that the Company's senior secured leverage ratio is less than 3.00 to 1 on a pro forma basis after giving effect to the incurrence of such indebtedness. As of January 2, 2016, the Company had $15,683 of standby and trade letters of credit issued and outstanding under the Revolving Loan Facility and $920,817 of borrowing availability.

The Senior Secured Credit Facility is guaranteed by substantially all of the Company's existing and future direct and indirect U.S. subsidiaries, with certain customary or agreed-upon exceptions for foreign subsidiaries and certain other subsidiaries. The Company and each of the guarantors under the Senior Secured Credit Facility have granted the lenders under the Senior Secured Credit Facility a valid and perfected first priority (subject to certain customary exceptions) lien and security interest in the following:

- the equity interests of substantially all of the Company's direct and indirect U.S. subsidiaries (other than U.S. subsidiaries directly or indirectly owned by foreign subsidiaries) and 65% of the voting securities of certain first tier foreign subsidiaries; and
- substantially all present and future property and assets, real and personal, tangible and intangible, of the Company and each guarantor, except for certain enumerated interests, and all proceeds and products of such property and assets.

Additionally, the Euro Term Loan is guaranteed by substantially all of the Company's subsidiary MFB International Holdings S.à r.l.'s ("MFB International Holdings") existing and future direct and indirect subsidiaries, with certain customary or agreed-upon exceptions for certain subsidiaries and secured by a pledge of 100% of the equity interests of MFB International Holdings and its direct subsidiaries, 100% of the equity interests owned by any subsidiary of MFB International Holdings that is domiciled in Luxembourg and substantially all present and future property and assets, real and personal, tangible and intangible, of each Luxembourg domiciled guarantor, except for certain enumerated interests, and all proceeds and products of such property and assets.

The Term Loan A, the Term Loan B and the Company's Euro Term Loan require the Company and its subsidiary Maidenform Luxembourg ("MF Lux"), as applicable, to prepay any outstanding Term Loans in connection with (i) the incurrence of certain indebtedness and (ii) non-ordinary course asset sales or other dispositions (including as a result of casualty or condemnation) that exceed certain thresholds in any period of twelve-consecutive months, with customary reinvestment provisions. The Term Loan B and the Euro Term Loan also require the Company and MF Lux, as applicable, to prepay any outstanding Term Loans under the Term Loan B and the Euro Term Loan in connection with excess cash flow, which percentage will be based upon the Company's leverage ratio during the relevant fiscal period. All such prepayments will be made on a pro rata basis under each of the applicable Term Loans that are subject to such prepayments.

At the Company's option, borrowings under the Revolving Loan Facility, the Term Loan A and the Term Loan B bear interest based on the LIBOR rate or the "base rate" plus, in each case, an applicable margin. The applicable margin for the Revolving Loan Facility and the Term Loan A is determined by reference to a leverage-based pricing grid set forth in the Senior Secured Credit Facility, ranging from a maximum of 2.00% in the case of LIBOR-based loans and 1.00% in the case of Base Rate loans if the Company's leverage ratio is greater than or equal to 4.00 to 1, and will step down in 0.25% increments to a minimum of 1.25% in the case of LIBOR-based loans and 0.25% in the case of Base Rate loans if the Company's leverage ratio is less than 2.50 to 1. The applicable margin under the Term Loan B is 2.50% in the case of LIBOR-based loans and 1.50% in the case of Base Rate loans.

The Senior Secured Credit Facility requires the Company to comply with customary affirmative, negative and financial covenants. The Senior Secured Credit Facility requires that the Company maintain a minimum interest coverage ratio and a maximum total debt to EBITDA (earnings before income taxes, depreciation expense and amortization, as computed pursuant to the Senior Secured Credit Facility), or leverage ratio. The interest coverage ratio covenant requires that the ratio of the Company's EBITDA for the preceding four fiscal quarters to its consolidated total interest expense for such period shall not be less than 3.0 to 1.0 for each fiscal quarter. The leverage ratio covenant requires that the ratio of the Company's total debt to EBITDA for the preceding four fiscal quarters will not be more than 4.0 to 1.0 for each fiscal quarter provided that, following a permitted acquisition in which the consideration is at least $200, such maximum leverage ratio covenant shall be increased to 4.5 to 1.0 for each fiscal quarter ending in the succeeding 12-month period following such permitted acquisition. The method of calculating all of the components used in the covenants is included in the Senior Secured Credit Facility.

In addition, the commitment fee for the unused portion of revolving loan commitments made by the Lenders is between 25 and 35 basis points based on the applicable commitment fee margin in effect from time to time. When the Leverage Ratio (as defined in the Senior Secured Credit Facility) is greater than or equal to 4.00 to 1.00, the commitment fee margin is 0.350%. When the Leverage Ratio is less than 4.00 to 1.00 but greater than or equal to 3.25 to 1.00, the applicable commitment fee margin is 0.300%. When the Leverage Ratio is less than 3.25 to 1.00, the applicable commitment fee margin is 0.250%.

The Senior Secured Credit Facility contains customary events of default, including nonpayment of principal when due; nonpayment of interest, fees or other amounts after stated grace period; material inaccuracy of representations and warranties; violations of covenants; certain bankruptcies and liquidations; any cross-default to material indebtedness; certain material judgments; certain events related to the ERISA, actual or asserted invalidity of any guarantee, security document or subordination provision or non-perfection of security interest, and a change in control (as defined in the Senior Secured Credit Facility). As of January 2, 2016 the Company was in compliance with all financial covenants.

Fair Value

Author's Note
In May 2015, FASB issued ASU No. 2015-07, *Fair Value Measurement (Topic 820): Disclosures for Investments in Certain Entities That Calculate Net Asset Value per Share (or Its Equivalent) (a consensus of the Emerging Issues Task Force)*. The amendments in this ASU remove the requirement to categorize within the fair value hierarchy all investments for which fair value is measured using the net asset value per share practical expedient. The amendments also remove the requirement to make certain disclosures for all investments that are eligible to be measured at fair value using the net asset value per share practical expedient. Rather, those disclosures are limited to investments for which the entity has elected to measure the fair value using that practical expedient. The ASU will be effective for public business entities for fiscal years beginning after December 15, 2015, and interim periods within those fiscal years. For all other entities, the amendments in this ASU are effective for fiscal years beginning after December 15, 2016, and interim periods within those fiscal years. A reporting entity should apply this ASU retrospectively to all periods presented. Early application is permitted. None of the examples that follow contain an example of these disclosures due to the effective date.

RECOGNITION AND MEASUREMENT

1.103 FASB ASC 820 defines fair value, establishes a framework for measuring fair value, and requires certain disclosures about fair value measurements. *Fair value* is defined as an exit price (that is, a price that would be received to sell, versus acquire, an asset or transfer a liability in an orderly transaction between market participants at the measurement date). Further, fair value is a market-based measurement, not an entity-specific measurement. It establishes a fair value hierarchy that distinguishes between assumptions developed based on market data obtained from independent external sources and the reporting entity's own assumptions. Further, fair value measurement should consider adjustment for risk, such as the risk inherent in a valuation technique or its inputs.

1.104 FASB ASC 820-10-35-10A provides that a fair value measurement of a nonfinancial asset takes into account a market participant's ability to generate economic benefits by using the asset in its highest and best use or by selling it to another market participant that would use the asset in its highest and best use. FASB ASC 820-10-35-10B states that the highest and best use for a nonfinancial asset takes into account the use of the asset that is physically possible, legally permissible, and financial feasible. FASB ASC 820-10-35-10E states that the highest and best use of a nonfinancial asset might provide maximum value to market participants through its use in combination with other assets as a group (as installed or otherwise configured for use) or in combination with other assets and liabilities. The highest and best use of a nonfinancial asset is determined from the perspective of market participants, even if the reporting entity intends a different use. Because the highest and best use of the asset is determined based on its use by market participants, the fair value measurement considers the assumptions that market participants would use in pricing the asset, whether using an in-use or an in-exchange valuation premise.

1.105 According to paragraphs 16–16AA of FASB ASC 820-10-35, a fair value measurement of a financial or nonfinancial liability or an instrument classified in a reporting entity's shareholders' equity is transferred to a market participant at the measurement date. Even when there is no observable market to provide pricing information about the transfer of a liability or an instrument classified in a reporting entity's shareholders' equity, there might be an observable market for such items if they are held by other parties as assets. In all cases, a reporting entity shall maximize the use of relevant observable inputs and minimize the use of unobservable inputs to meet the objective of a fair value measurement. A reporting entity is permitted, as a practical expedient, to estimate the fair value of an investment within the scope of paragraph 4 of FASB ASC 820-10-15 using the net asset value per share (or its equivalent) of the investment if the net asset value per share or its equivalent is calculated in a manner consistent with the measurement principles of FASB ASC 946, *Financial Services—Investment Companies*, as of the reporting entity's measurement date.

DISCLOSURE

1.106 For assets and liabilities measured at fair value, whether on a recurring or nonrecurring basis, FASB ASC 820-10-50 specifies the required disclosures concerning the inputs used to measure fair value. FASB ASC 820-10-50–1 explains that the reporting entity should disclose information that enables users of its financial statements to assess the following: (*a*) for assets and liabilities measured at fair value on a recurring basis in periods subsequent to initial recognition or measured on a nonrecurring basis in periods subsequent to initial recognition, the valuation techniques and inputs used to develop those measurements; and (*b*) for recurring fair value measurements using significant unobservable inputs (Level 3), the effect of the measurements on earnings for the period.

PRESENTATION AND DISCLOSURE EXCERPT

FAIR VALUE MEASUREMENTS

1.107 THE PRICELINE GROUP INC. (DEC)
NOTES TO CONSOLIDATED FINANCIAL STATEMENTS (in part)

2. Summary of Significant Accounting Policies (in part)

Fair Value of Financial Instruments—The Company's financial instruments, including cash, restricted cash, accounts receivable, accounts payable, accrued expenses and deferred merchant bookings, are carried at cost which approximates their fair value because of the short-term nature of these financial instruments. See Notes 4, 5, 10 and 12 for information on fair value for investments, derivatives, the Company's outstanding Senior Notes and redeemable noncontrolling interests.

Cash and Cash Equivalents—Cash and cash equivalents consists primarily of cash and highly liquid investment grade securities with an original maturity of three months or less.

Restricted Cash—Restricted cash at December 31, 2015 and 2014 collateralizes office leases and supplier obligations.

Investments—The Company has classified its investments in debt securities and equity securities with readily determinable fair value as available-for-sale securities. These securities are carried at estimated fair value with the aggregate unrealized gains and losses related to these investments, net of taxes, reflected as a part of "Accumulated other comprehensive income (loss)" within stockholders' equity.

The fair value of the investments is based on the specific quoted market price of the securities or comparable securities at the balance sheet dates. Investments in debt securities are considered to be impaired when a decline in fair value is judged to be other than temporary because the Company either intends to sell or it is more-likely-than not that it will have to sell the impaired security before recovery. Once a decline in fair value is determined to be other than temporary, an impairment charge is recorded and a new cost basis in the investment is established. If the Company does not intend to sell the debt security, but it is probable that the Company will not collect all amounts due, then only the impairment due to the credit risk would be recognized in earnings and the remaining amount of the impairment would be recognized in "Accumulated other comprehensive income (loss)" within stockholders' equity. Marketable securities are presented as current assets on the Company's Consolidated Balance Sheets if they are available to meet short-term working capital needs of the Company. Marketable debt securities not held to meet short-term working capital needs of the Company are classified as short-term or long-term investments on the Company's Consolidated Balance Sheets based on the maturity date of the debt security. See Notes 4 and 5 for further detail of investments.

Equity investments without readily determinable fair values, in companies over which the Company does not have the ability to exercise significant influence, are accounted for using the cost method of accounting and classified within "Other assets" in the Consolidated Balance Sheets. Under the cost method, investments are carried at cost and are adjusted to fair value only for other-than-temporary declines in fair value.

Goodwill—The Company accounts for acquired businesses using the purchase method of accounting which requires that the assets acquired and liabilities assumed be recorded at the date of acquisition at their respective fair values. Any excess of the purchase price over the estimated fair values of the net assets acquired is recorded as goodwill. The Company's Consolidated Financial Statements reflect an acquired business starting at the date of the acquisition.

Goodwill is not subject to amortization and is reviewed at least annually for impairment, or earlier if an event occurs or circumstances change and there is an indication of impairment. The Company tests goodwill at a reporting unit level. The fair value of the reporting unit is compared to its carrying value, including goodwill. Fair values are determined based on discounted cash flows, market multiples and/or appraised values and are based on market participant assumptions. An impairment is recorded to the extent that the implied fair value of goodwill is less than the carrying value of goodwill. See Note 9 for further information.

Stock-Based Compensation—Stock-based compensation is recognized in the financial statements based upon fair value. The fair value of performance share units and restricted stock units is determined based on the number of units or shares, as applicable, granted and the quoted price of the Company's common stock as of the grant date or acquisition date. Stock-based compensation related to performance share units reflects the estimated probable outcome at the end of the performance period. The fair value of employee stock options assumed in acquisitions was determined using the Black Scholes model and the market value of the Company's common stock at the respective acquisition dates. Fair value is recognized as expense on a straight line basis, net of estimated forfeitures, over the employee requisite service period.

3. Stock-Based Compensation

The Company's 1999 Omnibus Plan, as amended and restated effective June 6, 2013, (the "1999 Plan") is the primary stock compensation plan from which broad-based employee equity awards may be made. As of December 31, 2015, there were 2,425,519 shares of common stock available for future grant under the 1999 Plan. In addition, in connection with the acquisition of KAYAK in May 2013, Buuteeq, Inc. in June 2014, OpenTable in July 2014 and Rocket Travel, Inc. in February 2015, the Company assumed the KAYAK Software Corporation 2012 Equity Incentive Plan (the "KAYAK Plan"), the Buuteeq, Inc. Amended and Restated 2010 Stock Plan (the "Buuteeq Plan"), the OpenTable, Inc. 2009 Equity Incentive Award Plan (the "OpenTable Plan") and the Rocket Travel, Inc. 2012 Stock Incentive Plan (the "Rocketmiles Plan"). As of December 31, 2015, there were 145,392 shares of common stock available for future grant under the OpenTable Plan.

Stock-based compensation issued under the plans generally consists of restricted stock units, performance share units and stock options. Stock-based compensation is recognized in the financial statements based upon fair value. Fair value is recognized as expense on a straight-line basis, net of estimated forfeitures, over the employee's requisite service period. The fair value of restricted stock units and performance share units is determined based on the number of units granted and the quoted price of the Company's common stock as of the grant date. Stock-based compensation related to performance share units reflects the estimated probable outcome at the end of the performance period. The fair value of the employee stock options assumed in acquisitions was determined using the Black-Scholes model and the market value of the Company's common stock at their respective acquisition dates. Stock options granted to employees generally have a term of 10 years. Restricted stock units and performance share units generally vest over periods from 1 to 4 years. The Company issues new shares of common stock upon the issuance of restricted stock, the exercise of stock options and the vesting of restricted stock units and performance share units.

Stock-based compensation included in personnel expenses in the Consolidated Statements of Operations was approximately $247.4 million, $186.4 million and $140.5 million for the years ended December 31, 2015, 2014 and 2013, respectively. Stock-based compensation for the years ended December 31, 2015, 2014 and 2013 includes charges amounting to $22.6 million, $20.6 million and $24.1 million, respectively, representing the impact of adjusting the estimated probable outcome at the end of the performance period for outstanding unvested performance share units. Included in the stock-based compensation are approximately $2.6 million, $2.3 million, and $2.1 million for the years ended December 31, 2015, 2014, and 2013, respectively, for grants to non-employee directors. The related tax benefit for stock-based compensation is $52.9 million, $38.4 million and $18.5 million for the years ended December 31, 2015, 2014 and 2013, respectively.

Restricted Stock Units and Performance Share Units

The following table summarizes the activity of restricted stock units and performance share units ("share-based awards") during the years ended December 31, 2013, 2014 and 2015:

Share-Based Awards	Shares	Weighted Average Grant Date Fair Value
Unvested at December 31, 2012	540,128	$ 389.21
Granted	162,341	$ 730.47
Vested	(258,198)	$ 242.63
Performance Shares Adjustment	101,490	$ 681.13
Forfeited/Canceled	(11,442)	$ 579.71
Unvested at December 31, 2013	534,319	$ 615.10
Granted	128,484	$1,308.13
Assumed in an acquisition	43,993	$1,238.68
Vested	(195,730)	$ 492.22
Performance Shares Adjustment	68,499	$1,085.94
Forfeited/Canceled	(9,250)	$ 972.19
Unvested at December 31, 2014	570,315	$ 912.26
Granted	198,141	$1,226.41
Vested	(161,862)	$ 757.66
Performance Shares Adjustment	64,328	$1,238.30
Forfeited/Canceled	(33,665)	$1,151.70
Unvested at December 31, 2015	637,257	$1,070.10

Share-based awards granted by the Company during the years ended December 31, 2015, 2014 and 2013 had aggregate grant date fair values of approximately $243.0 million, $168.1 million and $118.6 million, respectively. Share-based awards that vested during the years ended December 31, 2015, 2014, and 2013 had grant date fair values of $122.6 million, $96.3 million and $62.6 million, respectively.

As of December 31, 2015, there was $336.5 million of total future compensation cost related to unvested share-based awards to be recognized over a weighted-average period of 1.9 years.

During the year ended December 31, 2015, the Company made broad-based grants of 90,518 restricted stock units that generally vest after three years, subject to certain exceptions for terminations other than for "cause," for "good reason" or on account of death or disability. These share-based awards had a total grant date fair value of $109.8 million based on a weighted-average grant date fair value per share of $1,213.18.

In addition, during the year ended December 31, 2015, the Company granted 107,623 performance share units to executives and certain other employees. The performance share units had a total grant date fair value of $133.2 million based upon a weighted-average grant date fair value per share of $1,237.53. The performance share units are payable in shares of the Company's common stock upon vesting. Subject to certain exceptions for terminations other than for "cause," for "good reason" or on account of death or disability, recipients of these performance share units generally must continue their service through the requisite service period in order to receive any shares. Stock-based compensation related to performance share units reflects the estimated probable outcome at the end of the performance period. The actual number of shares to be issued on the vesting date will be determined upon completion of the performance period, which, for most of these performance share units, ends December 31, 2017, assuming there is no accelerated vesting for, among other things, a termination of employment under certain circumstances. As of December 31, 2015, the estimated number of probable shares to be issued is a total of 164,857 shares. If the maximum performance thresholds are met at the end of the performance period, a maximum number of 254,643 total shares could be issued. If the minimum performance thresholds are not met, 51,621 shares would be issued at the end of the performance period.

2014 Performance Share Units

During the year ended December 31, 2014, the Company granted 72,277 performance share units with a grant date fair value of $96.1 million, based on a weighted-average grant date fair value per share of $1,329.11. The actual number of shares to be issued will be determined upon completion of the performance period which generally ends December 31, 2016.

At December 31, 2015, there were 63,484 unvested 2014 performance share units outstanding, net of performance share units that were forfeited or vested since the grant date. As of December 31, 2015, the number of shares estimated to be issued pursuant to these performance share units at the end of the performance period is a total of 104,241 shares. If the maximum thresholds are met at the end of the performance period, a maximum of 127,732 total shares could be issued pursuant to these performance share units. If the minimum performance thresholds are not met, 43,291 shares would be issued at the end of the performance period.

2013 Performance Share Units

During the year ended December 31, 2013, the Company granted 104,865 performance share units with a grant date fair value of $74.4 million, based on a weighted-average grant date fair value per share of $709.74. The actual number of shares to be issued will be determined based upon completion of the performance period which ended December 31, 2015.

At December 31, 2015, there were 97,296 unvested 2013 performance share units outstanding, net of performance share units that were forfeited or vested since the grant date. As of December 31, 2015, the total number of shares expected to be issued pursuant to these performance share units on the March 4, 2016 vesting date is 186,020 shares.

Stock Options

The following table summarizes the activity for the stock options during the years ended December 31, 2013, 2014 and 2015 :

Employee Stock Options	Number of Shares	Weighted Average Exercise Price	Aggregate Intrinsic Value (000's)	Weighted Average Remaining Contractual Term (in years)
Balance, December 31, 2012	71,001	$ 19.73	$ 42,647	1.3
Assumed in acquisitions	540,179	$260.96		
Exercised	(449,670)	$194.68		
Forfeited	(23,802)	$478.83		
Balance, December 31, 2013	137,708	$315.36	$116,686	6.6
Assumed in acquisitions	61,897	$457.67		
Exercised	(51,003)	$293.59		
Forfeited	(2,217)	$517.91		
Balance, December 31, 2014	146,385	$380.05	$111,277	6.5
Assumed in acquisitions	1,422	$230.37		
Exercised	(52,697)	$355.85		
Forfeited	(6,006)	$511.87		
Balance, December 31, 2015	89,104	$383.03	$ 79,474	5.4
Vested and exercisable as of December 31, 2015	72,654	$354.59	$ 66,868	5.0
Vested and exercisable as of December 31, 2015 and expected to vest thereafter, net of estimated forfeitures	88,687	$383.06	$ 79,099	5.4

The aggregate intrinsic value of employee stock options exercised during the years ended December 31, 2015, 2014 and 2013 was $46.3 million, $49.2 million and $281.8 million, respectively. During the years ended December 31, 2015, 2014 and 2013, stock options assumed in acquisitions vested for 38,689, 41,524 and 65,293 shares with an acquisition-date fair value of $24.4 million, $24.2 million and $30.9 million, respectively.

For the years ended December 31, 2015, 2014 and 2013, the Company recorded stock-based compensation expense related to employee stock options of $24.9 million, $24.7 million and $30.9 million, respectively. Employee stock options assumed in acquisitions during the year ended December 31, 2015 had a total acquisition-date fair value of $1.4 million based on a weighted-average acquisition date fair value of $1,015.81 per share. As of December 31, 2015, there was $9.7 million of total future compensation costs related to unvested employee stock options to be recognized over a weighted-average period of 1.3 years.

4. Investments

Short-term and Long-term Investments in Available for Sale Securities

The following table summarizes, by major security type, the Company's investments as of December 31, 2015 (in thousands):

	Cost	Gross Unrealized Gains	Gross Unrealized Losses	Fair Value
Short-term investments:				
Foreign government securities	$ 395,404	$ 497	$ (104)	$ 395,797
U.S. government securities	457,001	—	(507)	456,494
Corporate debt securities	305,654	25	(419)	305,260
Commercial paper	11,688	—	—	11,688
U.S. government agency securities	2,009	—	(2)	2,007
Total short-term investments	$1,171,756	$ 522	$ (1,032)	$1,171,246
Long-term investments:				
Foreign government securities	$ 718,947	$ 1,367	$ (683)	$ 719,631
U.S. government securities	580,155	277	(1,982)	578,450
Corporate debt securities	4,294,282	1,273	(18,941)	4,276,614
U.S. municipal securities	1,080	3	—	1,083
Ctrip convertible debt securities	1,250,000	158,600	(30,050)	1,378,550
Ctrip equity securities	630,311	346,724	—	977,035
Total long-term investments	$7,474,775	$508,244	$(51,656)	$7,931,363

The Company's investment policy seeks to preserve capital and maintain sufficient liquidity to meet operational and other needs of the business. As of December 31, 2015, the weighted-average life of the Company's fixed income investment portfolio, excluding the Company's investment in Ctrip convertible debt securities, was approximately 2.0 years with an average credit quality of A/A2/A.

The Company invests in foreign government securities with high credit quality. As of December 31, 2015, investments in foreign government securities principally included debt securities issued by the governments of Germany, the Netherlands, France, Belgium and Austria.

On May 26, 2015 and August 7, 2014, the Company invested $250 million and $500 million, respectively, in five-year senior convertible notes issued at par by Ctrip.com International Ltd. ("Ctrip"). On December 11, 2015, the Company invested $500 million in a ten-year senior convertible note issued at par value, which included a put option allowing the Company to require a prepayment in cash from Ctrip at the end of the sixth year of the note. As of December 31, 2015, the Company had also invested $630.3 million of its international cash in Ctrip American Depositary Shares ("ADSs"). The convertible debt and equity securities of Ctrip have been marked-to-market in accordance with the accounting guidance for available-for-sale securities.

In connection with the purchase of the convertible note in August 2014, Ctrip granted the Company the right to appoint an observer to Ctrip's board of directors and permission to acquire Ctrip shares (through the acquisition of Ctrip ADSs in the open market) over the twelve months following the purchase date, so that combined with ADSs issuable upon conversion of this note, the Company could hold up to 10% of Ctrip's outstanding equity. In connection with the purchase of the convertible note in May 2015, Ctrip granted the Company permission to acquire additional Ctrip shares (through the acquisition of Ctrip ADSs in the open market) over the twelve months following the purchase date, so that combined with ADSs issuable upon conversion of the August 2014 and May 2015 notes, the Company could hold up to an aggregate of 15% of Ctrip's outstanding equity. Under the terms of the December 2015 convertible note, the ADSs into which this debt could be converted will not be included in the aggregate 15% ownership holding. As of December 31, 2015, the Company did not have a significant influence over Ctrip. In addition, the Company may acquire the additional ADSs without a time limitation.

The following table summarizes, by major security type, the Company's investments as of December 31, 2014 (in thousands):

	Cost	Gross Unrealized Gains	Gross Unrealized Losses	Fair Value
Short-term investments:				
Foreign government securities	$ 52,524	$ —	$ (34)	$ 52,490
U.S. government securities	364,276	24	(34)	364,266
Corporate debt securities	582,160	15	(652)	581,523
Commercial paper	39,092	—	—	39,092
U.S. government agency securities	104,829	—	(18)	104,811
Total short-term investments	$1,142,881	$ 39	$ (738)	$1,142,182
Long-term investments:				
Foreign government securities	$ 12,707	$ —	$ (36)	$ 12,671
U.S. government securities	557,130	80	(762)	556,448
U.S. corporate debt securities	2,332,030	2,299	(5,296)	2,329,033
U.S. government agency securities	95,108	97	(111)	95,094
U.S. municipal securities	1,114	—	(12)	1,102
Ctrip corporate debt securities	500,000	—	(74,039)	425,961
Ctrip equity securities	421,930	—	(86,586)	335,344
Total long-term investments	$3,920,019	$2,476	$(166,842)	$3,755,653

The Company has classified its investments as available-for-sale securities. These securities are carried at estimated fair value with the aggregate unrealized gains and losses related to these investments, net of taxes, reflected as a part of "Accumulated other comprehensive income (loss)" in the Consolidated Balance Sheets. Classification as short-term or long-term is based upon the maturity of the debt securities.

The Company recognized $2.2 million of net realized gains related to investments for the year ended December 31, 2015. There were no significant realized gains or losses related to investments for the year ended December 31, 2014.

Cost Method Investments

The Company held investments in equity securities of private companies of approximately $62.3 million and $0.6 million as of December 31, 2015 and December 31, 2014, respectively. These investments are accounted for under the cost method and included in "Other assets" in the Company's Consolidated Balance Sheets. As of December 31, 2015, the Company did not estimate the fair value of these cost-method investments because there were no identified events or changes in circumstances that may have a significant adverse impact on the carrying values of these investments.

5. Fair Value Measurements

Financial assets and liabilities are carried at fair value as of December 31, 2015 and are classified in the categories described in the tables below (in thousands):

	Level 1	Level 2	Total
Assets:			
Cash equivalents:			
U.S. Treasury money market funds	$ 99,117	$ —	$ 99,117
Foreign government securities	—	10,659	10,659
U.S. government securities	—	90,441	90,441
Corporate debt securities	—	1,855	1,855
Commercial paper	—	335,663	335,663
Short-term investments:			
Foreign government securities	—	395,797	395,797
U.S. government securities	—	456,494	456,494
Corporate debt securities	—	305,260	305,260
Commercial paper	—	11,688	11,688
U.S. government agency securities	—	2,007	2,007
Foreign exchange derivatives	—	363	363
Long-term investments:			
Foreign government securities	—	719,631	719,631
U.S. government securities	—	578,450	578,450
Corporate debt securities	—	4,276,614	4,276,614
U.S. municipal securities	—	1,083	1,083
Ctrip convertible debt securities	—	1,378,550	1,378,550
Ctrip equity securities	977,035	—	977,035
Total assets at fair value	$1,076,152	$8,564,555	$9,640,707
Liabilities:			
Foreign exchange derivatives	$ —	$ 644	$ 644

Financial assets and liabilities are carried at fair value as of December 31, 2014 and are classified in the categories described in the tables below (in thousands):

	Level 1	Level 2	Total
Assets:			
Cash equivalents:			
U.S. Treasury money market funds	$155,608	$ —	$ 155,608
Foreign government securities	—	974,855	974,855
U.S. government securities	—	676,503	676,503
Corporate debt securities	—	45,340	45,340
Commercial paper	—	382,544	382,544
U.S. government agency securities	—	10,000	10,000
Short-term investments:			
Foreign government securities	—	52,490	52,490
U.S. government securities	—	364,266	364,266
Corporate debt securities	—	581,523	581,523
Commercial paper	—	39,092	39,092
U.S. government agency securities	—	104,811	104,811
Foreign exchange derivatives		336	336
Long-term investments:			
Foreign government securities	—	12,671	12,671
U.S. government securities	—	556,448	556,448
Corporate debt securities	—	2,329,033	2,329,033
U.S. government agency securities	—	95,094	95,094
U.S. municipal securities	—	1,102	1,102
Ctrip convertible debt securities	—	425,961	425,961
Ctrip equity securities	335,344	—	335,344
Total assets at fair value	$490,952	$6,652,069	$7,143,021
Liabilities:			
Foreign exchange derivatives	$ —	$ 129	$ 129

There are three levels of inputs to measure fair value. The definition of each input is described below:

Level 1: Quoted prices in active markets that are accessible by the Company at the measurement date for identical assets and liabilities.

Level 2: Inputs are observable, either directly or indirectly. Such prices may be based upon quoted prices for identical or comparable securities in active markets or inputs not quoted on active markets, but corroborated by market data.

Level 3: Unobservable inputs are used when little or no market data is available.

Investments in corporate debt securities, U.S. and foreign government securities, commercial paper, government agency securities, convertible debt securities and municipal securities are considered "Level 2" valuations because the Company has access to quoted prices, but does not have visibility to the volume and frequency of trading for all of these investments. For the Company's investments, a market approach is used for recurring fair value measurements and the valuation techniques use inputs that are observable, or can be corroborated by observable data, in an active marketplace.

The Company's derivative instruments are valued using pricing models. Pricing models take into account the contract terms as well as multiple inputs where applicable, such as interest rate yield curves, option volatility and currency rates.

Derivatives are considered "Level 2" fair value measurements. The Company's derivative instruments are typically short-term in nature.

As of December 31, 2015 and 2014, the Company's cash consisted of bank deposits and cash held in investment accounts. Other financial assets and liabilities, including restricted cash, accounts receivable, accounts payable, accrued expenses and deferred merchant bookings are carried at cost which approximates their fair value because of the short-term nature of these items. As of December 31, 2015, the Company held investments in equity securities of private companies of approximately $62.3 million and these investments are accounted for under the cost method of accounting (see Note 4). See Note 4 for information on the carrying value of investments and Note 10 for the estimated fair value of the Company's outstanding Senior Notes. See Note 19 for the Company's contingent liabilities associated with business acquisitions.

In the normal course of business, the Company is exposed to the impact of foreign currency fluctuations. The Company limits these risks by following established risk management policies and procedures, including the use of derivatives. See Note 2 for further information on our accounting policy for derivative financial instruments.

Derivatives Not Designated as Hedging Instruments—The Company is exposed to adverse movements in currency exchange rates as the operating results of its international operations are translated from local currency into U.S. Dollars upon consolidation. The Company's derivative contracts principally address short-term foreign exchange fluctuations for the Euro and British Pound Sterling versus the U.S.

Dollar. As of December 31, 2015 and 2014, there were no outstanding derivative contracts related to foreign currency translation risk. Foreign exchange losses of $6.6 million for the year ended December 31, 2015, and foreign exchange gains of $13.7 million and $0.3 million for the years ended December 31, 2014 and 2013, respectively, were recorded related to these derivatives in "Foreign currency transactions and other" in the Consolidated Statements of Operations.

The Company also enters into foreign currency forward contracts to hedge its exposure to the impact of movements in currency exchange rates on its transactional balances denominated in currencies other than the functional currency. Foreign exchange derivatives outstanding as of December 31, 2015 associated with foreign currency transaction risks resulted in a net liability of $0.3 million, with a liability in the amount of $0.7 million recorded in "Accrued expenses and other current liabilities" and an asset in the amount of $0.4 million recorded in "Prepaid expenses and other current assets" in the Consolidated Balance Sheet. Foreign exchange derivatives outstanding as of December 31, 2014 associated with foreign exchange transaction risks resulted in a net asset of $0.2 million, with an asset in the amount of $0.3 million recorded in "Prepaid expense and other current assets" and a liability in the amount of $0.1 million recorded in "Accrued expenses and other current liabilities" in the Consolidated Balance Sheet. Derivatives associated with these transaction risks resulted in foreign exchange losses of $15.3 million and $21.8 million for the years ended December 31, 2015 and 2014, respectively, and foreign exchange gains of $3.6 million for the year ended December 31, 2013. These mark-to-market adjustments on the derivative contracts, offset by the effect of changes in currency exchange rates on transactions denominated in currencies other than the functional currency, resulted in net losses of $13.8 million, $11.8 million and $5.5 million for the years ended December 31, 2015, 2014 and 2013, respectively. These net impacts are reported in "Foreign currency transactions and other" in the Consolidated Statements of Operations.

The settlement of derivative contracts not designated as hedging instruments resulted in net cash outflows of $33.9 million and $8.9 million for the years ended December 31, 2015 and 2014, respectively, and a net cash inflow of $4.4 million for the year ended December 31, 2013, respectively, and were reported within "Net cash provided by operating activities" in the Consolidated Statements of Cash Flows.

Derivatives Designated as Hedging Instruments—The Company had no foreign currency forward contracts designated as hedges of its net investment in a foreign subsidiary outstanding as of December 31, 2015 and 2014 . A net cash inflow of $5.2 million for the year ended December 31, 2015 and net cash outflows of $80.3 million and $78.6 million for the years ended December 31, 2014 and 2013, respectively, were reported within "Net cash used in investing activities" in the Consolidated Statements of Cash Flows.

10. Debt (in part)

Outstanding Debt

Outstanding debt as of December 31, 2015 consisted of the following (in thousands):

December 31, 2015	Outstanding Principal Amount	Unamortized Debt Discount and Debt Issuance Cost	Carrying Value
Long-term Debt:			
1.0% Convertible Senior Notes due March 2018	$1,000,000	$ (58,929)	$ 941,071
0.35% Convertible Senior Notes due June 2020	1,000,000	(114,898)	885,102
0.9% Convertible Senior Notes due September 2021	1,000,000	(125,258)	874,742
2.375% (€1 Billion) Senior Notes due September 2024	1,086,957	(14,688)	1,072,269
3.65% Senior Notes due March 2025	500,000	(4,160)	495,840
1.8% (€1 Billion) Senior Notes due March 2027	1,086,957	(6,200)	1,080,757
2.15% (€750 Million) Senior Notes due November 2022	815,217	(6,555)	808,662
Total long-term debt	$6,489,131	$(330,688)	$6,158,443

Outstanding debt as of December 31, 2014 consisted of the following (in thousands):

December 31, 2014	Outstanding Principal Amount	Unamortized Debt Discount and Debt Issuance Cost See Note 2	Carrying Value See Note 2
Short-term Debt:			
1.25% Convertible Senior Notes due March 2015	$ 37,524	$ (374)	$ 37,150
Long-term Debt:			
1.0% Convertible Senior Notes due March 2018	$1,000,000	$ (84,708)	$ 915,292
0.35% Convertible Senior Notes due June 2020	1,000,000	(138,786)	861,214
0.9% Convertible Senior Notes due September 2021	1,000,000	(145,311)	854,689
2.375% (€1 Billion) Senior Notes due September 2024	1,210,068	(17,393)	1,192,675
Total long-term debt	$4,210,068	$(386,198)	$3,823,870

The 2015 Notes (as defined below) became convertible on December 15, 2014, at the option of the holders, and remained convertible until the scheduled trading day immediately preceding the maturity date of March 15, 2015. Since these notes were convertible at the option of the holders and the principal amount is required to be paid in cash, the difference between the principal amount and the carrying value was reflected as convertible debt in the mezzanine section in the Company's Consolidated Balance Sheet as of December 31, 2014. Therefore, with respect to the 2015 Notes, the Company reclassified the unamortized debt discount for these 1.25% Notes in the amount of $0.3 million before tax as of December 31, 2014, from additional paid-in capital to convertible debt in the mezzanine section in the Company's Consolidated Balance Sheet.

Based upon the closing price of the Company's common stock for the prescribed measurement periods during the year ended December 31, 2015 and December 31, 2014, the respective contingent conversion thresholds of the 2018 Notes (as defined below), the 2020 Notes (as defined below) and the 2021 Notes (as defined below) were not exceeded and therefore these notes are reported as non-current liabilities in the Consolidated Balance Sheets.

Fair Value of Debt

As of December 31, 2015 and 2014, the estimated market value of the outstanding Senior Notes was approximately $7.0 billion and $4.8 billion, respectively, and was considered a "Level 2" fair value measurement (see Note 5). Fair value was estimated based upon actual trades at the end of the reporting period or the most recent trade available as well as the Company's stock price at the end of the reporting period. A substantial portion of the market value of the Company's debt in excess of the outstanding principal amount relates to the conversion premium on the Convertible Senior Notes.

Convertible Debt

If the note holders exercise their option to convert, the Company delivers cash to repay the principal amount of the notes and delivers shares of common stock or cash, at its option, to satisfy the conversion value in excess of the principal amount. In cases where holders decide to convert prior to the maturity date, the Company charges the proportionate amount of remaining debt issuance costs to interest expense.

Description of Senior Convertible Notes

In August 2014, the Company issued in a private placement $1.0 billion aggregate principal amount of Convertible Senior Notes due September 15, 2021, with an interest rate of 0.9% (the "2021 Notes"). The Company paid $11.0 million in debt issuance costs during the year ended December 31, 2014, related to this offering. The 2021 Notes are convertible, subject to certain conditions, into the Company's common stock at a conversion price of approximately $2,055.50 per share. The 2021 Notes are convertible, at the option of the holder, prior to September 15, 2021, upon the occurrence of specific events, including but not limited to a change in control, or if the closing sales price of the Company's common stock for at least 20 trading days in the period of 30 consecutive trading days ending on the last trading day of the immediately preceding calendar quarter is more than 150% of the applicable conversion price in effect for the notes on the last trading day of the immediately preceding quarter. In the event that all or substantially all of the Company's common stock is acquired on or prior to the maturity of the 2021 Notes in a transaction in which the consideration paid to holders of the Company's common stock consists of all or substantially all cash, the Company would be required to make additional payments in the form of additional shares of common stock to the holders of the 2021 Notes in an aggregate value ranging from $0 to approximately $375 million depending upon the date of the transaction and the then current stock price of the Company. As of June 15, 2021, holders will have the right to convert all or any portion of the 2021 Notes. The 2021 Notes may not be redeemed by the Company prior to maturity. The holders may require the Company to repurchase the 2021 Notes for cash in certain circumstances. Interest on the 2021 Notes is payable on March 15 and September 15 of each year.

In May 2013, the Company issued in a private placement $1.0 billion aggregate principal amount of Convertible Senior Notes due June 15, 2020, with an interest rate of 0.35% (the "2020 Notes"). The 2020 Notes were Issued with an initial discount of $20.0 million. The Company paid $1.0 million in debt issuance costs during the year ended December 31, 2013, related to this offering. The 2020 Notes are convertible, subject to certain conditions, into the Company's common stock at a conversion price of approximately $1,315.10 per share. The 2020 Notes are convertible, at the option of the holder, prior to June 15, 2020, upon the occurrence of specific events, including but not limited to a change in control, or if the closing sales price of the Company's common stock for at least 20 trading days in the period of 30 consecutive trading days ending on the last trading day of the immediately preceding calendar quarter is more than 150% of the applicable conversion price in effect for the notes on the last trading day of the immediately preceding quarter. In the event that all or substantially all of the Company's common stock is acquired on or prior to the maturity of the 2020 Notes in a transaction in which the consideration paid to holders of the Company's common stock consists of all or substantially all cash, the Company would be required to make additional payments in the form of additional shares of common stock to the holders of the 2020 Notes in an aggregate value ranging from $0 to approximately $397 million depending upon the date of the transaction and the then current stock price of the Company. As of March 15, 2020, holders will have the right to convert all or any portion of the 2020 Notes. The 2020 Notes may not be redeemed by the Company prior to maturity. The holders may require the Company to repurchase the 2020 Notes for cash in certain circumstances. Interest on the 2020 Notes is payable on June 15 and December 15 of each year.

In March 2012, the Company issued in a private placement $1.0 billion aggregate principal amount of Convertible Senior Notes due March 15, 2018, with an interest rate of 1.0% (the "2018 Notes"). The Company paid $20.9 million in debt issuance costs during the year ended December 31, 2012, related to this offering. The 2018 Notes are convertible, subject to certain conditions, into the Company's common stock at a conversion price of approximately $944.61 per share. The 2018 Notes are convertible, at the option of the holder, prior to March 15, 2018, upon the occurrence of specific events, including but not limited to a change in control, or if the closing sales price of the Company's common stock for at least 20 trading days in the period of 30 consecutive trading days ending on the last trading day of the immediately preceding calendar quarter is more than 150% of the applicable conversion price in effect for the notes on the last trading day of the immediately preceding quarter. In the event that all or substantially all of the Company's common stock is acquired on or prior to the maturity of the 2018 Notes in a transaction in which the consideration paid to holders of the Company's common stock consists of all or substantially all cash, the Company would be required to make additional payments in the form of additional shares of common stock to the holders of the 2018 Notes in aggregate value ranging from $0 to approximately $344 million depending upon the date of the transaction and the then current stock price of the Company. As of December 15, 2017, holders will have the right to convert all or any portion of the 2018 Notes. The 2018 Notes may not be redeemed by the Company prior to maturity. The holders may require the Company to repurchase the 2018 Notes for cash in certain circumstances. Interest on the 2018 Notes is payable on March 15 and September 15 of each year.

In March 2010, the Company issued in a private placement $575.0 million aggregate principal amount of Convertible Senior Notes due March 15, 2015, with an interest rate of 1.25% (the "2015 Notes"). The Company paid $13.3 million in debt issuance costs associated with the 2015 Notes for the year ended December 31, 2010. The 2015 Notes were convertible, subject to certain conditions, into the Company's common stock at a conversion price of approximately $303.06 per share. In March 2015, in connection with the maturity or conversion prior to maturity of the remaining outstanding 1.25% Convertible Senior Notes, the Company paid $37.5 million to satisfy the aggregate principal amount due and paid an additional $110.1 million in satisfaction of the conversion value in excess of the principal amount, which was charged to additional paid-in capital. During the year ended December 31, 2014, the Company delivered cash of $122.9 million to repay the aggregate principal amount and issued 300,256 shares of its common stock and paid cash of $2.2 million in satisfaction of the conversion value in excess of the principal amount associated with 1.25% Convertible Senior Notes due March 2015 that were converted prior to maturity. In the year ended December 31, 2013, the Company delivered cash of $414.6 million to repay the principal amount and issued 972,235 shares of its common stock in satisfaction of the conversion value in excess of the principal amount for convertible debt that was converted prior to maturity.

Accounting guidance requires that cash-settled convertible debt, such as the Company's Convertible Senior Notes, be separated into debt and equity components at issuance and each be assigned a value. The value assigned to the debt component is the estimated fair value, as of the issuance date, of a similar bond without the conversion feature. The difference between the bond cash proceeds and this estimated fair value, representing the value assigned to the equity component, is recorded as a debt discount. Debt discount is amortized using the effective interest method over the period from the origination date through the stated maturity date. The Company estimated the straight debt borrowing rates at debt origination to be 3.50% for the 2018 Notes, 3.13% for the 2020 Notes and 3.18% for the 2021 Notes. The yield to maturity was estimated at an at-market coupon priced at par.

Debt discount after tax of $82.5 million ($142.9 million before tax) net of financing costs associated with the equity component of convertible debt of $1.6 million after tax were recorded in additional paid-in capital related to the 2021 Notes at December 31, 2014. Debt discount after tax of $92.4 million ($154.3 million before tax) net of financing costs associated with the equity component of convertible debt of $0.1 million after tax were recorded in additional paid-in capital related to the 2020 Notes at June 30, 2013. Debt discount after tax of $80.9 million ($135.2 million before tax) net of financing costs associated with the equity component of convertible debt of $2.8 million after tax were recorded in additional paid-in capital related to the 2018 Notes in March 2012. Debt discount after tax of $69.1 million ($115.2 million before tax) net of financing costs associated with the equity component of convertible debt of $1.6 million after tax were recorded in additional paid-in capital related to the 2015 Notes in March 2010.

For the years ended December 31, 2015, 2014 and 2013, the Company recognized interest expense of $92.7 million, $75.3 million and $78.2 million, respectively, related to convertible notes, comprised of $22.6 million, $17.1 million and $17.7 million, respectively, for the contractual coupon interest, $65.6 million, $54.4 million and $55.7 million, respectively, related to the amortization of debt discount and $4.5 million, $3.8 million and $4.8 million, respectively, related to the amortization of debt issuance costs. For the years ended December 31, 2015, 2014 and 2013, included in the amortization of debt discount mentioned above was $2.7 million, $2.6 million and $1.5 million, respectively, of original issuance discount amortization related to the 2020 Notes. In addition, the Company incurred interest expense for the write-off of unamortized debt issuance costs related to debt conversions of $0.5 million and $2.4 million for the years ended December 31, 2014 and 2013, respectively. The remaining period for amortization of debt discount and debt issuance costs is the period until the stated maturity date for the respective debt. The weighted-average effective interest rates for the years ended December 31, 2015, 2014, and 2013 are 3.4%, 3.5% and 4.4%, respectively.

In addition, if the Company's convertible debt is redeemed or converted prior to maturity, a gain or loss on extinguishment is recognized. The gain or loss is the difference between the fair value of the debt component immediately prior to extinguishment and its carrying value. To estimate the fair value of the debt at the conversion date, the Company estimated its straight debt borrowing rate, considering its credit rating and straight debt of comparable corporate issuers. For the years ended December 31, 2014 and 2013, the Company recognized non-cash losses of $6.3 million ($3.8 million after tax) and $26.7 million ($16.2 million after tax), respectively, in "Foreign currency transactions and other" in the Consolidated Statements of Operations in connection with the conversion of the 2015 Notes.

Other Long-term Debt

In November 2015, the Company issued Senior Notes due November 25, 2022, with an interest rate of 2.15% (the "2022 Notes") for an aggregate principal amount of 750 million Euros. The 2022 Notes were issued with an initial discount of 2.2 million Euros. In addition, the Company paid $3.7 million in debt issuance costs during the year ended December 31, 2015. Interest on the 2022 Notes is payable annually on November 25, beginning November 25, 2016. Subject to certain limited exceptions, all payments of interest and principal, including payments made upon any redemption of the 2022 Notes will be made in Euros.

In March 2015, the Company issued Senior Notes due March 15, 2025, with an interest rate of 3.65% (the "2025 Notes") for an aggregate principal amount of $500 million. The 2025 Notes were issued with an initial discount of $1.3 million. In addition, the Company paid $3.2 million in debt issuance costs during the year ended December 31, 2015. Interest on the 2025 Notes is payable semi-annually on March 15 and September 15, beginning September 15, 2015.

In March 2015, the Company issued Senior Notes due March 3, 2027, with an interest rate of 1.8% (the "2027 Notes") for an aggregate principal amount of 1.0 billion Euros. The 2027 Notes were issued with an initial discount of 0.3 million Euros. In addition, the Company paid $6.3 million in debt issuance costs during the year ended December 31, 2015. Interest on the 2027 Notes is payable annually on March 3, beginning March 3, 2016. Subject to certain limited exceptions, all payments of interest and principal for the 2027 Notes will be made in Euros.

In September 2014, the Company issued Senior Notes due September 23, 2024, with an interest rate of 2.375% (the "2024 Notes") for an aggregate principal amount of 1.0 billion Euros. The 2024 Notes were issued with an initial discount of 9.4 million Euros. In addition, the Company paid $6.5 million in debt issuance costs during the year ended December 31, 2014. Interest on the 2024 Notes is payable annually on September 23, beginning September 23, 2015. Subject to certain limited exceptions, all payments of interest and principal, including payments made upon any redemption of the 2024 Notes, will be made in Euros.

The aggregate principal value of the 2022 Notes, 2024 Notes and 2027 Notes and accrued interest thereon are designated as a hedge of the Company's net investment in certain Euro functional currency subsidiaries. The foreign currency transaction gains or losses on these liabilities are measured based upon changes in spot rates and are recorded in "Accumulated other comprehensive income (loss)" in the Consolidated Balance Sheets. The Euro-denominated net assets of the subsidiary are translated into U.S. Dollars at each balance sheet date, with effects of foreign currency changes also reported in "Accumulated other comprehensive income (loss)" in the Consolidated Balance Sheets. Since the notional amount of the recorded Euro-denominated debt and related interest are not greater than the notional amount of the Company's net investment, the Company does not expect to incur any ineffectiveness on this hedge.

Debt discount is amortized using the effective interest method over the period from the origination date through the stated maturity date. The Company estimated the effective interest rates at debt origination to be 2.20% for the 2022 Notes, 3.68% for the 2025 Notes, 1.80% for the 2027 Notes and 2.48% for the 2024 Notes.

For the years ended December 31, 2015 and 2014, the Company recognized interest expense of $61.5 million and $8.6 million, respectively, related to other long-term debt which was comprised of $59.0 million and $8.1 million, respectively, for the contractual coupon interest, $1.1 million and $0.3 million, respectively, related to the amortization of debt discount and $1.4 million and $0.2 million, respectively, related to the amortization of debt issuance costs. The remaining period for amortization of debt discount and debt issuance costs is the stated maturity date for this debt.

12. Redeemable Noncontrolling Interests

On May 18, 2010, the Company, through its wholly-owned subsidiary, priceline.com International Ltd. ("PIL"), paid $108.5 million, net of cash acquired, to purchase a controlling interest of the outstanding equity of TravelJigsaw Holdings Limited (now known as rentalcars.com), a Manchester, U.K.-based international rental car reservation service. Certain key members of rentalcars.com's management team retained a noncontrolling ownership interest in rentalcars.com. In addition, certain key members of the management team of Booking.com purchased a 3% ownership interest in rentalcars.com from PIL in June 2010 (together with rentalcars.com management's investment, the "Redeemable Shares"). The holders of the Redeemable Shares had the right to put their shares to PIL and PIL had the right to call the shares in each case at a purchase price reflecting the fair value of the Redeemable Shares at the time of exercise. Subject to certain exceptions, one-third of the Redeemable Shares were subject to the put and call options in each of 2011, 2012 and 2013, respectively, during specified option exercise periods.

In April 2012 and 2011, in connection with the exercise of call and put options, PIL purchased a portion of the shares underlying redeemable noncontrolling interests for an aggregate purchase price of approximately $61.1 million and $13.0 million, respectively. As a result of the April 2011 purchase, the redeemable noncontrolling interests in rentalcars.com were reduced from 24.4% to 19.0%. As a result of the April 2012 purchase, the redeemable noncontrolling interests in rentalcars.com were further reduced to 12.7%. In April 2013, in connection with the exercise of the March 2013 call and put options, PIL purchased the remaining outstanding shares underlying redeemable noncontrolling interests for an aggregate purchase price of approximately $192.5 million.

Redeemable noncontrolling interests were measured at fair value, both at the date of acquisition and subsequently at each reporting period. The redeemable noncontrolling interests were reported in the Consolidated Balance Sheets in mezzanine equity in "Redeemable noncontrolling interests."

A reconciliation of redeemable noncontrolling interests for the year ended December 31, 2013 is as follows (in thousands):

	2013
Balance, beginning of period	$ 160,287
Net income attributable to noncontrolling interests	135
Fair value adjustments[1]	42,522
Purchase of subsidiary shares at fair value[1]	(192,530)
Currency translation adjustments	(10,414)
Balance, end of period	$ —

[1] The fair value of the redeemable noncontrolling interests was determined by industry peer comparable analysis and a discounted cash flow valuation model.

Subsequent Events

RECOGNITION AND MEASUREMENT

1.108 The FASB ASC glossary defines *subsequent events* as events or transactions that occur subsequent to the balance sheet date but before financial statements are issued or are available to be issued. FASB ASC 855, *Subsequent Events*, includes general guidance applicable to all entities on accounting for, and disclosure of, events after the reporting period (subsequent events) that are not addressed specifically in other topics within FASB ASC. The following are the two types of subsequent events: the first type existed at the balance sheet date and includes the estimates inherent in the process of preparing financial statements (recognized subsequent events); the second type did not exist at the balance sheet date but arose subsequent to that date (nonrecognized subsequent events). The first type of subsequent event should be recognized in the entity's financial statements.

1.109 FASB ASC 855-10-25-1 requires an entity to recognize the effects of events that provide evidence of conditions that existed at the balance sheet date, including accounting estimates. FASB ASC 855-10-25-1A indicates that an SEC filer or a conduit bond obligor for conduit debt securities that are traded in a public market (a domestic or foreign stock exchange or an over-the-counter market, including local or regional markets) should evaluate subsequent events through the date the financial statements are issued. In addition, FASB ASC 855-10-25-2 requires all other entities that do not meet the criteria outlined in FASB ASC 855-10-25-1A to evaluate such events through the date the financial statements are available to be issued. As defined in the FASB ASC glossary, financial statements are considered available to be issued when they are complete in a form and format that complies with GAAP and all approvals necessary for issuance have been obtained, for example, from management, the board of directors, and all significant shareholders.

1.110 FASB ASC 855-10-25-3 prohibits an entity from recognizing subsequent events that provide evidence about conditions that did not exist at the date of the balance sheet but which arose after that date but before the financial statements are issued or are available to be issued.

1.111 FASB ASC 855-10-25-4 also addresses the potential for reissue of the financial statements in reports filed with regulatory agencies. In this circumstance, an entity should not recognize events occurring between the time the financial statements were originally issued or were available to be issued and the time the financial statements were reissued, unless GAAP or regulatory requirements require the adjustment. Similarly, an entity should not recognize events or transactions occurring after the financial statements were issued or were available to be issued in financial statements that are later reissued in comparative form along with financial statements of subsequent periods, unless the adjustment meets the criteria previously stated.

DISCLOSURE

1.112 FASB ASC 855-10-50-3 requires an entity to consider supplementing the historical financial statements with pro forma financial data when an unrecognized subsequent event occurs. An entity should present pro forma financial data when an unrecognized subsequent event is sufficiently significant that pro forma information provides the best disclosure. In preparing pro forma data, an entity should include the event as if it had occurred on the balance sheet date. An entity should also consider presenting pro forma statements, usually a statement of financial position only, in columnar form on the face of the historical statements.

1.113 Paragraphs 1 and 4 of FASB ASC 855-10-50 state that an entity, except an SEC registrant, should disclose the date through which subsequent events have been evaluated, as well as whether that date is the date the financial statements were issued or the date the financial statements were available to be issued. An entity, except an SEC registrant, should also disclose in the revised financial statements the date through which subsequent events have been evaluated in both the originally issued financial statements and the reissued financial statements.

PRESENTATION AND DISCLOSURE EXCERPTS

DEBT FINANCING

1.114 THE MANITOWOC COMPANY, INC. (DEC)
NOTES TO CONSOLIDATED FINANCIAL STATEMENTS (in part)

27. Subsequent Events

In connection with the previously announced spin-off (the "Spin-Off") of Manitowoc Foodservice, Inc. ("MFS") from Manitowoc the company entered into the following material agreements related to the debt financing for MFS and Manitowoc.

Foodservice Escrow Agreement

On February 5, 2016, in connection with the Spin-Off of MFS from Manitowoc, MFS entered into an escrow agreement (the "Escrow Agreement") among MFS, its subsidiary Enodis Holdings Limited, a corporation organized under the laws of the United Kingdom (the "UK Borrower"), the lenders party thereto, and JPMorgan Chase Bank, N.A., as administrative agent and as escrow agent, pursuant to which the parties thereto have delivered in escrow executed signature pages to a credit agreement (the "Credit Agreement") for a new senior secured revolving credit facility in an aggregate principal amount of $225 million (the "Revolving Facility") and a senior secured term loan B facility in an aggregate principal amount of $975 million (the "Term Loan Facility," and together with the Revolving Facility, the "Credit Facilities") with JPMorgan Chase Bank, N.A., as administrative agent and collateral agent, J.P. Morgan Securities LLC, Goldman Sachs Bank USA, HSBC Securities (USA) Inc., and Citigroup Global Markets Inc., on behalf of certain of its affiliates, as joint lead arrangers and joint bookrunners, and certain lenders, as lenders. The Revolving Facility will include (i) a $20 million sublimit for the issuance of letters of credit on customary terms, and (ii) a $40 million sublimit for swingline loans on customary terms. Pursuant to the Escrow Agreement, the executed signature pages will be released from escrow only upon written notice from MFS and the UK Borrower to JPMorgan Chase Bank, N.A., in its capacity as escrow agent under the Escrow Agreement. The escrowed Credit Agreement will become effective upon delivery of such notice. MFS expects to enter into security and other agreements relating to the Credit Agreement governing the Revolving Facility and the Term Loan Facility.

The Term Loan Facility proceeds will be used in part to repay existing debt, and for the payment of a cash dividend to Manitowoc in an amount sufficient to repay certain of Manitowoc existing debt and credit facilities (the "Foodservice Dividend") in connection with the contribution of certain assets to MFS immediately prior to the completion of the Spin-Off. Any proceeds remaining after the payment of the Foodservice Dividend will be used by MFS for general corporate purposes.

Borrowings under the Credit Facilities are expected to bear interest at a rate per annum equal to, at the option of MFS, (i) LIBOR plus the applicable margin of approximately 4.75% for term loans subject to a 1.00% LIBOR floor and 1.50% to 2.75% for revolving loans, based on consolidated total leverage, or (ii) an alternate base rate plus the applicable margin, which will be 1.00% lower than for LIBOR loans.

Foodservice Notes Purchase Agreement

On February 18, 2016, in connection with the previously announced Spin-Off, MFS's wholly owned subsidiary, MTW Foodservice Escrow Corp. (the "Foodservice Escrow Issuer"), entered into an indenture (the "Foodservice Indenture") with Wells Fargo Bank, National Association, as trustee (in such capacity, the "Foodservice Trustee"). Pursuant to the Foodservice Indenture, on the same date, the Foodservice Escrow Issuer issued $425 million in aggregate principal amount of the Foodservice Escrow Issuer's 9.500% senior notes due 2024 (the "Foodservice Notes"). The Foodservice Notes bear interest at a rate of 9.500% per year, payable in cash semi-annually on February 15 and August 15 of each year, commencing on August 15, 2016. The Foodservice Notes will mature on February 15, 2024, unless earlier repurchased or redeemed. The Foodservice Notes have not been registered under the Securities Act of 1933, as amended (the "Securities Act"), and will be resold by the initial purchasers (the "Foodservice Purchasers") to qualified institutional buyers pursuant to Rule 144A (and outside the United States in reliance on Regulation S) under the Securities Act.

Following the issuance of the Foodservice Notes, the Foodservice Escrow Issuer and MFS deposited the proceeds from the Foodservice Notes, together with an amount sufficient to fund a special mandatory redemption, as described below, into a segregated escrow account (the "Foodservice Escrow Account"). The funds will be released from escrow (the "Foodservice Escrow Release") upon the delivery of an officers' certificate to the escrow agent certifying, among other things, that substantially concurrently with the Foodservice Escrow Release, the following conditions will be satisfied:

- the Spin-Off will be consummated within five business days and no later than July 1, 2016;
- MFS will use the escrowed funds to (i) pay a cash dividend to Manitowoc in an amount sufficient, together with Manitowoc's other cash on hand, to repay certain of Manitowoc's existing debt and credit facilities (the "Foodservice Dividend") and (ii) pay certain fees and expenses, and Manitowoc will use the proceeds from the Foodservice Dividend accordingly;
- substantially concurrently with the Foodservice Escrow Release, the lenders under MFS's new senior secured term loan B facility (the "Term Loan Facility") will fund the term loan thereunder in an aggregate principal amount of at least $975 million, less any applicable discounts, fees and expenses;
- immediately prior to the Foodservice Escrow Release, the Foodservice Escrow Issuer will be merged with and into MFS (the "Foodservice Escrow Merger");
- immediately prior to the Foodservice Escrow Release, MFS and each of its domestic restricted subsidiaries that is a borrower or a guarantor under the Term Loan Facility and MFS's new senior secured revolving credit facility (the "Foodservice Guarantors") will have executed a supplemental indenture pursuant to which MFS will assume the Foodservice Escrow Issuer's obligations under the Foodservice Notes and the Foodservice Indenture and the Foodservice Guarantors will guarantee the Foodservice Notes as of the date of the Foodservice Escrow Release;
- immediately prior to the Foodservice Escrow Release, MFS and the Foodservice Guarantors will execute a joinder to a related registration rights agreement;
- MFS, the Foodservice Escrow Issuer and the Foodservice Guarantors will deliver certain opinions of counsel to the Foodservice Trustee and the Foodservice Purchasers, as required under the Foodservice Indenture and the purchase agreement related to the Foodservice Notes; and
- no event of default under the Foodservice Indenture shall have occurred and be continuing (or would result therefrom).

If (x) by July 1, 2016, the escrow agent and the Foodservice Trustee have not received the officers' certificate regarding the conditions for the Foodservice Escrow Release described above or (y) at any time prior to the Foodservice Escrow Release, (i) the Foodservice Escrow Issuer notifies the Foodservice Trustee in writing that the board of directors of Manitowoc has determined, in its sole and absolute discretion, that the Spin-Off is not in the best interests of Manitowoc or its shareholders or is otherwise not advisable and that Manitowoc will not pursue the completion of the Spin-Off, (ii) Manitowoc, in its sole discretion, publicly announces that it will not pursue the completion of the Spin-Off or (iii) the Foodservice Escrow Issuer notifies the Foodservice Trustee in writing that the conditions for the Foodservice Escrow Release cannot be satisfied on or prior to July 1, 2016, the Foodservice Escrow Issuer will be required to notify noteholders and redeem the Foodservice Notes within five business days thereafter at a special mandatory redemption price equal to 100% of the principal amount of the Foodservice Notes, together with the interest accrued on the Foodservice Notes from the issue date to but excluding the date of redemption.

From and after the Foodservice Escrow Release, the Foodservice Notes will be fully and unconditionally guaranteed, jointly and severally, on an unsecured basis by the Foodservice Guarantors. Prior to the Foodservice Escrow Release, the Foodservice Notes will be secured by a first-priority lien on and security interest in the Foodservice Escrow Account and the escrowed funds therein. From and after the Foodservice Escrow Release, the Foodservice Notes and the subsidiary guarantees will be senior unsecured obligations.

The Foodservice Escrow Issuer or, after the Foodservice Escrow Merger, MFS may redeem some or all of the Foodservice Notes from time to time at a redemption price equal to the principal amount of the notes to be redeemed plus certain premiums as set forth in the Foodservice Indenture. The Foodservice Escrow Issuer or, after the Foodservice Escrow Merger, MFS must generally offer to repurchase all of the outstanding Foodservice Notes upon the occurrence of certain specific change of control events at a purchase price equal to 101% of the principal amount of Foodservice Notes purchased plus accrued and unpaid interest to the date of purchase.

The Foodservice Indenture provides for customary events of default, including with respect to the escrow arrangements. Generally, if an event of default occurs (subject to certain exceptions), the Foodservice Trustee or the holders of at least 25% in aggregate principal amount of the then-outstanding Foodservice Notes may declare all the Foodservice Notes to be due and payable immediately.

Among other things, the Foodservice Indenture also limits the ability of MFS and its subsidiaries to engage in certain activities, including: incurring additional indebtedness or issuing certain preferred stock; paying dividends or making certain other restricted payments; incurring liens; entering into certain types of transactions with affiliates; and consolidating or merging with or into other companies or undergoing certain other fundamental changes (excluding the Foodservice Escrow Merger and the Spin-Off). If, in the future, the Foodservice Notes have investment grade credit ratings and no default or event of default exists under the Foodservice Indenture, certain of these covenants will no longer apply to the Foodservice Notes for so long as the Foodservice Notes are rated investment grade. These and other covenants contained in the Indenture are subject to important exceptions and qualifications.

Cranes Indenture

On February 18, 2016, also in connection with the Spin-Off, Manitowoc's wholly owned subsidiary, MTW Cranes Escrow Corp. (the "Cranes Escrow Issuer"), entered into an indenture (the "Cranes Indenture") with Wells Fargo Bank, National Association, as trustee (in such capacity, the "Cranes Trustee") and as collateral agent. Pursuant to the Cranes Indenture, on the same date, the Cranes Escrow Issuer issued $260 million in aggregate principal amount of its 12.75% in aggregate principal amount of its 12.75% per year, payable in cash semi-annually on February 15 and August 15 of each year, commencing on August 15, 2016. The Cranes Notes will mature on August 15, 2021, unless earlier repurchased or redeemed. The Cranes Notes have not been registered under the Securities Act, and will be resold by the initial purchasers (the "Cranes Purchasers") to qualified institutional buyers pursuant to Rule 144A (and outside the United States in reliance on Regulation S) under the Securities Act.

Following the issuance of the Cranes Notes, the Cranes Escrow Issuer and Manitowoc deposited the net proceeds from the Cranes Notes, together with an amount sufficient to fund a special mandatory redemption, as described below, into a segregated escrow account (the "Cranes Escrow Account"). The funds will be released from escrow (the "Cranes Escrow Release") upon the delivery of an officer's certificate to the escrow agent certifying, among other things, that substantially concurrently with the Cranes Escrow Release the following conditions will be satisfied:

* the Spin-Off will be consummated within five business days and no later than July 1, 2016;
* Manitowoc will use the escrowed funds, together with the proceeds of the Foodservice Dividend and other borrowings, to (i) repay all of Manitowoc's outstanding $600 million aggregate principal amount of 8.50% senior notes due 2020 and all of Manitowoc's $300 million aggregate principal amount of 5.875% senior notes due 2022; (ii) repay all amounts outstanding under, and to terminate, Manitowoc's existing revolving credit facility and term loan facilities; (iii) repay certain other debt of Manitowoc's subsidiaries; and (iv) pay certain fees and expenses;
* immediately prior to the Cranes Escrow Release, the Cranes Escrow Issuer will be merged with and into Manitowoc (the "Cranes Escrow Merger");
* immediately prior to the Cranes Escrow Release, Manitowoc and each of Manitowoc's domestic restricted subsidiaries that is a borrower or a guarantor under an asset-based revolving credit facility that Manitowoc expects to enter into on or about the date of the Cranes Escrow Release (the "Cranes Guarantors") will have executed a supplemental indenture, pursuant to which Manitowoc will assume the Cranes Escrow Issuer's obligations under the Cranes Notes and the Cranes Indenture and the Cranes Guarantors will guarantee the Cranes Notes as of the date of the Cranes Escrow Release;
* Manitowoc, the Cranes Escrow Issuer and the Cranes Guarantors will deliver certain opinions of counsel to the Cranes Trustee and the Cranes Purchasers, as required under the Cranes Indenture and the purchase agreement related to the Cranes Notes; and
* no event of default under the Cranes Indenture shall have occurred and be continuing (or would result therefrom).

If (x) by July 1, 2016, the escrow agent and the Cranes Trustee have not received the officers' certificate regarding the conditions for the Cranes Escrow Release described above or (y) at any time prior to the Cranes Escrow Release, (i) the Cranes Escrow Issuer notifies the Cranes Trustee in writing that the board of directors of Manitowoc has determined, in its sole and absolute discretion, that the Spin-Off is not in the best interests of Manitowoc or its shareholders or is otherwise not advisable and that Manitowoc will not pursue the completion of the Spin-Off, (ii) Manitowoc, in its sole discretion, publicly announces that it will not pursue the completion of the Spin-Off or (iii) the Cranes

Escrow Issuer notifies the Cranes Trustee in writing that the conditions for the Cranes Escrow Release cannot be satisfied on or prior to July 1, 2016, the Cranes Escrow Issuer will be required to notify noteholders and redeem the Cranes Notes within five business days thereafter at a special mandatory redemption price equal to 100% of the issue price of the Cranes Notes, together with the interest accrued on the Cranes Notes from the issue date to but excluding the date of redemption.

Prior to the Cranes Escrow Release, the Cranes Notes will be secured by a first-priority lien on and security interest in the Cranes Escrow Account and the escrowed funds therein. From and after the Cranes Escrow Release, the Cranes Notes will be fully and unconditionally guaranteed, jointly and severally, on a senior secured second lien basis by each of the Cranes Guarantors. From and after the Cranes Escrow Release, the Cranes Notes and the related guarantees will be secured by, and noteholders will have a second-priority security interest in, all capital stock held by Manitowoc and the Cranes Guarantors and substantially all of the other property and assets held by Manitowoc and the Cranes Guarantors, except for certain specific excluded assets.

The Cranes Escrow Issuer or, after the Cranes Escrow Merger, Manitowoc may redeem some or all of the Cranes Notes from time to time at a redemption price equal to the principal amount of the notes to be redeemed plus certain premiums as set forth in the Cranes Indenture. The Cranes Escrow Issuer or, after the Cranes Escrow Merger, Manitowoc must generally offer to repurchase all of the outstanding Cranes Notes upon the occurrence of certain specific change of control events at a purchase price equal to 101% of the principal amount of Cranes Notes purchased plus accrued and unpaid interest to the date of purchase.

The Cranes Indenture provides for customary events of default, including with respect to the escrow arrangements. Generally, if an event of default occurs (subject to certain exceptions), the Cranes Trustee or the holders of at least 25% in aggregate principal amount of the then-outstanding Cranes Notes may declare all the Cranes Notes to be due and payable immediately.

Among other things, the Cranes Indenture also limits the ability of Manitowoc and its subsidiaries to engage in certain activities, including: incurring additional indebtedness or issuing certain preferred stock; paying dividends or making certain other restricted payments; incurring liens; entering into certain types of transactions with affiliates; and consolidating or merging with or into other companies (excluding the Cranes Escrow Merger and the Spin-Off). These and other covenants contained in the Indenture are subject to important exceptions and qualifications.

SEPARATION TRANSACTION

1.115 W. R. GRACE & CO. (DEC)
NOTES TO CONSOLIDATED FINANCIAL STATEMENTS (in part)

1. Basis of Presentation and Summary of Significant Accounting and Financial Reporting Policies (in part)

W. R. Grace & Co., through its subsidiaries, is engaged in specialty chemicals and specialty materials businesses on a global basis through three operating segments: Grace Catalysts Technologies, which includes catalysts and related products and technologies used in refining, petrochemical and other chemical manufacturing applications; Grace Materials Technologies, which includes packaging technologies and engineered materials used in consumer, industrial, coatings, and pharmaceutical applications; and Grace Construction Products, which includes specialty construction chemicals and specialty building materials used in commercial, infrastructure and residential construction.

W. R. Grace & Co. conducts all of its business through a single wholly owned subsidiary, W. R. Grace & Co.—Conn. ("Grace—Conn."). Grace—Conn. owns all of the assets, properties and rights of W. R. Grace & Co. on a consolidated basis, either directly or through subsidiaries.

As used in these notes, the term "Company" refers to W. R. Grace & Co. The term "Grace" refers to the Company and/or one or more of its subsidiaries and, in certain cases, their respective predecessors.

Separation Transaction On February 5, 2015, Grace announced a plan to separate into two independent, publicly traded companies, intended to improve Grace's strategic focus, simplify its operating structure, and allow for more efficient capital allocation. On January 27, 2016, Grace entered into a separation agreement with GCP Applied Technologies Inc., then a wholly-owned subsidiary of Grace ("GCP"), pursuant to which Grace agreed to transfer its Grace Construction Products operating segment and the packaging technologies business, operated under the "Darex" name, of its Grace Materials Technologies operating segment to GCP (the "Separation"). The Separation occurred on February 3, 2016, by means of a pro rata distribution to Grace stockholders of all of the outstanding shares of GCP common stock (the "Distribution"). Under the Distribution, one share of GCP common stock was distributed for each share of Grace common stock held as of the close of business on January 27, 2016. No fractional shares were distributed. As a result of the Distribution, GCP is now an independent public company and its common stock is listed under the symbol "GCP" on the New York Stock Exchange.

5. Debt (in part)

Credit Agreement (in part)

On February 3, 2014, Grace entered into a Credit Agreement (the "Credit Agreement") in connection with its exit financing. The Credit Agreement provides for:
- (a) a $700 million term loan due in 2021, with interest at LIBOR + 225 bps with a 75 bps floor;
- (b) a €150 million term loan due in 2021, with interest at EURIBOR + 250 bps with a 75 bps floor;
- (c) a $400 million revolving credit facility due in 2019, with interest at LIBOR + 175 bps; and
- (d) a $250 million delayed draw term loan facility available for 12 months, with amounts drawn due in 2021, with interest at LIBOR + 225 bps with a 75 bps floor.

During the fourth quarter, Grace entered into an amendment to the Credit Agreement to permit the Separation. The amendment, which became effective upon completion of the Separation, revised certain covenants, reduced the revolving credit facility limit to $300 million and extended the facility's term to November 1, 2020.

In connection with the Separation, GCP distributed $750 million to Grace. Using a portion of these proceeds, Grace repaid $500 million of its euro and U.S. dollar term loans. See Note 21 for information related to the Separation.

7. Income Taxes (in part)

Unrepatriated Foreign Earnings (in part)

As of December 31, 2014, Grace had the intent and ability to indefinitely reinvest undistributed earnings of its foreign subsidiaries outside the United States. In the 2015 first quarter, Grace announced its plan to separate into two publicly traded companies and has subsequently reassessed the capital structure and financial requirements of both Grace and GCP. Further, in connection with the Separation, Grace repatriated a total of $173.1 million of foreign earnings from foreign subsidiaries transferred to GCP pursuant to the Separation. Such amount was determined based on an analysis of each non-U.S. subsidiary's requirements for working capital, debt repayment and strategic initiatives. Grace also considered local country legal and regulatory restrictions. In 2015, Grace included tax expense of $19.0 million in its effective tax rate for repatriation attributable to both current and prior years' earnings. The tax effect of the repatriation is determined by several variables including the tax rate applicable to the entity making the distribution, the cumulative earnings and associated foreign taxes of the entity and the extent to which those earnings may have already been taxed in the U.S. Grace anticipates that the tax consequences of other transactions pursuant to the Separation may require recognition of additional tax expense for deemed repatriation of undistributed earnings of our foreign subsidiaries. Such tax consequences will be recorded in the 2016 first quarter.

Grace believes that the Separation is a one-time, non-recurring event, and that recognition of deferred taxes of undistributed earnings during 2015 would not have occurred if not for the Separation. Subsequent to separation, Grace expects undistributed prior-year earnings of its foreign subsidiaries to remain permanently reinvested except in certain instances where repatriation of such earnings would result in minimal or no tax. Grace bases this assertion on:
- (1) the expectation that it will satisfy its U.S. cash obligations in the foreseeable future without requiring the repatriation of prior-year foreign earnings;
- (2) plans for significant and continued reinvestment of foreign earnings in organic and inorganic growth initiatives outside the U.S.; and
- (3) remittance restrictions imposed by local governments.

Grace will continually analyze and evaluate its cash needs to determine the appropriateness of its indefinite reinvestment assertion.

21. Subsequent Event

On February 3, 2016, (the "Distribution Date"), Grace completed the separation of GCP. As a result, beginning in the 2016 first quarter, GCP's historical financial results through the Distribution Date will be reflected in Grace's Consolidated Financial Statements as a discontinued operation. To effect the Separation, Grace distributed to its stockholders one share of GCP common stock, par value $0.01 per share, for each share of Company common stock, par value $0.01 per share outstanding as of 5:00 p.m. on January 27, 2016, the record date for the Distribution. In lieu of fractional shares of GCP, Grace stockholders received cash, which generally will be subject to income tax.

In connection with the Separation, GCP distributed $750 million to Grace. Grace used $500 million of those funds to repay $426.9 million of its U.S. dollar term loan and €67.3 million of its euro term loan. In connection with the financing GCP entered into related to the Separation, mortgages or deeds of trust will be executed with respect to GCP properties in Chicago, Illinois, and Mount Pleasant, Tennessee. Grace will have no obligations with respect to such mortgages or deeds of trust.

ACQUISITIONS

1.116 ATMEL CORPORATION (DEC)
NOTES TO CONSOLIDATED FINANCIAL STATEMENTS (in part)

Note 1. Business and Summary of Significant Accounting Policies (in part)

Pending Acquisition of Atmel by Microchip Technology

On January 19, 2016, Atmel entered into an Agreement and Plan of Merger (the "Merger Agreement") with Microchip Technology Incorporated ("Microchip"), and Hero Acquisition Corporation, a wholly-owned subsidiary of Microchip ("Merger Sub"), after terminating a previously announced merger agreement with Dialog Semiconductor plc.

Under the terms of the Merger Agreement, the acquisition of Atmel will be accomplished through a merger of Merger Sub with and into Atmel (the "Merger"), with Atmel being the surviving corporation (the "Surviving Corporation").

At the effective time of the Merger (the "Effective Time"), each share of Atmel's common stock issued and outstanding immediately prior to the Merger (other than dissenting shares and shares held by Microchip, Merger Sub, Atmel or any of their respective subsidiaries) will be converted into the right to receive (1) $7.00 in cash and (2) a fraction of a share of Microchip common stock having a value of $1.15, based on a ten-day average of the closing price of Microchip's common stock measured as of the day before the closing of the Merger (with cash being substituted for Microchip common stock to the extent that the aggregate number of shares of Microchip stock issued in exchange for Atmel stock would exceed 13 million shares) (the "Merger Consideration").

Each of Microchip's and Atmel's respective obligation to consummate the Merger is subject to a number of conditions specified in the Merger Agreement, including the following: (1) adoption of the Merger Agreement by Atmel's stockholders, (2) effectiveness under the Securities Act of 1933 of the Registration Statement on Form S-4 to be filed with the U.S. Securities and Exchange Commission (the "SEC") by Microchip in connection with the Microchip common stock issuable to Atmel stockholders in the Merger; (3) approval for listing on The NASDAQ Stock Market of the Microchip common stock issuable to Atmel stockholders in the Merger; (4) expiration or termination of the waiting period under the Hart-Scott-Rodino Antitrust Improvements Act of 1976 and receipt of antitrust clearances in Germany and South Korea (the "Antitrust Condition"); (5) absence of laws, orders, judgments and injunctions that enjoin or otherwise prohibit consummation of the Merger and any proceedings instituted by a governmental entity with competent jurisdiction seeking any of the foregoing; (6) subject to certain materiality-related standards contained in the Merger Agreement, the accuracy of the respective representations and warranties made by Atmel and Microchip and material compliance with the respective covenants of Atmel and Microchip in the Merger Agreement and (7) the absence of a material adverse effect with respect to the other party. The consummation of the Merger is not subject to a financing condition.

The Merger Agreement contains customary representations, warranties and covenants by the parties and requires the payment of termination fees under specified conditions.

The foregoing description of the Merger and the Merger Agreement does not purport to be complete and is qualified in its entirety by reference to the Merger Agreement.

In the year ended December 31, 2015, Atmel recorded transaction-related costs of approximately $11.6 million, principally for outside financial advisory, legal, and related fees and expenses associated with the strategic transaction process. These costs were recorded in selling, general and administrative expense included in the Consolidated Statements of Operations for the year ended December 31, 2015. Additional transaction-related costs are expected to be incurred through the closing of the Merger.

Related Party Transactions

DISCLOSURE

1.117 FASB ASC 850, *Related Party Disclosures,* specifies the nature of information that should be disclosed in financial statements about related-party transactions and certain common control relationships. FASB ASC 850-10-50-1 requires an entity to disclose material related party transactions but exempts compensation arrangements, expense allowances, and other similar items in the ordinary course of business from disclosure requirements. However, Item 402, "Executive Compensation," of SEC Regulation S-K requires SEC registrants to provide compensation information outside the financial statements for specified members of management. The disclosures should include the nature of the relationship(s) involved, a description of the transactions, the dollar amounts of the transactions, and amounts due to or from related parties for each period for which the entity presents an income statement. FASB ASC 740-10-50-17 also includes guidance for entities with separately issued financial statements that are members of a consolidated tax return and the additional disclosures that are required. Further, if the reporting entity and one or more other companies are under common ownership or management control, and the existence of that control could result in operating results or a financial position of the reporting entity significantly different from those that would have been obtained if the companies were autonomous, FASB ASC 850-10-50-6 requires the nature of the control relationship to be disclosed even if there are no transactions between the entities.

PRESENTATION AND DISCLOSURE EXCERPTS

TRANSACTIONS WITH RELATED PARTIES

1.118 UNIFI, INC. (JUN)
NOTES TO CONSOLIDATED FINANCIAL STATEMENTS (in part)

25. Related Party Transactions

Related party receivables consist of the following:

	June 28, 2015	June 29, 2014
Cupron, Inc.	$72	$ 1
Salem Global Logistics, Inc.	3	12
Dillon Yarn Corporation	—	4
Total related party receivables (included within receivables, net)	$75	$17

Related party payables consist of the following:

	June 28, 2015	June 29, 2014
Cupron, Inc.	$506	$525
Salem Leasing Corporation	277	272
Dillon Yarn Corporation[1]	117	131
Total related party payables (included within accounts payable)	$900	$928

[1] Excludes amounts related to the contingent consideration, as detailed in "Note 18. Fair Value of Financial Instruments and Non-Financial Assets and Liabilities"

Related party transactions consist of the matters in the table below and the following paragraphs:

Affiliated Entity	Transaction Type	For the Fiscal Years Ended		
		June 28, 2015	June 29, 2014	June 30, 2013
Dillon Yarn Corporation	Yarn purchases	$2,000	$3,042	$2,523
Dillon Yarn Corporation	Sales service agreement costs	—	—	349
Dillon Yarn Corporation	Sales	—	1,237	182
Dillon Yarn Corporation	Reimbursement of equipment relocation costs	—	—	75
American Drawtech Company, Inc.	Sales	—	—	884
American Drawtech Company, Inc.	Yarn purchases	—	—	56
Salem Leasing Corporation	Transportation equipment costs	3,633	3,607	3,077
Salem Global Logistics	Freight services	179	25	—
Cupron, Inc.	Sales	925	486	236
Cupron, Inc.	Yarn purchases	281	8	—
Invemed Associates LLC	Brokerage services	3	23	11

Through April 24, 2015, Mr. Mitchel Weinberger was a member of the Company's Board, President and Chief Operating Officer of Dillon and an Executive Vice President and a director of ADC. In fiscal year 2007, the Company purchased the polyester and nylon texturing operations of Dillon and entered into an agreement under which the Company agreed to pay Dillon for certain sales and services to be provided by Dillon's sales staff and executive management. That agreement expired pursuant to its terms on December 31, 2012. In addition, the Company recorded sales and service income from Dillon and has purchased products from Dillon.

On April 8, 2013, the Company entered a commissioning agreement with Dillon. Under the terms of the agreement, the Company agreed to move Dillon's draw winding equipment from Dillon's facility in Dillon, South Carolina and install it in the Company's polyester texturing facility in Yadkinville, North Carolina. Pursuant to the exercise of an option granted to the Company under the terms of the commissioning agreement, the Company acquired the draw winding equipment and associated business from Dillon on December 2, 2013, as described in "Note 4. Acquisition."

On March 22, 2013, the Company entered into a Stock Purchase Agreement with Dillon. Pursuant to the Stock Purchase Agreement, the Company repurchased 500 shares of the Company's common stock from Dillon for an aggregate amount of $8,500. The Company and Dillon negotiated the $17.00 per share price based on an approximately 10% discount to the closing price of the stock on March 20, 2013.

On November 1, 2013, the Company entered into a second Stock Purchase Agreement with Dillon, pursuant to which the Company purchased 150 shares of the Company's common stock from Dillon, at a negotiated price of $23.00 per share, for $3,450. The purchase price was equal to an approximately 6% discount to the closing price of the common stock on October 31, 2013.

On June 18, 2015, the Company entered into a third Stock Purchase Agreement with Dillon. In connection therewith, the Company repurchased 200 shares of the Company's common stock from Dillon for an aggregate amount of $6,200. The Company and Dillon negotiated the $31.00 per share price based on an approximately 3% discount to the closing price of the stock on June 17, 2015.

The Board approved these stock repurchase transactions in accordance with its related persons transactions policy. Mr. Weinberger was not involved in any decisions by the Board, or any committee thereof, with respect to these stock repurchase transactions.

Mr. Kenneth G. Langone, a member of the Board, is a director, stockholder and non-executive Chairman of the Board of Salem Holding Company. The Company leases tractors and trailers from Salem Leasing Corporation, a wholly-owned subsidiary of Salem Holding Company. In addition to the monthly operating lease payments, the Company also incurs expenses for routine repair and maintenance, fuel and other expenses. These leases do not contain renewal, purchase options or escalation clauses with respect to the minimum lease charges.

Salem Global Logistics, Inc. is also a wholly-owned subsidiary of Salem Holding Company. During fiscal years 2015 and 2014, the Company earned income by providing for-hire freight services for Salem Global Logistics, Inc.

On November 19, 2012, the Company entered into a capital lease with Salem Leasing Corporation for certain transportation equipment. The present value of the fifteen-year lease was $1,234 and payments are made monthly. The implicit annual interest rate under the lease is approximately 4.6%. The balance of the capital lease obligation as of June 28, 2015 was $1,081.

Mr. William J. Armfield, IV, a member of the Board, holds an indirect minority equity interest in (and is non-executive Chairman of the Board of) Cupron, Inc. ("Cupron") and is also a director.

Mr. Langone is also the President and Chief Executive Officer of Invemed Associates LLC ("Invemed"). During fiscal years 2015, 2014 and 2013, Invemed provided brokerage services to the Company for the Company's repurchase of 149, 1,149 and 568 shares of its common stock, respectively, through open market transactions. The Company paid a commission of $.02 per share to Invemed.

On December 3, 2013, certain of the Company's executive officers exercised options to purchase shares of the Company's common stock under previously granted option awards. Pursuant to authorization from the Company's Board, and as part of the 2013 SRP, the Company repurchased 225 shares of common stock issued in those option exercises at a negotiated price of $25.59 per share (which was equal to the average of the closing trade prices of the Company's common stock for the 30 days ending December 2, 2013 and represented a 7.1% discount to the $27.56 closing price of the common stock on December 2, 2013).

1.119 CHARTER COMMUNICATIONS, INC. (DEC)
NOTES TO CONSOLIDATED FINANCIAL STATEMENTS (in part)

(dollars in millions, except share or per share data or where indicated)

17. Related Party Transactions

The following sets forth certain transactions in which the Company and the directors, executive officers, and affiliates of the Company are involved or, in the case of the management arrangements, subsidiaries that are debt issuers that pay certain of their parent companies for services.

Charter is a party to management arrangements with Charter Holdco and certain of its subsidiaries. Under these agreements, Charter and Charter Holdco provide management services for the cable systems owned or operated by their subsidiaries. Costs associated with providing these services are charged directly to the Company's operating subsidiaries. All other costs incurred on behalf of Charter's operating subsidiaries are considered a part of the management fee. These costs are recorded as a component of operating costs and expenses, in the accompanying consolidated financial statements. The management fee charged to the Company's operating subsidiaries approximated the expenses incurred by Charter Holdco and Charter on behalf of the Company's operating subsidiaries in 2015, 2014, and 2013.

Equity Investments

On May 1, 2015, the Company acquired a 35% equity interest in ActiveVideo Networks ("AVN") for $55 million in cash representing the initial investment, a capital call and associated transaction fees. AVN is the developer of CloudTV, a cloud-based software platform enabling service providers, content aggregators, and consumer electronic manufacturers to deploy new services by virtualizing consumer premise equipment functions in the cloud. AVN's software platform is one of the key technologies enabling the development and deployment of the Company's cloud-based user interface, Spectrum Guide ®. The Company applies the equity method of accounting to this investment which is recorded in other noncurrent assets in the consolidated balance sheet as of December 31, 2015. For the year ended December 31, 2015, the Company recorded equity losses for AVN and other investments of $7 million in other expense, net. The Company has agreements with AVN and other equity investments pursuant to which the Company made related party transaction payments to investees totaling approximately $28 million during the year ended December 31, 2015.

Liberty Broadband

On May 23, 2015, in connection with the execution of the Merger Agreement and the amendment of the Contribution Agreement, Charter entered into the Amended and Restated Stockholders Agreement with Liberty Broadband, A/N and New Charter (the "Stockholders Agreement"). The Stockholders Agreement replaced Charter's existing stockholders agreement with Liberty Broadband, dated September 29, 2014, and superseded the amended and restated stockholders agreement among Charter, New Charter, Liberty Broadband and A/N, dated March 31, 2015. Charter's existing stockholders agreement with Liberty Broadband (as amended by an investment agreement between Liberty Broadband, Charter and New Charter, dated as of May 23, 2015) will remain in effect until the closing of the TWC Transaction or the Bright House Transaction, whichever occurs earlier, and, in the event the Stockholders Agreement is terminated, will revive and continue in full force and effect. Certain provisions of the Stockholders Agreement became effective upon its execution. See Note 3 for additional information.

Under the terms of the Stockholders Agreement, the number of New Charter directors will be fixed at 13, and will include New Charter's chief executive officer. Upon the closing of the Bright House Transaction, two designees selected by A/N and three designees selected by Liberty Broadband will become members of the board of directors of New Charter. The remaining eight directors (other than the chief executive officer, who is expected to become chairman of the board) will be independent directors selected by the nominating committee of the New Charter board by the approval of both a majority of the nominating committee and a majority of the directors that were not appointed by either A/N or Liberty Broadband. Thereafter, Liberty Broadband will be entitled to designate three nominees to be elected as directors and A/N will be entitled to designate two nominees to be elected as directors, in each case provided that each maintains certain specified voting or equity ownership thresholds, provided that each nominee must meet any applicable requirements or qualifications. Each of A/N and Liberty Broadband will be entitled to nominate at least one director to each of the committees of the Charter board of directors, subject to applicable stock exchange listing rules and certain specified voting or equity ownership thresholds for each of A/N and Liberty Broadband, and provided that the nominating and compensation committees will have at least a majority of directors independent from A/N, Liberty Broadband and New Charter (referred to as the "unaffiliated directors"). The nominating committee will be comprised of three unaffiliated directors, and one designee of each of A/N and Liberty Broadband. A/N and Liberty Broadband also will have certain other committee designation and other governance rights. Mr. Thomas Rutledge, the Company's Chief Executive Officer ("CEO"), will be offered the positions of CEO and chairman of New Charter.

The Company is aware that Dr. Malone may be deemed to have a 36.8% voting interest in Liberty Interactive and is Chairman of the board of directors, an executive officer position, of Liberty Interactive. Liberty Interactive owns 38.0% of the common stock of HSN, Inc. ("HSN") and has the right to elect 20% of the board members of HSN. Liberty Interactive wholly owns QVC, Inc ("QVC"). The Company has programming relationships with HSN and QVC which pre-date the Liberty Media Transaction. For the years ended December 31, 2015 and 2014 and nine months ended December 31, 2013, the Company recorded payments in aggregate of approximately $17 million, $14 million and $10 million, respectively, from HSN and QVC as part of channel carriage fees and revenue sharing arrangements for home shopping sales made to customers in Charter's footprint.

Dr. Malone also serves on the board of directors of Discovery Communications, Inc., ("Discovery") and the Company is aware that Dr. Malone owns 4.8% in the aggregate of the common stock of Discovery and has a 28.7% voting interest in Discovery for the election of directors. In addition, Dr. Malone owns approximately 10.8% in the aggregate of the common stock of Starz and has 47.2% of the voting power. Mr. Gregory Maffei, a member of Charter's board of directors, is a non-executive Chairman of the board of Starz. The Company purchases programming from both Discovery and Starz pursuant to agreements entered into prior to Dr. Malone and Mr. Maffei joining Charter's board of directors. Based on publicly available information, the Company does not believe that either Discovery or Starz would currently be considered related parties. The amounts paid in aggregate to Discovery and Starz represent less than 3% of total operating costs and expenses for the years ended December 31, 2015 and 2014 and nine months ended December 31, 2013.

1.120 IDT CORPORATION (JUL)
NOTES TO CONSOLIDATED FINANCIAL STATEMENTS (in part)

Note 20—Related Party Transactions

The Company entered into various agreements with Straight Path prior to the Straight Path Spin-Off including (1) a Separation and Distribution Agreement to effect the separation and provide a framework for the Company's relationship with Straight Path after the spin-off, (2) a Tax Separation Agreement, which sets forth the responsibilities of the Company and Straight Path with respect to, among other things, liabilities for federal, state, local and foreign taxes for periods before and including the spin-off, the preparation and filing of tax returns for such periods and disputes with taxing authorities regarding taxes for such periods, and (3) a Transition Services Agreement, which provides for certain services to be performed by the Company to facilitate Straight Path's transition into a separate publicly-traded company. These agreements provide for, among other things, the allocation between the Company and Straight Path of employee benefits, taxes and other liabilities and obligations attributable to periods prior to the spin-off, and provision of certain services by the Company to Straight Path following the spin-off, including services relating to human resources and employee benefits administration, treasury, accounting, tax, external reporting, and legal. Straight Path transitioned accounting and external reporting services from the Company to a third party in the first quarter of fiscal 2015. In addition, the Company and Straight Path have entered into a license agreement whereby each of the Company, Straight Path and their subsidiaries granted and will grant a license to the other to utilize patents held by each entity.

The Separation and Distribution Agreement also includes that the Company is obligated to reimburse Straight Path for the payment of any liabilities of Straight Path arising or related to the period prior to the Straight Path Spin-Off. The following table summarizes the change in the balance of the Company's estimated liability to Straight Path, which is included in "Other current liabilities" in the accompanying consolidated balance sheet:

(In thousands) Year Ended July 31	2015	2014
Balance at beginning of year	$1,860	$ 931
Additional liability	1,793	1,930
Adjustments	(556)	—
Payments	(2,811)	(1,001)
Balance at end of year	$ 286	$1,860

Pursuant to the Separation and Distribution Agreement, the Company indemnifies Straight Path and Straight Path indemnifies the Company for losses related to the failure of the other to pay, perform or otherwise discharge, any of the liabilities and obligations set forth in the agreement. Pursuant to the Tax Separation Agreement, the Company indemnifies Straight Path from all liability for taxes of Straight Path or any of its subsidiaries or relating to the Straight Path business with respect to taxable periods ending on or before the Straight Path Spin-Off, from all liability for taxes of the Company, other than Straight Path and its subsidiaries, for any taxable period, and from all liability for taxes due to the Straight Path Spin-Off.

The Company charged Straight Path $1.1 million and $0.8 million in fiscal 2015 and fiscal 2014, respectively, for services provided pursuant to the Transition Services Agreement and other items. At July 31, 2015 and 2014, other current assets reported in the Company's consolidated balance sheet included receivables from Straight Path of nil and $29,000, respectively.

In July 2015, the Company received 64,624 shares of Straight Path Class B common stock in connection with the lapsing of restrictions on awards of Straight Path restricted stock to certain of the Company's employees (see Note 4). As part of the Straight Path Spin-Off, holders of the Company's restricted Class B common stock received, in respect of those restricted shares, one share of Straight Path's Class B common stock for every two restricted shares of the Company that they held as of the record date for the Straight Path Spin-Off. The Company received the Straight Path shares in exchange for the payment of an aggregate of $2.1 million for the employees' tax withholding obligations upon the vesting event. The number of shares was determined based on their fair market value on the trading day immediately prior to the vesting date.

The Company entered into various agreements with Genie prior to the Genie Spin-Off including a Separation and Distribution Agreement to effect the separation and provide a framework for the Company's relationship with Genie after the spin-off, and a Transition Services Agreement, which provides for certain services to be performed by the Company and Genie to facilitate Genie's transition into a separate publicly-traded company. These agreements provide for, among other things, (1) the allocation between the Company and Genie of employee benefits, taxes and other liabilities and obligations attributable to periods prior to the spin-off, (2) transitional services to be provided by the Company relating to human resources and employee benefits administration, (3) the allocation of responsibilities relating to employee compensation and benefit plans and programs and other related matters, (4) finance, accounting, tax, internal audit, facilities, external reporting, investor relations and legal services to be provided by the Company to Genie following the spin-off and (5) specified administrative services to be provided by Genie to certain of the Company's foreign subsidiaries. In addition, the Company entered into a Tax Separation Agreement with Genie, which sets forth the responsibilities of the Company and Genie with respect to, among other things, liabilities for federal, state, local and foreign taxes for periods before and including the spin-off, the preparation and filing of tax returns for such periods and disputes with taxing authorities regarding taxes for such periods.

Pursuant to the Separation and Distribution Agreement, the Company indemnifies Genie and Genie indemnifies the Company for losses related to the failure of the other to pay, perform or otherwise discharge, any of the liabilities and obligations set forth in the agreement. Pursuant to the Tax Separation Agreement, the Company indemnifies Genie from all liability for the Company's taxes with respect to any taxable period, and Genie indemnifies the Company from all liability for taxes of Genie and its subsidiaries with respect to any taxable period, including, without limitation, the ongoing tax audits related to Genie's business.

The Company's Chairman of the Board and former Chief Executive Officer, Howard S. Jonas, is the controlling stockholder and Chairman of the Board of Genie. The Company charged Genie $3.6 million, $3.1 million and $3.8 million in fiscal 2015, fiscal 2014 and fiscal 2013, respectively, for services provided pursuant to the Transition Services Agreement and other items, net of the amounts charged by Genie to the Company. At July 31, 2015 and 2014, other current assets reported in the Company's consolidated balance sheet included receivables from Genie of $0.5 million.

IDT Energy, Inc., a subsidiary of Genie, supplied electricity to the Company's facilities in Piscataway, New Jersey, and Newark, New Jersey through January 2013. IDT Energy also supplied natural gas to the Company's Newark, New Jersey building until April 2013, and IDT Energy supplies natural gas to the Company's facility in Piscataway, New Jersey. In fiscal 2014 and fiscal 2013, IDT Energy, Inc. billed the Company $16,000 and $21,000, respectively.

The Company provides office space, certain connectivity and other services to Jonas Media Group, a publishing firm owned by Howard Jonas. Billings for such services were $21,000, $18,000 and $27,000 in fiscal 2015, fiscal 2014 and fiscal 2013, respectively. The balance owed to the Company by Jonas Media Group was $7,000 and $4,000 as of July 31, 2015 and 2014, respectively.

The Company obtains insurance policies from several insurance brokers, one of which is IGM Brokerage Corp. ("IGM"). IGM was, until his death in October 2009, owned by Irwin Jonas, father of Howard Jonas, and the Company's General Counsel, Joyce J. Mason. IGM is currently owned by Irwin Jonas' widow—the mother of Howard Jonas and Joyce Mason. Jonathan Mason, husband of Joyce Mason and brother-in-law of Howard Jonas, provides insurance brokerage services via IGM. Based on information the Company received from IGM, the Company believes that IGM received commissions and fees from payments made by the Company to third party brokers in the aggregate amounts of $20,000 in fiscal 2015, $20,000 in fiscal 2014 and $15,000 in fiscal 2013, which fees and commissions inured to the benefit of Mr. Mason. Neither Howard Jonas nor Joyce Mason has any ownership or other interest in IGM or the commissions paid to IGM other than via the familial relationships with their mother and Jonathan Mason.

Mason and Company Consulting, LLC ("Mason and Co."), a company owned solely by Jonathan Mason, receives an annual fee for the insurance brokerage referral and placement of the Company's health benefit plan with Brown & Brown Metro, Inc. Based on information the

Company received from Jonathan Mason, the Company believes that Mason and Co. received from Brown & Brown Metro, Inc. commissions and fees from payments made by the Company in the amount of $18,000 in fiscal 2015, $18,000 in fiscal 2014 and $24,000 in fiscal 2013. Neither Howard Jonas nor Joyce Mason has any ownership or other interest in Mason and Co. or the commissions paid to Mason and Co., other than via the familial relationships with Jonathan Mason.

Since August 2009, IDT Domestic Telecom, Inc., a subsidiary of the Company, has leased space in a building in the Bronx, New York. Howard Jonas and Shmuel Jonas, the Company's Chief Executive Officer, and the son of Howard Jonas, are members of the limited liability company that owns the building. For the six month period from May 1, 2012 to October 31, 2012, IDT Domestic Telecom was charged aggregate rent of $34,512. The parties entered into a new lease, which became effective November 1, 2012 and had a one-year term, with a one-year renewal option for IDT Domestic Telecom with the same terms. Aggregate annual rent under the new lease was $69,025.

The Company had net loans receivable outstanding from employees aggregating $0.3 million and $0.2 million at July 31, 2015 and 2014, respectively, which are included in "Other current assets" in the accompanying consolidated balance sheets.

Inflationary Accounting

DISCLOSURE

1.121 FASB ASC 255, *Changing Prices*, states that entities are encouraged to disclose supplementary information on the effects of changing prices (inflation). Entities are not discouraged from experimenting with other forms of disclosure.

1.122 However, Item 303 of the SEC's Regulation S-K requires that registrants discuss in "Management's Discussion and Analysis of Financial Condition and Results of Operations" the effects of inflation and other changes in prices when considered material. The SEC also encourages experimentation with these disclosures in order to provide the most meaningful presentation of the impact of price changes on the registrant's financial statements.

PRESENTATION AND DISCLOSURE EXCERPT

INFLATIONARY ACCOUNTING

1.123 THE COCA-COLA COMPANY (DEC)
NOTES TO CONSOLIDATED FINANCIAL STATEMENTS (in part)

Note 1: Business and Summary of Significant Accounting Policies (in part)

Summary of Significant Accounting Policies (in part)

Hyperinflationary Economies

A hyperinflationary economy is one that has cumulative inflation of 100 percent or more over a three-year period. In accordance with U.S. GAAP, local subsidiaries in hyperinflationary economies are required to use the U.S. dollar as their functional currency and remeasure the monetary assets and liabilities not denominated in U.S. dollars using the rate applicable to conversion of a currency for purposes of dividend remittances. All exchange gains and losses resulting from remeasurement are recognized currently in income.

Venezuela has been designated as a hyperinflationary economy. In February 2013, the Venezuelan government devalued its currency to an official rate of exchange ("official rate") of 6.3 bolivars per U.S. dollar. At that time, the Company remeasured the net monetary assets of our Venezuelan subsidiary at the official rate. As a result of the devaluation, we recognized a loss of $140 million from remeasurement in the line item other income (loss)—net in our consolidated statement of income.

Beginning in the first quarter of 2014, the Venezuelan government recognized three legal exchange rates to convert bolivars to the U.S. dollar: (1) the official rate of 6.3 bolivars per U.S. dollar; (2) SICAD 1, which was available to foreign investments and designated industry sectors to exchange a limited volume of bolivars for U.S. dollars using a bid rate established at weekly auctions; and (3) SICAD 2, which applied to transactions that did not qualify for either the official rate or SICAD 1. As of March 28, 2014, the three legal exchange rates were

6.3 (official rate), 10.8 (SICAD 1) and 50.9 (SICAD 2). We determined that the SICAD 1 rate was the most appropriate rate to use for remeasurement given our circumstances and estimates of the applicable rate at which future transactions could be settled, including the payment of dividends. Therefore, as of March 28, 2014, we remeasured the net monetary assets of our Venezuelan subsidiary using an exchange rate of 10.8 bolivars per U.S. dollar, resulting in a charge of $226 million recorded in the line item other income (loss)—net in our consolidated statement of income.

In December 2014, due to the continued lack of liquidity and increasing economic uncertainty, the Company reevaluated the rate that should be used to remeasure the monetary assets and liabilities of our Venezuelan subsidiary. As of December 31, 2014, we determined that the SICAD 2 rate of 50 bolivars per U.S. dollar was the most appropriate legally available rate and remeasured the net monetary assets of our Venezuelan subsidiary, resulting in a charge of $146 million recorded in the line item other income (loss)—net in our consolidated statement of income.

In February 2015, the Venezuelan government merged SICAD 1 and SICAD 2 into a single mechanism called SICAD and introduced a new open market exchange rate system, SIMADI. As a result, management determined that the SIMADI rate was the most appropriate legally available rate and remeasured the net monetary assets of our Venezuelan subsidiary, resulting in a charge of $27 million recorded in the line item other income (loss)—net in our consolidated statement of income.

In addition to the foreign currency exchange exposure related to our Venezuelan subsidiary's net monetary assets, we also sell concentrate to our bottling partner in Venezuela from outside the country. These sales are denominated in U.S. dollars. During the years ended December 31, 2015 and December 31, 2014, as a result of the continued lack of liquidity and our revised assessment of the U.S. dollar value we expect to realize upon the conversion of Venezuelan bolivars into U.S. dollars by our bottling partner to pay our concentrate sales receivables, we recorded write-downs of $56 million and $296 million, respectively, recorded in the line item other operating charges in our consolidated statements of income.

We also have certain U.S. dollar denominated intangible assets associated with products sold in Venezuela. As a result of the Company's revised expectations regarding the convertibility of the local currency, we recognized impairment charges of $55 million and $18 million, respectively, during the years ended December 31, 2015 and December 31, 2014. These charges were recorded in the line item other operating charges in our consolidated statements of income.

During the year ended December 31, 2015, the Company continued to use the SIMADI rate to remeasure the net monetary assets of our Venezuelan subsidiary. As of December 31, 2015, the combined value of the net monetary assets of our Venezuelan subsidiary, the receivables from our bottling partner in Venezuela and the intangible assets associated with products sold in Venezuela was $100 million. Included in this combined value is $15 million of cash and cash equivalents. Despite the additional currency conversion mechanisms, the Company's ability to pay dividends from Venezuela is still restricted due to the low volume of U.S. dollars available for conversion.

In February 2016, the Venezuelan government devalued its currency and changed its official and most preferential exchange rate, which will continue to be used for purchases of certain essential goods, to 10 bolivars per U.S. dollar from 6.3. The Venezuelan government announced it will reduce its three-tier system of exchange rates to two tiers by eliminating the SICAD rate. Additionally, the government announced that the SIMADI rate will be allowed to float freely beginning at a rate of 203 bolivars per U.S. dollar. As a result, the Company expects to continue to record losses on foreign currency exchange, may incur additional write-downs of receivables or impairment charges and will continue to record our proportionate share of any charges recorded by our equity method investee that has operations in Venezuela.

Note 17: Significant Operating and Nonoperating Items (in part)

Other Operating Charges (in part)

In 2015, the Company incurred other operating charges of $1,657 million. These charges primarily consisted of $691 million due to the Company's productivity and reinvestment program and $292 million due to the integration of our German bottling operations. In addition, the Company recorded impairment charges of $418 million primarily due to the discontinuation of the energy products in the glacéau portfolio as a result of the Monster Transaction and incurred a charge of $100 million due to a cash contribution we made to The Coca-Cola Foundation. The Company also incurred a charge of $111 million due to the write-down of receivables from our bottling partner in Venezuela and an impairment of a Venezuelan trademark primarily due to changes in exchange rates as a result of the establishment of the new open market exchange system. Refer to Note 18 for additional information on the Company's productivity, integration and restructuring initiatives. Refer to Note 2 for additional information on the Monster Transaction. Refer to Note 1 for additional information on the Venezuelan currency change. Refer to Note 19 for the impact these charges had on our operating segments.

In 2014, the Company incurred other operating charges of $1,183 million. These charges primarily consisted of $601 million due to the Company's productivity and reinvestment program and $208 million due to the integration of our German bottling operations. In addition, the Company incurred a charge of $314 million due to a write-down we recorded related to receivables from our bottling partner in Venezuela and an impairment of a Venezuelan trademark primarily due to changes in exchange rates. The write-down was recorded as a result of limited government-approved exchange rate conversion mechanisms. The Company also recorded a loss of $36 million as a result of the restructuring and transition of the Company's Russian juice operations to an existing joint venture with an unconsolidated bottling partner. Refer to Note 18 for additional information on our productivity and reinvestment program as well as the Company's other productivity, integration and restructuring initiatives. Refer to Note 1 for additional information on the Venezuelan currency change. Refer to Note 19 for the impact these charges had on our operating segments.

Other Nonoperating Items (in part)

Other Income (Loss)—Net (in part)

In 2015, the Company recorded a net gain of $1,403 million as a result of the Monster Transaction and charges of $1,006 million due to the refranchising of certain territories in North America. In addition, the Company recognized a foreign currency exchange gain of $300 million associated with our foreign-denominated debt partially offset by a charge of $27 million due to the remeasurement of the net monetary assets of our Venezuelan subsidiary using the SIMADI exchange rate. Refer to Note 2 for additional information related to the Monster Transaction and North America refranchising. Refer to Note 1 for additional information related to the charge due to the remeasurement in Venezuela. Refer to Note 19 for the impact these items had on our operating segments.

In 2014, the Company recorded charges of $799 million due to the refranchising of certain territories in North America. The Company also incurred a charge of $372 million due to the remeasurement of the net monetary assets of our Venezuelan subsidiary using the SICAD 2 exchange rate. Refer to Note 2 for more information related to the North America refranchising, Note 1 for more information related to the charge due to the remeasurement in Venezuela and Note 19 for the impact these charges had on our operating segments.

In 2013, the Company recorded a charge of $140 million due to the Venezuelan government announcing a currency devaluation. As a result of this devaluation, the Company remeasured the net monetary assets related to its operations in Venezuela. Refer to Note 19 for the impact this charge had on our operating segments. The Company also recognized a gain of $139 million due to Coca-Cola FEMSA issuing additional shares of its own stock at a per share amount greater than the carrying value of the Company's per share investment. Accordingly, the Company is required to treat this type of transaction as if the Company sold a proportionate share of its investment in Coca-Cola FEMSA. Refer to Note 16 for additional information on the measurement of the gain and Note 19 for the impact this gain had on our operating segments.

General Balance Sheet Considerations

PRESENTATION

2.01 FASB *Accounting Standards Codification*® (ASC) describes the benefits of presenting comparative financial statements instead of single-period financial statements and addresses the required disclosures and how the comparative information should be presented. SEC Regulation S-X, together with Financial Reporting Releases and Staff Accounting Bulletins, prescribe the form and content of, and requirements for, financial statements filed with the SEC. However, those requirements are modified for smaller reporting companies, as defined by SEC Regulation S-K, in Article 8 of Regulation S-X.

2.02 FASB ASC 810, *Consolidation*, and Rule 3A-02 of Regulation S-X state that a presumption exists that consolidated financial statements are more meaningful than separate financial statements and that they are usually necessary for a fair presentation when one of the entities in the consolidated group directly or indirectly has a controlling financial interest in the other entities. Rule 3-01(a) of Regulation S-X requires an entity to present consolidated balance sheets as of the end of each of the two most recent fiscal years. If the entity has been in existence for less than one fiscal year, the entity is required to file an audited balance sheet as of a date within 135 days of the date of filing the registration statement.

2.03 FASB ASC does not require an entity to present a classified balance sheet or mandate any particular ordering of balance sheet accounts. However, FASB ASC 210-10-05-4 states that entities usually present a classified balance sheet to facilitate calculation of working capital. FASB ASC 210-10-05-5 indicates that in the statements of manufacturing, trading, and service entities, assets and liabilities are generally classified and segregated. Financial institutions generally present unclassified balance sheets. The FASB ASC glossary includes definitions of *current assets* and *current liabilities* for when an entity presents a classified balance sheet. FASB ASC 210-10-45 provides additional guidance for determining these classifications.

DISCLOSURE

2.04 FASB ASC sets forth disclosure guidelines regarding capital structure and other balance sheet items. SEC regulations also contain additional requirements for disclosures that registrants should provide outside the financial statements.

2.05 FASB ASC 205-10-50 states that reclassifications or other changes in the manner of, or basis for, presenting corresponding items for two or more periods should be explained. This conforms to the well-recognized principle that any change that affects comparability of financial statements should be disclosed.

Cash and Cash Equivalents

PRESENTATION

2.06 Cash is commonly considered to consist of currency and demand deposits. The FASB ASC glossary defines *cash equivalents* as short-term, highly liquid investments that are both readily convertible into known amounts of cash and so near their maturity that they present an insignificant risk of changes in value because of changes in interest rates. Generally, only investments with original maturities of three months or less qualify under that definition.

DISCLOSURE

2.07 Rule 5-02.1 of Regulation S-X states that separate disclosure should be made of the cash and cash items that are restricted regarding withdrawal or usage. The provisions of any restrictions should be described in a note to the financial statements. Restrictions may include legally restricted deposits held as compensating balances against short-term borrowing arrangements, contracts entered into with others, or company statements of intention with regard to particular deposits; however, time deposits and short-term certificates of deposit are not generally included in legally restricted deposits. Compensating balance arrangements that do not legally restrict the use of cash should be described in the notes to the financial statements; the amount involved, if determinable, for the most recent audited balance sheet and any subsequent unaudited balance sheet should be disclosed. Compensating balances maintained under an agreement to assure future credit availability should be disclosed, along with the amount and terms of such agreement.

Marketable Securities

RECOGNITION AND MEASUREMENT

2.08 FASB ASC 320, *Investments—Debt and Equity Securities*, provides guidance on accounting for and reporting investments in equity securities that have readily determinable fair values and all investments in debt securities.

2.09 FASB ASC 320-10-25-1 requires that at acquisition, entities classify certain debt and equity securities into one of three categories: held-to-maturity, trading, or available-for-sale. Investments in debt securities that the entity has the positive intent and ability to hold to maturity are classified as held-to-maturity and reported at amortized cost in the statement of financial position. Securities that are bought and held principally for the purpose of selling them in the near term (thus held for only a short period of time) are classified as trading securities and reported at fair value. Trading generally reflects active and frequent buying and selling, and trading securities are generally used with the objective of generating profits on short-term differences in price. Investments not classified as either held-to-maturity or trading securities are classified as available-for-sale securities and reported at fair value. FASB ASC 320-10-35-1 explains that unrealized holding gains and losses are included in earnings for trading securities and other comprehensive income for available-for-sale securities with the exception of an available-for-sale security designated as being hedged in a fair value hedge. All or a portion of that unrealized gain or loss should be recognized in earnings during the period of the hedge in accordance with paragraphs 1–4 of FASB ASC 815-25-35.

2.10 FASB ASC 320 indicates when certain investments are considered impaired, whether that impairment is other than temporary, and the measurement and recognition of an impairment loss. FASB ASC 320 also provides guidance on accounting considerations for debt securities subsequent to the recognition of an other-than-temporary impairment and requires certain disclosures about unrealized losses that have not been recognized as other-than-temporary impairments.

PRESENTATION

2.11 Under FASB ASC 320-10-45-2, an entity that presents a classified balance sheet should report individual held-to-maturity securities, individual available-for-sale securities, and individual trading securities as either current or noncurrent.

DISCLOSURE

2.12 FASB ASC 320-10-50 includes detailed disclosure requirements for various marketable securities, including matters such as the nature and risks of the securities; cost, fair value, contractual maturities; impairment of securities; and certain transaction information.

2.13 By definition, investments in debt and equity securities are financial instruments. FASB ASC 825, *Financial Instruments*, requires disclosure of the fair value of those investments for which it is practicable to estimate that value, the methods and assumptions used in estimating the fair value of marketable securities, and a description of any changes in the methods and assumptions during the period. Under FASB ASC 825-10-50-3, the fair value disclosures are optional for certain nonpublic entities with assets less than $100 million.

2.14 FASB ASC 820, *Fair Value Measurement*, defines *fair value*, establishes a framework for measuring fair value, and requires certain disclosures about fair value measurements. *Fair value* is defined as the price that would be received to sell an asset or paid to transfer a liability in an orderly transaction between market participants at the measurement date. Further, fair value is a market-based measurement, not an entity-specific measurement. It establishes a fair value hierarchy that distinguishes between assumptions developed based on market data obtained from independent external sources and the reporting entity's own assumptions. Fair value measurement should consider adjustment for risk, such as the risk inherent in a valuation technique or its inputs.

2.15 For assets and liabilities measured at fair value, whether on a recurring or nonrecurring basis, FASB ASC 820 specifies the required disclosures concerning the inputs used to measure fair value. FASB ASC 820-10-50-1 explains that the reporting entity should disclose information that enables users of its financial statements to assess the following: (*a*) for assets and liabilities measured at fair value on a recurring or nonrecurring basis in the statement of financial position after initial recognition, the valuation techniques and inputs used to develop those measurements and (*b*) for recurring fair value measurements using significant unobservable inputs (Level 3), the effect of the measurements on earnings or other comprehensive income for the period.

2.16 FASB ASC 820-10-50-2 states that the reporting entity should disclose all of the following information for each interim and annual period separately for each class of assets and liabilities:

a. The fair value measurement at the reporting date.
b. The level within the fair value hierarchy in which the fair value measurement in its entirety falls (quoted prices in active markets for identical assets or liabilities—Level 1, significant other observable inputs—Level 2; significant unobservable inputs—Level 3).
c. The amounts of significant transfers between Level 1 and Level 2 and the reasons for the transfers.
d. For Level 3 measurements, a reconciliation of beginning and ending balances showing gains and losses for the period (realized and unrealized), purchases, sales, issuances, and settlements, and transfers in or out of Level 3 and reasons for those transfers.
e. For Level 3 measurements, the amount of total gains or losses for the period that are attributable to the change in unrealized gains or losses relating to those assets and liabilities still held at the reporting date and a description of where those unrealized gains or losses are reported in the statement of income (or activities).
f. For Level 2 and Level 3 measurements, a description of the valuation technique and the inputs used in determining the fair values of each class of assets or liabilities.
g. For recurring fair value measurements in Level 3, a narrative description of the sensitivity of the fair value measurement to changes in unobservable inputs if a change in those inputs to a different amount might result in a significantly higher or lower fair value measurement.
h. For recurring and nonrecurring fair value measurements, if the highest and best use of a nonfinancial asset differs from its current use, the reason why the asset is being used in a manner that differs from its highest and best use.

2.17 FASB ASC 825 permits entities to choose to measure at fair value many financial instruments and certain other items that are not currently required to be measured at fair value. Further, under FASB ASC 825, a business entity should report unrealized gains and losses on eligible items for which the fair value option has been elected in earnings at each subsequent reporting date. The irrevocable election of the fair value option is made on an instrument-by-instrument basis, with certain exceptions, and applied to the entire instrument, not only to specified risks, specific cash flows, or portions of that instrument. FASB ASC 825 also establishes presentation and disclosure requirements designed to facilitate comparison between entities that choose different measurement attributes for similar types of assets and liabilities. The required disclosures are optional for certain nonpublic entities.

PRESENTATION AND DISCLOSURE EXCERPTS

MARKETABLE SECURITIES—AVAILABLE-FOR-SALE SECURITIES

2.18 CATERPILLAR INC. (DEC)
MANAGEMENT'S DISCUSSION AND ANALYSIS OF FINANCIAL CONDITION AND RESULTS OF OPERATIONS (in part)

Critical Accounting Policies (in part)

Impairment of available-for-sale securities —Available-for-sale securities, primarily at Insurance Services, are reviewed at least quarterly to identify fair values below cost which may indicate that a security is impaired and should be written down to fair value.

For debt securities, once a security's fair value is below cost we utilize data gathered by investment managers, external sources and internal research to monitor the performance of the security to determine whether an other-than-temporary impairment has occurred. These reviews, which include an analysis of whether it is more likely than not that we will be required to sell the security before its anticipated recovery, consist of both quantitative and qualitative analysis and require a degree of management judgment. Securities in a loss position are monitored and assessed at least quarterly based on severity and timing of loss and may be deemed other-than-temporarily impaired at any time. Once a security's fair value has been 20 percent or more below its original cost for six consecutive months, the security will be other-than-temporarily impaired unless there are sufficient facts and circumstances supporting otherwise.

For equity securities in a loss position, determining whether a security is other-than-temporarily impaired requires an analysis of that security's historical sector return as well as the volatility of that return. This information is utilized to estimate a security's future fair value and to assess whether the security has the ability to recover to its original cost over a reasonable period of time. Both historical annualized sector returns and the volatility of those returns are applied over a two year period to arrive at these estimates.

For both debt and equity securities, qualitative factors are also considered in determining whether a security is other-than-temporarily impaired. These include reviews of the following: significant changes in the regulatory, economic or technological environment of the investee, significant changes in the general market condition of either the geographic area or the industry in which the investee operates, and length of time and the extent to which the fair value has been less than cost. These qualitative factors are subjective and require a degree of management judgment.

NOTES TO CONSOLIDATED FINANCIAL STATEMENTS (in part)

11. Available-for-sale Securities

We have investments in certain debt and equity securities, primarily at Insurance Services, that have been classified as available-for-sale and recorded at fair value. These investments are primarily included in Other assets in Statement 3. Unrealized gains and losses arising from the revaluation of available-for-sale securities are included, net of applicable deferred income taxes, in equity (Accumulated other comprehensive income (loss) in Statement 3). Realized gains and losses on sales of investments are generally determined using the specific identification method for debt and equity securities and are included in Other income (expense) in Statement 1.

The cost basis and fair value of available-for-sale securities were as follows:

	December 31, 2015			December 31, 2014		
(Millions of dollars)	Cost Basis	Unrealized Pretax Net Gains (Losses)	Fair Value	Cost Basis	Unrealized Pretax Net Gains (Losses)	Fair Value
Government debt						
U.S. treasury bonds	$ 9	$—	$ 9	$ 10	$ —	$ 10
Other U.S. and non-U.S. government bonds	71	1	72	94	—	94
Corporate bonds						
Corporate bonds	701	7	708	677	16	693
Asset-backed securities	129	—	129	103	2	105
Mortgage-backed debt securities						
U.S. governmental agency	291	1	292	292	2	294
Residential	12	—	12	15	—	15
Commercial	59	2	61	63	4	67
Equity securities						
Large capitalization value	243	30	273	150	83	233
Real estate investment trust (REIT)	25	—	25	—	—	—
Smaller company growth	37	17	54	17	26	43
Total	$1,577	$ 58	$1,635	$1,421	$133	$1,554

Investments in an unrealized loss position that are not other-than-temporarily impaired:

	December 31, 2015					
	Less than 12 months[1]		12 months or more[1]		Total	
(Millions of dollars)	Fair Value	Unrealized Losses	Fair Value	Unrealized Losses	Fair Value	Unrealized Losses
Corporate bonds						
Corporate bonds	$242	$ 3	$27	$1	$269	$ 4
Asset-backed securities	84	1	10	1	94	2
Mortgage-backed debt securities						
U.S. governmental agency	135	1	57	1	192	2
Equity securities						
Large capitalization value	97	8	2	—	99	8
Smaller company growth	14	1	—	—	14	1
Total	$572	$14	$96	$3	$668	$17

| (Millions of dollars) | December 31, 2014 | | | | | |
| | Less than 12 months[1] | | 12 months or more[1] | | Total | |
	Fair Value	Unrealized Losses	Fair Value	Unrealized Losses	Fair Value	Unrealized Losses
Corporate bonds						
Corporate bonds	$195	$ 1	$ 32	$—	$227	$1
Mortgage-backed debt securities						
U.S. governmental agency	34	—	140	3	174	3
Equity securities						
Large capitalization value	15	2	1	—	16	2
Total	$244	$ 3	$173	$ 3	$417	$6

[1] Indicates length of time that individual securities have been in a continuous unrealized loss position.

Corporate Bonds. The unrealized losses on our investments in corporate bonds and asset-backed securities relate to changes in interest rates and credit-related yield spreads since time of purchase. We do not intend to sell the investments and it is not likely that we will be required to sell the investments before recovery of their amortized cost basis. We do not consider these investments to be other-than-temporarily impaired as of December 31, 2015.

Mortgage-Backed Debt Securities. The unrealized losses on our investments in mortgage-backed securities relate to changes in interest rates and credit-related yield spreads since time of purchase. We do not intend to sell the investments and it is not likely that we will be required to sell these investments before recovery of their amortized cost basis. We do not consider these investments to be other-than-temporarily impaired as of December 31, 2015.

Equity Securities. The unrealized losses on our investments in equity securities relate to inherent risks of individual holdings and/or their respective sectors. We do not consider these investments to be other-than-temporarily impaired as of December 31, 2015.

The cost basis and fair value of the available-for-sale debt securities at December 31, 2015, by contractual maturity, is shown below. Expected maturities will differ from contractual maturities because borrowers may have the right to prepay and creditors may have the right to call obligations.

| (Millions of dollars) | December 31, 2015 | |
	Cost Basis	Fair Value
Due in one year or less	$ 124	$ 124
Due after one year through five years	709	716
Due after five years through ten years	49	50
Due after ten years	28	28
U.S. governmental agency mortgage-backed securities	291	292
Residential mortgage-backed securities	12	12
Commercial mortgage-backed securities	59	61
Total debt securities—available-for-sale	$1,272	$1,283

| (Millions of dollars) | Years Ended December 31, | | |
Sales of Securities:	2015	2014	2013
Proceeds from the sale of available-for-sale securities	$351	$434	$449
Gross gains from the sale of available-for-sale securities	$ 64	$ 38	$ 22
Gross losses from the sale of available-for-sale securities	$ 2	$ 2	$ 2

18. Fair Value Disclosures (in part)

A. Fair Value Measurements (in part)

The guidance on fair value measurements defines fair value as the exchange price that would be received for an asset or paid to transfer a liability (an exit price) in the principal or most advantageous market for the asset or liability in an orderly transaction between market participants. This guidance also specifies a fair value hierarchy based upon the observability of inputs used in valuation techniques. Observable inputs (highest level) reflect market data obtained from independent sources, while unobservable inputs (lowest level) reflect internally developed market assumptions. In accordance with this guidance, fair value measurements are classified under the following hierarchy:

Level 1—Quoted prices for identical instruments in active markets.

Level 2—Quoted prices for similar instruments in active markets; quoted prices for identical or similar instruments in markets that are not active; and model-derived valuations in which all significant inputs or significant value-drivers are observable in active markets.

Level 3—Model-derived valuations in which one or more significant inputs or significant value-drivers are unobservable.

When available, we use quoted market prices to determine fair value, and we classify such measurements within Level 1. In some cases where market prices are not available, we make use of observable market based inputs to calculate fair value, in which case the measurements are classified within Level 2. If quoted or observable market prices are not available, fair value is based upon valuations in which one or more significant inputs are unobservable, including internally developed models that use, where possible, current market-based parameters such as interest rates, yield curves and currency rates. These measurements are classified within Level 3.

Fair value measurements are classified according to the lowest level input or value-driver that is significant to the valuation. A measurement may therefore be classified within Level 3 even though there may be significant inputs that are readily observable.

Fair value measurement includes the consideration of nonperformance risk. Nonperformance risk refers to the risk that an obligation (either by a counterparty or Caterpillar) will not be fulfilled. For financial assets traded in an active market (Level 1 and certain Level 2), the nonperformance risk is included in the market price. For certain other financial assets and liabilities (certain Level 2 and Level 3), our fair value calculations have been adjusted accordingly.

Available-for-sale securities

Our available-for-sale securities, primarily at Insurance Services, include a mix of equity and debt instruments (see Note 11 for additional information). Fair values for our U.S. treasury bonds and large capitalization value and smaller company growth equity securities are based upon valuations for identical instruments in active markets. The fair value of our investment in a real estate investment trust (REIT) is based on the net asset value (NAV) of the investment. Fair values for other government bonds, corporate bonds and mortgage-backed debt securities are based upon models that take into consideration such market-based factors as recent sales, risk-free yield curves and prices of similarly rated bonds.

Assets and liabilities measured on a recurring basis at fair value, primarily related to Financial Products, included in Statement 3 as of December 31, 2015 and 2014 are summarized below:

| (Millions of dollars) | December 31, 2015 | | | |
	Level 1	Level 2	Level 3	Total Assets/ Liabilities, at Fair Value
Assets				
Available-for-sale securities				
Government debt				
U.S. treasury bonds	$ 9	$ —	$—	$ 9
Other U.S. and non-U.S. government bonds	—	72	—	72
Corporate bonds				
Corporate bonds	—	708	—	708
Asset-backed securities	—	129	—	129
Mortgage-backed debt securities				
U.S. governmental agency	—	292	—	292
Residential	—	12	—	12
Commercial	—	61	—	61
Equity securities				
Large capitalization value	273	—	—	273
REIT	—	—	25	25
Smaller company growth	54	—	—	54
Total available-for-sale securities	336	1,274	25	1,635
Derivative financial instruments, net	—	49	—	49
Total Assets	$336	$1,323	$ 25	$1,684

| | December 31, 2014 | | | |
(Millions of dollars)	Level 1	Level 2	Level 3	Total Assets/ Liabilities, at Fair Value
Assets				
Available-for-sale securities				
Government debt				
U.S. treasury bonds	$ 10	$ —	$—	$ 10
Other U.S. and non-U.S. government bonds	—	94	—	94
Corporate bonds				
Corporate bonds	—	693	—	693
Asset-backed securities	—	105	—	105
Mortgage-backed debt securities				
U.S. governmental agency	—	294	—	294
Residential	—	15	—	15
Commercial	—	67	—	67
Equity securities				
Large capitalization value	233	—	—	233
Smaller company growth	43	—	—	43
Total available-for-sale securities	286	1,268	—	1,554
Total Assets	$286	$1,268	$—	$1,554
Liabilities				
Derivative financial instruments, net	$—	$ 86	$—	$ 86
Total Liabilities	$—	$ 86	$—	$ 86

Please refer to the table below for the fair values of our financial instruments.

TABLE III—Fair Values of Financial Instruments

| | 2015 | | 2014 | | | |
(Millions of dollars)	Carrying Amount	Fair Value	Carrying Amount	Fair Value	Fair Value Levels	Reference
Assets at December 31,						
Cash and short-term investments	$ 6,460	$ 6,460	$ 7,341	$ 7,341	1	Statement 3
Restricted cash and short-term investments	52	52	62	62	1	Statement 3
Available-for-sale securities	1,635	1,635	1,554	1,554	1, 2 & 3	Notes 11 & 19
Finance receivables—net (excluding finance leases[1])	16,515	16,551	16,426	16,159	3	Notes 6 & 19
Wholesale inventory receivables—net (excluding finance leases[1])	1,821	1,775	1,774	1,700	3	Notes 6 & 19
Foreign currency contracts—net	13	13	—	—	2	Notes 3 & 19
Interest rate swaps—net	48	48	71	71	2	Notes 3 & 19
Liabilities at December 31,						
Short-term borrowings	6,967	6,967	4,708	4,708	1	Note 13
Long-term debt (including amounts due within one year):						
Machinery, Energy & Transportation	9,521	10,691	10,003	11,973	2	Note 14
Financial Products	21,605	21,904	24,574	25,103	2	Note 14
Foreign currency contracts—net	—	—	143	143	2	Notes 3 & 19
Commodity contracts—net	12	12	14	14	2	Notes 3 & 19
Guarantees	12	12	12	12	3	Note 21

[1] Total excluded items have a net carrying value at December 31, 2015 and 2014 of $6,452 million and $7,638 million, respectively.

MARKETABLE SECURITIES—HELD-TO-MATURITY (HTM) SECURITIES

2.19 BB&T CORPORATION (DEC)
CONSOLIDATED BALANCE SHEETS (in part)

(Dollars in millions, except per share data, shares in thousands)

	December 31,	
	2015	2014
Assets (in part)		
Cash and due from banks	$ 2,123	$ 1,639
Interest-bearing deposits with banks	1,435	529
Federal funds sold and securities purchased under resale agreements or similar arrangements	153	157
Restricted cash	456	374
AFS securities at fair value	25,297	20,907
HTM securities (fair value of $18,519 and $20,313 at December 31, 2015 and December 31, 2014, respectively)	18,530	20,240
LHFS at fair value	1,035	1,423
Loans and leases	135,951	119,884
ALLL	(1,460)	(1,474)
Loans and leases, net of ALLL	134,491	118,410

Note 1. Summary of Significant Accounting Policies (in part)

Securities

BB&T classifies marketable investment securities as HTM, AFS or trading. Interest income and dividends on securities are recognized in income on an accrual basis. Premiums and discounts on debt securities are amortized as an adjustment to interest income using the interest method.

Debt securities are classified as HTM where BB&T has both the intent and ability to hold the securities to maturity. These securities are reported at amortized cost.

Debt securities, which may be sold to meet liquidity needs arising from unanticipated deposit and loan fluctuations, changes in regulatory capital requirements, or unforeseen changes in market conditions, are classified as AFS. AFS securities are reported at estimated fair value, with unrealized gains and losses reported in AOCI, net of deferred income taxes, in the shareholders' equity section of the Consolidated Balance Sheets. Gains or losses realized from the sale of AFS securities are determined by specific identification and are included in noninterest income.

Each HTM and AFS security in a loss position is evaluated for OTTI. BB&T considers such factors as the length of time and the extent to which the fair value has been below amortized cost, long term expectations and recent experience regarding principal and interest payments, BB&T's intent to sell and whether it is more likely than not that the Company would be required to sell those securities before the anticipated recovery of the amortized cost basis. The credit component of an OTTI loss is recognized in earnings and the non-credit component is recognized in AOCI in situations where BB&T does not intend to sell the security and it is more-likely-than-not that BB&T will not be required to sell the security prior to recovery. Subsequent to recognition of OTTI, an increase in expected cash flows is recognized as a yield adjustment over the remaining expected life of the security based on an evaluation of the nature of the increase.

Trading account securities, which include both debt and equity securities, are reported at fair value and included in other assets in the Consolidated Balance Sheets. Unrealized fair value adjustments, fees, and realized gains or losses from trading account activities (determined by specific identification) are included in noninterest income. Interest income on trading account securities is included in interest on other earning assets.

Note 3. Securities

(Dollars in millions) December 31, 2015	Amortized Cost	Gross Unrealized Gains	Gross Unrealized Losses	Fair Value
AFS securities:				
U.S. Treasury	$ 1,836	$ 2	$ 6	$ 1,832
GSE	51	—	—	51
Agency MBS	20,463	22	439	20,046
States and political subdivisions	2,025	94	40	2,079
Non-agency MBS	198	23	—	221
Other	4	—	—	4
Acquired from FDIC	772	292	—	1,064
Total AFS securities	$25,349	$433	$485	$25,297
HTM securities:				
U.S. Treasury	$ 1,097	$ 22	$—	$ 1,119
GSE	5,045	16	98	4,963
Agency MBS	12,267	70	22	12,315
States and political subdivisions	63	—	—	63
Other	58	2	1	59
Total HTM securities	$18,530	$110	$121	$18,519

(Dollars in millions) December 31, 2014	Amortized Cost	Gross Unrealized		Fair Value
		Gains	Losses	
AFS securities:				
U.S. Treasury	$ 1,230	$ 1	$ —	$ 1,231
Agency MBS	16,358	93	297	16,154
States and political subdivisions	1,913	120	59	1,974
Non-agency MBS	232	32	—	264
Other	41	—	—	41
Acquired from FDIC	886	357	—	1,243
Total AFS securities	$20,660	$603	$356	$20,907
HTM securities:				
U.S. Treasury	$ 1,096	$ 23	$ —	$ 1,119
GSE	5,394	17	108	5,303
Agency MBS	13,120	137	12	13,245
States and political subdivisions	22	2	—	24
Other	608	14	—	622
Total HTM securities	$20,240	$193	$120	$20,313

BB&T transferred $517 million of HTM securities to AFS during the third quarter of 2015. These securities, which were sold by the end of the third quarter, represented investments in student loans for which there was a significant increase in risk weighting as a result of the implementation of Basel III.

The fair value of securities acquired from the FDIC included non-agency MBS of $768 million and $931 million as of December 31, 2015 and December 31, 2014, respectively, and states and political subdivisions securities of $296 million and $312 million as of December 31, 2015 and December 31, 2014, respectively. Effective October 1, 2014, securities subject to the commercial loss sharing agreement with the FDIC related to the Colonial acquisition were no longer covered by loss sharing; however, any gains on the sale of these securities through September 30, 2017 would be shared with the FDIC. Since these securities are in a significant unrealized gain position, they continue to be effectively covered as any declines in the unrealized gains of the securities down to a contractually specified amount would reduce the liability to the FDIC at the applicable percentage. The contractually-specified amount is the acquisition date fair value less any paydowns, redemptions or maturities and OTTI and totaled approximately $492 million at December 31, 2015. Any further declines below the contractually-specified amount would not be covered.

Certain investments in marketable debt securities and MBS issued by FNMA and FHLMC exceeded 10% of shareholders' equity at December 31, 2015. The FNMA investments had total amortized cost and fair value of $12.2 billion and $12.0 billion, respectively. The FHLMC investments had total amortized cost and fair value of $5.8 billion and $5.7 billion, respectively.

The following table reflects changes in credit losses on securities with OTTI (excluding securities acquired from the FDIC) where a portion of the unrealized loss was recognized in OCI:

(Dollars in millions)	Year Ended December 31,		
	2015	2014	2013
Balance at beginning of period	$ 64	$ 78	$ 98
Credit losses on securities without previous OTTI	—	6	—
Credit losses on securities for which OTTI was previously recognized	4	—	—
Reductions for securities sold/settled during the period	(22)	(17)	(20)
Credit recoveries through yield	(4)	(3)	—
Balance at end of period	$ 42	$ 64	$ 78

The amortized cost and estimated fair value of the securities portfolio by contractual maturity are shown in the following table. The expected life of MBS may differ from contractual maturities because borrowers have the right to prepay the underlying mortgage loans with or without prepayment penalties.

(Dollars in millions) December 31, 2015	AFS		HTM	
	Amortized Cost	Fair Value	Amortized Cost	Fair Value
Due in one year or less	$ 265	$ 264	$ 1	$ 1
Due after one year through five years	1,661	1,667	2,097	2,101
Due after five years through ten years	971	992	4,062	3,998
Due after ten years	22,452	22,374	12,370	12,419
Total debt securities	$25,349	$25,297	$18,530	$18,519

The following tables present the fair values and gross unrealized losses of investments based on the length of time that individual securities have been in a continuous unrealized loss position:

(Dollars in millions) December 31, 2015	Less than 12 Months		12 Months or More		Total	
	Fair Value	Unrealized Losses	Fair Value	Unrealized Losses	Fair Value	Unrealized Losses
AFS securities:						
U.S. Treasury securities	$ 1,211	$ 6	$ —	$ —	$ 1,211	$ 6
Agency MBS	12,052	199	5,576	240	17,628	439
States and political subdivisions	64	1	329	39	393	40
Total	$13,327	$206	$5,905	$279	$19,232	$485
HTM securities:						
GSE	$ 2,307	$ 41	$1,743	$ 57	$ 4,050	$ 98
Agency MBS	3,992	21	124	1	4,116	22
Other securities	56	1	—	—	56	1
Total	$ 6,355	$ 63	$1,867	$ 58	$ 8,222	$121

(Dollars in millions) December 31, 2014	Less than 12 Months		12 Months or More		Total	
	Fair Value	Unrealized Losses	Fair Value	Unrealized Losses	Fair Value	Unrealized Losses
AFS securities:						
Agency MBS	$2,285	$ 19	$6,878	$278	$9,163	$297
States and political subdivisions	13	—	449	59	462	59
Total	$2,298	$ 19	$7,327	$337	$9,625	$356
HTM securities:						
GSE	$ 896	$ 5	$3,968	$103	$4,864	$108
Agency MBS	1,329	5	800	7	2,129	12
Total	$2,225	$ 10	$4,768	$110	$6,993	$120

Periodic reviews are conducted to identify and evaluate each investment with an unrealized loss for OTTI. An unrealized loss exists when the current fair value of an individual security is less than its amortized cost basis. Unrealized losses that are determined to be temporary in nature are recorded, net of tax, in AOCI for AFS securities. The unrealized losses on GSE securities and agency MBS were the result of increases in market interest rates compared to the date the securities were acquired rather than the credit quality of the issuers.

Cash flow modeling is used to evaluate non-agency MBS in an unrealized loss position for potential credit impairment. These models give consideration to long-term macroeconomic factors applied to current security default rates, prepayment rates and recovery rates and security-level performance. At December 31, 2015, one non-agency MBS had an immaterial amount of other than temporary credit impairment.

At December 31, 2015, $39 million of the unrealized loss on municipal securities was the result of fair value hedge basis adjustments that are a component of amortized cost. Municipal securities in an unrealized loss position are evaluated for credit impairment through a qualitative analysis of issuer performance and the primary source of repayment. At December 31, 2015, the evaluation of municipal securities did not indicate any municipal securities with other than temporary credit impairment.

MARKETABLE SECURITIES—TRADING SECURITIES

2.20 CITIGROUP INC. (DEC)
CONSOLIDATED BALANCE SHEET (in part)

	December 31,	
In millions of dollars	2015	2014
Assets		
Cash and due from banks (including segregated cash and other deposits)	$ 20,900	$ 32,108
Deposits with banks	112,197	128,089
Federal funds sold and securities borrowed or purchased under agreements to resell (including $137,964 and $144,191 as of December 31, 2015 and December 31, 2014, respectively, at fair value)	219,675	242,570
Brokerage receivables	27,683	28,419
Trading account assets (including $92,123 and $106,217 pledged to creditors at December 31, 2015 and December 31, 2014, respectively)	249,956	296,786
Investments:		
Available for sale (including $10,698 and $13,808 pledged to creditors as of December 31, 2015 and December 31, 2014, respectively)	299,136	300,143
Held to maturity (including $3,630 and $2,974 pledged to creditors as of December 31, 2015 and December 31, 2014, respectively)	36,215	23,921
Non-marketable equity securities (including $2,088 and $2,758 at fair value as of December 31, 2015 and December 31, 2014, respectively)	7,604	9,379
Total investments	$ 342,955	$ 333,443

(continued)

In millions of dollars	December 31, 2015	December 31, 2014
Loans:		
Consumer (including $34 and $43 as of December 31, 2015 and December 31, 2014, respectively, at fair value)	329,783	369,970
Corporate (including $4,971 and $5,858 as of December 31, 2015 and December 31, 2014, respectively, at fair value)	287,834	274,665
Loans, net of unearned income	$ 617,617	$ 644,635
Allowance for loan losses	(12,626)	(15,994)
Total loans, net	$ 604,991	$ 628,641
Goodwill	22,349	23,592
Intangible assets (other than MSRs)	3,721	4,566
Mortgage servicing rights (MSRs)	1,781	1,845
Other assets (including $6,121 and $7,762 as of December 31, 2015 and December 31, 2014, respectively, at fair value)	125,002	122,122
Total assets	$1,731,210	$1,842,181

The following table presents certain assets of consolidated variable interest entities (VIEs), which are included in the Consolidated Balance Sheet above. The assets in the table below include those assets that can only be used to settle obligations of consolidated VIEs, presented on the following page, and are in excess of those obligations. Additionally, the assets in the table below include third-party assets of consolidated VIEs only and exclude intercompany balances that eliminate in consolidation.

In millions of dollars	December 31, 2015	December 31, 2014
Assets of consolidated VIEs to be used to settle obligations of consolidated VIEs		
Cash and due from banks	$ 153	$ 300
Trading account assets	583	671
Investments	5,263	8,014
Loans, net of unearned income		
Consumer	58,772	66,383
Corporate	22,008	29,596
Loans, net of unearned income	$80,780	$ 95,979
Allowance for loan losses	(2,135)	(2,793)
Total loans, net	$78,645	$ 93,186
Other assets	150	619
Total assets of consolidated VIEs to be used to settle obligations of consolidated VIEs	$84,794	$102,790

In millions of dollars, except shares and per share amounts	December 31, 2015	December 31, 2014
Liabilities		
Non-interest-bearing deposits in U.S. offices	$ 139,249	$ 128,958
Interest-bearing deposits in U.S. offices (including $923 and $994 as of December 31, 2015 and December 31, 2014, respectively, at fair value)	280,234	284,978
Non-interest-bearing deposits in offices outside the U.S.	71,577	70,925
Interest-bearing deposits in offices outside the U.S. (including $667 and $690 as of December 31, 2015 and December 31, 2014, respectively, at fair value)	416,827	414,471
Total deposits	$ 907,887	$ 899,332
Federal funds purchased and securities loaned or sold under agreements to repurchase (including $36,843 and $36,725 as of December 31, 2015 and December 31, 2014, respectively, at fair value)	146,496	173,438
Brokerage payables	53,722	52,180
Trading account liabilities	117,512	139,036
Short-term borrowings (including $1,207 and $1,496 as of December 31, 2015 and December 31, 2014, respectively, at fair value)	21,079	58,335
Long-term debt (including $25,293 and $26,180 as of December 31, 2015 and December 31, 2014, respectively, at fair value)	201,275	223,080
Other liabilities (including $1,624 and $1,776 as of December 31, 2015 and December 31, 2014, respectively, at fair value)	60,147	85,084
Total liabilities	$1,508,118	$1,630,485
Stockholders' equity		
Preferred stock ($1.00 par value; authorized shares: 30 million), issued shares: 668,720 as of December 31, 2015 and 418,720 as of December 31, 2014, at aggregate liquidation value	$ 16,718	$ 10,468
Common stock ($0.01 par value; authorized shares: 6 billion), issued shares: 3,099,482,042 as of December 31, 2015 and 3,082,037,568 as of December 31, 2014	31	31
Additional paid-in capital	108,288	107,979
Retained earnings	133,841	117,852
Treasury stock, at cost: December 31, 2015—146,203,311 shares and December 31, 2014—58,119,993 shares	(7,677)	(2,929)
Accumulated other comprehensive income (loss)	(29,344)	(23,216)
Total Citigroup stockholders' equity	$ 221,857	$ 210,185
Noncontrolling interest	1,235	1,511
Total equity	$ 223,092	$ 211,696
Total liabilities and equity	$1,731,210	$1,842,181

The following table presents certain liabilities of consolidated VIEs, which are included in the Consolidated Balance Sheet above. The liabilities in the table below include third-party liabilities of consolidated VIEs only and exclude intercompany balances that eliminate in consolidation. The liabilities also exclude amounts where creditors or beneficial interest holders have recourse to the general credit of Citigroup.

	December 31,	
In millions of dollars	2015	2014
Liabilities of consolidated VIEs for which creditors or beneficial interest holders do not have recourse to the general credit of Citigroup		
Short-term borrowings	$11,965	$20,254
Long-term debt	31,273	40,078
Other liabilities	2,099	901
Total liabilities of consolidated VIEs for which creditors or beneficial interest holders do not have recourse to the general credit of Citigroup	$45,337	$61,233

NOTES TO CONSOLIDATED FINANCIAL STATEMENTS (in part)

1. Summary of Significant Accounting Policies (in part)

Trading Account Assets and Liabilities

Trading account assets include debt and marketable equity securities, derivatives in a receivable position, residual interests in securitizations and physical commodities inventory. In addition, as described in Note 26 to the Consolidated Financial Statements, certain assets that Citigroup has elected to carry at fair value under the fair value option, such as loans and purchased guarantees, are also included in *Trading account assets*.

Trading account liabilities include securities sold, not yet purchased (short positions) and derivatives in a net payable position, as well as certain liabilities that Citigroup has elected to carry at fair value (as described in Note 26 to the Consolidated Financial Statements).

Other than physical commodities inventory, all trading account assets and liabilities are carried at fair value. Revenues generated from trading assets and trading liabilities are generally reported in *Principal transactions* and include realized gains and losses as well as unrealized gains and losses resulting from changes in the fair value of such instruments. Interest income on trading assets is recorded in *Interest revenue* reduced by interest expense on trading liabilities.

Physical commodities inventory is carried at the lower of cost or market with related losses reported in *Principal transactions*. Realized gains and losses on sales of commodities inventory are included in *Principal transactions*. Investments in unallocated precious metals accounts (gold, silver, platinum and palladium) are accounted for as hybrid instruments containing a debt host contract and an embedded non-financial derivative instrument indexed to the price of the relevant precious metal. The embedded derivative instrument is separated from the debt host contract and accounted for at fair value. The debt host contract is accounted for at fair value under the fair value option, as described in Note 26 to the Consolidated Financial Statements.

Derivatives used for trading purposes include interest rate, currency, equity, credit, and commodity swap agreements, options, caps and floors, warrants, and financial and commodity futures and forward contracts. Derivative asset and liability positions are presented net by counterparty on the Consolidated Balance Sheet when a valid master netting agreement exists and the other conditions set out in ASC 210-20, *Balance Sheet—Offsetting,* are met. See Note 23 to the Consolidated Financial Statements.

The Company uses a number of techniques to determine the fair value of trading assets and liabilities, which are described in Note 25 to the Consolidated Financial Statements.

Securitizations

The Company primarily securitizes credit card receivables and mortgages. Other types of securitized assets include corporate debt instruments (in cash and synthetic form).

There are two key accounting determinations that must be made relating to securitizations. Citi first makes a determination as to whether the securitization entity must be consolidated. Second, it determines whether the transfer of financial assets to the entity is considered a sale under GAAP. If the securitization entity is a VIE, the Company consolidates the VIE if it is the primary beneficiary (as discussed in "Variable Interest Entities" above). For all other securitization entities determined not to be VIEs in which Citigroup participates, consolidation is based on which party has voting control of the entity, giving consideration to removal and liquidation rights in certain partnership structures. Only securitization entities controlled by Citigroup are consolidated.

Interests in the securitized and sold assets may be retained in the form of subordinated or senior interest-only strips, subordinated tranches, spread accounts and servicing rights. In credit card securitizations, the Company retains a seller's interest in the credit card receivables transferred to the trusts, which is not in securitized form. In the case of consolidated securitization entities, including the credit card trusts, these retained interests are not reported on Citi's Consolidated Balance Sheet. The securitized loans remain on the balance sheet. Substantially all of the Consumer loans sold or securitized through non-consolidated trusts by Citigroup are U.S. prime residential mortgage loans. Retained interests in non-consolidated mortgage securitization trusts are classified as *Trading account assets*, except for MSRs, which are included in *Mortgage servicing rights* on Citigroup's Consolidated Balance Sheet.

Risk Management Activities—Derivatives Used for Hedging Purposes (in part)

The Company manages its exposures to market rate movements outside its trading activities by modifying the asset and liability mix, either directly or through the use of derivative financial products, including interest-rate swaps, futures, forwards, and purchased options, as well as foreign-exchange contracts. These end-user derivatives are carried at fair value in *Other assets, Other liabilities, Trading account assets* and *Trading account liabilities*.

13. Trading Account Assets and Liabilities

Trading account assets and *Trading account liabilities* are carried at fair value, other than physical commodities accounted for at the lower of cost or fair value, and consist of the following:

In millions of dollars	December 31, 2015	December 31, 2014
Trading Account Assets		
Mortgage-backed securities[1]		
U.S. government-sponsored agency guaranteed	$ 24,767	$ 27,053
Prime	803	1,271
Alt-A	543	709
Subprime	516	1,382
Non-U.S. residential	523	1,476
Commercial	2,855	4,343
Total mortgage-backed securities	$ 30,007	$ 36,234
U.S. Treasury and federal agency securities		
U.S. Treasury	$ 15,791	$ 18,906
Agency obligations	2,005	1,568
Total U.S. Treasury and federal agency securities	$ 17,796	$ 20,474
State and municipal securities	$ 2,696	$ 3,402
Foreign government securities	56,609	64,937
Corporate	14,437	27,797
Derivatives[2]	56,184	67,957
Equity securities	56,495	57,846
Asset-backed securities[1]	3,956	4,546
Other trading assets[3]	11,776	13,593
Total trading account assets	$249,956	$296,786
Trading Account Liabilities		
Securities sold, not yet purchased	$ 57,827	$ 70,944
Derivatives[2]	57,592	68,092
Other trading liabilities[3]	2,093	—
Total trading account liabilities	$117,512	$139,036

[1] The Company invests in mortgage-backed and asset-backed securities. These securitizations are generally considered VIEs. The Company's maximum exposure to loss from these VIEs is equal to the carrying amount of the securities, which is reflected in the table above. For mortgage-backed and asset-backed securitizations in which the Company has other involvement, see Note 22 to the Consolidated Financial Statements.

[2] Presented net, pursuant to enforceable master netting agreements. See Note 23 to the Consolidated Financial Statements for a discussion regarding the accounting and reporting for derivatives.

[3] Includes positions related to investments in unallocated precious metals, as discussed in Note 26 to the Consolidated Financial Statements. Also includes physical commodities accounted for at the lower of cost or fair value.

22. Securitizations and Variable Interest Entities (in part)

Consolidated VIEs

The Company engages in on-balance sheet securitizations, which are securitizations that do not qualify for sales treatment; thus, the assets remain on the Company's Consolidated Balance Sheet, and any proceeds received are recognized as secured liabilities. The consolidated VIEs included in the tables below represent hundreds of separate entities with which the Company is involved. In general, the third-party investors in the obligations of consolidated VIEs have legal recourse only to the assets of the respective VIEs and do not have such recourse to the Company, except where the Company has provided a guarantee to the investors or is the counterparty to certain derivative transactions involving the VIE. Thus, the Company's maximum legal exposure to loss related to consolidated VIEs is significantly less than the carrying value of the consolidated VIE assets due to outstanding third-party financing. Intercompany assets and liabilities are excluded from the table. All VIE assets are restricted from being sold or pledged as collateral. The cash flows from these assets are the only source used to pay down the associated liabilities, which are non-recourse to the Company's general assets.

The following table presents the carrying amounts and classifications of consolidated assets that are collateral for consolidated VIE obligations:

In billions of dollars	December 31, 2015	December 31, 2014
Cash	$ 0.2	$ 0.3
Trading account assets	0.6	0.7
Investments	5.3	8.0
Total loans, net of allowance	78.6	93.2
Other	0.1	0.6
Total assets	$84.8	$102.8
Short-term borrowings	$14.0	$ 22.7
Long-term debt	31.3	40.1
Other liabilities	2.1	0.9
Total liabilities[1]	$47.4	$ 63.7

(1) The total liabilities of consolidated VIEs for which creditors or beneficial interest holders do not have recourse to the general credit of Citi were $45.3 billion and $61.2 billion as of December 31, 2015 and 2014, respectively. Liabilities of consolidated VIEs for which creditors or beneficial interest holders have recourse to the general credit of Citi comprise two items included in the above table: (i) credit enhancements provided to consolidated Citi-administered commercial paper conduits in the form of letters of credit of $1.9 billion and $2.3 billion at December 31, 2015 and 2014, respectively; and (ii) credit guarantees provided by Citi to certain consolidated municipal tender option bond trusts of $82 million and $198 million at December 31, 2015 and 2014, respectively.

Significant Interests in Unconsolidated VIEs—Balance Sheet Classification

The following table presents the carrying amounts and classification of significant variable interests in unconsolidated VIEs:

In billions of dollars	December 31, 2015	December 31, 2014
Cash	$ 0.1	$ —
Trading account assets	6.2	7.6
Investments	3.0	2.6
Total loans, net of allowance	28.4	25.0
Other	1.8	2.0
Total assets	$39.5	$37.2

23. Derivatives Activities (in part)

In the ordinary course of business, Citigroup enters into various types of derivative transactions. These derivative transactions include:
- *Futures and forward contracts,* which are commitments to buy or sell at a future date a financial instrument, commodity or currency at a contracted price and may be settled in cash or through delivery.
- *Swap contracts,* which are commitments to settle in cash at a future date or dates that may range from a few days to a number of years, based on differentials between specified indices or financial instruments, as applied to a notional principal amount.
- *Option contracts,* which give the purchaser, for a premium, the right, but not the obligation, to buy or sell within a specified time a financial instrument, commodity or currency at a contracted price that may also be settled in cash, based on differentials between specified indices or prices.

Swaps and forwards and some option contracts are over-the-counter (OTC) derivatives that are bilaterally negotiated with counterparties and settled with those counterparties, except for swap contracts that are novated and "cleared" through central counterparties (CCPs). Futures contracts and other option contracts are standardized contracts that are traded on an exchange with a CCP as the counterparty from the inception of the transaction. Citigroup enters into these derivative contracts relating to interest rate, foreign currency, commodity and other market/credit risks for the following reasons:
- *Trading Purposes:* Citigroup trades derivatives as an active market maker. Citigroup offers its customers derivatives in connection with their risk management actions to transfer, modify or reduce their interest rate, foreign exchange and other market/credit risks or for their own trading purposes. Citigroup also manages its derivative risk positions through offsetting trade activities, controls focused on price verification, and daily reporting of positions to senior managers.
- *Hedging:* Citigroup uses derivatives in connection with its risk management activities to hedge certain risks or reposition the risk profile of the Company. For example, Citigroup issues fixed-rate long-term debt and then enters into a receive-fixed, pay-variable-rate interest rate swap with the same tenor and notional amount to convert the interest payments to a net variable-rate basis. This strategy

is the most common form of an interest rate hedge, as it minimizes net interest cost in certain yield curve environments. Derivatives are also used to manage risks inherent in specific groups of on-balance sheet assets and liabilities, including AFS securities and borrowings, as well as other interest-sensitive assets and liabilities. In addition, foreign-exchange contracts are used to hedge non-U.S.-dollar-denominated debt, foreign-currency-denominated AFS securities and net investment exposures.

Information pertaining to Citigroup's derivative activity, based on notional amounts is presented in the table below. Derivative notional amounts are reference amounts from which contractual payments are derived and do not represent a complete and accurate measure of Citi's exposure to derivative transactions. Rather, as discussed above, Citi's derivative exposure arises primarily from market fluctuations (i.e., market risk), counterparty failure (i.e., credit risk) and/or periods of high volatility or financial stress (i.e., liquidity risk), as well as any market valuation adjustments that may be required on the transactions. Moreover, notional amounts do not reflect the netting of offsetting trades (also as discussed above). For example, if Citi enters into an interest rate swap with $100 million notional, and offsets this risk with an identical but opposite position with a different counterparty, $200 million in derivative notionals is reported, although these offsetting positions may result in de minimis overall market risk. Aggregate derivative notional amounts can fluctuate from period to period in the normal course of business based on Citi's market share, levels of client activity and other factors.

Derivative Notionals

In millions of dollars	Hedging Instruments Under ASC 815[1][2] December 31, 2015	December 31, 2014	Other Derivative Instruments Trading Derivatives December 31, 2015	December 31, 2014	Management Hedges[3] December 31, 2015	December 31, 2014
Interest Rate Contracts						
Swaps	$166,576	$163,348	$22,208,794	$31,906,549	$ 28,969	$ 31,945
Futures and forwards	—	—	6,868,340	7,044,990	38,421	42,305
Written options	—	—	3,033,617	3,311,904	2,606	3,913
Purchased options	—	—	2,887,605	3,171,184	4,575	4,910
Total interest rate contract notionals	$166,576	$163,348	$34,998,356	$45,434,627	$ 74,571	$ 83,073
Foreign exchange contracts						
Swaps	$ 23,007	$ 25,157	$ 4,765,687	$ 4,567,977	$ 23,960	$ 23,990
Futures, forwards and spot[4]	72,124	73,219	2,563,649	3,003,295	3,034	7,069
Written options	448	—	1,125,664	1,343,520	—	432
Purchased options	819	—	1,131,816	1,363,382	—	432
Total foreign exchange contract notionals	$ 96,398	$ 98,376	$ 9,586,816	$10,278,174	$ 26,994	$ 31,923
Equity Contracts						
Swaps	$ —	$ —	$ 180,963	$ 131,344	$ —	$ —
Futures and forwards	—	—	33,735	30,510	—	—
Written options	—	—	298,876	305,627	—	—
Purchased options	—	—	265,062	275,216	—	—
Total equity contract notionals	$ —	$ —	$ 778,636	$ 742,697	$ —	$ —
Commodity and Other Contracts						
Swaps	$ —	$ —	$ 70,561	$ 90,817	$ —	$ —
Futures and forwards	789	1,089	106,474	106,021	—	—
Written options	—	—	72,648	104,581	—	—
Purchased options	—	—	66,051	95,567	—	—
Total commodity and other contract notionals	$ 789	$ 1,089	$ 315,734	$ 396,986	$ —	$ —
Credit Derivatives[5]						
Protection sold	$ —	$ —	$ 950,922	$ 1,063,858	$ —	$ —
Protection purchased	—	—	981,586	1,100,369	23,628	16,018
Total credit derivatives	$ —	$ —	$ 1,932,508	$ 2,164,227	$ 23,628	$ 16,018
Total derivative notionals	$263,763	$262,813	$47,612,050	$59,016,711	$125,193	$131,014

[1] The notional amounts presented in this table do not include hedge accounting relationships under ASC 815 where Citigroup is hedging the foreign currency risk of a net investment in a foreign operation by issuing a foreign-currency-denominated debt instrument. The notional amount of such debt was $2,102 million and $3,752 million at December 31, 2015 and December 31, 2014, respectively.

[2] Derivatives in hedge accounting relationships accounted for under ASC 815 are recorded in either *Other assets/Other liabilities* or *Trading account assets/Trading account liabilities* on the Consolidated Balance Sheet.

[3] Management hedges represent derivative instruments used to mitigate certain economic risks, but for which hedge accounting is not applied. These derivatives are recorded in either *Other assets/Other liabilities* or *Trading account assets/Trading account liabilities* on the Consolidated Balance Sheet.

[4] Foreign exchange notional contracts include spot contract notionals of $335 billion and $849 billion at December 31, 2015 and December 31, 2014, respectively. Previous presentations of foreign exchange derivative notional contracts did not include spot contracts. There was no impact to the Consolidated Financial Statements related to this updated presentation.

[5] Credit derivatives are arrangements designed to allow one party (protection buyer) to transfer the credit risk of a "reference asset" to another party (protection seller). These arrangements allow a protection seller to assume the credit risk associated with the reference asset without directly purchasing that asset. The Company enters into credit derivative positions for purposes such as risk management, yield enhancement, reduction of credit concentrations and diversification of overall risk.

The following tables present the gross and net fair values of the Company's derivative transactions, and the related offsetting amounts permitted under ASC 210-20-45 and ASC 815-10-45, as of December 31, 2015 and December 31, 2014. Under ASC 210-20-45, gross positive fair values are offset against gross negative fair values by counterparty pursuant to enforceable master netting agreements. Under ASC 815-10-45, payables and receivables in respect of cash collateral received from or paid to a given counterparty pursuant to a credit support annex are included in the offsetting amount if a legal opinion supporting enforceability of netting and collateral rights has been obtained. GAAP does not permit similar offsetting for security collateral. The tables also include amounts that are not permitted to be offset under ASC 210-20-45 and ASC 815-10-45, such as security collateral posted or cash collateral posted at third-party custodians, but which would be eligible for offsetting to the extent an event of default occurred and a legal opinion supporting enforceability of the netting and collateral rights has been obtained.

Derivative Mark-to-Market (MTM) Receivables/Payables

In Millions of Dollars at December 31, 2015	Derivatives Classified in Trading Account Assets/Liabilities[1][2][3]		Derivatives Classified in Other Assets/Liabilities[2][3]	
	Assets	Liabilities	Assets	Liabilities
Derivatives instruments designated as ASC 815 hedges				
Over-the-counter	$ 262	$ 105	$ 2,328	$ 106
Cleared	4,607	1,471	5	—
Interest rate contracts	$ 4,869	$ 1,576	$ 2,333	$ 106
Over-the-counter	$ 2,688	$ 364	$ 95	$ 677
Foreign exchange contracts	$ 2,688	$ 364	$ 95	$ 677
Total derivative instruments designated as ASC 815 hedges	$ 7,557	$ 1,940	$ 2,428	$ 783
Derivatives instruments not designated as ASC 815 hedges				
Over-the-counter	$ 289,124	$ 267,761	$ 182	$ 12
Cleared	120,848	126,532	244	216
Exchange traded	53	35	—	—
Interest rate contracts	$ 410,025	$ 394,328	$ 426	$ 228
Over-the-counter	$ 126,474	$ 133,361	$ —	$ 66
Cleared	134	152	—	—
Exchange traded	21	36	—	—
Foreign exchange contracts	$ 126,629	$ 133,549	$ —	$ 66
Over-the-counter	$ 14,560	$ 20,107	$ —	$ —
Cleared	28	3	—	—
Exchange traded	7,297	6,406	—	—
Equity contracts	$ 21,885	$ 26,516	$ —	$ —
Over-the-counter	$ 16,794	$ 18,641	$ —	$ —
Exchange traded	1,216	1,912	—	—
Commodity and other contracts	$ 18,010	$ 20,553	$ —	$ —
Over-the-counter	$ 31,072	$ 30,608	$ 711	$ 245
Cleared	3,803	3,560	131	318
Credit derivatives[4]	$ 34,875	$ 34,168	$ 842	$ 563
Total derivatives instruments not designated as ASC 815 hedges	$ 611,424	$ 609,114	$ 1,268	$ 857
Total derivatives	$ 618,981	$ 611,054	$ 3,696	$1,640
Cash collateral paid/received[5][6]	$ 4,911	$ 13,628	$ 8	$ 37
Less: Netting agreements[7]	(524,481)	(524,481)	—	—
Less: Netting cash collateral received/paid[8]	(43,227)	(42,609)	(1,949)	(53)
Net receivables/payables included on the consolidated balance sheet[9]	$ 56,184	$ 57,592	$ 1,755	$1,624
Additional amounts subject to an enforceable master netting agreement but not offset on the Consolidated Balance Sheet				
Less: Cash collateral received/paid	$ (779)	$ (2)	$ —	$ —
Less: Non-cash collateral received/paid	(9,855)	(5,131)	(270)	—
Total net receivables/payables[9]	$ 45,550	$ 52,459	$ 1,485	$1,624

[1] The trading derivatives fair values are presented in Note 13 to the Consolidated Financial Statements.

[2] Derivative mark-to-market receivables/payables related to management hedges are recorded in either *Other assets/Other liabilities* or *Trading account assets/Trading account liabilities*.

[3] Over-the-counter (OTC) derivatives are derivatives executed and settled bilaterally with counterparties without the use of an organized exchange or central clearing house. Cleared derivatives include derivatives executed bilaterally with a counterparty in the OTC market but then novated to a central clearing house, whereby the central clearing house becomes the counterparty to both of the original counterparties. Exchange traded derivatives include derivatives executed directly on an organized exchange that provides pre-trade price transparency.

[4] The credit derivatives trading assets comprise $17,957 million related to protection purchased and $16,918 million related to protection sold as of December 31, 2015. The credit derivatives trading liabilities comprise $16,968 million related to protection purchased and $17,200 million related to protection sold as of December 31, 2015.

[5] For the trading account assets/liabilities, reflects the net amount of the $47,520 million and $56,855 million of gross cash collateral paid and received, respectively. Of the gross cash collateral paid, $42,609 million was used to offset trading derivative liabilities and, of the gross cash collateral received, $43,227 million was used to offset trading derivative assets.

[6] For cash collateral paid with respect to non-trading derivative assets, reflects the net amount of $61 million of gross cash collateral paid, of which $53 million is netted against non-trading derivative positions within *Other liabilities*. For cash collateral received with respect to non-trading derivative liabilities, reflects the net amount of $1,986 million of gross cash collateral received, of which $1,949 million is netted against OTC non-trading derivative positions within *Other assets*.

[7] Represents the netting of derivative receivable and payable balances with the same counterparty under enforceable netting agreements. Approximately $391 billion, $126 billion and $7 billion of the netting against trading account asset/liability balances is attributable to each of the OTC, cleared and exchange-traded derivatives, respectively.

[8] Represents the netting of cash collateral paid and received by counterparty under enforceable credit support agreements. Substantially all cash collateral received and paid is netted against OTC derivative assets and liabilities, respectively.

[9] The net receivables/payables include approximately $10 billion of derivative asset and $10 billion of derivative liability fair values not subject to enforceable master netting agreements, respectively.

In Millions of Dollars at December 31, 2014	Derivatives Classified in Trading Account Assets/Liabilities[1][2][3]		Derivatives Classified in Other Assets/Liabilities[2][3]	
	Assets	Liabilities	Assets	Liabilities
Derivatives instruments designated as ASC 815 hedges				
Over-the-counter	$ 1,508	$ 204	$ 3,117	$ 414
Cleared	4,300	868	—	25
Interest rate contracts	$ 5,808	$ 1,072	$ 3,117	$ 439
Over-the-counter	$ 3,885	$ 743	$ 678	$ 588
Foreign exchange contracts	$ 3,885	$ 743	$ 678	$ 588
Total derivative instruments designated as ASC 815 hedges	$ 9,693	$ 1,815	$ 3,795	$1,027
Derivatives instruments not designated as ASC 815 hedges				
Over-the-counter	$ 376,778	$ 359,689	$ 106	$ —
Cleared	255,847	261,499	6	21
Exchange traded	20	22	141	164
Interest rate contracts	$ 632,645	$ 621,210	$ 253	$ 185
Over-the-counter	$ 151,736	$ 157,650	$ —	$ 17
Cleared	366	387	—	—
Exchange traded	7	46	—	—
Foreign exchange contracts	$ 152,109	$ 158,083	$ —	$ 17
Over-the-counter	$ 20,425	$ 28,333	$ —	$ —
Cleared	16	35	—	—
Exchange traded	4,311	4,101	—	—
Equity contracts	$ 24,752	$ 32,469	$ —	$ —
Over-the-counter	$ 19,943	$ 23,103	$ —	$ —
Exchange traded	3,577	3,083	—	—
Commodity and other contracts	$ 23,520	$ 26,186	$ —	$ —
Over-the-counter	$ 39,412	$ 39,439	$ 265	$ 384
Cleared	4,106	3,991	13	171
Credit derivatives[4]	$ 43,518	$ 43,430	$ 278	$ 555
Total derivatives instruments not designated as ASC 815 hedges	$ 876,544	$ 881,378	$ 531	$ 757
Total derivatives	$ 886,237	$ 883,193	$ 4,326	$1,784
Cash collateral paid/received[5][6]	$ 6,523	$ 9,846	$ 123	$ 7
Less: Netting agreements[7]	(777,178)	(777,178)	—	—
Less: Netting cash collateral received/paid[8]	(47,625)	(47,769)	(1,791)	(15)
Net receivables/payables included on the Consolidated Balance Sheet[9]	$ 67,957	$ 68,092	$ 2,658	$1,776
Additional amounts subject to an enforceable master netting agreement but not offset on the Consolidated Balance Sheet				
Less: Cash collateral received/paid	$ (867)	$ (11)	$ —	$ —
Less: Non-cash collateral received/paid	(10,043)	(6,264)	(1,293)	—
Total net receivables/payables[9]	$ 57,047	$ 61,817	$ 1,365	$1,776

[1] The trading derivatives fair values are presented in Note 13 to the Consolidated Financial Statements.

[2] Derivative mark-to-market receivables/payables related to management hedges are recorded in either *Other assets/Other liabilities* or *Trading account assets/Trading account liabilities*.

[3] Over-the-counter (OTC) derivatives include derivatives executed and settled bilaterally with counterparties without the use of an organized exchange or central clearing house. Cleared derivatives include derivatives executed bilaterally with a counterparty in the OTC market but then novated to a central clearing house, whereby the central clearing house becomes the counterparty to both of the original counterparties. Exchange traded derivatives include derivatives executed directly on an organized exchange that provides pre-trade price transparency.

[4] The credit derivatives trading assets comprise $18,430 million related to protection purchased and $25,088 million related to protection sold as of December 31, 2014. The credit derivatives trading liabilities comprise $25,972 million related to protection purchased and $17,458 million related to protection sold as of December 31, 2014.

[5] For the trading account assets/liabilities, reflects the net amount of the $54,292 million and $57,471 million of gross cash collateral paid and received, respectively. Of the gross cash collateral paid, $47,769 million was used to offset derivative liabilities and, of the gross cash collateral received, $47,625 million was used to offset derivative assets.

[6] For cash collateral paid with respect to non-trading derivative assets, reflects the net amount of $138 million of the gross cash collateral paid, of which $15 million is netted against non-trading derivative positions within *Other liabilities*. For cash collateral received with respect to non-trading derivative liabilities, reflects the net amount of $1,798 million of gross cash collateral received of which $1,791 million is netted against non-trading derivative positions within *Other assets*.

[7] Represents the netting of derivative receivable and payable balances with the same counterparty under enforceable netting agreements. Approximately $510 billion, $264 billion and $3 billion of the netting against trading account asset/liability balances is attributable to each of the OTC, cleared and exchange-traded derivatives, respectively.

[8] Represents the netting of cash collateral paid and received by counterparty under enforceable credit support agreements. Substantially all cash collateral received is netted against OTC derivative assets. Cash collateral paid of approximately $46 billion and $2 billion is netted against OTC and cleared derivative liabilities, respectively.

[9] The net receivables/payables include approximately $11 billion of derivative asset and $10 billion of liability fair values not subject to enforceable master netting agreements.

24. Concentrations of Credit Risk

Concentrations of credit risk exist when changes in economic, industry or geographic factors similarly affect groups of counterparties whose aggregate credit exposure is material in relation to Citigroup's total credit exposure. Although Citigroup's portfolio of financial instruments is broadly diversified along industry, product, and geographic lines, material transactions are completed with other financial institutions, particularly in the securities trading, derivatives and foreign exchange businesses.

In connection with the Company's efforts to maintain a diversified portfolio, the Company limits its exposure to any one geographic region, country or individual creditor and monitors this exposure on a continuous basis. At December 31, 2015, Citigroup's most significant concentration of credit risk was with the U.S. government and its agencies. The Company's exposure, which primarily results from trading assets and investments issued by the U.S. government and its agencies, amounted to $223.0 billion and $216.3 billion at December 31, 2015 and 2014, respectively. The Mexican and United Kingdom governments and their agencies, which are rated investment grade by both Moody's and S&P, were the next largest exposures. The Company's exposure to Mexico amounted to $22.5 billion and $29.7 billion at December 31, 2015 and 2014, respectively, and was composed of investment securities, loans and trading assets. The Company's exposure to the United Kingdom amounted to $20.4 billion and $18.0 billion at December 31, 2015 and 2014, respectively, and was composed of investment securities, loans and trading assets.

The Company's exposure to states and municipalities amounted to $29.3 billion and $31.0 billion at December 31, 2015 and 2014, respectively, and was composed of trading assets, investment securities, derivatives and lending activities.

25. Fair Value Measurement (in part)

ASC 820-10 *Fair Value Measurement*, defines fair value, establishes a consistent framework for measuring fair value and requires disclosures about fair value measurements. Fair value is defined as the price that would be received to sell an asset or paid to transfer a liability in an orderly transaction between market participants at the measurement date. Among other things, the standard requires the Company to maximize the use of observable inputs and minimize the use of unobservable inputs when measuring fair value.

Under ASC 820-10, the probability of default of a counterparty is factored into the valuation of derivative and other positions as well as the impact of Citigroup's own credit risk on derivatives and other liabilities measured at fair value.

Fair Value Hierarchy (in part)

ASC 820-10 specifies a hierarchy of inputs based on whether the inputs are observable or unobservable. Observable inputs are developed using market data and reflect market participant assumptions, while unobservable inputs reflect the Company's market assumptions. These two types of inputs have created the following fair value hierarchy:
  • Level 1: Quoted prices for *identical* instruments in active markets.
  • Level 2: Quoted prices for *similar* instruments in active markets; quoted prices for identical or similar instruments in markets that are not active; and model-derived valuations in which all significant inputs and significant value drivers are *observable* in active markets.
  • Level 3: Valuations derived from valuation techniques in which one or more significant inputs or significant value drivers are *unobservable*.

As required under the fair value hierarchy, the Company considers relevant and observable market inputs in its valuations where possible. The frequency of transactions, the size of the bid-ask spread and the amount of adjustment necessary when comparing similar transactions are all factors in determining the liquidity of markets and the relevance of observed prices in those markets.

The Company's policy with respect to transfers between levels of the fair value hierarchy is to recognize transfers into and out of each level as of the end of the reporting period.

Trading Account Assets and Liabilities—Trading Securities and Trading Loans

When available, the Company uses quoted market prices in active markets to determine the fair value of trading securities; such items are classified as Level 1 of the fair value hierarchy. Examples include government securities and exchange-traded equity securities.

For bonds and secondary market loans traded over the counter, the Company generally determines fair value utilizing valuation techniques, including discounted cash flows, price-based and internal models, such as Black-Scholes and Monte Carlo simulation. Fair value estimates from these internal valuation techniques are verified, where possible, to prices obtained from independent sources, including third-party vendors. Vendors compile prices from various sources and may apply matrix pricing for similar bonds or loans where no price is observable. A price-based methodology utilizes, where available, quoted prices or other market information obtained from recent trading activity of assets with similar characteristics to the bond or loan being valued. The yields used in discounted cash flow models are derived from the same price information. Trading securities and loans priced using such methods are generally classified as Level 2. However, when less liquidity exists for a security or loan, a quoted price is stale, a significant adjustment to the price of a similar security or loan is necessary to reflect differences in the terms of the actual security or loan being valued, or prices from independent sources are insufficient to corroborate valuation, a loan or security is generally classified as Level 3. The price input used in a price-based methodology may be zero for a security, such as a subprime CDO, that is not receiving any principal or interest and is currently written down to zero.

When the Company's principal market for a portfolio of loans is the securitization market, the Company uses the securitization price to determine the fair value of the portfolio. The securitization price is determined from the assumed proceeds of a hypothetical securitization in the current market, adjusted for transformation costs (i.e., direct costs other than transaction costs) and securitization uncertainties such as market conditions and liquidity. As a result of the severe reduction in the level of activity in certain securitization markets since the second half of 2007, observable securitization prices for certain directly comparable portfolios of loans have not been readily available. Therefore, such portfolios of loans are generally classified as Level 3 of the fair value hierarchy. However, for other loan securitization markets, such as commercial real estate loans, price verification of the hypothetical securitizations has been possible, since these markets have remained active. Accordingly, this loan portfolio is classified as Level 2 of the fair value hierarchy.

For most of the lending and structured direct subprime exposures, fair value is determined utilizing observable transactions where available, other market data for similar assets in markets that are not active and other internal valuation techniques. The valuation of certain asset-backed security (ABS) CDO positions utilizes prices based on the underlying assets of the ABS CDO.

Trading Account Assets and Liabilities—Derivatives

Exchange-traded derivatives, measured at fair value using quoted (i.e., exchange) prices in active markets, where available, are classified as Level 1 of the fair value hierarchy.

Derivatives without a quoted price in an active market and derivatives executed over the counter are valued using internal valuation techniques. These derivative instruments are classified as either Level 2 or Level 3 depending upon the observability of the significant inputs to the model.

The valuation techniques and inputs depend on the type of derivative and the nature of the underlying instrument. The principal techniques used to value these instruments are discounted cash flows and internal models, including Black-Scholes and Monte Carlo simulation.

The key inputs depend upon the type of derivative and the nature of the underlying instrument and include interest rate yield curves, foreign-exchange rates, volatilities and correlation. The Company uses overnight indexed swap (OIS) curves as fair value measurement inputs for the valuation of certain collateralized derivatives. Citi uses the relevant benchmark curve for the currency of the derivative (e.g., the London Interbank Offered Rate for U.S. dollar derivatives) as the discount rate for uncollateralized derivatives.

As referenced above, during the third quarter of 2014, Citi incorporated FVA into the fair value measurements due to what it believes to be an industry migration toward incorporating the market's view of funding risk premium in OTC derivatives. The charge incurred in connection with the implementation of FVA was reflected in *Principal transactions* as a change in accounting estimate. Citi's FVA methodology leverages the existing CVA methodology to estimate a funding exposure profile. The calculation of this exposure profile considers collateral agreements where the terms do not permit the firm to reuse the collateral received, including where counterparties post collateral to third-party custodians.

Alt-A Mortgage Securities

The Company classifies its Alt-A mortgage securities as held-to-maturity, available-for-sale or trading investments. The securities classified as trading and available-for-sale are recorded at fair value with changes in fair value reported in current earnings and AOCI, respectively. For these purposes, Citi defines Alt-A mortgage securities as non-agency residential mortgage-backed securities (RMBS) where (i) the underlying collateral has weighted average FICO scores between 680 and 720 or (ii) for instances where FICO scores are greater than 720, RMBS have 30% or less of the underlying collateral composed of full documentation loans.

Similar to the valuation methodologies used for other trading securities and trading loans, the Company generally determines the fair values of Alt-A mortgage securities utilizing internal valuation techniques. Fair value estimates from internal valuation techniques are verified, where possible, to prices obtained from independent vendors. Consensus data providers compile prices from various sources. Where available, the Company may also make use of quoted prices for recent trading activity in securities with the same or similar characteristics to the security being valued.

The valuation techniques used for Alt-A mortgage securities, as with other mortgage exposures, are price-based and yield analysis. The primary market-derived input is yield. Cash flows are based on current collateral performance with prepayment rates and loss projections reflective of current economic conditions of housing price change, unemployment rates, interest rates, borrower attributes and other market indicators.

Alt-A mortgage securities that are valued using these methods are generally classified as Level 2. However, Alt-A mortgage securities backed by Alt-A mortgages of lower quality or subordinated tranches in the capital structure are mostly classified as Level 3 due to the reduced liquidity that exists for such positions, which reduces the reliability of prices available from independent sources.

Items Measured at Fair Value on a Recurring Basis

The following tables present for each of the fair value hierarchy levels the Company's assets and liabilities that are measured at fair value on a recurring basis at December 31, 2015 and December 31, 2014. The Company's hedging of positions that have been classified in the Level 3 category is not limited to other financial instruments (hedging instruments) that have been classified as Level 3, but also instruments classified as Level 1 or Level 2 of the fair value hierarchy. The effects of these hedges are presented gross in the following tables:

Fair Value Levels

In Millions of Dollars at December 31, 2015	Level 1[(1)]	Level 2[(1)]	Level 3	Gross Inventory	Netting[(2)]	Net Balance
Assets						
Federal funds sold and securities borrowed or purchased under agreements to resell	$ —	$ 177,538	$ 1,337	$ 178,875	$ (40,911)	$137,964
Trading non-derivative assets						
Trading mortgage-backed securities						
U.S. government-sponsored agency guaranteed	—	24,023	744	24,767	—	24,767
Residential	—	1,059	1,326	2,385	—	2,385
Commercial	—	2,338	517	2,855	—	2,855
Total trading mortgage-backed securities	$ —	$ 27,420	$ 2,587	$ 30,007	$ —	$ 30,007
U.S. Treasury and federal agency securities	$ 14,208	$ 3,587	$ 1	$ 17,796	$ —	$ 17,796
State and municipal	—	2,345	351	2,696		2,696
Foreign government	35,715	20,697	197	56,609	—	56,609
Corporate	302	13,759	376	14,437	—	14,437
Equity securities	50,429	2,382	3,684	56,495	—	56,495
Asset-backed securities	—	1,217	2,739	3,956	—	3,956
Other trading assets	—	9,293	2,483	11,776	—	11,776
Total trading non-derivative assets	$100,654	$ 80,700	$12,418	$ 193,772	$ —	$193,772
Trading derivatives						
Interest rate contracts	$ 9	$ 412,802	$ 2,083	$ 414,894		
Foreign exchange contracts	5	128,189	1,123	129,317		
Equity contracts	2,422	17,866	1,597	21,885		
Commodity contracts	204	16,706	1,100	18,010		
Credit derivatives	—	31,082	3,793	34,875		
Total trading derivatives	$ 2,640	$ 606,645	$ 9,696	$ 618,981		
Cash collateral paid[(3)]				$ 4,911		
Netting agreements					$(524,481)	
Netting of cash collateral received					(43,227)	
Total trading derivatives	$ 2,640	$ 606,645	$ 9,696	$ 623,892	$(567,708)	$ 56,184
Investments						
Mortgage-backed securities						
U.S. government-sponsored agency guaranteed	$ —	$ 39,575	$ 139	$ 39,714	$ —	$ 39,714
Residential	—	5,982	4	5,986	—	5,986
Commercial	—	569	2	571	—	571
Total investment mortgage-backed securities	$ —	$ 46,126	$ 145	$ 46,271	$ —	$ 46,271
U.S. Treasury and federal agency securities	$111,536	$ 11,375	$ 4	$ 122,915	$ —	$122,915
State and municipal	—	9,267	2,192	11,459	—	11,459
Foreign government	42,073	49,868	260	92,201	—	92,201
Corporate	3,605	11,595	603	15,803	—	15,803
Equity securities	430	71	124	625	—	625
Asset-backed securities	—	8,578	596	9,174	—	9,174
Other debt securities	—	688	—	688	—	688
Non-marketable equity securities[(4)]	—	58	1,135	1,193	—	1,193
Total investments	$157,644	$ 137,626	$ 5,059	$ 300,329	$ —	$300,329
Loans[(5)]	$ —	$ 2,839	$ 2,166	$ 5,005	$ —	$ 5,005
Mortgage servicing rights	—	—	1,781	1,781	—	1,781
Non-trading derivatives and other financial assets measured on a recurring basis, gross	$ —	$ 7,882	$ 180	$ 8,062		
Cash collateral paid[(6)]				8		
Netting of cash collateral received					$ (1,949)	

(continued)

In Millions of Dollars at December 31, 2015	Level 1[1]	Level 2[1]	Level 3	Gross Inventory	Netting[2]	Net Balance
Non-trading derivatives and other financial assets measured on a recurring basis	$ —	$ 7,882	$ 180	$ 8,070	$ (1,949)	$ 6,121
Total assets	$260,938	$1,013,230	$32,637	$1,311,724	$(610,568)	$701,156
Total as a percentage of gross assets[7]	20.0%	77.5%	2.5%			
Liabilities						
Interest-bearing deposits	$ —	$ 1,156	$ 434	$ 1,590	$ —	$ 1,590
Federal funds purchased and securities loaned or sold under agreements to repurchase	—	76,507	1,247	77,754	(40,911)	36,843
Trading account liabilities						
Securities sold, not yet purchased	$ 48,452	$ 9,176	$ 199	$ 57,827	$ —	$ 57,827
Other trading liabilities	—	2,093	—	2,093	—	2,093
Total trading liabilities	$ 48,452	$ 11,269	$ 199	$ 59,920	$ —	$ 59,920
Trading derivatives						
Interest rate contracts	$ 5	$ 393,321	$ 2,578	$ 395,904		
Foreign exchange contracts	6	133,404	503	133,913		
Equity contracts	2,244	21,875	2,397	26,516		
Commodity contracts	263	17,329	2,961	20,553		
Credit derivatives	—	30,682	3,486	34,168		
Total trading derivatives	$ 2,518	$ 596,611	$11,925	$ 611,054		
Cash collateral received[8]				$ 13,628		
Netting agreements					$(524,481)	
Netting of cash collateral paid					(42,609)	
Total trading derivatives	$ 2,518	$ 596,611	$11,925	$ 624,682	$(567,090)	$ 57,592
Short-term borrowings	$ —	$ 1,198	$ 9	$ 1,207	$ —	$ 1,207
Long-term debt	—	18,342	6,951	25,293	—	25,293
Non-trading derivatives and other financial liabilities measured on a recurring basis, gross	$ —	$ 1,626	$ 14	$ 1,640		
Cash collateral received[9]				37		
Netting of cash collateral paid					$ (53)	
Total non-trading derivatives and other financial liabilities measured on a recurring basis	$ —	$ 1,626	$ 14	$ 1,677	$ (53)	$ 1,624
Total liabilities	$ 50,970	$ 706,709	$20,779	$ 792,123	$(608,054)	$184,069
Total as a percentage of gross liabilities[7]	6.5%	90.8%	2.7%			

[1] In 2015, the Company transferred assets of approximately $3.3 billion from Level 1 to Level 2, respectively, primarily related to foreign government securities and equity securities not traded in active markets. In 2015, the Company transferred assets of approximately $4.4 billion from Level 2 to Level 1, respectively, primarily related to foreign government bonds and equity securities traded with sufficient frequency to constitute a liquid market. In 2015, the Company transferred liabilities of approximately $0.6 billion from Level 2 to Level 1. In 2015, the Company transferred liabilities of approximately $0.4 billion from Level 1 to Level 2.

[2] Represents netting of: (i) the amounts due under securities purchased under agreements to resell and the amounts owed under securities sold under agreements to repurchase; and (ii) derivative exposures covered by a qualifying master netting agreement and cash collateral offsetting.

[3] Reflects the net amount of $47,520 million of gross cash collateral paid, of which $42,609 million was used to offset trading derivative liabilities.

[4] Amounts exclude $0.9 billion investments measured at Net Asset Value (NAV) in accordance with ASU No. 2015-07, *Fair Value Measurement (Topic 820): Disclosures for Investments in Certain Entities That Calculate Net Asset Value per Share (or Its Equivalent)*. See Note 1 to the Consolidated Financial Statements.

[5] There is no allowance for loan losses recorded for loans reported at fair value.

[6] Reflects the net amount of $61 million of gross cash collateral paid, of which $ 53 million was used to offset non-trading derivative liabilities.

[7] Because the amount of the cash collateral paid/received has not been allocated to the Level 1, 2 and 3 subtotals, these percentages are calculated based on total assets and liabilities measured at fair value on a recurring basis, excluding the cash collateral paid/received on derivatives.

[8] Reflects the net amount of $56,855 million of gross cash collateral received, of which $43,227 million was used to offset trading derivative assets.

[9] Reflects the net amount of $1,986 million of gross cash collateral received, of which $1,949 million was used to offset non-trading derivative assets.

Fair Value Levels

In Millions of Dollars at December 31, 2014	Level 1[1]	Level 2[1]	Level 3	Gross Inventory	Netting[2]	Net Balance
Assets						
Federal funds sold and securities borrowed or purchased under agreements to resell	$ —	$ 187,922	$ 3,398	$ 191,320	$ (47,129)	$144,191
Trading non-derivative assets						
Trading mortgage-backed securities						
U.S. government-sponsored agency guaranteed	—	25,968	1,085	27,053	—	27,053
Residential	—	2,158	2,680	4,838	—	4,838
Commercial	—	3,903	440	4,343	—	4,343
Total trading mortgage-backed securities	$ —	$ 32,029	$ 4,205	$ 36,234	$ —	$ 36,234

(continued)

In Millions of Dollars at December 31, 2014	Level 1[1]	Level 2[1]	Level 3	Gross Inventory	Netting[2]	Net Balance
U.S. Treasury and federal agency securities	$ 15,991	$ 4,483	$ —	$ 20,474	$ —	$ 20,474
State and municipal	—	3,161	241	3,402	—	3,402
Foreign government	37,995	26,736	206	64,937	—	64,937
Corporate	1,337	25,640	820	27,797	—	27,797
Equity securities	51,346	4,281	2,219	57,846	—	57,846
Asset-backed securities	—	1,252	3,294	4,546	—	4,546
Other trading assets	—	9,221	4,372	13,593	—	13,593
Total trading non-derivative assets	$106,669	$ 106,803	$15,357	$ 228,829	$ —	$228,829
Trading derivatives						
Interest rate contracts	$ 74	$ 634,318	$ 4,061	$ 638,453		
Foreign exchange contracts	—	154,744	1,250	155,994		
Equity contracts	2,748	19,969	2,035	24,752		
Commodity contracts	647	21,850	1,023	23,520		
Credit derivatives	—	40,618	2,900	43,518		
Total trading derivatives	$ 3,469	$ 871,499	$11,269	$ 886,237		
Cash collateral paid[3]				$ 6,523		
Netting agreements					$(777,178)	
Netting of cash collateral received[4][8]					(47,625)	
Total trading derivatives	$ 3,469	$ 871,499	$11,269	$ 892,760	$(824,803)	$ 67,957
Investments						
Mortgage-backed securities						
U.S. government-sponsored agency guaranteed	$ —	$ 36,053	$ 38	$ 36,091	$ —	$ 36,091
Residential	—	8,355	8	8,363	—	8,363
Commercial	—	553	1	554	—	554
Total investment mortgage-backed securities	$ —	$ 44,961	$ 47	$ 45,008	$ —	$ 45,008
U.S. Treasury and federal agency securities	$110,710	$ 12,974	$ 6	$ 123,690	$ —	$123,690
State and municipal	—	10,519	2,180	12,699	—	12,699
Foreign government	37,280	52,739	678	90,697	—	90,697
Corporate	1,739	9,746	672	12,157	—	12,157
Equity securities	1,770	274	681	2,725	—	2,725
Asset-backed securities	—	11,957	549	12,506	—	12,506
Other debt securities	—	661	—	661	—	661
Non-marketable equity securities[5]	—	233	1,460	1,693	—	1,693
Total investments	$151,499	$ 144,064	$ 6,273	$ 301,836	$ —	$301,836
Loans[6]	$ —	$ 2,793	$ 3,108	$ 5,901	$ —	$ 5,901
Mortgage servicing rights	—	—	1,845	1,845	—	1,845
Non-trading derivatives and other financial assets measured on a recurring basis, gross	$ —	$ 9,352	$ 78	$ 9,430		
Cash collateral paid[7]				123		
Netting of cash collateral received[8]					$ (1,791)	
Non-trading derivatives and other financial assets measured on a recurring basis	$ —	$ 9,352	$ 78	$ 9,553	$ (1,791)	$ 7,762
Total assets	$261,637	$1,322,433	$41,328	$1,632,044	$(873,723)	$758,321
Total as a percentage of gross assets[7]	16.1%	81.4%	2.5%			
Liabilities						
Interest-bearing deposits	$ —	$ 1,198	$ 486	$ 1,684	$ —	$ 1,684
Federal funds purchased and securities loaned or sold under agreements to repurchase	—	82,811	1,043	83,854	(47,129)	36,725
Trading account liabilities						
Securities sold, not yet purchased	59,463	11,057	424	70,944	—	70,944
Other trading liabilities	—	—	—	—	—	—
Total trading liabilities	$ 59,463	$ 11,057	$ 424	$ 70,944	$ —	$ 70,944
Trading account derivatives						
Interest rate contracts	$ 77	$ 617,933	$ 4,272	$ 622,282		
Foreign exchange contracts	—	158,354	472	158,826		
Equity contracts	2,955	26,616	2,898	32,469		
Commodity contracts	669	22,872	2,645	26,186		
Credit derivatives	—	39,787	3,643	43,430		
Total trading derivatives	$ 3,701	$ 865,562	$13,930	$ 883,193		
Cash collateral received[8]				$ 9,846		
Netting agreements					$(777,178)	
Netting of cash collateral paid[3]					(47,769)	
Total trading derivatives	$ 3,701	$ 865,562	$13,930	$ 893,039	$(824,947)	$ 68,092
Short-term borrowings	$ —	$ 1,152	$ 344	$ 1,496	$ —	$ 1,496
Long-term debt	—	18,890	7,290	26,180	—	26,180

(continued)

In Millions of Dollars at December 31, 2014	Level 1[1]	Level 2[1]	Level 3	Gross Inventory	Netting[2]	Net Balance
Non-trading derivatives and other financial liabilities measured on a recurring basis, gross	$ —	$ 1,777	$ 7	$ 1,784		
Cash collateral received[9]				7		
Netting of cash collateral paid[7]					$ (15)	
Non-trading derivatives and other financial liabilities measured on a recurring basis	$ —	$ 1,777	$ 7	$ 1,791	$ (15)	$ 1,776
Total liabilities	$ 63,164	$ 982,447	$23,524	$1,078,988	$(872,091)	$206,897
Total as a percentage of gross liabilities[4]	5.9%	91.9%	2.2%			

[1] In 2014, the Company transferred assets of approximately $4.1 billion from Level 1 to Level 2, primarily related to foreign government securities not traded with sufficient frequency to constitute an active market and Citi refining its methodology for certain equity contracts to reflect the prevalence of off-exchange trading. In 2014, the Company transferred assets of approximately $4.2 billion from Level 2 to Level 1, primarily related to foreign government bonds traded with sufficient frequency to constitute a liquid market. In 2014, the Company transferred liabilities of approximately $1.4 billion from Level 1 to Level 2, as Citi refined its methodology for certain equity contracts to reflect the prevalence of off-exchange trading. In 2014, there were no material liability transfers from Level 2 to Level 1.

[2] Represents netting of (i) the amounts due under securities purchased under agreements to resell and the amounts owed under securities sold under agreements to repurchase; and (ii) derivative exposures covered by a qualifying master netting agreement and cash collateral offsetting.

[3] Reflects the net amount of $54,292 million of gross cash collateral paid, of which $47,769 million was used to offset trading derivative liabilities.

[4] Because the amount of the cash collateral paid/received has not been allocated to the Level 1, 2 and 3 subtotals, these percentages are calculated based on total assets and liabilities measured at fair value on a recurring basis, excluding the cash collateral paid/received on derivatives.

[5] Amounts exclude $1.1 billion investments measured at Net Asset Value (NAV) in accordance with ASU No. 2015-07, *Fair Value Measurement (Topic 820): Disclosures for Investments in Certain Entities That Calculate Net Asset Value per Share (or Its Equivalent)*. See Note 1 to the Consolidated Financial Statements.

[6] There is no allowance for loan losses recorded for loans reported at fair value.

[7] Reflects the net amount of $138 million of gross cash collateral paid, of which $15 million was used to offset non-trading derivative liabilities.

[8] Reflects the net amount of $57,471 million of gross cash collateral received, of which $47,625 million was used to offset trading derivative assets.

[9] Reflects the net amount of $1,798 million of gross cash collateral received, of which $1,791 million was used to offset non-trading derivative assets.

Changes in Level 3 Fair Value Category

The following tables present the changes in the Level 3 fair value category for the years ended December 31, 2015 and 2014. As discussed above, the Company classifies financial instruments as Level 3 of the fair value hierarchy when there is reliance on at least one significant unobservable input to the valuation model. In addition to these unobservable inputs, the valuation models for Level 3 financial instruments typically also rely on a number of inputs that are readily observable either directly or indirectly. The gains and losses presented below include changes in the fair value related to both observable and unobservable inputs.

The Company often hedges positions with offsetting positions that are classified in a different level. For example, the gains and losses for assets and liabilities in the Level 3 category presented in the tables below do not reflect the effect of offsetting losses and gains on hedging instruments that have been classified by the Company in the Level 1 and Level 2 categories. In addition, the Company hedges items classified in the Level 3 category with instruments also classified in Level 3 of the fair value hierarchy. The effects of these hedges are presented gross in the following tables:

Level 3 Fair Value Rollforward

In millions of dollars	Dec. 31, 2014	Principal Trans-actions	Other[1][2]	Into Level 3	Out of Level 3	Pur-chases	Issu-ances	Sales	Settle-ments	Dec. 31, 2015	Unrealized Gains (Losses) Still Held[3]
Assets											
Federal funds sold and securities borrowed or purchased under agreements to resell	$ 3,398	$ (147)	$ —	$ 279	$(2,856)	$ 784	$ —	$ —	$ (121)	$ 1,337	$ (5)
Trading non-derivative assets											
Trading mortgage-backed securities											
U.S. government-sponsored agency guaranteed	1,085	24	—	872	(1,277)	796	—	(756)	—	744	(4)
Residential	2,680	254	—	370	(480)	1,574	—	(3,072)	—	1,326	(101)
Commercial	440	18	—	252	(157)	697	—	(733)	—	517	(7)
Total trading mortgage-backed securities	$ 4,205	$ 296	$ —	$1,494	$(1,914)	$ 3,067	$ —	$ (4,561)	$ —	$ 2,587	$(112)

(continued)

In millions of dollars	Dec. 31, 2014	Principal Trans-actions	Other[1][2]	Into Level 3	Out of Level 3	Purchases	Issuances	Sales	Settle-ments	Dec. 31, 2015	Unrealized Gains (Losses) Still Held[3]
U.S. Treasury and federal agency securities	$ —	$ —	$ —	$ 2	$ (1)	$ 1	$ —	$ (1)	$ —	$ 1	$ —
State and municipal	241	—	—	67	(35)	183	—	(105)	—	351	(7)
Foreign government	206	(10)	—	53	(100)	271	—	(169)	(54)	197	6
Corporate	820	111	—	186	(288)	802	—	(1,244)	(11)	376	(29)
Equity securities	2,219	547	—	344	(371)	1,377	—	(432)	—	3,684	464
Asset-backed securities	3,294	141	—	663	(282)	4,426	—	(5,503)	—	2,739	(174)
Other trading assets	4,372	180	—	968	(3,290)	2,504	51	(2,110)	(192)	2,483	(45)
Total trading non-derivative assets	$15,357	$1,265	$ —	$3,777	$(6,281)	$12,631	$ 51	$(14,125)	$ (257)	$12,418	$ 103
Trading derivatives, net[4]											
Interest rate contracts	$ (211)	$ (492)	$ —	$ (124)	$ 15	$ 24	$ —	$ 141	$ 152	$ (495)	$ 553
Foreign exchange contracts	778	(245)	—	(11)	27	393	—	(381)	59	620	(12)
Equity contracts	(863)	148	—	(126)	66	496	—	(334)	(187)	(800)	41
Commodity contracts	(1,622)	(753)	—	214	(28)	—	—	—	328	(1,861)	(257)
Credit derivatives	(743)	555	—	9	61	1	—	(3)	427	307	442
Total trading derivatives, net[4]	$ (2,661)	$ (787)	$ —	$ (38)	$ 141	$ 914	$ —	$ (577)	$ 779	$ (2,229)	$ 767
Investments											
Mortgage-backed securities											
U.S. government-sponsored agency guaranteed	$ 38	$ —	$ 29	$ 171	$ (118)	$ 62	$ —	$ (43)	$ —	$ 139	$ (2)
Residential	8	—	(1)	4	—	11	—	(18)	—	4	—
Commercial	1	—	—	4	(3)	—	—	—	—	2	—
Total investment mortgage-backed securities	$ 47	$ —	$ 28	$ 179	$ (121)	$ 73	$ —	$ (61)	$ —	$ 145	$ (2)
U.S. Treasury and federal agency securities	$ 6	$ —	$ —	$ —	$ —	$ 6	$ —	$ (8)	$ —	$ 4	$ —
State and municipal	2,180	—	(23)	834	(721)	842	—	(671)	(249)	2,192	9
Foreign government	678	—	45	(5)	(270)	601	—	(519)	(270)	260	(1)
Corporate	672	—	(7)	15	(52)	144	—	(134)	(35)	603	(4)
Equity securities	681	—	(22)	12	(14)	7	—	(540)	—	124	(120)
Asset-backed securities	549	—	(17)	45	(58)	202	—	(125)	—	596	14
Other debt securities	—	—	—	—	—	10	—	(10)	—	—	—
Non-marketable equity securities	1,460	—	(50)	76	6	5	—	(58)	(304)	1,135	26
Total investments	$ 6,273	$ —	$ (46)	$1,156	$(1,230)	$ 1,890	$ —	$ (2,126)	$ (858)	$ 5,059	$ (78)
Loans	$ 3,108	$ —	$(303)	$ 689	$ (805)	$ 1,190	$ 461	$ (807)	$(1,367)	$ 2,166	$ 24
Mortgage servicing rights	1,845	—	110	—	—	—	214	(38)	(350)	1,781	(390)
Other financial assets measured on a recurring basis	78	—	100	201	(66)	6	208	(85)	(262)	180	582
Liabilities											
Interest-bearing deposits	$ 486	$ —	$ 10	$ 1	$ (1)	$ —	$ 36	$ —	$ (78)	$ 434	$(154)
Federal funds purchased and securities loaned or sold under agreements to repurchase	1,043	(23)	—	—	—	—	—	302	(121)	1,247	134
Trading account liabilities											
Securities sold, not yet purchased	424	88	—	311	(231)	—	—	385	(602)	199	(25)
Short-term borrowings	344	11	—	23	(30)	—	1	—	(318)	9	(4)
Long-term debt	7,290	539	—	2,311	(3,958)	—	3,407	—	(1,560)	6,951	(347)
Other financial liabilities measured on a recurring basis	7	—	(11)	10	(4)	(5)	5	2	(12)	14	(4)

(1) Changes in fair value for available-for-sale investments are recorded in *Accumulated other comprehensive income (loss)*, unless related to other-than-temporary impairment, while gains and losses from sales are recorded in *Realized gains (losses) from sales of investments* on the Consolidated Statement of Income.

(2) Unrealized gains (losses) on MSRs are recorded in *Other revenue* on the Consolidated Statement of Income.

(3) Represents the amount of total gains or losses for the period, included in earnings (and *Accumulated other comprehensive income (loss)* for changes in fair value of available-for-sale investments), attributable to the change in fair value relating to assets and liabilities classified as Level 3 that are still held at December 31, 2015.

(4) Total Level 3 derivative assets and liabilities have been netted in these tables for presentation purposes only.

In millions of dollars	Dec. 31, 2013	Net Realized/ Unrealized Gains (Losses) Incl. in Principal Trans-actions	Other[1][2]	Transfers Into Level 3	Transfers Out of Level 3	Purchases	Issuances	Sales	Settle-ments	Dec. 31, 2014	Unrealized Gains (Losses) Still Held[3]
Assets											
Federal funds sold and securities borrowed or purchased under agreements to resell	$ 3,566	$ (61)	$ —	$ 84	$ (8)	$ 75	$ —	$ —	$ (258)	$ 3,398	$ 133
Trading non-derivative assets											
Trading mortgage-backed securities											
U.S. government-sponsored agency guaranteed	1,094	117	—	854	(966)	714	26	(695)	(59)	1,085	8
Residential	2,854	457	—	442	(514)	2,582	—	(3,141)	—	2,680	132
Commercial	256	17	—	187	(376)	758	—	(402)	—	440	(4)
Total trading mortgage-backed securities	$ 4,204	$ 591	$ —	$1,483	$(1,856)	$ 4,054	$ 26	$ (4,238)	$ (59)	$ 4,205	$ 136
U.S. Treasury and federal agency securities	$ —	$ 3	$ —	$ —	$ —	$ 7	$ —	$ (10)	$ —	$ —	$ —
State and municipal	222	10	—	150	(105)	34	—	(70)	—	241	1
Foreign government	416	(56)	—	130	(253)	676	—	(707)	—	206	5
Corporate	1,835	(127)	—	465	(502)	1,988	—	(2,839)	—	820	(139)
Equity securities	1,057	87	—	142	(209)	1,437	—	(295)	—	2,219	337
Asset-backed securities	4,342	876	—	158	(332)	3,893	—	(5,643)	—	3,294	3
Other trading assets	3,184	269	—	2,637	(2,278)	5,427	—	(4,490)	(377)	4,372	31
Total trading non-derivative assets	$15,260	$ 1,653	$ —	$5,165	$(5,535)	$17,516	$ 26	$(18,292)	$ (436)	$15,357	$ 374
Trading derivatives, net[4]											
Interest rate contracts	$ 839	$ (818)	$ —	$ 24	$ (98)	$ 113	$ —	$ (162)	$ (109)	$ (211)	$ (414)
Foreign exchange contracts	695	92	—	47	(39)	59	—	(59)	(17)	778	56
Equity contracts	(858)	482	—	(916)	766	435	—	(279)	(493)	(863)	(274)
Commodity contracts	(1,393)	(338)	—	92	(12)	—	—	—	29	(1,622)	(174)
Credit derivatives	(274)	(567)	—	4	(156)	103	—	(3)	150	(743)	(369)
Total trading derivatives, net[4]	$ (991)	$(1,149)	$ —	$ (749)	$ 461	$ 710	$ —	$ (503)	$ (440)	$(2,661)	$(1,175)
Investments											
Mortgage-backed securities											
U.S. government-sponsored agency guaranteed	$ 187	$ —	$ 52	$ 60	$ (203)	$ 17	$ —	$ (73)	$ (2)	$ 38	$ (8)
Residential	102	—	33	31	(2)	17	—	(173)	—	8	—
Commercial	—	—	(6)	4	(7)	10	—	—	—	1	—
Total investment mortgage-backed securities	$ 289	$ —	$ 79	$ 95	$ (212)	$ 44	$ —	$ (246)	$ (2)	$ 47	$ (8)
U.S. Treasury and federal agency securities	$ 8	$ —	$ —	$ —	$ —	$ —	$ —	$ (2)	$ —	$ 6	$ —
State and municipal	1,643	—	(64)	811	(584)	923	—	(549)	—	2,180	49
Foreign government	344	—	(27)	286	(105)	851	—	(490)	(181)	678	(17)
Corporate	285	—	(6)	26	(143)	728	—	(218)	—	672	(4)
Equity securities	815	—	111	19	(19)	10	—	(255)	—	681	(78)
Asset-backed securities	1,960	—	41	—	(47)	95	—	(195)	(1,305)	549	(18)
Other debt securities	50	—	(1)	—	—	116	—	(115)	(50)	—	—
Non-marketable equity securities	2,508	—	211	67	—	416	—	(768)	(974)	1,460	81
Total investments	$ 7,902	$ —	$ 344	$1,304	$(1,110)	$ 3,183	$ —	$ (2,838)	$(2,512)	$ 6,273	$ 5
Loans	$ 4,143	$ —	$(233)	$ 92	$ 6	$ 951	$ 197	$ (895)	$(1,153)	$ 3,108	$ 37
Mortgage servicing rights	2,718	—	(390)	—	—	—	217	(317)	(383)	1,845	(390)
Other financial assets measured on a recurring basis	181	—	100	(83)	—	3	178	(18)	(283)	78	14

(continued)

In millions of dollars	Dec. 31, 2013	Net Realized/Unrealized Gains (Losses) Incl. in		Transfers		Purchases	Issuances	Sales	Settle-ments	Dec. 31, 2014	Unrealized Gains (Losses) Still Held[3]
		Principal Trans-actions	Other[1][2]	Into Level 3	Out of Level 3						
Liabilities											
Interest-bearing deposits	$ 890	$ —	$ 357	$ 5	$ (12)	$ —	$ 127	$ —	$ (167)	$ 486	$ (69)
Federal funds purchased and securities loaned or sold under agreements to repurchase	902	(6)	—	54	—	78	—	220	(217)	1,043	(34)
Trading account liabilities											
Securities sold, not yet purchased	590	(81)	—	79	(111)	—	—	534	(749)	424	(58)
Short-term borrowings	29	(31)	—	323	(12)	—	49	—	(76)	344	(8)
Long-term debt	7,621	109	49	2,701	(4,206)	—	3,893	—	(2,561)	7,290	(446)
Other financial liabilities measured on a recurring basis	10	—	(5)	7	(3)	(2)	1	(3)	(8)	7	(4)

(1) Changes in fair value of available-for-sale investments are recorded in *Accumulated other comprehensive income (loss)*, unless related to other-than-temporary impairment, while gains and losses from sales are recorded in *Realized gains (losses) from sales of investments* on the Consolidated Statement of Income.

(2) Unrealized gains (losses) on MSRs are recorded in *Other revenue* on the Consolidated Statement of Income.

(3) Represents the amount of total gains or losses for the period, included in earnings (and *Accumulated other comprehensive income (loss)* for changes in fair value of available-for-sale invest-ments), attributable to the change in fair value relating to assets and liabilities classified as Level 3 that are still held at December 31, 2014.

(4) Total Level 3 derivative assets and liabilities have been netted in these tables for presentation purposes only.

Level 3 Fair Value Rollforward

The following were the significant Level 3 transfers for the period December 31, 2014 to December 31, 2015:
- Transfers of *Federal Funds sold and securities borrowed or purchased under agreements to resell* of $2.9 billion from Level 3 to Level 2 related to shortening of the remaining tenor of certain reverse repos. There is more transparency and observability for repo curves used in the valuation of structured reverse repos with tenors up to five years; thus, these positions are generally classified as Level 2.
- Transfers of U.S. government-sponsored agency guaranteed MBS in *Trading account assets* of $0.9 billion from Level 2 to Level 3, and of $1.3 billion from Level 3 to Level 2 primarily related to changes in observability due to market trading activity.
- Transfers of other trading assets of $1.0 billion from Level 2 to Level 3, and of $3.3 billion from Level 3 to Level 2 primarily related to trading loans for which there were changes in volume of and transparency into market quotations.
- Transfers of *Long-term debt* of $2.3 billion from Level 2 to Level 3, and of $4.0 billion from Level 3 to Level 2, mainly related to structured debt, reflecting certain unobservable inputs becoming less significant and certain underlying market inputs being more observable.

The following were the significant Level 3 transfers for the period December 31, 2013 to December 31, 2014:
- Transfers of *Long-term debt* of $2.7 billion from Level 2 to Level 3, and of $4.2 billion from Level 3 to Level 2, mainly related to structured debt, reflecting changes in the significance of unobservable inputs as well as certain underlying market inputs becoming less or more observable.
- Transfers of other trading assets of $2.6 billion from Level 2 to Level 3, and of $2.3 billion from Level 3 to Level 2, related to trading loans, reflecting changes in the volume of market quotations.

Valuation Techniques and Inputs for Level 3 Fair Value Measurements

The Company's Level 3 inventory consists of both cash securities and derivatives of varying complexity. The valuation methodologies used to measure the fair value of these positions include discounted cash flow analysis, internal models and comparative analysis. A position is classified within Level 3 of the fair value hierarchy when at least one input is unobservable and is considered significant to its valuation. The specific reason an input is deemed unobservable varies. For example, at least one significant input to the pricing model is not observable in the market, at least one significant input has been adjusted to make it more representative of the position being valued, or the price quote available does not reflect sufficient trading activities.

The following tables present the valuation techniques covering the majority of Level 3 inventory and the most significant unobservable inputs used in Level 3 fair value measurements. Differences between this table and amounts presented in the Level 3 Fair Value Rollforward table represent individually immaterial items that have been measured using a variety of valuation techniques other than those listed.

Valuation Techniques and Inputs for Level 3 Fair Value Measurements

As of December 31, 2015	Fair value[1] (In millions)	Methodology	Input	Low[2][3]	High[2][3]	Weighted average[4]
Assets						
Federal funds sold and securities borrowed or purchased under agreements to resell	$1,337	Model-based	IR log-normal volatility	29.02%	137.02%	37.90%
			Interest rate	—%	2.03%	0.27%
Mortgage-backed securities	$1,287	Price-based	Price	$ 3.45	$ 109.21	$ 78.25
	1,377	Yield analysis	Yield	0.50%	14.07%	4.83%
State and municipal, foreign government, corporate and other debt securities	$3,761	Price-based	Price	$ —	$ 217.00	$ 79.41
	1,719	Cash flow	Credit spread	20 bps	600 bps	251 bps
Equity securities[5]	$3,499	Model-based	WAL	1.5 years	1.5 years	1.5 years
			Redemption rate	41.21%	41.21%	41.21%
Asset-backed securities	$3,075	Price-based	Price	$ 5.55	$ 100.21	$ 71.57
Non-marketable equity	$ 633	Comparables analysis	EBITDA multiples	6.80x	10.80x	9.05x
	473	Price-based	Discount to price	—%	90.00%	10.89%
			Price-to-book ratio	0.19x	1.09x	0.60x
			Price	$ —	$ 132.78	$ 46.66
Derivatives—gross[6]						
Interest rate contracts (gross)	$4,553	Model-based	IR log-normal volatility	17.41%	137.02%	37.60%
			Mean reversion	(5.52)%	20.00%	0.71%
Foreign exchange contracts (gross)	$1,326	Model-based	Foreign exchange (FX) volatility	0.38%	25.73%	11.63%
	275	Cash flow	Interest rate	7.50%	7.50%	7.50%
			Forward price	1.48%	138.09%	56.80%
			Credit spread	3 bps	515 bps	235 bps
			IR-IR correlation	(51.00)%	77.94%	32.91%
			IR-FX correlation	(20.30)%	60.00%	48.85%
Equity contracts (gross)[7]	$3,976	Model-based	Equity volatility	11.87%	49.57%	27.33%
			Equity-FX correlation	(88.17)%	65.00%	(21.09)%
			Equity forward	82.72%	100.53%	95.20%
			Equity-equity correlation	(80.54)%	100.00%	49.54%
Commodity contracts (gross)	$4,061	Model-based	Forward price	35.09%	299.32%	112.98%
			Commodity volatility	5.00%	83.00%	24.00%
			Commodity correlation	(57.00)%	91.00%	30.00%
Credit derivatives (gross)	$5,849	Model-based	Recovery rate	1.00%	75.00%	32.49%
	1,424	Price-based	Credit correlation	5.00%	90.00%	43.48%
			Price	$ 0.33	$ 101.00	$ 61.52
			Credit spread	1 bps	967 bps	133 bps
			Upfront points	7.00%	99.92%	66.75%
Nontrading derivatives and other financial assets and liabilities measured on a recurring basis (gross)[6]	$ 194	Model-based	Recovery rate	7.00%	40.00%	10.72%
			Redemption rate	27.00%	99.50%	74.80%
			Interest rate	5.26%	5.28%	5.27%
Loans	$ 750	Price-based	Yield	1.50%	4.50%	2.52%
	892	Model-based	Price	$ —	$ 106.98	$ 40.69
	524	Cash flow	Credit spread	29 bps	500 bps	105 bps
Mortgage servicing rights	$1,690	Cash flow	Yield	—%	23.32%	6.83%
			WAL	3.38 years	7.48 years	5.5 years
Liabilities						
Interest-bearing deposits	$ 434	Model-based	Equity-IR correlation	23.00%	39.00%	34.51%
			Forward price	35.09%	299.32%	112.72%
			Commodity correlation	(57.00)%	91.00%	30.00%
			Commodity volatility	5.00%	83.00%	24.00%
Federal funds purchased and securities loaned or sold under agreements to repurchase	$1,245	Model-based	Interest rate	1.27%	2.02%	1.92%
Trading account liabilities						
Securities sold, not yet purchased	$ 152	Price-based	Price	$ —	$ 217.00	$ 87.78
Short-term borrowings and long-term debt	$7,004	Model-based	Mean reversion	(5.52)%	20.00%	7.80%
			Equity volatility	9.55%	42.56%	22.26%
			Equity forward	82.72%	100.80%	94.48%
			Equity-equity correlation	(80.54)%	100.00%	49.16%
			Forward price	35.09%	299.32%	106.32%
			Equity-FX correlation	(88.20)%	56.85%	(31.76)%

As of December 31, 2014	Fair value[1] (In millions)	Methodology	Input	Low[2][3]	High[2][3]	Weighted average[4]
Assets						
Federal funds sold and securities borrowed or purchased under agreements to resell	$3,156	Model-based	Interest rate	1.27%	1.97%	1.80%
Mortgage-backed securities	$2,874	Price-based	Price	$ —	$ 127.87	$ 81.43
	1,117	Yield analysis	Yield	0.01%	19.91%	5.89%
State and municipal, foreign government, corporate and other debt securities	$5,937	Price-based	Price	$ —	$ 124.00	$ 90.62
	1,860	Cash flow	Credit spread	25 bps	600 bps	233 bps
Equity securities[5]	$2,163	Price-based	Price[5]	$ —	$ 141.00	$ 91.00
	679	Cash flow	Yield	4.00%	5.00%	4.50%
			WAL	0.01 years	3.14 years	1.07 years
Asset-backed securities	$3,607	Price-based	Price	$ —	$ 105.50	$ 67.01
Non-marketable equity	$1,224	Price-based	Discount to price	—%	90.00%	4.04%
	1,055	Comparables analysis	EBITDA multiples	2.90x	13.10x	9.77x
			PE ratio	8.10x	13.10x	8.43x
			Price-to-book ratio	0.99x	1.56x	1.15x
Derivatives—gross[6]						
Interest rate contracts (gross)	$8,309	Model-based	Interest rate (IR) log-normal volatility	18.05%	90.65%	30.21%
			Mean reversion	1.00%	20.00%	10.50%
Foreign exchange contracts (gross)	$1,428	Model-based	Foreign exchange (FX) volatility	0.37%	58.40%	8.57%
	294	Cash flow	Interest rate	3.72%	8.27%	5.02%
			IR-FX correlation	40.00%	60.00%	50.00%
Equity contracts (gross)[7]	$4,431	Model-based	Equity volatility	9.56%	82.44%	24.61%
	502	Price-based	Equity forward	84.10%	100.80%	94.10%
			Equity-FX correlation	(88.20)%	48.70%	(25.17)%
			Equity-equity correlation	(66.30)%	94.80%	36.87%
			Price	$ 0.01	$ 144.50	$ 93.05
Commodity contracts (gross)	$3,606	Model-based	Commodity volatility	5.00%	83.00%	24.00%
			Commodity correlation	(57.00)%	91.00%	30.00%
			Forward price	35.34%	268.77%	101.74%
Credit derivatives (gross)	$4,944	Model-based	Recovery rate	13.97%	75.00%	37.62%
	1,584	Price-based	Credit correlation	—%	95.00%	58.76%
			Price	$ 1.00	$ 144.50	$ 53.86
			Credit spread	1 bps	3,380 bps	180 bps
			Upfront points	0.39	100.00	52.26
Non-trading derivatives and other financial assets and liabilities measured on a recurring basis (gross)[6]	$ 74	Model-based	Redemption rate	13.00%	99.50%	68.73%
			Forward Price	107.00%	107.10%	107.05%
Loans	$1,095	Cash flow	Yield	1.60%	4.50%	2.23%
	832	Model-based	Price	$ 4.72	$ 106.55	$ 98.56
	740	Price-based	Credit spread	35 bps	500 bps	199 bps
	441	Yield analysis				
Mortgage servicing rights	$1,750	Cash flow	Yield	5.19%	21.40%	10.25%
			WAL	3.31 years	7.89 years	5.17 years
Liabilities						
Interest-bearing deposits	$ 486	Model-based	Equity-IR correlation	34.00%	37.00%	35.43%
			Commodity correlation	(57.00)%	91.00%	30.00%
			Commodity volatility	5.00%	83.00%	24.00%
			Forward price	35.34%	268.77%	101.74%
Federal funds purchased and securities loaned or sold under agreements to repurchase	$1,043	Model-based	Interest rate	0.74%	2.26%	1.90%
Trading account liabilities						
Securities sold, not yet purchased	$ 251	Model-based	Credit-IR correlation	(70.49)%	8.81%	47.17%
	$ 142	Price-based	Price	$ —	$ 117.00	$ 70.33
Short-term borrowings and long-term debt	$7,204	Model-based	IR log-normal volatility	18.05%	90.65%	30.21%
			Mean reversion	1.00%	20.00%	10.50%
			Equity volatility	10.18%	69.65%	23.72%
			Credit correlation	87.50%	87.50%	87.50%
			Equity forward	89.50%	100.80%	95.80%
			Forward price	35.34%	268.77%	101.80%
			Commodity correlation	(57.00)%	91.00%	30.00%
			Commodity volatility	5.00%	83.00%	24.00%

[1] The fair value amounts presented in these tables represent the primary valuation technique or techniques for each class of assets or liabilities.

[2] Some inputs are shown as zero due to rounding.

[3] When the low and high inputs are the same, there is either a constant input applied to all positions, or the methodology involving the input applies to only one large position.

[4] Weighted averages are calculated based on the fair values of the instruments.

[5] For equity securities, the price and fund NAV inputs are expressed on an absolute basis, not as a percentage of the notional amount.

[6] Both trading and nontrading account derivatives—assets and liabilities—are presented on a gross absolute value basis.

[7] Includes hybrid products.

Current Receivables

PRESENTATION

2.21 FASB ASC 310, *Receivables*, indicates that loans or trade receivables may be presented on the balance sheet as aggregate amounts. However, major categories of loans or trade receivables should be presented separately either in the balance sheet or in the notes to the financial statements. Also, any such receivables held for sale should be a separate balance sheet category. Receivables from officers, employees, or affiliated companies should be shown separately and not included under a general heading, such as accounts receivable. Valuation allowance for credit losses or doubtful accounts and any unearned income included in the face amount of receivables should be shown as a deduction from the related receivables.

DISCLOSURE

2.22 FASB ASC 310 states that allowances for doubtful accounts should be deducted from the related receivables and appropriately disclosed. FASB ASC 310-10-50-4 requires, as applicable, any unearned income, unamortized premiums and discounts, and net unamortized deferred fees and costs be disclosed in the financial statements. Under FASB ASC 825, fair value disclosure is not required for trade receivables when the carrying amount of the trade receivable approximates its fair value.

PRESENTATION AND DISCLOSURE EXCERPT

FINANCE RECEIVABLES

2.23 CISCO SYSTEMS, INC. (JUL)
CONSOLIDATED BALANCE SHEETS (in part)

(in millions, except par value)

	July 25, 2015	July 26, 2014
Assets (in part)		
Current assets:		
Cash and cash equivalents	$ 6,877	$ 6,726
Investments	53,539	45,348
Accounts receivable, net of allowance for doubtful accounts of $302 at July 25, 2015 and $265 at July 26, 2014	5,344	5,157
Inventories	1,627	1,591
Financing receivables, net	4,491	4,153
Deferred tax assets	2,915	2,808
Other current assets	1,490	1,331
Total current assets	76,283	67,114

NOTES TO CONSOLIDATED FINANCIAL STATEMENTS (in part)

2. Summary of Significant Accounting Policies (in part)

(f) Financing Receivables and Guarantees The Company provides financing arrangements, including leases, financed service contracts, and loans, for certain qualified end-user customers to build, maintain, and upgrade their networks. Lease receivables primarily represent sales-type and direct-financing leases. Leases have on average a four -year term and are usually collateralized by a security interest in the underlying assets, while loan receivables generally have terms of up to three years. Financed service contracts typically have terms of one to three years and primarily relate to technical support services.

The Company determines the adequacy of its allowance for credit loss by assessing the risks and losses inherent in its financing receivables by portfolio segment. The portfolio segment is based on the types of financing offered by the Company to its customers: lease receivables, loan receivables, and financed service contracts and other.

The Company assesses the allowance for credit loss related to financing receivables on either an individual or a collective basis. The Company considers various factors in evaluating lease and loan receivables and the earned portion of financed service contracts for possible impairment on an individual basis. These factors include the Company's historical experience, credit quality and age of the receivable balances, and economic conditions that may affect a customer's ability to pay. When the evaluation indicates that it is probable that all amounts due pursuant to the contractual terms of the financing agreement, including scheduled interest payments, are unable to be collected, the financing receivable is considered impaired. All such outstanding amounts, including any accrued interest, will be assessed and fully reserved at the customer level. The Company's internal credit risk ratings are categorized as 1 through 10, with the lowest credit risk rating representing the highest quality financing receivables. Typically, the Company also considers receivables with a risk rating of 8 or higher to be impaired and will include them in the individual assessment for allowance. The Company evaluates the remainder of its financing receivables portfolio for impairment on a collective basis and records an allowance for credit loss at the portfolio segment level. When evaluating the financing receivables on a collective basis, the Company uses expected default frequency rates published by a major third-party credit-rating agency as well as its own historical loss rate in the event of default, while also systematically giving effect to economic conditions, concentration of risk, and correlation.

Expected default frequency rates are published quarterly by a major third-party credit-rating agency, and the internal credit risk rating is derived by taking into consideration various customer-specific factors and macroeconomic conditions. These factors, which include the strength of the customer's business and financial performance, the quality of the customer's banking relationships, the Company's specific historical experience with the customer, the performance and outlook of the customer's industry, the customer's legal and regulatory environment, the potential sovereign risk of the geographic locations in which the customer is operating, and independent third-party evaluations, are updated regularly or when facts and circumstances indicate that an update is deemed necessary.

Financing receivables are written off at the point when they are considered uncollectible, and all outstanding balances, including any previously earned but uncollected interest income, will be reversed and charged against the allowance for credit loss. The Company does not typically have any partially written-off financing receivables.

Outstanding financing receivables that are aged 31 days or more from the contractual payment date are considered past due. The Company does not accrue interest on financing receivables that are considered impaired or more than 90 days past due unless either the receivable has not been collected due to administrative reasons or the receivable is well secured and in the process of collection. Financing receivables may be placed on nonaccrual status earlier if, in management's opinion, a timely collection of the full principal and interest becomes uncertain. After a financing receivable has been categorized as nonaccrual, interest will be recognized when cash is received. A financing receivable may be returned to accrual status after all of the customer's delinquent balances of principal and interest have been settled, and the customer remains current for an appropriate period.

The Company facilitates arrangements for third-party financing extended to channel partners, consisting of revolving short-term financing, generally with payment terms ranging from 60 to 90 days. In certain instances, these financing arrangements result in a transfer of the Company's receivables to the third party. The receivables are derecognized upon transfer, as these transfers qualify as true sales, and the Company receives a payment for the receivables from the third party based on the Company's standard payment terms. These financing arrangements facilitate the working capital requirements of the channel partners, and, in some cases, the Company guarantees a portion of these arrangements. The Company also provides financing guarantees for third-party financing arrangements extended to end-user customers related to leases and loans, which typically have terms of up to three years. The Company could be called upon to make payments under these guarantees in the event of nonpayment by the channel partners or end-user customers. Deferred revenue relating to these financing arrangements is recorded in accordance with revenue recognition policies or for the fair value of the financing guarantees.

7. Financing Receivables and Operating Leases (in part)

(a) Financing Receivables (in part)

Financing receivables primarily consist of lease receivables, loan receivables, and financed service contracts and other. Lease receivables represent sales-type and direct-financing leases resulting from the sale of the Company's and complementary third-party products and are typically collateralized by a security interest in the underlying assets. Loan receivables represent financing arrangements related to the sale of the Company's products and services, which may include additional funding for other costs associated with network installation and integration of the Company's products and services. Lease receivables consist of arrangements with terms of four years on average, while loan receivables generally have terms of up to three years. The financed service contracts and other category includes financing receivables related to technical support and advanced services, as well as receivables related to financing of certain indirect costs associated with leases. Revenue related to the technical support services is typically deferred and included in deferred service revenue and is recognized ratably over the period during which the related services are to be performed, which typically ranges from one to three years.

A summary of the Company's financing receivables is presented as follows (in millions):

July 25, 2015	Lease Receivables	Loan Receivables	Financed Service Contracts and Other	Total
Gross	$3,361	$1,763	$3,573	$8,697
Residual value	224	—	—	224
Unearned income	(190)	—	—	(190)
Allowance for credit loss	(259)	(87)	(36)	(382)
Total, net	$3,136	$1,676	$3,537	$8,349
Reported as:				
Current	$1,468	$856	$2,167	$4,491
Noncurrent	1,668	820	1,370	3,858
Total, net	$3,136	$1,676	$3,537	$8,349

July 26, 2014	Lease Receivables	Loan Receivables	Financed Service Contracts and Other	Total
Gross	$3,532	$1,683	$3,210	$8,425
Residual value	233	—	—	233
Unearned income	(238)	—	—	(238)
Allowance for credit loss	(233)	(98)	(18)	(349)
Total, net	$3,294	$1,585	$3,192	$8,071
Reported as:				
Current	$1,476	$728	$1,949	$4,153
Noncurrent	1,818	857	1,243	3,918
Total, net	$3,294	$1,585	$3,192	$8,071

As of July 25, 2015 and July 26, 2014, the deferred service revenue related to "Financed Service Contracts and Other" was $1,853 million and $1,843 million, respectively.

(b) Credit Quality of Financing Receivables

Gross receivables less unearned income categorized by the Company's internal credit risk rating as of July 25, 2015 and July 26, 2014 are summarized as follows (in millions):

July 25, 2015	Internal Credit Risk Rating			
	1 to 4	5 to 6	7 and Higher	Total
Lease receivables	$1,688	$1,342	$141	$3,171
Loan receivables	788	823	152	1,763
Financed service contracts and other	2,133	1,389	51	3,573
Total	$4,609	$3,554	$344	$8,507

July 26, 2014	Internal Credit Risk Rating			
	1 to 4	5 to 6	7 and Higher	Total
Lease receivables	$1,615	$1,538	$141	$3,294
Loan receivables	953	593	137	1,683
Financed service contracts and other	1,744	1,367	99	3,210
Total	$4,312	$3,498	$377	$8,187

The Company determines the adequacy of its allowance for credit loss by assessing the risks and losses inherent in its financing receivables by portfolio segment. The portfolio segment is based on the types of financing offered by the Company to its customers, which consist of the following: lease receivables, loan receivables, and financed service contracts and other.

The Company's internal credit risk ratings of 1 through 4 correspond to investment-grade ratings, while credit risk ratings of 5 and 6 correspond to non-investment grade ratings. Credit risk ratings of 7 and higher correspond to substandard ratings.

In circumstances when collectibility is not deemed reasonably assured, the associated revenue is deferred in accordance with the Company's revenue recognition policies, and the related allowance for credit loss, if any, is included in deferred revenue. The Company also records deferred revenue associated with financing receivables when there are remaining performance obligations, as it does for financed service contracts. Total allowances for credit loss and deferred revenue as of July 25, 2015 and July 26, 2014 were $2,253 million and $2,220 million, respectively, and they were associated with total financing receivables before allowance for credit loss of $8,731 million and $8,420 million as of their respective period ends.

The following tables present the aging analysis of gross receivables less unearned income as of July 25, 2015 and July 26, 2014 (in millions):

| July 25, 2015 | Days Past Due (Includes Billed and Unbilled) | | | | | | Nonaccrual Financing Receivables | Impaired Financing Receivables |
	31–60	61–90	91 +	Total Past Due	Current	Total		
Lease receivables	$ 90	$ 27	$185	$ 302	$2,869	$3,171	$ 73	$ 73
Loan receivables	21	3	25	49	1,714	1,763	32	32
Financed service contracts and other	396	152	414	962	2,611	3,573	29	9
Total	$507	$182	$624	$1,313	$7,194	$8,507	$134	$114

| July 26, 2014 | Days Past Due (Includes Billed and Unbilled) | | | | | | Nonaccrual Financing Receivables | Impaired Financing Receivables |
	31–60	61–90	91 +	Total Past Due	Current	Total		
Lease receivables	$ 63	$ 46	$202	$ 311	$2,983	$3,294	$48	$41
Loan receivables	3	21	27	51	1,632	1,683	19	19
Financed service contracts and other	268	230	220	718	2,492	3,210	12	9
Total	$334	$297	$449	$1,080	$7,107	$8,187	$79	$69

Past due financing receivables are those that are 31 days or more past due according to their contractual payment terms. The data in the preceding tables is presented by contract, and the aging classification of each contract is based on the oldest outstanding receivable, and therefore past due amounts also include unbilled and current receivables within the same contract. The balances of either unbilled or current financing receivables included in the category of 91 days plus past due for financing receivables were $496 million and $334 million as of July 25, 2015 and July 26, 2014, respectively.

As of July 25, 2015, the Company had financing receivables of $70 million, net of unbilled or current receivables from the same contract, that were in the category of 91 days plus past due but remained on accrual status as they are well secured and in the process of collection. Such balance was $78 million as of July 26, 2014.

(c) Allowance for Credit Loss Rollforward

The allowances for credit loss and the related financing receivables are summarized as follows (in millions):

| | Credit Loss Allowances | | | |
	Lease Receivables	Loan Receivables	Financed Service Contracts and Other	Total
Allowance for credit loss as of July 26, 2014	$ 233	$ 98	$ 18	$ 349
Provisions	45	(8)	20	57
Recoveries (write-offs), net	(7)	1	(1)	(7)
Foreign exchange and other	(12)	(4)	(1)	(17)
Allowance for credit loss as of July 25, 2015	$ 259	$ 87	$ 36	$ 382
Financing receivables as of July 25, 2015[1]	$3,395	$1,763	$3,573	$8,731

| | Credit Loss Allowances | | | |
	Lease Receivables	Loan Receivables	Financed Service Contracts and Other	Total
Allowance for credit loss as of July 27, 2013	$ 238	$ 86	$ 20	$ 344
Provisions	4	9	1	14
Recoveries (write-offs), net	(11)	5	(3)	(9)
Foreign exchange and other	2	(2)	—	—
Allowance for credit loss as of July 26, 2014	$ 233	$ 98	$ 18	$ 349
Financing receivables as of July 26, 2014[1]	$3,527	$1,683	$3,210	$8,420

| | Credit Loss Allowances | | | |
	Lease Receivables	Loan Receivables	Financed Service Contracts and Other	Total
Allowance for credit loss as of July 28, 2012	$ 247	$ 122	$ 11	$ 380
Provisions	21	(20)	10	11
Recoveries (write-offs), net	(30)	(15)	(1)	(46)
Foreign exchange and other	—	(1)	—	(1)
Allowance for credit loss as of July 27, 2013	$ 238	$ 86	$ 20	$ 344
Financing receivables as of July 27, 2013[1]	$3,507	$1,649	$3,136	$8,292

[1] Total financing receivables before allowance for credit loss.

Receivables Sold or Collateralized

RECOGNITION AND MEASUREMENT

2.24 FASB ASC 860, *Transfers and Servicing*, establishes criteria for determining whether a transfer of financial assets in exchange for cash or other consideration should be accounted for as a sale or pledge of collateral in a secured borrowing. FASB ASC 860 also establishes the criteria for accounting for securitizations and other transfers of financial assets and collateral and requires certain disclosures.

2.25 FASB ASC 860 requires that all separately recognized servicing assets and liabilities be initially measured at fair value. Further, FASB ASC 860 permits, but does not require, the subsequent measurement of servicing assets and liabilities at fair value.

2.26 FASB ASC 860, *Transfers and Servicing*, provides guidance for certain transactions involving (*a*) a transfer of a financial asset accounted for as a sale and (*b*) an agreement with the same transferee entered into in contemplation of the initial transfer that results in the transferor retaining substantially all the exposure to the economic return on the transferred financial asset throughout the term of the transaction.

DISCLOSURE

2.27 FASB ASC 860 requires additional disclosures and separate balance sheet presentation of the carrying amounts of servicing assets and liabilities that are subsequently measured at fair value. FASB ASC 860-50-50-2 requires disclosures including (*a*) a description of the risks inherent in servicing assets and servicing liabilities, (*b*) the amount of contractually specified servicing fees, late fees, and ancillary fees earned for each period, including a description of where each amount is reported in the statement of income, and(c) quantitative and qualitative information about the assumptions used to estimate fair value.

2.28 FASB ASC 860-30-50-7 includes additional requirement disclosures to provide an understanding of the nature and risks of short-term collateralized financing obtained through repurchase agreements, securities lending transactions, and repurchase-to-maturity transactions that are accounted for as secured borrowings at the reporting date.

PRESENTATION AND DISCLOSURE EXCERPTS

RECEIVABLES SOLD OR COLLATERALIZED

2.29 COMMERCIAL METALS COMPANY (AUG)
NOTES TO CONSOLIDATED FINANCIAL STATEMENTS (in part)

Note 5. Sales of Accounts Receivable

During the fourth quarter of fiscal 2014, the Company entered into a third amended $200.0 million U.S. sale of accounts receivable program which expires on August 15, 2017. Under the program, Commercial Metals Company contributes, and several of its subsidiaries sell without recourse, certain eligible trade accounts receivable to CMC Receivables, Inc. ("CMCRV"), a wholly owned subsidiary of CMC. CMCRV is structured to be a bankruptcy-remote entity and was formed for the sole purpose of buying and selling trade accounts receivable generated by the Company. CMCRV sells the trade accounts receivable in their entirety to three financial institutions. Under the amended U.S. sale of accounts receivable program, with the consent of both CMCRV and the program's administrative agent, the amount advanced by the financial institutions can be increased to a maximum of $300.0 million for all trade accounts receivable sold. The remaining portion of the purchase price of the trade accounts receivable takes the form of subordinated notes from the respective financial institutions. These notes will be satisfied from the ultimate collection of the trade accounts receivable after payment of certain fees and other costs. The Company accounts for sales of the trade accounts receivable as true sales, and the trade accounts receivable balances that are sold are removed from the consolidated balance sheets. The cash advances received are reflected as cash provided by operating activities on the Company's consolidated statements of cash flows. Additionally, the U.S. sale of accounts receivable program contains certain cross-default provisions whereby a termination event could occur if the Company defaulted under certain of its credit arrangements. The covenants contained in the receivables purchase agreement are consistent with the credit facility described in Note 11, Credit Arrangements.

At August 31, 2015 and 2014, under its U.S. sale of accounts receivable program, the Company had sold $274.3 million and $389.6 million of trade accounts receivable, respectively, to the financial institutions. At August 31, 2015, the Company had no advance payments outstanding on the sale of its trade accounts receivable. At August 31, 2014 the Company had $55.0 million in advance payments outstanding on the sale of its trade accounts receivable.

In addition to the U.S. sale of accounts receivable program described above, the Company's international subsidiaries in Europe and Australia sell trade accounts receivable to financial institutions without recourse. These arrangements constitute true sales, and once the trade accounts receivable are sold, they are no longer available to the Company's creditors in the event of bankruptcy. In the third quarter of fiscal 2015, the Company phased out its existing European program and entered into a new, two year renewable, trade accounts receivable sales program with a different financial institution. The new agreement increased the facility limit from PLN 200.0 million to PLN 220.0 million. The European program allows the Company's European subsidiaries to obtain an advance of up to 90% of eligible trade accounts receivable sold under the terms of the arrangement. During the first quarter of fiscal 2014, the Company phased out its existing Australian program and entered into a new, one year renewable, trade accounts receivable sales program with a different financial institution. In October 2014, the Company entered into a first amendment to its Australian program, which extended the maturity date to October 2016. Under the new Australian program, trade accounts receivable balances are sold to a special purpose vehicle, which in turn sells 100% of the eligible trade accounts receivable of Commercial Metals Pty. Ltd., CMC Steel Distribution Pty. Ltd. and G.A.M. Steel Pty. Ltd. to the financial institution. In August 2015, the Company entered into a second amendment to its Australian program, which reduced the facility limit from A$75.0 million to A$40.0 million. The financial institution will fund up to the facility limit for all trade accounts receivable sold, and the remaining portion of the purchase price of the trade accounts receivable is in the form of a subordinated note from the financial institution. This note will be satisfied from the ultimate collection of the trade accounts receivable after payment of certain fees and other costs. The Company accounts for sales of the trade accounts receivable as true sales, and the trade accounts receivable balances that are sold are removed from the consolidated balance sheets. The cash advances received are reflected as cash provided by operating activities on the Company's consolidated statements of cash flows.

At August 31, 2015 and 2014, under its European and Australian programs, the Company had sold $97.9 million and $147.3 million of trade accounts receivable, respectively, to third-party financial institutions and received advance payments of $27.7 million and $90.5 million, respectively.

For the years ended August 31, 2015, 2014 and 2013, cash proceeds from the U.S. and international sale of accounts receivable programs were $596.4 million, $688.2 million and $1.0 billion, respectively, and cash payments to the owners of accounts receivable were $714.2 million, $567.2 million and $1.1 billion, respectively. For a nominal servicing fee, the Company is responsible for servicing the accounts receivable for the U.S. and Australian programs. Discounts on U.S. and international sales of trade accounts receivable were $2.4 million, $3.9 million and $3.9 million for the years ended August 31, 2015, 2014 and 2013, respectively, and are included in selling, general and administrative expenses in the Company's consolidated statements of earnings.

The deferred purchase price on the Company's U.S. and international sale of trade accounts receivable programs are included in accounts receivable on the Company's consolidated balance sheets. The following tables summarize the activity of the deferred purchase price receivables for the U.S. and international sale of accounts receivable programs:

(In thousands)	Total	U.S.	Australia*	Europe
Balance at September 1, 2012	$ 515,481	$ 396,919	$ 70,073	$ 48,489
Transfers of accounts receivable	4,423,952	3,570,922	408,530	444,500
Collections	(4,486,181)	(3,609,019)	(413,607)	(463,555)
Balance at August 31, 2013	$ 453,252	$ 358,822	$ 64,996	$ 29,434
Transfers of accounts receivable	4,243,471	3,347,103	487,583	408,785
Collections	(4,239,242)	(3,376,128)	(446,196)	(416,918)
Program termination	(72,312)	—	(72,312)	—
Balance at August 31, 2014	$ 385,169	$ 329,797	$ 34,071	$ 21,301
Transfers of accounts receivable	3,574,283	2,944,627	298,179	331,477
Collections	(3,619,905)	(3,004,646)	(314,212)	(301,047)
Balance at August 31, 2015	$ 339,547	$ 269,778	$ 18,038	$ 51,731

* Includes the sale of accounts receivable activities related to businesses sold or held for sale (transfer of accounts receivable of $180.0 million and collections of $209.2 million) for the year ended August 31, 2015.

2.30 ARCHER-DANIELS-MIDLAND COMPANY (DEC)
NOTES TO CONSOLIDATED FINANCIAL STATEMENTS (in part)

Note 1. Summary of Significant Accounting Policies (in part)

Receivables

The Company records accounts receivable at net realizable value. This value includes an allowance for estimated uncollectible accounts of $70 million and $81 million at December 31, 2015 and 2014, respectively, to reflect any loss anticipated on the accounts receivable balances. The Company estimates this allowance based on its history of write-offs, level of past-due accounts, and its relationships with, and the economic status of, its customers. Portions of the allowance for uncollectible accounts are recorded in trade receivables, other current assets, and other assets.

Credit risk on receivables is minimized as a result of the large and diversified nature of the Company's worldwide customer base. The Company manages its exposure to counter-party credit risk through credit analysis and approvals, credit limits, and monitoring procedures. Collateral is generally not required for the Company's receivables.

Accounts receivable due from unconsolidated affiliates as of December 31, 2015 and 2014 was $35 million and $15 million, respectively.

Note 10. Debt Financing Arrangements (in part)

The Company has accounts receivable securitization programs (the "Programs"). The Programs provide the Company with up to $1.6 billion in funding resulting from the sale of accounts receivable. As of December 31, 2015, the Company utilized $1.2 billion of its facility under the Programs (see Note 20 for more information on the Programs).

Note 20. Sale of Accounts Receivable

Since March 2012, the Company has had an accounts receivable securitization program (the "Program") with certain commercial paper conduit purchasers and committed purchasers (collectively, the "Purchasers"). Under the Program, certain U.S.-originated trade accounts receivable are sold to a wholly-owned bankruptcy-remote entity, ADM Receivables, LLC ("ADM Receivables"). ADM Receivables in turn transfers such purchased accounts receivable in their entirety to the Purchasers pursuant to a receivables purchase agreement. In exchange for the transfer of the accounts receivable, ADM Receivables receives a cash payment of up to $1.3 billion, as amended, and an additional amount upon the collection of the accounts receivable (deferred consideration). The Program terminates on June 24, 2016, unless extended.

In March 2014, the Company entered into a second accounts receivable securitization program (the "Second Program") with certain commercial paper conduit purchasers and committed purchasers (collectively, the "Second Purchasers"). Under the Second Program, certain non-U.S.-originated trade accounts receivable are sold to a wholly-owned bankruptcy-remote entity, ADM Ireland Receivables Company ("ADM Ireland Receivables"). ADM Ireland Receivables in turn transfers such purchased accounts receivable in their entirety to the Second Purchasers pursuant to a receivables purchase agreement. In exchange for the transfer of the accounts receivable, ADM Ireland Receivables receives a cash payment of up to $0.3 billion and an additional amount upon the collection of the accounts receivable (deferred consideration). The Second Program terminates on March 18, 2016, unless extended.

Under the Program and Second Program (collectively, the "Programs"), ADM Receivables and ADM Ireland Receivables use the cash proceeds from the transfer of receivables to the Purchasers and Second Purchasers and other consideration to finance the purchase of receivables from the Company and the ADM subsidiaries originating the receivables.

The Company accounts for these transfers as sales. The Company has no retained interests in the transferred receivables, other than collection and administrative responsibilities and its right to the deferred consideration. At December 31, 2015 and 2014, the Company did not record a servicing asset or liability related to its retained responsibility, based on its assessment of the servicing fee, market values for similar transactions and its cost of servicing the receivables sold.

As of December 31, 2015 and 2014, the fair value of trade receivables transferred to the Purchasers under the Programs and derecognized from the Company's consolidated balance sheet was $1.7 billion and $2.1 billion, respectively. In exchange for the transfer as of December 31, 2015 and 2014, the Company received cash of $1.2 billion and $1.6 billion and recorded a receivable for deferred consideration included in other current assets $513 million and $511 million, respectively. Cash collections from customers on receivables sold were $40.7 billion, $36.4 billion, and $39.8 billion for the years ended December 31, 2015, 2014, and 2013, respectively. Of this amount, $40.3 billion, $35.1 billion, and $39.8 billion pertain to cash collections on the deferred consideration for the years ended December 31, 2015, 2014, and 2013, respectively. Deferred consideration is paid to the Company in cash on behalf of the Purchasers as receivables are collected; however, as this is a revolving facility, cash collected from the Company's customers is reinvested by the Purchasers daily in new receivable purchases under the Program.

The Company's risk of loss following the transfer of accounts receivable under the Program is limited to the deferred consideration outstanding. The Company carries the deferred consideration at fair value determined by calculating the expected amount of cash to be received and is principally based on observable inputs (a Level 2 measurement under the applicable accounting standards) consisting mainly of the face amount of the receivables adjusted for anticipated credit losses and discounted at the appropriate market rate. Payment of deferred consideration is not subject to significant risks other than delinquencies and credit losses on accounts receivable transferred under the program which have historically been insignificant.

Transfers of receivables under the Program during the years ended December 31, 2015, 2014, and 2013 resulted in an expense for the loss on sale of $5 million, $5 million, and $4 million, respectively, which is classified as selling, general, and administrative expenses in the consolidated statements of earnings.

The Company reflects all cash flows related to the Program as operating activities in its consolidated statements of cash flows because the cash received from the Purchasers upon both the sale and collection of the receivables is not subject to significant interest rate risk given the short-term nature of the Company's trade receivables.

ACCOUNTS RECEIVABLE FACTORING AND SECURITIZATION

2.31 MERITOR, INC. (SEP)
NOTES TO CONSOLIDATED FINANCIAL STATEMENTS (in part)

2. Significant Accounting Policies (in part)

Concentration of Credit Risk

In the normal course of business, the company provides credit to customers. The company limits its credit risk by performing ongoing credit evaluations of its customers and maintaining reserves for potential credit losses and through accounts receivable factoring programs. The company's accounts receivable is due from medium- and heavy-duty truck OEMs, specialty vehicle manufacturers, aftermarket customers, and trailer producers. The company's ten largest customers accounted for 75 percent and 76 percent of sales in fiscal year 2015 and 2014, respectively. Sales to the company's top three customers were 55 percent and 57 percent of total sales in fiscal 2015 and 2014, respectively. At September 30, 2015 and 2014, 21 percent of the company's trade accounts receivable were from the company's three largest customers.

7. Accounts Receivable Factoring and Securitization

Off-balance Sheet Arrangements

Swedish Factoring Facility: The company has an arrangement to sell trade receivables from AB Volvo through one of its European subsidiaries. Under this arrangement, which was recently renewed and now terminates on June 28, 2016, the company can sell up to, at any point in time, €150 million ($168 million) of eligible trade receivables. The receivables under this program are sold at face value and are excluded from the consolidated balance sheet. The company had utilized €108 million ($121 million) and €99 million ($127 million) of this accounts receivable factoring facility as of September 30, 2015 and 2014, respectively.

U.S. Factoring Facility: The company has an arrangement to sell trade receivables from AB Volvo and its subsidiaries to Nordea Bank. Under this arrangement, which was recently renewed and now terminates on February 28, 2016, the company can sell up to, at any point in time, €65 million ($73 million) of eligible trade receivables. In December 2014, the company amended this agreement to allow for the sale of trade receivables to exceed Nordea Bank's commitment at Nordea Bank's discretion. The receivables under this program are sold at face value and are excluded from the consolidated balance sheet. The company had utilized €74 million ($83 million) and €64 million ($81 million) of this accounts receivable factoring facility as of September 30, 2015 and 2014, respectively. As of September 30, 2015, the company had utilized more than the committed eligible trade receivable amount of €65 million ($73 million) based on approval from the bank.

The above facilities are backed by 364 -day liquidity commitments from Nordea Bank which extend through May 2016. The commitments are subject to standard terms and conditions for these types of arrangements.

United Kingdom Factoring Facility: The company has an arrangement to sell trade receivables from AB Volvo and its European subsidiaries through one of its United Kingdom subsidiaries. Under this arrangement, which expires in February 2018, the company can sell up to, at any point in time, €25 million ($28 million) of eligible trade receivables. The receivables under this program are sold at face value and are excluded from the consolidated balance sheet. The company had utilized €8 million ($8 million) and €6 million ($7 million) of this accounts receivable factoring facility as of September 30, 2015 and 2014, respectively. The agreement is subject to standard terms and conditions for these types of arrangements including a sole discretion clause whereby the purchasing bank retains the right to not purchase receivables, which has not been invoked since the inception of the program.

Italy Factoring Facility: The company has an arrangement to sell trade receivables from AB Volvo and its European subsidiaries through one of its Italian subsidiaries. Under this arrangement, which expires in June 2017, the company can sell up to, at any point in time, €30 million ($34 million) of eligible trade receivables. The receivables under this program are sold at face value and are excluded from the consolidated balance sheet. The company had utilized €22 million ($24 million) and €8 million ($10 million) of this accounts receivable factoring facility as of September 30, 2015 and 2014, respectively. The agreement is subject to standard terms and conditions for these types of arrangements including a sole discretion clause whereby the purchasing bank retains the right to not purchase receivables, which has not been invoked since the inception of the program.

In addition, several of the company's subsidiaries, primarily in Europe, factor eligible accounts receivable with financial institutions. Certain receivables are factored without recourse to the company and are excluded from accounts receivable in the consolidated balance sheet. The amount of factored receivables excluded from accounts receivable was $18 million and $19 million at September 30, 2015 and 2014, respectively.

Total costs associated with these off-balance sheet arrangements described above were $6 million, $8 million and $6 million in fiscal years 2015, 2014 and 2013, respectively, and are included in selling, general and administrative expenses in the consolidated statement of operations.

On-balance Sheet Arrangements

The company has a $100 million U.S. accounts receivables securitization facility. On October 15, 2014, the company entered into an amendment which extended the facility expiration date to October 15, 2017 and set the maximum permitted priority-debt-to-EBITDA ratio as of the last day of each fiscal quarter under the U.S. securitization facility at 2.25 to 1.00. This program is provided by PNC Bank, National Association, as Administrator and Purchaser, and the other Purchasers and Purchaser Agents from time to time (participating lenders), which are party to the agreement. Under this program, the company has the ability to sell an undivided percentage ownership interest in substantially all of its trade receivables (excluding the receivables due from AB Volvo and subsidiaries eligible for sale under the U.S. accounts receivable factoring facility) of certain U.S. subsidiaries to ArvinMeritor Receivables Corporation (ARC), a wholly-owned, special purpose subsidiary. ARC funds these purchases with borrowings from participating lenders under a loan agreement. This program also includes a letter of credit facility pursuant to which ARC may request the issuance of letters of credit issued for the company's U.S. subsidiaries (originators) or their designees, which when issued will constitute a utilization of the facility for the amount of letters of credit issued. Amounts outstanding under this agreement are collateralized by eligible receivables purchased by ARC and are reported as short-term debt in the consolidated balance sheet. At September 30, 2015 and 2014, no amounts, including letters of credit, were outstanding under this program. This securitization program contains a cross-default to the revolving credit facility. At certain times during any given month, the company may sell eligible accounts receivable under this program to fund intra-month working capital needs. In such months, the company would then typically utilize the cash received from customers throughout the month to repay the borrowings under the program. Accordingly, during any given month, the company may borrow under this program in amounts exceeding the amounts shown as outstanding at fiscal year ends.

Inventory

Author's Note
In July 2015, FASB issued ASU No. 2015-11, *Inventory (Topic 330): Simplifying the Measurement of Inventory*. The amendments in this ASU do not apply to inventory that is measured using last-in, first-out (LIFO) or the retail inventory method. The amendments apply to all other inventory, which includes inventory that is measured using first-in, first-out (FIFO) or average cost. An entity should measure inventory within the scope of this ASU at the lower of cost and net realizable value. *Net realizable value* is the estimated selling prices in the ordinary course of business, less reasonably predictable costs of completion, disposal, and transportation. For public business entities, the amendments in this ASU are effective for fiscal years beginning after December 15, 2016, including interim periods within those fiscal years. For all other entities, the amendments in this ASU are effective for fiscal years beginning after December 15, 2016, and interim periods within fiscal years beginning after December 15, 2017. The amendments in this ASU should be applied prospectively, with earlier application permitted as of the beginning of an interim or annual reporting period. Due to the effective date, none of the examples that follow contain an example of these disclosures.

RECOGNITION AND MEASUREMENT

2.32 FASB ASC 330, *Inventory*, states that the primary basis of accounting for inventories is cost, but a departure from the cost basis of pricing the inventory is required when the utility of the goods is no longer as great as their cost. FASB ASC 330-10-35-1 requires an entity to measure inventories at the lower of cost or market. *Market*, as defined in the FASB ASC glossary, means current replacement cost, with the constraint that market should not exceed net realizable value and should not be lower than net realizable value less an allowance for an approximately normal profit margin.

2.33 FASB ASC 330-10-35-14 states that if inventories are written down below cost at the close of a fiscal year, such reduced amount is to be considered the cost for subsequent accounting purposes. Similarly, the Topic 5(BB), "Inventory Valuation Allowances," of the SEC's *Codification of Staff Accounting Bulletins* indicates that a write-down of inventory creates a new cost basis that subsequently cannot be marked up.

PRESENTATION

2.34 Rule 5-02.6 of Regulation S-X requires separate presentation in the balance sheet or notes of the amounts of major classes of inventory, such as finished goods, work in process, raw materials, and supplies. Additional disclosures are required for amounts related to long-term contracts or programs.

DISCLOSURE

2.35 FASB ASC 330 requires disclosure of the basis for stating inventories. Rule 5-02.6 of Regulation S-X requires disclosure of the method by which amounts are removed from inventory (for example, average cost; first-in, first-out (FIFO); last-in, first-out (LIFO); estimated average cost per unit).

2.36 Rule 5-02.6(c) of Regulation S-X requires that registrants using LIFO disclose the excess of replacement or current cost over stated LIFO value, if material.

PRESENTATION AND DISCLOSURE EXCERPTS

FIRST-IN FIRST-OUT

2.37 STANLEY BLACK & DECKER, INC. (DEC)
MANAGEMENT'S DISCUSSION AND ANALYSIS OF FINANCIAL CONDITION AND RESULTS OF OPERATIONS (in part)

Other Matters (in part)

INVENTORIES—LOWER OF COST OR MARKET, SLOW MOVING AND OBSOLETE—Inventories in the U.S. are predominantly valued at the lower of Last-In First-Out ("LIFO") cost or market, while non-U.S. inventories are valued at the lower of First-In, First-Out ("FIFO") cost or market. The calculation of LIFO reserves, and therefore the net inventory valuation, is affected by inflation and deflation in inventory components. The Company ensures all inventory is valued at the lower of cost or market, and continually reviews the carrying value of discontinued product lines and stock-keeping-units ("SKUs") to determine that these items are properly valued. The Company also continually evaluates the composition of its inventory and identifies obsolete and/or slow-moving inventories. Inventory items identified as obsolete and/or slow-moving are evaluated to determine if write-downs are required. The Company assesses the ability to dispose of these inventories at a price greater than cost. If it is determined that cost is less than market value, cost is used for inventory valuation. If market value is less than cost, the Company writes down the related inventory to that value. If a write-down to the current market value is necessary, the market value cannot be greater than the net realizable value, or ceiling (defined as selling price less costs to sell and dispose), and cannot be lower than the net realizable value less a normal profit margin, also called the floor. If the Company is not able to achieve its expectations regarding net realizable value of inventory at its current value, further write-downs would be recorded.

CONSOLIDATED BALANCE SHEETS (in part)

(Millions of Dollars)

	2015	2014
Assets (in part)		
Current Assets		
Cash and cash equivalents	$ 465.4	$ 496.6
Accounts and notes receivable, net	1,331.8	1,396.7
Inventories, net	1,526.4	1,562.7
Prepaid expenses	177.4	180.5
Assets held for sale	—	29.5
Other current assets	161.1	282.8
Total Current Assets	3,662.1	3,948.8

NOTES TO CONSOLIDATED FINANCIAL STATEMENTS (in part)

A. Significant Accounting Policies (in part)

INVENTORIES — U.S. inventories are predominantly valued at the lower of Last-In First-Out ("LIFO") cost or market because the Company believes it results in better matching of costs and revenues. Other inventories are valued at the lower of First-In, First-Out ("FIFO") cost or market because LIFO is not permitted for statutory reporting outside the U.S. See *Note C, Inventories*, for a quantification of the LIFO impact on inventory valuation.

New Accounting Standards (in part)

In July 2015, the FASB issued ASU 2015-11, "Inventory (Topic 330): Simplifying the Measurement of Inventory." This ASU changes the measurement principle for certain inventory methods from the lower of cost or market to the lower of cost and net realizable value. Net realizable value is defined as the estimated selling price in the ordinary course of business, less reasonably predictable costs of completion, disposal, and transportation. This ASU does not apply to inventory that is measured using Last-in First-out ("LIFO") or the retail inventory method. The provisions of ASU 2015-11 are effective for fiscal years beginning after December 15, 2016, including interim periods within those fiscal years. The Company is currently evaluating this guidance to determine the impact it may have on its consolidated financial statements.

C. Inventories

(Millions of Dollars)	2015	2014
Finished products	$1,085.0	$1,105.0
Work in process	136.1	141.4
Raw materials	305.3	316.3
Total	$1,526.4	$1,562.7

Net inventories in the amount of $651.0 million at January 2, 2016 and $600.4 million at January 3, 2015 were valued at the lower of LIFO cost or market. If the LIFO method had not been used, inventories would have been $26.7 million higher than reported at January 2, 2016 and $34.9 million higher than reported at January 3, 2015.

LAST-IN FIRST-OUT

2.38 PRECISION CASTPARTS CORP. (MAR)

MANAGEMENT'S DISCUSSION AND ANALYSIS OF FINANCIAL CONDITION AND RESULTS OF OPERATIONS (in part)

(in millions, except per share data)

Critical Accounting Policies (in part)

Valuation of Inventories

All inventories are stated at the lower of their cost or market value, with the market value being determined based on sales in the ordinary course of business. Cost for inventories at a significant number of our operations is determined on a last-in, first-out ("LIFO") basis. The average inventory cost method is utilized for most other inventories. We regularly review inventory quantities on hand and record a provision for excess or obsolete inventory equal to the difference between the cost of the inventory and the estimated market value based on the age, historical usage or assumptions about future demand for the inventory.

We also regularly review inventory balances on a LIFO basis to ensure the balances are stated at the lower of cost or market as of the balance sheet date. For those inventories valued using LIFO, their carrying value may be higher or lower than current replacement costs for such inventory, since the LIFO costing assumption matches current costs with current sales, not with current inventory values. When the LIFO cost is greater than the current cost, there is an increased likelihood that our inventories could be subject to write-downs to market value. As of March 29, 2015, the LIFO cost of our inventories exceeds the current cost by $679 million. If actual demand is significantly less than the future demand that we have projected, inventory write-downs may be required, which could have a material adverse effect on the value of our inventories and reported operating results. In the fourth quarter of fiscal 2015, we recognized a non-cash inventory impairment charge of $120 million, pre-tax, primarily in our oil & gas, pipe and associated raw material operations, reflecting the more challenging environment, declines in market value, and size or quality characteristics that impact marketability. The projections of future demand by management are based upon firm orders (including long-term agreements), forecasted demand from customers, and macro-economic industry data.

The key drivers that are causing our LIFO inventory costs to exceed current costs are as follows:
- Decreases in raw material prices in recent fiscal years, including nickel, titanium, cobalt, rutile, titanium sponge and revert
- Reduced variable manufacturing costs as a result of operational efficiencies and improved labor productivity
- Decreased fixed costs per unit of inventory due to cost controls and increasing production volumes
- Inventory added through acquisitions that are valued at fair market value (typically higher than historical cost) that remains in the LIFO cost basis unless liquidated through quantity reductions

As we acquire additional businesses, management first determines if the acquired business should account for inventory on a LIFO basis due to the nature of the business and materiality of the inventory balances. If LIFO treatment is deemed appropriate, management then determines whether to incorporate the acquired inventories into existing LIFO pools or create a new LIFO pool based on several factors. Those factors include, but are not limited to:
- Similarity or dissimilarity of nature of operations, including raw materials used, product produced and cost structure, to existing businesses. The more similar businesses are, the more likely they will have common LIFO pools
- Location of the business as LIFO pools do not typically include operations in more than one country for tax, functional currency and other reasons
- The size of the acquisition in relation to the existing pool(s). Smaller businesses are often incorporated into existing LIFO pools

CONSOLIDATED BALANCE SHEETS (in part)

(In millions, except share data)	March 29, 2015	March 30, 2014
Assets (in part)		
Current assets:		
Cash and cash equivalents	$ 474	$ 361
Receivables, net of allowance of $12 in 2015 and $7 in 2014	1,710	1,568
Inventories	3,640	3,426
Prepaid expenses and other current assets	81	105
Income tax receivable	37	5
Deferred income taxes	2	13
Discontinued operations	28	29
Total current assets	5,972	5,507

NOTES TO CONSOLIDATED FINANCIAL STATEMENTS (in part)

(In millions, except option share and per share data)

6. Inventories

Inventories consisted of the following:

	March 29, 2015	March 30, 2014
Finished goods	$ 544	$ 498
Work-in-process	1,262	1,325
Raw materials and supplies	1,155	1,037
	2,961	2,860
Excess of LIFO cost over current cost	679	566
Total	$3,640	$3,426

Approximately 96 percent of total inventories were valued on a LIFO basis at March 29, 2015 and March 30, 2014. During fiscal 2015 and 2014, certain LIFO inventory quantities were reduced. The liquidation of LIFO inventory quantities carried at costs paid in prior years increased cost of goods sold by $13 million in fiscal 2015 and $8 million in fiscal 2014. Refer to Note 20—Restructuring, asset impairment and other non-recurring charges for discussion of a non-cash inventory impairment charge recognized in fiscal 2015.

20. Restructuring, Asset Impairment and Other Non-Recurring Charges (in part)

In the fourth quarter of fiscal 2015, we recognized a non-cash inventory and other asset impairment charge of $127 million, pre-tax, primarily in our oil & gas, pipe and associated raw material operations, reflecting the more challenging environment, declines in market value, and size or quality characteristics that impact marketability. In addition, to improve our cost structure and in response to the current market conditions, we implemented headcount reductions at impacted operations, which resulted in a pre-tax charge of $8 million in the fourth quarter of fiscal 2015. These restructuring plans provided for terminations of approximately 490 employees in the fourth quarter of fiscal 2015 and the first quarter of fiscal 2016. The restructuring and asset impairment charges recorded by segment are as follows:

Fiscal	2015
Investment Cast Products	$ 4
Forged Products	127
Airframe Products	4
	$135

Restructuring, inventory and other asset impairment, and other non-recurring charges incurred in fiscal 2015 were recorded in the Consolidated Statement of Income as follows:

Fiscal	2015
Cost of goods sold	$127
Restructuring expense	8
Equity in loss of unconsolidated affiliates	174
	$309

AVERAGE COST

2.39 RALPH LAUREN CORPORATION (MAR)

CONSOLIDATED BALANCE SHEETS (in part)

(Millions)	March 28, 2015	March 29, 2014
Assets (in part)		
Current assets:		
Cash and cash equivalents	$ 500	$ 797
Short-term investments	644	488
Accounts receivable, net of allowances of $251 million and $270 million	655	588
Inventories	1,042	1,020
Income tax receivable	57	62
Deferred tax assets	145	150
Prepaid expenses and other current assets	281	224
Total current assets	3,324	3,329

NOTES TO CONSOLIDATED FINANCIAL STATEMENTS (in part)

3. Summary of Significant Accounting Policies (in part)

Inventories

The Company holds inventory that is sold through wholesale distribution channels to major department stores and specialty retail stores, including the Company's own retail stores. The Company also holds retail inventory that is sold in its own stores and e-commerce sites directly to consumers. Wholesale and retail inventories are stated at the lower of cost or estimated realizable value, with cost primarily determined on a weighted-average cost basis.

The estimated realizable value of inventory is determined based on an analysis of historical sales trends of the Company's individual product lines, the impact of market trends and economic conditions, and a forecast of future demand, giving consideration to the value of current in-house orders for future sales of inventory, as well as plans to sell inventory through the Company's factory stores, among other liquidation channels. Estimates may differ from actual results due to the quantity, quality, and mix of products in inventory, consumer and retailer preferences, and market conditions. Reserves for inventory shrinkage, representing the risk of physical loss of inventory, are estimated based on historical experience and are adjusted based upon physical inventory counts. The Company's historical estimates of these costs and its related provisions have not differed materially from actual results.

6. Inventories

Inventories consist of the following:

(Millions)	March 28, 2015	March 29, 2014
Raw materials	$ 3	$ 3
Work-in-process	2	2
Finished goods	1,037	1,015
Total inventories	$1,042	$1,020

RETAIL METHOD

2.40 TARGET CORPORATION (JAN)
CONSOLIDATED STATEMENTS OF FINANCIAL POSITION (in part)

(Millions, except footnotes)	January 31, 2015	February 1, 2014
Assets (in part)		
Cash and cash equivalents, including short-term investments of $1,520 and $3	$ 2,210	$ 670
Inventory	8,790	8,278
Assets of discontinued operations	1,333	793
Other current assets	1,754	1,832
Total current assets	14,087	11,573

NOTES TO CONSOLIDATED FINANCIAL STATEMENTS (in part)

10. Inventory

The majority of our inventory is accounted for under the retail inventory accounting method (RIM) using the last-in, first-out (LIFO) method. Inventory is stated at the lower of LIFO cost or market. The cost of our inventory includes the amount we pay to our suppliers to acquire inventory, freight costs incurred in connection with the delivery of product to our distribution centers and stores, and import costs, reduced by vendor income and cash discounts. The majority of our distribution center operating costs, including compensation and benefits, are expensed in the period incurred. Inventory is also reduced for estimated losses related to shrink and markdowns. The LIFO provision is calculated based on inventory levels, markup rates and internally measured retail price indices.

Under RIM, inventory cost and the resulting gross margins are calculated by applying a cost-to-retail ratio to the inventory retail value. RIM is an averaging method that has been widely used in the retail industry due to its practicality. The use of RIM will result in inventory being valued at the lower of cost or market because permanent markdowns are taken as a reduction of the retail value of inventory.

Certain other inventory is recorded at the lower of cost or market using the cost method. The valuation allowance for inventory valued under a cost method was not material to our Consolidated Financial Statements as of the end of fiscal 2014 or 2013.

We routinely enter into arrangements with vendors whereby we do not purchase or pay for merchandise until the merchandise is ultimately sold to a guest. Activity under this program is included in sales and cost of sales in the Consolidated Statements of Operations, but the merchandise received under the program is not included in inventory in our Consolidated Statements of Financial Position because of the virtually simultaneous purchase and sale of this inventory. Sales made under these arrangements totaled $2,040 million, $1,833 million and $1,800 million in 2014, 2013 and 2012, respectively.

Other Current Assets

PRESENTATION

2.41 Rule 5-02.8 of Regulation S-X requires that any amount of current assets in excess of 5 percent of total current assets be stated separately on the balance sheet or disclosed in the notes.

2.42 ALLIANCE ONE INTERNATIONAL, INC. (MAR)

CONSOLIDATED BALANCE SHEETS (in part)

(In thousands)	March 31, 2015	March 31, 2014
Assets (in part)		
Current assets		
Cash and cash equivalents	$ 143,849	$ 234,742
Trade and other receivables, net	200,403	176,459
Accounts receivable, related parties	41,816	44,869
Inventories	772,608	760,607
Advances to tobacco suppliers	38,589	49,598
Recoverable income taxes	5,257	4,789
Current deferred taxes	15,587	10,013
Prepaid expenses	23,541	27,667
Current derivative asset	1,373	—
Other current assets	13,233	12,053
Total current assets	1,256,256	1,320,797

NOTES TO CONSOLIDATED FINANCIAL STATEMENTS (in part)

(in thousands)

Note 1—Significant Accounting Policies (in part)

Income Taxes

The Company uses the asset and liability method to account for income taxes. The objective of the asset and liability method is to establish deferred tax assets and liabilities for the temporary differences between the financial reporting basis and the income tax basis of the Company's assets and liabilities at enacted tax rates expected to be in effect when such amounts are realized or settled.

The Company's annual tax rate is based on its income, statutory tax rates and tax planning opportunities available to it in the various jurisdictions in which it operates. Tax laws are complex and subject to different interpretations by the taxpayer and respective governmental taxing authorities. Significant judgment is required in determining tax expense and in evaluating tax positions, including evaluating uncertainties. The Company reviews its tax positions quarterly and adjusts the balances as new information becomes available.

Deferred income tax assets represent amounts available to reduce income taxes payable on taxable income in future years. Such assets arise because of temporary differences between the financial reporting and tax bases of assets and liabilities, as well as from net operating loss and tax credit carryforwards. The Company evaluates the recoverability of these future tax deductions by assessing the adequacy of future expected taxable income from all sources, including reversal of taxable temporary differences, forecasted operating earnings and available tax planning strategies. These sources of income inherently rely on estimates. The Company uses historical experience and short and long-range business forecasts to provide insight. The Company believes it is more likely than not that a portion of the deferred income tax assets may expire unused and has established a valuation allowance against them. Although realization is not assured for the remaining deferred income tax assets, the Company believes it is more likely than not the deferred tax assets will be fully recoverable within the applicable statutory expiration periods. However, deferred tax assets could be reduced in the near term if estimates of taxable income are significantly reduced or available tax planning strategies are no longer viable. See Note 12 "Income Taxes" to the "Notes to Consolidated Financial Statements" for further information.

Note 12—Income Taxes

Accounting for Uncertainty in Income Taxes

As of March 31, 2015, 2014 and 2013, the Company's unrecognized tax benefits totaled $16,201, $10,152 and $7,874, respectively, of which $7,127 would impact the Company's effective tax rate if recognized. The following table presents the changes to unrecognized tax benefits during the years ended March 31, 2015, 2014 and 2013:

	2015	2014	2013
Balance at April 1	$10,152	$ 7,874	$11,804
Increase for current year tax positions	6,959	2,512	1,661
Reduction for prior year tax positions	(161)	(111)	(1,960)
Impact of changes in exchange rates	(749)	(123)	(131)
Reduction for settlements	—	—	(3,500)
Balance at March 31	$16,201	$10,152	$ 7,874

The Company recognizes interest and penalties related to unrecognized tax benefits in income tax expense. During the years ended March 31, 2015 and 2014, the Company accrued (reduced) interest, penalties and related exchange losses related to unrecognized tax benefits by $(98) and $(233), respectively. As of March 31, 2015, accrued interest and penalties totaled $797 and $901, respectively. During the year ending March 31, 2015, the Company reduced its accrued interest and penalties for $22 related to the expiration of statute of limitations. As of March 31, 2014, accrued interest and penalties totaled $771 and $1,025, respectively.

During the fiscal year ending March 31, 2015, the Company's total liability for unrecognized tax benefits, including the related interest and penalties, increased from $11,948 to $17,899. The change in the liability for unrecognized tax benefits relates to expiration of statute of limitations of approximately $185, decreases related to current period activity of approximately $824 and increases related to the adoption of new positions of approximately $6,959.

The Company expects to continue accruing interest expenses related to the remaining unrecognized tax benefits. Additionally, the Company may be subject to fluctuations in the unrecognized tax liability due to currency exchange rate movements.

It is reasonably possible that the Company's unrecognized tax benefits may decrease in the next twelve months by $867 due to the expiration of the statute of limitations but the Company must acknowledge circumstances can change due to unexpected developments in the law. In certain jurisdictions, tax authorities have challenged positions that the Company has taken that resulted in recognizing benefits that are material to its financial statements. The Company believes it is more likely than not that it will prevail in these situations and accordingly have not recorded liabilities for these positions. The Company expects the challenged positions to be settled at a time greater than twelve months from its balance sheet date.

The Company and its subsidiaries file a U.S. federal consolidated income tax return as well as returns in several U.S. states and a number of foreign jurisdictions. As of March 31, 2015, the Company's earliest open tax year for U.S. federal income tax purposes was its fiscal year ended March 31, 2012; however, the Company's net operating loss carryovers from prior periods remain subject to adjustment. Open tax years in state and foreign jurisdictions generally range from three to six years.

Income Tax Provision

The components of income before income taxes, equity in net income of investee companies and minority interests consisted of the following:

	Years Ended March 31,		
	2015	2014	2013
U.S.	$(24,749)	$(91,290)	$(44,731)
Non-U.S.	29,268	43,170	95,798
Total	$ 4,519	$(48,120)	$ 51,067

The details of the amount shown for income taxes in the Consolidated Statements of Operations follow:

	Years Ended March 31,		
	2015	2014	2013
Current			
Federal	$ —	$ —	$ (2,723)
State	—	—	—
Non-U.S.	20,374	22,877	5,999
	$20,374	$22,877	$ 3,276
Deferred			
Federal	$ —	$ —	$ 3,466
State	—	—	—
Non-U.S.	2,565	16,065	21,250
	$ 2,565	$16,065	$24,716
Total	$22,939	$38,942	$27,992

The reasons for the difference between income tax expense based on income before income taxes, equity in net income of investee companies and minority interests and the amount computed by applying the U.S. statutory federal income tax rate to such income are as follows:

| | Years Ended March 31, | | |
	2015	2014	2013
Tax expense at U.S. statutory rate	$ 1,582	$(16,842)	$ 17,873
Effect of non-U.S. income taxes	(2,754)	4,209	(1,921)
U.S. taxes on non-U.S. income	22,043	—	—
Change in valuation allowance	(20,701)	23,732	26,598
Increase (decrease) in reserves for uncertain tax positions	5,951	2,046	(11,781)
Exchange effects and currency translation	14,208	26,885	(1,482)
Permanent items	2,610	(1,088)	(1,295)
Actual tax expense	$ 22,939	$ 38,942	$ 27,992

The deferred tax liabilities (assets) are comprised of the following:

	March 31, 2015	March 31, 2014
Deferred tax liabilities:		
Unremitted earnings of foreign subsidiaries	$ 22,043	$ —
Intangible assets	6,415	7,048
Fixed assets	3,488	5,608
Total deferred tax liabilities	$ 31,946	$ 12,656
Deferred tax assets:		
Reserves and accruals	$ (29,610)	$ (35,747)
Tax credits	(55,744)	(52,624)
Tax loss carryforwards	(102,103)	(115,280)
Derivative transactions	(567)	(1,567)
Postretirement and other benefits	(34,388)	(31,040)
Unrealized exchange loss	(10,057)	(1,522)
Other	(7,694)	(3,097)
Gross deferred tax assets	(240,163)	(240,877)
Valuation allowance	170,937	188,752
Total deferred tax assets	$ (69,226)	$ (52,125)
Net deferred tax asset	$ (37,280)	$ (39,469)

The following table presents the breakdown between current and non-current (assets) liabilities:

	March 31, 2015	March 31, 2014
Current asset	$(15,587)	$(10,013)
Current liability	4,672	5,682
Non-current asset	(31,649)	(40,926)
Non-current liability	5,284	5,788
Net deferred tax asset	$(37,280)	$(39,469)

The current portion of deferred tax liability is included in income taxes.

During the year ended March 31, 2015, the net deferred tax asset balance increased by $372 for certain adjustments not included in the deferred tax expense (benefit), primarily for deferred tax assets related to pension accruals recorded in equity as part of Other Comprehensive Income (Loss) and currency translation adjustments.

For the year ended March 31, 2015, the valuation allowance decreased by $17,815 which is inclusive of $3,999 related to adjustments in other comprehensive income and $(1,112) related primarily to currency translation adjustments. The valuation allowance decreased primarily due to the accrual of a deferred liability on unremitted foreign earnings and the accrual of an additional liability for unrecognized tax benefits netted against tax loss carryovers. The valuation allowance is based on the Company's assessment that it is more likely than not that certain deferred tax assets, primarily foreign tax credits and net operating loss carryovers, will not be realized in the foreseeable future. Recent years' cumulative losses incurred in the United States as of March 31, 2015, combined with the effects of certain changes in the market, provide significant objective negative evidence in the evaluation of whether the U.S. entity will generate sufficient taxable income to realize the tax benefits of the deferred tax assets. This negative evidence carries greater weight than the more subjective positive evidence of favorable future projected income in the assessment of whether realization of the tax benefits of the deferred tax assets is more likely than not. Therefore, based on the weight of presently objectively verifiable positive and negative evidence, it is management's judgment that realization of the tax benefits of the deferred tax assets is less than more likely than not.

At March 31, 2015, the Company has U.S federal tax loss carryovers of $246,408, non-U.S. tax loss carryovers of $52,348, and U.S. state tax loss carryovers of $372,895. The U.S. federal tax loss carryovers will expire in 2030 and thereafter. Of the non-U.S. tax loss carryovers, $23,080 will expire within the next five years, $23,583 will expire in later years, and $5,685 can be carried forward indefinitely. Of the U.S. state tax loss carryovers, $82,838 will expire within the next five years and $290,056 will expire thereafter. At March 31, 2015, the Company has foreign tax credit carryovers in the United States of $51,932 that will substantially expire in 2016.

Realization of deferred tax assets is dependent on generating sufficient taxable income prior to expiration of the loss carryovers. Although realization is not assured, management believes it is more likely than not that all of the deferred tax assets, net of applicable valuation allowances, will be realized. The amount of the deferred tax assets considered realizable could be reduced or increased if estimates of future taxable income change during the carryover period.

A provision of $22,043 has been made for U.S. on foreign taxes that may result from future remittances of foreign earnings of $60,318. No provision has been made for U.S. or foreign taxes that may result from future remittances of approximately $409,505 at March 31, 2015 and $408,424 at March 31, 2014 of undistributed earnings of foreign subsidiaries because management expects that such earnings will be reinvested overseas indefinitely. Determination of the amount of any unrecognized deferred income tax liability on these unremitted earnings is not practicable.

ADVANCES

2.43 UNIVERSAL CORPORATION (MAR)
CONSOLIDATED BALANCE SHEETS (in part)

	March 31,	
(In thousands of dollars)	2015	2014
Assets (in part)		
Current assets		
Cash and cash equivalents	$ 248,783	$ 163,532
Accounts receivable, net	434,362	468,015
Advances to suppliers, net	114,883	134,621
Accounts receivable—unconsolidated affiliates	1,907	7,375
Inventories—at lower of cost or market:		
Tobacco	636,488	639,812
Other	62,195	67,219
Prepaid income taxes	17,811	27,866
Deferred income taxes	36,611	22,052
Other current assets	81,570	142,755
Total current assets	1,634,610	1,673,247

NOTES TO CONSOLIDATED FINANCIAL STATEMENTS (in part)

(All dollar amounts are in thousands, except per share amounts or as otherwise noted.)

Note 1. Nature of Operations and Significant Accounting Policies (in part)

Advances to Suppliers

In many sourcing origins where the Company operates, it provides agronomy services and seasonal advances of seed, fertilizer, and other supplies to tobacco farmers for crop production, or makes seasonal cash advances to farmers for the procurement of those inputs. These advances are short term, are repaid upon delivery of tobacco to the Company, and are reported in advances to suppliers in the consolidated balance sheets. In several origins, the Company has made long-term advances to tobacco farmers to finance curing barns and other farm infrastructure. In some years, due to low crop yields and other factors, individual farmers may not deliver sufficient volumes of tobacco to fully repay their seasonal advances, and the Company may extend repayment of those advances into future crop years. The long-term portion of advances is included in other noncurrent assets in the consolidated balance sheets. Both the current and the long-term portions of advances to suppliers are reported net of allowances recorded when the Company determines that amounts outstanding are not likely to be collected. Short-term and long-term advances to suppliers totaled approximately $156 million at March 31, 2015 and $190 million at March 31, 2014. The related valuation allowances totaled $35 million at March 31, 2015, and $46 million at March 31, 2014, and were estimated based on the Company's historical loss information and crop projections. The allowances were increased by net provisions for estimated uncollectible amounts of approximately $3.7 million in fiscal year 2015, $5.5 million in fiscal year 2014, and $1.6 million in fiscal year 2013.

These provisions are included in selling, general, and administrative expenses in the consolidated statements of income. Interest on advances is recognized in earnings upon the farmers' delivery of tobacco in payment of principal and interest. Advances on which interest accrual had been discontinued totaled approximately $15 million at March 31, 2015, and $23 million at March 31, 2014.

ASSETS HELD FOR SALE

2.44 NEWELL RUBBERMAID INC. (DEC)
CONSOLIDATED BALANCE SHEETS (in part)

(Amounts in millions, except par values)

December 31,	2015	2014
Assets (in part)		
Current Assets:		
Cash and cash equivalents	$ 274.8	$ 199.4
Accounts receivable, net of allowances of $22.0 for 2015 and $25.3 for 2014	1,250.7	1,248.2
Inventories, net	721.8	708.5
Prepaid expenses and other	147.8	136.1
Assets held for sale	98.4	—
Total Current Assets	2,493.5	2,292.2

NOTES TO CONSOLIDATED FINANCIAL STATEMENTS (in part)

Footnote 3 (in part)

Divestitures and Planned Divestitures

Based on the Company's strategy to allocate resources to its businesses relative to their growth potential and those with the greater right to win in the marketplace, the Company determined that certain businesses as described below did not align with the Company's long-term growth plans, which led to the decisions to divest or cease operations of these businesses.

Held for Sale

In October 2015, the Company determined that the Levolor ® and Kirsch ® window coverings brands ("Décor") did not align with the Company's long-term growth plans and therefore, announced its intention to divest the Décor business. The Décor business did not meet the criteria for reporting the business as discontinued operations; thus, the Company has continued to include the Décor business in continuing operations as part of the Home Solutions segment. The Company expects to complete the sale of Décor during 2016 and anticipates realizing net proceeds greater than the net assets upon sale. The Décor business generated 5.1%, 5.5% and 5.7% of the Company's consolidated net sales for the years ended December 31, 2015, 2014 and 2013, respectively. The following table presents information related to the major classes of Décor's assets and liabilities that were classified as assets and liabilities held for sale in the Consolidated Balance Sheet as of December 31, 2015 (*in millions*):

	2015
Inventories, net	$35.3
Prepaid expenses and other	2.0
Property, plant and equipment, net	18.2
Goodwill	19.2
Other intangible assets, net	23.7
Total Assets	$98.4
Accounts payable	$34.8
Other accrued liabilities	8.5
Total Liabilities	$43.3

COSTS AND ESTIMATED EARNINGS IN EXCESS OF BILLINGS

2.45 TUTOR PERINI CORPORATION (DEC)
CONSOLIDATED BALANCE SHEETS (in part)

(in thousands, except share data)

	As of December 31,	
	2015	2014
Assets		
Current Assets:		
Cash, including cash equivalents of $1,696 and $12,044	$ 75,452	$ 135,583
Restricted cash	45,853	44,370
Accounts receivable, including retainage of $484,255 and $382,891	1,473,615	1,479,504
Costs and estimated earnings in excess of billings	905,175	726,402
Deferred income taxes	26,306	17,962
Other current assets	108,844	68,735
Total current assets	2,635,245	2,472,556

1. Summary of Significant Accounting Policies (in part)

(d) Construction Contracts

The Company and its affiliated entities recognize construction contract revenue using the percentage-of-completion method, based primarily on contract cost incurred to date compared to total estimated contract cost. Cost of revenue includes an allocation of depreciation and amortization. Pre-contract costs are expensed as incurred. Changes to total estimated contract cost or losses, if any, are recognized in the period in which they are determined.

The Company generally provides limited warranties for work performed under its construction contracts with periods typically extending for a limited duration following substantial completion of the Company's work on a project. Historically, warranty claims have not resulted in material costs incurred.

The Company classifies construction-related receivables and payables that may be settled in periods exceeding one year from the balance sheet date as current, consistent with the length of time of its project operating cycle. For example:
- Costs and estimated earnings in excess of billings represent the excess of contract costs and profits (or contract revenue) over the amount of contract billings to date and are classified as a current asset.
- Billings in excess of costs and estimated earnings represent the excess of contract billings to date over the amount of contract costs and profits (or contract revenue) recognized to date and are classified as a current liability.

Costs and estimated earnings in excess of billings result when either: 1) costs are incurred related to certain claims and unapproved change orders, or 2) the appropriate contract revenue amount has been recognized in accordance with the percentage-of-completion accounting method, but a portion of the revenue recorded cannot be billed currently due to the billing terms defined in the contract. Claims occur when there is a dispute regarding both a change in the scope of work and the price associated with that change. Unapproved change orders occur when there is a dispute regarding only the price associated with a change in scope of work. For both claims and unapproved change orders, the Company recognizes revenue, but not profit, when it is determined that recovery of incurred cost is probable and the amounts can be reliably estimated. For claims, these requirements are satisfied under ASC 605-35-25 when the contract or other evidence provides a legal basis for the claim, additional costs were caused by circumstances that were unforeseen at the contract date and not the result of deficiencies in the Company's performance, claim-related costs are identifiable and considered reasonable in view of the work performed, and evidence supporting the claim or change order is objective and verifiable.

Reported costs and estimated earnings in excess of billings consists of the following

	As of December 31,	
(In thousands)	2015	2014
Claims	$407,164	$311,949
Unapproved change orders	270,019	161,375
Other unbilled costs and profits	227,992	253,078
Total costs and estimated earnings in excess of billings	$905,175	$726,402

The prerequisite for billing claims and unapproved change orders is the final resolution and agreement between the parties. The prerequisite for billing other unbilled costs and profits is provided in the defined billing terms of each of the applicable contracts. The amount of costs and estimated earnings in excess of billings as of December 31, 2015 estimated by management to be collected beyond one year is approximately $353.2 million.

DERIVATIVES

2.46 INTEL CORPORATION (DEC)
CONSOLIDATED BALANCE SHEETS (in part)

(In Millions, Except Par Value)	Dec 26, 2015	Dec 27, 2014
Assets (in part)		
Current assets:		
Cash and cash equivalents	$15,308	$ 2,561
Short-term investments	2,682	2,430
Trading assets	7,323	9,063
Accounts receivable, net of allowance for doubtful accounts of $40 ($38 in 2014)	4,787	4,427
Inventories	5,167	4,273
Deferred tax assets	2,036	1,958
Other current assets	3,053	3,018
Total current assets	40,356	27,730

NOTES TO CONSOLIDATED FINANCIAL STATEMENTS (in part)

Note 2: Accounting Policies (in part)

Derivative Financial Instruments

Our primary objective for holding derivative financial instruments is to manage currency exchange rate risk and interest rate risk, and, to a lesser extent, equity market risk, commodity price risk, and credit risk. When possible, we enter into master netting arrangements with counterparties to mitigate credit risk in derivative transactions. A master netting arrangement may allow counterparties to net settle amounts owed to each other as a result of multiple, separate derivative transactions. Generally, our master netting agreements allow for net settlement in case of certain triggering events such as bankruptcy or default of one of the counterparties to the transaction. We may also elect to exchange cash collateral with certain of our counterparties on a regular basis. For presentation on our consolidated balance sheets, we do not offset fair value amounts recognized for derivative instruments under master netting arrangements. Our derivative financial instruments are recorded at fair value and are included in other current assets, other long-term assets, other accrued liabilities, or other long-term liabilities.

Our accounting policies for derivative financial instruments are based on whether they meet the criteria for hedge accounting designation.

A designated hedge with exposure to variability in the functional currency equivalent of the future foreign currency cash flows of a forecasted transaction or variability in the functional currency equivalent cash flows of a recognized asset or liability are examples of cash flow hedges. The criteria for designating a derivative as a cash flow hedge include the assessment of the instrument's effectiveness in risk reduction, matching of the derivative instrument to its underlying transaction, and the assessment of the probability that the underlying transaction will occur. For derivatives with cash flow hedge accounting designation, we report the after-tax gain or loss from the effective portion of the hedge as a component of accumulated other comprehensive income (loss) and reclassify it into earnings in the same period or periods in which the hedged transaction affects earnings, and in the same line item on the consolidated statements of income as the impact of the hedged transaction. Derivatives that we designate as cash flow hedges are classified in the consolidated statements of cash flows in the same section as the underlying item, primarily within cash flows from operating activities.

A designated hedge with exposure to changes in the fair value of a recognized asset or liability that are attributable to the changes in the benchmark interest rate is one example of a fair value hedge. For derivatives with fair value hedge accounting designation, the gains and losses of the hedge as well as the offsetting gains and losses attributable to the changes in the benchmark interest rate on the underlying hedged item are recognized in earnings in the current period. Derivatives that we designated as fair value hedges are classified in the consolidated statements of cash flows in the same section as the underlying item, primarily within cash flows from financing activities.

We recognize gains and losses from changes in fair value of derivatives that are not designated as hedges for accounting purposes in the line item on the consolidated statements of income most closely associated with the related exposures, primarily in interest and other, net and gains (losses) on equity investments, net. As part of our strategic investment program, we also acquire equity derivative instruments, such as equity conversion rights associated with debt instruments, which we do not designate as hedging instruments. We recognize the gains or losses from changes in fair value of these equity derivative instruments in gains (losses) on equity investments, net. Realized gains and losses from derivatives not designated as hedges are classified in the consolidated statements of cash flows within cash flows from operating activities or investing activities, depending on the activity the exposure is most closely associated with.

Measurement of Effectiveness

- *Effectiveness for forwards* is generally measured by comparing the cumulative change in the fair value of the hedge contract with the cumulative change in the fair value of the forecasted cash flows of the hedged item. For currency forward contracts used in cash flow hedging strategies related to capital purchases, forward points are excluded, and effectiveness is measured using spot rates to value both the hedge contract and the hedged item. For currency forward contracts used in cash flow hedging strategies related to operating expenditures, forward points are included, and effectiveness is measured using forward rates to value both the hedge contract and the hedged item.
- *Effectiveness for options* is generally measured by comparing the cumulative change in the intrinsic value of the hedge contract with the cumulative change in the intrinsic value of an option instrument representing the hedged risks in the hedged item. Time value is excluded and effectiveness is measured using spot rates to value both the hedge contract and the hedged item.
- *Effectiveness for interest rate swaps and commodity swaps* is generally measured by comparing the cumulative change in fair value of the swap with the cumulative change in the fair value of the hedged item.

If a cash flow hedge is discontinued because it is probable that the original hedged transaction will not occur as previously anticipated, the cumulative unrealized gain or loss on the related derivative is reclassified from accumulated other comprehensive income (loss) into earnings. Subsequent gains or losses on the related derivative instrument are recognized in interest and other, net in each period until the instrument matures, is terminated, is re-designated as a qualified cash flow hedge, or is sold. Ineffective portions of cash flow hedges, as well as amounts excluded from the assessment of effectiveness, are recognized in earnings in interest and other, net. For further discussion of our derivative instruments and risk management programs, see " Note 6: Derivative Financial Instruments."

Note 6: Derivative Financial Instruments

Our primary objective for holding derivative financial instruments is to manage currency exchange rate risk and interest rate risk, and, to a lesser extent, equity market risk, commodity price risk, and credit risk.

Currency Exchange Rate Risk

We are exposed to currency exchange rate risk, and generally hedge our exposures with currency forward contracts, currency interest rate swaps, or currency options. Substantially all of our revenue is transacted in U.S. dollars. However, a significant portion of our operating expenditures and capital purchases is incurred in or exposed to other currencies, primarily the euro, the Chinese yuan, the Japanese yen, and the Israeli shekel. We have established balance sheet and forecasted transaction currency risk management programs to protect against fluctuations in the fair value and the volatility of the functional currency equivalent of future cash flows caused by changes in exchange rates. Our non-U.S.-dollar-denominated investments in debt instruments and loans receivable are generally hedged with offsetting currency forward contracts or currency interest rate swaps. We may also hedge currency risk arising from funding foreign currency-denominated forecasted investments. These programs reduce, but do not eliminate, the impact of currency exchange movements.

Our currency risk management programs include:
- *Currency derivatives with cash flow hedge accounting designation* that utilize currency forward contracts and currency options to hedge exposures to the variability in the U.S.-dollar equivalent of anticipated non-U.S.-dollar-denominated cash flows. These instruments generally mature within 12 months. For these derivatives, we report the after-tax gain or loss from the effective portion of the hedge as a component of accumulated other comprehensive income (loss), and we reclassify it into earnings in the same period or periods in which the hedged transaction affects earnings, and in the same line item on the consolidated statements of income as the impact of the hedged transaction. We utilize currency interest rate swaps to hedge exposures to the variability in the U.S.-dollar equivalent of coupon and principal payments associated with our non-U.S.-dollar-denominated indebtedness.
- *Currency derivatives without hedge accounting designation* that utilize currency forward contracts or currency interest rate swaps to economically hedge the functional currency equivalent cash flows of recognized monetary assets and liabilities, non-U.S.-dollar-denominated debt instruments classified as trading assets, and hedges of non-U.S.-dollar-denominated loans receivable recognized at fair value. A substantial majority of these instruments mature within 12 months. Changes in the functional currency equivalent cash flows of the underlying assets and liabilities are approximately offset by the changes in the fair value of the related derivatives. We record net gains or losses in the line item on the consolidated statements of income most closely associated

with the related exposures, primarily in interest and other, net, except for equity-related gains or losses, which we primarily record in gains (losses) on equity investments, net.

Interest Rate Risk

Our primary objective for holding investments in debt instruments is to preserve principal while maximizing yields. We generally swap the returns on our investments in fixed-rate debt instruments with remaining maturities longer than six months into U.S. dollar three-month LIBOR-based returns, unless management specifically approves otherwise. We may elect to swap fixed coupon payments on our debt issuances for floating rate coupon payments. These swaps are settled at various interest payment times involving cash payments at each interest and principal payment date, with the majority of the contracts having quarterly payments.

Our interest rate risk management programs include:
- *Interest rate derivatives with cash flow hedge accounting designation* that utilize interest rate swap agreements to modify the interest characteristics of debt instruments. For these derivatives, we report the after-tax gain or loss from the effective portion of the hedge as a component of accumulated other comprehensive income (loss), and we reclassify it into earnings in the same period or periods in which the hedged transaction affects earnings, and in the same line item on the consolidated statements of income as the impact of the hedged transaction.
- *Interest rate derivatives with fair value hedge accounting designation* that utilize interest rate swap agreements to hedge against changes in fair value on certain fixed rate debt due to fluctuations in the benchmark interest rate. For these derivatives, we recognize gains and losses in interest and other, net, along with the offsetting gains and losses attributable to the changes in the benchmark interest rate on the underlying hedged items.
- *Interest rate derivatives without hedge accounting designation* that utilize interest rate swaps and currency interest rate swaps in economic hedging transactions, including hedges of non-U.S.-dollar-denominated debt instruments classified as trading assets and hedges of non-U.S.-dollar-denominated loans receivable recognized at fair value. Floating interest rates on the swaps generally reset on a quarterly basis. Changes in the fair value of the debt instruments classified as trading assets and loans receivable recognized at fair value are generally offset by changes in the fair value of the related derivatives, both of which are recorded in interest and other, net.

Equity Market Risk

Our investments include marketable equity securities and equity derivative instruments. We typically do not attempt to reduce or eliminate our equity market exposure through hedging activities at the inception of our investments. Before we enter into hedge arrangements, we evaluate legal, market, and economic factors, as well as the expected timing of disposal, to determine whether hedging is appropriate. Our equity market risk management program may include equity derivatives with or without hedge accounting designation that utilize warrants, equity options, or other equity derivatives. We recognize changes in the fair value of such derivatives in gains (losses) on equity investments, net.

We also utilize total return swaps to offset changes in liabilities related to the equity market risks of certain deferred compensation arrangements. Gains and losses from changes in fair value of these total return swaps are generally offset by the losses and gains on the related liabilities, both of which are recorded in cost of sales and operating expenses. Deferred compensation liabilities were $1.3 billion as of December 26, 2015 ($1.2 billion as of December 27, 2014), and are included in other accrued liabilities.

Commodity Price Risk

We operate facilities that consume commodities and have established forecasted transaction risk management programs to protect against fluctuations in the fair value and the volatility of future cash flows caused by changes in commodity prices, such as those for natural gas. These programs reduce, but do not always eliminate, the impact of commodity price movements.

Our commodity price risk management program may include commodity derivatives with cash flow hedge accounting designation that utilize commodity swap contracts to hedge future cash flow exposures to the variability in commodity prices. These instruments generally mature within 12 months. For these derivatives, we report the after-tax gain (loss) from the effective portion of the hedge as a component of accumulated other comprehensive income (loss) and reclassify it into earnings in the same period or periods in which the hedged transaction affects earnings, and in the same line item on the consolidated statements of income as the impact of the hedged transaction.

Volume of Derivative Activity

Total gross notional amounts for outstanding derivatives (recorded at fair value) at the end of each period were as follows:

(In Millions)	Dec 26, 2015	Dec 27, 2014	Dec 28, 2013
Currency forwards	$11,212	$15,578	$13,404
Currency interest rate swaps	5,509	5,446	4,377
Embedded debt derivatives	3,600	3,600	3,600
Interest rate swaps	5,212	1,347	1,377
Total return swaps	1,061	1,056	914
Other	61	49	67
Total	$26,655	$27,076	$23,739

The gross notional amounts for currency forwards and currency interest rate swaps (presented by currency) at the end of each period were as follows:

(In Millions)	Dec 26, 2015	Dec 27, 2014	Dec 28, 2013
Chinese yuan	$ 2,231	$ 3,097	$ 1,116
Euro	6,084	7,486	6,874
Israeli shekel	1,674	2,489	2,244
Japanese yen	2,663	3,779	4,116
Other	4,069	4,173	3,431
Total	$16,721	$21,024	$17,781

During the fourth quarter of 2014, we entered into $1.5 billion of forward contracts to hedge our anticipated equity funding of the UniSpreadtrum investment. The hedges were designated as cash flow hedges and the related gains and losses attributable to changes in the spot rates were recognized in accumulated other comprehensive income (loss). Hedge gains and losses attributable to changes in the forward rates were recognized in interest and other, net. During 2015, we discontinued cash flow hedge accounting treatment for $478 million of forward contracts since we could no longer assert that funding is probable to occur within the initially specified timeline. Hedge losses accumulated in other comprehensive income and subsequently released to interest and other, net, related to these de-designated forward contracts were insignificant.

During 2015, we entered into $4.4 billion of interest rate swap agreements to hedge against changes in the fair value attributable to the benchmark interest rates related to $4.4 billion of our outstanding senior notes. These hedges were designated as fair value hedges. During 2015, we entered into $577 million of currency interest rate swap agreements to hedge against the variability in the U.S.-dollar equivalent of coupon and principal payments associated with our non-U.S.-dollar-denominated indebtedness. These hedges were designated as cash flow hedges.

Fair Value of Derivative Instruments in the Consolidated Balance Sheets

The fair value of our derivative instruments at the end of each period were as follows:

(In Millions)	December 26, 2015				December 27, 2014			
	Other Current Assets	Other Long-Term Assets	Other Accrued Liabilities	Other Long-Term Liabilities	Other Current Assets	Other Long-Term Assets	Other Accrued Liabilities	Other Long-Term Liabilities
Derivatives designated as hedging instruments:								
Currency forwards	$ 20	$ 3	$ 83	$ 2	$ 6	$ 1	$497	$ 9
Interest rate swaps	—	1	—	14	—	—	—	—
Currency interest rate swaps	—	7	—	—	—	—	—	—
Total derivatives designated as hedging instruments	20	11	83	16	6	1	497	9
Derivatives not designated as hedging instruments:								
Currency forwards	20	—	63	—	207	—	44	—
Currency interest rate swaps	370	18	52	—	344	34	7	—
Embedded debt derivatives	—	—	—	17	—	—	4	8
Interest rate swaps	2	—	12	—	3	—	11	—
Total return swaps	32	—	2	—	—	—	—	—
Other	1	11	—	—	1	22	—	—
Total derivatives not designated as hedging instruments	425	29	129	17	555	56	66	8
Total derivatives	$445	$40	$212	$33	$561	$57	$563	$17

Amounts Offset in the Consolidated Balance Sheets

The gross amounts of our derivative instruments and reverse repurchase agreements subject to master netting arrangements with various counterparties, and cash and non-cash collateral posted under such agreements at the end of each period were as follows:

(In Millions)	December 26, 2015					
				Gross Amounts Not Offset in the Balance Sheet		
	Gross Amounts Recognized	Gross Amounts Offset in the Balance Sheet	Net Amounts Presented in the Balance Sheet	Financial Instruments	Cash and Non-Cash Collateral Received or Pledged	Net Amount
Assets:						
Derivative assets subject to master netting arrangements	$ 482	$—	$ 482	$(201)	$ (188)	$93
Reverse repurchase agreements	3,368	—	3,368	—	(3,368)	—
Total assets	3,850	—	3,850	(201)	(3,556)	93
Liabilities:						
Derivative liabilities subject to master netting arrangements	242	—	242	(201)	(27)	14
Total liabilities	$ 242	$—	$ 242	$(201)	$ (27)	$14

(In Millions)	December 27, 2014					
				Gross Amounts Not Offset in the Balance Sheet		
	Gross Amounts Recognized	Gross Amounts Offset in the Balance Sheet	Net Amounts Presented in the Balance Sheet	Financial Instruments	Cash and Non-Cash Collateral Received or Pledged	Net Amount
Assets:						
Derivative assets subject to master netting arrangements	$ 559	$—	$ 559	$(365)	$ (78)	$116
Reverse repurchase agreements	718	—	718	—	(718)	—
Total assets	1,277	—	1,277	(365)	(796)	116
Liabilities:						
Derivative liabilities subject to master netting arrangements	559	—	559	(365)	(80)	114
Total liabilities	$ 559	$—	$ 559	$(365)	$ (80)	$114

We obtain and secure available collateral from counterparties against obligations, including securities lending transactions and reverse repurchase agreements, when we deem it appropriate.

Derivatives in Cash Flow Hedging Relationships

The before-tax gains (losses), attributed to the effective portion of cash flow hedges, recognized in other comprehensive income (loss) for each period were as follows:

(In Millions)	Gains (Losses) Recognized in OCI on Derivatives (Effective Portion)		
Years Ended	Dec 26, 2015	Dec 27, 2014	Dec 28, 2013
Currency forwards	$(305)	$(587)	$(167)
Currency interest rate swaps and other	7	(2)	1
Total	$(298)	$(589)	$(166)

Gains and losses on derivative instruments in cash flow hedging relationships related to hedge ineffectiveness and amounts excluded from effectiveness testing were insignificant during all periods presented in the preceding tables. Additionally, for all periods presented, there was an insignificant impact on results of operations from discontinued cash flow hedges, which arises when forecasted transactions are probable of not occurring.

For information on the unrealized holding gains (losses) on derivatives reclassified out of accumulated other comprehensive income into the consolidated statements of income, see "Note 24: Other Comprehensive Income (Loss)."

Derivatives in Fair Value Hedging Relationships

The effects of derivative instruments designated as fair value hedges, recognized in interest and other, net for each period were as follows:

(In Millions)	Gains (Losses) Recognized in Statement of Income on Derivatives		
Years Ended	Dec 26, 2015	Dec 27, 2014	Dec 28, 2013
Interest rate swap	$(13)	$—	$—
Hedged item	13	—	—
Total	$—	$—	$—

There was no ineffectiveness during all periods presented in the preceding table.

Derivatives Not Designated as Hedging Instruments

The effects of derivative instruments not designated as hedging instruments on the consolidated statements of income for each period were as follows:

(In Millions) Years Ended	Location of Gains (Losses) Recognized in Income on Derivatives	Dec 26, 2015	Dec 27, 2014	Dec 28, 2013
Currency forwards	Interest and other, net	$ (50)	$144	$ 44
Currency interest rate swaps	Interest and other, net	346	456	29
Interest rate swaps	Interest and other, net	(6)	(3)	—
Total return swaps	Various	(27)	68	140
Other	Gains (losses) on equity investments, net	(11)	(6)	6
Other	Interest and other, net	(2)	—	—
Total		$250	$659	$219

PREPAID EXPENSES

2.47 WILLIAMS-SONOMA, INC. (JAN)
CONSOLIDATED BALANCE SHEETS (in part)

In thousands, except per share amounts	Feb. 1, 2015	Feb. 2, 2014
Assets		
Current assets		
Cash and cash equivalents	$ 222,927	$ 330,121
Restricted cash	0	14,289
Accounts receivable, net	67,465	60,330
Merchandise inventories, net	887,701	813,160
Prepaid catalog expenses	33,942	33,556
Prepaid expenses	36,265	35,309
Deferred income taxes, net	130,618	121,486
Other assets	13,005	10,852
Total current assets	1,391,923	1,419,103

NOTES TO CONSOLIDATED FINANCIAL STATEMENTS (in part)

Note A: Summary of Significant Accounting Policies (in part)

Advertising and Prepaid Catalog Expenses

Advertising expenses consist of media and production costs related to catalog mailings, e-commerce advertising and other direct marketing activities. All advertising costs are expensed as incurred, or upon the release of the initial advertisement, with the exception of prepaid catalog expenses. Prepaid catalog expenses consist primarily of third party incremental direct costs, including creative design, paper, printing, postage and mailing costs for all of our direct response catalogs. Such costs are capitalized as prepaid catalog expenses and are amortized over their expected period of future benefit. Such amortization is based upon the ratio of estimated e-commerce revenues for the period to the total estimated e-commerce revenues over the life of the catalog on an individual catalog basis. Estimated e-commerce revenues over the life of the catalog are based upon various factors such as the total number of catalogs and pages circulated, the probability and magnitude of consumer response and the assortment of merchandise offered. Each catalog is generally fully amortized over a six to nine month period, with the majority of the amortization occurring within the first four to five months. Prepaid catalog expenses are evaluated for realizability on a monthly basis by comparing the carrying amount associated with each catalog to the estimated probable future profitability (net revenues less merchandise cost of goods sold, selling expenses and catalog-related costs) of that catalog. If the estimated future profitability of the catalog is below its carrying amount, the catalog is impaired accordingly.

Total advertising expenses (including catalog advertising, e-commerce advertising and all other advertising costs) were approximately $330,070,000, $325,708,000 and $318,338,000 in fiscal 2014, fiscal 2013 and fiscal 2012, respectively.

CONTRACTS

2.48 L-3 COMMUNICATIONS HOLDINGS, INC. (DEC)
CONSOLIDATED BALANCE SHEETS (in part)

(in millions, except share data)

	December 31,	
	2015	**2014**
Assets (in part)		
Current assets:		
Cash and cash equivalents	$ 207	$ 442
Billed receivables, net of allowances of $15 in 2015 and $13 in 2014	746	803
Contracts in process	2,081	2,148
Inventories	333	288
Other current assets	201	175
Assets held for sale	—	547
Assets of discontinued operations	664	1,262
Total current assets	4,232	5,665

NOTES TO CONSOLIDATED FINANCIAL STATEMENTS (in part)

2. Summary of Significant Accounting Policies (in part)

Revenue Recognition: Substantially all of the Company's sales are generated from written contractual (revenue) arrangements. The sales price for the Company's revenue arrangements are either fixed-price, cost-plus or time-and-material type. Depending on the contractual scope of work, the Company utilizes either contract accounting standards or accounting standards for revenue arrangements with commercial customers to account for these contracts. Approximately 49% of the Company's 2015 sales were accounted for under contract accounting standards, of which approximately 41% were fixed-price type contracts and approximately 8% were cost-plus type contracts. For contracts that are accounted for under contract accounting standards, sales and profits are recognized based on: (1) a Percentage-of-Completion (POC) method of accounting (fixed-price contracts), (2) allowable costs incurred plus the estimated profit on those costs (cost-plus contracts), or (3) direct labor hours expended multiplied by the contractual fixed rate per hour plus incurred costs for material (time-and-material contracts). Aggregate net changes in contract estimates amounted to increases of $49 million, or 10% of consolidated operating income (6% of segment operating income) for the year ended December 31, 2015, increases of $72 million, or 7% of consolidated operating income for the year ended December 31, 2014, and increases of $106 million, or 9% of consolidated operating income for the year ended December 31, 2013.

Sales and profits on fixed-price type contracts covered by contract accounting standards are substantially recognized using POC methods of accounting. Sales and profits on fixed-price production contracts under which units are produced and delivered in a continuous or sequential process are recorded as units are delivered based on their contractual selling prices (the "units-of-delivery" method). Sales and profits on each fixed-price production contract under which units are not produced and delivered in a continuous or sequential process, or under which a relatively few number of units are produced, are recorded based on the ratio of actual cumulative costs incurred to the total estimated costs at completion of the contract, multiplied by the total estimated contract revenue, less cumulative sales recognized in prior periods (the "cost-to-cost" method). Under both POC methods of accounting, a single estimated total profit margin is used to recognize profit for each contract over its entire period of performance, which can exceed one year. Losses on contracts are recognized in the period in which they become evident. The impact of revisions of contract estimates, which may result from contract modifications, performance or other reasons, are recognized on a cumulative catch-up basis in the period in which the revisions are made.

Sales and profits on cost-plus type contracts covered by contract accounting standards are recognized as allowable costs are incurred on the contract, at an amount equal to the allowable costs plus the estimated profit on those costs. The estimated profit on a cost-plus type contract is fixed or variable based on the contractual fee arrangement. Incentive and award fees are the primary variable fee contractual arrangements. Incentive and award fees on cost-plus type contracts are included as an element of total estimated contract revenues and are recorded as sales when a basis exists for the reasonable prediction of performance in relation to established contractual targets and the Company is able to make reasonably dependable estimates for them.

Sales and profits on time-and-material type contracts are recognized on the basis of direct labor hours expended multiplied by the contractual fixed rate per hour, plus the actual costs of materials and other direct non-labor costs.

Sales on arrangements for (1) fixed-price type contracts that require us to perform services that are not related to the production of tangible assets (Fixed-Price Service Contracts) and (2) certain commercial customers are recognized in accordance with accounting standards for revenue arrangements with commercial customers. Sales for the Company's businesses whose customers are primarily commercial business enterprises are substantially all generated from single element revenue arrangements. Sales are recognized when there is persuasive evidence of an arrangement, delivery has occurred or services have been performed, the selling price to the buyer is fixed or determinable and collectability is reasonably assured. Sales for Fixed-Price Service Contracts that do not contain measurable units of work performed are generally recognized on a straight-line basis over the contractual service period, unless evidence suggests that the revenue is earned, or obligations fulfilled, in a different manner. Sales for Fixed-Price Service Contracts that contain measurable units of work performed are generally recognized when the units of work are completed. Sales and profit on cost-plus and time-and-material type contracts to perform services are recognized in the same manner as those within the scope of contract accounting standards, except for incentive and award fees. Cost-based incentive fees are recognized when they are realizable in the amount that would be due under the contractual termination provisions as if the contract was terminated. Performance based incentive fees and award fees are recorded as sales when objective evidence exists that the fees have been earned.

For contracts with multiple deliverables, the Company applies the separation and allocation guidance under the accounting standard for revenue arrangements with multiple deliverables, unless all the deliverables are covered by contract accounting standards, in which case the Company applies the separation and allocation guidance under contract accounting standards. Revenue arrangements with multiple deliverables are evaluated to determine if the deliverables should be separated into more than one unit of accounting. The Company recognizes revenue for each unit of accounting based on the revenue recognition policies discussed above.

Sales and cost of sales in connection with contracts to provide services to the U.S. Government that contain collection risk because the contracts are incrementally funded and subject to the availability of funds appropriated, are deferred until a contract modification is obtained, indicating that adequate funds are available to the contract or task order.

Contracts in Process: Contracts in Process include unbilled contract receivables and inventoried contract costs for which sales and profits are recognized primarily using a POC method of accounting. Unbilled Contract Receivables represent accumulated incurred costs and earned profits on contracts in process that have been recorded as sales, primarily using the cost-to-cost method, but have not been billed to customers. Inventoried Contract Costs primarily represent incurred costs on contracts using the units-of-delivery method of accounting and include direct costs and indirect costs, including overhead costs, and materials acquired for U.S. Government service contracts. As discussed in Note 4, the Company's inventoried contract costs for U.S. Government contracts, and contracts with prime contractors or subcontractors of the U.S. Government include allocated general and administrative costs (G&A), IRAD costs and B&P costs. Contracts in Process contain amounts relating to contracts and programs with long performance cycles, a portion of which may not be realized within one year. For contracts in a loss position, the unrecoverable costs expected to be incurred in future periods are recorded in Estimated Costs in Excess of Estimated Contract Value to Complete Contracts in Process in a Loss Position, which is a component of Other Current Liabilities. Under the terms of certain revenue arrangements (contracts) with the U.S. Government, the Company is entitled to receive progress payments as costs are incurred or milestone payments as work is performed. The U.S. Government has a security interest in the Unbilled Contract Receivables and Inventoried Contract Costs to which progress payments have been applied, and such progress payments are reflected as a reduction of the related amounts. Milestone payments that have been received in excess of contract costs incurred and related estimated profits are reported on the Company's balance sheet as Advance Payments and Billings in Excess of Costs Incurred.

The Company values its acquired contracts in process in connection with business acquisitions on the date of acquisition at contract value less the Company's estimated costs to complete the contract and a reasonable profit allowance on the Company's completion effort.

4. Contracts in Process

The components of contracts in process are presented in the table below. The unbilled contract receivables, inventoried contract costs and unliquidated progress payments principally relate to contracts with the U.S. Government and prime contractors or subcontractors of the U.S. Government. In connection with contracts in process assumed by the Company in its business acquisitions, the underlying contractual customer relationships are separately recognized as identifiable intangible assets at the date of acquisition, and are discussed and presented in Note 6.

(In millions)	December 31, 2015	December 31, 2014
Unbilled contract receivables, gross	$2,097	$2,149
Unliquidated progress payments	(869)	(887)
Unbilled contract receivables, net	1,228	1,262
Inventoried contract costs, gross	975	981
Unliquidated progress payments	(122)	(95)
Inventoried contract costs, net	853	886
Total contracts in process	$2,081	$2,148

Unbilled Contract Receivables. Unbilled contract receivables represent accumulated incurred costs and earned profits on contracts (revenue arrangements), which have been recorded as sales, but have not yet been billed to customers. Unbilled contract receivables arise from the cost-to-cost method of revenue recognition that is used to record sales on certain fixed-price contracts. Unbilled contract receivables from fixed-price type contracts are converted to billed receivables when amounts are invoiced to customers according to contractual billing terms, which generally occur when deliveries or other performance milestones are completed. Unbilled contract receivables also arise from cost-plus type contracts, time-and-material type contracts and fixed-price service type contracts for revenue amounts that have not been billed by the end of the accounting period due to the timing of preparation of invoices to customers. The Company believes that approximately 92% of the unbilled contract receivables, net at December 31, 2015 will be billed and collected within one year.

Unliquidated Progress Payments. Unliquidated progress payments arise from fixed-price type contracts with the U.S. Government that contain progress payment clauses, and represent progress payments on invoices that have been collected in cash, but have not yet been liquidated. Progress payment invoices are billed to the customer as contract costs are incurred at an amount generally equal to 75% to 80% of incurred costs. Unliquidated progress payments are liquidated as deliveries or other contract performance milestones are completed, at an amount equal to a percentage of the contract sales price for the items delivered or work performed, based on a contractual liquidation rate. Therefore, unliquidated progress payments are a contra asset account, and are classified against unbilled contract receivables if revenue for the underlying contract is recorded using the cost-to-cost method, and against inventoried contract costs if revenue is recorded using the units-of-delivery method.

Inventoried Contract Costs. In accordance with contract accounting standards, the Company's U.S. Government contractor businesses account for the portion of their G&A, IRAD and B&P costs that are allowable and reimbursable indirect contract costs under U.S. Government procurement regulations on their U.S. Government contracts (revenue arrangements) as inventoried contract costs. G&A, IRAD and B&P costs are allocated to contracts for which the U.S. Government is the end customer and are charged to costs of sales when sales on the related contracts are recognized. The Company's U.S. Government contractor businesses record the unallowable portion of their G&A, IRAD and B&P costs to expense as incurred, and do not include them in inventoried contract costs.

The table below presents a summary of G&A, IRAD and B&P costs included in inventoried contract costs and the changes to them, including amounts charged to cost of sales by the Company's U.S. Government contractor businesses for the periods presented.

(In millions)	Year Ended December 31, 2015	Year Ended December 31, 2014	Year Ended December 31, 2013
Amounts included in inventoried contract costs at beginning of the year	$ 135	$ 133	$ 104
Contract costs incurred:			
IRAD and B&P	280	266	279
Other G&A	812	805	817
Total	1,092	1,071	1,096
Amounts charged to cost of sales	(1,065)	(1,069)	(1,067)
Amounts included in inventoried contract costs at end of the year	$ 162	$ 135	$ 133

The table below presents a summary of selling, general and administrative expenses and research and development expenses for the Company's commercial businesses, which are expensed as incurred and included in cost of sales on the Consolidated Statements of Operations.

(In millions)	Year Ended December 31, 2015	Year Ended December 31, 2014	Year Ended December 31, 2013
Selling, general and administrative expenses	$259	$295	$310
Research and development expenses	56	67	76
Total	$315	$362	$386

Property, Plant, and Equipment

RECOGNITION AND MEASUREMENT

2.49 *Property, plant, and equipment* are the long-lived, physical assets of the entity acquired for use in the entity's normal business operations and not intended for resale by the entity. FASB ASC 360, *Property, Plant, and Equipment*, states that these assets are initially recorded at historical cost, which includes the costs necessarily incurred to bring them to the condition and location necessary for their intended use. FASB ASC 835-20 establishes standards for capitalizing interest cost as part of the historical cost of acquiring assets constructed by an entity for its own use or produced for the entity by others for which deposits or progress payments have been made.

2.50 An entity may acquire or develop computer software either for internal use or for sale or lease to others. If for internal use, FASB ASC 350-40 provides guidance on accounting for the costs of computer software and for determining whether the software is for internal use. Under FASB ASC 350-40, internal and external costs incurred to develop internal-use software during the application development stage should be capitalized and amortized over the software's estimated useful life. The accounting for costs of software to be sold, leased, or marketed is addressed by FASB ASC 985-20. Whether for internal use or sale or lease, FASB ASC refers to capitalized software costs as amortizable intangible assets.

PRESENTATION

2.51 FASB ASC 210-10-45-4 indicates that property, plant, and equipment should be classified as noncurrent when a classified balance sheet is presented. Under FASB ASC 805-20-55-37, some use rights acquired in a business combination may have characteristics of tangible, rather than intangible, assets. An example is mineral rights.

2.52 Under FASB ASC 985-20-45-2, capitalized costs related to software for sale or lease having a life of more than one year or one operating cycle should be presented as an other asset. Under FASB ASC 985-20, amortization expense should be on a product-by-product basis and charged to cost of sales or a similar expense category because it relates to a software product that is marketed to others. Presentations of capitalized computer software costs by survey entities vary.

DISCLOSURE

2.53 FASB ASC 360-10-50-1 requires the following disclosures in the financial statements or notes thereto:
   a. Depreciation expense for the period
   b. Balances of major classes of depreciable assets, by nature or function, at the balance sheet date
   c. Accumulated depreciation, either by major classes of depreciable assets or in total, at the balance sheet date
   d. A general description of the method(s) used in computing depreciation with respect to major classes of depreciable assets.

2.54 Additionally, FASB ASC 360-10-50-3 states that for any period in which a long-lived asset (disposal group) either has been disposed of or is classified as held for sale (see FASB ASC 360-10-45-9) an entity shall disclose all of the following in the notes to financial statements:
   a. A description of the facts and circumstances leading to the disposal or the expected disposal.
   b. The expected manner and timing of that disposal.
   c. The gain or loss recognized in accordance with paragraphs 37–45 of FASB ASC 360-10-35 and FASB ASC 360-10-40-5.
   d. If not separately presented on the face of the statement where net income is reported (or in the statement of activities for a not-for-profit entity), the caption in the statement where net income is reported (or in the statement of activities for a not-for-profit entity) that includes that gain or loss.
   e. If not separately presented on the face of the statement of financial position, the carrying amount(s) of the major classes of assets and liabilities included as part of a disposal group classified as held for sale. Any loss recognized on the disposal group classified as held for sale in accordance with paragraphs 37–45 of FASB ASC 360-10-35-37 and FASB ASC 360-10-40-5 shall not be allocated to the major classes of assets and liabilities of the disposal group.
   f. If applicable, the segment in which the long-lived asset (disposal group) is reported under FASB ASC 280 on segment reporting.

2.55 Rule 5-02 of Regulation S-X requires that registrants state the basis of determining the amounts of property, plant, and equipment.

PRESENTATION AND DISCLOSURE EXCERPTS

PROPERTY, PLANT, AND EQUIPMENT

2.56 CENTURYLINK, INC. (DEC)

CONSOLIDATED BALANCE SHEETS (in part)

	As of December 31,	
(Dollars in millions and shares in thousands)	2015	2014
Assets		
Current Assets		
Cash and cash equivalents	$ 126	128
Accounts receivable, less allowance of $152 and $162	1,943	1,988
Other	581	580
Total current assets	2,650	2,696
Net Property, Plant and Equipment		
Property, plant and equipment	38,785	36,718
Accumulated depreciation	(20,716)	(18,285)
Net property, plant and equipment	18,069	18,433
Goodwill and Other Assets		
Goodwill	20,742	20,755
Customer relationships, net	3,928	4,893
Other intangible assets, net	1,555	1,647
Other, net	660	679
Total goodwill and other assets	26,885	27,974
Total Assets	$ 47,604	49,103

NOTES TO CONSOLIDATED FINANCIAL STATEMENTS (in part)

(1) Basis of Presentation and Summary of Significant Accounting Policies (in part)

Connect America Fund Support Payments (in part)

Changes in Estimates

As a result of our annual reviews to evaluate the reasonableness of the depreciable lives for our property, plant and equipment, effective January 2014, we changed the estimates of the remaining economic lives of certain switch and circuit network equipment. These changes resulted in a net increase in depreciation expense of approximately $78 million for the year ended December 31, 2014. This net increase in depreciation expense, net of tax, reduced consolidated net income by approximately $48 million, or $0.08 per basic and diluted common share, for the year ended December 31, 2014.

Additionally, during the third quarter of 2014, we developed a plan to migrate customers from one of our networks to another over a one-year period beginning in the fourth quarter of 2014. As a result, we implemented changes in estimates that reduced the remaining economic lives of certain network assets. The increase in depreciation expense from the changes in estimates was more than fully offset by decreases in depreciation expense resulting from normal aging of our property, plant and equipment. These changes in the estimated remaining economic lives resulted in an increase in depreciation expense of approximately $48 million and $12 million for the years ended December 31, 2015 and 2014, respectively. This increase in depreciation expense, net of tax, reduced consolidated net income by approximately $32 million, or $0.06 per basic and diluted common share and $7 million, or $0.01 per basic and diluted common share, for the years ended December 31, 2015 and 2014, respectively.

Summary of Significant Accounting Policies (in part)

Property, Plant and Equipment

Property, plant and equipment acquired in connection with our acquisitions was recorded based on its estimated fair value as of its acquisition date plus the estimated value of any associated legally or contractually required retirement obligations. Purchased and constructed property, plant and equipment is recorded at cost, plus the estimated value of any associated legally or contractually required retirement obligations. Property, plant and equipment is depreciated primarily using the straight-line group method. Under the straight-line group method, assets dedicated to providing telecommunications services (which comprise the majority of our property, plant and equipment) that have similar physical characteristics, use and expected useful lives are pooled for purposes of depreciation and tracking.

The equal life group procedure is used to establish each pool's average remaining useful life. Generally, under the straight-line group method, when an asset is sold or retired in the course of normal business activities, the cost is deducted from property, plant and equipment and charged to accumulated depreciation without recognition of a gain or loss. A gain or loss is recognized in our consolidated statements of operations only if a disposal is abnormal or unusual. Leasehold improvements are amortized over the shorter of the useful lives of the assets or the expected lease term. Expenditures for maintenance and repairs are expensed as incurred. Interest is capitalized during the construction phase of network and other internal-use capital projects. Employee-related costs for construction of network and other internal use assets are also capitalized during the construction phase. Property, plant and equipment supplies used internally are carried at average cost, except for significant individual items for which cost is based on specific identification.

We perform annual internal reviews to evaluate the reasonableness of the depreciable lives for our property, plant and equipment. Our reviews utilize models that take into account actual usage, physical wear and tear, replacement history, assumptions about technology evolution and, in certain instances, actuarially determined probabilities to estimate the remaining useful life of our asset base. Our remaining useful life assessments anticipate the loss in service value of assets that may precede the physical retirement. Assets shared among many customers may lose service value as those customers leave the network. However, the asset is not retired until all customers no longer utilize the asset and we determine there is no alternative use for the asset.

We have asset retirement obligations associated with the legally or contractually required removal of a limited group of property, plant and equipment assets from leased properties and the disposal of certain hazardous materials present in our owned properties. When an asset retirement obligation is identified, usually in association with the acquisition of the asset, we record the fair value of the obligation as a liability. The fair value of the obligation is also capitalized as property, plant and equipment and then amortized over the estimated remaining useful life of the associated asset. Where the removal obligation is not legally binding, the net cost to remove assets is expensed in the period in which the costs are actually incurred.

We review long-lived tangible assets for impairment whenever facts and circumstances indicate that the carrying amounts of the assets may not be recoverable. For assessment purposes, long-lived assets are grouped with other assets and liabilities at the lowest level for which identifiable cash flows are largely independent of the cash flows of other assets and liabilities, absent a material change in operations. An impairment loss is recognized only if the carrying amount of the asset group is not recoverable and exceeds its fair value. Recoverability of the asset group to be held and used is assessed by comparing the carrying amount of the asset group to the estimated undiscounted future net cash flows expected to be generated by the asset group. If the asset group's carrying value is not recoverable, an impairment charge is recognized for the amount by which the carrying amount of the asset group exceeds its fair value. We determine fair values by using a combination of comparable market values and discounted cash flows, as appropriate.

(5) Property, Plant and Equipment

Net property, plant and equipment is composed of the following:

		As of December 31,	
(Dollars in millions)	Depreciable Lives	2015	2014
Land	n/a	$ 571	575
Fiber, conduit and other outside plant[1]	15–45	16,166	15,151
Central office and other network electronics[2]	3–10	14,144	13,248
Support assets[3]	3–30	7,000	6,578
Construction in progress[4]	n/a	904	1,166
Gross property, plant and equipment		38,785	36,718
Accumulated depreciation		(20,716)	(18,285)
Net property, plant and equipment		$ 18,069	18,433

[1] Fiber, conduit and other outside plant consists of fiber and metallic cable, conduit, poles and other supporting structures.
[2] Central office and other network electronics consists of circuit and packet switches, routers, transmission electronics and electronics providing service to customers.
[3] Support assets consist of buildings, data centers, computers and other administrative and support equipment.
[4] Construction in progress includes inventory held for construction and property of the aforementioned categories that has not been placed in service as it is still under construction.

We recorded depreciation expense of $2.836 billion, $2.958 billion and $2.952 billion for the years ended December 31, 2015, 2014 and 2013, respectively.

In 2014, we recorded an impairment charge of $17 million in connection with a sale-leaseback transaction involving an office building which closed in the fourth quarter of 2014. This impairment charge is included in selling, general and administrative expense in our consolidated statement of operations for the year ended December 31, 2014.

Additionally, in 2014 we sold an office building for $12 million.

Asset Retirement Obligations

At December 31, 2015, our asset retirement obligations balance was primarily related to estimated future costs of removing equipment from leased properties and estimated future costs of properly disposing of asbestos and other hazardous materials upon remodeling or demolishing buildings. Asset retirement obligations are included in other long-term liabilities on our consolidated balance sheets.

The following table provides asset retirement obligation activity:

	Years Ended December 31,		
(Dollars in millions)	2015	2014	2013
Balance at beginning of year	$107	106	106
Accretion expense	7	7	7
Liabilities incurred	—	6	—
Liabilities settled	(2)	(2)	(4)
Change in estimate	(21)	(10)	(3)
Balance at end of year	$ 91	107	106

During 2015, 2014 and 2013, we revised our estimates for the cost of removal of network equipment, asbestos remediation, and other obligations by $21 million, $10 million and $3 million, respectively. These revisions resulted in a reduction of the asset retirement obligation and offsetting reduction to gross property, plant and equipment and revisions to assets specifically identified are recorded as a reduction to accretion expense.

2.57 BERKSHIRE HATHAWAY INC. (DEC)
CONSOLIDATED BALANCE SHEETS (in part)

(dollars in millions)

	December 31,	
	2015	2014
Assets		
Insurance and Other:		
Cash and cash equivalents	$ 61,181	$ 57,974
Investments:		
Fixed maturity securities	25,988	27,397
Equity securities	110,212	115,529
Other	15,998	16,346
Investments in The Kraft Heinz Company	23,424	11,660
Receivables	23,303	21,852
Inventories	11,916	10,236
Property, plant and equipment	15,540	14,153
Goodwill	37,188	34,959
Other intangible assets	9,148	9,203
Deferred charges reinsurance assumed	7,687	7,772
Other	6,697	6,748
	348,282	333,829
Railroad, Utilities and Energy:		
Cash and cash equivalents	3,437	3,001
Property, plant and equipment	120,279	115,054
Goodwill	24,178	24,418
Regulatory assets	4,285	4,253
Other	12,833	11,817
	165,012	158,543
Finance and Financial Products:		
Cash and cash equivalents	7,112	2,294
Investments in equity and fixed maturity securities	411	1,299
Other investments	5,719	5,978
Loans and finance receivables	12,772	12,566
Property, plant and equipment and assets held for lease	9,347	8,037
Goodwill	1,342	1,337
Other	2,260	1,984
	38,963	33,495
	$552,257	$525,867

(1) Significant Accounting Policies and Practices (in part)

(i) Property, Plant and Equipment and Leased Assets

Additions to property, plant and equipment used in operations and leased assets are recorded at cost and consist of major additions, improvements and betterments. With respect to constructed assets, all construction related material, direct labor and contract services as well as certain indirect costs are capitalized. Indirect costs include interest over the construction period. With respect to constructed assets of certain of our regulated utility and energy subsidiaries that are subject to authoritative guidance for regulated operations, capitalized costs also include an equity allowance for funds used during construction, which represents the cost of equity funds used to finance the construction of the regulated facilities. Also see Note 1(q).

Normal repairs and maintenance and other costs that do not improve the property, extend the useful life or otherwise do not meet capitalization criteria are charged to expense as incurred. Rail grinding costs related to our railroad properties are expensed as incurred.

Property, plant and equipment and leased assets are depreciated to estimated salvage value primarily using the straight-line method over estimated useful lives or mandated recovery periods as prescribed by regulatory authorities. Depreciation of assets of our regulated utilities and railroad is generally determined using group depreciation methods where rates are based on periodic depreciation studies approved by the applicable regulator. Under group depreciation, a single depreciation rate is applied to the gross investment in a particular class of property, despite differences in the service life or salvage value of individual property units within the same class. When our regulated utilities or railroad retires or sells a component of the assets accounted for using group depreciation methods, no gain or loss is recognized. Gains or losses on disposals of all other assets are recorded through earnings.

Our businesses evaluate property, plant and equipment for impairment when events or changes in circumstances indicate that the carrying value of such assets may not be recoverable or the assets are being held for sale. Upon the occurrence of a triggering event, we assess whether the estimated undiscounted cash flows expected from the use of the asset and the residual value from the ultimate disposal of the asset exceeds the carrying value. If the carrying value exceeds the estimated recoverable amounts, we write down the asset to the estimated fair value. Impairment losses are included in earnings, except with respect to impairment of assets of our regulated utility and energy subsidiaries when the impacts of regulation are considered in evaluating the carrying value of regulated assets.

(10) Property, Plant and Equipment and Assets Held for Lease

A summary of property, plant and equipment of our insurance and other businesses follows (in millions).

		December 31,	
	Ranges of Estimated Useful Life	2015	2014
Land	—	$ 1,689	$ 1,171
Buildings and improvements	2–40 years	7,329	6,600
Machinery and equipment	3–25 years	17,054	16,413
Furniture, fixtures and other	1–30 years	3,545	3,136
		29,617	27,320
Accumulated depreciation		(14,077)	(13,167)
		$ 15,540	$ 14,153

A summary of property, plant and equipment of our railroad and our utilities and energy businesses follows (in millions).

		December 31,	
	Ranges of Estimated Useful Life	2015	2014
Railroad:			
Land	—	$ 6,037	$ 5,983
Track structure and other roadway	7–100 years	45,967	42,588
Locomotives, freight cars and other equipment	6–40 years	11,320	9,493
Construction in progress	—	1,031	1,292
		64,355	59,356
Accumulated depreciation		(4,845)	(3,550)
		$ 59,510	$ 55,806
Utilities and energy:			
Utility generation, transmission and distribution systems	5–80 years	$ 69,248	$ 64,645
Interstate natural gas pipeline assets	3–80 years	6,755	6,660
Independent power plants and other assets	3–30 years	5,626	5,035
Construction in progress	—	2,627	5,194
		84,256	81,534
Accumulated depreciation		(23,487)	(22,286)
		$ 60,769	$ 59,248

The utility generation, transmission and distribution systems and interstate natural gas pipeline assets are owned by regulated public utility and natural gas pipeline subsidiaries.

Assets held for lease and property, plant and equipment of our finance and financial products businesses are summarized below (in millions).

		December 31,	
	Ranges of Estimated Useful Life	2015	2014
Assets held for lease	5–30 years	$11,317	$ 9,810
Land	—	220	227
Buildings, machinery and other	3–50 years	1,207	1,179
		12,744	11,216
Accumulated depreciation		(3,397)	(3,179)
		$ 9,347	$ 8,037

Assets held for lease includes railcars, intermodal tank containers, cranes, over-the-road trailers, storage units and furniture. As of December 31, 2015, the minimum future lease rentals to be received on assets held for lease (including rail cars leased from others) were as follows (in millions): 2016—$1,256; 2017—$1,035; 2018—$809; 2019—$589; 2020—$410; and thereafter—$593.

Depreciation expense for each of the three years ending December 31, 2015 is summarized below (in millions).

	2015	2014	2013
Insurance and other	$1,680	$1,632	$1,691
Railroad, utilities and energy	4,383	3,981	3,232
Finance and financial products	610	602	495
	$6,673	$6,215	$5,418

Equity Method and Joint Ventures

RECOGNITION AND MEASUREMENT

2.58 FASB ASC 323, *Investments—Equity Method and Joint Ventures*, stipulates that the equity method should be used to account for investments in corporate joint ventures and certain other noncontrolled entities when an investor has the ability to exercise significant influence over operating and financial policies of an investee, even though the investor holds 50 percent or less of the common stock. FASB ASC 323 considers that an investment (direct or indirect) of 20 percent or more of the voting stock of an investee should lead to a presumption that in the absence of predominant evidence to the contrary an investor has the ability to exercise significant influence. FASB ASC 323 also specifies the criteria for applying the equity method of accounting to 50 percent or less owned entities and lists circumstances under which, despite 20 percent ownership, an investor may not be able to exercise significant influence.

PRESENTATION

2.59 Under the equity method, FASB ASC 323-10-45-1 requires that an investment in common stock be shown in the balance sheet of an investor as a single amount.

DISCLOSURE

2.60 Under FASB ASC 323-10-50-2, the significance of an equity method investment to the investor's financial position and results of operations should be considered in evaluating the extent of disclosures of the financial position and results of operations of an investee. If the investor has more than one investment in common stock, disclosures wholly or partly on a combined basis may be appropriate. FASB ASC 323-10-50-3 details disclosures required for equity method investments, including name and percentage of ownership of the investee, investor accounting policies, any difference between the amount at which an investment is carried and the amount of underlying equity in net assets, and the accounting treatment of the difference.

EQUITY METHOD

2.61 THE COCA-COLA COMPANY (DEC)

CONSOLIDATED BALANCE SHEETS (in part)

(In millions except par value) December 31,	2015	2014
Assets		
Current Assets		
Cash and cash equivalents	$ 7,309	$ 8,958
Short-term investments	8,322	9,052
Total Cash, Cash Equivalents and Short-Term Investments	15,631	18,010
Marketable securities	4,269	3,665
Trade accounts receivable, less allowances of $352 and $331, respectively	3,941	4,466
Inventories	2,902	3,100
Prepaid expenses and other assets	2,752	3,066
Assets held for sale	3,900	679
Total Current Assets	33,395	32,986
Equity Method Investments	12,318	9,947
Other Investments	3,470	3,678
Other Assets	4,207	4,407
Property, Plant and Equipment—net	12,571	14,633
Trademarks With Indefinite Lives	5,989	6,533
Bottlers' Franchise Rights With Indefinite Lives	6,000	6,689
Goodwill	11,289	12,100
Other Intangible Assets	854	1,050
Total Assets	$90,093	$92,023

NOTES TO CONSOLIDATED FINANCIAL STATEMENTS (in part)

Note 1: Business and Summary of Significant Accounting Policies (in part)

Summary of Significant Accounting Policies (in part)

Basis of Presentation

Our consolidated financial statements are prepared in accordance with accounting principles generally accepted in the United States ("U.S. GAAP"). The preparation of our consolidated financial statements requires us to make estimates and assumptions that affect the reported amounts of assets, liabilities, revenues and expenses and the disclosure of contingent assets and liabilities in our consolidated financial statements and accompanying notes. Although these estimates are based on our knowledge of current events and actions we may undertake in the future, actual results may ultimately differ from these estimates and assumptions. Furthermore, when testing assets for impairment in future periods, if management uses different assumptions or if different conditions occur, impairment charges may result.

We use the equity method to account for investments in companies, if our investment provides us with the ability to exercise significant influence over operating and financial policies of the investee. Our consolidated net income includes our Company's proportionate share of the net income or loss of these companies. Our judgment regarding the level of influence over each equity method investment includes considering key factors such as our ownership interest, representation on the board of directors, participation in policy-making decisions and material intercompany transactions.

We eliminate from our financial results all significant intercompany transactions, including the intercompany transactions with consolidated variable interest entities ("VIEs") and the intercompany portion of transactions with equity method investees.

Investments in Equity and Debt Securities (in part)

We use the equity method to account for our investments in equity securities if our investment gives us the ability to exercise significant influence over operating and financial policies of the investee. We include our proportionate share of earnings and/or losses of our equity method investees in equity income (loss)—net in our consolidated statements of income. The carrying value of our equity investments is reported in equity method investments in our consolidated balance sheets. Refer to Note 6.

We account for investments in companies that we do not control or account for under the equity method either at fair value or under the cost method, as applicable. Investments in equity securities, other than investments accounted for under the equity method, are carried at fair value if the fair value of the security is readily determinable. Equity investments carried at fair value are classified as either trading or available-for-sale securities with their cost basis determined by the specific identification method. Realized and unrealized gains and losses on trading securities and realized gains and losses on available-for-sale securities are included in other income (loss)—net in our consolidated statements of income. Unrealized gains and losses, net of deferred taxes, on available-for-sale securities are included in our consolidated balance sheets as a component of accumulated other comprehensive income (loss) ("AOCI"), except for the change in fair value attributable to the currency risk being hedged, if applicable, which is included in other income (loss)—net in our consolidated statements of income. Trading securities are reported as either marketable securities or other assets in our consolidated balance sheets. Securities classified as available-for-sale are reported as either marketable securities, other investments or other assets in our consolidated balance sheets, depending on the length of time we intend to hold the investment. Refer to Note 3.

Investments in equity securities that we do not control or account for under the equity method and do not have readily determinable fair values for are accounted for under the cost method. Cost method investments are originally recorded at cost, and we record dividend income when applicable dividends are declared. Cost method investments are reported as other investments in our consolidated balance sheets, and dividend income from cost method investments is reported in the line item other income (loss)—net in our consolidated statements of income.

Note 2: Acquisitions and Divestitures

Acquisitions

During 2015, our Company's acquisitions of businesses, equity method investments and nonmarketable securities totaled $2,491 million, which primarily related to our strategic partnership with Monster Beverage Corporation ("Monster") and an investment in a bottling partner in Indonesia that is accounted for under the equity method of accounting. The bottling partner in Indonesia is a subsidiary of Coca-Cola Amatil Limited, an equity method investee. We also acquired the remaining outstanding shares of a bottling partner in South Africa ("South African bottler"), which was previously accounted for as an equity method investment. We remeasured our previously held equity interest in the South African bottler to fair value upon the close of the transaction and recorded a loss on the remeasurement of $19 million during the year ended December 31, 2015. This bottler will be included in the Coca-Cola Beverages Africa Limited transaction discussed further below.

During 2014, our Company's acquisitions of businesses, equity method investments and nonmarketable securities totaled $389 million and primarily included a joint investment with one of our bottling partners in a dairy company in Ecuador, which is accounted for under the equity method of accounting.

During 2013, our Company's acquisitions of businesses, equity method investments and nonmarketable securities totaled $353 million, which primarily included our acquisition of the majority of the remaining outstanding shares of Fresh Trading Ltd. ("innocent") and a majority interest in bottling operations in Myanmar. The Company previously accounted for our investment in innocent under the equity method of accounting. We remeasured our equity interest in innocent to fair value upon the close of the transaction. The resulting gain on the remeasurement was not significant to our consolidated financial statements.

Monster Beverage Corporation

On August 14, 2014, the Company and Monster entered into definitive agreements for a long-term strategic relationship in the global energy drink category. The transaction contemplated under these agreements ("Monster Transaction") closed on June 12, 2015. As a result of the Monster Transaction, (1) the Company purchased newly issued shares of Monster common stock representing approximately 17 percent of the outstanding shares of Monster common stock (after giving effect to the new issuance); (2) the Company sold its global energy drink business (including NOS, Full Throttle, Burn, Mother, Play and Power Play, and Relentless) to Monster, and the Company acquired Monster's non-energy drink business (including Hansen's Natural Sodas, Peace Tea, Hubert's Lemonade and Hansen's Juice Products); and (3) the parties amended their distribution coordination agreements to expand distribution of Monster products into additional territories pursuant to long-term agreements with the Company's existing network of Company-owned or -controlled bottling operations and distribution partners. The Coca-Cola system also became Monster's preferred global distribution partner. The Company made a net cash payment of $2,150 million to Monster, of which $125 million is being held in escrow, subject to release upon achievement of milestones relating to the transfer of Monster's domestic distribution rights to our distribution network.

The Monster Transaction consisted of multiple elements including the purchase of common stock, the acquisition and divestiture of businesses and the expansion of distribution territories. When consideration transferred is not solely in the form of cash, measurement is based on either the cost to the acquiring entity (the fair value of the assets given) or the fair value of the assets acquired, whichever is more clearly evident and, thus, more reliably measurable. As the majority of the consideration transferred was cash, we believe the fair value of the consideration transferred is more reliably measurable. The consideration transferred consists of $2,150 million of cash (including $125 million in escrow) and the fair value of our global energy business of $2,046 million, which we determined using discounted cash flow analyses, resulting in total consideration transferred of $4,196 million. As such, we have allocated the total consideration transferred to the individual assets and business acquired based on a relative fair value basis, using the closing date fair values of each element, as follows (in millions):

	June 12, 2015
Equity investment in Monster	$3,066
Expansion of distribution territories	1,035
Monster non-energy drink business	95
Total assets and business acquired	$4,196

In addition to our ownership interest in Monster's outstanding common stock, the Company is represented by two directors on Monster's 10 member Board of Directors. Based on our equity ownership percentage, the significance that our expanded distribution and coordination agreements have on Monster's operations, and our representation on Monster's Board of Directors, the Company is accounting for its interest in Monster as an equity method investment.

As a result of the Monster Transaction, the North America Coca-Cola system obtained the right to distribute Monster products in territories for which it was not previously the authorized distributor ("expanded territories"). These distribution rights are governed by an agreement with an initial term of 20 years, after which it will continue to remain in effect unless otherwise terminated by either party and there are no future costs of renewal. As such, these rights were determined to be indefinite-lived intangible assets and are classified in the line item bottlers' franchise rights with indefinite lives in our consolidated balance sheet. CCR is the distributor in the majority of the expanded territories. The remainder of the territories are serviced by independent bottling partners. Of the $1,035 million allocated to the expanded distribution rights, the Company derecognized $341 million related to the expanded territories serviced by the independent bottling partners upon the close of the transaction. As consideration for these rights, the Company received an up-front payment of $28 million related to these territories, and we will receive a payment per case on all future sales made by these independent bottlers for the duration of the distribution agreements. As these payments are dependent on future sales, they are a form of contingent consideration. We elected to account for this consideration in the same manner as the contingent consideration to be received in the North America refranchising, discussed below. This resulted in a net loss of $313 million recorded in the line item other income (loss)—net in our consolidated statement of income during the year ended December 31, 2015.

During the year ended December 31, 2015, the Company recognized a gain of $1,715 million on the sale of our global energy drink business, primarily due to the difference in the recorded carrying value of the assets transferred, including an allocated portion of goodwill, compared to the value of the total assets and business acquired. After considering the loss resulting from the derecognition of the expanded territory rights serviced by the independent bottling partners, the net gain recognized on the Monster Transaction was $1,403 million, which was recorded in the line item other income (loss)—net in our consolidated statement of income. Additionally, under the terms of the Monster Transaction, we were required to discontinue selling energy products under certain trademarks, including one trademark in the glacéau portfolio. The Company recognized an impairment charge of $380 million upon closing, primarily related to the discontinuation of the energy products in the glacéau portfolio, which was recorded in the line item other operating charges in our consolidated statement of income.

During the year ended December 31, 2015, based on the relative fair values of the total assets and business acquired, $1,620 million of the $2,150 million cash payment made was classified in the line item acquisitions of businesses, equity method investments and nonmarketable securities in our consolidated statement of cash flows. The remaining $530 million was classified in the line item other investing activities in our consolidated statement of cash flows.

Keurig Green Mountain, Inc.

In February 2014, the Company purchased newly issued shares in Keurig Green Mountain, Inc. ("Keurig") for $1,265 million, including transaction costs of $14 million. In May 2014, the Company purchased additional shares of Keurig in the market for $302 million, which represented an additional 2 percent equity position in Keurig.

Subsequent to these purchases, the Company entered into an agreement with Credit Suisse Capital LLC ("CS") to purchase additional shares of Keurig which would increase the Company's equity position to a 16 percent interest based on the total number of issued and outstanding shares of Keurig as of May 1, 2014. Under the agreement, the Company was to purchase from CS, on a date selected by CS no later than February 2015, the lesser of (1) 6.5 million shares of Keurig or (2) the number of shares that shall cause our ownership to equal 16 percent. The purchase price per share was the average of the daily volume-weighted average price per share from May 15, 2014, to the date selected by CS, as adjusted in certain circumstances specified in the agreement. CS had exclusive ownership and control over any such shares until delivered to the Company. In February 2015, the Company purchased 6.4 million shares from CS under this agreement for a total purchase price of $830 million. As this agreement qualified as a derivative, we recognized a loss of $58 million in the line item other income (loss)—net in our consolidated statement of income during the year ended December 31, 2015. The Company recognized a cumulative loss of $47 million in the line item other income (loss)—net in our consolidated statement of income over the term of the agreement.

We account for the investment in Keurig as an available-for-sale security, which is included in the line item other investments in our consolidated balance sheet. These purchases of the shares were included in the line item purchases of investments in our consolidated statement of cash flows, net of any related derivative impact.

German Bottling Operations

In conjunction with the Company's acquisition of German bottling operations in 2007, the former owners received put options to sell their respective shares in the operations back to the Company in January 2014. During the year ended December 31, 2014, the Company paid $503 million to purchase these shares, which was included in the line item other financing activities in our consolidated statement of cash flows, resulting in 100 percent ownership of our German bottling operations.

Divestitures

During 2015, proceeds from disposals of businesses, equity method investments and nonmarketable securities totaled $565 million, which included proceeds from the refranchising of certain of our territories in North America and proceeds from the sale of a 10 percent interest in a Brazilian bottling partner as a result of the majority owners exercising their right to acquire additional shares from us.

During 2014, proceeds from disposals of businesses, equity method investments and nonmarketable securities totaled $148 million, which primarily represented the proceeds from the refranchising of certain of our territories in North America.

During 2013, proceeds from disposals of businesses, equity method investments and nonmarketable securities totaled $872 million. These proceeds primarily included the sale of a majority ownership interest in our previously consolidated bottling operations in the Philippines ("Philippine bottling operations"), and separately, the deconsolidation of our bottling operations in Brazil ("Brazilian bottling operations").

North America Refranchising

In conjunction with implementing a new beverage partnership model in North America, the Company refranchised territories that were previously managed by CCR to certain of our unconsolidated bottling partners. These territories generally border these bottlers' existing territories, allowing each bottler to better service local customers and provide more efficient execution. By entering into comprehensive beverage agreements ("CBAs") with each of the bottlers, we granted certain exclusive territory rights for the distribution, promotion, marketing and sale of Company-owned and licensed beverage products as defined by the CBA. In some cases, the Company has entered into, or agreed to enter into, manufacturing agreements that authorize certain bottlers that have executed a CBA to manufacture certain beverage products. If a bottler has not entered into a specific manufacturing agreement, then under the CBA for these territories, CCR retains the rights to produce these beverage products and the bottlers will purchase from CCR (or other Company-authorized manufacturing bottlers) substantially all of the related finished products needed in order to service the customers in these territories.

Each CBA generally has a term of 10 years and is renewable, in most cases by the bottler and in some cases by the Company, indefinitely for successive additional terms of 10 years each. Under the CBA, the bottlers will make ongoing quarterly payments to the Company based on their gross profit in the refranchised territories throughout the term of the CBA, including renewals, in exchange for the grant of the exclusive territory rights.

Contemporaneously with the grant of these rights, the Company sold the distribution assets, certain working capital items, and the exclusive rights to distribute certain beverage brands not owned by the Company, but distributed by CCR, in each of these territories to the respective bottlers in exchange for cash. These rights include, where applicable, the recently acquired Monster distribution rights discussed above. During the years ended December 31, 2015 and December 31, 2014, cash proceeds from these sales totaled $362 million and $143 million, respectively. Included in the cash proceeds for the years ended December 31, 2015 and December 31, 2014 was $83 million and $42 million, respectively, from Coca-Cola Bottling Co. Consolidated, an equity method investee. Under the applicable accounting guidance, we were required to derecognize all of the tangible assets sold as well as the intangible assets transferred, including distribution rights, customer relationships and an allocated portion of goodwill related to these territories.

Additionally, in September 2015, the Company announced the formation of a new National Product Supply System ("NPSS") which will facilitate optimal operation of the U.S. product supply system. Under the NPSS, the Company and several of its existing independent producing bottlers will administer key national product supply activities for these bottlers, which currently represent approximately 95 percent of the U.S. produced volume. As part of the NPSS, it is anticipated that each of these bottlers will acquire certain production facilities from CCR in exchange for cash, subject to the parties reaching definitive agreements. The transition of these production facilities is anticipated to take place by the end of 2017.

We recognized noncash losses of $1,006 million and $799 million during the years ended December 31, 2015 and December 31, 2014, respectively. These losses primarily related to the derecognition of the intangible assets transferred or reclassified as held for sale, and were included in the line item other income (loss)—net in our consolidated statements of income. See further discussion of assets and liabilities held for sale below. We expect to recover the value of the intangible assets transferred to the bottlers under the CBAs through the future quarterly payments; however, as the payments for the territory rights are dependent on the bottlers' future gross profit in these territories, they are considered a form of contingent consideration.

There is diversity in practice as it relates to the accounting for contingent consideration by the seller. The seller can account for the future contingent payments received as a gain contingency, recognizing the amounts in the income statement only after the related contingencies are resolved and the gain is realized, which in this arrangement will be quarterly as the bottlers earn gross profit in the transferred territories. Alternatively, the seller can record a receivable for the contingent consideration at fair value on the date of sale and record any future differences between the payments received and this receivable in the income statement as they occur. We elected the gain contingency treatment since the quarterly payments will be received throughout the terms of the CBAs, including all subsequent renewals, regardless of the cumulative amount received as compared to the value of the intangible assets transferred.

Philippine Bottling Operations

On January 25, 2013, the Company sold a 51 percent interest in our Philippine bottling operations to Coca-Cola FEMSA, an equity method investee. The Company accounts for our remaining 49 percent ownership interest in the Philippine bottling operations under the equity method of accounting. As a result of this transaction, we remeasured our remaining investment in the Philippine bottling operations to fair value taking into consideration the sale price of the majority ownership interest. Coca-Cola FEMSA has an option to purchase our remaining ownership interest in the Philippine bottling operations at any time during the seven years following closing based on the initial purchase price plus a defined return. Coca-Cola FEMSA also has an option exercisable during the sixth year after closing to sell its ownership interest back to the Company at a price not to exceed the initial purchase price.

Brazilian Bottling Operations

On July 3, 2013, the Company combined our Brazilian bottling operations with an independent bottler in Brazil in a transaction involving a disposition of shares for cash and an exchange of shares for a 44 percent minority ownership interest in the newly combined entity, which was recorded at fair value. This combination resulted in the deconsolidation of our Brazilian bottling operations. As a result of this transaction, the Company recognized a gain of $615 million in the line item other income (loss)—net in our consolidated statement of income during the year ended December 31, 2013.

The owners of the majority interest have the option to acquire up to 24 percent of the new entity's outstanding shares from us at any time for a period of six years beginning December 31, 2013, based on an agreed-upon formula. In December 2014, the Company received notification that the owners of the majority interest had exercised their option to acquire from us a 10 percent interest in the entity's outstanding shares. During the year ended December 31, 2014, we recorded an estimated loss of $32 million as a result of the exercise price being lower than our carrying value. The transaction closed in January 2015, and the Company recorded an additional loss of $6 million during the year ended December 31, 2015, calculated based on the final option price. As a result of this transaction, the Company's ownership was reduced to 34 percent of the entity's outstanding shares. The owners of the majority interest have a remaining option to acquire an additional 14 percent interest of the entity's outstanding shares at any time through December 31, 2019, based on an agreed-upon formula.

Assets and Liabilities Held for Sale

North America Refranchising

As of December 31, 2015, the Company had entered into agreements to refranchise additional territories in North America. These territories met the criteria to be classified as held for sale. Additionally, to the extent that the parties have reached definitive agreements related to the transfer of production assets in conjunction with the new NPSS, and the related transfer is anticipated to close within a year, the related assets also met the criteria to be classified as held for sale. As such, we were required to record the related assets and liabilities at the lower of carrying value or fair value less any costs to sell based on the agreed-upon sale price. The Company expects these transactions to close at various times throughout 2016.

Coca-Cola European Partners

In August 2015, the Company entered into an agreement to merge our German bottling operations with Coca-Cola Enterprises, Inc. ("CCE") and Coca-Cola Iberian Partners SA ("CCIP") to create Coca-Cola European Partners ("CCEP"). At closing, the Company will own 18 percent of CCEP, which we anticipate accounting for as an equity method investment based on our equity ownership percentage, our representation on CCEP's Board of Directors and other governance rights. The Boards of Directors of the Company, CCE and CCIP have approved the transaction. The proposed merger is subject to approval by CCE's shareowners, receipt of regulatory clearances and other customary conditions. The merger is expected to close in the second quarter of 2016. As a result of this agreement, our German bottling operations met the criteria to be classified as held for sale as of December 31, 2015. We were not required to record the related assets and liabilities at fair value less any costs to sell because their fair value exceeded our carrying value.

Coca-Cola Beverages Africa Limited

In November 2014, the Company, SAB Miller plc, and Gutsche Family Investments entered into an agreement to combine the bottling operations of each of the parties' nonalcoholic ready-to-drink beverage businesses in Southern and East Africa. Upon completion of the proposed merger, the Company will have an ownership of 11 percent in the bottler which will be called Coca-Cola Beverages Africa Limited. The Company will also acquire or license several brands in exchange for cash as a result of the transaction. As of December 31, 2015, our South African bottling operations and related equity method investments met the criteria to be classified as held for sale, but we were not required to record these assets and liabilities at fair value less any costs to sell because their fair value exceeded our carrying value. The Company expects the transaction to close in the second quarter of 2016, subject to regulatory approval. Based on the proposed governance structure, the Company expects to account for its resulting interest in the new entity as an equity method investment.

The following table presents information related to the major classes of assets and liabilities that were classified as held for sale in our consolidated balance sheet (in millions):

	December 31, 2015	December 31, 2014
Cash, cash equivalents and short-term investments	$ 143	$ 30
Trade accounts receivable, less allowances	485	100
Inventories	276	54
Prepaid expenses and other assets	83	7
Equity method investments	92	141
Other assets	25	3
Property, plant and equipment—net	2,021	303
Bottlers' franchise rights with indefinite lives	1,020	410
Trademarks	—	43
Goodwill	333	46
Other intangible assets	115	36
Allowance for reduction of assets held for sale	(693)	(494)
Total assets	$3,900[1]	$679[3]
Accounts payable and accrued expenses	$ 712	$ 48
Current maturities of long-term debt	12	—
Accrued income taxes	4	—
Long-term debt	74	—
Other liabilities	79	6
Deferred income taxes	252	4
Total liabilities	$1,133[2]	$ 58[4]

[1] Consists of total assets relating to CCEP of $2,894 million, North America refranchising of $589 million, Coca-Cola Beverages Africa Limited of $398 million and other assets held for sale of $19 million, which are included in the Europe, North America, Eurasia and Africa, Bottling Investments and Corporate operating segments.

[2] Consists of total liabilities relating to CCEP of $924 million, North America refranchising of $123 million and Coca-Cola Beverages Africa Limited of $86 million, which are included in the Europe, North America, Eurasia and Africa, and Bottling Investments operating segments.

[3] Consists of total assets relating to North America refranchising of $223 million, Coca-Cola Beverages Africa Limited of $333 million, the Monster Transaction of $43 million and other assets held for sale of $80 million, which are included in the North America, Eurasia and Africa, Bottling Investments and Corporate operating segments.

[4] Consists of total liabilities relating to North America refranchising of $22 million and Coca-Cola Beverages Africa Limited of $36 million, which are included in the North America, Eurasia and Africa, and Bottling Investments operating segments.

We determined that the operations included in the table above did not meet the criteria to be classified as discontinued operations under the applicable guidance.

Note 6: Equity Method Investments

Our consolidated net income includes our Company's proportionate share of the net income or loss of our equity method investees. When we record our proportionate share of net income, it increases equity income (loss)—net in our consolidated statements of income and our carrying value in that investment. Conversely, when we record our proportionate share of a net loss, it decreases equity income (loss)—net in our consolidated statements of income and our carrying value in that investment. The Company's proportionate share of the net income or loss of our equity method investees includes significant operating and nonoperating items recorded by our equity method investees. These items can have a significant impact on the amount of equity income (loss)—net in our consolidated statements of income and our carrying value in those investments. Refer to Note 17 for additional information related to significant operating and nonoperating items recorded by our equity method investees. The carrying values of our equity method investments are also impacted by our proportionate share of items impacting the equity investee's AOCI.

We eliminate from our financial results all significant intercompany transactions, including the intercompany portion of transactions with equity method investees.

The Company's equity method investments include our ownership interests in Coca-Cola FEMSA, Coca-Cola Hellenic, Coca-Cola Amatil Limited and Monster. As of December 31, 2015, we owned approximately 28 percent, 24 percent, 29 percent and 17 percent, respectively, of these companies' outstanding shares. As of December 31, 2015, our investment in our equity method investees in the aggregate exceeded our proportionate share of the net assets of these equity method investees by $4,306 million. This difference is not amortized.

A summary of financial information for our equity method investees in the aggregate is as follows (in millions):

Year Ended December 31, [1]	2015	2014	2013
Net operating revenues	$47,498	$52,627	$53,038
Cost of goods sold	28,749	31,810	32,377
Gross profit	$18,749	$20,817	$20,661
Operating income	$ 4,483	$ 4,489	$ 4,380
Consolidated net income	$ 2,299	$ 2,440	$ 2,364
Less: Net income attributable to noncontrolling interests	65	74	62
Net income attributable to common shareowners	$ 2,234	$ 2,366	$ 2,302
Equity income (loss)—net	$ 489	$ 769	$ 602

[1] The financial information represents the results of the equity method investees during the Company's period of ownership.

December 31,	2015	2014
Current assets	$17,524	$16,184
Noncurrent assets	36,498	40,080
Total assets	$54,022	$56,264
Current liabilities	$11,820	$12,477
Noncurrent liabilities	14,467	16,657
Total liabilities	$26,287	$29,134
Equity attributable to shareowners of investees	$26,854	$26,363
Equity attributable to noncontrolling interests	881	767
Total equity	$27,735	$27,130
Company equity investment	$12,318	$ 9,947

Net sales to equity method investees, the majority of which are located outside the United States, were $8,984 million, $10,063 million and $9,178 million in 2015, 2014 and 2013, respectively. Total payments, primarily marketing, made to equity method investees were $1,380 million, $1,605 million and $1,807 million in 2015, 2014 and 2013, respectively. In addition, purchases of beverage products from equity method investees were $1,131 million, $381 million and $415 million in 2015, 2014 and 2013, respectively. The increase in purchases of beverage products in 2015 is primarily due to purchases from Monster. Refer to Note 2 for additional information.

If valued at the December 31, 2015 quoted closing prices of shares actively traded on stock markets, the value of our equity method investments in publicly traded bottlers would have exceeded our carrying value by $7,225 million.

Net Receivables and Dividends from Equity Method Investees

Total net receivables due from equity method investees were $1,399 million and $1,448 million as of December 31, 2015 and 2014, respectively. The total amount of dividends received from equity method investees was $367 million, $398 million and $401 million for the years ended December 31, 2015, 2014 and 2013, respectively. The amount of consolidated reinvested earnings that represents undistributed earnings of investments accounted for under the equity method as of December 31, 2015 was $3,389 million.

COST METHOD

2.62 COMCAST CORPORATION (DEC)
CONSOLIDATED BALANCE SHEET (in part)

December 31 (in millions, except share data)	2015	2014
Assets		
Current Assets:		
Cash and cash equivalents	$ 2,295	$ 3,910
Investments	106	602
Receivables, net	6,896	6,321
Programming rights	1,213	839
Other current assets	1,793	1,859
Total current assets	12,303	13,531
Film and television costs	5,855	5,727
Investments	3,224	3,135
Property and equipment, net	33,665	30,953
Franchise rights	59,364	59,364
Goodwill	32,945	27,316
Other intangible assets, net	16,946	16,980
Other noncurrent assets, net	2,272	2,180
Total assets	$166,574	$159,186

NOTES TO CONSOLIDATED FINANCIAL STATEMENTS (in part)

Note 7: Investments (in part)

December 31 (in millions)	2015	2014
Fair Value Method	$ 167	$ 662
Equity Method:		
The Weather Channel	—	335
Hulu	184	167
Other	494	517
	678	1,019
Cost Method:		
AirTouch	1,583	1,568
Other	902	488
	2,485	2,056
Total investments	3,330	3,737
Less: Current investments	106	602
Noncurrent investments	$3,224	$3,135

Investment Income (Loss), Net

Year Ended December 31 (in millions)	2015	2014	2013
Gains on sales and exchanges of investments, net	$ 12	$192	$ 484
Investment impairment losses	(59)	(50)	(29)
Unrealized gains on securities underlying prepaid forward sale agreements	42	66	1,601
Mark to market adjustments on derivative component of prepaid forward sale agreements and indexed debt instruments	(42)	(56)	(1,604)
Interest and dividend income	115	116	111
Other, net	13	28	13
Investment income (loss), net	$ 81	$296	$ 576

Equity Method (in part)

Hulu

In July 2013, we entered into an agreement to provide capital contributions totaling $247 million to Hulu, LLC ("Hulu"), which we had previously accounted for as a cost method investment. This represented an agreement to provide our first capital contribution to Hulu since we acquired our interest in it as part of our acquisition of a controlling interest in NBCUniversal Holdings in 2011 (the "NBCUniversal transaction"); therefore, we began to apply the equity method of accounting for this investment. The change in the method of accounting for this investment required us to recognize our proportionate share of Hulu's accumulated losses from the date of the NBCUniversal transaction through July 2013.

In 2015, 2014 and 2013, we recognized our proportionate share of losses of $106 million, $20 million and $142 million, respectively, related to our investment in Hulu.

Cost Method

We use the cost method to account for investments not accounted for under the fair value method or the equity method.

Vox and BuzzFeed

In September 2015, NBCUniversal made an additional investment in Vox Media, Inc. ("Vox Media") and acquired an interest in BuzzFeed, Inc. ("BuzzFeed") for $200 million each in cash. Vox Media is a digital media company comprised of eight distinct brands. BuzzFeed is a global media company that produces and distributes original news, entertainment and videos.

AirTouch

We hold two series of preferred stock of Verizon Americas, Inc., formerly known as AirTouch Communications, Inc. ("AirTouch"), a subsidiary of Verizon Communications Inc., which are redeemable in April 2020. As of both December 31, 2015 and 2014, the estimated fair value of the AirTouch preferred stock was $1.7 billion.

The dividend and redemption activity of the AirTouch preferred stock determines the dividend and redemption payments associated with substantially all of the preferred shares issued by one of our consolidated subsidiaries, which is a VIE. The subsidiary has three series of preferred stock outstanding with an aggregate redemption value of $1.75 billion. Substantially all of the AirTouch preferred stock is redeemable in April 2020 at a redemption value of $1.65 billion. As of both December 31, 2015 and 2014, the two series of redeemable subsidiary preferred shares were recorded at $1.6 billion, and those amounts are included in other noncurrent liabilities. As of both December 31, 2015 and 2014, the liability related to the redeemable subsidiary preferred shares had an aggregate estimated fair value of $1.7 billion. The estimated fair values of the AirTouch preferred stock and redeemable subsidiary preferred shares are based on Level 2 inputs that use pricing models whose inputs are derived primarily from or corroborated by observable market data through correlation or other means for substantially the full term of the financial instrument. The one nonredeemable series of subsidiary preferred shares was recorded at $100 million as of both December 31, 2015 and 2014, and those amounts are included in noncontrolling interests in our consolidated balance sheet. The carrying amount of the nonredeemable subsidiary preferred stock approximates its fair value.

Impairment Testing of Investments

We review our investment portfolio each reporting period to determine whether there are identified events or circumstances that would indicate there is a decline in the fair value that would be considered other than temporary. For our nonpublic investments, if there are no identified events or circumstances that would have a significant adverse effect on the fair value of the investment, then the fair value is not estimated. If an investment is deemed to have experienced an other-than-temporary decline below its cost basis, we reduce the carrying amount of the investment to its quoted or estimated fair value, as applicable, and establish a new cost basis for the investment. For our AFS and cost method investments, we record the impairment to investment income (loss), net. For our equity method investments, we record the impairment to other income (expense), net. In 2013, we recorded $249 million of impairment charges to our equity method investments, which primarily related to a regional sports cable network based in Houston, Texas.

FAIR VALUE

2.63 TEXAS INSTRUMENTS INCORPORATED (DEC)

CONSOLIDATED BALANCE SHEETS (in part)

(Millions of dollars, except share amounts)	December 31, 2015	December 31, 2014
Assets		
Current assets:		
Cash and cash equivalents	$ 1,000	$ 1,199
Short-term investments	2,218	2,342
Accounts receivable, net of allowances of ($7) and ($12)	1,165	1,246
Raw materials	109	101
Work in process	846	896
Finished goods	736	787
Inventories	1,691	1,784
Prepaid expenses and other current assets	1,000	850
Total current assets	7,074	7,421
Property, plant and equipment at cost	5,465	6,266
Accumulated depreciation	(2,869)	(3,426)
Property, plant and equipment, net	2,596	2,840
Long-term investments	221	224
Goodwill, net	4,362	4,362
Acquisition-related intangibles, net	1,583	1,902
Deferred income taxes	201	180
Capitalized software licenses, net	46	83
Overfunded retirement plans	85	127
Other assets	62	233
Total assets	$16,230	$17,372

NOTES TO FINANCIAL STATEMENTS (in part)

2. Basis of Presentation and Significant Accounting Policies and Practices (in part)

Significant Accounting Policies and Practices (in part)

Investments

We present investments on our Consolidated Balance Sheets as cash equivalents, short-term investments or long-term investments. Specific details are as follows:

- *Cash equivalents and short-term investments:* We consider investments in debt securities with maturities of 90 days or less from the date of our investment to be cash equivalents. We consider investments in debt securities with maturities beyond 90 days from the date of our investment as being available for use in current operations and include them in short-term investments. The primary objectives of our cash equivalent and short-term investment activities are to preserve capital and maintain liquidity while generating appropriate returns.
- *Long-term investments:* Long-term investments consist of mutual funds, venture capital funds and non-marketable equity securities.
- *Classification of investments:* Depending on our reasons for holding the investment and our ownership percentage, we classify our investments as either available for sale, trading, equity method or cost method, which are more fully described in Note 8. We determine cost or amortized cost, as appropriate, on a specific identification basis.

7. Financial Instruments and Risk Concentration (in part)

Financial Instruments

We hold derivative financial instruments such as forward foreign currency exchange contracts, the fair value of which was not material as of December 31, 2015. Our forward foreign currency exchange contracts outstanding as of December 31, 2015, had a notional value of $464 million to hedge our non-U.S. dollar net balance sheet exposures, including $175 million to sell Japanese yen and $139 million to sell euros.

Our investments in cash equivalents, short-term investments and certain long-term investments, as well as our postretirement plan assets and deferred compensation liabilities, are carried at fair value. The carrying values for other current financial assets and liabilities, such as accounts receivable and accounts payable, approximate fair value due to the short maturity of such instruments. The carrying value of our long-term debt approximates the fair value as measured using broker-dealer quotes, which are Level 2 inputs. See Note 8 for a description of fair value and the definition of Level 2 inputs.

8. Valuation of Debt and Equity Investments and Certain Liabilities

Debt and Equity Investments

We classify our investments as either available for sale, trading, equity method or cost method. Most of our investments are classified as available for sale.

Available-for-sale and trading securities are stated at fair value, which is generally based on market prices or broker quotes. See the fair-value discussion below. Unrealized gains and losses on available-for-sale securities are recorded as an increase or decrease, net of taxes, in AOCI on our Consolidated Balance Sheets. We record other-than-temporary impairments on available-for-sale securities in OI&E in our Consolidated Statements of Income.

We classify certain mutual funds as trading securities. These mutual funds hold a variety of debt and equity investments intended to generate returns that offset changes in certain deferred compensation liabilities. We record changes in the fair value of these mutual funds and the related deferred compensation liabilities in SG&A.

Our other investments are not measured at fair value but are accounted for using either the equity method or cost method. These investments consist of interests in venture capital funds and other non-marketable equity securities. Gains and losses from equity-method investments are reflected in OI&E based on our ownership share of the investee's financial results. Gains and losses on cost-method investments are recorded in OI&E when realized or when an impairment of the investment's value is warranted based on our assessment of the recoverability of each investment.

Details of our investments are as follows:

	December 31, 2015			December 31, 2014		
	Cash and Cash Equivalents	Short-Term Investments	Long-Term Investments	Cash and Cash Equivalents	Short-Term Investments	Long-Term Investments
Measured at Fair Value:						
Available-for-sale securities:						
Money market funds	$ 395	$ —	$ —	$ 522	$ —	$ —
Corporate obligations	132	285	—	97	390	—
U.S. Government agency and Treasury securities	245	1,933	—	365	1,952	—
Trading securities:						
Mutual funds	—	—	187	—	—	185
Total	772	2,218	187	984	2,342	185
Other Measurement Basis:						
Equity-method investments	—	—	25	—	—	27
Cost-method investments	—	—	9	—	—	12
Cash on hand	228	—	—	215	—	—
Total	$1,000	$2,218	$221	$1,199	$2,342	$224

At December 31, 2015 and 2014, unrealized gains and losses associated with our available-for-sale investments were not material. We did not recognize any credit losses related to available-for-sale investments for the years ended December 31, 2015, 2014 and 2013.

For the years ended December 31, 2015, 2014 and 2013, the proceeds from sales, redemptions and maturities of short-term available-for-sale investments were $2.89 billion, $2.97 billion and $4.25 billion, respectively. Gross realized gains and losses from these sales were not material.

The following table presents the aggregate maturities of investments in debt securities classified as available for sale at December 31, 2015:

Due	Fair Value
One year or less	$2,970
One to two years	20

Gross realized gains and losses from sales of long-term investments were not material for 2015, 2014 and 2013. Other-than-temporary declines and impairments in the values of these investments recognized in OI&E were not material in 2015, 2014 and 2013.

Fair-Value Considerations

We measure and report certain financial assets and liabilities at fair value on a recurring basis. Fair value is defined as the price that would be received to sell an asset or paid to transfer a liability (an exit price) in the principal or most advantageous market for the asset or liability in an orderly transaction between market participants on the measurement date.

The three-level hierarchy discussed below indicates the extent and level of judgment used to estimate fair-value measurements.

- Level 1—Uses unadjusted quoted prices that are available in active markets for identical assets or liabilities as of the reporting date.
- Level 2—Uses inputs other than Level 1 that are either directly or indirectly observable as of the reporting date through correlation with market data, including quoted prices for similar assets and liabilities in active markets and quoted prices in markets that are not active. Level 2 also includes assets and liabilities that are valued using models or other pricing methodologies that do not require significant judgment since the input assumptions used in the models, such as interest rates and volatility factors, are corroborated by readily observable data. We utilize a third-party data service to provide Level 2 valuations. We verify these valuations for reasonableness relative to unadjusted quotes obtained from brokers or dealers based on observable prices for similar assets in active markets.
- Level 3—Uses inputs that are unobservable, supported by little or no market activity and reflect the use of significant management judgment. These values are generally determined using pricing models that utilize management estimates of market participant assumptions. As of December 31, 2015 and 2014, we had no Level 3 assets or liabilities, other than certain assets held by our postretirement plans.

The following are our assets and liabilities that were accounted for at fair value on a recurring basis as of December 31, 2015 and 2014. These tables do not include cash on hand, assets held by our postretirement plans, or assets and liabilities that are measured at historical cost or any basis other than fair value.

	Fair Value December 31, 2015	Level 1	Level 2
Assets:			
Money market funds	$ 395	$ 395	$ —
Corporate obligations	417	—	417
U.S. Government agency and Treasury securities	2,178	1,828	350
Mutual funds	187	187	—
Total assets	$3,177	$2,410	$767
Liabilities:			
Deferred compensation	$ 198	$ 198	$ —
Total liabilities	$ 198	$ 198	$ —

	Fair Value December 31, 2014	Level 1	Level 2
Assets:			
Money market funds	$ 522	$ 522	$ —
Corporate obligations	487	—	487
U.S. Government agency and Treasury securities	2,317	1,762	555
Mutual funds	185	185	—
Total assets	$3,511	$2,469	$1,042
Liabilities:			
Deferred compensation	$ 202	$ 202	$ —
Total liabilities	$ 202	$ 202	$ —

Noncurrent Receivables

PRESENTATION

2.64 FASB ASC 210, *Balance Sheet*, states that the concept of current assets excludes receivables arising from unusual transactions that are not expected to be collected within 12 months, such as the sale of capital assets or loans or advances to affiliates, officers, or employees.

2.65 FASB ASC 825 includes noncurrent receivables as financial instruments. FASB ASC 820 requires disclosure of both the fair value and bases for estimating the fair value of noncurrent receivables, unless it is not practicable to estimate that value. However, FASB ASC 825-10-50-14 indicates that for trade receivables and payables, fair value disclosure is not required if the carrying amount approximates fair value.

LONG-TERM RECEIVABLES

2.66 SNAP-ON INCORPORATED (DEC)
CONSOLIDATED BALANCE SHEETS (in part)

	Fiscal Year End	
(Amounts in millions, except share data)	2015	2014
Assets		
Current assets:		
Cash and cash equivalents	$ 92.8	$ 132.9
Trade and other accounts receivable—net	562.5	550.8
Finance receivables—net	447.3	402.4
Contract receivables—net	82.1	74.5
Inventories—net	497.8	475.5
Deferred income tax assets	109.9	101.0
Prepaid expenses and other assets	106.3	121.5
Total current assets	1,898.7	1,858.6
Property and equipment—net	413.5	404.5
Deferred income tax assets	106.3	93.2
Long-term finance receivables—net	772.7	650.5
Long-term contract receivables—net	266.6	242.0
Goodwill	790.1	810.7
Other intangibles—net	195.0	203.3
Other assets	44.0	47.3
Total assets	$4,486.9	$4,310.1

NOTES TO CONSOLIDATED FINANCIAL STATEMENTS (in part)

Note 1: Summary of Accounting Policies (in part)

Financial services revenue: Snap-on also generates revenue from various financing programs that include: (i) installment sales and lease contracts arising from franchisees' customers and Snap-on's industrial and other customers for the purchase or lease of tools and diagnostic and equipment products on an extended-term payment plan; and (ii) business loans and vehicle leases to franchisees. These financing programs are offered through Snap-on's wholly owned finance subsidiaries. Financial services revenue consists primarily of interest income on finance and contract receivables and is recognized over the life of the underlying contracts, with interest computed primarily on the average daily balances of the underlying contracts.

The decision to finance through Snap-on or another financing entity is solely at the election of the customer. When assessing customers for potential financing, Snap-on considers various factors regarding ability to pay including customers' financial condition, collateral, debt-servicing ability, past payment experience, credit bureau information and proprietary credit models. For finance and contract receivables, Snap-on assesses these factors through the use of credit quality indicators consisting primarily of customer credit risk scores combined with internal credit risk grades, collection experience and other internal metrics.

Receivables and allowances for doubtful accounts: All trade, finance and contract receivables are reported on the Consolidated Balance Sheets at their outstanding principal balance adjusted for any charge-offs and net of allowances for doubtful accounts. Finance and contract receivables also include accrued interest and contract acquisition costs, net of contract acquisition fees.

Snap-on maintains allowances for doubtful accounts to absorb probable losses inherent in its portfolio of receivables. The allowances for doubtful accounts represent management's estimate of the losses inherent in the company's receivables portfolio based on ongoing assessments and evaluations of collectability and historical loss experience. In estimating losses inherent in each of its receivable portfolios (trade, finance and contract receivables), Snap-on uses historical loss experience rates by portfolio and applies them to a related aging analysis. Determination of the proper level of allowances by portfolio requires management to exercise significant judgment about the timing, frequency and severity of credit losses that could materially affect the provision for credit losses and, therefore, net earnings. The allowances for doubtful accounts takes into consideration numerous quantitative and qualitative factors, by receivable type, including historical loss experience, collection experience, delinquency trends, economic conditions and credit risk quality as follows:
  • Snap-on evaluates the collectability of receivables based on a combination of various financial and qualitative factors that may affect the customers' ability to pay. These factors may include customers' financial condition, collateral, debt-servicing ability, past payment experience and credit bureau information.

- For finance and contract receivables, Snap-on assesses quantitative and qualitative factors through the use of credit quality indicators consisting primarily of collection experience and other internal metrics as follows:
  — Collection experience—Snap-on conducts monthly reviews of credit and collection performance for each of its finance and contract receivable portfolios focusing on data such as delinquency trends, non-performing assets, and charge-off and recovery activity. These reviews allow for the formulation of collection strategies and potential collection policy modifications in response to changing risk profiles in the finance and contract receivable portfolios.
  — Other internal metrics—Snap-on maintains a system that aggregates credit exposure by customer, risk classification and geographical area, among other factors, to further monitor changing risk profiles.

Management performs detailed reviews of its receivables on a monthly and/or quarterly basis to assess the adequacy of the allowances based on historical and current trends and other factors affecting credit losses and to determine if any impairment has occurred. A receivable is impaired when it is probable that all amounts related to the receivable will not be collected according to the contractual terms of the agreement. Additions to the allowances for doubtful accounts are maintained through adjustments to the provision for credit losses, which are charged to current period earnings; amounts determined to be uncollectable are charged directly against the allowances, while amounts recovered on previously charged-off accounts increase the allowances. Net charge-offs include the principal amount of losses charged-off as well as charged-off interest and fees. Recovered interest and fees previously charged-off are recorded through the allowances for doubtful accounts and increase the allowances. Finance receivables are assessed for charge-off when an account becomes 120 days past due and are charged-off typically within 60 days of asset repossession. Contract receivables related to equipment leases are generally charged-off when an account becomes 150 days past due, while contract receivables related to franchise finance and van leases are generally charged-off up to 180 days past the asset return date. For finance and contract receivables, customer bankruptcies are generally charged-off upon notification that the associated debt is not being reaffirmed or, in any event, no later than 180 days past due.

Snap-on does not believe that its trade accounts, finance or contract receivables represent significant concentrations of credit risk because of the diversified portfolio of individual customers and geographical areas. See Note 3 for further information on receivables and allowances for doubtful accounts.

Other accrued liabilities: Supplemental balance sheet information for "Other accrued liabilities" as of 2015 and 2014 year end is as follows:

(Amounts in millions)	2015	2014
Income taxes	$ 28.5	$ 15.2
Accrued restructuring	4.1	6.5
Accrued warranty	16.4	17.3
Deferred subscription revenue	40.7	34.1
Accrued property, payroll and other taxes	39.7	41.8
Accrued selling and promotion expense	23.3	24.5
Other	143.6	158.9
Total other accrued liabilities	$296.3	$298.3

Note 3: Receivables

Trade and Other Accounts Receivable

Snap-on's trade and other accounts receivable primarily arise from the sale of tools and diagnostic and equipment products to a broad range of industrial and commercial customers and to Snap-on's independent franchise van channel on a non-extended-term basis with payment terms generally ranging from 30 to 120 days.

The components of Snap-on's trade and other accounts receivable as of 2015 and 2014 year end are as follows:

(Amounts in millions)	2015	2014
Trade and other accounts receivable	$579.2	$567.0
Allowances for doubtful accounts	(16.7)	(16.2)
Total trade and other accounts receivable—net	$562.5	$550.8

Finance and Contract Receivables

Snap-on Credit LLC ("SOC"), the company's financial services operation in the United States, originates extended-term finance and contract receivables on sales of Snap-on's products through the U.S. franchisee and customer network and to Snap-on's industrial and other customers; Snap-on's foreign finance subsidiaries provide similar financing internationally. Interest income on finance and contract receivables is included in "Financial services revenue" on the accompanying Consolidated Statements of Earnings.

Snap-on's finance receivables are comprised of extended-term installment payment contracts to both technicians and independent shop owners (i.e., franchisees' customers) to enable them to purchase tools and diagnostic and equipment products on an extended-term payment plan, generally with expected average payment terms of approximately three years. Contract receivables, with payment terms of up to 10 years, are comprised of extended-term installment payment contracts to a broad base of industrial and other customers worldwide, including shop owners, both independents and national chains, for their purchase of tools and diagnostic and equipment products. Contract receivables also include extended-term installment loans to franchisees to meet a number of financing needs, including working capital loans, loans to enable new franchisees to fund the purchase of the franchise and van leases. Finance and contract receivables are generally secured by the underlying tools and/or diagnostic or equipment products financed and, for installment loans to franchisees, other franchisee assets.

The components of Snap-on's current finance and contract receivables as of 2015 and 2014 year end are as follows:

(Amounts in millions)	2015	2014
Finance receivables, net of unearned finance charges of $16.9 million and $15.6 million, respectively	$460.7	$414.6
Contract receivables, net of unearned finance charges of $15.1 million and $13.9 million, respectively	83.5	75.5
Total	544.2	490.1
Allowances for doubtful accounts:		
Finance receivables	(13.4)	(12.2)
Contract receivables	(1.4)	(1.0)
Total	(14.8)	(13.2)
Total current finance and contract receivables—net	$529.4	$476.9
Finance receivables—net	$447.3	$402.4
Contract receivables—net	82.1	74.5
Total current finance and contract receivables—net	$529.4	$476.9

The components of Snap-on's finance and contract receivables with payment terms beyond one year as of 2015 and 2014 year end are as follows:

(Amounts in millions)	2015	2014
Finance receivables, net of unearned finance charges of $10.9 million and $9.9 million, respectively	$ 797.5	$671.0
Contract receivables, net of unearned finance charges of $21.1 million and $19.4 million, respectively	269.6	244.5
Total	1,067.1	915.5
Allowances for doubtful accounts:		
Finance receivables	(24.8)	(20.5)
Contract receivables	(3.0)	(2.5)
Total	(27.8)	(23.0)
Total long-term finance and contract receivables—net	$1,039.3	$892.5
Finance receivables—net	$772.7	$650.5
Contract receivables—net	266.6	242.0
Total long-term finance and contract receivables—net	$1,039.3	$892.5

Long-term finance and contract receivables installments, net of unearned finance charges, as of 2015 and 2014 year end are scheduled as follows:

(Amounts in millions) Due in Months:	2015 Finance Receivables	2015 Contract Receivables	2014 Finance Receivables	2014 Contract Receivables
13–24	$361.0	$65.1	$320.2	$58.7
25–36	252.8	56.6	212.0	50.1
37–48	137.8	46.5	106.2	41.7
49–60	45.9	35.0	32.6	31.6
Thereafter	—	66.4	—	62.4
Total	$797.5	$269.6	$671.0	$244.5

Delinquency is the primary indicator of credit quality for finance and contract receivables. Receivable balances are considered delinquent when contractual payments become 30 days past due.

Finance receivables are generally placed on nonaccrual status (nonaccrual of interest and other fees) (i) when a customer is placed on repossession status; (ii) upon receipt of notification of bankruptcy; (iii) upon notification of the death of a customer; or (iv) in other instances in which management concludes collectability is not reasonably assured. Finance receivables that are considered nonperforming include receivables that are on nonaccrual status and receivables that are generally more than 90 days past due.

Contract receivables are generally placed on nonaccrual status (i) when a receivable is more than 90 days past due or at the point a customer's account is placed on terminated status regardless of its delinquency status; (ii) upon notification of the death of a customer; or (iii) in other instances in which management concludes collectability is not reasonably assured. Contract receivables that are considered nonperforming include receivables that are on nonaccrual status and receivables that are generally more than 90 days past due.

The accrual of interest and other fees is resumed when the finance or contract receivable becomes contractually current and collection of all remaining contractual amounts due is reasonably assured. Finance and contract receivables are evaluated for impairment on a collective basis. A receivable is impaired when it is probable that all amounts related to the receivable will not be collected according to the contractual terms of the applicable agreement. Impaired receivables are covered by the company's finance and contract allowances for doubtful accounts reserves and are charged-off against the reserves when appropriate. As of 2015 and 2014 year end, there were $18.2 million and $15.5 million, respectively, of impaired finance receivables, and there were $1.7 million and $1.5 million, respectively, of impaired contract receivables.

It is the general practice of Snap-on's financial services business to not engage in contract or loan modifications. In limited instances, Snap-on's financial services business may modify certain impaired receivables in troubled debt restructurings. The amount and number of restructured finance and contract receivables as of 2015 and 2014 year end were immaterial to both the financial services portfolio and the company's results of operations and financial position.

The aging of finance and contract receivables as of 2015 and 2014 year end is as follows:

(Amounts in millions)	30–59 Days Past Due	60–90 Days Past Due	Greater Than 90 Days Past Due	Total Past Due	Total Not Past Due	Total	Greater Than 90 Days Past Due and Accruing
2015 year end:							
Finance receivables	$12.1	$7.6	$11.9	$31.6	$1,226.6	$1,258.2	$9.1
Contract receivables	1.3	0.7	1.3	3.3	349.8	353.1	0.3
2014 year end:							
Finance receivables	$ 9.8	$6.7	$10.4	$26.9	$1,058.7	$1,085.6	$7.7
Contract receivables	0.9	0.7	1.1	2.7	317.3	320.0	0.1

The amount of performing and nonperforming finance and contract receivables based on payment activity as of 2015 and 2014 year end is as follows:

(Amounts in millions)	2015 Finance Receivables	2015 Contract Receivables	2014 Finance Receivables	2014 Contract Receivables
Performing	$1,240.0	$351.4	$1,070.1	$318.5
Nonperforming	18.2	1.7	15.5	1.5
Total	$1,258.2	$353.1	$1,085.6	$320.0

The amount of finance and contract receivables on nonaccrual status as of 2015 and 2014 year end is as follows:

(Amounts in millions)	2015	2014
Finance receivables	$9.3	$7.9
Contract receivables	1.5	1.5

The following is a rollforward of the allowances for credit losses for finance and contract receivables for 2015 and 2014:

(Amounts in millions)	2015 Finance Receivables	2015 Contract Receivables	2014 Finance Receivables	2014 Contract Receivables
Allowances for credit losses:				
Beginning of year	$32.7	$3.5	$27.8	$3.3
Provision for bad debt expense	31.6	2.5	27.4	1.9
Charge-offs	(31.7)	(1.9)	(27.5)	(2.0)
Recoveries	5.9	0.4	5.1	0.4
Currency translation	(0.3)	(0.1)	(0.1)	(0.1)
End of year	$38.2	$4.4	$32.7	$3.5

The following is a rollforward of the combined allowances for doubtful accounts related to trade and other accounts receivable, as well as finance and contract receivables, for 2015, 2014 and 2013:

(Amounts in millions)	Balance at Beginning of Year	Expenses	Deductions[1]	Balance at End of Year
Allowances for doubtful accounts:				
2015	$52.4	$45.1	$(38.2)	$59.3
2014	46.0	41.7	(35.3)	52.4
2013	48.7	30.7	(33.4)	46.0

[1] Represents write-offs of bad debts, net of recoveries, and the net impact of currency translation.

Intangible Assets

RECOGNITION AND MEASUREMENT

2.67 FASB ASC 350, *Intangibles—Goodwill and Other*, specifies that goodwill and intangible assets that have indefinite lives are not subject to amortization but, rather, should be tested at least annually for impairment. In addition, FASB ASC 350 provides specific guidance on how to determine and measure impairment of goodwill and intangible assets not subject to amortization. Intangible assets that have finite useful lives should be amortized over their useful lives.

2.68 FASB ASC 350-20-35 delineates a comprehensive two-step approach to impairment testing of a reporting unit that includes goodwill. If an entity chooses, it may assess qualitative factors to determine whether it is more likely than not that the fair value of a reporting unit is less than its carrying amount; the entity may use this determination as a basis for deciding whether it is necessary to perform the two-step goodwill impairment test. The *more-likely-than-not threshold* is defined as having a likelihood of more than 50 percent. An entity has an unconditional option to bypass the qualitative assessment described for any reporting unit in any period and proceed directly to performing the first step of the goodwill impairment test. An entity may resume performing the qualitative assessment in any subsequent period.

2.69 If the entity decides that the quantitative impairment test is required, then the first step is to compare the fair value of a reporting unit with its carrying amount, including goodwill. When the carrying amount is greater than zero and its fair value exceeds its carrying amount, the entity should not consider the goodwill of the reporting unit to be impaired and the second step is unnecessary. When the carrying amount of the reporting unit exceeds its fair value, an entity should proceed to step two to measure the loss by comparing the implied fair value of the goodwill with its carrying value. When the carrying amount of the reporting unit is zero or negative, an entity should proceed to step two to measure an impairment loss, if any, when it is more likely than not that a goodwill impairment exists. An entity should evaluate whether there are adverse qualitative factors in making that "more likely than not" assessment. FASB ASC 350-20-35-3C (a)–(g) provide examples of such qualitative factors. If the carrying amount of reporting unit goodwill exceeds the implied fair value of that goodwill, an impairment loss should be recognized in an amount equal to that excess. The loss recognized cannot exceed the carrying amount of goodwill. After a goodwill impairment loss is recognized, the adjusted carrying amount of goodwill should be its new accounting basis. Subsequent reversal of a previously recognized goodwill impairment loss is prohibited once the measurement of that loss is recognized.

2.70 FASB 350-20-35 provides an accounting alternative for the subsequent measurement of goodwill for nonpublic companies. The goodwill relating to each business combination or reorganization event may be amortized on a straight-line basis over 10 years, or less than 10 years, if the entity demonstrated that another useful life is more important.

2.71 FASB ASC 350 also provides guidance on accounting for the cost of computer software developed or obtained for internal use and website development costs.

PRESENTATION

2.72 FASB ASC 350-20-45-1 requires that the aggregate amount of goodwill be presented as a separate line item in the balance sheet. Under FASB ASC 350-30-45-1, at minimum, all intangible assets should be aggregated and presented as a separate line item in the balance sheet. However, that requirement does not preclude presentation of individual intangible assets or classes of intangible assets as separate line items. Rule 5-02 of Regulation S-X also calls for separately stating each class of intangible assets in excess of 5 percent of total assets and for separate presentation of the amount of accumulated amortization of intangible assets.

DISCLOSURE

2.73 FASB ASC 350 requires additional disclosures for each period for which a balance sheet is presented, including information about gross carrying amounts and changes therein of goodwill and other intangible assets, accumulated amortization for amortizable assets, and estimates about intangible asset amortization expense for each of the five succeeding fiscal years. For intangibles, the balance sheet disclosures should be in total and by major intangible asset class.

PRESENTATION AND DISCLOSURE EXCERPTS

GOODWILL

2.74 KINDER MORGAN, INC. (DEC)
CONSOLIDATED BALANCE SHEETS (in part)

(In Millions, Except Share and Per Share Amounts)

Assets	December 31, 2015	December 31, 2014
Current assets		
Cash and cash equivalents	$ 229	$ 315
Accounts receivable, net	1,315	1,641
Fair value of derivative contracts	507	535
Inventories	407	459
Deferred income taxes	—	56
Other current assets	366	746
Total current assets	2,824	3,752
Property, plant and equipment, net	40,547	38,564
Investments	6,040	6,036
Goodwill	23,790	24,654
Other intangibles, net	3,551	2,302
Deferred income taxes	5,323	5,651
Deferred charges and other assets	2,029	2,090
Total Assets	$84,104	$83,049

NOTES TO CONSOLIDATED FINANCIAL STATEMENTS (in part)

2. Summary of Significant Accounting Policies (in part)

Goodwill

Goodwill is the cost of an acquisition in excess of the fair value of acquired assets and liabilities and is recorded as an asset on our balance sheet. Goodwill is not subject to amortization but must be tested for impairment at least annually. This test requires us to assign goodwill to an appropriate reporting unit and to determine if the implied fair value of the reporting unit's goodwill is less than its carrying amount.

We evaluate goodwill for impairment on May 31 of each year. For this purpose, we have seven reporting units as follows: (i) Products Pipelines (excluding associated terminals); (ii) Products Pipelines Terminals (evaluated separately from Products Pipelines for goodwill purposes); (iii) Natural Gas Pipelines Regulated; (iv) Natural Gas Pipelines Non-Regulated; (v) CO2; (vi) Terminals; and (vii) Kinder Morgan Canada. We also evaluate goodwill for impairment to the extent events or conditions indicate a risk of possible impairment during the interim periods subsequent to our annual impairment test. Generally, the evaluation of goodwill for impairment involves a two-step test, although under certain circumstance an initial qualitative evaluation may be sufficient to conclude that goodwill is not impaired without conducting the quantitative test.

Step 1 involves comparing the estimated fair value of each respective reporting unit to its carrying value, including goodwill. If the estimated fair value exceeds the carrying value, the reporting unit's goodwill is not considered impaired. If the carrying value exceeds the estimated fair value, step 2 must be performed to determine whether goodwill is impaired and, if so, the amount of the impairment. Step 2 involves calculating an implied fair value of goodwill by performing a hypothetical allocation of the estimated fair value of the reporting unit determined in step 1 to the respective tangible and intangible net assets of the reporting unit. The remaining implied goodwill is then compared to the actual carrying amount of the goodwill for the reporting unit. To the extent the carrying amount of goodwill exceeds the implied goodwill, the difference is the amount of the goodwill impairment.

A large portion of our goodwill is non-deductible for tax purposes, and as such, to the extent there are impairments, all or a portion of the impairment may not result in a corresponding tax benefit.

Refer to Note 8 for further information.

4. Impairments and Disposals (in part)

We recognized the following non-cash pre-tax impairment charges and losses (gains) on disposals of assets (in millions):

	Year Ended December 31,		
	2015	2014	2013
Natural Gas Pipelines			
Impairment of goodwill	$1,150	$—	$—
Impairments of long-lived assets[a]	79	—	—
Losses (gains) on disposals of long-lived assets	43	5	(28)
Impairment of equity investments[b]	26	—	65
CO2			
Impairments of long-lived assets[c]	606	243	—
Impairment at equity investee[d]	26	—	—
Terminals			
Impairments of long-lived assets[e]	188	—	—
Losses (gains) on disposals of long-lived assets	3	29	(73)
Impairment of equity investments[e]	4	—	—
Other (gains) losses on disposals of long-lived assets	—	(3)	3
Total losses (gains) on impairments and disposals	$2,125	$274	$(33)

[a] Represents $47 million and $32 million of project write-offs in our non-regulated midstream and regulated natural gas pipelines assets, respectively.

[b] 2015 amount is primarily related to an investment in a gathering and processing asset in Oklahoma and the 2013 amount is related to an investment in our regulated natural gas pipelines.

[c] 2015 amount includes (i) $399 million related to oil and gas properties and (ii) $207 million related to the certain CO2 source and transportation project write-offs. 2014 amount is primarily related to oil and gas properties.

[d] 2015 amount is a loss on impairment recorded by an investee and included in "Earnings from equity investments" in our accompanying consolidated statement of income.

[e] 2015 amount is primarily related to certain terminals with significant coal operations, including a $175 million impairment ($84 million net after-tax impact to common stockholders) of a terminal facility reflecting the impact of an agreement to adjust certain payment terms under a contract with a coal customer in February 2016.

Impairment of Goodwill

Due to recent events and conditions, interim goodwill impairment testing was performed during December 2015, which resulted in a partial impairment of goodwill in our Natural Gas Pipelines Non-Regulated reporting unit of approximately $1,150 million. See Note 8 for further information.

8. Goodwill

Changes in the amounts of our goodwill for each of the years ended December 31, 2015 and 2014 are summarized by reporting unit as follows (in millions):

	Natural Gas Pipelines Regulated	Natural Gas Pipelines Non-Regulated	CO2	Products Pipelines	Products Pipelines Terminals	Terminals	Kinder Morgan Canada	Total
Historical Goodwill	$17,527	$5,637	$1,528	$1,908	$221	$1,486	$610	$28,917
Accumulated impairment losses	(1,643)	(447)	—	(1,197)	(70)	(679)	(377)	(4,413)
December 31, 2013	15,884	5,190	1,528	711	151	807	233	24,504
Acquisitions[a]	—	82	—	—	—	89	—	171
Currency translation	—	—	—	—	—	—	(19)	(19)
Divestiture	—	—	—	—	—	(2)	—	(2)
December 31, 2014	15,884	5,272	1,528	711	151	894	214	24,654
Acquisitions[b]	—	93	—	217	—	11	—	321
Currency translation	—	—	—	—	—	—	(35)	(35)
Impairment	—	(1,150)	—	—	—	—	—	(1,150)
December 31, 2015	$15,884	$4,215	$1,528	$928	$151	$905	$179	$23,790

[a] 2014 includes $82 million related to the May 2013 Copano acquisition in Natural Gas Pipelines Non-Regulated and $89 million related to Terminals' acquisitions of APT tankers in January 2014 and Crowley tankers in November 2014, as discussed in Note 3.

[b] 2015 includes $93 million and $217 million, respectively, related to the February 2015 acquisition of Hiland by Natural Gas Pipelines Non-Regulated and Products Pipelines, and $7 million related to the February 2015 acquisition of Vopak terminal assets by Terminals, all of which are discussed in Note 3.

Refer to Note 2 "Summary of Significant Accounting Policies— *Goodwill*" for a description of our accounting for goodwill and Note 4 for further discussion regarding impairments.

We determined the fair value of each reporting unit as of May 31, 2015, based primarily on a market approach utilizing a median dividend/distribution yield of comparable companies. The value of each reporting unit was determined on a stand-alone basis from the perspective of a market participant and represented the price estimated to be received in a sale of the reporting unit in an orderly transaction between market participants at the measurement date. The results of our annual test during the second quarter indicated fair value in excess of carrying value for each of our reporting units. We noted no significant events or conditions during the third quarter of 2015 that would have affected the conclusions from our annual assessment in the prior quarter.

During the month of December 2015, consistent with decreases in certain market indices which track the market sectors in which we operate, the Company's market capitalization decreased by approximately 36% after experiencing declines earlier in the quarter. During the fourth quarter 2015, many energy companies also indicated their dividends/distributions may be impacted by the ongoing effect of commodity prices on market conditions in the energy sector. As discussed above, our step 1 test performed as of May 31, 2015, used market valuations primarily based on dividend/distribution yields. This indicated that our prior step 1 valuations required re-evaluation. Based on these indicators and related factors, we conducted an interim test of the recoverability of goodwill as of December 31, 2015.

Our step 1 test as of December 31, 2015, utilized both a market approach and income approach to estimate the fair values of our reporting units. The market approach was based on enterprise value (EV) to estimated EBITDA multiples. We believe these multiples appropriately reflect fair value for purposes of our step 1 goodwill impairment test because EV/EBITDA is not dependent on dividend/distribution policy, capital structure or tax profile. For our Natural Gas Pipelines Regulated and Non-Regulated and our CO2 reporting units, we also conducted a discounted cash flow analysis (income approach) to evaluate the fair value of these reporting units to provide additional indication of fair value based on the present value of cash flows these reporting units are expected to generate in the future. We weighted the market and income approaches for these reporting units to arrive at an estimated fair value of these respective reporting units giving more weighting on the income approach and less on the market approach as we believed the values indicated using the income approach are more representative of the value that could be received from a market participant. With the exception of our Natural Gas Pipelines Non-Regulated reporting unit, each of our reporting units indicated a fair value in excess of their respective carrying values. The amount of excess fair value over the carrying value ranged from approximately 3% for our Natural Gas Pipelines Regulated reporting unit to 104% for our Products Pipelines Terminals. If the fair value of the Natural Gas Pipelines Regulated reporting unit decreased by approximately 3%, it could indicate a possible failure of the step 1 test. The primary assumptions in our step 1 market approach test include the following:

- We selected a peer group of midstream companies with large market capitalizations with comparable operations, economic characteristics, and assets which generally include significant holdings of interstate transmission pipelines, midstream gathering and processing systems, and/or terminal operations. We use this peer group for all of our reporting units with the exception of our CO2 reporting unit. We estimated the median enterprise value to EBITDA multiple to be approximately 12.7 x, without consideration of any control premium.
- For our CO2 reporting unit, we utilized a group of large independent oil and gas exploration and production companies which generally have operations similar to ours and include assets in the Permian basin where we operate and may have enhanced oil recovery operations similar to ours. We estimated the median enterprise value to EBITDA multiple for this peer group to be approximately 7.9 x, without consideration of any control premium.
- In calculating the market multiples, we used estimates of enterprise value as of December 31, 2015, and consensus estimates of the 2015 EBITDA for each company in the peer group obtained from a third party provider of financial data. Estimates of enterprise value were calculated based on market capitalization plus net debt utilizing the most recent data available as of December 31, 2015. EV/EBITDA multiples are sensitive to changes in the components that comprise the ratio, including EBITDA, market capitalizations, and debt of the peer group companies.
- We assessed the reasonableness of the control premium implied by the above market valuations as the market multiples include equity values on a non-controlling basis. As such, we considered the implied control premium as part of our reconciliation of our total reporting unit estimated fair value to our market capitalization which indicated an implied control premium of 34%, which we considered to be reasonable.

For our CO2 reporting unit, the above market approach indicated a fair value of approximately 7.9 x EBITDA. Management concluded because of current commodity price conditions, the fair value based on the market approach should be given partial weighting with a discounted cash flow analysis. The discounted cash flow analysis indicated a fair value of approximately 4.1 x EBITDA. Based on a weighting of the market and income approaches, we determined a fair value of the CO2 reporting unit of approximately 5.1 x EBITDA. If the fair value of the CO2 reporting unit decreased by approximately 12%, this could indicate a possible impairment of goodwill requiring a step 2 analysis.

Applying the market approach to our Natural Gas Pipeline Non-Regulated reporting unit indicated an 18% deficit of fair value as compared to carrying value. We also applied an income approach to this reporting unit, which indicated a deficit of fair value of approximately 4% as compared to the carrying value. The results of our step 1 test of our Natural Gas Pipelines Non-Regulated reporting unit indicated that our carrying value exceeded the fair value thereby requiring us to perform a step 2 evaluation. The primary assumptions in our step 1 income approach for this reporting unit include the following:

- Based on the weighted-average cost of capital of the peer group, we determined the appropriate rate at which to discount the cash flows is 8%. Each 100 basis points change in the discount rate changes the estimated fair value by approximately 5%.
- We used a five -year forward commodity price curve which assumed $38 crude and $2.50 natural gas in 2016 gradually increasing over the following five years to $65 and $3.50, respectively, and then remaining flat. Management developed this price curve based on the year-end NYMEX price curve and a third party median consensus five year forward price curve.
- We estimated cash flows based on 6 years of projections and applied exit multiples, ranging from 10x to 15x based on management's expectations of those that would be applied by a market participant and market transactions for comparable assets, to year 6 cash flows. These cash flows have various assumptions on volumes and prices based on management's expectations for each underlying component asset within the reporting unit.
- We estimated ethane fractionation spreads based on the relationship between ethane and natural gas prices. Our estimates assumed $(0.01) for 2016-2017, increasing to $0.15 in 2018 through 2021 based on a trailing five-year average spreads as management expects demand to increase commensurate with expected petrochemical capacity and export facilities coming online around that time.
- Consistent with how we evaluate potential acquisitions and we believe a market participant would do, we assumed a certain amount of capital expenditure, including for projects that are already in progress, and consistent with historical levels as adjusted for commodity prices assumptions and customer activity. We assumed an approximate 12% return on this invested capital beginning in the years the assets are expected to be placed in service.

After considering the market and income approaches, we determined the $19.0 billion carrying value of this reporting unit exceeded the estimated fair value of $17.2 billion, and therefore conducted a step 2 analysis. The fair value was estimated based on a weighting of the market and income approaches for this reporting unit. This implies an EBITDA valuation of approximately 14.0 x. Management believes this is a reasonable estimate of fair value based on comparable sales transactions and the fact that it implies a reasonable control premium at the reporting unit level.

Below is a hypothetical allocation of the fair value to the assets and liabilities of this reporting unit, including goodwill. The amount of implied goodwill is then compared to the carrying value of goodwill to determine the amount of impairment (in millions).

Allocation of Fair Value:	
Working capital, net	$ 232
Property, plant and equipment	9,627
Other intangible assets	3,121
Other liabilities, net	(7)
Goodwill	4,215
Estimated Reporting Unit Fair Value	$17,188
Prior carrying amount of goodwill	$ 5,365
Goodwill impairment	$ 1,150

The key assumptions used in determining the fair value of the assets and liabilities of the reporting unit are as follows:

- Working capital and other liabilities were assumed to have fair values that approximate carrying value as these generally relate to monetary assets and liabilities that settle in the short-term, derivative positions that are recorded at fair value, and inventory which has been subjected to lower of cost or market adjustments in a declining commodity price environment.
- With respect to property, plant and equipment, and other intangibles, the company based its determination of fair values on previously completed fair value studies conducted for these assets as updated for developments subsequent to the date of the initial studies.
- The fair value allocation assumed the reporting unit would be sold in a taxable transaction.

The result of our step 2 analysis was a partial impairment of goodwill in our Natural Gas Pipelines Non-Regulated reporting unit of approximately $1,150 million. The above fair value estimates are based on Level 3 Inputs of the fair value hierarchy.

The sustained decrease and the long-term outlook in commodity prices have adversely impacted our customers and their future capital and operating plans. A continued or prolonged period of lower commodity prices could result in further deterioration of market multiples, comparable sales transactions prices, weighted average costs of capital, and our cash flow estimates. A significant change to any one or combination of these factors would result in a change to the reporting unit fair values discussed above which could lead to further impairment charges. This would negatively impact our estimates of the fair values of our reporting units and could cause impairments of long-lived assets, equity method investments, and/or goodwill. Such non-cash impairments from one or both, or any, of these reportable units could have a significant effect on our results of operations, which would be recognized in the period in which the carrying value exceeds fair value.

TRADENAMES

2.75 TUPPERWARE BRANDS CORPORATION (DEC)

CONSOLIDATED BALANCE SHEETS (in part)

(In millions, except share amounts)	December 26, 2015	December 27, 2014
Assets		
Cash and cash equivalents	$ 79.8	$ 77.0
Accounts receivable, less allowances of $32.7 and $34.5, respectively	142.7	168.1
Inventories	254.6	306.0
Non-trade amounts receivable, net	45.5	61.8
Prepaid expenses and other current assets	27.9	21.6
Total current assets	550.5	634.5
Deferred income tax benefits, net	524.9	525.3
Property, plant and equipment, net	253.6	290.3
Long-term receivables, less allowances of $11.2 and $13.1, respectively	13.2	17.3
Tradenames, net	82.7	104.2
Other intangible assets, net	—	1.5
Goodwill	146.3	164.7
Other assets, net	27.0	32.0
Total assets	$1,598.2	$1,769.8

NOTES TO THE CONSOLIDATED FINANCIAL STATEMENTS (in part)

Note 1: Summary of Significant Accounting Policies (in part)

Intangible Assets. Intangible assets are recorded at their fair market values at the date of acquisition and definite-lived intangibles are amortized over their estimated useful lives. The intangible assets included in the Company's Consolidated Financial Statements at December 26, 2015 and December 27, 2014 were related to the acquisition of the Sara Lee direct-to-consumer businesses in December 2005. The weighted average estimated useful lives of the Company's intangible assets were as follows:

	Weighted Average Estimated Useful Life
Indefinite-lived tradenames	Indefinite
Definite-lived tradenames	10 years
Sales force relationships	6–10 years

The Company's indefinite-lived tradename intangible assets are evaluated for impairment annually similarly to goodwill. The annual process for assessing the carrying value of indefinite-lived tradename intangible assets begins with a qualitative assessment that is similar to the assessment performed for goodwill. When the Company determines it is appropriate, the quantitative impairment evaluation for the Company's indefinite-lived tradenames involves comparing the estimated fair value of the assets to the carrying amounts, to determine if fair value is lower and a write-down required. If the carrying amount of a tradename exceeds its estimated fair value, an impairment charge is recognized in an amount equal to the excess. The fair value of these assets is determined using the relief from royalty method, which is a form of the income approach. In this method, the value of the asset is calculated by selecting royalty rates, which estimate the amount a company would be willing to pay for the use of the asset. These rates are applied to the Company's projected revenue, tax affected and discounted to present value using an appropriate rate.

The Company's definite-lived intangible assets consist of the value of the acquired independent sales forces, as well as the Fuller tradename since August 2013. The Fuller tradename is being amortized over the period that it is estimated that the tradename will contribute directly to the Company's revenue. The sales force relationships have been fully amortized as of the end of 2015. Definite-lived intangible assets are reviewed for impairment in a similar manner as property, plant and equipment as discussed above. Amortization related to definite-lived intangible assets is included in DS&A on the Consolidated Statements of Income.

Intangible assets are further discussed in Note 6 to the Consolidated Financial Statements.

Note 6: Goodwill and Intangible Assets (in part)

The Company's goodwill and intangible assets relate primarily to the December 2005 acquisition of the direct-to-consumer businesses of Sara Lee Corporation.

In the third quarters of 2015 and 2014, the Company completed the annual impairment assessments for all of its reporting units and indefinite-lived intangible assets, concluding there were no impairments. The Company only considers the goodwill balances of

$88.6 million and $23.5 million associated with the Fuller Mexico and NaturCare reporting units, respectively, to be significant relative to total equity.

The Company performed in 2015, step 1 impairment evaluations for the goodwill associated with the Fuller Mexico and NaturCare reporting units as prescribed under ASC 350, *Intangibles—Goodwill and Other*. The fair value analysis for Fuller Mexico and NaturCare were completed using a combination of the income and market approach with a 75 percent weighting on the income approach. The significant assumptions used in the income approach included estimates regarding future operations and the ability to generate cash flows, including projections of revenue, costs, utilization of assets and capital requirements. The income approach, or discounted cash flow approach, also requires an estimate as to the appropriate discount rate to be used for each entity. The most sensitive estimate in this valuation is the projection of operating cash flows, as these provide the basis for the estimate of fair market value. The Company's cash flow model used a forecast period of 10 years and a terminal value. The growth rates were determined by reviewing historical results of the respective operating units and the historical results of the Company's other similar business units, along with the expected contribution from growth strategies being implemented in the respective reporting units. The market approach relies on an analysis of publicly-traded companies similar to Tupperware and deriving a range of revenue and profit multiples. The publicly-traded companies used in the market approach were selected based on their having similar product lines of consumer goods, beauty products and/or companies using a direct-to-consumer distribution method. The resulting multiples were then applied to the respective reporting units to determine fair value.

The significant assumptions for the Fuller Mexico step 1 analysis included annual revenue growth rates ranging from negative 2.0 to positive 5.0 percent with an average growth rate of 3.0 percent, including a 3.0 percent growth rate used in calculating the terminal value. The discount rate used for Fuller Mexico was 14.6 percent. As the forecasted results of Fuller Mexico were below the expectations for the step 1 analysis done in 2014, the amount by which the estimated fair value of the Fuller Mexico reporting unit exceeded its carrying value, at 13 percent, was smaller in the third quarter of 2015 than in the 2014 assessment. This decrease reflected lower than expected additions of sales force members in light of high field manager turnover. Along with a difficult competitive environment, this led to worse 2015 operating performance than foreseen in 2014. This was partially offset by a lower discount rate and a lower entity carrying value from amortization of the definite lived Fuller tradename asset that began in the third quarter of 2013. Though the estimated fair value of the reporting unit exceeded its carrying value in the annual assessment, a smaller sales force size and/or operating performance significantly below current expectations, including changes in projected future revenue, profitability and cash flow, as well as higher working capital, interest rates or cost of capital, could have a further negative effect on the fair value of the reporting unit and therefore reduce the fair value below the carrying value. This could result in recording an impairment to the goodwill of Fuller Mexico.

The significant assumptions for the NaturCare step 1 analysis included annual revenue changes ranging from 3.0 to 5.0 percent with an average growth rate of 4.0 percent, as well as a 3.0 percent growth rate used in calculating the terminal value. The discount rate used for Naturcare was 10.0 percent. The estimated fair value of the NaturCare reporting unit exceeded the carrying value by 130 percent. Based on the Company's evaluation of the assumptions and sensitivities associated with the step 1 analysis for NaturCare, the Company concluded that the fair value substantially exceeded its carrying value as of the end of the third quarter of 2015.

In August of 2013, the Company concluded it should reclassify its Fuller tradename from indefinite-lived to definite-lived. This conclusion was primarily reached in light of a long-term transition in the Fuller Mexico business to a new brand name. The reclassification of the Fuller tradename from an indefinite-lived to definite-lived asset triggered an impairment review similar to that performed during an annual assessment, as described above. The results of the impairment evaluation demonstrated that the estimated fair value of the Fuller tradename exceeded its carrying value. As a result of this transition, the Company has estimated that the Fuller tradename has a 10 year useful life with amortization to be recorded on a straight-line basis. Amortization expense recorded in 2015, 2014 and 2013 related to the Fuller tradename was $8.8 million, $10.2 million, and $3.4 million, respectively.

The gross carrying amount and accumulated amortization of the Company's intangible assets, other than goodwill, were as follows:

(In millions)	December 26, 2015		
	Gross Carrying Value	Accumulated Amortization	Net
Indefinite-lived tradenames	$ 20.1	$ —	$20.1
Definite-lived tradenames	81.7	19.1	62.6
Sales force relationships	46.6	46.6	—
Total intangible assets	$148.4	$65.7	$82.7

(In millions)	December 27, 2014		
	Gross Carrying Value	Accumulated Amortization	Net
Indefinite-lived tradenames	$ 22.2	$ —	$ 22.2
Definite-lived tradenames	94.6	12.6	82.0
Sales force relationships	49.6	48.1	1.5
Total intangible assets	$166.4	$60.7	$105.7

A summary of the identifiable intangible asset account activity is as follows:

(In millions)	Year Ended	
	December 26, 2015	December 27, 2014
Beginning balance	$166.4	$184.4
Effect of changes in exchange rates	(18.0)	(18.0)
Ending balance	$148.4	$166.4

Amortization expense was $10.2 million, $11.8 million and $4.8 million in 2015, 2014 and 2013, respectively. The estimated annual amortization expense associated with the above intangibles for each of the five succeeding years is $8.2 million.

CUSTOMER RELATIONSHIPS

2.76 CHARTER COMMUNICATIONS, INC. (DEC)
CONSOLIDATED BALANCE SHEETS (in part)

(dollars in millions, except share data)

	December 31, 2015	December 31, 2014
Assets		
Current Assets:		
Cash and cash equivalents	$ 5	$ 3
Accounts receivable, less allowance for doubtful accounts of $21 and $22, respectively	279	285
Prepaid expenses and other current assets	61	57
Total current assets	345	345
Restricted Cash and Cash Equivalents	22,264	7,111
Investment in Cable Properties:		
Property, plant and equipment, net of accumulated depreciation of $6,518 and $5,484, respectively	8,345	8,373
Franchises	6,006	6,006
Customer relationships, net	856	1,105
Goodwill	1,168	1,168
Total investment in cable properties, net	16,375	16,652
Other Noncurrent Assets	332	280
Total assets	$39,316	$24,388

NOTES TO CONSOLIDATED FINANCIAL STATEMENTS (in part)

(dollars in millions, except share or per share data or where indicated)

6. Franchises, Goodwill and Other Intangible Assets (in part)

Customer relationships are recorded at fair value as of the date acquired less accumulated amortization. Customer relationships, for valuation purposes, represent the value of the business relationship with existing customers (less the anticipated customer churn), and are calculated by projecting the discrete future after-tax cash flows from these customers, including the right to deploy and market additional services to these customers. The present value of these after-tax cash flows yields the fair value of the customer relationships. The use of different valuation assumptions or definitions of franchises or customer relationships, such as our inclusion of the value of selling additional services to our current customers within customer relationships versus franchises, could significantly impact our valuations and any resulting impairment. Customer relationships are amortized on an accelerated sum of years' digits method over useful lives of 8–15 years based on the period over which current customers are expected to generate cash flows. The Company periodically evaluates the remaining useful lives of its customer relationships to determine whether events or circumstances warrant revision to the remaining periods of amortization. Customer relationships are evaluated for impairment upon the occurrence of events or changes in circumstances indicating that the carrying amount of an asset may not be recoverable. Customer relationships are deemed impaired when the carrying value exceeds the projected undiscounted future cash flows associated with the customer relationships. No impairment of customer relationships was recorded in the years ended December 31, 2015, 2014 or 2013.

As of December 31, 2015 and 2014, indefinite lived and finite-lived intangible assets are presented in the following table:

| | December 31, | | | | | |
| | 2015 | | | 2014 | | |
	Gross Carrying Amount	Accumulated Amortization	Net Carrying Amount	Gross Carrying Amount	Accumulated Amortization	Net Carrying Amount
Indefinite lived intangible assets:						
Franchises	$6,006	$ —	$6,006	$6,006	$ —	$6,006
Goodwill	1,168	—	1,168	1,168	—	1,168
Trademarks	159	—	159	159	—	159
Other intangible assets	4	—	4	4	—	4
	$7,337	$ —	$7,337	$7,337	$ —	$7,337
Finite-lived intangible assets:						
Customer relationships	$2,616	$1,760	$ 856	$2,616	$1,511	$1,105
Other intangible assets	173	82	91	151	60	91
	$2,789	$1,842	$ 947	$2,767	$1,571	$1,196

Amortization expense related to customer relationships and other intangible assets for the years ended December 31, 2015, 2014 and 2013 was $271 million, $299 million and $299 million, respectively.

The Company expects amortization expense on its finite-lived intangible assets will be as follows.

2016	$237
2017	204
2018	169
2019	133
2020	95
Thereafter	109
	$947

Actual amortization expense in future periods could differ from these estimates as a result of new intangible asset acquisitions or divestitures, changes in useful lives, impairments and other relevant factors.

TECHNOLOGY

2.77 AUTODESK, INC. (JAN)
CONSOLIDATED BALANCE SHEETS (in part)

(In millions, except per share data)

	January 31, 2015	January 31, 2014
Assets		
Current assets:		
Cash and cash equivalents	$1,410.6	$1,853.0
Marketable securities	615.8	414.1
Accounts receivable, net	458.9	423.7
Deferred income taxes, net	85.1	56.8
Prepaid expenses and other current assets	100.9	87.4
Total current assets	2,671.3	2,835.0
Marketable securities	273.0	277.3
Computer equipment, software, furniture, and leasehold improvements, net	159.2	130.3
Developed technologies, net	86.5	63.1
Goodwill	1,456.2	1,009.9
Deferred income taxes, net	100.0	131.1
Other assets	167.6	148.3
Total assets	$4,913.8	$4,595.0

(Tables in millions of dollars, except per share data, unless otherwise indicated)

1. Business and Summary of Significant Accounting Policies (in part)

Other Intangible Assets, Net

Other intangible assets include developed technologies, customer relationships, trade names, patents, user lists, and the related accumulated amortization. These assets are shown as "Developed technologies, net" and as part of "Other assets" in the Consolidated Balance Sheet. The majority of Autodesk's other intangible assets are amortized to expense over the estimated economic life of the product, which ranges from one to ten years. Amortization expense for developed technologies, customer relationships, trade names, patents, and user lists was $92.9 million in fiscal 2015, $80.7 million in fiscal 2014 and $82.0 million in fiscal 2013.

Other intangible assets and related accumulated amortization at January 31 were as follows:

	2015	2014
Developed technologies, at cost	$538.4	$462.4
Customer relationships, trade names, patents, and user lists, at cost[1]	348.9	268.1
	887.3	730.5
Less: Accumulated amortization	(715.4)	(626.2)
Other intangible assets, net	$171.9	$104.3

[1] Included as a net balance in "Other assets" in the Consolidated Balance Sheet. Customer relationships and trade names include the effects of foreign currency translation.

The weighted average amortization period for developed technologies, customer relationships, and trade names during fiscal 2015 was 4.2 years. Expected future amortization expense for developed technologies, customer relationships, trade names, patents, and user lists for each of the fiscal years ended thereafter is as follows:

	Fiscal Year Ended January 31,
2016	$ 73.2
2017	49.7
2018	24.0
2019	15.5
2020	5.3
Thereafter	4.2
Total	$171.9

SOFTWARE

2.78 FIDELITY NATIONAL INFORMATION SERVICES, INC. (DEC)
CONSOLIDATED BALANCE SHEETS (in part)

(In millions, except per share amounts)

	2015	2014
Assets		
Current assets:		
Cash and cash equivalents	$ 687.6	$ 492.8
Settlement deposits	370.9	393.9
Trade receivables, net	1,701.2	1,126.4
Settlement receivables	161.9	153.7
Other receivables	196.6	31.5
Due from Brazilian venture partner	30.5	33.6
Prepaid expenses and other current assets	262.9	167.0
Deferred income taxes	99.8	67.4
Assets held for sale	—	6.8
Total current assets	3,511.4	2,473.1
Property and equipment, net	610.7	483.3
Goodwill	14,744.7	8,877.6
Intangible assets, net	5,159.2	1,268.0
Computer software, net	1,583.6	893.4
Deferred contract costs	253.0	213.2
Other noncurrent assets	406.2	311.9
Total assets	$26,268.8	$14,520.5

(2) Summary of Significant Accounting Policies (in part)

(j) Computer Software

Computer software includes software acquired in business combinations, purchased software and capitalized software development costs. Software acquired in business combinations is generally valued using the relief-from-royalty method, a Level 3 type measurement. Purchased software is recorded at cost and amortized using the straight-line method over its estimated useful life and software acquired in business combinations is recorded at its fair value and amortized using straight-line or accelerated methods over its estimated useful life, ranging from five to 10 years.

The capitalization of software development costs is governed by FASB ASC Subtopic 985-20 if the software is to be sold, leased or otherwise marketed, or by FASB ASC Subtopic 350-40 if the software is for internal use. After the technological feasibility of the software has been established (for software to be marketed), or at the beginning of application development (for internal-use software), software development costs, which primarily include salaries and related payroll costs and costs of independent contractors incurred during development, are capitalized. Research and development costs incurred prior to the establishment of technological feasibility (for software to be marketed), or prior to application development (for internal-use software), are expensed as incurred. Software development costs are amortized on a product-by-product basis commencing on the date of general release (for software to be marketed) or the date placed in service (for internal-use software). Software development costs for software to be marketed are amortized using the greater of (1) the straight-line method over its estimated useful life, which ranges from three to 10 years, or (2) the ratio of current revenues to total anticipated revenues over its useful life.

(10) Computer Software

Computer software as of December 31, 2015 and 2014 consists of the following (in millions):

	2015	2014
Software from business acquisitions	$1,188.8	$ 519.2
Capitalized software development costs	984.7	953.1
Purchased software	126.0	120.3
Computer software	2,299.5	1,592.6
Accumulated amortization	(715.9)	(699.2)
Computer software, net of accumulated amortization	$1,583.6	$ 893.4

Amortization expense for computer software was $228.6 million, $209.7 million and $195.8 million for the years ended December 31, 2015, 2014 and 2013, respectively.

FRANCHISE RIGHTS

2.79 COMCAST CORPORATION (DEC)
CONSOLIDATED BALANCE SHEET (in part)

December 31 (in millions, except share data)	2015	2014
Assets		
Current Assets:		
Cash and cash equivalents	$ 2,295	$ 3,910
Investments	106	602
Receivables, net	6,896	6,321
Programming rights	1,213	839
Other current assets	1,793	1,859
Total current assets	12,303	13,531
Film and television costs	5,855	5,727
Investments	3,224	3,135
Property and equipment, net	33,665	30,953
Franchise rights	59,364	59,364
Goodwill	32,945	27,316
Other intangible assets, net	16,946	16,980
Other noncurrent assets, net	2,272	2,180
Total assets	$166,574	$159,186

Note 2: Accounting Policies (in part)

Our consolidated financial statements are prepared in accordance with GAAP, which requires us to select accounting policies, including in certain cases industry-specific policies, and make estimates that affect the reported amount of assets, liabilities, revenue and expenses, and the related disclosure of contingent assets and contingent liabilities. Actual results could differ from these estimates. We believe that the judgments and related estimates for the following items are critical in the preparation of our consolidated financial statements:

- valuation and impairment testing of cable franchise rights (see Note 9)
- film and television costs (see Note 6)

In addition, the following accounting policies are specific to the industries in which we operate:

- capitalization and amortization of film and television costs (see Note 6)
- installation revenue and costs for connecting customers to our cable systems (see revenue recognition below and Note 8)

Information on our other accounting policies and methods that are used in the preparation of our consolidated financial statements are included, where applicable, in their respective footnotes that follow. Below is a discussion of accounting policies and methods used in our consolidated financial statements that are not presented within other footnotes.

Note 9: Goodwill and Intangible Assets (in part)

Intangible Assets

		2015		2014	
December 31 (in millions)	**Weighted-Average Original Useful Life as of December 31, 2015**	**Gross Carrying Amount**	**Accumulated Amortization**	**Gross Carrying Amount**	**Accumulated Amortization**
Indefinite-Lived Intangible Assets:					
Franchise rights	N/A	$59,364		$59,364	
Trade names	N/A	2,857		3,083	
FCC licenses	N/A	651		651	
Finite-Lived Intangible Assets:					
Customer relationships	19 years	13,396	$(4,442)	15,129	$ (5,495)
Software	4 years	6,008	(3,429)	5,040	(2,832)
Cable franchise renewal costs and contractual operating rights	9 years	1,499	(849)	1,418	(792)
Patents and other technology rights	7 years	409	(350)	373	(330)
Other agreements and rights	18 years	1,994	(798)	1,456	(721)
Total		$86,178	$(9,868)	$ 86,514	$(10,170)

Indefinite-Lived Intangible Assets

Indefinite-lived intangible assets consist primarily of our cable franchise rights, as well as trade names and FCC licenses. Our cable franchise rights represent the values we attributed to agreements with state and local authorities that allow access to homes and businesses in cable service areas acquired in business combinations. We do not amortize our cable franchise rights because we have determined that they meet the definition of indefinite-lived intangible assets since there are no legal, regulatory, contractual, competitive, economic or other factors which limit the period over which these rights will contribute to our cash flows. We reassess this determination periodically or whenever events or substantive changes in circumstances occur. Costs we incur in negotiating and renewing cable franchise agreements are included in other intangible assets and are generally amortized on a straight-line basis over the term of the franchise agreement.

We assess the recoverability of our cable franchise rights and other indefinite-lived intangible assets annually, or more frequently whenever events or substantive changes in circumstances indicate that the assets might be impaired. Our three Cable Communications divisions represent the unit of account we use to test for impairment for our cable franchise rights. We evaluate the unit of account used to test for impairment of our cable franchise rights and other indefinite-lived intangible assets periodically or whenever events or substantive changes in circumstances occur to ensure impairment testing is performed at an appropriate level. The assessment of recoverability may first consider qualitative factors to determine whether it is more likely than not that the fair value of an indefinite-lived intangible asset is less than its carrying amount. A quantitative assessment is performed if the qualitative assessment results in a more-likely-than-not determination or if a qualitative assessment is not performed. When performing a quantitative assessment, we estimate the fair value of our cable franchise rights and other indefinite-lived intangible assets primarily based on a discounted cash flow analysis that involves significant judgment. When analyzing the fair values indicated under the discounted cash flow models, we also consider multiples of operating income before depreciation and amortization generated by the underlying assets, current market transactions, and profitability information. If the fair value of our cable franchise rights or other indefinite-lived intangible assets were less than the carrying amount, we would recognize an impairment charge for the difference between the estimated fair value and the carrying value of the assets. Unless presented separately, the impairment charge is included as a component of amortization expense. We did not recognize any material impairment charges in any of the periods presented.

Finite-Lived Intangible Assets

Estimated Amortization Expense of Finite-Lived Intangible Assets

(In millions)	
2016	$1,785
2017	$1,612
2018	$1,365
2019	$1,039
2020	$ 902

Finite-lived intangible assets are subject to amortization and consist primarily of customer relationships acquired in business combinations, software, cable franchise renewal costs, contractual operating rights and intellectual property rights. Our finite-lived intangible assets are amortized primarily on a straight-line basis over their estimated useful life or the term of the associated agreement.

We capitalize direct development costs associated with internal-use software, including external direct costs of material and services and payroll costs for employees devoting time to these software projects. We also capitalize costs associated with the purchase of software licenses. We include these costs in other intangible assets and generally amortize them on a straight-line basis over a period not to exceed five years. We expense maintenance and training costs, as well as costs incurred during the preliminary stage of a project, as they are incurred. We capitalize initial operating system software costs and amortize them over the life of the associated hardware.

We evaluate the recoverability of our finite-lived intangible assets whenever events or substantive changes in circumstances indicate that the carrying amount may not be recoverable. The evaluation is based on the cash flows generated by the underlying asset groups, including estimated future operating results, trends or other determinants of fair value. If the total of the expected future undiscounted cash flows were less than the carrying amount of the asset group, we would recognize an impairment charge to the extent the carrying amount of the asset group exceeded its estimated fair value. Unless presented separately, the impairment charge is included as a component of amortization expense.

PURCHASED INTANGIBLE ASSETS

2.80 AGCO CORPORATION (DEC)
NOTES TO CONSOLIDATED FINANCIAL STATEMENTS (in part)

1. Operations and Summary of Significant Accounting Policies (in part)

Goodwill, Other Intangible Assets and Long-Lived Assets (in part)

The Company amortizes certain acquired identifiable intangible assets primarily on a straight-line basis over their estimated useful lives, which range from five to 50 years. The acquired intangible assets have a weighted average useful life as follows:

Intangible Asset	Weighted-Average Useful Life
Patents and technology	13 years
Customer relationships	14 years
Trademarks and trade names	20 years
Land use rights	45 years

For the years ended December 31, 2015, 2014 and 2013, acquired intangible asset amortization was $42.7 million, $41.0 million and $47.8 million, respectively. The Company estimates amortization of existing intangible assets will be $42.1 million for 2016, $41.9 million for 2017, $41.9 million for 2018, $41.9 million for 2019, and $41.3 million for 2020.

The Company has previously determined that two of its trademarks have an indefinite useful life. The Massey Ferguson trademark has been in existence since 1952 and was formed from the merger of Massey-Harris (established in the 1890's) and Ferguson (established in the 1930's). The Massey Ferguson brand is currently sold in over 140 countries worldwide, making it one of the most widely sold tractor brands in the world. The Company also has identified the Valtra trademark as an indefinite-lived asset. The Valtra trademark has been in existence since the late 1990's, but is a derivative of the Valmet trademark which has been in existence since 1951. The Valmet name transitioned to the Valtra name over a period of time in the marketplace. The Valtra brand is currently sold in approximately 50 countries around the world. Both the Massey Ferguson brand and the Valtra brand are primary product lines of the Company's business, and the Company plans to use these trademarks for an indefinite period of time. The Company plans to continue to make investments in product development to enhance the value of these brands into the future. There are no legal, regulatory, contractual, competitive, economic or other factors that the Company is aware of or that the Company believes would limit the useful lives of the trademarks. The Massey Ferguson and Valtra trademark registrations can be renewed at a nominal cost in the countries in which the Company operates.

Changes in the carrying amount of acquired intangible assets during 2015 and 2014 are summarized as follows (in millions):

	Trademarks and Trade Names	Customer Relationships	Patents and Technology	Land Use Rights	Total
Gross carrying amounts:					
Balance as of December 31, 2013	$118.6	$502.7	$89.1	$14.9	$725.3
Acquisition	7.0	28.0	11.3	—	46.3
Settlement of purchase consideration	—	—	—	(4.8)	(4.8)
Foreign currency translation	(2.1)	(16.9)	(6.4)	(0.4)	(25.8)
Balance as of December 31, 2014	123.5	513.8	94.0	9.7	741.0
Acquisition	1.9	4.1	3.6	—	9.6
Foreign currency translation	(3.2)	(25.6)	(5.1)	(0.6)	(34.5)
Balance as of December 31, 2015	$122.2	$492.3	$92.5	$ 9.1	$716.1

	Trademarks and Trade Names	Customer Relationships	Patents and Technology	Land Use Rights	Total
Accumulated amortization:					
Balance as of December 31, 2013	$31.0	$160.7	$59.0	$2.7	$253.4
Amortization expense	6.2	31.4	3.2	0.2	41.0
Foreign currency translation	(0.8)	(11.3)	(6.1)	—	(18.2)
Balance as of December 31, 2014	36.4	180.8	56.1	2.9	276.2
Amortization expense	6.6	32.0	3.9	0.2	42.7
Foreign currency translation	(1.1)	(19.0)	(4.9)	(0.2)	(25.2)
Balance as of December 31, 2015	$41.9	$193.8	$55.1	$2.9	$293.7

	Trademarks and Trade Names
Indefinite-lived intangible assets:	
Balance as of December 31, 2013	$93.7
Foreign currency translation	(4.7)
Balance as of December 31, 2014	89.0
Foreign currency translation	(3.7)
Balance as of December 31, 2015	$85.3

2. Acquisitions

On April 17, 2015, the Company acquired Farmer Automatic GmbH & Co. KG ("Farmer Automatic") for approximately $17.9 million, net of cash acquired of approximately $0.1 million. Farmer Automatic, headquartered in Laer, Germany, manufactures and supplies poultry housing and related products, including egg production cages and broiler production equipment. The acquisition was financed with available cash on hand. The Company allocated the purchase price to the assets acquired and liabilities assumed based on preliminary estimates of their fair values as of the acquisition date. The acquired net assets primarily consisted of accounts receivable, inventories, accounts payable and accrued expenses, property, plant and equipment, and customer relationship, technology and trademark identifiable intangible assets. The Company recorded approximately $9.6 million of customer relationship, technology and trademark identifiable intangible assets and approximately $10.0 million of goodwill associated with the acquisition. The results of operations of Farmer Automatic have been included in the Company's Consolidated Financial Statements as of and from the date of the acquisition.

The acquired identifiable intangible assets of Farmer Automatic as of the date of the acquisition are summarized in the following table (in millions):

Intangible Asset	Amount	Weighted-Average Useful Life
Customer relationships	$4.1	10 years
Technology	3.6	10 years
Trademarks	1.9	10 years
	$9.6	

On September 11, 2014, the Company acquired the remaining 39% interest of Santal Equipamentos S.A. Comércio e Indústria ("Santal") for approximately R $9.0 million (or approximately $3.7 million). Santal is headquartered in Ribeirão Preto, Brazil, and manufactures and distributes sugarcane planting, harvesting, handling and transportation equipment as well as replacement parts across Brazil. Due to the fact that the Company and the seller each had a call option and put option, respectively, with varying dates with respect to the remaining 39% interest in Santal, the fair value of the redeemable noncontrolling interest had previously been recorded within "Temporary equity" in the Company's Consolidated Balance Sheets. The acquisition of the remaining interest was funded with available cash on hand. The redemption and related amounts settled were reflected in "Additional paid-in capital" in the Company's Consolidated Balance Sheets.

On August 1, 2014, the Company acquired Intersystems Holdings, Inc. ("Intersystems") for approximately $134.4 million, net of cash acquired of approximately $4.1 million (or approximately $130.3 million, net). Intersystems, headquartered in Omaha, Nebraska, designs and manufactures commercial material handling solutions, primarily for the agricultural, biofuels and food and feed processing industries. The acquisition was financed with available cash on hand and the Company's credit facility (Note 7). The Company allocated the purchase price to the assets acquired and liabilities assumed based on preliminary estimates of their fair values as of the acquisition date. The acquired net assets primarily consisted of accounts receivable, inventories, accounts payable and accrued expenses, property, plant and equipment, and customer relationship, technology and trademark identifiable intangible assets. The Company recorded approximately $46.3 million of customer relationship, technology and trademark identifiable intangible assets and approximately $89.6 million of goodwill associated with the acquisition. The goodwill was reported within the Company's North American geographical reportable segment. The results of operations of Intersystems have been included in the Company's Consolidated Financial Statements as of and from the date of acquisition.

The acquired identifiable intangible assets of Intersystems as of the date of the acquisition are summarized in the following table (in millions):

Intangible Asset	Amount	Weighted-Average Useful Life
Customer relationships	$28.0	15 years
Technology	11.3	15 years
Trademarks	7.0	16 years
	$46.3	

Other Noncurrent Assets

RECOGNITION AND MEASUREMENT

2.81 FASB ASC 210 indicates that the concept of current assets excludes resources such as the following:
- Cash restricted regarding withdrawal or use for other than current operations, designated for expenditure in the acquisition or construction of noncurrent assets, or segregated for the liquidation of long-term debts
- Investments or advances for the purposes of control, affiliation, or other continuing business advantage
- Certain receivables (see the "Noncurrent Receivables" section)
- Cash surrender value of life insurance policies
- Land and other natural resources
- Long-term prepayments chargeable to operations over several years

DISCLOSURE

2.82 Rule 5-02 of Regulation S-X requires that any item not classed in another Regulation S-X caption and in excess of 5 percent of total assets be stated separately on the balance sheet or disclosed in the notes.

PRESENTATION AND DISCLOSURE EXCERPTS

ASSETS HELD FOR SALE

2.83 FLOWERS FOODS, INC. (DEC)

CONSOLIDATED BALANCE SHEETS (in part)

(Amounts in thousands, except share data)	January 2, 2016	January 3, 2015
Assets		
Current Assets:		
Cash and cash equivalents	$ 14,378	$ 7,523
Accounts and notes receivable, net of allowances of $1,341 and $2,723, respectively	269,683	235,911
Inventories:		
Raw materials	42,336	33,579
Packaging materials	21,853	19,591
Finished goods	46,988	39,930
	111,177	93,100
Spare parts and supplies	57,288	54,058
Deferred taxes	37,207	26,823
Other	47,782	43,148
Total current assets	537,515	460,563
Property, Plant and Equipment:		
Land	93,115	93,314
Buildings	455,626	441,444
Machinery and equipment	1,162,314	1,115,129
Furniture, fixtures and transportation equipment	131,875	124,173
Construction in progress	38,334	18,566
	1,881,264	1,792,626
Less: accumulated depreciation	(1,076,296)	(985,168)
	804,968	807,458
Notes Receivable	154,311	161,905
Assets Held for Sale	36,191	39,108
Other Assets	11,791	12,011
Goodwill	464,926	282,960
Other Intangible Assets, net	875,466	644,969
Total assets	$2,885,168	$2,408,974

NOTES TO CONSOLIDATED FINANCIAL STATEMENTS (in part)

Note 2. Summary of Significant Accounting Policies (in part)

Revenue Recognition (in part)

The company repurchases distribution rights from and sells distribution rights to independent distributors from time to time. At the time the company purchases a distribution right from an independent distributor, the fair value purchase price of the distribution right is recorded as "Assets Held for Sale". Upon the sale of the distribution rights to a new independent distributor, generally a note receivable of up to ten years is recorded for the sales price of the distribution right (for those situations when the company provides direct financing to the independent distributor) with a corresponding credit to assets held for sale to relieve the carrying amount of the territory. Any difference between the amount of the note receivable (i.e., the sales price) and the distribution rights' carrying value, if any, is recorded as a gain or a loss in selling, distribution and administrative expenses because the company considers the independent distributor activity a cost of distribution. Since the independent distributor has the right to require the company to repurchase the distribution rights at the original purchase price within the first six-month period following the date of sale, no gain is recorded on the sale of the distribution rights until after the six-month period is completed and a liability is established (except that gains of $5,000 or less are recognized immediately upon the sale). The company is not required to repay interest paid by the distributor during such six-month period. Upon expiration of the six-month period, the amount of the deferred gain is recorded into income over the remaining term of the note. In instances where a distribution right is sold for less than its carrying value, a loss is recorded at the date of sale and any impairment of a distribution right held for sale is recorded at such time when the impairment occurs. The deferred gains were $26.2 million and $30.1 million at January 2, 2016 and January 3, 2015, respectively, and are recorded in other short and long-term liabilities on the Consolidated Balance Sheet. The company recorded net gains of $4.1 million during fiscal 2015, $3.8 million during fiscal 2014, and $5.5 million during fiscal 2013 related to the sale of distribution rights as a component of selling, distribution and administrative expenses.

Goodwill. The company accounts for goodwill in a purchase business combination as the excess of the cost over the fair value of net assets acquired. Goodwill is allocated to the DSD and Warehouse Segments based on the segment assignment for the acquisition. The company tests goodwill for impairment on an annual basis (or an interim basis if an event occurs that indicates the fair value of a reporting unit may be below its carrying value) using a two-step method. This analysis is performed for both of our segments. Goodwill is recorded at the segment level primarily because of reciprocal baking arrangements for plants within each segment. We have elected not to perform the qualitative approach. The company conducts this review during the fourth quarter of each fiscal year absent any triggering events. We use the following four material assumptions in our fair value analysis: (a) weighted average cost of capital; (b) long-term sales growth rates; (c) forecasted operating margins; and (d) market multiples. No impairment resulted from the annual review performed in fiscal years 2015, 2014, or 2013. During the second quarter of fiscal 2014, we recorded an impairment of $2.6 million related to the disposition of certain assets as described in Note 6, *Assets Held For Sale*. This goodwill impairment represented the share of goodwill for the disposed assets. See Note 7, *Goodwill and Other Intangible Assets*, for additional disclosure.

Note 6. Assets Held for Sale

The company purchases distribution rights from and sells distribution rights to independent distributors from time to time. The company repurchases distribution rights from independent distributors in circumstances when the company decides to exit a territory or when the independent distributor elects to terminate the relationship with the company. In the event the company decides to exit a territory or stop using the independent distribution model in a territory, the company is contractually required to purchase the distribution rights from the independent distributor. In the event an independent distributor terminates his or her relationship with the company, the company, although not legally obligated, may repurchase and operate those distribution rights as a company-owned territory. The independent distributors may also sell their distribution rights to another person or entity. Distribution rights purchased from independent distributors and operated as company-owned territories are recorded on the company's Consolidated Balance Sheet in the line item "Assets Held for Sale" while the company actively seeks another independent distributor to purchase the distribution rights for the territory.

Distribution rights held for sale and operated by the company are sold to independent distributors at the fair market value of the distribution rights. In accordance with the terms of the applicable Distributor Agreement, within the six-month period following the date of sale, the independent distributor has the right to require the company to repurchase the distribution rights and truck, if applicable, at the original purchase price paid by the independent distributor. The company records a liability for this amount during the six-month period. The company is not required to repay interest paid by the independent distributor during such six-month period. If the independent distributor's truck is leased, the company will assume the lease payment (but not the lease) if the distribution rights are repurchased during the six-month period. Should the independent distributor wish to sell the distribution rights after the six-month period has expired, the company has the right of first refusal but is not legally required to purchase the distribution rights. After the six-month period the liability is recorded as deferred income and will be recognized over the term of the distribution rights notes receivable.

The company is also selling certain manufacturing facilities and depots from the Acquired Hostess Bread Assets purchased in July 2013. These assets were originally recorded as held and used in the purchase price allocation in Note 8, *Acquisitions*. Subsequent to the acquisition of the Acquired Hostess Bread Assets, we determined that some of the acquired manufacturing facilities and depots do not meet our long-term strategy and we are actively marketing them. There are certain other properties not associated with the Acquired Hostess Bread Assets that are also in the process of being sold. These assets are recorded on the Consolidated Balance Sheets in the line item "Assets Held for Sale" and are included in the "Other" line item in the summary table below. During fiscal 2015, the company received $9.1 million on the sale of five Acquired Hostess Bread Asset depots and manufacturing facilities. During fiscal 2014, the company received $24.2 million on the sale of 22 Acquired Hostess Bread Assets depots and manufacturing facilities.

During the second quarter of fiscal 2014, we decided to sell certain assets at our Ft. Worth, Texas, tortilla facility (the "disposal group"). The company relocated our flour tortilla equipment to an existing manufacturing facility and continues to sell these products through our DSD Segment. The disposal group sale closed on August 13, 2014 for a sale price of $8.4 million in cash. The carrying value of the assets sold was $7.6 million. Assets not included in the disposal group were either transferred to other plants or were scrapped shortly after closing. We recognized an impairment of $2.3 million and $5.8 million for assets held for sale during fiscal years 2015 and 2014, respectively. We recognized an impairment loss on goodwill of $2.6 million and an additional impairment loss of $1.9 million for the scrapped assets during the second quarter of fiscal 2014. These impairments are recorded on the Consolidated Statements of Income in the line item "Impairment of assets". The total gain on the divestiture was $1.8 million, of which $0.8 million related to property, plant and equipment recorded as held for sale in our second quarter of fiscal 2014, and was recorded on the Consolidated Statements of Income in the line item "Selling, distribution and administrative expenses". We also incurred costs of $0.8 million included in the Consolidated Statements of Income line item "Materials, supplies, labor, and other production costs, excluding depreciation" relating to severance and inventory. The total costs for fiscal 2014 relating to the divestiture were $3.5 million.

In addition to the impairments described above, during the fourth quarter of our fiscal 2014, we recognized an impairment loss of $5.8 million for the difference between the carrying value and the fair value of certain Acquired Hostess Bread Assets classified as held for sale.

Additional assets recorded in assets held for sale are for property, plant and equipment exclusive of the amounts disclosed as part of the Acquired Hostess Bread Assets and the disposal group discussed above. The carrying values of assets held for sale are not amortized and are evaluated for impairment as required. The table below presents the assets held for sale as of January 2, 2016 and January 3, 2015, respectively (amounts in thousands):

	January 2, 2016	January 3, 2015
Distribution rights	$28,325	$20,491
Acquired Hostess Bread Assets plants and depots	3,082	13,406
Other	4,784	5,211
Total assets held for sale	$36,191	$39,108

PENSION ASSETS

2.84 W. R. GRACE & CO. (DEC)
CONSOLIDATED BALANCE SHEETS (in part)

(In millions, except par value and shares)	December 31, 2015	December 31, 2014
Assets		
Current Assets		
Cash and cash equivalents	$ 329.9	$ 557.5
Restricted cash and cash equivalents	9.4	—
Trade accounts receivable, less allowance of $7.7 (2014—$5.8)	458.1	481.1
Inventories	304.1	332.8
Other current assets	83.0	84.1
Total Current Assets	1,184.5	1,455.5
Properties and equipment, net of accumulated depreciation and amortization of $1,746.5 (2014—$1,818.4)	842.4	833.5
Goodwill	439.0	452.9
Technology and other intangible assets, net	260.8	288.0
Deferred income taxes	746.3	845.8
Overfunded defined benefit pension plans	26.1	44.1
Investment in unconsolidated affiliate	103.2	113.1
Other assets	73.7	60.7
Total Assets	$3,676.0	$4,093.6

NOTES TO CONSOLIDATED FINANCIAL STATEMENTS (in part)

1. Basis of Presentation and Summary of Significant Accounting and Financial Reporting Policies (in part)

Pension Benefits Grace's method of accounting for actuarial gains and losses relating to its global defined benefit pension plans is referred to as "mark-to-market accounting." Under mark-to-market accounting, Grace's pension costs consist of two elements: 1) ongoing costs recognized quarterly, which include service and interest costs, expected returns on plan assets, and amortization of prior service costs/credits; and 2) mark-to-market gains and losses recognized annually in the fourth quarter resulting from changes in actuarial assumptions, such as discount rates and the difference between actual and expected returns on plan assets. Should a significant event occur, Grace's pension obligation and plan assets would be remeasured at an interim period, and the gains or losses on remeasurement would be recognized in that period.

8. Pension Plans and Other Postretirement Benefit Plans

Pension Plans The following table presents the funded status of Grace's fully-funded, underfunded, and unfunded pension plans:

(In millions)	December 31, 2015	December 31, 2014
Overfunded defined benefit pension plans	$ 26.1	$ 44.1
Underfunded defined benefit pension plans	(118.9)	(79.5)
Unfunded defined benefit pension plans	(337.6)	(378.0)
Total underfunded and unfunded defined benefit pension plans	(456.5)	(457.5)
Pension liabilities included in other current liabilities	(15.3)	(15.6)
Net funded status	$(445.7)	$(429.0)

Fully-funded plans include several advance-funded plans where the fair value of the plan assets exceeds the projected benefit obligation ("PBO"). This group of plans was overfunded by $26.1 million as of December 31, 2015, and the overfunded status is reflected as "overfunded defined benefit pension plans" in the Consolidated Balance Sheets. Underfunded plans include a group of advance-funded plans that are underfunded on a PBO basis. Unfunded plans include several plans that are funded on a pay-as-you-go basis, and therefore, the entire PBO is unfunded. The combined balance of the underfunded and unfunded plans was $471.8 million as of December 31, 2015.

Grace maintains defined benefit pension plans covering current and former employees of certain business units and divested business units who meet age and service requirements. Benefits are generally based on final average salary and years of service. Grace funds its U.S. qualified pension plans ("U.S. qualified pension plans") in accordance with U.S. federal laws and regulations. Non-U.S. pension plans ("non-U.S. pension plans") are funded under a variety of methods, as required under local laws and customs.

Grace also provides, through nonqualified plans, supplemental pension benefits in excess of U.S. qualified pension plan limits imposed by federal tax law. These plans cover officers and higher-level employees and serve to increase the combined pension amount to the level that they otherwise would have received under the U.S. qualified pension plans in the absence of such limits. The nonqualified plans are unfunded and Grace pays the costs of benefits as they are due to the participants.

At the December 31, 2015, measurement date for Grace's defined benefit pension plans, the PBO was $1,900.2 million as measured under U.S. GAAP compared with $2,027.7 million as of December 31, 2014. The PBO basis reflects the present value (using a 4.31% weighted average discount rate for U.S. plans and a 3.00% weighted average discount rate for non-U.S. plans as of December 31, 2015) of vested and non-vested benefits earned from employee service to date, based upon current services and estimated future pay increases for active employees.

On an annual basis a full remeasurement of pension assets and pension liabilities is performed based on Grace's estimates and actuarial valuations. These valuations reflect the terms of the plan and use participant-specific information as well as certain key assumptions provided by management.

Postretirement Benefits Other Than Pensions Grace has provided postretirement health care and life insurance benefits for retired employees of certain U.S. business units and certain divested business units. The postretirement medical plan provided various levels of benefits to employees hired before 1993 who retired from Grace after age 55 with at least 10 years of service. These plans are unfunded and Grace pays a portion of the costs of benefits under these plans as they are incurred. Grace applies ASC 715 "Compensation-Retirement Benefits" to these plans, which requires that the future costs of postretirement health care and life insurance benefits be accrued over the employees' years of service. Actuarial gains and losses are recognized in the Consolidated Balance Sheets as a component of Shareholders' Equity, with amortization of the net actuarial gains and losses that exceed 10 percent of the accumulated postretirement benefit obligation recognized each quarter in the Consolidated Statements of Operations over the average future service period of active employees.

In June 2014, Grace announced that it would discontinue its postretirement medical plan for all U.S. employees effective October 31, 2014, and eliminate certain postretirement life insurance benefits. As a result of these actions, Grace recognized a gain of $41.9 million in other comprehensive income in the 2014 second quarter. Grace amortized $39.5 million from accumulated other comprehensive income into the Consolidated Statement of Operations during the five -month period from June to October 2014.

The postretirement plan was further remeasured as of September 30, 2015, due to a plan amendment to eliminate certain other postretirement life insurance benefits, which resulted in a curtailment gain of $4.5 million.

Defined Contribution Retirement Plan Grace sponsors a defined contribution retirement plan for its employees in the United States. This plan is qualified under section 401(k) of the U.S. tax code. Currently, Grace contributes an amount equal to 100% of employee contributions, up to 6% of an individual employee's salary or wages. Grace's cost related to this benefit plan was $15.2 million, $13.8 million, and $13.2 million for the years ended December 31, 2015, 2014, and 2013, respectively.

Analysis of Plan Accounting and Funded Status The following table summarizes the changes in benefit obligations and fair values of retirement plan assets during 2015 and 2014:

(In Millions)	Defined Benefit Pension Plans						Other Post-Retirement Plans	
	U.S.		Non-U.S.		Total			
Change in Financial Status of Retirement Plans	2015	2014	2015	2014	2015	2014	2015	2014
Change in Projected Benefit Obligation (PBO):								
Benefit obligation at beginning of year	$1,437.3	$1,326.8	$ 590.4	$ 546.4	$2,027.7	$1,873.2	$ 2.4	$ 57.2
Service cost	25.7	23.5	11.7	10.7	37.4	34.2	—	0.1
Interest cost	55.1	60.0	16.1	22.2	71.2	82.2	0.1	1.1
Plan participants' contributions	—	—	0.5	0.6	0.5	0.6	—	—
Amendments	(3.6)	—	—	—	(3.6)	—	(2.1)	(51.5)
Settlements/curtailments	—	—	(1.0)	—	(1.0)	—	—	—
Actuarial (gain) loss	(63.0)	131.4	(11.4)	92.4	(74.4)	223.8	0.4	(1.0)
Medicare subsidy receipts	—	—	—	—	—	—	1.0	0.2
Benefits paid	(87.0)	(104.4)	(20.7)	(25.8)	(107.7)	(130.2)	(1.1)	(3.7)
Currency exchange translation adjustments	—	—	(49.9)	(56.1)	(49.9)	(56.1)	—	—
Benefit obligation at end of year	$1,364.5	$1,437.3	$ 535.7	$ 590.4	$1,900.2	$2,027.7	$ 0.7	$ 2.4
Change in Plan Assets:								
Fair value of plan assets at beginning of year	$1,262.6	$1,145.2	$ 336.1	$ 306.5	$1,598.7	$1,451.7	$ —	$ —
Actual return on plan assets	(34.6)	112.1	2.9	59.1	(31.7)	171.2	—	—
Employer contributions	7.3	109.7	10.5	18.1	17.8	127.8	0.1	3.5
Plan participants' contributions	—	—	0.5	0.6	0.5	0.6	—	—
Settlements	—	—	(1.5)	—	(1.5)	—	—	—
Medicare subsidy receipts	—	—	—	—	—	—	1.0	0.2
Benefits paid	(87.0)	(104.4)	(20.7)	(25.8)	(107.7)	(130.2)	(1.1)	(3.7)
Currency exchange translation adjustments	—	—	(21.6)	(22.4)	(21.6)	(22.4)	—	—
Fair value of plan assets at end of year	$1,148.3	$1,262.6	$ 306.2	$ 336.1	$1,454.5	$1,598.7	$ —	$ —
Funded status at end of year (PBO basis)	$ (216.2)	$ (174.7)	$ (229.5)	$ (254.3)	$ (445.7)	$ (429.0)	$ (0.7)	$ (2.4)
Amounts recognized in the Consolidated Balance Sheets consist of:								
Noncurrent assets	$ —	$ —	$ 26.1	$ 44.1	$ 26.1	$ 44.1	$ —	$ —
Current liabilities	(7.1)	(7.1)	(8.2)	(8.5)	(15.3)	(15.6)	—	(0.1)
Noncurrent liabilities	(209.1)	(167.6)	(247.4)	(289.9)	(456.5)	(457.5)	(0.7)	(2.3)
Net amount recognized	$ (216.2)	$ (174.7)	$ (229.5)	$ (254.3)	$ (445.7)	$ (429.0)	$ (0.7)	$ (2.4)
Amounts recognized in Accumulated Other Comprehensive Loss consist of:								
Accumulated actuarial loss	$ —	$ —	$ —	$ —	$ —	$ —	$ 5.9	$ 6.2
Prior service (credit) cost	(3.1)	0.8	(0.3)	(0.3)	(3.4)	0.5	(7.1)	(12.9)
Net amount recognized	$ (3.1)	$ 0.8	$ (0.3)	$ (0.3)	$ (3.4)	$ 0.5	$ (1.2)	$ (6.7)
Weighted Average Assumptions Used to Determine Benefit Obligations as of December 31:								
Discount rate	4.31%	3.95%	3.00%	2.97%	NM	NM	4.40%	4.18%
Rate of compensation increase	4.70%	4.70%	3.35%	3.24%	NM	NM	NM	NM
Weighted Average Assumptions Used to Determine Net Periodic Benefit Cost for Years Ended December 31:								
Discount rate	3.95%	4.76%	2.97%	4.25%	NM	NM	4.18%	4.26%
Expected return on plan assets	5.75%	6.00%	4.11%	5.06%	NM	NM	NM	NM
Rate of compensation increase	4.70%	4.70%	3.24%	3.41%	NM	NM	NM	NM

NM—Not meaningful

Components of Net Periodic Benefit Cost (Income) and Other Amounts Recognized in Other Comprehensive (Income) Loss	2015			2014			2013		
(In millions)	U.S.	Non-U.S.	Other	U.S.	Non-U.S.	Other	U.S.	Non-U.S.	Other
Net Periodic Benefit Cost (Income)									
Service cost	$25.7	$11.7	$ —	$ 23.5	$10.7	$ 0.1	$ 25.2	$11.1	$ 0.2
Interest cost	55.1	16.1	0.1	60.0	22.2	1.1	51.9	20.6	2.2
Expected return on plan assets	(70.4)	(13.0)	—	(69.9)	(15.2)	—	(68.0)	(14.0)	—
Amortization of prior service cost (credit)	0.3	—	(3.4)	0.7	—	(2.4)	0.7	—	—
Amortization of net deferred actuarial loss	—	—	0.7	—	—	—	—	—	0.4
Annual mark-to-market adjustment	42.0	(0.1)	—	89.2	45.4	—	(65.8)	11.0	—
Gain on termination and curtailment of postretirement plans	—	—	(4.5)	—	—	(39.5)	—	—	—
Net curtailment and settlement gain	—	—	—	—	—	—	—	(0.1)	—
Net periodic benefit cost (income)	$52.7	$14.7	$(7.1)	$103.5	$63.1	$(40.7)	$(56.0)	$28.6	$ 2.8

(continued)

Components of Net Periodic Benefit Cost (Income) and Other Amounts Recognized in Other Comprehensive (Income) Loss

(In millions)	2015 U.S.	2015 Non-U.S.	2015 Other	2014 U.S.	2014 Non-U.S.	2014 Other	2013 U.S.	2013 Non-U.S.	2013 Other
Other Changes in Plan Assets and Benefit Obligations Recognized in Other Comprehensive (Income) Loss									
Net deferred actuarial loss (gain)	$ —	$ —	$ 0.4	$ —	$ —	$ (1.0)	$ —	$ —	$(4.3)
Net prior service credit	(3.6)	—	(2.1)	—	—	(13.6)	—	—	(1.7)
Amortization of prior service cost (credit)	(0.3)	—	3.4	(0.7)	—	2.4	(0.7)	—	—
Amortization of net deferred actuarial loss	—	—	(0.7)	—	—	—	—	—	(0.4)
Loss on termination and curtailment of postretirement plans	—	—	4.5	—	—	12.2	—	—	—
Total recognized in other comprehensive (income) loss	(3.9)	—	5.5	(0.7)	—	—	(0.7)	—	(6.4)
Total recognized in net periodic benefit cost (income) and other comprehensive (income) loss	$48.8	$14.7	$(1.6)	$102.8	$63.1	$(40.7)	$(56.7)	$28.6	$(3.6)

The estimated prior service credit for the defined benefit pension plans that will be amortized from accumulated other comprehensive loss into net periodic benefit cost (income) over the next fiscal year is $0.2 million. The estimated net deferred actuarial loss and prior service credit for the other postretirement plans that will be amortized from accumulated other comprehensive loss into net periodic benefit cost (income) over the next fiscal year are $0.6 million and $2.6 million, respectively.

Funded Status of U.S. Pension Plans	Fully-Funded U.S. Qualified Pension Plans[1]		Underfunded U.S. Qualified Pension Plans[1]		Unfunded Pay-As-You-Go U.S. Nonqualified Plans[2]	
(In millions)	2015	2014	2015	2014	2015	2014
Projected benefit obligation	$—	$—	$1,257.5	$1,329.8	$ 107.0	$ 107.5
Fair value of plan assets	—	—	1,148.3	1,262.6		
Funded status (PBO basis)	$—	$—	$ (109.2)	$ (67.2)	$(107.0)	$(107.5)
Benefits paid	$—	$—	$ (79.7)	$ (69.7)	$ (7.3)	$ (34.7)

Funded Status of Non-U.S. Pension Plans	Fully-Funded Non-U.S. Pension Plans[1]		Underfunded Non-U.S. Pension Plans[1]		Unfunded Pay-As-You-Go Non-U.S. Pension Plans[2]	
(In millions)	2015	2014	2015	2014	2015	2014
Projected benefit obligation	$240.3	$245.8	$49.5	$ 58.5	$ 245.9	$ 286.1
Fair value of plan assets	266.4	289.9	39.8	46.2	—	—
Funded status (PBO basis)	$ 26.1	$ 44.1	$(9.7)	$(12.3)	$(245.9)	$(286.1)
Benefits paid	$ (11.3)	$ (12.3)	$(2.3)	$ (4.7)	$ (7.1)	$ (8.8)

[1] Plans intended to be advance-funded.
[2] Plans intended to be pay-as-you-go.

The accumulated benefit obligation for all defined benefit pension plans was approximately $1,804 million and $1,933 million as of December 31, 2015 and 2014, respectively.

Pension Plans with Underfunded or Unfunded Accumulated Benefit Obligation	U.S.		Non-U.S.		Total	
(In millions)	2015	2014	2015	2014	2015	2014
Projected benefit obligation	$1,364.4	$352.6	$260.8	$306.0	$1,625.2	$658.6
Accumulated benefit obligation	1,314.1	351.8	229.1	274.5	1,543.2	626.3
Fair value of plan assets	1,148.2	220.8	7.4	9.4	1,155.6	230.2

Estimated Expected Future Benefit Payments Reflecting Future Service and Medicare Subsidy Receipts for the Fiscal Years Ending (In millions)	Pension Plans U.S. Benefit Payments[2]	Pension Plans Non-U.S.[1] Benefit Payments	Other Postretirement Plans Benefit Payments	Other Postretirement Plans Medicare Subsidy Receipts	Total Payments Net of Subsidy
2013 (actual)	$ 79.2	$ 22.1	$4.5	$(1.4)	$104.4
2014 (actual)[2]	104.4	25.8	3.7	(0.2)	133.7
2015 (actual)	87.0	20.7	1.1	(1.0)	107.8
2016	85.7	21.8	—	—	107.5
2017	86.0	20.6	—	—	106.6
2018	87.0	21.2	—	—	108.2
2019	87.9	22.1	—	—	110.0
2020	89.1	23.0	—	—	112.1
2021–2025	457.5	126.1	0.2	—	583.8

[1] Non-U.S. estimated benefit payments for 2016 and future periods have been translated at the applicable December 31, 2015, exchange rates.
[2] Includes approximately $28 million of benefit payments from nonqualified plans that were previously restricted by the Bankruptcy Court while the Company was in Chapter 11 and were paid in 2014.

Discount Rate Assumption   The assumed discount rate for pension plans reflects the market rates for high-quality corporate bonds currently available and is subject to change based on changes in overall market interest rates. For the U.S. qualified pension plans, the assumed weighted average discount rate of 4.31% as of December 31, 2015, was selected by Grace, in consultation with its independent actuaries, based on a yield curve constructed from a portfolio of high quality bonds for which the timing and amount of cash outflows approximate the estimated payouts of the plan.

As of December 31, 2015 and 2014, the United Kingdom pension plan and German pension plans combined represented approximately 87% and 86%, respectively, of the benefit obligation of the non-U.S. pension plans. The assumed weighted average discount rates as of December 31, 2015, for the United Kingdom (3.00%) and Germany (2.57%) were selected by Grace, in consultation with its independent actuaries, based on yield curves constructed from a portfolio of sterling- and euro-denominated high quality bonds for which the timing and amount of cash outflows approximate the estimated payouts of the plans. The assumed discount rates for the remaining non-U.S. pension plans were determined based on the nature of the liabilities, local economic environments and available bond indices.

As of December 31, 2015, Grace changed the approach used to determine the service and interest cost components of defined benefit pension expense. Previously, Grace estimated service and interest costs using a single weighted average discount rate derived from the same yield curve used to measure the projected benefit obligation. For 2016, Grace elected to measure service and interest costs by applying the specific spot rates along that yield curve to the plans' liability cash flows. Grace believes the new approach provides a more precise measurement of service and interest costs by aligning the timing of the plans' liability cash flows to the corresponding spot rates on the yield curve. This change does not affect the measurement of the projected benefit obligation at year-end. Grace considers this a change in accounting estimate, which will be accounted for prospectively beginning in 2016.

Investment Guidelines for Advance-Funded Pension Plans   The investment goal for the U.S. qualified pension plans subject to advance funding is to earn a long-term rate of return consistent with the related cash flow profile of the underlying benefit obligation. The plans are pursuing a well-defined risk management strategy designed to reduce investment risks as their funded status improves.

The U.S. qualified pension plans have adopted a diversified set of portfolio management strategies to optimize the risk reward profile of the plans:

- Liability hedging portfolio: primarily invested in intermediate-term and long-term investment grade corporate bonds in actively managed strategies.
- Growth portfolio: invested in a diversified set of assets designed to deliver performance in excess of the underlying liabilities with controls regarding the level of risk.
    — U.S. equity securities: the portfolio contains domestic equities that are passively managed to the S&P 500 and Russell 2000 benchmark and an allocation to an active portfolio benchmarked to the Russell 2000.
    — Non-U.S. equity securities: the portfolio contains non-U.S. equities in an actively managed strategy. Currency futures and forward contracts may be held for the sole purpose of hedging existing currency risk in the portfolio.
- Other investments: may include (a) high yield bonds: fixed income portfolio of securities below investment grade including up to 30% of the portfolio in non-U.S. issuers; and (b) global real estate securities: portfolio of diversified REIT and other liquid real estate related securities. These portfolios combine income generation and capital appreciation opportunities from developed markets globally.
- Liquidity portfolio: invested in short-term assets intended to pay periodic plan benefits and expenses.

For 2015, the expected long-term rate of return on assets for the U.S. qualified pension plans was 5.75%. Average annual returns over one-, three-, five-, and ten-year periods were approximately (3)%, 4%, 6%, and 5%, respectively.

The expected return on plan assets for the U.S. qualified pension plans for 2015 was selected by Grace, in consultation with its independent actuaries, using an expected return model. The model determines the weighted average return for an investment portfolio based on the target asset allocation and expected future returns for each asset class, which were developed using a building block approach based on observable inflation, available interest rate information, current market characteristics, and historical results.

The target allocation of investment assets at December 31, 2015, and the actual allocation at December 31, 2015 and 2014, for Grace's U.S. qualified pension plans are as follows:

U.S. Qualified Pension Plans Asset Category	Target Allocation 2015	Percentage of Plan Assets December 31, 2015	Percentage of Plan Assets December 31, 2014
U.S. equity securities	11%	11%	11%
Non-U.S. equity securities	7%	7%	6%
Short-term debt securities	6%	6%	10%
Intermediate-term debt securities	28%	28%	26%
Long-term debt securities	46%	46%	45%
Other investments	2%	2%	2%
Total	100%	100%	100%

The following tables present the fair value hierarchy for the U.S. qualified pension plan assets measured at fair value as of December 31, 2015 and 2014.

(In millions)	Total	Fair Value Measurements at December 31, 2015, Using — Quoted Prices in Active Markets for Identical Assets or Liabilities (Level 1)	Significant Other Observable Inputs (Level 2)	Significant Unobservable Inputs (Level 3)
U.S. equity group trust funds	$ 120.1	$—	$ 120.1	$—
Non-U.S. equity group trust funds	81.8	—	81.8	—
Corporate bond group trust funds—intermediate-term	320.4	—	320.4	—
Corporate bond group trust funds—long-term	525.6	—	525.6	—
Other fixed income group trust funds	25.4	—	25.4	—
Common/collective trust funds	57.3	—	57.3	—
Annuity and immediate participation contracts	17.7	—	17.7	—
Total Assets	$1,148.3	$—	$1,148.3	$—

(In millions)	Total	Fair Value Measurements at December 31, 2014, Using — Quoted Prices in Active Markets for Identical Assets or Liabilities (Level 1)	Significant Other Observable Inputs (Level 2)	Significant Unobservable Inputs (Level 3)
U.S. equity group trust funds	$ 134.2	$—	$ 134.2	$—
Non-U.S. equity group trust funds	76.8	—	76.8	—
Corporate bond group trust funds—intermediate-term	324.9	—	324.9	—
Corporate bond group trust funds—long-term	567.1	—	567.1	—
Other fixed income group trust funds	23.7	—	23.7	—
Common/collective trust funds	118.8	—	118.8	—
Annuity and immediate participation contracts	17.1	—	17.1	—
Total Assets	$1,262.6	$—	$1,262.6	$—

Non-U.S. pension plans accounted for approximately 21% of total global pension assets at December 31, 2015 and 2014. Each of these plans, where applicable, follows local requirements and regulations. Some of the local requirements include the establishment of a local pension committee, a formal statement of investment policy and procedures, and routine valuations by plan actuaries.

The target allocation of investment assets for non-U.S. pension plans varies depending on the investment goals of the individual plans. The plan assets of the United Kingdom pension plan represent approximately 85% and 84% of the total non-U.S. pension plan assets at December 31, 2015 and 2014, respectively. In determining the expected rate of return for the U.K. pension plan, the trustees' strategic investment policy has been considered together with long-term historical returns and investment community forecasts for each asset class. The expected return by sector has been combined with the actual asset allocation to determine the 2015 expected long-term return assumption of 3.75%.

The target allocation of investment assets at December 31, 2015, and the actual allocation at December 31, 2015 and 2014, for the U.K. pension plan are as follows:

United Kingdom Pension Plan Asset Category	Target Allocation 2015	Percentage of Plan Assets December 31, 2015	Percentage of Plan Assets December 31, 2014
Diversified growth funds	10%	10%	11%
U.K. gilts	29%	29%	42%
U.K. corporate bonds	8%	8%	47%
Insurance contracts	53%	53%	—%
Total	100%	100%	100%

The plan assets of the Canadian pension plan represent approximately 9% and 10% of the total non-U.S. pension plan assets at December 31, 2015 and 2014, respectively. The expected long-term rate of return on assets for the Canadian pension plan was 5.25% for 2015.

The target allocation of investment assets at December 31, 2015, and the actual allocation at December 31, 2015 and 2014, for the Canadian pension plan are as follows:

Canadian Pension Plan Asset Category	Target Allocation 2015	Percentage of Plan Assets December 31, 2015	Percentage of Plan Assets December 31, 2014
Equity securities	27%	28%	27%
Bonds	58%	57%	58%
Other investments	15%	15%	15%
Total	100%	100%	100%

The plan assets of the other country plans represent approximately 6% in the aggregate (with no country representing more than 3% individually) of total non-U.S. pension plan assets at December 31, 2015 and 2014.

The following table presents the fair value hierarchy for the non-U.S. pension plan assets measured at fair value as of December 31, 2015.

(In millions)	Total	Fair Value Measurements at December 31, 2015, Using — Quoted Prices in Active Markets for Identical Assets or Liabilities (Level 1)	Fair Value Measurements at December 31, 2015, Using — Significant Other Observable Inputs (Level 2)	Fair Value Measurements at December 31, 2015, Using — Significant Unobservable Inputs (Level 3)
Common/collective trust funds	$159.8	$—	$159.8	$ —
Government and agency securities	2.5	—	2.5	—
Corporate bonds	1.4	—	1.4	—
Insurance contracts and other investments[1]	141.8	—	3.3	138.5
Cash	0.7	0.7	—	—
Total Assets	$306.2	$0.7	$167.0	$138.5

[1] In October 2015, the trustees of the U.K. pension plan entered into a contract with an insurance company to secure the benefits for current retirees and hedge the risk of future inflation and changes in longevity with a buy-in contract. At December 31, 2015, the fair value of the insurance contract has been determined using a discounted cash flow approach that maximizes observable inputs, such as current yields on similar instruments, but includes adjustments for certain risks that may not be observable, such as credit and liquidity risks.

The following table presents a summary of the changes in the fair value of the plans' Level 3 assets for the year ended December 31, 2015.

(In millions)	Insurance Contracts
Balance, December 31, 2014	$ —
Actual return on plan assets relating to assets still held at year-end	(1.2)
Purchases, sales, and settlements, net	145.6
Transfers out for benefit payments	(1.7)
Currency exchange translation adjustments	(4.2)
Balance, December 31, 2015	$138.5

The following table presents the fair value hierarchy for the non-U.S. pension plan assets measured at fair value as of December 31, 2014.

| (In millions) | Total | Fair Value Measurements at December 31, 2014, Using | | |
		Quoted Prices in Active Markets for Identical Assets or Liabilities (Level 1)	Significant Other Observable Inputs (Level 2)	Significant Unobservable Inputs (Level 3)
Common/collective trust funds	$326.7	$—	$326.7	$—
Government and agency securities	2.6	—	2.6	—
Corporate bonds	1.1	—	1.1	—
Insurance contracts and other investments	4.6	—	4.6	—
Cash	1.1	1.1	—	—
Total Assets	$336.1	$1.1	$335.0	$—

Plan Contributions and Funding Grace intends to satisfy its funding obligations under the U.S. qualified pension plans and to comply with all of the requirements of the Employee Retirement Income Security Act of 1974 ("ERISA"). For ERISA purposes, funded status is calculated on a different basis than under U.S. GAAP. Based on the U.S. qualified pension plans' status as of December 31, 2015, there are no minimum required payments under ERISA for 2016.

Grace intends to fund non-U.S. pension plans based on applicable legal requirements and actuarial and trustee recommendations. Grace expects to contribute approximately $12 million to its non-U.S. pension plans in 2016.

RESTRICTED CASH

2.85 BALL CORPORATION (DEC)

CONSOLIDATED BALANCE SHEETS (in part)

| ($ in millions) | December 31, | |
	2015	2014
Assets		
Current assets		
Cash and cash equivalents	$ 224.0	$ 191.4
Receivables, net	885.4	957.1
Inventories, net	898.4	1,016.7
Deferred taxes and other current assets	176.2	148.3
Total current assets	2,184.0	2,313.5
Noncurrent assets		
Property, plant and equipment, net	2,685.9	2,430.7
Goodwill	2,176.5	2,254.5
Restricted cash	2,154.4	—
Intangibles and other assets, net	576.2	572.3
Total assets	$9,777.0	$7,571.0

NOTES TO THE CONSOLIDATED FINANCIAL STATEMENTS (in part)

4. Acquisitions (in part)

Rexam PLC (Rexam)

On February 19, 2015, the company and Rexam PLC (Rexam) announced the terms of a recommended offer by the company to acquire all of the outstanding shares of Rexam in a cash and stock transaction. Under the terms of the offer, for each Rexam share, Rexam shareholders will receive 407 pence in cash and 0.04568 shares of the company. The transaction valued Rexam at 610 pence per share based on the company's 90-day volume weighted average stock price as of February 17, 2015, and an exchange rate of US $1.54: £1 on that date representing an equity value of £4.3 billion ($6.6 billion). The actual value of the transaction will be determined based on the exchange rate and the company's stock price at the time of the closing of the transaction. As described below, the company has entered into collar and option contracts to partially mitigate its currency exchange risk with regard to the cash component of the purchase price.

By way of compensation for any loss suffered by Rexam in connection with the preparation and negotiation of the offer, the co-operation agreement and any other document relating to the acquisition, Ball has undertaken in the co-operation agreement that, on the occurrence of a break payment event Ball will pay, or procure the payment to Rexam of an amount in cash in British pounds. As discussed below, Ball's shareholders approved the issuance of Ball common stock to shareholders of Rexam as partial consideration for the proposed acquisition. As a result, the amount of the break payment would be £302 million.

A special meeting of Ball's shareholders was held on July 28, 2015, to approve the issuance of Ball common stock to shareholders of Rexam as partial consideration for the proposed acquisition. Both Ball and Rexam's boards of directors unanimously support the transaction, and the consummation of the transaction remains subject to approval from Rexam's shareholders, certain regulatory approvals and other customary closing conditions. Subject to the satisfaction of all such conditions, Ball currently expects to complete the acquisition during the first half of 2016.

Ball currently expects to complete the Rexam acquisition during the first half of 2016, subject to final regulatory approval by the European Commission (EC), Brazil's Council for Economic Defence (CADE) and the Federal Trade Commission (FTC), the completion of the Rexam acquisition divestitures required by the regulators and other customary closing conditions; however, there can be no assurances that the Rexam acquisition or the Rexam acquisition divestitures will be completed by such time, or on the terms described herein, or at all. The European Commission (EC) and Brazil's Council for Economic Defence (CADE) have provided conditional clearance of the proposed acquisition, subject to their approval of the proposed buyer of the divested assets and other customary regulatory processes.

Ball owned interests in a joint venture company (Latapack-Ball) organized and operating in Brazil. During October and November 2015, Ball and its joint venture partners reached an agreement to exchange all of their interest in Latapack-Ball for a total of approximately 5.7 million treasury shares of Ball common stock and $17.4 million of cash. The acquisition of the noncontrolling interests in the joint venture was completed in December 2015, and Latapack-Ball is now a wholly owned subsidiary of Ball.

Long-Term Debt (in part)

In February 2015, the company entered into a £3.3 billion unsecured, committed bridge loan agreement, pursuant to which lending institutions have agreed, subject to limited conditions, to provide the financing necessary to pay the cash portion of the consideration payable to Rexam's shareholders upon consummation of the announced, proposed acquisition of Rexam along with related fees and expenses. In December 2015, the company issued senior notes totaling $1 billion, €400 million and €700 million due 2020, 2020, and 2023, respectively, with rates of 4.375 percent, 3.5 percent and 4.375 percent, respectively. Pursuant to the terms of the unsecured bridge loan agreement, the company deposited the net proceeds from the issuance of such notes into escrow accounts, recorded as restricted cash, (from which proceeds would be released, subject to certain conditions, to pay a portion of the cash consideration payable to Rexam shareholders and related fees and expenses), which reduced the commitments under the unsecured bridge loan agreement to £1.9 billion. If the Rexam acquisition is not consummated on or prior to November 15, 2016, we will be required to effect the redemption of all of the outstanding notes from the December 2015 senior note issuances at the redemption price applicable to each series. This would result in the use of restricted cash and other available funds to redeem these senior notes and pay any additional fees. However, the senior note offerings are not conditioned upon the Rexam acquisition. See Note 13 for further details related to these transactions.

5. Business Consolidation and Other Activities (in part)

Corporate (in part)

During the year ended December 31, 2015, the company recorded charges of $97.9 million for professional services and other costs associated with the proposed acquisition of Rexam announced in February 2015. Also during the year ended December 31, 2015, the company recognized losses of $41.0 million associated with the change in fair value of its collar and option contracts entered into to reduce its exposure to currency exchange rate changes in connection with the British pound denominated cash portion of the announced, proposed acquisition of Rexam, further discussed in Note 19.

During 2015, the company recorded charges of $14.2 million for net foreign currency gains and losses from the revaluation of foreign currency denominated restricted cash held to pay a portion of the cash component of the proposed Rexam acquisition purchase price and the revaluation of the euro-denominated debt issuance in December 2015. The company also recognized $7.4 million for cross-currency swaps in connection with the December 2015 issuance of the $1 billion senior notes due 2020 to more effectively match the future cash flows of our business. See Note 19 for additional information.

10. Restricted Cash

In December 2015, the company issued €400 million of 3.5 percent senior notes due in December 2020 and €700 million of 4.375 percent senior notes due in December 2023. Subsequent to the issuance, the company converted the net euro proceeds to British pounds. The company elected to restrict the funds in an acquisition escrow account, which enabled the reduction of its unsecured, committed bridge loan agreement capacity from £3.3 billion to £1.9 billion. The company issued additional senior notes due in December 2020 for $1 billion. At December 31, 2015, £792 million ($1,167 million) was held in a British pound denominated escrow account and $987.5 million was held in a U.S. dollar escrow account. The funds in the escrow accounts will be used to pay a portion of the cash component of the announced, proposed acquisition price of Rexam and was therefore recorded as noncurrent restricted cash. There was no noncurrent restricted cash balance at December 31, 2014. Subsequent to December 31, 2015, the company converted the U.S. dollars into British pounds.

13. Debt and Interest Costs (in part)

In December 2015, the company issued $1 billion of 4.375 percent senior notes, €400 million of 3.5 percent senior notes, all due in December 2020, and €700 million of 4.375 percent senior notes, due in December 2023. The company intends to use the proceeds to pay a portion of the cash consideration payable in the proposed Rexam acquisition. Until the Rexam acquisition is consummated, the interest on these senior notes is recorded in debt refinancing and other costs, which totaled $4.6 million. In the event the Rexam acquisition is not consummated on or prior to November 15, 2016, these senior notes will be callable by the lender, requiring the company to effect the redemption of all of the outstanding notes of each series at the applicable redemption price of face value plus accrued and unpaid interest. This would result in use of restricted cash to redeem these senior notes and pay any additional fees.

CASH SURRENDER VALUE OF LIFE INSURANCE

2.86 WINNEBAGO INDUSTRIES, INC. (AUG)
CONSOLIDATED BALANCE SHEETS (in part)

(In thousands, except per share data)	August 29, 2015	August 30, 2014
Assets		
Current assets:		
Cash and cash equivalents	$ 70,239	$ 57,804
Receivables, less allowance for doubtful accounts ($120 and $127, respectively)	66,936	69,699
Inventories	112,165	112,848
Investment in operating leases	—	15,978
Prepaid expenses and other assets	6,882	5,723
Deferred income taxes	9,995	9,641
Total current assets	266,217	271,693
Property, plant and equipment, net	37,250	25,135
Investment in life insurance	26,172	25,126
Deferred income taxes	21,994	24,029
Goodwill	1,228	1,228
Other assets	9,313	11,091
Total assets	$362,174	$358,302

NOTES TO CONSOLIDATED FINANCIAL STATEMENTS (in part)

Note 9: Employee and Retiree Benefits (in part)

Supplemental Executive Retirement Plan (SERP)

The primary purpose of this plan was to provide our officers and managers with supplemental retirement income for a period of 15 years after retirement. We have not offered this plan on a continuing basis to members of management since 1998. The plan was funded with individual whole life insurance policies (Split Dollar Program) owned by the named insured officer or manager. We initially paid the life insurance premiums on the life of the individual and the individual would receive life insurance and supplemental cash payment during the 15 years following retirement. In October 2008, the plan was amended as a result of changes in the tax and accounting regulations and rising administrative costs. Under the redesigned SERP, the underlying life insurance policies previously owned by the insured individual became COLI by a release of all interests by the participant and assignment to us as a prerequisite to participation in the SERP and transition from the Split Dollar Program. Total SERP liabilities were $2.6 million and $3.0 million at August 29, 2015 and August 30, 2014, respectively. This program remains closed to new employee participation.

To assist in funding the deferred compensation and SERP liabilities, we have invested in COLI policies. The cash surrender value of these policies is presented as investment in life insurance in the accompanying balance sheets and consists of the following:

(In thousands)	August 29, 2015	August 30, 2014
Cash value	$58,501	$55,982
Borrowings	(32,329)	(30,856)
Investment in life insurance	$26,172	$25,126

DERIVATIVES

2.87 INTERNATIONAL BUSINESS MACHINES CORPORATION (DEC)
CONSOLIDATED STATEMENT OF FINANCIAL POSITION (in part)

($ in millions except per share amounts)

At December 31:	Notes	2015	2014
Assets			
Current assets			
Cash and cash equivalents		$ 7,686	$ 8,476
Marketable securities	D	508	0
Notes and accounts receivable—trade (net of allowances of $367 in 2015 and $336 in 2014)		8,333	9,090
Short-term financing receivables (net of allowances of $490 in 2015 and $452 in 2014)	F	19,020	19,835
Other accounts receivable (net of allowances of $51 in 2015 and $40 in 2014)		1,201	2,906
Inventories	E	1,551	2,103
Prepaid expenses and other current assets		4,205	4,967
Total current assets		42,504	47,377*
Property, plant and equipment	G	29,342	39,034
Less: Accumulated depreciation	G	18,615	28,263
Property, plant and equipment—net	G	10,727	10,771
Long-term financing receivables (net of allowances of $118 in 2015 and $126 in 2014)	F	10,013	11,109
Prepaid pension assets	S	1,734	2,160
Deferred taxes	N	4,822	6,675*
Goodwill	I	32,021	30,556
Intangible assets—net	I	3,487	3,104
Investments and sundry assets	H	5,187	5,520**
Total assets		$110,495	$117,271***

Amounts may not add due to rounding.

* Reclassified to reflect adoption of the FASB guidance on deferred taxes in consolidated financial statements. Refer to note B, "Accounting Changes," for additional information.

** Reclassified to reflect adoption of the FASB guidance on debt issuance costs in consolidated financial statements. Refer to note B, "Accounting Changes," for additional information.

The accompanying notes on pages 82 through 146 are an integral part of the financial statements.

NOTES TO CONSOLIDATED FINANCIAL STATEMENTS (in part)

Note A. Significant Accounting Policies (in part)

Derivative Financial Instruments

Derivatives are recognized in the Consolidated Statement of Financial Position at fair value and are reported in prepaid expenses and other current assets, investments and sundry assets, other accrued expenses and liabilities or other liabilities. Classification of each derivative as current or noncurrent is based upon whether the maturity of the instrument is less than or greater than 12 months. To qualify for hedge accounting, the company requires that the instruments be effective in reducing the risk exposure that they are designated to hedge. For instruments that hedge cash flows, hedge designation criteria also require that it be probable that the underlying transaction will occur. Instruments that meet established accounting criteria are formally designated as hedges. These criteria demonstrate that the derivative is expected to be highly effective at offsetting changes in fair value or cash flows of the underlying exposure both at inception of the hedging relationship and on an ongoing basis. The method of assessing hedge effectiveness and measuring hedge ineffectiveness is formally documented at hedge inception. The company assesses hedge effectiveness and measures hedge ineffectiveness at least quarterly throughout the designated hedge period.

Where the company applies hedge accounting, the company designates each derivative as a hedge of: (1) the fair value of a recognized financial asset or liability, or of an unrecognized firm commitment (fair value hedge attributable to interest rate or foreign currency risk); (2) the variability of anticipated cash flows of a forecasted transaction, or the cash flows to be received or paid related to a recognized financial asset or liability (cash flow hedge attributable to interest rate or foreign currency risk); or (3) a hedge of a long-term investment (net investment hedge) in a foreign operation. In addition, the company may enter into derivative contracts that economically hedge certain of its risks, even though hedge accounting does not apply or the company elects not to apply hedge accounting. In these cases, there exists a natural hedging relationship in which changes in the fair value of the derivative, which are recognized currently in net income, act as an economic offset to changes in the fair value of the underlying hedged item(s).

Changes in the fair value of a derivative that is designated as a fair value hedge, along with offsetting changes in the fair value of the underlying hedged exposure, are recorded in earnings each period. For hedges of interest rate risk, the fair value adjustments are recorded as adjustments to interest expense and cost of financing in the Consolidated Statement of Earnings. For hedges of currency risk associated with recorded financial assets or liabilities, derivative fair value adjustments are recognized in other (income) and expense in the Consolidated Statement of Earnings. Changes in the fair value of a derivative that is designated as a cash flow hedge are recorded, net of applicable taxes, in OCI, in the Consolidated Statement of Comprehensive Income. When net income is affected by the variability of the underlying cash flow, the applicable offsetting amount of the gain or loss from the derivative that is deferred in AOCI is released to net income and reported in interest expense, Cost, SG&A expense or other (income) and expense in the Consolidated Statement of Earnings based on the nature of the underlying cash flow hedged. Effectiveness for net investment hedging derivatives is measured on a spot-to-spot basis. The effective portion of changes in the fair value of net investment hedging derivatives and other non-derivative financial instruments designated as net investment hedges are recorded as foreign currency translation adjustments in OCI. Changes in the fair value of the portion of a net investment hedging derivative excluded from the effectiveness assessment are recorded in interest expense. If the underlying hedged item in a fair value hedge ceases to exist, all changes in the fair value of the derivative are included in net income each period until the instrument matures. When the derivative transaction ceases to exist, a hedged asset or liability is no longer adjusted for changes in its fair value except as required under other relevant accounting standards.

Derivatives that are not designated as hedges, as well as changes in the fair value of derivatives that do not effectively offset changes in the fair value of the underlying hedged item throughout the designated hedge period (collectively, "ineffectiveness"), are recorded in net income for each period and are primarily reported in other (income) and expense. When a cash flow hedging relationship is discontinued, the net gain or loss in AOCI must generally remain in AOCI until the item that was hedged affects earnings. However, when it is probable that a forecasted transaction will not occur by the end of the originally specified time period or within an additional two-month period thereafter, the net gain or loss in AOCI must be reclassified into earnings immediately.

The company reports cash flows arising from derivative financial instruments designated as fair value or cash flow hedges consistent with the classification of cash flows from the underlying hedged items that these derivatives are hedging. Accordingly, the cash flows associated with derivatives designated as fair value or cash flow hedges are classified in cash flows from operating activities in the Consolidated Statement of Cash Flows. Cash flows from derivatives designated as net investment hedges and derivatives that do not qualify as hedges are reported in cash flows from investing activities in the Consolidated Statement of Cash Flows. For currency swaps designated as hedges of foreign currency denominated debt (included in the company's debt risk management program as addressed in note D, "Financial Instruments," on pages 101 through 105), cash flows directly associated with the settlement of the principal element of these swaps are reported in payments to settle debt in cash flows from financing activities in the Consolidated Statement of Cash Flows.

Note D. Financial Instruments (in part)

Derivative Financial Instruments

The company operates in multiple functional currencies and is a significant lender and borrower in the global markets. In the normal course of business, the company is exposed to the impact of interest rate changes and foreign currency fluctuations, and to a lesser extent equity and commodity price changes and client credit risk. The company limits these risks by following established risk management policies and procedures, including the use of derivatives, and, where cost effective, financing with debt in the currencies in which assets are denominated. For interest rate exposures, derivatives are used to better align rate movements between the interest rates associated with the company's lease and other financial assets and the interest rates associated with its financing debt. Derivatives are also used to manage the related cost of debt. For foreign currency exposures, derivatives are used to better manage the cash flow volatility arising from foreign exchange rate fluctuations.

As a result of the use of derivative instruments, the company is exposed to the risk that counterparties to derivative contracts will fail to meet their contractual obligations. To mitigate the counterparty credit risk, the company has a policy of only entering into contracts with carefully selected major financial institutions based upon their overall credit profile. The company's established policies and procedures for mitigating credit risk on principal transactions include reviewing and establishing limits for credit exposure and continually assessing the creditworthiness of counterparties. The right of set-off that exists under certain of these arrangements enables the legal entities of the company subject to the arrangement to net amounts due to and from the counterparty reducing the maximum loss from credit risk in the event of counterparty default.

The company is also a party to collateral security arrangements with most of its major derivative counterparties. These arrangements require the company to hold or post collateral (cash or U.S. Treasury securities) when the derivative fair values exceed contractually established thresholds. Posting thresholds can be fixed or can vary based on credit default swap pricing or credit ratings received from the major credit agencies. The aggregate fair value of all derivative instruments under these collateralized arrangements that were in a liability position at December 31, 2015 and 2014 was $28 million and $21 million, respectively, for which no collateral was posted at either date. Full collateralization of these agreements would be required in the event that the company's credit rating falls below investment grade or if its credit default swap spread exceeds 250 basis points, as applicable, pursuant to the terms of the collateral security arrangements. The aggregate fair value of derivative instruments in net asset positions as of December 31, 2015 and 2014 was $994 million and $1,432 million, respectively. This amount represents the maximum exposure to loss at the reporting date as a result of the counterparties failing to perform as contracted. This exposure was reduced by $139 million and $97 million at December 31, 2015 and 2014, respectively, of liabilities included in master netting arrangements with those counterparties. Additionally, at December 31, 2015 and 2014, this exposure was reduced by $90 million and $487 million of cash collateral and $40 million and $31 million of non-cash collateral in U.S. Treasury securities, respectively, received by the company. At December 31, 2015 and 2014, the net exposure related to derivative assets recorded in the Statement of Financial Position was $726 million and $817 million, respectively. At December 31, 2015 and 2014, the net amount related to derivative liabilities recorded in the Statement of Financial Position was $47 million and $99 million, respectively.

In the Consolidated Statement of Financial Position, the company does not offset derivative assets against liabilities in master netting arrangements nor does it offset receivables or payables recognized upon payment or receipt of cash collateral against the fair values of the related derivative instruments. No amount was recognized in other receivables at December 31, 2015 and 2014 for the right to reclaim cash collateral. The amount recognized in accounts payable for the obligation to return cash collateral totaled $90 million and $487 million at December 31, 2015 and 2014, respectively. The company restricts the use of cash collateral received to rehypothecation, and therefore reports it in prepaid expenses and other current assets in the Consolidated Statement of Financial Position. No amount was rehypothecated at December 31, 2015 and 2014.

The company may employ derivative instruments to hedge the volatility in stockholders' equity resulting from changes in currency exchange rates of significant foreign subsidiaries of the company with respect to the U.S. dollar. These instruments, designated as net investment hedges, expose the company to liquidity risk as the derivatives have an immediate cash flow impact upon maturity which is not offset by a cash flow from the translation of the underlying hedged equity. The company monitors this cash loss potential on an ongoing basis, and may discontinue some of these hedging relationships by de-designating or terminating the derivative instrument in order to manage the liquidity risk. Although not designated as accounting hedges, the company may utilize derivatives to offset the changes in the fair value of the de-designated instruments from the date of de-designation until maturity.

In its hedging programs, the company uses forward contracts, futures contracts, interest-rate swaps, cross-currency swaps and options depending upon the underlying exposure. The company is not a party to leveraged derivative instruments.

A brief description of the major hedging programs, categorized by underlying risk, follows.

Interest Rate Risk

Fixed and Variable Rate Borrowings

The company issues debt in the global capital markets, principally to fund its financing lease and loan portfolio. Access to cost-effective financing can result in interest rate mismatches with the underlying assets. To manage these mismatches and to reduce overall interest cost, the company uses interest rate swaps to convert specific fixed-rate debt issuances into variable-rate debt (i.e., fair value hedges) and to convert specific variable-rate debt issuances into fixed-rate debt (i.e., cash flow hedges). At December 31, 2015 and 2014, the total notional amount of the company's interest rate swaps was $7.3 billion and $5.8 billion, respectively. The weighted-average remaining maturity of these instruments at December 31, 2015 and 2014 was approximately 7.2 years and 8.7 years, respectively.

Forecasted Debt Issuance

The company is exposed to interest rate volatility on future debt issuances. To manage this risk, the company may use forward-starting interest rate swaps to lock in the rate on the interest payments related to the forecasted debt issuance. These swaps are accounted for as cash flow hedges. The company did not have any derivative instruments relating to this program outstanding at December 31, 2015 and 2014.

At December 31, 2015 and 2014, net gains of less than $1 million (before taxes), respectively, were recorded in accumulated other comprehensive income/(loss) in connection with cash flow hedges of the company's borrowings. Within these amounts, less than $1 million of gains, respectively, are expected to be reclassified to net income within the next 12 months, providing an offsetting economic impact against the underlying transactions.

Foreign Exchange Risk

Long-Term Investments in Foreign Subsidiaries (Net Investment)

A large portion of the company's foreign currency denominated debt portfolio is designated as a hedge of net investment in foreign subsidiaries to reduce the volatility in stockholders' equity caused by changes in foreign currency exchange rates in the functional currency of major foreign subsidiaries with respect to the U.S. dollar. The company also uses cross-currency swaps and foreign exchange forward contracts for this risk management purpose. At December 31, 2015 and 2014, the total notional amount of derivative instruments designated as net investment hedges was $5.5 billion and $2.2 billion, respectively. The weighted-average remaining maturity of these instruments at December 31, 2015 and 2014 was approximately 0.2 years for both periods.

Anticipated Royalties and Cost Transactions

The company's operations generate significant nonfunctional currency, third-party vendor payments and intercompany payments for royalties and goods and services among the company's non-U.S. subsidiaries and with the parent company. In anticipation of these foreign currency cash flows and in view of the volatility of the currency markets, the company selectively employs foreign exchange forward contracts to manage its currency risk. These forward contracts are accounted for as cash flow hedges. The maximum length of time over which the company is hedging its exposure to the variability in future cash flows is four years. At December 31, 2015 and 2014, the total notional amount of forward contracts designated as cash flow hedges of forecasted royalty and cost transactions was $8.2 billion and $9.3 billion, respectively, with a weighted-average remaining maturity of 0.7 years for both periods.

At December 31, 2015 and 2014, in connection with cash flow hedges of anticipated royalties and cost transactions, the company recorded net gains of $147 million and net gains of $602 million (before taxes), respectively, in accumulated other comprehensive income/(loss). Within these amounts $121 million of gains and $572 million of gains, respectively, are expected to be reclassified to net income within the next 12 months, providing an offsetting economic impact against the underlying anticipated transactions.

Foreign Currency Denominated Borrowings

The company is exposed to exchange rate volatility on foreign currency denominated debt. To manage this risk, the company employs cross-currency swaps to convert fixed-rate foreign currency denominated debt to fixed-rate debt denominated in the functional currency of the borrowing entity. These swaps are accounted for as cash flow hedges. The maximum length of time over which the company hedges its exposure to the variability in future cash flows is approximately seven years. At December 31, 2015 and December 31, 2014, no amounts were outstanding under this program.

At December 31, 2015 and 2014, in connection with cash flow hedges of foreign currency denominated borrowings, the company recorded net losses of $2 million (before taxes), respectively, in accumulated other comprehensive income/(loss). Within these amounts, less than $1 million of losses, respectively, are expected to be reclassified to net income within the next 12 months, providing an offsetting economic impact against the underlying exposure.

Subsidiary Cash and Foreign Currency

Asset/Liability Management

The company uses its Global Treasury Centers to manage the cash of its subsidiaries. These centers principally use currency swaps to convert cash flows in a cost-effective manner. In addition, the company uses foreign exchange forward contracts to economically hedge, on a net basis, the foreign currency exposure of a portion of the company's nonfunctional currency assets and liabilities. The terms of these forward and swap contracts are generally less than one year. The changes in the fair values of these contracts and of the underlying hedged exposures are generally offsetting and are recorded in other (income) and expense in the Consolidated Statement of Earnings. At December 31, 2015 and 2014, the total notional amount of derivative instruments in economic hedges of foreign currency exposure was $11.7 billion and $13.1 billion, respectively.

Equity Risk Management

The company is exposed to market price changes in certain broad market indices and in the company's own stock primarily related to certain obligations to employees. Changes in the overall value of these employee compensation obligations are recorded in SG&A expense in the Consolidated Statement of Earnings. Although not designated as accounting hedges, the company utilizes derivatives, including equity swaps and futures, to economically hedge the exposures related to its employee compensation obligations. The derivatives are linked to the total return on certain broad market indices or the total return on the company's common stock. They are recorded at fair value with gains or losses also reported in SG&A expense in the Consolidated Statement of Earnings. At December 31, 2015 and 2014, the total notional amount of derivative instruments in economic hedges of these compensation obligations was $1.2 billion and $1.3 billion, respectively.

Other Risks

The company may hold warrants to purchase shares of common stock in connection with various investments that are deemed derivatives because they contain net share or net cash settlement provisions. The company records the changes in the fair value of these warrants in other (income) and expense in the Consolidated Statement of Earnings. The company did not have any warrants qualifying as derivatives outstanding at December 31, 2015 and 2014.

The company is exposed to a potential loss if a client fails to pay amounts due under contractual terms. The company may utilize credit default swaps to economically hedge its credit exposures. These derivatives have terms of one year or less. The swaps are recorded at fair value with gains and losses reported in other (income) and expense in the Consolidated Statement of Earnings. The company did not have any derivative instruments relating to this program outstanding at December 31, 2015 and 2014.

The company is exposed to market volatility on certain investment securities. The company may utilize options or forwards to economically hedge its market exposure. The derivatives are recorded at fair value with gains and losses reported in other (income) and expense in the Consolidated Statement of Earnings. At December 31, 2015 and 2014, the total notional amount of derivative instruments in economic hedges of investment securities was less than $0.1 billion for both periods.

The following tables provide a quantitative summary of the derivative and non-derivative instrument-related risk management activity as of December 31, 2015 and 2014, as well as for the years ended December 31, 2015, 2014 and 2013, respectively.

Fair Values of Derivative Instruments in the Consolidated Statement of Financial Position

($ in millions)

At December 31:	Fair Value of Derivative Assets			Fair Value of Derivative Liabilities		
	Balance Sheet Classification	2015	2014	Balance Sheet Classification	2015	2014
Designated as hedging instruments						
Interest rate contracts	Prepaid expenses and other current assets	$ —	$ 5	Other accrued expenses and liabilities	$ —	$ 0
	Investments and sundry assets	656	628	Other liabilities	3	—
Foreign exchange contracts	Prepaid expenses and other current assets	197	632	Other accrued expenses and liabilities	70	50
	Investments and sundry assets	5	17	Other liabilities	19	21
	Fair value of derivative assets	$858	$1,281	Fair value of derivative liabilities	$ 92	$ 72
Not designated as hedging instruments						
Foreign exchange contracts	Prepaid expenses and other current assets	$ 90	$ 90	Other accrued expenses and liabilities	$ 75	$ 101
	Investments and sundry assets	40	37	Other liabilities	—	4
Equity contracts	Prepaid expenses and other current assets	6	24	Other accrued expenses and liabilities	19	14
	Investments and sundry assets	—	0	Other liabilities	—	5
	Fair value of derivative assets	$136	$151	Fair value of derivative liabilities	$94	$125
Total debt designated as hedging instruments						
Short-term debt		N/A	N/A		$—	$ 0
Long-term debt		N/A	N/A		$7,945	$7,747
Total		$994	$1,432		$8,131	$7,944

* Reclassified to reflect adoption of the FASB guidance on debt issuance costs in consolidated financial statements. Refer to note B, "Accounting Changes," for additional information.
N/A—Not applicable

The Effect of Derivative Instruments in the Consolidated Statement of Earnings

($ in millions)

For the Year Ended December 31:	Consolidated Statement of Earnings Line Item	Gain/(Loss) Recognized in Earnings					
		Recognized on Derivatives[1]			Attributable to Risk Being Hedged[2]		
		2015	2014	2013	2015	2014	2013
Derivative instruments in fair value hedges[5]							
Interest rate contracts	Cost of financing	$108	$231	$(109)	$ (1)	$(127)	$202
	Interest expense	94	206	(74)	(1)	(114)	138
Derivative instruments not designated as hedging instruments[1]							
Foreign exchange contracts	Other (income) and expense	127	(776)	(328)	N/A	N/A	N/A
Interest rate contracts	Other (income) and expense	(1)	34	—	N/A	N/A	N/A
Equity contracts	SG&A expense	(27)	51	164	N/A	N/A	N/A
	Other (income) and expense	(9)	(9)	—	N/A	N/A	N/A
Total		$291	$(263)	$(347)	$ (1)	$(241)	$340

($ in millions)

For the year ended December 31:	Gain/(Loss) Recognized in Earnings and Other Comprehensive Income									
	Effective Portion Recognized in OCI			Consolidated Statement of Earnings Line Item	Effective Portion Reclassified from AOCI			Ineffectiveness and Amounts Excluded from Effectiveness Testing[3]		
	2015	2014	2013		2015	2014	2013	2015	2014	2013
Derivative instruments in cash flow hedges										
Interest rate contracts	$ —	$ —	$ —	Interest expense	$ 0	$ (1)	$—	$—	$—	$—
Foreign exchange contracts	618	958	43	Other (income) and expense	731	98	162	5	(1)	0
				Cost of sales	192	(15)	(34)	—	—	—
				SG&A expense	149	15	39	—	—	—
Instruments in net investment hedges[4]										
Foreign exchange contracts	889	1,136	173	Interest expense	—	—	—	13	0	3
Total	$1,507	$2,095	$216		$1,072	$97	$167	$ 18	$ (1)	$ 3

[1] The amount includes changes in clean fair values of the derivative instruments in fair value hedging relationships and the periodic accrual for coupon payments required under these derivative contracts.

[2] The amount includes basis adjustments to the carrying value of the hedged item recorded during the period and amortization of basis adjustments recorded on de-designated hedging relationships during the period.

[3] The amount of gain/(loss) recognized in income represents ineffectiveness on hedge relationships.

[4] Instruments in net investment hedges include derivative and non-derivative instruments.

[5] For the years ended December 31, 2015 and December 31, 2014, fair value hedges resulted in a loss of $2 million and a gain of $4 million in ineffectiveness, respectively. There were no amounts recorded as ineffectiveness on fair value hedges for the year ended December 31, 2013.

N/A—Not applicable

For the 12 months ending December 31, 2015, 2014 and 2013, there were no significant gains or losses recognized in earnings representing hedge ineffectiveness or excluded from the assessment of hedge effectiveness (for fair value hedges), or associated with an underlying exposure that did not or was not expected to occur (for cash flow hedges); nor are there any anticipated in the normal course of business.

SOFTWARE

2.88 ANN INC. (JAN)
CONSOLIDATED BALANCE SHEETS (in part)

(In thousands, except share amounts)	January 31, 2015	February 1, 2014
Assets		
Current assets		
Cash	$ 207,711	$ 201,707
Accounts receivable	20,360	22,448
Merchandise inventories	265,022	239,667
Refundable income taxes	9,270	7,252
Deferred income taxes	26,046	28,854
Prepaid expenses and other current assets	72,489	61,287
Total current assets	600,898	561,215
Property and equipment, net	426,729	443,086
Deferred income taxes	12,119	6,599
Other assets	21,760	22,060
Total assets	$1,061,506	$1,032,960

1. Summary of Significant Accounting Policies (in part)

Property and Equipment

Property and equipment are presented at cost less accumulated depreciation and amortization. Depreciation and amortization are computed on a straight-line basis over the following estimated useful lives:

Building	40 years
Leasehold improvements	10 years or term of lease, if shorter
Furniture, fixtures and equipment	2–10 years
Software	5 years

When assets are sold or retired, the related cost and accumulated depreciation are removed from their respective accounts and any resulting gain or loss is recorded to the same income statement line item as the related depreciation expense was charged. Expenditures for maintenance and repairs which do not improve or extend the useful life of the respective assets are expensed as incurred.

Internal-Use Software Development Costs

The Company capitalizes certain external and internal computer software and software development costs incurred during the application development stage. The application development stage generally includes software design and configuration, coding, testing and installation activities. Capitalized costs include only external direct cost of materials and services consumed in developing or obtaining internal-use software, and payroll and payroll-related costs for employees who are directly associated with and devote time to the internal-use software project. Capitalization of such costs ceases no later than the point at which the project is substantially complete and ready for its intended use. Training and maintenance costs are expensed as incurred, while upgrades and enhancements are capitalized if it is probable that such expenditures will result in additional functionality. Capitalized software costs are depreciated on a straight-line basis over five years.

4. Property and Equipment

Property and equipment consists of the following:

(In thousands)	January 31, 2015	February 1, 2014
Land	$ 1,056	$ 1,056
Buildings	12,395	13,464
Leasehold improvements	653,091	638,807
Furniture and fixtures	340,971	330,981
Computer equipment and software	251,619	243,558
Assets under construction or development	13,186	21,803
	1,272,318	1,249,669
Less accumulated depreciation and amortization	(845,589)	(806,583)
Net property and equipment	$ 426,729	$ 443,086

Depreciation and amortization expense was approximately $111.1 million, $106.6 million and $97.8 million in Fiscal 2014, Fiscal 2013 and Fiscal 2012, respectively.

INSURANCE CLAIMS

2.89 HONEYWELL INTERNATIONAL INC. (DEC)
CONSOLIDATED BALANCE SHEET (in part)

	December 31,	
(Dollars in millions)	2015	2014
Assets		
Current assets:		
Cash and cash equivalents	$ 5,455	$ 6,959
Accounts, notes and other receivables	8,075	7,960
Inventories	4,420	4,405
Deferred income taxes	—	722
Investments and other current assets	2,103	2,145
Total current assets	20,053	22,191

(continued)

(Dollars in millions)	December 31,	
	2015	2014
Investments and long-term receivables	517	465
Property, plant and equipment—net	5,789	5,383
Goodwill	15,895	12,788
Other intangible assets—net	4,577	2,208
Insurance recoveries for asbestos related liabilities	426	454
Deferred income taxes	283	404
Other assets	1,776	1,558
Total assets	$49,316	$45,451

NOTES TO FINANCIAL STATEMENTS (in part)

(Dollars in millions, except per share amounts)

Note 1. Summary of Significant Accounting Policies (in part)

Asbestos Related Contingencies and Insurance Recoveries —We recognize a liability for any asbestos related contingency that is probable of occurrence and reasonably estimable. In connection with the recognition of liabilities for asbestos related matters, we record asbestos related insurance recoveries that are deemed probable. For additional information, see Note 19 Commitments and Contingencies.

Note 19. Commitments and Contingencies (in part)

Asbestos Matters

Honeywell is a defendant in asbestos related personal injury actions related to two predecessor companies:

- North American Refractories Company (NARCO), which was sold in 1986, produced refractory products (bricks and cement used in high temperature applications). Claimants consist largely of individuals who allege exposure to NARCO asbestos-containing refractory products in an occupational setting.
- Bendix Friction Materials (Bendix) business, which was sold in 2014, manufactured automotive brake parts that contained chrysotile asbestos in an encapsulated form. Claimants consist largely of individuals who allege exposure to asbestos from brakes from either performing or being in the vicinity of individuals who performed brake replacements.

The following tables summarize information concerning NARCO and Bendix asbestos related balances:

Asbestos Related Liabilities

	Year Ended December 31, 2015			Year Ended December 31, 2014			Year Ended December 31, 2013		
	Bendix	NARCO	Total	Bendix	NARCO	Total	Bendix	NARCO	Total
Beginning of year	$623	$929	$1,552	$656	$955	$1,611	$653	$1,119	$1,772
Accrual for update to estimated liability	180	8	188	195	4	199	180	5	185
Change in estimated cost of future claims	11	—	11	(1)	—	(1)	16	—	16
Update of expected resolution values for pending claims	1	—	1	2	—	2	(5)	—	(5)
Asbestos related liability payments	(193)	(16)	(209)	(229)	(30)	(259)	(188)	(169)	(357)
End of year	$622	$921	$1,543	$623	$929	$1,552	$656	$ 955	$1,611

Insurance Recoveries for Asbestos Related Liabilities

	Year Ended December 31, 2015			Year Ended December 31, 2014			Year Ended December 31, 2013		
	Bendix	NARCO	Total	Bendix	NARCO	Total	Bendix	NARCO	Total
Beginning of year	$135	$350	$485	$141	$531	$672	$138	$569	$707
Probable insurance recoveries related to estimated liability	21	—	21	24	—	24	27	—	27
Insurance receipts for asbestos related liabilities	(33)	(30)	(63)	(24)	(187)	(211)	(24)	(34)	(58)
Insurance receivables settlements and write offs	1	6	7	(6)	7	1	—	(6)	(6)
Other	—	(1)	(1)	—	(1)	(1)	—	2	2
End of year	$124	$325	$449	$135	$350	$485	$141	$531	$672

NARCO and Bendix asbestos related balances are included in the following balance sheet accounts:

	December 31,	
	2015	2014
Other current assets	$ 23	$ 31
Insurance recoveries for asbestos related liabilities	426	454
	$ 449	$ 485
Accrued liabilities	$ 292	$ 352
Asbestos related liabilities	1,251	1,200
	$1,543	$1,552

NARCO Products —In connection with NARCO's emergence from bankruptcy on April 30, 2013, a federally authorized 524(g) trust (NARCO Trust) was established for the evaluation and resolution of all existing and future NARCO asbestos claims. Both Honeywell and NARCO are protected by a permanent channeling injunction barring all present and future individual actions in state or federal courts and requiring all asbestos related claims based on exposure to NARCO asbestos-containing products to be made against the NARCO Trust. The NARCO Trust reviews submitted claims and determines award amounts in accordance with established Trust Distribution Procedures approved by the Bankruptcy Court which set forth the criteria claimants must meet to qualify for compensation including, among other things, exposure and medical criteria that determine the award amount. In addition, Honeywell provided, and continues to provide, input to the design of control procedures for processing NARCO claims, and has on-going audit rights to review and monitor the claims processors' adherence to the established requirements of the Trust Distribution Procedures.

Honeywell is obligated to fund NARCO asbestos claims submitted to the NARCO Trust which qualify for payment under the Trust Distribution Procedures (Annual Contribution Claims), subject to annual caps of $140 million in the years 2016 through 2018 and $145 million for each year thereafter. However, the initial $100 million of claims processed through the NARCO Trust (the Initial Claims Amount) will not count against the annual cap and any unused portion of the Initial Claims Amount will roll over to subsequent years until fully utilized. In 2015, Honeywell filed suit against the NARCO Trust in Bankruptcy Court alleging breach of certain provisions of the Trust Agreement and Trust Distribution Procedures. The proceeding is ongoing. As of December 31, 2015, Honeywell has not made any payments to the NARCO Trust for Annual Contribution Claims.

Honeywell is also responsible for payments due to claimants pursuant to settlement agreements reached during the pendency of the NARCO bankruptcy proceedings that provide for the right to submit claims to the NARCO Trust subject to qualification under the terms of the settlement agreements and Trust Distribution Procedures criteria (Pre-established Unliquidated Claims), which amounts are estimated at $150 million and are expected to be paid during the initial years of trust operations ($5 million of which has been paid since the effective date of the NARCO Trust). Such payments are not subject to the annual cap described above.

Our consolidated financial statements reflect an estimated liability for pre-established unliquidated claims ($145 million), unsettled claims pending as of the time NARCO filed for bankruptcy protection ($33 million) and for the estimated value of future NARCO asbestos claims expected to be asserted against the NARCO Trust through 2018 ($743 million). In the absence of actual trust experience on which to base the estimate, Honeywell projected the probable value of asbestos related future liabilities, including trust claim handling costs, based on a commonly accepted methodology used by numerous bankruptcy courts addressing 524(g) trusts. Some critical assumptions underlying this methodology include claims filing rates, disease criteria and payment values contained in the Trust Distribution Procedures, estimated approval rates of claims submitted to the NARCO Trust and epidemiological studies estimating disease instances. This projection resulted in a range of estimated liability of $743 million to $961 million. We believe that no amount within this range is a better estimate than any other amount and accordingly, we have recorded the minimum amount in the range. In light of the uncertainties inherent in making long-term projections and in connection with the recent implementation of the Trust Distribution Procedures by the NARCO Trust, as well as the stay of all NARCO asbestos claims which remained in place throughout NARCO's Chapter 11 case, we do not believe that we have a reasonable basis for estimating NARCO asbestos claims beyond 2018.

Our insurance receivable corresponding to the estimated liability for pending and future NARCO asbestos claims reflects coverage which reimburses Honeywell for portions of NARCO-related indemnity and defense costs and is provided by a large number of insurance policies written by dozens of insurance companies in both the domestic insurance market and the London excess market. We conduct analyses to estimate the probable amount of insurance that is recoverable for asbestos claims. While the substantial majority of our insurance carriers are solvent, some of our individual carriers are insolvent, which has been considered in our analysis of probable recoveries. We made judgments concerning insurance coverage that we believe are reasonable and consistent with our historical dealings and our knowledge of any pertinent solvency issues surrounding insurers.

Projecting future events is subject to many uncertainties that could cause the NARCO-related asbestos liabilities or assets to be higher or lower than those projected and recorded. Given the uncertainties, we review our estimates periodically, and update them based on our experience and other relevant factors. Similarly, we will reevaluate our projections concerning our probable insurance recoveries in light of any changes to the projected liability or other developments that may impact insurance recoveries.

Friction Products —The following tables present information regarding Bendix related asbestos claims activity:

Claims Activity	Years Ended December 31,	
	2015	2014
Claims Unresolved at the beginning of year	9,267	12,302
Claims Filed	2,862	3,694
Claims Resolved[1]	(4,350)	(6,729)
Claims Unresolved at the end of year	7,779	9,267

[1] Claims resolved in 2014 include 2,110 cancer claims which were determined to have no value. Also, claims resolved in 2015 and 2014 include significantly aged (i.e., pending for more than six years) claims totaling 153 and 1,266.

Disease Distribution of Unresolved Claims	December 31,	
	2015	2014
Mesothelioma and Other Cancer Claims	3,772	3,933
Nonmalignant Claims	4,007	5,334
Total Claims	7,779	9,267

Honeywell has experienced average resolution values per claim excluding legal costs as follows:

(In whole dollars)	Years Ended December 31,				
	2015	2014	2013	2012	2011
Malignant claims	$44,000	$53,500	$51,000	$49,000	$48,000
Nonmalignant claims	$ 100	$ 120	$ 850	$ 1,400	$ 1,000

It is not possible to predict whether resolution values for Bendix-related asbestos claims will increase, decrease or stabilize in the future.

Our consolidated financial statements reflect an estimated liability for resolution of pending (claims actually filed as of the financial statement date) and future Bendix-related asbestos claims. We have valued Bendix pending and future claims using average resolution values for the previous five years. We update the resolution values used to estimate the cost of Bendix pending and future claims during the fourth quarter each year.

The liability for future claims represents the estimated value of future asbestos related bodily injury claims expected to be asserted against Bendix over the next five years. Such estimated cost of future Bendix-related asbestos claims is based on historic claims filing experience and dismissal rates, disease classifications, and resolution values in the tort system for the previous five years. In light of the uncertainties inherent in making long-term projections, as well as certain factors unique to friction product asbestos claims, we do not believe that we have a reasonable basis for estimating asbestos claims beyond the next five years. The methodology used to estimate the liability for future claims is similar to that used to estimate the liability for future NARCO-related asbestos claims.

Our insurance receivable corresponding to the liability for settlement of pending and future Bendix asbestos claims reflects coverage which is provided by a large number of insurance policies written by dozens of insurance companies in both the domestic insurance market and the London excess market. Based on our ongoing analysis of the probable insurance recovery, insurance receivables are recorded in the financial statements simultaneous with the recording of the estimated liability for the underlying asbestos claims. This determination is based on our analysis of the underlying insurance policies, our historical experience with our insurers, our ongoing review of the solvency of our insurers, judicial determinations relevant to our insurance programs, and our consideration of the impacts of any settlements reached with our insurers.

Honeywell believes it has sufficient insurance coverage and reserves to cover all pending Bendix-related asbestos claims and Bendix-related asbestos claims estimated to be filed within the next five years. Although it is impossible to predict the outcome of either pending or future Bendix-related asbestos claims, we do not believe that such claims would have a material adverse effect on our consolidated financial position in light of our insurance coverage and our prior experience in resolving such claims. If the rate and types of claims filed, the average resolution value of such claims and the period of time over which claim settlements are paid (collectively, the Variable Claims Factors) do not substantially change, Honeywell would not expect future Bendix-related asbestos claims to have a material adverse effect on our results of operations or operating cash flows in any fiscal year. No assurances can be given, however, that the Variable Claims Factors will not change.

Short-Term Debt

PRESENTATION

2.90 FASB ASC 470, *Debt*, addresses classification determination for specific debt obligations, such as the following:
- Short-term obligations expected to be refinanced on a long-term basis
- Due on demand loan arrangements
- Callable debt
- Sales of future revenue
- Increasing-rate debt
- Debt that includes covenants
- Revolving credit agreements subject to lock-box arrangements and subjective acceleration clauses

DISCLOSURE

2.91 Rule 5-02 of Regulation S-X calls for disclosure of the amount and terms of unused lines of credit for short-term financing, if significant. The weighted average interest rate on short-term borrowings outstanding as of the date of each balance sheet presented should be furnished. Further, the amount of these lines of credit that support commercial paper or similar borrowing arrangements should be separately identified.

2.92 By definition, *short-term notes payable*, *loans payable*, and *commercial paper* are financial instruments. FASB ASC 825 requires disclosure of both the fair value and bases for estimating the fair value of short-term notes payable, loans payable, and commercial paper, unless it is not practicable to estimate that value.

2.93 "Pending Content" in FASB ASC 405-40-50-01 lists the required disclosures for obligations resulting from joint and several liability arrangements. Among these required disclosures are the nature of the arrangement; the total outstanding amount under the arrangement; the carrying amount, if any, of an entity's liability and the carrying amount of a receivable recognized, if any; the nature of any recourse provisions that would enable recovery from other entities; and the corresponding entry and where the entry was recorded in the financial statements in the period the liability is initially recognized and measured or in a period the measurement changes significantly.

PRESENTATION AND DISCLOSURE EXCERPTS

SHORT-TERM DEBT

2.94 CISCO SYSTEMS, INC. (JUL)
CONSOLIDATED BALANCE SHEETS (in part)

(in millions, except par value)

	July 25, 2015	July 26, 2014
Liabilities And Equity (in part)		
Current liabilities:		
Short-term debt	$ 3,897	$ 508
Accounts payable	1,104	1,032
Income taxes payable	62	159
Accrued compensation	3,049	3,181
Deferred revenue	9,824	9,478
Other current liabilities	5,687	5,451
Total current liabilities	23,623	19,809

10. Borrowings

(a) Short-Term Debt

The following table summarizes the Company's short-term debt (in millions, except percentages):

	July 25, 2015		July 26, 2014	
	Amount	Effective Rate	Amount	Effective Rate
Current portion of long-term debt	$3,894	2.48%	$500	3.11%
Other notes and borrowings	3	2.44%	8	2.67%
Total short-term debt	$3,897		$508	

The effective interest rate on the current portion of long-term debt includes the impact of interest rate swaps, as discussed further in "(b) Long-Term Debt." Other notes and borrowings consist of the short-term portion of secured borrowings associated with customer financing arrangements. These notes and credit facilities were subject to various terms and foreign currency market interest rates pursuant to individual financial arrangements between the financing institution and the applicable foreign subsidiary.

The Company repaid the fixed-rate notes (2.90%) due on November 17, 2014 for an aggregate principal amount of $500 million upon maturity.

The Company repaid the floating-rate notes due on September 3, 2015 for an aggregate principal amount of $850 million upon maturity.

In fiscal 2011, the Company established a short-term debt financing program of up to $3.0 billion through the issuance of commercial paper notes. The Company uses the proceeds from the issuance of commercial paper notes for general corporate purposes. The Company did not have any commercial paper notes outstanding as of each of July 25, 2015 and July 26, 2014.

(b) Long-Term Debt

The following table summarizes the Company's long-term debt (in millions, except percentages):

	Maturity Date	July 25, 2015		July 26, 2014	
		Amount	Effective Rate	Amount	Effective Rate
Senior notes:					
Floating-rate notes:					
Three-month LIBOR plus 0.05%	September 3, 2015	$ 850	0.43%	$ 850	0.35%
Three-month LIBOR plus 0.28%	March 3, 2017	1,000	0.63%	1,000	0.56%
Three-month LIBOR plus 0.31%	June 15, 2018[1]	900	0.65%	—	—
Three-month LIBOR plus 0.50%	March 1, 2019	500	0.84%	500	0.78%
Fixed-rate notes:					
2.90%	November 17, 2014	—	—	500	3.11%
5.50%	February 22, 2016	3,000	3.07%	3,000	3.04%
1.10%	March 3, 2017	2,400	0.59%	2,400	0.56%
3.15%	March 14, 2017	750	0.85%	750	0.79%
1.65%	June 15, 2018[1]	1,600	1.72%	—	—
4.95%	February 15, 2019	2,000	4.70%	2,000	4.69%
2.125%	March 1, 2019	1,750	0.80%	1,750	0.77%
4.45%	January 15, 2020	2,500	3.01%	2,500	2.98%
2.45%	June 15, 2020[1]	1,500	2.54%	—	—
2.90%	March 4, 2021	500	0.96%	500	0.93%
3.00%	June 15, 2022[1]	500	1.21%	—	—
3.625%	March 4, 2024	1,000	1.08%	1,000	1.05%
3.50%	June 15, 2025[1]	500	1.37%	—	—
5.90%	February 15, 2039	2,000	6.11%	2,000	6.11%
5.50%	January 15, 2040	2,000	5.67%	2,000	5.67%
Other long-term debt		1	2.08%	4	2.39%
Total		25,251		20,754	
Unaccreted discount/issuance costs		(131)		(127)	
Hedge accounting fair value adjustments		231		210	
Total		$25,351		$20,837	
Reported as:					
Current portion of long-term debt		$3,894		$500	
Long-term debt		21,457		20,337	
Total		$25,351		$20,837	

[1] In June 2015, the Company issued senior notes for an aggregate principal amount of $5.0 billion.

To achieve its interest rate risk management objectives, the Company entered into interest rate swaps in prior periods with an aggregate notional amount of $11.4 billion designated as fair value hedges of certain of its fixed-rate senior notes. In effect, these swaps convert the fixed interest rates of the fixed-rate notes to floating interest rates based on the London InterBank Offered Rate (LIBOR). The gains and losses related to changes in the fair value of the interest rate swaps substantially offset changes in the fair value of the hedged portion of the underlying debt that are attributable to the changes in market interest rates. For additional information, see Note 11.

The effective rates for the fixed-rate debt include the interest on the notes, the accretion of the discount, and, if applicable, adjustments related to hedging. Interest is payable semiannually on each class of the senior fixed-rate notes and payable quarterly on the floating-rate notes. Each of the senior fixed-rate notes is redeemable by the Company at any time, subject to a make-whole premium.

The senior notes rank at par with the commercial paper notes that may be issued in the future pursuant to the Company's short-term debt financing program, as discussed above under "(a) Short-Term Debt." As of July 25, 2015, the Company was in compliance with all debt covenants.

As of July 25, 2015, future principal payments for long-term debt, including the current portion, are summarized as follows (in millions):

Fiscal Year	Amount
2016	$ 3,850
2017	4,151
2018	2,500
2019	4,250
2020	4,000
Thereafter	6,500
Total	$25,251

(c) Credit Facility

On May 15, 2015, the Company entered into a credit agreement with certain institutional lenders that provides for a $3.0 billion unsecured revolving credit facility that is scheduled to expire on May 15, 2020. Any advances under the credit agreement will accrue interest at rates that are equal to, based on certain conditions, either (i) the highest of (a) the Federal Funds rate plus 0.50%, (b) Bank of America's "prime rate" as announced from time to time, or (c) LIBOR, or a comparable or successor rate that is approved by the Administrative Agent ("Eurocurrency Rate"), for an interest period of one-month plus 1.00%, or (ii) the Eurocurrency Rate, plus a margin that is based on the Company's senior debt credit ratings as published by Standard & Poor's Financial Services, LLC and Moody's Investors Service, Inc., provided that in no event will the Eurocurrency Rate be less than zero. The credit agreement requires the Company to comply with certain covenants, including that it maintain an interest coverage ratio as defined in the agreement.

The Company may also, upon the agreement of either the then-existing lenders or additional lenders not currently parties to the agreement, increase the commitments under the credit facility by up to an additional $2.0 billion and/or extend the expiration date of the credit facility up to May 15, 2022. As of July 25, 2015, the Company was in compliance with the required interest coverage ratio and the other covenants, and the Company had not borrowed any funds under the credit facility.

This credit facility replaces the Company's prior credit facility that was entered into on February 17, 2012, which was terminated in connection with its entering into the new credit facility.

CONVERTIBLE DEBT

2.95 YAHOO! INC. (DEC)
CONSOLIDATED BALANCE SHEETS (in part)

(In thousands, except par values)	December 31, 2014	December 31, 2015
Liabilities And Equity (in part)		
Current liabilities		
Accounts payable	$ 238,018	$ 208,691
Income taxes payable related to sale of Alibaba Group ADSs	3,282,293	—
Other accrued expenses and current liabilities	657,709	934,658
Deferred revenue	336,963	134,031
Total current liabilities	4,514,983	1,277,380
Convertible notes	1,170,423	1,233,485
Long-term deferred revenue	20,774	27,801
Other long-term liabilities	143,095	118,689
Deferred tax liabilities related to investment in Alibaba Group	16,154,906	12,611,867
Deferred and other long-term tax liabilities	917,563	855,324
Total liabilities	22,921,744	16,124,546

Note 11. Convertible Notes

0.00% Convertible Senior Notes

As of December 31, 2015, the Company had $1.4 billion principal amount of Notes outstanding. In 2013, the Company issued the Notes. The Notes were sold under a purchase agreement, dated November 20, 2013, with J.P. Morgan Securities LLC and Goldman, Sachs & Co., as representatives of the several initial purchasers named therein (collectively, the "Initial Purchasers"). The Notes were sold to the Initial Purchasers for resale to qualified institutional buyers pursuant to Rule 144 A under the Securities Act of 1933, as amended.

In connection with the issuance of the Notes, the Company entered into an indenture (the "Indenture") with respect to the Notes with The Bank of New York Mellon Trust Company, N.A., as trustee. Under the Indenture, the Notes are senior unsecured obligations of Yahoo, the Notes do not bear regular interest. The Notes mature on December 1, 2018, unless previously purchased or converted in accordance with their terms prior to such date. The Company may not redeem Notes prior to maturity. However, holders of the Notes may convert them at certain times and upon the occurrence of certain events in the future, as outlined in the indenture governing the Notes (the "Indenture"). Holders of the Notes who convert in connection with a "make-whole fundamental change," as defined in the Indenture, may require Yahoo to purchase for cash all or any portion of their Notes at a purchase price equal to 100 percent of the principal amount, plus accrued and unpaid special interest as defined in the Indenture, if any. The Notes are convertible, subject to certain conditions, into shares of Yahoo common stock at an initial conversion rate of 18.7161 shares per $1,000 principal amount of Notes (which is equivalent to an initial conversion price of approximately $53.43 per share), subject to adjustment upon the occurrence of certain events. Certain corporate events described in the Indenture may increase the conversion rate for holders who elect to convert their Notes in connection with such corporate event should they occur. Upon conversion of the Notes, holders will receive cash, shares of Yahoo's common stock, or a combination thereof, at Yahoo's election. The Company's intent is to settle the principal amount of the Notes in cash upon conversion. If the conversion value exceeds the principal amount, the Company will deliver shares of its common stock in respect to the remainder of its conversion obligation in excess of the aggregate principal amount (conversion spread). The conversion spread will be included in the denominator for the computation of diluted net income per common share, using the treasury stock method. As of December 31, 2015, none of the conditions allowing holders of the Notes to convert had been met.

In accounting for the issuance of the Notes, the Company separated the Notes into liability and equity components. The carrying amount of the liability component was calculated by measuring the estimated fair value of a similar liability that does not have an associated convertible feature. The carrying amount of the equity component representing the conversion option was determined by deducting the fair value of the liability component from the face value of the Notes as a whole. The excess of the principal amount of the liability component over its carrying amount ("debt discount") is amortized to interest expense over the term of the Notes using the effective interest method with an effective interest rate of 5.26 percent per annum. The equity component is not remeasured as long as it continues to meet the conditions for equity classification.

In accounting for the transaction costs related to the Note issuance, the Company allocated the total amount incurred to the liability and equity components based on their relative values. Issuance costs attributable to the $1.4 billion liability component are being amortized to expense over the term of the Notes, and issuance costs attributable to the $306 million equity component were included with the equity component in stockholders' equity. Additionally, the Company recorded a deferred tax liability of $37 million on a portion of the equity component transaction costs which are deductible for tax purposes.

The Notes consist of the following (in thousands):

	December 31, 2014	December 31, 2015
Liability component:		
Principal	$1,437,500	$1,437,500
Less: note discount	(267,077)	(204,015)
Net carrying amount	$1,170,423	$1,233,485
Equity component[(*)]	$ 305,569	$ 305,569

[(*)] Recorded on the consolidated balance sheet within additional paid-in capital.

The following table sets forth total interest expense recognized related to the Notes (in thousands):

	Years Ended December 31,		
	2013	2014	2015
Accretion of convertible note discount	$ 4,846	$59,838	$63,061

The estimated fair value of the Notes, which was determined based on inputs that are observable in the market (Level 2), and the carrying value of debt instruments (the carrying value excludes the equity component of the Notes classified in equity) were as follows (in thousands):

	December 31, 2014		December 31, 2015	
	Fair Value	Carrying Value	Fair Value	Carrying Value
Convertible senior notes	$1,175,240	$1,170,423	$1,250,124	$1,233,485

Note Hedge Transactions and Warrant Transactions

The Company entered into note hedge transactions with certain option counterparties (the "Option Counterparties") to reduce the potential dilution with respect to Yahoo's common stock upon conversion of the Notes or offset any cash payment the Company is required to make in excess of the principal amount of converted Notes. For the year ended December 31, 2013, the Company paid $206 million for the note hedge transactions. Separately, the Company also entered into privately negotiated warrant transactions with the Option Counterparties giving them the right to purchase common stock from the Company. The warrant transactions will have a dilutive effect with respect to Yahoo's common stock to the extent that the market price per share of its common stock exceeds the strike price of $71.24 per share of the warrants on or prior to the expiration date of the warrants. The warrants begin to expire in March 2019. For the year ended December 31, 2013, the Company received $125 million in proceeds from the issuance of warrants. The note hedges and warrants are not marked to market. The value of the note hedges and warrants were initially recorded in stockholders' equity and continue to be classified as stockholders' equity.

Trade Accounts Payable

RECOGNITION AND MEASUREMENT

2.96 FASB ASC 210 states that current liabilities generally include obligations for items that have entered into the operating cycle, such as payables incurred in the acquisition of materials and supplies to be used in the production of goods or in providing services to be offered for sale.

PRESENTATION

2.97 Rule 5.02 of Regulation S-X requires that amounts payable to trade creditors be separately stated.

DISCLOSURE

2.98 Under FASB ASC 825, fair value disclosure is not required for trade payables when the carrying amount of the trade payable approximates its fair value.

Employee-Related Liabilities

PRESENTATION

2.99 FASB ASC 715, *Compensation—Retirement Benefits*, requires that an entity recognize the overfunded or underfunded status of a single-employer defined benefit postretirement plan as an asset or a liability in its statement of financial position. FASB ASC 715 also requires an employer presenting a classified balance sheet to classify the liability for an underfunded plan as a current liability, a noncurrent liability, or a combination of both. The current portion (determined on a plan-by-plan basis) is the amount by which the actuarial present value of benefits included in the benefit obligation that is payable in the next 12 months, or operating cycle if longer, exceeds the fair value of plan assets. The asset for an overfunded plan should be classified as a noncurrent asset in a classified balance sheet. The amount classified as a current liability is limited to the amount of the plan's unfunded status recognized in the employer's balance sheet.

DISCLOSURE

2.100 FASB ASC 715 requires that employers recognize changes in that funded status in comprehensive income and disclose in the notes to financial statements additional information about plan assets, the benefit obligation, reconciliations of beginning and ending balances of both plan assets and obligations, and net periodic benefit cost.

2.101 FASB ASC 715-80 requires additional disclosures related to multiemployer plans. An entity should include details in these disclosures including plan names and identifying numbers for significant multiemployer plans, the level of employer's participation in the plans, the financial health of the plans, and the nature of the employer commitments to the plans.

PRESENTATION AND DISCLOSURE EXCERPTS

EMPLOYEE-RELATED LIABILITIES

2.102 INSPERITY, INC. (DEC)
CONSOLIDATED BALANCE SHEETS (in part)

(In thousands)

Liabilities And Stockholders' Equity (in part)	December 31, 2015	December 31, 2014
Current liabilities:		
Accounts payable	$ 5,381	$ 4,674
Payroll taxes and other payroll deductions payable	205,393	176,341
Accrued worksite employee payroll cost	161,917	192,396
Accrued health insurance costs	13,643	18,329
Accrued workers' compensation costs	39,053	45,592
Accrued corporate payroll and commissions	39,103	32,644
Other accrued liabilities	20,250	22,444
Income tax payable	2,971	4,031
Total current liabilities	487,711	496,451
Noncurrent liabilities:		
Accrued workers' compensation costs	124,746	92,048
Total noncurrent liabilities	124,746	92,048

NOTES TO CONSOLIDATED FINANCIAL STATEMENTS (in part)

1. Accounting Policies (in part)

Health Insurance Costs

We provide group health insurance coverage to our worksite employees through a national network of carriers including UnitedHealthcare ("United"), UnitedHealthcare of California, Kaiser Permanente, Blue Shield of California, HMSA BlueCross BlueShield and Tufts, all of which provide fully insured policies or service contracts. In 2015, we terminated our relationship with Unity Health Plan.

The policy with United provides the majority of our health insurance coverage. As a result of certain contractual terms, we have accounted for this plan since its inception using a partially self-funded insurance accounting model. Accordingly, we record the cost of the United portion of the plan, including an estimate of the incurred claims, taxes and administrative fees (collectively the "Plan Costs") as benefits expense in the Consolidated Statements of Operations. The estimated incurred claims are based upon: (i) the level of claims processed during each quarter; (ii) estimated completion rates based upon recent claim development patterns under the plan; and (iii) the number of participants in the plan, including both active and COBRA enrollees. Each reporting period, changes in the estimated ultimate costs resulting from claim trends, plan design and migration, participant demographics and other factors are incorporated into the benefits costs.

Additionally, since the plan's inception, under the terms of the contract, United establishes cash funding rates 90 days in advance of the beginning of a reporting quarter. If the Plan Costs for a reporting quarter are greater than the premiums paid and owed to United, a deficit in the plan would be incurred and a liability for the excess costs would be accrued in our Consolidated Balance Sheets. On the other hand, if the Plan Costs for the reporting quarter are less than the premiums paid and owed to United, a surplus in the plan would be incurred and we would record an asset for the excess premiums in our Consolidated Balance Sheets. The terms of the arrangement require us to maintain an accumulated cash surplus in the plan of $9.0 million, which is reported as long-term prepaid insurance. In addition, United requires a deposit equal to approximately one day of claims funding activity, which was $3.5 million as of December 31, 2015, and is reported as a long-term asset. As of December 31, 2015, Plan Costs were less than the net premiums paid and owed to United by $2.2 million. As this amount is less than the agreed-upon $9.0 million surplus maintenance level, the $6.8 million difference is included in accrued health insurance costs, a current liability, in our Consolidated Balance Sheets. In addition, the premiums owed to United at December 31, 2015, were $3.1 million, which is also included in accrued health insurance costs, a current liability in our Consolidated Balance Sheets.

Workers' Compensation Costs

Our workers' compensation coverage has been provided through an arrangement with the ACE Group of Companies ("the ACE Program") since 2007. The ACE Program is fully insured in that ACE has the responsibility to pay all claims incurred regardless of whether we satisfy our responsibilities. Under the ACE Program, we bear the economic burden for the first $1 million layer of claims per occurrence, and effective October 1, 2010, we also bear the economic burden for a maximum aggregate amount of $5 million per policy year for claim amounts that exceed the first $1 million. ACE bears the economic burden for all claims in excess of these levels.

Because we bear the economic burden for claims up to the levels noted above, such claims, which are the primary component of our workers' compensation costs, are recorded in the period incurred. Workers' compensation insurance includes ongoing health care and indemnity coverage whereby claims are paid over numerous years following the date of injury. Accordingly, the accrual of related incurred costs in each reporting period includes estimates, which take into account the ongoing development of claims and therefore requires a significant level of judgment.

We employ a third party actuary to estimate our loss development rate, which is primarily based upon the nature of worksite employees' job responsibilities, the location of worksite employees, the historical frequency and severity of workers compensation claims, and an estimate of future cost trends. Each reporting period, changes in the actuarial assumptions resulting from changes in actual claims experience and other trends are incorporated into our workers' compensation claims cost estimates. During the years ended December 31, 2015 and 2014, we reduced accrued workers' compensation costs by $1.3 million and $2.9 million, respectively, for changes in estimated losses related to prior reporting periods. Workers' compensation cost estimates are discounted to present value at a rate based upon the U.S. Treasury rates that correspond with the weighted average estimated claim payout period (the average discount rate utilized in both 2015 and 2014 was 1.0%) and are accreted over the estimated claim payment period and included as a component of direct costs in our Consolidated Statements of Operations.

The following table provides the activity and balances related to incurred but not reported workers' compensation claims:

	Year ended December 31,	
(In thousands)	2015	2014
Beginning balance	$136,088	$120,833
Accrued claims	67,559	55,971
Present value discount	(3,095)	(1,998)
Paid claims	(38,368)	(38,718)
Ending balance	$162,184	$136,088
Current portion of accrued claims	$37,438	$44,040
Long-term portion of accrued claims	124,746	92,048
	$162,184	$136,088

The current portion of accrued workers' compensation costs at December 31, 2015 and 2014 includes $1.6 million of workers' compensation administrative fees in both periods.

As of December 31, the undiscounted accrued workers' compensation costs were $172.3 million in 2015 and $145.8 million in 2014.

At the beginning of each policy period, the insurance carrier establishes monthly funding requirements comprised of premium costs and funds to be set aside for payment of future claims ("claim funds"). The level of claim funds is primarily based upon anticipated worksite employee payroll levels and expected workers' compensation loss rates, as determined by the insurance carrier. Monies funded into the program for incurred claims expected to be paid within one year are recorded as restricted cash, a short-term asset, while the remainder of claim funds are included in deposits, a long-term asset in our Consolidated Balance Sheets. In 2015, we received $5.3 million for the return of excess claim funds related to the workers' compensation program, which decreased deposits. As of December 31, 2015, we had restricted cash of $37.4 million and deposits of $136.5 million.

Our estimate of incurred claim costs expected to be paid within one year is included in short-term liabilities, while our estimate of incurred claim costs expected to be paid beyond one year are included in long-term liabilities on our Consolidated Balance Sheets.

4. Deposits

The contractual arrangement with United for health insurance coverage requires us to maintain an accumulated cash surplus in the plan of $9.0 million, which is reported as long-term prepaid health insurance. Please read Note 1, "Accounting Policies," for a discussion of our accounting policies for health insurance costs.

As of December 31, 2015, we had $3.7 million in health insurance long-term deposits. Please read Note 1, "Accounting Policies," for a discussion of our accounting policies for health insurance costs.

As of December 31, 2015, we had $136.5 million in workers' compensation long-term deposits. Please read Note 1, "Accounting Policies," for a discussion of our accounting policies for workers' compensation costs.

2.103 ALLEGHENY TECHNOLOGIES INCORPORATED (DEC)
CONSOLIDATED BALANCE SHEETS (in part)

(In millions, except share and per share amounts)	December 31, 2015	December 31, 2014
Liabilities and Stockholders' Equity (in part)		
Accounts payable	$ 380.8	$ 556.7
Accrued liabilities	301.8	323.2
Short-term debt and current portion of long-term debt	3.9	17.8
Total Current Liabilities	686.5	897.7
Long-term debt	1,491.8	1,498.2
Accrued postretirement benefits	359.2	415.8
Pension liabilities	833.8	739.3
Deferred income taxes	75.6	143.1
Other long-term liabilities	108.3	156.2
Total Liabilities	3,555.2	3,850.3

NOTES TO CONSOLIDATED FINANCIAL STATEMENTS (in part)

Note 12. Pension Plans and Other Postretirement Benefits

The Company has defined benefit pension plans or defined contribution retirement plans covering substantially all employees. Benefits under the defined benefit pension plans are generally based on years of service and/or final average pay. The Company funds the U.S. pension plans in accordance with the Employee Retirement Income Security Act of 1974, as amended, and the Internal Revenue Code ("Code").

The Company also sponsors several postretirement plans covering certain salaried and hourly employees. The plans provide health care and life insurance benefits for eligible retirees. In most retiree health care plans, Company contributions towards premiums are capped based on the cost as of a certain date, thereby creating a defined contribution. For the non-collectively bargained plans, the Company maintains the right to amend or terminate the plans at its discretion.

In December 2014, the Company announced several significant changes to its retirement benefit programs. These changes are part of the Company's ongoing initiatives to create an integrated and aligned business with a market competitive, cost competitive, and consistent health, welfare and retirement benefit structure across its operations. These changes included:
- Freezing all future benefit accruals to its U.S. qualified defined benefit pension plan (U.S. Plan), and to the Company's non-qualified defined benefit pension plans, including the executive Supplemental Pension Plan, effective December 31, 2014.
- Implementing a consistent defined contribution retirement plan with a base 6.5% company contribution and up to 3% in Company matching contributions across all U.S. operations effective January 1, 2015.
- Ending Company-provided salaried retiree life insurance benefits effective January 1, 2015.
- Ending all remaining Company-provided salaried retiree medical benefits on January 1, 2016. The salaried retiree medical benefit plan being ended was assumed as part of the 2011 Ladish acquisition. Certain participants in the retiree medical plan will have transition provisions through the end of 2016.
- These changes to pension, retiree life insurance and medical benefits do not affect benefits for those employees or retirees covered by collective bargaining contracts or other contractual employment agreements.

The components of pension and other postretirement benefit expense for the Company's defined benefit plans included the following:

(In millions)	Pension Benefits			Other Postretirement Benefits		
	2015	2014	2013	2015	2014	2013
Service cost—benefits earned during the year	$ 22.8	$ 29.4	$ 39.0	$ 2.7	$ 2.9	$ 3.2
Interest cost on benefits earned in prior years	121.0	133.6	122.8	17.9	24.0	22.4
Expected return on plan assets	(168.3)	(184.2)	(176.0)	(0.1)	(0.3)	(0.5)
Amortization of prior service cost (credit)	1.3	2.3	3.0	4.9	(3.0)	(18.2)
Amortization of net actuarial loss	60.4	74.0	111.8	14.6	14.1	17.2
Curtailment (gain) loss	—	0.5	—	—	(25.5)	—
Termination benefits	—	0.3	4.8	—	—	1.3
Total retirement benefit expense	$ 37.2	$ 55.9	$ 105.4	$40.0	$ 12.2	$ 25.4

Other postretirement benefit costs for a defined contribution plan were $2.6 million and $4.6 million for the fiscal years ended December 31, 2014 and 2013, respectively. The curtailment loss for pension benefits recorded in 2014 relates to unamortized prior service cost recognized as a result of the freezing of pension benefit accruals in the fourth quarter of 2014, as discussed above. The curtailment gain for other postretirement benefits recorded in 2014 relates to the changes to salaried retiree life insurance and medical benefits in the fourth quarter of 2014 as discussed above. Special termination benefits recorded in 2014 relate to the acceptance of an early retirement benefit in the Forged Products business. Special termination benefits recorded in 2013 relate largely to the closure of the Flat Rolled Product segment's Wallingford, CT finishing facility, and these costs were reported in restructuring costs for segment reporting (see Notes 16 and 17).

Actuarial assumptions used to develop the components of defined benefit pension expense and other postretirement benefit expense were as follows:

	Pension Benefits			Other Postretirement Benefits		
	2015	2014	2013	2015	2014	2013
Discount rate[a]	4.25%	5.15%	4.25–4.95%	4.10%	5.15%	4.25%
Rate of increase in future compensation levels	3.0–3.50%	3.0–3.50%	3.0–3.50%	—	—	—
Expected long-term rate of return on assets	8.00%	8.25%	8.25%	4.0%	8.3%	8.3%

[a] Pension expense for 2013 was initially measured at a 4.25% discount rate. The U.S. Plan was remeasured using a 4.95% discount rate as of October 31, 2013, following the sale of the tungsten materials business.

Actuarial assumptions used for the valuation of defined benefit pension and other postretirement benefit obligations at the end of the respective periods were as follows:

	Pension Benefits		Other Postretirement Benefits	
	2015	2014	2015	2014
Discount rate	4.65%	4.25%	4.50%	4.10%
Rate of increase in future compensation levels	3.0–3.5%	3.0–3.5%	—	—

A reconciliation of the funded status for the Company's defined benefit pension and other postretirement benefit plans at December 31, 2015 and 2014 was as follows:

(In millions)	Pension Benefits		Other Postretirement Benefits	
	2015	2014	2015	2014
Change in benefit obligations:				
Benefit obligation at beginning of year	$2,953.9	$2,698.2	$466.1	$506.7
Service cost	22.8	29.4	2.7	2.9
Interest cost	121.0	133.6	17.9	24.0
Benefits paid	(207.4)	(269.9)	(53.4)	(54.3)
Subsidy paid	—	—	0.7	1.0
Participant contributions	0.3	0.3	—	—
Effect of currency rates	(4.8)	(4.9)	—	—
Net actuarial (gains) losses – discount rate change	(124.4)	288.5	(14.1)	39.5
– other	44.5	78.4	(19.1)	(19.5)
Plan curtailments	—	—	—	(7.2)
Plan settlements	—	—	—	(27.0)
Special termination benefits	—	0.3	—	—
Benefit obligation at end of year	$2,805.9	$2,953.9	$400.8	$466.1

Pension benefit payments in 2014 include approximately $52 million associated with a one-time, voluntary lump sum cash out offer to terminated vested participants in the U.S. Plan. Changes in the pension benefit obligation for 2014 include the effects of updated estimates of participant life expectancy, including consideration of the impacts of the updated 2014 U.S. Society of Actuaries projections and Company-specific experience. These mortality assumption changes increased the pension benefit obligation at December 31, 2014 by approximately $90 million.

(In millions)	Pension Benefits		Other Postretirement Benefits	
	2015	2014	2015	2014
Change in plan assets:				
Fair value of plan assets at beginning of year	$2,204.4	$2,329.8	$ 2.9	$ 4.0
Actual returns on plan assets and plan expenses	(41.1)	136.8	(1.0)	(0.9)
Employer contributions	10.3	11.5	—	—
Participant contributions	0.3	0.3	—	—
Effect of currency rates	(4.2)	(4.1)	—	—
Benefits paid	(207.4)	(269.9)	(0.1)	(0.2)
Fair value of plan assets at end of year	$1,962.3	$2,204.4	$ 1.8	$ 2.9
Amounts recognized in the consolidated balance sheet:				
Current liabilities	(9.8)	(10.2)	(39.8)	(47.3)
Noncurrent liabilities	(833.8)	(739.3)	(359.2)	(415.8)
Total amount recognized	$ (843.6)	$ (749.5)	$(399.0)	$(463.1)

Changes to accumulated other comprehensive loss related to pension and other postretirement benefit plans in 2015 and 2014 were as follows:

(In millions)	Pension Benefits		Other Postretirement Benefits	
	2015	2014	2015	2014
Beginning of year accumulated other comprehensive loss	$(1,352.1)	$(1,016.4)	$(152.9)	$(151.5)
Amortization of net actuarial loss	60.4	74.0	14.6	14.1
Amortization of prior service cost (credit)	1.3	2.3	4.9	(3.0)
Remeasurements	(127.8)	(412.0)	32.0	(12.5)
End of year accumulated other comprehensive loss	$(1,418.2)	$(1,352.1)	$(101.4)	$(152.9)
Net change in accumulated other comprehensive loss	$ (66.1)	$ (335.7)	$ 51.5	$ (1.4)

Amounts included in accumulated other comprehensive loss at December 31, 2015 and 2014 were as follows:

(In millions)	Pension Benefits		Other Postretirement Benefits	
	2015	2014	2015	2014
Prior service cost	$ (3.6)	$ (4.9)	$ (6.9)	$ (11.8)
Net actuarial loss	(1,414.6)	(1,347.2)	(94.5)	(141.1)
Accumulated other comprehensive loss	(1,418.2)	(1,352.1)	(101.4)	(152.9)
Deferred tax effect	529.9	514.7	38.5	58.8
Accumulated other comprehensive loss, net of tax	$ (888.3)	$ (837.4)	$ (62.9)	$ (94.1)

Retirement benefit expense for 2016 for defined benefit plans is estimated to be approximately $98 million, comprised of $64 million for pension expense and $34 million of expense for other postretirement benefits. As a result of the pension freeze effective December 31, 2014 and the resultant determination of inactive status, beginning in 2015, the U.S. Plan and the non-qualified U.S. pension plans changed the amortization period for accumulated other comprehensive loss recognition to the average remaining life expectancy, which is approximately 18 years on a weighted average basis, rather than the average remaining service period of 10 years, which was used in 2014 and prior periods.

Amounts in accumulated other comprehensive loss that are expected to be recognized as components of net periodic benefit cost in 2016 are:

(In millions)	Pension Benefits	Other Postretirement Benefits	Total
Amortization of prior service cost	$ 1.3	$ 4.9	$ 6.2
Amortization of net actuarial loss	65.4	9.5	74.9
Amortization of accumulated other comprehensive loss	$66.7	$14.4	$81.1

The accumulated benefit obligation for all defined benefit pension plans was $2,767.0 million and $2,917.3 million at December 31, 2015 and 2014, respectively. Additional information for pension plans with accumulated benefit obligations in excess of plan assets:

(In millions)	Pension Benefits	
	2015	2014
Projected benefit obligation	$2,805.9	$2,953.9
Accumulated benefit obligation	$2,767.0	$2,917.3
Fair value of plan assets	$1,962.3	$2,204.4

Based upon current regulations and actuarial studies, the Company does not expect to be required to make significant cash contributions to its U.S. Plan for 2016. However, the Company may elect, depending upon the investment performance of the pension plan assets and other factors, to make voluntary cash contributions to this pension plan in the future. For 2016, the Company expects to fund benefits of approximately $10 million for its U.S. nonqualified benefit pension plans and its U.K. defined benefit plan.

The following table summarizes expected benefit payments from the Company's various pension and other postretirement benefit defined benefit plans through 2025, and also includes estimated Medicare Part D subsidies projected to be received during this period based on currently available information.

(In millions)	Pension Benefits	Other Postretirement Benefits	Medicare Part D Subsidy
2016	$200.2	$ 42.6	$1.1
2017	195.0	35.7	1.0
2018	194.4	34.5	1.0
2019	191.7	34.2	1.0
2020	190.5	34.3	0.9
2021–2025	917.8	144.6	3.9

The annual assumed rate of increase in the per capita cost of covered benefits (the health care cost trend rate) for health care plans was 8.0% in 2016 and is assumed to gradually decrease to 4.5% in the year 2038 and remain at that level thereafter. Assumed health care cost trend rates have a significant effect on the amounts reported for the health care plans. A one percentage point change in assumed health care cost trend rates would have the following effects:

(In millions)	One Percentage Point Increase	One Percentage Point Decrease
Effect on total of service and interest cost components for the year ended December 31, 2015	$0.5	$(0.4)
Effect on other postretirement benefit obligation at December 31, 2015	$7.6	$(6.8)

The plan assets for the U.S. Plan represent approximately 96% of total pension plan assets at December 31, 2015. The U.S. Plan invests in a diversified portfolio consisting of an array of asset classes that attempts to maximize returns while minimizing volatility. These asset classes include U.S. domestic equities, developed market equities, emerging market equities, private equity, global high quality and high yield fixed income, floating rate debt and real estate. The Company continually monitors the investment results of these asset classes and its fund managers, and explores other potential asset classes for possible future investment.

U.S. Plan assets at December 31, 2015 and 2014 included 3.0 million shares of ATI common stock with a fair value of $33.2 million and $102.7 million, respectively. Dividends of $1.8 million and $2.1 million were received by the U.S. Plan in 2015 and 2014, respectively, on the ATI common stock held by this plan.

The fair values of the Company's pension plan assets at December 31, 2015 by asset category and by the level of inputs used to determine fair value, were as follows:

(In millions) Asset category	Total	Quoted Prices in Active Markets for Identical Assets (Level 1)	Significant Observable Inputs (Level 2)	Significant Unobservable Inputs (Level 3)
Equity securities:				
ATI common stock	$ 33.2	$ 33.2	$ —	$ —
Other U.S. equities[a]	522.0	254.1	267.9	—
International equities[b]	239.8	—	239.8	—
Global debt securities and cash:[c]				
Fixed income and cash equivalents	369.7	0.2	361.0	8.5
Floating rate	358.0	—	—	358.0
Private equity	201.2	—	—	201.2
Hedge funds	51.9	—	—	51.9
Real estate and other	186.5	—	5.9	180.6
Total assets	$1,962.3	$287.5	$874.6	$800.2

[a] Includes investments in commingled funds that invest in U.S. equity securities, comprised of approximately 90% large-cap U.S. companies and 10% small-cap U.S. companies.

[b] Includes investments in commingled funds that invest in non-U.S. equity securities, comprised of approximately 90% developed countries and 10% emerging market economies.

[c] Global debt securities include both fixed interest rate and floating interest rate instruments. These are comprised of actively managed investments which include U.S. government and U.S. government agency securities, foreign government securities, corporate bonds, mortgage-backed securities and other debt securities, and include both investment grade and non-investment grade debt, public and private debt, and secured and unsecured debt investments. To mitigate risk, investment managers have limitations regarding the amount of investment in particular securities and the credit quality of such investments.

The fair values of the Company's pension plan assets at December 31, 2014 by asset category and by the level of inputs used to determine fair value, were as follows:

(In millions) Asset category	Total	Quoted Prices in Active Markets for Identical Assets (Level 1)	Significant Observable Inputs (Level 2)	Significant Unobservable Inputs (Level 3)
Equity securities:				
ATI common stock	$ 102.7	$102.7	$ —	$ —
Other U.S. equities[a]	673.8	306.1	367.7	—
International equities[b]	238.2	—	238.2	—
Global debt securities and cash:[c]				
Fixed income and cash equivalents	383.5	0.7	373.9	8.9
Floating rate	392.3	—	—	392.3
Private equity	172.6	—	—	172.6
Hedge funds	84.7	—	—	84.7
Real estate and other	156.6	—	5.4	151.2
Total assets	$2,204.4	$409.5	$985.2	$809.7

[a] Includes investments in commingled funds that invest in U.S. equity securities, comprised of approximately 90% large-cap U.S. companies and 10% small-cap U.S. companies.

[b] Includes investments in commingled funds that invest in non-U.S. equity securities, comprised of approximately 80% developed countries and 20% emerging market economies.

[c] Global debt securities include both fixed interest rate and floating interest rate instruments. These are comprised of actively managed investments which include U.S. government and U.S. government agency securities, foreign government securities, corporate bonds, mortgage-backed securities and other debt securities, and include both investment grade and non-investment grade debt, public and private debt, and secured and unsecured debt investments. To mitigate risk, investment managers have limitations regarding the amount of investment in particular securities and the credit quality of such investments.

Changes in the fair value of Level 3 pension plan assets for the year ended December 31, 2015 were as follows:

(In millions)	January 1, 2015 Balance	Net Realized and Unrealized Gains (Losses)	Net Purchases, Issuances and Settlements	Net Transfers Into (Out Of) Level 3	December 31, 2015 Balance
Global debt securities and cash:					
Fixed income and cash equivalents	$ 8.9	$ —	$ (0.4)	$—	$ 8.5
Floating rate debt	392.3	6.8	(41.1)	—	358.0
Private equity	172.6	11.7	16.9	—	201.2
Hedge funds	84.7	2.5	(35.3)	—	51.9
Real estate and other	151.2	22.5	6.9	—	180.6
Total	$809.7	$43.5	$(53.0)	$—	$800.2

Changes in the fair value of Level 3 pension plan assets for the year ended December 31, 2014 were as follows:

(In millions)	January 1, 2014 Balance	Net Realized and Unrealized Gains (Losses)	Net Purchases, Issuances and Settlements	Net Transfers Into (Out Of) Level 3	December 31, 2014 Balance
Global debt securities and cash:					
Fixed income and cash equivalents	$ 0.8	$ 0.1	$ 8.0	$—	$ 8.9
Floating rate debt	294.5	4.6	93.2	—	392.3
Private equity	123.0	20.5	29.1	—	172.6
Hedge funds	111.2	4.5	(31.0)	—	84.7
Real estate and other	125.8	13.7	11.7	—	151.2
Total	$655.3	$43.4	$111.0	$—	$809.7

A financial instrument's categorization within the valuation hierarchy is based upon the lowest level of input that is significant to the fair value measurement. Investments in U.S. and International equities, and Fixed Income are predominantly held in common/collective trust funds and registered investment companies. These investments are public investment vehicles valued using the net asset value (NAV) provided by the administrator of the fund. The NAV is based on the value of the underlying assets owned by the fund, minus its liabilities, and then divided by the number of shares outstanding. In certain cases NAV is a quoted price in a market that is not active, and valuation is based on quoted prices for similar assets and liabilities in active markets, and these investments are classified within Level 2 of the valuation hierarchy. Investments that are not actively traded, such as non-publicly traded real estate funds, are classified within Level 3 of the valuation hierarchy, as the NAV is based on significant unobservable information.

Hedge fund investments are made either (1) as a limited partner in a portfolio of underlying hedge funds managed by a general partner or (2) through commingled institutional funds (CIFs) that in-turn invest in various portfolios of hedge funds whereby the allocation of the Plan's investments to each CIF is managed by a third party Investment Manager. All hedge fund investments are classified within Level 3 of the valuation hierarchy, as the valuations are substantially based on unobservable information.

Private equity investments include both Direct Funds and Fund-of-Funds. All private equity investments are classified as Level 3 in the valuation hierarchy, as the valuations are substantially based upon unobservable information. Direct Funds are investments in Limited Partnership (LP) interests. Fund-of-Funds are investments in private equity funds that invest in other private equity funds or LPs.

Real estate investments are made either (1) as a limited partner in a portfolio of properties managed by a general partner or (2) through a CIF that invests in a portfolio of real estate funds.

For certain investments classified as Level 3 which have formal financial valuations reported on a one-quarter lag, fair value is determined utilizing net asset values adjusted for subsequent cash flows, estimated financial performance and other significant events.

For 2016, the expected long-term rate of returns on defined benefit pension assets will be 8.0%. In developing the expected long-term rate of return assumptions, the Company evaluated input from its third party pension plan asset managers and actuaries, including reviews of their asset class return expectations and long-term inflation assumptions. The expected long-term rate of return is based on expected asset allocations within ranges for each investment category, and includes consideration of both historical and projected annual compound returns, weighted on a 65%/35% basis, respectively. The Company's actual returns on pension assets for the last five years have been 1.2% for 2015, 6.5% for 2014, 14.3% for 2013, 8.0% for 2012, and 0.3% for 2011.

The target asset allocations for pension plans for 2016, by major investment category, are:

Asset category	Target asset allocation range
Equity securities:	
U. S. equities	18%–40%
International equities	7%–17%
Global debt securities and cash	35%–55%
Private equity*	0%–10%
Hedge funds*	0%–10%
Real estate and other*	0%–10%

* Have a combined target allocation of 18% and a 20% limit.

At December 31, 2015, other postretirement benefit plan assets of $1.8 million are primarily invested in private equity investments, which are classified as Level 3 in the valuation hierarchy, as the valuations are substantially based upon unobservable information. For 2016, the expected long-term rate of returns on these other postretirement benefit assets will be 4.0%.

Costs for defined contribution plans were $41.2 million in 2015, $21.9 million in 2014, and $24.3 million in 2013. Company contributions to these defined contribution plans are funded with cash. Higher contributions in 2015 were the result of the implementation of the Company's defined contribution retirement plan accross all U.S. operations in 2015 in conjunction with the freeze of the U.S. qualified defined benefit pension plan.

Labor agreements with USW-represented employees require the Company to make contributions to VEBA trusts based upon the attainment of a certain level of profitability. The Company expects to make approximately $7 million of contributions, tied to profitability levels, to these VEBA trusts in 2016.

The Company contributes to several multiemployer defined benefit pension plans under collective bargaining agreements that cover certain of its union-represented employees. The risks of participating in such plans are different from the risks of single-employer plans, in the following respects:

  a. Assets contributed to a multiemployer plan by one employer may be used to provide benefits to employees of other participating employers.
  b. If a participating employer ceases to contribute to the plan, the unfunded obligations of the plan may be borne by the remaining participating employers.
  c. If the Company ceases to have an obligation to contribute to the multiemployer plan in which it had been a contributing employer, it may be required to pay to the plan an amount based on the underfunded status of the plan and on the history of the Company's participation in the plan prior to the cessation of its obligation to contribute. The amount that an employer that has ceased to have an obligation to contribute to a multiemployer plan is required to pay to the plan is referred to as a withdrawal liability.

The Company's participation in multiemployer plans for the years ended December 31, 2015, 2014 and 2013 is reported in the following table. The Company's contributions to the Steelworkers Western Independent Shops Pension Plan exceed 5% of this plan's total contributions for the plan year ended September 30, 2014, which is the most recent information available from the Plan Administrator.

| Pension Fund | EIN/Pension Plan Number | Pension Protection Act Zone Status[1] | | FIP/RP Status Pending/ Implemented[2] | In Millions Company Contributions | | | Surcharge Imposed[3] | Expiration Dates of Collective Bargaining Agreements |
		2015	2014		2015	2014	2013		
Steelworkers Western Independent Shops Pension Plan	90-0169564/001	Green	Green	N/A	$0.7	$1.1	$1.0	No	6/30/2015
Boilermakers-Blacksmiths National Pension Trust	48-6168020/ 001	Yellow	Yellow	Yes	1.8	2.0	2.2	No	9/30/2018
IAM National Pension Fund	51-6031295/ 002	Green	Green	N/A	1.5	1.6	1.8	No	Various between 2018-2019[4]
Total contributions					$4.0	$4.7	$5.0		

[1] The most recent Pension Protection Act Zone Status available for ATI's fiscal years 2015 and 2014 is for plan years ending in calendar years 2014 and 2013, respectively. The zone status is based on information provided to ATI and other participating employers by each plan and is certified by the plan's actuary. A plan in the "red" zone had been determined to be in "critical status", based on criteria established by the Code, and is generally less than 65% funded. A plan in the "yellow" zone has been determined to be in "endangered status", based on criteria established under the Code, and is generally less than 80% funded. A plan in the "green" zone has been determined to be neither in "critical status" nor in "endangered status", and is generally at least 80% funded.

[2] The "FIP / RP status Pending / Implemented" column indicates whether a Funding Improvement Plan, as required under the Code by plans in the "yellow" zone, or a Rehabilitation Plan, as required under the Code to be adopted by plans in the "red" zone, is pending or has been implemented as of the end of the plan year that ended in 2015.

[3] The "Surcharge Imposed" column indicates whether ATI's contribution rate for 2015 included an amount in addition to the contribution rate specified in the applicable collective bargaining agreement, as imposed by a plan in "critical status", in accordance with the requirements of the Code.

[4] The Company is party to five separate bargaining agreements that require contributions to this plan. Expiration dates of these collective bargaining agreements range between February 25, 2018 and July 14, 2019.

Income Tax Liability

PRESENTATION

2.104 FASB ASC 210 provides general guidance for classification of accounts in balance sheets. FASB 740-10-45 addresses classification matters applicable to income tax accounts and is incremental to the general guidance.

DISCLOSURE

2.105 FASB ASC 740-10-50 provides detailed disclosures for income taxes, including the components of the net deferred tax liability or asset recognized in an entity's balance sheet.

PRESENTATION AND DISCLOSURE EXCERPT

INCOME TAXES PAYABLE

2.106 POLARIS INDUSTRIES INC. (DEC)
CONSOLIDATED BALANCE SHEETS (in part)

(In thousands, except per share data)

	December 31, 2015	December 31, 2014
Liabilities and Shareholders' Equity (in part)		
Current liabilities:		
Current portion of debt, capital lease obligations, and notes payable	$ 5,059	$ 2,528
Accounts payable	299,660	343,470
Accrued expenses:		
Compensation	106,486	102,379
Warranties	56,474	53,104
Sales promotions and incentives	141,057	138,630
Dealer holdback	123,276	120,093
Other	88,030	79,262
Income taxes payable	6,741	11,344

(continued)

	December 31, 2015	December 31, 2014
Total current liabilities	826,783	850,810
Long-term income taxes payable	23,416	10,568
Capital lease obligations	19,660	23,620
Long-term debt	438,560	200,000
Deferred tax liabilities	13,733	18,191
Other long-term liabilities	74,188	96,951
Total liabilities	$1,396,340	$1,200,140

NOTES TO CONSOLIDATED FINANCIAL STATEMENTS (in part)

Note 6. Income Taxes

Polaris' income from continuing operations before income taxes was generated from its United States and foreign operations as follows (in thousands):

	For the Years Ended December 31,		
	2015	2014	2013
United States	$640,604	$666,323	$535,265
Foreign	45,133	32,994	39,164
Income from continuing operations before income taxes	$685,737	$699,317	$574,429

Components of Polaris' provision for income taxes for continuing operations are as follows (in thousands):

	For the Years Ended December 31,		
	2015	2014	2013
Current:			
Federal	$211,017	$255,299	$167,690
State	16,609	20,438	12,942
Foreign	20,733	21,584	15,457
Deferred	(17,983)	(52,033)	(2,729)
Total provision for income taxes for continuing operations	$230,376	$245,288	$193,360

Reconciliation of the Federal statutory income tax rate to the effective tax rate is as follows:

	For the Years Ended December 31,		
	2015	2014	2013
Federal statutory rate	35.0%	35.0%	35.0%
State income taxes, net of federal benefit	1.5	1.5	1.5
Domestic manufacturing deduction	(0.8)	(1.1)	(1.0)
Research and development tax credit	(3.1)	(1.1)	(2.2)
Valuation allowance for foreign subsidiaries net operating losses	0.2	—	0.3
Other permanent differences	0.8	0.8	0.1
Effective income tax rate for continuing operations	33.6%	35.1%	33.7%

In December 2015, the President of the United States signed the Consolidated Appropriations Act, 2016, which retroactively reinstated the research and development tax credit for 2015, and also made the research and development tax credit permanent. In addition to the 2015 research and development credits, the Company filed amended returns to claim additional credits related to qualified research expenditures incurred in prior years. In January 2013, the President of the United States signed the American Taxpayers Relief Act of 2012, which reinstated the research and development tax credit. As a result, the impact of both the 2012 and 2013 research and development tax credits were recorded in the 2013 tax provision.

Undistributed earnings relating to certain non-U.S. subsidiaries of approximately $143,284,000 and $105,782,000 at December 31, 2015 and 2014, respectively, are considered to be permanently reinvested; accordingly, no provision for U.S. federal income taxes has been provided thereon. If the Company were to distribute these earnings, it would be subject to both U.S. income taxes (subject to an adjustment for foreign tax credits reflecting the amounts paid to non-U.S. taxing authorities) and withholding taxes payable to the non-U.S. countries. Determination of the unrecognized deferred U.S. income tax liability related to these undistributed earnings is not practicable due to the complexities associated with this hypothetical calculation.

Polaris utilizes the liability method of accounting for income taxes whereby deferred taxes are determined based on the estimated future tax effects of differences between the financial statement and tax bases of assets and liabilities given the provisions of enacted tax laws.

In November 2015, the FASB issued ASU No. 2015-17, *Balance Sheet Classification of Deferred Taxes*. This ASU requires entities to present deferred tax assets and deferred tax liabilities as noncurrent in the consolidated balance sheet. The Company has early adopted the requirements of ASU No. 2015-17, and applied the amended provisions prospectively. The net deferred income taxes consist of the following (in thousands):

	December 31,	
	2015	**2014**
Current deferred income taxes:		
Inventories	—	$ 9,034
Accrued expenses	—	104,279
Derivative instruments	—	864
Total current	—	114,177
Noncurrent deferred income taxes:		
Inventories	$ 10,047	—
Accrued expenses	107,767	—
Derivative instruments	(1,112)	—
Cost in excess of net assets of business acquired	(7,956)	(13,111)
Property and equipment	(28,853)	(28,921)
Compensation payable in common stock	67,222	58,446
Net operating loss carryforwards and impairments	12,374	12,693
Valuation allowance	(6,684)	(6,097)
Total noncurrent	152,805	23,010
Total net deferred income tax asset	$152,805	$137,187

At December 31, 2015, the Company had available unused international and acquired federal net operating loss carryforwards of $38,039,000. The net operating loss carryforwards will expire at various dates from 2016 to 2034, with certain jurisdictions having indefinite carryforward terms.

Polaris classified liabilities related to unrecognized tax benefits as long-term income taxes payable in the accompanying consolidated balance sheets in accordance with ASC Topic 740. Polaris recognizes potential interest and penalties related to income tax positions as a component of the provision for income taxes on the consolidated statements of income. Reserves related to potential interest are recorded as a component of long-term income taxes payable. The entire balance of unrecognized tax benefits at December 31, 2015, if recognized, would affect the Company's effective tax rate. The Company does not anticipate that total unrecognized tax benefits will materially change in the next twelve months. Tax years 2009 through 2015 remain open to examination by certain tax jurisdictions to which the Company is subject. A reconciliation of the beginning and ending amounts of unrecognized tax benefits is as follows (in thousands):

	For the Years Ended December 31,	
	2015	**2014**
Balance at January 1,	$ 9,836	$13,199
Gross increases for tax positions of prior years	9,683	55
Gross increases for tax positions of current year	4,961	1,456
Decreases due to settlements and other prior year tax positions	(178)	(2,346)
Decreases for lapse of statute of limitations	(1,364)	(1,586)
Currency translation effect on foreign balances	(429)	(942)
Balance at December 31,	22,509	9,836
Reserves related to potential interest at December 31,	907	732
Unrecognized tax benefits at December 31,	$23,416	$10,568

Current Amount of Long-Term Debt

PRESENTATION

2.107 As noted in 2.90, FASB ASC 470 addresses classification determination for specific debt obligations.

DISCLOSURE

2.108 FASB ASC 470 includes disclosures required for long-term debt (see the "Long-Term Debt" section). FASB ASC 825 requires disclosure of both the fair value and bases for estimating the fair value of the current amount of long-term debt, unless it is not practicable to estimate that value.

PRESENTATION AND DISCLOSURE EXCERPT

CURRENT AMOUNT OF LONG-TERM DEBT

2.109 NACCO INDUSTRIES, INC. (DEC)
CONSOLIDATED BALANCE SHEETS (in part)

	December 31	
(In thousands, except share data)	2015	2014
Liabilities And Equity (in part)		
Current liabilities		
Accounts payable	$100,300	$133,668
Revolving credit agreements of subsidiaries—not guaranteed by the parent company	8,365	55,000
Current maturities of long-term debt of subsidiaries—not guaranteed by the parent company	1,504	1,467
Accrued income taxes	1,935	4,015
Accrued payroll	40,854	23,567
Accrued cooperative advertising	10,676	9,899
Other current liabilities	28,112	27,065
Total current liabilities	191,746	254,681
Long-term debt of subsidiaries—not guaranteed by the parent company	160,113	191,431
Asset retirement obligations	39,780	37,399
Pension and other postretirement obligations	10,046	10,616
Other long-term liabilities	52,585	64,919
Total liabilities	454,270	559,046

NOTES TO CONSOLIDATED FINANCIAL STATEMENTS (in part)

(Tabular Amounts in Thousands, Except Per Share and Percentage Data)

Note 8—Current and Long-Term Financing (in part)

Financing arrangements are obtained and maintained at the subsidiary level. NACCO has not guaranteed any borrowings of its subsidiaries.

The following table summarizes the Company's available and outstanding borrowings:

	December 31	
	2015	2014
Total outstanding borrowings:		
Revolving credit agreements:		
NACoal	$100,000	$180,000
HBB	57,513	52,845
KC	—	—
	$157,513	$232,845
Capital lease obligations and other term loans—NACoal	$ 11,617	$ 14,445
Other debt—HBB	852	608
Total debt outstanding	$169,982	$247,898
Current portion of borrowings outstanding:		
NACoal	$ 1,504	$ 56,467
HBB	8,365	—
KC	—	—
	$ 9,869	$ 56,467
Long-term portion of borrowings outstanding:		
NACoal	$110,113	$137,978
HBB	50,000	53,453
	$160,113	$191,431
Total available borrowings, net of limitations, under revolving credit agreements:		
NACoal	$223,795	$223,995
HBB	111,590	112,105
KC	18,299	22,596
	$353,684	$358,696

(continued)

	December 31	
	2015	2014
Unused revolving credit agreements:		
NACoal	$123,795	$ 43,995
HBB	54,077	59,260
KC	18,299	22,596
	$196,171	$125,851
Weighted average stated interest rate on total borrowings:		
NACoal	2.4%	2.5%
HBB	2.3%	2.0%
KC	N/A	N/A
Weighted average effective interest rate on total borrowings (including interest rate swap agreements):		
NACoal	3.3%	3.1%
HBB	2.7%	2.5%
KC	N/A	N/A

Annual maturities of total debt, excluding capital leases, are as follows:

2016	$ —
2017	—
2018	100,000
2019	59,811
2020	—
Thereafter	—
	$159,811

Including swap settlements, interest paid on total debt was $6.5 million, $7.4 million and $5.3 million during 2015, 2014 and 2013, respectively. Interest capitalized was less than $0.1 million in 2015 and $0.3 million in 2014.

NACoal: NACoal has an unsecured revolving line of credit of up to $225.0 million (the "NACoal Facility") that expires in November 2018. Borrowings outstanding under the NACoal Facility were $100.0 million at December 31, 2015. At December 31, 2015, the excess availability under the NACoal Facility was $123.8 million, which reflects a reduction for outstanding letters of credit of $1.2 million.

The NACoal Facility has performance-based pricing, which sets interest rates based upon NACoal achieving various levels of debt to EBITDA ratios, as defined in the NACoal Facility. Borrowings bear interest at a floating rate plus a margin based on the level of debt to EBITDA ratio achieved. The applicable margins, effective December 31, 2015, for base rate and LIBOR loans were 1.00% and 2.00%, respectively. The NACoal Facility has a commitment fee which is based upon achieving various levels of debt to EBITDA ratios. The commitment fee was 0.35% on the unused commitment at December 31, 2015. The weighted average interest rate applicable to the NACoal Facility at December 31, 2015 was 3.39% including the floating rate margin and the effect of the interest rate swap agreements.

The NACoal Facility contains restrictive covenants, which require, among other things, NACoal to maintain a maximum debt to EBITDA ratio of 3.50 to 1.00 and an interest coverage ratio of not less than 4.00 to 1.00. The NACoal Facility provides the ability to make loans, dividends and advances to NACCO, with some restrictions based on maintaining a maximum debt to EBITDA ratio of 3.00 to 1.00 in conjunction with maintaining unused availability thresholds of borrowing capacity, as defined in the NACoal Facility, of $15.0 million. At December 31, 2015, NACoal was in compliance with all financial covenants in the NACoal Facility.

NACoal has a demand note payable to Coteau, one of the unconsolidated subsidiaries, which bears interest based on the applicable quarterly federal short-term interest rate as announced from time to time by the Internal Revenue Service. At December 31, 2015, the balance of the note was $1.4 million and the interest rate was 0.55%.

NACoal incurred fees and expenses of $1.2 million in the year ended December 31, 2013 related to the NACoal Facility. These fees were deferred and are being amortized as interest expense in the Consolidated Statements of Operations over the term of the NACoal Facility. No similar fees were incurred in 2015 and 2014.

Other Current Liabilities

PRESENTATION

2.110 Rule 5-02 of Regulation S-X requires that any items in excess of 5 percent of total current liabilities be stated separately on the balance sheet or disclosed in the notes. In addition, registrants should state separately amounts payable to the following:

- Banks for borrowings
- Factors or other financial institutions for borrowings
- Holders of commercial paper
- Trade creditors
- Related parties
- Underwriters, promoters, and employees (other than related parties)
- Others

Amounts applicable to the first three categories may be stated separately in the balance sheet or in a note thereto.

PRESENTATION AND DISCLOSURE EXCERPTS

DEPOSITS

2.111 THE GOLDMAN SACHS GROUP, INC. (DEC)

CONSOLIDATED STATEMENTS OF FINANCIAL CONDITION (in part)

	As of December	
$ in millions, except per share amounts	2015	2014
Liabilities and Shareholders' Equity (in part)		
Deposits (includes $14,680 and $13,523 at fair value as of December 2015 and December 2014, respectively)	$ 97,519	$ 82,880
Collateralized financings:		
Securities sold under agreements to repurchase, at fair value	86,069	88,215
Securities loaned (includes $466 and $765 at fair value as of December 2015 and December 2014, respectively)	3,614	5,570
Other secured financings (includes $23,207 and $21,450 at fair value as of December 2015 and December 2014, respectively)	24,753	22,809
Payables:		
Brokers, dealers and clearing organizations	5,406	6,636
Customers and counterparties	204,956	206,936
Financial instruments sold, but not yet purchased, at fair value	115,248	132,083
Unsecured short-term borrowings, including the current portion of unsecured long-term borrowings (includes $17,743 and $18,826 at fair value as of December 2015 and December 2014, respectively)	42,787	44,539
Unsecured long-term borrowings (includes $22,273 and $16,005 at fair value as of December 2015 and December 2014, respectively)	175,422	167,302
Other liabilities and accrued expenses (includes $1,253 and $831 at fair value as of December 2015 and December 2014, respectively)	18,893	16,075
Total liabilities	774,667	773,045

NOTES TO CONSOLIDATED FINANCIAL STATEMENTS (in part)

Note 8. Fair Value Option (in part)

Deposits. The significant inputs to the valuation of time deposits are interest rates and the amount and timing of future cash flows. The inputs used to value the embedded derivative component of hybrid financial instruments are consistent with the inputs used to value the firm's other derivative instruments. See Note 7 for further information about derivatives. See Note 14 for further information about deposits.

The firm's deposits that are included in level 3 are hybrid financial instruments. As the significant unobservable inputs used to value hybrid financial instruments primarily relate to the embedded derivative component of these deposits, these inputs are incorporated in the firm's derivative disclosures related to unobservable inputs in Note 7.

Note 14. Deposits

The table below presents deposits held in U.S. and non-U.S. offices, substantially all of which were interest-bearing. Substantially all U.S. deposits were held at Goldman Sachs Bank USA (GS Bank USA) and substantially all non-U.S. deposits were held at Goldman Sachs International Bank (GSIB).

	As of December	
$ in millions	2015	2014
U.S. offices	$81,920	$69,142
Non-U.S. offices	15,599	13,738
Total	$97,519	$82,880

The table below presents maturities of time deposits held in U.S. and non-U.S. offices.

	As of December 2015		
$ in millions	U.S.	Non-U.S.	Total
2016	$ 8,572	$8,692	$17,264
2017	6,213	119	6,332
2018	3,975	7	3,982
2019	3,931	—	3,931
2020	3,191	—	3,191
2021–thereafter	8,196	116	8,312
Total	$34,078[1]	$8,934[2]	$43,012[3]

[1] Includes $1.92 billion greater than $100,000, of which $741 million matures within three months, $730 million matures within three to six months, $326 million matures within six to twelve months, and $127 million matures after twelve months.

[2] Includes $6.98 billion greater than $100,000.

[3] Includes $14.68 billion of time deposits accounted for at fair value under the fair value option. See Note 8 for further information about deposits accounted for at fair value.

As of December 2015 and December 2014, deposits include $54.51 billion and $49.29 billion, respectively, of savings and demand deposits, which have no stated maturity, and were recorded based on the amount of cash received plus accrued interest, which approximates fair value. In addition, the firm designates certain derivatives as fair value hedges to convert substantially all of its time deposits not accounted for at fair value from fixed-rate obligations into floating-rate obligations. Accordingly, the carrying value of time deposits approximated fair value as of December 2015 and December 2014. While these savings and demand deposits and time deposits are carried at amounts that approximate fair value, they are not accounted for at fair value under the fair value option or at fair value in accordance with other U.S. GAAP and therefore are not included in the firm's fair value hierarchy in Notes 6 through 8. Had these deposits been included in the firm's fair value hierarchy, they would have been classified in level 2 as of December 2015 and December 2014.

PRODUCT WARRANTIES

2.112 FIRST SOLAR, INC. (DEC)
CONSOLIDATED BALANCE SHEETS (in part)

(In thousands, except share data)

	December 31,	
	2015	2014
Liabilities And Stockholders' Equity (in part)		
Current liabilities:		
Accounts payable	$337,668	$ 214,656
Income taxes payable	1,330	1,727
Accrued expenses	409,452	388,156
Current portion of long-term debt	38,090	51,399
Billings in excess of costs and estimated earnings	87,942	195,346
Payments and billings for deferred project costs	28,580	60,591
Other current liabilities	57,738	88,664
Total current liabilities	960,800	1,000,539

NOTES TO CONSOLIDATED FINANCIAL STATEMENTS (in part)

2. Summary of Significant Accounting Policies (in part)

Product Warranties. We provide a limited PV solar module warranty covering defects in materials and workmanship under normal use and service conditions for 10 years following the transfer of title to our modules. We also typically warrant that modules installed in accordance with agreed-upon specifications will produce at least 97% of their labeled power output rating during the first year, with the warranty coverage reducing by 0.7% every year thereafter throughout the 25-year performance warranty period. Prior to 2014, we warranted that modules installed in accordance with agreed-upon specifications would produce at least 90% of their labeled power output rating during the first 10 years following installation and at least 80% of their labeled power output rating during the following 15 years. In resolving claims under both the defect and power output warranties, we have the option of either repairing or replacing the covered modules or, under the power output warranty, providing additional modules to remedy the power shortfall. We also have the option to make a payment for the then current market price of modules to resolve the claims. Such limited module warranties are standard for module sales and are automatically transferred from the original purchasers of the solar modules to subsequent purchasers upon resale.

As an alternative form of our standard limited module power output warranty, we also offer an aggregated or system level limited module performance warranty. This system level limited module performance warranty is designed for utility-scale systems and provides 25-year system level energy degradation protection. In addition, this warranty represents a practical expedient to address the challenge of identifying, from the potential millions of modules installed in a utility-scale system, individual modules that may be performing below warranty thresholds by focusing on the aggregate energy generated by the system rather than the power output of individual modules. The system level module performance warranty typically is calculated as a percentage of a system's expected energy production, adjusted for certain actual site conditions, with the warranted level of performance declining each year in a linear fashion, but never falling below 80% during the term of the warranty. In resolving claims under the system level limited module performance warranty to restore the system to warranted performance levels, we first must validate that the root cause of the issue is due to module performance; we then have the option of either repairing or replacing the covered modules, providing supplemental modules, or making a cash payment. Consistent with our limited module power output warranty, when we elect to satisfy a warranty claim by providing replacement or supplemental modules under the system level module performance warranty, we do not have any obligation to pay for the labor to remove or install modules.

In addition to our limited solar module warranty described above, for PV solar power systems built by us, we typically provide a limited product warranty on BoS parts for defects in engineering design, installation, and workmanship for a period of one to two years following the substantial completion of a system. In resolving claims under such BoS warranties, we have the option of remedying the defect through repair or replacement.

When we recognize revenue for module or systems sales, we accrue liabilities for the estimated future costs of meeting our limited warranty obligations. We make and revise these estimates based primarily on the number of our solar modules under warranty installed at customer locations, our historical experience with warranty claims, our monitoring of field installation sites, our internal testing of and the expected future performance of our solar modules and BoS components, and our estimated per-module replacement costs.

From time to time, we have taken remediation actions with respect to affected modules beyond our limited warranties, and we may elect to do so in the future, in which case we would incur additional expenses. Such potential voluntary future remediation actions beyond our limited warranty obligations could be material to our consolidated statement of operations if we commit to any such remediation actions.

9. Consolidated Balance Sheet Details (in part)

Accrued Expenses

Accrued expenses consisted of the following at December 31, 2015 and 2014 (in thousands):

	2015	2014
Accrued compensation and benefits	$ 63,699	$ 43,072
Accrued property, plant and equipment	7,808	30,723
Accrued inventory and balance of systems parts	53,542	36,233
Accrued project assets and deferred project costs	145,695	113,012
Product warranty liability[1]	38,468	69,656
Accrued expenses in excess of normal product warranty liability and related expenses[1]	5,040	7,800
Other	95,200	87,660
Accrued expenses	$409,452	$388,156

[1] See Note 16 "Commitments and Contingencies" to our consolidated financial statements for further discussion of "Product warranty liability" and "Accrued expenses in excess of normal product warranty liability and related expenses."

16. Commitments and Contingencies (in part)

Product Warranties

When we recognize revenue for module or systems sales, we accrue liabilities for the estimated future costs of meeting our limited warranty obligations for both modules and the balance of the systems. We make and revise these estimates based primarily on the number of our solar modules under warranty installed at customer locations, our historical experience with warranty claims, our monitoring of field installation sites, our internal testing of and the expected future performance of our solar modules and BoS components, and our estimated replacement costs.

From time to time, we have taken remediation actions with respect to affected modules beyond our limited warranties, and we may elect to do so in the future, in which case we would incur additional expenses. Such potential voluntary future remediation actions beyond our limited warranty obligations could be material to our consolidated statements of operations if we commit to any such remediation actions.

Product warranty activities during the years ended December 31, 2015, 2014, and 2013 were as follows (in thousands):

	2015	2014	2013
Product warranty liability, beginning of period	$223,057	$198,041	$191,596
Accruals for new warranties issued	50,040	40,599	35,985
Settlements	(13,392)	(16,721)	(33,499)
Changes in estimate of product warranty liability	(27,954)	1,138	3,959
Product warranty liability, end of period	$231,751	$223,057	$198,041
Current portion of warranty liability	$ 38,468	$ 69,656	$ 67,097
Noncurrent portion of warranty liability	$193,283	$153,401	$130,944

We have historically estimated our limited product warranty liability for power output and defects in materials and workmanship under normal use and service conditions to have a warranty return rate of approximately 3% of modules covered under warranty. A 1% change in the estimated warranty return rate would change our module warranty liability by $71.5 million, and a 1% change in the estimated warranty return rate for BoS components would not have a material impact on the associated warranty liability.

Accrued Expenses in Excess of Product Warranty

We may also accrue expenses for the cost of any voluntary remediation programs beyond our normal product warranty. As of December 31, 2015 and 2014, accrued expenses in excess of our product warranty were $24.6 million and $30.9 million, respectively, of which $5.0 million and $7.8 million, respectively, were classified as current and included in "Accrued expenses" on our consolidated balance sheets and $19.6 million and $23.1 million, respectively, were classified as noncurrent and included in "Other liabilities" on our consolidated balance sheets. Our estimates for such remediation programs are based on an evaluation of available information including the estimated number of potentially affected solar modules, historical experience related to our remediation efforts, customer-provided data related to potentially affected systems, estimated costs for performing removal, replacement, and logistical services, and any post-sale expenses covered under our voluntary remediation program. If any of our estimates prove incorrect, we could be required to accrue additional expenses.

BILLINGS IN EXCESS OF COSTS AND ESTIMATED EARNINGS

2.113 NATIONAL OILWELL VARCO, INC. (DEC)
CONSOLIDATED BALANCE SHEETS (in part)

(In millions, except share data)

	December 31,	
	2015	2014
Liabilities And Stockholders' Equity (in part)		
Current liabilities:		
Accounts payable	$ 623	$1,189
Accrued liabilities	2,284	3,518
Billings in excess of costs	785	1,775
Current portion of long-term debt and short-term borrowings	2	152
Accrued income taxes	264	431
Deferred income taxes	291	309
Total current liabilities	4,249	7,374

2. Summary of Significant Accounting Policies (in part)

Revenue Recognition

The Company's products and services are sold based upon purchase orders or contracts with the customer that include fixed or determinable prices and that do not generally include right of return or other similar provisions or other significant post delivery obligations. Except for certain construction contracts and drill pipe sales described below, the Company records revenue at the time its manufacturing process is complete, the customer has been provided with all proper inspection and other required documentation, title and risk of loss has passed to the customer, collectability is reasonably assured and the product has been delivered. Customer advances or deposits are deferred and recognized as revenue when the Company has completed all of its performance obligations related to the sale. The Company also recognizes revenue as services are performed. The amounts billed for shipping and handling cost are included in revenue and related costs are included in cost of sales.

Revenue Recognition under Long-term Construction Contracts

The Company uses the percentage-of-completion method to account for certain long-term construction contracts in the Rig Systems and Completion & Production Solutions segments. These long-term construction contracts include the following characteristics:
- the contracts include custom designs for customer specific applications;
- the structural design is unique and requires significant engineering efforts; and
- construction projects often have progress payments.

This method requires the Company to make estimates regarding the total costs of the project, progress against the project schedule and the estimated completion date, all of which impact the amount of revenue and gross margin the Company recognizes in each reporting period. The Company prepares detailed cost estimates at the beginning of each project. Significant projects and their related costs and profit margins are updated and reviewed at least quarterly by senior management. Factors that may affect future project costs and margins include shipyard access, weather, production efficiencies, availability and costs of labor, materials and subcomponents and other factors. These factors can impact the accuracy of the Company's estimates and materially impact the Company's current and future reported earnings.

The asset, "Costs in excess of billings," represents revenues recognized in excess of amounts billed. The liability, "Billings in excess of costs," represents billings in excess of revenues recognized.

8. Costs and Estimated Earnings on Uncompleted Contracts

Costs and estimated earnings on uncompleted contracts consist of (in millions):

	December 31,	
	2015	2014
Costs incurred on uncompleted contracts	$ 9,082	$10,442
Estimated earnings	4,080	4,699
	13,162	15,141
Less: Billings to date on uncompleted contracts	12,697	15,038
	$ 465	$ 103
Costs and estimated earnings in excess of billings on uncompleted contracts	$ 1,250	$ 1,878
Billings in excess of costs and estimated earnings on uncompleted contracts	(785)	(1,775)
	$ 465	$ 103

DISCONTINUED OPERATIONS

2.114 AVON PRODUCTS, INC. (DEC)

CONSOLIDATED BALANCE SHEETS (in part)

(In millions, except per share data) December 31	2015	2014
Liabilities and Shareholders' (Deficit) Equity (in part)		
Current Liabilities		
Debt maturing within one year	$ 55.2	$ 121.7
Accounts payable	774.2	806.3
Accrued compensation	157.6	174.9
Other accrued liabilities	419.6	539.1
Sales and taxes other than income	174.9	160.8
Income taxes	23.9	36.8
Payable to discontinued operations	100.0	100.0
Current liabilities of discontinued operations	489.7	207.6
Total current liabilities	2,195.1	2,147.2

NOTES TO CONSOLIDATED FINANCIAL STATEMENTS (in part)

(U.S. dollars in millions, except per share and share data)

Note 1. Description of the Business and Summary of Significant Accounting Policies (in part)

Business

When used in these notes, the terms "Avon," "Company," "we," "our" or "us" mean Avon Products, Inc.

We are a global manufacturer and marketer of beauty and related products. Our business is conducted primarily in one channel, direct selling. Our reportable segments are based on geographic operations in three regions: Latin America; Europe, Middle East & Africa; and Asia Pacific. In addition, we operate our business in North America, which has been presented as discontinued operations for all periods presented and is discussed further below. Our product categories are Beauty and Fashion & Home. Beauty consists of skincare (which includes personal care), fragrance and color (cosmetics). Fashion & Home consists of fashion jewelry, watches, apparel, footwear, accessories, gift and decorative products, housewares, entertainment and leisure products, children's products and nutritional products. Sales are made to the ultimate consumer principally by independent Representatives.

In December 2015, we entered into definitive agreements with affiliates controlled by Cerberus Capital Management ("Cerberus"), which include a $435 investment in Avon by an affiliate of Cerberus through the purchase of our convertible preferred stock and the separation of the North America business from Avon into a privately-held company that will be majority-owned and managed by an affiliate of Cerberus. Avon will retain approximately 20% ownership in this new privately-held company. The transactions are expected to close concurrently in the first half of 2016. North America was previously its own reportable segment and has been presented as discontinued operations for all periods presented. Refer to Note 3, Discontinued Operations and Divestitures for additional information regarding the investment by an affiliate of Cerberus and the separation of the North America business.

Note 3. Discontinued Operations and Divestitures

Discontinued Operations

North America

On December 17, 2015, the Company entered into definitive agreements with affiliates controlled by Cerberus. The agreements include a an investment agreement providing for a $435 investment by Cleveland Apple Investor LLC ("Cleveland Investor") (an affiliate of Cerberus) in the Company through the purchase of perpetual convertible preferred stock and a separation and investment agreement providing for the separation of the Company's North America business, which represents the Company's operations in the United States, Canada and Puerto Rico, from the Company into a privately-held company ("NewCo") that will be majority-owned and managed by Cleveland NA Investor LLC ("Cleveland NA") (an affiliate of Cerberus) as a result of the issuance to Cleveland NA of ownership interests in NewCo. Cleveland NA will contribute $170 of cash into NewCo in exchange for 80.1% of its ownership interests. We will contribute the North America business, certain pension and postretirement liabilities and $100 of cash into NewCo and will own 19.9% of NewCo's ownership interests.

The $435 investment by Cleveland Investor in the Company will be in exchange for perpetual convertible preferred stock with an optional conversion price for holders of $5.00 per share and a dividend that accrues at a rate of 5% per annum, subject to increase upon certain events. The dividend is payable at the Company's option in (i) cash, (ii) subject to certain conditions, in common shares or (iii) subject to certain conditions, upon conversion of shares in Series C Preferred Stock, in shares of our non-voting, non-convertible Series D Preferred Stock, par value $1.00 per share (the "Series D Preferred Stock"). Any such shares of Series D Preferred Stock issued would have similar preferential rights. At the close of these transactions, the Company will make changes to its Board of Directors, including certain current directors stepping down and other directors joining from Cerberus. In addition, new independent directors jointly selected by the Company and Cerberus will be appointed at or as soon as practicable after the close of the transactions. The transactions are expected to close concurrently in the first half of 2016. Proceeds from the sale of the perpetual convertible preferred stock are intended to be used to fund the $100 cash contribution into NewCo, approximately $250 may be used to reduce debt, and the remainder will be used for restructuring and reinvestment in the business. The Company considered that the transactions with affiliates of Cerberus should help to drive enhanced focus on Avon's international markets, revitalize the North America business and deliver long-term value to shareholders.

The North America business was previously its own reportable segment and has been presented as discontinued operations for all periods presented as the separation represented a significant strategic shift and was determined to have a major effect on our operations and financial results. Amounts previously allocated from Global Expenses to North America have been moved to Global Expenses for all periods presented, as these represent costs associated with functions of the Company's continuing operations.

As the carrying value exceeded the estimated fair value less costs to sell, in the fourth quarter of 2015, we recorded an estimated loss on sale of discontinued operations of approximately $340 before tax (approximately $340 after tax). The estimated loss on sale represents the net assets to be contributed into NewCo, including certain pension and postretirement benefit plan liabilities and amounts in AOCI associated with the North America business, which were primarily unrecognized losses associated with our U.S. defined benefit pension plan, and costs to sell, as compared to the implied value of our ownership interests in NewCo which will be $43. The actual total loss on sale will be dependent on a number of factors including discount rates and the actual return on plan assets. Post-separation, the Company will account for its ownership interests in NewCo using the equity method of accounting, which will result in the Company recognizing its proportionate share of NewCo's income or loss.

NewCo will enter into a perpetual, irrevocable royalty-free licensing agreement with the Company for the use of the Avon brand and certain other intellectual property. There will also be transition services agreements which include, among other things, information technology, human resources and supply chain services and other commercial agreements, including research and development and manufacturing.

The major classes of financial statement components comprising the loss on discontinued operations, before tax for North America are shown below:

	Year Ended December 31,		
	2015	2014	2013
Total revenue	$1,012.5	$1,203.4	$1,458.2
Cost of sales	404.0	492.4	599.7
Selling, general and administrative expenses[1]	606.2	745.2	971.1
Operating income (loss)[1]	2.3	(34.2)	(112.6)
Other expense items	3.2	2.4	2.7
Loss from discontinued operations, before tax[1]	(.9)	(36.6)	(115.3)
Loss on sale of discontinued operations, before tax	(340.0)	—	—
Loss from discontinued operations, before tax[1]	$ (340.9)	$ (36.6)	$ (115.3)

[1] Includes a capitalized software impairment charge of $117.2 during 2013, as discussed below.

The carrying amount of the major classes of assets and liabilities for North America discontinued operations at December 31, 2015 and 2014 are shown below:

	2015	2014
Cash and cash equivalents	$ (2.2)	$ 24.1
Receivable from continuing operations[2]	100.0	100.0
Accounts receivable, net	41.4	47.9
Inventories	128.2	114.5
Prepaid expenses and other	23.7	27.6
Current assets of discontinued operations	$291.1	$314.1
Property, plant and equipment, net	$171.8	$194.2
Other assets	8.3	17.7
Noncurrent assets of discontinued operations	$180.1	$211.9

(continued)

	2015	2014
Debt maturing within one year	$ 5.9	$ 15.4
Accounts payable	78.4	89.1
Accrued compensation	18.2	35.6
Other accrued liabilities[3]	380.6	59.7
Other classes of current liabilities that are not major	6.6	7.8
Current liabilities of discontinued operations	$489.7	$207.6
Long-term debt	$ 29.3	$ 35.2
Employee benefit plans	228.2	252.2
Other liabilities	.2	7.0
Other classes of noncurrent liabilities that are not major	2.5	2.6
Noncurrent liabilities of discontinued operations	$260.2	$297.0

[2] Represents the expected cash contribution by the Company into NewCo to be made at close of the transactions.
[3] Includes the accrual for the estimated loss on sale at December 31, 2015.

As of December 31, 2015 and December 31, 2014, there were also approximately $19.4 and $15.6 of net deferred tax assets with $19.4 and $9.1 of related valuation allowances reflected in discontinued operations associated with the separation of North America.

In December 2013, we decided to halt further roll-out of our Service Model Transformation ("SMT") project. SMT was a global program initiated in 2009 to improve our order management system and enable changes to the way Representatives interact with us. SMT was piloted in Canada during 2013, and caused significant business disruption in that market. This decision to halt the further roll-out of SMT was made in light of the potential risk of further disruption. In addition, SMT did not show a clear return on investment.

As Canada was the only market expected to utilize the capitalized software associated with SMT ("SMT asset"), the accounting guidance requires the impairment assessment to consider the cash flows of the Canadian business, which includes the ongoing costs associated with SMT. These expected cash flows were not sufficient to supporting the carrying value of the associated asset group, which includes the SMT asset. In the fourth quarter of 2013, we recorded a non-cash impairment charge of $117.2 before tax ($74.1 after tax), reflecting the write-down of capitalized software.

The fair value of the SMT asset was determined using a risk-adjusted DCF model under the relief-from-royalty method. The impairment analysis performed for the asset group, which includes the SMT asset, required several estimates, including revenue and cash flow projections, and royalty and discount rates. As a result of this impairment charge, the remaining carrying amount of the SMT asset is not material.

INSURANCE

2.115 UNIVERSAL HEALTH SERVICES, INC. (DEC)
NOTES TO CONSOLIDATED FINANCIAL STATEMENTS (in part)

1) Business and Summary of Significant Accounting Policies (in part)

L) Self-Insured/Other Insurance Risks: We provide for self-insured risks, primarily general and professional liability claims and workers' compensation claims. Our estimated liability for self-insured professional and general liability claims is based on a number of factors including, among other things, the number of asserted claims and reported incidents, estimates of losses for these claims based on recent and historical settlement amounts, estimate of incurred but not reported claims based on historical experience, and estimates of amounts recoverable under our commercial insurance policies. All relevant information, including our own historical experience is used in estimating the expected amount of claims. While we continuously monitor these factors, our ultimate liability for professional and general liability claims could change materially from our current estimates due to inherent uncertainties involved in making this estimate. Our estimated self-insured reserves are reviewed and changed, if necessary, at each reporting date and changes are recognized currently as additional expense or as a reduction of expense. See Note 8 for discussion of adjustments to our prior year reserves for claims related to our self-insured general and professional liability and workers' compensation liability.

In addition, we also: (i) own commercial health insurers headquartered in Nevada and Puerto Rico, and; (ii) maintain self-insured employee benefits programs for employee healthcare and dental claims. The ultimate costs related to these programs/operations include expenses for claims incurred and paid in addition to an accrual for the estimated expenses incurred in connection with claims incurred but not yet reported. Given our significant insurance-related exposure, there can be no assurance that a sharp increase in the number and/or severity of claims asserted against us will not have a material adverse effect on our future results of operations.

8) Commitments and Contingencies (in part)

Professional and General Liability, Workers' Compensation Liability and Property Insurance

Professional and General Liability and Workers Compensation Liability:

Effective November, 2010, excluding certain subsidiaries acquired since 2010 as discussed below, the vast majority of our subsidiaries are self-insured for professional and general liability exposure up to $10 million and $3 million per occurrence, respectively. Our subsidiaries were provided with several excess policies through commercial insurance carriers which provide for coverage in excess of the applicable per occurrence self-insured retention (either $3 million or $10 million) up to $250 million per occurrence and in the aggregate for claims incurred in 2015 and 2014 and up to $200 million per occurrence and in the aggregate for claims incurred from 2011 through 2013. We remain liable for 10% of the claims paid pursuant to the commercially insured coverage in excess of $10 million up to $60 million per occurrence and in the aggregate.

Since our acquisition of Psychiatric Solutions, Inc. ("PSI") in November, 2010, the former PSI subsidiaries are self-insured for professional and general liability exposure up to $3 million per occurrence. The nine behavioral health facilities acquired from Ascend Health Corporation ("Ascend") in October, 2012 have general and professional liability policies through commercial insurance carriers which provide for up to $12 million of aggregate coverage, subject to a $100,000 per occurrence deductible. The 21 behavioral health care facilities located in the U.K. have policies through a commercial insurance carrier located in the U. K. that provides for £10 million of professional liability coverage and £25 million of general liability coverage. The facilities acquired from PSI, Ascend and the facilities located in the U.K., like our other facilities, are also provided excess coverage through commercial insurance carriers for coverage in excess of the underlying commercial policy limitations, as mentioned above.

Our estimated liability for self-insured professional and general liability claims is based on a number of factors including, among other things, the number of asserted claims and reported incidents, estimates of losses for these claims based on recent and historical settlement amounts, estimates of incurred but not reported claims based on historical experience, and estimates of amounts recoverable under our commercial insurance policies. While we continuously monitor these factors, our ultimate liability for professional and general liability claims could change materially from our current estimates due to inherent uncertainties involved in making this estimate. Given our significant self-insured exposure for professional and general liability claims, there can be no assurance that a sharp increase in the number and/or severity of claims asserted against us will not have a material adverse effect on our future results of operations.

As of December 31, 2015, the total accrual for our professional and general liability claims was $204 million, of which $48 million is included in current liabilities. As of December 31, 2014, the total accrual for our professional and general liability claims was $193 million, of which $51 million is included in current liabilities.

Below is a schedule showing the changes in our general and professional liability and workers' compensation reserves during the three years ended December 31, 2015 (amount in thousands):

	General and Professional Liability	Workers' Compensation	Total
Balance at January 1, 2013	$278,599	$ 65,954	$344,553
Plus: Accrued insurance expense, net of commercial premiums paid[(a)]	(35,182)	31,361	(3,821)
Less: Payments made in settlement of self-insured claims	(37,127)	(33,517)	(70,644)
Balance at January 1, 2014	206,290	63,798	270,088
Plus: Accrued insurance expense, net of commercial premiums paid[(a)]	22,601	36,675	59,276
Less: Payments made in settlement of self-insured claims	(35,987)	(33,659)	(69,646)
Balance at January 1, 2015	192,904	66,814	259,718
Plus: Accrued insurance expense, net of commercial premiums paid	58,460	32,435	90,895
Less: Payments made in settlement of self-insured claims	(47,391)	(31,746)	(79,137)
Balance at December 31, 2015	$203,973	$ 67,503	$271,476

[(a)] General and professional liability amounts are net of adjustments recorded during 2014 and 2013, as discussed below.

The adjustments recorded during 2015 to our prior year reserves for professional and general liability claims did not have a material impact on our 2015 consolidated results of operations. We recorded reductions to our professional and general liability self-insurance reserves (relating to prior years) amounting to $20 million during 2014, and $81 million during 2013. The favorable change recorded during 2014 resulted from favorable changes in our estimated future claims payments pursuant to a reserve analysis. The favorable change in our estimated future claims payments recorded during 2013, relating to years prior to 2013, were due primarily to: (i) an increased weighting given to company-specific metrics (to 100% from 75%), and decreased general industry metrics (to 0% from 25%), related to projected incidents per exposure, historical claims experience and loss development factors; (ii) historical data which measured the realized favorable impact of medical malpractice tort reform experienced in several states in which we operate, and; (iii) a decrease in claims related to certain higher risk specialties (such as obstetrical) due to a continuation of the company-wide patient safety initiative undertaken during the last several years. As the number of our facilities and our patient volumes have increased, thereby providing for a statistically significant data group, and taking into consideration our long-history of company-specific risk management programs and claims experience, our reserve analyses have included a greater emphasis on our historical professional and general liability experience which has developed favorably as compared to general industry trends.

As of December 31, 2015, the total accrual for our workers' compensation liability claims was $68 million, of which $34 million is included in current liabilities. As of December 31, 2014, the total accrual for our workers' compensation liability claims was $67 million, of which $32 million is included in current liabilities. The adjustments recorded during the last three years to our prior year reserves for workers' compensation claims did not have a material impact on our consolidated results of operations for the years ended December 31, 2015, 2014 or 2013.

Although we are unable to predict whether or not our future financial statements will include adjustments to our prior year reserves for self-insured general and professional and workers' compensation claims, given the relatively unpredictable nature of the these potential liabilities and the factors impacting these reserves, as discussed above, it is reasonably likely that our future financial results may include material adjustments to prior period reserves.

Property Insurance:

We have commercial property insurance policies for our properties covering catastrophic losses, including windstorm damage, up to a $1 billion policy limit per occurrence, subject to a deductible ranging from $50,000 to $250,000 per occurrence. Losses resulting from named windstorms are subject to deductibles between 3% and 5% of the declared total insurable value of the property. In addition, we have commercial property insurance policies covering catastrophic losses resulting from earthquake and flood damage, each subject to aggregated loss limits (as opposed to per occurrence losses). Our earthquake limit is $250 million, subject to a deductible of $250,000, except for facilities located within documented fault zones. Earthquake losses that affect facilities located in fault zones within the United States are subject to a $100 million limit and will have applied deductibles ranging from 1% to 5% of the declared total insurable value of the property. The earthquake limit in Puerto Rico is $25 million, subject to a $25,000 deductible. Non-critical flood losses have either a $250,000 or $500,000 deductible, based upon the location of the facility. Since certain of our facilities have been designated by our insurer as flood prone, we have elected to purchase policies from The National Flood Insurance Program to cover a substantial portion of the applicable deductible. Property insurance for the facilities acquired from Cygnet are provided on an all risk basis up to a £180 million limit that includes coverage for real and personal property as well as business interruption losses.

DEFERRED REVENUE

2.116 EQUIFAX INC. (DEC)
CONSOLIDATED BALANCE SHEETS (in part)

	December 31,	
(In millions, except par values)	2015	2014
Assets		
Current assets:		
Cash and cash equivalents	$ 93.3	$ 128.3
Trade accounts receivable, net of allowance for doubtful accounts of $7.5 and $7.2 at December 31, 2015 and 2014, respectively	349.8	337.2
Prepaid expenses	39.3	35.7
Other current assets	79.2	89.3
Total current assets	561.6	590.5
Property and equipment:		
Capitalized internal-use software and system costs	212.5	257.3
Data processing equipment and furniture	247.8	203.3
Land, buildings and improvements	194.6	194.8
Total property and equipment	654.9	655.4
Less accumulated depreciation and amortization	(288.1)	(354.8)
Total property and equipment, net	366.8	300.6
Goodwill	2,571.0	2,606.8
Indefinite-lived intangible assets	94.7	95.2
Purchased intangible assets, net	827.9	953.9
Other assets, net	87.0	114.0
Total assets	$4,509.0	$4,661.0

(continued)

(In millions, except par values)	December 31, 2015	December 31, 2014
Liabilities And Equity		
Current liabilities:		
Short-term debt and current maturities	$ 49.3	$ 380.4
Accounts payable	40.6	20.3
Accrued expenses	112.7	85.5
Accrued salaries and bonuses	139.2	101.9
Deferred revenue	96.8	73.4
Other current liabilities	165.2	161.6
Total current liabilities	603.8	823.1

NOTES TO CONSOLIDATED FINANCIAL STATEMENTS (in part)

1. Summary of Significant Accounting Policies (in part)

Revenue Recognition and Deferred Revenue. Revenue is recognized when persuasive evidence of an arrangement exists, collectibility of arrangement consideration is reasonably assured, the arrangement fees are fixed or determinable and delivery of the product or service has been completed. A significant portion of our revenue is derived from the provision of information services to our customers on a transaction basis, in which case revenue is recognized, assuming all other revenue recognition criteria are met, when the services are provided. A smaller portion of our revenues relates to subscription-based contracts under which a customer pays a preset fee for a predetermined or unlimited number of transactions or services provided during the subscription period, generally one year. Revenue related to subscription-based contracts having a preset number of transactions is recognized as the services are provided, using an effective transaction rate as the actual transactions are completed. Any remaining revenue related to unfulfilled units is not recognized until the end of the related contract's subscription period. Revenue related to subscription-based contracts having an unlimited volume is recognized ratably during the contract term. Revenue is recorded net of sales taxes.

If at the outset of an arrangement, we determine that collectibility is not reasonably assured, revenue is deferred until the earlier of when collectibility becomes probable or the receipt of payment. If there is uncertainty as to the customer's acceptance of our deliverables, revenue is not recognized until the earlier of receipt of customer acceptance or expiration of the acceptance period. If at the outset of an arrangement, we determine that the arrangement fee is not fixed or determinable, revenue is deferred until the arrangement fee becomes fixed or determinable, assuming all other revenue recognition criteria have been met.

The determination of certain of our tax management services revenue requires the use of estimates, principally related to transaction volumes in instances where these volumes are reported to us by our clients on a monthly basis in arrears. In these instances, we estimate transaction volumes based on average actual volumes reported in the past. Differences between our estimates and actual final volumes reported are recorded in the period in which actual volumes are reported. We have not experienced significant variances between our estimates and actual reported volumes in the past. We monitor actual volumes to ensure that we will continue to make reasonable estimates in the future. If we determine that we are unable to make reasonable future estimates, revenue may be deferred until actual customer data is obtained. Also within our Workforce Solutions operating segment, the fees for certain of our tax credits and incentives revenue are based on a portion of the credit delivered to our clients. Revenue for these arrangements is recognized based on the achievement of milestones, upon calculation of the credit, or when the credit is utilized by our client, depending on the provisions of the client contract.

We have certain offerings that are sold as multiple element arrangements. The multiple elements may include consumer or commercial information, file updates for certain solutions, services provided by our decisioning technologies personnel, training services, statistical models and other services. To account for each of these elements separately, the delivered elements must have stand-alone value to our customer. For certain customer contracts, the total arrangement fee is allocated to the undelivered elements. If we are unable to unbundle the arrangement into separate units of accounting, we apply one of the accounting policies described above. This may lead to the arrangement consideration being recognized as the final contract element is delivered to our customer or ratably over the contract.

Many of our multiple element arrangements involve the delivery of services generated by a combination of services provided by one or more of our operating segments. No individual information service impacts the value or usage of other information services included in an arrangement and each service can be sold alone or, in most cases, purchased from another vendor without affecting the quality of use or value to the customer of the other information services included in the arrangement. Some of our products require the development of interfaces or platforms by our decisioning technologies personnel that allow our customers to interact with our proprietary information databases. These development services do not meet the requirement for having stand-alone value, thus any related development fees are deferred when billed and are recognized over the expected period that the customer will benefit from the related decisioning technologies service. Revenue from the provision of statistical models is recognized as the service is provided and accepted, assuming all other revenue recognition criteria are met. The direct costs of set up of a customer are capitalized and amortized as a cost of service during the term of the related customer contract.

We have some multiple element arrangements that include software. We recognize the elements for which we have established vendor specific objective evidence at fair value upon delivery, in accordance with the applicable guidance.

We record revenue on a net basis for those sales in which we have in substance acted as an agent or broker in the transaction.

The debt collections and recovery management revenue is calculated as a percentage of debt collected on behalf of the customer and, as such, is primarily recognized when the cash is collected assuming all other revenue recognition criteria are met.

Deferred revenue consists of amounts billed in excess of revenue recognized on sales of our information services relating generally to the deferral of subscription fees and arrangement consideration from elements not meeting the criteria for having stand-alone value discussed above. Deferred revenues are subsequently recognized as revenue in accordance with our revenue recognition policies.

ENVIRONMENT

2.117 POLYONE CORPORATION (DEC)
CONSOLIDATED BALANCE SHEETS (in part)

	Year Ended December 31,	
(In millions, except par value per share)	2015	2014
Liabilities And Shareholders' Equity (in part)		
Current liabilities:		
Short-term and current portion of long-term debt	$ 18.6	$ 61.7
Accounts payable	351.6	365.9
Accrued expenses and other liabilities	127.9	172.9
Total current liabilities	498.1	600.5

NOTES TO CONSOLIDATED FINANCIAL STATEMENTS (in part)

Note 1—Description of Business and Summary of Significant Accounting Policies (in part)

Environmental Costs

We expense costs that are associated with managing hazardous substances and pollution in ongoing operations on a current basis. Costs associated with environmental contamination are accrued when it becomes probable that a liability has been incurred and our proportionate share of the cost can be reasonably estimated. Any such provision is recognized using the Company's best estimate of the amount of loss incurred, or at the lower end of an estimated range, when a single best estimate is not determinable. In some cases, the Company may be able to recover a portion of the costs relating to these obligations from insurers or other third parties; however, the Company records such amounts only when it is probable that they will be collected.

Note 13—Commitments and Contingencies (in part)

Environmental —We have been notified by federal and state environmental agencies and by private parties that we may be a potentially responsible party (PRP) in connection with the environmental investigation and remediation of certain sites. While government agencies frequently assert that PRPs are jointly and severally liable at these sites, in our experience, the interim and final allocations of liability costs are generally made based on the relative contribution of waste. We may also initiate corrective and preventive environmental projects of our own to ensure safe and lawful activities at our operations. We believe that compliance with current governmental regulations at all levels will not have a material adverse effect on our financial position, results of operations or cash flows.

In September 2007, we were informed of rulings by the United States District Court for the Western District of Kentucky on several pending motions in the case of Westlake Vinyls, Inc. v. Goodrich Corporation, et al., which had been pending since 2003. The Court held that PolyOne must pay the remediation costs at the former Goodrich Corporation Calvert City facility (now largely owned and operated by Westlake Vinyls), together with certain defense costs of Goodrich Corporation. The rulings also provided that PolyOne can seek indemnification for contamination attributable to Westlake Vinyls.

The environmental obligation at the site arose as a result of an agreement between The B.F.Goodrich Company (n/k/a Goodrich Corporation) and our predecessor, The Geon Company, at the time of the initial public offering in 1993, by which the Geon Company became a public company, to indemnify Goodrich Corporation for environmental costs at the site. At the time, neither PolyOne nor The Geon Company ever owned or operated the facility. Following the Court rulings, the parties to the litigation entered into settlement negotiations and agreed to settle all claims regarding past environmental costs incurred at the site. The settlement agreement provides a mechanism to pursue allocation of future remediation costs at the Calvert City site to Westlake Vinyls. While we do not currently assume any allocation of costs in our current reserve, we will adjust our reserve, in the future, consistent with any such future allocation of costs.

A remedial investigation and feasibility study (RIFS) is underway at the Calvert City site. During the third quarter of 2013, we submitted a remedial investigation report to the United States Environmental Protection Agency (USEPA).

Utilizing the preliminary results of a ground water modeling study that we obtained in the fourth quarter of 2013, we were able to develop estimates for potential remedies at Calvert City. Based upon this information, we recorded a $47.0 million charge in the fourth quarter of 2013 associated with the anticipated remedy. The EPA provided a final remedial investigation report in the third quarter of 2015. Additionally, in the third quarter of 2015, the USEPA assumed responsibility for the completion of the feasibility study. We continue to pursue available insurance coverage related to this matter and recognize gains as we receive reimbursement. No receivable has been recognized for future recoveries.

On March 13, 2013, PolyOne acquired Spartech. One of Spartech's subsidiaries, Franklin-Burlington Plastics, Inc. (Franklin-Burlington), operated a plastic resin compounding facility in Kearny, New Jersey, located adjacent to the Passaic River. The USEPA has requested that companies located in the area of the lower Passaic River, including Franklin-Burlington, cooperate in an investigation of contamination of the lower Passaic River. In response, Franklin-Burlington and approximately 70 other companies (collectively, the Cooperating Parties) agreed, pursuant to an Administrative Order of Consent with the USEPA, to assume responsibility for development of a RIFS of the lower Passaic River. The RIFS costs are exclusive of any costs that may ultimately be required to remediate the lower Passaic River area being studied or costs associated with natural resource damages that may be assessed. By agreeing to bear a portion of the cost of the RIFS, Franklin-Burlington did not admit to any liability or agree to bear any such remediation or natural resource damage costs.

In April 2014, the USEPA released a Focused Feasibility Study for public comment for a portion of the lower Passaic River. The Cooperating Parties, along with other interested parties, have submitted comments, and the USEPA is currently reviewing the comments. In February 2015, the Cooperating Parties submitted to the USEPA a remedial investigation report for the lower Passaic River. In March 2015, Franklin-Burlington, along with nine other PRPs, submitted a de minimis settlement petition to the USEPA, asserting the ten entities contributed little or no impact to the lower Passaic River and seeking a meeting to commence settlement discussions. The USEPA has stated that it views the issuance of a Record of Decision as the appropriate time for de minimis discussions. It is uncertain when such discussions will take place. In April 2015, the Cooperating Parties submitted a feasibility study to the USEPA. The feasibility study does not contemplate who is responsible for remediation nor does it determine how such costs will be allocated to PRPs. The CPG is currently revising its RIFS, which has not yet been approved by the USEPA, as part of continuing technical discussions with the USEPA.

As of December 31, 2015, we have not accrued for remedial costs related to the lower Passaic River. We believe Franklin-Burlington, based on the currently available information, contributed little to no contamination to the lower Passaic River. We are unable to estimate a liability, if any, given the uncertainties related to this matter, including the fact that the final remedial actions and scope, an allocation to Franklin-Burlington, if any, and a final resolution of the de minimis petition or the appropriate legal actions, have not been determined.

Based on our estimates, we had accruals totaling $119.9 million and $121.1 million as of December 31, 2015 and 2014, respectively, for probable future environmental expenditures relating to previously contaminated sites. These accruals are undiscounted and included in *Accrued expenses and other liabilities* and *Other non-current liabilities* on the accompanying Consolidated Balance Sheets. The accruals represent our best estimate of probable future costs that we can reasonably estimate, based upon information and technology that is currently available and our view of the most likely remedy. Depending upon the results of future testing, completion and results of remedial investigation and feasibility studies, the ultimate remediation alternatives undertaken, changes in regulations, new information, newly discovered conditions and other factors, it is reasonably possible that we could incur additional costs in excess of the amount accrued at December 31, 2015. However, such additional costs, if any, cannot be currently estimated.

We believe that the probability is remote that losses in excess of amounts we have accrued would be materially adverse to our financial position, results of operations or cash flows.

The following table details the changes in the environmental accrued liabilities:

(In millions)	2015	2014	2013
Balance at beginning of the year	$121.1	$125.9	$ 75.4
Environmental expenses	9.3	10.3	61.2
Net cash payments	(9.8)	(14.7)	(14.3)
Currency translation and other	(0.7)	(0.4)	3.6
Balance at end of year	$119.9	$121.1	$125.9

Included in *Cost of sales* in the accompanying Consolidated Statements of Income are insurance recoveries received for previously incurred environmental costs of $3.5 million, $3.7 million and $23.5 million in 2015, 2014 and 2013, respectively. Such insurance recoveries are recognized as a gain when received.

CONTINGENT CONSIDERATION

2.118 BOSTON SCIENTIFIC CORPORATION (DEC)
NOTES TO THE CONSOLIDATED FINANCIAL STATEMENTS (in part)

Note A—Significant Accounting Policies (in part)

Valuation of Business Combinations

We allocate the amounts we pay for each acquisition to the assets we acquire and liabilities we assume based on their fair values at the dates of acquisition, including identifiable intangible assets and in-process research and development which either arise from a contractual or legal right or are separable from goodwill. We base the fair value of identifiable intangible assets acquired in a business combination, including in-process research and development, on detailed valuations that use information and assumptions provided by management, which consider management's best estimates of inputs and assumptions that a market participant would use. We allocate any excess purchase price over the fair value of the net tangible and identifiable intangible assets acquired to goodwill. Transaction costs associated with these acquisitions are expensed as incurred through selling, general and administrative costs.

In those circumstances where an acquisition involves a contingent consideration arrangement, we recognize a liability equal to the fair value of the contingent payments we expect to make as of the acquisition date. We re-measure this liability each reporting period and record changes in the fair value through a separate line item within our consolidated statements of operations. Increases or decreases in the fair value of the contingent consideration liability can result from changes in discount periods and rates, as well as changes in the timing and amount of revenue estimates or in the timing or likelihood of achieving regulatory, revenue or commercialization-based milestones.

Note B—Acquisitions and Strategic Investments (in part)

Our consolidated financial statements include the operating results for each acquired entity from its respective date of acquisition. We do not present pro forma financial information for these acquisitions given their results are not material to our consolidated financial statements. Transaction costs associated with these acquisitions were expensed as incurred and are not material for the years ended December 31, 2015, 2014, and 2013.

2015 Acquisitions

Interventional Radiology Business of CeloNova Biosciences

On December 31, 2015, we completed the acquisition of the interventional radiology business of CeloNova Biosciences (CeloNova), for an upfront payment of $70 million and additional payments contingent on regulatory and sales milestones. The acquisition includes drug-eluting microspheres designed to be loaded with chemotherapy drugs for delivery to cancerous tumors, and spherical embolic products used to treat uterine fibroids and other conditions. We are in the process of integrating CeloNova into our Peripheral Interventions business.

AMS Portfolio Acquisition

On August 3, 2015, we completed the acquisition of the American Medical Systems male urology portfolio (AMS Portfolio Acquisition), which includes the men's health and prostate health businesses, from Endo International plc. Total consideration was comprised of $1.616 billion in up-front cash plus related fees and expenses, and a potential additional $50 million in consideration based on 2016 sales. The AMS male urology portfolio is being integrated with our formerly named Urology and Women's Health business, and the joint businesses have become Urology and Pelvic Health. In addition, as part of the acquisition agreement, we made a $60 million Series B non-voting preferred stock investment in the women's health business of Endo Health Solutions, a wholly owned subsidiary of Endo International, plc., representing the remaining Women's Health business of the American Medical Systems' Portfolio. This investment was subsequently repaid in the fourth quarter of 2015.

Xlumena, Inc.

On April 2, 2015, we acquired Xlumena, Inc. (Xlumena), a medical device company that developed minimally invasive devices for Endoscopic Ultrasound (EUS) guided transluminal drainage of targeted areas within the gastrointestinal tract. The purchase agreement called for an upfront payment of $63 million, an additional payment of $13 million upon FDA clearance of the HOT AXIOS™ product, and further sales-based milestones based on sales achieved through 2018. We are in the process of integrating Xlumena into our Endoscopy business, and expect the integration to be substantially complete by the end of 2016.

In addition, we completed other acquisitions during 2015 for total consideration of $6 million in cash at closing plus contingent consideration of up to $1 million.

Purchase Price Allocation

We accounted for these acquisitions as business combinations and, in accordance with Financial Accounting Standards Board (FASB) Accounting Standards Codification® (ASC) Topic 805, *Business Combinations*, we have recorded the assets acquired and liabilities assumed at their respective fair values as of the acquisition dates. The components of the aggregate preliminary purchase prices are as follows (in millions):

Cash, net of cash acquired	$1,734
Fair value of contingent consideration	63
	$1,797

The following summarizes the aggregate preliminary purchase price allocation for the 2015 acquisitions as of December 31, 2015 (in millions):

Goodwill	$ 573
Amortizable intangible assets	1,073
Indefinite-lived intangible assets	7
Inventory	103
Property, Plant and Equipment	43
Other net assets	43
Deferred income taxes	(45)
	$1,797

We allocated a portion of the preliminary purchase price to specific intangible asset categories as follows:

	Amount Assigned (in millions)	Weighted Average Amortization Period (in years)	Range of Risk-Adjusted Discount Rates used in Purchase Price Allocation
Amortizable Intangible Assets:			
Technology-related	$ 431	11–13	13.5%–23%
Customer relationships	624	12–13	13.5%–15%
Other intangible assets	18	13	13.5%
Indefinite-Lived Intangible Assets:			
In-process research & development	$ 7	N/A	17%
	$1,080		

2014 Acquisitions

Interventional Business of Bayer AG

On August 29, 2014, we completed the acquisition of the Interventional Division of Bayer AG (Bayer), for a total cash consideration of $414 million. We believe that this acquisition enhances our ability to offer physicians and healthcare systems a more complete portfolio of solutions to treat challenging vascular conditions. The transaction includes the AngioJet® Thrombectomy System and the Fetch® 2 Aspiration Catheter, which are used in endovascular procedures to remove blood clots from blocked arteries and veins, and the JetStream® Atherectomy System, used to remove plaque and thrombi from diseased arteries. We are integrating the operations of the Bayer business with our Peripheral Interventions and Interventional Cardiology divisions and expect integration to be substantially completed by the middle of 2016.

IoGyn, Inc.

On May 7, 2014, we completed the acquisition of the remaining fully diluted equity of IoGyn, Inc. (IoGyn). Prior to the acquisition, we held a 28 percent minority interest in IoGyn in addition to notes receivable of approximately $8 million. Total consideration was comprised of a net cash payment of $65 million at closing to acquire the remaining 72 percent of IoGyn equity and repay outstanding debt. IoGyn has developed the Symphion™ System, a next generation system for hysteroscopic intrauterine tissue removal including fibroids (myomas) and polyps. In March 2014, IoGyn received U.S. Food & Drug Administration (FDA) approval for the system and in October 2014, we began a limited market release of the system in the United States. We have integrated the operations of the IoGyn business into our Urology and Pelvic Health business.

In addition, we completed other acquisitions during 2014 for total consideration of $7 million cash at closing plus contingent consideration of up to $4 million.

Purchase Price Allocation

We accounted for these acquisitions as business combinations and, in accordance with ASC Topic 805, *Business Combination*, we have recorded the assets acquired and liabilities assumed at their respective fair values as of the acquisition date. The components of the aggregate purchase price for the Bayer and IoGyn acquisitions are as follows (in millions):

Cash, net of cash acquired	$479
Fair value of prior interests	31
	$510

In addition, prior to the acquisition of IoGyn, we had an equity interest in IoGyn and held $8 million of notes receivables. We re-measured our previously-held investments to their estimated acquisition-date fair value of $31 million and recorded a gain of $19 million in other, net, in the accompanying consolidated statements of operations during the second quarter of 2014. We measured the fair values of the previously-held investments based on the liquidation preferences and priority of the equity interest and debt, including accrued interest.

The following summarizes the aggregate purchase price allocation for Bayer and IoGyn as of December 31, 2014:

Goodwill	$210
Amortizable intangible assets	263
Inventory	23
Property, Plant and Equipment	17
Prepaid Transaction Service Agreement	5
Other net assets	(1)
Deferred income taxes	(7)
	$510

We allocated a portion of the purchase price to specific intangible asset categories as follows:

	Amount Assigned (in millions)	Weighted Average Amortization Period (in years)	Range of Risk-Adjusted Discount Rates used in Purchase Price Allocation
Amortizable Intangible Assets:			
Technology-related	$233	10–14	14–18%
Customer Relationships	29	10	18%
Other intangible assets	1	2	14%
	$263		

2013 Acquisition

On November 1, 2013, we completed the acquisition of the electrophysiology business of C.R. Bard Inc. (Bard EP), for $274 million in cash. This acquisition added a strong commercial team and complementary portfolio of ablation catheters, diagnostic tools, and electrophysiology recording systems, which we believe will allow us to better serve the global Electrophysiology market through a more comprehensive portfolio offering and sales infrastructure.

Purchase Price Allocation

We accounted for this acquisition as a business combination and, in accordance with ASC Topic 805, *Business Combinations*, we have recorded the assets acquired and liabilities assumed at their respective fair values as of the acquisition date. The following summarizes the aggregate purchase price allocation for the Bard EP acquisition (in millions):

Goodwill	$140
Amortizable intangible assets	112
Other net assets	19
Deferred income taxes	3
	$274

We allocated a portion of the purchase price to specific intangible asset categories as of the acquisition date as follows:

	Amount Assigned (in millions)	Weighted Average Amortization Period (in years)	Range of Risk-Adjusted Discount Rates used in Purchase Price Allocation
Amortizable Intangible Assets:			
Technology-related	$ 82	10	11.5%
Customer relationships	30	7	11.5%
	$112		

For our 2015, 2014 and 2013 acquisitions, our technology-related intangible assets consist of technical processes, intellectual property, and institutional understanding with respect to products and processes that we will leverage in future products or processes and will carry forward from one product generation to the next. We used the income approach and relief from royalty approach to derive the fair value of the technology-related intangible assets, and are amortizing them on a straight-line basis over their assigned estimated useful lives.

In-process research and development represents the estimated fair value of acquired in-process research and development projects that have not yet reached technological feasibility. These indefinite-lived intangible assets are tested for impairment on an annual basis, or more frequently if impairment indicators are present, in accordance with U.S. GAAP and our accounting policies. Upon completion of the associated research and development efforts, we will determine the useful life of the technology and begin amortizing the assets to reflect their use over their remaining lives. The primary basis for determining the technological feasibility or completion of these projects is obtaining regulatory approval to market the underlying products.

Customer relationships represent the estimated fair value of non-contractual customer and distributor relationships. Customer relationships are direct relationships with physicians and hospitals performing procedures with the acquired products, and distributor relationships are relationships with third parties used to sell products, both as of the acquisition date. These relationships were valued separately from goodwill because there is a history and pattern of conducting business with customers and distributors. We used the income approach or the replacement cost and lost profits methodology to derive the fair value of the customer relationships. The customer relationships intangible assets are amortized on a straight-line basis over their assigned estimated useful lives.

Other intangible assets primarily include acquired tradenames. These tradenames include brand names that we expect to continue using in our product portfolio and related marketing materials. The tradenames are valued using a relief from royalty methodology and are amortized on a straight-line basis over their assigned estimated useful lives.

We believe that the estimated intangible asset values represent the fair value at the date of acquisition and do not exceed the amount a third party would pay for the assets. These fair value measurements are based on significant unobservable inputs, including management estimates and assumptions and, accordingly, are classified as Level 3 within the fair value hierarchy prescribed by FASB ASC Topic 820, *Fair Value Measurements and Disclosures*.

We recorded the excess of the aggregate purchase price over the estimated fair values of the identifiable assets acquired as goodwill. Goodwill was established due primarily to synergies expected to be gained from leveraging our existing operations as well as revenue and cash flow projections associated with future technologies, and has been allocated to our reportable segments based on the relative expected benefit. Of the goodwill recorded, approximately $453 million related to our 2015 acquisitions is deductible for tax purposes. Of the goodwill recorded related to our 2014 and 2013 acquisitions, $160 million and $131 million, respectively, is deductible for tax purposes. See *Note D—Goodwill and Other Intangible Assets* for more information related to goodwill allocated to our reportable segments.

Contingent Consideration

Certain of our acquisitions involve contingent consideration arrangements. Payment of additional consideration is generally contingent on the acquired company reaching certain performance milestones, including attaining specified revenue levels, achieving product development targets or obtaining regulatory approvals. In accordance with U.S. GAAP, we recognize a liability equal to the fair value of the contingent payments we expect to make as of the acquisition date. We re-measure this liability each reporting period and record changes in the fair value through a separate line item within our consolidated statements of operations.

We recorded a net expense related to the change in fair value of our contingent consideration liabilities of $123 million during 2015, a net benefit related to the change in fair value of our contingent consideration liabilities of $85 million during 2014, and a net expense related to the change in fair value of our contingent consideration liabilities of $4 million during 2013. We made contingent consideration payments of $213 million, $137 million and $165 million in 2015, 2014 and 2013, respectively.

Changes in our contingent consideration liability were as follows (in millions):

Balance as of December 31, 2013	$ 501
Amounts recorded related to new acquisitions	3
Other amounts recorded related to prior acquisitions	(8)
Fair value adjustment	(85)
Contingent payments related to prior period acquisition	(137)
Balance as of December 31, 2014	$ 274
Amounts recorded related to new acquisitions	63
Other amounts recorded related to prior acquisitions	(1)
Fair value adjustment	123
Contingent payments related to prior period acquisition	(213)
Balance as of December 31, 2015	$ 246

As of December 31, 2015, the maximum amount of future contingent consideration (undiscounted) that we could be required to make associated with our acquisitions is approximately $1.918 billion.

Increases or decreases in the fair value of our contingent consideration liability can result from changes in discount periods and rates, as well as changes in the timing and amount of revenue estimates or in the timing or likelihood of achieving regulatory-, revenue- or commercialization-based milestones. The recurring Level 3 fair value measurements of our contingent consideration liability include the following significant unobservable inputs:

Contingent Consideration Liability	Fair Value as of December 31, 2015	Valuation Technique	Unobservable Input	Range
R&D and Commercialization-based Milestone	$19 million	Discounted Cash Flow	Discount Rate	2%–3.5%
			Probability of Payment	32%–95%
			Projected Year of Payment	2017–2021
Revenue-based Payments	$125 million	Discounted Cash Flow	Discount Rate	11%–15%
			Projected Year of Payment	2016–2022
	$102 million	Monte Carlo	Revenue Volatility	15%
			Risk Free Rate	LIBOR Term Structure
			Projected Year of Payment	2016–2018

Contingent consideration liabilities are remeasured to fair value each reporting period using projected revenues, discount rates, probabilities of payment and projected payment dates. Projected contingent payment amounts related to R&D, regulatory- and commercialization-based milestones and certain revenue-based milestones are discounted back to the current period using a discounted cash flow model. Other revenue-based payments are valued using a monte carlo valuation model, which simulates future revenues during the earn out-period using management's best estimates. Projected revenues are based on our most recent internal operational budgets and long-range strategic plans. Increases in projected revenues and probabilities of payment may result in higher fair value measurements. Increases in discount rates and the time to payment may result in lower fair value measurements. Increases or decreases in any of those inputs together, or in isolation, may result in a significantly lower or higher fair value measurement.

Note I—Supplemental Balance Sheet Information (in part)

Components of selected captions in our accompanying consolidated balance sheets are as follows:

Accrued Expenses

(In millions)	As of	
	December 31, 2015	December 31, 2014
Legal reserves	$ 773	$ 694
Payroll and related liabilities	504	512
Accrued contingent consideration	119	158
Other	574	586
	$1,970	$1,950

Other Long-Term Liabilities

(In millions)	As of	
	December 31, 2015	December 31, 2014
Accrued income taxes	$1,253	$1,231
Legal reserves	1,163	883
Accrued contingent consideration	127	116
Other long-term liabilities	431	436
	$2,974	$2,666

LITIGATION

2.119 MASTERCARD INCORPORATED (DEC)

CONSOLIDATED BALANCE SHEET (in part)

(In millions, except per share data)	December 31,	
	2015	2014
Liabilities And Equity (in part)		
Accounts payable	$ 472	$ 419
Settlement due to customers	866	1,142
Restricted security deposits held for customers	895	950
Accrued litigation	709	771
Accrued expenses	2,763	2,439
Other current liabilities	564	501
Total Current Liabilities	6,269	6,222

NOTES TO CONSOLIDATED FINANCIAL STATEMENTS (in part)

Note 1. Summary of Significant Accounting Policies (in part)

Litigation—The Company is a party to certain legal and regulatory proceedings with respect to a variety of matters. The Company evaluates the likelihood of an unfavorable outcome of all legal or regulatory proceedings to which it is a party and accrues a loss contingency when the loss is probable and reasonably estimable. These judgments are subjective based on the status of the legal or regulatory proceedings, the merits of its defenses and consultation with in-house and external legal counsel. Legal costs are expensed as incurred and recorded in general and administrative expenses.

Restricted cash—The Company classifies cash as restricted when the cash is unavailable for withdrawal or usage for general operations. Restrictions may include legally restricted deposits, contracts entered into with others, or the Company's statements of intention with regard to particular deposits. In December 2012, the Company made a payment into a qualified cash settlement fund related to its U.S. merchant class litigation. The Company has presented these funds as restricted cash for litigation settlement since the use of the funds under the qualified cash settlement fund is restricted for payment under the settlement agreement.

Note 10. Accrued Expenses and Accrued Litigation

Accrued expenses consisted of the following at December 31:

(In millions)	2015	2014
Customer and merchant incentives	$1,748	$1,433
Personnel costs	473	531
Advertising	114	154
Income and other taxes	143	105
Other	285	216
Total accrued expenses	$2,763	$2,439

As of December 31, 2015 and 2014, personnel costs included a restructuring accrual with a remaining balance of $25 million and $84 million, respectively. This accrual relates to a restructuring charge of $87 million recorded in general and administrative expenses in 2014. The Company restructured its organization to align with its strategic priorities and to best meet the Company's continued growth. The Company is substantially complete with these restructuring activities. The decrease in the balance was primarily due to payments and lower than expected severance actions.

As of December 31, 2015 and 2014, the Company's provision related to U.S. merchant litigations was $709 million and $771 million, respectively. These amounts are not included in the accrued expenses table above and are separately reported as accrued litigation on the consolidated balance sheet. During 2015 and 2014, MasterCard executed settlement agreements with a number of opt-out merchants and no adjustment to the amount previously recorded was deemed necessary. See Note 18 (Legal and Regulatory Proceedings) for further discussion of the U.S. merchant class litigation.

Note 18. Legal and Regulatory Proceedings (in part)

MasterCard is a party to legal and regulatory proceedings with respect to a variety of matters in the ordinary course of business. Some of these proceedings are based on complex claims involving substantial uncertainties and unascertainable damages. Accordingly, except as discussed below, it is not possible to determine the probability of loss or estimate damages, and therefore, MasterCard has not established reserves for any of these proceedings. When the Company determines that a loss is both probable and reasonably estimable, MasterCard records a liability and discloses the amount of the liability if it is material. When a material loss contingency is only reasonably possible, MasterCard does not record a liability, but instead discloses the nature and the amount of the claim, and an estimate of the loss or range of loss, if such an estimate can be made. Unless otherwise stated below with respect to these matters, MasterCard cannot provide an estimate of the possible loss or range of loss based on one or more of the following reasons: (1) actual or potential plaintiffs have not claimed an amount of monetary damages or the amounts are unsupportable or exaggerated, (2) the matters are in early stages, (3) there is uncertainty as to the outcome of pending appeals or motions, (4) there are significant factual issues to be resolved, (5) the existence in many such proceedings of multiple defendants or potential defendants whose share of any potential financial responsibility has yet to be determined, and/or (6) there are novel legal issues presented. Furthermore, except as identified with respect to the matters below, MasterCard does not believe that the outcome of any individual existing legal or regulatory proceeding to which it is a party will have a material adverse effect on its results of operations, financial condition or overall business. However, an adverse judgment or other outcome or settlement with respect to any proceedings discussed below could result in fines or payments by MasterCard and/or could require MasterCard to change its business practices. In addition, an adverse outcome in a regulatory proceeding could lead to the filing of civil damage claims and possibly result in significant damage awards. Any of these events could have a material adverse effect on MasterCard's results of operations, financial condition and overall business.

Interchange Litigation and Regulatory Proceedings (in part)

MasterCard's interchange fees and other practices are subject to regulatory and/or legal review and/or challenges in a number of jurisdictions, including the proceedings described below. When taken as a whole, the resulting decisions, regulations and legislation with respect to interchange fees and acceptance practices may have a material adverse effect on the Company's prospects for future growth and its overall results of operations, financial position and cash flows.

United States. In June 2005, the first of a series of complaints were filed on behalf of merchants (the majority of the complaints were styled as class actions, although a few complaints were filed on behalf of individual merchant plaintiffs) against MasterCard International, Visa U.S.A., Inc., Visa International Service Association and a number of financial institutions. Taken together, the claims in the complaints were generally brought under both Sections 1 and 2 of the Sherman Act, which prohibit monopolization and attempts or conspiracies to monopolize a particular industry, and some of these complaints contain unfair competition law claims under state law. The complaints allege, among other things, that MasterCard, Visa, and certain financial institutions conspired to set the price of interchange fees, enacted point of sale acceptance rules (including the no surcharge rule) in violation of antitrust laws and engaged in unlawful tying and bundling of certain products and services. The cases were consolidated for pre-trial proceedings in the U.S. District Court for the Eastern District of New York in MDL No. 1720. The plaintiffs filed a consolidated class action complaint that seeks treble damages.

In July 2006, the group of purported merchant class plaintiffs filed a supplemental complaint alleging that MasterCard's initial public offering of its Class A Common Stock in May 2006 (the "IPO") and certain purported agreements entered into between MasterCard and financial institutions in connection with the IPO: (1) violate U.S. antitrust laws and (2) constituted a fraudulent conveyance because the financial institutions allegedly attempted to release, without adequate consideration, MasterCard's right to assess them for MasterCard's litigation liabilities. The class plaintiffs sought treble damages and injunctive relief including, but not limited to, an order reversing and unwinding the IPO.

In February 2011, MasterCard and MasterCard International entered into each of: (1) an omnibus judgment sharing and settlement sharing agreement with Visa Inc., Visa U.S.A. Inc. and Visa International Service Association and a number of financial institutions; and (2) a MasterCard settlement and judgment sharing agreement with a number of financial institutions. The agreements provide for the apportionment of certain costs and liabilities which MasterCard, the Visa parties and the financial institutions may incur, jointly and/or severally, in the event of an adverse judgment or settlement of one or all of the cases in the merchant litigations. Among a number of scenarios addressed by the agreements, in the event of a global settlement involving the Visa parties, the financial institutions and MasterCard, MasterCard would pay 12% of the monetary portion of the settlement. In the event of a settlement involving only MasterCard and the financial institutions with respect to their issuance of MasterCard cards, MasterCard would pay 36% of the monetary portion of such settlement.

In October 2012, the parties entered into a definitive settlement agreement with respect to the merchant class litigation (including with respect to the claims related to the IPO) and the defendants separately entered into a settlement agreement with the individual merchant plaintiffs. The settlements included cash payments that were apportioned among the defendants pursuant to the omnibus judgment sharing and settlement sharing agreement described above. MasterCard also agreed to provide class members with a short-term reduction in default credit interchange rates and to modify certain of its business practices, including its No Surcharge Rule. Objections to the settlement were filed by both merchants and certain competitors, including Discover. Discover's objections include a challenge to the settlement on the grounds that certain of the rule changes agreed to in the settlement constitute a restraint of trade in violation of Section 1 of the Sherman Act. The court granted final approval of the settlement in December 2013. Objectors to the settlement appealed the decision, and an oral argument was heard on the appeal in September 2015. Separately, the objectors filed a motion in July 2015 to set aside the approval order, contending that the merchant class was inadequately represented and the settlement was insufficient because a counsel for several individual merchant plaintiffs improperly exchanged communications with a defense counsel who at the time was representing MasterCard.

Merchants representing slightly more than 25% of the MasterCard and Visa purchase volume over the relevant period chose to opt out of the class settlement. MasterCard anticipates that most of the larger merchants who opted out of the settlement will initiate separate actions seeking to recover damages, and over 30 opt-out complaints have been filed on behalf of numerous merchants in various jurisdictions. The defendants have consolidated all of these matters (except for one state court action in New Mexico) in front of the same federal district court that is overseeing the approval of the settlement. In July 2014, the district court denied the defendants' motion to dismiss the opt-out merchant complaints for failure to state a claim.

MasterCard recorded a pre-tax charge of $770 million in the fourth quarter of 2011 and an additional $20 million pre-tax charge in the second quarter of 2012 relating to the settlement agreements described above. In 2012, MasterCard paid $790 million with respect to the settlements, of which $726 million was paid into a qualified cash settlement fund related to the merchant class litigation. As of December 31, 2015 and December 31, 2014, MasterCard had $541 million and $540 million, in the qualified cash settlement fund classified as restricted cash on its balance sheet. The class settlement agreement provided for a return to the defendants of a portion of the class cash settlement fund, based upon the percentage of purchase volume represented by the opt-out merchants. This resulted in $164 million from the cash settlement fund being returned to MasterCard in January 2014 and reclassified at that time from restricted cash to cash and cash equivalents. In the fourth quarter of 2013, MasterCard recorded an incremental net pre-tax charge of $95 million related to the opt-out merchants, representing a change in its estimate of probable losses relating to these matters. MasterCard has executed settlement agreements with a number of opt-out merchants and no adjustment to the amount previously recorded was deemed necessary. As of December 31, 2015, MasterCard had accrued a liability of $709 million as a reserve for both the merchant class litigation and the filed and anticipated opt-out merchant cases.

The portion of the accrued liability relating to the opt-out merchants does not represent an estimate of a loss, if any, if the opt-out merchant matters were litigated to a final outcome, in which case MasterCard cannot estimate the potential liability. MasterCard's estimate involves significant judgment and may change depending on progress in settlement negotiations or depending upon decisions in any opt-out merchant cases. In addition, in the event that the merchant class litigation settlement approval is overturned, a negative outcome in the litigation could have a material adverse effect on MasterCard's results of operations, financial position and cash flows.

DERIVATIVES

2.120 REGAL BELOIT CORPORATION (DEC)
CONSOLIDATED BALANCE SHEETS (in part)

(Dollars in Millions)

Liabilities and Equity (in part)	January 2, 2016	January 3, 2015
Current Liabilities:		
Accounts Payable	$336.2	$312.2
Dividends Payable	10.3	9.8
Hedging Obligations	44.7	29.7
Accrued Compensation and Employee Benefits	80.6	75.7
Other Accrued Expenses	134.7	125.5
Current Maturities of Long-Term Debt	6.3	7.8
Total Current Liabilities	612.8	560.7

NOTES TO THE CONSOLIDATED FINANCIAL STATEMENTS (in part)

(3) Accounting Policies (in part)

Derivative Financial Instruments

Derivative instruments are recorded on the Consolidated Balance Sheets at fair value. Any fair value changes are recorded in Net Income or Accumulated Other Comprehensive Loss as determined under accounting guidance that establishes criteria for designation and effectiveness of the hedging relationships.

The Company uses derivative instruments to manage its exposure to fluctuations in certain raw material commodity pricing, fluctuations in the cost of forecasted foreign currency transactions, and variability in interest rate exposure on floating rate borrowings. The majority of derivative instruments have been designated as cash flow hedges (see also Note 13 of Notes to the Consolidated Financial Statements).

(13) Derivative Financial Instruments

The Company is exposed to certain risks relating to its ongoing business operations. The primary risks managed using derivative instruments are commodity price risk, currency exchange risk, and interest rate risk. Forward contracts on certain commodities are entered into to manage the price risk associated with forecasted purchases of materials used in the Company's manufacturing process. Forward contracts on certain currencies are entered into to manage forecasted cash flows in certain foreign currencies. Interest rate swaps are entered into to manage interest rate risk associated with the Company's floating rate borrowings.

The Company is exposed to credit losses in the event of non-performance by the counterparties to various financial agreements, including its commodity hedging transactions, foreign currency exchange contracts and interest rate swap agreements. Exposure to counterparty credit risk is managed by limiting counterparties to major international banks and financial institutions meeting established credit guidelines and continually monitoring their compliance with the credit guidelines. The Company does not obtain collateral or other security to support financial instruments subject to credit risk. The Company does not anticipate non-performance by its counterparties, but cannot provide assurances.

The Company recognizes all derivative instruments as either assets or liabilities at fair value in the statement of financial position. The Company designates commodity forward contracts as cash flow hedges of forecasted purchases of commodities, currency forward contracts as cash flow hedges of forecasted foreign currency cash flows and interest rate swaps as cash flow hedges of forecasted LIBOR-based interest payments. There were no significant collateral deposits on derivative financial instruments as of January 2, 2016.

For derivative instruments that are designated and qualify as a cash flow hedge, the effective portion of the gain or loss on the derivative is reported as a component of AOCI and reclassified into earnings in the same period or periods during which the hedged transaction affects earnings. Gains and losses on the derivative representing either hedge ineffectiveness or changes in market value of derivatives not designated as hedges are recognized in current earnings. At January 2, 2016 and January 3, 2015 the Company had $(7.4) million and $(2.2) million, net of tax, of derivative losses on closed hedge instruments in AOCI that will be realized in earnings when the hedged items impact earnings.

The Company had outstanding the following notional amounts to hedge forecasted purchases of commodities (in millions):

	January 2, 2016	January 3, 2015
Copper	$59.4	$137.4
Aluminum	4.2	5.2

As of January 2, 2016, the maturities of commodity forward contracts extended through June 2017.

The Company had outstanding the following notional amounts of currency forward contracts (in millions):

	January 2, 2016	January 3, 2015
Mexican Peso	$339.4	$324.1
Chinese Renminbi	233.9	206.1
Indian Rupee	54.5	51.7
Euro	68.5	17.8
Canadian Dollar	6.2	8.6
Australian Dollar	10.8	4.3
Thai Baht	3.7	3.5
Japanese Yen	2.7	—
Great Britain Pound	4.8	—
Singapore Dollar	0.5	—

As of January 2, 2016, the maturities of currency forward contracts extended through December 2018.

As of January 2, 2016 and January 3, 2015, the total notional amount of the Company's receive-variable/pay-fixed interest rate swap was $100.0 million (with maturities extending to August 2017).

Fair values of derivative instruments were (in millions):

	January 2, 2016			
	Prepaid Expenses	Other Noncurrent Assets	Hedging Obligations (Current)	Hedging Obligations (Noncurrent)
Designated as hedging instruments:				
Interest rate swap contracts	$—	$—	$ —	$ 7.8
Currency contracts	0.7	0.4	29.9	19.5
Commodity contracts	0.1	—	8.7	—
Not designated as hedging instruments:				
Currency contracts	0.5	0.6	0.9	0.3
Commodity contracts	5.1	—	5.2	—
Total Derivatives	$6.4	$1.0	$44.7	$27.6

	January 3, 2015			
	Prepaid Expenses	Other Noncurrent Assets	Hedging Obligations (Current)	Hedging Obligations (Noncurrent)
Designated as hedging instruments:				
Interest rate swap contracts	$ —	$—	$—	$11.9
Currency contracts	1.6	—	15.9	10.3
Commodity contracts	—	—	9.8	0.1
Not designated as hedging instruments:				
Currency contracts	—	—	1.6	0.2
Commodity contracts	2.3	—	2.4	—
Total Derivatives	$3.9	$—	$29.7	$22.5

Derivatives Designated as Cash Flow Hedging Instruments

The effect of derivative instruments on the consolidated statements of income and comprehensive income for fiscal 2015, 2014 and 2013 were (in millions):

	Fiscal 2015			
	Commodity Forwards	Currency Forwards	Interest Rate Swaps	Total
Gain (Loss) recognized in Other Comprehensive Income (Loss)	$(22.3)	$(46.5)	$(1.1)	$(69.9)
Amounts reclassified from Other Comprehensive Income (Loss):				
Gain recognized in Net Sales	—	0.2	—	0.2
Loss recognized in Cost of Sales	(19.8)	(18.5)	—	(38.3)
Loss recognized in Interest Expense	—	—	(5.2)	(5.2)

	Fiscal 2014			
	Commodity Forwards	Currency Forwards	Interest Rate Swaps	Total
Gain (Loss) recognized in Other Comprehensive Income (Loss)	$(18.8)	$(25.2)	$ (0.5)	$(44.5)
Amounts reclassified from Other Comprehensive Income (Loss):				
(Loss) Gain recognized in Cost of Sales	(7.1)	7.6	—	0.5
Loss recognized in Interest Expense	—	—	(10.3)	(10.3)

	Fiscal 2013			
	Commodity Forwards	Currency Forwards	Interest Rate Swaps	Total
Gain (Loss) recognized in Other Comprehensive Income (Loss)	$(11.3)	$ 8.8	$ 0.7	$ (1.8)
Amounts reclassified from Other Comprehensive Income (Loss):				
Loss recognized in Net Sales	—	(0.9)	—	(0.9)
(Loss) Gain recognized in Cost of Sales	(8.3)	7.5	—	(0.8)
Loss recognized in Interest Expense	—	—	(12.8)	(12.8)

The ineffective portion of hedging instruments recognized was immaterial for all periods presented.

Derivatives Not Designated as Cash Flow Hedging Instruments

The effect of derivative instruments on the consolidated statements of income for fiscal 2015, 2014 and 2013 were (in millions):

	Fiscal 2015		
	Commodity Forwards	Currency Forwards	Total
Loss recognized in Operating Expenses	$—	$(8.8)	$(8.8)

	Fiscal 2014		
	Commodity Forwards	Currency Forwards	Total
Loss recognized in Cost of Sales	$—	$(1.3)	$(1.3)

	Fiscal 2013		
	Commodity Forwards	Currency Forwards	Total
(Loss) Gain recognized in Cost of Sales	$(0.1)	$0.5	$0.4

The net AOCI balance related to hedging activities of $(47.5) million losses at January 2, 2016 includes $(26.6) million of net deferred losses expected to be reclassified to the Statement of Income in the next twelve months. There were no gains or losses reclassified from AOCI to earnings based on the probability that the forecasted transaction would not occur.

The Company's commodity and currency derivative contracts are subject to master netting agreements with the respective counterparties which allow the Company to net settle transactions with a single net amount payable by one party to another party. The Company has elected to present the derivative assets and derivative liabilities on the Consolidated Balance Sheets on a gross basis for the periods ended January 2, 2016 and January 3, 2015.

The following table presents the derivative assets and derivative liabilities presented on a net basis under enforceable master netting agreements (in millions):

| | January 2, 2016 | | |
	Gross Amounts as Presented in the Consolidated Balance Sheet	Derivative Contract Amounts Subject to Right of Offset	Derivative Contracts as Presented on a Net Basis
Prepaid Expenses and Other Current Assets:			
Derivative Currency Contracts	$ 1.2	$(1.2)	$ —
Derivative Commodity Contracts	5.2	(5.2)	—
Other Noncurrent Assets:			
Derivative Currency Contracts	1.0	(1.0)	—
Hedging Obligations Current:			
Derivative Currency Contracts	30.8	(1.2)	29.6
Derivative Commodity Contracts	13.9	(5.2)	8.7
Hedging Obligations:			
Derivative Currency Contracts	19.8	(1.0)	18.8

| | January 3, 2015 | | |
	Gross Amounts as Presented in the Consolidated Balance Sheet	Derivative Contract Amounts Subject to Right of Offset	Derivative Contracts as Presented on a Net Basis
Prepaid Expenses and Other Current Assets:			
Derivative Currency Contracts	$ 1.6	$(1.3)	$ 0.3
Derivative Commodity Contracts	2.3	(2.3)	—
Hedging Obligations Current:			
Derivative Currency Contracts	17.5	(1.3)	16.2
Derivative Commodity Contracts	12.2	(2.3)	9.9
Hedging Obligations:			
Derivative Currency Contracts	10.5	—	10.5
Derivative Commodity Contracts	0.1	—	0.1

CLAIMS AND DISCOUNTS

2.121 CVS HEALTH CORPORATION (DEC)

CONSOLIDATED BALANCE SHEETS (in part)

| | December 31, | |
In millions, except per share amounts	2015	2014
Liabilities (in part):		
Accounts payable	$ 7,490	$ 6,547
Claims and discounts payable	7,653	5,404
Accrued expenses	6,829	5,816
Short-term debt	—	685
Current portion of long-term debt	1,197	575
Total current liabilities	23,169	19,027

NOTES TO CONSOLIDATED FINANCIAL STATEMENTS (in part)

1. Significant Accounting Policies (in part)

Revenue Recognition

Pharmacy Services Segment—The PSS sells prescription drugs directly through its mail service dispensing pharmacies and indirectly through its retail pharmacy network. The PSS recognizes revenue from prescription drugs sold by its mail service dispensing pharmacies and under retail pharmacy network contracts where it is the principal using the gross method at the contract prices negotiated with its clients. Net revenues include: (i) the portion of the price the client pays directly to the PSS, net of any volume-related or other discounts paid back to the client (see "Drug Discounts" below), (ii) the price paid to the PSS by client plan members for mail order prescriptions ("Mail Co-Payments") and the price paid to retail network pharmacies by client plan members for retail prescriptions ("Retail Co-Payments"), and (iii) administrative fees for retail pharmacy network contracts where the PSS is not the principal as discussed below. Sales taxes are not included in revenue.

Revenue is recognized when: (i) persuasive evidence of an arrangement exists, (ii) delivery has occurred or services have been rendered, (iii) the seller's price to the buyer is fixed or determinable, and (iv) collectability is reasonably assured. The following revenue recognition policies have been established for the PSS:

- Revenues generated from prescription drugs sold by mail service dispensing pharmacies are recognized when the prescription is delivered. At the time of delivery, the PSS has performed substantially all of its obligations under its client contracts and does not experience a significant level of returns or reshipments.
- Revenues generated from prescription drugs sold by third party pharmacies in the PSS' retail pharmacy network and associated administrative fees are recognized at the PSS' point-of-sale, which is when the claim is adjudicated by the PSS online claims processing system.

The PSS determines whether it is the principal or agent for its retail pharmacy network transactions on a contract by contract basis. In the majority of its contracts, the PSS has determined it is the principal due to it: (i) being the primary obligor in the arrangement, (ii) having latitude in establishing the price, changing the product or performing part of the service, (iii) having discretion in supplier selection, (iv) having involvement in the determination of product or service specifications, and (v) having credit risk. The PSS' obligations under its client contracts for which revenues are reported using the gross method are separate and distinct from its obligations to the third party pharmacies included in its retail pharmacy network contracts. Pursuant to these contracts, the PSS is contractually required to pay the third party pharmacies in its retail pharmacy network for products sold, regardless of whether the PSS is paid by its clients. The PSS' responsibilities under its client contracts typically include validating eligibility and coverage levels, communicating the prescription price and the co-payments due to the third party retail pharmacy, identifying possible adverse drug interactions for the pharmacist to address with the prescriber prior to dispensing, suggesting generic alternatives where clinically appropriate and approving the prescription for dispensing. Although the PSS does not have credit risk with respect to Retail Co-Payments or inventory risk related to retail network claims, management believes that all of the other applicable indicators of gross revenue reporting are present. For contracts under which the PSS acts as an agent, revenue is recognized using the net method.

Drug Discounts—The PSS deducts from its revenues any rebates, inclusive of discounts and fees, earned by its clients. Rebates are paid to clients in accordance with the terms of client contracts, which are normally based on fixed rebates per prescription for specific products dispensed or a percentage of manufacturer discounts received for specific products dispensed. The liability for rebates due to clients is included in "Claims and discounts payable" in the accompanying consolidated balance sheets.

Medicare Part D—The PSS, through its SilverScript subsidiary, participates in the federal government's Medicare Part D program as a Prescription Drug Plan ("PDP"). Net revenues include insurance premiums earned by the PDP, which are determined based on the PDP's annual bid and related contractual arrangements with the Centers for Medicare and Medicaid Services ("CMS"). The insurance premiums include a direct premium paid by CMS and a beneficiary premium, which is the responsibility of the PDP member, but which is subsidized by CMS in the case of low-income members. Premiums collected in advance are initially deferred in accrued expenses and are then recognized in net revenues over the period in which members are entitled to receive benefits.

In addition to these premiums, net revenues include co-payments, coverage gap benefits, deductibles and co-insurance (collectively, the "Member Co-Payments") related to PDP members' actual prescription claims. In certain cases, CMS subsidizes a portion of these Member Co-Payments and pays the PSS an estimated prospective Member Co-Payment subsidy amount each month. The prospective Member Co-Payment subsidy amounts received from CMS are also included in net revenues. SilverScript assumes no risk for these amounts. If the prospective Member Co-Payment subsidies received differ from the amounts based on actual prescription claims, the difference is recorded in either accounts receivable or accrued expenses.

The PSS accounts for CMS obligations and Member Co-Payments (including the amounts subsidized by CMS) using the gross method consistent with its revenue recognition policies for Mail Co-Payments and Retail Co-Payments (discussed previously in this document).

Retail/LTC Segment

Retail Pharmacy—The retail drugstores recognize revenue at the time the customer takes possession of the merchandise. Customer returns are not material. Revenue generated from the performance of services in the RLS' health care clinics is recognized at the time the services are performed. Sales taxes are not included in revenue.

Long-term Care—Revenue is recognized when products are delivered or services are rendered or provided to the customer, prices are fixed and determinable, and collection is reasonably assured. A significant portion of our revenues from sales of pharmaceutical and medical products are reimbursed by the federal Medicare Part D program and, to a lesser extent, state Medicaid programs. Payments for services rendered to patients covered by these programs are generally less than billed charges. The Company monitors its revenues and receivables from these reimbursement sources, as well as other third party insurance payors, and record an estimated contractual allowance for sales and receivable balances at the revenue recognition date, to properly account for anticipated differences between billed and reimbursed amounts. Accordingly, the total net sales and receivables reported in the Company's consolidated financial statements are recorded at the amount expected to be ultimately received from these payors. Since billing functions for a portion of the Company's revenue systems are largely computerized, enabling on-line adjudication at the time of sale to record net revenues, the Company's exposure in connection with estimating contractual allowance adjustments is limited primarily to unbilled and initially rejected Medicare, Medicaid and third party claims (typically approved for reimbursement once additional information is provided to the payor). For the remaining portion of the Company's revenue systems, the contractual allowance is estimated for all billed, unbilled and initially rejected Medicare, Medicaid and third party claims. The Company evaluates several criteria in developing the estimated contractual allowances on a monthly basis, including historical trends based on actual claims paid, current contract and reimbursement terms, and changes in customer base and payor/product mix. Contractual allowance estimates are adjusted to actual amounts as cash is received and claims are settled, and the aggregate impact of these resulting adjustments was not significant to our results of operations for any of the periods presented.

Patient co-payments associated with Medicare Part D, certain state Medicaid programs, Medicare Part B and certain third party payors are typically not collected at the time products are delivered or services are rendered, but are billed to the individuals as part of our normal billing procedures and subject to our normal accounts receivable collections procedures.

Health Care Clinics—For services provided by our health care clinics, revenue recognition occurs for completed services provided to patients, with adjustments taken for third party payor contractual obligations and patient direct bill historical collection rates.

Loyalty Program—The Company's customer loyalty program, ExtraCare®, is comprised of two components, ExtraSavings TM and ExtraBucks® Rewards. ExtraSavings coupons redeemed by customers are recorded as a reduction of revenues when redeemed. ExtraBucks® Rewards are accrued as a charge to cost of revenues when earned, net of estimated breakage. The Company determines breakage based on historical redemption patterns.

See Note 13 for additional information about the revenues of the Company's business segments.

Cost of Revenues

Pharmacy Services Segment—The PSS' cost of revenues includes: (i) the cost of prescription drugs sold during the reporting period directly through its mail service dispensing pharmacies and indirectly through its retail pharmacy network, (ii) shipping and handling costs, and (iii) the operating costs of its mail service dispensing pharmacies and client service operations and related information technology support costs including depreciation and amortization. The cost of prescription drugs sold component of cost of revenues includes: (i) the cost of the prescription drugs purchased from manufacturers or distributors and shipped to members in clients' benefit plans from the PSS' mail service dispensing pharmacies, net of any volume-related or other discounts (see "Vendor allowances and purchase discounts" below) and (ii) the cost of prescription drugs sold (including Retail Co-Payments) through the PSS' retail pharmacy network under contracts where it is the principal, net of any volume-related or other discounts.

Retail/LTC Segment—The RLS' cost of revenues includes: the cost of merchandise sold during the reporting period and the related purchasing costs, warehousing and delivery costs (including depreciation and amortization) and actual and estimated inventory losses.

See Note 13 for additional information about the cost of revenues of the Company's business segments.

Vendor Allowances and Purchase Discounts

The Company accounts for vendor allowances and purchase discounts as follows:

Pharmacy Services Segment—The PSS receives purchase discounts on products purchased. The PSS' contractual arrangements with vendors, including manufacturers, wholesalers and retail pharmacies, normally provide for the PSS to receive purchase discounts from established list prices in one, or a combination, of the following forms: (i) a direct discount at the time of purchase, (ii) a discount for the prompt payment of invoices, or (iii) when products are purchased indirectly from a manufacturer (e.g., through a wholesaler or retail pharmacy), a discount (or rebate) paid subsequent to dispensing. These rebates are recognized when prescriptions are dispensed and are generally calculated and billed to manufacturers within 30 days of the end of each completed quarter. Historically, the effect of adjustments resulting from the reconciliation of rebates recognized to the amounts billed and collected has not been material to the PSS' results of operations. The PSS accounts for the effect of any such differences as a change in accounting estimate in the period the reconciliation is completed. The PSS also receives additional discounts under its wholesaler contracts if it exceeds contractually defined annual purchase volumes. In addition, the PSS receives fees from pharmaceutical manufacturers for administrative services. Purchase discounts and administrative service fees are recorded as a reduction of "Cost of revenues".

Retail/LTC Segment—Vendor allowances received by the RLS reduce the carrying cost of inventory and are recognized in cost of revenues when the related inventory is sold, unless they are specifically identified as a reimbursement of incremental costs for promotional programs and/or other services provided. Amounts that are directly linked to advertising commitments are recognized as a reduction of advertising expense (included in operating expenses) when the related advertising commitment is satisfied. Any such allowances received in excess of the actual cost incurred also reduce the carrying cost of inventory. The total value of any upfront payments received from vendors that are linked to purchase commitments is initially deferred. The deferred amounts are then amortized to reduce cost of revenues over the life of the contract based upon purchase volume. The total value of any upfront payments received from vendors that are not linked to purchase commitments is also initially deferred. The deferred amounts are then amortized to reduce cost of revenues on a straight-line basis over the life of the related contract. The total amortization of these upfront payments was not material to the accompanying consolidated financial statements.

ASSET RETIREMENT OBLIGATIONS

2.122 ANADARKO PETROLEUM CORPORATION (DEC)
CONSOLIDATED BALANCE SHEETS (in part)

	December 31,	
millions	2015	2014
Liabilities and Equity (in part)		
Current Liabilities		
Accounts payable	$ 2,850	$ 3,683
Current asset retirement obligations	309	257
Interest payable	247	247
Other taxes payable	318	332
Accrued expenses	424	505
Short-term debt	33	—
Tronox-related contingent liability	—	5,210
Total	4,181	10,234
Long-term Debt	15,718	15,092
Other Long-term Liabilities		
Deferred income taxes	5,400	8,527
Asset retirement obligations	1,750	1,796
Other	3,908	3,000
Total	11,058	13,323

NOTES TO CONSOLIDATED FINANCIAL STATEMENTS (in part)

1. Summary of Significant Accounting Policies (in part)

Asset Retirement Obligations Asset retirement obligations (AROs) associated with the retirement of tangible long-lived assets are recognized as liabilities with an increase to the carrying amounts of the related long-lived assets in the period incurred. The cost of the tangible asset, including the asset retirement cost, is depreciated over the useful life of the asset. AROs are recorded at estimated fair value, measured by reference to the expected future cash outflows required to satisfy the retirement obligations discounted at the Company's credit-adjusted risk-free interest rate. Accretion expense is recognized over time as the discounted liabilities are accreted to their expected settlement value and is included in DD&A in the Company's Consolidated Statements of Income. If estimated future costs of AROs change, an adjustment is recorded to both the asset retirement obligation and the long-lived asset. Revisions to estimated AROs can result from changes in retirement cost estimates, revisions to estimated inflation rates, and changes in the estimated timing of abandonment. See *Note 13—Asset Retirement Obligations*.

13. Asset Retirement Obligations

The majority of Anadarko's AROs relate to the plugging of wells and the related abandonment of oil and gas properties. Revisions in estimated liabilities during the period relate primarily to changes in estimates of asset retirement costs and include, but are not limited to, revisions of estimated inflation rates, changes in property lives, and the expected timing of settlement. The following summarizes changes in the Company's AROs:

Millions	2015	2014
Carrying amount of asset retirement obligations at January 1	$2,053	$2,022
Liabilities incurred	104	119
Property dispositions	(108)	(70)
Liabilities settled	(298)	(443)
Accretion expense	102	93
Revisions in estimated liabilities	206	332
Carrying amount of asset retirement obligations at December 31	$2,059	$2,053

Long-Term Debt

Author's Note

In April 2015, FASB issued ASU No. 2015-03, *Interest—Imputation of Interest (Subtopic 835-30): Simplifying the Presentation of Debt Issuance Costs*. The amendments in this ASU require that debt issuance costs related to a recognized debt liability be presented in the balance sheet as a direct deduction from the carrying amount of that debt liability, consistent with debt discounts. For public business entities, the amendments in this ASU are effective for fiscal years beginning after December 15, 2015, including interim periods within those fiscal years. For all other entities, the amendments in this ASU are effective for financial statements issued for fiscal years beginning after December 15, 2015, and interim periods within fiscal years beginning after December 15, 2016. Early adoption is permitted for financial statements that have not been previously issued. Due to the effective date, none of the examples that follow contain an example of these disclosures.

In February 2016, FASB issued ASU No. 2016-02, *Leases (Topic 842)*. FASB issued this ASU to increase transparency and comparability among organizations by recognizing lease assets and lease liabilities on the balance sheet and disclosing key information about leasing arrangements. To meet that objective, FASB amended the FASB ASC and created FASB ASC 842, *Leases*. The amendments in this ASU are effective for fiscal years beginning after December 15, 2018, including interim periods within those fiscal years, for any of the following: a public business entity, a not-for-profit entity that has issued, or is a conduit bond obligor for, securities that are traded, listed, or quoted on an exchange or an over-the-counter market, and for an employee benefit plan that files financial statements with the SEC. For all other entities, the amendments in this ASU are effective for fiscal years beginning after December 15, 2019, and interim periods within fiscal years beginning after December 15, 2020. Early application of the amendments in this ASU is permitted for all entities.

PRESENTATION

2.123 FASB ASC 470 addresses classification determination for specific debt obligations. FASB ASC 470-10-45-11 states that the current liability classification is intended to include long-term obligations that are or will be callable by the creditor either because the debtor's violation of a provision of the debt agreement at the balance sheet date makes the obligation callable, or because the violation, if not cured within a specified grace period, will make the obligation callable. Accordingly, such callable obligations should be classified as current liabilities, unless one of the following conditions is met:

- The creditor has waived or subsequently lost the right to demand repayment for more than one year, or operating cycle if longer, from the balance sheet date. For example, the debtor may have cured the violation after the balance sheet date, and the obligation is not callable at the time the financial statements are issued or available to be issued.
- For long-term obligations containing a grace period within which the debtor may cure the violation, it is probable that the violation will be cured within that period, thus preventing the obligation from becoming callable.

DISCLOSURE

2.124 FASB ASC 470 requires, for each of the five years following the date of the latest balance sheet presented, disclosure of the combined aggregate amount of maturities and sinking fund requirements for all long-term borrowings. In addition, FASB ASC 440, *Commitments*, requires disclosure of terms and conditions provided in loan agreements, such as assets pledged as collateral and covenants to limit additional debt, maintain working capital, and restrict dividends. Regulation S-X has similar or expanded requirements for matters such as debt details, assets subject to lien, defaults, dividend restrictions, and changes in long-term debt.

2.125 FASB ASC 825 requires disclosure of both the fair value and bases for estimating the fair value of long-term debt, unless it is not practicable to estimate the value.

PRESENTATION AND DISCLOSURE EXCERPTS

UNSECURED

2.126 LEAR CORPORATION (DEC)
CONSOLIDATED BALANCE SHEETS (in part)

(In millions, except share data)

December 31,	2015	2014
Liabilities and Equity (in part)		
Current Liabilities:		
Accounts payable and drafts	$2,504.4	$2,525.3
Accrued liabilities	1,312.1	1,179.3
Current portion of long-term debt	23.1	240.5
Total current liabilities	3,839.6	3,945.1
Long-Term Liabilities:		
Long-term debt	1,931.7	1,454.0
Other	616.8	684.7
Total long-term liabilities	2,548.5	2,138.7

NOTES TO CONSOLIDATED FINANCIAL STATEMENTS (in part)

(3) Acquisition (in part)

Eagle Ottawa

On January 5, 2015, the Company completed the acquisition of 100% of the outstanding equity interests of Everett Smith Group, Ltd., the parent company of Eagle Ottawa, LLC ("Eagle Ottawa"). Eagle Ottawa is a leading provider of leather for the automotive industry, with annual sales of approximately $1 billion, including annual sales to Lear of approximately $200 million. The purchase price of $843.9 million (net of purchase price adjustments received in the second quarter of 2015 of $8.0 million) consists of cash paid of $815.3 million, net of cash acquired, and contingent consideration of $28.6 million. In addition, the Company incurred transaction costs related to advisory services of $8.6 million, which were expensed as incurred and are recorded in selling, general and administrative expenses in the accompanying consolidated statement of income for the year ended December 31, 2015. The acquisition was financed with $350 million of restricted cash proceeds from the Company's offering of $650 million in aggregate principal amount of senior unsecured notes due 2025 at a stated coupon rate of 5.25% in November 2014 and borrowings under a $500 million delayed-draw term loan facility ("Term Loan Facility") established in November 2014 under the Company's amended and restated senior secured credit agreement (the "Credit Agreement") (Note 6, "Debt").

(6) Debt (in part)

Long-Term Debt

A summary of long-term debt, net of unamortized debt issuance costs, and the related weighted average interest rates is shown below (in millions):

December 31,	2015				2014			
Debt Instrument	Long-Term Debt	Debt Issuance Costs[1]	Long-Term Debt, Net	Weighted Average Interest Rate	Long-Term Debt	Debt Issuance Costs[1]	Long-Term Debt, Net	Weighted Average Interest Rate
Credit Agreement — Term Loan Facility	$ 490.6	$ (2.2)	$ 488.4	1.78%	$ —	$ (2.7)	$ (2.7)	N/A
8.125% Senior Notes due 2020	—	—	—	N/A	243.7	(3.2)	240.5	8.25%
4.75% Senior Notes due 2023	500.0	(5.5)	494.5	4.75%	500.0	(6.4)	493.6	4.75%
5.375% Senior Notes due 2024	325.0	(3.2)	321.8	5.375%	325.0	(3.6)	321.4	5.375%
5.25% Senior Notes due 2025	650.0	(7.5)	642.5	5.25%	650.0	(8.3)	641.7	5.25%
Other	7.6	—	7.6	N/A	—	—	—	N/A
	$1,973.2	$(18.4)	1,954.8		$1,718.7	$(24.2)	1,694.5	
Less — Current portion			(23.1)				(240.5)	
Long-term debt			$1,931.7				$1,454.0	

[1] Unamortized portion

Senior Notes (in part)

As of December 31, 2015, the Company's senior notes consist of $500 million in aggregate principal amount of senior unsecured notes due 2023 at a stated coupon rate of 4.75% (the "2023 Notes"), $325 million in aggregate principal amount of senior unsecured notes due 2024 at a stated coupon rate of 5.375% (the "2024 Notes") and $650 million in aggregate principal amount of senior unsecured notes due 2025 at a stated coupon rate of 5.25% (the "2025 Notes" and together with the 2023 Notes and 2024 Notes, the "Notes").

2023 Notes

The 2023 Notes were issued in January 2013 and mature on January 15, 2023. Interest is payable on January 15 and July 15 of each year. The 2023 Notes were offered and sold in a private transaction to qualified institutional buyers under Rule 144 A and, outside of the United States, pursuant to Regulation S of the Securities Act of 1933, as amended (the "Securities Act"). In accordance with the registration rights agreement entered into at the time of the issuance of the 2023 Notes, the Company completed an exchange offer to exchange the 2023 Notes for substantially identical notes registered under the Securities Act in the second quarter of 2014. The proceeds from the offering of $500 million, net of related issuance costs of $7.4 million, together with the Company's existing sources of liquidity, were used for general corporate purposes, including, without limitation, the redemption of $70 million in aggregate principal amount of the Company's 7.875% senior unsecured notes due 2018 (the "2018 Notes") and the 8.125% senior unsecured notes due 2020 (the "2020 Notes"), investments in additional component capabilities and emerging markets and share repurchases under the Company's common stock share repurchase program (Note 9, " Capital Stock and Equity "). In connection with the partial redemption of the 2018 Notes and 2020 Notes, the Company paid $72.1 million and recognized a loss of $3.6 million on the partial extinguishment of debt in the year ended December 31, 2013.

The Company may redeem the 2023 Notes, in whole or in part, on or after January 15, 2018, at the redemption prices set forth below, plus accrued and unpaid interest to the redemption date.

Twelve-Month Period Commencing January 15,	2023 Notes
2018	102.375%
2019	101.583%
2020	100.792%
2021 and thereafter	100.000%

Prior to January 15, 2018, the Company may redeem the 2023 Notes, in whole or in part, at a redemption price equal to 100% of the aggregate principal amount thereof, plus a "make-whole" premium as of, and accrued and unpaid interest to, the redemption date.

COLLATERALIZED

2.127 TENET HEALTHCARE CORPORATION (DEC)
CONSOLIDATED BALANCE SHEETS (in part)

Dollars in Millions

	December 31, 2015	December 31, 2014
Liabilities and Equity (in part)		
Current liabilities:		
Current portion of long-term debt	$ 127	$ 112
Accounts payable	1,380	1,179
Accrued compensation and benefits	880	852
Professional and general liability reserves	177	189
Accrued interest payable	205	194
Liabilities held for sale	101	—
Accrued legal settlement costs	294	45
Other current liabilities	1,144	1,006
Total current liabilities	4,308	3,577
Long-term debt, net of current portion	14,383	11,505
Professional and general liability reserves	578	492
Defined benefit plan obligations	595	633
Other long-term liabilities	594	558
Total liabilities	20,458	16,765

Note 6. Short-Term Borrowings and Long-Term Debt and Lease Obligations (in part)

Long-Term Debt and Lease Obligations

The table below shows our long-term debt as of December 31, 2015 and 2014:

	December 31, 2015	December 31, 2014
Senior notes:		
5%, due 2019	$ 1,100	$ 1,100
5$\frac{1}{2}$%, due 2019	500	500
6$\frac{3}{4}$%, due 2020	300	300
8%, due 2020	750	750
8$\frac{1}{8}$%, due 2022	2,800	2,800
6$\frac{3}{4}$%, due 2023	1,900	—
6$\frac{7}{8}$%, due 2031	430	430
Senior secured notes:		
6$\frac{1}{4}$%, due 2018	1,041	1,041
4$\frac{3}{4}$%, due 2020	500	500
6%, due 2020	1,800	1,800
Floating % due 2020	900	—
4$\frac{1}{2}$%, due 2021	850	850
4$\frac{3}{8}$%, due 2021	1,050	1,050
Credit facility due 2020	—	220
Capital leases and mortgage notes	852	487
Unamortized issue costs, note discounts and premium	(263)	(211)
Total long-term debt	14,510	11,617
Less current portion	127	112
Long-term debt, net of current portion	$14,383	$11,505

Letter of Credit Facility

On March 7, 2014, we entered into a new letter of credit facility agreement ("LC Facility") that provides for the issuance of standby and documentary letters of credit (including certain letters of credit issued under our existing Credit Agreement, which we transferred to the LC Facility (the "Existing Letters of Credit")), from time to time, in an aggregate principal amount of up to $180 million (subject to increase to up to $200 million). The LC Facility has a scheduled maturity date of March 7, 2017, and obligations thereunder are guaranteed by and secured by a first priority pledge of the capital stock and other ownership interests of certain of our hospital subsidiaries on an equal ranking basis with our existing senior secured notes.

Drawings under any letter of credit issued under the LC Facility (including the Existing Letters of Credit) that we have not reimbursed within three business days after notice thereof will accrue interest at a base rate plus a margin equal to 0.875% per annum. An unused commitment fee is payable at an initial rate of 0.50% per annum with a step down to 0.375% per annum based on the secured debt to EBITDA ratio of 3.00 to 1.00 . A per annum fee on the aggregate outstanding amount of issued but undrawn letters of credit (including Existing Letters of Credit) will accrue at a rate of 1.875% per annum. An issuance fee equal to 0.125% per annum of the aggregate face amount of each outstanding letter of credit is payable to the account of the issuer of the related letter of credit. At December 31, 2015, we had approximately $105 million of standby letters of credit outstanding under the LC Facility.

Senior Notes and Senior Secured Notes

In June 2015, we sold $900 million aggregate principal amount of floating rate senior secured notes, which will mature on June 15, 2020 (the "Secured Notes"), and assumed $1 .9 billion aggregate principal amount of 6$\frac{3}{4}$% senior notes, which will mature on June 15, 2023 (the "Unsecured Notes" and, together with the Secured Notes, the "Notes"), issued by THC Escrow Corporation II. We will pay interest on the Secured Notes quarterly in arrears on March 15, June 15, September 15 and December 15 of each year, which payments commenced on September 15, 2015. The Secured Notes accrue interest at a rate per annum, reset quarterly, equal to LIBOR plus 3$\frac{1}{2}$%. We will pay interest on the Unsecured Notes semi-annually in arrears on June 15 and December 15 of each year, commencing on December 15, 2015. The proceeds from the sale of the Notes were used to repay borrowings outstanding under our Interim Loan Agreement and Credit Agreement, as well as to refinance the debt of USPI and to pay the cash consideration in respect of our USPI joint venture and Aspen acquisition.

In September 2014, we sold $500 million aggregate principal amount of $5\frac{1}{2}$% senior notes, which will mature on March 1, 2019. We will pay interest on the notes semi-annually in arrears on March 1 and September 1 of each year, commencing on March 1, 2015. The proceeds from the sale of the notes were used for general corporate purposes, including the repayment of indebtedness and drawings under our Credit Agreement, related transaction fees and expenses, and acquisitions.

In June and March 2014, we sold $500 million and $600 million aggregate principal amount, respectively, of 5% senior notes, which will mature on March 1, 2019. We will pay interest on the notes semi-annually in arrears on March 1 and September 1 of each year, which payments commenced on September 1, 2014. The net proceeds from the sale of the notes in June 2014 were used to redeem our $9\frac{1}{4}$% senior notes due 2015 in July 2014. In connection with the redemption, we recorded a loss from early extinguishment of debt of approximately $24 million, primarily related to the difference between the redemption price and the par value of the notes, as well as the write-off of associated unamortized note discounts and issuance costs. The net proceeds from the sale of the notes in March 2014 were used for general corporate purposes, including the repayment of borrowings under our Credit Agreement.

In October 2013, we sold $2.8 billion aggregate principal amount of $8\frac{1}{8}$% senior notes, which will mature on April 1, 2022, and $1.8 billion aggregate principal amount of 6% senior secured notes, which will mature on October 1, 2020. We will pay interest on the $8\frac{1}{8}$% senior notes and 6% senior secured notes semi-annually in arrears on April 1 and October 1 of each year, commencing on April 1, 2014. The proceeds from the sale of the notes were used to finance the acquisition of Vanguard.

In May 2013, we sold $1.050 billion aggregate principal amount of $4\frac{3}{8}$% senior secured notes, which will mature on October 1, 2021. We will pay interest on the $4\frac{3}{8}$% senior secured notes semi-annually in arrears on January 1 and July 1 of each year, which payments commenced on January 1, 2014. We used a portion of the proceeds from the sale of the notes to purchase approximately $767 million aggregate principal amount outstanding of our $8\frac{7}{8}$% senior secured notes due 2019 in a tender offer and to call approximately $158 million of the remaining aggregate principal amount outstanding of those notes. In connection with the purchase, we recorded a loss from early extinguishment of debt of $171 million, primarily related to the difference between the purchase prices and the par values of the purchased notes, as well as the write-off of unamortized note discounts and issuance costs.

In February 2013, we sold $850 million aggregate principal amount of $4\frac{1}{2}$% senior secured notes, which will mature on April 1, 2021. We will pay interest on the $4\frac{1}{2}$% senior secured notes semi-annually in arrears on April 1 and October 1 of each year, which payments commenced on October 1, 2013. We used a portion of the proceeds from the sale of the notes to purchase approximately $645 million aggregate principal amount outstanding of our 10% senior secured notes due 2018 in a tender offer and to call approximately $69 million of the remaining aggregate principal amount outstanding of those notes. In connection with the purchase, we recorded a loss from early extinguishment of debt of $177 million, primarily related to the difference between the purchase prices and the par values of the purchased notes, as well as the write-off of unamortized note discounts and issuance costs. The remaining net proceeds were used for general corporate purposes, including the repayment of borrowings under our senior secured revolving credit facility.

All of our senior notes are general unsecured senior debt obligations that rank equally in right of payment with all of our other unsecured senior indebtedness, but are effectively subordinated to our senior secured notes described below, the obligations of our subsidiaries and any obligations under our Credit Agreement to the extent of the collateral. We may redeem any series of our senior notes, in whole or in part, at any time at a redemption price equal to 100% of the principal amount of the notes redeemed, plus a make-whole premium specified in the applicable indenture, together with accrued and unpaid interest to the redemption date.

All of our senior secured notes are guaranteed by certain of our hospital company subsidiaries and secured by a first-priority pledge of the capital stock and other ownership interests of those subsidiaries. All of our senior secured notes and the related subsidiary guarantees are our and the subsidiary guarantors' senior secured obligations. All of our senior secured notes rank equally in right of payment with all of our other senior secured indebtedness. Our senior secured notes rank senior to any subordinated indebtedness that we or such subsidiary guarantors may incur; they are effectively senior to our and such subsidiary guarantors' existing and future unsecured indebtedness and other liabilities to the extent of the value of the collateral securing the notes and the subsidiary guarantees; they are effectively subordinated to our and such subsidiary guarantors' obligations under our Credit Agreement to the extent of the value of the collateral securing borrowings thereunder; and they are structurally subordinated to all obligations of our non-guarantor subsidiaries.

The indentures setting forth the terms of our senior secured notes contain provisions governing our ability to redeem the notes and the terms by which we may do so. At our option, we may redeem our senior secured notes, in whole or in part, at any time at a redemption price equal to 100% of the principal amount of the notes redeemed plus the make-whole premium set forth in the related indenture, together with accrued and unpaid interest thereon, if any, to the redemption date.

In addition, we may be required to purchase for cash all or any part of each series of our senior secured notes upon the occurrence of a change of control (as defined in the applicable indentures) for a cash purchase price of 101% of the aggregate principal amount of the notes, plus accrued and unpaid interest.

Covenants (in part)

Senior Secured Notes. The indentures governing our senior secured notes contain covenants that, among other things, restrict our ability and the ability of our subsidiaries to incur liens, consummate asset sales, enter into sale and lease-back transactions or consolidate, merge or sell all or substantially all of our or their assets, other than in certain transactions between one or more of our wholly owned subsidiaries. These restrictions, however, are subject to a number of important exceptions and qualifications. In particular, there are no restrictions on our ability or the ability of our subsidiaries to incur additional indebtedness, make restricted payments, pay dividends or make distributions in respect of capital stock, purchase or redeem capital stock, enter into transactions with affiliates or make advances to, or invest in, other entities (including unaffiliated entities). In addition, the indentures governing our senior secured notes contain a covenant that neither we nor any of our subsidiaries will incur secured debt, unless at the time of and after giving effect to the incurrence of such debt, the aggregate amount of all such secured debt (including the aggregate principal amount of senior secured notes outstanding at such time) does not exceed the greater of (i) $3.2 billion or (ii) the amount that would cause the secured debt ratio (as defined in the indentures) to exceed 4.0 to 1.0; provided that the aggregate amount of all such debt secured by a lien on par to the lien securing the senior secured notes may not exceed the greater of (a) $2.6 billion or (b) the amount that would cause the secured debt ratio to exceed 3.0 to 1.0.

Secured Notes. The indenture governing the Secured Notes contains covenants and terms (including terms regarding mandatory redemption) that are similar to those in the indentures governing our senior secured notes described above, except we are permitted under the indenture governing the Secured Notes to incur secured debt so long as, at the time of and after giving effect to the incurrence of such debt, the aggregate amount of all such secured debt (including the aggregate principal amount of Secured Notes outstanding at such time) does not exceed the greater of (i) $8.5 billion or (ii) the amount that would cause the secured debt ratio (as defined in the indenture) to exceed 4.0 to 1.0 and, provided further, that the aggregate amount of all such debt secured by a lien on par to the lien securing the Secured Notes does not exceed the greater of (a) $6.4 billion or (b) the amount that would cause the secured debt ratio to exceed 3.0 to 1.0. In addition, pursuant to the Secured Notes indenture, we may, at our option, redeem the Secured Notes, in whole or in part, at any time prior to June 15, 2016 at a redemption price equal to 100% of the principal amount of the notes being redeemed plus the make-whole premium set forth in the Secured Notes indenture, together with accrued and unpaid interest thereon, if any, to the redemption date. From and after June 15, 2016, we may, at our option, redeem the Secured Notes in whole or in part at the redemption prices specified in the Secured Notes indenture.

All of our senior secured notes are guaranteed by certain of our domestic hospital company subsidiaries and secured by a first-priority pledge of the capital stock and other ownership interests of those subsidiaries. All of our senior secured notes and the related subsidiary guarantees are our and the subsidiary guarantors' senior secured obligations. All of our senior secured notes rank equally in right of payment with all of our other senior secured indebtedness. Our senior secured notes rank senior to any subordinated indebtedness that we or such subsidiary guarantors may incur; they are effectively senior to our and such subsidiary guarantors' existing and future unsecured indebtedness and other liabilities to the extent of the value of the collateral securing the notes and the subsidiary guarantees; they are effectively subordinated to our and such subsidiary guarantors' obligations under our Credit Agreement and the LC Facility to the extent of the value of the collateral securing borrowings thereunder; and they are structurally subordinated to all obligations of our nonguarantor subsidiaries.

CONVERTIBLE

2.128 LAM RESEARCH CORPORATION (JUN)
CONSOLIDATED BALANCE SHEETS (in part)

(in thousands, except per share data)

	June 28, 2015	June 29, 2014
Liabilities and Stockholders' Equity (in part)		
Trade accounts payable	$ 300,203	$ 223,515
Accrued expenses and other current liabilities	649,438	604,296
Deferred profit	322,070	235,923
Current portion of convertible notes and capital leases	1,359,650	518,267
Total current liabilities	2,631,361	1,582,001
Senior notes, convertible notes, and capital leases, less current portion	1,001,382	817,202
Income taxes payable	202,930	258,357
Other long-term liabilities	184,023	122,662
Total liabilities	4,019,696	2,780,222
Commitments contingencies		
Temporary equity, convertible notes	241,808	183,349

Note 14: Long Term Debt and Other Borrowings (in part)

Convertible Senior Notes

In May 2011, the Company issued and sold $450 million in aggregate principal amount of 0.50% Convertible Senior Notes due May 2016 (the "2016 Notes") at par. At the same time, the Company issued and sold $450 million in aggregate principal amount of 1.25% Convertible Senior Notes due May 2018 (the "2018 Notes") at par. The Company pays cash interest at an annual rate of 0.5% and 1.25%, respectively, on the 2016 Notes and the 2018 Notes, on a semi-annual basis on May 15 and November 15 of each year.

In June 2012, with the acquisition of Novellus, the Company assumed $700 million in aggregate principal amount of 2.625% Convertible Senior Notes due May 2041 (the "2041 Notes," collectively with the 2016 Notes and the 2018 Notes, the "Convertible Notes"). The Company pays cash interest at an annual rate of 2.625%, on a semi-annual basis on May 15 and November 15 of each year on the 2041 Notes. The 2041 Notes also have a contingent interest payment provision that may require the Company to pay additional interest, up to 0.60% per year, based on certain thresholds, beginning with the semi-annual interest payment on May 15, 2021, and upon the occurrence of certain events, as outlined in the indenture governing the 2041 Notes.

The Company separately accounts for the liability and equity components of the Convertible Notes. The initial liability components of the Convertible Notes were valued based on the present value of the future cash flows using the Company's borrowing rate at the date of the issuance or assumption for similar debt instruments without the conversion feature, which equals the effective interest rate on the liability component disclosed in the following table, respectively. The equity component was initially valued equal to the principle value of the notes, less the present value of the future cash flows using the Company's borrowing rate at the date of the issuance or assumption for similar debt instruments without a conversion feature, which equated to the initial debt discount.

Under certain circumstances, the Convertible Notes may be converted into shares of the Company's Common Stock. The number of shares each debenture is convertible into is based on conversion rates, disclosed in the following table. The conversion rates are adjusted for certain corporate events, including dividends on the Company's Common Stock. At June 28, 2015, the market value of the Company's Common Stock was greater than 130% of the Convertible Notes conversion prices for 20 or more of the 30 consecutive trading days preceding the quarter end. As a result, the Convertible Notes are convertible at the option of the bondholder. The carrying amount of the Convertible Notes was classified in current liabilities and a portion of the equity component, representing the unamortized debt discount, was classified in temporary equity on the Company's Consolidated Balance Sheets. Upon closure of the conversion period, the 2018 and 2041 Notes not converted will be reclassified back into noncurrent liabilities, the 2016 Notes will remain in current liabilities due to its scheduled maturity, and the temporary equity will be reclassified into permanent equity. At June 29, 2014 the 2041 Notes were convertible at the option of the bondholder.

As of June 28, 2015 and June 29, 2014, the Convertible Notes consisted of the following:

(In thousands, except years, percentages, conversion rate, and conversion price)	June 28, 2015			June 29, 2014		
	2016 Notes	2018 Notes	2041 Notes	2016 Notes	2018 Notes	2041 Notes
Carrying value, long-term	$ —	$ —	$ —	$419,561	$387,338	$ —
Carrying value, current portion	435,493	402,320	520,313	—	—	516,586
Unamortized discount	14,507	47,680	179,622	30,439	62,662	183,349
Principal amount	$450,000	$450,000	$ 699,935	$450,000	$450,000	$699,935
Carrying amount of permanent equity component, net of tax	$ 61,723	$ 57,215	$ 148,487	$ 76,230	$104,895	$144,760
Carrying amount of temporary equity component, net of tax	$ 14,507	$ 47,679	$ 179,622	$ —	$ —	$183,349
Remaining amortization period (years)	0.9	2.9	25.9			
Effective interest rate on liability component	4.29%	5.27%	4.28%			
Fair Value of Notes (Level 2)	$604,004	$643,500	$1,679,844			
Conversion rate (shares of common stock per $1,000 principal amount of notes)	16.0806	16.0806	28.8585			
Conversion price (per share of common stock)	$ 62.19	$ 62.19	$ 34.65			
If-converted value in excess of par value	$149,598	$149,598	$ 973,758			

Convertible Note Hedges and Warrants

Concurrent with the issuance of the 2016 Notes and 2018 Notes, the Company purchased a convertible note hedge and sold warrants. At expiration, the Company may, at its option, elect to settle the warrants on a net share basis. As of June 28, 2015, the warrants had not been exercised and remained outstanding. The exercise price is adjusted for certain corporate events, including dividends on the Company's Common Stock.

In conjunction with the convertible note hedge, counterparties agreed to sell to the Company shares of Common Stock equal to the number of shares issuable upon conversion of the 2016 Notes and 2018 Notes in full. The convertible note hedge transactions will be settled in net shares and will terminate upon the earlier of the maturity date or the first day none of the respective notes remain outstanding due to conversion or otherwise. Settlement of the convertible note hedge in net shares, based on the number of shares issued upon conversion of the 2016 and 2018 Notes, on the expiration date would result in the Company receiving net shares equivalent to the number of shares issuable by the Company upon conversion of the 2016 Notes and 2018 Notes. The exercise price is adjusted for certain corporate events, including dividends on the Company's Common Stock.

The following table presents the details of the warrants and convertible note hedge arrangements as of June 28, 2015:

(Shares in thousands)	2016 Notes	2018 Notes
Warrants:		
Number of shares to be delivered upon exercise	7,236	7,236
Exercise price	$70.40	$75.10
Expiration date range	August 15–October 21, 2016	August 15–October 23, 2018
Convertible Note Hedge:		
Number of shares available from counterparties	7,236	7,236
Exercise price	$62.19	$62.19

Interest Cost

The following table presents the amount of interest cost recognized relating to both the contractual interest coupon and amortization of the debt discount, issuance costs, and effective portion of interest rate contracts with respect to the Senior Notes and the Convertible Notes during the twelve months ended June 29, 2015, June 28, 2014, and June 30, 2013.

(In thousands)	Twelve Months Ended		
	June 28, 2015	June 29, 2014	June 30, 2013
Contractual interest coupon	$36,074	$26,248	$26,248
Amortization of interest discount	34,886	33,065	31,560
Amortization of issuance costs	2,435	2,362	2,362
Amortization of interest rate contract	113	—	—
Total interest cost recognized	$73,508	$61,675	$60,170

Contractual Obligations

The Company's contractual cash obligations relating to its Convertible Notes and other long-term debt as of June 28, 2015 were as follows:

(In thousands)	Long-Term Debt
Payments due by period:	
2016*	$1,599,935
2017	—
2018	—
2019	—
2020	500,000
Thereafter	500,000
Total	2,599,935
Current portion of long-term debt	1,599,935
Long-term debt	$1,000,000

* As noted above, the conversion periods for the Convertible Notes are open as of June 28, 2015. As there is the potential for conversion at the option of the holder, the principal balance of the 2018 and 2041 Notes have been included in the one year payment period. As of August 6, 2015, none of the Convertible Notes have been converted during fiscal year 2015 or 2014.

Credit Agreements

DISCLOSURE

2.129 Regulation S-X requires disclosure of the amounts and terms, including commitment fees and conditions for draw-downs, of unused commitments for short-term and long-term financing.

PRESENTATION AND DISCLOSURE EXCERPTS

CREDIT AGREEMENTS

2.130 HARMAN INTERNATIONAL INDUSTRIES, INCORPORATED (JUN)
CONSOLIDATED BALANCE SHEETS (in part)

	June 30,	
(In thousands)	2015	2014
Liabilities and Equity (in part)		
Current liabilities		
Current portion of long-term debt	$ 4,550	$ 35,625
Short-term debt	1,021	3,736
Accounts payable	918,910	697,553
Accrued liabilities	956,425	566,722
Accrued warranties	163,331	155,472
Income taxes payable	76,131	26,544
Total current liabilities	2,120,368	1,485,652
Borrowings under revolving credit facility	283,125	300,000
Long-term debt	797,542	219,407
Pension liability	186,662	186,352
Other non-current liabilities	149,229	141,158
Total liabilities	3,536,926	2,332,569

NOTES TO THE CONSOLIDATED FINANCIAL STATEMENTS (in part)

(Dollars in thousands, except per share data and unless otherwise indicated)

Note 9—Debt (in part)

2015 Credit Agreement

On March 26, 2015 we and our wholly-owned subsidiary Harman Holding GmbH & Co. KG ("Harman KG"), entered into the 2015 Credit Agreement with a group of banks. The 2015 Credit Agreement provides for a five-year unsecured multi-currency revolving credit facility in the amount of $1.2 billion (the "Aggregate Commitment") with availability in currencies other than the United States Dollar of up to $750.0 million. Up to $50.0 million of the Aggregate Commitment is available for letters of credit. Subject to certain conditions set forth in the 2015 Credit Agreement, the Aggregate Commitment may be increased by up to $500.0 million. However, there is presently no commitment for this additional borrowing ability. We may select interest rates for borrowings under the 2015 Credit Agreement equal to (i) the LIBO rate plus an applicable margin, (ii) the EURIBO rate plus an applicable margin, or (iii) a base rate plus an applicable margin, which in each case is based on ratings which are established by Standard & Poor's Ratings Services ("S&P") and Moody's Investor Services ("Moody's"). We pay a facility fee on the Aggregate Commitment, whether drawn or undrawn, which is also determined based on our ratings which are established by S&P and Moody's. Any proceeds from borrowings under the 2015 Credit Agreement may be used for general corporate purposes.

The 2015 Credit Agreement includes certain financial condition covenants, including covenants that do not permit us to allow (i) our ratio of consolidated EBITDA to consolidated cash interest expense to be less than 3.5:1.0 or (ii) our ratio of consolidated total debt to consolidated EBITDA to exceed 3.5:1.0, or following certain acquisitions, 4.0:1.0, each calculated as of the end of the applicable fiscal quarter on a rolling four-quarter basis. The terms "consolidated EBITDA," "consolidated cash interest expense," and "consolidated total debt" are defined in the 2015 Credit Agreement.

The 2015 Credit Agreement also contains certain negative covenants that limit, among other things, the ability of certain of our subsidiaries to incur debt and our ability and the ability of our subsidiaries to incur liens, make fundamental changes (including selling all or substantially all of our assets), undertake transactions with affiliates and undertake sale and leaseback transactions. The 2015 Credit

Agreement is subject to acceleration upon certain specified events of default, including failure to make timely payments, breaches of representations or covenants, or a "change of control", as such term is defined in the 2015 Credit Agreement. As of June 30, 2015, we were in compliance with all the financial covenants of the 2015 Credit Agreement and we believe we will be in compliance for the next 12 months.

Upon the signing of the 2015 Credit Agreement, we voluntarily terminated the Multi-Currency Credit Agreement, dated as of October 10, 2012 (the "2013 Credit Agreement") with a group of banks. No early termination penalties were incurred by us as a result of the termination of the 2013 Credit Agreement. All of the approximately $4.0 million of letters of credit that were previously outstanding under the 2013 Credit Agreement were deemed to be issued and outstanding under the 2015 Credit Agreement.

At June 30, 2015, there was approximately $283.1 million of outstanding borrowings, which are included in our Consolidated Balance Sheet as Borrowings under revolving credit facility and $4.8 million of outstanding letters of credit under the 2015 Credit Agreement. At June 30, 2015, unused available credit under the 2015 Credit Agreement was $912.1 million. In connection with the 2015 Credit Agreement, we incurred $3.0 million of fees and other expenses, which are included within Other assets in our Consolidated Balance Sheet at June 30, 2015. These costs are amortized over the term of the 2015 Credit Agreement to Interest expense, net in our Consolidated Statement of Income on a straight-line basis. In addition, during the fiscal year ended June 30, 2015, we wrote off $0.6 million of debt issuance costs to Interest expense, net, associated with the 2013 Credit Agreement, which represented the portion of these costs that were attributed to the 2013 Credit Agreement.

At June 30, 2014, there was $300.0 million of outstanding borrowings and approximately $4.6 million of outstanding letters of credit under the revolving credit facility of the 2013 Credit Agreement and $255.0 million of outstanding borrowings under the five-year unsecured United States Dollar term loan facility (the "Term Facility") of the 2013 Credit Agreement, of which $35.6 million is included in our Consolidated Balance Sheet as Current portion of long-term debt and $219.4 million is classified as Long-term debt.

Long-Term Debt and Current Portion of Long-Term-Debt

At June 30, 2015 and 2014, long-term debt and current portion of long-term debt consisted of the following:

	Fair Value at June 30, 2015[1]	Book Value at June 30, 2015	Fair Value at June 30, 2014	Book Value at June 30, 2014
4.150 Percent Senior Notes	$ 393,160	$ 400,000	$ 0	$ 0
2.000 Percent Senior Notes	379,200	389,883	0	0
Borrowings under revolving credit facility[2]	283,125	283,125	300,000	300,000
Term facility	0	0	255,000	255,000
Capital lease obligations	16,325	16,325	32	32
Total debt	1,071,810	1,089,333	555,032	555,032
Current portion of long-term debt	(4,550)	(4,550)	(35,625)	(35,625)
Unamortized debt discount on 4.150 Percent Senior Notes	(2,626)	(2,626)	0	0
Unamortized debt discount on 2.000 Percent Senior Notes	(1,490)	(1,490)	0	0
Total long-term debt	$1,063,144	$1,080,667	$519,407	$519,407

[1] The estimated fair value of the 2.000 Percent Senior Notes and the 4.150 Senior Notes were based on a broker quotation (Level 2). Under fair value accounting guidance Level 2 is based on inputs that are observable for the asset or liability, either directly or indirectly through market corroboration, for substantially the full term of the financial instrument.

[2] At June 30, 2015, the borrowings were outstanding under the 2015 Credit Agreement. At June 30, 2014, the borrowings were outstanding under the 2013 Credit Agreement.

2.131 SPX CORPORATION (DEC)
CONSOLIDATED BALANCE SHEETS (in part)

(in millions, except share data)

	December 31, 2015	December 31, 2014
Liabilities and Equity (in part)		
Current liabilities:		
Accounts payable	$ 176.9	$ 210.0
Accrued expenses	403.7	440.2
Income taxes payable	1.7	8.3
Short-term debt	22.1	156.5
Current maturities of long-term debt	9.1	29.1
Liabilities held for sale	41.3	—
Liabilities of discontinued operations	—	765.8
Total current liabilities	654.8	1,609.9
Long-term debt	342.6	547.5
Deferred and other income taxes	55.2	69.1
Other long-term liabilities	820.4	823.7
Liabilities of discontinued operations	—	1,032.2
Total long-term liabilities	1,218.2	2,472.5

(All currency and share amounts are in millions, except per share and par value data)

(12) Indebtedness

The following summarizes our debt activity (both current and non-current) for the year ended December 31, 2015:

	December 31, 2014	Borrowings	Repayments	Spin-Off[6]	Other[7]	December 31, 2015
Revolving loans:						
Prior SPX facilities[1]	$ 133.0	$ 430.0	$ (563.0)	$ —	$ —	$ —
Current SPX facilities	—	29.0	(29.0)	—	—	—
Current SPX FLOW facilities	—	55.0	—	(55.0)	—	—
Term loans:						
Prior SPX facilities[1]	575.0	—	(575.0)	—	—	—
Current SPX facilities[2]	—	350.0	—	—	—	350.0
Current SPX FLOW facilities	—	400.0	—	(400.0)	—	—
6.875% senior notes[3]	600.0	—	—	(600.0)	—	—
Trade receivables financing arrangement[4]	10.0	156.0	(166.0)	—	—	—
Other indebtedness[3][5]	51.7	27.4	(16.9)	(36.7)	(1.7)	23.8
Total debt	1,369.7	$1,447.4	$(1,349.9)	$(1,091.7)	$(1.7)	373.8
Less: Amounts included in discontinued operations[3]	(636.6)					—
Total debt—continuing operations	733.1					373.8
Less: short-term debt	156.5					22.1
Less: current maturities of long-term debt	29.1					9.1
Total long-term debt—continuing operations	$ 547.5					$342.6

[1] As noted below, both SPX and SPX FLOW entered into separate credit agreements in connection with the Spin-Off. On September 24, 2015, the lenders provided the initial funding under each of these credit agreements. The proceeds from the initial funding were used in part to repay indebtedness under SPX's prior credit facilities, with such repayments totaling $224.0 for the revolving loans and $560.6 for the term loan.

[2] The term loan is repayable in quarterly installments of 5.0% annually, beginning in the third fiscal quarter of 2016. The remaining balance is repayable in full on September 24, 2020.

[3] In connection with the Spin-Off, the 6.875% senior notes became an obligation of SPX FLOW. Accordingly, the related balance of $600.0 has been reflected in "Liabilities of discontinued operations—non current" in the consolidated balance sheet as of December 31, 2014. In addition, there is "Other indebtedness" related to SPX FLOW totaling $36.6 at December 31, 2014, with such balance reflected in "Liabilities of discontinued operations—current" and "Liabilities of discontinued operations—non current" in the consolidated balance sheet as of December 31, 2014.

[4] Under this arrangement, we can borrow, on a continuous basis, up to $50.0, as available. At December 31, 2015, we had $40.1 of available borrowing capacity under this facility.

[5] Primarily included capital lease obligations of $1.7 and $13.6, balances under purchase card programs of $4.8 and $32.1, and other borrowings under a line of credit in China of $17.3 and $0, at December 31, 2015 and 2014, respectively. The purchase card program allows for payment beyond the normal payment terms for goods and services acquired under the program. As this arrangement extends the payment of these purchases beyond their normal payment terms through third-party lending institutions, we have classified these amounts as short-term debt.

[6] Represents debt of SPX FLOW that is no longer an obligation of SPX as a result of the Spin-Off.

[7] "Other" primarily included foreign currency translation on debt instruments denominated in currencies other than the U.S. dollar, partially offset by debt assumed.

Maturities of long-term debt payable during each of the five years subsequent to December 31, 2015 are $9.1, $18.0, $17.8, $17.8 and $288.9, respectively.

Senior Credit Facilities

In connection with the Spin-Off, we entered into a credit agreement (the "Credit Agreement"), dated September 1, 2015, ("Effective Date") with a syndicate of lenders that provided for committed senior secured financing in the aggregate amount of $1,200.0, consisting of the following (each with a final maturity of September 24, 2020):

- A term loan facility in an aggregate principle amount of $350.0;
- A domestic revolving credit facility, available for loans and letters of credit, in an aggregate principal amount up to $200.0;
- A global revolving credit facility, available for loans in Euros, GBP and other currencies, in an aggregate principal amount up to the equivalent of $150.0;
- A participation foreign credit instrument facility, available for performance letters of credit and guarantees, in an aggregate principal amount up to the equivalent of $300.0; and
- A bilateral foreign credit instrument facility, available for performance letters of credit and guarantees, in an aggregate principal amount up to the equivalent of $200.0.

In addition, SPX FLOW entered into a credit agreement, dated September 1, 2015, with a syndicate of lenders that provided for committed senior secured financing in the aggregate amount of $1,350.0 (the "SPX FLOW Credit Agreement"). As a result of the Spin-Off, we have no obligations under the SPX FLOW Credit Agreement.

On September 24, 2015, the lenders provided the initial funding under the Credit Agreement and the SPX FLOW Credit Agreement. The proceeds of the initial borrowings were used in part to repay indebtedness outstanding under our amended and restated credit agreement, dated December 31, 2013 (the "December 2013 Credit Agreement"). The December 2013 Credit Agreement terminated on September 24, 2015 upon the repayment of such indebtedness.

The term loan under the Credit Agreement is repayable in quarterly installments (with annual aggregate repayments, as a percentage of the initial principal amount of $350.0, of 5.0%, beginning in the third calendar quarter of 2016), with the remaining balance repayable in full on September 24, 2020.

We also may seek additional commitments, without consent from the existing lenders, to add an incremental term loan facility and/or increase the commitments in respect of the domestic revolving credit facility, the global revolving credit facility, the participation foreign credit instrument facility and/or the bilateral foreign credit instrument facility by an aggregate principal amount not to exceed (i) $300.0 plus (ii) an unlimited amount so long as, immediately after giving effect thereto, our Consolidated Senior Secured Leverage Ratio (as defined in the Credit Agreement generally as the ratio of consolidated total debt (excluding the face amount undrawn letters of credit, bank undertakings, or analogous instruments and net of cash and cash equivalents in excess of $50.0) at the date of determination secured by liens to consolidated adjusted EBITDA for the four fiscal quarters ended most recently before such date) does not exceed 2.75:1.00 plus (iii) an amount equal to all voluntary prepayments of the term loan facility and voluntary prepayments accompanied by permanent commitment reductions of revolving credit facilities and foreign credit instrument facilities.

We are the borrower under each of the above facilities, and certain of our foreign subsidiaries are (and we may designate other foreign subsidiaries to be) borrowers under the global revolving credit facility and the foreign credit instrument facilities. All borrowings and other extensions of credit under the Credit Agreement are subject to the satisfaction of customary conditions, including absence of defaults and accuracy in material respects of representations and warranties.

The letters of credit under the domestic revolving credit facility are stand-by letters of credit requested by SPX on behalf of any of our subsidiaries or certain joint ventures. The foreign credit instrument facility is used to issue foreign credit instruments, including bank undertakings to support our foreign operations.

The interest rates applicable to loans under the Credit Agreement are, at our option, equal to either (i) an alternate base rate (the highest of (a) the federal funds effective rate plus 0.5%, (b) the prime rate of Bank of America, N.A., and (c) the one-month LIBOR rate plus 1.0%) or (ii) a reserve-adjusted LIBOR rate for dollars (Eurodollars) plus, in each case, an applicable margin percentage, which varies based on our Consolidated Leverage Ratio (as defined in the Credit Agreement generally as the ratio of consolidated total debt (excluding the face amount of undrawn letters of credit, bank undertakings and analogous instruments and net of cash and cash equivalents in excess of $ 50.0) at the date of determination to consolidated adjusted EBITDA for the four fiscal quarters ended most recently before such date). We may elect interest periods of one, two, three or six months (and, if consented to by all relevant lenders, twelve months) for Eurodollar borrowings. The per annum fees charged and the interest rate margins applicable to Eurodollar and alternate base rate loans are as follows:

Consolidated Leverage Ratio	Domestic Revolving Commitment Fee	Global Revolving Commitment Fee	Letter of Credit Fee	Foreign Credit Commitment Fee	Foreign Credit Instrument Fee	LIBOR Rate Loans	ABR Loans
Greater than or equal to 3.00 to 1.0	0.350%	0.350%	2.000%	0.350%	1.250%	2.000%	1.000%
Between 2.00 to 1.0 and 3.00 to 1.0	0.300%	0.300%	1.750%	0.300%	1.000%	1.750%	0.750%
Between 1.50 to 1.0 and 2.00 to 1.0	0.275%	0.275%	1.500%	0.275%	0.875%	1.500%	0.500%
Between 1.00 to 1.0 and 1.50 to 1.0	0.250%	0.250%	1.375%	0.250%	0.800%	1.375%	0.375%
Less than 1.00 to 1.0	0.225%	0.225%	1.250%	0.225%	0.750%	1.250%	0.250%

The weighted-average interest rate of outstanding borrowings under our senior credit facilities was approximately 2.2% at December 31, 2015.

The fees and bilateral foreign credit commitments are as specified above for foreign credit commitments unless otherwise agreed with the bilateral foreign issuing lender. We also pay fronting fees on the outstanding amounts of letters of credit and foreign credit instruments (in the participation facility) at the rates of 0.125% per annum and 0.25% per annum, respectively.

The Credit Agreement requires mandatory prepayments in amounts equal to the net proceeds from the sale or other disposition of, including from any casualty to, or governmental taking of, property in excess of specified values (other than in the ordinary course of business and subject to other exceptions) by SPX or our subsidiaries. Mandatory prepayments will be applied to repay, first, amounts outstanding under any term loans and, then, amounts (or cash collateralize letters of credit) outstanding under the global revolving credit facility and the domestic revolving credit facility (without reducing the commitments thereunder). No prepayment is required generally to the extent the net proceeds are reinvested (or committed to be reinvested) in permitted acquisitions, permitted investments or assets to be used in our business within 360 days (and if committed to be reinvested, actually reinvested within 180 days after the end of such 360-day period) of the receipt of such proceeds.

We may voluntarily prepay loans under the Credit Agreement, in whole or in part, without premium or penalty. Any voluntary prepayment of loans will be subject to reimbursement of the lenders' breakage costs in the case of a prepayment of Eurodollar rate borrowings other than on the last day of the relevant interest period. Indebtedness under the Credit Agreement is guaranteed by:
- Each existing and subsequently acquired or organized domestic material subsidiary with specified exceptions; and
- SPX with respect to the obligations of our foreign borrower subsidiaries under the global revolving credit facility, the participation foreign credit instrument facility and the bilateral foreign credit instrument facility.

Indebtedness under the Credit Agreement is secured by a first priority pledge and security interest in 100% of the capital stock of our domestic subsidiaries (with certain exceptions) held by SPX or our domestic subsidiary guarantors and 65% of the capital stock of our material first-tier foreign subsidiaries (with certain exceptions). If SPX obtains a corporate credit rating from Moody's and S&P and such corporate credit rating is less than "Ba2" (or not rated) by Moody's and less than "BB" (or not rated) by S&P, then SPX and our domestic subsidiary guarantors are required to grant security interests, mortgages and other liens on substantially all of their assets. If SPX's corporate credit rating is "Baa3" or better by Moody's or "BBB-" or better by S&P and no defaults would exist, then all collateral security will be released and the indebtedness under the Credit Agreement will be unsecured.

The Credit Agreement requires that SPX maintain:
- A Consolidated Interest Coverage Ratio (as defined in the Credit Agreement generally as the ratio of consolidated adjusted EBITDA for the four fiscal quarters ended on such date to consolidated cash interest expense for such period) as of the last day of any fiscal quarter of at least 3.50 to 1.00; and
- A Consolidated Leverage Ratio as of the last day of any fiscal quarter of not more than 3.25 to 1.00 (or 3.50 to 1.00 for the four fiscal quarters after certain permitted acquisitions).

The Credit Agreement also contains covenants that, among other things, restrict our ability to incur additional indebtedness, grant liens, make investments, loans, guarantees, or advances, make restricted junior payments, including dividends, redemptions of capital stock, and voluntary prepayments or repurchase of certain other indebtedness, engage in mergers, acquisitions or sales of assets, enter into sale and leaseback transactions, or engage in certain transactions with affiliates, and otherwise restrict certain corporate activities. The Credit Agreement contains customary representations, warranties, affirmative covenants and events of default.

We are permitted under the Credit Agreement to repurchase our capital stock and pay cash dividends in an unlimited amount if our Consolidated Leverage Ratio is (after giving pro forma effect to such payments) less than 2.50 to 1.00. If our Consolidated Leverage Ratio is (after giving pro forma effect to such payments) greater than or equal to 2.50 to 1.00, the aggregate amount of such repurchases and dividend declarations cannot exceed (A) $50.0 in any fiscal year plus (B) an additional amount for all such repurchases and dividend declarations made after the Effective Date equal to the sum of (i) $100.0 plus (ii) a positive amount equal to 50% of cumulative Consolidated Net Income (as defined in the Credit Agreement generally as consolidated net income subject to certain adjustments solely for the purposes of determining this basket) during the period from the Effective Date to the end of the most recent fiscal quarter preceding the date of such repurchase or dividend declaration for which financial statements have been (or were required to be) delivered (or, in case such Consolidated Net Income is a deficit, minus 100% of such deficit) plus (iii) certain other amounts.

At December 31, 2015, we had $301.9 of available borrowing capacity under our revolving credit facilities after giving effect to $48.1 reserved for outstanding letters of credit. In addition, at December 31, 2015, we had $224.1 of available issuance capacity under our foreign credit instrument facilities after giving effect to $275.9 reserved for outstanding letters of credit.

At December 31, 2015, we were in compliance with all covenants of our Credit Agreement.

Other Borrowings and Financing Activities

Certain of our businesses purchase goods and services under purchase card programs allowing for payment beyond their normal payment terms. As of December 31, 2015 and 2014, the participating businesses had $4.8 and $32.10, respectively, outstanding under these arrangements.

We are party to a trade receivables financing agreement, whereby we can borrow, on a continuous basis, up to $50.00. Availability of funds may fluctuate over time given changes in eligible receivable balances, but will not exceed the $50.0 program limit. The facility contains representations, warranties, covenants and indemnities customary for facilities of this type. The facility does not contain any covenants that we view as materially constraining to the activities of our business.

Long-Term Leases

RECOGNITION AND MEASUREMENT

2.132 FASB ASC 840 establishes standards of financial accounting and reporting for leases on the financial statements of lessees and lessors. FASB ASC 840 classifies leases as capital or operating. Capital leases are accounted for as the acquisition of an asset and the incurrence of an obligation by the lessee and as a sale or financing by the lessor. All other leases are accounted for as operating leases.

PRESENTATION

2.133 Under FASB ASC 840-30-45-1, lessees should separately identify on the balance sheet or notes thereto assets recorded under capital leases, the accumulated amortization thereon, and obligations. Capital lease obligations are subject to the same considerations as other obligations in classifying them with current and noncurrent liabilities in classified balance sheets. Similarly, a lessor's net investment in a sales-type or direct financing lease is also subject to the same considerations as other assets in classification as current or noncurrent assets.

2.134 FASB ASC 840-20-45-2 requires that lessors include property subject to operating leases with or near property, plant, and equipment in the balance sheet. Accumulated depreciation should be deducted by lessors from the investments in the leased property, as explained in FASB ASC 840-20-45-3.

DISCLOSURE

2.135 FASB ASC 840-20-50 and 840-30-50 contain detailed disclosure requirements for lessors and lessees under operating and capital leases, respectively.

PRESENTATION AND DISCLOSURE EXCERPTS

LESSEE LEASES

2.136 PEABODY ENERGY CORPORATION (DEC)
NOTES TO CONSOLIDATED FINANCIAL STATEMENTS (in part)

(1) Summary of Significant Accounting Policies (in part)

Accounting Standards Not Yet Implemented (in part)

Lease accounting. In February 2016, FASB issued accounting guidance that will require a lessee to recognize in is balance sheet a liability to make lease payments and a right-of-use asset representing its right to use the underlying asset for the lease term for leases with lease terms of more than 12 months. Consistent with current U.S. GAAP, the recognition, measurement, and presentation of expenses and cash flows arising from a lease by a lessee primarily will depend on its classification as a finance or operating lease. Additional qualitative disclosures along with specific quantitative disclosures will also be required. The new guidance will take effect for public companies for fiscal years, and interim periods within those fiscal years, beginning after Dec. 15, 2018 (January 1, 2019 for the Company), with early adoption permitted. Upon adoption, the Company will be required to recognize and measure leases at the beginning of the earliest period presented using a modified retrospective approach. The Company is in the process of evaluating the impact that the adoption of this guidance will have on its results of operations, financial condition, cash flows and financial statement presentation.

(12) Long-term Debt (in part)

The Company's total indebtedness as of December 31, 2015 and 2014 consisted of the following:

	December 31,	
(Dollars in millions)	2015	2014
2013 Term Loan Facility due September 2020	$1,164.9	$1,175.1
7.375% Senior Notes due November 2016	—	650.0
6.00% Senior Notes due November 2018	1,518.8	1,518.8
6.50% Senior Notes due September 2020	650.0	650.0
6.25% Senior Notes due November 2021	1,339.6	1,339.6
10.00% Senior Secured Second Lien Notes due March 2022	978.4	—
7.875% Senior Notes due November 2026	247.7	247.6
Convertible Junior Subordinated Debentures due December 2066	385.2	382.3
Capital lease obligations	30.3	22.2
Other	0.7	1.2
Total	$6,315.6	$5,986.8

Capital Lease Obligations

Refer to Note 13. "Leases" for additional information associated with the Company's capital leases, which pertain to the financing of mining equipment used in operations.

Debt Maturities, Interest Paid and Financing Costs

The aggregate amounts of long-term debt maturities (including unamortized debt discounts) subsequent to December 31, 2015, including capital lease obligations, were as follows:

Year of Maturity	(Dollars in millions)
2016	$5,930.4
2017	—
2018	—
2019	—
2020	—
2021 and thereafter	385.2
Total	$6,315.6

Interest paid on long-term debt was $414.2 million, $404.4 million and $388.2 million for the years ended December 31, 2015, 2014 and 2013, respectively.

Financing costs incurred with the issuance of the Company's debt are being amortized to interest expense over the remaining term of the associated debt. The remaining balance at December 31, 2015 was $94.8 million, of which $70.6 million will be amortized to interest expense over the next five years.

(13) Leases

The Company leases equipment and facilities under various noncancelable lease agreements. Certain lease agreements are subject to the restrictive covenants of the Company's credit facilities and include cross-acceleration provisions, under which the lessor could require certain remedies including, but not limited to, immediate recovery of the present value of any remaining lease payments. Rental expense under operating leases, including expense related to short-term operating leases, was $290.1 million, $306.0 million and $305.9 million for the years ended December 31, 2015, 2014 and 2013, respectively. One of the Company's operating lease agreements for underground mining equipment in Australia entered into in 2013 requires contingent rent to be paid only if and when certain coal is mined at a specified margin as defined in the agreements. There was no contingent expense related to that arrangement for the years ended December 31, 2015, 2014 and 2013. The gross value of property, plant, and equipment under capital leases was $125.6 million and $175.1 million as of December 31, 2015 and 2014, respectively, related primarily to the leasing of mining equipment. The accumulated depreciation for these items was $111.4 million and $138.4 million at December 31, 2015 and 2014, respectively, and changes thereto have been included in "Depreciation, depletion and amortization" in the consolidated statements of operations.

The Company also leases coal reserves under agreements that require royalties to be paid as the coal is mined. Certain agreements also require minimum annual royalties to be paid regardless of the amount of coal mined during the year. Total royalty expense was $444.5 million, $507.8 million and $546.0 million for the years ended December 31, 2015, 2014 and 2013, respectively.

A substantial amount of the coal mined by the Company is produced from mineral reserves leased from the owner. One of the major lessors is the U.S. government, from which the Company leases substantially all of the coal it mines in Wyoming under terms set by Congress and administered by the U.S. Bureau of Land Management. These leases are generally for an initial term of ten years but may be extended by diligent development and mining of the reserves until all economically recoverable reserves are depleted. The Company has met the diligent development requirements for substantially all of these federal leases either directly through production, by including the lease as a part of a logical mining unit with other leases upon which development has occurred, or by paying an advance royalty in lieu of continued operations. Annual production on these federal leases must total at least 1.0% of the leased reserve or the original amount of coal in the entire logical mining unit in which the leased reserve resides. In addition, royalties are payable monthly at a rate of 12.5% of the gross realization from the sale of the coal mined using surface mining methods and at a rate of 8.0% of the gross realization for coal produced using underground mining methods. The Company also leases coal reserves in Arizona from The Navajo Nation and the Hopi Tribe under leases that are administered by the U.S. Department of the Interior. These leases expire upon exhaustion of the leased reserves or upon the permanent ceasing of all mining activities on the related reserves as a whole. The royalty rates are also generally based upon a percentage of the gross realization from the sale of coal. These rates are subject to redetermination every ten years under the terms of the leases. The remainder of the leased coal is generally leased from state governments, land holding companies and various individuals. The duration of these leases varies greatly. Typically, the lease terms are automatically extended as long as active mining continues. Royalty payments are generally based upon a specified rate per ton or a percentage of the gross realization from the sale of the coal.

Mining and exploration in Australia is generally conducted under leases, licenses or permits granted by state governments. Mining and exploration licenses and their associated environmental protection approvals contain conditions relating to such matters as minimum annual expenditures, environmental compliance, restoration and rehabilitation. Royalties are paid to the state government as a percentage of the sales price (less certain allowable deductions in some cases). Generally landowners do not own the mineral rights or have the ability to grant rights to mine those minerals. These rights are retained by state governments. Compensation is often payable to landowners, occupiers and Aboriginal traditional owners with residual native title rights and interests for the loss of access to the land from the proposed mining activities. The amount and type of compensation and the ability to proceed to grant of a mining tenement may be determined by agreement or court determination, as provided by law.

Future minimum lease and royalty payments as of December 31, 2015 are as follows:

(Dollars in millions) Year Ending December 31,	Capital Leases	Operating Leases	Coal Lease and Royalty Obligations
2016	$12.9	$191.5	$254.3
2017	7.3	173.8	20.3
2018	8.8	109.4	19.9
2019	0.5	64.2	19.4
2020	0.5	23.4	18.9
2021 and thereafter	10.1	36.5	30.8
Total minimum lease payments	40.1	$598.8	$363.6
Less interest	9.8		
Present value of minimum capital lease payments	$30.3		

As of December 31, 2015, certain of the Company's coal lease obligations were secured by outstanding surety bonds totaling $110.5 million

2.137 DOLLAR GENERAL CORPORATION (JAN)
NOTES TO CONSOLIDATED FINANCIAL STATEMENTS (in part)

1. Basis of Presentation and Accounting Policies (in part)

Operating Leases and Related Liabilities

Rent expense is recognized over the term of the lease. The Company records minimum rental expense on a straight-line basis over the base, non-cancelable lease term commencing on the date that the Company takes physical possession of the property from the landlord, which normally includes a period prior to the store opening to make necessary leasehold improvements and install store fixtures. When a lease contains a predetermined fixed escalation of the minimum rent, the Company recognizes the related rent expense on a straight-line basis and records the difference between the recognized rental expense and the amounts payable under the lease as deferred rent. Tenant allowances, to the extent received, are recorded as deferred incentive rent and are amortized as a reduction to rent expense over the term of the lease. The difference between the calculated expense and the amounts paid result in a liability, with the current portion in Accrued expenses and other and the long-term portion in Other liabilities in the consolidated balance sheets, and totaled approximately $54.6 million and $49.5 million at January 30, 2015 and January 31, 2014, respectively.

The Company recognizes contingent rental expense when the achievement of specified sales targets is considered probable. The amount expensed but not paid as of January 30, 2015 and January 31, 2014 was approximately $4.8 million and $6.0 million, respectively, and is included in Accrued expenses and other in the consolidated balance sheets.

8. Commitments and Contingencies (in part)

Leases (in part)

As of January 30, 2015, the Company was committed under operating lease agreements for most of its retail stores. Many of the Company's stores are subject to build-to-suit arrangements with landlords which typically carry a primary lease term of up to 15 years with multiple renewal options. The Company also has stores subject to shorter-term leases and many of these leases have renewal options. Certain of the Company's leased stores have provisions for contingent rentals based upon a specified percentage of defined sales volume.

The land and buildings of the Company's DCs in Fulton, Missouri and Indianola, Mississippi are subject to operating lease agreements and the leased Ardmore, Oklahoma DC is subject to a financing arrangement. The entities involved in the ownership structure underlying these leases meet the accounting definition of a Variable Interest Entity ("VIE"). The Company is not the primary beneficiary of these VIEs and, accordingly, has not included these entities in its consolidated financial statements. Certain leases contain restrictive covenants that, individually, are not material to the Company. As of January 30, 2015, the Company is not aware of any material violations of such covenants.

In January 2014, the Company sold 233 store locations for cash and concurrent with the sale transaction, the Company leased the properties back for a period of 15 years. The transaction resulted in cash proceeds of approximately $281.6 million and a deferred gain of $67.2 million which is being recognized as a reduction of rent expense over the 15-year initial lease term of the properties.

In January 1999, the Company sold its DC located in Ardmore, Oklahoma for cash and concurrent with the sale transaction, the Company leased the property back for a period of 23 years. The transaction is accounted for as a financing obligation rather than a sale as a result of, among other things, the lessor's ability to put the property back to the Company under certain circumstances. The property and equipment, along with the related lease obligation associated with this transaction are recorded in the consolidated balance sheets. In August 2007, the Company purchased a secured promissory note (the "Ardmore Note") from an unrelated third party with a face value of $34.3 million at the date of purchase which approximated the remaining financing obligation. The Ardmore Note represents debt issued by the third party entity from which the Company leases the Ardmore DC and therefore the Company holds the debt instrument pertaining to its lease financing obligation. Because a legal right of offset exists, the Company is accounting for the Ardmore Note as a reduction of its outstanding financing obligation in its consolidated balance sheets.

Future minimum payments as of January 30, 2015 for operating leases are as follows:

(In thousands)	
2015	$ 793,274
2016	751,044
2017	703,892
2018	648,120
2019	584,508
Thereafter	3,145,663
Total minimum payments	$6,626,501

Rent expense under all operating leases is as follows:

(In thousands)	2014	2013	2012
Minimum rentals[a]	$776,103	$674,849	$599,138
Contingent rentals	9,099	12,058	15,150
	$785,202	$686,907	$614,288

[a] Excludes amortization of leasehold interests of $5.8 million, $11.9 million and $16.9 million included in rent expense for the years ended January 30, 2015, January 31, 2014, and February 1, 2013, respectively.

LESSOR LEASES

2.138 VERIZON COMMUNICATIONS INC. (DEC)
NOTES TO CONSOLIDATED FINANCIAL STATEMENTS VERIZON COMMUNICATIONS INC. AND SUBSIDIARIES (in part)

Note 6—Leasing Arrangements

As Lessor

We are the lessor in leveraged and direct financing lease agreements for commercial aircraft and power generating facilities, which comprise the majority of our leasing portfolio along with telecommunications equipment, commercial real estate property and other equipment. These leases have remaining terms of up to 23 years as of December 31, 2015. In addition, we lease space on certain of our cell towers to other wireless carriers. Minimum lease payments receivable represent unpaid rentals, less principal and interest on third-party nonrecourse debt relating to leveraged lease transactions. Since we have no general liability for this debt, which is secured by a senior security interest in the leased equipment and rentals, the related principal and interest have been offset against the minimum lease payments. All recourse debt is reflected in our consolidated balance sheets.

At each reporting period, we monitor the credit quality of the various lessees in our portfolios. Regarding the leveraged lease portfolio, external credit reports are used where available and where not available we use internally developed indicators. These indicators or internal credit risk grades factor historic loss experience, the value of the underlying collateral, delinquency trends, and industry and general economic conditions. The credit quality of our lessees varies from A to CCC $+$. For each reporting period, the leveraged leases within the portfolio are reviewed for indicators of impairment where it is probable the rent due according to the contractual terms of the lease will not be collected. All significant accounts, individually or in the aggregate, are current and none are classified as impaired.

Finance lease receivables, which are included in Prepaid expenses and other and Other assets in our consolidated balance sheets, are comprised of the following:

	At December 31,					
	2015			**2014**		
(Dollars in millions)	**Leveraged Leases**	**Direct Finance Leases**	**Total**	**Leveraged Leases**	**Direct Finance Leases**	**Total**
Minimum lease payments receivable	$ 778	$ 7	$ 785	$1,095	$ 8	$1,103
Estimated residual value	496	2	498	600	2	602
Unearned income	(309)	(2)	(311)	(535)	(2)	(537)
Total	$ 965	$ 7	$ 972	$1,160	$ 8	$1,168
Allowance for doubtful accounts			(78)			(78)
Finance lease receivables, net			$ 894			$1,090
Prepaid expenses and other			$ 3			$4
Other assets			891			1,086
			$ 894			$1,090

Accumulated deferred taxes arising from leveraged leases, which are included in Deferred income taxes, amounted to $0.8 billion at December 31, 2015 and $0.9 billion at December 31, 2014.

The future minimum lease payments to be received from noncancelable capital leases (direct financing and leveraged leases), net of nonrecourse loan payments related to leveraged leases and allowances for doubtful accounts, along with expected receipts relating to operating leases for the periods shown at December 31, 2015, are as follows:

(Dollars in millions) Years	Capital Leases	Operating Leases
2016	$ 93	$128
2017	94	103
2018	52	82
2019	44	51
2020	72	23
Thereafter	430	12
Total	$785	$399

Other Noncurrent Liabilities

PRESENTATION

2.139 FASB ASC 210 indicates that liabilities classified as noncurrent (that is, beyond the operating cycle) include long-term deferments of the delivery of goods or services, such as the issuance of a long-term warranty or the advance receipt by a lessor of rent for the final period of a 10-year lease. Similarly, a loan on a life insurance policy with the intent that it will not be paid but will be liquidated by deduction from the proceeds of the policy upon maturity or cancellation should be excluded from current liabilities.

2.140 FASB ASC 480, *Distinguishing Liabilities from Equity*, requires that an issuer classify certain financial instruments with characteristics of both liabilities and equity as liabilities. Some issuances of stock, such as mandatorily redeemable preferred stock, impose unconditional obligations requiring the issuer to transfer assets or issue its equity shares. FASB ASC 480 requires an issuer to classify such financial instruments as liabilities, not present them between the "Liabilities" and "Equity" sections of the balance sheet. Rule 5-02 of Regulation S-X includes matters related to redeemable preferred stocks to be stated on the face of the balance sheet or included in the notes.

2.141 Rule 5-02 of Regulation S-X requires that any item not classed in another Regulation S-X liability caption and in excess of 5 percent of total liabilities be stated separately on the balance sheet or disclosed in the notes. Regulation S-X also requires that deferred income taxes, deferred tax credits, and material items of deferred income be stated separately in the balance sheet.

2.142 Rule 5-02 of Regulation S-X includes a balance sheet caption for commitments and contingent liabilities. When commitments or contingent liabilities exist and are disclosed in footnotes, registrants customarily include a caption on the balance sheet without an amount but with a reference to the related footnote.

PRESENTATION AND DISCLOSURE EXCERPTS

DEFERRED INCOME TAXES

2.143 FIDELITY NATIONAL INFORMATION SERVICES, INC. (DEC)
CONSOLIDATED BALANCE SHEETS (in part)

(In millions, except per share amounts)

	2015	2014
Liabilities and Equity (in part)		
Current liabilities:		
Accounts payable and accrued liabilities	$ 1,186.4	$ 730.3
Settlement payables	537.7	558.4
Deferred revenues	615.3	279.4
Current portion of long-term debt	15.3	13.1
Due to Brazilian venture partner	9.2	13.3
Liabilities held for sale	—	4.4
Total current liabilities	2,363.9	1,598.9
Long-term debt, excluding current portion	11,497.8	5,054.6
Deferred income taxes	2,658.4	874.4
Due to Brazilian venture partner	24.0	29.6
Deferred revenues	30.4	26.1
Other long-term liabilities	287.5	245.4
Total liabilities	16,862.0	7,829.0

NOTES TO CONSOLIDATED FINANCIAL STATEMENTS (in part)

(2) Summary of Significant Accounting Policies (in part)

(m) Income Taxes

The Company recognizes deferred income tax assets and liabilities for temporary differences between the financial reporting basis and the tax basis of the Company's assets and liabilities and expected benefits of using net operating loss and credit carryforwards. Deferred income tax assets and liabilities are measured using enacted tax rates expected to apply to taxable income in the years in which those temporary differences are expected to be recovered or settled. The impact on deferred income taxes of changes in tax rates and laws, if any, is reflected in the Consolidated Financial Statements in the period enacted. A valuation allowance is established for any portion of a deferred income tax asset for which management believes it is more likely than not that the Company will not be able to realize the benefits of all or a portion of that deferred income tax asset.

(14) Income Taxes

Income tax expense (benefit) attributable to continuing operations for the years ended December 31, 2015, 2014 and 2013 consists of the following (in millions):

	2015	2014	2013
Current provision:			
Federal	$248.4	$248.2	$232.2
State	32.5	32.1	27.2
Foreign	51.8	63.7	49.3
Total current provision	$332.7	$344.0	$308.7
Deferred provision (benefit):			
Federal	$ 49.8	$ (3.6)	$ 0.2
State	5.5	(2.3)	(1.1)
Foreign	(9.2)	(3.0)	1.1
Total deferred provision	46.1	(8.9)	0.2
Total provision for income taxes	$378.8	$335.1	$308.9

The provision for income taxes is based on pre-tax income from continuing operations, which is as follows for the years ended December 31, 2015, 2014 and 2013 (in millions):

	2015	2014	2013
United States	$ 863.5	$ 789.3	$753.8
Foreign	173.4	264.1	69.7
Total	$1,036.9	$1,053.4	$823.5

Total income tax expense for the years ended December 31, 2015, 2014 and 2013 is allocated as follows (in millions):

	2015	2014	2013
Tax expense per statements of earnings	$378.8	$335.1	$308.9
Tax expense attributable to discontinued operations	(1.8)	(3.9)	2.3
Unrealized (benefit)/loss gain on investments and derivatives	(5.1)	1.0	0.4
Unrealized (loss) gain on foreign currency translation	(0.2)	(4.6)	(5.8)
Other components of other comprehensive income	—	(3.1)	(0.1)
Total income tax expense (benefit) allocated to other comprehensive income	(5.3)	(6.7)	(5.5)
Tax benefit from exercise of stock options	(28.6)	(39.5)	(40.4)
Total income tax expense	$343.1	$285.0	$265.3

A reconciliation of the federal statutory income tax rate to the Company's effective income tax rate for the years ended December 31, 2015, 2014 and 2013 is as follows:

	2015	2014	2013
Federal statutory income tax rate	35.0%	35.0%	35.0%
State income taxes	4.6	4.6	4.6
Federal benefit of state taxes	(1.6)	(1.6)	(1.6)
Foreign rate differential	(2.6)	(2.6)	(2.5)
Capco contingent consideration	—	—	5.9
Other	1.1	(3.6)	(3.9)
Effective income tax rate	36.5%	31.8%	37.5%

The significant components of deferred income tax assets and liabilities as of December 31, 2015 and 2014 consist of the following (in millions):

	2015	2014
Deferred income tax assets:		
Net operating loss carryforwards	$ 228.2	$ 183.2
Employee benefit accruals	98.0	55.5
State taxes	44.4	11.8
Foreign currency translation adjustment	30.0	28.9
Foreign tax credit carryforwards	13.6	12.7
Accruals	13.5	27.1
Allowance for doubtful accounts	10.6	3.6
Deferred revenue	—	43.7
Interest rate swaps	—	0.5
Total gross deferred income tax assets	438.3	367.0
Less valuation allowance	(166.9)	(121.7)
Total deferred income tax assets	271.4	245.3
Deferred income tax liabilities:		
Amortization of goodwill and intangible assets	2,606.1	899.5
Deferred contract costs	102.7	91.1
Depreciation	60.9	48.4
Deferred revenue	27.5	—
Prepaid expenses	10.5	6.6
Other	1.6	0.9
Total deferred income tax liabilities	2,809.3	1,046.5
Net deferred income tax liability	$2,537.9	$ 801.2

Deferred income taxes have been classified in the Consolidated Balance Sheets as of December 31, 2015 and 2014 as follows (in millions):

	2015	2014
Current assets	$ 99.8	$ 67.4
Noncurrent assets (included in other noncurrent assets)	22.6	9.5
Total deferred income tax assets	122.4	76.9
Current liabilities (included in accounts payable and accrued liabilities)	(1.9)	(3.7)
Noncurrent liabilities	(2,658.4)	(874.4)
Net deferred income tax liability	$(2,537.9)	$(801.2)

We believe that based on our historical pattern of taxable income, projections of future income, tax planning strategies and other relevant evidence, the Company will produce sufficient income in the future to realize its deferred income tax assets. A valuation allowance is established for any portion of a deferred income tax asset for which we believe it is more likely than not that the Company will not be able to realize the benefits of all or a portion of that deferred income tax asset. We also receive periodic assessments from taxing authorities challenging our positions that must be taken into consideration in determining our tax accruals. Resolving these assessments, which may or may not result in additional taxes due, may require an extended period of time. Adjustments to the valuation allowance will be made if there is a change in our assessment of the amount of deferred income tax asset that is realizable.

As a result of provisional purchase price allocations associated with the SunGard acquisition, acquired deferred revenue was adjusted to its fair value, which was determined to be significantly lower than its historical book value. As a result of this adjustment, the tax basis of deferred revenue now exceeds the book basis, resulting in a deferred tax liability as of December 31, 2015 as compared to a deferred tax asset as of December 31, 2014.

As of December 31, 2015 and 2014, the Company had income taxes receivable of $138.6 million and $12.0 million, respectively. These amounts are included in other receivables in the Consolidated Balance Sheets.

As of December 31, 2015 and 2014, the Company has federal, state and foreign net operating loss carryforwards resulting in deferred tax assets of $228.2 million and $183.2 million, respectively. The federal and state net operating losses result in deferred tax assets as of December 31, 2015 and 2014 of $52.8 million and $26.1 million, respectively, which expire between 2020 and 2035. The Company has a valuation allowance related to these deferred tax assets for net operating loss carryforwards in the amounts of $34.8 million and $8.8 million as of December 31, 2015 and 2014. The Company has foreign net operating loss carryforwards resulting in deferred tax assets as of December 31, 2015 and 2014 of $175.4 million and $157.1 million, respectively. The Company has valuation allowances related to these net operating losses as of December 31, 2015 and 2014 of $132.1 million and $112.9 million, respectively. As of December 31, 2015 and 2014, the Company had foreign tax credit carryforwards of $13.6 million and $12.7 million, respectively, which expire between 2020 and 2025.

The Company participates in the IRS' Compliance Assurance Process (CAP), which is a real-time continuous audit. The IRS has completed its review for years through 2011. Currently, we believe the ultimate resolution of the IRS examinations will not result in a material adverse effect to the Company's financial position or results of operations. Substantially all material foreign income tax return matters have been concluded through 2008. Substantially all state income tax returns have been concluded through 2012.

The Company provides for United States income taxes on earnings of foreign subsidiaries unless they are considered permanently reinvested outside the United States. As of December 31, 2015, U.S. income taxes have not been provided on a cumulative total of $673.5 million of such earnings. At this time, a determination of the amount of unrecognized deferred tax liability is not practicable.

As of December 31, 2015 and 2014, the Company had gross unrecognized tax benefits of $98.0 million and $18.4 million of which $75.3 million and $13.1 million would favorably impact our income tax rate in the event that the unrecognized tax benefits are recognized.

The following table reconciles the gross amounts of unrecognized tax benefits at the beginning and end of the period (in millions):

	Gross Amount
Amounts of unrecognized tax benefits as of January 1, 2014	$ 29.2
Amount of decreases due to lapse of the applicable statute of limitations	(2.4)
Amount of decreases due to settlements	(14.1)
Increases as a result of tax positions taken in the current period	2.6
Increases as a result of tax positions taken in a prior period	3.1
Amount of unrecognized tax benefit as of December 31, 2014	18.4
Amount of decreases due to lapse of the applicable statute of limitations	(5.3)
Assumed in SunGard acquisition	81.7
Increases as a result of tax positions taken in the current period	0.7
Increases as a result of tax positions taken in a prior period	2.5
Amount of unrecognized tax benefit as of December 31, 2015	$ 98.0

The total amount of interest expense recognized in the Consolidated Statements of Earnings for unpaid taxes is $1.8 million, $1.8 million and $3.1 million for the years ended December 31, 2015, 2014 and 2013, respectively. The total amount of interest and penalties included in the Consolidated Balance Sheets is $26.7 million and $7.9 million as of December 31, 2015 and 2014, respectively. Interest and penalties are recorded as a component of income tax expense in the Consolidated Statements of Earnings.

Due to the expiration of various statutes of limitation in the next twelve months, an estimated $3.9 million of gross unrecognized tax benefits may be recognized during that twelve month period.

UNRECOGNIZED TAX BENEFITS

2.144 MOLSON COORS BREWING COMPANY (DEC)
CONSOLIDATED BALANCE SHEETS (in part)

(In Millions, Except Par Value)

	As of	
	December 31, 2015	December 31, 2014
Liabilities and equity (in part)		
Current liabilities:		
Accounts payable and other current liabilities (includes affiliate payable amounts of $10.6 and $21.4, respectively)	$1,184.4	$1,305.0
Deferred tax liabilities	—	164.8
Current portion of long-term debt and short-term borrowings	28.7	849.0
Discontinued operations	4.1	6.1
Total current liabilities	1,217.2	2,324.9
Long-term debt	2,908.7	2,321.3
Pension and postretirement benefits	201.9	542.9
Deferred tax liabilities	799.8	784.3
Unrecognized tax benefits	8.4	25.4
Other liabilities	66.9	79.7
Discontinued operations	10.3	15.5
Total liabilities	5,213.2	6,094.0

1. Basis of Presentation and Summary of Significant Accounting Policies (in part)

Income Taxes

Deferred income taxes are provided for the temporary differences between the financial reporting basis and the tax basis of our assets, liabilities, and certain unrecognized gains and losses recorded in accumulated other comprehensive income (loss). Intraperiod tax allocation rules require that we allocate our provision for income taxes between continuing operations and other categories of earnings, such as discontinued operations and other comprehensive income (loss). The application of these rules indicated that no additional tax expense should be allocated outside of continuing operations for all years presented. We provide for taxes that may be payable if undistributed earnings of overseas subsidiaries were to be remitted to the U.S., except for those earnings that we consider to be permanently reinvested. Interest, penalties and offsetting positions related to unrecognized tax benefits are recognized as a component of income tax expense. Our deferred tax valuation allowances are primarily the result of uncertainties regarding the future realization of recorded tax benefits on tax loss carryforwards from operations in various jurisdictions. These valuation allowances are primarily related to deferred tax assets generated from net operating losses.

6. Income Tax

Our income (loss) from continuing operations before income taxes on which the provision for income taxes was computed is as follows:

	For the Years Ended		
(In millions)	December 31, 2015	December 31, 2014	December 31, 2013
Domestic	$ 746.1	$ 736.2	$ 809.7
Foreign	(335.4)	(149.9)	(155.2)
Total	$ 410.7	$ 586.3	$ 654.5

Income tax expense (benefit) includes the following current and deferred provisions:

	For the Years Ended		
(In millions)	December 31, 2015	December 31, 2014	December 31, 2013
Current:			
Federal	$ 116.1	$ 78.4	$ 39.1
State	11.8	12.9	11.8
Foreign	25.2	(22.5)	50.7
Total current tax expense (benefit)	$ 153.1	$ 68.8	$101.6
Deferred:			
Federal	$ (26.1)	$ 27.6	$ 59.6
State	(5.8)	2.0	5.1
Foreign	(69.4)	(29.4)	(82.3)
Total deferred tax expense (benefit)	$(101.3)	$ 0.2	$ (17.6)
Total income tax expense (benefit) from continuing operations	$ 51.8	$ 69.0	$ 84.0

The decrease in income tax expense in 2015 was primarily due to lower pretax income versus the prior year. The decrease in pretax income was due to an increased foreign pretax loss, driven by unfavorable movements in foreign currency rates, increased special charges versus the prior year and the impact from the loss of major business contracts in 2015. The decrease in income tax expense in 2014 versus 2013 was primarily driven by lower pretax income due to an increase in special charges versus 2013, as well as the release of unrecognized tax benefits and an approximate $21 million income tax benefit related to the finalization of the bilateral advanced pricing agreement ("BAPA") between the U.S. and Canada tax authorities in 2014.

Our effective tax rate varies from the U.S. federal statutory income tax rate as follows:

	For the Years Ended		
	December 31, 2015	December 31, 2014	December 31, 2013
Statutory Federal income tax rate	35.0%	35.0%	35.0%
State income taxes, net of federal benefits	1.6%	2.5%	1.3%
Effect of foreign tax rates and tax planning	(29.2)%	(24.3)%	(27.4)%
Effect of unrecognized tax benefits	(3.5)%	(3.9)%	3.3%
Change in valuation allowance	8.2%	0.4%	(1.5)%
Other, net	0.5%	2.1%	2.1%
Effective tax rate	12.6%	11.8%	12.8%

Our effective tax rates were significantly lower than the federal statutory rate of 35% primarily due to the impact of lower effective income tax rates applicable to our foreign businesses, driven by lower local statutory income tax rates and tax planning impacts on statutory taxable income. The statutory tax rates in the countries in Europe which we operate range from 9% in Montenegro to 20% in the U.K. Canada has a statutory tax rate of approximately 26%. In addition to these lower effective foreign tax rates, during 2015 and 2014, our effective tax rate was also positively impacted by the favorable resolution of unrecognized tax benefits in various taxing jurisdictions as further discussed below. Our effective tax rates were also positively impacted by the above mentioned finalization of the BAPA between the U.S. and Canada tax authorities in 2014, and the related BAPA renewal application which was formally submitted during the first quarter of 2015. The BAPA renewal submission covers both historical and future tax years and is subject to approval by both taxing authorities.

The table below summarizes our deferred tax assets and liabilities:

	As of	
(In millions)	December 31, 2015	December 31, 2014
Current deferred tax assets:		
Compensation related obligations	$—	$ 2.8
Accrued liabilities and other	—	15.8
Valuation allowance	—	(4.9)
Balance sheet reserves and accruals	—	10.7
Other	—	7.8
Total current deferred tax assets	$—	$ 32.2
Current deferred tax liabilities:		
Partnership investments	—	169.8
Total current deferred tax liabilities	$—	$169.8
Net current deferred tax assets	—	—
Net current deferred tax liabilities	$—	$137.6

	As of	
(In millions)	December 31, 2015	December 31, 2014
Non-current deferred tax assets:		
Compensation related obligations	$ 19.3	$ 8.0
Pension and postretirement benefits	61.2	118.7
Tax credit carryforwards	1.5	1.5
Tax loss carryforwards	897.9	166.8
Intercompany financing	3.2	6.8
Partnership investments	—	27.2
Accrued liabilities and other	32.3	1.0
Other	6.8	10.4
Valuation allowance	(824.9)	(100.5)
Total non-current deferred tax assets	$ 197.3	$ 239.9
Non-current deferred tax liabilities:		
Fixed assets	69.7	107.3
Partnership investments	169.7	—
Foreign exchange gain/loss	48.7	13.7
Intangible assets	644.0	789.1
Hedging	4.0	12.5
Other	9.9	5.5
Total non-current deferred tax liabilities	$ 946.0	$ 928.1
Net non-current deferred tax assets	—	—
Net non-current deferred tax liabilities	$ 748.7	$ 688.2

As discussed in Note 2, "New Accounting Pronouncements", during the fourth quarter of 2015, we elected to early adopt the FASB's recently issued guidance requiring all deferred tax assets and deferred tax liabilities to be presented as non-current on the consolidated balance sheet. Adoption of this guidance resulted in the reclassification of our current deferred tax assets and liabilities to non-current in our consolidated balance sheet as of December 31, 2015. This guidance has been adopted on a prospective basis, and therefore, prior periods have not been retrospectively adjusted and continue to reflect current and non-current classification as historically presented.

Additionally, during 2015, we recorded tax loss carryforwards in certain European jurisdictions in the aggregate of $713.7 million, primarily driven by investment losses recognized based on local statutory accounting requirements. As the carryforwards were generated in jurisdictions where we do not have operations, we concluded that it was more likely than not that the net operating losses will not be realized, and thus recorded a full valuation allowance on the associated deferred tax assets. The recognition of these deferred tax assets and fully offsetting valuation allowance resulted in a zero net impact to the consolidated statement of operations, balance sheet and statement of cash flows.

The measurement of deferred tax assets is reduced by a valuation allowance if, based upon available evidence, it is more likely than not that the deferred tax assets will not be realized. We have evaluated the realizability of our deferred tax assets in each jurisdiction by assessing the adequacy of expected taxable income, including the reversal of existing temporary differences, historical and projected operating results and the availability of prudent and feasible tax planning strategies. Based on this analysis, we have determined that the valuation allowances recorded in each period presented are appropriate.

We have deferred tax assets for U.S. tax carryforwards that expire between 2016 and 2032 of $4.5 million and $8.6 million at December 31, 2015, and December 31, 2014, respectively. We have foreign tax loss carryforwards that expire between 2016 and 2035 of $160.5 million and $142.1 million as of December 31, 2015, and December 31, 2014, respectively. We have foreign tax loss carryforwards that do not expire of $734.4 million and $17.6 million as of December 31, 2015, and December 31, 2014, respectively. The significant increase in foreign tax loss carryforwards that do not expire is primarily driven by the tax loss carryforwards related to certain European jurisdictions specifically mentioned above.

The following table presents our deferred tax assets and liabilities on a net basis:

| (In millions) | As of | |
	December 31, 2015	December 31, 2014
Domestic net current deferred tax liabilities	$ —	$164.6
Foreign net current deferred tax liabilities	—	0.2
Foreign net current deferred tax assets	—	27.2
Net current deferred tax liabilities	$ —	$137.6
Domestic net non-current deferred tax assets	$ —	$ 23.1
Domestic net non-current deferred tax liabilities	195.0	—
Foreign net non-current deferred tax assets	20.2	35.1
Foreign net non-current deferred tax liabilities	573.9	746.4
Net non-current deferred tax liabilities	$748.7	$688.2

The 2015 and 2014 amounts above exclude $30.9 million and $37.9 million, respectively, of unrecognized tax benefits that have been recorded as a reduction of non-current deferred tax assets, which is presented within non-current deferred tax liabilities due to jurisdictional netting on the consolidated balance sheets, as a result of the FASB's recently issued guidance related to the presentation of these items which was adopted in 2014.

A reconciliation of the beginning and ending amount of unrecognized tax benefits, excluding interest and penalties, is as follows:

| (In millions) | For the Years Ended | | |
	December 31, 2015	December 31, 2014	December 31, 2013
Balance at beginning of year	$ 59.8	$137.9	$109.2
Additions for tax positions related to the current year	1.8	2.2	3.7
Additions for tax positions of prior years	2.2	20.4	59.2
Reductions for tax positions of prior years	(5.5)	(19.4)	(3.2)
Settlements	(0.9)	(55.4)	(2.6)
Release due to statute expiration and legislative changes	(9.6)	(18.4)	(24.9)
Foreign currency adjustment	(8.3)	(7.5)	(3.5)
Balance at end of year	$39.5	$59.8	$137.9

During 2015, we had a net reduction in unrecognized tax benefits of $20.3 million. This reduction was primarily driven by the release of the remaining $8.1 million unrecognized tax benefit that was established during the second quarter of 2014 as further discussed below, as well as the release of other unrecognized tax benefits in domestic and foreign jurisdictions, and foreign exchange rate movements.

During the second quarter of 2014, we identified that we had incorrectly omitted recognizing a liability for uncertain tax positions related to fiscal year 2010 that resulted in an immaterial misstatement of income tax expense within the consolidated statement of operations for the year ended December 25, 2010, as well as the liability for unrecognized tax benefits and retained earnings within the consolidated balance sheets at December 31, 2013, December 29, 2012, December 31, 2011, and December 25, 2010. Accordingly, during 2014, we revised our presentation of these amounts to correct for this error, which resulted in an increase in current unrecognized tax benefits of $19.3 million and non-current unrecognized tax benefits of $14.4 million as of December 31, 2013. During the third quarter of 2014, we filed an amendment to certain historical U.S. tax returns and concurrently fully settled the current $19.3 million unrecognized tax benefit resulting from this adjustment. This settlement amount is included in the table above but did not impact our 2014 effective tax rate as it was settled for the amount of the liability. Additionally, upon expiration of certain statutes of limitations during the third quarter of 2014, we released a portion of the non-current unrecognized tax benefit adjustment, which resulted in a $6.3 million benefit to our 2014 income tax expense. As discussed above, the remainder of this unrecognized tax benefit adjustment was released in the third quarter of 2015 upon expiration of the statute of limitations, resulting in an $8.1 million benefit to 2015 income tax expense.

In addition to the $25.6 million decrease in 2014 unrecognized tax benefits discussed above, the overall decrease in unrecognized tax positions during 2014 was further driven by the $34.9 million settlement of a tax audit and the impact of the resolution of the BAPA in Canada that were offset by the intended utilization of deferred tax assets and therefore did not impact our effective tax rate, the favorable resolution of tax audits resolved in Europe resulting in the release of $16.2 million of unrecognized tax positions and the release of unrecognized tax benefits due to expiration of the statute of limitations in Europe and Canada.

Our remaining unrecognized tax benefits as of December 31, 2015, relate to tax years that are currently open, and amounts may differ from those to be determined upon closing of the positions. Annual tax provisions include amounts considered sufficient to pay assessments that may result from examination of prior year tax returns; however, the amount ultimately paid upon resolution of issues may differ materially from the amount accrued.

During 2016, we anticipate that approximately $1 million to $4 million of unrecognized tax benefits will be released due to settlements as well as the closing of statutes of limitation in the U.S., Canada and Europe.

| (In millions) | For the Years Ended | | |
Reconciliation of Unrecognized Tax Benefits Balance	December 31, 2015	December 31, 2014	December 31, 2013
Estimated interest and penalties	$ 5.3	$ 7.2	$ 15.5
Offsetting positions	(3.7)	(3.7)	(3.8)
Unrecognized tax positions	39.5	59.8	137.9
Total unrecognized tax benefits	$41.1	$63.3	$149.6
Presented net against non-current deferred tax assets	$30.9	$37.9	$ —
Current (included in accounts payable and other current liabilities)	1.8	—	42.5
Non-current	8.4	25.4	107.1
Total unrecognized tax benefits	$41.1	$63.3	$149.6
Amount of unrecognized tax benefits that would impact the effective tax rate[1]	$39.5	$59.8	$137.9

[1] Amounts exclude the potential effects of valuation allowances, which may fully or partially offset the impact to the effective tax rate.

We file income tax returns in most of the federal, state and provincial jurisdictions in the U.S., Canada and various countries in Europe. Tax years through 2011 are closed in the U.S. In Canada, tax years through the year ended 2010 are closed or have been effectively settled through examination except for issues relating to intercompany cross-border transactions. The statute of limitations for intercompany cross-border transactions is closed through tax year 2007. Tax years through 2007 are closed for most countries in European jurisdictions with statutes of limitations varying from 3–7 years.

We annually receive cash from our foreign subsidiaries' current year earnings. Separately, we treat all accumulated foreign subsidiary earnings through December 31, 2015, as indefinitely reinvested under the accounting guidance and accordingly, have not provided for any U.S. or foreign tax thereon. In order to arrive at this conclusion, we considered factors including, but not limited to, past experience, domestic cash requirements and distributions from MillerCoors, as well as cash requirements to satisfy the ongoing operations, capital expenditures and other financial obligations of our foreign subsidiaries. As of December 31, 2015, approximately $20 million of undistributed earnings and profits attributable to foreign subsidiaries was considered to be indefinitely invested. Our intention is to permanently reinvest the earnings outside of the U.S. It is not practicable to determine the amount of incremental taxes that might arise were these earnings to be remitted. The amount of tax payable could be impacted by the jurisdiction in which a distribution was made, the amount of the distribution, foreign withholding taxes under applicable tax laws when distributed, relevant tax treaties and foreign tax credits. While it is not practical to determine the amount of tax, we believe that U.S. foreign tax credits and tax planning strategies would allow us to make remittances in a tax efficient manner.

2.145 REPUBLIC SERVICES, INC. (DEC)
CONSOLIDATED BALANCE SHEETS (in part)

(in millions, except per share data)

	December 31, 2015	December 31, 2014
Liabilities and Stockholders' Equity (in part)		
Current liabilities:		
Accounts payable	$ 577.4	$ 527.3
Notes payable and current maturities of long-term debt	5.5	10.4
Deferred revenue	313.9	306.3
Accrued landfill and environmental costs, current portion	149.8	164.3
Accrued interest	71.6	67.0
Other accrued liabilities	716.6	750.7
Total current liabilities	1,834.8	1,826.0
Long-term debt, net of current maturities	7,568.7	7,050.8
Accrued landfill and environmental costs, net of current portion	1,677.9	1,677.5
Deferred income taxes and other long-term tax liabilities	1,131.8	1,149.0
Insurance reserves, net of current portion	278.1	298.0
Other long-term liabilities	309.3	344.9

NOTES TO CONSOLIDATED FINANCIAL STATEMENTS (in part)

2. Summary of Significant Accounting Policies (in part)

Insurance Reserves

Our insurance programs for workers' compensation, commercial general and auto liability, environmental and remediation liability, and employee-related health care benefits are subject to high deductible insurance policies. Accruals for insurance reserves are based on claims filed and estimates of claims incurred but not reported. We consider our past claims experience, including both frequency and settlement amount of claims, in determining these estimates. It is possible that recorded reserves may not be adequate to cover the future payment of claims. Adjustments, if any, to estimates recorded resulting from ultimate claim payments will be reflected in the consolidated statements of income in the periods in which such adjustments are known.

In general, our insurance reserves are recorded on an undiscounted basis; however, the insurance liabilities we acquired in the Allied acquisition have been recorded at estimated fair value, and therefore have been discounted to present value based on our estimate of the timing of the related cash flows.

7. Other Liabilities

Other Accrued Liabilities

A summary of other accrued liabilities as of December 31 follows:

	2015	2014
Accrued payroll and benefits	$187.8	$180.2
Accrued fees and taxes	126.5	125.6
Insurance reserves, current portion	127.7	118.6
Ceded insurance reserves, current portion	12.5	12.4
Accrued dividends	103.7	98.7
Current tax liabilities	0.5	16.3
Fuel hedge liabilities	41.0	35.3
Accrued professional fees and legal settlement reserves	44.2	61.2
Withdrawal liability—Central States Pension and Other Funds	—	15.9
Other	72.7	86.5
Total	$716.6	$750.7

Other Long-Term Liabilities

A summary of other long-term liabilities as of December 31 follows:

	2015	2014
Deferred compensation plan	$ 83.3	$ 76.3
Pension and other post-retirement liabilities	12.1	11.0
Legal settlement reserves	24.7	10.8
Ceded insurance reserves	44.0	48.4
Withdrawal liability—Central States Pension and Other Funds	6.1	139.6
Contingent consideration and acquisition holdbacks	78.0	—
Other	61.1	58.8
Total	$309.3	$344.9

Insurance Reserves

Our liabilities for unpaid and incurred but not reported claims as of December 31, 2015 and 2014 (which include claims for workers' compensation, commercial general and auto liability, and employee-related health care benefits) were $405.8 million and $416.6 million, respectively, under our risk management program and are included in other accrued liabilities and insurance reserves, net of current portion, in our consolidated balance sheets. While the ultimate amount of claims incurred depends on future developments, we believe the recorded reserves are adequate to cover the future payment of claims; however, it is possible that these recorded reserves may not be adequate to cover the future payment of claims. Adjustments, if any, to estimates recorded resulting from ultimate claim payments will be reflected in our consolidated statements of income in the periods in which such adjustments are known. The following table summarizes the activity in our insurance reserves for the years ended December 31:

	2015	2014	2013
Balance at beginning of year	$416.6	$431.5	$426.4
Additions charged to expense	360.4	354.8	379.1
Payments	(373.1)	(372.2)	(377.2)
Accretion expense	1.9	2.5	3.2
Balance at end of year	405.8	416.6	431.5
Less: current portion	(127.7)	(118.6)	(136.6)
Long-term portion	$278.1	$298.0	$294.9

DISCONTINUED OPERATIONS

2.146 CENVEO, INC. (DEC)
CONSOLIDATED BALANCE SHEETS (in part)

(in thousands, except par values)

	2015	2014
Liabilities and Shareholders' Deficit (in part)		
Current liabilities:		
Current maturities of long-term debt	$ 5,373	$ 3,872
Accounts payable	200,120	213,040
Accrued compensation and related liabilities	31,961	35,055
Other current liabilities	86,703	84,777
Liabilities of discontinued operations—current	22,268	24,203
Total current liabilities	346,425	360,947
Long-term debt	1,203,250	1,206,508
Other liabilities	198,926	197,421
Liabilities of discontinued operations—long-term	1,153	3,520

NOTES TO CONSOLIDATED FINANCIAL STATEMENTS (in part)

1. Summary of Significant Accounting Policies (in part)

Basis of Presentation (in part):

As a result of exploring opportunities to divest certain non-strategic or underperforming businesses within its manufacturing platform, during the first quarter of 2016 the Company completed the sale of its folded carton and shrink sleeve packaging businesses, along with its one top-sheet lithographic print operation (collectively, the "Packaging Business"). See Note 3 for information regarding the completion of sale of the Packaging Business. In accordance with the guidance in Accounting Standards Codification ("ASC") 205-20 *Presentation of Financial Statements—Discontinued Operations* and ASC 360 *Property, Plant & Equipment*, the financial results of the Packaging Business have been accounted for as discontinued operations for all periods presented.

The Company completed the sale of its Custom Envelope Group ("Custom Envelope") during the third quarter of 2013. Additionally, during the second quarter of 2013, the Company decided to exit the San Francisco market and closed a manufacturing facility. Collectively with the Packaging Business, the Company refers to these businesses as the "Discontinued Operations." As a result, the Company's historical consolidated balance sheets, statements of comprehensive income (loss) ("statement of operations") and statements of cash flows have been retroactively adjusted to give recognition to the Discontinued Operations for all periods presented.

New Accounting Pronouncements (in part): In April 2014, the Financial Accounting Standards Board ("FASB") issued ASU 2014-08, " *Presentation of Financial Statements (Topic 205) and Property, Plant, and Equipment (Topic 360): Reporting Discontinued Operations and Disclosures of Disposals of Components of an Entity*." The amendments in the ASU change the criteria for reporting discontinued operations while enhancing related disclosures. The amendments in the ASU were effective in the first quarter of 2015. The Company adopted this new guidance effective December 28, 2014. The new guidance was only applied prospectively to new disposals and new classifications of disposal groups held for sale after such date. As a result, this guidance did not have any impact on the Company's previously reported financial statements or related disclosures upon adoption.

3. Discontinued Operations (in part)

During the second and third quarters of 2015, the Company began actively marketing for sale its Packaging Business to multiple strategic parties. As of the end of the third quarter, management was given the appropriate authority to move forward with these strategic parties on a potential sale of the Packaging Business. In accordance with the guidance in ASC 205-20 *Presentation of Financial Statements—Discontinued Operations* and ASC 360 *Property, Plant & Equipment*, at that time, the financial results of the Packaging Business were accounted for as discontinued operations.

On January 19, 2016, the Company completed the sale of the Packaging Business. The Company received total cash proceeds of approximately $86.6 million, net of transaction costs of approximately $6.4 million. In the fourth quarter of 2015, the Company recorded a non-cash loss on sale of $5.0 million. The Company recorded a non-cash goodwill impairment charge of $9.9 million related to this transaction. This loss was based on the executed purchase agreement and the net assets of the Packaging Business. In addition to the proceeds, $5.0 million of purchase price consideration has been held in escrow ("the Holdback Amount") and will be paid to the Company subject to the satisfaction of certain conditions, which is expected to be completed within 90 days of the closing date. Any amount received from the Holdback Amount will be recognized as income when received.

During the fourth quarter of 2013, the Company made the decision to retire a certain indefinite lived trade name during 2014 as a result of rebranding the Company's packaging business line. Accordingly, based on its evaluation using a relief-from-royalty and other discounted cash flow methodologies, the Company concluded that the trade name asset was impaired. An impairment charge of $8.9 million was recorded to reduce the carrying value to the estimated fair value. The trade name was fully amortized during 2014. The non-cash impairment charge was reported in discontinued operations in the Company's consolidated financial statements.

On September 28, 2013, the Company completed the sale of Custom Envelope. The Company received total net cash proceeds of approximately $47.0 million, of which $2.2 million was received in 2014. This resulted in the recognition of a total after-tax gain of $16.5 million, of which $14.9 million was recognized in the year ended 2013. The operating results of Custom Envelope are reported in discontinued operations in the Company's financial statements for all periods presented herein.

During the second quarter of 2013, the Company decided to exit the San Francisco market and closed a manufacturing facility within its print segment. The operating results of this manufacturing facility are reported in discontinued operations in the Company's consolidated financial statements for all periods presented herein.

The following table shows the components of assets and liabilities that are classified as discontinued operations in the Company's consolidated balance sheets as of January 2, 2016, and December 27, 2014 (in thousands):

	2015	2014
Accounts receivable, net	$23,244	$ 29,344
Inventories	18,603	18,119
Other current assets	6,719	5,106
Assets of discontinued operations—current	48,566	52,569
Property, plant and equipment, net	48,244	54,585
Goodwill and other long-term assets	14,607	32,028
Assets of discontinued operations—long-term	62,851	86,613
Accounts payable	17,917	19,145
Other current liabilities	4,351	5,058
Liabilities of discontinued operations—current	22,268	24,203
Long-term debt and other liabilities	1,153	3,520
Liabilities of discontinued operations—long-term	1,153	3,520
Net assets of discontinued operations	$87,996	$111,459

WARRANTY

2.147 CUMMINS INC. (DEC)
CONSOLIDATED BALANCE SHEETS (in part)

	December 31,	
In millions, except par value	2015	2014
Liabilities (in part)		
Current liabilities		
Accounts payable (principally trade)	$1,706	$1,881
Loans payable (Note 11)	24	86
Accrued compensation, benefits and retirement costs	409	508
Current portion of accrued product warranty (Note 12)	359	363
Current portion of deferred revenue	403	401
Other accrued expenses	863	759
Current maturities of long-term debt (Note 11)	39	23
Total current liabilities	3,803	4,021
Long-term liabilities		
Long-term debt (Note 11)	1,576	1,577
Postretirement benefits other than pensions (Note 10)	349	369
Pensions (Note 10)	298	289
Other liabilities and deferred revenue (Note 13)	1,358	1,415
Total liabilities	$7,384	$7,671

NOTES TO CONSOLIDATED FINANCIAL STATEMENTS (in part)

Note 1. Summary of Significant Accounting Policies (in part)

Warranty

We charge the estimated costs of warranty programs, other than product recalls, to cost of sales at the time products are sold and revenue is recognized. We use historical experience to develop the estimated liability for our various warranty programs. As a result of the uncertainty surrounding the nature and frequency of product recall programs, the liability for such programs is recorded when we commit to a recall action or when a recall becomes probable and estimable, which generally occurs when it is announced. The liability for these programs is reflected in the provision for warranties issued. We review and assess the liability for these programs on a quarterly basis. We also assess our ability to recover certain costs from our suppliers and record a receivable when we believe a recovery is probable. In addition to costs incurred on warranty and recall programs, from time to time we also incur costs related to customer satisfaction programs for items not covered by warranty. We accrue for these costs when agreement is reached with a specific customer. These costs are not included in the provision for warranties but are included in cost of sales.

In addition, we sell extended warranty coverage on most of our engines. The revenue collected is initially deferred and is recognized as revenue in proportion to the costs expected to be incurred in performing services over the contract period. We compare the remaining deferred revenue balance quarterly to the estimated amount of future claims under extended warranty programs and provide an additional accrual when the deferred revenue balance is less than expected future costs. See NOTE 12, "PRODUCT WARRANTY LIABILITY," for additional information.

Note 12. Product Warranty Liability

A tabular reconciliation of the product warranty liability, including the deferred revenue related to our extended warranty coverage and accrued recall programs was as follows:

	December 31,	
In millions	2015	2014
Balance, beginning of year	$1,283	$1,129
Provision for warranties issued	391	411
Deferred revenue on extended warranty contracts sold	290	263
Payments	(389)	(404)
Amortization of deferred revenue on extended warranty contracts	(179)	(148)
Changes in estimates for pre-existing warranties	20	41
Foreign currency translation	(12)	(9)
Balance, end of year	$1,404	$1,283

Warranty related deferred revenue, supplier recovery receivables and the long-term portion of the warranty liability on our *Consolidated Balance Sheets* were as follows:

	December 31,		
In millions	2015	2014	Balance Sheet Location
Deferred revenue related to extended coverage programs			
Current portion	$189	$170	Deferred revenue
Long-term portion	529	438	Other liabilities and deferred revenue
Total	$718	$608	
Receivables related to estimated supplier recoveries			
Current portion	$ 6	$ 12	Trade and other receivables
Long-term portion	4	4	Other assets
Total	$ 10	$ 16	
Long-term portion of warranty liability	$327	$312	Other liabilities and deferred revenue

Note 13. Other Liabilities and Deferred Revenue

Other liabilities and deferred revenue included the following:

	December 31,	
In millions	2015	2014
Deferred revenue	$ 583	$ 513
Accrued warranty	327	312
Accrued compensation	199	215
Other long-term liabilities	249	375
Other liabilities and deferred revenue	$1,358	$1,415

ENVIRONMENTAL

2.148 ALCOA INC. (DEC)
CONSOLIDATED BALANCE SHEET (in part)

(in millions)

December 31,	2015	2014
Liabilities		
Current liabilities:		
Short-term borrowings (K & X)	$ 38	$ 54
Accounts payable, trade	2,889	3,152
Accrued compensation and retirement costs	850	937
Taxes, including income taxes	239	265
Other current liabilities	1,174	1,021
Long-term debt due within one year (K & X)	21	29
Total current liabilities	5,211	5,458
Long-term debt, less amount due within one year (K & X)	9,044	8,769
Accrued pension benefits (W)	3,298	3,291
Accrued other postretirement benefits (W)	2,106	2,155
Other noncurrent liabilities and deferred credits (L)	2,738	2,896
Total liabilities	22,397	22,569

(dollars in millions, except per-share amounts)

A. Summary of Significant Accounting Policies (in part)

Environmental Matters. Expenditures for current operations are expensed or capitalized, as appropriate. Expenditures relating to existing conditions caused by past operations, which will not contribute to future revenues, are expensed. Liabilities are recorded when remediation costs are probable and can be reasonably estimated. The liability may include costs such as site investigations, consultant fees, feasibility studies, outside contractors, and monitoring expenses. Estimates are generally not discounted or reduced by potential claims for recovery. Claims for recovery are recognized as agreements are reached with third parties. The estimates also include costs related to other potentially responsible parties to the extent that Alcoa has reason to believe such parties will not fully pay their proportionate share. The liability is continuously reviewed and adjusted to reflect current remediation progress, prospective estimates of required activity, and other factors that may be relevant, including changes in technology or regulations.

L. Other Noncurrent Liabilities and Deferred Credits

December 31,	2015	2014
Environmental remediation (N)	$ 554	$ 473
Asset retirement obligations (C)	551	587
Income taxes (T)	521	377
Accrued compensation and retirement costs	329	346
Fair value of derivative contracts (X)	208	376
Liability related to the resolution of a legal matter (N)	148	222
Contingent payment related to an acquisition (F)	130	130
Deferred alumina sales revenue	84	93
Deferred credit related to derivative contract (X)	—	62
Other	213	230
	$2,738	$2,896

N. Contingencies and Commitments (in part)

Contingencies (in part)

Environmental Matters. Alcoa participates in environmental assessments and cleanups at more than 100 locations. These include owned or operating facilities and adjoining properties, previously owned or operating facilities and adjoining properties, and waste sites, including Superfund (Comprehensive Environmental Response, Compensation and Liability Act (CERCLA)) sites.

A liability is recorded for environmental remediation when a cleanup program becomes probable and the costs can be reasonably estimated. As assessments and cleanups proceed, the liability is adjusted based on progress made in determining the extent of remedial actions and related costs. The liability can change substantially due to factors such as the nature and extent of contamination, changes in remedial requirements, and technological changes, among others.

Alcoa's remediation reserve balance was $604 and $543 at December 31, 2015 and 2014 (of which $50 and $70 was classified as a current liability), respectively, and reflects the most probable costs to remediate identified environmental conditions for which costs can be reasonably estimated.

In 2015, the remediation reserve was increased by $115 due to a charge of $52 related to the planned demolition of the remaining structures at the Massena East smelter location (see Note D), a charge of $29 related to the planned demolition of the Poços de Caldas smelter and the Anglesea power station (see Note D), a charge of $12 related to the Mosjøen location (see below), a charge of $7 related to the Portovesme location (see below), and a net charge of $15 associated with a number of other sites. In 2014, the remediation reserve was increased by $61 due to a charge of $42 related to the planned demolition of certain structures at the Massena East, NY, Point Henry and Yennora, Australia, and Portovesme, Italy locations (see Note D), a charge of $3 related to the Portovesme location (see below), and a net charge of $16 associated with a number of other sites. Of the changes to the remediation reserve in 2015 and 2014, $86 and $47, respectively, was recorded in Restructuring and other charges, while the remainder was recorded in Cost of goods sold on the accompanying Statement of Consolidated Operations.

Payments related to remediation expenses applied against the reserve were $43 and $46 in 2015 and 2014, respectively. These amounts include expenditures currently mandated, as well as those not required by any regulatory authority or third party. In 2015, the change in the reserve also reflects a decrease of $16 due to the effects of foreign currency translation and an increase of $5 related to the acquisition of Firth Rixson (see Note F). In 2014, the change in the reserve also reflects an increase of $19 due to the effects of foreign currency translation and a reclassification of amounts included in other reserves within Other noncurrent liabilities and deferred credits on Alcoa's Consolidated Balance Sheet as of December 31, 2013.

Included in annual operating expenses are the recurring costs of managing hazardous substances and environmental programs. These costs are estimated to be approximately 2% of cost of goods sold.

The following discussion provides details regarding the current status of certain significant reserves related to current or former Alcoa sites.

Massena West, NY— Alcoa has an ongoing remediation project related to the Grasse River, which is adjacent to Alcoa's Massena plant site. Many years ago, it was determined that sediments and fish in the river contain varying levels of polychlorinated biphenyls (PCBs). The project, which was selected by the U.S. Environmental Protection Agency (EPA) in a Record of Decision (ROD) issued in April 2013, is aimed at capping PCB contaminated sediments with concentration in excess of one part per million in the main channel of the river and dredging PCB contaminated sediments in the near-shore areas where total PCBs exceed one part per million. At December 31, 2015 and 2014, the reserve balance associated with this matter was $234 and $239, respectively. Alcoa is in the planning and design phase, which is expected to be completed in 2017. Subsequently in 2017, the actual remediation fieldwork is expected to commence and take approximately four years. The majority of the project funding is expected to be spent between 2017 and 2021.

Sherwin, TX— In connection with the sale of the Sherwin alumina refinery, which was required to be divested as part of the Reynolds merger in 2000, Alcoa agreed to retain responsibility for the remediation of the then existing environmental conditions, as well as a pro rata share of the final closure of the active bauxite residue waste disposal areas (known as the Copano facility). Alcoa's share of the closure costs is proportional to the total period of operation of the active waste disposal areas. At December 31, 2015 and 2014, the reserve balance associated with Sherwin was $30 and $32, respectively. Approximately half of the project funding is expected to be spent through 2019. The remainder is not expected to be spent in the foreseeable future as it is dependent upon the operating life of the active waste disposal areas.

East St. Louis, IL— Alcoa has an ongoing remediation project related to an area used for the disposal of bauxite residue from former alumina refining operations. The project, which was selected by the EPA in a ROD issued in July 2012, is aimed at implementing a soil cover over the affected area. On November 1, 2013, the U.S. Department of Justice lodged a consent decree on behalf of the EPA for Alcoa to conduct the work outlined in the ROD. This consent decree was entered as final in February 2014 by the U.S. Department of Justice. As a result, Alcoa began construction in March 2014; this project is expected to be completed by the end of March 2016 (Alcoa has a second project in East St. Louis that is separate from the matter presented herein on which Alcoa is expecting an EPA decision in 2016 — any resulting liability is not expected to be material). At December 31, 2015 and 2014, the reserve balance associated with this matter was $8 and $15, respectively.

Fusina and Portovesme, Italy— In 1996, Alcoa acquired the Fusina smelter and rolling operations and the Portovesme smelter, both of which are owned by Alcoa's subsidiary Alcoa Trasformazioni S.r.l. ("Trasformazioni"), from Alumix, an entity owned by the Italian Government. At the time of the acquisition, Alumix indemnified Alcoa for pre-existing environmental contamination at the sites. In 2004, the Italian Ministry of Environment and Protection of Land and Sea (MOE) issued orders to Trasformazioni and Alumix for the development of a clean-up plan related to soil contamination in excess of allowable limits under legislative decree and to institute emergency actions and pay natural resource damages. Trasformazioni appealed the orders and filed suit against Alumix, among others, seeking indemnification for these liabilities under the provisions of the acquisition agreement. In 2009, Ligestra S.r.l. ("Ligestra"), Alumix's successor, and Trasformazioni agreed to a stay of the court proceedings while investigations were conducted and negotiations advanced towards a possible settlement.

In December 2009, Trasformazioni and Ligestra reached an initial agreement for settlement of the liabilities related to Fusina while negotiations continued related to Portovesme (see below). The agreement outlined an allocation of payments to the MOE for emergency action and natural resource damages and the scope and costs for a proposed soil remediation project, which was formally presented to the MOE in mid-2010. The agreement was contingent upon final acceptance of the remediation project by the MOE. As a result of entering into this agreement, Alcoa increased the reserve by $12 in 2009 for Fusina. Based on comments received from the MOE and local and regional environmental authorities, Trasformazioni submitted a revised remediation plan in the first half of 2012; however, such revisions did not require any change to the existing reserve. In October 2013, the MOE approved the project submitted by Alcoa, resulting in no adjustment to the reserve.

In January 2014, in anticipation of Alcoa reaching a final administrative agreement with the MOE, Alcoa and Ligestra entered into a final agreement related to Fusina for allocation of payments to the MOE for emergency action and natural resource damages and the costs for the approved soil remediation project. The agreement resulted in Ligestra assuming 50% to 80% of all payments and remediation costs. On February 27, 2014, Alcoa and the MOE reached a final administrative agreement for conduct of work. The agreement includes both a soil and groundwater remediation project estimated to cost $33 (€24) and requires payments of $25 (€18) to the MOE for emergency action and natural resource damages. The remediation projects are slated to begin as soon as Alcoa receives final approval from the Ministry of Infrastructure. Based on the final agreement with Ligestra, Alcoa's share of all costs and payments is $17 (€12), of which $9 (€6) related to the damages will be paid annually over a 10-year period, which began in April 2014, and was previously fully reserved.

Separately, in 2009, due to additional information derived from the site investigations conducted at Portovesme, Alcoa increased the reserve by $3. In November 2011, Trasformazioni and Ligestra reached an agreement for settlement of the liabilities related to Portovesme, similar to the one for Fusina. A proposed soil remediation project for Portovesme was formally presented to the MOE in June 2012. Neither the agreement with Ligestra nor the proposal to the MOE resulted in a change to the reserve for Portovesme. In November 2013, the MOE rejected the proposed soil remediation project and requested a revised project be submitted. In May 2014, Trasformazioni and Ligestra submitted a revised soil remediation project that addressed certain stakeholders' concerns. Alcoa increased the reserve by $3 in 2014 to reflect the estimated higher costs associated with the revised soil remediation project, as well as current operating and maintenance costs of the Portovesme site.

In October 2014, the MOE required a further revised project be submitted to reflect the removal of a larger volume of contaminated soil than what had been proposed, as well as design changes for the cap related to the remaining contaminated soil left in place and the expansion of an emergency containment groundwater pump and treatment system that was previously installed. Trasformazioni and Ligestra submitted the further revised soil remediation project in February 2015. As a result, Alcoa increased the reserve by $7 in March 2015 to reflect the increase in the estimated costs of the project. In October 2015, Alcoa received a final ministerial decree approving the February 2015 revised soil remediation project. Work on the soil remediation project will commence in 2016 and is expected to be completed in 2019. Alcoa and Ligestra are now working on a final groundwater remediation project, which will be submitted to the MOE for review during 2016. The ultimate outcome of this matter may result in a change to the existing reserve for Portovesme.

Baie Comeau, Quebec, Canada— In August 2012, Alcoa presented an analysis of remediation alternatives to the Quebec Ministry of Sustainable Development, Environment, Wildlife and Parks (MDDEP), in response to a previous request, related to known PCBs and polycyclic aromatic hydrocarbons (PAHs) contained in sediments of the Anse du Moulin bay. As such, Alcoa increased the reserve for Baie Comeau by $25 in 2012 to reflect the estimated cost of Alcoa's recommended alternative, consisting of both dredging and capping of the contaminated sediments. In July 2013, Alcoa submitted the Environmental Impact Assessment for the project to the MDDEP. The MDDEP notified Alcoa that the project as it was submitted was approved and a final mistrial decree was issued in July 2015. As a result, no further adjustment to the reserve was required in 2015. The decree provides final approval for the project and allows Alcoa to start work on the final project design, which is expected to be completed in 2016 with construction on the project expected to begin in 2017. Completion of the final project design and bidding of the project may result in additional liability in a future period.

Mosjøen, Norway— In September 2012, Alcoa presented an analysis of remediation alternatives to the Norwegian Environmental Agency (NEA) (formerly the Norwegian Climate and Pollution Agency, or "Klif"), in response to a previous request, related to known PAHs in the sediments located in the harbor and extending out into the fjord. As such, Alcoa increased the reserve for Mosjøen by $20 in 2012 to reflect the estimated cost of the baseline alternative for dredging of the contaminated sediments. A proposed project reflecting this alternative was formally presented to the NEA in June 2014, and was resubmitted in late 2014 to reflect changes by the NEA. The revised proposal did not result in a change to the reserve for Mosjøen.

In April 2015, the NEA notified Alcoa that the revised project was approved and required submission of the final project design before issuing a final order. Alcoa completed and submitted the final project design, which identified a need to stabilize the related wharf structure to allow for the sediment dredging in the harbor. As a result, Alcoa increased the reserve for Mosjøen by $11 in June 2015 to reflect the estimated cost of the wharf stabilization. Also in June 2015, the NEA issued a final order approving the project as well as the final project design. In September 2015, Alcoa increased the reserve by $1 to reflect the potential need (based on prior experience with similar projects) to perform additional dredging if the results of sampling, which is required by the order, don't achieve the required cleanup levels. Project construction will commence in 2016 and is expected to be completed by the end of 2017.

ASSET RETIREMENT OBLIGATIONS

2.149 NACCO INDUSTRIES, INC. (DEC)

CONSOLIDATED BALANCE SHEETS (in part)

(In thousands, except share data)	December 31 2015	December 31 2014
Liabilities And Equity (in part)		
Current liabilities		
Accounts payable	$100,300	$133,668
Revolving credit agreements of subsidiaries—not guaranteed by the parent company	8,365	55,000
Current maturities of long-term debt of subsidiaries—not guaranteed by the parent company	1,504	1,467
Accrued income taxes	1,935	4,015
Accrued payroll	40,854	23,567
Accrued cooperative advertising	10,676	9,899
Other current liabilities	28,112	27,065
Total current liabilities	191,746	254,681
Long-term debt of subsidiaries—not guaranteed by the parent company	160,113	191,431
Asset retirement obligations	39,780	37,399
Pension and other postretirement obligations	10,046	10,616
Other long-term liabilities	52,585	64,919
Total liabilities	454,270	559,046

NOTES TO CONSOLIDATED FINANCIAL STATEMENTS (in part)

(Tabular Amounts in Thousands, Except Per Share and Percentage Data)

Note 2—Significant Accounting Policies (in part)

Property, Plant and Equipment, Net: Property, plant and equipment are initially recorded at cost. Depreciation, depletion and amortization are provided in amounts sufficient to amortize the cost of the assets, including assets recorded under capital leases, over their estimated useful lives using the straight-line method. Buildings and building improvements are depreciated using a 40 year life or, at NACoal, over the life of the mine, which is 30 years. Estimated lives for machinery and equipment range from three to 15 years. Leasehold improvements are depreciated over the shorter of the estimated useful life or the term of the lease. The units-of-production method is used to amortize certain tooling for sourced products and certain coal-related assets based on estimated recoverable tonnages. Repairs and maintenance costs are generally expensed when incurred. Asset retirement costs associated with asset retirement obligations are capitalized with the carrying amount of the related long-lived asset and depreciated over the asset's estimated useful life.

Note 3—Other Transactions (in part)

NACoal : On July 31, 2015, NACoal's management and Board of Directors approved cessation of coal production at its Centennial mines in Alabama. NACoal ceased coal production at Centennial during the fourth quarter of 2015. The decision was made as a result of worsening conditions in the Alabama and global coal markets and the adverse effect regulatory changes had on Centennial's business. As a result of this decision, revisions were made to Centennial's asset retirement obligations due to revised estimated cash flows and the timing of those cash flows, resulting in a $7.5 million charge during the third quarter of 2015. Also as a result of this decision, the Company recognized a $0.6 million charge for severance and other employee benefit costs in 2015. Both of these charges are included in Cost of sales. See Note 7 for further discussion of the Company's asset retirement obligations.

Note 7—Asset Retirement Obligations

NACoal's asset retirement obligations are principally for costs to dismantle certain mining equipment at the end of the life of the mine as well as for costs to close its surface mines and reclaim the land it has disturbed as a result of its normal mining activities. The Company determined the amounts of these obligations based on estimates adjusted for inflation, projected to the estimated closure dates, and then discounted using a credit-adjusted risk-free interest rate. The accretion of the liability is being recognized over the estimated life of each individual asset retirement obligation and is recorded in the line "Cost of sales" in the accompanying Consolidated Statements of Operations. The associated asset is recorded in "Property, Plant and Equipment, net" in the accompanying Consolidated Balance Sheets.

On July 31, 2015, NACoal's management and Board of Directors approved cessation of coal production at its Centennial mines in Alabama. NACoal ceased coal production at Centennial during the fourth quarter of 2015. The decision was made as a result of worsening conditions in the Alabama and global coal markets and the adverse effect regulatory changes had on Centennial's business. As a result of this decision, revisions were made to Centennial's asset retirement obligations due to revised estimated cash flows and the timing of those cash flows, resulting in a $7.5 million charge during the third quarter of 2015.

Bellaire Corporation ("Bellaire") is a non-operating subsidiary of the Company with legacy liabilities relating to closed mining operations, primarily former Eastern U.S. underground coal mining operations. These legacy liabilities include obligations for water treatment and other environmental remediation that arose as part of the normal course of closing these underground mining operations. The Company determined the amounts of these obligations based on estimates adjusted for inflation and then discounted the amounts using a credit-adjusted risk-free interest rate. The accretion of the liability is recognized over the estimated life of the asset retirement obligation and is recorded in the line "Closed mine obligations" in the accompanying Consolidated Statements of Operations. Since Bellaire's properties are no longer active operations, no associated asset has been capitalized.

In connection with Bellaire's normal permit renewal with the Pennsylvania Department of Environmental Protection ("DEP"), Bellaire was notified during 2004 that in order to obtain renewal of the permit Bellaire would be required to establish a mine water treatment trust (the "Mine Water Treatment Trust"). On October 1, 2010, Bellaire executed a Post-Mining Treatment Trust Consent Order and Agreement with the DEP which established the Mine Water Treatment Trust to provide a financial assurance mechanism in order to assure the long-term treatment of post-mining discharges. Bellaire funded the Mine Water Treatment Trust with $5.0 million. The fair value of the Mine Water Treatment assets are $7.2 million at December 31, 2015 and are legally restricted for purposes of settling the Bellaire asset retirement obligation. See Note 10 for further fair value disclosure.

A reconciliation of the Company's beginning and ending aggregate carrying amount of the asset retirement obligations are as follows:

	NACCO Consolidated
Balance at January 1, 2014	$32,415
Liabilities acquired during the period	7,297
Liabilities settled during the period	(1,509)
Accretion expense	1,562
Revision of estimated cash flows	2,054
Balance at December 31, 2014	$41,819
Liabilities settled during the period	(7,835)
Accretion expense	2,361
Revision of estimated cash flows	7,247
Balance at December 31, 2015	$43,592

Asset retirement obligations totaled $43.6 million at December 31, 2015, of which, $3.8 million is included on the line "Other current liabilities" and $39.8 million on the line "Asset retirement obligations" in the Consolidated Balance Sheets.

LITIGATION

2.150 ITT CORPORATION (DEC)
CONSOLIDATED BALANCE SHEETS (in part)

(in Millions, except per share amounts) December 31	2015	2014
Liabilities and Shareholders' Equity (in part)		
Current liabilities:		
Short-term loans and current maturities of long-term debt	$ 245.7	$ 1.5
Accounts payable	314.7	309.6
Accrued liabilities	392.7	464.3
Total current liabilities	953.1	775.4
Asbestos-related liabilities	954.8	1,116.6
Postretirement benefits	260.4	249.7
Other non-current liabilities	189.9	269.5
Total non-current liabilities	1,405.1	1,635.8
Total liabilities	2,358.2	2,411.2

Note 1. Description of Business, Basis of Presentation and Summary of Significant Accounting Policies (in part)

Significant Accounting Policies (in part)

Asbestos-Related Liabilities and Assets

ITT has been named as a defendant in numerous product liability lawsuits alleging personal injury due to asbestos exposure. We accrue the estimated value of pending claims and unasserted claims estimated to be filed over the next 10 years, including legal fees, on an undiscounted basis, due to the inability to reliably forecast the timing of future cash flows. Assumptions utilized in estimating the liability for both pending and unasserted claims include: disease type, average settlement costs, percentage of claims settled or dismissed, the number of claims estimated to be filed against the Company in the future and the costs to defend such claims.

The Company has also recorded an asbestos-related asset, composed of insurance receivables. The asbestos-related asset represents our best estimate of probable recoveries from third parties for pending claims, as well as unasserted claims estimated to be filed over the next 10 years. In developing this estimate, the Company considers coverage-in-place and other settlement agreements with its insurers, as well as a review of expected levels of future cost recovery, the financial viability of the insurance companies, the method by which losses will be allocated to the various insurance policies and the years covered by those policies, and interpretation of the various policy and contract terms and limits and their interrelationships. Consistent with the asbestos liability, the asbestos-related asset has not been discounted to present value due to the inability to reliably forecast the timing of future cash flows. Under coverage-in-place agreements, an insurer's policies remain in force and the insurer undertakes to provide coverage for the Company's pending and future asbestos claims on specified terms and conditions. Insurance payments under coverage-in-place agreements are made to the Company as asbestos claims are settled or adjudicated. The Company's buyout agreements provide an agreed upon amount of available coverage for future asbestos claims under the subject policies to be paid to a Qualified Settlement Fund (QSF) on a specific schedule as agreed upon by the Company and its insurer. However, assets in the QSF are only available and distributed when qualifying asbestos expenditures are submitted for reimbursement as defined in the QSF agreement. Therefore, recovery of insurance reimbursements under these types of agreements is dependent on the timing of the payment of the liability and, consistent with the asbestos liability, have not been discounted to present value.

In the third quarter each year we conduct an asbestos remeasurement with the assistance of outside consultants to review and update, as appropriate, the underlying assumptions used to estimate our asbestos liability and related assets, including a reassessment of the time horizon over which a reasonable estimate of unasserted claims can be projected. In addition, as part of our ongoing review of our net asbestos exposure, each quarter we assess the most recent data available for the key inputs and assumptions, comparing the data to the expectations on which the most recent annual liability and asset estimates were based. Provided the quarterly review does not indicate a more detailed evaluation of our asbestos exposure is required, each quarter we record a net asbestos expense to maintain a rolling 10-year time horizon.

Note 18—Commitments and Contingencies (in part)

From time to time, we are involved in legal proceedings that are incidental to the operation of our businesses. Some of these proceedings allege damages relating to environmental exposures, intellectual property matters, copyright infringement, personal injury claims, employment and employee benefit matters, government contract issues and commercial or contractual disputes, sometimes related to acquisitions or divestitures. We will continue to defend vigorously against all claims. Although the ultimate outcome of any legal matter cannot be predicted with certainty, based on present information including our assessment of the merits of the particular claim, as well as our current reserves and insurance coverage, we do not expect that such legal proceedings will have any material adverse impact on our financial statements, unless otherwise noted below.

Asbestos Matters

ITT, including its subsidiary Goulds Pumps, Inc., has been sued, along with many other companies in product liability lawsuits alleging personal injury due to asbestos exposure. These claims generally allege that certain products sold by us or our subsidiaries prior to 1985 contained a part manufactured by a third party (e.g., a gasket) which contained asbestos. To the extent these third-party parts may have contained asbestos, it was encapsulated in the gasket (or other) material and was non-friable. As of December 31, 2015, there were 37 thousand pending active claims against ITT, including Goulds Pumps, filed in various state and federal courts alleging injury as a result of exposure to asbestos. Activity related to these asserted asbestos claims during the period was as follows:

(In thousands)	2015	2014	2013
Pending claims—Beginning	62	79	96
New claims	4	4	5
Settlements	(1)	(2)	(3)
Dismissals	(28)	(19)	(19)
Pending claims—Ending	37	62	79
Pending inactive claims[a]	—	13	13
Pending active claims	37	49	66

[a] Inactive claims represent pending claims in Mississippi filed in 2004 or prior, which have been excluded from our asbestos measurement because the plaintiffs cannot demonstrate a significant compensable loss. As of December 31, 2015, all inactive claims have been dismissed.

Frequently, plaintiffs are unable to identify any ITT or Goulds Pumps product as a source of asbestos exposure. Our experience to date is that a majority of resolved claims are dismissed without any payment from the Company. Management believes that a large majority of the pending claims have little or no value. In addition, because claims are sometimes dismissed in large groups, the average cost per resolved claim, as well as the number of open claims, can fluctuate significantly from period to period. ITT expects more asbestos-related suits will be filed in the future, and ITT will aggressively defend or seek a reasonable resolution, as appropriate.

Estimating the Liability and Related Asset

The Company records an asbestos liability, including legal fees, for costs estimated to be incurred to resolve all pending claims, as well as unasserted claims estimated to be filed against the Company over the next ten years. The asbestos liability has not been discounted to present value due to an inability to reliably forecast the timing of future cash flows. The methodology used to estimate our asbestos liability for pending claims and claims estimated to be filed over the next 10 years relies on and includes the following:
- interpretation of a widely accepted forecast of the population likely to have been exposed to asbestos in the workplace;
- widely accepted epidemiological studies estimating the number of people likely to develop mesothelioma and lung cancer from exposure to asbestos;
- the Company's historical experience with the filing of non-malignant claims against it and the historical relationship between non-malignant and malignant claims filed against the Company;
- analysis of the number of likely asbestos personal injury claims to be filed against the Company based on such epidemiological and historical data and the Company's recent claims experience;
- analysis of the Company's pending cases, by disease type;
- analysis of the Company's recent experience to determine the average settlement value of claims, by disease type;
- analysis of the Company's recent experience in the ratio of settled claims to total resolved claims, by disease type;
- analysis of the Company's defense costs in relation to its indemnity costs and agreements in place with external counsel;
- adjustment for inflation in the average settlement value of claims and defense costs estimated to be paid in the future; and
- analysis of the Company's recent experience with regard to the length of time to resolve asbestos claims.

Asbestos litigation is a unique form of litigation. Frequently, the plaintiff sues a large number of defendants and does not state a specific claim amount. After filing of the complaint, the plaintiff engages defendants in settlement negotiations to establish a settlement value based on certain criteria, including the number of defendants in the case. Rarely do the plaintiffs seek to collect all damages from one defendant. Rather, they seek to spread the liability, and thus the payments, among many defendants. As a result, the Company is unable to estimate the maximum potential exposure to pending claims and claims estimated to be filed over the next 10 years.

The forecast period used to estimate our potential liability to pending and projected asbestos claims is a judgment based on a number of factors, including the number and type of claims filed, recent experience with pending claims activity and whether that experience is expected to continue into the future, the jurisdictions where claims are filed, the effect of any legislative or judicial developments, and the likelihood of any comprehensive asbestos legislation at the federal level. These factors have both positive and negative effects on the dynamics of asbestos litigation in the tort system and, accordingly, our estimate of the asbestos exposure. Developments related to asbestos tend to be long-cycle, changing over multi-year periods. Accordingly, we monitor these and other factors and periodically assess whether an alternative forecast period is appropriate.

The Company retains a consulting firm to assist management in estimating the potential liability for pending asbestos claims and for claims estimated to be filed over the next 10 years based on the methodology described above. Our methodology determines a point estimate based on our assessment of the value of each underlying assumption, rather than a range of reasonably possible outcomes. Projecting future asbestos costs is subject to numerous variables and uncertainties that are inherently difficult to predict. In addition to the uncertainties surrounding the key assumptions discussed above, additional uncertainty related to asbestos claims and estimated costs arises from the long latency period prior to the manifestation of an asbestos-related disease, changes in available medical treatments and changes in medical costs, changes in plaintiff behavior resulting from bankruptcies of other companies that are or could be co-defendants, uncertainties surrounding the litigation process from jurisdiction to jurisdiction and from case to case, and the impact of potential legislative or judicial changes. At December 31, 2015, approximately 28% of the recorded asbestos liability relates to pending claims, with the remainder relating to claims estimated to be filed over the next 10 years.

We record a corresponding undiscounted asbestos-related asset that represents our best estimate of probable recoveries from our insurers for the estimated asbestos liabilities. In developing this estimate, the Company considers coverage-in-place and other agreements with its insurers, as well as a number of additional factors. These additional factors reviewed include the financial viability of our insurance carriers and any related solvency issues, the method by which losses will be allocated to the various insurance policies and the years covered by those policies, the extent to which settlement and defense costs will be reimbursed by the insurance policies and interpretation of the various policy and contract terms and limits and their interrelationships, and various judicial determinations relevant to our insurance programs. The timing and amount of reimbursements will vary due to a time lag between when ITT pays an amount to defend or settle a claim and when a reimbursement is received from an insurer, differing policy terms and certain gaps in our insurance coverage as a result of uninsured periods, insurer insolvencies, and prior insurance settlements. Approximately 83% of our estimated receivables are due from insurers that had credit ratings of A- or better from A.M. Best as of December 31, 2015.

In addition, the Company retains an insurance consulting firm to assist management in estimating probable recoveries for pending asbestos claims and for claims estimated to be filed over the next 10 years based on the analysis of policy terms, the likelihood of recovery provided by external legal counsel, and incorporating risk mitigation judgments where policy terms or other factors are not certain. The aggregate amount of insurance available to the Company for asbestos-related claims was acquired over many years and from many different carriers. Amounts deemed not recoverable generally are due from insurers that are insolvent, or result from disagreements with the insurers over policy terms, coverage limits or coverage disputes. Such limitations in our insurance coverage are expected to result in projected payments to claimants substantially exceeding the probable insurance recovery.

The Company has negotiated with certain of its insurers to reimburse the Company for a portion of its indemnity and defense costs through "coverage-in-place" agreements or policy buyout agreements. The agreements are designed to facilitate the collection of ITT's insurance portfolio, to mitigate issues that insurers may raise regarding their responsibility to respond to claims, and to promote an orderly exhaustion of the policies. As of December 31, 2015, approximately 53% of our asbestos-related assets were related to coverage-in-place agreements and buyout agreements with insurers.

After reviewing our portfolio of insurance policies, with consideration given to applicable deductibles, retentions and policy limits, the solvency and historical payment experience of various insurance carriers, existing insurance settlements, and the advice of outside counsel with respect to the applicable insurance coverage law relating to the terms and conditions of its insurance policies, ITT believes that its recorded receivable for insurance recoveries is probable of collection.

Estimating our exposure to pending asbestos claims and those that may be filed in the future is subject to significant uncertainty and risk as there are multiple variables that can affect the timing, severity, quality, quantity and resolution of claims. Any predictions with respect to the variables impacting the estimate of the asbestos liability and related asset are subject to even greater uncertainty as the projection period lengthens. In light of the uncertainties and variables inherent in the long-term projection of the Company's asbestos exposures, although it is probable that the Company will incur additional costs for asbestos claims filed beyond the next 10 years which could be material to the financial statements, we do not believe there is a reasonable basis for estimating those costs at this time.

The asbestos liability and related receivables reflect management's best estimate of future events. However, future events affecting the key factors and other variables for either the asbestos liability or the related receivables could cause actual costs or recoveries to be materially higher or lower than currently estimated. Due to these uncertainties, as well as our inability to reasonably estimate any additional asbestos liability for claims which may be filed beyond the next 10 years, it is difficult to predict the ultimate cost of resolving all pending and unasserted asbestos claims. We believe it is possible that future events affecting the key factors and other variables within the next 10 years, as well as the cost of asbestos claims filed beyond the next 10 years, net of expected recoveries, could have a material adverse effect on our financial statements.

Settlement Agreements

During 2015, ITT entered into settlement agreements with insurers to settle responsibility for certain insured claims through a series of payments into a Qualified Settlement Fund (QSF) to be paid over the next three years, resulting in a benefit of $8.9. During 2014, ITT executed a final settlement agreement with an insurer to settle responsibility for multiple insurance claims, resulting in a one-time lump sum payment to a QSF of $2.2 in 2015. During 2013, ITT executed a final settlement agreement (the 2013 Settlement) with an insurer to settle responsibility for multiple categories of insured claims, including pending and future product liability claims. Under the terms of the 2013 Settlement, the insurer agreed to a specified series of payments into a QSF over the course of the next five years, resulting in a one-time benefit of $31.0.

Defense Cost Adjustment

During 2015, the Company changed its asbestos defense strategy to retain a single firm to defend the Company in asbestos litigation. This long-term strategy streamlines the Company's management of cases and significantly reduces defense costs. Our agreement with the defense firm is currently limited to a certain set of claims and the remaining claims are expected to be transitioned to the firm within the next four years. Based on the terms of the agreement, the Company adjusted its asbestos liability and related assets and recognized a net benefit of $100.7 in 2015 for the revised estimate of the cost to defend pending claims and claims expected to be filed over the next 10 years.

Income Statement Charges

The table below summarizes the total net asbestos charge for the years ended December 31, 2015, 2014 and 2013 .

	2015	2014	2013
Asbestos provision	$ 63.0	$ 64.9	$ 63.3
Defense cost adjustment	(100.7)	—	—
Asbestos remeasurement, net	(44.8)	(58.8)	0.5
Settlement agreements	(8.9)	(2.2)	(31.0)
Net asbestos (benefit) charge, net	(91.4)	3.9	32.8

Changes in Financial Position

The following table provides a rollforward of the estimated asbestos liability and related assets for the years ended December 31, 2015 and 2014

	2015			2014		
	Liability	Asset	Net	Liability	Asset	Net
Balance as of January 1	$1,223.2	$476.4	$746.8	$1,264.7	$517.8	$746.9
Changes in estimate	(103.6)	(21.1)	(82.5)	32.4	26.3	6.1
Settlement agreements	—	8.9	(8.9)	—	2.2	(2.2)
Net cash activity and other	(76.8)	(52.2)	(24.6)	(73.9)	(69.9)	(4.0)
Balance as of December 31	$1,042.8	$412.0	$630.8	$1,223.2	$476.4	$746.8
Current portion	88.0	74.5		106.6	102.4	
Noncurrent portion	954.8	337.5		1,116.6	374.0	

DERIVATIVES

2.151 CHESAPEAKE ENERGY CORPORATION (DEC)
CONSOLIDATED BALANCE SHEETS (in part)

	December 31,	
	2015	2014
Current Liabilities:		
Accounts payable	$ 944	$ 2,049
Current maturities of long-term debt, net	381	381
Accrued interest	101	150
Short-term derivative liabilities	40	15
Other current liabilities ($8 and $15 attributable to our VIE)	2,219	3,061
Total Current Liabilities	3,685	5,656
Long-Term Liabilities:		
Long-term debt, net	10,354	11,154
Deferred income tax liabilities	—	4,392
Long-term derivative liabilities	60	218
Asset retirement obligations, net of current portion	452	447
Other long-term liabilities	409	679
Total Long-Term Liabilities	11,275	16,890

1. Basis of Presentation and Summary of Significant Accounting Policies (in part)

Derivatives

Derivative instruments are recorded on our consolidated balance sheets as derivative assets or derivative liabilities at fair value, and changes in a derivative's fair value are recognized currently in earnings unless specific hedge accounting criteria are followed. For qualifying commodity derivative instruments designated as cash flow hedges, changes in fair value, to the extent the hedge is effective, are recognized in other comprehensive income until the hedged item is recognized in earnings. Any change in fair value resulting from ineffectiveness is recognized immediately in earnings. Locked-in gains and losses of settled cash flow hedges are recorded in accumulated other comprehensive income and are transferred to earnings in the month of production. Changes in the fair value of interest rate derivative instruments designated as fair value hedges are recorded on the consolidated balance sheets as assets or liabilities, and the debt's carrying value amount is adjusted by the change in the fair value of the debt subsequent to the initiation of the derivative. Differences between the changes in the fair values of the hedged item and the derivative instrument, if any, represent hedge ineffectiveness and are recognized currently in earnings. Locked-in gains and losses related to settled fair value hedges are amortized as an adjustment to interest expense over the remaining term of the related debt instrument. We have elected not to designate any of our qualifying commodity and interest rate derivatives as cash flow or fair value hedges. Therefore, changes in fair value of these derivatives that occur prior to their maturity (i.e., temporary fluctuations in value) are recognized in our consolidated statements of operations within oil, natural gas and NGL sales and interest expense, respectively.

From time to time and in the normal course of business, our marketing subsidiary enters into supply contracts under which we commit to deliver a predetermined quantity of natural gas to certain counterparties in an attempt to earn attractive margins. Under certain contracts, we receive a sales price that is based on the price of a product other than natural gas, thereby creating an embedded derivative requiring bifurcation. The changes in fair value of the embedded derivative and the settlements are recognized in our consolidated statements of operations within marketing, gathering and compression sales.

Derivative instruments reflected as current in the consolidated balance sheets represent the estimated fair value of derivatives scheduled to settle over the next twelve months based on market prices/rates as of the respective balance sheet dates. Cash settlements of our derivative instruments are generally classified as operating cash flows unless the derivatives are deemed to contain, for accounting purposes, a significant financing element at contract inception, in which case these cash settlements are classified as financing cash flows in the accompanying consolidated statement of cash flows. All of our derivative instruments are subject to master netting arrangements by contract type (i.e., commodity, interest rate and cross currency contracts) which provide for the offsetting of asset and liability positions within each contract type, as well as related cash collateral if applicable, by counterparty. Therefore, we net the value of our derivative instruments by contract type with the same counterparty in the accompanying consolidated balance sheets.

We have established the fair value of our derivative instruments using established index prices, volatility curves and discount factors. These estimates are compared to our counterparty values for reasonableness. The values we report in our financial statements are as of a point in time and subsequently change as these estimates are revised to reflect actual results, changes in market conditions and other factors. Derivative transactions are subject to the risk that counterparties will be unable to meet their obligations. This non-performance risk is considered in the valuation of our derivative instruments, but to date has not had a material impact on the values of our derivatives. See Note 11 for further discussion of our derivative instruments.

11. Derivative and Hedging Activities (in part)

Chesapeake uses commodity derivative instruments to secure attractive pricing and margins on its share of expected production, to reduce its exposure to fluctuations in future commodity prices and to protect its expected operating cash flow against significant market movements or volatility. Chesapeake also uses derivative instruments to mitigate a portion of its exposure to interest rate and foreign currency exchange rate fluctuations. All of our commodity derivative instruments are net settled based on the difference between the fixed-price payment and the floating-price payment, resulting in a net amount due to or from the counterparty.

Oil and Natural Gas Derivatives

As of December 31, 2015 and 2014, our oil and natural gas derivative instruments consisted of the following types of instruments:
- *Swaps*: Chesapeake receives a fixed price and pays a floating market price to the counterparty for the hedged commodity. In exchange for higher fixed prices on certain of our swap trades, we granted options that allow the counterparty to double the notional amount.

- *Options*: Chesapeake sells, and occasionally buys, call options in exchange for a premium. At the time of settlement, if the market price exceeds the fixed price of the call option, Chesapeake pays the counterparty the excess on sold call options and Chesapeake receives the excess on bought call options. If the market price settles below the fixed price of the call option, no payment is due from either party.
- *Basis Protection Swaps*: These instruments are arrangements that guarantee a fixed price differential to NYMEX from a specified delivery point. Chesapeake receives the fixed price differential and pays the floating market price differential to the counterparty for the hedged commodity.

The estimated fair values of our oil and natural gas derivative instrument assets (liabilities) as of December 31, 2015 and 2014 are provided below.

	December 31, 2015		December 31, 2014	
	Volume	Fair Value ($ in millions)	Volume	Fair Value ($ in millions)
Oil (mmbbl):				
Fixed-price swaps	13.5	$144	12.5	$ 471
Three-way collars	—	—	4.4	40
Call options	19.2	(7)	35.8	(89)
Basis protection swaps	—	—	—	—
Total oil	32.7	$137	52.7	$ 422
Natural Gas (tbtu):				
Fixed-price swaps	500	$229	275	$ 281
Three-way collars	—	—	207	165
Call options	295	(99)	193	(170)
Basis protection swaps	57	—	60	23
Total natural gas	852	$130	735	$ 299
Total estimated fair value		$267		$ 721

We have terminated certain commodity derivative contracts that were previously designated as cash flow hedges for which the hedged production is still expected to occur. See further discussion below under *Effect of Derivative Instruments—Accumulated Other Comprehensive Income (Loss)*.

Interest Rate Derivatives

As of December 31, 2015, there were no interest rate derivatives outstanding. As of December 31, 2014, our interest rate derivative instruments consisted of swaps. We enter into fixed-to-floating interest rate swaps (we receive a fixed interest rate and pay a floating market rate) to mitigate our exposure to changes in the fair value of our senior notes. We enter into floating-to-fixed interest rate swaps (we receive a floating market rate and pay a fixed interest rate) to manage our interest rate exposure related to our revolving credit facility borrowings.

The notional amount of our interest rate derivatives associated with our long-term debt as of December 31, 2014 was $850 million. The estimated fair value of our interest rate derivative liabilities as of December 31, 2014 was $17 million.

We have terminated certain fair value hedges related to certain of our senior notes. Gains and losses related to these terminated hedges will be amortized as an adjustment to interest expense over the remaining term of the related senior notes. Over the next six years, we will recognize $7 million in net gains related to these transactions.

Foreign Currency Derivatives

We are party to cross currency swaps to mitigate our exposure to foreign currency exchange rate fluctuations. In December 2015, we exchanged in privately negotiated transactions and subsequently retired €42 million in aggregate principal amount of these senior notes, and we simultaneously unwound the cross currency swaps for the same principal amount at a cost of $8 million. As a result, we realized a loss of $8 million which was included in losses on purchases or exchanges of debt. Under the terms of the remaining cross currency swaps, on each semi-annual interest payment date, the counterparties pay us €9 million and we pay the counterparties $15 million, which yields an annual dollar-equivalent interest rate of 7.491%. Upon maturity of the notes, the counterparties will pay us €302 million and we will pay the counterparties $403 million. The terms of the cross currency swaps were based on the dollar/euro exchange rate on the issuance date of $1.3325 to €1.00. The swaps are designated as cash flow hedges and, because they are entirely effective in having eliminated any potential variability in our expected cash flows related to changes in foreign exchange rates, changes in their fair value do not impact earnings. The fair values of the cross currency swaps are recorded on the consolidated balance sheets as liabilities of $52 million and $53 million as of December 31, 2015 and 2014, respectively. The euro-denominated debt in long-term debt has been adjusted to $329 million as of December 31, 2015, using an exchange rate of $1.0862 to €1.00.

Supply Contract Derivatives

From time to time and in the normal course of business, our marketing subsidiary enters into supply contracts under which we commit to deliver a predetermined quantity of natural gas to certain counterparties in an attempt to earn attractive margins. Under certain contracts, we receive a sales price that is based on the price of a product other than natural gas, thereby creating an embedded derivative requiring bifurcation. In one of these supply contracts, we are committed to supply a minimum of 90 bbtu per day of natural gas through March 2025. In 2015, we recorded revenues of approximately $96 million for settlements of this embedded derivative. The bifurcated derivative was measured at fair value resulting in an unrealized gain of $297 million in 2015. Both settlements and mark-to-market gains (losses) are included in marketing, gathering and compression revenues in our consolidated statements of operations.

Effect of Derivative Instruments—Consolidated Balance Sheets

The following table presents the fair value and location of each classification of derivative instrument included in the consolidated balance sheets as of December 31, 2015 and 2014 on a gross basis and after same-counterparty netting:

($ in millions) Balance Sheet Classification	Gross Fair Value	Amounts Netted in Consolidated Balance Sheet	Net Fair Value Presented in Consolidated Balance Sheet
As of December 31, 2015			
Commodity Contracts:			
Short-term derivative asset	$ 381	$(66)	$ 315
Long-term derivative asset	—	—	—
Short-term derivative liability	(106)	66	(40)
Long-term derivative liability	(8)	—	(8)
Total commodity contracts	267	—	267
Foreign Currency Contracts:[a]			
Long-term derivative liability	(52)	—	(52)
Total foreign currency contracts	(52)	—	(52)
Supply Contracts:			
Short-term derivative asset	51	—	51
Long-term derivative asset	246	—	246
Total supply contracts	297	—	297
Total derivatives	$ 512	$—	$ 512
As of December 31, 2014			
Commodity Contracts:			
Short-term derivative asset	$ 973	$(95)	$ 878
Long-term derivative asset	16	(10)	6
Short-term derivative liability	(105)	95	(10)
Long-term derivative liability	(163)	10	(153)
Total commodity contracts	721	—	721
Interest Rate Contracts:			
Short-term derivative liability	(5)	—	(5)
Long-term derivative liability	(12)	—	(12)
Total interest rate contracts	(17)	—	(17)
Foreign Currency Contracts:[a]			
Long-term derivative liability	(53)	—	(53)
Total foreign currency contracts	(53)	—	(53)
Supply Contracts:			
Short-term derivative asset	1	—	1
Long-term derivative asset	—	—	—
Total supply contracts	1	—	1
Total derivatives	$ 652	$—	$ 652

[a] Designated as cash flow hedging instruments.

As of December 31, 2015 and 2014, we did not have any cash collateral balances for these derivatives.

Effect of Derivative Instruments—Consolidated Statements of Operations

The components of oil, natural gas and NGL revenues for the years ended December 31, 2015, 2014 and 2013 are presented below.

($ in millions)	Years Ended December 31,		
	2015	2014	2013
Oil, natural gas and NGL revenues	$4,767	$ 9,336	$8,497
Gains (losses) on undesignated oil and natural gas derivatives	661	1,055	443
Losses on terminated cash flow hedges	(37)	(37)	(314)
Total oil, natural gas and NGL revenues	$5,391	$10,354	$8,626

The components of marketing, gathering and compression revenues for the years ended December 31, 2015, 2014 and 2013 are presented below.

($ in millions)	Years Ended December 31,		
	2015	2014	2013
Marketing, gathering and compression revenues	$7,077	$12,224	$9,559
Gains on undesignated supply contract derivatives	296	1	—
Total marketing, gathering and compression revenues	$7,373	$12,225	$9,559

The components of interest expense for the years ended December 31, 2015, 2014 and 2013 are presented below.

($ in millions)	Years Ended December 31,		
	2015	2014	2013
Interest expense on senior notes	$ 682	$ 704	$ 740
Interest expense on term loan	—	36	116
Amortization of loan discount, issuance costs and other	59	42	91
Interest expense on credit facilities	12	28	38
Gains on terminated fair value hedges	(3)	(3)	(5)
(Gains) losses on undesignated interest rate derivatives	(9)	(81)	63
Capitalized interest	(424)	(637)	(816)
Total interest expense	$ 317	$ 89	$ 227

Effect of Derivative Instruments—Accumulated Other Comprehensive Income (Loss)

A reconciliation of the changes in accumulated other comprehensive income (loss) in our consolidated statements of stockholders' equity related to our cash flow hedges is presented below.

($ in millions)	Years Ended December 31,					
	2015		2014		2013	
	Before Tax	After Tax	Before Tax	After Tax	Before Tax	After Tax
Balance, beginning of period	$(231)	$(143)	$(269)	$(167)	$(304)	$(189)
Net change in fair value	32	20	1	1	3	2
Losses reclassified to income	39	24	37	23	32	20
Balance, end of period	$(160)	$ (99)	$(231)	$(143)	$(269)	$(167)

Approximately $113 million of the $99 million of accumulated other comprehensive loss as of December 31, 2015 represented the net deferred loss associated with commodity derivative contracts that were previously designated as cash flow hedges for which the hedged production is still expected to occur. Deferred gain or loss amounts will be recognized in earnings in the month in which the originally forecasted hedged production occurs. As of December 31, 2015, we expect to transfer approximately $21 million of net loss included in accumulated other comprehensive income to net income (loss) during the next 12 months. The remaining amounts will be transferred by December 31, 2022.

Credit Risk Considerations

Over-the-counter traded derivative instruments and our supply contracts expose us to our counterparties' credit risk. To mitigate this risk, we enter into derivative contracts only with counterparties that are rated investment grade and deemed by management to be competent and competitive market makers, and we attempt to limit our exposure to non-performance by any single counterparty. As of December 31, 2015, our oil, natural gas, foreign currency and supply contract derivative instruments were spread among 16 counterparties.

Hedging Arrangements

As of December 31, 2015, our secured commodity hedging facility with three counterparties provided approximately 94 mmboe of hedging capacity for oil, natural gas and NGL price derivatives and 94 mmboe for basis derivatives with an aggregate mark-to-market capacity of $1.5 billion. The facility, which was terminated in February 2016, was secured by proved reserves, the value of which covered the fair value of the transactions outstanding under the facility by at least 1.65 times at semi-annual collateral redetermination dates and 1.30 times in between those dates, and guarantees by certain subsidiaries that also guarantee our revolving credit facility and indentures. The counterparties' obligations under the facility were required to be secured by cash or short-term U.S. treasury instruments to the extent that any mark-to-market amounts owed to us exceed defined thresholds. As of December 31, 2015, we had hedged under the facility 1.2 mmboe of our future production with price derivatives.

In 2015, we also began entering into bilateral hedging agreements with the intention of replacing and terminating the respective counterparties' positions in the secured hedging facility. We also entered into bilateral arrangements that reduced the aggregate mark-to-market capacity under the secured hedging facility from $16.5 billion to $1.5 billion. The counterparties' and our obligations under certain of the bilateral hedging agreements must be secured by cash or letters of credit to the extent that any mark-to-market amounts owed to us or by us exceed defined thresholds. Our obligations under other bilateral hedging agreements are secured by the same collateral securing our revolving credit facility. As of December 31, 2015, we had hedged under bilateral agreements 164.0 mmboe of our future production with price derivatives and 9.5 mmboe with basis derivatives.

DEFERRED REVENUE

2.152 APPLE INC. (SEP)
CONSOLIDATED BALANCE SHEETS (in part)

(In millions, except number of shares which are reflected in thousands and par value)

Liabilities and Shareholders' Equity (in part):	September 26, 2015	September 27, 2014
Current liabilities:		
Accounts payable	$ 35,490	$ 30,196
Accrued expenses	25,181	18,453
Deferred revenue	8,940	8,491
Commercial paper	8,499	6,308
Current portion of long-term debt	2,500	0
Total current liabilities	80,610	63,448
Deferred revenue, non-current	3,624	3,031
Long-term debt	53,463	28,987
Other non-current liabilities	33,427	24,826
Total liabilities	171,124	120,292

NOTES TO CONSOLIDATED FINANCIAL STATEMENTS (in part)

Note 1—Summary of Significant Accounting Policies (in part)

Revenue Recognition

Net sales consist primarily of revenue from the sale of hardware, software, digital content and applications, accessories, and service and support contracts. The Company recognizes revenue when persuasive evidence of an arrangement exists, delivery has occurred, the sales price is fixed or determinable and collection is probable. Product is considered delivered to the customer once it has been shipped and title, risk of loss and rewards of ownership have been transferred. For most of the Company's product sales, these criteria are met at the time the product is shipped. For online sales to individuals, for some sales to education customers in the U.S., and for certain other sales, the Company defers revenue until the customer receives the product because the Company retains a portion of the risk of loss on these sales during transit. For payment terms in excess of the Company's standard payment terms, revenue is recognized as payments become due unless the Company has positive evidence that the sales price is fixed or determinable, such as a successful history of collection, without concession, on comparable arrangements. The Company recognizes revenue from the sale of hardware products, software bundled with hardware that is essential to the functionality of the hardware and third-party digital content sold on the iTunes Store in accordance with general revenue recognition accounting guidance. The Company recognizes revenue in accordance with industry specific software accounting guidance for the following types of sales transactions: (i) standalone sales of software products, (ii) sales of software upgrades and (iii) sales of software bundled with hardware not essential to the functionality of the hardware.

For the sale of most third-party products, the Company recognizes revenue based on the gross amount billed to customers because the Company establishes its own pricing for such products, retains related inventory risk for physical products, is the primary obligor to the customer and assumes the credit risk for amounts billed to its customers. For third-party applications sold through the App Store and Mac App Store and certain digital content sold through the iTunes Store, the Company does not determine the selling price of the products and is not the primary obligor to the customer. Therefore, the Company accounts for such sales on a net basis by recognizing in net sales only the commission it retains from each sale. The portion of the gross amount billed to customers that is remitted by the Company to third-party app developers and certain digital content owners is not reflected in the Company's Consolidated Statements of Operations.

The Company records deferred revenue when it receives payments in advance of the delivery of products or the performance of services. This includes amounts that have been deferred for unspecified and specified software upgrade rights and non-software services that are attached to hardware and software products. The Company sells gift cards redeemable at its retail and online stores, and also sells gift cards redeemable on iTunes Store, App Store, Mac App Store and iBooks Store for the purchase of digital content and software. The Company records deferred revenue upon the sale of the card, which is relieved upon redemption of the card by the customer. Revenue from AppleCare service and support contracts is deferred and recognized over the service coverage periods. AppleCare service and support contracts typically include extended phone support, repair services, web-based support resources and diagnostic tools offered under the Company's standard limited warranty.

The Company records reductions to revenue for estimated commitments related to price protection and other customer incentive programs. For transactions involving price protection, the Company recognizes revenue net of the estimated amount to be refunded. For the Company's other customer incentive programs, the estimated cost of these programs is recognized at the later of the date at which the Company has sold the product or the date at which the program is offered. The Company also records reductions to revenue for expected future product returns based on the Company's historical experience. Revenue is recorded net of taxes collected from customers that are remitted to governmental authorities, with the collected taxes recorded as current liabilities until remitted to the relevant government authority.

Revenue Recognition for Arrangements with Multiple Deliverables

For multi-element arrangements that include hardware products containing software essential to the hardware product's functionality, undelivered software elements that relate to the hardware product's essential software, and undelivered non-software services, the Company allocates revenue to all deliverables based on their relative selling prices. In such circumstances, the Company uses a hierarchy to determine the selling price to be used for allocating revenue to deliverables: (i) vendor-specific objective evidence of fair value ("VSOE"), (ii) third-party evidence of selling price ("TPE") and (iii) best estimate of selling price ("ESP"). VSOE generally exists only when the Company sells the deliverable separately and is the price actually charged by the Company for that deliverable. ESPs reflect the Company's best estimates of what the selling prices of elements would be if they were sold regularly on a stand-alone basis. For multi-element arrangements accounted for in accordance with industry specific software accounting guidance, the Company allocates revenue to all deliverables based on the VSOE of each element, and if VSOE does not exist revenue is recognized when elements lacking VSOE are delivered.

For sales of qualifying versions of iPhone, iPad and iPod touch ("iOS devices"), Mac, Apple Watch and Apple TV, the Company has indicated it may from time to time provide future unspecified software upgrades to the device's essential software and/or non-software services free of charge. The Company has identified up to three deliverables regularly included in arrangements involving the sale of these devices. The first deliverable, which represents the substantial portion of the allocated sales price, is the hardware and software essential to the functionality of the hardware device delivered at the time of sale. The second deliverable is the embedded right included with qualifying devices to receive on a when-and-if-available basis, future unspecified software upgrades relating to the product's essential software. The third deliverable is the non-software services to be provided to qualifying devices. The Company allocates revenue between these deliverables using the relative selling price method. Because the Company has neither VSOE nor TPE for these deliverables, the allocation of revenue is based on the Company's ESPs. Revenue allocated to the delivered hardware and the related essential software is recognized at the time of sale provided the other conditions for revenue recognition have been met. Revenue allocated to the embedded unspecified software upgrade rights and the non-software services is deferred and recognized on a straight-line basis over the estimated period the software upgrades and non-software services are expected to be provided. Cost of sales related to delivered hardware and related essential software, including estimated warranty costs, are recognized at the time of sale. Costs incurred to provide non-software services are recognized as cost of sales as incurred, and engineering and sales and marketing costs are recognized as operating expenses as incurred.

The Company's process for determining its ESP for deliverables without VSOE or TPE considers multiple factors that may vary depending upon the unique facts and circumstances related to each deliverable including, where applicable, prices charged by the Company and market trends in the pricing for similar offerings, product specific business objectives, length of time a particular version of a device has been available, estimated cost to provide the non-software services and the relative ESP of the upgrade rights and non-software services as compared to the total selling price of the product.

Beginning in September 2015, the Company reduced the combined ESPs for iOS devices and Mac between $5 and $10 to reflect the increase in competitive offers for similar products at little to no cost for users, which reduces the amount the Company could reasonably charge for these deliverables on a standalone basis.

Accumulated Other Comprehensive Income

PRESENTATION

2.153 FASB ASC 220, *Comprehensive Income*, requires that a separate caption for accumulated other comprehensive income be presented in the "Equity" section of a balance sheet. An entity should disclose accumulated balances for each classification in that separate component of equity on the face of a balance sheet or in notes to the financial statements.

PRESENTATION AND DISCLOSURE EXCERPTS

ACCUMULATED OTHER COMPREHENSIVE INCOME—EQUITY SECTION OF BALANCE SHEET

2.154 THE BRINK'S COMPANY (DEC)
CONSOLIDATED BALANCE SHEETS

	December 31,	
(In millions, except for per share amounts)	2015	2014
Assets		
Current assets:		
Cash and cash equivalents	$ 198.3	176.2
Accounts receivable (net of allowance: 2015—$9.1; 2014—$10.0)	478.1	530.5
Prepaid expenses and other	101.3	129.0
Deferred income taxes	—	71.9
Total current assets	777.7	907.6
Property and equipment, net	549.0	669.5
Goodwill	185.3	215.7
Other intangibles	28.5	39.8
Deferred income taxes	329.8	289.5
Other	76.4	69.9
Total assets	$1,946.7	2,192.0
Liabilities and Equity		
Current liabilities:		
Short-term borrowings	$ 29.1	59.4
Current maturities of long-term debt	43.3	34.1
Accounts payable	155.3	168.6
Accrued liabilities	414.1	466.3
Total current liabilities	641.8	728.4
Long-term debt	358.1	373.1
Accrued pension costs	219.4	219.0
Retirement benefits other than pensions	259.2	257.1
Deferred income taxes	8.1	10.8
Other	129.5	129.8
Total liabilities	1,616.1	1,718.2
Commitments and contingent liabilities (notes 3, 4, 13, 15, 18, 22 and 23)		
Equity:		
The Brink's Company ("Brink's") shareholders:		
Common stock, par value $1 per share:		
Shares authorized: 100.0		
Shares issued and outstanding: 2015—48.9; 2014—48.6	48.9	48.6
Capital in excess of par value	599.6	584.5
Retained earnings	561.3	592.9
Accumulated other comprehensive income (loss):		
Benefit plan adjustments	(570.5)	(571.7)
Foreign currency translation	(322.6)	(222.1)

(continued)

(In millions, except for per share amounts)	December 31, 2015	December 31, 2014
Unrealized gains on available-for-sale securities	1.1	1.4
Gains on cash flow hedges	0.1	0.4
Accumulated other comprehensive loss	(891.9)	(792.0)
Brink's shareholders	317.9	434.0
Noncontrolling interests	12.7	39.8
Total equity	330.6	473.8
Total liabilities and equity	$1,946.7	2,192.0

See accompanying notes to consolidated financial statements.

NOTES TO CONSOLIDATED FINANCIAL STATEMENTS (in part)

Note 9—Accumulated Other Comprehensive Income (Loss)

The following tables provide the components of other comprehensive income (loss), including the amounts reclassified from accumulated other comprehensive income (loss) into earnings:

(In millions)	Amounts Arising During the Current Period		Amounts Reclassified to Net Income (Loss)		Total Other Comprehensive Income (Loss)
	Pretax	Income Tax	Pretax	Income Tax	
2015					
Amounts attributable to Brink's:					
Benefit plan adjustments	$ (57.1)	20.4	58.1	(20.2)	1.2
Foreign currency translation adjustments	(106.2)	0.3	5.7	—	(100.2)
Unrealized gains (losses) on available-for-sale securities	0.6	(0.2)	(1.1)	0.4	(0.3)
Gains (losses) on cash flow hedges	3.3	—	(3.6)	—	(0.3)
	(159.4)	20.5	59.1	(19.8)	(99.6)
Amounts attributable to noncontrolling interests:					
Benefit plan adjustments	(0.7)	—	0.5	—	(0.2)
Foreign currency translation adjustments	(3.6)	—	—	—	(3.6)
	(4.3)	—	0.5	—	(3.8)
Total					
Benefit plan adjustments[a]	(57.8)	20.4	58.6	(20.2)	1.0
Foreign currency translation adjustments[b]	(109.8)	0.3	5.7	—	(103.8)
Unrealized gains (losses) on available-for-sale securities[c]	0.6	(0.2)	(1.1)	0.4	(0.3)
Gains (losses) on cash flow hedges[d]	3.3	—	(3.6)	—	(0.3)
	$(163.7)	20.5	59.6	(19.8)	(103.4)
2014					
Amounts attributable to Brink's:					
Benefit plan adjustments	$(231.2)	78.1	95.3	(35.9)	(93.7)
Foreign currency translation adjustments	(82.2)	—	1.3	0.3	(80.6)
Unrealized gains (losses) on available-for-sale securities	0.1	—	(0.5)	0.2	(0.2)
Gains (losses) on cash flow hedges	0.7	—	(0.9)	—	(0.2)
	(312.6)	78.1	95.2	(35.4)	(174.7)
Amounts attributable to noncontrolling interests:					
Benefit plan adjustments	(1.4)	0.4	0.4	(0.1)	(0.7)
Foreign currency translation adjustments	(6.1)	—	—	—	(6.1)
	(7.5)	0.4	0.4	(0.1)	(6.8)
Total					
Benefit plan adjustments[a][b]	(232.6)	78.5	95.7	(36.0)	(94.4)
Foreign currency translation adjustments[b]	(88.3)	—	1.3	0.3	(86.7)
Unrealized gains (losses) on available-for-sale securities[c]	0.1	—	(0.5)	0.2	(0.2)
Gains (losses) on cash flow hedges[d]	0.7	—	(0.9)	—	(0.2)
	$(320.1)	78.5	95.6	(35.5)	(181.5)
2013					
Amounts attributable to Brink's:					
Benefit plan adjustments	$ 251.9	(114.1)	76.4	(27.1)	187.1
Foreign currency translation adjustments	(30.9)	—	(0.5)	0.1	(31.3)
Unrealized gains (losses) on available-for-sale securities	(0.3)	0.1	0.4	(0.2)	—
Gains (losses) on cash flow hedges	2.9	—	(2.3)	—	0.6
	223.6	(114.0)	74.0	(27.2)	156.4

(continued)

(In millions)	Amounts Arising During the Current Period		Amounts Reclassified to Net Income (Loss)		Total Other Comprehensive Income (Loss)
	Pretax	Income Tax	Pretax	Income Tax	
Amounts attributable to noncontrolling interests:					
Benefit plan adjustments	(0.9)	0.3	0.3	(0.1)	(0.4)
Foreign currency translation adjustments	(1.4)	—	—	—	(1.4)
	(2.3)	0.3	0.3	(0.1)	(1.8)
Total					
Benefit plan adjustments[a]	251.0	(113.8)	76.7	(27.2)	186.7
Foreign currency translation adjustments[b]	(32.3)	—	(0.5)	0.1	(32.7)
Unrealized gains (losses) on available-for-sale securities[c]	(0.3)	0.1	0.4	(0.2)	—
Gains (losses) on cash flow hedges[d]	2.9	—	(2.3)	—	0.6
	$ 221.3	(113.7)	74.3	(27.3)	154.6

[a] The amortization of prior experience losses and prior service cost is part of total net periodic retirement benefit cost when reclassified to net income (loss). Net periodic retirement benefit cost also includes service cost, interest cost, expected returns on assets, and settlement costs. The total pretax expense is allocated between cost of revenues and selling, general and administrative expenses on a plan-by-plan basis:

	December 31,		
(In millions)	2015	2014	2013
Total net periodic retirement benefit cost included in:			
Cost of revenues	$36.1	68.0	66.8
Selling, general and administrative expenses	14.3	29.5	17.5

[b] Reclassification of foreign currency translation amounts in 2015 relate primarily to the sale of our Russian cash management operations. These amounts are included in other operating income (expense). Pretax benefit plan adjustments of $8 million (including related deferred tax component) and foreign currency translation adjustments reclassified to the consolidated statements of operations in 2014 relate to the sale of CIT operations in the Netherlands. Reclassification of foreign currency translation amounts in 2013 relate to the sale of ICD Limited and its affiliates, as well as CIT operations in Hungary and Poland. The 2014 and 2013 amounts are included in loss from discontinued operations in the consolidated statements of operations.

[c] Gains and losses on sales of available-for-sale securities are reclassified from accumulated other comprehensive loss to the consolidated statements of operations when the gains or losses are realized. Pretax amounts are classified in the consolidated statements of operations as interest and other income (expense).

[d] Pretax gains and losses on cash flow hedges are classified in the consolidated statements of operations as
- other operating income (expense) ($4.1 million gains in 2015, $1.9 million gains in 2014 and $3.3 million gains in 2013)
- interest and other income (expense) ($0.5 million losses in 2015 and $1.0 million losses in 2014 and 2013.)

The changes in accumulated other comprehensive loss attributable to Brink's are as follows:

(In millions)	Benefit Plan Adjustments	Foreign Currency Translation Adjustments	Unrealized Gains (Losses) on Available-for-Sale Securities	Gains (Losses) on Cash Flow Hedges	Total
Balance as of December 31, 2012	$(665.1)	(109.9)	1.6	—	(773.4)
Other comprehensive income (loss) before reclassifications	137.8	(30.9)	(0.2)	2.9	109.6
Amounts reclassified from accumulated other comprehensive loss	49.3	(0.4)	0.2	(2.3)	46.8
Other comprehensive income (loss) attributable to Brink's	187.1	(31.3)	—	0.6	156.4
Acquisitions of noncontrolling interests	—	(0.3)	—	—	(0.3)
Balance as of December 31, 2013	(478.0)	(141.5)	1.6	0.6	(617.3)
Other comprehensive income (loss) before reclassifications	(153.1)	(82.2)	0.1	0.7	(234.5)
Amounts reclassified from accumulated other comprehensive loss	59.4	1.6	(0.3)	(0.9)	59.8
Other comprehensive income (loss) attributable to Brink's	(93.7)	(80.6)	(0.2)	(0.2)	(174.7)
Balance as of December 31, 2014	(571.7)	(222.1)	1.4	0.4	(792.0)
Other comprehensive income (loss) before reclassifications	(36.7)	(105.9)	0.4	3.3	(138.9)
Amounts reclassified from accumulated other comprehensive loss	37.9	5.7	(0.7)	(3.6)	39.3
Other comprehensive income (loss) attributable to Brink's	1.2	(100.2)	(0.3)	(0.3)	(99.6)
Acquisitions of noncontrolling interests	—	(0.3)	—	—	(0.3)
Balance as of December 31, 2015	$(570.5)	(322.6)	1.1	0.1	(891.9)

2.155 THE PRICELINE GROUP INC. (DEC)

CONSOLIDATED STATEMENTS OF CHANGES IN STOCKHOLDERS' EQUITY

(In thousands)

	Common Stock		Treasury Stock		Additional Paid-in Capital	Accumulated Earnings	Accumulated Other Comprehensive Income (Loss)	Total
	Shares	Amount	Shares	Amount				
Balance, December 31, 2012	58,056	$450	(8,185)	$(1,060,607)	$2,612,197	$2,368,611	$ (23,676)	$ 3,896,975
Net income applicable to common stockholders	—	—	—	—	—	1,892,663	—	1,892,663
Unrealized gain (loss) on marketable securities, net of tax benefit of $43	—	—	—	—	—	—	21	21
Foreign currency translation adjustments, net of tax benefit of $55,001	—	—	—	—	—	—	108,384	108,384
Redeemable noncontrolling interests fair value adjustments	—	—	—	—	—	(42,522)	—	(42,522)
Reclassification adjustment for convertible debt in mezzanine	—	—	—	—	46,122	—	—	46,122
Exercise of stock options and vesting of restricted stock units and performance share units	715	6	—	—	91,601	—	—	91,607
Repurchase of common stock	—	—	(1,030)	(883,515)	—	—	—	(883,515)
Stock-based compensation and other stock-based payments	—	—	—	—	142,098	—	—	142,098
Issuance of senior convertible notes					93,402			93,402
Common stock issued in an acquisition	1,522	12			1,281,122			1,281,134
Vested stock options assumed in an acquisition					264,423			264,423
Conversion of debt	972	8	—	—	1,224	—	—	1,232
Settlement of conversion spread hedges	—	—	(42)	(43,085)	43,104	—	—	19
Excess tax benefits on stock-based awards	—	—	—	—	17,686	—	—	17,686
Balance, December 31, 2013	61,265	$476	(9,257)	$(1,987,207)	$4,592,979	$4,218,752	$ 84,729	$ 6,909,729
Net income applicable to common stockholders	—	—	—	—	—	2,421,753	—	2,421,753
Unrealized gain (loss) on marketable securities, net of tax benefit of $7,621	—	—	—	—	—	—	(157,275)	(157,275)
Foreign currency translation adjustment, net of tax of $55,597	—	—	—	—	—	—	(187,356)	(187,356)
Reclassification adjustment for convertible debt in mezzanine	—	—	—	—	8,204	—	—	8,204
Exercise of stock options and vesting of restricted stock units and performance share units	256	2	—	—	16,389	—	—	16,391
Repurchase of common stock	—	—	(631)	(750,378)	—	—	—	(750,378)
Stock-based compensation and other stock-based payments	—	—	—	—	189,292	—	—	189,292
Conversion of debt	300	2	—	—	(1,658)	—	—	(1,656)
Issuance of senior convertible notes	—	—	—	—	80,873	—	—	80,873
Stock options and restricted stock units assumed in acquisitions	—	—	—	—	13,751	—	—	13,751
Excess tax benefits on stock-based awards	—	—	—	—	23,366	—	—	23,366
Balance, December 31, 2014	61,821	$480	(9,888)	$(2,737,585)	$4,923,196	$6,640,505	$(259,902)	$ 8,566,694
Net income applicable to common stockholders	—	—	—	—	—	2,551,360	—	2,551,360
Unrealized gain (loss) on marketable securities, net of tax of $1,551	—	—	—	—	—	—	619,259	619,259
Foreign currency translation adjustment, net of tax of $60,418	—	—	—	—	—	—	(114,505)	(114,505)
Reclassification adjustment for convertible debt in mezzanine	—	—	—	—	329	—	—	329
Exercise of stock options and vesting of restricted stock units and performance share units	219	2	—	—	20,849	—	—	20,851
Repurchase of common stock	—	—	(2,540)	(3,089,055)	—	—	—	(3,089,055)
Stock-based compensation and other stock-based payments	—	—	—	—	249,133	—	—	249,133
Conversion of debt	—	—	—	—	(110,105)	—	—	(110,105)
Excess tax benefits on stock-based awards	—	—	—	—	101,508	—	—	101,508
Balance, December 31, 2015	62,040	$482	(12,428)	$(5,826,640)	$5,184,910	$9,191,865	$ 244,852	$ 8,795,469

See Notes to Consolidated Financial Statements.

13. Accumulated Other Comprehensive Income (Loss)

The table below provides the balances for each classification of accumulated other comprehensive income (loss) as of December 31, 2015 and 2014 (in thousands):

	December 31, 2015	December 31, 2014
Foreign currency translation adjustments, net of tax[1]	$(217,263)	$(102,758)
Net unrealized gain (loss) on marketable securities, net of tax[2]	462,115	(157,144)
Accumulated other comprehensive income (loss)	$ 244,852	$(259,902)

[1] Foreign currency translation adjustments, net of tax, includes net losses from fair value adjustments of $34.8 million after tax ($52.6 million before tax) and $37.8 million after tax ($57.8 million before tax) associated with derivatives designated as net investment hedges at December 31, 2015 and 2014, respectively (see Note 5).

Foreign currency translation adjustments, net of tax, includes foreign currency transaction gains at December 31, 2015 of $126.8 million after tax ($220.5 million before tax) associated with the Company's 2022 Notes, 2024 Notes and 2027 Notes and foreign currency transaction gains at December 31, 2014 of $48.3 million after tax ($83.8 million before tax) associated with the Company's 2024 Notes. The 2022 Notes, 2024 Notes and 2027 Notes are Euro-denominated debt and are designated as hedges of certain of the Company's Euro-denominated net assets (see Note 10).

The remaining balance in foreign currency translation adjustments excludes income taxes as a result of the Company's intention to indefinitely reinvest the earnings of its international subsidiaries outside of the United States.

[2] The unrealized gains before tax at December 31, 2015 were $456.1 million, of which unrealized gains of $481.3 million were exempt from tax in the Netherlands and unrealized losses of $25.2 million were taxable. The unrealized losses before tax at December 31, 2014 were $164.7 million, of which unrealized losses of $134.6 million were exempt from tax in the Netherlands and unrealized losses of $30.1 million were taxable.

ACCUMULATED OTHER COMPREHENSIVE INCOME—NOTES TO CONSOLIDATED FINANCIAL STATEMENTS

2.156 AIR PRODUCTS AND CHEMICALS, INC. (SEP)

CONSOLIDATED BALANCE SHEETS

(Millions of dollars, except for share data) 30 September	2015	2014
Assets		
Current Assets		
Cash and cash items	$ 206.4	$ 336.6
Trade receivables, net	1,406.2	1,486.0
Inventories	657.8	706.0
Contracts in progress, less progress billings	110.8	155.4
Prepaid expenses	67.3	87.8
Other receivables and current assets	462.3	523.0
Total Current Assets	2,910.8	3,294.8
Investment in net assets of and advances to equity affiliates	1,265.7	1,257.9
Plant and equipment, net	9,636.9	9,532.1
Goodwill, net	1,131.3	1,237.3
Intangible assets, net	508.3	615.8
Noncurrent capital lease receivables	1,350.2	1,414.9
Other noncurrent assets	634.9	426.3
Total Noncurrent Assets	14,527.3	14,484.3
Total Assets	$17,438.1	$17,779.1
Liabilities and Equity		
Current Liabilities		
Payables and accrued liabilities	$ 1,662.4	$ 1,591.0
Accrued income taxes	55.8	78.0
Short-term borrowings	1,494.3	1,228.7
Current portion of long-term debt	435.6	65.3
Total Current Liabilities	3,648.1	2,963.0
Long-term debt	3,949.1	4,824.5
Other noncurrent liabilities	1,556.5	1,187.5
Deferred income taxes	903.3	995.5
Total Noncurrent Liabilities	6,408.9	7,007.5
Total Liabilities	10,057.0	9,970.5

(continued)

(Millions of dollars, except for share data) 30 September	2015	2014
Commitments and Contingencies—See Note 17		
Redeemable Noncontrolling Interest	—	287.2
Common stock (par value $1 per share; issued 2015 and 2014—249,455,584 shares)	249.4	249.4
Capital in excess of par value	904.7	842.0
Retained earnings	10,580.4	9,993.2
Accumulated other comprehensive loss	(2,125.9)	(1,241.9)
Treasury stock, at cost (2015—34,096,471 shares; 2014—35,917,440 shares)	(2,359.6)	(2,476.9)
Total Air Products Shareholders' Equity	7,249.0	7,365.8
Noncontrolling Interests	132.1	155.6
Total Equity	7,381.1	7,521.4
Total Liabilities and Equity	$17,438.1	$17,779.1

NOTES TO THE CONSOLIDATED FINANCIAL STATEMENTS (in part)

(Millions of dollars, except for share data)

20. Accumulated Other Comprehensive Loss

The table below summarizes changes in accumulated other comprehensive loss (AOCL), net of tax, attributable to Air Products:

	Net Loss on Derivatives Qualifying as Hedges	Foreign Currency Translation Adjustments	Pension and Postretirement Benefits	Total
Balance at 30 September 2012	$(18.9)	$ (38.8)	$(1,291.1)	$(1,348.8)
Other comprehensive income (loss) before reclassifications	35.0	(25.0)	231.9	241.9
Amounts reclassified from AOCL	(20.2)	.6	104.9	85.3
Net current period other comprehensive income (loss)	$ 14.8	$ (24.4)	$ 336.8	$ 327.2
Amount attributable to noncontrolling interest	—	(1.7)	.7	(1.0)
Balance at 30 September 2013	$ (4.1)	$ (61.5)	$ (955.0)	$(1,020.6)
Other comprehensive income (loss) before reclassifications	(15.2)	(213.1)	(74.2)	(302.5)
Amounts reclassified from AOCL	(9.1)	—	84.7	75.6
Net current period other comprehensive income (loss)	$(24.3)	$(213.1)	$ 10.5	$ (226.9)
Amount attributable to noncontrolling interest	.1	(5.9)	.2	(5.6)
Balance at 30 September 2014	$(28.5)	$(268.7)	$ (944.7)	$(1,241.9)
Other comprehensive income (loss) before reclassifications	(35.0)	(699.3)	(278.5)	(1,012.8)
Amounts reclassified from AOCL	20.8	—	97.0	117.8
Net current period other comprehensive income (loss)	$(14.2)	$(699.3)	$ (181.5)	$ (895.0)
Amount attributable to noncontrolling interest	.2	(11.5)	.3	(11.0)
Balance at 30 September 2015	$(42.9)	$(956.5)	$(1,126.5)	$(2,125.9)

The table below summarizes the reclassifications out of accumulated other comprehensive loss and the affected line item on the consolidated income statements:

	2015	2014	2013
(Gain) Loss on Cash Flow Hedges, net of tax			
Sales/Cost of sales	$ .6	$ .7	$ 1.0
Other income (expense), net	16.9	(8.7)	(21.5)
Interest expense	3.3	(1.1)	.3
Total (Gain) Loss on Cash Flow Hedges, net of tax	$20.8	$ (9.1)	$ (20.2)
Pension and Postretirement Benefits, net of tax[A]	$97.0	$84.7	$104.9
Currency Translation Adjustment[B]	$ —	$ —	$ .6

[A] The components include items such as prior service cost amortization, actuarial loss amortization, and settlements and are reflected in net periodic benefit cost. Refer to Note 16, Retirement Benefits.

[B] The impact is reflected in Income from Discontinued Operations, net of tax.

Income Statement Format

PRESENTATION

3.01 Either a single-step or multi-step format is acceptable for preparing a statement of income. In a single-step format, the operating and non-operating revenues are grouped and totaled and the operating and non-operating expenses are grouped and totaled. Then there is one subtraction of the combined expenses from the combined revenues. In a multi-step format, either costs are deducted from sales to show the gross margin or costs and expenses are deducted from sales to show operating income. The multi-step income statement is divided into two main sections: the operating section and the non-operating sections. Net income should reflect all items of profit and loss recognized during the period, except for certain entities (investment companies, insurance entities, and certain not-for-profit entities) and with the sole exception of error corrections, as discussed in FASB *Accounting Standards Codification* (ASC) 250, *Accounting Changes and Error Corrections*.

3.02 FASB ASC 220, *Comprehensive Income*, requires that comprehensive income and its components be reported in a financial statement. Comprehensive income and its components can be reported in an income statement or a separate statement of comprehensive income.

PRESENTATION AND DISCLOSURE EXCERPT

RECLASSIFICATIONS

3.03 THE WENDY'S COMPANY (DEC)
NOTES TO CONSOLIDATED FINANCIAL STATEMENTS (in part)

(In Thousands Except Per Share Amounts)

(1) Summary of Significant Accounting Policies (in part)

Reclassifications

Certain reclassifications have been made to prior year presentation to conform to the current year presentation.

During the second quarter of 2015, the Company early adopted an amendment requiring debt issuance costs to be presented in the balance sheet as a direct reduction of the related debt liability rather than as an asset. The adoption of this guidance resulted in the reclassification of debt issuance costs of $8,243 from "Other assets" to "Long-term debt" in our consolidated balance sheet as of December 28, 2014. Refer to Note 12 and "New Accounting Standards Adopted" below for further information.

Prior to fiscal 2015, the Company reported its system optimization initiative as a discrete event and separately included the related gain or loss on sales of restaurants, impairment losses and other associated costs, along with other restructuring initiatives, in "Facilities action (income) charges, net." In February 2015, the Company announced plans to reduce its ongoing company-owned restaurant ownership to approximately 5% of the total system and further emphasized that restaurant dispositions and acquisitions are a continuous and integrated part of the overall strategy to optimize its restaurant portfolio. As a result, commencing with the first quarter of 2015, all gains and losses on dispositions are included on a separate line in our consolidated statements of operations, "System optimization gains, net" and impairment losses recorded in connection with the sale or anticipated sale of restaurants ("System Optimization Remeasurement") are reclassified to "Impairment of long-lived assets." In addition, the Company retitled the line, "Facilities action (income) charges, net" to "Reorganization and realignment costs" in our consolidated statements of operations to better describe the current and historical initiatives included given the reclassifications described above. The Company believes the new presentation will aid users in understanding its results of operations. The prior periods reflect reclassifications to conform to the current year presentation. All amounts being reclassified in our statements of operations were separately disclosed in the notes to our consolidated financial statements included in our Annual Report on Form 10-K for the fiscal year ended December 28, 2014. Such reclassifications had no impact on operating profit, net income or net income per share.

The following table illustrates the reclassifications made to the consolidated statements of operations for the years ended December 28, 2014 and December 29, 2013:

	As Previously Reported[b]	Year Ended December 28, 2014 Reclassifications Gain on Dispositions, Net[c]	System Optimization Remeasurement[d]	As Currently Reported
System optimization gains, net	$ —	$(91,510)	$ —	$(91,510)
Reorganization and realignment costs[a]	(29,100)	69,631	(8,628)	31,903
Impairment of long-lived assets	10,985	—	8,628	19,613
Other operating expense, net	4,329	21,879	—	26,208
	$(13,786)	$ —	$ —	$(13,786)

	As Previously Reported[b]	Year Ended December 29, 2013 Reclassifications Gain on Dispositions, Net[c]	System Optimization Remeasurement[d]	As Currently Reported
System optimization gains, net	$ —	$(51,276)	$ —	$(51,276)
Reorganization and realignment costs[a]	10,856	46,667	(20,506)	37,017
Impairment of long-lived assets	15,879	—	20,506	36,385
Other operating expense, net	341	4,609	—	4,950
	$27,076	$ —	$ —	$ 27,076

[a] Previously titled "Facilities action (income) charges, net."

[b] "As Previously Reported," reflects adjustments to reclassify the Bakery's other operating income, net of $65 and $96 from "Other operating expense, net" to "Income (loss) from discontinued operations, net of income taxes."

[c] Reclassified the gain on sales of restaurants, net, previously included in "Facilities action (income) charges, net" and the gain on disposal of assets, net, which included sales of restaurants and other assets, and was previously reported in "Other operating expense, net" to a separate line in our consolidated statements of operations, "System optimization gains, net."

[d] Reclassified impairment losses recorded in connection with the sale or anticipated sale of restaurants ("System Optimization Remeasurement"), previously included in "Facilities action charges (income), net" to "Impairment of long-lived assets."

Derivative Instruments

The Company used interest rate swap agreements to manage its exposure to changes in interest rates as well as to maintain an appropriate mix of fixed and variable rate debt. In May 2015, the Company terminated its floating to fixed interest rate swap agreements which were accounted for as cash flow hedges. Changes in the fair value of the cash flow hedging instruments were recorded as an adjustment to "Accumulated other comprehensive loss" to the extent of the effectiveness of such hedging instruments and subsequently reclassified into "Interest expense" in the period that the hedged forecasted transaction affects earnings. In October 2013, the Company terminated its fixed to floating interest rate swap agreements which were accounted for as fair value hedges. Changes in the fair value of fair value hedging instruments were recorded as an adjustment to the underlying debt balance being hedged to the extent of the effectiveness of such hedging instruments. There was no ineffectiveness from the fair value hedges through their termination.

(3) System Optimization Gains, Net

In July 2013, the Company announced a system optimization initiative, as part of its brand transformation, which includes a shift from company-owned restaurants to franchised restaurants over time, through acquisitions and dispositions, as well as helping to facilitate franchisee-to-franchisee restaurant transfers. In February 2015, the Company announced plans to sell approximately 540 additional restaurants to franchisees and reduce its ongoing company-owned restaurant ownership to approximately 5% of the total system by the end of 2016. During 2015, 2014 and 2013, the Company completed the sale of 327, 255 and 244 company-owned restaurants to franchisees, respectively, which included the sale of all of its company-owned restaurants in Canada. In addition, during 2015 the Company helped facilitate the transfer of 71 restaurants between franchisees. The Company expects to complete its plan to reduce its company-owned restaurant ownership to approximately 5% with the sale of approximately 315 restaurants during 2016, of which 99 restaurants were classified as held for sale as of January 3, 2016.

Gains and losses recognized on dispositions are recorded to "System optimization gains, net" in our consolidated statements of operations. Costs related to our system optimization initiative are recorded to "Reorganization and realignment costs," and include severance and employee related costs, professional fees and other associated costs, which are further described in Note 5.

The following is a summary of the disposition activity recorded as a result of our system optimization initiative:

	Year Ended		
	2015	2014[a][b]	2013[a]
Number of restaurants sold to franchisees	327	237	244
Proceeds from sales of restaurants	$193,860	$128,292	$130,154
Net assets sold[c]	(86,493)	(53,043)	(60,895)
Goodwill related to sales of restaurants	(29,970)	(18,032)	(20,578)
Net (unfavorable) favorable leases[d]	(846)	34,335	(57)
Other[e]	(5,499)	(5,692)	(1,957)
	71,052	85,860	46,667
Post-closing adjustments on sales of restaurants[f]	1,285	(1,280)	—
Gain on sales of restaurants, net	72,337	84,580	46,667
Gain on sales of other assets, net[g]	1,672	5,089	4,609
System optimization gains, net	$ 74,009	$ 89,669	$ 51,276

[a] Reclassifications have been made to the prior year presentation to include sales of restaurants previously reported in "Other operating expense, net" to conform to the current year presentation. Reclassifications have also been made to reflect the Bakery's gain on sales of other assets as discontinued operations. See Note 1 for further details.

[b] In addition, during 2014 Wendy's acquired and immediately sold 18 restaurants to a franchisee for cash proceeds of $15,779 and recognized a gain on sale of $1,841. No goodwill was recognized on this acquisition and as a result no goodwill was allocated to the sale. See Note 4 for further details.

[c] Net assets sold consisted primarily of cash, inventory and equipment.

[d] During 2015, 2014 and 2013, the Company recorded favorable lease assets of $34,437, $63,120 and $37,749, respectively, and unfavorable lease liabilities of $35,283, $28,785 and $37,806, respectively, as a result of leasing and/or subleasing land, buildings, and/or leasehold improvements to franchisees, in connection with sales of restaurants.

[e] 2015 includes a deferred gain of $4,568 on the sale of 17 restaurants to franchisees during 2015 as a result of certain contingencies related to the extension of lease terms. 2014 includes a deferred gain of $1,995 (C$2,300) on the sale of eight Canadian restaurants to a franchisee as a result of Wendy's providing a guarantee to a lender on behalf of the franchisee. See Note 21 for further information on the guarantee.

[f] During 2015, notes receivable from franchisees received in connection with sales of restaurants in 2014 were repaid and as a result, we recognized the related gain on the sales of restaurants of $4,492.

[g] During 2015, 2014 and 2013, Wendy's received cash proceeds of $10,478, $17,263 and $18,844, respectively, primarily from the sale of surplus properties as well as from the sale of a company-owned aircraft during 2014 and franchisees exercising options to purchase previously leased properties in 2013.

Assets Held for Sale

	January 3, 2016	December 28, 2014[a]
Number of restaurants classified as held for sale	99	106
Net restaurant assets held for sale[b]	$50,262	$25,266
Other assets held for sale[b]	$ 7,124	$13,469

[a] Reclassifications have been made to the prior year presentation to include restaurants previously excluded from our system optimization initiative to conform to the current year presentation. See Note 1 for further details.

[b] Net restaurant assets held for sale include company-owned restaurants and consist primarily of cash, inventory, equipment and an estimate of allocable goodwill. Other assets held for sale primarily consist of surplus properties. Assets held for sale are included in "Prepaid expenses and other current assets."

Subsequent to January 3, 2016, the Company completed the sale of certain assets used in the operation of 17 Wendy's company-owned restaurants for cash proceeds of approximately $7,900, subject to customary purchase price adjustments.

(13) Fair Value Measurements (in part)

Derivative Instruments (in part)

The Company's primary objective for entering into interest rate swap agreements was to manage its exposure to changes in interest rates, as well as to maintain an appropriate mix of fixed and variable rate debt.

Our derivative instruments for the periods presented included seven forward starting interest rate swaps designated as cash flow hedges to change the floating rate interest payments associated with $350,000 and $100,000 in borrowings under the Term A Loans and Term B Loans, respectively, to fixed rate interest payments beginning June 30, 2015 and maturing on December 31, 2017. In May 2015, the Company terminated these interest rate swaps and paid $7,275, which was recorded against the derivative liability. In addition, the Company incurred $62 in fees to terminate the interest rate swaps which was included in "Loss on early extinguishment of debt." See Note 12 for further information. The unrealized loss on the cash flow hedges at termination of $7,275 is being reclassified on a straight-line basis from "Accumulated other comprehensive loss" to "Interest expense" beginning June 30, 2015, the original effective date of the interest rate swaps through December 31, 2017, the original maturity date of the interest rate swaps. As a result, the year ended January 3, 2016 includes the reclassification of unrealized losses on the cash flow hedges of $1,487 from "Accumulated other comprehensive loss" to "Interest expense."

(15) Stockholders' Equity (in part)

Accumulated Other Comprehensive Loss

The following table provides a rollforward of the components of accumulated other comprehensive income (loss) attributable to The Wendy's Company, net of tax as applicable:

	Foreign Currency Translation	Cash Flow Hedges[a]	Pension	Total
Balance at December 30, 2012	$ 7,197	$ —	$(1,216)	$ 5,981
Current-period other comprehensive (loss) income	(17,000)	744	(62)	(16,318)
Balance at December 29, 2013	(9,803)	744	(1,278)	(10,337)
Current-period other comprehensive (loss) income	(18,560)	(2,788)	391	(20,957)
Balance at December 28, 2014	(28,363)	(2,044)	(887)	(31,294)
Current-period other comprehensive (loss) income	(37,800)	(1,527)	(202)	(39,529)
Balance at January 3, 2016	$(66,163)	$(3,571)	$(1,089)	$(70,823)

[a] Current-period other comprehensive (loss) income includes the effect of changes in unrealized losses on cash flow hedges, net of tax, for all periods presented. In addition, 2015 includes the reclassification of unrealized losses on cash flow hedges of $915 from "Accumulated other comprehensive loss" to our consolidated statements of operations consisting of $1,487 recorded to "Interest expense," net of the related income tax benefit of $572 recorded to "Provision for income taxes." See Note 13 for more information.

The cumulative gains and losses on these items are included in "Accumulated other comprehensive loss" in the consolidated balance sheets and consolidated statements of stockholders' equity.

Revenues and Gains

Author's Note

In May 2014, FASB issued Accounting Standards Update (ASU) No. 2014-09, *Revenue from Contracts with Customers (Topic 606)*, which creates FASB ASC 606, *Revenue from Contracts with Customers*, and supersedes the revenue recognition requirements in FASB ASC 605, *Revenue Recognition*, including most industry-specific revenue recognition guidance throughout the industry topics of the codification. In addition, the ASU supersedes some cost guidance in FASB ASC 605-35 and creates FASB ASC 340-40. The core principle of FASB ASC 606 is that an entity recognizes revenue to depict the transfer of promised goods or services to customers in an amount that reflects the consideration to which the entity expects to be entitled in exchange for those goods or services. Entities are required to apply the amendments in this ASU for annual reporting periods beginning after December 15, 2016, including interim periods within that reporting period. Early adoption is not permitted. For nonpublic entities, the amendments are effective for annual reporting periods beginning after December 15, 2017, and interim periods within annual periods beginning after December 15, 2018 . A nonpublic entity may elect to apply this guidance earlier, however only as of the following:

1. An annual reporting period beginning after December 15, 2016, including interim periods within that reporting period
2. An annual reporting period beginning after December 15, 2016, and interim periods within annual periods beginning after December 15, 2017
3. An annual reporting period beginning after December 15, 2017, including interim periods within that reporting period.

Given the effective date of this ASU, no survey entity will have adopted these requirements in its 2015 financial statements.

In September 2015, FASB issued ASU No. 2015-16, *Business Combinations (Topic 805): Simplifying the Accounting for Measurement-Period Adjustments*. The amendments in this ASU require an entity to present separately on the face of the income statement or disclose in the notes the portion of the amount recorded in current-period earnings by line item that would have been recorded in previous reporting periods if the adjustment to the provisional amounts had been recognized as of the acquisition date. For public business entities, the amendments in this ASU are effective for fiscal years beginning after December 15, 2015, including interim periods within those fiscal years. For all other entities, the amendments in this ASU are effective for fiscal years beginning after December 15, 2016, and interim periods within fiscal years beginning after December 15, 2017. The amendments in this ASU should be applied prospectively to adjustments to provisional amounts that occur after the effective date of this ASU with earlier application permitted for financial statements that have not yet been made available for issuance. Given the effective date of this ASU, no survey entity will have adopted these requirements in its 2015 financial statements.

RECOGNITION AND MEASUREMENT

3.04 As explained by FASB ASC 605-10-25-1, the recognition of revenue and gains of an entity during a period involves consideration of the following two factors, with sometimes one and sometimes the other being the more important consideration:

- *Being realized or realizable.* Revenue and gains generally are not recognized until realized or realizable. Paragraph 83(a) of FASB Concepts Statement No. 5, *Recognition and Measurement in Financial Statements of Business Enterprises,* states that revenue and gains are realized when products (goods or services), merchandise, or other assets are exchanged for cash or claims to cash. That paragraph states that revenue and gains are realizable when related assets received or held are readily convertible to known amounts of cash or claims to cash.
- *Being earned.* Paragraph 83(b) of FASB Concepts Statement No. 5 states that revenue is not recognized until earned. That paragraph states that an entity's revenue-earning activities involve delivering or producing goods, rendering services, or other activities that constitute its ongoing major or central operations, and revenues are considered to have been earned when the entity has substantially accomplished what it must do to be entitled to the benefits represented by the revenues. That paragraph states that gains commonly result from transactions and other events that involve no earning process, and for recognizing gains, being earned is generally less significant than being realized or realizable.

3.05 FASB ASC 605-25 contains guidance on segmenting of transactions, referred to as *multiple element arrangements,* for both recognition and measurement. FASB ASC 605-25-25-2 requires that an entity divide revenue arrangements with multiple deliverables into separate units of accounting if both the delivered item(s) have value to the customer on a standalone basis and, if the arrangement includes a general right of return, delivery or performance of the undelivered item(s) is probable and substantially in the vendor's control. FASB ASC 605-25-30-2 requires an entity to allocate the arrangement consideration at the inception of the arrangement to all deliverables based on their relative selling price (relative selling price method), except when another Topic in the FASB ASC requires a unit of accounting in the arrangement to be recorded at fair value or the amount that can be allocated to a unit of accounting is limited to an amount that is not contingent on delivery of additional deliverables or specified performance conditions. When a vendor applies the relative selling price method, an entity should determine the selling price using vendor-specific objective evidence of selling price, if it exists. Otherwise, the vendor should use its best estimate of selling price for that deliverable. Vendors should not ignore information that is reasonably available without undue cost and effort.

DISCLOSURE

3.06 FASB ASC 605-25-50 requires an entity to provide specific disclosures regarding multiple element arrangements, including the accounting policy for such arrangements (for example, whether deliverables are separable into units of accounting) and the nature of such arrangements (for example, provisions for performance, termination, or cancellation of the arrangements). FASB ASC 605-25-50-1 explains that the objective of the disclosure guidance is to provide both qualitative and quantitative information about a vendor's revenue arrangements and about the significant judgments made about the application of FASB ASC 605-25, changes in those judgments, or the application of FASB ASC 605-25 that may significantly affect the timing or amount of revenue recognition. Therefore, in addition to the required disclosures, a vendor shall also disclose other qualitative and quantitative information as necessary to comply with this objective. FASB ASC 605-25-50-2 requires a vendor to disclose specific information by similar arrangements including the nature of multiple deliverable arrangements; significant deliverables and the general timing of delivery or performance of service; contract provisions including performance, termination, and refund-type; discussion of significant factors, inputs, assumptions, and methods used to determine selling price; information about whether significant deliverables qualify as separate units of accounting; general timing of revenue recognition for significant deliverables; and effects of changes in selling price or methods for determining selling price.

PRESENTATION AND DISCLOSURE EXCERPTS

REVENUES

3.07 ANN INC. (JAN)
CONSOLIDATED STATEMENTS OF OPERATIONS (in part)

	Fiscal Year Ended		
(In thousands, except per share amounts)	**January 31, 2015**	**February 1, 2014**	**February 2, 2013**
Net sales	$2,533,460	$2,493,491	$2,375,509
Cost of sales	1,242,506	1,150,183	1,073,167
Gross margin	1,290,954	1,343,308	1,302,342
Selling, general and administrative expenses	1,161,838	1,173,234	1,135,551
Restructuring charge	17,303	—	—
Operating income	111,813	170,074	166,791

1. Summary of Significant Accounting Policies (in part)

Revenue Recognition

The Company records revenue as merchandise is sold to clients. Sales from the Company's Websites are recorded as merchandise is shipped to clients based on the date clients receive the merchandise. Amounts related to shipping and handling billed to clients in a sales transaction are classified as revenue and the costs related to shipping product to clients (billed and accrued) are classified as Cost of sales. A reserve for estimated returns is established when sales are recorded based upon an analysis of actual historical returns and current sales and gross margin rate performance. The Company excludes sales taxes collected from clients from "Net sales" in its Consolidated Statements of Operations.

The following table sets forth certain product-level sales information for the past three fiscal years:

	Fiscal Year Ended					
	January 31, 2015		February 1, 2014		February 2, 2013	
($ in thousands)	Sales	% of Sales	Sales	% of Sales	Sales	% of Sales
Apparel	$2,253,994	89%	$2,244,618	90%	$2,146,173	90%
Accessories	171,564	7%	164,897	7%	157,852	7%
Shoes	44,207	2%	44,536	2%	44,331	2%
Other	63,695	2%	39,440	1%	27,153	1%
Total	$2,533,460	100%	$2,493,491	100%	$2,375,509	100%

Gift cards and merchandise credits issued by the Company do not have expiration dates and the Company honors all gift cards and merchandise credits presented by clients, regardless of the length of time that passes from issuance to redemption. The Company records a liability for unredeemed gift cards and merchandise credits at the time gift cards are sold or merchandise credits are issued. The Company recognizes revenue and relieves the corresponding gift card and/or merchandise credit liability when the cards are redeemed by clients.

In cases where the Company has determined that it has a legal obligation to remit the value of unredeemed gift cards and merchandise credits to any state, the value of these cards is escheated to the appropriate state in accordance with that state's unclaimed property laws. In certain jurisdictions, the Company is permitted to retain a portion of the escheated value of unredeemed gift cards and merchandise credits, which is immaterial and is recorded in "Net sales" in the Company's Consolidated Statements of Operations.

In cases where the Company has determined that, under applicable state unclaimed property laws, there is no legal obligation to escheat the value of unredeemed gift cards and merchandise credits and the likelihood of redemption is considered remote, the Company recognizes the unredeemed value of gift cards and merchandise credits as revenue over time based upon an analysis of actual historical redemption patterns. In Fiscal 2014, Fiscal 2013 and Fiscal 2012, the Company recognized $1.2 million, $2.1 million and $6.6 million in gift card and merchandise credit "breakage," respectively, which is included in Net sales in the Company's Consolidated Statements of Operations. Fiscal 2012 was the first period during which the Company recognized gift card and merchandise credit breakage, and therefore included the breakage income related to gift cards sold and merchandise credits issued since inception of these programs.

The Company has a credit card program that offers eligible clients in the U.S. the choice of a private label or co-branded credit card. All cardholders are automatically enrolled in the exclusive rewards program, which is designed to recognize and promote client loyalty. The Company provides the sponsoring bank with marketing support of the program, and uses its sales force to process credit card applications for both the private label and co-branded credit cards. On December 2, 2013, the Company entered into an eight-year agreement with the sponsoring bank, which amended and restated the original agreement that began in October 2008. As with the original agreement, the Company received an upfront signing bonus from the sponsoring bank and also receives ongoing payments for new accounts activated as well as a share of finance charges collected by the sponsoring bank. These revenue streams are accounted for as a single unit of accounting and accordingly, are recognized as revenue ratably based on the total projected revenues over the term of the agreement.

Certain judgments and estimates underlie the Company's projected revenues and related expenses under the credit card program, including projected future store counts, the number of applications processed, the Company's projected sales growth and points breakage, among other things. During Fiscal 2014, Fiscal 2013 and Fiscal 2012, the Company recognized approximately $47.1 million, $18.8 million, and $17.8 million of revenue related to the credit card program, respectively. Partially offsetting this revenue are costs, net of points breakage, related to the client loyalty program. These costs are included in either "Cost of sales" or in "Net sales" as a sales discount, as appropriate. The cost of sales impact was approximately $12.0 million, $5.2 million and $5.7 million and the sales discount impact was approximately $20.0 million, $6.8 million and $6.8 million in Fiscal 2014, Fiscal 2013 and Fiscal 2012, respectively.

The Company recognizes revenue generated from its franchise operations in Mexico on a net basis, since it operates as an agent and receives a percentage of the franchise partner's net merchandise sales. Revenue recognized from franchise operations during Fiscal 2014, the first year of such operations, was immaterial and is included in "Net sales" in the Company's Consolidated Statements of Operations.

Recent Accounting Pronouncements

In May 2014, the Financial Accounting Standards Board issued Accounting Standard Update ("ASU") 2014-09, "*Revenue from Contracts with Customers*," which supersedes the revenue recognition requirements in Accounting Standards Codification ("ASC") 605, "*Revenue Recognition*," as well as various other sections of the ASC, such as, but not limited to, ASC 340-20, "*Other Assets and Deferred Costs-Capitalized Advertising Costs.*" The core principle of ASU 2014-09 is that an entity should recognize revenue in a way that depicts the transfer of promised goods or services to customers in an amount that reflects the consideration to which the entity expects to be entitled in exchange for those goods or services. ASU 2014-09 also includes a cohesive set of disclosure requirements that would result in an entity providing users of financial statements with comprehensive information about the nature, amount, timing and uncertainty of revenue and cash flows arising from the entity's contracts with customers. ASU 2014-09 is effective for fiscal years, and interim periods within those years, beginning after December 15, 2016, and is to be applied either retrospectively to each prior reporting period presented or with the cumulative effect recognized at the date of initial adoption as an adjustment to the opening balance of retained earnings (or other appropriate components of equity or net assets on the balance sheet). Early adoption is not permitted. The Company is in the process of evaluating ASU 2014-09, including the choice of retrospective application upon adoption, and does not currently anticipate it will have a material impact on the Company's Consolidated Financial Statements.

3.08 TEREX CORPORATION (DEC)
CONSOLIDATED STATEMENT OF INCOME (in part)

(In millions, except per share data)

	Year Ended December 31,		
	2015	**2014**	**2013**
Net sales	$ 6,543.1	$ 7,308.9	$ 7,084.0
Cost of goods sold	(5,234.6)	(5,855.4)	(5,644.5)
Gross profit	1,308.5	1,453.5	1,439.5
Selling, general and administrative expenses	(918.6)	(1,030.4)	(1,020.4)
Goodwill and intangible asset impairment	(34.7)	—	—
Income (loss) from operations	355.2	423.1	419.1

NOTES TO CONSOLIDATED FINANCIAL STATEMENTS (in part)

(Dollar amounts in millions, unless otherwise noted, except per share amounts)

Note B—Basis of Presentation (in part)

Revenue Recognition. Revenue and related costs are generally recorded when products are shipped and invoiced to either independently owned and operated dealers or to end-customers.

Revenue generated in the United States is recognized when title and risk of loss pass from the Company to its customers which generally occurs upon shipment depending upon the shipping terms negotiated. The Company also has a policy which requires it to meet certain criteria in order to recognize revenue, including satisfaction of the following requirements:

a) Persuasive evidence that an arrangement exists;
b) The price to the buyer is fixed or determinable;
c) Collectability is reasonably assured; and
d) The Company has no significant obligations for future performance.

In the United States, the Company has the ability to enter into a security agreement and receive a security interest in the product by filing an appropriate Uniform Commercial Code ("UCC") financing statement. However, a significant portion of the Company's revenue is generated outside of the United States. In many countries outside of the United States, as a matter of statutory law, a seller retains title to a product until payment is made. The laws do not provide for a seller's retention of a security interest in goods in the same manner as established in the UCC. In these countries, the Company retains title to goods delivered to a customer until the customer makes payment so that the Company can recover the goods in the event of customer default on payment. In these circumstances, where the Company only retains title to secure its recovery in the event of customer default, the Company also has a policy requiring it to meet certain criteria in order to recognize revenue, including satisfaction of the following requirements:

a) Persuasive evidence that an arrangement exists;
b) Delivery has occurred or services have been rendered;
c) The price to the buyer is fixed or determinable;
d) Collectability is reasonably assured;
e) The Company has no significant obligations for future performance; and
f) The Company is not entitled to direct the disposition of the goods, cannot rescind the transaction, cannot prohibit the customer from moving, selling, or otherwise using the goods in the ordinary course of business and has no other rights of holding title that rest with a titleholder of property that is subject to a lien under the UCC.

In circumstances where the sales transaction requires acceptance by the customer for items such as testing on site, installation, trial period or performance criteria, revenue is not recognized unless the following criteria have been met:

a) Persuasive evidence that an arrangement exists;
b) Delivery has occurred or services have been rendered;
c) The price to the buyer is fixed or determinable;
d) Collectability is reasonably assured; and
e) The customer has given their acceptance, the time period has elapsed or the Company has otherwise objectively demonstrated that the criteria specified in the acceptance provisions have been satisfied.

In addition to performance commitments, the Company analyzes factors such as the reason for the purchase to determine if revenue should be recognized. This analysis is done before the product is shipped and includes the evaluation of factors that may affect the conclusion related to the revenue recognition criteria as follows:

a) Persuasive evidence that an arrangement exists;
b) Delivery has occurred or services have been rendered;
c) The price to the buyer is fixed or determinable; and
d) Collectability is reasonably assured.

Revenue from sales-type leases is recognized at the inception of the lease. Income from operating leases is recognized ratably over the term of the lease. The Company routinely sells equipment subject to operating leases and the related lease payments. If the Company does not retain a substantial risk of ownership in the equipment, the transaction is recorded as a sale. If the Company does retain a substantial risk of ownership, the transaction is recorded as a borrowing, the operating lease payments are recognized as revenue over the term of the lease and the debt is amortized over a similar period.

The Company, from time to time, issues buyback guarantees in conjunction with certain sales agreements. These primarily relate to trade value agreements ("TVAs") in which a customer may trade in equipment in the future at a stated price/credit if the customer meets certain conditions. The trade-in price/credit is determined at the time of the original sale of equipment. In conjunction with the trade-in, these conditions include a requirement to purchase new equipment at fair market value at the time of trade-in, which fair value is required to be of equal or greater value than the original equipment cost. Other conditions also include the general functionality and state of repair of the machine. The Company has concluded that any credit provided to customers under a TVA/buyback guarantee, which is expected to be equal to or less than the fair value of the equipment returned on the trade-in date, is a guarantee to be accounted for in accordance with Accounting Standards Codification ("ASC") 460, "Guarantees" ("ASC 460").

The original sale of equipment, accompanied by a buyback guarantee, is a multiple element transaction wherein the Company offers its customer the right, after some period of time, for a limited period of time, to exchange purchased equipment for a fixed price trade-in credit toward another of our products. The fixed price trade-in credit is accounted for under the guidance provided by ASC 460. Pursuant to this right, the Company has agreed to make a payment (in the form of a trade-in credit) to the customer contingent upon the customer exercising its right to trade in the original purchased equipment. Under the guidance of ASC 460, the Company records the fixed price trade-in credit at its fair value. Accordingly, as noted above, the Company has accounted for the trade-in credit as a separate deliverable in a multiple element arrangement.

When a sales transaction includes multiple deliverables, such as sales of multiple products or sales of products and services that are delivered over multiple reporting periods, the multiple deliverables are evaluated to determine the units of accounting, and the entire fee from the arrangement is allocated to each unit of accounting based on the relative selling price. The selling price of a unit of accounting is determined using a selling price hierarchy. Vendor-specific objective evidence ("VSOE") is established based upon the price charged for products and services that are sold separately in standalone transactions. If VSOE cannot be established, third-party evidence ("TPE") is evaluated based on competitor prices for similar deliverables when sold separately. If neither VSOE or TPE is available, management's best estimate of selling price is established based upon the price at which the Company would sell the product on a standalone basis taking into consideration factors including, but not limited to, internal costs, gross margin objectives, pricing practices and market conditions. Revenue is recognized when the revenue recognition criteria for each unit of accounting are met.

Recent Accounting Pronouncements (in part). In May 2014, the Financial Accounting Standards Board ("FASB") issued Accounting Standards Update ("ASU") 2014-09, "Revenue from Contracts with Customers," ("ASU 2014-09"). ASU 2014-09 outlines a new, single comprehensive model for entities to use in accounting for revenue arising from contracts with customers and supersedes most current revenue recognition guidance, including industry-specific guidance. This new revenue recognition model provides a five-step analysis in determining when and how revenue is recognized. The new model will require revenue recognition to depict the transfer of promised goods or services to customers in an amount that reflects the consideration a company expects to receive in exchange for those goods or services. The ASU also requires additional disclosure about the nature, amount, timing and uncertainty of revenue and cash flows arising from customer contracts, including significant judgments and changes in judgments and assets recognized from costs incurred to obtain or fulfill a contract. In August 2015, the FASB issued ASU 2015-14, Deferral of the Effective Date, which amends ASU 2014-09. As a result, the effective date will be the first quarter of fiscal year 2018 with early adoption permitted in the first quarter of fiscal year 2017. The adoption will use one of two retrospective application methods. The Company is evaluating the impact that adoption of this new standard will have on its consolidated financial statements and footnote disclosures.

NET INVESTMENT GAINS

3.09 METLIFE, INC. (DEC)
CONSOLIDATED STATEMENTS OF OPERATIONS (in part)

(In millions, except per share data)

	2015	2014	2013
Revenues			
Premiums	$38,545	$39,067	$37,674
Universal life and investment-type product policy fees	9,507	9,946	9,451
Net investment income	19,281	21,153	22,232
Other revenues	1,983	2,030	1,920
Net investment gains (losses):			
Other-than-temporary impairments on fixed maturity securities	(84)	(43)	(106)
Other-than-temporary impairments on fixed maturity securities transferred to other comprehensive income (loss)	(6)	(17)	(60)
Other net investment gains (losses)	687	(137)	327
Total net investment gains (losses)	597	(197)	161
Net derivative gains (losses)	38	1,317	(3,239)
Total revenues	69,951	73,316	68,199

NOTES TO THE CONSOLIDATED FINANCIAL STATEMENTS (in part)

1. Business, Basis of Presentation and Summary of Significant Accounting Policies (in part)

Investments (in part)

Net Investment Income and Net Investment Gains (Losses)

Income from investments is reported within net investment income, unless otherwise stated herein. Gains and losses on sales of investments, impairment losses and changes in valuation allowances are reported within net investment gains (losses), unless otherwise stated herein.

Fixed Maturity and Equity Securities (in part)

The majority of the Company's fixed maturity and equity securities are classified as available-for-sale ("AFS") and are reported at their estimated fair value. Unrealized investment gains and losses on these securities are recorded as a separate component of other comprehensive income (loss) ("OCI"), net of policy-related amounts and deferred income taxes. All security transactions are recorded on a trade date basis. Investment gains and losses on sales are determined on a specific identification basis.

FVO and Trading Securities

FVO and trading securities are stated at estimated fair value and include investments for which the FVO has been elected ("FVO Securities") and investments that are actively purchased and sold ("Actively traded securities"). FVO Securities include:

- fixed maturity and equity securities held-for-investment by the general account to support asset and liability management strategies for certain insurance products and investments in certain separate accounts ("FVO general account securities"); and
- contractholder-directed investments supporting unit-linked variable annuity type liabilities which do not qualify for presentation and reporting as separate account summary total assets and liabilities. These investments are primarily mutual funds and, to a lesser extent, fixed maturity and equity securities, short-term investments and cash and cash equivalents. The investment returns on these investments inure to contractholders and are offset by a corresponding change in Policyholder account balances through interest credited to policyholder account balances ("FVO contractholder-directed unit-linked investments").

Actively traded securities principally include fixed maturity securities and short sale agreement liabilities, which are included in other liabilities.

Changes in estimated fair value of these securities are included in net investment income, except for certain securities included in FVO Securities where changes are included in net investment gains (losses).

Mortgage Loans Held-For-Investment

Mortgage loans held-for-investment are stated at unpaid principal balance, adjusted for any unamortized premium or discount, deferred fees or expenses, and are net of valuation allowances. Interest income and prepayment fees are recognized when earned. Interest income is recognized using an effective yield method giving effect to amortization of premiums and accretion of discounts.

Also included in mortgage loans held-for-investment are commercial mortgage loans held by consolidated securitization entities ("CSEs") and residential mortgage loans for which the FVO was elected, which are stated at estimated fair value. Changes in estimated fair value are recognized in net investment gains (losses) for commercial mortgage loans held by CSEs—FVO, and net investment income for residential mortgage loans—FVO.

Foreign Currency

Assets, liabilities and operations of foreign affiliates and subsidiaries are recorded based on the functional currency of each entity. The determination of the functional currency is made based on the appropriate economic and management indicators. For most of the Company's foreign operations, the local currency is the functional currency. For certain other foreign operations, such as Japan, the local currency and one or more other currencies qualify as functional currencies. Assets and liabilities of foreign affiliates and subsidiaries are translated from the functional currency to U.S. dollars at the exchange rates in effect at each year-end and revenues and expenses are translated at the average exchange rates during the year. The resulting translation adjustments are charged or credited directly to OCI, net of applicable taxes. Gains and losses from foreign currency transactions, including the effect of re-measurement of monetary assets and liabilities to the appropriate functional currency, are reported as part of net investment gains (losses) in the period in which they occur.

8. Investments (in part)

Net Investment Gains (Losses)

Components of Net Investment Gains (Losses)

The components of net investment gains (losses) were as follows:

(In millions)	Years Ended December 31,		
	2015	2014	2013
Total gains (losses) on fixed maturity securities:			
Total OTTI losses recognized—by sector and industry:			
U.S. and foreign corporate securities—by industry:			
Consumer	$ (28)	$ (7)	$ (11)
Utility	(21)	—	(48)
Industrial	(5)	—	—

(continued)

(In millions)	Years Ended December 31,		
	2015	**2014**	**2013**
Transportation	—	(2)	(3)
Finance	—	—	(10)
Communications	—	—	(2)
Total U.S. and foreign corporate securities	(54)	(9)	(74)
RMBS	(30)	(31)	(80)
CMBS	—	(13)	(12)
ABS	—	(7)	—
State and political subdivision	(6)	—	—
OTTI losses on fixed maturity securities recognized in earnings	(90)	(60)	(166)
Fixed maturity securities—net gains (losses) on sales and disposals	204	598	561
Total gains (losses) on fixed maturity securities	114	538	395
Total gains (losses) on equity securities:			
Total OTTI losses recognized—by sector:			
Common stock	(39)	(13)	(6)
Non-redeemable preferred stock	(1)	(23)	(20)
OTTI losses on equity securities recognized in earnings	(40)	(36)	(26)
Equity securities—net gains (losses) on sales and disposals	61	101	31
Total gains (losses) on equity securities	21	65	5
FVO and trading securities—FVO general account securities	—	9	15
Mortgage loans	(105)	(36)	22
Real estate and real estate joint ventures	531	222	(19)
Other limited partnership interests	(67)	(78)	(48)
Other	(6)	(110)	22
Subtotal	488	610	392
FVO CSEs:			
Commercial mortgage loans	(7)	(13)	(52)
Securities	—	—	2
Long-term debt—related to commercial mortgage loans	4	19	85
Long-term debt—related to securities	—	(1)	(2)
Non-investment portfolio gains (losses)[1]	112	(812)	(264)
Subtotal	109	(807)	(231)
Total net investment gains (losses)	$ 597	$(197)	$ 161

[1] Non-investment portfolio gains (losses) for the year ended December 31, 2014 includes a loss of $633 million related to the disposition of MAL as more fully described in Note 3.

See "—Variable Interest Entities" for discussion of CSEs.

Gains (losses) from foreign currency transactions included within net investment gains (losses) were $46 million, ($183) million and $171 million for the years ended December 31, 2015, 2014 and 2013, respectively.

Sales or Disposals and Impairments of Fixed Maturity and Equity Securities

Investment gains and losses on sales of securities are determined on a specific identification basis. Proceeds from sales or disposals of fixed maturity and equity securities and the components of fixed maturity and equity securities net investment gains (losses) were as shown in the table below.

(In millions)	Years Ended December 31,					
	2015	**2014**	**2013**	**2015**	**2014**	**2013**
	Fixed Maturity Securities			**Equity Securities**		
Proceeds	$115,395	$82,075	$76,070	$358	$544	$746
Gross investment gains	$ 1,262	$ 1,165	$ 1,326	$ 99	$112	$ 56
Gross investment losses	(1,058)	(567)	(765)	(38)	(11)	(25)
OTTI losses	(90)	(60)	(166)	(40)	(36)	(26)
Net investment gains (losses)	$ 114	$ 538	$ 395	$ 21	$ 65	$ 5

3.10 CUMMINS INC. (DEC)

CONSOLIDATED STATEMENTS OF INCOME (in part)

In millions, except per share amounts	Years Ended December 31,		
	2015	2014	2013
Net Sales (a)	$19,110	$19,221	$17,301
Cost of sales	14,163	14,360	13,021
Gross Margin	4,947	4,861	4,280
Operating Expenses And Income			
Selling, general and administrative expenses	2,092	2,095	1,817
Research, development and engineering expenses	735	754	713
Equity, royalty and interest income from investees (Note 2)	315	370	361
Impairment of light-duty diesel assets (Note 3)	211	—	—
Restructuring actions and other charges (Note 4)	90	—	—
Other operating expense, net	(77)	(17)	(10)
Operating Income	2,057	2,365	2,101

NOTES TO CONSOLIDATED FINANCIAL STATEMENTS (in part)

Note 1. Summary of Significant Accounting Policies (in part)

Investments in Equity Investees

We use the equity method to account for our investments in joint ventures, affiliated companies and alliances in which we have the ability to exercise significant influence, generally represented by equity ownership or partnership equity of at least 20 percent but not more than 50 percent. Generally, under the equity method, original investments in these entities are recorded at cost and subsequently adjusted by our share of equity in income or losses after the date of acquisition. Investment amounts in excess of our share of an investee's net assets are amortized over the life of the related asset creating the excess. If the excess is goodwill, then it is not amortized. Equity in income or losses of each investee is recorded according to our level of ownership; if losses accumulate, we record our share of losses until our investment has been fully depleted. If our investment has been fully depleted, we recognize additional losses only when we are the primary funding source. We eliminate (to the extent of our ownership percentage) in our *Consolidated Financial Statements* the profit in inventory held by our equity method investees that has not yet been sold to a third-party. Our investments are classified as "Investments and advances related to equity method investees" in our *Consolidated Balance Sheets.* Our share of the results from joint ventures, affiliated companies and alliances is reported in our *Consolidated Statements of Income* as "Equity, royalty and interest income from investees," and is reported net of all applicable income taxes.

Our foreign equity investees are presented net of applicable foreign income taxes in our *Consolidated Statements of Income.* Our remaining United States (U.S.) equity investees are partnerships (non-taxable), thus there is no difference between gross or net of tax presentation as the investees are not taxed. See NOTE 2, " INVESTMENTS IN EQUITY INVESTEES," for additional information.

Note 2. Investments in Equity Investees

Investments in and advances to equity investees and our ownership percentage was as follows:

In millions	Ownership%	December 31,	
		2015	2014
Komatsu alliances	20–50%	$173	$160
Beijing Foton Cummins Engine Co., Ltd.	50%	172	117
Dongfeng Cummins Engine Company, Ltd.	50%	118	136
Chongqing Cummins Engine Company, Ltd.	50%	80	92
Cummins-Scania XPI Manufacturing, LLC	50%	66	85
Tata Cummins, Ltd.	50%	60	57
North American distributors[1]	50%	15	41
Other	Various	291	293
Total		$975	$981

[1] Current ownership percentage of North American distributor investments as of December 31, 2015.

Equity, royalty and interest income from investees, net of applicable taxes, was as follows:

In millions	Years Ended December 31,		
	2015	2014	2013
Distribution Entities			
North American distributors	$ 33	$107	$129
Komatsu Cummins Chile, Ltda.	31	29	25
All other distributors	3	4	1
Manufacturing Entities			
Beijing Foton Cummins Engine Co., Ltd.	62	(2)	(4)
Dongfeng Cummins Engine Company, Ltd.	51	67	63
Chongqing Cummins Engine Company, Ltd.	41	51	58
All other manufacturers	52	74	53
Cummins share of net income	273	330	325
Royalty and interest income	42	40	36
Equity, royalty and interest income from investees	$315	$370	$361

Distribution Entities

We have an extensive worldwide distributor and dealer network through which we sell and distribute our products and services. Generally, our distributors are divided by geographic region with some of our distributors being wholly-owned by Cummins, some partially-owned and the majority independently owned. We consolidate all wholly-owned distributors and partially-owned distributors where we are the primary beneficiary and account for other partially-owned distributors using the equity method of accounting.

- *North American Distributors* —At December 31, 2015, our distribution channel in North America included one unconsolidated distributor with a 50 percent ownership interest and one consolidated distributor in which we had more than a 50 percent ownership interest. While each distributor is a separate legal entity, the business of each is substantially the same as that of our wholly-owned distributors based in other parts of the world. All of our distributors, irrespective of their legal structure or ownership, offer the full range of our products and services to customers and end-users in their respective markets.
- *Komatsu Cummins Chile, Ltda.* —Komatsu Cummins Chile, Ltda. is a joint venture with Komatsu America Corporation. The joint venture is a distributor that offers the full range of our products and services to customers and end-users in the Chilean and Peruvian markets.

We are contractually obligated to repurchase new engines, parts and components, special tools and signage from our North American distributors following an ownership transfer or termination of the distributor. In addition, in certain cases where we own a partial interest in a distributor, we are obligated to purchase the other equity holders' interests if certain events occur (such as the death or resignation of the distributor principal or a change in control of Cummins Inc.). The purchase consideration of the equity interests is determined based on the fair value of the distributor's assets. Outside of North America, repurchase obligations and practices vary by region. All distributors that are partially-owned are considered to be related parties in our *Consolidated Financial Statements*.

Manufacturing Entities

Our manufacturing joint ventures have generally been formed with customers and generally are intended to allow us to increase our market penetration in geographic regions, reduce capital spending, streamline our supply chain management and develop technologies. Our largest manufacturing joint ventures are based in China and are included in the list below. Our engine manufacturing joint ventures are supplied by our Components segment in the same manner as it supplies our wholly-owned Engine segment and Power Generation segment manufacturing facilities. Our Components segment joint ventures and wholly owned entities provide fuel systems, filtration, aftertreatment systems and turbocharger products that are used in our engines as well as some competitors' products. The results and investments in our joint ventures in which we have 50 percent or less ownership interest are included in "Equity, royalty and interest income from investees" and "Investments and advances related to equity method investees" in our *Consolidated Statements of Income* and *Consolidated Balance Sheets*, respectively.

- *Dongfeng Cummins Engine Company, Ltd.* —Dongfeng Cummins Engine Company, Ltd. (DCEC) is a joint venture in China with Dongfeng Automotive Co. Ltd., a subsidiary of Dongfeng Motor Corporation (Dongfeng), one of the largest medium-duty and heavy-duty truck manufacturers in China. DCEC produces Cummins 4- to 13-liter mechanical engines, full-electric diesel engines, with a power range from 125 to 545 horsepower, and natural gas engines.
- *Chongqing Cummins Engine Company, Ltd.* —Chongqing Cummins Engine Company, Ltd. is a joint venture in China with Chongqing Machinery and Electric Co. Ltd. This joint venture manufactures several models of our heavy-duty and high-horsepower diesel engines, primarily serving the industrial and stationary power markets in China.
- *Beijing Foton Cummins Engine Co., Ltd.* —Beijing Foton Cummins Engine Co., Ltd. is a joint venture in China with Beiqi Foton Motor Co., Ltd., a commercial vehicle manufacturer, which consists of two distinct lines of business, a light-duty business and a heavy-duty

business. The light-duty business produces ISF 2.8 liter and ISF 3.8 liter families of our high performance light-duty diesel engines in Beijing. These engines are used in light-duty commercial trucks, pickup trucks, buses, multipurpose and sport utility vehicles with main markets in China, Brazil and Russia. Certain types of marine, small construction equipment and industrial applications are also served by these engine families. The heavy-duty business produces ISG 10.5 liter and ISG 11.8 liter families of our high performance heavy-duty diesel engines in Beijing. These engines are used in heavy-duty commercial trucks in China and will be used in world wide markets. Certain types of construction equipment and industrial applications will also be served by these engine families in the future.

Equity Investee Financial Summary

We have approximately $501 million in our investment account at December 31, 2015, that represents cumulative undistributed income in our equity investees. Dividends received from our unconsolidated equity investees were $248 million, $227 million and $271 million in 2015, 2014 and 2013, respectively. Summary financial information for our equity investees was as follows:

	At and for the years ended December 31,		
In millions	2015	2014	2013
Net sales	$ 5,946	$ 7,426	$7,799
Gross margin	1,265	1,539	1,719
Net income	521	630	690
Cummins share of net income	$ 273	$ 330	$ 325
Royalty and interest income	42	40	36
Total equity, royalty and interest from investees	$ 315	$ 370	$ 361
Current assets	$ 2,458	$ 2,476	
Non-current assets	1,539	1,667	
Current liabilities	(1,796)	(1,875)	
Non-current liabilities	(284)	(420)	
Net assets	$ 1,917	$ 1,848	
Cummins share of net assets	$ 958	$ 956	

EQUITY IN EARNINGS OF JOINT VENTURES

3.11 AECOM (SEP)
CONSOLIDATED STATEMENTS OF OPERATIONS (in part)

(In thousands, except per share data)

	Fiscal Year Ended		
	September 30, 2015	September 30, 2014	September 30, 2013
Revenue	$17,989,880	$8,356,783	$8,153,495
Cost of revenue	17,454,692	7,953,607	7,703,507
Gross profit	535,188	403,176	449,988
Equity in earnings of joint ventures	106,245	57,924	24,319
General and administrative expenses	(113,975)	(80,908)	(97,318)
Acquisition and integration expenses	(398,440)	(27,310)	—
Income from operations	129,018	352,882	376,989

NOTES TO CONSOLIDATED FINANCIAL STATEMENTS (in part)

1. Significant Accounting Policies (in part)

Principles of Consolidation and Presentation—The consolidated financial statements include the accounts of all majority-owned subsidiaries and material joint ventures in which the Company is the primary beneficiary. All inter-company accounts have been eliminated in consolidation. Also see Note 7 regarding joint ventures and variable interest entities.

Noncontrolling Interests—Noncontrolling interests represent the equity investments of the minority owners in our joint ventures and other subsidiary entities that we consolidate in our financial statements.

7. Joint Ventures and Variable Interest Entities

The Company's joint ventures provide architecture, engineering, program management, construction management and operations and maintenance services. Joint ventures, the combination of two or more partners, are generally formed for a specific project. Management of the joint venture is typically controlled by a joint venture executive committee, comprised of representatives from the joint venture partners. The joint venture executive committee normally provides management oversight and controls decisions which could have a significant impact on the joint venture.

Some of the Company's joint ventures have no employees and minimal operating expenses. For these joint ventures, the Company's employees perform work for the joint venture, which is then billed to a third-party customer by the joint venture. These joint ventures function as pass through entities to bill the third-party customer. For consolidated joint ventures of this type, the Company records the entire amount of the services performed and the costs associated with these services, including the services provided by the other joint venture partners, in the Company's result of operations. For certain of these joint ventures where a fee is added by an unconsolidated joint venture to client billings, the Company's portion of that fee is recorded in equity in earnings of joint ventures.

The Company also has joint ventures that have their own employees and operating expenses, and to which the Company generally makes a capital contribution. The Company accounts for these joint ventures either as consolidated entities or equity method investments based on the criteria further discussed below.

The Company follows guidance issued by the FASB on the consolidation of variable interest entities (VIEs) that requires companies to utilize a qualitative approach to determine whether it is the primary beneficiary of a VIE. The process for identifying the primary beneficiary of a VIE requires consideration of the factors that indicate a party has the power to direct the activities that most significantly impact the joint ventures' economic performance, including powers granted to the joint venture's program manager, powers contained in the joint venture governing board and, to a certain extent, a company's economic interest in the joint venture. The Company analyzes its joint ventures and classifies them as either:

- a VIE that must be consolidated because the Company is the primary beneficiary or the joint venture is not a VIE and the Company holds the majority voting interest with no significant participative rights available to the other partners; or
- a VIE that does not require consolidation and is treated as an equity method investment because the Company is not the primary beneficiary or the joint venture is not a VIE and the Company does not hold the majority voting interest.

As part of the above analysis, if it is determined that the Company has the power to direct the activities that most significantly impact the joint venture's economic performance, the Company considers whether or not it has the obligation to absorb losses or rights to receive benefits of the VIE that could potentially be significant to the VIE.

Contractually required support provided to the Company's joint ventures is discussed in Note 19.

A summary of unaudited financial information of the consolidated joint ventures is as follows:

(In millions)	September 30, 2015	September 30, 2014
Current assets	$ 727.8	$314.1
Non-current assets	282.8	106.2
Total assets	$1,010.6	$420.3
Current liabilities	$ 441.5	$229.1
Non-current liabilities	0.2	—
Total liabilities	441.7	229.1
Total AECOM equity	354.7	116.6
Noncontrolling interests	214.2	74.6
Total owners' equity	568.9	191.2
Total liabilities and owners' equity	$1,010.6	$420.3

Total revenue of the consolidated joint ventures was $2,368.0 million, $614.5 million and $490.9 million for the years ended September 30, 2015, 2014 and 2013, respectively. The assets of the Company's consolidated joint ventures are restricted for use only by the particular joint venture and are not available for the general operations of the Company.

Summary of unaudited financial information of the unconsolidated joint ventures is as follows:

(In millions)	September 30, 2015	September 30, 2014
Current assets	$1,200.7	$539.6
Non-current assets	527.3	273.7
Total assets	$1,728.0	$813.3
Current liabilities	$ 936.7	$397.9
Non-current liabilities	87.0	91.0
Total liabilities	1,023.7	488.9
Joint venturers' equity	704.3	324.4
Total liabilities and joint venturers' equity	$1,728.0	$813.3
AECOM's investment in joint ventures	$ 321.6	$142.9

(In millions)	Twelve Months Ended	
	September 30, 2015	September 30, 2014
Revenue	$4,754.6	$2,017.8
Cost of revenue	4,476.8	1,960.1
Gross profit	$ 277.8	$ 57.7
Net income	$ 231.2	$ 57.7

Summary of AECOM's equity in earnings of unconsolidated joint ventures is as follows:

(In millions)	Fiscal Year Ended		
	September 30, 2015	September 30, 2014	September 30, 2013
Pass through joint ventures	$ 26.2	$10.2	$ 6.4
Other joint ventures	80.0	47.7	17.9
Total	$106.2	$57.9	$24.3

Included in equity in earnings above is a $37.4 million gain recognized upon change in control ($23.4 million, net of tax) of an unconsolidated joint venture in the year ended September 30, 2014. The Company obtained control of the joint venture through modifications to the joint venture's operating agreement, which required the Company to consolidate the joint venture. The acquisition date fair value of the previously held equity interest was $58.0 million, excluding the control premium. The measurement of the fair value of the equity interest immediately before obtaining control of the joint venture resulted in the pre-tax gain of $37.4 million. The Company utilized income and market approaches, in addition to obtaining an independent third party valuation, in determining the joint venture's fair value, which includes making assumptions about variables such as revenue growth rates, profitability, discount rates, and industry market multiples. These assumptions are subject to a high degree of judgment. Total assets and liabilities of this entity included in the accompanying consolidated balance sheet at the acquisition date were $207.8 million and $48.1 million, respectively. This acquisition did not meet the quantitative thresholds to require pro forma disclosures of operating results based on the Company's consolidated assets, investments and net income. This joint venture performs engineering and program management services in the Middle East and is included in the Company's DCS segment.

GAIN ON ASSET DISPOSALS

3.12 THE WENDY'S COMPANY (DEC)
CONSOLIDATED STATEMENTS OF OPERATIONS (in part)

(In Thousands Except Per Share Amounts)

	Year Ended		
	January 3, 2016	December 28, 2014	December 29, 2013
Revenues:			
Sales	$1,438,802	$1,608,455	$2,102,881
Franchise revenues	431,495	390,047	320,788
	1,870,297	1,998,502	2,423,669
Costs and expenses:			
Cost of sales	1,184,073	1,355,086	1,780,931
General and administrative	256,553	260,732	291,544
Depreciation and amortization	145,051	153,882	175,391
System optimization gains, net	(74,009)	(91,510)	(51,276)
Reorganization and realignment costs	21,910	31,903	37,017
Impairment of long-lived assets	25,001	19,613	36,385
Impairment of goodwill	—	—	9,397
Other operating expense, net	37,248	26,208	4,950
	1,595,827	1,755,914	2,284,339
Operating profit	274,470	242,588	139,330
Interest expense	(86,067)	(51,994)	(68,644)
Loss on early extinguishment of debt	(7,295)	—	(28,563)
Investment income, net	52,214	1,199	23,565
Other income (expense), net	806	747	(2,096)
Income from continuing operations before income taxes and noncontrolling interests	234,128	192,540	63,592
Provision for income taxes	(94,149)	(76,116)	(16,057)
Income from continuing operations	139,979	116,424	47,535
Discontinued operations:			
Income (loss) from discontinued operations, net of income taxes	10,494	5,010	(2,903)
Gain on disposal of discontinued operations, net of income taxes	10,669	—	—
Net income (loss) from discontinued operations	21,163	5,010	(2,903)
Net income	161,142	121,434	44,632

(In Thousands Except Per Share Amounts)

(2) Discontinued Operations (in part)

Sale of the Bakery

On May 31, 2015, Wendy's completed the sale of 100% of its membership interest in the Bakery to East Balt US, LLC (the "Buyer") for $78,500 in cash (subject to customary purchase price adjustments). The Company also assigned certain capital leases for transportation equipment to the Buyer but retained the related obligation. Pursuant to the sale agreement, the Company was obligated to continue to provide health insurance benefits to the Bakery's employees at the Company's expense through December 31, 2015. The Company recorded a pre-tax gain on the disposal of the Bakery of $25,529 during the year ended January 3, 2016, which included transaction closing costs and a reduction of goodwill. The Company recognized income tax expense associated with the gain on disposal of $14,860 during the year ended January 3, 2016, which included the impact of the disposal of non-deductible goodwill.

In conjunction with the Bakery sale, Wendy's entered into a transition services agreement with the Buyer, pursuant to which Wendy's will provide certain continuing corporate and shared services to the Buyer through March 31, 2016 for no additional consideration. A purchasing cooperative, Quality Supply Chain Co-op, Inc., established by Wendy's and its franchisees, agreed to continue to source sandwich buns from the Bakery, for a specified time period following the sale of the Bakery. As a result, Wendy's paid the Buyer $8,358 for the purchase of sandwich buns during the period from June 1, 2015 through January 3, 2016, which has been recorded to "Cost of sales."

Information related to the Bakery has been reflected in the accompanying consolidated financial statements as follows:

- Balance sheets—As a result of our sale of the Bakery on May 31, 2015, there are no remaining Bakery assets and liabilities. The Bakery's assets and liabilities as of December 28, 2014 have been presented as discontinued operations.
- Statements of operations—The Bakery's results of operations for the period from December 29, 2014 through May 31, 2015 and the years ended December 28, 2014 and December 29, 2013 have been presented as discontinued operations. In addition, the gain on disposal of the Bakery has been included in "Net income (loss) from discontinued operations" for the year ended January 3, 2016.
- Statements of cash flows—The Bakery's cash flows prior to its sale (for the period from December 29, 2014 through May 31, 2015 and for the years ended December 28, 2014 and December 29, 2013) have been included in, and not separately reported from, our consolidated cash flows. The consolidated statement of cash flows for the year ended January 3, 2016 also includes the effects of the sale of the Bakery.

The following table presents the Bakery's results of operations and the gain on disposal which have been included in discontinued operations:

	Year Ended		
	2015	2014	2013
Revenues[a]	$ 25,885	$ 62,561	$ 63,741
Cost of sales[b]	(7,543)	(45,710)	(58,809)
	18,342	16,851	4,932
General and administrative	(1,093)	(2,525)	(2,248)
Depreciation and amortization[c]	(2,297)	(5,471)	(6,968)
Other expense, net[d]	(19)	(126)	(256)
Income (loss) from discontinued operations before income taxes	14,933	8,729	(4,540)
(Provision for) benefit from income taxes	(4,439)	(3,719)	1,903
Income (loss) from discontinued operations, net of income taxes	10,494	5,010	(2,637)
Gain on disposal of discontinued operations before income taxes	25,529	—	—
Provision for income taxes on gain on disposal	(14,860)	—	—
Gain on disposal of discontinued operations, net of income taxes	10,669	—	—
Net income (loss) from discontinued operations	$ 21,163	$ 5,010	$ (2,637)

[a] Includes sales of sandwich buns and related products previously reported in "Sales" as well as rental income.

[b] The year ended January 3, 2016 includes employee separation-related costs of $791 as a result of the sale of the Bakery. In addition, includes a $13,500 charge to cost of sales during the year ended December 29, 2013 resulting from the Bakery's withdrawal from a multiemployer pension plan and the subsequent reversal during the year ended January 3, 2016 of $12,486. See Note 19 for further discussion.

[c] Included in "Depreciation and amortization" in our consolidated statements of cash flows for the periods presented.

[d] Includes net gains on sales of other assets. During 2015, 2014 and 2013, the Bakery received cash proceeds of $50, $52 and $114, respectively, resulting in net gains on sales of other assets of $32, $69 and $96, respectively.

The Bakery's capital expenditures were $2,693, $2,613 and $3,106 for the years ended January 3, 2016, December 28, 2014 and December 29, 2013, respectively, which are included in "Capital expenditures" in our consolidated statements of cash flows.

The following table summarizes the gain on the disposal of our Bakery, which has been included in discontinued operations:

	Year Ended 2015
Proceeds from sale of the Bakery[a]	$ 78,408
Net working capital[b]	(5,655)
Net properties sold[c]	(30,664)
Goodwill allocated to the sale of the Bakery	(12,067)
Other[d]	(2,684)
	27,338
Post-closing adjustments on the sale of the Bakery	(1,809)
	25,529
Provision for income taxes[e]	(14,860)
Gain on disposal of discontinued operations, net of income taxes	$ 10,669

[a] Represents net proceeds received, which includes the purchase price of $78,500 less transaction closing costs paid directly by the Buyer on the Company's behalf.
[b] Primarily represents accounts receivable, inventory, prepaid expenses and accounts payable.
[c] Net properties sold consisted primarily of buildings, equipment and capital leases for transportation equipment.
[d] Primarily includes the recognition of the Company's obligation, pursuant to the sale agreement, to provide health insurance benefits to the Bakery's employees through December 31, 2015 of $1,993 and transaction closing costs paid directly by the Company.
[e] Includes the impact of non-deductible goodwill disposed of as a result of the sale.

GAIN ON BUSINESS COMBINATION

3.13 COHERENT, INC. (SEP)
CONSOLIDATED STATEMENTS OF OPERATIONS (in part)

(In thousands, except per share data)

	Year Ended		
	October 3, 2015	September 27, 2014	September 28, 2013
Net sales	$802,460	$794,639	$810,126
Cost of sales	467,061	481,249	487,855
Gross profit	335,399	313,390	322,271
Operating expenses:			
Research and development	81,455	79,070	82,785
Selling, general and administrative	149,829	154,030	149,513
Gain on business combination	(1,316)	—	—
Impairment of investment	2,017	—	—
Amortization of intangible assets	2,667	3,424	5,074
Total operating expenses	234,652	236,524	237,372
Income from operations	100,747	76,866	84,899

NOTES TO CONSOLIDATED FINANCIAL STATEMENTS (in part)

3. Business Combinations (in part)

Fiscal 2015 Acquisitions (in part)

Tinsley Optics

On July 27, 2015, we acquired the assets and certain liabilities of the Tinsley Optics ("Tinsley") business from L-3 Communications Corporation for approximately $4.3 million, excluding transaction costs. Tinsley is a specialized manufacturer of high precision optical components and subsystems sold primarily in the aerospace and defense industry. Tinsley manufactures the large form factor optics for our excimer laser annealing systems. Tinsley has been included in our Specialty Lasers and Systems segment.

Our preliminary allocation of the purchase price is as follows (in thousands):

Tangible assets:	
Inventories	$ 2,263
Accounts receivable	2,240
Prepaid expenses and other assets	1,132
Property and equipment	2,451
Liabilities assumed	(1,702)
Deferred tax liabilities	(768)
Gain on business combination	(1,316)
Total	$ 4,300

The purchase price was lower than the fair value of net assets purchased, resulting in a gain of $1.3 million recorded as a separate line item in our consolidated statements of operations for our fiscal year 2015. The Company reassessed the recognition and measurement of identifiable assets acquired and liabilities assumed and concluded that all acquired assets and assumed liabilities were recognized and that the valuation procedures and resulting measures were appropriate.

Results of operations for the business have been included in our consolidated financial statements subsequent to the date of acquisition and pro forma results of operations in accordance with authoritative guidance for prior periods have not been presented because the effect of the acquisition was not material to our prior period consolidated financial results.

The gain from the bargain purchase is not subject to income taxation.

We expensed $0.4 million of acquisition-related costs as selling, general and administrative expenses in our consolidated statements of operations for our fiscal year 2015.

LITIGATION

3.14 CORNING INCORPORATED (DEC)
NOTES TO CONSOLIDATED FINANCIAL STATEMENTS (in part)

7. Investments (in part)

Pittsburgh Corning Corporation and Asbestos Litigation (in part).

Total Estimated Liability for the Amended PCC Plan and the Non-PCC Asbestos Claims

The liability for the Amended PCC Plan and the non-PCC asbestos claims was estimated to be $678 million at December 31, 2015, compared with an estimate of liability of $681 million at December 31, 2014. The $678 million liability is comprised of $238 million of the fair value of PCE, $290 million for the fixed series of payments, and $150 million for the non-PCC asbestos claims, all referenced in the preceding paragraphs. With respect to the PCE liability, at December 31, 2015 and 2014, the fair value of $238 million and $241 million of our interest in PCE significantly exceeded its carrying value of $154 million and $162 million, respectively. There have been no impairment indicators for our investment in PCE and we continue to recognize equity earnings of this affiliate. At the time Corning recorded this liability, it determined it lacked the ability to recover the carrying amount of its investment in PCC and its investment was other than temporarily impaired. As a result, we reduced our investment in PCC to zero. As the fair value in PCE is significantly higher than book value, management believes that the risk of an additional loss in an amount materially higher than the fair value of the liability is remote. With respect to the liability for other asbestos litigation, the liability for non-PCC asbestos claims was estimated based upon industry data for asbestos claims since Corning does not have recent claim history due to the Stay issued by the Bankruptcy Court. The estimated liability represents the undiscounted projection of claims and related legal fees over the next 20 years. The amount may need to be adjusted in future periods as more data becomes available; however, we cannot estimate any additional losses at this time. For the years ended December 31, 2015 and 2014, Corning recorded asbestos litigation income of $15 million and expense of $9 million, respectively. At December 31, 2015, $440 million of the obligation, consisting of the $290 million for the fixed series of payments and $150 million for the non-PCC asbestos claims, is classified as a non-current liability, as installment payments for the cash portion of the obligation are not planned to commence until more than 12 months after the Amended PCC Plan becomes effective. The amount of the obligation related to the fair value of PCE, $238 million, was reclassified to a current liability in the fourth quarter of 2015, as the contribution of the assets is expected to be made within the next twelve months.

3.15 METLIFE, INC. (DEC)

CONSOLIDATED STATEMENTS OF OPERATIONS (in part)

(In millions, except per share data)

	2015	2014	2013
Revenues			
Premiums	$38,545	$39,067	$37,674
Universal life and investment-type product policy fees	9,507	9,946	9,451
Net investment income	19,281	21,153	22,232
Other revenues	1,983	2,030	1,920
Net investment gains (losses):			
Other-than-temporary impairments on fixed maturity securities	(84)	(43)	(106)
Other-than-temporary impairments on fixed maturity securities			
transferred to other comprehensive income (loss)	(6)	(17)	(60)
Other net investment gains (losses)	687	(137)	327
Total net investment gains (losses)	597	(197)	161
Net derivative gains (losses)	38	1,317	(3,239)
Total revenues	69,951	73,316	68,199
Expenses			
Policyholder benefits and claims	38,714	39,102	38,107
Interest credited to policyholder account balances	5,610	6,943	8,179
Policyholder dividends	1,388	1,376	1,259
Other expenses	16,769	17,091	16,602
Total expenses	62,481	64,512	64,147
Income (loss) from continuing operations before provision for income tax	7,470	8,804	4,052

NOTES TO THE CONSOLIDATED FINANCIAL STATEMENTS (in part)

1. Business, Basis of Presentation and Summary of Significant Accounting Policies (in part)

Derivatives

Freestanding Derivatives

Freestanding derivatives are carried on the Company's balance sheet either as assets within other invested assets or as liabilities within other liabilities at estimated fair value. The Company does not offset the estimated fair value amounts recognized for derivatives executed with the same counterparty under the same master netting agreement.

Accruals on derivatives are generally recorded in accrued investment income or within other liabilities. However, accruals that are not scheduled to settle within one year are included with the derivatives carrying value in other invested assets or other liabilities.

If a derivative is not designated as an accounting hedge or its use in managing risk does not qualify for hedge accounting, changes in the estimated fair value of the derivative are reported in net derivative gains (losses) except as follows:

Statement of Operations Presentation:	Derivative:
Policyholder benefits and claims	• Economic hedges of variable annuity guarantees included in future policy benefits
Net investment income	• Economic hedges of equity method investments in joint ventures • All derivatives held in relation to trading portfolios • Derivatives held within contractholder-directed unit-linked investments

Hedge Accounting

To qualify for hedge accounting, at the inception of the hedging relationship, the Company formally documents its risk management objective and strategy for undertaking the hedging transaction, as well as its designation of the hedge. Hedge designation and financial statement presentation of changes in estimated fair value of the hedging derivatives are as follows:
- Fair value hedge (a hedge of the estimated fair value of a recognized asset or liability)—in net derivative gains (losses), consistent with the change in estimated fair value of the hedged item attributable to the designated risk being hedged.
- Cash flow hedge (a hedge of a forecasted transaction or of the variability of cash flows to be received or paid related to a recognized asset or liability)—effectiveness in OCI (deferred gains or losses on the derivative are reclassified into the statement of operations

when the Company's earnings are affected by the variability in cash flows of the hedged item); ineffectiveness in net derivative gains (losses).

- Net investment in a foreign operation hedge—effectiveness in OCI, consistent with the translation adjustment for the hedged net investment in the foreign operation; ineffectiveness in net derivative gains (losses).

The changes in estimated fair values of the hedging derivatives are exclusive of any accruals that are separately reported on the statement of operations within interest income or interest expense to match the location of the hedged item. Accruals on derivatives in net investment hedges are recognized in OCI.

In its hedge documentation, the Company sets forth how the hedging instrument is expected to hedge the designated risks related to the hedged item and sets forth the method that will be used to retrospectively and prospectively assess the hedging instrument's effectiveness and the method that will be used to measure ineffectiveness. A derivative designated as a hedging instrument must be assessed as being highly effective in offsetting the designated risk of the hedged item. Hedge effectiveness is formally assessed at inception and at least quarterly throughout the life of the designated hedging relationship. Assessments of hedge effectiveness and measurements of ineffectiveness are also subject to interpretation and estimation and different interpretations or estimates may have a material effect on the amount reported in net income.

The Company discontinues hedge accounting prospectively when: (i) it is determined that the derivative is no longer highly effective in offsetting changes in the estimated fair value or cash flows of a hedged item; (ii) the derivative expires, is sold, terminated, or exercised; (iii) it is no longer probable that the hedged forecasted transaction will occur; or (iv) the derivative is de-designated as a hedging instrument.

When hedge accounting is discontinued because it is determined that the derivative is not highly effective in offsetting changes in the estimated fair value or cash flows of a hedged item, the derivative continues to be carried on the balance sheet at its estimated fair value, with changes in estimated fair value recognized in net derivative gains (losses). The carrying value of the hedged recognized asset or liability under a fair value hedge is no longer adjusted for changes in its estimated fair value due to the hedged risk, and the cumulative adjustment to its carrying value is amortized into income over the remaining life of the hedged item. Provided the hedged forecasted transaction is still probable of occurrence, the changes in estimated fair value of derivatives recorded in OCI related to discontinued cash flow hedges are released into the statement of operations when the Company's earnings are affected by the variability in cash flows of the hedged item.

When hedge accounting is discontinued because it is no longer probable that the forecasted transactions will occur on the anticipated date or within two months of that date, the derivative continues to be carried on the balance sheet at its estimated fair value, with changes in estimated fair value recognized currently in net derivative gains (losses). Deferred gains and losses of a derivative recorded in OCI pursuant to the discontinued cash flow hedge of a forecasted transaction that is no longer probable are recognized immediately in net derivative gains (losses).

In all other situations in which hedge accounting is discontinued, the derivative is carried at its estimated fair value on the balance sheet, with changes in its estimated fair value recognized in the current period as net derivative gains (losses).

Embedded Derivatives

The Company sells variable annuities and issues certain insurance products and investment contracts and is a party to certain reinsurance agreements that have embedded derivatives. The Company assesses each identified embedded derivative to determine whether it is required to be bifurcated. The embedded derivative is bifurcated from the host contract and accounted for as a freestanding derivative if:

- the combined instrument is not accounted for in its entirety at estimated fair value with changes in estimated fair value recorded in earnings;
- the terms of the embedded derivative are not clearly and closely related to the economic characteristics of the host contract; and
- a separate instrument with the same terms as the embedded derivative would qualify as a derivative instrument.

Such embedded derivatives are carried on the balance sheet at estimated fair value with the host contract and changes in their estimated fair value are generally reported in net derivative gains (losses), except for those in policyholder benefits and claims related to ceded reinsurance of GMIB. If the Company is unable to properly identify and measure an embedded derivative for separation from its host contract, the entire contract is carried on the balance sheet at estimated fair value, with changes in estimated fair value recognized in the current period in net investment gains (losses) or net investment income. Additionally, the Company may elect to carry an entire contract on the balance sheet at estimated fair value, with changes in estimated fair value recognized in the current period in net investment gains (losses) or net investment income if that contract contains an embedded derivative that requires bifurcation. At inception, the Company attributes to the embedded derivative a portion of the projected future guarantee fees to be collected from the policyholder equal to the present value of projected future guaranteed benefits. Any additional fees represent "excess" fees and are reported in universal life and investment-type product policy fees.

9. Derivatives

Accounting for Derivatives

See Note 1 for a description of the Company's accounting policies for derivatives and Note 10 for information about the fair value hierarchy for derivatives.

Derivative Strategies

The Company is exposed to various risks relating to its ongoing business operations, including interest rate, foreign currency exchange rate, credit and equity market. The Company uses a variety of strategies to manage these risks, including the use of derivatives.

Derivatives are financial instruments with values derived from interest rates, foreign currency exchange rates, credit spreads and/or other financial indices. Derivatives may be exchange-traded or contracted in the over-the-counter ("OTC") market. Certain of the Company's OTC derivatives are cleared and settled through central clearing counterparties ("OTC-cleared"), while others are bilateral contracts between two counterparties ("OTC-bilateral"). The types of derivatives the Company uses include swaps, forwards, futures and option contracts. To a lesser extent, the Company uses credit default swaps and structured interest rate swaps to synthetically replicate investment risks and returns which are not readily available in the cash market.

Interest Rate Derivatives

The Company uses a variety of interest rate derivatives to reduce its exposure to changes in interest rates, including interest rate swaps, caps, floors, swaptions, futures and forwards.

Interest rate swaps are used by the Company primarily to reduce market risks from changes in interest rates and to alter interest rate exposure arising from mismatches between assets and liabilities (duration mismatches). In an interest rate swap, the Company agrees with another party to exchange, at specified intervals, the difference between fixed rate and floating rate interest amounts as calculated by reference to an agreed notional amount. The Company utilizes interest rate swaps in fair value, cash flow and nonqualifying hedging relationships.

The Company uses structured interest rate swaps to synthetically create investments that are either more expensive to acquire or otherwise unavailable in the cash markets. These transactions are a combination of a derivative and a cash instrument such as a U.S. Treasury, agency, or other fixed maturity security. Structured interest rate swaps are included in interest rate swaps and are not designated as hedging instruments.

The Company purchases interest rate caps and floors primarily to protect its floating rate liabilities against rises in interest rates above a specified level, and against interest rate exposure arising from mismatches between assets and liabilities, as well as to protect its minimum rate guarantee liabilities against declines in interest rates below a specified level, respectively. In certain instances, the Company locks in the economic impact of existing purchased caps and floors by entering into offsetting written caps and floors. The Company utilizes interest rate caps and floors in nonqualifying hedging relationships.

In exchange-traded interest rate (Treasury and swap) futures transactions, the Company agrees to purchase or sell a specified number of contracts, the value of which is determined by the different classes of interest rate securities, and to post variation margin on a daily basis in an amount equal to the difference in the daily market values of those contracts. The Company enters into exchange-traded futures with regulated futures commission merchants that are members of the exchange. Exchange-traded interest rate (Treasury and swap) futures are used primarily to hedge mismatches between the duration of assets in a portfolio and the duration of liabilities supported by those assets, to hedge against changes in value of securities the Company owns or anticipates acquiring, to hedge against changes in interest rates on anticipated liability issuances by replicating Treasury or swap curve performance, and to hedge minimum guarantees embedded in certain variable annuity products offered by the Company. The Company utilizes exchange-traded interest rate futures in nonqualifying hedging relationships.

Swaptions are used by the Company to hedge interest rate risk associated with the Company's long-term liabilities and invested assets. A swaption is an option to enter into a swap with a forward starting effective date. In certain instances, the Company locks in the economic impact of existing purchased swaptions by entering into offsetting written swaptions. The Company pays a premium for purchased swaptions and receives a premium for written swaptions. The Company utilizes swaptions in nonqualifying hedging relationships. Swaptions are included in interest rate options.

The Company enters into interest rate forwards to buy and sell securities. The price is agreed upon at the time of the contract and payment for such a contract is made at a specified future date. The Company utilizes interest rate forwards in cash flow hedging relationships.

Foreign Currency Exchange Rate Derivatives

The Company uses foreign currency exchange rate derivatives, including foreign currency swaps, foreign currency forwards, currency options and exchange-traded currency futures, to reduce the risk from fluctuations in foreign currency exchange rates associated with its assets and liabilities denominated in foreign currencies. The Company also uses foreign currency derivatives to hedge the foreign currency exchange rate risk associated with certain of its net investments in foreign operations.

In a foreign currency swap transaction, the Company agrees with another party to exchange, at specified intervals, the difference between one currency and another at a fixed exchange rate, generally set at inception, calculated by reference to an agreed upon notional amount. The notional amount of each currency is exchanged at the inception and termination of the currency swap by each party. The Company utilizes foreign currency swaps in fair value, cash flow and nonqualifying hedging relationships.

In a foreign currency forward transaction, the Company agrees with another party to deliver a specified amount of an identified currency at a specified future date. The price is agreed upon at the time of the contract and payment for such a contract is made at the specified future date. The Company utilizes foreign currency forwards in fair value, net investment in foreign operations and nonqualifying hedging relationships.

The Company enters into currency options that give it the right, but not the obligation, to sell the foreign currency amount in exchange for a functional currency amount within a limited time at a contracted price. The contracts may also be net settled in cash, based on differentials in the foreign currency exchange rate and the strike price. The Company uses currency options to hedge against the foreign currency exposure inherent in certain of its variable annuity products. The Company also uses currency options as an economic hedge of foreign currency exposure related to the Company's international subsidiaries. The Company utilizes currency options in net investment in foreign operations and nonqualifying hedging relationships.

To a lesser extent, the Company uses exchange-traded currency futures to hedge currency mismatches between assets and liabilities, and to hedge minimum guarantees embedded in certain variable annuity products offered by the Company. The Company utilizes exchange-traded currency futures in nonqualifying hedging relationships.

Credit Derivatives

The Company enters into purchased credit default swaps to hedge against credit-related changes in the value of its investments. In a credit default swap transaction, the Company agrees with another party to pay, at specified intervals, a premium to hedge credit risk. If a credit event occurs, as defined by the contract, the contract may be cash settled or it may be settled gross by the delivery of par quantities of the referenced investment equal to the specified swap notional amount in exchange for the payment of cash amounts by the counterparty equal to the par value of the investment surrendered. Credit events vary by type of issuer but typically include bankruptcy, failure to pay debt obligations, repudiation, moratorium, involuntary restructuring or governmental intervention. In each case, payout on a credit default swap is triggered only after the Credit Derivatives Determinations Committee of the International Swaps and Derivatives Association, Inc. ("ISDA") deems that a credit event has occurred. The Company utilizes credit default swaps in nonqualifying hedging relationships.

The Company enters into written credit default swaps to synthetically create credit investments that are either more expensive to acquire or otherwise unavailable in the cash markets. These transactions are a combination of a derivative and one or more cash instruments, such as U.S. Treasury securities, agency securities or other fixed maturity securities. These credit default swaps are not designated as hedging instruments.

The Company also enters into certain purchased and written credit default swaps held in relation to trading portfolios for the purpose of generating profits on short-term differences in price. These credit default swaps are not designated as hedging instruments.

The Company enters into forwards to lock in the price to be paid for forward purchases of certain securities. The price is agreed upon at the time of the contract and payment for the contract is made at a specified future date. When the primary purpose of entering into these transactions is to hedge against the risk of changes in purchase price due to changes in credit spreads, the Company designates these transactions as credit forwards. The Company utilizes credit forwards in cash flow hedging relationships.

Equity Derivatives

The Company uses a variety of equity derivatives to reduce its exposure to equity market risk, including equity index options, equity variance swaps, exchange-traded equity futures and total rate of return swaps ("TRRs").

Equity index options are used by the Company primarily to hedge minimum guarantees embedded in certain variable annuity products offered by the Company. To hedge against adverse changes in equity indices, the Company enters into contracts to sell the equity index within a limited time at a contracted price. The contracts will be net settled in cash based on differentials in the indices at the time of exercise and the strike price. Certain of these contracts may also contain settlement provisions linked to interest rates. In certain instances, the Company may enter into a combination of transactions to hedge adverse changes in equity indices within a pre-determined range through the purchase and sale of options. The Company utilizes equity index options in nonqualifying hedging relationships.

Equity variance swaps are used by the Company primarily to hedge minimum guarantees embedded in certain variable annuity products offered by the Company. In an equity variance swap, the Company agrees with another party to exchange amounts in the future, based on changes in equity volatility over a defined period. The Company utilizes equity variance swaps in nonqualifying hedging relationships.

In exchange-traded equity futures transactions, the Company agrees to purchase or sell a specified number of contracts, the value of which is determined by the different classes of equity securities, and to post variation margin on a daily basis in an amount equal to the difference in the daily market values of those contracts. The Company enters into exchange-traded futures with regulated futures commission merchants that are members of the exchange. Exchange-traded equity futures are used primarily to hedge minimum guarantees embedded in certain variable annuity products offered by the Company. The Company utilizes exchange-traded equity futures in nonqualifying hedging relationships.

TRRs are swaps whereby the Company agrees with another party to exchange, at specified intervals, the difference between the economic risk and reward of an asset or a market index and the LIBOR, calculated by reference to an agreed notional amount. No cash is exchanged at the outset of the contract. Cash is paid and received over the life of the contract based on the terms of the swap. The Company uses TRRs to hedge its equity market guarantees in certain of its insurance products. TRRs can be used as hedges or to synthetically create investments. The Company utilizes TRRs in nonqualifying hedging relationships.

Primary Risks Managed by Derivatives

The following table presents the gross notional amount, estimated fair value and primary underlying risk exposure of the Company's derivatives, excluding embedded derivatives, held at:

		December 31,					
		2015			2014		
		Gross Notional	Estimated Fair Value		Gross Notional	Estimated Fair Value	
(In millions)	Primary Underlying Risk Exposure	Amount	Assets	Liabilities	Amount	Assets	Liabilities
Derivatives Designated as Hedging Instruments							
Fair value hedges:							
Interest rate swaps	Interest rate	$ 5,528	$ 2,215	$ 12	$ 6,044	$ 2,064	$ 21
Foreign currency swaps	Foreign currency exchange rate	2,154	62	159	2,708	65	100
Foreign currency forwards	Foreign currency exchange rate	1,685	—	52	2,335	—	291
Subtotal		9,367	2,277	223	11,087	2,129	412
Cash flow hedges:							
Interest rate swaps	Interest rate	2,190	487	—	2,560	528	—
Interest rate forwards	Interest rate	105	23	—	225	63	—
Foreign currency swaps	Foreign currency exchange rate	23,661	1,303	1,803	18,325	563	930
Subtotal		25,956	1,813	1,803	21,110	1,154	930
Foreign operations hedges:							
Foreign currency forwards	Foreign currency exchange rate	3,916	63	12	4,097	295	11
Currency options	Foreign currency exchange rate	7,569	205	36	6,419	415	—
Subtotal		11,485	268	48	10,516	710	11
Total qualifying hedges		46,808	4,358	2,074	42,713	3,993	1,353

(continued)

(In millions)	Primary Underlying Risk Exposure	December 31,					
		2015			2014		
		Gross Notional Amount	Estimated Fair Value		Gross Notional Amount	Estimated Fair Value	
			Assets	Liabilities		Assets	Liabilities
Derivatives Not Designated or Not Qualifying as Hedging Instruments							
Interest rate swaps	Interest rate	89,336	5,111	2,247	93,266	4,570	2,051
Interest rate floors	Interest rate	23,837	311	48	55,645	440	199
Interest rate caps	Interest rate	68,928	105	3	49,128	145	1
Interest rate futures	Interest rate	5,808	4	7	2,707	4	9
Interest rate options	Interest rate	30,234	1,177	30	48,078	1,241	75
Interest rate forwards	Interest rate	43	1	—	—	—	—
Synthetic GICs	Interest rate	4,216	—	—	4,298	—	—
Foreign currency swaps	Foreign currency exchange rate	11,081	766	431	11,041	447	385
Foreign currency forwards	Foreign currency exchange rate	11,724	154	220	13,206	127	791
Currency futures	Foreign currency exchange rate	930	—	—	522	2	—
Currency options	Foreign currency exchange rate	9,590	466	189	8,324	585	340
Credit default swaps—purchased	Credit	1,870	28	34	2,830	8	34
Credit default swaps—written	Credit	10,311	78	13	10,527	181	6
Equity futures	Equity market	7,206	63	18	6,073	65	2
Equity index options	Equity market	55,682	1,542	1,041	39,345	1,426	1,036
Equity variance swaps	Equity market	23,437	195	636	24,598	196	639
TRRs	Equity market	3,803	47	58	3,297	22	101
Total non-designated or nonqualifying derivatives		358,036	10,048	4,975	372,885	9,459	5,669
Total		$404,844	$14,406	$7,049	$415,598	$13,452	$7,022

Based on gross notional amounts, a substantial portion of the Company's derivatives was not designated or did not qualify as part of a hedging relationship at both December 31, 2015 and 2014. The Company's use of derivatives includes (i) derivatives that serve as macro hedges of the Company's exposure to various risks and that generally do not qualify for hedge accounting due to the criteria required under the portfolio hedging rules; (ii) derivatives that economically hedge insurance liabilities that contain mortality or morbidity risk and that generally do not qualify for hedge accounting because the lack of these risks in the derivatives cannot support an expectation of a highly effective hedging relationship; (iii) derivatives that economically hedge embedded derivatives that do not qualify for hedge accounting because the changes in estimated fair value of the embedded derivatives are already recorded in net income; and (iv) written credit default swaps that are used to synthetically create credit investments and that do not qualify for hedge accounting because they do not involve a hedging relationship. For these nonqualified derivatives, changes in market factors can lead to the recognition of fair value changes on the statement of operations without an offsetting gain or loss recognized in earnings for the item being hedged.

Net Derivative Gains (Losses)

The components of net derivative gains (losses) were as follows:

(In millions)	Years Ended December 31,		
	2015	2014	2013
Freestanding derivatives and hedging gains (losses)[1]	$ 277	$1,638	$(8,343)
Embedded derivatives gains (losses)	(239)	(321)	5,104
Total net derivative gains (losses)	$ 38	$1,317	$(3,239)

[1] Includes foreign currency transaction gains (losses) on hedged items in cash flow and nonqualifying hedging relationships, which are not presented elsewhere in this note.

The following table presents earned income on derivatives:

(In millions)	Years Ended December 31,		
	2015	2014	2013
Qualifying hedges:			
Net investment income	$ 219	$ 158	$ 135
Interest credited to policyholder account balances	25	101	150
Other expenses	(6)	(3)	(6)
Nonqualifying hedges:			
Net investment income	(5)	(4)	(6)
Net derivative gains (losses)	1,024	828	328
Policyholder benefits and claims	16	40	(292)
Total	$1,273	$1,120	$ 309

Nonqualifying Derivatives and Derivatives for Purposes Other Than Hedging

The following table presents the amount and location of gains (losses) recognized in income for derivatives that were not designated or qualifying as hedging instruments:

(In millions)	Net Derivative Gains (Losses)	Net Investment Income[1]	Policyholder Benefits and Claims[2]
Year Ended December 31, 2015			
Interest rate derivatives	$ (421)	$—	$ 5
Foreign currency exchange rate derivatives	547	—	—
Credit derivatives—purchased	7	(3)	—
Credit derivatives—written	(83)	—	—
Equity derivatives	(816)	(14)	(25)
Total	$ (766)	$(17)	$ (20)
Year Ended December 31, 2014			
Interest rate derivatives	$ 1,545	$—	$ 42
Foreign currency exchange rate derivatives	(344)	—	—
Credit derivatives—purchased	(12)	—	—
Credit derivatives—written	21	—	—
Equity derivatives	(634)	(18)	(288)
Total	$ 576	$(18)	$(246)
Year Ended December 31, 2013			
Interest rate derivatives	$(3,458)	$—	$ (27)
Foreign currency exchange rate derivatives	(1,716)	—	—
Credit derivatives—purchased	(21)	(14)	—
Credit derivatives—written	130	1	—
Equity derivatives	(3,663)	(25)	(727)
Total	$(8,728)	$(38)	$(754)

[1] Changes in estimated fair value related to economic hedges of equity method investments in joint ventures, derivatives held in relation to trading portfolios and derivatives held within contractholder-directed unit-linked investments.

[2] Changes in estimated fair value related to economic hedges of variable annuity guarantees included in future policy benefits.

Fair Value Hedges

The Company designates and accounts for the following as fair value hedges when they have met the requirements of fair value hedging: (i) interest rate swaps to convert fixed rate assets and liabilities to floating rate assets and liabilities; (ii) foreign currency swaps to hedge the foreign currency fair value exposure of foreign currency denominated assets and liabilities; and (iii) foreign currency forwards to hedge the foreign currency fair value exposure of foreign currency denominated investments.

The Company recognizes gains and losses on derivatives and the related hedged items in fair value hedges within net derivative gains (losses). The following table presents the amount of such net derivative gains (losses):

Derivatives in Fair Value Hedging Relationships	Hedged Items in Fair Value Hedging Relationships	Net Derivative Gains (Losses) Recognized for Derivatives	Net Derivative Gains (Losses) Recognized for Hedged Items (In millions)	Ineffectiveness Recognized in Net Derivative Gains (Losses)
Year Ended December 31, 2015				
Interest rate swaps:	Fixed maturity securities	$ 5	$ —	$ 5
	Policyholder liabilities[1]	(2)	(8)	(10)
Foreign currency swaps:	Foreign-denominated fixed maturity securities	15	(7)	8
	Foreign-denominated policyholder account balances[2]	(240)	232	(8)
Foreign currency forwards:	Foreign-denominated fixed maturity securities	(75)	68	(7)
Total		$(297)	$ 285	$(12)
Year Ended December 31, 2014				
Interest rate swaps:	Fixed maturity securities	$ 5	$ (1)	$ 4
	Policyholder liabilities[1]	681	(667)	14
Foreign currency swaps:	Foreign-denominated fixed maturity securities	13	(11)	2
	Foreign-denominated policyholder account balances[2]	(283)	270	(13)
Foreign currency forwards:	Foreign-denominated fixed maturity securities	(359)	330	(29)
Total		$ 57	$ (79)	$(22)
Year Ended December 31, 2013				
Interest rate swaps:	Fixed maturity securities	$ 42	$ (43)	$ (1)
	Policyholder liabilities[1]	(830)	835	5
Foreign currency swaps:	Foreign-denominated fixed maturity securities	13	(12)	1
	Foreign-denominated policyholder account balances[2]	(97)	110	13
Foreign currency forwards:	Foreign-denominated fixed maturity securities	(109)	102	(7)
Total		$(981)	$ 992	$ 11

[1] Fixed rate liabilities reported in policyholder account balances or future policy benefits.

[2] Fixed rate or floating rate liabilities.

For the Company's foreign currency forwards, the change in the estimated fair value of the derivative related to the changes in the difference between the spot price and the forward price is excluded from the assessment of hedge effectiveness. For all other derivatives, all components of each derivative's gain or loss were included in the assessment of hedge effectiveness. For the years ended December 31, 2015, 2014 and 2013, the component of the change in estimated fair value of derivatives that was excluded from the assessment of hedge effectiveness was ($11) million, $3 million and ($2) million, respectively.

Cash Flow Hedges

The Company designates and accounts for the following as cash flow hedges when they have met the requirements of cash flow hedging: (i) interest rate swaps to convert floating rate assets and liabilities to fixed rate assets and liabilities; (ii) foreign currency swaps to hedge the foreign currency cash flow exposure of foreign currency denominated assets and liabilities; (iii) interest rate forwards and credit forwards to lock in the price to be paid for forward purchases of investments; (iv) interest rate swaps and interest rate forwards to hedge the forecasted purchases of fixed-rate investments; and (v) interest rate swaps and interest rate forwards to hedge forecasted fixed-rate borrowings.

In certain instances, the Company discontinued cash flow hedge accounting because the forecasted transactions were no longer probable of occurring. Because certain of the forecasted transactions also were not probable of occurring within two months of the anticipated date, the Company reclassified amounts from AOCI into net derivative gains (losses). These amounts were $11 million, ($15) million and ($1) million for the years ended December 31, 2015, 2014 and 2013, respectively.

At December 31, 2015 and 2014, the maximum length of time over which the Company was hedging its exposure to variability in future cash flows for forecasted transactions did not exceed five years and six years, respectively.

At December 31, 2015 and 2014, the balance in AOCI associated with cash flow hedges was $2.4 billion and $1.8 billion, respectively.

The following table presents the effects of derivatives in cash flow hedging relationships on the consolidated statements of operations and the consolidated statements of equity:

Derivatives in Cash Flow Hedging Relationships	Amount of Gains (Losses) Deferred in AOCI on Derivatives (Effective Portion)	Amount and Location of Gains (Losses) Reclassified from AOCI into Income (Loss) (Effective Portion)			Amount and Location of Gains (Losses) Recognized in Income (Loss) on Derivatives (Ineffective Portion)
		Net Derivative Gains (Losses)	Net Investment Income	Other Expenses	Net Derivative Gains (Losses)
		(In millions)			
Year Ended December 31, 2015					
Interest rate swaps	$ 91	$ 85	$12	$—	$ 3
Interest rate forwards	(1)	6	5	2	—
Foreign currency swaps	(109)	(720)	(1)	1	9
Credit forwards	—	1	1	—	—
Total	$ (19)	$(628)	$17	$3	$12
Year Ended December 31, 2014					
Interest rate swaps	$ 722	$ 42	$ 9	$—	$ 3
Interest rate forwards	86	(7)	4	2	—
Foreign currency swaps	(139)	(768)	(2)	2	1
Credit forwards	—	—	1	—	—
Total	$ 669	$(733)	$12	$ 4	$ 4
Year Ended December 31, 2013					
Interest rate swaps	$(635)	$ 20	$ 8	$—	$ (3)
Interest rate forwards	(59)	10	3	(1)	1
Foreign currency swaps	(165)	(3)	(3)	1	3
Credit forwards	(4)	—	1	—	—
Total	$(863)	$ 27	$ 9	$—	$ 1

All components of each derivative's gain or loss were included in the assessment of hedge effectiveness.

At December 31, 2015, $50 million of deferred net gains (losses) on derivatives in AOCI was expected to be reclassified to earnings within the next 12 months.

Hedges of Net Investments in Foreign Operations

The Company uses foreign currency exchange rate derivatives, which may include foreign currency forwards and currency options, to hedge portions of its net investments in foreign operations against adverse movements in exchange rates. The Company measures ineffectiveness on these derivatives based upon the change in forward rates.

When net investments in foreign operations are sold or substantially liquidated, the amounts in AOCI are reclassified to the statement of operations.

The following table presents the effects of derivatives in net investment hedging relationships on the consolidated statements of operations and the consolidated statements of equity:

	Amount of Gains (Losses) Deferred in AOCI (Effective Portion)		
Derivatives in Net Investment Hedging Relationships[1],[2]	Years Ended December 31,		
(In millions)	2015	2014	2013
Foreign currency forwards	$ 255	$407	$ 69
Currency options	(138)	222	262
Total	$ 117	$629	$331

[1] During the years ended December 31, 2015 and 2013, there were no sales or substantial liquidations of net investments in foreign operations that would have required the reclassification of gains or losses from AOCI into earnings. In May 2014, the Company sold its interest in MAL, which was a hedged item in a net investment hedging relationship. See Note 3. As a result, during the year ended December 31, 2014, the Company released losses of $77 million from AOCI into earnings upon the sale.

[2] There was no ineffectiveness recognized for the Company's hedges of net investments in foreign operations. All components of each derivative's gain or loss were included in the assessment of hedge effectiveness.

At December 31, 2015 and 2014, the cumulative foreign currency translation gain (loss) recorded in AOCI related to hedges of net investments in foreign operations was $1.1 billion and $940 million, respectively.

Credit Derivatives

In connection with synthetically created credit investment transactions and credit default swaps held in relation to the trading portfolio, the Company writes credit default swaps for which it receives a premium to insure credit risk. Such credit derivatives are included within the nonqualifying derivatives and derivatives for purposes other than hedging table. If a credit event occurs, as defined by the contract, the contract may be cash settled or it may be settled gross by the Company paying the counterparty the specified swap notional amount in exchange for the delivery of par quantities of the referenced credit obligation. The Company's maximum amount at risk, assuming the value of all referenced credit obligations is zero, was $10.3 billion and $10.5 billion at December 31, 2015 and 2014, respectively. The Company can terminate these contracts at any time through cash settlement with the counterparty at an amount equal to the then current estimated fair value of the credit default swaps. At December 31, 2015 and 2014, the Company would have received $65 million and $175 million, respectively, to terminate all of these contracts.

The following table presents the estimated fair value, maximum amount of future payments and weighted average years to maturity of written credit default swaps at:

	December 31,					
	2015			2014		
Rating Agency Designation of Referenced Credit Obligations[1]	Estimated Fair Value of Credit Default Swaps	Maximum Amount of Future Payments under Credit Default Swaps	Weighted Average Years to Maturity[2]	Estimated Fair Value of Credit Default Swaps	Maximum Amount of Future Payments under Credit Default Swaps	Weighted Average Years to Maturity[2]
	(In millions)			(In millions)		
Aaa/Aa/A						
Single name credit default swaps (corporate)	$ 6	$ 661	2.5	$ 10	$ 677	2.4
Credit default swaps referencing indices	6	1,635	3.4	10	1,700	2.6
Subtotal	12	2,296	3.2	20	2,377	2.6

(continued)

Rating Agency Designation of Referenced Credit Obligations[1]	December 31,						
	2015			2014			
	Estimated Fair Value of Credit Default Swaps (In millions)	Maximum Amount of Future Payments under Credit Default Swaps	Weighted Average Years to Maturity[2]	Estimated Fair Value of Credit Default Swaps (In millions)	Maximum Amount of Future Payments under Credit Default Swaps	Weighted Average Years to Maturity[2]	
Baa							
Single name credit default swaps (corporate)	8	1,349	2.5	23	1,591	2.8	
Credit default swaps referencing indices	37	5,863	4.8	94	5,774	4.7	
Subtotal	45	7,212	4.4	117	7,365	4.3	
Ba							
Single name credit default swaps (corporate)	(2)	64	2.3	—	60	3.0	
Credit default swaps referencing indices	(1)	100	1.0	(1)	100	2.0	
Subtotal	(3)	164	1.5	(1)	160	2.4	
B							
Single name credit default swaps (corporate)	—	—	—	—	—	—	
Credit default swaps referencing indices	11	639	4.9	39	625	4.9	
Subtotal	11	639	4.9	39	625	4.9	
Total	$65	$10,311	4.1	$175	$10,527	3.9	

[1] The rating agency designations are based on availability and the midpoint of the applicable ratings among Moody's Investors Service ("Moody's"), S&P and Fitch Ratings. If no rating is available from a rating agency, then an internally developed rating is used.

[2] The weighted average years to maturity of the credit default swaps is calculated based on weighted average gross notional amounts.

The Company has also entered into credit default swaps to purchase credit protection on certain of the referenced credit obligations in the table above. As a result, the maximum amounts of potential future recoveries available to offset the $10.3 billion and $10.5 billion from the table above were $80 million and $75 million at December 31, 2015 and 2014, respectively.

Written credit default swaps held in relation to the trading portfolio amounted to $20 million and $15 million in gross notional amount and ($2) million and $1 million in estimated fair value at December 31, 2015 and 2014, respectively.

Credit Risk on Freestanding Derivatives

The Company may be exposed to credit-related losses in the event of nonperformance by its counterparties to derivatives. Generally, the current credit exposure of the Company's derivatives is limited to the net positive estimated fair value of derivatives at the reporting date after taking into consideration the existence of master netting or similar agreements and any collateral received pursuant to such agreements.

The Company manages its credit risk related to derivatives by entering into transactions with creditworthy counterparties and establishing and monitoring exposure limits. The Company's OTC-bilateral derivative transactions are generally governed by ISDA Master Agreements which provide for legally enforceable set-off and close-out netting of exposures to specific counterparties in the event of early termination of a transaction, which includes, but is not limited to, events of default and bankruptcy. In the event of an early termination, the Company is permitted to set off receivables from the counterparty against payables to the same counterparty arising out of all included transactions. Substantially all of the Company's ISDA Master Agreements also include Credit Support Annex provisions which require both the pledging and accepting of collateral in connection with its OTC-bilateral derivatives.

The Company's OTC-cleared derivatives are effected through central clearing counterparties and its exchange-traded derivatives are effected through regulated exchanges. Such positions are marked to market and margined on a daily basis (both initial margin and variation margin), and the Company has minimal exposure to credit-related losses in the event of nonperformance by counterparties to such derivatives.

See Note 10 for a description of the impact of credit risk on the valuation of derivatives.

The estimated fair values of the Company's net derivative assets and net derivative liabilities after the application of master netting agreements and collateral were as follows at:

Derivatives Subject to a Master Netting Arrangement or a Similar Arrangement	December 31,			
	2015		2014	
	Assets	Liabilities	Assets	Liabilities
	(In millions)			
Gross estimated fair value of derivatives:				
OTC-bilateral[1]	$13,017	$ 5,848	$12,256	$ 6,017
OTC-cleared[1]	1,600	1,217	1,380	1,054
Exchange-traded	67	25	71	11
Total gross estimated fair value of derivatives[1]	14,684	7,090	13,707	7,082
Amounts offset on the consolidated balance sheets	—	—	—	—
Estimated fair value of derivatives presented on the consolidated balance sheets[1]	14,684	7,090	13,707	7,082
Gross amounts not offset on the consolidated balance sheets:				
Gross estimated fair value of derivatives:[2]				
OTC-bilateral	(4,368)	(4,368)	(4,082)	(4,082)
OTC-cleared	(1,200)	(1,200)	(989)	(989)
Exchange-traded	(1)	(1)	(5)	(5)
Cash collateral:[3], [4]				
OTC-bilateral	(6,140)	(7)	(4,153)	(133)
OTC-cleared	(378)	(10)	(386)	(62)
Exchange-traded	—	(20)	—	(4)
Securities collateral:[5]				
OTC-bilateral	(2,078)	(1,395)	(3,768)	(1,700)
OTC-cleared	—	—	—	(3)
Exchange-traded	—	(3)	—	(2)
Net amount after application of master netting agreements and collateral	$ 519	$ 86	$ 324	$ 102

[1] At December 31, 2015 and 2014, derivative assets included income or expense accruals reported in accrued investment income or in other liabilities of $278 million and $255 million, respectively, and derivative liabilities included income or expense accruals reported in accrued investment income or in other liabilities of $41 million and $60 million, respectively.

[2] Estimated fair value of derivatives is limited to the amount that is subject to set-off and includes income or expense accruals.

[3] Cash collateral received by the Company for OTC-bilateral and OTC-cleared derivatives is included in cash and cash equivalents, short-term investments or in fixed maturity securities, and the obligation to return it is included in payables for collateral under securities loaned and other transactions on the balance sheet. In certain instances, cash collateral pledged to the Company as initial margin for OTC-bilateral derivatives is held in separate custodial accounts and is not recorded on the Company's balance sheet because the account title is in the name of the counterparty (but segregated for the benefit of the Company). The amount of this off-balance sheet collateral was $0 and $263 million at December 31, 2015 and 2014, respectively.

[4] The receivable for the return of cash collateral provided by the Company is inclusive of initial margin on exchange-traded and OTC-cleared derivatives and is included in premiums, reinsurance and other receivables on the balance sheet. The amount of cash collateral offset in the table above is limited to the net estimated fair value of derivatives after application of netting agreements. At December 31, 2015 and 2014, the Company received excess cash collateral of $89 million and $87 million (including $0 and $36 million off-balance sheet cash collateral held in separate custodial accounts), respectively, and provided excess cash collateral of $204 million and $192 million, respectively, which is not included in the table above due to the foregoing limitation.

[5] Securities collateral received by the Company is held in separate custodial accounts and is not recorded on the balance sheet. Subject to certain constraints, the Company is permitted by contract to sell or re-pledge this collateral, but at December 31, 2015 none of the collateral had been sold or re-pledged. Securities collateral pledged by the Company is reported in fixed maturity securities on the balance sheet. Subject to certain constraints, the counterparties are permitted by contract to sell or re-pledge this collateral. The amount of securities collateral offset in the table above is limited to the net estimated fair value of derivatives after application of netting agreements and cash collateral. At December 31, 2015 and 2014, the Company received excess securities collateral with an estimated fair value of $100 million and $395 million, respectively, for its OTC-bilateral derivatives, which are not included in the table above due to the foregoing limitation. At December 31, 2015 and 2014, the Company provided excess securities collateral with an estimated fair value of $150 million and $117 million, respectively, for its OTC-bilateral derivatives, $315 million and $199 million, respectively, for its OTC-cleared derivatives, and $224 million and $245 million, respectively, for its exchange-traded derivatives, which are not included in the table above due to the foregoing limitation.

The Company's collateral arrangements for its OTC-bilateral derivatives generally require the counterparty in a net liability position, after considering the effect of netting agreements, to pledge collateral when the estimated fair value of that counterparty's derivatives reaches a pre-determined threshold. Certain of these arrangements also include credit-contingent provisions that provide for a reduction of these thresholds (on a sliding scale that converges toward zero) in the event of downgrades in the credit ratings of the Company and/or the counterparty. In addition, certain of the Company's netting agreements for derivatives contain provisions that require both the Company and the counterparty to maintain a specific investment grade credit rating from each of Moody's and S&P. If a party's credit ratings were to fall below that specific investment grade credit rating, that party would be in violation of these provisions, and the other party to the derivatives could terminate the transactions and demand immediate settlement and payment based on such party's reasonable valuation of the derivatives.

The following table presents the estimated fair value of the Company's OTC-bilateral derivatives that are in a net liability position after considering the effect of netting agreements, together with the estimated fair value and balance sheet location of the collateral pledged. The table also presents the incremental collateral that the Company would be required to provide if there was a one notch downgrade in the Company's credit rating at the reporting date or if the Company's credit rating sustained a downgrade to a level that triggered full overnight collateralization or termination of the derivative position at the reporting date. OTC-bilateral derivatives that are not subject to collateral agreements are excluded from this table.

| (In millions) | December 31, | | | | | |
| | 2015 | | | 2014 | | |
	Derivatives Subject to Credit-Contingent Provisions	Derivatives Not Subject to Credit-Contingent Provisions	Total	Derivatives Subject to Credit-Contingent Provisions	Derivatives Not Subject to Credit-Contingent Provisions	Total
Estimated fair value of derivatives in a net liability position[1]	$1,270	$207	$1,477	$1,832	$ 84	$1,916
Estimated Fair Value of Collateral Provided						
Fixed maturity securities	$1,365	$174	$1,539	$1,750	$ 65	$1,815
Cash	$ 4	$ 4	$ 8	$ 131	$ 2	$ 133
Fair Value of Incremental Collateral Provided Upon						
One notch downgrade in the company's credit rating	$ 1	$ —	$ 1	$ 5	$—	$ 5
Downgrade in the company's credit rating to a level that triggers full overnight collateralization or termination of the derivative position	$ 1	$ —	$ 1	$ 7	$—	$ 7

[1] After taking into consideration the existence of netting agreements.

Embedded Derivatives

The Company issues certain products or purchases certain investments that contain embedded derivatives that are required to be separated from their host contracts and accounted for as freestanding derivatives. These host contracts principally include: variable annuities with guaranteed minimum benefits, including GMWBs, GMABs and certain GMIBs; ceded reinsurance of guaranteed minimum benefits related to certain GMIBs; assumed reinsurance of guaranteed minimum benefits related to GMWBs and GMABs; funding agreements with equity or bond indexed crediting rates; funds withheld on assumed and ceded reinsurance; fixed annuities with equity-indexed returns; and certain debt and equity securities.

The following table presents the estimated fair value and balance sheet location of the Company's embedded derivatives that have been separated from their host contracts at:

| (In millions) | Balance Sheet Location | December 31, | |
		2015	2014
Net embedded derivatives within asset host contracts:			
Ceded guaranteed minimum benefits	Premiums, reinsurance and other receivables	$ 356	$ 324
Funds withheld on assumed reinsurance	Other invested assets	35	53
Options embedded in debt or equity securities	Investments	(220)	(217)
Net embedded derivatives within asset host contracts		$ 171	$ 160
Net embedded derivatives within liability host contracts:			
Direct guaranteed minimum benefits	Policyholder account balances and Future policy benefits	$ (20)	$(1,126)
Assumed guaranteed minimum benefits	Policyholder account balances	965	973
Funds withheld on ceded reinsurance	Other liabilities	(14)	83
Other	Policyholder account balances	4	24
Net embedded derivatives within liability host contracts		$ 935	$ (46)

The following table presents changes in estimated fair value related to embedded derivatives:

| (In millions) | Years Ended December 31, | | |
	2015	2014	2013
Net derivative gains (losses)[1]	$(239)	$(321)	$5,104
Policyholder benefits and claims	$ 21	$ 87	$ (139)

[1] The valuation of guaranteed minimum benefits includes a nonperformance risk adjustment. The amounts included in net derivative gains (losses) in connection with this adjustment were $163 million, $13 million and ($952) million for the years ended December 31, 2015, 2014 and 2013, respectively.

CHANGE IN VALUE OF INVESTMENTS

3.16 ANTHEM, INC. (DEC)
CONSOLIDATED STATEMENTS OF INCOME (in part)

(In millions, except per share data)	Years Ended December 31		
	2015	2014	2013
Revenues			
Premiums	$73,385.1	$68,389.8	$66,119.1
Administrative fees	4,976.6	4,590.6	4,031.9
Other revenue	43.1	41.3	40.4
Total operating revenue	78,404.8	73,021.7	70,191.4
Net investment income	677.6	724.4	659.1
Net realized gains on investments	157.5	177.0	271.9
Other-than-temporary impairment losses on investments:			
Total other-than-temporary impairment losses on investments	(99.9)	(56.2)	(100.6)
Portion of other-than-temporary impairment losses recognized in other comprehensive income	16.5	7.2	1.7
Other-than-temporary impairment losses recognized in income	(83.4)	(49.0)	(98.9)
Total revenues	79,156.5	73,874.1	71,023.5

NOTES TO CONSOLIDATED FINANCIAL STATEMENTS (in part)

(In Millions, Except Per Share Data or As Otherwise Stated Herein)

2. Basis of Presentation and Significant Accounting Policies (in part)

Investments: Certain Financial Accounting Standards Board, or FASB, other-than-temporary impairment, or OTTI, guidance applies to fixed maturity securities and provides guidance on the recognition, presentation of, and disclosures for OTTIs. If a fixed maturity security is in an unrealized loss position and we have the intent to sell the fixed maturity security, or it is more likely than not that we will have to sell the fixed maturity security before recovery of its amortized cost basis, the decline in value is deemed to be other-than-temporary and is presented within the Other-than-temporary impairment losses recognized in income line item on our consolidated statements of income. For impaired fixed maturity securities that we do not intend to sell or it is more likely than not that we will not have to sell such securities, but we expect that we will not fully recover the amortized cost basis, the credit component of the OTTI is presented within the Other-than-temporary impairment losses recognized in income line item on our consolidated statements of income and the non-credit component of the OTTI is recognized in other comprehensive income. Furthermore, unrealized losses entirely caused by non-credit related factors related to fixed maturity securities for which we expect to fully recover the amortized cost basis continue to be recognized in accumulated other comprehensive income, or AOCI.

The credit component of an OTTI is determined primarily by comparing the net present value of projected future cash flows with the amortized cost basis of the fixed maturity security. The net present value is calculated by discounting our best estimate of projected future cash flows at the effective interest rate implicit in the fixed maturity security at the date of acquisition. For mortgage-backed and asset-backed securities, cash flow estimates are based on assumptions regarding the underlying collateral including prepayment speeds, vintage, type of underlying asset, geographic concentrations, default rates, recoveries and changes in value. For all other debt securities, cash flow estimates are driven by assumptions regarding probability of default, including changes in credit ratings, and estimates regarding timing and amount of recoveries associated with a default.

The unrealized gains or losses on our current and long-term equity securities classified as available-for-sale are included in accumulated other comprehensive income as a separate component of shareholders' equity, unless the decline in value is deemed to be other-than-temporary and we do not have the intent and ability to hold such equity securities until their full cost can be recovered, in which case such equity securities are written down to fair value and the loss is charged to other-than-temporary impairment losses recognized in income.

We maintain various rabbi trusts to account for the assets and liabilities under certain deferred compensation plans. Under these plans, the participants can defer certain types of compensation and elect to receive a return on the deferred amounts based on the changes in fair value of various investment options, primarily a variety of mutual funds. We have corporate-owned life insurance policies on certain participants in the deferred compensation plans. The cash surrender value of the corporate-owned life insurance policies is reported in other invested assets, long-term, in the consolidated balance sheets. The remaining rabbi trust assets are generally invested according to the participant's investment election, and are classified as trading, which are reported in other invested assets, current, in the consolidated balance sheets.

We use the equity method of accounting for investments in companies in which our ownership interest enables us to influence the operating or financial decisions of the investee company. Our proportionate share of equity in net income of these unconsolidated affiliates is reported with net investment income.

For asset-backed securities included in fixed maturity securities, we recognize income using an effective yield based on anticipated prepayments and the estimated economic life of the securities. When estimates of prepayments change, the effective yield is recalculated to reflect actual payments to date and anticipated future payments. The net investment in the securities is adjusted to the amount that would have existed had the new effective yield been applied since the acquisition of the securities. Such adjustments are reported with net investment income.

Investment income is recorded when earned. All securities sold resulting in investment gains and losses are recorded on the trade date. Realized gains and losses are determined on the basis of the cost or amortized cost of the specific securities sold.

We participate in securities lending programs whereby marketable securities in our investment portfolio are transferred to independent brokers or dealers in exchange for cash and securities collateral. Under FASB guidance related to accounting for transfers and servicing of financial assets and extinguishments of liabilities, we recognize the collateral as an asset, which is reported as "Securities lending collateral" on our consolidated balance sheets and we record a corresponding liability for the obligation to return the collateral to the borrower, which is reported as "Securities lending payable." The securities on loan are reported in the applicable investment category on our consolidated balance sheets. Unrealized gains or losses on securities lending collateral are included in accumulated other comprehensive income as a separate component of shareholders' equity. The market value of loaned securities and that of the collateral pledged can fluctuate in non-synchronized fashions. To the extent the loaned securities' value appreciates faster or depreciates slower than the value of the collateral pledged, we are exposed to the risk of the shortfall. As a primary mitigating mechanism, the loaned securities and collateral pledged are marked to market on a daily basis and the shortfall, if any, is collected accordingly. Secondarily, the collateral level is set at 102% of the value of the loaned securities, which provides a cushion before any shortfall arises. The investment of the cash collateral is subject to market risk, which is managed by limiting the investments to higher quality and shorter duration instruments.

4. Investments (in part)

A summary of current and long-term investments, available-for-sale, at December 31, 2015 and 2014 is as follows:

	Cost or Amortized Cost	Gross Unrealized Gains	Gross Unrealized Losses Less than 12 Months	12 Months or Greater	Estimated Fair Value	Non-Credit Component of Other-Than-Temporary Impairments Recognized in AOCI
December 31, 2015						
Fixed maturity securities:						
United States Government securities	$ 349.5	$ 2.0	$ (1.6)	$ —	$ 349.9	$ —
Government sponsored securities	75.6	0.5	(0.1)	(0.1)	75.9	—
States, municipalities and political subdivisions, tax-exempt	5,976.7	284.1	(4.0)	(5.2)	6,251.6	—
Corporate securities	8,209.7	61.1	(267.2)	(110.5)	7,893.1	(15.4)
Residential mortgage-backed securities	1,724.5	41.2	(7.6)	(7.2)	1,750.9	—
Commercial mortgage-backed securities	407.6	1.4	(4.3)	(0.4)	404.3	—
Other debt securities	756.8	4.1	(5.8)	(2.6)	752.5	—
Total fixed maturity securities	17,500.4	394.4	(290.6)	(126.0)	17,478.2	$(15.4)
Equity securities	1,083.1	420.6	(30.9)	—	1,472.8	
Total investments, available-for-sale	$18,583.5	$ 815.0	$(321.5)	$(126.0)	$18,951.0	
December 31, 2014						
Fixed maturity securities:						
United States Government securities	$ 315.7	$ 4.6	$ (0.3)	$ —	$ 320.0	$ —
Government sponsored securities	94.6	0.8	—	(0.4)	95.0	—
States, municipalities and political subdivisions, tax-exempt	5,451.4	287.0	(1.8)	(3.0)	5,733.6	—
Corporate securities	8,335.9	162.9	(123.1)	(43.2)	8,332.5	(6.8)
Options embedded in convertible securities	98.7	—	—	—	98.7	
Residential mortgage-backed securities	2,099.7	68.9	(1.0)	(8.6)	2,159.0	—
Commercial mortgage-backed securities	504.8	6.1	(0.6)	(0.4)	509.9	—
Other debt securities	720.3	6.1	(1.7)	(1.6)	723.1	—
Total fixed maturity securities	17,621.1	536.4	(128.5)	(57.2)	17,971.8	$ (6.8)
Equity securities	1,330.7	618.5	(11.1)	—	1,938.1	
Total investments, available-for-sale	$18,951.8	$1,154.9	$(139.6)	$ (57.2)	$19,909.9	

At December 31, 2015, we owned $2,155.2 of mortgage-backed securities and $698.6 of asset-backed securities out of a total available-for-sale investment portfolio of $18,951.0. These securities included sub-prime and Alt-A securities with fair values of $30.9 and $58.2, respectively. These sub-prime and Alt-A securities had accumulated net unrealized gains of $1.0 and $3.3, respectively. The average credit rating of the sub-prime and Alt-A securities was "CCC" and "CC", respectively.

At December 31, 2015, we owned $777.2 of energy sector fixed maturity securities out of a total available-for-sale investment portfolio of $18,951.0. These energy sector securities had accumulated net unrealized losses of $172.0.

For available-for-sale securities in an unrealized loss position at December 31, 2015 and 2014, the following table summarizes the aggregate fair values and gross unrealized losses by length of time those securities have continuously been in an unrealized loss position.

(Securities are whole amounts)	Less than 12 Months			12 Months or Greater		
	Number of Securities	Estimated Fair Value	Gross Unrealized Loss	Number of Securities	Estimated Fair Value	Gross Unrealized Loss
December 31, 2015						
Fixed maturity securities:						
United States Government securities	48	$ 248.4	$ (1.6)	2	$ 0.9	$ —
Government sponsored securities	13	18.3	(0.1)	6	8.2	(0.1)
States, municipalities and political subdivisions, tax-exempt	198	467.8	(4.0)	43	83.0	(5.2)
Corporate securities	2,492	4,912.3	(267.2)	372	447.0	(110.5)
Residential mortgage-backed securities	298	668.3	(7.6)	119	186.3	(7.2)
Commercial mortgage-backed securities	66	263.0	(4.3)	17	38.5	(0.4)
Other debt securities	153	488.2	(5.8)	28	77.0	(2.6)
Total fixed maturity securities	3,268	7,066.3	(290.6)	587	840.9	(126.0)
Equity securities	792	261.1	(30.9)	—	—	—
Total fixed maturity and equity securities	4,060	$7,327.4	$(321.5)	587	$ 840.9	$(126.0)
December 31, 2014						
Fixed maturity securities:						
United States Government securities	17	$ 145.3	$ (0.3)	2	$ 0.9	$ —
Government sponsored securities	2	0.3	—	16	29.3	(0.4)
States, municipalities and political subdivisions, tax-exempt	136	315.6	(1.8)	80	174.3	(3.0)
Corporate securities	1,802	3,213.3	(123.1)	314	514.6	(43.2)
Residential mortgage-backed securities	78	155.0	(1.0)	186	398.3	(8.6)
Commercial mortgage-backed securities	43	156.2	(0.6)	10	33.2	(0.4)
Other debt securities	79	270.6	(1.7)	21	65.0	(1.6)
Total fixed maturity securities	2,157	4,256.3	(128.5)	629	1,215.6	(57.2)
Equity securities	407	125.4	(11.1)	—	—	—
Total fixed maturity and equity securities	2,564	$4,381.7	$(139.6)	629	$1,215.6	$ (57.2)

The amortized cost and fair value of available-for-sale fixed maturity securities at December 31, 2015, by contractual maturity, are shown below. Expected maturities may differ from contractual maturities because the issuers of the securities may have the right to prepay obligations.

	Amortized Cost	Estimated Fair Value
Due in one year or less	$ 276.6	$ 278.6
Due after one year through five years	4,872.9	4,792.3
Due after five years through ten years	5,392.0	5,390.1
Due after ten years	4,826.8	4,862.0
Mortgage-backed securities	2,132.1	2,155.2
Total available-for-sale fixed maturity securities	$17,500.4	$17,478.2

The major categories of net investment income (loss) for the years ended December 31 are as follows:

	2015	2014	2013
Fixed maturity securities	$679.0	$644.1	$638.9
Equity securities	61.7	57.7	45.9
Cash equivalents	0.7	0.8	1.0
Other	(22.6)	66.3	19.8
Investment income	718.8	768.9	705.6
Investment expense	(41.2)	(44.5)	(46.5)
Net investment income	$677.6	$724.4	$659.1

Net realized investment gains/losses and net change in unrealized appreciation/depreciation in investments for the years ended December 31 are as follows:

	2015	2014	2013
Net realized gains (losses) on investments:			
Fixed maturity securities:			
Gross realized gains from sales	$ 135.9	$198.2	$ 225.9
Gross realized losses from sales	(182.1)	(50.6)	(125.7)
Net realized (losses) gains from sales of fixed maturity securities	(46.2)	147.6	100.2
Equity securities:			
Gross realized gains from sales	233.4	93.5	189.6
Gross realized losses from sales	(45.1)	(13.9)	(13.4)
Net realized gains from sales of equity securities	188.3	79.6	176.2
Other investments:			
Gross realized gains from sales	139.8	14.4	107.2
Gross realized losses from sales	(124.4)	(64.6)	(111.7)
Net realized gains (losses) from sales of other investments	15.4	(50.2)	(4.5)
Net realized gains on investments	157.5	177.0	271.9
Other-than-temporary impairment losses recognized in income:			
Fixed maturity securities	(31.2)	(22.3)	(42.5)
Equity securities	(35.6)	(13.5)	(13.9)
Other invested assets, long-term	(16.6)	(13.2)	(42.5)
Other-than-temporary impairment losses recognized in income	(83.4)	(49.0)	(98.9)
Change in net unrealized (losses) gains on investments:			
Fixed maturity securities	(372.9)	145.2	(679.8)
Equity securities	(217.7)	36.5	225.4
Other invested assets, long-term	(4.1)	—	—
Total change in net unrealized (losses) gains on investments	(594.7)	181.7	(454.4)
Deferred income tax benefit (expense)	210.4	(63.1)	159.7
Net change in net unrealized (losses) gains on investments	(384.3)	118.6	(294.7)
Net realized gains on investments, other-than-temporary impairment losses recognized in income and net change in net unrealized (losses) gains on investments	$(310.2)	$246.6	$(121.7)

A primary objective in the management of our fixed maturity and equity portfolios is to maximize total return relative to underlying liabilities and respective liquidity needs. In achieving this goal, assets may be sold to take advantage of market conditions or other investment opportunities as well as tax considerations. Sales will generally produce realized gains and losses. In the ordinary course of business, we may sell securities at a loss for a number of reasons, including, but not limited to: (i) changes in the investment environment; (ii) expectations that the fair value could deteriorate further; (iii) desire to reduce exposure to an issuer or an industry; (iv) changes in credit quality; or (v) changes in expected cash flow.

Proceeds from fixed maturity securities, equity securities and other invested assets and the related gross realized gains and gross realized losses for the years ended December 31 are as follows:

	2015	2014	2013
Proceeds	$11,779.8	$10,255.9	$13,662.8
Gross realized gains	509.1	306.1	522.7
Gross realized losses	(351.6)	(129.1)	(250.8)

A significant judgment in the valuation of investments is the determination of when an other-than-temporary decline in value has occurred. We follow a consistent and systematic process for recognizing impairments on securities that sustain other-than-temporary declines in value. We have established a committee responsible for the impairment review process. The decision to impair a security incorporates both quantitative criteria and qualitative information. The impairment review process considers a number of factors including, but not limited to: (i) the length of time and the extent to which the fair value has been less than book value, (ii) the financial condition and near term prospects of the issuer, (iii) our intent and ability to retain impaired investments for a period of time sufficient to allow for any anticipated recovery in fair value, (iv) our intent to sell or the likelihood that we will need to sell a fixed maturity security before recovery of its amortized cost basis, (v) whether the debtor is current on interest and principal payments, (vi) the reasons for the decline in value (i.e., credit event compared to liquidity, general credit spread widening, currency exchange rate or interest rate factors) and (vii) general market conditions and industry or sector specific factors. For securities that are deemed to be other-than-temporarily impaired, the security is adjusted to fair value and the resulting losses are recognized in the consolidated statements of income. The new cost basis of the impaired securities is not increased for future recoveries in fair value.

Other-than-temporary impairments recorded in 2015, 2014 and 2013 were primarily the result of the continued credit deterioration on specific issuers in the bond markets and the fair values of certain equity securities remaining below cost for an extended period of time. There were no individually significant OTTI losses on investments by issuer during 2015, 2014 or 2013.

Investment securities are exposed to various risks, such as interest rate, market and credit. Due to the level of risk associated with certain investment securities and the level of uncertainty related to changes in the value of investment securities, it is possible that changes in these risk factors in the near term could have an adverse material impact on our results of operations or shareholders' equity.

The changes in the amount of the credit component of OTTI losses on fixed maturity securities recognized in income, for which a portion of the OTTI losses was recognized in other comprehensive income, was not material for the years ended December 31, 2015, 2014 or 2013.

At December 31, 2015 and 2014, no investments exceeded 10% of shareholders' equity.

At December 31, 2015 and 2014, the carrying value of fixed maturity investments that did not produce income during the years then ended were $0.2 and $9.2, respectively.

As of December 31, 2015 we had committed approximately $662.3 to future capital calls from various third-party investments in exchange for an ownership interest in the related entities.

At December 31, 2015 and 2014, securities with carrying values of approximately $558.2 and $504.4, respectively, were deposited by our insurance subsidiaries under requirements of regulatory authorities.

In the tables above, certain amounts for the years ended December 31, 2014 and 2013 have been reclassified to conform to the current year presentation. The reclassifications do not impact amounts presented in the financial statements.

INSURANCE RECOVERIES

3.17 ASHLAND INC. (SEP)
NOTES TO CONSOLIDATED FINANCIAL STATEMENTS (in part)

Note C—Discontinued Operations (in part)

In previous periods, Ashland has divested certain businesses that have qualified as discontinued operations. The operating results from these divested businesses and subsequent adjustments related to ongoing assessments of certain retained liabilities and tax items have been recorded within the discontinued operations caption in the Statements of Consolidated Comprehensive Income for all periods presented and are discussed further within this note.

Ashland is subject to liabilities from claims alleging personal injury caused by exposure to asbestos. Such claims result primarily from indemnification obligations undertaken in 1990 in connection with the sale of Riley, a former subsidiary, which qualified as a discontinued operation and from the acquisition during 2009 of Hercules, a wholly-owned subsidiary of Ashland. Adjustments to the recorded litigation reserves and related insurance receivables are recorded within the discontinued operations caption and continue periodically. During 2015, Ashland recorded an after-tax gain of $120 million within discontinued operations due to the January 2015 asbestos insurance settlement. See Note N for further discussion of Ashland's asbestos-related activity.

Note N—Litigation, Claims and Contingencies (in part)

Asbestos Litigation (in part)

Ashland and Hercules have liabilities from claims alleging personal injury caused by exposure to asbestos. To assist in developing and annually updating independent reserve estimates for future asbestos claims and related costs given various assumptions, Ashland retained Hamilton, Rabinovitz & Associates, Inc. (HR&A). The methodology used by HR&A to project future asbestos costs is based largely on recent experience, including claim-filing and settlement rates, disease mix, enacted legislation, open claims and litigation defense. The claim experience of Ashland and Hercules are separately compared to the results of previously conducted third party epidemiological studies estimating the number of people likely to develop asbestos-related diseases. Those studies were undertaken in connection with national analyses of the population expected to have been exposed to asbestos. Using that information, HR&A estimates a range of the number of future claims that may be filed, as well as the related costs that may be incurred in resolving those claims. Changes in asbestos-related liabilities and receivables are recorded on an after-tax basis within the discontinued operations caption in the Statements of Consolidated Comprehensive Income.

Ashland asbestos-related litigation

The claims alleging personal injury caused by exposure to asbestos asserted against Ashland result primarily from indemnification obligations undertaken in 1990 in connection with the sale of Riley, a former subsidiary. The amount and timing of settlements and number of open claims can fluctuate from period to period. A summary of Ashland asbestos claims activity, excluding Hercules claims, follows.

(In thousands)	2015	2014	2013
Open claims—beginning of year	65	65	66
New claims filed	2	2	2
Claims settled	—	(1)	(1)
Claims dismissed	(7)	(1)	(2)
Open claims—end of year	60	65	65

Ashland asbestos-related liability

From the range of estimates, Ashland records the amount it believes to be the best estimate of future payments for litigation defense and claim settlement costs, which generally approximates the mid-point of the estimated range of exposure from model results. Ashland reviews this estimate and related assumptions quarterly and annually updates the results of a non-inflated, non-discounted approximate 50-year model developed with the assistance of HR&A.

During the most recent update, completed during 2015, it was determined that the liability for Ashland asbestos claims did not need to be adjusted. Total reserves for asbestos claims were $409 million at September 30, 2015 compared to $438 million at September 30, 2014.

A progression of activity in the asbestos reserve is presented in the following table.

(In millions)	2015	2014	2013
Asbestos reserve—beginning of year	$438	$463	$522
Reserve adjustment	—	4	(28)
Amounts paid	(29)	(29)	(31)
Asbestos reserve—end of year	$409	$438	$463

Ashland asbestos-related receivables

Ashland has insurance coverage for certain litigation defense and claim settlement costs incurred in connection with its asbestos claims, and coverage-in-place agreements exist with the insurance companies that provide substantially all of the coverage that will be accessed.

For the Ashland asbestos-related obligations, Ashland has estimated the value of probable insurance recoveries associated with its asbestos reserve based on management's interpretations and estimates surrounding the available or applicable insurance coverage, including an assumption that all solvent insurance carriers remain solvent. Substantially all of the estimated receivables from insurance companies are expected to be due from domestic insurers. Approximately 45% of the receivable is from insurance companies rated by A.M. Best, all of which have a credit rating of A- or higher as of September 30, 2015.

In October 2012, Ashland and Hercules initiated various arbitration proceedings against Underwriters at Lloyd's, certain London companies and/or Chartis (AIG) member companies seeking to enforce these insurers' contractual obligations to provide indemnity for asbestos liabilities and defense costs under existing coverage-in-place agreements. In addition, Ashland and Hercules initiated a lawsuit in Kentucky state court against certain Berkshire Hathaway entities (National Indemnity Company and Resolute Management, Inc.) on grounds that these Berkshire Hathaway entities had wrongfully interfered with Underwriters' and Chartis' performance of their respective contractual obligations to provide asbestos coverage by directing the insurers to reduce and delay certain claim payments.

On January 13, 2015, Ashland and Hercules entered into a comprehensive settlement agreement related to certain insurance coverage for asbestos bodily injury claims with Underwriters at Lloyd's, certain London companies and Chartis (AIG) member companies, along with National Indemnity Company and Resolute Management, Inc., under which Ashland and Hercules received a total of $398 million. In exchange, all claims were released against these entities for past, present and future coverage obligations arising out of the asbestos coverage-in-place agreements that were the subject of the pending arbitration proceedings. In addition, as part of this settlement, Ashland and Hercules released all claims against National Indemnity Company and Resolute Management, Inc. in the Kentucky state court action. As a result, the arbitration proceedings and the Kentucky state court action have been terminated.

As a result of this settlement, Ashland recorded an after-tax gain of $120 million within the discontinued operations caption of the Statements of Consolidated Comprehensive Income during 2015. The Ashland insurance receivable balance was also reduced as a result of this settlement by $227 million within the Consolidated Balance Sheets.

In addition, Ashland placed $335 million of the settlement funds received into a renewable annual trust restricted for the purpose of paying for ongoing and future litigation defense and claim settlement costs incurred in conjunction with asbestos claims.

At September 30, 2015, Ashland's receivable for recoveries of litigation defense and claim settlement costs from insurers amounted to $150 million (excluding the Hercules receivable for asbestos claims), of which $12 million relates to costs previously paid. Receivables from insurers amounted to $402 million at September 30, 2014. During 2015, the annual update of the model used for purposes of valuing the asbestos reserve and its impact on valuation of future recoveries from insurers, was completed. This model update resulted in a $3 million decrease in the receivable for probable insurance recoveries.

A progression of activity in the Ashland insurance receivable is presented in the following table.

(In millions)	2015	2014	2013
Insurance receivable—beginning of year	$402	$408	$423
Receivable adjustment	(3)	22	(3)
Insurance settlement	(227)	—	—
Amounts collected	(22)	(28)	(12)
Insurance receivable—end of year	$150	$402	$408

GAINS ON EXTINGUISHMENT OF DEBT

3.18 CLIFFS NATURAL RESOURCES INC. (DEC)
STATEMENTS OF CONSOLIDATED OPERATIONS (in part)

	Year Ended December 31,		
(In Millions, Except Per Share Amounts)	2015	2014	2013
Revenues From Product Sales And Services			
Product	$ 1,832.4	$ 3,095.2	$ 3,631.8
Freight and venture partners' cost reimbursements	180.9	278.0	259.0
	2,013.3	3,373.2	3,890.8
Cost Of Goods Sold And Operating Expenses	(1,776.8)	(2,487.5)	(2,406.4)
Sales Margin	236.5	885.7	1,484.4
Other Operating Income (Expense)			
Selling, general and administrative expenses	(110.0)	(154.7)	(163.8)
Impairment of goodwill and other long-lived assets	(3.3)	(635.5)	(14.3)
Miscellaneous—net	28.1	34.6	74.0
	(85.2)	(755.6)	(104.1)
Operating Income	151.3	130.1	1,380.3
Other Income (Expense)			
Interest expense, net	(228.5)	(176.7)	(186.4)
Gain on extinguishment of debt	392.9	16.2	—
Other non-operating income (expense)	(2.6)	10.7	(3.0)
	161.8	(149.8)	(189.4)
Income (Loss) From Continuing Operations Before Income Taxes And Equity Loss From Ventures	313.1	(19.7)	1,190.9
Income Tax Benefit (Expense)	(169.3)	86.0	(237.6)
Equity Loss From Ventures, net of tax	(0.1)	(9.9)	(74.4)
Income From Continuing Operations	143.7	56.4	878.9
Loss From Discontinued Operations, net of tax	(892.1)	(8,368.0)	(517.1)
Net Income (Loss)	(748.4)	(8,311.6)	361.8

NOTES TO CONSOLIDATED FINANCIAL STATEMENTS (in part)

Note 5—Debt and Credit Facilities (in part)

The following represents a summary of our long-term debt as of December 31, 2015 and 2014:

($ in Millions) Debt Instrument	Type	December 31, 2015 Annual Effective Interest Rate	Final Maturity	Total Principal Amount	Total Debt
$700 Million 4.875% 2021 Senior Notes	Fixed	4.89%	2021	$ 412.5	$ 410.6[1]
$1.3 Billion Senior Notes:					
$500 Million 4.80% 2020 Senior Notes	Fixed	4.83%	2020	306.7	305.2[2]
$800 Million 6.25% 2040 Senior Notes	Fixed	6.34%	2040	492.8	482.7[3]
$400 Million 5.90% 2020 Senior Notes	Fixed	5.98%	2020	290.8	288.9[4]
$500 Million 3.95% 2018 Senior Notes	Fixed	6.30%	2018	311.2	309.1[5]
$540 Million 8.25% 2020 First Lien Notes	Fixed	9.97%	2020	540.0	497.4[6]
$544.2 Million 7.75% 2020 Second Lien Notes	Fixed	15.55%	2020	544.2	403.2[7]
$550 Million ABL Facility:					
ABL Facility	Variable	N/A	2020	550.0	—[8]
Fair Value Adjustment to Interest Rate Hedge					2.3
Total debt				$3,448.2	$2,699.4

(continued)

($ in Millions) Debt Instrument	Type	Annual Effective Interest Rate	Final Maturity	Total Face Amount	Total Debt
$700 Million 4.875% 2021 Senior Notes	Fixed	4.89%	2021	$ 690.0	$ 686.0[1]
$1.3 Billion Senior Notes:					
$500 Million 4.80% 2020 Senior Notes	Fixed	4.83%	2020	490.0	487.2[2]
$800 Million 6.25% 2040 Senior Notes	Fixed	6.34%	2040	800.0	783.3[3]
$400 Million 5.90% 2020 Senior Notes	Fixed	5.98%	2020	395.0	391.9[4]
$500 Million 3.95% 2018 Senior Notes	Fixed	5.17%	2018	480.0	475.3[5]
$1.125 Billion Credit Facility:					
Revolving Credit Agreement	Variable	2.94%	2017	1,125.0	—[9]
Fair Value Adjustment to Interest Rate Hedge					2.8
Long-term debt				$3,980.0	$2,826.5

[1] During the third quarter of 2015, we purchased $10.7 million of outstanding 4.875 percent senior notes that were trading at 50.0 percent of par which resulted in a gain on extinguishment of $5.3 million. In addition, during the first quarter of 2015, we purchased $58.3 million of outstanding 4.875 percent senior notes that were trading at 52.0 percent of par, which resulted in a gain on extinguishment of $20.0 million. Also during the first quarter, on March 27, 2015, we exchanged as part of a tender offer $208.5 million of the 4.875 percent senior notes for $170.3 million of the 7.75 percent second lien notes at a discount of $46.0 million based on an imputed interest rate of 15.55 percent, resulting in a gain on extinguishment of $83.1 million, net of amounts expensed for unamortized original issue discount and deferred origination fees.

During the fourth quarter of 2014, we purchased $10.0 million of outstanding 4.875 percent senior notes that were trading at a discount of 40.5 percent which resulted in a gain on the extinguishment of debt of $4.1 million.

As of December 31, 2015, the $700.0 million 4.875 percent senior notes were recorded at a par value of $412.5 million less debt issuance costs of $1.7 million and unamortized discounts of $0.2 million, based on an imputed interest rate of 4.89 percent. As of December 31, 2014, the $700.0 million 4.875 percent senior notes were recorded at a par value of $690.0 million less debt issuance costs of $3.5 million and unamortized discounts of $0.5 million, based on an imputed interest rate of 4.89 percent.

[2] During the third quarter of 2015, we purchased $1.8 million of outstanding 4.80 percent senior notes that were trading at 50.0 percent of par, which resulted in a gain on extinguishment of $0.9 million. In addition, during the first quarter of 2015, we purchased $43.8 million of outstanding 4.80 percent senior notes that were trading at 54.3 percent of par, which resulted in a gain on extinguishment of $15.6 million. Also during the first quarter, on March 27, 2015, we exchanged as part of a tender offer $137.8 million of the 4.80 percent senior notes for $112.9 million of the 7.75 percent second lien notes at a discount of $30.5 million based on an imputed interest rate of 15.55 percent, resulting in a gain on extinguishment of $54.6 million, net of amounts expensed for unamortized original issue discount and deferred origination fees.

During the fourth quarter of 2014, we purchased $10.0 million of outstanding 4.80 percent senior notes that were trading at a discount of 40.25 percent which resulted in a gain on the extinguishment of debt of $4.0 million.

As of December 31, 2015, the $500.0 million 4.80 percent senior notes were recorded at a par value of $306.7 million less debt issuance costs of $1.1 million and unamortized discounts of $0.4 million, based on an imputed interest rate of 4.83 percent. As of December 31, 2014, the $500.0 million 4.80 percent senior notes were recorded at a par value of $490.0 million less debt issuance costs of $2.2 million and unamortized discounts of $0.6 million, based on an imputed interest rate of 4.83 percent.

[3] During the first quarter of 2015, we purchased $45.9 million of outstanding 6.25 percent senior notes that were trading at 52.5 percent of par, which resulted in a gain on extinguishment of $15.0 million. Also during the first quarter, on March 27, 2015, we exchanged as part of a tender offer $261.3 million of the 6.25 percent senior notes for $203.5 million of the 7.75 percent second lien notes at a discount of $55.0 million based on an imputed interest rate of 15.55 percent, resulting in a gain on extinguishment of $107.3 million, net of amounts expensed for unamortized original issue discount and deferred origination fees.

As of December 31, 2015, the $800.0 million 6.25 percent senior notes were recorded at par value of $492.8 million less debt issuance costs of $4.3 million and unamortized discounts of $5.8 million, based on an imputed interest rate of 6.34 percent. As of December 31, 2014, the $800.0 million 6.25 percent senior notes were recorded at par value of $800.0 million less debt issuance costs of $7.2 million and unamortized discounts of $9.5 million, based on an imputed interest rate of 6.34 percent.

[4] During the third quarter of 2015, we purchased $36.0 million of outstanding 5.90 percent senior notes that were trading at 50.0 percent of par, which resulted in a gain on extinguishment of $18.0 million. In addition, during the first quarter of 2015, we purchased $1.3 million of outstanding 5.90 percent senior notes that were trading at 58.0 percent of par, which resulted in a gain on extinguishment of $0.3 million. Also during the first quarter, on March 27, 2015, we exchanged as part of a tender offer $67.0 million of the 5.90 percent senior notes for $57.5 million of the 7.75 percent second lien notes at a discount of $15.5 million based on an imputed interest rate of 15.55 percent, resulting in a gain on extinguishment of $24.5 million, net of amounts expensed for unamortized original issue discount and deferred origination fees.

During the fourth quarter of 2014, we purchased $5.0 million of outstanding 5.90 percent senior notes that were trading at a discount of 38.125 percent which resulted in a gain on the extinguishment of debt of $1.9 million.

As of December 31, 2015, the $400.0 million 5.90 percent senior notes were recorded at a par value of $290.8 million less debt issuance costs of $1.1 million and unamortized discounts of $0.8 million, based on an imputed interest rate of 5.98 percent. As of December 31, 2014, the $400.0 million 5.90 percent senior notes were recorded at a par value of $395.0 million less debt issuance costs of $1.8 million and unamortized discounts of $1.3 million, based on an imputed interest rate of 5.98 percent.

[5] During the third quarter, on August 28, 2015, we purchased for cash as part of a tender offer, $124.8 million of the 3.95 percent senior notes for $68.6 million, resulting in a gain on extinguishment of $54.9 million, net of amounts expensed for reacquisition costs, unamortized original issue discount and deferred origination fees. In addition, during the first quarter of 2015, we purchased $44.0 million of outstanding 3.95 percent senior notes that were trading at 77.5 percent of par, which resulted in a gain on the extinguishment of debt of $7.1 million.

During the fourth quarter of 2014, we purchased $20.0 million of outstanding 3.95 percent senior notes that were trading at a discount of 30.875 percent which resulted in a gain on the extinguishment of debt of $6.2 million.

As of December 31, 2015, the $500.0 million 3.95 percent senior notes were recorded at a par value of $311.2 million less debt issuance cost of $0.9 million and unamortized discounts of $1.2 million, based on an imputed interest rate of 6.30 percent. As of December 31, 2014, the $500.0 million 3.95 percent senior notes were recorded at a par value of $480.0 million less debt issuance costs of $2.1 million and unamortized discounts of $2.6 million, based on an imputed interest rate of 5.17 percent.

[6] As of December 31, 2015, the $540.0 million 8.25 percent first lien notes were recorded at a par value of $540.0 million less debt issuance costs of $10.5 million and unamortized discounts of $32.1 million, based on an imputed interest rate of 9.97 percent.

[7] As of December 31, 2015, the $544.2 million 7.75 percent second lien notes were recorded at a par value of $544.2 million less debt issuance costs of $9.5 million and unamortized discounts of $131.5 million, based on an imputed interest rate of 15.55 percent. See NOTE 6—FAIR VALUE OF FINANCIAL INSTRUMENTS for further discussion of unamortized discount as a result of the exchange offers.

[8] As of December 31, 2015, no loans were drawn under the $550.0 million ABL Facility and we had total availability of $366.0 million as a result of borrowing base limitations. As of December 31, 2015, the principal amount of letter of credit obligations totaled $186.3 million and commodity hedge obligations totaled $0.5 million, thereby further reducing available borrowing capacity on our ABL Facility to $179.2 million.

[9] As of December 31, 2014, we had no revolving loans drawn under the revolving credit agreement, which had total availability of $1.125 billion as of December 31, 2014. As of December 31, 2014, the principal amount of letter of credit obligations totaled $149.5 million, thereby reducing available borrowing capacity to $975.5 million.

Expenses and Losses

PRESENTATION

3.19 Paragraphs 80 and 83 of FASB Concepts Statement No. 6, *Elements of Financial Statements—a replacement of FASB Concepts Statement No. 3 (incorporating an amendment of FASB Concepts Statement No. 2)*, define expenses and losses as follows:

> 80. Expenses are outflows or other using up of assets or incurrences of liabilities (or a combination of both) from delivering or producing goods, rendering services, or carrying out other activities that constitute the entity's ongoing major or central operations.

> 83. Losses are decreases in equity (net assets) from peripheral or incidental transactions of an entity and from all other transactions and other events and circumstances affecting the entity except those that result from expenses or distributions to owners.

PRESENTATION AND DISCLOSURE EXCERPTS

SELLING, GENERAL, AND ADMINISTRATIVE

3.20 KOHL'S CORPORATION (JAN)
CONSOLIDATED STATEMENTS OF INCOME (in part)

(In Millions, Except per Share Data)

	2014	2013	2012
Net sales	$19,023	$19,031	$19,279
Cost of merchandise sold	12,098	12,087	12,289
Gross margin	6,925	6,944	6,990
Operating expenses:			
Selling, general and administrative	4,350	4,313	4,267
Depreciation and amortization	886	889	833
Operating income	1,689	1,742	1,890

NOTES TO CONSOLIDATED FINANCIAL STATEMENTS (in part)

1. Business and Summary of Accounting Policies (in part)

Cost of Merchandise Sold and Selling, General and Administrative Expenses

The following table illustrates the primary costs classified in Cost of Merchandise Sold and Selling, General and Administrative Expenses:

Cost of Merchandise Sold	Selling, General and Administrative Expenses

• Total cost of products sold including product development costs, net of vendor payments other than reimbursement of specific, incremental and identifiable costs
• Inventory shrink
• Markdowns
• Freight expenses associated with moving merchandise from our vendors to our distribution centers
• Shipping and handling expenses of sales generated on-line
• Terms cash discount
	• Compensation and benefit costs including:
	  — Stores
	  — Corporate headquarters, including buying and merchandising
	  — Distribution centers
	• Occupancy and operating costs of our retail, distribution and corporate facilities
	• Net revenues from the Kohl's credit card program
	• Freight expenses associated with moving merchandise from our distribution centers to our retail stores and between distribution and retail facilities
	• Advertising expenses, offset by vendor payments for reimbursement of specific, incremental and identifiable costs
	• Other administrative revenues and expenses

The classification of these expenses varies across the retail industry.

RESEARCH AND DEVELOPMENT

3.21 JOHNSON & JOHNSON (DEC)
CONSOLIDATED STATEMENTS OF EARNINGS (in part)

(Dollars and Shares in Millions Except Per Share Amounts) (Note 1)

	2015	2014	2013
Sales to customers	$70,074	74,331	71,312
Cost of products sold	21,536	22,746	22,342
Gross profit	48,538	51,585	48,970
Selling, marketing and administrative expenses	21,203	21,954	21,830
Research and development expense	9,046	8,494	8,183
In-process research and development	224	178	580
Interest income	(128)	(67)	(74)
Interest expense, net of portion capitalized (Note 4)	552	533	482
Other (income) expense, net	(2,064)	(70)	2,498
Restructuring (Note 22)	509	—	—
Earnings before provision for taxes on income	19,196	20,563	15,471
Provision for taxes on income (Note 8)	3,787	4,240	1,640
Net earnings	$15,409	16,323	13,831

NOTES TO CONSOLIDATED FINANCIAL STATEMENTS (in part)

1. Summary of Significant Accounting Policies (in part)

Research and Development

Research and development expenses are expensed as incurred. Upfront and milestone payments made to third parties in connection with research and development collaborations are expensed as incurred up to the point of regulatory approval. Payments made to third parties subsequent to regulatory approval are capitalized and amortized over the remaining useful life of the related product. Amounts capitalized for such payments are included in other intangibles, net of accumulated amortization.

The Company enters into collaborative arrangements, typically with other pharmaceutical or biotechnology companies, to develop and commercialize drug candidates or intellectual property. These arrangements typically involve two (or more) parties who are active participants in the collaboration and are exposed to significant risks and rewards dependent on the commercial success of the activities. These collaborations usually involve various activities by one or more parties, including research and development, marketing and selling and distribution. Often, these collaborations require upfront, milestone and royalty or profit share payments, contingent upon the occurrence of certain future events linked to the success of the asset in development. Amounts due from collaborative partners related to development activities are generally reflected as a reduction of research and development expense because the performance of contract development services is not central to the Company's operations. In general, the income statement presentation for these collaborations is as follows:

Nature/Type of Collaboration	Statement of Earnings Presentation
Third-party sale of product	Sales to customers
Royalties/milestones paid to collaborative partner (post-regulatory approval)*	Cost of products sold
Royalties received from collaborative partner	Other income (expense), net
Upfront payments & milestones paid to collaborative partner (pre-regulatory approval)	Research and development expense
Research and development payments to collaborative partner	Research and development expense
Research and development payments received from collaborative partner	Reduction of Research and development expense

* Milestones are capitalized as intangible assets and amortized to cost of goods sold over the useful life.

For all years presented, there was no individual project that represented greater than 5% of the total annual consolidated research and development expense.

The Company has a number of products and compounds developed in collaboration with strategic partners including XARELTO®, co-developed with Bayer HealthCare AG and IMBRUVICA®, developed in collaboration and co-marketed with Pharmacyclics LLC, an AbbVie company.

3.22 ANADARKO PETROLEUM CORPORATION (DEC)

CONSOLIDATED STATEMENTS OF INCOME (in part)

Millions except per-share amounts	Years Ended December 31,		
	2015	2014	2013
Revenues and Other			
Oil and condensate sales	$ 5,420	$ 9,748	$ 9,178
Natural-gas sales	2,007	3,849	3,388
Natural-gas liquids sales	833	1,572	1,262
Gathering, processing, and marketing sales	1,226	1,206	1,039
Gains (losses) on divestitures and other, net	(788)	2,095	(286)
Total	8,698	18,470	14,581
Costs and Expenses			
Oil and gas operating	1,014	1,171	1,092
Oil and gas transportation	1,117	1,116	981
Exploration	2,644	1,639	1,329
Gathering, processing, and marketing	1,054	1,030	869
General and administrative	1,176	1,316	1,090
Depreciation, depletion, and amortization	4,603	4,550	3,927
Other taxes	553	1,244	1,077
Impairments	5,075	836	794
Other operating expense	271	165	89
Total	17,507	13,067	11,248
Operating Income (Loss)	(8,809)	5,403	3,333

NOTES TO CONSOLIDATED FINANCIAL STATEMENTS (in part)

1. Summary of Significant Accounting Policies (in part)

Oil and Gas Properties The Company applies the successful efforts method of accounting for oil and gas properties. Exploration costs, such as exploratory geological and geophysical costs, delay rentals, and exploration overhead, are charged against earnings as incurred. If an exploratory well provides evidence to justify potential completion as a producing well, drilling costs associated with the well are initially capitalized, or suspended, pending a determination as to whether a commercially sufficient quantity of proved reserves can be attributed to the area as a result of drilling. This determination may take longer than one year in certain areas (generally in deepwater and international locations) depending on, among other things, the amount of hydrocarbons discovered, the outcome of planned geological and engineering studies, the need for additional appraisal drilling activities to determine whether the discovery is sufficient to support an economic development plan, and government sanctioning of development activities in certain international locations. At the end of each quarter, management reviews the status of all suspended exploratory drilling costs in light of ongoing exploration activities, in particular, whether the Company is making sufficient progress in its ongoing exploration and appraisal efforts or, in the case of discoveries requiring government sanctioning, analyzing whether development negotiations are underway and proceeding as planned. If management determines that future appraisal drilling or development activities are unlikely to occur, associated suspended exploratory well costs are expensed.

Acquisition costs of unproved properties are periodically assessed for impairment and are transferred to proved oil and gas properties to the extent the costs are associated with successful exploration activities. Significant undeveloped leases are assessed individually for impairment, based on the Company's current exploration plans, and a valuation allowance is provided if impairment is indicated. Unproved oil and gas properties with individually insignificant lease acquisition costs are amortized on a group basis (thereby establishing a valuation allowance) over the average lease terms at rates that provide for full amortization of unsuccessful leases upon lease expiration or abandonment. Costs of expired or abandoned leases are charged against the valuation allowance, while costs of productive leases are transferred to proved oil and gas properties. Costs of maintaining and retaining unproved properties, as well as amortization of individually insignificant leases and impairment of unsuccessful leases, are included in exploration expense in the Company's Consolidated Statements of Income.

5. Impairments (in part)

Impairments of Unproved Properties Impairments of unproved properties are included in exploration expense in the Company's Consolidated Statements of Income. In 2015, the Company recognized a $935 million impairment of unproved Greater Natural Buttes properties and a $66 million impairment of an unproved Gulf of Mexico property as a result of lower commodity prices. Also in 2015, the Company recognized a $109 million impairment of unproved Utica properties resulting from an assignment of mineral interests in settlement of a legal matter.

6. Suspended Exploratory Well Costs

The following summarizes the changes in suspended exploratory well costs at December 31 for each of the last three years. Additions pending the determination of proved reserves excludes amounts capitalized and subsequently charged to expense within the same year.

Millions	2015	2014	2013
Balance at January 1	$1,522	$2,232	$2,062
Additions pending the determination of proved reserves	461	421	848
Divestitures and other[1]	(33)	(913)	(48)
Reclassifications to proved properties	(104)	(100)	(507)
Charges to exploration expense[2]	(722)	(118)	(123)
Balance at December 31	$1,124	$1,522	$2,232

[1] Includes $(744) million during 2014 related to the Company's sale of a 10% working interest in Offshore Area 1 in Mozambique.

[2] Includes $(565) million during 2015 related to Brazil. Given the current oil-price environment and other considerations, the Company does not expect to have substantive exploration and development activities in Brazil in the foreseeable future.

The following provides an aging of suspended well balances at December 31:

Millions	2015	2014	2013
Exploratory well costs capitalized for a period of one year or less	$ 452	$ 393	$ 836
Exploratory well costs capitalized for a period greater than one year	672	1,129	1,396
Balance at December 31	$1,124	$1,522	$2,232

The following summarizes a further aging by geographic area of those exploratory well costs that have been capitalized for a period greater than one year since the completion of drilling at December 31, 2015:

Millions except projects	Number of Projects	Total	2014	2013	2012 and Prior
United States—Onshore	18	$ 55	$ 34	$11	$ 10
United States—Offshore	4	314	77	80	157
International	7	303	119	3	181
	29	$672	$230	$94	$348

Projects with suspended exploratory well costs are those identified by management as exhibiting sufficient quantities of hydrocarbons to justify potential development and where management is actively pursuing efforts to assess whether reserves can be attributed to these projects. Suspended exploratory well costs capitalized for a period greater than one year after completion of drilling at December 31, 2015, primarily related to the Gulf of Mexico, Ghana, and Mozambique.

For projects located in the Gulf of Mexico, the majority of exploratory well costs capitalized greater than one year are related to the Shenandoah discovery. Well costs have been suspended pending further appraisal activities, including drilling and analysis of well results. Appraisal activities undertaken at the Shenandoah discovery include the acquisition of whole-core across the primary reservoir interval, the processing and analysis of seismic data, reservoir simulation modeling, and analysis of well results. Remaining activities required to classify the associated reserves as proved for the Shenandoah discovery include completion of geologic, reservoir, and economic modeling; product development testing; and pre-front-end engineering and design (FEED) and FEED engineering studies.

For projects located in Ghana, exploratory well costs that have been capitalized greater than one year are pending development plan approval. During the fourth quarter of 2015, the Company and its partners submitted the Jubilee full field development plan for the Mahogany East and Teak areas. Remaining activities required to classify the associated reserves as proved include approval of development plans and project sanctioning.

For projects located in Mozambique, the majority of exploratory well costs capitalized greater than one year are related to the Orca, Tubarão, and Tubarão Tigre discoveries. Well costs have been suspended pending further appraisal activities, including analysis of well results and seismic reprocessing. During 2015, drilling and evaluation operations at the Tubarão Tigre-2 appraisal well were completed. Anadarko is continuing to appraise the Orca, Tubarão, and Tubarão Tigre discoveries in accordance with the appraisal programs provided to the government of Mozambique in the first quarter of 2015.

If additional information becomes available that raises substantial doubt as to the economic or operational viability of any of these projects, the associated costs will be expensed at that time.

3.23 NIKE, INC. (MAY)
CONSOLIDATED STATEMENTS OF INCOME (in part)

(In millions, except per share data)	Year Ended May 31,		
	2015	**2014**	**2013**
Income from continuing operations:			
Revenues	$30,601	$27,799	$25,313
Cost of sales	16,534	15,353	14,279
Gross profit	14,067	12,446	11,034
Demand creation expense	3,213	3,031	2,745
Operating overhead expense	6,679	5,735	5,051
Total selling and administrative expense	9,892	8,766	7,796
Interest expense (income), net (Notes 6, 7 and 8)	28	33	(3)
Other (income) expense, net (Note 17)	(58)	103	(15)
Income before income taxes	4,205	3,544	3,256

NOTES TO CONSOLIDATED FINANCIAL STATEMENTS (in part)

Note 1—Summary of Significant Accounting Policies (in part)

Demand Creation Expense

Demand creation expense consists of advertising and promotion costs, including costs of endorsement contracts, television, digital and print advertising, brand events and retail brand presentation. Advertising production costs are expensed the first time an advertisement is run. Advertising communication costs are expensed when the advertisement appears. Costs related to brand events are expensed when the event occurs. Costs related to retail brand presentation are expensed when the presentation is completed and delivered.

A significant amount of the Company's promotional expenses result from payments under endorsement contracts. Accounting for endorsement payments is based upon specific contract provisions. Generally, endorsement payments are expensed on a straight-line basis over the term of the contract after giving recognition to periodic performance compliance provisions of the contracts. Prepayments made under contracts are included in *Prepaid expenses and other current assets* or *Deferred income taxes and other assets* depending on the period to which the prepayment applies.

Certain contracts provide for contingent payments to endorsers based upon specific achievements in their sports (e.g., winning a championship). The Company records demand creation expense for these amounts when the endorser achieves the specific goal.

Certain contracts provide for variable payments based upon endorsers maintaining a level of performance in their sport over an extended period of time (e.g., maintaining a specified ranking in a sport for a year). When the Company determines payments are probable, the amounts are reported in demand creation expense ratably over the contract period based on our best estimate of the endorser's performance. In these instances, to the extent that actual payments to the endorser differ from the Company's estimate due to changes in the endorser's performance, increased or decreased demand creation expense may be recorded in a future period.

Certain contracts provide for royalty payments to endorsers based upon a predetermined percent of sales of particular products. The Company expenses these payments in *Cost of sales* as the related sales occur. In certain contracts, the Company offers minimum guaranteed royalty payments. For contracts for which the Company estimates it will not meet the minimum guaranteed amount of royalty fees through sales of product, the Company records the amount of the guaranteed payment in excess of that earned through sales of product in *Demand creation expense* uniformly over the guarantee period.

Through cooperative advertising programs, the Company reimburses retail customers for certain costs of advertising the Company's products. The Company records these costs in *Demand creation expense* at the point in time when it is obligated to its customers for the costs. This obligation may arise prior to the related advertisement being run.

Total advertising and promotion expenses were $3,213 million, $3,031 million and $2,745 million for the years ended May 31, 2015, 2014 and 2013, respectively. Prepaid advertising and promotion expenses totaled $455 million and $516 million at May 31, 2015 and 2014, respectively, and were recorded in *Prepaid expenses and other current assets* and *Deferred income taxes and other assets* depending on the period to which the prepayment applies.

3.24 EXXON MOBIL CORPORATION (DEC)

CONSOLIDATED STATEMENT OF INCOME (in part)

(Millions of dollars)	Note Reference Number	2015	2014	2013
Revenues and other income				
Sales and other operating revenue[1]		259,488	394,105	420,836
Income from equity affiliates	7	7,644	13,323	13,927
Other income		1,750	4,511	3,492
Total revenues and other income		268,882	411,939	438,255
Costs and other deductions				
Crude oil and product purchases		130,003	225,972	244,156
Production and manufacturing expenses		35,587	40,859	40,525
Selling, general and administrative expenses		11,501	12,598	12,877
Depreciation and depletion		18,048	17,297	17,182
Exploration expenses, including dry holes		1,523	1,669	1,976
Interest expense		311	286	9
Sales-based taxes[1]	19	22,678	29,342	30,589
Other taxes and duties	19	27,265	32,286	33,230
Total costs and other deductions		246,916	360,309	380,544
Income before income taxes		21,966	51,630	57,711
Income taxes	19	5,415	18,015	24,263
Net income including noncontrolling interests		16,551	33,615	33,448
Net income attributable to noncontrolling interests		401	1,095	868
Net income attributable to ExxonMobil		16,150	32,520	32,580
Earnings per common share *(dollars)*	12	3.85	7.60	7.37
Earnings per common share—assuming dilution *(dollars)*	12	3.85	7.60	7.37

[1] Sales and other operating revenue includes sales-based taxes of $22,678 million for 2015, $29,342 million for 2014 and $30,589 million for 2013.

NOTES TO CONSOLIDATED FINANCIAL STATEMENTS (in part)

1. Summary of Accounting Policies (in part)

Sales-Based Taxes. The Corporation reports sales, excise and value-added taxes on sales transactions on a gross basis in the Consolidated Statement of Income (included in both revenues and costs).

2. Accounting Changes (in part)

In May 2014, the Financial Accounting Standards Board issued a new standard, *Revenue from Contracts with Customers*. The standard establishes a single revenue recognition model for all contracts with customers, eliminates industry specific requirements, and expands disclosure requirements. The standard is required to be adopted beginning January 1, 2018.

"Sales and Other Operating Revenue" on the Consolidated Statement of Income includes sales, excise and value-added taxes on sales transactions. When the Corporation adopts the standard, revenue will exclude sales-based taxes collected on behalf of third parties. This change in reporting will not impact earnings.

19. Income, Sales-Based and Other Taxes (in part)

(Millions of dollars)	2015			2014			2013		
	U.S.	Non-U.S.	Total	U.S.	Non-U.S.	Total	U.S.	Non-U.S.	Total
Income tax expense									
Federal and non-U.S.									
Current	—	7,126	7,126	1,456	14,755	16,211	1,073	22,115	23,188
Deferred—net	(1,166)	(571)	(1,737)	900	1,398	2,298	(116)	757	641
U.S. tax on non-U.S. operations	38	—	38	5	—	5	37	—	37
Total federal and non-U.S.	(1,128)	6,555	5,427	2,361	16,153	18,514	994	22,872	23,866
State[1]	(12)	—	(12)	(499)	—	(499)	397	—	397
Total income tax expense	(1,140)	6,555	5,415	1,862	16,153	18,015	1,391	22,872	24,263
Sales-based taxes	6,402	16,276	22,678	6,310	23,032	29,342	5,992	24,597	30,589
All other taxes and duties									
Other taxes and duties	162	27,103	27,265	378	31,908	32,286	955	32,275	33,230
Included in production and manufacturing expenses	1,157	828	1,985	1,454	1,179	2,633	1,318	1,182	2,500
Included in SG&A expenses	150	390	540	155	441	596	150	516	666
Total other taxes and duties	1,469	28,321	29,790	1,987	33,528	35,515	2,423	33,973	36,396
Total	6,731	51,152	57,883	10,159	72,713	82,872	9,806	81,442	91,248

[1] In 2014, state taxes included a favorable adjustment of deferred taxes of approximately $830 million.

All other taxes and duties include taxes reported in production and manufacturing and selling, general and administrative (SG&A) expenses. The above provisions for deferred income taxes include a net charge of $177 million in 2015 and net credits of $40 million in 2014 and $310 million in 2013 for the effect of changes in tax laws and rates.

PROVISION FOR LOSSES

3.25 HARLEY-DAVIDSON, INC. (DEC)
CONSOLIDATED STATEMENTS OF INCOME (in part)

(In thousands, except per share amounts)

	2015	2014	2013
Revenue:			
Motorcycles and Related Products	$5,308,744	$5,567,681	$5,258,290
Financial Services	686,658	660,827	641,582
Total revenue	5,995,402	6,228,508	5,899,872
Costs and expenses:			
Motorcycles and Related Products cost of goods sold	3,356,284	3,542,601	3,395,918
Financial Services interest expense	161,983	164,476	165,491
Financial Services provision for credit losses	101,345	80,946	60,008
Selling, administrative and engineering expense	1,220,095	1,159,502	1,124,753
Total costs and expenses	4,839,707	4,947,525	4,746,170
Operating income	1,155,695	1,280,983	1,153,702

NOTES TO CONSOLIDATED FINANCIAL STATEMENTS (in part)

1. Summary of Significant Accounting Policies (in part)

Finance Receivables, Net—Finance receivables include both retail and wholesale finance receivables, net, including amounts held by VIEs. Finance receivables are recorded in the financial statements at amortized cost net of an allowance for credit losses. The provision for credit losses on finance receivables is charged to earnings in amounts sufficient to maintain the allowance for credit losses at a level that is adequate to cover estimated losses of principal inherent in the existing portfolio. Portions of the allowance for credit losses are specified to cover estimated losses on finance receivables specifically identified for impairment. The unspecified portion of the allowance covers estimated losses on finance receivables which are collectively reviewed for impairment. Finance receivables are considered impaired when management determines it is probable that the Company will be unable to collect all amounts due according to the terms of the loan agreement.

The retail portfolio primarily consists of a large number of small balance, homogeneous finance receivables. The Company performs a periodic and systematic collective evaluation of the adequacy of the retail allowance for credit losses. The Company utilizes loss forecast models which consider a variety of factors including, but not limited to, historical loss trends, origination or vintage analysis, known and inherent risks in the portfolio, the value of the underlying collateral, recovery rates and current economic conditions including items such as unemployment rates. Retail finance receivables are not evaluated individually for impairment prior to charge-off and therefore are not reported as impaired loans.

The wholesale portfolio is primarily composed of large balance, non-homogeneous loans. The Company's wholesale allowance evaluation is first based on a loan-by-loan review. A specific allowance for credit losses is established for wholesale finance receivables determined to be individually impaired when management concludes that the borrower will not be able to make full payment of contractual amounts due based on the original terms of the loan agreement. The impairment is determined based on the cash that the Company expects to receive discounted at the loan's original interest rate or the fair value of the collateral, if the loan is collateral-dependent. In establishing the allowance, management considers a number of factors including the specific borrower's financial performance as well as ability to repay. Finance receivables in the wholesale portfolio that are not individually evaluated for impairment are segregated, based on similar risk characteristics, according to the Company's internal risk rating system and collectively evaluated for impairment. The related allowance is based on factors such as the Company's past loan loss experience, current economic conditions as well as the value of the underlying collateral.

Impaired finance receivables also include loans that have been modified in troubled debt restructurings as a concession to borrowers experiencing financial difficulty. Generally, it is the Company's policy not to change the terms and conditions of finance receivables. However, to minimize the economic loss, the Company may modify certain impaired finance receivables in troubled debt restructurings. Total restructured finance receivables are not significant.

Repossessed inventory representing recovered collateral on impaired finance receivables is recorded at the lower of cost or net realizable value. In the period during which the collateral is repossessed, the related finance receivable is adjusted to the fair value of the collateral through a charge to the allowance for credit losses and reclassified to repossessed inventory. Repossessed inventory is included in other current assets and was $17.7 million and $13.4 million at December 31, 2015 and 2014, respectively.

5. Finance Receivables

Finance receivables, net at December 31 for the past five years were as follows (in thousands):

	2015	2014	2013	2012	2011
Wholesale					
United States	$ 965,379	$ 903,380	$ 800,491	$ 776,633	$ 778,320
Canada	58,481	48,941	44,721	39,771	46,320
Total wholesale	1,023,860	952,321	845,212	816,404	824,640
Retail					
United States	5,803,071	5,398,006	5,051,245	4,850,450	4,858,781
Canada	188,400	209,918	213,799	222,665	228,709
Total retail	5,991,471	5,607,924	5,265,044	5,073,115	5,087,490
	7,015,331	6,560,245	6,110,256	5,889,519	5,912,130
Allowance for credit losses	(147,178)	(127,364)	(110,693)	(107,667)	(125,449)
Total finance receivables, net	$6,868,153	$6,432,881	$5,999,563	$5,781,852	$5,786,681

HDFS offers wholesale financing to the Company's independent dealers. Wholesale loans to dealers are generally secured by financed inventory or property and are originated in the U.S. and Canada. Wholesale finance receivables are related primarily to motorcycles and related parts and accessories sales.

HDFS provides retail financial services to customers of the Company's independent dealers in the U.S. and Canada. The origination of retail loans is a separate and distinct transaction between HDFS and the retail customer, unrelated to the Company's sale of product to its dealers. Retail finance receivables consist of secured promissory notes and secured installment contracts and are primarily related to sales of motorcycles to the dealers' customers. HDFS holds either titles or liens on titles to vehicles financed by promissory notes and installment sales contracts. As of December 31, 2015 and 2014, approximately 12% of gross outstanding finance receivables were originated in Texas; there were no other states that accounted for more than 10%.

Unused lines of credit extended to the Company's wholesale finance customers totaled $1.27 billion and $1.01 billion at December 31, 2015 and 2014, respectively. Approved but unfunded retail finance loans totaled $169.6 million and $168.7 million at December 31, 2015 and 2014, respectively.

Wholesale finance receivables are generally contractually due within one year. On December 31, 2015, contractual maturities of finance receivables were as follows (in thousands):

	United States	Canada	Total
2016	$1,991,614	$ 93,539	$2,085,153
2017	1,104,233	37,415	1,141,648
2018	1,234,333	41,339	1,275,672
2019	1,379,791	45,673	1,425,464
2020	1,024,927	28,915	1,053,842
Thereafter	33,552	—	33,552
Total	$6,768,450	$246,881	$7,015,331

The allowance for credit losses on finance receivables is comprised of individual components relating to wholesale and retail finance receivables. Changes in the allowance for credit losses on finance receivables by portfolio for the year ended December 31 were as follows (in thousands):

	2015		
	Retail	Wholesale	Total
Balance, beginning of period	$ 122,025	$5,339	$ 127,364
Provision for credit losses	98,826	2,519	101,345
Charge-offs	(123,911)	—	(123,911)
Recoveries	42,380	—	42,380
Balance, end of period	$ 139,320	$7,858	$ 147,178

	2014		
	Retail	Wholesale	Total
Balance, beginning of period	$ 106,063	$4,630	$ 110,693
Provision for credit losses	80,237	709	80,946
Charge-offs	(102,831)	—	(102,831)
Recoveries	38,556	—	38,556
Balance, end of period	$ 122,025	$5,339	$ 127,364

	2013		
	Retail	Wholesale	Total
Balance, beginning of period	$ 101,442	$ 6,225	$ 107,667
Provision for credit losses	61,603	(1,595)	60,008
Charge-offs	(97,928)	—	(97,928)
Recoveries	40,946	—	40,946
Balance, end of period	$ 106,063	$ 4,630	$ 110,693

There were no finance receivables individually evaluated for impairment on December 31, 2014 or 2015. The allowance for credit losses and finance receivables by portfolio collectively evaluated for impairment, at December 31 were as follows (in thousands):

	2015		
	Retail	Wholesale	Total
Allowance for credit losses, ending balance:			
Individually evaluated for impairment	$ —	$ —	$ —
Collectively evaluated for impairment	139,320	7,858	147,178
Total allowance for credit losses	$ 139,320	$ 7,858	$ 147,178
Finance receivables, ending balance:			
Individually evaluated for impairment	$ —	$ —	$ —
Collectively evaluated for impairment	5,991,471	1,023,860	7,015,331
Total finance receivables	$5,991,471	$1,023,860	$7,015,331

	2014		
	Retail	Wholesale	Total
Allowance for credit losses, ending balance:			
Individually evaluated for impairment	$ —	$ —	$ —
Collectively evaluated for impairment	122,025	5,339	127,364
Total allowance for credit losses	$ 122,025	$ 5,339	$ 127,364
Finance receivables, ending balance:			
Individually evaluated for impairment	$ —	$ —	$ —
Collectively evaluated for impairment	5,607,924	952,321	6,560,245
Total finance receivables	$5,607,924	$952,321	$6,560,245

Finance receivables are considered impaired when management determines it is probable that the Company will be unable to collect all amounts due according to the loan agreement. As retail finance receivables are collectively and not individually reviewed for impairment, this portfolio does not have specifically impaired finance receivables. At December 31, 2015 and 2014, there were no wholesale finance receivables that were on non-accrual status or individually deemed to be impaired under ASC Topic 310, "Receivables".

An analysis of the aging of past due finance receivables at December 31 was as follows (in thousands):

	2015					
	Current	31–60 Days Past Due	61–90 Days Past Due	Greater than 90 Days Past Due	Total Past Due	Total Finance Receivables
Retail	$5,796,003	$118,996	$43,680	$32,792	$195,468	$5,991,471
Wholesale	1,022,365	888	530	77	1,495	1,023,860
Total	$6,818,368	$119,884	$44,210	$32,869	$196,963	$7,015,331

	2014					
	Current	31–60 Days Past Due	61–90 Days Past Due	Greater than 90 Days Past Due	Total Past Due	Total Finance Receivables
Retail	$5,427,719	$113,007	$38,486	$28,712	$180,205	$5,607,924
Wholesale	951,660	383	72	206	661	952,321
Total	$6,379,379	$113,390	$38,558	$28,918	$180,866	$6,560,245

The recorded investment of retail and wholesale finance receivables, excluding non-accrual status finance receivables, that were contractually past due 90 days or more at December 31 for the past five years was as follows (in thousands):

	2015	2014	2013	2012	2011
United States	$31,677	$27,800	$23,770	$26,500	$27,171
Canada	1,192	1,118	1,031	1,533	1,207
Total	$32,869	$28,918	$24,801	$28,033	$28,378

A significant part of managing the Company's finance receivable portfolios includes the assessment of credit risk associated with each borrower. As the credit risk varies between the retail and wholesale portfolios, the Company utilizes different credit risk indicators for each portfolio.

The Company manages retail credit risk through its credit approval policy and ongoing collection efforts. The Company uses FICO scores, a standard credit rating measurement, to differentiate the expected default rates of retail credit applicants enabling the Company to better evaluate credit applicants for approval and to tailor pricing according to this assessment. Retail loans with a FICO score of 640 or above at origination are considered prime, and loans with a FICO score below 640 are considered sub-prime. These credit quality indicators are determined at the time of loan origination and are not updated subsequent to the loan origination date.

The recorded investment of retail finance receivables, by credit quality indicator, at December 31 was as follows (in thousands):

	2015	2014
Prime	$4,777,448	$4,435,352
Sub-prime	1,214,023	1,172,572
Total	$5,991,471	$5,607,924

The Company's credit risk on the wholesale portfolio is different from that of the retail portfolio. Whereas the retail portfolio represents a relatively homogeneous pool of retail finance receivables that exhibit more consistent loss patterns, the wholesale portfolio exposures are less consistent. The Company utilizes an internal credit risk rating system to manage credit risk exposure consistently across wholesale borrowers and evaluates credit risk factors for each borrower. The Company uses the following internal credit quality indicators, based on an internal risk rating system, listed from highest level of risk to lowest level of risk, for the wholesale portfolio: Doubtful, Substandard, Special Mention, Medium Risk and Low Risk. Based upon management's review, the dealers classified in the Doubtful category are the dealers with the greatest likelihood of being charged-off, while the dealers classified as Low Risk are least likely to be charged-off. The internal rating system considers factors such as the specific borrower's ability to repay and the estimated value of any collateral. Dealer risk rating classifications are reviewed and updated on a quarterly basis.

The recorded investment of wholesale finance receivables, by internal credit quality indicator, at December 31 was as follows (in thousands):

	2015	2014
Doubtful	$ 5,169	$ 954
Substandard	21,774	7,025
Special Mention	6,271	—
Medium Risk	11,494	11,557
Low Risk	979,152	932,785
Total	$1,023,860	$952,321

WARRANTY

3.26 HOVNANIAN ENTERPRISES, INC. (OCT)
CONSOLIDATED STATEMENTS OF OPERATIONS (in part)

	Year Ended		
(In thousands except per share data)	October 31, 2015	October 31, 2014	October 31, 2013
Revenues:			
Homebuilding:			
Sale of homes	$2,088,129	$2,013,013	$1,784,327
Land sales and other revenues	3,686	7,953	19,199
Total homebuilding	2,091,815	2,020,966	1,803,526
Financial services	56,665	42,414	47,727
Total revenues	2,148,480	2,063,380	1,851,253

(continued)

(In thousands except per share data)	Year Ended		
	October 31, 2015	October 31, 2014	October 31, 2013
Expenses:			
Homebuilding:			
Cost of sales, excluding interest	1,722,038	1,615,199	1,442,044
Cost of sales interest	59,613	53,966	52,230
Inventory impairment loss and land option write-offs	12,044	5,224	4,965
Total cost of sales	1,793,695	1,674,389	1,499,239
Selling, general and administrative	188,403	191,537	165,809
Total homebuilding expenses	1,982,098	1,865,926	1,665,048
Financial services	31,972	28,616	29,059
Corporate general and administrative	62,506	63,375	54,357
Other interest	91,835	87,378	91,344
Other operations	6,003	4,647	790
Total expenses	2,174,414	2,049,942	1,840,598
Loss on extinguishment of debt	—	(1,155)	(760)
Income from unconsolidated joint ventures	4,169	7,897	12,040
(Loss) income before income taxes	(21,765)	20,180	21,935

NOTES TO CONSOLIDATED FINANCIAL STATEMENTS (in part)

3. Summary of Significant Accounting Policies (in part)

Post-Development Completion, Warranty Costs and *Insurance Deductible Reserves*—In those instances where a development is substantially completed and sold and we have additional construction work to be incurred, an estimated liability is provided to cover the cost of such work. We accrue for warranty costs that are covered under our existing general liability and construction defect policy as part of our general liability insurance deductible. This accrual is expensed as selling, general and administrative costs. For homes delivered in fiscal 2015 and 2014, our deductible under our general liability insurance is a $20 million aggregate for construction defect and warranty claims. For bodily injury claims, our deductible per occurrence in fiscal 2015 and 2014 is $0.25 million, up to a $5 million limit. Our aggregate retention in fiscal 2015 and 2014 is $21 million for construction defect, warranty and bodily injury claims. We do not have a deductible on our worker's compensation insurance. Reserves for estimated losses for construction defects, warranty and bodily injury claims have been established using the assistance of a third-party actuary. We engage a third-party actuary that uses our historical warranty and construction defect data to assist our management in estimating our unpaid claims, claim adjustment expenses and incurred but not reported claims reserves for the risks that we are assuming under the general liability and construction defect programs. The estimates include provisions for inflation, claims handling and legal fees. These estimates are subject to a high degree of variability due to uncertainties such as trends in construction defect claims relative to our markets and the types of products we build, claim settlement patterns, insurance industry practices and legal interpretations, among others. Because of the high degree of judgment required in determining these estimated liability amounts, actual future costs could differ significantly from our currently estimated amounts. In addition, we establish a warranty accrual for lower cost-related issues to cover home repairs, community amenities and land development infrastructure that are not covered under our general liability and construction defect policy. We accrue an estimate for these warranty costs as part of cost of sales at the time each home is closed and title and possession have been transferred to the homebuyer. See Note 16 for additional information on the amount of warranty costs recognized in cost of goods sold and administrative expenses.

16. Warranty Costs

General liability insurance for homebuilding companies and their suppliers and subcontractors is very difficult to obtain. The availability of general liability insurance is limited due to a decreased number of insurance companies willing to underwrite for the industry. In addition, those few insurers willing to underwrite liability insurance have significantly increased the premium costs. To date, we have been able to obtain general liability insurance but at higher premium costs with higher deductibles. Our subcontractors and suppliers have advised us that they have also had difficulty obtaining insurance that also provides us coverage. As a result, we have an owner controlled insurance program for certain of our subcontractors whereby the subcontractors pay us an insurance premium (through a reduction of amounts we would otherwise owe such subcontractors for their work on our homes) based on the risk type of the trade. We absorb the liability associated with their work on our homes as part of our overall general liability insurance at no additional cost to us because our existing general liability and construction defect insurance policy and related reserves for amounts under our deductible covers construction defects regardless of whether we or our subcontractors are responsible for the defect. For the fiscal years ended October 31, 2015 and 2014, we received $3.1 million and $2.3 million, respectively, from subcontractors related to the owner controlled insurance program, which we accounted for as a reduction to inventory.

We accrue for warranty costs that are covered under our existing general liability and construction defect policy as part of our general liability insurance deductible. This accrual is expensed as selling, general and administrative costs. For homes delivered in fiscal 2015 and 2014, our deductible under our general liability insurance is a $20 million aggregate for construction defect and warranty claims. For bodily injury claims, our deductible per occurrence in fiscal 2015 and 2014 is $0.25 million, up to a $5 million limit. Our aggregate retention in fiscal 2015 and 2014 is $21 million for construction defect, warranty and bodily injury claims. In addition, we establish a warranty accrual for lower cost related issues to cover home repairs, community amenities and land development infrastructure that are not covered under our general liability and construction defect policy. We accrue an estimate for these warranty costs as part of cost of sales at the time each home is closed and title and possession have been transferred to the homebuyer. Additions and charges in the warranty reserve and general liability reserve for the fiscal years ended October 31, 2015 and 2014 were as follows:

| | Year Ended October 31, | |
	2015	2014
(In thousands)		
Balance, beginning of period	$178,008	$131,028
Additions—Selling, general and administrative	18,013	18,839
Additions—Cost of sales	15,308	11,115
Charges incurred during the period	(49,131)	(18,241)
Changes to pre-existing reserves	(17,125)	(2,600)
Changes to reserves where corresponding amounts are recorded as receivables from insurance carriers	(10,020)	37,867
Balance, end of period	$135,053	$178,008

Warranty accruals are based upon historical experience. We engage a third-party actuary that uses our historical warranty and construction defect data to assist our management in estimating our unpaid claims, claim adjustment expenses and incurred but not reported claims reserves for the risks that we are assuming under the general liability and construction defect programs. The estimates include provisions for inflation, claims handling and legal fees. As a result of reductions in our construction defect claims over the last two years and the impact of those reductions on the actuarial analysis of our total reserves, we recorded a $15.2 million reduction in our construction defect reserves during the fourth quarter of fiscal 2015. We also had minor reductions in our warranty accruals based on recent history. These reductions are reflected in the changes to pre-existing reserves in the table above.

Charges incurred during the period noted in the table above include the $21.0 million settlement regarding the D'Andrea litigation discussed in Note 18. Also included is the settlement of several other less significant construction defect claims, in addition to the usual construction defect charges incurred repairing homes.

Insurance claims paid by our insurance carriers, excluding insurance deductibles paid, were $32.0 million and $6.4 million for the fiscal years ended October 31, 2015 and 2014, respectively, for prior year deliveries. During fiscal year 2015 we settled the D'Andrea class action suit with the majority of the settlement being paid by our insurance carriers and we settled the dispute with our XL insurance carrier which resulted in a payment to the Company in full settlement of certain policy years. See Note 18. For the fiscal year ended October 31, 2014, we settled construction defect claims relating to the Northeast and West segments which made up the majority of the payments.

INTEREST

3.27 UNIFI, INC. (JUN)
CONSOLIDATED STATEMENTS OF INCOME (in part)

(amounts in thousands, except per share amounts)

| | For the Fiscal Years Ended | | |
	June 28, 2015	June 29, 2014	June 30, 2013
Net sales	$687,121	$687,902	$713,962
Cost of sales	596,416	604,640	640,858
Gross profit	90,705	83,262	73,104
Selling, general and administrative expenses	49,672	46,203	47,386
Provision (benefit) for bad debts	947	287	(154)
Other operating expense, net	1,600	5,289	3,409
Operating income	38,486	31,483	22,463
Interest income	(916)	(1,790)	(698)
Interest expense	4,025	4,329	4,489
Loss on extinguishment of debt	1,040	—	1,102
Other non-operating expense	—	126	—
Equity in earnings of unconsolidated affiliates	(19,475)	(19,063)	(11,444)
Income before income taxes	53,812	47,881	29,014

2. Summary of Significant Accounting Policies (in part)

Debt Financing Fees

The Company capitalizes costs associated with the financing of its debt obligations. These costs are amortized as additional interest expense following either the effective interest method or the straight-line method. In the event of any prepayment of its debt obligations, the Company accelerates the recognition of a pro-rata amount of issuance costs and records an extinguishment of debt.

8. Property, Plant and Equipment, Net (in part)

Depreciation expense, including the amortization of assets under capital leases, internal software development costs amortization, repairs and maintenance expenses, and capitalized interest were as follows:

	For the Fiscal Years Ended		
	June 28, 2015	June 29, 2014	June 30, 2013
Depreciation expense	$ 15,276	$ 15,031	$ 21,597
Internal software development costs amortization	146	143	128
Repair and maintenance expenses	17,741	18,319	18,649
Capitalized interest	191	172	36

12. Long-Term Debt (in part)

Type-Debt Obligations

The following table presents the total balances outstanding for the Company's debt obligations, their scheduled maturity dates and the weighted average interest rates for borrowings as well as the applicable current portion of long-term debt:

	Scheduled Maturity Date	Weighted Average Interest Rate as of June 28, 2015[1]	Principal Amounts as of	
			June 28, 2015	June 29, 2014
ABL Revolver	March 2020	1.7%	$ 5,000	$26,000
ABL Term Loan	March 2020	2.2%	82,125	68,000
Term loan from unconsolidated affiliate	August 2016	3.0%	1,250	1,250
Capital lease obligations	[2]	[3]	15,735	4,238
Total debt			104,110	99,488
Current portion of long-term debt			(12,385)	(7,215)
Total long-term debt			$ 91,725	$92,273

[1] The weighted average interest rate as of June 28, 2015 for the ABL Term Loan includes the effects of the interest rate swap with a notional balance of $50,000.

[2] Scheduled maturity dates for capital lease obligations range from January 2017 to November 2027.

[3] Fixed interest rates for capital lease obligations range from 2.3% to 4.6%.

On March 26, 2015, the Company and its subsidiary, Unifi Manufacturing, Inc., entered into an Amended and Restated Credit Agreement (the "Amended Credit Agreement") for a $200,000 senior secured credit facility (the "ABL Facility") with a syndicate of lenders. The ABL Facility consists of a $100,000 revolving credit facility (the "ABL Revolver") and an $84,375 term loan that can be reset up to a maximum amount of $100,000 if certain future conditions are met (the "ABL Term Loan"). The ABL Facility has a maturity date of March 26, 2020. The Company paid $750 to the lenders in connection with the Amended Credit Agreement.

The Amended Credit Agreement replaced a previous senior secured credit facility dated May 24, 2012 with a similar syndicate of lenders, which, after multiple amendments, would have matured on March 28, 2019 and consisted of a $100,000 revolving credit facility and a $90,000 term loan. As used herein, the terms "ABL Facility," "ABL Revolver" and "ABL Term Loan" shall mean the senior secured credit facility, the revolving credit facility or the term loan, respectively, under the Amended Credit Agreement or the previous senior secured credit facility, as applicable.

ABL Facility

The ABL Facility is secured by a first-priority perfected security interest in substantially all owned property and assets (together with proceeds and products) of Unifi, Inc., Unifi Manufacturing, Inc. and certain subsidiary guarantors (the "Loan Parties"). It is also secured by a first-priority security interest in all (or 65% in the case of certain first tier controlled foreign corporations, as required by the lenders) of the stock of (or other ownership interests in) each of the Loan Parties (other than the Company) and certain subsidiaries of the Loan Parties, together with all proceeds and products thereof.

The Amended Credit Agreement includes representations and warranties made by the Loan Parties, affirmative and negative covenants and events of default that are usual and customary for financings of this type. If excess availability under the ABL Revolver falls below the defined Trigger Level, a financial covenant requiring the Loan Parties to maintain a fixed charge coverage ratio on a monthly basis of at least 1.05 to 1.0 becomes effective. The Trigger Level as of June 28, 2015 was $22,766. In addition, the ABL Facility contains restrictions on certain payments and investments, including restrictions on the payment of dividends and share repurchases. Subject to certain provisions, the ABL Term Loan may be prepaid at par, in whole or in part, at any time before the maturity date, at the Company's discretion.

ABL Facility borrowings bear interest at the London Interbank Offer Rate ("LIBOR") plus an applicable margin of 1.50% to 2.00%, or the Base Rate plus an applicable margin of 0.50% to 1.00%, with interest currently being paid on a monthly basis. The applicable margin is based on (a) the excess availability under the ABL Revolver and (b) the consolidated leverage ratio, calculated by fiscal quarter. The Base Rate means the greater of (i) the prime lending rate as publicly announced from time to time by Wells Fargo, (ii) the Federal Funds Rate plus 0.5%, and (iii) LIBOR plus 1.0%. The Company's ability to borrow under the ABL Revolver is limited to a borrowing base equal to specified percentages of eligible accounts receivable and inventory and is subject to certain conditions and limitations. There is also a monthly unused line fee under the ABL Revolver of 0.25%.

The ABL Term Loan is currently subject to quarterly amortizing payments of $2,250. Additionally, principal increases are available at the Company's discretion, resetting the loan balance up to a maximum amount of $100,000, once per fiscal year upon satisfaction of certain conditions, beginning October 1, 2015.

As of June 28, 2015, the Company was in compliance with all financial covenants; the excess availability under the ABL Revolver was $75,933; the consolidated leverage ratio was 1.6 to 1.0; the fixed charge coverage ratio was 3.0 to 1.0; and the Company had $235 of standby letters of credit, none of which have been drawn upon.

Term Loan from Unconsolidated Affiliate

On August 30, 2012, a foreign subsidiary of the Company entered into an unsecured loan agreement under which it borrowed $1,250 from the Company's unconsolidated affiliate, U.N.F. Industries Ltd. The loan does not amortize and bears interest at 3%, payable semi-annually. The entire principal balance is due August 30, 2016, the revised maturity date.

Capital Lease Obligations

During fiscal year 2015, the Company entered into six capital leases with an aggregate present value of $12,784. Fixed interest rates and maturity dates for these capital leases range from 3.1% to 3.8% and August 2019 to August 2020, respectively.

During fiscal year 2014, the Company entered into four capital leases with an aggregate present value of $3,353.

Scheduled Debt Maturities

The following table presents the scheduled maturities of the Company's outstanding debt obligations for the following five fiscal years and thereafter:

	Scheduled Maturities on a Fiscal Year Basis					
	2016	2017	2018	2019	2020	Thereafter
ABL Revolver	$ —	$ —	$ —	$ —	$ 5,000	$ —
ABL Term Loan	9,000	9,000	9,000	9,000	46,125	—
Capital lease obligations	3,385	3,463	3,301	3,200	1,652	734
Term loan from unconsolidated affiliate	—	1,250	—	—	—	—
Total	$12,385	$13,713	$12,301	$12,200	$52,777	$734

Debt Financing Fees

Debt financing fees are classified within other non-current assets and consist of the following:

	June 28, 2015	June 29, 2014
Balance at beginning of year	$ 2,093	$2,117
Additions	1,063	400
Amortization charged to interest expense	(505)	(424)
Loss on extinguishment of debt	(1,040)	—
Balance at end of year	$ 1,611	$2,093

Interest Expense

Interest expense consists of the following:

	For the Fiscal Years Ended		
	June 28, 2015	June 29, 2014	June 30, 2013
Interest on ABL Facility	$3,290	$3,292	$3,673
Interest on a prior term loan	—	—	722
Other	273	192	107
Subtotal of interest on debt obligations	3,563	3,484	4,502
Reclassification adjustment for interest rate swap	231	554	322
Amortization of debt financing fees	505	424	632
Mark-to-market adjustment for interest rate swap	(83)	39	(931)
Interest capitalized to property, plant and equipment, net	(191)	(172)	(36)
Subtotal of other components of interest expense	462	845	(13)
Total interest expense	$4,025	$4,329	$4,489

18. Fair Value of Financial Instruments and Non-Financial Assets and Liabilities (in part)

Interest Rate Swap

On May 18, 2012, the Company entered into a five year, $50,000 interest rate swap with Wells Fargo to provide a hedge against the variability of cash flows related to LIBOR-based variable rate borrowings under the Company's ABL Facility. It increased to $85,000 in May 2013 (when certain other interest rate swaps terminated) and has decreased $5,000 per quarter since August 2013 to the current notional balance of $50,000, where it will remain through the life of the instrument. This interest rate swap allows the Company to fix LIBOR at 1.06% and terminates on May 24, 2017.

On November 26, 2012, the Company de-designated the interest rate swap as a cash flow hedge. See "Note 19. Accumulated Other Comprehensive Loss" for detail regarding the reclassifications of amounts from accumulated other comprehensive loss related to the interest rate swap.

The Company's financial assets and liabilities accounted for at fair value on a recurring basis and the level within the fair value hierarchy used to measure these items are as follows:

As of June 28, 2015	Notional Amount		USD Equivalent	Balance Sheet Location	Fair Value Hierarchy	Fair Value
Foreign currency contracts	EUR	—	$ —	—	Level 2	$ —
Interest rate swap	USD	$50,000	$50,000	Other long-term liabilities	Level 2	$ (280)
Contingent consideration		—	—	Accrued expenses and other long-term liabilities	Level 3	$(2,207)

As of June 29, 2014	Notional Amount		USD Equivalent	Balance Sheet Location	Fair Value Hierarchy	Fair Value
Foreign currency contracts	EUR	495	$ 668	Other current assets	Level 2	$ 7
Interest rate swap	USD	$65,000	$65,000	Other long-term liabilities	Level 2	$ (363)
Contingent consideration		—	—	Accrued expenses and other long-term liabilities	Level 3	$(2,563)

(EUR represents the Euro)

Estimates for the fair value of the Company's foreign currency forward contracts and interest rate swaps are obtained from month-end market quotes for contracts with similar terms.

The effects of marked to market hedging derivative instruments are as follows:

Derivatives not Designated as Hedges:	Classification:	For the Fiscal Years Ended		
		June 28, 2015	June 29, 2014	June 30, 2013
Foreign currency contracts—EUR/USD	Other operating expense, net	$ 7	$(10)	$ —
Foreign currency contracts—MXN/USD	Other operating expense, net	—	(3)	46
Interest rate swap	Interest expense	(83)	39	(931)
Total (gain) loss recognized in income		$(76)	$ 26	$(885)

(EUR represents the Euro; MXN represents the Mexican Peso)

INTEREST AND PENALTIES

3.28 RITE AID CORPORATION (FEB)
CONSOLIDATED STATEMENTS OF OPERATIONS (in part)

(In thousands, except per share amounts)

	Year Ended		
	February 28, 2015 (52 Weeks)	March 1, 2014 (52 Weeks)	March 2, 2013 (52 Weeks)
Revenues	$26,528,377	$25,526,413	$25,392,263
Costs and expenses:			
Cost of goods sold	18,951,645	18,202,679	18,073,987
Selling, general and administrative expenses	6,695,642	6,561,162	6,600,765
Lease termination and impairment charges	41,945	41,304	70,859
Interest expense	397,612	424,591	515,421
Loss on debt retirements, net	18,512	62,443	140,502
Gain on sale of assets, net	(3,799)	(15,984)	(16,776)
	26,101,557	25,276,195	25,384,758
Income before income taxes	426,820	250,218	7,505
Income tax (benefit) expense	(1,682,353)	804	(110,600)
Net income	$ 2,109,173	$ 249,414	$ 118,105

NOTES TO CONSOLIDATED FINANCIAL STATEMENTS (in part)

(In thousands, except per share amounts)

7. Income Taxes (in part)

A reconciliation of the beginning and ending amount of unrecognized tax benefits was as follows:

	2015	2014	2013
Unrecognized tax benefits	$10,143	$ 30,020	$ 247,722
Increases to prior year tax positions	1,003	—	6,305
Decreases to tax positions in prior periods	(984)	(3,215)	(196,214)
Increases to current year tax positions	123	—	—
Settlements	(681)	—	(3,655)
Lapse of statute of limitations	(90)	(16,662)	(24,138)
Unrecognized tax benefits balance	$ 9,514	$ 10,143	$ 30,020

The amount of the above unrecognized tax benefits at February 28, 2015, March 1, 2014 and March 2, 2013 which would impact the Company's effective tax rate, if recognized, was $440, $876 and $14,651, respectively. Additionally, any impact on the effective rate may be mitigated by the valuation allowance that is remaining against the Company's net deferred tax assets.

The Company is indemnified by Jean Coutu Group for certain tax liabilities incurred for all years ended up to and including the acquisition date of June 4, 2007, related to the Brooks Eckerd acquisition. Although the Company is indemnified by Jean Coutu Group, the Company remains the primary obligor to the tax authorities with respect to any tax liability arising for the years prior to the acquisition. Accordingly, as of February 28, 2015, March 1, 2014 and March 2, 2013, the Company had a corresponding recoverable indemnification asset of $0, $195 and $30,710 from Jean Coutu Group, included in the "Other Assets" line of the Consolidated Balance Sheets, to reflect the indemnification for such liabilities.

While it is expected that the amount of unrecognized tax benefits will change in the next twelve months, management does not expect the change to have a significant impact on the results of operations or the financial position of the company.

The Company recognizes interest and penalties related to tax contingencies as income tax expense. Prior to the adoption of ASC 740, "Income Taxes," the Company included interest as income tax expense and penalties as an operating expense. The Company recognized a benefit for interest and penalties in connection with tax matters of ($5,250), ($16,833) and ($43,069) for fiscal years 2015, 2014 and 2013, respectively. As of February 28, 2015 and March 1, 2014 the total amount of accrued income tax-related interest and penalties was $115 and $5,364, respectively.

The Company files U.S. federal income tax returns as well as income tax returns in those states where it does business. The consolidated federal income tax returns are closed for examination thru fiscal year 2011. However, any net operating losses that were generated in these prior closed years may be subject to examination by the IRS upon utilization. Tax examinations by various state taxing authorities could generally be conducted for a period of three to five years after filing of the respective return. However, as a result of filing amended returns, the Company has statutes open in some states from fiscal year 2005.

ACCRETION ON ASSET RETIREMENT OBLIGATION

3.29 APACHE CORPORATION (DEC)

STATEMENT OF CONSOLIDATED OPERATIONS (in part)

	For the Year Ended December 31,		
(In millions, except per common share data)	2015	2014	2013
Revenues And Other:			
Oil and gas production revenues:			
Oil revenues	$ 4,999	$10,040	$11,853
Gas revenues	1,157	1,983	2,266
Natural gas liquids revenues	227	668	652
	6,383	12,691	14,771
Other	(17)	110	(333)
	6,366	12,801	14,438
Operating Expenses:			
Depreciation, depletion, and amortization:			
Oil and gas property and equipment			
Recurring	3,531	4,388	4,534
Additional	25,517	5,001	995
Other assets	324	331	337
Asset retirement obligation accretion	145	154	211
Lease operating expenses	1,854	2,238	2,650
Gathering and transportation	211	273	288
Taxes other than income	282	577	772
Impairments	1,920	1,919	—
General and administrative	377	451	481
Transaction, reorganization, and separation	132	67	33
Financing costs, net	299	211	229
	34,592	15,610	10,530
Net Income (Loss) From Continuing Operations Before Income Taxes	(28,226)	(2,809)	3,908
Current income tax provision	309	1,177	1,619
Deferred income tax provision (benefit)	(5,778)	(514)	309
Net Income (Loss) From Continuing Operations			
Including Noncontrolling Interest	(22,757)	(3,472)	1,980
Net income (loss) from discontinued operations, net of tax	(771)	(1,588)	308
Net Income (Loss) Including Noncontrolling Interest	(23,528)	(5,060)	2,288
Preferred stock dividends	—	—	44
Net income (loss) attributable to noncontrolling interest	(409)	343	56
Net Income (Loss) Attributable To Common Stock	$(23,119)	$ (5,403)	$ 2,188

NOTES TO CONSOLIDATED FINANCIAL STATEMENTS (in part)

1. Summary of Significant Accounting Policies (in part)

Property and Equipment (in part)

Asset Retirement Costs and Obligations

The initial estimated asset retirement obligation related to property and equipment is recorded as a liability at its fair value, with an offsetting asset retirement cost recorded as an increase to the associated property and equipment on the consolidated balance sheet. If the fair value of the recorded asset retirement obligation changes, a revision is recorded to both the asset retirement obligation and the asset retirement cost. Revisions in estimated liabilities can result from changes in estimated inflation rates, changes in service and equipment costs and changes in the estimated timing of an asset's retirement. Asset retirement costs are depreciated using a systematic and rational method similar to that used for the associated property and equipment. Accretion expense on the liability is recognized over the estimated productive life of the related assets.

5. Asset Retirement Obligation

The following table describes changes to the Company's asset retirement obligation (ARO) liability for the years ended December 31, 2015 and 2014:

(In millions)	2015	2014
Asset retirement obligation at beginning of year	$3,085	$3,222
Liabilities incurred	68	171
Liabilities divested	(623)	(471)
Liabilities settled	(90)	(146)
Accretion expense	158	181
Revisions in estimated liabilities	—	128
Asset retirement obligation at end of year	2,598	3,085
Less current portion	(36)	(37)
Asset retirement obligation, long-term	$2,562	$3,048

The ARO liability reflects the estimated present value of the amount of dismantlement, removal, site reclamation, and similar activities associated with Apache's oil and gas properties. The Company utilizes current retirement costs to estimate the expected cash outflows for retirement obligations. The Company estimates the ultimate productive life of the properties, a risk-adjusted discount rate, and an inflation factor in order to determine the current present value of this obligation. To the extent future revisions to these assumptions impact the present value of the existing ARO liability, a corresponding adjustment is made to the oil and gas property balance.

Accretion expense for 2015 and 2014 includes discontinued operations of $13 million and $27 million, respectively, which are included in "Net income (loss) from discontinued operations, net of tax" on the statement of consolidated operations.

During 2015 and 2014, the Company recorded $68 million and $171 million, respectively, in abandonment liabilities resulting from Apache's active exploration and development capital program. Liabilities settled primarily relate to individual properties, platforms, and facilities plugged and abandoned during the period.

IMPAIRMENT OF INVESTMENT

3.30 EQUIFAX INC. (DEC)
CONSOLIDATED STATEMENTS OF INCOME (in part)

	Twelve Months Ended December 31,		
(In millions, except per share amounts)	2015	2014	2013
Operating revenue	$2,663.6	$2,436.4	$2,303.9
Operating expenses:			
Cost of services (exclusive of depreciation and amortization below)	887.4	844.7	787.3
Selling, general and administrative expenses	884.3	751.7	715.8
Depreciation and amortization	198.0	201.8	189.6
Total operating expenses	1,969.7	1,798.2	1,692.7
Operating income	693.9	638.2	611.2
Interest expense	(63.8)	(68.6)	(70.2)
Other income (expense), net	6.5	4.6	(10.6)
Consolidated income from continuing operations before income taxes	636.6	574.2	530.4

NOTES TO CONSOLIDATED FINANCIAL STATEMENTS (in part)

1. Summary of Significant Accounting Policies (in part)

Basis of Consolidation (in part). Our Consolidated Financial Statements and the accompanying notes, which are prepared in accordance with U.S. generally accepted accounting principles, or GAAP, include Equifax and all its subsidiaries. We consolidate all majority-owned and controlled subsidiaries as well as variable interest entities in which we are the primary beneficiary. Other parties' interests in consolidated entities are reported as noncontrolling interests. We use the equity method of accounting for investments in which we are able to exercise significant influence and use the cost method for all other investments. All significant intercompany transactions and balances are eliminated.

Other Assets. Other assets on our Consolidated Balance Sheets primarily represents our investment in unconsolidated affiliates, our cost method investment in Boa Vista Servicos ("BVS"), assets related to life insurance policies covering certain officers of the Company, employee benefit trust assets, and debt issuance costs.

Impairment of Cost Method Investment. We monitor the status of our cost method investment in order to determine if conditions exist or events and circumstances indicate that it may be impaired in that its carrying amount may exceed the fair value of the investment. Significant factors that are considered that could be indicative of an impairment include: changes in business strategy, market conditions, underperformance relative to historical or expected future operating results; and negative industry or economic trends. If potential indicators of impairment exist, we estimate the fair value of the investment using a combination of a discounted cash flow analysis and an evaluation of EBITDA and transaction multiples for comparable companies. If the carrying value of the investment exceeds the estimated fair value, an impairment loss is recorded based on the amount by which the investment's carrying amount exceeds its fair value. There were no indicators of impairment for 2014. We recorded an impairment of our cost method investment in 2015 and 2013. See Note 2 for further discussion.

2. Cost Method Investment

We hold a 15% equity interest in BVS, which is the second largest consumer and commercial credit information company in Brazil. This investment is recorded in other assets, net, on the Consolidated Balance Sheets and is accounted for using the cost method. As of December 31, 2012, our investment in BVS was valued at 130 million Brazilian Reais, which was the same as the initial fair value. The initial fair value was determined by a third-party using income, market and transaction approaches.

During the fourth quarter of 2013, management of BVS updated financial projections in connection with a request for additional financing. The financial projections reflected the effects of reduced near-term market expectations for consumer credit and for credit information services in Brazil and increased investment to achieve the strategic objectives and capitalize on future market opportunities, such as positive data, resulting in reduced expected cash flows. The request for financing, the projections received, along with the near-term weakness in the Brazilian consumer and small commercial credit markets were considered indicators of impairment. Management of Equifax performed an analysis to estimate the fair value of our investment at December 31, 2013 and estimated that value to be 90 million Reais ($38.2 million). As a result, we wrote-down the carrying value of our investment and recorded a loss of 40 million Reais ($17.0 million) which is included in other income (expense) in the Consolidated Statements of Income.

At December 31, 2014, we estimated the fair value of the investment approximated the fair value of the investment recorded.

During the second quarter of 2015, management updated the financial projections. The updated projections, along with the continued weakness in the Brazilian consumer and small commercial credit markets were considered indicators of impairment. Management of Equifax prepared an analysis to estimate the fair value of our investment at June 30, 2015 and estimated that value to be 44 million Brazilian Reais ($14.1 million). As a result, we decreased the carrying value of our investment and recorded a loss of 46 million Brazilian Reais ($14.8 million) which is included in other income (expense), net, in the Consolidated Statements of Income. Additionally, the carrying value has decreased by $39.0 million related to the foreign exchange impact since 2011, which is included in the foreign currency translation adjustments in accumulated other comprehensive income. As of December 31, 2015, our investment in BVS, recorded at 44 million Brazilian Reais ($11.5 million), approximated the fair value.

RESTRUCTURING

3.31 THE DOW CHEMICAL COMPANY (DEC)
CONSOLIDATED STATEMENTS OF INCOME (in part)

(In millions, except per share amounts) **For the Years Ended December 31**	2015	2014	2013
Net Sales	$48,778	$58,167	$57,080
Cost of sales	37,836	47,464	47,594
Research and development expenses	1,598	1,647	1,747
Selling, general and administrative expenses	2,971	3,106	3,024
Amortization of intangibles	419	436	461
Goodwill and other intangible asset impairment losses	—	50	—
Restructuring charges (credits)	415	(3)	(22)
Asbestos-related charge	—	78	—
Equity in earnings of nonconsolidated affiliates	674	835	1,034
Sundry income (expense)—net	4,592	(27)	2,554
Interest income	71	51	41
Interest expense and amortization of debt discount	946	983	1,101
Income Before Income Taxes	9,930	5,265	6,804

Note 3—Restructuring

On April 29, 2015, Dow's Board of Directors approved actions to further streamline the organization and optimize the Company's footprint as a result of the separation of a significant portion of Dow's chlorine value chain. These actions, which will further accelerate Dow's value growth and productivity targets, will result in a reduction of approximately 1,750 positions across a number of businesses and functions and adjustments to the Company's asset footprint to enhance competitiveness. These actions are expected to be completed primarily by March 31, 2017.

As a result of these actions, the Company recorded pretax restructuring charges of $375 million in the second quarter of 2015 consisting of costs associated with exit or disposal activities of $10 million, severance costs of $196 million and asset write-downs and write-offs of $169 million. In the fourth quarter of 2015, the Company recorded restructuring charge adjustments of $40 million, including severance costs of $39 million for the separation of approximately 500 additional positions as part of the Company's efforts to further streamline the organization, and $1 million of costs associated with exit and disposal activities. The impact of these charges is shown as "Restructuring charges (credits)" in the consolidated statements of income and reflected in the Company's segment results as shown in the following table. The Company also recorded $14 million of "Net loss attributable to noncontrolling interests" for noncontrolling interests' portion of the restructuring charges.

2015 Restructuring Charges by Operating Segment In millions	Costs Associated with Exit or Disposal Activities	Severance Costs	Impairment of Long-Lived Assets, Investments and Other Assets	Total
Agricultural Sciences	$ 6	$ —	$ 8	$ 14
Consumer Solutions	2	—	65	67
Infrastructure Solutions	2	—	25	27
Performance Plastics	—	—	12	12
Corporate	—	196	59	255
2015 Restructuring Charges	$ 10	$196	$169	$375
Adjustments to 2015 Restructuring Charges:				
Agricultural Sciences	1	—	1	2
Infrastructure Solutions	—	—	(1)	(1)
Corporate	—	39	—	39
Total 2015 Restructuring Charges	$ 11	$235	$169	$415

Details regarding the components of the 2015 restructuring charges are discussed below:

Costs Associated with Exit and Disposal Activities

The restructuring charges for costs associated with exit and disposal activities, primarily environmental remediation and contract penalties, totaled $10 million in the second quarter of 2015, impacting Agricultural Sciences ($6 million), Consumer Solutions ($2 million) and Infrastructure Solutions ($2 million). In the fourth quarter of 2015, the Company increased the restructuring reserve for costs associated with exit and disposal activities by $1 million, impacting Agricultural Sciences.

Severance Costs

The restructuring charges recorded in the second quarter of 2015 included severance of $196 million for the separation of approximately 1,750 employees under the terms of the Company's ongoing benefit arrangements. In the fourth quarter of 2015, the Company recorded an additional charge of $39 million related to the separation of approximately 500 additional employees, primarily by March 31, 2017. These costs were charged against Corporate. At December 31, 2015, severance of $92 million was paid, leaving a liability of $143 million for approximately 1,250 employees.

Impairment of Long-Lived Assets, Investments and Other Assets

The restructuring charges related to the write-down and write-off of assets in the second quarter of 2015 totaled $169 million. Details regarding the write-downs and write-offs are as follows:
- As a result of changing market dynamics in certain end-use markets, select manufacturing facilities and non-core assets aligned with the Dow Electronic Materials business will be shut down. The assets impacted include certain display films and metalorganic precursors, including a metalorganic materials manufacturing site in North Andover, Massachusetts, and related operations in

Taoyuan, Taiwan, as well as certain display films' manufacturing assets aligned with SKC Haas Display Films Co., Ltd., a majority-owned joint venture located in Cheonan, South Korea. In the second quarter of 2015, the Company recorded a $51 million charge for asset write-downs and write-offs in the Dow Electronic Materials business, which is reflected in the Consumer Solutions segment. The facilities and assets associated with these charges are expected to be shut down primarily by the end of 2016.

- The Company will shut down and/or consolidate manufacturing capacity in the Dow Building & Construction business. As a result, the Company recorded a charge of $15 million in the second quarter of 2015 for asset write-offs which is reflected in the Infrastructure Solutions segment. The impacted facilities are expected to be shut down by the end of the third quarter of 2016.
- A Consumer Care manufacturing facility in Institute, West Virginia, was shut down in the fourth quarter of 2015. As a result, an asset write-down of $14 million was recorded against the Consumer Solutions segment.
- A Dow Packaging and Specialty Plastics plant in Schkopau, Germany, was permanently shut down in the second quarter of 2015, resulting in an asset write-off of $12 million against the Performance Plastics segment.
- Select operations in Agricultural Sciences were shut down, closed or idled in the second half of 2015, resulting in a pretax charge of $8 million for the write-down of assets. In the fourth quarter of 2015, the Company recorded an additional charge of $1 million related to the impairment of long-lived assets and other assets.
- A decision was made to shut down a number of small manufacturing and administrative facilities to optimize the Company's asset footprint. Write-downs of $14 million were recorded in the second quarter of 2015, impacting Infrastructure Solutions ($10 million) and Corporate ($4 million). These facilities will be shut down no later than the second quarter of 2016. During the fourth quarter of 2015, the Company recorded a favorable adjustment to the restructuring charge related to the impairment of long-lived assets of $1 million, impacting Infrastructure Solutions.
- Due to a change in the Company's strategy to monetize and exit certain Venture Capital portfolio investments, a write-down of $55 million was recorded in the second quarter of 2015, reflected in Corporate.

The following table summarizes the activities related to the Company's 2015 restructuring reserve, which is included in "Accrued and other current liabilities" and "Other noncurrent obligations" in the consolidated balance sheets as shown in the following table.

2015 Restructuring Activities In millions	Costs Associated with Exit and Disposal Activities	Severance Costs	Impairment of Long- Lived Assets, Investments and Other Assets	Total
Restructuring Charges recognized in the second quarter of 2015	$ 10	$196	$ 169	$ 375
Charges against the reserve	—	—	(169)	(169)
Adjustments to the reserve	1	39	—	40
Impact of currency	(1)	—	—	(1)
Cash payments	—	(92)	—	(92)
Reserve balance at Dec 31, 2015	$ 10	$143	$ —	$ 153

Dow expects to incur additional costs in the future related to its restructuring activities, as the Company continually looks for ways to enhance the efficiency and cost effectiveness of its operations, and to ensure competitiveness across its businesses and geographic areas. Future costs are expected to include demolition costs related to closed facilities and restructuring plan implementation costs; these costs will be recognized as incurred. The Company also expects to incur additional employee-related costs, including involuntary termination benefits, related to its other optimization activities. These costs cannot be reasonably estimated at this time.

2014 Adjustments to the 4Q12 Restructuring Plan

In 2014, the Company reduced the 4Q12 Restructuring reserve related to contract cancellation fees by $3 million. The impact of this adjustment is shown as "Restructuring charges (credits)" in the consolidated statements of income and reflected in Performance Materials & Chemicals.

2013 Adjustments to the 1Q12 and 4Q12 Restructuring Plans

In 2013, the Company reduced the 4Q12 Restructuring reserve related to contract cancellation fees by $6 million, impacting Performance Plastics. The Company also reduced the 1Q12 Restructuring reserve related to the adjustment of contract cancellation fees and asbestos abatement costs by $16 million, impacting Infrastructure Solutions ($1 million) and Performance Materials & Chemicals ($15 million). These adjustments are shown as "Restructuring charges (credits)" in the consolidated statements of income.

INTANGIBLE ASSET AMORTIZATION

3.32 ARCBEST CORPORATION (DEC)

NOTES TO CONSOLIDATED FINANCIAL STATEMENTS (in part)

Note B—Accounting Policies (in part)

Computer Software Developed or Obtained for Internal Use, Including Web Site Development Costs: The Company capitalizes the costs of software acquired from third parties and qualifying internal computer software costs incurred during the application development stage. Costs incurred in the preliminary project stage and postimplementation-operation stage, which includes maintenance and training costs, are expensed as incurred. For financial reporting purposes, capitalized software costs are amortized by the straight line method generally over 2 to 3 years with some applications, including the acquired software of Panther, having longer lives (primarily up to 7 years) as applicable. The amount of costs capitalized within any period is dependent on the nature of software development activities and projects in each period.

Assets to be disposed of are reclassified as assets held for sale at the lower of their carrying amount or fair value less cost to sell. Assets held for sale primarily represent ABF Freight's nonoperating properties, older ABF Freight and Panther revenue equipment, and other equipment. Adjustments to write down assets to fair value less the amount of costs to sell are reported in operating income. Assets held for sale are expected to be disposed of by selling the assets within the next 12 months. Gains and losses on property and equipment are reported in operating income. Assets held for sale of $2.1 million and $0.3 million are reported within other noncurrent assets as of December 31, 2015 and 2014, respectively. At December 31, 2015 and 2014, management was not aware of any events or circumstances indicating the Company's long-lived assets would not be recoverable.

Goodwill and Intangible Assets: Goodwill represents the excess of the purchase price in a business combination over the fair value of net tangible and intangible assets acquired. Goodwill is not amortized, but rather is evaluated for impairment annually or more frequently if indicators of impairment exist. The Company's measurement of goodwill impairment involves a comparison of the estimated fair value of a reporting unit to its carrying value. If the estimated fair value of the reporting unit is less than the carrying value, an estimate of the current fair values of all assets and liabilities is made to determine the amount of implied goodwill and, consequently, the amount of any goodwill impairment. Fair value is derived using a combination of valuation methods, including earnings before interest, taxes, depreciation, and amortization (EBITDA) and revenue multiples (market approach) and the present value of discounted cash flows (income approach).

Indefinite-lived intangible assets are also not amortized but rather are evaluated for impairment annually or more frequently if indicators of impairment exist. If the carrying amount of the intangible asset exceeds its fair value, an impairment loss shall be recognized in an amount equal to that excess. Fair values are determined based on a discounted cash flow model, similar to the goodwill analysis.

The Company's annual impairment testing is performed as of October 1.

The Company amortizes finite-lived intangible assets over their respective estimated useful lives. Finite-lived intangible assets are also evaluated for impairment whenever events or changes in circumstances indicate that the carrying value may not be recoverable. In reviewing finite-lived intangible assets for impairment, the carrying amount of the asset is compared to the estimated undiscounted future cash flows expected from the use of the asset and its eventual disposition. If such cash flows are not sufficient to support the recorded value, an impairment loss to reduce the carrying value of the asset to its estimated fair value shall be recognized in operating income.

Note D—Goodwill and Intangible Assets (in part)

Intangible assets consisted of the following as of December 31:

	Weighted-Average Amortization Period (In years)	2015			2014		
		Cost	Accumulated Amortization (In thousands)	Net Value	Cost	Accumulated Amortization (In thousands)	Net Value
Finite-lived intangible assets							
Customer relationships[1]	13	$52,221	$11,331	$40,890	$44,242	$ 7,971	$36,271
Driver network	3	3,200	3,200	—	3,200	2,711	489
Other	8	1,032	257	775	1,032	105	927
	13	56,453	14,788	41,665	48,474	10,787	37,687
Indefinite-lived intangible assets							
Trade name	N/A	32,300	N/A	32,300	32,300	N/A	32,300
Other	N/A	2,822	N/A	2,822	2,822	N/A	2,822
		35,122		35,122	35,122		35,122
Total intangible assets	N/A	$91,575	$14,788	$76,787	$83,596	$10,787	$72,809

[1] Customer relationships include $7.3 million related to the December 1, 2015 acquisition of Bear. The fair value assessment of assets and liabilities acquired with Bear was based on preliminary information as of December 31, 2015.

Amortization expense on intangible assets totaled $4.0 million, $4.4 million, and $4.2 million for the year ended December 31, 2015, 2014, and 2013 respectively. As of December 31, 2015, amortization expense on intangible assets (excluding acquired software which is reported within property, plant and equipment) is anticipated to range between $4.0 million and $4.2 million per year for the years ended December 31, 2016 through 2020. Acquired software (reported in property, plant and equipment) is being amortized on a straight-line basis over seven years, which resulted in $4.5 million of amortization expense in 2015 and 2014 and is expected to result in $4.5 million of annual amortization expense for the years ended December 31, 2016 through 2018 and $2.1 million for the year ended December 31, 2019.

Annual impairment evaluations of goodwill and indefinite-lived intangible assets were performed as of October 1, 2015 and 2014, and it was determined that there was no impairment of the recorded balances.

FOREIGN CURRENCY

3.33 NATIONAL OILWELL VARCO, INC. (DEC)
QUANTITATIVE AND QUALITATIVE DISCLOSURES ABOUT MARKET RISK (in part)

We are exposed to changes in foreign currency exchange rates and interest rates. Additional information concerning each of these matters follows:

Foreign Currency Exchange Rates

We have extensive operations in foreign countries. The net assets and liabilities of these operations are exposed to changes in foreign currency exchange rates, although such fluctuations generally do not affect income since their functional currency is typically the local currency. These operations also have net assets and liabilities not denominated in the functional currency, which exposes us to changes in foreign currency exchange rates that impact income. During the years ended December 31, 2015, 2014 and 2013, the Company reported foreign currency gains (losses) of ($47) million, $20 million and ($24) million, respectively. Gains and losses are primarily due to exchange rate fluctuations related to monetary asset balances denominated in currencies other than the functional currency and adjustments to our hedged positions as a result of changes in foreign currency exchange rates. Strengthening of currencies against the U.S. dollar may create losses in future periods to the extent we maintain net assets and liabilities not denominated in the functional currency of our subsidiaries using the local currency as their functional currency.

Some of our revenues in foreign countries are denominated in U.S. dollars, and therefore, changes in foreign currency exchange rates impact our earnings to the extent that costs associated with those U.S. dollar revenues are denominated in the local currency. Similarly some of our revenues are denominated in foreign currencies, but have associated U.S. dollar costs, which also give rise to foreign currency exchange rate exposure. In order to mitigate that risk, we may utilize foreign currency forward contracts to better match the currency of our revenues and associated costs. We do not use foreign currency forward contracts for trading or speculative purposes.

The following table details the Company's foreign currency exchange risk grouped by functional currency and their expected maturity periods as of December 31, 2015 (in millions except for rates):

	December 31, 2015			December 31,
Functional Currency	2016	2017	Total	2014
CAD Buy USD/Sell CAD:				
Notional amount to buy (in Canadian dollars)	10	—	10	66
Average USD to CAD contract rate	1.3759	—	1.3759	1.1632
Fair Value at December 31, 2015 in U.S. dollars	—	—	—	—
Sell USD/Buy CAD:				
Notional amount to sell (in Canadian dollars)	136	—	136	285
Average USD to CAD contract rate	1.3554	—	1.3554	1.1511
Fair Value at December 31, 2015 in U.S. dollars	(2)	—	(2)	(3)
EUR Buy USD/Sell EUR:				
Notional amount to buy (in Euros)	10	1	11	4
Average USD to EUR contract rate	0.8516	0.8843	0.8528	0.7933
Fair Value at December 31, 2015 in U.S. dollars	1	—	1	—
Sell USD/Buy EUR:				
Notional amount to buy (in Euros)	198	1	199	430
Average USD to EUR contract rate	0.8954	0.8771	0.8953	0.7832
Fair Value at December 31, 2015 in U.S. dollars	(5)	—	(5)	(25)
KRW Sell USD/Buy KRW:				
Notional amount to buy (in South Korean won)	23,613	—	23,613	143,488
Average USD to KRW contract rate	1,181	—	1,181	1,104
Fair Value at December 31, 2015 in U.S. dollars	—	—	—	—

(continued)

Functional Currency	December 31, 2015			December 31, 2014
	2016	2017	Total	
GBP Buy USD/Sell GBP:				
Notional amount to buy (in British Pounds Sterling)	2	—	2	—
Average USD to GBP contract rate	0.6416	—	0.6416	—
Fair Value at December 31, 2015 in U.S. dollars	—	—	—	—
GBP Sell USD/Buy GBP:				
Notional amount to buy (in British Pounds Sterling)	170	—	170	205
Average USD to GBP contract rate	0.6613	—	0.6613	0.6201
Fair Value at December 31, 2015 in U.S. dollars	(5)	—	(5)	(6)
USD Buy CAD/Sell USD:				
Notional amount to buy (in U.S. dollars)	7	—	7	16
Average CAD to USD contract rate	0.7635	—	0.7635	0.9431
Fair Value at December 31, 2015 in U.S. dollars	—	—	—	(1)
Buy DKK/Sell USD:				
Notional amount to buy (in U.S. dollars)	24	—	24	75
Average DKK to USD contract rate	0.1553	—	0.1553	0.1813
Fair Value at December 31, 2015 in U.S. dollars	(1)	—	(1)	(6)
Buy EUR/Sell USD:				
Notional amount to buy (in U.S. dollars)	278	—	278	884
Average EUR to USD contract rate	1.1925	—	1.1925	1.3411
Fair Value at December 31, 2015 in U.S. dollars	(23)	—	(23)	(77)
Buy GBP/Sell USD:				
Notional amount to buy (in U.S. dollars)	20	—	20	147
Average GBP to USD contract rate	1.5568	—	1.5568	1.5779
Fair Value at December 31, 2015 in U.S. dollars	(1)	—	(1)	(3)
Buy NOK/Sell USD:				
Notional amount to buy (in U.S. dollars)	1,216	285	1,501	1,961
Average NOK to USD contract rate	0.1380	0.1252	0.1353	0.1642
Fair Value at December 31, 2015 in U.S. dollars	(214)	(25)	(239)	(276)
Buy SGD/Sell USD:				
Notional amount to buy (in U.S. dollars)	7	5	12	36
Average SGD to USD contract rate	0.7716	0.7262	0.7534	0.7966
Fair Value at December 31, 2015 in U.S. dollars	(1)	—	(1)	(1)
Sell DKK/Buy USD:				
Notional amount to buy (in U.S. dollars)	8	—	8	22
Average DKK to USD contract rate	0.1510	—	0.1510	1.3625
Fair Value at December 31, 2015 in U.S. dollars	—	—	—	1
Sell EUR/Buy USD:				
Notional amount to sell (in U.S. dollars)	89	—	89	251
Average EUR to USD contract rate	1.1075	—	1.1075	1.3109
Fair Value at December 31, 2015 in U.S. dollars	1	—	1	7
Sell GBP/Buy USD:				
Notional amount to sell (in U.S. dollars)	3	—	3	—
Average GBP to USD contract rate	1.4961	—	1.4961	—
Fair Value at December 31, 2015 in U.S. dollars	—	—	—	—
Sell NOK/Buy USD:				
Notional amount to sell (in U.S. dollars)	107	3	110	348
Average NOK to USD contract rate	0.1325	0.1187	0.1321	0.1634
Fair Value at December 31, 2015 in U.S. dollars	15	—	15	44
Sell RUB/Buy USD:				
Notional amount to sell (in U.S. dollars)	30	—	30	—
Average RUB to USD contract rate	0.0139	—	0.0139	—
Fair Value at December 31, 2015 in U.S. dollars	1	—	1	—
Sell SGD/Buy USD:				
Notional amount to sell (in U.S. dollars)	2	—	2	2
Average SGD to USD contract rate	0.7082	—	0.7082	0.7678
Fair Value at December 31, 2015 in U.S. dollars	—	—	—	—
BRL Buy EUR/Sell BRL:				
Notional amount to sell (in U.S. dollars)	199	—	199	—
Average EUR to BRL contract rate	4.3679	—	4.3679	—
Fair Value at December 31, 2015 in U.S. dollars	1	—	1	—
Sell EUR/Buy BRL:				
Notional amount to sell (in U.S. dollars)	427	—	427	—
Average EUR to BRL contract rate	4.6985	—	4.6985	—
Fair Value at December 31, 2015 in U.S. dollars	4	—	4	—

(continued)

Functional Currency	December 31, 2015			December 31,
	2016	2017	Total	2014
DKK Sell DKK/Buy USD:				
Notional amount to buy (in U.S. dollars)	1,396	—	1,396	59
Average DKK to USD contract rate	6.5618	—	6.5618	5.9300
Fair Value at December 31, 2015 in U.S. dollars	(8)	—	(8)	—
Other Currencies				
Fair Value at December 31, 2015 in U.S. dollars	2	—	2	—
Total Fair Value at December 31, 2015 in U.S. dollars	(235)	(25)	(260)	(346)

The Company had other financial market risk sensitive instruments denominated in foreign currencies for transactional exposures totaling $157 million and translation exposures totaling $323 million as of December 31, 2015, excluding trade receivables and payables, which approximate fair value. These market risk sensitive instruments consisted of cash balances and overdraft facilities. The Company estimates that a hypothetical 10% movement of all applicable foreign currency exchange rates on the transactional exposures financial market risk sensitive instruments could affect net income by $10 million and the translational exposures financial market risk sensitive instruments could affect the future fair value by $32 million.

The counterparties to forward contracts are major financial institutions. The credit ratings and concentration of risk of these financial institutions are monitored on a continuing basis. In the event that the counterparties fail to meet the terms of a foreign currency contract, our exposure is limited to the foreign currency rate differential.

Historically, the Venezuelan government has devalued the country's currency. During the first quarters of 2015 and 2013, the Venezuelan government again officially devalued the Venezuelan bolivar against the U.S. dollar. As a result, the Company incurred approximately $9 million and $12 million in devaluation charges in the first quarter of 2015 and 2013, respectively. The reporting currency of all of the Company's Venezuelan entities is the U.S. dollar. The Company's remaining net investment in Venezuela, which is largely U.S. dollar, was $25 million at December 31, 2015.

During the fourth quarter of 2015, the Argentinian government officially devalued the Argentine peso against the U.S. dollar. As a result, the Company incurred approximately $7 million of devaluation charges in the fourth quarter of 2015. The reporting currency of all of the Company's Argentinian entities is the Argentine peso.

SOFTWARE AMORTIZATION

3.34 XEROX CORPORATION (DEC)
CONSOLIDATED STATEMENTS OF INCOME (in part)

(In millions, except per-share data)	Year Ended December 31,		
	2015	2014	2013
Revenues			
Sales	$ 4,748	$ 5,288	$ 5,582
Outsourcing, maintenance and rentals	12,951	13,865	13,941
Financing	346	387	483
Total Revenues	18,045	19,540	20,006
Costs and Expenses			
Cost of sales	2,961	3,269	3,550
Cost of outsourcing, maintenance and rentals	9,691	9,885	9,808
Cost of financing	130	140	163
Research, development and engineering expenses	563	577	603
Selling, administrative and general expenses	3,559	3,788	4,073
Restructuring and asset impairment charges	186	128	115
Amortization of intangible assets	310	315	305
Other expenses, net	233	232	146
Total Costs and Expenses	17,633	18,334	18,763
Income Before Income Taxes and Equity Income	412	1,206	1,243

(in millions, except per-share data and where otherwise noted)

Note 1—Basis of Presentation and Summary of Significant Accounting Policies (in part)

Use of Estimates

The preparation of our Consolidated Financial Statements requires that we make estimates and assumptions that affect the reported amounts of assets and liabilities, as well as the disclosure of contingent assets and liabilities at the date of the financial statements, and the reported amounts of revenues and expenses during the reporting period. Future events and their effects cannot be predicted with certainty; accordingly, our accounting estimates require the exercise of judgment. The accounting estimates used in the preparation of our Consolidated Financial Statements will change as new events occur, as more experience is acquired, as additional information is obtained and as our operating environment changes. Our estimates are based on management's best knowledge of current events, historical experience, actions that the company may undertake in the future and on various other assumptions that are believed to be reasonable under the circumstances. As a result, actual results may be different from these estimates.

The following table summarizes certain recurring type costs and expenses that require management estimates for the three years ended December 31, 2015:

| | Year Ended December 31, | | |
Expense/(Income)	2015	2014	2013
Provisions for restructuring and asset impairments—continuing operations	$186	$128	$115
Provisions for restructuring and asset impairments—discontinued operations	—	2	7
Provision for receivables	58	53	123
Provisions for litigation and regulatory matters	16	11	(34)
Provisions for obsolete and excess inventory	30	26	35
Provision for product warranty liability	22	25	28
Depreciation and obsolescence of equipment on operating leases	286	297	283
Depreciation of buildings and equipment[1]	277	324	332
Amortization of internal use software[1]	135	139	137
Amortization of product software	69	62	43
Amortization of acquired intangible assets[1]	310	315	305
Amortization of customer contract costs[1]	113	128	100
Defined pension benefits—net periodic benefit cost	142	82	267
Retiree health benefits—net periodic benefit cost	2	3	1
Income tax (benefit) expense—continuing operations	(23)	215	253
Income tax expense—discontinued operations	81	6	27

[1] Excludes amounts related to our ITO business, which was reported as a discontinued operation through its date of sale on June 30, 2015. Refer to Note 4—Divestitures for additional information regarding this sale.

Other Significant Accounting Policies (in part)

Software—Internal Use and Product

We capitalize direct costs associated with developing, purchasing or otherwise acquiring software for internal use and amortize these costs on a straight-line basis over the expected useful life of the software, beginning when the software is implemented (Internal Use Software). Costs incurred for upgrades and enhancements that will not result in additional functionality are expensed as incurred. Amounts expended for Internal Use Software are included in Cash Flows from Investing.

We also capitalize certain costs related to the development of software solutions to be sold to our customers upon reaching technological feasibility (Product Software). These costs are amortized on a straight-line basis over the estimated economic life of the software. Amounts expended for Product Software are included in Cash Flows from Operations. We perform periodic reviews to ensure that unamortized Product Software costs remain recoverable from estimated future operating profits (net realizable value or NRV). Costs to support or service licensed software are charged to Costs of services as incurred.

Refer to Note 8—Land, Buildings, Equipment and Software, Net for further information.

Note 8—Land, Buildings, Equipment and Software, Net (in part)

Internal Use and Product Software

	Year Ended December 31,		
Additions to:	2015	2014	2013
Internal use software	$91	$82	$77
Product software	23	23	28

	December 31,	
Capitalized Costs, Net:	2015	2014
Internal use software	$383	$434
Product software	115	307

Useful lives of our internal use and product software generally vary from three to ten years.

Included within product software at December 31, 2015 and 2014 is approximately $55 and $250, respectively, of capitalized costs associated with software system platforms developed for use in certain of our government services businesses. During 2015, as a result of our decision to discontinue certain future implementations of these software system platforms (*Government Healthcare Strategy Change*), we recorded impairment charges associated with these software platforms of approximately $160. Our impairment review of the remaining balance at December 31, 2015 indicated that the costs would be recoverable from estimated future operating profits; however, those future operating profits are dependent on our ability to successfully complete existing contracts as well as obtain future contracts.

LITIGATION

3.35 COMPUTER SCIENCES CORPORATION (MAR)
CONSOLIDATED STATEMENTS OF OPERATIONS (in part)

	Twelve Months Ended		
(Amounts in millions, except per-share amounts)	April 3, 2015	March 28, 2014	March 29, 2013
Revenues	$12,173	$12,998	$14,195
Costs of services (excludes depreciation and amortization and restructuring costs)	9,534	9,272	11,293
Selling, general and administrative (excludes SEC settlement related charges and restructuring costs)	1,340	1,220	1,197
Selling, general and administrative—SEC settlement related charges	197	—	—
Depreciation and amortization	977	1,018	1,070
Restructuring costs	261	76	264
Interest expense	148	147	183
Interest income	(20)	(16)	(22)
Other expense (income), net	12	18	(25)
Total costs and expenses	12,449	11,735	13,960
(Loss) income from continuing operations, before taxes	(276)	1,263	235

NOTES TO CONSOLIDATED FINANCIAL STATEMENTS (in part)

Note 2—Settlement of SEC Investigation (in part)

As previously disclosed, on January 28, 2011, the Company was notified by the Division of Enforcement of the SEC that it had commenced a formal civil investigation. That investigation covered a range of matters as previously disclosed by the Company, including the Company's prior use in fiscal years 2009-2012 of the terms of ongoing contract negotiations with the U.K. National Health Service (the NHS) in developing its assumptions and judgments with respect to the margin used in recognizing profit under the percentage of completion accounting method and in evaluating the recoverability of NHS contract assets, as well as the Company's prior disclosures concerning such matters. On May 2, 2011, the Audit Committee commenced an independent investigation and, in August 2012, determined in that its independent investigation was complete. The Audit Committee instructed its independent counsel to cooperate with the SEC's Division of Enforcement by completing production of documents and providing any further information requested by the SEC's Division of Enforcement.

As a result of findings by the Audit Committee's independent investigation, the Company has previously acknowledged certain historic errors and irregularities relating to accounting entries arising from the Nordics region, Australia, and the Company's contractual relationship with the NHS, self-reported these errors and irregularities to the SEC's Division of Enforcement, and made out of period adjustments to its financial statements as reported in its past filings. In addition, as previously disclosed, certain personnel in certain foreign operations were reprimanded, suspended, terminated and/or resigned and additional controls were implemented. Based on recommendations from the Audit Committee's independent investigation and discussions with the SEC's staff concerning the SEC's investigation, the Company also instituted comprehensive enhancements beginning in 2011 to its compliance, financial and disclosure controls, and to the function of internal audit. In doing so, the Company made significant changes to prevent the type of misconduct identified by the Audit Committee's independent investigation from recurring. The Company also previously took significant steps to enhance its compliance culture and to remediate any deficiencies.

During the third quarter of fiscal 2015, the Company reached an understanding with the staff of the SEC regarding a settlement of a formal civil investigation by the SEC that commenced on January 28, 2011 and covered a range of matters, as previously disclosed, including certain of the Company's prior disclosures and accounting determinations. As part of the Company's understanding with the staff of the SEC regarding terms of the settlement, the Company agreed to pay a penalty of $190 million and to implement a review of its compliance policies through an independent compliance consultant. The Company recorded a pre-tax charge of $197 million for the penalty and related expenses in fiscal 2015.

During the first quarter of fiscal 2016, the agreed-upon settlement with the SEC was formally approved by the SEC and became effective on June 5, 2015 and the Company has agreed, in addition to the payment of the fine and the engagement of the compliance consultant referenced above, to cease and desist from further violations of the anti-fraud, reporting, and books-and-records provisions of the U.S. securities laws. As part of the settlement, the Company has neither admitted nor denied the SEC's allegations concerning such matters. Further, as part of the settlement, on June 5, 2015, the Company filed its Form 10-K/A in respect of its fiscal year ended March 28, 2014 in order to restate its financial statements for fiscal 2012 and its summary financial results for fiscal 2011 and 2010 reflected in the five year financial data table, all as previously set forth in the Company's originally filed Form 10-K for its 2014 fiscal year. The restatement had no impact on the Company's Consolidated Balance Sheets, Statements of Operations, Statements of Comprehensive Income (Loss), Statements of Cash Flows and Statements of Changes in Equity for fiscal 2013 or fiscal 2014 or on its financial statements for fiscal 2015.

Note 22—Commitments and Contingencies (in part)

Contingencies (in part)

As previously disclosed, on January 28, 2011, the Company was notified by the Division of Enforcement of the SEC that it had commenced a formal civil investigation. That investigation covered a range of matters as previously disclosed by the Company, including certain of the Company's prior disclosures and accounting determinations. During the first quarter of fiscal 2016, the Company's previously agreed upon settlement with the SEC was formally approved by the SEC and became effective on June 5, 2015. For additional information, see Note 2.

EQUITY IN LOSSES OF AFFILIATES

3.36 PEABODY ENERGY CORPORATION (DEC)
CONSOLIDATED STATEMENTS OF OPERATIONS (in part)

	Year Ended December 31,		
(Dollars in millions, except per share data)	2015	2014	2013
Revenues			
Sales	$ 5,138.3	$6,132.7	$6,380.0
Other revenues	470.9	659.5	633.7
Total revenues	5,609.2	6,792.2	7,013.7
Costs and Expenses			
Operating costs and expenses (exclusive of items shown separately below)	5,007.7	5,716.9	5,729.1
Depreciation, depletion and amortization	572.2	655.7	740.3
Asset retirement obligation expenses	45.5	81.0	66.5
Selling and administrative expenses	176.4	227.1	244.2
Restructuring and pension settlement charges	23.5	26.0	11.9
Other operating (income) loss:			
Net gain on disposal of assets	(45.0)	(41.4)	(52.6)
Asset impairment	1,277.8	154.4	528.3
Settlement charges related to the Patriot bankruptcy reorganization	—	—	30.6
Loss from equity affiliates	15.9	107.6	40.2
Operating loss	(1,464.8)	(135.1)	(324.8)

(1) Summary of Significant Accounting Policies (in part)

Equity and Cost Method Investments

The Company accounts for its investments in less than majority owned corporate joint ventures under either the equity or cost method. The Company applies the equity method to investments in joint ventures when it has the ability to exercise significant influence over the operating and financial policies of the joint venture. Investments accounted for under the equity method are initially recorded at cost and any difference between the cost of the Company's investment and the underlying equity in the net assets of the joint venture at the investment date is amortized over the lives of the related assets that gave rise to the difference. The Company's pro-rata share of the operating results of joint ventures and basis difference amortization is reported in the consolidated statements of operations in "Loss from equity affiliates." Similarly, the Company's pro-rata share of the cumulative foreign currency translation adjustment of its equity method investments whose functional currency is not the U.S. dollar is reported in the consolidated balance sheet as a component of "Accumulated other comprehensive loss," with periodic changes thereto reflected in the consolidated statements of comprehensive income.

The Company monitors its equity and cost method investments for indicators that a decrease in investment value has occurred that is other than temporary. Examples of such indicators include a sustained history of operating losses and adverse changes in earnings and cash flow outlook. In the absence of quoted market prices for an investment, discounted cash flow projections are used to assess fair value, the underlying assumptions to which are generally considered unobservable Level 3 inputs under the fair value hierarchy. If the fair value of an investment is determined to be below its carrying value and that loss in fair value is deemed other than temporary, an impairment loss is recognized. Refer to Note 2. "Asset Impairment" and Note 5. "Investments" for details regarding other-than-temporary impairment losses of $276.5 million and $43.2 million recorded during the years ended December 31, 2015 and 2013, respectively, related to certain of the Company's equity and cost method investments. No such impairment losses were recorded during the year ended December 31, 2014.

(5) Investments (in part)

Equity Method Investments

The Company's equity method investments include its joint venture interest in Middlemount, which was acquired in connection with the 2011 acquisition of PEA-PCI (formerly Macarthur Coal Limited), in addition to certain other equity method investments. The table below summarizes the book value of those investments, which is reported in "Investments and other assets" in the consolidated balance sheets, and the related loss from equity affiliates:

(Dollars in millions)	Book Value at December 31,		Loss from Equity Affiliates for the Year Ended December 31,		
	2015	2014	2015	2014	2013
Equity interest in Middlemount Coal Pty Ltd	$—	$58.0	$ 7.0	$ 98.5	$33.5
Other equity method investments	4.7	7.3	8.9	9.1	6.7
Total equity method investments	$4.7	$65.3	$15.9	$107.6	$40.2

During the years ended December 31, 2015, 2014 and 2013, Middlemount generated revenues of approximately $160 million, $165 million and $157 million (on a 50% basis). During the year ended December 31, 2015, due to sustained weakness in seaborne metallurgical coal prices that had persisted longer than the Company had previously anticipated, a history of operating losses at the mine and the magnitude of the difference between the estimated fair value and the carrying value of its equity investment, the Company determined the carrying value of its equity investment in Middlemount to be other-than-temporarily impaired. Correspondingly, the Company recorded an impairment charge of $46.6 million to write down the carrying value of its equity investment. The Company determined its Subordinated Loans to Middlemount were also fully impaired resulting in an additional impairment charge of $229.9 million. A total impairment charge related to Middlemount of $276.5 million was reflected in "Asset impairment" in the consolidated statement of operations for year ended December 31, 2015. Refer to Note 2. "Asset Impairment" for additional background surrounding the impairment charge recognized in 2015. At December 31, 2015, the Company had priority loans related to Middlemount with a carrying value of $65.2 million reflected in "Investments and other assets". Refer to Note 8. "Financing Receivables" for additional background on the Company's loans with Middlemount as of December 31, 2015.

In 2014, the Company recorded to "Loss from equity affiliates" its pro-rata share of a valuation allowance of $52.3 million on Middlemount's Australian net deferred tax assets. Based on a Middlemount's history of operating losses driven by sustained weakness in seaborne metallurgical coal prices, and considering available sources of taxable income, it was determined in 2014 that the net deferred tax assets are no longer considered more likely than not of being realized.

There is no remaining unamortized basis difference as of December 31, 2015 between the amount at which the Company's equity investment in Middlemount is carried and the amount of underlying equity in net assets of Middlemount. Middlemount had current assets, noncurrent assets, current liabilities and noncurrent liabilities of $31.7 million, $348.0 million, $362.2 million and $10.5 million, respectively, as of December 31, 2015 and $27.8 million, $424.4 million, $382.9 million and $11.3 million, respectively, as of December 31, 2014 (on a 50% basis).

In addition to its equity method investment, the Company periodically makes loans to Middlemount pursuant to the related shareholders' agreement. Refer to Note 8. "Financing Receivables" for additional details surrounding those loans.

ENVIRONMENTAL

3.37 CONOCOPHILLIPS (DEC)
MANAGEMENT'S DISCUSSION AND ANALYSIS OF FINANCIAL CONDITION AND RESULTS OF OPERATIONS (in part)

Contingencies (in part)

Environmental

We are subject to the same numerous international, federal, state and local environmental laws and regulations as other companies in our industry. The most significant of these environmental laws and regulations include, among others, the:
- U.S. Federal Clean Air Act, which governs air emissions.
- U.S. Federal Clean Water Act, which governs discharges to water bodies.
- European Union Regulation for Registration, Evaluation, Authorization and Restriction of Chemicals (REACH).
- U.S. Federal Comprehensive Environmental Response, Compensation and Liability Act (CERCLA), which imposes liability on generators, transporters and arrangers of hazardous substances at sites where hazardous substance releases have occurred or are threatening to occur.
- U.S. Federal Resource Conservation and Recovery Act (RCRA), which governs the treatment, storage and disposal of solid waste.
- U.S. Federal Oil Pollution Act of 1990 (OPA90), under which owners and operators of onshore facilities and pipelines, lessees or permittees of an area in which an offshore facility is located, and owners and operators of vessels are liable for removal costs and damages that result from a discharge of oil into navigable waters of the United States.
- U.S. Federal Emergency Planning and Community Right-to-Know Act (EPCRA), which requires facilities to report toxic chemical inventories with local emergency planning committees and response departments.
- U.S. Federal Safe Drinking Water Act, which governs the disposal of wastewater in underground injection wells.
- U.S. Department of the Interior regulations, which relate to offshore oil and gas operations in U.S. waters and impose liability for the cost of pollution cleanup resulting from operations, as well as potential liability for pollution damages.
- European Union Trading Directive resulting in European Emissions Trading Scheme.

These laws and their implementing regulations set limits on emissions and, in the case of discharges to water, establish water quality limits. They also, in most cases, require permits in association with new or modified operations. These permits can require an applicant to collect substantial information in connection with the application process, which can be expensive and time consuming. In addition, there can be delays associated with notice and comment periods and the agency's processing of the application. Many of the delays associated with the permitting process are beyond the control of the applicant.

Many states and foreign countries where we operate also have, or are developing, similar environmental laws and regulations governing these same types of activities. While similar, in some cases these regulations may impose additional, or more stringent, requirements that can add to the cost and difficulty of marketing or transporting products across state and international borders.

The ultimate financial impact arising from environmental laws and regulations is neither clearly known nor easily determinable as new standards, such as air emission standards, water quality standards and stricter fuel regulations, continue to evolve. However, environmental laws and regulations, including those that may arise to address concerns about global climate change, are expected to continue to have an increasing impact on our operations in the United States and in other countries in which we operate. Notable areas of potential impacts include air emission compliance and remediation obligations in the United States and Canada.

An example is the use of hydraulic fracturing, an essential completion technique that facilitates production of oil and natural gas otherwise trapped in lower permeability rock formations. A range of local, state, federal or national laws and regulations currently govern hydraulic fracturing operations, with hydraulic fracturing currently prohibited in some jurisdictions. Although hydraulic fracturing has been conducted for many decades, a number of new laws, regulations and permitting requirements are under consideration by the U.S. Environmental Protection Agency (EPA), the U.S. Department of the Interior, and others which could result in increased costs, operating restrictions, operational delays and/or limit the ability to develop oil and natural gas resources. Governmental restrictions on hydraulic fracturing could impact the overall profitability or viability of certain of our oil and natural gas investments. We have adopted operating principles that incorporate established industry standards designed to meet or exceed government requirements. Our practices continually evolve as technology improves and regulations change.

We also are subject to certain laws and regulations relating to environmental remediation obligations associated with current and past operations. Such laws and regulations include CERCLA and RCRA and their state equivalents. Longer-term expenditures are subject to considerable uncertainty and may fluctuate significantly.

We occasionally receive requests for information or notices of potential liability from the EPA and state environmental agencies alleging we are a potentially responsible party under CERCLA or an equivalent state statute. On occasion, we also have been made a party to cost recovery litigation by those agencies or by private parties. These requests, notices and lawsuits assert potential liability for remediation costs at various sites that typically are not owned by us, but allegedly contain wastes attributable to our past operations. As of December 31, 2015, there were 14 sites around the United States in which we were identified as a potentially responsible party under CERCLA and comparable state laws.

For most Superfund sites, our potential liability will be significantly less than the total site remediation costs because the percentage of waste attributable to us, versus that attributable to all other potentially responsible parties, is relatively low. Although liability of those potentially responsible is generally joint and several for federal sites and frequently so for state sites, other potentially responsible parties at sites where we are a party typically have had the financial strength to meet their obligations, and where they have not, or where potentially responsible parties could not be located, our share of liability has not increased materially. Many of the sites at which we are potentially responsible are still under investigation by the EPA or the state agencies concerned. Prior to actual cleanup, those potentially responsible normally assess site conditions, apportion responsibility and determine the appropriate remediation. In some instances, we may have no liability or attain a settlement of liability. Actual cleanup costs generally occur after the parties obtain EPA or equivalent state agency approval. There are relatively few sites where we are a major participant, and given the timing and amounts of anticipated expenditures, neither the cost of remediation at those sites nor such costs at all CERCLA sites, in the aggregate, is expected to have a material adverse effect on our competitive or financial condition.

Expensed environmental costs were $485 million in 2015 and are expected to be about $478 million per year in 2016 and 2017. Capitalized environmental costs were $303 million in 2015 and are expected to be about $250 million per year in 2016 and 2017.

Accrued liabilities for remediation activities are not reduced for potential recoveries from insurers or other third parties and are not discounted (except those assumed in a purchase business combination, which we do record on a discounted basis).

Many of these liabilities result from CERCLA, RCRA and similar state or international laws that require us to undertake certain investigative and remedial activities at sites where we conduct, or once conducted, operations or at sites where ConocoPhillips-generated waste was disposed. The accrual also includes a number of sites we identified that may require environmental remediation, but which are not currently the subject of CERCLA, RCRA or other agency enforcement activities. If applicable, we accrue receivables for probable insurance or other third-party recoveries. In the future, we may incur significant costs under both CERCLA and RCRA.

Remediation activities vary substantially in duration and cost from site to site, depending on the mix of unique site characteristics, evolving remediation technologies, diverse regulatory agencies and enforcement policies, and the presence or absence of potentially liable third parties. Therefore, it is difficult to develop reasonable estimates of future site remediation costs.

At December 31, 2015, our balance sheet included total accrued environmental costs of $258 million, compared with $344 million at December 31, 2014, for remediation activities in the U.S., Canada and the U.K. We expect to incur a substantial amount of these expenditures within the next 30 years.

Notwithstanding any of the foregoing, and as with other companies engaged in similar businesses, environmental costs and liabilities are inherent concerns in our operations and products, and there can be no assurance that material costs and liabilities will not be incurred. However, we currently do not expect any material adverse effect upon our results of operations or financial position as a result of compliance with current environmental laws and regulations.

Note 1—Accounting Policies (in part)

Asset Retirement Obligations and Environmental Costs—(in part)

Environmental expenditures are expensed or capitalized, depending upon their future economic benefit. Expenditures relating to an existing condition caused by past operations, and those having no future economic benefit, are expensed. Liabilities for environmental expenditures are recorded on an undiscounted basis (unless acquired in a purchase business combination) when environmental assessments or cleanups are probable and the costs can be reasonably estimated. Recoveries of environmental remediation costs from other parties are recorded as assets when their receipt is probable and estimable.

Note 10—Asset Retirement Obligations and Accrued Environmental Costs (in part)

Asset retirement obligations and accrued environmental costs at December 31 were:

Millions of Dollars	2015	2014
Asset retirement obligations	$ 9,911	10,939
Accrued environmental costs	258	344
Total asset retirement obligations and accrued environmental costs	10,169	11,283
Asset retirement obligations and accrued environmental costs due within one year*	(589)	(636)
Long-term asset retirement obligations and accrued environmental costs	$ 9,580	10,647

Classified as a current liability on the balance sheet under "Other accruals."

Accrued Environmental Costs

Total accrued environmental costs at December 31, 2015 and 2014, were $258 million and $344 million, respectively.

We had accrued environmental costs of $184 million and $250 million at December 31, 2015 and 2014, respectively, related to remediation activities in the United States and Canada. We had also accrued in Corporate and Other $57 million and $79 million of environmental costs associated with sites no longer in operation at December 31, 2015 and 2014, respectively. In addition, $17 million and $15 million were included at both December 31, 2015 and 2014, respectively, where the company has been named a potentially responsible party under the Federal Comprehensive Environmental Response, Compensation and Liability Act, or similar state laws. Accrued environmental liabilities are expected to be paid over periods extending up to 30 years.

Expected expenditures for environmental obligations acquired in various business combinations are discounted using a weighted-average 5 percent discount factor, resulting in an accrued balance for acquired environmental liabilities of $105 million at December 31, 2015. The expected future undiscounted payments related to the portion of the accrued environmental costs that have been discounted are: $12 million in 2016, $13 million in 2017, $9 million in 2018, $6 million in 2019, $4 million in 2020, and $117 million for all future years after 2020.

Note 13—Contingencies and Commitments (in part)

A number of lawsuits involving a variety of claims arising in the ordinary course of business have been made against ConocoPhillips. We also may be required to remove or mitigate the effects on the environment of the placement, storage, disposal or release of certain chemical, mineral and petroleum substances at various active and inactive sites. We regularly assess the need for accounting recognition or disclosure of these contingencies. In the case of all known contingencies (other than those related to income taxes), we accrue a liability when the loss is probable and the amount is reasonably estimable. If a range of amounts can be reasonably estimated and no amount within the range is a better estimate than any other amount, then the minimum of the range is accrued. We do not reduce these liabilities for potential insurance or third-party recoveries. If applicable, we accrue receivables for probable insurance or other third-party recoveries. With respect to income tax-related contingencies, we use a cumulative probability-weighted loss accrual in cases where sustaining a tax position is less than certain. See Note 19—Income Taxes, for additional information about income tax-related contingencies.

Based on currently available information, we believe it is remote that future costs related to known contingent liability exposures will exceed current accruals by an amount that would have a material adverse impact on our consolidated financial statements. As we learn new facts concerning contingencies, we reassess our position both with respect to accrued liabilities and other potential exposures. Estimates particularly sensitive to future changes include contingent liabilities recorded for environmental remediation, tax and legal matters.

Estimated future environmental remediation costs are subject to change due to such factors as the uncertain magnitude of cleanup costs, the unknown time and extent of such remedial actions that may be required, and the determination of our liability in proportion to that of other responsible parties. Estimated future costs related to tax and legal matters are subject to change as events evolve and as additional information becomes available during the administrative and litigation processes.

Environmental

We are subject to international, federal, state and local environmental laws and regulations. When we prepare our consolidated financial statements, we record accruals for environmental liabilities based on management's best estimates, using all information that is available at the time. We measure estimates and base liabilities on currently available facts, existing technology, and presently enacted laws and regulations, taking into account stakeholder and business considerations. When measuring environmental liabilities, we also consider our prior experience in remediation of contaminated sites, other companies' cleanup experience, and data released by the U.S. Environmental Protection Agency (EPA) or other organizations. We consider unasserted claims in our determination of environmental liabilities, and we accrue them in the period they are both probable and reasonably estimable.

Although liability of those potentially responsible for environmental remediation costs is generally joint and several for federal sites and frequently so for other sites, we are usually only one of many companies cited at a particular site. Due to the joint and several liabilities, we could be responsible for all cleanup costs related to any site at which we have been designated as a potentially responsible party. We have been successful to date in sharing cleanup costs with other financially sound companies. Many of the sites at which we are potentially responsible are still under investigation by the EPA or the agency concerned. Prior to actual cleanup, those potentially responsible normally assess the site conditions, apportion responsibility and determine the appropriate remediation. In some instances, we may have no liability or may attain a settlement of liability. Where it appears that other potentially responsible parties may be financially unable to bear their proportional share, we consider this inability in estimating our potential liability, and we adjust our accruals accordingly. As a result of various acquisitions in the past, we assumed certain environmental obligations. Some of these environmental obligations are mitigated by indemnifications made by others for our benefit, and some of the indemnifications are subject to dollar limits and time limits.

We are currently participating in environmental assessments and cleanups at numerous federal Superfund and comparable state and international sites. After an assessment of environmental exposures for cleanup and other costs, we make accruals on an undiscounted basis (except those acquired in a purchase business combination, which we record on a discounted basis) for planned investigation and remediation activities for sites where it is probable future costs will be incurred and these costs can be reasonably estimated. We have not reduced these accruals for possible insurance recoveries. In the future, we may be involved in additional environmental assessments, cleanups and proceedings. See Note 10—Asset Retirement Obligations and Accrued Environmental Costs, for a summary of our accrued environmental liabilities.

SALE OF RECEIVABLES

3.38 ALLIANCE ONE INTERNATIONAL, INC. (MAR)
STATEMENTS OF CONSOLIDATED OPERATIONS (in part)

	Years Ended March 31,		
(In thousands, except per share data)	2015	2014	2013
Sales and other operating revenues	$2,065,850	$2,354,956	$2,243,816
Cost of goods and services sold	1,810,771	2,114,929	1,958,570
Gross profit	255,079	240,027	285,246
Selling, general and administrative expenses	137,020	134,087	145,750
Other income	1,894	18,230	20,721
Restructuring and asset impairment charges (recoveries)	9,118	5,111	(55)
Operating income	110,835	119,059	160,272

NOTES TO CONSOLIDATED FINANCIAL STATEMENTS (in part)

(in thousands)

Note 1—Significant Accounting Policies (in part)

Other Income (in part)

Other Income consists primarily of gains on sales of property, plant and equipment and assets held for sale. This caption also includes expenses related to the Company's sale of receivables. See Note 17 "Sale of Receivables" to the "Notes to Consolidated Financial Statements" for further information.

The following table summarizes the significant components of Other Income.

	Years Ending March 31,		
	2015	2014	2013
Turkey other property sales	$ —	$ 2,700	$ —
Brazil 51% subsidiary investment sale	—	20,369	—
Brazil excise tax benefit	—	—	24,142
Other sales of assets and expenses	9,319	2,138	4,892
Losses on sale of receivables	(7,425)	(6,977)	(8,313)
	$ 1,894	$18,230	$20,721

Sale of Accounts Receivable

The Company is currently engaged in three revolving trade accounts receivable securitization arrangements to sell receivables. The Company records the transaction as a sale of receivables, removes such receivables from its financial statements and records a receivable for the beneficial interest in such receivables. The losses on the sale of receivables are recognized in Other Income. As of March 31, 2015 and 2014, respectively, accounts receivable sold and outstanding were $235,162 and $204,364. See Note 17 "Sale of Receivables" and Note 18 "Fair Value Measurements" to the "Notes to Consolidated Financial Statements" for further information.

Note 17—Sale of Receivables

The Company sells trade receivables to unaffiliated financial institutions under three accounts receivable securitization programs. Under the first program, the Company continuously sells a designated pool of trade receivables to a special purpose entity, which in turn sells 100% of the receivables to an unaffiliated financial institution. This program allows the Company to receive a cash payment and a deferred purchase price receivable for sold receivables. Following the sale and transfer of the receivables to the special purpose entity, the receivables are isolated from the Company and its affiliates, and upon the sale and transfer of the receivables from the special purpose entity to the unaffiliated financial institutions effective control of the receivables is passed to the unaffiliated financial institution, which has all rights, including the right to pledge or sell the receivables. The investment limit is $250,000, which was reduced to $150,000 on April 30, 2015. The Company incurred program costs of $1,642 and $1,675 during the years ending March 31, 2015 and 2014 which were included in Other Income in the Statements of Consolidated Operations. The program requires a minimum level of deferred purchase price to be retained by the Company in connection with the sales. The Company continues to service, administer and collect the receivables on behalf of the special purpose entity and receives a servicing fee of 0.5% of serviced receivables per annum. As the Company estimates the fee it receives in return for its obligation to service these receivables is at fair value, no servicing assets or liabilities are recognized. Servicing fees recognized were not material and are recorded as a reduction of Selling, General and Administrative Expenses within the Statements of Consolidated Operations.

The agreement for the second securitization program previously executed on September 28, 2011, as amended November 30, 2013, expired December 31, 2014. This securitization program was replaced by a securitization program with the same financial institution executed on March 31, 2015. The agreement for the third securitization program was executed on March 28, 2013, amended and restated March 25, 2014. These programs also allow the Company to receive a cash payment and a deferred purchase price receivable for sold receivables. These are uncommitted programs, whereby the Company offers receivables for sale to the respective unaffiliated financial institution, which are then subject to acceptance by the unaffiliated financial institution. Following the sale and transfer of the receivables to the unaffiliated financial institution, the receivables are isolated from the Company and its affiliates, and effective control of the receivables is passed to the unaffiliated financial institution, which has all rights, including the right to pledge or sell the receivables. The Company receives no servicing fee from the unaffiliated financial institution and as a result, has established a servicing liability based upon unobservable inputs, primarily discounted cash flow. For the years ended March 31, 2015 and 2014, the expense for the servicing liability was $178 and $184 which is included in Other Income in the Statements of Consolidated Operations. The liability is recorded in Accrued Expenses and other Current Liabilities in the Consolidated Balance Sheets. As receivables sold under these facilities were settled in fiscal 2015 and 2014, the servicing liability was reduced by $115 and $281 and is included in Selling, General and Administrative Expenses in the Statements of Consolidated Operations. The investment limits under the second and third agreements are $35,000 and $100,000 respectively. The cost for entering the third program was $1,220 and is included in Other Income in the Statements of Consolidated Operations in fiscal 2013.

Under the programs, all of the receivables sold for cash are removed from the Consolidated Balance Sheets and the net cash proceeds received by the Company are included as cash provided by operating activities in the Statements of Consolidated Cash Flows. A portion of the purchase price for the receivables is paid by the unaffiliated financial institutions in cash and the balance is a deferred purchase price receivable, which is paid as payments on the receivables are collected from account debtors. The deferred purchase price receivable represents a continuing involvement and a beneficial interest in the transferred financial assets and is recognized at fair value as part of the sale transaction. The deferred purchase price receivables are included in Trade and Other Receivables, Net in the Consolidated Balance Sheets and are valued using unobservable inputs (i.e., level three inputs), primarily discounted cash flow. As servicer of these facilities, the Company may receive funds that are due to the unaffiliated financial institutions which are net settled on the next settlement date. As of March 31, 2015 and 2014, Trade and Other Receivables, Net in the Consolidated Balance Sheets has been reduced by $20,396 and $16,575 as a result of the net settlement. See Note 18 "Fair Value Measurements" to the "Notes to Consolidated Financial Statements" for further information.

The difference between the carrying amount of the receivables sold under these programs and the sum of the cash and fair value of the other assets received at the time of transfer is recognized as a loss on sale of the related receivables and recorded in Other Income in the Statements of Consolidated Operations.

The following table summarizes the Company's accounts receivable securitization information as of March 31:

	2015	2014
Receivables outstanding in facility as of March 31:	$235,162	$ 204,364
Beneficial interest as of March 31	$ 40,712	$ 35,559
Servicing Liability as of March 31	$ 131	$ 69
Cash proceeds for the twelve months ended March 31:		
Cash purchase price	$622,844	$ 801,480
Deferred purchase price	229,573	268,650
Service fees	589	572
Total	$853,006	$1,070,702

MERGERS

3.39 BAKER HUGHES INCORPORATED (DEC)
NOTES TO CONSOLIDATED FINANCIAL STATEMENTS (in part)

Note 2. Halliburton Merger Agreement

On November 16, 2014, Baker Hughes, Halliburton Company ("Halliburton") and a wholly owned subsidiary of Halliburton ("Merger Sub"), entered into an Agreement and Plan of Merger (the "Merger Agreement"), under which Halliburton will acquire all of the outstanding shares of Baker Hughes through a merger of Baker Hughes with and into Merger Sub (the "Merger"). Subject to certain specified exceptions, at the effective time of the Merger, each share of Baker Hughes common stock will be converted into the right to receive (i) 1.12 shares of Halliburton common stock and (ii) $19.00 in cash.

On March 27, 2015, Halliburton's stockholders approved the proposal to issue shares of Halliburton common stock as contemplated by the Merger Agreement. In addition, Baker Hughes' stockholders adopted the Merger Agreement and thereby approved the proposed combination of the two companies. The obligation of the parties to consummate the Merger is still subject to additional customary closing conditions, including: (i) applicable regulatory approvals; (ii) the absence of legal restraints and prohibitions; and (iii) other customary closing conditions. Halliburton is required to take all actions necessary to obtain regulatory approvals (including agreeing to divestitures) unless the assets, businesses or product lines subject to such actions would account for more than $7.5 billion of 2013 revenue.

Under the U.S. Hart-Scott-Rodino Antitrust Improvements Act of 1976, as amended (the "HSR Act") and the rules promulgated thereunder by the Federal Trade Commission (the "FTC"), the Merger cannot be completed until each of Halliburton and Baker Hughes has filed a notification and report form with the FTC and the Antitrust Division of the Department of Justice (the "DOJ") under the HSR Act and the applicable waiting period has expired or been terminated. Each of Halliburton and Baker Hughes filed an initial notification and report form on December 8, 2014. Halliburton withdrew its filing on January 7, 2015 and refiled on January 9, 2015 in order to provide the FTC and the DOJ with an additional 30-day period to review the filings. On February 9, 2015, the DOJ issued a request for additional information under the HSR Act (the "Second Request"). On July 10, 2015, Halliburton and Baker Hughes entered into a timing agreement with the DOJ, and on September 28, 2015, Halliburton and Baker Hughes announced an amendment to the timing agreement which extended the period for the DOJ's review of the Merger to the later of December 15, 2015 or 30 days following the date on which both companies have certified final, substantial compliance with the Second Request.

On December 16, 2015, Baker Hughes' and Halliburton's timing agreement with the DOJ expired without reaching a settlement or the DOJ initiating litigation to block the pending Merger. The companies intend to continue their discussions with the DOJ and other competition agencies that have expressed an interest in the transaction, and remain focused on completing the Merger as early as possible in 2016. In that regard, Baker Hughes and Halliburton have agreed to extend the period for the parties to obtain required competition approvals to April

30, 2016, as permitted under the Merger Agreement, though the parties would proceed with closing prior to such date if all relevant competition approvals have been obtained. If review by the relevant competition authorities extends beyond April 30, 2016, the Merger Agreement does not terminate automatically; the parties may continue to seek relevant competition approvals or either of the parties may terminate the Merger Agreement. Baker Hughes cannot predict with certainty when, or if, the Merger will be completed because completion of the Merger is subject to conditions beyond the control of Baker Hughes.

Baker Hughes and Halliburton each made customary representations, warranties and covenants in the Merger Agreement, including, among others, covenants by each of Baker Hughes and Halliburton to, subject to certain exceptions, conduct its business in the ordinary course. In particular, among other restrictions and subject to certain exceptions, Baker Hughes agreed to generally refrain from acquiring new businesses, incurring new indebtedness, repurchasing shares, issuing new common stock or equity awards (other than equity awards granted to employees, officers and directors materially consistent with historical long-term incentive awards granted), or entering into new material contracts or commitments outside the normal course of business, without the consent of Halliburton, during the period between the execution of the Merger Agreement and the consummation of the Merger. With respect to equity awards granted after the Merger Agreement to officers and employees, such awards will not vest solely as a result of the Merger but will be converted to an equivalent Halliburton equity award. However, they will vest entirely if an officer or employee is terminated within one year following the closing of the Merger with Halliburton. Baker Hughes and Halliburton are each permitted to pay regular quarterly cash dividends during such period. In addition, under the terms of the Merger Agreement, Halliburton and Baker Hughes have agreed to coordinate the declaration and payment of dividends in respect of each party's common stock including record dates and payment dates relating thereto, which we expect to be in the third month of each quarter. Under the Merger Agreement, we have agreed not to increase the quarterly dividend while the Merger is pending.

In the event the Merger Agreement is terminated by (i) either party as a result of the failure of the Merger to occur on or before the end date (as it may be extended) due to the failure to achieve certain specified antitrust-related approvals when all other closing conditions (other than receipt of antitrust and other specified regulatory approvals and conditions that by their nature cannot be satisfied until the closing but subject to such conditions being capable of being satisfied if the closing date were the date of termination) have been satisfied, (ii) either party as a result of any antitrust-related final, non-appealable order or injunction prohibiting the closing, or (iii) Baker Hughes as a result of Halliburton's material breach of its obligations to obtain regulatory approval such that the antitrust-related condition to closing is incapable of being satisfied, then in each case Halliburton would be required to pay Baker Hughes a termination fee of $3.5 billion.

Baker Hughes incurred costs related to the Merger of $295 million during 2015, including costs under our retention program and obligations for minimum incentive compensation costs, which, based on meeting eligibility criteria, have been treated as Merger related expenses.

ACQUISITION-RELATED COSTS

3.40 HARRIS CORPORATION (JUN)
CONSOLIDATED STATEMENT OF INCOME (in part)

	Fiscal Years Ended		
(In millions, except per share amounts)	2015	2014	2013
Revenue from product sales and services			
Revenue from product sales	$ 3,311	$ 3,189	$ 3,204
Revenue from services	1,772	1,823	1,908
	5,083	5,012	5,112
Cost of product sales and services			
Cost of product sales	(1,969)	(1,857)	(1,919)
Cost of services	(1,393)	(1,453)	(1,466)
	(3,362)	(3,310)	(3,385)
Engineering, selling and administrative expenses	(1,008)	(820)	(914)
Non-operating income (loss)	(108)	4	(41)
Interest income	2	3	2
Interest expense	(130)	(94)	(109)
Income from continuing operations before income taxes	477	795	665

NOTES TO CONSOLIDATED FINANCIAL STATEMENTS (in part)

Note 1: Significant Accounting Policies (in part)

Long-Lived Assets, Including Finite-Lived Intangible Assets—Long-lived assets, including finite-lived intangible assets, are amortized on a straight-line basis over their useful lives. We assess the recoverability of the carrying value of our long-lived assets, including finite-lived intangible assets, whenever events or changes in circumstances indicate the carrying amount of the assets may not be recoverable. We evaluate the recoverability of such assets based on the expectations of undiscounted cash flows from such assets. If the sum of the expected future undiscounted cash flows were less than the carrying amount of the asset, a loss would be recognized for the difference between the fair value and the carrying amount. See *Note 7: Property, Plant and Equipment* and *Note 9: Intangible Assets* for additional information regarding long-lived assets and intangible assets.

In the fourth quarter of fiscal 2015, we recorded impairment charges totaling $38 million related to long-lived assets, consisting of $32 million and $6 million included as a component of the "Engineering, selling and administrative expenses" and "Cost of product sales" line items, respectively, in our Consolidated Statement of Income. These charges included an impairment in our Integrated Network Solutions segment related to an intangible asset associated with the Navy/Marine Corps Intranet ("NMCI") program due to the loss of the contract and the inability to obtain replacement work on the successor program to the NMCI program (the Next Generation Enterprise Network program); an impairment in our Integrated Network Solutions segment related to fixed assets in Harris CapRock Communications due to a combination of soft market conditions and obsolescence; and impairments of capitalized software acquired in connection with our acquisition of Exelis Inc. and its subsidiaries (collectively, "Exelis"—see *Note 4: Business Combinations* for more information) based on our decision to use alternative software.

In the fourth quarter of fiscal 2013, we recorded impairment charges totaling $35 million related to long-lived assets. These included an impairment in our Integrated Network Solutions segment related to intangible assets recorded in connection with our acquisition of Carefx Corporation ("Carefx") in the fourth quarter of fiscal 2011, primarily resulting from a shift in strategy away from Carefx's legacy products; an impairment in our Integrated Network Solutions segment related to an IT services contract vehicle, primarily based on impacts of sequestration and a new rule incorporated into the contract vehicle limiting bid opportunities for large businesses; and an impairment of other Company-owned assets based on recent market indications.

Restructuring Costs—We record restructuring charges for sales or terminations of product lines, closures or relocations of business activities, changes in management structure, and fundamental reorganizations that affect the nature and focus of operations. Such costs include one-time termination benefits, contract termination costs and costs to consolidate facilities or relocate employees. We record these charges at their fair value when incurred. In cases where employees are required to render service until they are terminated in order to receive the termination benefits and will be retained beyond the minimum retention period, we record the expense ratably over the future service period. These charges are included as a component of the "Cost of product sales" and "Engineering, selling and administrative expenses" line items in our Consolidated Statement of Income.

In connection with the Exelis acquisition and Company-wide restructuring and other actions in the fourth quarter of fiscal 2015 to align resources with our business outlook, we incurred restructuring costs of $57 million for workforce reductions (including severance and other employee-related exit costs) and $14 million for facility consolidation and contract terminations, substantially all of which were included as a component of the "Engineering, selling and administrative expenses" line item in our Consolidated Statement of Income. This resulted in charges of $65 million recorded at our corporate headquarters (related to the Exelis acquisition), $3 million in our RF Communications segment, and $3 million in our Integrated Network Solutions segment. As of the end of fiscal 2015, we had recorded liabilities of $68 million associated with these restructuring actions, of which the majority will be paid within the next twelve months.

In connection with Company-wide restructuring and other actions in the fourth quarter of fiscal 2013 to align resources with our business outlook and challenging fiscal environment, we incurred restructuring costs, net of government cost reimbursement, of $17 million for workforce reductions (including severance and other employee-related exit costs) and $12 million for facility consolidation. This resulted in charges of $9 million, $7 million and $13 million recorded in our RF Communications and Government Communications Systems segments and at our corporate headquarters, respectively. As of the end of fiscal 2013, we had recorded liabilities of $26 million associated with these restructuring actions, of which the majority was paid during fiscal 2014.

Acquisition-Related Charges—In fiscal 2015, in connection with the Exelis acquisition, we recorded $281 million of charges at our corporate headquarters, consisting of financing, restructuring, integration, transaction and other costs as follows:
- $146 million of financing costs, primarily consisting of $118 million of charges associated with our optional redemption on May 27, 2015 of our 5.95% Notes due December 1, 2017 and 6.375% Notes due June 15, 2019 (see *Note 21: Non-Operating Income (Loss)* for additional information) and $18 million of debt issuance costs related to financing commitments for a senior unsecured bridge loan facility (see *Note 18: Interest Expense* for additional information);
- $65 million of restructuring costs as discussed in the "Restructuring Costs" section above;
- $34 million of integration costs, recognized as incurred;
- $23 million of transaction costs, recognized as incurred; and
- $13 million of other costs, including impairments of capitalized software (see "Long-Lived Assets, Including Finite-Lived Intangible Assets" in this Note above for additional information).

All of the costs above were recorded in the "Engineering, selling and administrative expenses" line item in our Consolidated Statement of Income, except for the $146 million of financing costs.

Note 18: Interest Expense

Total interest expense was $130 million, $94 million and $109 million in fiscal 2015, 2014 and 2013, respectively. Fiscal 2015 interest expense includes $18 million of debt issuance costs related to financing commitments for a senior unsecured bridge loan facility established (and subsequently terminated when we secured permanent financing) in connection with our acquisition of Exelis. Interest paid was $89 million, $93 million and $110 million in fiscal 2015, 2014 and 2013, respectively. The increase in the difference between interest expense and interest paid in fiscal 2015 was primarily due to the timing of the new debt issued during the fourth quarter of fiscal 2015 in connection with our acquisition of Exelis.

Note 21: Non-Operating Income (Loss)

The components of non-operating income (loss) were as follows:

(In millions)	2015	2014	2013
Loss on prepayment of long-term debt[1][2]	$(118)	$—	$(33)
Impairment of cost-method investment	—	—	(11)
Impairment of investment in joint venture	—	—	(7)
Gain on sale of securities available-for-sale	—	—	9
Gain on sale of business	9	—	—
Net income related to intellectual property matters	1	4	1
	$(108)	$ 4	$(41)

[1] The loss in fiscal 2015 reflected charges associated with our optional redemption on May 27, 2015 of the entire outstanding $400 million principal amount of our 5.95% Notes due December 1, 2017 and the entire outstanding $350 million principal amount of our 6.375% Notes due June 15, 2019.

[2] The loss in fiscal 2013 reflected a charge associated with our optional redemption on May 28, 2013 of the entire outstanding $300 million principal amount of our 5% Notes due October 1, 2015.

CHANGE IN FAIR VALUE OF DERIVATIVES

3.41 COMMERCIAL METALS COMPANY (AUG)
CONSOLIDATED STATEMENTS OF EARNINGS (in part)

	Year Ended August 31,		
(In thousands, except share data)	2015	2014	2013
Net sales	$5,988,605	$6,790,438	$6,601,070
Costs and expenses:			
Cost of goods sold	5,213,203	6,109,338	5,951,870
Selling, general and administrative expenses	443,275	448,943	439,571
Impairment of assets	9,839	3,305	4,576
Interest expense	77,760	77,037	68,439
Gain on sale of cost method investment	—	—	(26,088)
	5,744,077	6,638,623	6,438,368
Earnings from continuing operations before income taxes	244,528	151,815	162,702
Income taxes	83,206	42,724	57,979
Earnings from continuing operations	161,322	109,091	104,723
Earnings (loss) from discontinued operations before income taxes	(20,124)	15,005	(26,094)
Income taxes (benefit)	(436)	8,544	1,310
Earnings (loss) from discontinued operations	(19,688)	6,461	(27,404)
Net earnings	141,634	115,552	77,319

NOTES TO CONSOLIDATED FINANCIAL STATEMENTS (in part)

Note 12. Derivatives and Risk Management

The Company's global operations and product lines expose it to risks from fluctuations in metal commodity prices, foreign currency exchange rates, natural gas prices and interest rates. One objective of the Company's risk management program is to mitigate these risks using derivative instruments. The Company enters into (i) metal commodity futures and forward contracts to mitigate the risk of unanticipated changes in gross margin due to the volatility of the commodities' prices, (ii) foreign currency forward contracts that match the expected settlements for purchases and sales denominated in foreign currencies and (iii) natural gas forward contracts to mitigate the risk of unanticipated changes in operating cost due to the volatility of natural gas prices. When sales commitments to customers include a fixed price freight component, the Company occasionally enters into freight forward contracts to reduce the effects of the volatility of ocean freight rates.

At August 31, 2015, the notional values of the Company's foreign currency contract commitments and its commodity contract commitments were $390.8 million and $37.7 million, respectively. At August 31, 2014, the notional values of the Company's foreign currency contract commitments and its commodity contract commitments were $406.6 million and $59.6 million, respectively.

The Company designates only those contracts which closely match the terms of the underlying transaction as hedges for accounting purposes. These hedges resulted in substantially no ineffectiveness in the Company's consolidated statements of earnings, and there were no components excluded from the assessment of hedge effectiveness for the years ended August 31, 2015 and 2014. Certain foreign currency and commodity contracts were not designated as hedges for accounting purposes, although management believes they are essential economic hedges.

The following tables summarize activities related to the Company's derivative instruments and hedged items recognized in the consolidated statements of earnings:

Derivatives Not Designated as Hedging Instruments		Year Ended August 31,		
(In thousands)	Location	2015	2014	2013
Commodity	Cost of goods sold	$ 7,746	$ 2,504	$2,456
Foreign exchange	Net sales	3,016	473	—
Foreign exchange	Cost of goods sold	4,996	(1,078)	—
Foreign exchange	SG&A expenses	23,105	(4,135)	5,089
Other	Cost of goods sold	—	—	9
Gain (loss) before income taxes		$38,863	$(2,236)	$7,554

The Company's fair value hedges are designated for accounting purposes with the gains or losses on the hedged items offsetting the gains or losses on the related derivative transactions. Hedged items relate to firm commitments on commercial sales and purchases and capital expenditures.

Derivatives Designated as Fair Value Hedging Instruments		Year Ended August 31,		
(In thousands)	Location	2015	2014	2013
Foreign exchange	Net sales	$(105)	$ 93	$ (151)
Foreign exchange	Cost of goods sold	881	(1,465)	2,241
Gain (loss) before income taxes		$ 776	$(1,372)	$2,090

Hedged Items Designated as Fair Value Hedging Instruments		Year Ended August 31,		
(In thousands)	Location	2015	2014	2013
Foreign exchange	Net sales	$ 105	$ (91)	$ 153
Foreign exchange	Cost of goods sold	(881)	1,469	(2,241)
Gain (loss) before income taxes		$(776)	$1,378	$(2,088)

Effective Portion of Derivatives Designated as Cash Flow Hedging Instruments Recognized in Accumulated Other Comprehensive Income (Loss)	August 31,		
(In thousands)	2015	2014	2013
Commodity	$ (635)	$ (54)	$(218)
Foreign exchange	(1,832)	(1,794)	439
Gain (loss), net of income taxes	$(2,467)	$(1,848)	$ 221

Effective Portion of Derivatives Designated as Cash Flow Hedging Instruments Reclassified from Accumulated Other Comprehensive Income (Loss)		Year Ended August 31,		
(In thousands)	Location	2015	2014	2013
Commodity	Cost of goods sold	$ (665)	$ (160)	$(260)
Foreign exchange	Net sales	124	(213)	73
Foreign exchange	Cost of goods sold	(2,774)	(1,717)	18
Foreign exchange	SG&A expenses	76	53	17
Interest rate	Interest expense	532	532	617
Gain (loss) before income taxes		(2,707)	(1,505)	465
Income tax (expense) benefit	Income taxes	949	237	(128)
Gain (loss), net of income taxes		$(1,758)	$(1,268)	$ 337

The Company enters into derivative agreements that include provisions to allow the set-off of certain amounts. Derivative instruments are presented on a gross basis on the Company's consolidated balance sheets. The asset and liability balances in the tables below reflect the gross amounts of derivative instruments at August 31, 2015 and 2014. The fair value of the Company's derivative instruments on the consolidated balance sheets was as follows:

	August 31,	
Derivative Assets (In thousands)	2015	2014
Commodity—designated for hedge accounting	$ 19	$ 42
Commodity—not designated for hedge accounting	846	869
Foreign exchange—designated for hedge accounting	1,500	136
Foreign exchange—not designated for hedge accounting	3,088	1,853
Derivative assets (other current assets)*	$5,453	$2,900

	August 31,	
Derivative Liabilities (In thousands)	2015	2014
Commodity—designated for hedge accounting	$ 129	$ 6
Commodity—not designated for hedge accounting	537	162
Foreign exchange—designated for hedge accounting	874	325
Foreign exchange—not designated for hedge accounting	1,263	1,010
Derivative liabilities (accrued expenses and other payables)*	$2,803	$1,503

* Derivative assets and liabilities do not include the hedged items designated as fair value hedges.

As of August 31, 2015 and 2014, all of the Company's derivative instruments designated to hedge exposure to the variability in future cash flows of the forecasted transactions will mature within twelve months.

All of the instruments are highly liquid and were not entered into for trading purposes.

IMPAIRMENTS OF INTANGIBLE ASSETS AND GOODWILL

3.42 CABOT CORPORATION (SEP)
CONSOLIDATED STATEMENTS OF OPERATIONS (in part)

	Years Ended September 30		
(In millions, except per share amounts)	2015	2014	2013
Net sales and other operating revenues	$2,871	$3,647	$3,456
Cost of sales	2,286	2,926	2,823
Gross profit	585	721	633
Selling and administrative expenses	282	326	297
Research and technical expenses	58	60	68
Purification Solutions long-lived assets impairment charge (Note G)	210	—	—
Purification Solutions goodwill impairment charge (Note G)	352	—	—
(Loss) income from operations	(317)	335	268

NOTES TO CONSOLIDATED FINANCIAL STATEMENTS (in part)

Note A. Significant Accounting Policies (in part)

Intangible Assets and Goodwill Impairment

The Company records tangible and intangible assets acquired and liabilities assumed in business combinations under the acquisition method of accounting. Amounts paid for an acquisition are allocated to the assets acquired and liabilities assumed based on their fair values at the date of acquisition. Goodwill is comprised of the purchase price of business acquisitions in excess of the fair value assigned to the net tangible and identifiable intangible assets acquired. Goodwill is not amortized, but is reviewed for impairment annually as of May 31, or when events or changes in the business environment indicate that the carrying value of the reporting unit may exceed its fair value. A reporting unit, for the purpose of the impairment test, is at or below the operating segment level, and constitutes a business for which discrete financial information is available and regularly reviewed by segment management. The reporting units with goodwill balances are Reinforcement Materials, Purification Solutions, and Fumed Metal Oxides. The separate businesses included within Performance Chemicals are considered separate reporting units. As such, the goodwill balance relative to Performance Chemicals is recorded in the Fumed Metal Oxides reporting unit.

For the purpose of the goodwill impairment test, the Company first assesses qualitative factors to determine whether it is more likely than not that the fair value of a reporting unit is less than its carrying amount. If an initial qualitative assessment identifies that it is more likely than not that the carrying value of a reporting unit exceeds its estimated fair value, an additional quantitative evaluation is performed under the two-step impairment test. Alternatively, the Company may elect to proceed directly to the quantitative goodwill impairment test. If based on the quantitative evaluation the fair value of the reporting unit is less than its carrying amount, the Company performs an analysis of the fair value of all assets and liabilities of the reporting unit. If the implied fair value of the reporting unit's goodwill is determined to be less than its carrying amount, an impairment is recognized for the difference. The fair value of a reporting unit is based on discounted estimated future cash flows. The fair value is also benchmarked against a market approach using the guideline public companies method. The assumptions used to estimate fair value include management's best estimates of future growth rates, operating cash flows, capital expenditures and discount rates over an estimate of the remaining operating period at the reporting unit level. Should the fair value of any of the Company's reporting units decline below its carrying amount because of reduced operating performance, market declines, changes in the discount rate, or other conditions, charges for impairment may be necessary. Based on the Company's most recent annual goodwill impairment test performed as of May 31, 2015, the fair values of the Reinforcement Materials and Fumed Metal Oxides reporting units were substantially in excess of their carrying values. The fair value of the Purification Solutions reporting unit was less than its carrying amount. Refer to Note G for details on the Purification Solutions goodwill impairment test and the resulting impairment charge recorded in the third fiscal quarter of 2015. Due to the impairment recorded, the fair value of the Purification Solutions reporting unit was insignificantly higher than its carrying value. No events occurred in the fourth fiscal quarter of 2015 that would suggest that it is more likely than not that the carrying values of any of our reporting units exceeded its fair value.

The Company uses assumptions and estimates in determining the fair value of assets acquired and liabilities assumed in a business combination. The determination of the fair value of intangible assets requires the use of significant judgment with regard to assumptions used in the valuation model. The Company estimates the fair value of identifiable acquisition-related intangible assets principally based on projections of cash flows that will arise from these assets. The projected cash flows are discounted to determine the fair value of the assets at the dates of acquisition.

Definite-lived intangible assets, which are comprised of customer relationships and developed technologies, are amortized over their estimated useful lives and are reviewed for impairment when indication of potential impairment exists, such as a significant reduction in cash flows associated with the assets. The Company evaluates indefinite-lived intangible assets, which are comprised of the trademarks of Purification Solutions, for impairment annually or when events occur or circumstances change that may reduce the fair value of the asset below its carrying amount. The annual review is performed as of May 31. The Company may first perform a qualitative assessment to determine whether it is necessary to perform the quantitative impairment test or bypass the qualitative assessment and proceed directly to performing the quantitative impairment test. The quantitative impairment test is based on discounted estimated future cash flows. The assumptions used to estimate fair value include management's best estimates of future growth rates and discount rates over an estimate of the remaining operating period at the unit of accounting level. Refer to Note G for details on the impairment test performed on intangible assets of the Purification Solutions reporting unit and the resulting impairment charges recorded. Effective in the third quarter of 2015 and as a part of the impairment assessment performed, the Company determined that the trademarks for Purification Solutions no longer have an indefinite life.

Long-Lived Assets Impairment

The Company's long-lived assets primarily include property, plant and equipment, intangible assets, long-term investments and assets held for rent. The carrying values of long-lived assets are reviewed for impairment whenever events or changes in business circumstances indicate that the carrying amount of an asset may not be recoverable.

To test for impairment of assets, the Company generally uses a probability-weighted estimate of the future undiscounted net cash flows of the assets over their remaining lives to determine if the value of the asset is recoverable. Long-lived assets are grouped with other assets and liabilities at the lowest level for which independent identifiable cash flows are determinable.

An asset impairment is recognized when the carrying value of the asset is not recoverable based on the analysis described above, in which case the asset is written down to its fair value. If the asset does not have a readily determinable market value, a discounted cash flow model may be used to determine the fair value of the asset. In circumstances when an asset does not have separate identifiable cash flows, an impairment charge is recorded when the Company no longer intends to use the asset. Refer to Note G regarding the results of the impairment test performed on the long-lived assets of the Purification Solutions segment.

Note G. Purification Solutions Goodwill and Long-Lived Assets Impairment Charges

During fiscal 2015 and as a result of the impairment tests performed on goodwill and long-lived assets of the Purification Solutions reporting unit, the Company recorded impairment charges and an associated tax benefit in the Consolidated Statements of Operations as follows:

(Dollars in millions)	Year Ended September 30, 2015
Purification Solutions goodwill impairment charge	$352
Purification Solutions long-lived assets impairment charge	210
Provision (benefit) for income taxes	(80)
Impairment charges, after tax	$482

The future growth in the Purification Solutions segment is highly dependent on achieving the expected volumes and margins in the activated carbon based mercury removal business. These volumes and margins are highly dependent on demand for mercury removal products and the Company's successful realization of its anticipated share of volumes in this business. The expected demand for mercury removal products significantly depends on: (1) the implementation and enforcement of environmental laws and regulations, particularly those that would require U.S. based coal-fired electric utilities to reduce the quantity of air pollutants they release, including mercury, to comply with the Mercury and Air Toxics Standards ("MATS") issued by the U.S. Environmental Protection Agency ("EPA") and (2) other factors such as the anticipated usage of activated carbon in the coal-fired energy units. In November 2014, the U.S. Supreme Court agreed to consider whether the EPA appropriately considered costs in determining whether it is necessary and appropriate to regulate hazardous air pollutants emitted by electric utilities. On June 29, 2015, the U.S. Supreme Court held that the EPA unreasonably failed to consider costs in determining whether it is necessary and appropriate to regulate hazardous air pollutants emitted by coal-fired utilities, and remanded the case back to the U.S. Court of Appeals for the District of Columbia Circuit further proceedings.

The implementation period for the MATS regulations began in April 2015. With this recent implementation and associated customer and industry developments during the third fiscal quarter, as well as the U.S. Supreme Court's ruling, the Company reassessed its previous estimates for expected growth in volumes, prices and margins in the Purification Solutions reporting unit. The main drivers of growth, including the size of the overall mercury removal industry, utility adoption rates, usage levels, and pricing, among others, were lowered from previous estimates. Based on these revised estimates and as part of step one of the annual impairment test, the Company determined that the estimated fair value of the Purification Solutions reporting unit was lower than the reporting unit's carrying value. As such, the reporting unit failed step one of the goodwill impairment test.

In determining the fair value of the Purification Solutions reporting unit, the Company used an income approach (a discounted cash flow analysis) which incorporated significant estimates and assumptions related to future periods, including timing of MATS implementation, the anticipated size of the mercury removal industry, and growth rates and pricing assumptions of activated carbon, among others. The Company assumed a two year delay in the final MATS implementation due to the U.S. Supreme Court's ruling. Total charges incurred could be higher if the rulings of the U.S. Court of Appeals for the District of Columbia Circuit on remand result in a delay in the implementation of MATS that is longer than two years. In addition, an estimate of the reporting unit's weighted average cost of capital ("WACC") is used to discount future estimated cash flows to their present value. The WACC was based upon externally available data considering market participants' cost of equity and debt, capital structure and risk factors specific to the Purification Solutions reporting unit.

Step two of the goodwill impairment test requires the Company to perform a theoretical purchase price allocation for the reporting unit to determine the implied fair value of goodwill and to compare the implied fair value of goodwill to the recorded amount of goodwill. The estimate of fair value is complex and requires significant judgment. Accounting guidance provides that a company should recognize an estimated impairment charge to the extent that it determines that it is probable that an impairment loss has occurred and such impairment can be reasonably estimated. As of June 30, 2015, we recorded a pre-tax goodwill impairment charge in the amount of $353 million. We completed the step two analysis in the fourth quarter of fiscal 2015, which resulted in recording a credit of $1 million to the pre-tax goodwill impairment charge. Therefore, for the year ended September 30, 2015, the pre-tax goodwill impairment charge was $352 million.

Based on the same factors leading to goodwill impairment, the Company also considered whether the reporting unit's carrying values of definite-lived intangible assets and property, plant and equipment may not be recoverable or whether the carrying value of certain indefinite-lived intangible assets were impaired. The Company used the income approach to determine the fair value of the indefinite-lived intangible assets, which are the trademarks of Purification Solutions, and determined that the fair value of these intangible assets was lower than their carrying value. As such, an impairment loss was recorded in the amount of $39 million. Subsequent to this impairment analysis, the Company concluded that such assets no longer had an indefinite life and began amortizing these assets over their estimated useful life. The Company also performed an impairment analysis to assess if definite-lived intangible assets and property, plant and equipment were recoverable based on the estimated undiscounted cash flows of the reporting unit, and these cash flows were not sufficient to recover the carrying value of the long-lived assets over their remaining useful lives. Accordingly, an impairment charge was recorded based on the lower of the carrying amount or fair value of the long-lived assets. The Company used the income approach to determine the fair value of the definite-lived intangible assets and a combination of the cost and market approaches to fair value its property, plant and equipment. The Company recorded impairment charges of $119 million and $51 million, to its definite-lived intangible assets and property, plant and equipment, respectively. We completed the impairment analysis in the fourth quarter of fiscal year 2015 which resulted in increasing the property, plant and equipment impairment charge by $1 million to $52 million. Therefore, for the year ended September 30, 2015, the long-lived assets impairment charge was $210 million.

In connection with the long-lived assets impairment charges, the Company recorded a deferred tax benefit of $80 million to its income tax provision.

The performance of the Purification Solutions reporting unit will continue to be monitored. If the reporting unit does not achieve the financial performance that the Company expects or events or circumstances change, it is possible that additional impairment charges may result.

Note H. Goodwill and Intangible Assets

Cabot had goodwill balances of $154 million and $536 million at September 30, 2015 and September 30, 2014, respectively. The carrying amount of goodwill attributable to each reportable segment with goodwill balances and the changes in those balances during the period ended September 30, 2015 are as follows:

(Dollars in millions)	Reinforcement Materials	Performance Chemicals	Purification Solutions	Total
Balance at September 30, 2014	$ 68	$ 10	$ 458	$ 536
Impairment charge	—	—	(352)	(352)
Foreign currency impact	(13)	(1)	(16)	(30)
Balance at September 30, 2015	$ 55	$ 9	$ 90	$ 154

(Dollars in millions)	Reinforcement Materials	Performance Chemicals	Purification Solutions	Total
Accumulated impairment losses at September 30, 2014	—	—	—	—
Accumulated impairment losses at September 30, 2015	$—	$—	$(352)	$(352)

Goodwill impairment tests are performed at least annually. The Company performed its most recent annual impairment assessment as of May 31, 2015 and determined there was an impairment of the assets attributable to the Purification Solutions reporting unit. Refer to Note G.

The following table provides information regarding the Company's intangible assets:

(Dollars in millions)	September 30, 2015			September 30, 2014		
	Gross Carrying Value	Accumulated Amortization	Net Intangible Assets	Gross Carrying Value	Accumulated Amortization	Net Intangible Assets
Intangible assets with finite lives[1]						
Developed technologies	$ 48	$ (1)	$ 47	$152	$(16)	$136
Trademarks	16	—	16	57	—	57
Customer relationships	96	(6)	90	171	(17)	154
Total intangible assets	$160	$ (7)	$153	$380	$(33)	$347

[1] Refer to Note G for intangible assets impairment charges recorded in fiscal 2015.

Intangible assets are amortized over their estimated useful lives, which range from fourteen to twenty-five years, with a weighted average amortization period of approximately nineteen years. Amortization expense for the years ended September 30, 2015, 2014 and 2013 was $14 million, $17 million and $14 million, respectively, and is included in Cost of sales and Selling and administrative expenses in the Consolidated Statements of Operations. Total amortization expense is estimated to be approximately $9 million each year for the next five fiscal years.

LOSS ON EXTINGUISHMENT OF DEBT

3.43 CENVEO, INC. (DEC)
CONSOLIDATED STATEMENTS OF COMPREHENSIVE INCOME (LOSS) (in part)

(in thousands, except per share data)

	For The Years Ended		
	2015	2014	2013
Net sales	$1,741,779	$1,761,315	$1,588,702
Cost of sales	1,450,876	1,491,488	1,325,365
Selling, general and administrative expenses	186,749	196,343	186,435
Amortization of intangible assets	7,785	9,184	7,782
Restructuring and other charges	12,576	21,526	12,586
Impairment of intangible assets	—	—	24,493
Operating income	83,793	42,774	32,041
Gain on bargain purchase	—	—	(17,262)
Interest expense, net	100,805	106,661	112,579
Loss on early extinguishment of debt, net	1,252	27,449	11,324
Other income, net	(3,196)	(442)	(2,485)
Loss from continuing operations before income taxes	(15,068)	(90,894)	(72,115)

NOTES TO CONSOLIDATED FINANCIAL STATEMENTS (in part)

8. Long-Term Debt (in part)

2015 Extinguishments

During the year ended 2015, the Company recorded a total loss on early extinguishment of debt of $1.3 million. During the year ended 2015, the Company paid in full its existing equipment loan, which had a remaining principal balance at the time of $12.3 million. In connection with this extinguishment, the Company recorded a loss on early extinguishment of $0.7 million, of which $0.2 million related to prepayment fees and $0.5 million related to the write-off of unamortized debt issuance costs. During the year ended 2015, the Company recorded a loss on early extinguishment of debt of $0.6 million related to the repurchase of $22.6 million of its 11.5% Notes, of which $0.2 million related to the write-off of unamortized debt issuance costs, $0.2 million related to the write-off of original issuance discount, and $0.2 million related to a premium paid over the principal amount upon repurchase.

2014 Extinguishments

During the year ended 2014, the Company recorded a total loss on extinguishment of $27.4 million. In 2014, the Company extinguished a total of $2.7 million of its 11.5% Notes. In connection with these retirements, the Company recorded a total loss on early extinguishment of debt of $0.1 million. The Company extinguished $2.0 million of its 8.500% Notes. In connection with the extinguishment, the Company recorded a gain on early extinguishment of debt of $0.4 million. In connection with the exchange of $3.0 million of its 7% Notes, the Company incurred a non-cash induced conversion expense of $1.1 million, which has been recorded in loss on early extinguishment of debt, net. The Company extinguished its Term Loan Facility and its 8.875% Notes. In connection with this extinguishment, the Company recorded a loss on early extinguishment of debt of approximately $9.0 million, of which $5.8 million related to the write-off of unamortized debt issuance costs, and $3.2 million related to the write-off of original issuance discount. Additionally, in connection with the issuance of the 6.000% Notes and 8.500% Notes, the Company expensed debt issuance costs of $16.5 million, of which $1.6 million related to fees paid to third parties. The Company also used cash on hand of $9.4 million to repay in full the remaining principal balance on the Unsecured Term Loan. In connection with the extinguishment of the Unsecured Term Loan, the Company recorded a loss on early extinguishment of debt of approximately $1.0 million, of which $0.6 million related to the write-off of unamortized debt issuance costs, and $0.4 million related to the write-off of original issuance discount.

2013 Extinguishments

During the year ended 2013, the Company recorded a total loss on early extinguishment of debt of $11.3 million. In connection with the Refinanced Facility, the Company recorded a loss on early extinguishment of debt of approximately $6.4 million, of which $4.1 million related to consent fees paid to consenting lenders, $2.1 million related to the write-off of unamortized debt issuance costs and $0.2 million related to the write-off of original issuance discount. The Company recorded a loss on early extinguishment of debt of approximately $4.0 million related to the extinguishment of $40.0 million of its Unsecured Term Loan, of which $2.2 million related to the write-off of unamortized debt issuance costs and $1.8 million related to the write-off of original issuance discount. In connection with the extinguishment of $28.2 million of its Term Loan Facility, the Company recorded a loss on early extinguishment of debt of approximately $0.8 million, of which $0.5 million related to the write-off of unamortized debt issuance costs and $0.3 million related to the write-off of original issuance discount.

Pensions and Other Postretirement Benefits

RECOGNITION AND MEASUREMENT

3.44 FASB ASC 715, *Compensation—Retirement Benefits*, requires that an entity recognize the overfunded or underfunded status of a single-employer defined benefit postretirement plan as an asset or a liability in its statement of financial position, recognize changes in that funded status in comprehensive income, and disclose in the notes to the financial statements additional information about net periodic benefit cost. FASB ASC 715 requires an entity to recognize as components of other comprehensive income the gains or losses and prior service costs or credits that arise during a period but are not recognized in the income statement as components of net periodic benefit cost of a period. Those amounts recognized in accumulated other comprehensive income are adjusted as they are subsequently recognized in the income statement as components of net periodic benefit cost. Additionally, FASB ASC 715 requires that an entity measure plan assets and benefit obligations as of the date of its fiscal year-end statement of financial position. An employer whose equity securities are publicly traded is required to initially recognize the funded status of a defined benefit postretirement plan.

DISCLOSURE

3.45 FASB ASC 715 states the disclosure requirements for pensions and other postretirement benefits, including disclosures about the assets, obligations, cash flows, investment strategy, and net periodic benefit cost of defined pension and postretirement plans. FASB ASC 715 also includes disclosures related to multiemployer plans. FASB ASC 715-20 calls for different disclosures about defined benefit plans for public and nonpublic entities.

3.46 The disclosure requirements of FASB ASC 715 include, but are not limited to, the actuarial gains and losses, the assumed health care cost trend rate for other postretirement benefits, the allocation by major category of plan assets, the inputs and valuation techniques used to measure the fair value of plan assets, the effect of fair value measurements using significant unobservable inputs (level 3) on changes in plan assets for the period, and significant concentrations of risk within plan assets.

3.47 FASB ASC 715-80 explains the additional disclosures required for multiemployer plans. An entity should include details in these disclosures, including plan names and identifying numbers for significant multiemployer plans, the level of employers' participation in the plans, the financial health of the plans, and the nature of the employer commitments to the plans.

PRESENTATION AND DISCLOSURE EXCERPTS

PENSIONS AND OTHER POSTRETIREMENT BENEFITS

3.48 AXIALL CORPORATION (DEC)
NOTES TO CONSOLIDATED FINANCIAL STATEMENTS (in part)

1. Summary of Significant Accounting Policies and Nature of Business (in part)

Pension Plans and Other Post-Retirement Employment Benefit ("OPEB") Plans. Accounting for employee pension and OPEB plans involves estimating the cost of benefits that are to be provided in the future and attempting to match, for each employee, that estimated cost to the period worked. To accomplish this, we make assumptions about discount rates, expected long-term rates of return on plan assets, salary increases, employee turnover and mortality rates, amongst others. We reevaluate all assumptions annually with our independent actuaries taking into consideration existing and forecasted economic conditions and our investment policy and strategy with regard to managing the plans. We believe our estimates, the most significant of which are presented in Note 14 to the Notes to the Consolidated Financial Statements, to be reasonable.

During the year ended December 31, 2015, the Company changed the accounting method used to estimate the interest and service cost components of net periodic cost for its U.S. Pension and OPEB plans. See Note 14 for a discussion of this change.

14. Employee Retirement Plans (in part)

Defined Benefit Plans

The Company sponsors and contributes to pension plans ("Pension Plans") and OPEB plans covering many of our United States ("U.S.") employees, in whole or in part based on meeting certain eligibility criteria. In addition, the Company and its subsidiaries have various pension plans and other forms of OPEB arrangements outside the United States, namely in Canada and Taiwan.

The Pension Plans provide benefits to certain employees and retirees and are closed to new hires. Effective January 31, 2014, amendments to the Pension Plans for U.S. non-bargained employees froze all future benefit accruals for non-bargained employees who were not already frozen. The financial impact of these amendments to the Pension Plans was recognized in the fourth quarter of 2013.

During 2014, the U.S. Pension Plans were amended to provide a one-time voluntary lump-sum distribution offer to terminated vested participants. Payments were made during December 2014 and a settlement charge of $5.8 million was recognized at December 31, 2014.

The OPEB Plans are unfunded and provide medical and life insurance benefits for certain employees and their dependents.

Recently approved amendments to the OPEB plans were made to further deliver retiree medical benefits through health reimbursement account contributions and to further limit life insurance benefits. Effective January 1, 2016, the majority of Medicare and non-Medicare eligible retirees will receive retiree medical benefits through health reimbursement account contributions. In addition, effective January 1, 2016, most life insurance benefits for non-bargained retirees were eliminated and a sunset period was provided for life insurance benefits for the majority of other retirees. These OPEB benefit changes were approved and communicated to participants in August 2015 and the quantitative financial impact is reflected in the year ended December 31, 2015. These changes reduced the OPEB benefit obligation by $29.8 million and the resulting prior service credit will be amortized through 2025.

In connection with the OPEB plan amendments, the benefit obligation was remeasured using current assumptions as of that date, including the Society of Actuaries' ("SOA") mortality tables "RPH-2014" and an alternative generational improvement scale published by the SOA "BB-2D". The discount rate used to remeasure the OPEB plan obligation was 3.59 percent at September 1, 2015 compared to 3.90 percent at December 31, 2014.

For the U.S. Pension Plans, benefit obligations continue to be measured using the SOA's base mortality table ("RP-2014"), with collar adjustments by plan. The generational improvement scale was updated to use the same consistently with the scale used for the OPEB plans.

In the third quarter of 2015, we changed the accounting method used to estimate the service and interest components of net periodic benefit cost for the U.S. postretirement benefits. This new estimation approach discounts the individual expected cash flows underlying the service cost and interest cost using the applicable spot rates derived from the yield curve used to discount the cash flows used to measure the benefit obligation. Historically, we estimated these service and interest cost components utilizing a single weighted-average discount rate derived from the yield curve used to measure the benefit obligation at the beginning of the period.

We have made this change to provide a more precise measurement of service and interest costs by improving the correlation between projected benefit cash flows to the corresponding spot yield curve rates. We have accounted for this change as a change in accounting estimate that is inseparable from a change in accounting principle and accordingly have accounted for it prospectively. While the benefit obligation measured under this approach is unchanged, the more granular application of the spot rates reduced the service and interest cost for the OPEB plan for the last four months of fiscal 2015 by $0.2 million. For the OPEB plan, the spot rates used to determine service and interest costs ranged from 0.65 percent to 5.01 percent and 0.65 percent to 5.01 percent, respectively. Under the Company's prior methodology, these rates would have resulted in weighted-average rates for service and interest costs of 3.59 percent and 3.59 percent, respectively. The new approach will be used to measure the service and interest cost for our other U.S. pension plans in 2016. For the U.S. OPEB and pension plans, the spot rates that will be used to determine 2016 service and interest costs range from 0.92 percent to 4.97 percent and 0.92 percent to 4.97 percent, respectively. Under the Company's prior methodology, these rates would have resulted in a single weighted-average rate of 4.37 percent for both service and interest costs. Based on current economic conditions, we estimate the service cost and interest cost for the pension plans will be reduced by approximately $7.0 million in 2016 as a result of the change.

Benefit Obligations. The reconciliation of the beginning and ending balances of the projected benefit obligation for defined benefit plans is as follows:

| (In millions) | Pension Benefits | | OPEB | |
| | As of December 31, | | | |
	2015	2014	2015	2014
Change in Benefit Obligation				
Benefit obligation, beginning of year	$786.8	$673.4	$111.7	$ 97.9
Service costs	4.3	3.6	0.9	0.8
Interest cost	30.7	31.7	3.5	4.4
Actuarial loss (gain)	(44.1)	141.3	(8.7)	16.7
Foreign currency translation adjustment	(2.5)	(1.5)	(0.5)	(0.3)
Plan participants' contributions	—	—	1.4	1.4
Gross benefits paid	(37.7)	(38.2)	(9.2)	(9.2)
Plan amendments	—	—	(29.8)	—
Settlements	(0.5)	(24.0)	—	—
Other	—	0.5	—	—
Benefit obligation, end of year	$737.0	$786.8	$ 69.3	$111.7
Accumulated benefit obligation, end of year	$734.6	$784.0	NA	NA

The accumulated benefit obligation is defined as the actuarial present value of pension benefits (whether vested or unvested) attributed to employee services rendered before December 31, 2015 and 2014, respectively, and based on employee service and compensation prior to the applicable date.

Plan Assets. The summary and reconciliation of the beginning and ending balances of the fair value of the plans' assets were as follows:

| (In millions) | Pension Benefits | | OPEB | |
| | As of December 31, | | | |
	2015	2014	2015	2014
Change in Plan Assets				
Fair value of plan assets, beginning of year	$638.2	$659.4	$ —	$ —
Actual return (loss) on plan assets	(5.3)	40.1	—	—
Foreign currency translation adjustment	(1.9)	(1.1)	—	—
Employer contribution	2.0	2.0	7.8	7.8
Plan participants' contributions	—	—	1.4	1.4
Gross benefits paid	(37.7)	(38.2)	(9.2)	(9.2)
Settlements	(0.5)	(24.0)	—	—
Fair value of plan assets, end of year	$594.8	$638.2	$ —	$ —

Investments are classified based on the lowest level of input that is significant to the fair value measurement. The following table sets forth, by level within the fair value hierarchy, a summary of the investments measured at fair value and the target and current asset allocations.

(In millions, except percentages) Asset Category	Target Allocation 2016	Percentage of Plan Assets, December 31, 2015	Total	Quoted Prices in Active Markets for Identical Assets (Level 1)	Significant Observable Inputs (Level 2)
Short-term investment fund	—%	1%	$ 8.5	$ —	$ 8.5
U.S. equity securities:					
Consumer discretionary sector			2.8	2.8	—
Consumer staples sector			4.3	4.3	—
Energy sector			0.2	0.2	—
Finance sector			0.4	0.4	—
Health care sector			4.6	4.6	—
Index funds			117.8	—	117.8
Industrials sector			1.3	1.3	—
Information technology sector			3.5	3.5	—
Capital appreciation mutual fund			56.1	56.1	—
Small cap growth mutual fund			7.0	7.0	—
Pooled equity fund			55.7	—	55.7
Total U.S. equity securities	44%	43%	253.7	80.2	173.5
U.S. fixed income securities:					
Western assets total return funds			80.6	—	80.6
Blackrock investments, institutional			68.7	—	68.7
Other fixed income securities			69.8	69.6	0.2

(continued)

(In millions, except percentages) Asset Category	Target Allocation 2016	Percentage of Plan Assets, December 31, 2015	Total	Quoted Prices in Active Markets for Identical Assets (Level 1)	Significant Observable Inputs (Level 2)
Total fixed income securities	37%	37%	219.1	69.6	149.5
International securities:					
Equity securities			53.6	6.7	46.9
Equity securities measured at net asset value[1]			3.6	—	—
Euro pacific growth fund			49.8	49.8	—
Fixed income securities			1.6	1.6	—
Fixed income securities measured at net asset value[1]			4.8	—	—
Total international securities	19%	19%	113.4	58.1	46.9
Real estate partnership, measured at net asset value[1]	—%	—%	0.1	—	—
Total			$ 594.8	$207.9	$378.4

[1] In accordance with Subtopic 820-10, certain investments that are measured at fair value using the net asset value per share (or its equivalent) practical expedient have not been classified in the fair value hierarchy. The fair value amounts presented in this table are intended to permit reconciliation of the fair value hierarchy to the amounts presented in the statement of financial position. See Note 5 for more details.

(In millions, except percentages) Asset Category	Target Allocation 2015	Percentage of Plan Assets, December 31, 2014	Total	Quoted Prices in Active Markets for Identical Assets (Level 1)	Significant Observable Inputs (Level 2)
Short-term investment fund	—%	2%	$ 10.2	$ —	$ 10.2
U.S. equity securities:					
Consumer discretionary sector			4.3	4.3	—
Consumer staples sector			6.1	6.1	—
Energy sector			1.3	1.3	—
Finance sector			2.3	2.3	—
Health care sector			9.9	9.9	—
Index funds			141.3	—	141.3
Industrials sector			3.5	3.5	—
Information technology sector			3.7	3.7	—
Capital appreciation mutual fund			39.4	39.4	—
Small cap growth mutual fund			7.2	7.2	—
Pooled equity fund			55.5	—	55.5
Other			1.3	1.3	—
Total U.S. equity securities	41%	43%	275.8	79.0	196.8
U.S. fixed income securities:					
Western assets total return funds			85.5	—	85.5
Blackrock investments, institutional			70.8	—	70.8
Other fixed income securities			71.4	—	71.4
Total fixed income securities	38%	36%	227.7	—	227.7
International securities:					
Equity securities		12%	76.5	8.0	68.5
Equity securities measured at net asset value[1]			5.0	—	—
Euro pacific growth fund		6%	35.4	35.4	—
Fixed income securities			2.0	2.0	—
Fixed income securities measured at net asset value[1]			4.2	—	—
Total international securities	18%	19%	123.1	45.4	68.5
Long-biased hedge fund, measured at net asset value[1]	3%	—%	0.2	—	—
Real estate partnership, measured at net asset value[1]	—%	—%	1.2	—	—
Total			$638.2	$124.4	$503.2

[1] In accordance with Subtopic 820-10, certain investments that are measured at fair value using the net asset value per share (or its equivalent) practical expedient have not been classified in the fair value hierarchy. The fair value amounts presented in this table are intended to permit reconciliation of the fair value hierarchy to the amounts presented in the statement of financial position. See Note 5 for more details.

Funded Status. The following table shows the funded status of the pension and other OPEB benefits, reconciled to the amounts reported on the consolidated balance sheets:

(In millions)	Pension Benefits		OPEB	
	As of December 31,			
	2015	2014	2015	2014
Funded status, end of year:				
Fair value of plan assets	$ 594.8	$ 638.2	$ —	$ —
Benefit obligations	737.0	786.8	69.3	111.7
Unfunded status	$(142.2)	$(148.6)	$(69.3)	$(111.7)
Amounts recognized in the balance sheets consist of:				
Current liability	$ (1.5)	$ (1.5)	$ (7.2)	$ (8.7)
Noncurrent liability	(140.7)	(147.1)	(62.1)	(103.0)
Amount recognized, end of year	$(142.2)	$(148.6)	$(69.3)	$(111.7)
Gross amount recognized in accumulated other comprehensive income (loss) consist of:				
Net actuarial gain (loss)	(135.1)	$(131.5)	(3.4)	$ (12.3)
Prior service credit (cost)	(0.1)	(0.1)	90.7	71.2
Amount recognized, end of year	$(135.2)	$(131.6)	$ 87.3	$ 58.9

Our pension plans have projected benefit obligations in excess of the fair value of plan assets. For these plans, the projected benefit obligations and the fair value of plan assets were as follows:

(In millions)	Pension Benefits As of December 31,	
	2015	2014
Projected benefit obligation, end of year	$737.0	$786.8
Fair value of plan assets, end of year	594.8	638.2

Our pension plans have accumulated benefit obligations in excess of the fair value of plan assets. For these plans, the accumulated benefit obligations and the fair value of plan assets were as follows:

(In millions)	Pension Benefits As of December 31,	
	2015	2014
Accumulated benefit obligation, end of year	$725.2	$784.0
Fair value of plan assets, end of year	585.2	638.2

Changes in Other Comprehensive Income (Loss). The following table summarizes the changes in plan assets and benefit obligations which were recognized in other comprehensive income (loss):

End of year (in millions):	Pension Benefits			OPEB		
	As of December 31,					
	2015	2014	2013	2015	2014	2013
Current year actuarial gain (loss)	$(6.2)	$(142.5)	$102.2	$ 8.8	$(16.6)	$ 4.2
Amortization of actuarial loss (gain)	2.6	(0.4)	(13.3)	0.1	0.1	—
Current year prior service credit	—	—	—	29.8	—	82.6
Amortization of prior service credit	—	—	—	(10.2)	(9.2)	(2.3)
Total recognized in other comprehensive income (loss)	$(3.6)	$(142.9)	$ 88.9	$ 28.5	$(25.7)	$84.5
Total recognized in net periodic benefit cost and other comprehensive income (loss)	$ 4.0	$(137.1)	$106.2	$ 34.2	$(21.9)	$78.5

The following table summarizes the estimated amount that will be amortized from accumulated other comprehensive income (loss) into net periodic benefit cost in 2016:

(In millions)	Pension Benefits	OPEB
Prior service credit	$ —	$12.2
Actuarial loss	(2.8)	(0.1)
Total	$(2.8)	$12.1

Net Periodic Benefit Income (Expense). Net periodic benefit income (expense) for the years ended December 31, 2015, 2014 and 2013 includes the following:

(In millions)	Pension Benefits Year Ended December 31,			OPEB Year Ended December 31,		
	2015	2014	2013	2015	2014	2013
Components of Net Periodic Benefit Income (Expense):						
Interest cost	$(30.7)	$(31.7)	$(28.0)	$(3.5)	$(4.4)	$(6.4)
Service cost	(4.3)	(3.6)	(6.6)	(0.9)	(0.8)	(2.0)
Expected return on assets	45.2	47.0	38.5	—	—	—
Amortization of:						
Prior service credit	—	—	—	10.2	9.2	2.3
Actuarial gain (loss)	(2.6)	0.4	(2.1)	(0.1)	(0.1)	—
Total amortization	(2.6)	0.4	(2.1)	10.1	9.1	2.3
Settlement loss	—	(5.8)	-	—	—	—
Curtailment gain	—	—	15.5	—	—	—
Other components of net periodic pension cost	—	(0.5)	—	—	—	—
Total net periodic benefit income (expense)	$ 7.6	$ 5.8	$ 17.3	$5.7	$ 3.9	$(6.1)

Assumptions for Defined Benefit Obligations. Mortality is a key assumption used to determine the benefit obligation for our defined benefit pension and OPEB plans. The Company continues to measure year-end benefit obligations using the SAO's RP-2014 base mortality table, with adjustments by plan. The Company selected the Scale BB-2D generational mortality projection scale to reflect mortality improvement rates for purposes of measuring pension and OPEB benefit obligations at year-end.

The discount rate reflects the rate at which pension benefit obligations could be effectively settled. For the U.S. and Canadian plans, we determined our discount rate by matching the expected cash flows of our pension and OPEB obligations to a yield curve generated from a broad portfolio of high-quality fixed rate debt instruments. For Taiwan, a government bond yield was used to determine the discount rate. The rate of compensation is based on projected salary increases for our plan participants. The healthcare cost trend assumption is based on a number of factors including our actual healthcare cost increases, the design of our benefit programs, the demographics of our active and retiree populations and external expectations of future medical cost inflation rates. The weighted average assumptions used for determining our benefit obligations as of December 31, 2015, 2014 and 2013 are as follows:

	Pension Benefits			OPEB		
	2015	2014	2013	2015	2014	2013
Discount rate	4.34%	3.98%	4.81%	3.61%	3.90%	4.65%
Rate of compensation increase	3.01%	3.01%	3.00%	NA	NA	3.00%
Health care cost trend rate						
— Initial rate	NA	NA	NA	7.47%	7.00%	7.49%
— Ultimate rate	NA	NA	NA	4.50%	4.50%	4.50%
— Years to ultimate	NA	NA	NA	12	9	10

Assumptions for Net Periodic Costs. The rate of compensation increase for our OPEB plans was not applicable in 2014 and 2015 due to benefit changes made to the U.S. OPEB plans, eliminating the salary-based life insurance benefit for future non-bargained retirees, subsequent to 2014. The following weighted average assumptions were used to determine the net periodic costs for the defined benefit pension and OPEB plans for the years presented:

	Pension Benefits			OPEB		
	2015	2014	2013	2015	2014	2013
Discount rate	3.97%[1]	4.81%	4.16%	3.60%[1]	4.65%	4.39%
Expected long-term rate of return on plan assets	7.39%	7.42%	6.91%	NA	NA	NA
Rate of compensation increase	3.01%	3.00%	3.14%	NA	NA	3.11%
Health care cost trend rate						
— Initial rate	NA	NA	NA	7.00%	7.49%	6.63%
— Ultimate rate	NA	NA	NA	4.50%	4.50%	4.50%
— Years to ultimate	NA	NA	NA	9	10	11

[1] The weighted average spot rate selected for pension benefit and OPEB plans, respectively, in 2015.

In selecting the rates for our current and long-term healthcare cost assumptions, we take into consideration a number of factors including our actual healthcare cost increases, the design of our benefit programs, the demographics of our active and retiree populations and external expectations of future medical cost inflation rates. If the assumed healthcare cost trend rates were 1 percent higher or 1 percent lower, the estimated OPEB cost for 2015 would increase by $0.1 million or decrease by $0.1 million, respectively.

The expected long-term rate of return on plan assets assumption is based on historical and projected rates of return for current and planned asset classes in the plan's investment portfolio. Projected rates of return for each of the plans' projected asset classes were selected after analyzing historical experience and future expectations of the returns and volatility of the various asset classes. Based on the target asset allocation for each asset class, the overall expected rate of return for the portfolio was developed and adjusted for historical and expected experience of active portfolio management results compared to the benchmark returns and for the effect of expenses paid from plan assets.

Our investment committee establishes investment policies and strategies and regularly monitors the performance of the plans' funds. Our investment strategy with respect to U.S. pension plan assets is to invest the assets in accordance with the "prudent investor" guidelines contained in the Employee Retirement Income Security Act of 1974 and fiduciary standards. Our policy on funding is to contribute an amount within the range of the minimum required and the maximum tax-deductible contribution.

Expected Cash Flows. During 2016, we expect to make contributions of $2.0 million to our pension plans and $7.3 million to our unfunded OPEB plans for benefit payments. We do not expect any federal subsidy with regards to our OPEB plans. Expected benefit payments for all pension and OPEB plans are as follows:

(In millions)	Pension Benefits	OPEB (Gross)
Expected Benefit Payments:		
2016	$ 39.2	$ 7.3
2017	40.3	7.0
2018	41.3	6.9
2019	42.4	6.9
2020	43.8	6.9
2021–2025	230.8	32.9

DEFINED CONTRIBUTION PLANS

3.49 ORBITAL ATK, INC. (MAR)
NOTES TO THE CONSOLIDATED FINANCIAL STATEMENTS (in part)

(Amounts in thousands except share and per share data and unless otherwise indicated)

10. Employee Benefit Plans (in part)

The Company provides defined benefit pension plans and defined contribution plans for the majority of its employees. The Company has tax-qualified defined benefit plans, a supplemental (nonqualified) defined benefit pension plan, a defined contribution plan and a supplemental (non-qualified) defined contribution plan. A qualified plan meets the requirements of certain sections of the Internal Revenue Code and, generally, contributions to qualified plans are tax deductible. A qualified plan typically provides benefits to a broad group of employees and may not discriminate in favor of highly compensated employees in coverage, benefits or contributions. In addition, the Company provides medical and life insurance benefits to certain retirees and their eligible dependents through its postretirement plans.

Defined Contribution Plan

The Company also sponsors two defined contribution plans—the Alliant Techsystems Inc. 401(k) Plan and the Deferred Salary and Profit Sharing Plan for Employees of Orbital Sciences Corporation. Participation in these plans is available to substantially all U.S. employees.

The Alliant Techsystems Inc. 401(k) Plan is a 401(k) plan, with an employee stock ownership ("ESOP") feature, to which employees may contribute up to 50% of their pay (highly compensated employees are subject to limitations). Employee contributions are invested, at the employees' direction, among a variety of investment alternatives including a Company common stock fund. Participants may transfer amounts into and out of the investment alternatives at any time, except for the Company common stock fund. Any dividends declared on the Company common stock can be either reinvested within the Company common stock fund or provided as a cash payment. Effective January 1, 2013 employees no longer had the option to invest in the Company common stock fund, other than for the reinvestment of dividends paid on the Company common stock in participants' accounts. Balances in the fund prior to January 1, 2013 remain in the fund unless distributed or transferred. Effective January 1, 2004, the Company matching contribution and non-elective contribution to this plan depends on a participant's years of service, pension plan participation and certain other factors. Participants receive:
- a matching contribution of 100% of the first 3% of the participant's contributed pay plus 50% of the next 2% of the participant's contributed pay, or
- a matching contribution of 50% of the first 6% of the participant's contributed pay, or

- a matching contribution of 100% of the first 3% of the participant's contributed pay plus 50% of the next 3% of the participant's contributed pay (subject to one-year vesting) and a non-elective contribution based on recognized compensation, age and service (subject to three-year vesting), or
- an automatic enrollment of a 6% pre-tax contribution rate (of which the participant can either change or opt out) along with a matching contribution of 100% of the first 3% of the participant's contributed pay plus 50% of the next 3% of the participant's contributed pay (subject to one-year vesting) and a non-elective contribution based on recognized compensation, age and service (subject to three-year vesting), or
- a non-elective contribution based on the recognized compensation, age and service (subject to three-year vesting), or
- no matching contribution

The Company's contributions to the plan were $51,205 in fiscal 2015, $48,379 in fiscal 2014 and $37,377 in fiscal 2013.

As of March 31, 2015, the Company had approximately 9,000 U.S. employees eligible under the plan. The Company has union-represented employees at five locations, comprising less than 20% of its total workforce. One location has two separate bargaining units, each with its own collective bargaining agreement ("CBA"). One location is currently negotiating its initial CBA with the Company. The Company's current CBAs expire in calendar years 2015, 2016 and 2017.

The Deferred Salary and Profit Sharing Plan for Employees of Orbital Sciences Corporation is a 401(k) plan to which employees may contribute up to 30% of their pay (highly compensated employees are subject to limitations). Employee contributions are invested, at the employees' direction, among a variety of investment alternatives including the Company common stock fund. Participants may transfer amounts into and out of the investment alternatives at any time, except for the Company common stock fund. Any dividends declared on the Company common stock can be reinvested within the Company common stock fund. Effective February 9, 2015, employees no longer had the option to invest in the Company common stock fund, other than for the reinvestment of dividends paid on the Company common stock in participants' accounts. Balances in the fund prior to February 9, 2015 remain in the fund unless distributed or transferred. Participants receive a matching contribution of 100% of the first 5% of the participant's contributed pay. The company may also make an annual discretionary profit sharing contribution based on the participant's compensation. The Company's contributions to the plan were $2,778 in fiscal 2015.

SUPPLEMENTAL RETIREMENT PLANS (SERP)

3.50 GUESS?, INC. (JAN)
NOTES TO CONSOLIDATED FINANCIAL STATEMENTS (in part)

(12) Defined Benefit Plans (in part)

Supplemental Executive Retirement Plan

On August 23, 2005, the Board of Directors of the Company adopted a Supplemental Executive Retirement Plan ("SERP") which became effective January 1, 2006. The SERP provides select employees who satisfy certain eligibility requirements with certain benefits upon retirement, termination of employment, death, disability or a change in control of the Company, in certain prescribed circumstances. Paul Marciano, Chief Executive Officer and Vice Chairman of the Board, is the only active employee participating in the SERP.

In July 2013, the Company amended the SERP to limit the amount of eligible wages under the plan that count toward the SERP benefit for the active participant. As a result, the projected benefit obligation and unrecognized prior service cost were reduced by $4.5 million during fiscal 2014.

As a non-qualified pension plan, no dedicated funding of the SERP is required; however, the Company has made, and may continue to make, periodic payments into insurance policies held in a rabbi trust to fund the expected obligations arising under the non-qualified SERP. The amount of any future payments into the insurance policies may vary, depending on any changes to the estimates of final annual compensation levels and investment performance of the trust. The cash surrender values of the insurance policies were $53.6 million and $51.4 million as of January 31, 2015 and February 1, 2014, respectively, and were included in other assets in the Company's consolidated balance sheets. As a result of changes in the value of the insurance policy investments, the Company recorded unrealized gains of $2.2 million, $3.6 million and $3.4 million in other income during fiscal 2015, fiscal 2014 and fiscal 2013, respectively.

The components of net periodic defined benefit pension cost to comprehensive income (loss) for fiscal 2015, fiscal 2014 and fiscal 2013 related to the SERP were as follows (in thousands):

	Year Ended Jan 31, 2015	Year Ended Feb 1, 2014	Year Ended Feb 2, 2013
Interest cost	$ 2,289	$ 2,345	$ 2,392
Net amortization of unrecognized prior service (credit) cost	(233)	194	620
Net amortization of actuarial losses	938	1,108	3,340
Net periodic defined benefit pension cost	$ 2,994	$ 3,647	$ 6,352
Unrecognized prior service (credit) cost charged to comprehensive income (loss)	$ (233)	$ 194	$ 620
Unrecognized net actuarial loss charged to comprehensive income (loss)	938	1,108	3,340
Actuarial gains (losses)	(6,142)	1,751	3,508
Plan amendment	—	4,529	—
Related tax impact	2,080	(2,963)	(2,855)
Total periodic defined benefit pension cost and other charges to comprehensive income (loss)	$(3,357)	$ 4,619	$ 4,613

Included in accumulated other comprehensive income (loss), before tax, as of January 31, 2015 and February 1, 2014 were the following amounts that have not yet been recognized in net periodic defined benefit pension cost (in thousands):

	Jan 31, 2015	Feb 1, 2014
Unrecognized prior service credit[1]	$ (1,748)	$ (1,981)
Unrecognized net actuarial loss	18,178	12,974
Total included in accumulated other comprehensive loss	$16,430	$10,993

[1] During fiscal 2014, the Company amended the SERP to limit the amount of eligible wages under the plan that count toward the SERP benefit for the active participant. As a result, unrecognized prior service cost was reduced by $4.5 million during fiscal 2014.

The following chart summarizes the SERP's funded status and the amounts recognized in the Company's consolidated balance sheets (in thousands):

	Jan 31, 2015	Feb 1, 2014
Projected benefit obligation[1]	$(61,862)	$(54,704)
Plan assets at fair value[2]	—	—
Net liability	$(61,862)	$(54,704)

[1] The projected benefit obligation was included in accrued expenses and other long-term liabilities in the Company's consolidated balance sheets depending on the expected timing of payments.

[2] The SERP is a non-qualified pension plan and hence the insurance policies are not considered to be plan assets. Accordingly, the table above does not include the insurance policies with cash surrender values of $53.6 million and $51.4 million as of January 31, 2015 and February 1, 2014, respectively.

A reconciliation of the changes in the projected benefit obligation for fiscal 2015 and fiscal 2014 is as follows (in thousands):

	Projected Benefit Obligation
Balance at February 2, 2013	$58,639
Interest cost	2,345
Plan amendment	(4,529)
Actuarial gains	(1,751)
Balance at February 1, 2014	$54,704
Interest cost	2,289
Actuarial losses	6,142
Payments	(1,273)
Balance at January 31, 2015	$61,862

The Company assumed a discount rate of approximately 3.3% and 4.3% for the years ended January 31, 2015 and February 1, 2014, respectively, as part of the actuarial valuation performed to calculate the projected benefit obligation disclosed above, based on the timing of cash flows expected to be made in the future to the participants, applied to high quality yield curves. Compensation levels utilized in calculating the projected benefit obligation were derived from expected future compensation as outlined in employment contracts in effect at the time. In October 2014, the Society of Actuaries issued new mortality tables which reflected longer life expectancies than the previous tables. The Company considered these new tables in developing its best estimate of the expected mortality rates for its plan participants.

As of January 31, 2015, amounts included in comprehensive income (loss) that are expected to be recognized as components of net periodic defined benefit pension cost in fiscal 2016 consist of amortization of prior service credits of $0.2 million and actuarial losses of $1.7 million. Aggregate benefits projected to be paid in the next five fiscal years amount to $8.5 million with equal amounts expected to be paid during each of the years. Aggregate benefits projected to be paid in the following five fiscal years amount to $18.6 million.

3.51 UNITED PARCEL SERVICE, INC. (DEC)
NOTES TO CONSOLIDATED FINANCIAL STATEMENTS (in part)

Note 5. Multiemployer Employee Benefit Plans

We contribute to a number of multiemployer defined benefit plans under the terms of collective bargaining agreements that cover our union-represented employees. These plans generally provide for retirement, death and/or termination benefits for eligible employees within the applicable collective bargaining units, based on specific eligibility/participation requirements, vesting periods and benefit formulas. The risks of participating in these multiemployer plans are different from single-employer plans in the following aspects:

- Assets contributed to a multiemployer plan by one employer may be used to provide benefits to employees of other participating employers.
- If we negotiate to cease participating in a multiemployer plan, we may be required to pay that plan an amount based on our allocable share of its underfunded status, referred to as a "withdrawal liability". However, cessation of participation in a multiemployer plan and subsequent payment of any withdrawal liability is subject to the collective bargaining process.
- If any of the multiemployer pension plans in which we participate enter critical status, and our contributions are not sufficient to satisfy any rehabilitation plan funding schedule, we could be required under the Pension Protection Act of 2006 to make additional surcharge contributions to the multiemployer pension plan in the amount of five to ten percent of the existing contributions required by our labor agreement. Such surcharges would cease upon the ratification of a new collective bargaining agreement, and could not recur unless a plan re-entered critical status at a later date.

The discussion that follows sets forth the financial impact on our results of operations and cash flows for the years ended December 31, 2015, 2014 and 2013 from our participation in multiemployer benefit plans. As part of the overall collective bargaining process for wage and benefit levels, we have agreed to contribute certain amounts to the multiemployer benefit plans during the contract period. The multiemployer benefit plans set benefit levels and are responsible for benefit delivery to participants. Future contribution amounts to multiemployer benefit plans are determined only through collective bargaining, and we have no additional legal or constructive obligation to increase contributions beyond the agreed-upon amounts (except potential surcharges under the Pension Protection Act of 2006 as described above).

The number of employees covered by our multiemployer health and welfare plans increased during 2014, affecting the comparability of contributions with prior years, as a result of provisions of the new collective bargaining agreement with the International Brotherhood of Teamsters ("Teamsters") discussed below. The number of employees covered by our multiemployer pension plans has remained consistent over the past three years, and there have been no significant changes that affect the comparability of 2015, 2014 and 2013 contributions. We recognize expense for the contractually-required contribution for each period, and we recognize a liability for any contributions due and unpaid at the end of a reporting period.

Status of Collective Bargaining Agreements

As of December 31, 2015, we had approximately 266,000 employees employed under a national master agreement and various supplemental agreements with local unions affiliated with the Teamsters. During 2014, the Teamsters ratified a new national master agreement ("NMA") with UPS that will expire on July 31, 2018. The economic provisions in the NMA included wage rate increases, as well as increased contribution rates for healthcare and pension benefits. Most of these economic provisions were retroactive to August 1, 2013, which was the effective date of the NMA. In 2014 and 2015, we remitted $278 and $53 million, respectively, for these retroactive economic benefits; this payment had an immaterial impact on net income, as these retroactive economic benefits had been accrued since the July 31, 2013 expiration of the prior agreement.

In addition to the retroactive economic provisions of the NMA, there were certain changes to the delivery of healthcare benefits that were effective at various dates. These changes impact approximately 36,000 full-time and 73,000 part-time active employees covered by the NMA and the UPS Freight collective bargaining agreement (collectively referred to as the "NMA Group"), as well as approximately 16,000 employees covered by other collective bargaining agreements (the "Non-NMA Group"). These provisions are discussed further below in the "Changes to the Delivery of Active and Postretirement Healthcare Benefits" section.

We have approximately 2,600 pilots who are employed under a collective bargaining agreement with the Independent Pilots Association ("IPA"), which became amendable at the end of 2011. The ongoing contract negotiations between UPS and the IPA are in mediation by the National Mediation Board.

Our airline mechanics are covered by a collective bargaining agreement with Teamsters Local 2727, which became amendable November 1, 2013. In addition, approximately 3,100 of our auto and maintenance mechanics who are not employed under agreements with the Teamsters are employed under collective bargaining agreements with the International Association of Machinists and Aerospace Workers ("IAM") that will expire on July 31, 2019.

Multiemployer Pension Plans

The following table outlines our participation in multiemployer pension plans for the periods ended December 31, 2015, 2014 and 2013, and sets forth our calendar year contributions accrued for each plan. The "EIN/Pension Plan Number" column provides the Employer Identification Number ("EIN") and the three-digit plan number. The most recent Pension Protection Act zone status available in 2015 and 2014 relates to the plans' two most recent fiscal year-ends. The zone status is based on information that we received from the plans' administrators and is certified by each plan's actuary. Among other factors, plans certified in the red zone are generally less than 65% funded, plans certified in the orange zone are both less than 80% funded and have an accumulated funding deficiency or are expected to have a deficiency in any of the next six plan years, plans certified in the yellow zone are less than 80% funded, and plans certified in the green zone are at least 80% funded. The "FIP/RP Status Pending/Implemented" column indicates whether a financial improvement plan ("FIP") for yellow/orange zone plans, or a rehabilitation plan ("RP") for red zone plans, is either pending or has been implemented. As of December 31, 2015, all plans that have either a FIP or RP requirement have had the respective FIP or RP implemented.

Our collectively-bargained contributions satisfy the requirements of all implemented FIPs and RPs and do not currently require the payment of any surcharges. In addition, minimum contributions outside of the agreed upon contractual rate are not required. For the plans detailed in the following table, the expiration date of the associated collective bargaining agreements is July 31, 2018, with the exception of the Automotive Industries Pension Plan and the IAM National Pension Fund / National Pension Plan which both have a July 31, 2019 expiration date. For all plans detailed in the following table, we provided more than 5% of the total plan contributions from all employers for 2015, 2014 and 2013 (as disclosed in the Form 5500 for each respective plan).

Certain plans have been aggregated in the "all other multiemployer pension plans" line in the following table, as the contributions to each of these individual plans were not material.

Pension Fund	EIN/Pension Plan Number	Pension Protection Act Zone Status		FIP/RP Status Pending / Implemented	(In millions) UPS Contributions and Accruals			Surcharge Imposed
		2015	2014		2015	2014	2013	
Alaska Teamster-Employer Pension Plan	92-6003463-024	Red	Red	Yes/Implemented	$ 5	$ 5	$ 5	No
Automotive Industries Pension Plan	94-1133245-001	Red	Red	Yes/Implemented	4	5	4	No
Central Pennsylvania Teamsters Defined Benefit Plan	23-6262789-001	Green	Green	No	36	33	30	No
Eastern Shore Teamsters Pension Fund	52-0904953-001	Green	Green	No	4	4	4	No
Employer-Teamsters Local Nos. 175 & 505 Pension Trust Fund	55-6021850-001	Red	Red	Yes/Implemented	11	10	9	No
Hagerstown Motor Carriers and Teamsters Pension Fund	52-6045424-001	Red	Red	Yes/Implemented	7	6	5	No
I.A.M. National Pension Fund / National Pension Plan	51-6031295-002	Green	Green	No	29	27	27	No
International Brotherhood of Teamsters Union Local No. 710 Pension Fund	36-2377656-001	Green	Green	No	106	89	88	No
Local 705, International Brotherhood of Teamsters Pension Plan	36-6492502-001	Red	Red	Yes/Implemented	91	69	68	No
Local 804 I.B.T. & Local 447 I.A.M.—UPS Multiemployer Retirement Plan	51-6117726-001	Red	Red	Yes/Implemented	97	92	88	No
Milwaukee Drivers Pension Trust Fund	39-6045229-001	Green	Green	No	35	32	29	No
New England Teamsters & Trucking Industry Pension Fund	04-6372430-001	Red	Red	Yes/Implemented	110	108	102	No
New York State Teamsters Conference Pension and Retirement Fund	16-6063585-074	Red	Red	Yes/Implemented	86	81	72	No
Teamster Pension Fund of Philadelphia and Vicinity	23-1511735-001	Yellow	Yellow	Yes/Implemented	53	50	46	No
Teamsters Joint Council No. 83 of Virginia Pension Fund	54-6097996-001	Yellow	Yellow	Yes/Implemented	57	52	49	No
Teamsters Local 639—Employers Pension Trust	53-0237142-001	Green	Green	No	48	45	41	No
Teamsters Negotiated Pension Plan	43-6196083-001	Green	Yellow	No	30	27	26	No
Truck Drivers and Helpers Local Union No. 355 Retirement Pension Plan	52-6043608-001	Yellow	Yellow	Yes/Implemented	17	16	14	No

(continued)

Pension Fund	EIN/ Pension Plan Number	Pension Protection Act Zone Status		FIP/ RP Status Pending / Implemented	(in millions) UPS Contributions and Accruals			Surcharge Imposed
		2015	2014		2015	2014	2013	
United Parcel Service, Inc.—Local 177, I.B.T. Multiemployer Retirement Plan	13-1426500-419	Red	Red	Yes/Implemented	83	85	68	No
Western Conference of Teamsters Pension Plan	91-6145047-001	Green	Green	No	646	604	553	No
Western Pennsylvania Teamsters and Employers Pension Fund	25-6029946-001	Red	Red	Yes/Implemented	26	24	23	No
All Other Multiemployer Pension Plans					42	53	45	
				Total Contributions	$1,623	$1,517	$1,396	

Agreement with the New England Teamsters and Trucking Industry Pension Fund

In 2012, we reached an agreement with the New England Teamsters and Trucking Industry Pension Fund ("NETTI Fund"), a multiemployer pension plan in which UPS is a participant, to restructure the pension liabilities for approximately 10,200 UPS employees represented by the Teamsters. As of December 31, 2015 and 2014, we had $872 and $878 million, respectively, recognized in "other non-current liabilities" on our consolidated balance sheets representing the remaining balance of the NETTI Fund withdrawal liability. Based on the borrowing rates currently available to the Company for long-term financing of a similar maturity, the fair value of the NETTI Fund withdrawal liability as of December 31, 2015 and 2014 was $841 and $913 million. We utilized Level 2 inputs in the fair value hierarchy of valuation techniques to determine the fair value of this liability.

Multiemployer Health and Welfare Plans

We also contribute to several multiemployer health and welfare plans that cover both active and retired employees. Health care benefits are provided to participants who meet certain eligibility requirements as covered under the applicable collective bargaining unit. The following table sets forth our calendar year plan contributions and accruals. Certain plans have been aggregated in the "all other multiemployer health and welfare plans" line in the table, as the contributions to each of these individual plans are not material.

(In millions) Health and Welfare Fund	UPS Contributions and Accruals		
	2015	2014	2013
Central States, South East & South West Areas Health and Welfare Fund	$2,081	$1,306	$ 505
Teamsters Western Region & Local 177 Health Care Plan	515	239	—
Health & Welfare Insurance Fund Teamsters Local 653	6	5	—
Bay Area Delivery Drivers	34	32	29
Central Pennsylvania Teamsters Health & Pension Fund	23	21	20
Delta Health Systems—East Bay Drayage Drivers	27	24	24
Employer—Teamster Local Nos. 175 & 505	10	9	9
Joint Council #83 Health & Welfare Fund	28	26	24
Local 191 Teamsters Health Fund	11	11	9
Local 401 Teamsters Health & Welfare Fund	7	7	6
Local 804 Welfare Trust Fund	75	70	67
Milwaukee Drivers Pension Trust Fund—Milwaukee Drivers Health and Welfare Trust Fund	34	32	31
Montana Teamster Employers Trust	7	7	6
New York State Teamsters Health & Hospital Fund	53	51	46
North Coast Benefit Trust	8	9	8
Northern California General Teamsters (DELTA)	108	96	84
Northern New England Benefit Trust	42	39	35
Oregon/Teamster Employers Trust	31	29	28
Teamsters 170 Health & Welfare Fund	15	15	12
Teamsters Benefit Trust	36	40	38
Teamsters Local 251 Health & Insurance Plan	13	12	11
Teamsters Local 404 Health & Insurance Plan	7	7	6
Teamsters Local 638 Health Fund	39	35	32
Teamsters Local 639—Employers Health & Pension Trust Funds	26	26	24
Teamsters Local 671 Health Services & Insurance Plan	15	14	13
Teamsters Union 25 Health Services & Insurance Plan	46	44	37
Teamsters Union Local 677 Health Services & Insurance Plan	10	9	8
Truck Drivers and Helpers Local 355 Baltimore Area Health & Welfare Fund	15	15	13
Utah-Idaho Teamsters Security Fund	25	22	18
Washington Teamsters Welfare Trust	44	36	35
All Other Multiemployer Health and Welfare Plans	95	64	44
Total Contributions	$3,486	$2,352	$1,222

The increase in 2015 and 2014 contributions to the Central States, South East & South West Areas Health and Welfare Fund, the Teamsters Western Region & Local 177 Health Care Plan, and the Health & Welfare Insurance Fund Teamsters Local 653 plan are related to the changes to the delivery of active and postretirement healthcare benefits described below.

Changes to the Delivery of Active and Postretirement Healthcare Benefits

Prior to ratification, the NMA Group and Non-NMA Group employees received their healthcare benefits through UPS-sponsored active and postretirement health and welfare benefit plans. Effective June 1, 2014, we ceased providing healthcare benefits to active NMA Group employees through these UPS-sponsored benefit plans, and the responsibility for providing healthcare benefits for active employees was assumed by three separate multiemployer healthcare funds (the "Funds"). The responsibility for providing healthcare benefits for the active Non-NMA Group employees was also assumed by the Funds on various dates up to January 1, 2015, depending on the ratification date of the applicable collective bargaining agreement. We will make contributions to the Funds based on negotiated fixed hourly or monthly contribution rates for the duration of the NMA and other applicable collective bargaining agreements.

Additionally, the Funds assumed the obligation to provide postretirement healthcare benefits to the employees in the NMA Group who retire on or after January 1, 2014. The postretirement healthcare benefit obligation for the employees in the Non-NMA Group was assumed by the Funds for employees retiring on or after January 1, 2014 or January 1, 2015, depending on the applicable collective bargaining agreement. In exchange for the assumption of the obligation to provide postretirement healthcare benefits to the NMA Group and Non-NMA Group, we transferred cash totaling $2.271 billion to the Funds in the second quarter of 2014. UPS-sponsored health and welfare benefit plans retained responsibility for providing postretirement healthcare coverage for employees in the NMA Group who retired from UPS prior to January 1, 2014, and for employees in the Non-NMA Group who retired from UPS prior to the January 1, 2014 or January 1, 2015 effective date in the applicable collective bargaining agreement.

Accounting Impact of Health and Welfare Plan Changes

Income Statement Impact:

We recorded a pre-tax charge of $1.066 billion ($665 million after-tax) in the second quarter of 2014 for the health and welfare plan changes described above. The components of this charge, which was included in "compensation and benefits" expense in the statement of consolidated income, are as follows:
- *Partial Plan Curtailment:* We recorded a $112 million pre-tax curtailment loss due to the elimination of future service benefit accruals. This curtailment loss represents the accelerated recognition of unamortized prior service costs.
- *Remeasurement of Postretirement Obligation:* We recorded a $746 million pre-tax loss due to the remeasurement of the postretirement benefit obligations of the affected UPS-sponsored health and welfare benefit plans.
- *Settlement:* We recorded a $208 million pre-tax settlement loss, which represents the recognition of unamortized actuarial losses associated with the postretirement obligation for the NMA Group.

We recorded an additional pre-tax charge of $36 million ($22 million after-tax) in the fourth quarter of 2014 upon ratification of the collective bargaining agreements covering the Non-NMA Group, related to the remeasurement and settlement of the postretirement benefit obligation associated with those employees.

Balance Sheet and Cash Flow Impact:

During 2014, as part of the health and welfare plan changes described previously, we transferred cash totaling $2.271 billion to the Funds, which was accounted for as a settlement of our postretirement benefit obligations (see note 4). We received approximately $854 million of cash tax benefits (through reduced U.S. Federal and state quarterly income tax payments) in 2014.

For NMA Group employees who retired prior to January 1, 2014 and remained with the UPS-sponsored health and welfare plans, the changes to the contributions, benefits and cost sharing provisions in these plans resulted in an increase in the postretirement benefit obligation and a corresponding decrease in pre-tax AOCI of $13 million upon ratification.

PLAN AMENDMENT

3.52 FLUOR CORPORATION (DEC)
CONSOLIDATED STATEMENT OF EARNINGS (in part)

	Year Ended December 31,		
(In thousands, except per share amounts)	**2015**	**2014**	**2013**
Total Revenue	$18,114,048	$21,531,577	$27,351,573
Total Cost Of Revenue	17,019,352	20,132,544	25,986,382
Other (Income) And Expenses			
Gain related to a partial sale of a subsidiary	(68,162)	—	—
Pension settlement charge	239,896	—	—
Corporate general and administrative expense	168,329	182,711	175,148
Interest expense	44,770	29,681	26,887
Interest income	(16,689)	(18,268)	(14,443)
Total cost and expenses	17,387,496	20,326,668	26,173,974
Earnings From Continuing Operations Before Taxes	726,552	1,204,909	1,177,599

NOTES TO CONSOLIDATED FINANCIAL STATEMENTS (in part)

5. Retirement Benefits (in part)

The company sponsors contributory and non-contributory defined contribution retirement and defined benefit pension plans for eligible employees worldwide. Domestic and international defined contribution retirement plans are available to eligible salaried and craft employees. Contributions to defined contribution retirement plans are based on a percentage of the employee's eligible compensation. The company recognized expense of $146 million, $150 million and $151 million associated with contributions to its defined contribution retirement plans during 2015, 2014 and 2013, respectively. Certain defined benefit pension plans are available to eligible international salaried employees. A defined benefit pension plan was previously available to U.S. salaried and craft employees; however, the U.S. defined benefit pension plan (the "U.S. plan") was terminated on December 31, 2014 (see further discussion below). Contributions to defined benefit pension plans are at least the minimum amounts required by applicable regulations. Benefit payments under these plans are generally based upon length of service and/or a percentage of qualifying compensation.

The company's Board of Directors previously approved amendments to freeze the accrual of future service-related benefits for salaried participants of the U.S. plan as of December 31, 2011 and craft participants of the U.S. plan as of December 31, 2013. During the fourth quarter of 2014, the company's Board of Directors approved an amendment to terminate the U.S. plan effective December 31, 2014. In December 2015, the company settled the remaining obligations associated with the U.S. plan. Plan participants received vested benefits from the plan assets by electing either a lump-sum distribution, roll-over contribution to other defined contribution or individual retirement plans, or an annuity contract with a third-party provider. As a result of the settlement, the company was relieved of any further obligation. During 2015, the company recorded a pension settlement charge of $251 million, of which $11 million was reimbursable and included in "Total cost of revenue" and $240 million was recorded as "Pension settlement charge" in the Consolidated Statement of Earnings. The settlement charge consisted primarily of unrecognized actuarial losses included in AOCI. The settlement of the plan obligations did not have a material impact on the company's cash position.

The company's defined benefit pension plan in the Netherlands was closed to new participants on December 31, 2013. This change did not have a material impact on the pension obligation or the accumulated other comprehensive income balance of the plan. The company previously approved an amendment to freeze the accrual of future service-related benefits for eligible participants of the U.K. pension plan as of April 1, 2011.

Net periodic pension expense for the U.S. and non-U.S. defined benefit pension plans included the following components:

	U.S. Pension Plan Year Ended December 31,			Non-U.S. Pension Plans Year Ended December 31,		
(In thousands)	**2015**	**2014**	**2013**	**2015**	**2014**	**2013**
Service cost	$ 6,800	$ 3,800	$ 6,453	$ 20,517	$ 16,217	$ 15,390
Interest cost	16,116	31,675	29,100	26,511	34,536	32,176
Expected return on assets	(19,711)	(30,105)	(30,975)	(49,066)	(48,077)	(46,420)
Amortization of prior service cost/(credits)	867	750	103	(814)	—	—
Recognized net actuarial loss	9,714	4,435	6,039	7,681	7,738	6,788
Loss on settlement/(gain on curtailment)	250,946	—	(309)	390	—	—
Net periodic pension expense	$264,732	$ 10,555	$ 10,411	$ 5,219	$ 10,414	$ 7,934

Postemployment Benefits

RECOGNITION AND MEASUREMENT

3.53 FASB ASC 712, *Compensation—Nonretirement Postemployment Benefits*, requires that entities providing postemployment benefits to their employees accrue the cost of such benefits. FASB ASC 712 does not require that the amount of other postemployment benefits be disclosed.

PRESENTATION AND DISCLOSURE EXCERPT

POSTEMPLOYMENT BENEFITS

3.54 CATERPILLAR INC. (DEC)
CONSOLIDATED FINANCIAL POSITION (in part)

(Dollars in millions)	2015	2014
Liabilities		
Current liabilities:		
Short-term borrowings:		
Machinery, Energy & Transportation	$ 9	$ 9
Financial Products	6,958	4,699
Accounts payable	5,023	6,515
Accrued expenses	3,116	3,548
Accrued wages, salaries and employee benefits	1,994	2,438
Customer advances	1,146	1,697
Dividends payable	448	424
Other current liabilities	1,730	1,754
Long-term debt due within one year:		
Machinery, Energy & Transportation	517	510
Financial Products	5,362	6,283
Total current liabilities	26,303	27,877
Long-term debt due after one year:		
Machinery, Energy & Transportation	9,004	9,493
Financial Products	16,243	18,291
Liability for postemployment benefits	8,843	8,963
Other liabilities	3,219	3,231
Total liabilities	63,612	67,855

NOTES TO CONSOLIDATED FINANCIAL STATEMENTS (in part)

12. Postemployment Benefit Plans

We provide defined benefit pension plans, defined contribution plans and/or other postretirement benefit plans (retirement health care and life insurance) to employees in many of our locations throughout the world. Our defined benefit pension plans provide a benefit based on years of service and/or the employee's average earnings near retirement. Our defined contribution plans allow employees to contribute a portion of their salary to help save for retirement, and in certain cases, we provide a matching contribution. The benefit obligation related to our non-U.S. defined benefit pension plans are for employees located primarily in Europe, Japan and Brazil. For other postretirement benefits, substantially all of our benefit obligation is for employees located in the United States.

Our U.S. defined benefit pension plans for support and management employees were frozen for certain employees on December 31, 2010, and will freeze for remaining employees on December 31, 2019. On the respective transition dates employees move to a retirement benefit that provides a frozen pension benefit and a 401(k) plan that will include a matching contribution and a new annual employer contribution.

As discussed in Note 26, during 2015 the company offered a voluntary retirement enhancement program to qualifying U.S. employees. This voluntary program impacted employees participating in certain U.S. pension and other postretirement benefit plans and resulted in a curtailment loss of $86 million, recognized in Other operating (income) expenses in Statement 1.

At December 31, 2015, we changed our method for calculating the service and interest cost components of net periodic benefit cost. Historically, these components were determined utilizing a single weighted-average discount rate based on a yield curve used to measure the benefit obligation at the beginning of the period. Beginning in 2016, we have elected to utilize a full yield curve approach in the estimation of the service and interest costs by applying the specific spot rates along the yield curve used in the determination of the benefit obligation to the relevant projected cash flows. We have made this change to provide a more precise measurement of service and interest costs by improving the correlation between the projected cash flows to the corresponding spot rates along the yield curve. This change will have no impact on pension and other postretirement benefit liabilities and will be accounted for prospectively as a change in accounting estimate.

At January 1, 2016, we changed our accounting principle for recognizing actuarial gains and losses and expected return on plan assets for our pension and other postretirement benefit plans to a more preferable policy under U.S. GAAP. Prior to 2016, actuarial gains and losses were recognized as a component of Accumulated other comprehensive income (loss), and were generally amortized into earnings in future periods. Under the new principle, actuarial gains and losses will be immediately recognized through earnings upon the annual remeasurement in the fourth quarter, or on an interim basis as triggering events warrant remeasurement. In addition, we changed our policy for recognizing expected returns on plan assets from a market-related value method (based on a three-year smoothing of asset returns) to a fair value method. We believe that these changes are preferable as they provide greater transparency of our economic obligations in accounting results and better align with the fair value accounting principles by recognizing the effects of economic and interest rate changes on pension and other postretirement benefit assets and liabilities in the year in which the gains and losses are incurred. These changes will be applied retrospectively to prior years.

A. Benefit Obligations

(Millions of dollars)	U.S. Pension Benefits		Non-U.S. Pension Benefits		Other Postretirement Benefits	
	2015	2014	2015	2014	2015	2014
Change in Benefit Obligation:						
Benefit obligation, beginning of year	$16,249	$14,419	$4,801	$4,609	$4,938	$4,784
Service cost	181	157	110	109	101	82
Interest cost	608	648	146	185	181	213
Plan amendments	—	—	—	—	3	(1)
Actuarial losses (gains)	(384)	1,994	(167)	604	(626)	196
Foreign currency exchange rates	—	—	(292)	(436)	(42)	(30)
Participant contributions	—	—	8	9	52	61
Benefits paid—gross	(890)	(963)	(191)	(206)	(345)	(377)
Less: federal subsidy on benefits paid	—	—	—	—	11	14
Curtailments, settlements and termination benefits	28	(6)	(60)	(53)	40	(4)
Acquisitions, divestitures and other	—	—	—	(20)	—	—
Benefit obligation, end of year	$15,792	$16,249	$4,355	$4,801	$4,313	$4,938
Accumulated benefit obligation, end of year	$15,550	$15,701	$4,024	$4,408		
Weighted-Average Assumptions Used to Determine Benefit Obligation:						
Discount rate	4.2%	3.8%	3.2%	3.3%	4.1%	3.9%
Rate of compensation increase	4.0%	4.0%	3.8%	4.0%	4.0%	4.0%

Assumed health care cost trend rates have a significant effect on the amounts reported for the health care plans. A one-percentage-point change in assumed health care cost trend rates would have the following effects:

(Millions of dollars)	One-Percentage-Point Increase	One-Percentage-Point Decrease
Effect on 2015 service and interest cost components of other postretirement benefit cost	$ 37	$ (6)
Effect on accumulated postretirement benefit obligation	$244	$(202)

B. Plan Assets

(Millions of dollars)	U.S. Pension Benefits		Non-U.S. Pension Benefits		Other Postretirement Benefits	
	2015	2014	2015	2014	2015	2014
Change in Plan Assets:						
Fair value of plan assets, beginning of year	$12,530	$12,395	$4,100	$3,949	$ 776	$ 822
Actual return on plan assets	(225)	849	105	507	3	75
Foreign currency exchange rates	—	—	(232)	(352)	—	—
Company contributions	30	255	156	265	164	195
Participant contributions	—	—	8	9	52	61

(continued)

(Millions of dollars)	U.S. Pension Benefits		Non-U.S. Pension Benefits		Other Postretirement Benefits	
	2015	2014	2015	2014	2015	2014
Benefits paid	(890)	(963)	(191)	(206)	(345)	(377)
Settlements and termination benefits	(5)	(6)	(56)	(50)	—	—
Acquisitions, divestitures and other	—	—	—	(22)	—	—
Fair value of plan assets, end of year	$11,440	$12,530	$3,890	$4,100	$ 650	$ 776

In general, our strategy for both the U.S. and non-U.S. pensions includes further aligning our investments to our liabilities, while reducing risk in our portfolio. The current U.S. pension target asset allocations are 45 percent equities and 55 percent fixed income. These target allocations will be revisited periodically to ensure that they reflect our overall objectives. The non-U.S. pension weighted-average target allocations are 41 percent equities, 51 percent fixed income, 5 percent real estate and 3 percent other. The target allocations for each plan vary based upon local statutory requirements, demographics of plan participants and funded status. The non-U.S. plan assets are primarily invested in non-U.S. securities.

Our target allocations for the other postretirement benefit plans are 70 percent equities and 30 percent fixed income.

The U.S. plans are rebalanced to plus or minus 5 percentage points of the target asset allocation ranges on a monthly basis. The frequency of rebalancing for the non-U.S. plans varies depending on the plan. As a result of our diversification strategies, there are no significant concentrations of risk within the portfolio of investments.

The use of certain derivative instruments is permitted where appropriate and necessary for achieving overall investment policy objectives. The plans do not engage in derivative contracts for speculative purposes.

The accounting guidance on fair value measurements specifies a fair value hierarchy based upon the observability of inputs used in valuation techniques (Level 1, 2 and 3). See Note 18 for a discussion of the fair value hierarchy.

Fair values are determined as follows:
• Equity securities are primarily based on valuations for identical instruments in active markets.
• Fixed income securities are primarily based upon models that take into consideration such market-based factors as recent sales, risk-free yield curves and prices of similarly rated bonds.
• Real estate is stated at the fund's net asset value or at appraised value.
• Cash, short-term instruments and other are based on the carrying amount, which approximates fair value, or the fund's net asset value.

The fair value of the pension and other postretirement benefit plan assets by category is summarized below:

(Millions of dollars)	December 31, 2015			
	Level 1	Level 2	Level 3	Total Assets, at Fair Value
U.S. Pension				
Equity securities:				
U.S. equities	$2,976	$ —	$172	$ 3,148
Non-U.S. equities	2,044	5	1	2,050
Fixed income securities:				
U.S. corporate bonds	—	4,004	42	4,046
Non-U.S. corporate bonds	—	575	—	575
U.S. government bonds	—	526	—	526
U.S. governmental agency mortgage-backed securities	—	627	—	627
Non-U.S. government bonds	—	65	—	65
Real estate	—	—	9	9
Cash, short-term instruments and other	157	234	3	394
Total U.S. pension assets	$5,177	$6,036	$227	$11,440

(Millions of dollars)	December 31, 2014			
	Level 1	Level 2	Level 3	Total Assets, at Fair Value
U.S. Pension				
Equity securities:				
U.S. equities	$3,713	$ 1	$161	$ 3,875
Non-U.S. equities	2,291	12	1	2,304
Fixed income securities:				
U.S. corporate bonds	—	3,985	25	4,010
Non-U.S. corporate bonds	—	552	—	552
U.S. government bonds	—	528	—	528
U.S. governmental agency mortgage-backed securities	—	752	2	754
Non-U.S. government bonds	—	62	2	64
Real estate	—	—	9	9
Cash, short-term instruments and other	37	397	—	434
Total U.S. pension assets	$6,041	$6,289	$200	$12,530

(Millions of dollars)	December 31, 2015			
	Level 1	Level 2	Level 3	Total Assets, at Fair Value
Non-U.S. Pension				
Equity securities:				
U.S. equities	$ 426	$ 118	$—	$ 544
Non-U.S. equities	680	152	2	834
Global equities[1]	155	49	—	204
Fixed income securities:				
U.S. corporate bonds	—	135	3	138
Non-U.S. corporate bonds	—	400	2	402
U.S. government bonds	—	64	—	64
Non-U.S. government bonds	—	1,083	—	1,083
Global fixed income[1]	—	341	—	341
Real estate	—	172	—	172
Cash, short-term instruments and other[2]	61	47	—	108
Total non-U.S. pension assets	$1,322	$2,561	$ 7	$3,890

(Millions of dollars)	December 31, 2014			
	Level 1	Level 2	Level 3	Total Assets, at Fair Value
Non-U.S. Pension				
Equity securities:				
U.S. equities	$ 552	$ —	$—	$ 552
Non-U.S. equities	794	250	—	1,044
Global equities[1]	218	52	—	270
Fixed income securities:				
U.S. corporate bonds	—	81	9	90
Non-U.S. corporate bonds	—	503	2	505
U.S. government bonds	—	1	—	1
Non-U.S. government bonds	—	836	—	836
Global fixed income[1]	—	363	—	363
Real estate	—	182	48	230
Cash, short-term instruments and other[2]	159	50	—	209
Total non-U.S. pension assets	$1,723	$2,318	$ 59	$4,100

[1] Includes funds that invest in both U.S. and non-U.S. securities.
[2] Includes funds that invest in multiple asset classes, hedge funds and other.

(Millions of dollars)	December 31, 2015			
	Level 1	Level 2	Level 3	Total Assets, at Fair Value
Other Postretirement Benefits				
Equity securities:				
U.S. equities	$296	$ 1	$—	$297
Non-U.S. equities	136	—	—	136
Fixed income securities:				
U.S. corporate bonds	—	87	—	87
Non-U.S. corporate bonds	—	18	—	18
U.S. government bonds	—	31	—	31
U.S. governmental agency mortgage-backed securities	—	45	—	45
Non-U.S. government bonds	—	4	—	4
Cash, short-term instruments and other	17	15	—	32
Total other postretirement benefit assets	$449	$201	$—	$650

(Millions of dollars)	December 31, 2014			
	Level 1	Level 2	Level 3	Total Assets, at Fair Value
Other Postretirement Benefits				
Equity securities:				
U.S. equities	$392	$ —	$—	$392
Non-U.S. equities	158	1	—	159
Fixed income securities:				
U.S. corporate bonds	—	103	—	103
Non-U.S. corporate bonds	—	17	—	17
U.S. government bonds	—	30	—	30
U.S. governmental agency mortgage-backed securities	—	50	—	50
Non-U.S. government bonds	—	3	—	3
Cash, short-term instruments and other	9	13	—	22
Total other postretirement benefit assets	$559	$217	$—	$776

Below are roll-forwards of assets measured at fair value using Level 3 inputs for the years ended December 31, 2015 and 2014. These instruments were valued using pricing models that, in management's judgment, reflect the assumptions a market participant would use.

(Millions of dollars)	Equities	Fixed Income	Real Estate	Other
U.S. Pension				
Balance at December 31, 2013	$ 129	$ 54	$ 8	$—
Unrealized gains (losses)	1	—	1	—
Realized gains (losses)	19	3	—	—
Purchases, issuances and settlements, net	13	(23)	—	—
Transfers in and/or out of Level 3	—	(5)	—	—
Balance at December 31, 2014	$ 162	$ 29	$ 9	$—
Unrealized gains (losses)	(1)	(1)	—	—
Realized gains (losses)	14	—	—	—
Purchases, issuances and settlements, net	(2)	16	—	2
Transfers in and/or out of Level 3	—	(2)	—	1
Balance at December 31, 2015	$173	$ 42	$ 9	$ 3
Non-U.S. Pension				
Balance at December 31, 2013	$ —	$ 21	$111	$—
Unrealized gains (losses)	—	(1)	(23)	—
Realized gains (losses)	—	—	22	—
Purchases, issuances and settlements, net	—	(1)	(62)	—
Transfers in and/or out of Level 3	—	(8)	—	—
Balance at December 31, 2014	$ —	$ 11	$ 48	$—
Unrealized gains (losses)	—	(1)	(18)	—
Realized gains (losses)	—	—	15	—
Purchases, issuances and settlements, net	—	—	(45)	—
Transfers in and/or out of Level 3	2	(5)	—	—
Balance at December 31, 2015	$ 2	$ 5	$ —	$—

C. Funded Status

The funded status of the plans, reconciled to the amount reported on Statement 3, is as follows:

(Millions of dollars)	U.S. Pension Benefits		Non-U.S. Pension Benefits		Other Postretirement Benefits	
	2015	2014	2015	2014	2015	2014
End of Year						
Fair value of plan assets	$11,440	$12,530	$3,890	$4,100	$ 650	$ 776
Benefit obligations	15,792	16,249	4,355	4,801	4,313	4,938
Over (under) funded status recognized in financial position	$ (4,352)	$ (3,719)	$ (465)	$ (701)	$(3,663)	$(4,162)
Components of Net Amount Recognized in Financial Position:						
Other assets (non-current asset)	$ 6	$ 3	$ 163	$ 144	$ —	$ —
Accrued wages, salaries and employee benefits (current liability)	(32)	(28)	(19)	(24)	(161)	(160)
Liability for postemployment benefits (non-current liability)	(4,326)	(3,694)	(609)	(821)	(3,502)	(4,002)
Net liability recognized	$ (4,352)	$ (3,719)	$ (465)	$ (701)	$(3,663)	$(4,162)
Amounts Recognized in Accumulated Other Comprehensive Income (Pre-Tax) Consist of:						
Net actuarial loss (gain)	$ 6,245	$ 6,034	$1,300	$1,494	$ 171	$ 800
Prior service cost (credit)	1	2	1	9	39	(31)
Total	$ 6,246	$ 6,036	$1,301	$1,503	$ 210	$ 769

In 2016, we elected to make a change in accounting principle related to the recognition of actuarial gains and losses. Actuarial gains and losses will be immediately recognized upon the annual remeasurement in the fourth quarter, or on an interim basis as triggering events warrant remeasurement. Accordingly, there will be no actuarial gains and losses amortized from Accumulated other comprehensive income (loss) into net periodic benefit cost in 2016. This change will be effective in reporting periods after December 31, 2015 and will be applied retrospectively to prior years. The estimated amount of prior service cost (credit) that will be amortized from Accumulated other comprehensive income (loss) at December 31, 2015 into net periodic benefit cost (pre-tax) in 2016 are as follows:

(Millions of dollars)	U.S. Pension Benefits	Non-U.S. Pension Benefits	Other Postretirement Benefits
Prior service cost (credit)	$—	$—	$(30)
Total	$—	$—	$(30)

The following amounts relate to our pension plans with projected benefit obligations in excess of plan assets:

(Millions of dollars)	U.S. Pension Benefits at Year-end		Non-U.S. Pension Benefits at Year-end	
	2015	2014	2015	2014
Projected benefit obligation	$15,734	$16,182	$1,818	$4,539
Accumulated benefit obligation	$15,493	$15,634	$1,657	$4,148
Fair value of plan assets	$11,377	$12,460	$1,190	$3,695

The following amounts relate to our pension plans with accumulated benefit obligations in excess of plan assets:

(Millions of dollars)	U.S. Pension Benefits at Year-end		Non-U.S. Pension Benefits at Year-end	
	2015	2014	2015	2014
Projected benefit obligation	$15,734	$16,182	$1,363	$1,879
Accumulated benefit obligation	$15,493	$15,634	$1,320	$1,734
Fair value of plan assets	$11,377	$12,460	$ 793	$1,068

The accumulated postretirement benefit obligation exceeds plan assets for all of our other postretirement benefit plans for all years presented.

D. Expected Cash Flow

Information about the expected cash flow for the pension and other postretirement benefit plans is as follows:

(Millions of dollars)	U.S. Pension Benefits	Non-U.S. Pension Benefits	Other Postretirement Benefits
Employer Contributions:			
2016 (expected)	$ 30	$ 120	$ 200
Expected Benefit Payments:			
2016	$ 990	$ 220	$ 310
2017	990	170	320
2018	980	170	310
2019	980	170	310
2020	980	170	300
2021–2025	4,890	990	1,480
Total	$9,810	$1,890	$3,030

The above table reflects the total employer contributions and benefits expected to be paid from the plan or from company assets and does not include the participants' share of the cost. The expected benefit payments for our other postretirement benefits include payments for prescription drug benefits. Medicare Part D subsidy amounts expected to be received by the company which will offset other postretirement benefit payments are as follows:

(Millions of dollars)	2016	2017	2018	2019	2020	2021–2025	Total
Other postretirement benefits	$15	$15	$20	$20	$20	$100	$190

E. Net Periodic Cost

(Millions of dollars)	U.S. Pension Benefits			Non-U.S. Pension Benefits			Other Postretirement Benefits		
	2015	2014	2013	2015	2014	2013	2015	2014	2013
Components of Net Periodic Benefit Cost:									
Service cost	$ 181	$ 157	$ 196	$ 110	$ 109	$ 120	$ 101	$ 82	$ 108
Interest cost	608	648	581	146	185	166	181	213	195
Expected return on plan assets[1]	(879)	(885)	(832)	(260)	(258)	(225)	(53)	(52)	(56)
Other adjustments[2]	—	—	31	—	—	—	—	—	(22)
Curtailments, settlements and termination benefits[3]	52	—	—	14	14	2	32	(2)	—
Amortization of:									
Transition obligation (asset)	—	—	—	—	—	—	—	—	2
Prior service cost (credit)[4]	1	17	18	—	—	1	(54)	(55)	(73)
Net actuarial loss (gain)[5]	490	392	546	99	86	128	52	41	107
Total cost included in operating profit	$ 453	$ 329	$ 540	$ 109	$ 136	$ 192	$ 259	$227	$ 261
Other Changes in Plan Assets and Benefit Obligations Recognized in Other Comprehensive Income (pre-tax):									
Current year actuarial loss (gain)	$ 701	$2,030	$(2,344)	$ (95)	$ 207	$(406)	$(577)	$179	$(759)
Amortization of actuarial (loss) gain	(490)	(392)	(546)	(99)	(86)	(128)	(52)	(41)	(107)
Current year prior service cost (credit)	—	—	—	(8)	(4)	(7)	16	(2)	2
Amortization of prior service (cost) credit	(1)	(17)	(18)	—	—	(1)	54	55	73
Amortization of transition (obligation) asset	—	—	—	—	—	—	—	—	(2)
Total recognized in other comprehensive income	210	1,621	(2,908)	(202)	117	(542)	(559)	191	(793)
Total recognized in net periodic cost and other comprehensive income	$ 663	$1,950	$(2,368)	$ (93)	$ 253	$(350)	$(300)	$418	$(532)
Weighted-Average Assumptions Used to Determine Net Cost:									
Discount rate	3.8%	4.6%	3.7%	3.3%	4.1%	3.7%	3.9%	4.6%	3.7%
Expected rate of return on plan assets[6]	7.4%	7.8%	7.8%	6.8%	6.9%	6.8%	7.8%	7.8%	7.8%
Rate of compensation increase	4.0%	4.0%	4.5%	4.0%	4.2%	3.9%	4.0%	4.0%	4.4%

[1] Expected return on plan assets developed using calculated market-related value of plan assets which recognizes differences in expected and actual returns over a three-year period.

[2] Charge to recognize a previously unrecorded liability related to a subsidiary's pension plans and an adjustment to other postretirement benefits related to certain other benefits.

[3] Curtailments, settlements and termination benefits were recognized in Other operating (income) expenses in Statement 1.

[4] Prior service cost (credit) for both pension and other postretirement benefits are generally amortized using the straight-line method over the average remaining service period of active employees expected to receive benefits from the plan. For pension plans in which all or almost all of the plan's participants are inactive and other postretirement benefit plans in which all or almost all of the plan's participants are fully eligible for benefits under the plan, prior service cost (credit) are amortized using the straight-line method over the remaining life expectancy of those participants.

[5] Net actuarial loss (gain) for pension and other postretirement benefit plans are generally amortized using the straight-line method over the average remaining service period of active employees expected to receive benefits from the plan. For plans in which all or almost all of the plan's participants are inactive, net actuarial loss (gain) are amortized using the straight-line method over the remaining life expectancy of the inactive participants.

[6] The weighted-average rates for 2016 are 6.9 percent and 6.1 percent for U.S. and non-U.S. pension plans, respectively.

The assumed discount rate is used to discount future benefit obligations back to today's dollars. The U.S. discount rate is based on a benefit cash flow-matching approach and represents the rate at which our benefit obligations could effectively be settled as of our measurement date, December 31. The benefit cash flow-matching approach involves analyzing Caterpillar's projected cash flows against a high quality bond yield curve, calculated using a wide population of corporate Aa bonds available on the measurement date. The very highest and lowest yielding bonds (top and bottom 10 percent) are excluded from the analysis. A similar process is used to determine the assumed discount rate for our most significant non-U.S. plans. This rate is sensitive to changes in interest rates. A decrease in the discount rate would increase our obligation and future expense.

Our U.S. expected long-term rate of return on plan assets is based on our estimate of long-term passive returns for equities and fixed income securities weighted by the allocation of our pension assets. Based on historical performance, we increase the passive returns due to our active management of the plan assets. To arrive at our expected long-term return, the amount added for active management was 0.95 percent for 2015 and 1 percent for 2014 and 2013. A similar process is used to determine this rate for our non-U.S. plans.

The assumed health care trend rate represents the rate at which health care costs are assumed to increase. We assumed a weighted-average increase of 6.6 percent in our calculation of 2015 benefit expense. We expect a weighted-average increase of 6.5 percent during 2016. The 2016 rates are assumed to decrease gradually to the ultimate health care trend rate of 5 percent in 2021. This rate represents 3 percent general inflation plus 2 percent additional health care inflation.

F. Other Postemployment Benefit Plans

We offer long-term disability benefits, continued health care for disabled employees, survivor income benefit insurance and supplemental unemployment benefits to substantially all U.S. employees.

G. Defined Contribution Plans

We have both U.S. and non-U.S. employee defined contribution plans to help employees save for retirement. Our primary U.S. 401(k) plan allows eligible employees to contribute a portion of their cash compensation to the plan on a tax-deferred basis. Employees with frozen defined benefit pension accruals are eligible for matching contributions equal to 100 percent of employee contributions to the plan up to 6 percent of cash compensation and an annual employer contribution that ranges from 3 to 5 percent of cash compensation (depending on years of service and age). Employees that are still accruing benefits under a defined benefit pension plan are eligible for matching contributions equal to 50 percent of employee contributions up to 6 percent of cash compensation. These 401(k) plans include various investments funds, including a non-leveraged employee stock ownership plan (ESOP). As of December 31, 2015 and 2014 the ESOP held 26.4 million and 26.2 million shares, respectively. All of the shares held by the ESOP were allocated to participant accounts. Dividends paid to participants are automatically reinvested into company shares unless the participant elects to have all or a portion of the dividend paid to the participant. Various other U.S. and non-U.S. defined contribution plans allow eligible employees to contribute a portion of their salary to the plans, and in some cases, we provide a matching contribution to the funds.

Total company costs related to U.S. and non-U.S. defined contribution plans were as follows:

(Millions of dollars)	2015	2014	2013
U.S. plans	$267	$301	$308
Non-U.S. plans	76	85	64
	$343	$386	$372

H. Summary of Long-Term Liability:

	December 31,	
(Millions of dollars)	2015	2014
Pensions:		
U.S. pensions	$4,326	$3,694
Non-U.S. pensions	609	821
Total pensions	4,935	4,515
Postretirement benefits other than pensions	3,502	4,002
Other postemployment benefits	104	112
Defined contribution	302	334
	$8,843	$8,963

Employee Compensatory Plans

RECOGNITION AND MEASUREMENT

3.55 FASB ASC 718, *Compensation—Stock Compensation*, establishes accounting and reporting standards for share-based payment transactions with employees, including awards classified as equity, awards classified as liabilities, employee stock ownership plans, and employee stock purchase plans. FASB ASC 718 requires that share-based payment transactions be accounted for using a fair value based method. Thus, entities are required to recognize the cost of employee services received in exchange for award of equity instruments based on the grant-date fair value of those awards or the fair value of the liabilities incurred. FASB ASC 718 provides clarification and expanded guidance in several areas, including measuring fair value, classifying an award as equity or a liability, and attributing compensation cost to reporting periods.

PRESENTATION AND DISCLOSURE EXCERPTS

STOCK OPTION PLANS

3.56 NATIONAL OILWELL VARCO, INC. (DEC)
NOTES TO CONSOLIDATED FINANCIAL STATEMENTS (in part)

2. Summary of Significant Accounting Policies (in part)

Stock-Based Compensation

Compensation expense for the Company's stock-based compensation plans is measured using the fair value method required by ASC Topic 718 "Compensation—Stock Compensation" ("ASC Topic 718"). Under this guidance the fair value of stock option grants and restricted stock is amortized to expense using the straight-line method over the shorter of the vesting period or the remaining employee service period.

The Company provides compensation benefits to employees and non-employee directors under share-based payment arrangements, including various employee stock option plans.

13. Common Stock (in part)

Stock Options

Under the terms of National Oilwell Varco's Long-Term Incentive Plan, as amended, 39.5 million shares of common stock are authorized for the grant of options to officers, key employees, non-employee directors and other persons. Options granted under our stock option plan generally vest over a three-year period starting one year from the date of grant and expire ten years from the date of grant. The purchase price of options granted may not be less than the closing market price of National Oilwell Varco common stock on the date of grant. At December 31, 2015, approximately 6.2 million shares were available for future grants.

We also have inactive stock option plans that were acquired in connection with the acquisitions of Varco International, Inc. in 2005 and Grant Prideco in 2008. We converted the outstanding stock options under these plans to options to acquire our common stock and no further options are being issued under these plans. Stock option information summarized below includes amounts for the National Oilwell Varco Long-Term Incentive Plan and stock plans of acquired companies. Options outstanding at December 31, 2015 under the stock option plans have exercise prices between $12.15 and $77.99 per share, and expire at various dates from January 13, 2016 to February 26, 2025.

On June 2, 2014, as a result of the spin-off and pursuant to the terms of the Employee Matters Agreement and the Plan, outstanding NOV stock-based awards held by continuing NOV employees were adjusted to generally preserve the intrinsic value of the original award. Outstanding NOV stock-based awards held by employees of NOW were converted into similar NOW stock-based awards, each appropriately adjusted to generally preserve the intrinsic value of the original award. Adjustments to the awards are reflected in the following tables and did not have a material impact to compensation expense.

The following summarizes options activity:

| | Years Ended December 31, | | | | | |
| | 2015 | | 2014 | | 2013 | |
	Number of Shares	Average Exercise Price	Number of Shares	Average Exercise Price	Number of Shares	Average Exercise Price
Shares under option at beginning of year	10,881,133	$61.22	11,535,566	$58.36	10,274,477	$54.11
Granted	5,746,153	54.74	3,389,547	69.00	3,072,086	63.96
Spun-off	—	—	(1,567,348)	70.56	—	—
Cancelled	(886,356)	62.73	(498,967)	70.32	(329,002)	66.78
Exercised	(310,623)	22.56	(1,977,665)	53.56	(1,481,995)	38.75
Shares under option at end of year	15,430,307	$59.50	10,881,133	$61.22	11,535,566	$58.36
Exercisable at end of year	7,498,414	$60.30	5,903,712	$55.06	6,324,117	$49.29

The following summarizes information about stock options outstanding at December 31, 2015:

| Range of Exercise Price | Weighted-Avg Remaining Contractual Life | Options Outstanding | | Options Exercisable | |
		Shares	Weighted-Avg Exercise Price	Shares	Weighted-Avg Exercise Price
$12.15–$55.00	7.34	7,599,928	$48.99	2,148,275	$34.39
$55.01–$70.00	7.25	5,045,298	66.22	2,569,643	64.98
$70.01–$77.99	5.68	2,785,081	76.00	2,780,496	76.00
Total	7.01	15,430,307	$59.50	7,498,414	$60.30

The weighted-average fair value of options granted during 2015, 2014 and 2013, was approximately $15.41, $25.60 and $24.11 per share, respectively, as determined using the Black-Scholes option-pricing model. The total intrinsic value of options exercised during 2015 and 2014, was $9 million and $111 million, respectively.

The determination of fair value of share-based payment awards on the date of grant using an option-pricing model is affected by our stock price as well as assumptions regarding a number of highly complex and subjective variables. These variables include, but are not limited to, the expected stock price volatility over the term of the awards, and actual and projected employee stock option exercise activity. The use of the Black Scholes model requires the use of extensive actual employee exercise activity data and the use of a number of complex assumptions including expected volatility, risk-free interest rate, expected dividends and expected term.

| | Years Ended December 31, | | |
	2015	2014	2013
Valuation Assumptions:			
Expected volatility	49.1%	49.4%	50.1%
Risk-free interest rate	1.5%	1.5%	0.9%
Expected dividends	$3.36	$1.39	$0.75
Expected term (in years)	3.0	3.7	3.4

The Company used the actual volatility for traded options for the past 10 years prior to option date as the expected volatility assumption required in the Black Scholes model.

The risk-free interest rate assumption is based upon observed interest rates appropriate for the term of our employee stock options. The dividend yield assumption is based on the history and expectation of dividend payouts. The estimated expected term is based on actual employee exercise activity for the past ten years.

As stock-based compensation expense recognized in the Consolidated Statement of Income in 2015 is based on awards ultimately expected to vest, it has been reduced for estimated forfeitures. ASC Topic 718 requires forfeitures to be estimated at the time of grant and revised, if necessary, in subsequent periods if actual forfeitures differ from those estimates. Forfeitures were estimated based on historical experience.

The following summary presents information regarding outstanding options at December 31, 2015 and changes during 2015 with regard to options under all stock option plans:

	Shares	Weighted-Average Exercise Price	Weighted Average Remaining Contractual Term (Years)	Aggregate Intrinsic Value
Outstanding at December 31, 2014	10,881,133	$61.22	5.15	$85,503,217
Granted	5,746,153	$54.74		
Cancelled	(886,356)	$62.73		
Exercised	(310,623)	$22.56		
Outstanding at December 31, 2015	15,430,307	$59.50	7.01	$ 5,894,977
Vested or expected to vest	15,229,713	$59.50	7.01	$ 5,814,216
Exercisable at December 31, 2015	7,498,414	$60.30	5.16	$ 5,894,977

At December 31, 2015, total unrecognized compensation cost related to nonvested stock options was $95 million. This cost is expected to be recognized over a weighted-average period of two years. The total fair value of stock options vested in 2015, 2014 and 2013 was approximately $72 million, $67 million and $64 million, respectively. Cash received from option exercises for 2015, 2014 and 2013 was $7 million, $108 million and $58 million, respectively. The actual tax benefit realized for the tax deductions from option exercises totaled $7 million, $44 million and $39 million for 2015, 2014 and 2013, respectively. Cash used to settle equity instruments granted under all share-based payment arrangements for 2015, 2014 and 2013 was not material for any period.

STOCK AWARD PLANS

3.57 LOUISIANA-PACIFIC CORPORATION (DEC)
CONSOLIDATED STATEMENTS OF STOCKHOLDERS' EQUITY

Dollar and share amounts in millions, except per share amounts

	Common Stock		Treasury Stock		Additional Paid-In Capital	Retained Earnings	Accumulated Comprehensive Loss	Total Stockholders' Equity
	Shares	Amount	Shares	Amount				
Balance as of December 31, 2012	150.4	$150.4	11.9	$(252.9)	$533.6	$710.6	$(107.9)	$1,033.8
Net income (loss)						177.1		177.1
Issuance of shares for employee stock plans and stock-based compensation			(1.0)	20.7	(32.7)			(12.0)
Amortization of restricted stock grants					8.4			8.4
Exercise of stock warrants	1.6	1.6			(1.6)			—
Tax benefit of employee stock plan transactions					0.3			0.3
Other comprehensive gain							18.7	18.7
Balance as of December 31, 2013	152.0	152.0	10.9	(232.2)	508.0	887.7	(89.2)	1,226.3
Net income (loss)						(75.4)		(75.4)
Issuance of shares for employee stock plans and stock-based compensation			(0.4)	8.8	(9.5)			(0.7)
Amortization of restricted stock grants					2.1			2.1
Exercise of stock warrants	0.8	0.8			(0.8)			—
Compensation expense associated with stock awards					7.2			7.2
Taxes paid related to net settlements			0.1	(1.6)				(1.6)
Other comprehensive loss							(42.1)	(42.1)
Balance as of December 31, 2014	152.8	152.8	10.6	(225.0)	507.0	812.3	(131.3)	1,115.8
Net income (loss)						(88.1)		(88.1)
Issuance of shares for employee stock plans and stock-based compensation			(1.0)	20.5	(19.6)			0.9
Amortization of restricted stock grants					1.8			1.8
Exercise of stock warrants	0.2	0.2			(0.2)			—
Compensation expense associated with stock awards					7.5			7.5
Taxes paid related to net share settlement of equity awards			0.4	(6.1)	—			(6.1)
Other comprehensive loss							(14.8)	(14.8)
Balance as of December 31, 2015	153.0	$153.0	10.0	$(210.6)	$496.5	$724.2	$(146.1)	$1,017.0

1. Summary of Significant Accounting Policies (in part)

Stock-Based Compensation

LP recognizes the cost of employee services received in exchange for awards of equity instruments, such as stock options, performance shares, restricted stock or restricted stock units and stock settled stock appreciation rights (SSAR), based upon the fair value of those awards at the date of grant over the requisite service period. LP generally uses the Black-Scholes-Merton (Black-Scholes) option pricing model to determine the fair value of the SSAR awards. Stock-based compensation plans, related expenses and assumptions used in the Black-Scholes option pricing model are more fully described in Note 15. The fair market value of performance share awards are determined based on the fair value as of the date of grant times the number of shares adjusted for the weighted probability of the attainment of the relevant performance goals.

15. Stockholders' Equity (in part)

Common Stock Plan

LP has a stock-based compensation plan under which stock option, SSARs, incentive shares, restricted stock and performance shares awards are granted. At December 31, 2015, 4.2 million shares were available under the current plan for these awards. In 2015, 2014 and 2013, LP recognized compensation expense related to these awards of $9.3 million, $9.4 million and $8.8 million. LP received cash from stock option exercises of $0.7 million for the year ended December 31, 2015. LP paid $6.1 million, $1.5 million and $12.1 million associated with taxes related to the net share settlement of equity awards for the years ended December 31, 2015, 2014 and 2013.

LP recognizes these compensation costs, net of an estimated forfeiture rate and recognizes the compensation costs for only those shares expected to vest on a straight-line basis over the requisite service period of the award, which is generally the vesting term of three years. LP estimated the forfeiture rate for 2015, 2014 and 2013 based on its historical experience during the preceding three years.

Stock Settled Stock Appreciation Rights

LP grants SSARs to key employees. On exercise, LP generally issues these shares from treasury. The SSARs are granted at market price at the date of grant. SSARs become exercisable over three years and expire ten years after the date of grant. Prior to 2013, LP granted stock options to its Board of Directors. These options vested over a three year period. As of December 31, 2015, there were 0.2 million options outstanding. The following table sets out the weighted average assumptions used to estimate the fair value of the SSARs granted using the Black-Scholes option-pricing model:

	2015	2014	2013
Expected stock price volatility	54%	57%	69%
Expected dividend yield	—%	—%	—%
Risk-free interest rate	1.5%	1.5%	0.9%
Expected life of options (in years)	6.0 years	5.0 years	5.0 years
Weighted average fair value of options and SSARs granted	$8.80	$9.03	$11.68

Expected Stock Price Volatility: The fair values of stock-based payments were valued using the Black-Scholes valuation method with a volatility factor based on LP's historical stock prices.

Expected Dividend Yield: The Black-Scholes valuation model calls for a single expected dividend yield as an input. This is determined based upon current annual dividend as of the date of grant compared to the grant price.

Risk-Free Interest Rate: LP bases the risk-free interest rate used in the Black-Scholes valuation method on U.S. Treasury issues with an equivalent term. Where the expected term of LP's stock-based awards do not correspond with the terms for which interest rates are quoted, LP performed a straight-line interpolation to determine the rate from the available maturities.

Expected Life of SSARS: Expected life represents the period that LP's stock-based awards are expected to be outstanding and was determined based on historical experience of similar awards, giving consideration to the contractual terms of the stock-based awards, vesting schedules and expectations of future employee behavior as influenced by changes to the terms of its stock-based awards.

Estimated Pre-vesting Forfeitures: When estimating forfeitures, LP considers voluntary termination behavior as well as workforce reduction programs.

The following table summarizes stock options and SSARs outstanding as of December 31, 2015 as well as activity during the three year period then ended.

Share amounts in thousands	Options/ SSARs	Weighted Average Exercise Price	Weighted Average Contractual Term (In years)	Aggregate Intrinsic Value (In millions)
Options/SSARS outstanding at January 1, 2013	8,475	$12.88		
Options granted	343	$20.49		
Options/SSARS exercised	(1,861)	$ 9.06		
Options/SSARS canceled	(20)	$22.23		
Options/SSARS outstanding at December 31, 2013	6,937	$14.26		
Options granted	494	$18.09		
Options/SSARS exercised	(43)	$ 9.92		
Options/SSARS canceled	(384)	$21.14		
Options/SSARS outstanding at December 31, 2014	7,004	$14.19		
Options granted	378	$17.04		
Options/SSARS exercised	(1,334)	$10.76		
Options/SSARS canceled	(309)	$25.83		
Options/SSARS outstanding at December 31, 2015	5,739	$14.54	4.2	$29.8
Vested and expected to vest at December 31, 2015[1]	5,714	$14.54	4.2	$29.8
Options/SSARS exercisable at December 31, 2015	4,987	$14.04	3.6	$29.5

[1] Options or SSARS expected to vest based upon historical forfeiture rate

The aggregate intrinsic value in the table above represents the total pre-tax intrinsic value (the difference between LP's closing stock price on the last trading day of 2015 and the exercise price, multiplied by the number of in-the-money options and SSARs) that would have been received by the holders had all holders exercised their awards on December 31, 2015. This amount changes based on the market value of LP's stock as reported by the New York Stock Exchange.

As of December 31, 2015, there was $3.7 million of total unrecognized compensation costs related to stock options and SSARs. These costs are expected to be recognized over a weighted-average period of 1.27 years. LP recognized $3.6 million, $3.8 million and 3.4 million in compensation expense associated with these awards for the years ended December 31, 2015, 2014 and 2013 .

Incentive Share Awards

LP has granted incentive share stock awards (restricted stock units) to certain key employees and directors. The awards entitle the participant to receive a specified number of shares of LP common stock at no cost to the participant. Awards granted under this plan vest three years from the date of grant. The market value of these grants approximates the fair value. LP recorded compensation expense related to these awards in 2015, 2014 and 2013 of $3.5 million, $3.0 million and $2.7 million. As of December 31, 2015, there was $4.2 million of total unrecognized compensation cost related to unvested incentive share awards. This expense will be recognized over a weighted-average period of 1.2 years.

The following table summarizes incentive share awards outstanding as of December 31, 2015 as well as activity during the three-year period then ended.

	Shares	Weighted Average Contractual Term (In years)	Aggregate Intrinsic Value (In millions)
Incentive share awards outstanding at January 1, 2013	960,388		
Incentive shares awards granted	166,474		
Incentive share awards vested	(350,107)		
Incentive share awards canceled	(24,160)		
Incentive share awards outstanding at December 31, 2013	752,595		
Incentive shares awards granted	123,982		
Incentive share awards vested	(253,834)		
Incentive share awards canceled	(29,130)		
Incentive share awards outstanding at December 31, 2014	593,613		
Incentive shares awards granted	252,629		
Incentive share awards vested	(285,495)		
Incentive share awards canceled	(24,765)		
Incentive share awards outstanding at December 31, 2015	535,982	1.3	$9.7
Vested and expected to vest at December 31, 2015[1]	503,552	1.3	$9.1
Incentive share awards exercisable at December 31, 2015	—	—	—

[1] Incentive shares expected to vest based upon historical forfeitures rate

Restricted Stock

LP grants restricted stock to certain senior executive employees. The shares vest three years from the date of grant. During the vesting period, the participants have voting rights and receive dividends, but the shares may not be sold, assigned, transferred, pledged or otherwise encumbered. Additionally, granted but unvested shares are forfeited upon termination of employment. The fair value of the restricted shares on the date of the grant is amortized ratably over the vesting period which is generally three years. As of December 31, 2015, there was $1.7 million of total unrecognized compensation costs related to restricted stock. This expense will be recognized over the next 1.2 years.

The following table summarizes restricted stock awards outstanding as of December 31, 2015 as well as activity during the three year period then ended.

	Number of Shares	Weighted Average Grant Date Fair Value
Restricted stock awards outstanding at January 1, 2013	625,049	$ 8.46
Restricted stock awards granted	108,174	20.49
Restrictions lapsing	(221,138)	7.37
Restricted stock awards canceled	—	—
Restricted stock awards at December 31, 2013	512,085	11.48
Restricted stock awards granted	122,649	17.93
Restrictions lapsing	(170,567)	9.54
Restricted stock awards canceled	(11,021)	12.35
Restricted stock awards at December 31, 2014	453,146	13.93
Restricted stock awards granted	69,744	17.04
Restrictions lapsing	(225,645)	8.71
Restricted stock awards canceled	(14,544)	19.29
Restricted stock awards at December 31, 2015	282,701	$18.59

LP recorded compensation expense related to these awards in 2015, 2014 and 2013 of $1.7 million, $2.1 million, and $2.1 million.

Performance Share Awards

In connection with Mr. Stevens' appointment to Chief Executive Officer on May 4, 2012, he was awarded 300,000 performance shares. This award was granted pursuant to the terms of LP's 1997 Incentive Stock Award Plan. If pre-determined market-based performance goals are met, shares of LP's stock will be issued to Mr. Stevens based upon a pre-determined vesting schedule based upon the required service periods. The fair market value of this award was determined based on the fair value as of the date of grant times the number of shares adjusted for the weighted probability of the attainment of certain performance goals. LP recorded compensation expense related to these awards of $0.4 million in 2015. As of December 31, 2015, the performance target for 200,000 performance shares was met. As of December 31, 2015, there was $0.1 million of total unrecognized compensation expense related to this award. This expense will be recognized over the next 0.4 years.

In 2015, LP awarded performance shares to certain senior key employees. These performance shares are earned based upon LP attaining specified revenue growth rates associated with its SmartSide products as compared to the prior year and LP's overall revenue growth as compared to a predetermined peer group, in each case for 2015. The performance period is measured over 2015 with a subsequent two year vesting period. The Company issued 78,182 restricted stock units during 2015 with an aggregate value of $1.7 million. As of December 31, 2015, the Company deemed it improbable that the specified performance metrics would be achieved sufficient to earn any portion of the performance-based restricted stock units. As a result, $0.5 million of previously recorded stock-based compensation expense related to these performance-based restricted stock units was reversed.

SAVINGS AND INVESTMENT PLANS

3.58 POLARIS INDUSTRIES INC. (DEC)
NOTES TO CONSOLIDATED FINANCIAL STATEMENTS (in part)

Note 3. Employee Savings Plans

Employee Stock Ownership Plan (ESOP). Polaris sponsors a qualified non-leveraged ESOP under which a maximum of 7,200,000 shares of common stock can be awarded. The shares are allocated to eligible participants accounts based on total cash compensation earned during the calendar year. An employee's ESOP account vests equally after two and three years of service and requires no cash payments from the recipient. Participants may instruct Polaris to pay respective dividends directly to the participant in cash or reinvest the dividends into the participants ESOP accounts. Substantially all employees are eligible to participate in the ESOP, with the exception of Company officers.

Total expense related to the ESOP was $7,455,000, $10,789,000 and $9,224,000, in 2015, 2014 and 2013, respectively. As of December 31, 2015 there were 3,847,000 shares held in the plan.

Defined contribution plans. Polaris sponsors various defined contribution retirement plans covering substantially all U.S. employees. For the 401(k) defined contribution retirement plan which covers the majority of U.S. employees, the Company matches 100 percent of employee contributions up to a maximum of five percent of eligible compensation. All contributions vest immediately. The cost of these defined contribution retirement plans was $14,178,000, $12,486,000, and $10,651,000, in 2015, 2014 and 2013, respectively.

Supplemental Executive Retirement Plan (SERP). Polaris sponsors a SERP that provides executive officers of the Company an alternative to defer portions of their salary, cash incentive compensation, and Polaris matching contributions. The deferrals and contributions are held in a rabbi trust and are in funds to match the liabilities of the plan. The assets are recorded as trading assets. The assets of the rabbi trust are included in other long-term assets on the consolidated balance sheets and the SERP liability is included in other long-term liabilities on the consolidated balance sheets. The asset and liability balance are both $48,238,000 and $41,797,000 at December 31, 2015, and 2014, respectively.

In November 2013, Polaris amended the SERP to allow executive officers of the Company the opportunity to defer certain restricted stock awards beginning with the annual performance-based award, which vested on February 14, 2015. After a holding period, the executive officer has the option to diversify the vested award into other funds available under the SERP. The deferrals are held in a rabbi trust and are invested in funds to match the liabilities of the SERP. The awards are redeemable in Polaris stock or in cash based upon the occurrence of events not solely within the control of Polaris; therefore, awards probable of vesting, for which the executive has not yet made an election to defer, or awards that have been deferred but have not yet vested and are probable of vesting or have been diversified into other funds are reported as deferred compensation in the temporary equity section of the consolidated balance sheets. The awards recorded in temporary equity are recognized at fair value as though the reporting date is also the redemption date, with any difference from stock-based compensation recorded in retained earnings. At December 31, 2015, 112,215 shares are recorded at a fair value of $9,645,000 in temporary equity, which includes $10,372,000 of compensation cost and $(727,000) of cumulative fair value adjustment recorded through retained earnings.

EMPLOYEE STOCK PURCHASE PLANS (ESPP)

3.59 AIRGAS, INC. (MAR)
NOTES TO CONSOLIDATED FINANCIAL STATEMENTS (in part)

(1) Summary of Significant Accounting Policies (in part)

(v) Stock-Based Compensation

The Company grants stock-based compensation awards in connection with its equity incentive and employee stock purchase plans. Stock-based compensation expense is generally recognized on a straight-line basis over the stated vesting period for each award, with accelerated vesting for retirement-eligible employees in accordance with the provisions of the equity incentive plan. See Note 13 for additional disclosures relating to stock-based compensation.

(13) Stock-Based Compensation (in part)

The Company recognizes stock-based compensation expense for its equity incentive plan and Employee Stock Purchase Plan. The following table summarizes stock-based compensation expense recognized by the Company in each of the years in the three-year period ended March 31, 2015

	Years Ended March 31,		
(In thousands)	2015	2014	2013
Stock-Based Compensation Expense Related to:			
Equity Incentive Plan	$ 25,935	$ 24,892	$ 22,969
Employee Stock Purchase Plan—options to purchase stock	4,092	4,069	4,084
	30,027	28,961	27,053
Tax benefit	(10,624)	(10,392)	(9,338)
Stock-based compensation expense, net of tax	$ 19,403	$ 18,569	$ 17,715

Employee Stock Purchase Plan

The Company's Employee Stock Purchase Plan (the "ESPP") encourages and assists employees in acquiring an equity interest in the Company. As of March 31, 2015, the ESPP was authorized to issue up to 5.5 million shares of Company common stock, of which 1.1 million shares were available for issuance at March 31, 2015, 54,114 shares of which were issued on April 1, 2015.

Under the terms of the ESPP, eligible employees may elect to have up to 15% of their annual gross earnings withheld to purchase common stock at 85% of the market value. Employee purchases are limited in any calendar year to an aggregate market value of $25 thousand. Market value under the ESPP is defined as either the closing share price on the New York Stock Exchange as of an employee's enrollment date or the closing price on the first business day of a fiscal quarter when the shares are purchased, whichever is lower. An employee may lock-in a purchase price for up to 12 months. The ESPP effectively resets at the beginning of each fiscal year at which time employees are re-enrolled in the plan and a new 12 -month purchase price is established. The ESPP is designed to comply with the requirements of Sections 421 and 423 of the Internal Revenue Code.

Fair Value

Compensation expense is measured based on the fair value of the employees' option to purchase shares of common stock at the grant date and is recognized over the future periods in which the related employee service is rendered. The fair value per share of employee options to purchase shares under the ESPP was $20.44, $19.27 and $16.73 for the years ended March 31, 2015, 2014 and 2013, respectively. The fair value of the employees' option to purchase shares of common stock was estimated using the Black-Scholes model. The following assumptions were used by the Company in valuing the employees' option to purchase shares of common stock under the ESPP:

	Fiscal 2015	Fiscal 2014	Fiscal 2013
Expected volatility	17.1%	19.5%	23.2%
Expected dividend yield	2.07%	1.96%	2.19%
Expected term	3 to 9 months	3 to 9 months	3 to 6 months
Risk-free interest rate	0.06%	0.08%	0.10%

ESPP—Purchase Option Activity

The following table summarizes the activity of the ESPP during the three years ended March 31, 2015:

	Number of Purchase Options	Weighted- Average Exercise Price	Aggregate Intrinsic Value (In thousands)
Outstanding at March 31, 2012	79,208	$51.61	
Granted	244,122	$70.74	
Exercised	(261,193)	$65.42	
Outstanding at March 31, 2013	62,137	$68.74	$1,890
Granted	211,093	$82.88	
Exercised	(218,109)	$79.38	
Outstanding at March 31, 2014	55,121	$80.77	$1,419
Granted	200,030	$90.82	
Exercised	(201,037)	$89.24	
Outstanding at March 31, 2015	54,114	$86.47	$1,063

DEFERRED COMPENSATION PLANS

3.60 MORGAN STANLEY (DEC)
NOTES TO CONSOLIDATED FINANCIAL STATEMENTS (in part)

18. Deferred Compensation Plans

The Company maintains various deferred compensation plans for the benefit of certain current and former employees. The two principal forms of deferred compensation are granted under several stock-based compensation and cash-based compensation plans.

Stock-Based Compensation Plans.

Stock-Based Compensation Expense.

The components of the Company's stock-based compensation expense (net of cancellations) are presented below:

(Dollars in millions)	2015	2014	2013
Restricted stock units[1]	$1,080	$1,212	$1,140
Stock options	(3)	5	15
Performance-based stock units	26	45	29
Total	$1,103	$1,262	$1,184

[1] Amounts for 2015, 2014 and 2013 include $68 million, $31 million and $25 million, respectively, related to stock-based awards that were granted in 2016, 2015 and 2014, respectively, to employees who satisfied retirement-eligible requirements under award terms that do not contain a service period.

The tax benefit related to stock-based compensation expense was $369 million, $404 million and $371 million for 2015, 2014 and 2013, respectively.

At December 31, 2015, the Company had $720 million of unrecognized compensation cost related to unvested stock-based awards. Absent estimated or actual forfeitures or cancellations, this amount of unrecognized compensation cost will be recognized as $448 million in 2016, $228 million in 2017 and $44 million thereafter. These amounts do not include 2015 performance year awards granted in January 2016, which will begin to be amortized in 2016 (see "2015 Performance Year Deferred Compensation Awards" herein).

In connection with awards under its stock-based compensation plans, the Company is authorized to issue shares of its common stock held in treasury or newly issued shares. At December 31, 2015, approximately 96 million shares were available for future grants under these plans.

The Company generally uses treasury shares, if available, to deliver shares to employees and has an ongoing repurchase authorization that includes repurchases in connection with awards granted under its stock-based compensation plans. Share repurchases by the Company are subject to regulatory approval. See Note 15 for additional information on the Company's share repurchase program.

Restricted Stock Units.

RSUs are generally subject to vesting over time, generally one to three years from the date of grant, contingent upon continued employment and to restrictions on sale, transfer or assignment until conversion to common stock. All or a portion of an award may be canceled if employment is terminated before the end of the relevant vesting period, and after the relevant vesting period in certain situations. Recipients of RSUs may have voting rights, at the Company's discretion, and generally receive dividend equivalents.

Vested and Unvested RSU Activity.

	2015	
	Number of Shares (Shares in millions)	Weighted Average Grant Date Fair Value
RSUs at beginning of period	121	$25.52
Granted	34	34.76
Conversions to common stock	(47)	23.57
Canceled	(3)	28.72
RSUs at end of period[1]	105	29.26

[1] At December 31, 2015, approximately 98 million RSUs with a weighted average grant date fair value of $29.17 were vested or expected to vest.

The weighted average grant date fair value for RSUs granted during 2014 and 2013 was $32.58 and $22.72, respectively. At December 31, 2015, the weighted average remaining term until delivery for the Company's outstanding RSUs was approximately 1.1 years.

At December 31, 2015, the intrinsic value of RSUs vested or expected to vest was $3,144 million.

The total intrinsic value of RSUs converted to common stock during 2015, 2014 and 2013 was $1,646 million, $1,461 million and $939 million, respectively.

Unvested RSU Activity.

	2015	
	Number of Shares (Shares in millions)	Weighted Average Grant Date Fair Value
Unvested RSUs at beginning of period	87	$26.44
Granted	34	34.76
Vested	(48)	27.06
Canceled	(3)	28.72
Unvested RSUs at end of period[1]	70	29.91

[1] Unvested RSUs represent awards where recipients have yet to satisfy either the explicit vesting terms or retirement-eligible requirements. At December 31, 2015, approximately 63 million unvested RSUs with a weighted average grant date fair value of $29.84 were expected to vest.

The aggregate fair value of awards that vested during 2015, 2014 and 2013 was $1,693 million, $1,517 million and $842 million, respectively.

Stock Options.

Stock options generally have an exercise price not less than the fair value of the Company's common stock on the date of grant, vest and become exercisable over a three-year period and expire five to 10 years from the date of grant, subject to accelerated expiration upon certain terminations of employment. Stock options have vesting, restriction and cancellation provisions that are generally similar to those of RSUs. The weighted average fair value of the Company's stock options granted during 2013 was $5.41, utilizing the following weighted average assumptions.

Weighted Average Assumptions.

Grant Year	Risk-Free Interest Rate	Expected Life	Expected Stock Price Volatility	Expected Dividend Yield
2013	0.6%	3.9 years	32.0%	0.9%

No stock options were granted during 2015 or 2014.

The Company's expected option life has been determined based upon historical experience. The expected stock price volatility assumption was determined using the implied volatility of exchange-traded options, in accordance with accounting guidance for share-based payments. The risk-free interest rate was determined based on the yields available on U.S. Treasury zero-coupon issues.

Stock Option Activity.

	2015	
	Number of Options (Options in millions)	Weighted Average Exercise Price
Options outstanding at beginning of period	19	$51.30
Expired	(2)	45.32
Options outstanding at end of period[1]	17	52.26
Options exercisable at end of period	15	55.02

[1] At December 31, 2015, approximately 16 million options with a weighted average exercise price of $52.43 were vested.

The aggregate intrinsic value of stock options exercised in 2015 and 2014 was $2 million per year, with a weighted average exercise price of $30.01 and $24.68 for 2015 and 2014, respectively. No stock options were exercised during 2013. At December 31, 2015, the intrinsic value of in the money exercisable stock options was $28 million.

Stock Options Outstanding and Exercisable.

	At December 31, 2015					
	Options Outstanding			Options Exercisable		
Range of Exercise Prices	Number Outstanding	Weighted Average Exercise Price	Average Remaining Life (Years)	Number Exercisable	Weighted Average Exercise Price	Average Remaining Life (Years)
			(Options in millions)			
$22.00–$39.99	6	$26.85	2.0	4	$28.13	2.0
$50.00–$59.99	1	52.43	0.3	1	52.43	0.3
$60.00–$76.99	10	66.75	0.9	10	66.75	0.9
Total	17			15		

Performance-Based Stock Units.

PSUs will vest and convert to shares of common stock at the end of the performance period only if the Company satisfies predetermined performance and market-based conditions over the three-year performance period that began on January 1 of the grant year and ends three years later on December 31. Under the terms of the award, the number of PSUs that will actually vest and convert to shares will be based on the extent to which the Company achieves the specified performance goals during the performance period. PSUs have vesting, restriction and cancellation provisions that are generally similar to those of RSUs.

One-half of the award will be earned based on the Company's average return on equity, excluding the impact of the fluctuation in its credit spreads and other credit factors for certain of its long-term and short-term borrowings, primarily structured notes, that are accounted for at fair value, certain gains or losses associated with the sale of specified businesses, specified goodwill impairments, certain gains or losses associated with specified legal settlements related to business activities conducted prior to January 1, 2011 and specified cumulative catch-up adjustments resulting from changes in an existing, or application of a new, accounting principle that is not applied on a fully retrospective basis ("MS Average ROE"). The number of PSUs ultimately earned for this portion of the awards will be determined by applying a multiplier within the following ranges:

	Minimum		Maximum	
Grant Year	MS Average ROE	Multiplier	MS Average ROE	Multiplier
2015	Less than 5%	0.0	11.5% or more	1.5
2014	Less than 5%	0.0	11.5% or more	1.5
2013	Less than 5%	0.0	13% or more	2.0

On the date of award, the fair value per share of this portion was $34.58, $32.81 and $22.85 for 2015, 2014 and 2013, respectively.

One-half of the award will be earned based on the Company's total shareholder return, relative to the total shareholder return of the S&P 500 Financial Sectors Index ("Relative TSR"). The number of PSUs ultimately earned for this portion of the award will be determined by applying a multiplier within the following ranges:

	Minimum		Maximum	
Grant Year	Relative TSR	Multiplier	Relative TSR	Multiplier
2015	Less than—50%	0.0	25% or more	1.5
2014	Less than—50%	0.0	25% or more	1.5
2013	Less than—50%	0.0	50% or more	2.0

On the date of award, the fair value per share of this portion was $38.07, $37.72 and $34.65 for 2015, 2014 and 2013, respectively, estimated using a Monte Carlo simulation and the following assumptions:

Grant Year	Risk-Free Interest Rate	Expected Stock Price Volatility	Expected Dividend Yield
2015	0.9%	29.6%	0.0%
2014	0.8%	44.2%	0.0%
2013	0.4%	45.4%	0.0%

The risk-free interest rate was determined based on the yields available on U.S. Treasury zero-coupon issues. The expected stock price volatility was determined using historical volatility. The expected dividend yield was based on historical dividend payments. A correlation coefficient was developed based on historical price data of the Company and the S&P 500 Financial Sectors Index.

PSU Activity.

	2015
	Number of Shares
	(In millions)
PSUs at beginning of period	4
Awarded	2
Conversions to common stock	(2)
PSUs at end of period	4

Deferred Cash-Based Compensation Plans.

Deferred cash-based compensation plans generally provide a return to the plan participants based upon the performance of various referenced investments. The Company often invests directly, as a principal, in investments or other financial instruments to economically hedge its obligations under its deferred cash-based compensation plans. Changes in value of such investments made by the Company are recorded in Trading revenues and Investments revenues.

Deferred Compensation Expense.

The components of the Company's deferred compensation expense (net of cancellations) are presented below:

(Dollars in millions)	2015	2014	2013
Deferred cash-based awards[1]	$660	$1,757	$1,490
Return on referenced investments	112	408	772
Total	$772	$2,165	$2,262

[1] Amounts for 2015, 2014 and 2013 include $144 million, $92 million and $78 million, respectively, related to deferred cash-based awards that were granted in 2016, 2015 and 2014, respectively, to employees who satisfied retirement-eligible requirements under award terms that do not contain a service period.

At December 31, 2015, the Company had approximately $541 million of unrecognized compensation cost related to unvested deferred cash-based awards (excluding unrecognized expense for returns on referenced investments). Absent actual cancellations and any future return on referenced investments, this amount of unrecognized compensation cost will be recognized as $291 million in 2016, $103 million in 2017 and $147 million thereafter. These amounts do not include 2015 performance year awards granted in January 2016, which will begin to be amortized in 2016 (see below).

2015 Performance Year Deferred Compensation Awards.

In January 2016, the Company granted approximately $0.8 billion of stock-based awards and $1.0 billion of deferred cash-based awards related to the 2015 performance year that contain a future service requirement. Absent estimated or actual forfeitures or cancellations or accelerations, and any future return on referenced investments, the annual compensation cost for these awards will be recognized as follows:

Annual Compensation Cost for 2015 Performance Year Awards.

(Dollars in millions)	2016	2017	Thereafter	Total
Stock-based awards	$453	$198	$162	$ 813
Deferred cash-based awards	545	298	128	971
Total	$998	$496	$290	$1,784

INCENTIVE COMPENSATION PLANS

3.61 CVS HEALTH CORPORATION (DEC)
NOTES TO CONSOLIDATED FINANCIAL STATEMENTS (in part)

10. Stock Incentive Plans

Stock-based compensation expense is measured at the grant date based on the fair value of the award and is recognized as expense over the requisite service period of the stock award (generally three to five years) using the straight-line method.

Compensation expense related to stock options, which includes the Employee Stock Purchase Plan (the "ESPP") totaled $90 million, $103 million and $100 million for 2015, 2014 and 2013, respectively. The recognized tax benefit was $26 million, $33 million and $32 million for 2015, 2014 and 2013, respectively. Compensation expense related to restricted stock awards totaled $140 million, $62 million and $41 million for 2015, 2014 and 2013, respectively. Stock-based compensation for the year ended December 31, 2015 includes $38 million associated with accelerated vesting of restricted stock replacement awards issued to Omnicare executives who were terminated subsequent to the acquisition.

The ESPP provides for the purchase of up to 15 million shares of common stock. In March 2013, the Board of Directors approved an amendment to the ESPP to provide an additional 15 million shares of common stock for issuance. Under the ESPP, eligible employees may purchase common stock at the end of each six month offering period at a purchase price equal to 85% of the lower of the fair market value on the first day or the last day of the offering period. During 2015, approximately 1 million shares of common stock were purchased under the provisions of the ESPP at an average price of $72.21 per share. As of December 31, 2015, approximately 14 million shares of common stock were available for issuance under the ESPP.

The fair value of stock-based compensation associated with the ESPP is estimated on the date of grant (the first day of the six month offering period) using the Black-Scholes Option Pricing Model.

The following table is a summary of the assumptions used to value the ESPP awards for each of the respective periods:

	2015	2014	2013
Dividend yield[1]	0.71%	0.75%	0.86%
Expected volatility[2]	13.92%	14.87%	16.94%
Risk-free interest rate[3]	0.11%	0.08%	0.10%
Expected life *(in years)*[4]	0.5	0.5	0.5
Weighted-average grant date fair value	$18.72	$13.74	$10.08

[1] The dividend yield is calculated based on semi-annual dividends paid and the fair market value of the Company's stock at the grant date.
[2] The expected volatility is based on the historical volatility of the Company's daily stock market prices over the previous six month period.
[3] The risk-free interest rate is based on the Treasury constant maturity interest rate whose term is consistent with the expected term of ESPP options (i.e., 6 months).
[4] The expected life is based on the semi-annual purchase period.

The terms of the Company's Incentive Compensation Plan ("ICP") provide for grants of annual incentive and long-term performance awards to executive officers and other officers and employees of the Company or any subsidiary of the Company. Payment of such annual incentive and long-term performance awards will be in cash, stock, other awards or other property, at the discretion of the Management Planning and Development Committee of the Company's Board of Directors. The ICP allows for a maximum of 74 million shares to be reserved and available for grants. The ICP is the only compensation plan under which the Company grants stock options, restricted stock and other stock-based awards to its employees, with the exception of the Company's ESPP. In November 2012, the Company's Board of Directors approved an amendment to the ICP to eliminate the share recycling provision of the ICP. As of December 31, 2015, there were approximately 24 million shares available for future grants under the ICP.

The Company's restricted awards are considered nonvested share awards and require no payment from the employee. Compensation cost is recorded based on the market price of the Company's common stock on the grant date and is recognized on a straight-line basis over the requisite service period. The Company granted 2,695,000, 2,708,000 and 1,715,000 restricted stock units with a weighted average fair value of $100.81, $73.60 and $54.30 in 2015, 2014 and 2013, respectively. As of December 31, 2015, there was $268 million of total unrecognized compensation cost related to the restricted stock units that are expected to vest. These costs are expected to be recognized over a weighted-average period of 2.61 years. The total fair value of restricted shares vested during 2015, 2014 and 2013 was $164 million, $57 million and $41 million, respectively.

The following table is a summary of the restricted stock unit and restricted share award activity for the year ended December 31, 2015.

Units in thousands	Units	Weighted Average Grant Date Fair Value
Nonvested at beginning of year	4,677	$ 51.90
Granted	2,695	$100.81
Vested	(1,646)	$103.82
Forfeited	(308)	$ 73.61
Nonvested at end of year	5,418	$ 59.22

All grants under the ICP are awarded at fair value on the date of grant. The fair value of stock options is estimated using the Black-Scholes Option Pricing Model and stock-based compensation is recognized on a straight-line basis over the requisite service period. Stock options granted generally become exercisable over a four-year period from the grant date. Stock options generally expire seven years after the grant date.

Excess tax benefits of $127 million, $106 million and $62 million were included in financing activities in the accompanying consolidated statements of cash flow during 2015, 2014 and 2013, respectively. Cash received from stock options exercised, which includes the ESPP, totaled $299 million, $421 million and $500 million during 2015, 2014 and 2013, respectively. The total intrinsic value of stock options exercised was $394 million, $372 million and $282 million in 2015, 2014 and 2013, respectively. The total fair value of stock options vested during 2015, 2014 and 2013 was $334 million, $292 million and $329 million, respectively.

The fair value of each stock option is estimated using the Black-Scholes option pricing model based on the following assumptions at the time of grant:

	2015	2014	2013
Dividend yield[1]	1.37%	1.47%	1.65%
Expected volatility[2]	18.07%	19.92%	30.96%
Risk-free interest rate[3]	1.24%	1.35%	0.73%
Expected life *(in years)*[4]	4.2	4.0	4.7
Weighted-average grant date fair value	$14.01	$11.04	$12.50

[1] The dividend yield is based on annual dividends paid and the fair market value of the Company's stock at the grant date.
[2] The expected volatility is estimated using the Company's historical volatility over a period equal to the expected life of each option grant after adjustments for infrequent events such as stock splits.
[3] The risk-free interest rate is selected based on yields from U.S. Treasury zero-coupon issues with a remaining term equal to the expected term of the options being valued.
[4] The expected life represents the number of years the options are expected to be outstanding from grant date based on historical option holder exercise experience.

As of December 31, 2015, unrecognized compensation expense related to unvested options totaled $91 million, which the Company expects to be recognized over a weighted-average period of 1.72 years. After considering anticipated forfeitures, the Company expects approximately 12 million of the unvested stock options to vest over the requisite service period.

The following table is a summary of the Company's stock option activity for the year ended December 31, 2015:

Shares in thousands	Shares	Weighted Average Exercise Price	Weighted Average Remaining Contractual Term	Aggregate Intrinsic Value
Outstanding at December 31, 2014	28,166	$ 47.87		
Granted	3,772	$102.25		
Exercised	(6,425)	$ 40.68		
Forfeited	(902)	$ 66.81		
Expired	(270)	$ 38.03		
Outstanding at December 31, 2015	24,341	$ 57.60	3.88	$993,965,110
Exercisable at December 31, 2015	11,847	$ 42.17	2.66	$658,732,653
Vested at December 31, 2015 and expected to vest in the future	23,765	$ 56.96	3.84	$984,746,487

EMPLOYEE STOCK OWNERSHIP PLANS (ESOP)

3.62 STANLEY BLACK & DECKER, INC. (DEC)
CONSOLIDATED STATEMENTS OF CHANGES IN SHAREOWNERS' EQUITY

(Millions of Dollars, Except Per Share Amounts)

	Preferred Stock	Common Stock	Additional Paid In Capital	Retained Earnings	Accumulated Other Comprehensive Loss	ESOP	Treasury Stock	Non-Controlling Interests	Share-owners' Equity
Balance December 29, 2012	$ —	$442.3	$4,473.5	$3,299.5	$ (388.0)	$(62.8)	$(1,097.4)	$60.0	$6,727.1
Net earnings				490.3				(1.0)	489.3
Other comprehensive loss					(111.0)				(111.0)
Cash dividends declared—$1.98 per share				(307.1)					(307.1)
Issuance of common stock			(115.6)				250.1		134.5
Settlement of forward share repurchase contract			350.0				(350.0)		—
Equity units—non-cash stock contract fees			(40.2)						(40.2)
Equity units—offering fees			(9.2)						(9.2)
Net premium paid on equity option			(83.2)						(83.2)
Repurchase of common stock (2,225,732 shares)			217.9				(257.1)		(39.2)
Non-controlling interest buyout			(1.1)					(15.2)	(16.3)
Non-controlling interests of acquired businesses								37.5	37.5
Stock-based compensation related			66.4						66.4
Tax benefit related to stock options exercised			20.1						20.1
ESOP and related tax benefit				2.2		9.6			11.8
Balance December 28, 2013	$ —	$442.3	$4,878.6	$3,484.9	$ (499.0)	$(53.2)	$(1,454.4)	$81.3	$6,880.5

(continued)

	Preferred Stock	Common Stock	Additional Paid In Capital	Retained Earnings	Accumulated Other Comprehensive Loss	ESOP	Treasury Stock	Non-Controlling Interests	Share-owners' Equity
Net earnings				760.9				0.5	761.4
Other comprehensive loss					(771.2)				(771.2)
Cash dividends declared—$2.04 per share				(321.3)					(321.3)
Issuance of common stock			(69.4)				129.8		60.4
Forward obligation to purchase treasury shares			(150.0)						(150.0)
Repurchase of common stock (340,576 shares)							(28.2)		(28.2)
Non-controlling interest buyout								(0.6)	(0.6)
Non-controlling interests of acquired businesses								1.6	1.6
Stock-based compensation related			57.1						57.1
Tax benefit related to stock options exercised			10.8						10.8
ESOP and related tax benefit				1.8		9.6			11.4
Balance January 3, 2015	$ —	$442.3	$4,727.1	$3,926.3	$(1,270.2)	$(43.6)	$(1,352.8)	$82.8	$6,511.9
Net earnings				883.7				(1.6)	882.1
Other comprehensive loss					(424.0)				(424.0)
Cash dividends declared—$2.14 per share				(319.9)					(319.9)
Issuance of common stock			(96.1)				231.4		135.3
Forward obligation to purchase treasury shares			(350.0)						(350.0)
Repurchase of common stock (9,227,564 shares)			263.9				(913.7)		(649.8)
Issuance of preferred stock	632.5								632.5
Redemption and conversion of preferred stock	(632.5)		(220.1)				220.1		(632.5)
Non-controlling interest buyout			0.8					(33.6)	(32.8)
Stock-based compensation related			67.9						67.9
Tax benefit related to stock options exercised			28.2						28.2
ESOP and related tax benefit				1.6		8.7			10.3
Balance January 2, 2016	$ —	$442.3	$4,421.7	$4,491.7	$(1,694.2)	$(34.9)	$(1,815.0)	$47.6	$5,859.2

NOTES TO CONSOLIDATED FINANCIAL STATEMENTS (in part)

L. Employee Benefit Plans (in part)

Employee Stock Ownership Plan ("ESOP") Most U.S. employees may contribute from 1% to 25% of their eligible compensation to a tax-deferred 401(k) savings plan, subject to restrictions under tax laws. Employees generally direct the investment of their own contributions into various investment funds. An employer match benefit is provided under the plan equal to one-half of each employee's tax-deferred contribution up to the first 7% of their compensation. Participants direct the entire employer match benefit such that no participant is required to hold the Company's common stock in their 401(k) account. The employer match benefit totaled $21.1 million, $19.9 million and $18.8 million in 2015, 2014 and 2013, respectively.

In addition, approximately 7,200 U.S. salaried and non-union hourly employees are eligible to receive a non-contributory benefit under the Core benefit plan. Core benefit allocations range from 2% to 6% of eligible employee compensation based on age. Approximately 3,600 U.S. employees also receive a Core transition benefit, allocations of which range from 1% to 2% of eligible compensation based on age and date of hire. Approximately 1,500 U.S. employees are eligible to receive an additional average 1% contribution actuarially designed to replace previously curtailed pension benefits. Allocations for benefits earned under the Core plan were $22.1 million in 2015, $20.7 million in 2014 and $21.1 million in 2013. Assets held in participant Core accounts are invested in target date retirement funds which have an age-based allocation of investments.

Shares of the Company's common stock held by the ESOP were purchased with the proceeds of borrowings from the Company in 1991 ("1991 internal loan"). Shareowners' equity reflects a reduction equal to the cost basis of unearned (unallocated) shares purchased with the internal borrowings. In 2015, 2014 and 2013, the Company made additional contributions to the ESOP for $7.2 million, $9.4 million, and $9.5 million, respectively, which were used by the ESOP to make additional payments on the 1991 internal loan. These payments triggered the release of 184,753, 230,032 and 219,900 shares of unallocated stock, respectively.

Net ESOP activity recognized is comprised of the cost basis of shares released, the cost of the aforementioned Core and 401(k) match defined contribution benefits, less the fair value of shares released and dividends on unallocated ESOP shares. The Company's net ESOP activity resulted in expense of $0.8 million in 2015, $0.7 million in 2014 and $1.9 million in 2013. ESOP expense is affected by the market value of the Company's common stock on the monthly dates when shares are released. The market value of shares released averaged $101.79 in 2015, $88.05 per share in 2014 and $80.71 per share in 2013.

Unallocated shares are released from the trust based on current period debt principal and interest payments as a percentage of total future debt principal and interest payments. Dividends on both allocated and unallocated shares may be used for debt service and to credit participant accounts for dividends earned on allocated shares. Dividends paid on the shares acquired with the 1991 internal loan were used solely to pay internal loan debt service in all periods. Dividends on ESOP shares, which are charged to shareowners' equity as declared, were $9.7 million in 2015, $10.6 million in 2014 and $12.3 million in 2013, net of the tax benefit which is recorded within equity. Dividends on ESOP shares were utilized entirely for debt service in all years. Interest costs incurred by the ESOP on the 1991 internal loan, which have no earnings impact, were $3.8 million, $4.7 million and $6.1 million for 2015, 2014 and 2013, respectively. Both allocated and unallocated ESOP shares are treated as outstanding for purposes of computing earnings per share. As of January 2, 2016, the cumulative number of ESOP shares allocated to participant accounts was 13,661,101, of which participants held 2,482,944 shares, and the number of unallocated shares was 1,880,256. At January 2, 2016, there were 23,189 released shares in the ESOP trust holding account pending allocation. The Company made cash contributions totaling $4.4 million in 2015, $3.4 million in 2014 and $30.7 million in 2013 excluding additional contributions of $7.2 million, $9.4 million and $9.5 million in 2015, 2014 and 2013, respectively, as discussed previously.

PROFIT SHARING PLANS

3.63 TIFFANY & CO. (JAN)
NOTES TO CONSOLIDATED FINANCIAL STATEMENTS (in part)

C. Supplemental Cash Flow Information (in part)

Supplemental noncash investing and financing activities:

(In thousands)	Years Ended January 31,		
	2015	2014	2013
Issuance of Common Stock under the Employee Profit Sharing and Retirement Savings Plan	$3,925	$	$3,150

N. Employee Benefit Plans (in part)

Pensions and Other Postretirement Benefits (in part)

The Company maintains the following pension plans: a noncontributory defined benefit pension plan qualified in accordance with the Internal Revenue Service Code ("Qualified Plan") covering substantially all U.S. employees hired before January 1, 2006, a non-qualified unfunded retirement income plan ("Excess Plan") covering certain U.S. employees hired before January 1, 2006 and affected by Internal Revenue Service Code compensation limits, a non-qualified unfunded Supplemental Retirement Income Plan ("SRIP") covering certain executive officers of the Company hired before January 1, 2006 and noncontributory defined benefit pension plans in certain of its international locations ("Other Plans").

Qualified Plan benefits are based on (i) average compensation in the highest paid five years of the last 10 years of employment ("average final compensation") and (ii) the number of years of service. Participants with at least 10 years of service who retire after attaining age 55 may receive reduced retirement benefits. The Company funds the Qualified Plan's trust in accordance with regulatory limits to provide for current service and for the unfunded benefit obligation over a reasonable period and for current service benefit accruals. To the extent that these requirements are fully covered by assets in the Qualified Plan, the Company may elect not to make any contribution in a particular year. No cash contribution was required in 2014 and none is required in 2015 to meet the minimum funding requirements of the Employee Retirement Income Security Act. The Company periodically evaluates whether to make discretionary cash contributions to the Qualified Plan, and did not make such contributions in 2014 and currently does not anticipate making such contributions in 2015. This expectation is subject to change based on management's assessment of a variety of factors, including, but not limited to, asset performance, interest rates and changes in actuarial assumptions.

The Qualified Plan, Excess Plan and SRIP exclude all employees hired on or after January 1, 2006. Instead, employees hired on or after January 1, 2006 will be eligible to receive a defined contribution retirement benefit under the Employee Profit Sharing and Retirement Savings ("EPSRS") Plan (see "Employee Profit Sharing and Retirement Savings Plan" below). Employees hired before January 1, 2006 will continue to be eligible for and accrue benefits under the Qualified Plan.

Employee Profit Sharing and Retirement Savings ("EPSRS") Plan

The Company maintains an EPSRS Plan that covers substantially all U.S.-based employees. Under the profit-sharing feature of the EPSRS Plan, the Company made contributions, in the form of newly-issued Company Common Stock through 2014, to the employees' accounts based on the achievement of certain targeted earnings objectives established by, or as otherwise determined by, the Company's Board of Directors. Beginning in 2015, these contributions will be made in cash. The Company recorded expense of $3,075,000 in 2014, $3,925,000 in 2013 and recorded no expense in 2012. Under the retirement savings feature of the EPSRS Plan, employees who meet certain eligibility requirements may participate by contributing up to 50% of their annual compensation beginning in 2012, not to exceed Internal Revenue Service limits, and the Company may provide up to a 50% matching cash contribution up to 6% of each participant's total compensation. The Company recorded expense of $7,735,000, $7,088,000 and $7,278,000 in 2014, 2013 and 2012. Contributions to both features of the EPSRS Plan are made in the following year.

Under the profit-sharing feature of the EPSRS Plan, for contributions made in the Company's stock, the Company's stock contribution is required to be maintained in such stock until the employee has two or more years of service, at which time the employee may diversify his or her Company stock account into other investment options provided under the plan. For contributions made in cash, the contribution is allocated within the participant's account based on their investment elections under the EPSRS Plan. If the participant has made no election, the contribution will be invested in the appropriate default target fund as determined by each participant's date of birth. Under the retirement savings portion of the EPSRS Plan, the employees have the ability to elect to invest their contribution and the matching contribution in Company stock. At January 31, 2015, investments in Company stock represented 26% of total EPSRS Plan assets.

The EPSRS Plan provides a defined contribution retirement benefit ("DCRB") to eligible employees hired on or after January 1, 2006. Under the DCRB, the Company makes contributions each year to each employee's account at a rate based upon age and years of service. These contributions are deposited into individual accounts in each employee's name to be invested in a manner similar to the retirement savings portion of the EPSRS Plan. The Company recorded expense of $4,584,000, $3,640,000 and $3,387,000 in 2014, 2013 and 2012.

Depreciation Expense

RECOGNITION AND MEASUREMENT

3.64 FASB ASC 360, *Property, Plant, and Equipment*, defines *depreciation accounting* (the process of allocating the cost of productive facilities over the expected useful lives of the facilities) as a system of accounting that aims to distribute the cost or other basic value of tangible capital assets, less salvage (if any), over the estimated useful life of the unit, which may be a group of assets, in a systematic and rational manner. It is a process of allocation, not of valuation.

3.65 FASB ASC 250 requires that a change in depreciation, amortization, or depletion method for long-lived, nonfinancial assets be accounted for as a change in accounting estimate effected by a change in accounting principle. Changes in accounting estimate are accounted for prospectively, not retrospectively as is required for changes in accounting principle.

DISCLOSURE

3.66 FASB ASC 360 stipulates that both the amount of depreciation expense and method(s) of depreciation should be disclosed in the financial statements or notes thereto.

PRESENTATION AND DISCLOSURE EXCERPTS

STRAIGHT-LINE AND ACCELERATED METHODS

3.67 STANLEY BLACK & DECKER, INC. (DEC)

NOTES TO CONSOLIDATED FINANCIAL STATEMENTS (in part)

A. Significant Accounting Policies (in part)

Property, Plant and Equipment—The Company generally values property, plant and equipment ("PP&E"), including capitalized software, at historical cost less accumulated depreciation and amortization. Costs related to maintenance and repairs which do not prolong the asset's useful life are expensed as incurred. Depreciation and amortization are provided using straight-line methods over the estimated useful lives of the assets as follows:

	Useful Life (Years)
Land improvements	10–20
Buildings	40
Machinery and equipment	3–15
Computer software	3–5

Leasehold improvements are depreciated over the shorter of the estimated useful life or the term of the lease.

The Company reports depreciation and amortization of property, plant and equipment in cost of sales and selling, general and administrative expenses based on the nature of the underlying assets. Depreciation and amortization related to the production of inventory and delivery of services are recorded in cost of sales. Depreciation and amortization related to distribution center activities, selling and support functions are reported in selling, general and administrative expenses.

The Company assesses its long-lived assets for impairment when indicators that the carrying amounts may not be recoverable are present. In assessing long-lived assets for impairment, the Company groups its long-lived assets with other assets and liabilities at the lowest level for which identifiable cash flows are generated ("asset group") and estimates the undiscounted future cash flows that are directly associated with, and expected to be generated from, the use of and eventual disposition of the asset group. If the carrying value is greater than the undiscounted cash flows, an impairment loss must be determined and the asset group is written down to fair value. The impairment loss is quantified by comparing the carrying amount of the asset group to the estimated fair value, which is determined using weighted-average discounted cash flows that consider various possible outcomes for the disposition of the asset group.

D. Property, Plant and Equipment

(Millions of Dollars)	2015	2014
Land	$ 129.2	$ 136.3
Land improvements	36.0	34.9
Buildings	525.3	542.8
Leasehold improvements	98.9	89.8
Machinery and equipment	1,979.9	1,895.9
Computer software	397.5	381.0
Property, plant & equipment, gross	$ 3,166.8	$ 3,080.7
Less: accumulated depreciation and amortization	(1,716.6)	(1,626.6)
Property, plant & equipment, net	$ 1,450.2	$ 1,454.1

Depreciation and amortization expense associated with property, plant and equipment was as follows:

(Millions of Dollars)	2015	2014	2013
Depreciation	$219.2	$229.5	$208.7
Amortization	37.7	33.9	29.3
Depreciation and amortization expense	$256.9	$263.4	$238.0

The amounts above are inclusive of depreciation and amortization expense for discontinued operations amounting to $2.7 million in 2014 and $2.8 million in 2013.

3.68 ORBITAL ATK, INC. (MAR)

NOTES TO THE CONSOLIDATED FINANCIAL STATEMENTS (in part)

(Amounts in thousands except share and per share data and unless otherwise indicated)

6. Property, Plant and Equipment

Property, plant and equipment is stated at cost and depreciated over estimated useful lives. Machinery and equipment is depreciated using the double declining balance method at most of the Company's facilities, and using the straight-line method at other Company facilities. Other depreciable property is depreciated using the straight-line method. Machinery and equipment are depreciated over 1 to 30 years and buildings and improvements are depreciated over 1 to 45 years. Depreciation expense was $75,764 in fiscal 2015, $69,192 in fiscal 2014 and $77,605 in fiscal 2013.

The Company reviews property, plant and equipment for impairment when indicators of potential impairment are present. When such impairment is identified, it is recorded as a loss in that period. Maintenance and repairs are charged to expense as incurred. Major improvements that extend useful lives are capitalized and depreciated. The cost and accumulated depreciation of property, plant and equipment retired or otherwise disposed of are removed from the related accounts, and any residual values are charged or credited to income.

Property, plant and equipment consisted of the following:

	March 31	
	2015	2014
Land	$ 41,597	$ 31,239
Buildings and improvements	344,140	291,811
Machinery and equipment	1,312,073	1,019,403
Property not yet in service	58,346	60,575
Gross property, plant and equipment	1,756,156	1,403,028
Less accumulated depreciation	(949,099)	(894,573)
Net property, plant and equipment	$ 807,057	$ 508,455

UNITS-OF-PRODUCTION METHOD

3.69 FREEPORT-MCMORAN INC. (DEC)

CONSOLIDATED STATEMENTS OF OPERATIONS (in part)

	Years Ended December 31,		
(In millions, except per share amounts)	2015	2014	2013
Revenues	$15,877	$21,438	$20,921
Cost of sales:			
Production and delivery	11,545	11,898	11,837
Depreciation, depletion and amortization	3,497	3,863	2,797
Impairment of oil and gas properties	13,144	3,737	—
Copper and molybdenum inventory adjustments	338	6	3
Total cost of sales	28,524	19,504	14,637
Selling, general and administrative expenses	569	592	657
Mining exploration and research expenses	127	126	210
Environmental obligations and shutdown costs	78	119	66
Goodwill impairment	—	1,717	—
Net gain on sales of assets	(39)	(717)	—
Total costs and expenses	29,259	21,341	15,570
Operating (loss) income	(13,382)	97	5,351

Note 1. Summary of Significant Accounting Policies (in part)

Property, Plant, Equipment and Mining Development Costs. Property, plant, equipment and mining development costs are carried at cost. Mineral exploration costs, as well as drilling and other costs incurred for the purpose of converting mineral resources to proven and probable reserves or identifying new mineral resources at development or production stage properties, are charged to expense as incurred. Development costs are capitalized beginning after proven and probable mineral reserves have been established. Development costs include costs incurred resulting from mine pre-production activities undertaken to gain access to proven and probable reserves, including shafts, adits, drifts, ramps, permanent excavations, infrastructure and removal of overburden. Additionally, interest expense allocable to the cost of developing mining properties and to constructing new facilities is capitalized until assets are ready for their intended use.

Expenditures for replacements and improvements are capitalized. Costs related to periodic scheduled maintenance (*i.e.*, turnarounds) are charged to expense as incurred. Depreciation for mining and milling life-of-mine assets, infrastructure and other common costs is determined using the unit-of-production (UOP) method based on total estimated recoverable proven and probable copper reserves (for primary copper mines) and proven and probable molybdenum reserves (for primary molybdenum mines). Development costs and acquisition costs for proven and probable mineral reserves that relate to a specific ore body are depreciated using the UOP method based on estimated recoverable proven and probable mineral reserves for the ore body benefited. Depreciation, depletion and amortization using the UOP method is recorded upon extraction of the recoverable copper or molybdenum from the ore body, at which time it is allocated to inventory cost and then included as a component of cost of goods sold. Other assets are depreciated on a straight-line basis over estimated useful lives of up to 39 years for buildings and three to 25 years for machinery and equipment, and mobile equipment.

Included in property, plant, equipment and mining development costs is value beyond proven and probable mineral reserves (VBPP), primarily resulting from FCX's acquisition of FMC in 2007. The concept of VBPP may be interpreted differently by different mining companies. FCX's VBPP is attributable to (i) mineralized material, which includes measured and indicated amounts, that FCX believes could be brought into production with the establishment or modification of required permits and should market conditions and technical assessments warrant, (ii) inferred mineral resources and (iii) exploration potential.

Carrying amounts assigned to VBPP are not charged to expense until the VBPP becomes associated with additional proven and probable mineral reserves and the reserves are produced or the VBPP is determined to be impaired. Additions to proven and probable mineral reserves for properties with VBPP will carry with them the value assigned to VBPP at the date acquired, less any impairment amounts. Refer to Note 5 for further discussion.

Note 5. Property, Plant, Equipment and Mining Development Costs, Net

The components of net property, plant, equipment and mining development costs follow:

	December 31,	
	2015	2014
Proven and probable mineral reserves	$ 4,663	$ 4,651
VBPP	1,037	1,042
Mining development and other	5,184	4,712
Buildings and infrastructure	7,451	5,100
Machinery and equipment	13,759	11,251
Mobile equipment	4,158	3,926
Construction in progress	3,999	6,802
Property, plant, equipment and mining development costs	40,251	37,484
Accumulated depreciation, depletion and amortization	(12,742)	(11,264)
Property, plant, equipment and mining development costs, net	$ 27,509	$ 26,220

FCX recorded $2.2 billion for VBPP in connection with the FMC acquisition in 2007 and transferred $10 million to proven and probable mineral reserves during 2015, $2 million during 2014 and $784 million prior to 2014. Cumulative impairments of VBPP total $485 million, which were primarily recorded in 2008.

Capitalized interest, which primarily related to FCX's mining operations' capital projects, totaled $157 million in 2015, $148 million in 2014 and $105 million in 2013.

Because of a decline in commodity prices, FCX made adjustments to its operating plans for its mining operations in the third and fourth quarters of 2015. Although FCX's long-term strategy of developing its mining resources to their full potential remains in place, the decline in copper and molybdenum prices has limited FCX's ability to invest in growth projects and caused FCX to make adjustments to its near-term plans by revising its strategy to protect liquidity while preserving its mineral resources and growth options for the longer term. Accordingly, operating plans were revised primarily to reflect: (a) the suspension of mining operations at the Miami mine in Arizona; (b) a 50 percent reduction in mining rates at the Tyrone mine in New Mexico; (c) the suspension of production at the Sierrita mine in Arizona; (d) adjustments to mining rates at other North America copper mines; (e) an approximate 50 percent reduction in mining and stacking rates at the El Abra mine in Chile; (f) an approximate 65 percent reduction in molybdenum production volumes at the Henderson molybdenum mine in Colorado; (g) capital cost reductions, including project deferrals associated with future development and expansion opportunities at the Tenke Fungurume minerals district in the DRC; and (h) reductions in operating, administrative and exploration costs, including workforce reductions.

In connection with the decline in copper and molybdenum prices and the revised operating plans discussed above, FCX evaluated its long-lived assets (other than indefinite-lived intangible assets) for impairment during 2015 and as of December 31, 2015, as described in Note 1. FCX's evaluations of its copper mines at December 31, 2015, were based on near-term price assumptions reflecting prevailing copper future prices, which ranged from approximately $2.15 per pound to $2.17 per pound for COMEX and from $2.13 per pound to $2.16 per pound for LME, and a long-term average price of $3.00 per pound. FCX's evaluations of its molybdenum mines at December 31, 2015, were based on near-term price assumptions that are consistent with current market prices for molybdenum and a long-term average price of $10.00 per pound.

FCX's evaluations of long-lived assets (other than indefinite-lived intangible assets) resulted in the recognition of a charge to production costs for the impairment of the Tyrone mine totaling $37 million in 2015, net of a revision to Tyrone's ARO.

COMPOSITE METHOD OF DEPRECIATION

3.70 VALERO ENERGY CORPORATION (DEC)
CONSOLIDATED STATEMENTS OF INCOME (in part)

(Millions of Dollars, Except per Share Amounts)

	Year Ended December 31,		
	2015	2014	2013
Operating revenues (a)	$87,804	$130,844	$138,074
Costs and expenses:			
Cost of sales (excluding the lower of cost or market inventory valuation adjustment)	73,861	118,141	127,316
Lower of cost or market inventory valuation adjustment	790	—	—
Operating expenses	4,243	4,387	4,323
General and administrative expenses	710	724	758
Depreciation and amortization expense	1,842	1,690	1,720
Total costs and expenses	81,446	124,942	134,117
Operating income	6,358	5,902	3,957

NOTES TO CONSOLIDATED FINANCIAL STATEMENTS (in part)

1. Basis of Presentation and Significant Accounting Policies (in part)

Property, Plant, and Equipment

The cost of property, plant, and equipment (property assets) purchased or constructed, including betterments of property assets, is capitalized. However, the cost of repairs to and normal maintenance of property assets is expensed as incurred. Betterments of property assets are those that extend the useful life, increase the capacity or improve the operating efficiency of the asset, or improve the safety of our operations. The cost of property assets constructed includes interest and certain overhead costs allocable to the construction activities.

Our operations, especially those of our refining segment, are highly capital intensive. Each of our refineries comprises a large base of property assets, consisting of a series of interconnected, highly integrated and interdependent crude oil processing facilities and supporting logistical infrastructure (Units), and these Units are continuously improved. Improvements consist of the addition of new Units and betterments of existing Units. We plan for these improvements by developing a multi-year capital program that is updated and revised based on changing internal and external factors.

Depreciation of property assets used in our refining segment is recorded on a straight-line basis over the estimated useful lives of these assets primarily using the composite method of depreciation. We maintain a separate composite group of property assets for each of our refineries. We estimate the useful life of each group based on an evaluation of the property assets comprising the group, and such evaluations consist of, but are not limited to, the physical inspection of the assets to determine their condition, consideration of the manner in which the assets are maintained, assessment of the need to replace assets, and evaluation of the manner in which improvements impact the useful life of the group. The estimated useful lives of our composite groups range primarily from 25 to 30 years.

Under the composite method of depreciation, the cost of an improvement is added to the composite group to which it relates and is depreciated over that group's estimated useful life. We design improvements to our refineries in accordance with engineering specifications, design standards, and practices accepted in our industry, and these improvements have design lives consistent with our estimated useful lives. Therefore, we believe the use of the group life to depreciate the cost of improvements made to the group is reasonable because the estimated useful life of each improvement is consistent with that of the group. It should be noted, however, that factors such as competition, regulation, or environmental matters could cause us to change our estimates, thus impacting depreciation expense in the future.

Also under the composite method of depreciation, the historical cost of a minor property asset (net of salvage value) that is retired or replaced is charged to accumulated depreciation and no gain or loss is recognized in income. However, a gain or loss is recognized in income for a major property asset that is retired, replaced, or sold and for an abnormal disposition of a property asset (primarily involuntary conversions). Gains and losses are reflected in depreciation and amortization expense, unless such amounts are reported separately due to materiality.

Depreciation of property assets used in our ethanol segment and our former retail segment (see Note 3) is recorded on a straight-line basis over the estimated useful lives of the related assets. Leasehold improvements are amortized on a straight-line basis over the shorter of the lease term or the estimated useful life of the related asset. Assets acquired under capital leases are amortized on a straight-line basis over (i) the lease term if transfer of ownership does not occur at the end of the lease term or (ii) the estimated useful life of the asset if transfer of ownership does occur at the end of the lease term.

7. Property, Plant, and Equipment

Major classes of property, plant, and equipment, which include capital lease assets, consisted of the following (in millions):

	December 31,	
	2015	**2014**
Land	$ 400	$ 396
Crude oil processing facilities	28,278	27,629
Pipeline and terminal facilities	2,456	2,380
Grain processing equipment	792	779
Administrative buildings	789	789
Other	3,019	2,607
Construction in progress	1,173	1,353
Property, plant, and equipment, at cost	36,907	35,933
Accumulated depreciation	(10,204)	(9,198)
Property, plant, and equipment, net	$ 26,703	$26,735

We have various assets under capital leases that primarily support our refining operations totaling $134 million and $72 million as of December 31, 2015 and 2014, respectively. Accumulated amortization on assets under capital leases was $50 million and $40 million as of December 31, 2015 and 2014, respectively.

Depreciation expense for the years ended December 31, 2015, 2014, and 2013 was $1.3 billion, $1.2 billion, and $1.2 billion, respectively.

Income Taxes

RECOGNITION AND MEASUREMENT

3.71 FASB ASC 740, *Income Taxes*, clarifies the accounting for tax positions in an entity's financial statements. FASB ASC 740 prescribes a more-likely-than-not recognition threshold and measurement attribute for the financial statement recognition and measurement of a tax position taken or expected to be taken. Under FASB ASC 740, tax positions will be evaluated for recognition, derecognition, and measurement using consistent criteria. In addition, FASB ASC 740 provides guidance on classification and disclosure. FASB ASC 740 requires, except in certain specified situations, that undistributed earnings of a subsidiary included in consolidated income be accounted for as a temporary difference. Finally, the provisions of FASB ASC 740 provide more information about the uncertainty in income tax assets and liabilities.

PRESENTATION

3.72 FASB ASC 740-10-45 states that except as indicated in FASB ASC 740-10-45-10B and 740-10-45-12, an unrecognized tax benefit, or a portion of an unrecognized tax benefit, shall be presented in the financial statements as a reduction to a deferred tax asset for a net operating loss carryforward, a similar tax loss, or a tax credit carryforward.

DISCLOSURE

3.73 FASB ASC 740 sets forth standards for financial presentation and disclosure of income tax liabilities or assets and expense. These requirements vary for public and nonpublic entities. FASB ASC 740 states that amounts and expiration dates of operating loss and tax credit carryforwards for tax purposes should be disclosed. Any portion of the valuation allowance for deferred tax assets for which subsequently recognized tax benefits will be credited directly to contributed capital should also be disclosed. An entity's temporary difference and carryforward information require additional disclosure, which differs for public and nonpublic entities.

PRESENTATION AND DISCLOSURE EXCERPTS

EXPENSE PROVISION

3.74 RALPH LAUREN CORPORATION (MAR)

CONSOLIDATED STATEMENTS OF INCOME (in part)

	Fiscal Years Ended		
(Millions, except per share data)	**March 28, 2015**	**March 29, 2014**	**March 30, 2013**
Net sales	$ 7,451	$ 7,284	$ 6,763
Licensing revenue	169	166	182
Net revenues	7,620	7,450	6,945
Cost of goods sold (a)	(3,242)	(3,140)	(2,789)
Gross profit	4,378	4,310	4,156
Selling, general, and administrative expenses (a)	(3,301)	(3,142)	(2,971)
Amortization of intangible assets	(25)	(35)	(27)
Gain on acquisition of Chaps	—	16	—
Impairments of assets	(7)	(1)	(19)
Restructuring and other charges	(10)	(18)	(12)
Total other operating expenses, net	(3,343)	(3,180)	(3,029)
Operating income	1,035	1,130	1,127
Foreign currency losses	(26)	(8)	(12)
Interest expense	(17)	(20)	(22)
Interest and other income, net	6	3	6
Equity in losses of equity-method investees	(11)	(9)	(10)
Income before provision for income taxes	987	1,096	1,089
Provision for income taxes	(285)	(320)	(339)
Net income	$ 702	$ 776	$ 750

3. Summary of Significant Accounting Policies (in part)

Income Taxes

Income taxes are provided using the asset and liability method. Under this method, income taxes (i.e., deferred tax assets and liabilities, current taxes payable/refunds receivable, and tax expense) are recorded based on amounts refundable or payable in the current year and include the results of any difference between U.S. GAAP and tax reporting. Deferred income taxes reflect the tax effect of certain net operating losses, capital losses, general business credit carryforwards, and the net tax effects of temporary differences between the carrying amount of assets and liabilities for financial statement and income tax purposes, as determined under enacted tax laws and rates. The Company accounts for the financial effect of changes in tax laws or rates in the period of enactment.

In addition, valuation allowances are established when management determines that it is more likely than not that some portion or all of a deferred tax asset will not be realized. Tax valuation allowances are analyzed periodically and adjusted as events occur or circumstances change that warrant adjustments.

In determining the income tax provision for financial reporting purposes, the Company establishes a reserve for uncertain tax positions. If the Company considers that a tax position is more likely than not of being sustained upon audit, based solely on the technical merits of the position, it recognizes the tax benefit. The Company measures the tax benefit by determining the largest amount that is greater than 50% likely of being realized upon settlement, presuming that the tax position is examined by the appropriate taxing authority that has full knowledge of all relevant information. These assessments can be complex and the Company often obtains assistance from external advisors. To the extent that the Company's estimates change or the final tax outcome of these matters is different than the amounts recorded, such differences will impact the income tax provision in the period in which such determinations are made. If the initial assessment fails to result in the recognition of a tax benefit, the Company regularly monitors its position and subsequently recognizes the tax benefit if (i) there are changes in tax law or analogous case law that sufficiently raise the likelihood of prevailing on the technical merits of the position to more likely than not; (ii) the statute of limitations expires; or (iii) there is a completion of an audit resulting in a settlement of that tax year with the appropriate agency. Uncertain tax positions are classified as current only when the Company expects to pay cash within the next twelve months. Interest and penalties, if any, are recorded within the provision for income taxes in the Company's consolidated statements of income and are classified on the consolidated balance sheets together with the related liability for unrecognized tax benefits.

See Note 13 for further discussion of the Company's income taxes.

13. Income Taxes

Taxes on Income

Domestic and foreign pretax income are as follows:

(Millions)	Fiscal Years Ended		
	March 28, 2015	March 29, 2014	March 30, 2013
Domestic	$620	$ 710	$ 672
Foreign	367	386	417
Total income before provision for income taxes	$987	$1,096	$1,089

Provisions (benefits) for current and deferred income taxes are as follows:

(Millions)	Fiscal Years Ended		
	March 28, 2015	March 29, 2014	March 30, 2013
Current:			
Federal[a]	$161	$211	$189
State and local[a]	35	51	42
Foreign	78	57	94
	274	319	325
Deferred:			
Federal	22	(4)	9
State and local	3	1	5
Foreign	(14)	4	—
	11	1	14
Total provision for income taxes	$285	$320	$339

[a] Excludes federal, state, and local tax benefits of approximately $8 million, $34 million, and $41 million in Fiscal 2015, Fiscal 2014, and Fiscal 2013, respectively, resulting from stock-based compensation arrangements. Such amounts were recorded within equity.

Tax Rate Reconciliation

The differences between income taxes expected at the U.S. federal statutory income tax rate of 35% and income taxes provided are as set forth below:

(Millions)	Fiscal Years Ended		
	March 28, 2015	March 29, 2014	March 30, 2013
Provision for income taxes at the U.S. federal statutory rate	$346	$384	$381
Increase (decrease) due to:			
State and local income taxes, net of federal benefit	21	29	28
Foreign income taxed at different rates, net of U.S. foreign tax credits	(96)	(89)	(75)
Unrecognized tax benefits and settlements of tax examinations	11	(5)	6
Other	3	1	(1)
Total provision for income taxes	$285	$320	$339
Effective tax rate[a]	28.9%	29.2%	31.1%

[a] Effective tax rate is calculated by dividing the provision for income taxes by income before provision for income taxes.

The Company's effective tax rate is lower than the statutory rate principally as a result of the proportion of earnings generated in lower taxed foreign jurisdictions versus the U.S. In addition, during both Fiscal 2015 and Fiscal 2014, the effective tax rate was favorably impacted by tax reserve reductions associated with income tax benefits resulting from the legal entity restructurings of certain of the Company's foreign operations. The Company's effective tax rate for Fiscal 2014 also reflected tax reserve reductions associated with the conclusion of a tax examination. The Company's effective tax rate for Fiscal 2013 reflected tax reserve reductions associated with the conclusion of a separate tax examination, offset by the inclusion of a reserve for an interest assessment on a prior year withholding tax.

Deferred Taxes

Significant components of the Company's net deferred tax assets (liabilities) are as follows:

(Millions)	March 28, 2015	March 29, 2014
Current deferred tax assets:		
Receivable allowances and reserves	$ 64	$ 70
Deferred compensation	32	31
Inventory basis difference	24	30
Other	15	20
Valuation allowance	—	(1)
Net current deferred tax assets[a]	135	150
Non-current deferred tax assets (liabilities):		
Goodwill and other intangible assets	(209)	(219)
Property and equipment	(86)	(90)
Cumulative translation adjustment and hedges	(1)	(8)
Lease obligations	86	92
Deferred compensation	76	79
Unrecognized tax benefits	30	46
Net operating loss carryforwards	19	17
Deferred rent	18	19
Transfer pricing	14	16
Deferred income	12	18
Other	7	(1)
Valuation allowance	(8)	(11)
Net non-current deferred tax liabilities[b]	(42)	(42)
Net deferred tax assets	$ 93	$ 108

[a] The net current deferred tax balance as of March 28, 2015 included current deferred tax liabilities of $10 million recorded within accrued expenses and other current liabilities in the consolidated balance sheets.

[b] The net non-current deferred tax balances as of March 28, 2015 and March 29, 2014 were comprised of non-current deferred tax assets of $45 million and $39 million, respectively, recorded within deferred tax assets, and non-current deferred tax liabilities of $87 million and $81 million, respectively, recorded within other non-current liabilities in the consolidated balance sheets.

The Company has available state and foreign net operating loss carryforwards of $4 million and $72 million, respectively, for tax purposes to offset future taxable income. The net operating loss carryforwards expire beginning in Fiscal 2016.

The Company also has available state and foreign net operating loss carryforwards of $9 million and $11 million, respectively, for which no net deferred tax asset has been recognized. A full valuation allowance has been recorded against these carryforwards since management does not believe that the Company will more likely than not be able to utilize these carryforwards to offset future taxable income. Subsequent recognition of these deferred tax assets would result in an income tax benefit in the year of such recognition. The valuation allowance relating to state net operating loss carryforwards decreased $1 million primarily due to the expiration of certain net operating loss carryforwards. The valuation allowance relating to foreign net operating loss carryforwards decreased $40 million mainly as a result of the legal entity restructuring of certain of the Company's foreign operations during Fiscal 2015, which allows the Company to utilize these net operating loss carryforwards in the future.

Provision has not been made for U.S. or additional foreign taxes on $2.515 billion of undistributed earnings of foreign subsidiaries. Those historical earnings have been and are expected to continue to be permanently reinvested. These earnings could become subject to tax if they were remitted as dividends, if foreign earnings were lent to RLC, a subsidiary or a U.S. affiliate of RLC, or if the stock of the subsidiaries were sold. Determination of the amount of unrecognized deferred tax liability with respect to such earnings is not practical. Management believes that the amount of the additional taxes that might be payable on the earnings of foreign subsidiaries, if remitted, would be partially offset by U.S. foreign tax credits.

In September 2013, the Internal Revenue Service released final tangible property regulations that clarified and expanded Sections 162(a) and 263(a) of the Internal Revenue Code, which relate to the deduction and capitalization of expenditures associated with tangible property, as well as dispositions of tangible property. These regulations became effective for the Company as of the beginning of its Fiscal 2015 and did not have a material impact on its consolidated financial statements.

Uncertain Income Tax Benefits

Fiscal 2015, Fiscal 2014, and Fiscal 2013 Activity

Reconciliations of the beginning and ending amounts of unrecognized tax benefits, excluding interest and penalties, for Fiscal 2015, Fiscal 2014, and Fiscal 2013 are presented below:

(Millions)	Fiscal Years Ended		
	March 28, 2015	March 29, 2014	March 30, 2013
Unrecognized tax benefits beginning balance	$ 83	$100	$129
Additions related to current period tax positions	5	6	4
Additions related to prior period tax positions	10	12	12
Reductions related to prior period tax positions	(1)	(13)[b]	(32)[c]
Reductions related to expiration of statutes of limitations	(1)	(2)	(1)
Reductions related to settlements with taxing authorities	(25)[a]	(23)[b]	(10)[c]
Additions (reductions) related to foreign currency translation	(2)	3	(2)
Unrecognized tax benefits ending balance	$ 69	$ 83	$100

[a] Includes a $20 million decline in unrecognized tax benefits as a result of the Company's tax settlement agreement reached in Fiscal 2015 for the taxable years ended April 2, 2011 and April 3, 2012.

[b] Includes a $29 million decline in unrecognized tax benefits as a result of the Company's tax settlement agreement reached in Fiscal 2014 for the taxable years ended April 3, 2004 and April 2, 2005.

[c] Includes a $34 million decline in unrecognized tax benefits as a result of the Company's tax settlement agreement reached in Fiscal 2013 in connection with a tax examination for the taxable years ended March 29, 2008 through April 3, 2010.

The Company classifies interest and penalties related to unrecognized tax benefits as part of its provision for income taxes. Reconciliations of the beginning and ending amounts of accrued interest and penalties related to unrecognized tax benefits for Fiscal 2015, Fiscal 2014, and Fiscal 2013 are presented below:

(Millions)	Fiscal Years Ended		
	March 28, 2015	March 29, 2014	March 30, 2013
Accrued interest and penalties beginning balance	$49	$50	$39
Net additions charged to expense	6	6	22[a]
Reductions related to prior period tax positions	(1)	(4)	(10)
Reductions related to settlements with taxing authorities	(5)	(5)	(1)
Additions (reductions) related to foreign currency translation	(2)	2	—
Accrued interest and penalties ending balance	$47	$49	$50

[a] Includes a reserve of $17 million for an interest assessment on a prior year withholding tax. No underlying tax exposure exists. The interest assessed was not material to the Company's consolidated financial statements in any period.

The total amount of unrecognized tax benefits, including interest and penalties, was $116 million and $132 million as of March 28, 2015 and March 29, 2014, respectively, and is included within the non-current liability for unrecognized tax benefits in the consolidated balance sheets. The total amount of unrecognized tax benefits that, if recognized, would affect the Company's effective tax rate was $85 million and $86 million as of March 28, 2015 and March 29, 2014, respectively.

The total amount of unrecognized tax benefits relating to the Company's tax positions is subject to change based on future events including, but not limited to, settlements of ongoing tax audits and assessments and the expiration of applicable statutes of limitations. Although the outcomes and timing of such events are highly uncertain, the Company does not anticipate that the balance of gross unrecognized tax benefits, excluding interest and penalties, will change significantly during the next twelve months. However, changes in the occurrence, expected outcomes, and timing of such events could cause the Company's current estimate to change materially in the future.

The Company files a consolidated U.S. federal income tax return, as well as tax returns in various state, local, and foreign jurisdictions. The Company is generally no longer subject to examinations by the relevant tax authorities for years prior to its fiscal year ended April 1, 2006.

CREDIT PROVISION

3.75 PEABODY ENERGY CORPORATION (DEC)

CONSOLIDATED STATEMENTS OF OPERATIONS (in part)

	Year Ended December 31,		
(Dollars in millions, except per share data)	2015	2014	2013
Revenues			
Sales	$ 5,138.3	$6,132.7	$6,380.0
Other revenues	470.9	659.5	633.7
Total revenues	5,609.2	6,792.2	7,013.7
Costs and expenses			
Operating costs and expenses (exclusive of items shown separately below)	5,007.7	5,716.9	5,729.1
Depreciation, depletion and amortization	572.2	655.7	740.3
Asset retirement obligation expenses	45.5	81.0	66.5
Selling and administrative expenses	176.4	227.1	244.2
Restructuring and pension settlement charges	23.5	26.0	11.9
Other operating (income) loss:			
Net gain on disposal of assets	(45.0)	(41.4)	(52.6)
Asset impairment	1,277.8	154.4	528.3
Settlement charges related to the Patriot bankruptcy reorganization	—	—	30.6
Loss from equity affiliates	15.9	107.6	40.2
Operating loss	(1,464.8)	(135.1)	(324.8)
Interest expense	465.4	426.6	408.3
Loss on early debt extinguishment	67.8	1.6	16.9
Interest income	(7.7)	(15.4)	(15.7)
Loss from continuing operations before income taxes	(1,990.3)	(547.9)	(734.3)
Income tax (benefit) provision	(176.4)	201.2	(448.3)
Loss from continuing operations, net of income taxes	(1,813.9)	(749.1)	(286.0)
Loss from discontinued operations, net of income taxes	(175.0)	(28.2)	(226.6)
Net loss	(1,988.9)	(777.3)	(512.6)

NOTES TO CONSOLIDATED FINANCIAL STATEMENTS (in part)

(1) Summary of Significant Accounting Policies (in part)

Income Taxes

Income taxes are accounted for using a balance sheet approach. The Company accounts for deferred income taxes by applying statutory tax rates in effect at the reporting date of the balance sheet to differences between the book and tax basis of assets and liabilities. A valuation allowance is established if it is "more likely than not" that the related tax benefits will not be realized. Significant weight is given to evidence that can be objectively verified including history of tax attribute expiration and cumulative income or loss. In determining the appropriate valuation allowance, the Company considers the projected realization of tax benefits based on expected levels of future taxable income, available tax planning strategies, reversals of existing taxable temporary differences and taxable income in carryback years.

The Company recognizes the tax benefit from uncertain tax positions only if it is "more likely than not" the tax position will be sustained on examination by the taxing authorities based on the technical merits of the position. The tax benefits recognized from such a position are measured based on the largest benefit that has a greater than fifty percent likelihood of being realized upon ultimate settlement. To the extent the Company's assessment of such tax positions changes, the change in estimate will be recorded in the period in which the determination is made. Tax-related interest and penalties are classified as a component of income tax expense.

(10) Income Taxes

Loss from continuing operations before income taxes for the years ended December 31, 2015, 2014 and 2013 consisted of the following:

(Dollars in millions)	Year Ended December 31,		
	2015	2014	2013
U.S.	$ (515.9)	$ 268.9	$ 220.6
Non-U.S.	(1,474.4)	(816.8)	(954.9)
Total	$(1,990.3)	$(547.9)	$(734.3)

Total income tax (benefit) provision for the years ended December 31, 2015, 2014 and 2013 consisted of the following:

(Dollars in millions)	Year Ended December 31,		
	2015	2014	2013
Current:			
U.S. federal	$ (71.9)	$ 27.1	$ (47.9)
Non-U.S.	3.7	(61.1)	38.4
State	(0.6)	3.3	(4.7)
Total current	(68.8)	(30.7)	(14.2)
Deferred:			
U.S. federal	(117.4)	111.0	4.8
Non-U.S.	15.7	122.3	(440.3)
State	(5.9)	(1.4)	1.4
Total deferred	(107.6)	231.9	(434.1)
Total income tax (benefit) provision	$(176.4)	$ 201.2	$(448.3)

The following is a reconciliation of the expected statutory federal income tax benefit to the Company's income tax (benefit) provision for the years ended December 31, 2015, 2014 and 2013:

(Dollars in millions)	Year Ended December 31,		
	2015	2014	2013
Expected income tax benefit at U.S. federal statutory rate	$(696.6)	$(191.7)	$(257.0)
Changes in valuation allowance, income tax	462.0	569.4	(29.4)
Changes in tax reserves	(21.4)	(81.5)	8.8
Excess depletion	(53.7)	(65.3)	(72.7)
Foreign earnings repatriation	—	(71.4)	—
Foreign earnings provision differential	146.5	28.8	62.7
General business tax credits	(15.7)	(19.2)	(18.9)
Minerals resource rent tax, net of federal tax	—	16.1	(87.4)
Remeasurement of foreign income tax accounts	(0.5)	(2.7)	(44.3)
State income taxes, net of federal tax benefit	(20.1)	(2.3)	(0.2)
Other, net	23.1	21.0	(9.9)
Total income tax (benefit) provision	$(176.4)	$ 201.2	$(448.3)

Certain reconciliation items included in the above table exclude the remeasurement of foreign income tax accounts as these foreign currency effects are separately presented.

The tax effects of temporary differences that gave rise to significant portions of the deferred tax assets and liabilities as of December 31, 2015 and 2014 consisted of the following:

(Dollars in millions)	December 31,	
	2015	2014
Deferred tax assets:		
Tax credits and loss carryforwards	$1,817.4	$1,723.5
Accrued postretirement benefit obligations	372.4	372.3
Asset retirement obligations	160.9	167.0
Employee benefits	69.6	70.7
Payable to voluntary employee beneficiary association for certain Patriot retirees[1]	52.9	79.2
Hedge activities	26.6	44.2
Environmental contingencies	—	29.9
Deferred revenue	—	29.1
Financial guarantees	16.9	16.9
Workers' compensation obligations	13.7	6.2
Other	66.7	50.5
Total gross deferred tax assets	2,597.1	2,589.5

(continued)

(Dollars in millions)	December 31, 2015	December 31, 2014
Deferred tax liabilities:		
Property, plant, equipment and mine development, principally due to differences in depreciation, depletion and asset impairments	966.6	1,223.4
Unamortized discount on Convertible Junior Subordinated Debentures	130.3	131.0
Investments and other assets	70.1	73.4
Other	—	1.1
Total gross deferred tax liabilities	1,167.0	1,428.9
Valuation allowance, income tax	(1,447.3)	(1,169.0)
Net deferred tax liability	$ (17.2)	$ (8.4)
Deferred taxes are classified as follows:		
Current deferred income taxes	$ 49.7	$ 80.0
Noncurrent deferred income taxes	(66.9)	(88.4)
Net deferred tax liability	$ (17.2)	$ (8.4)

(1) Refer to Note 25. "Matters Related to the Bankruptcy of Patriot Coal Corporation" herein for additional details related to this transaction.

The Company's tax credits and tax effected loss carryforwards included U.S. alternative minimum tax (AMT) credits of $272.5 million, foreign tax credits of $247.0 million, tax general business credits of $105.4 million, U.S. capital losses of $65.9 million, federal net operating loss (NOL) carryforwards of $9.9 million, state NOL carryforwards of $41.3 million, charitable contribution carryforwards of $0.9 million and foreign NOL carryforwards of $1,074.5 million as of December 31, 2015. The AMT credits and foreign NOLs have no expiration date. The federal NOLs expire in 2036. The U.S. capital losses and state NOLs begin to expire in 2017 and 2018, respectively. The foreign tax credits and general business credits begin to expire in 2020 and 2027, respectively.

In assessing the near-term use of NOLs and tax credits and corresponding valuation allowance adjustments, the Company evaluated the expected level of future taxable income, available tax planning strategies, reversals of existing taxable temporary differences and taxable income in carryback years. During the year ended December 31, 2015, the Company continued to record valuation allowance against net deferred tax asset positions in the U.S. and Australia of $177.0 million and $101.3 million, respectively. Recognition of those valuation allowances was driven by recent cumulative book losses, as determined by considering all sources of available income (including items classified as discontinued operations or recorded directly to "Accumulated other comprehensive loss"), which limited the Company's ability to look to future taxable income in assessing the realizability of the related assets. Of the $177.0 million increase in U.S. valuation allowance during the year ended December 31, 2015, $182.7 million and $(5.7) million were reflected in "Income tax (benefit) provision" and "Accumulated other comprehensive loss," respectively.

Unrecognized Tax Benefits

Net unrecognized tax benefits (excluding interest and penalties) were recorded as follows in the consolidated balance sheets as of December 31, 2015 and 2014:

(Dollars in millions)	December 31, 2015	December 31, 2014
Accounts payable and accrued expenses	$ —	$ —
Deferred income taxes	7.9	6.2
Other noncurrent liabilities	11.7	34.7
Net unrecognized tax benefits	$19.6	$40.9
Gross unrecognized tax benefits	$22.9	$44.5

The amount of the Company's gross unrecognized tax benefits decreased by $21.6 million since January 1, 2015 due to the finalization of IRS audits on the 2009 through 2013 tax years, offset by additions for current positions. The amount of the net unrecognized tax benefits that, if recognized, would directly affect the effective tax rate was $19.6 million and $40.9 million at December 31, 2015 and 2014, respectively. A reconciliation of the beginning and ending amount of gross unrecognized tax benefits for the years ended December 31, 2015, 2014 and 2013 is as follows:

(Dollars in millions)	Year Ended December 31, 2015	Year Ended December 31, 2014	Year Ended December 31, 2013
Balance at beginning of period	$ 44.5	$ 143.9	$ 122.8
Additions for current year tax positions	2.3	12.0	6.3
(Reductions) additions for prior year tax positions	(23.5)	—	63.8
Reductions for settlements with tax authorities	(0.4)	(111.4)	—
Reductions for expirations of statutes of limitations	—	—	(49.0)
Balance at end of period	$ 22.9	$ 44.5	$ 143.9

The Company recognizes interest and penalties related to unrecognized tax benefits in its income tax provision. The Company reversed gross interest and penalties of $2.1 million, $8.0 million and $36.0 million for the years ended December 31, 2015, 2014 and 2013, respectively. The Company had $0.4 million and $3.4 million of accrued gross interest and penalties related to unrecognized tax benefits at December 31, 2015 and 2014, respectively.

The Company expects that during the next twelve months there will be no changes to its net unrecognized tax benefits due to potential audit settlements and the expiration of statutes of limitations.

Tax Returns Subject to Examination

The IRS completed its audit of 2009 through 2013 income tax years. The Company's state income tax returns for the tax years 1999 and thereafter remain potentially subject to examination by various state taxing authorities due to NOL carryforwards. The ATO completed its audit of the Company's Australian income tax returns for the tax years 2004 through 2009 as well as its review of the tax years 2010 through 2012. Australian income tax returns for tax years 2010 through 2013 continue to be subject to potential examinations by the ATO.

Foreign Earnings

The Company had immaterial undistributed earnings of foreign subsidiaries as of December 31, 2015. Historically, the Company has not provided for deferred taxes on undistributed earnings because such earnings are considered to be indefinitely reinvested outside of the U.S.

Tax Payments and Refunds

The following table summarizes the Company's income tax (refunds) payments, net for the years ended December 31, 2015, 2014 and 2013:

	Year Ended December 31,		
(Dollars in millions)	2015	2014	2013
U.S.—federal	$(38.1)	$ (7.7)	$ (0.8)
U.S.—state and local	0.4	(6.8)	2.9
Non-U.S.	11.9	(2.2)	79.8
Total income tax (refunds) payments, net	$(25.8)	$(16.7)	$81.9

OPERATING LOSS AND TAX CREDIT CARRYFORWARDS

3.76 TENET HEALTHCARE CORPORATION (DEC)
NOTES TO CONSOLIDATED FINANCIAL STATEMENTS (in part)

Note 1. Significant Accounting Policies (in part)

Income Taxes

We account for income taxes using the asset and liability method. This approach requires the recognition of deferred tax assets and liabilities for the expected future tax consequences of temporary differences between the carrying amounts and the tax bases of assets and liabilities. Income tax receivables and liabilities and deferred tax assets and liabilities are recognized based on the amounts that more likely than not will be sustained upon ultimate settlement with taxing authorities.

Developing our provision for income taxes and analysis of uncertain tax positions requires significant judgment and knowledge of federal and state income tax laws, regulations and strategies, including the determination of deferred tax assets and liabilities and, if necessary, any valuation allowances that may be required for deferred tax assets.

We assess the realization of our deferred tax assets to determine whether an income tax valuation allowance is required. Based on all available evidence, both positive and negative, and the weight of that evidence to the extent such evidence can be objectively verified, we determine whether it is more likely than not that all or a portion of the deferred tax assets will be realized. The main factors that we consider include:
- Cumulative profits/losses in recent years, adjusted for certain nonrecurring items;
- Income/losses expected in future years;
- Unsettled circumstances that, if unfavorably resolved, would adversely affect future operations and profit levels;
- The availability, or lack thereof, of taxable income in prior carryback periods that would limit realization of tax benefits; and
- The carryforward period associated with the deferred tax assets and liabilities.

We consider many factors when evaluating our uncertain tax positions, and such judgments are subject to periodic review. Tax benefits associated with uncertain tax positions are recognized in the period in which one of the following conditions is satisfied: (1) the more likely than not recognition threshold is satisfied; (2) the position is ultimately settled through negotiation or litigation; or (3) the statute of limitations for the taxing authority to examine and challenge the position has expired. Tax benefits associated with an uncertain tax position are derecognized in the period in which the more likely than not recognition threshold is no longer satisfied.

Note 17. Income Taxes

The provision for income taxes for continuing operations for the years ended December 31, 2015, 2014 and 2013 consists of the following:

	Years Ended December 31,		
	2015	2014	2013
Current tax expense (benefit):			
Federal	$ (2)	$(12)	$ 2
State	28	18	4
	26	6	6
Deferred tax expense (benefit):			
Federal	24	46	(56)
State	18	(3)	(15)
	42	43	(71)
	$68	$ 49	$(65)

A reconciliation between the amount of reported income tax expense (benefit) and the amount computed by multiplying income (loss) from continuing operations before income taxes by the statutory federal income tax rate is shown below. State income tax for the year ended December 31, 2015 includes $11 million of expense related to the write off of expired unutilized state net operating loss carryforwards for which a full valuation allowance had been provided in prior years. A corresponding tax benefit of $11 million is included for the year ended December 31, 2015 to reflect the reduction in the valuation allowance.

	Years Ended December 31,		
	2015	2014	2013
Tax expense at statutory federal rate of 35%	$ 50	$ 52	$(55)
State income taxes, net of federal income tax benefit	18	5	1
Expired state net operating losses, net of federal income tax benefit	11	34	—
Tax attributable to noncontrolling interests	(59)	(23)	(10)
Nondeductible goodwill	22	—	—
Nontaxable gains	(11)	—	—
Nondeductible litigation	44	—	—
Nondeductible acquisition costs	4	2	6
Nondeductible health insurance provider fee	2	3	—
Changes in valuation allowance	4	(20)	(2)
Change in tax contingency reserves, including interest	7	(2)	(7)
Amendment of prior-year tax returns	(17)	—	—
Prior-year provision to return adjustments and other changes in deferred taxes	(12)	(5)	3
Other items	5	3	(1)
	$ 68	$ 49	$(65)

Deferred income taxes reflect the tax effects of temporary differences between the carrying amount of assets and liabilities for financial reporting purposes and the amount used for income tax purposes. The following table discloses those significant components of our deferred tax assets and liabilities, including any valuation allowance:

	December 31, 2015		December 31, 2014	
	Assets	Liabilities	Assets	Liabilities
Depreciation and fixed-asset differences	$ —	$ 718	$ —	$ 847
Reserves related to discontinued operations and restructuring charges	15	—	28	—
Receivables (doubtful accounts and adjustments)	185	—	173	—
Deferred gain on debt exchanges	—	32	—	42
Accruals for retained insurance risks	318	—	329	—
Intangible assets	—	366	—	157
Other long-term liabilities	141	—	166	—
Benefit plans	459	—	451	—
Other accrued liabilities	99	—	83	—
Investments and other assets	—	69	—	4
Net operating loss carryforwards	715	—	659	—
Stock-based compensation	40	—	31	—
Other items	55	6	80	—
	2,027	1,191	2,000	1,050
Valuation allowance	(96)		(87)	
	$1,931	$1,191	$1,913	$1,050

Below is a reconciliation of the deferred tax assets and liabilities and the corresponding amounts reported in the accompanying Consolidated Balance Sheets.

	December 31,	
	2015	**2014**
Deferred income tax assets	$776	$863
Other long-term liabilities	(36)	—
Net deferred tax asset	$740	$863

During the year ended December 31, 2015, the valuation allowance increased by $9 million, $5 million due to the acquisition of USPI and $4 million due to changes in expected realizability of deferred tax assets. The balance in the valuation allowance as of December 31, 2015 is $96 million. During the year ended December 31, 2014, the valuation allowance decreased by $20 million, primarily due to the expiration of unutilized state net operating loss carryovers. During the year ended December 31, 2013, the valuation allowance increased by $51 million, $34 million due to the acquisition of Vanguard and $17 million primarily due to the adjustment of deferred tax assets for state net operating loss carryforwards that have a full valuation allowance.

We account for uncertain tax positions in accordance with ASC 740-10-25, which prescribes a comprehensive model for the financial statement recognition, measurement, presentation and disclosure of uncertain tax positions taken or expected to be taken in income tax returns. The table below summarizes the total changes in unrecognized tax benefits during the year ended December 31, 2015. The additions and reductions for tax positions include the impact of items for which the ultimate deductibility is highly certain, but for which there is uncertainty about the timing of such deductions. Such amounts include unrecognized tax benefits that have impacted deferred tax assets and liabilities at December 31, 2015, 2014 and 2013.

	Continuing Operations	Discontinued Operations	Total
Balance at December 31, 2012	31	1	32
Additions for prior-year tax positions	15	—	15
Additions for current-year tax positions	3	—	3
Reductions due to a lapse of statute of limitations	(6)	(1)	(7)
Balance at December 31, 2013	43	$—	43
Reductions for tax positions of prior years	(1)	—	(1)
Additions for current-year tax positions	1	—	1
Reductions due to a lapse of statute of limitations	(5)	—	(5)
Balance at December 31, 2014	$38	$—	$38
Additions for prior-year tax positions	1	—	1
Additions for current-year tax positions	5	—	5
Reductions due to a lapse of statute of limitations	(4)	—	(4)
Balance at December 31, 2015	$40	$—	$40

The total amount of unrecognized tax benefits as of December 31, 2015 was $40 million, of which $37 million, if recognized, would affect our effective tax rate and income tax expense (benefit) from continuing operations. Income tax expense in the year ended December 31, 2015 includes expense of $2 million in continuing operations attributable to a increase in our estimated liabilities for uncertain tax positions, net of related deferred tax effects. The total amount of unrecognized tax benefits as of December 31, 2014 was $38 million, of which $31 million, if recognized, would affect our effective tax rate and income tax expense (benefit) from continuing operations. Income tax expense in the year ended December 31, 2014 includes a benefit of $6 million in continuing operations attributable to a decrease in our estimated liabilities for uncertain tax positions, net of related deferred tax effects. The total amount of unrecognized tax benefits as of December 31, 2013 was $43 million, of which $34 million, if recognized, would affect our effective tax rate and income tax expense (benefit) from continuing and discontinued operations. Income tax expense in the year ended December 31, 2013 includes a benefit of $1 million in continuing operations attributable to a decrease in our estimated liabilities for uncertain tax positions, net of related deferred tax effects.

Our practice is to recognize interest and/or penalties related to income tax matters in income tax expense in our consolidated statements of operations. Approximately $3 million of interest and penalties related to accrued liabilities for uncertain tax positions related to continuing operations are included in the accompanying Consolidated Statement of Operations for the year ended December 31, 2015. Total accrued interest and penalties on unrecognized tax benefits as of December 31, 2015 were $6 million, all of which related to continuing operations.

The Internal Revenue Service ("IRS") has completed audits of our tax returns for all tax years ending on or before December 31, 2007, and of Vanguard's tax returns for fiscal years ending on or before June 30, 2004. All disputed issues with respect to these audits have been resolved and all related tax assessments (including interest) have been paid. Our tax returns for years ended after December 31, 2007, and Vanguard's tax returns for fiscal years ended after June 30, 2004 remain subject to examination by the IRS. Vanguard's tax returns for fiscal years ended June 30, 2013 and October 1, 2013 are currently under audit by the IRS. USPI tax returns for years ended after December 31, 2011 remain subject to audit.

As of December 31, 2015, approximately $7 million of unrecognized federal and state tax benefits, as well as reserves for interest and penalties, may decrease in the next 12 months as a result of the settlement of audits, the filing of amended tax returns or the expiration of statutes of limitations.

At December 31, 2015, our carryforwards available to offset future taxable income consisted of (1) federal net operating loss ("NOL") carryforwards of approximately $1.8 billion pretax expiring in 2024 to 2034, (2) approximately $28 million in alternative minimum tax credits with no expiration, (3) general business credit carryforwards of approximately $22 million expiring in 2023 through 2035, and (4) state NOL carryforwards of $3.1 billion expiring in 2014 through 2035 for which the associated deferred tax benefit, net of valuation allowance and federal tax impact, is $12 million. Our ability to utilize NOL carryforwards to reduce future taxable income may be limited under Section 382 of the Internal Revenue Code if certain ownership changes in our company occur during a rolling three-year period. These ownership changes include purchases of common stock under share repurchase programs (see Note 2), the offering of stock by us, the purchase or sale of our stock by 5% shareholders, as defined in the Treasury regulations, or the issuance or exercise of rights to acquire our stock. If such ownership changes by 5% shareholders result in aggregate increases that exceed 50 percentage points during the three-year period, then Section 382 imposes an annual limitation on the amount of our taxable income that may be offset by the NOL carryforwards or tax credit carryforwards at the time of ownership change.

3.77 VALERO ENERGY CORPORATION (DEC)
NOTES TO CONSOLIDATED FINANCIAL STATEMENTS (in part)

1. Basis of Presentation and Significant Accounting Policies (in part)

Income Taxes

Income taxes are accounted for under the asset and liability method. Under this method, deferred tax assets and liabilities are recognized for the future tax consequences attributable to differences between the financial statement carrying amounts of existing assets and liabilities and their respective tax bases. Deferred amounts are measured using enacted tax rates expected to apply to taxable income in the year those temporary differences are expected to be recovered or settled. Deferred tax assets are reduced by unrecognized tax benefits, if such items may be available to offset the unrecognized tax benefit.

We have elected to classify any interest expense and penalties related to the underpayment of income taxes in income tax expense.

New Accounting Pronouncements (in part)

In November 2015, the provisions of ASC Topic 740, "Income Taxes," were amended to simplify the presentation of deferred income taxes. The amendments require that deferred tax liabilities and assets be classified as noncurrent in a classified balance sheet. The amendments are effective for financial statements for annual periods beginning after December 15, 2016, and interim periods within those annual periods, with early adoption permitted as of the beginning of any interim or annual period. The amendments may be applied either prospectively to all deferred tax liabilities and assets or retrospectively to all periods presented. Entities applying the guidance retrospectively should disclose in the first interim and first annual period of adoption the nature of and reason for the change in accounting principle and quantitative information about the effects of the accounting change on prior periods. Effective January 1, 2016, the adoption of this guidance on a retrospective basis will not materially affect our financial position and will not impact our results of operations. Upon adoption, our current deferred income tax assets of $74 million and current deferred income tax liabilities of $366 million as of December 31, 2015 will be reclassified to noncurrent deferred income tax liabilities. Adoption of this guidance simplifies the future presentation of our deferred income tax assets and liabilities.

15. Income Taxes

Income Tax Expense

Income from continuing operations before income tax expense was as follows (in millions):

	Year Ended December 31,		
	2015	**2014**	**2013**
U.S. operations	$5,327	$4,677	$3,531
International operations	644	875	445
Income from continuing operations before income tax expense	$5,971	$5,552	$3,976

The following is a reconciliation of income tax expense computed by applying statutory income tax rates as reflected in the table below to actual income tax expense related to continuing operations (in millions):

| | Year Ended December 31, 2015 | | |
	U.S.	International	Total
Income tax expense at statutory rates	$1,864	$ 92	$1,956
U.S. state and Canadian provincial tax expense, net of federal income tax effect	45	73	118
Permanent differences:			
Manufacturing deduction	(102)	—	(102)
Other	(18)	(5)	(23)
Change in tax law	—	(17)	(17)
Tax effects of income associated with noncontrolling interests	(39)	—	(39)
Other, net	(25)	2	(23)
Income tax expense	$1,725	$145	$1,870

| | Year Ended December 31, 2014 | | |
	U.S.	International	Total
Income tax expense at statutory rates	$1,637	$145	$1,782
U.S. state and Canadian provincial tax expense, net of federal income tax effect	62	71	133
Permanent differences:			
Manufacturing deduction	(74)	—	(74)
Other	(16)	1	(15)
Tax effects of income associated with noncontrolling interests	(28)	—	(28)
Other, net	(22)	1	(21)
Income tax expense	$1,559	$218	$1,777

| | Year Ended December 31, 2013 | | |
	U.S.	International	Total
Income tax expense at statutory rates	$1,236	$ 84	$1,320
U.S. state and Canadian provincial tax expense, net of federal income tax effect	62	24	86
Permanent differences:			
Manufacturing deduction	(36)	—	(36)
Nontaxable gain on disposition (See Notes 3 and 10)	(114)	—	(114)
Other	10	(1)	9
Change in tax law	(10)	(22)	(32)
Tax effects of income associated with noncontrolling interests	(3)	—	(3)
Other, net	44	(20)	24
Income tax expense	$1,189	$ 65	$1,254

Statutory income tax rates applicable to the countries in which we operate were as follows:

| | Year Ended December 31, | | |
	2015	2014	2013
U.S.	35%	35%	35%
Canada	15%	15%	15%
U.K.	20%	21%	23%
Ireland	13%	13%	13%
Aruba	7%	7%	7%

There was no income tax expense or benefit related to discontinued operations for the years ended December 31, 2015, 2014, and 2013.

Components of income tax expense related to continuing operations were as follows (in millions):

| | Year Ended December 31, 2015 | | |
	U.S.	International	Total
Current:			
Country	$1,513	$ 64	$1,577
U.S. state/Canadian provincial	85	43	128
Total current	1,598	107	1,705
Deferred:			
Country	143	8	151
U.S. state/Canadian provincial	(16)	30	14
Total deferred	127	38	165
Income tax expense	$1,725	$145	$1,870

	Year Ended December 31, 2014		
	U.S.	International	Total
Current:			
Country	$1,196	$ 53	$1,249
U.S. state/Canadian provincial	59	24	83
Total current	1,255	77	1,332
Deferred:			
Country	268	94	362
U.S. state/Canadian provincial	36	47	83
Total deferred	304	141	445
Income tax expense	$1,559	$218	$1,777

	Year Ended December 31, 2013		
	U.S.	International	Total
Current:			
Country	$ 635	$ 53	$ 688
U.S. state/Canadian provincial	36	29	65
Total current	671	82	753
Deferred:			
Country	459	(12)	447
U.S. state/Canadian provincial	59	(5)	54
Total deferred	518	(17)	501
Income tax expense	$1,189	$ 65	$1,254

Deferred Income Tax Assets and Liabilities

The tax effects of significant temporary differences representing deferred income tax assets and liabilities were as follows (in millions):

	December 31,	
	2015	2014
Deferred income tax assets:		
Tax credit carryforwards	$ 33	$ 37
Net operating losses (NOLs)	423	436
Inventories	72	160
Compensation and employee benefit liabilities	331	358
Environmental liabilities	80	92
Other	139	178
Total deferred income tax assets	1,078	1,261
Less: Valuation allowance	(435)	(393)
Net deferred income tax assets	643	868
Deferred income tax liabilities:		
Property, plant, and equipment	6,725	6,682
Deferred turnaround costs	394	356
Inventories	287	426
Investments	226	152
Other	71	73
Total deferred income tax liabilities	7,703	7,689
Net deferred income tax liabilities	$7,060	$6,821

We had the following income tax credit and loss carryforwards as of December 31, 2015 (in millions):

	Amount	Expiration
U.S. state income tax credits	$ 51	2016 through 2027
U.S. state NOLs (gross amount)	7,302	2016 through 2035
International NOLs	1,465	Unlimited

We have recorded a valuation allowance as of December 31, 2015 and 2014 due to uncertainties related to our ability to utilize some of our deferred income tax assets, primarily consisting of certain U.S. state income tax credits and NOLs, and international NOLs, before they expire. The valuation allowance is based on our estimates of taxable income in the various jurisdictions in which we operate and the period over which deferred income tax assets will be recoverable. During 2015, the valuation allowance increased by $42 million, primarily due to increases in U.S. state NOLs. The realization of net deferred income tax assets recorded as of December 31, 2015 is primarily dependent upon our ability to generate future taxable income in certain U.S. states and international jurisdictions.

Should we ultimately recognize tax benefits related to the valuation allowance for deferred income tax assets as of December 31, 2015, such amounts will be allocated as follows (in millions):

Income tax benefit	$429
Additional paid-in capital	6
Total	$435

Deferred income taxes have not been provided on the future tax consequences attributable to differences between the financial statement carrying amounts of existing assets and liabilities and the respective tax bases of our international subsidiaries based on the determination that such differences are essentially permanent in duration in that the earnings of these subsidiaries are expected to be indefinitely reinvested in the international operations. As of December 31, 2015, the cumulative undistributed earnings of these subsidiaries were approximately $3.2 billion. If those earnings were not considered indefinitely reinvested, deferred income taxes would have been recorded after consideration of U.S. foreign tax credits. It is not practicable to estimate the amount of additional tax that might be payable on those earnings, if distributed.

Unrecognized Tax Benefits

The following is a reconciliation of the change in unrecognized tax benefits, excluding related penalties, interest (net of the U.S. federal and state income tax effects), and the U.S. federal income tax effect of state unrecognized tax benefits (in millions):

	Year Ended December 31,		
	2015	2014	2013
Balance as of beginning of year	$989	$950	$341
Additions based on tax positions related to the current year	36	35	64
Additions for tax positions related to prior years	83	118	576
Reductions for tax positions related to prior years	(82)	(67)	(26)
Reductions for tax positions related to the lapse of applicable statute of limitations	(3)	(1)	(4)
Settlements	(59)	(46)	(1)
Balance as of end of year	$964	$989	$950

As of December 31, 2015, the balance in unrecognized tax benefits includes $570 million of tax refunds that we intend to claim by amending various of our income tax returns for 2005 through 2015. We intend to propose that incentive payments received from the U.S. federal government for blending biofuels into refined products be excluded from taxable income during these periods. However, due to the complexity of this matter and uncertainties with respect to the interpretation of the Internal Revenue Code, we concluded that the refund claims included in the reconciliation below cannot be recognized in our financial statements. As a result, these amounts are not included in our uncertain tax position liabilities as of December 31, 2015, 2014, and 2013 even though they are reflected in the table above.

The following is a reconciliation of unrecognized tax benefits reflected in the table above to our uncertain tax position liabilities as of December 31, 2015 and 2014 that are reflected in Note 9 (in millions):

	December 31,	
	2015	2014
Unrecognized tax benefits	$ 964	$ 989
Tax refund claim not recognized in our financial statements	(570)	(554)
Reduction of deferred tax asset	(28)	—
Penalties, interest (net of U.S. federal and state income tax effect), and the U.S. federal income tax effect of state unrecognized tax benefits	25	49
Uncertain tax position liabilities	$ 391	$ 484

As of December 31, 2015 and 2014, there were $757 million and $768 million, respectively, of unrecognized tax benefits that if recognized would affect our annual effective tax rate.

During the years ended December 31, 2015, 2014, and 2013, we recognized $5 million, $2 million, and $12 million, respectively, in penalties and interest, which are reflected within income tax expense. Accrued penalties and interest totaled $117 million and $141 million as of December 31, 2015 and 2014, respectively, excluding the U.S. federal and state income tax effects related to interest.

During the next 12 months, it is reasonably possible that tax audit resolutions could reduce unrecognized tax benefits, excluding interest, by approximately $370 million, either because the tax positions are sustained on audit or because we agree to their disallowance. We do not expect these reductions to have a significant impact on our financial statements because such reductions would not significantly affect our annual effective rate.

Tax Returns Under Audit

As of December 31, 2015, our tax years for 2008 through 2011 were under audit by the IRS. The IRS has proposed adjustments to our taxable income for certain open years. We are protesting the proposed adjustments and do not expect that the ultimate disposition of these adjustments will result in a material change to our financial position, results of operations, or liquidity. We are continuing to work with the IRS to resolve these matters and we believe that they will be resolved for amounts consistent with recorded amounts of unrecognized tax benefits associated with these matters.

During the year ended December 31, 2015, we settled the audits related to our 2004 through 2007 tax years consistent with the recorded amounts of uncertain tax position liabilities associated with those audits.

TAXES ON UNDISTRIBUTED EARNINGS

3.78 HANESBRANDS INC. (DEC)
MANAGEMENT'S DISCUSSION AND ANALYSIS OF FINANCIAL CONDITION AND RESULTS OF OPERATIONS (in part)

Liquidity and Capital Resources (in part)

Undistributed Earnings from Foreign Subsidiaries

As of January 2, 2016, the cumulative amount of undistributed earnings from our foreign subsidiaries was approximately $2.7 billion, of which $319 million of cash and cash equivalents was held by foreign subsidiaries whose undistributed earnings are considered permanently reinvested, and less than $1 million of cash and cash equivalents was held by foreign subsidiaries whose undistributed earnings are not considered permanently reinvested. Our intention is to reinvest the cash and cash equivalents of those entities whose undistributed earnings we have previously asserted as being permanently reinvested in our international operations. We reassess our reinvestment assertions each reporting period and currently believe that we have sufficient other sources of liquidity to support our assertion that such undistributed earnings held by foreign subsidiaries may be considered to be reinvested permanently.

We repatriated $124 million, $15 million and $10 million in 2015, 2014 and 2013, respectively, from earnings generated in such years. The amount of the current year foreign earnings that we have repatriated in the past has been determined, and the amount that we expect to repatriate during 2016 will be determined, based upon a variety of factors including current year earnings of the foreign subsidiaries, foreign investment needs and the cash flow needs we have in the U.S., such as for the repayment of debt and other domestic obligations. The majority of our repatriation of the earnings of foreign subsidiaries has historically occurred at year-end, although we may always repatriate funds earlier in the year based on the needs of our business. When we repatriate funds to the U.S., we are required to pay taxes on these amounts based on applicable U.S. tax rates, net of any foreign tax that would be allowed to be deducted or taken as a credit against U.S. income tax. There was a cost of $43 million, $1 million and $1 million in additional U.S. federal income taxes in 2015, 2014 and 2013, respectively, as a result of repatriation of foreign earnings generated in such years.

Construction-Type and Production-Type Contracts

RECOGNITION AND MEASUREMENT

3.79 Accounting and disclosure requirements for construction-type and production-type contracts are discussed in FASB ASC 605-35. Two accounting methods commonly followed by contractors are the percentage-of-completion method and the completed-contract method. The two methods should be used in specific circumstances and should not be used as acceptable alternatives for the same circumstances. The use of either of the two generally accepted methods involves, to a greater or lesser extent, three key areas of estimates and uncertainties, including the extent of progress toward completion, contract revenues, and contract costs.

CONSTRUCTION- AND PRODUCTION-TYPE CONTRACTS

3.80 NORTHROP GRUMMAN CORPORATION (DEC)

CONSOLIDATED STATEMENTS OF EARNINGS AND COMPREHENSIVE INCOME (LOSS) (in part)

	Year Ended December 31		
$ in millions, except per share amounts	2015	2014	2013
Sales			
Product	$13,966	$14,015	$14,033
Service	9,560	9,964	10,628
Total sales	23,526	23,979	24,661
Operating costs and expenses			
Product	10,333	10,431	10,623
Service	7,551	7,947	8,659
General and administrative expenses	2,566	2,405	2,256
Operating income	3,076	3,196	3,123
Other (expense) income			
Interest expense	(301)	(282)	(257)
Other, net	15	23	(3)
Earnings before income taxes	2,790	2,937	2,863
Federal and foreign income tax expense	800	868	911
Net earnings	$ 1,990	$ 2,069	$ 1,952

NOTES TO CONSOLIDATED FINANCIAL STATEMENTS (in part)

1. Summary of Significant Accounting Policies (in part)

Revenue Recognition

The majority of our sales are derived from long-term contracts with the U.S. Government for the production of goods, the provision of services, or in some cases, a combination of both. In accounting for these contracts, we utilize either the cost-to-cost method or the units-of-delivery method of percentage-of-completion accounting, with cost-to-cost being the predominant method. Generally, sales under cost-reimbursement contracts and construction-type contracts that provide for deliveries at lower volume rates per year or a small number of units are accounted for using the cost-to-cost method. Under this method, sales, including estimated profits, are recorded as costs are incurred. Generally, sales under contracts that provide for deliveries at higher volume rates per year or a large number of units are accounted for using the units-of-delivery method. Under this method, cost and sales are recognized as units are delivered to the customer. The company estimates profit on contracts as the difference between total estimated sales and total estimated cost at completion and recognizes that profit either as costs are incurred (cost-to-cost) or as units are delivered (units-of-delivery). The company classifies sales as product or service depending upon the predominant attributes of the contract.

Contract sales may include estimated amounts not contractually agreed to by the customer, including cost or performance incentives (such as award and incentive fees), un-priced change orders, claims and requests for equitable adjustment (REAs). Further, as contracts are performed, change orders can be a regular occurrence and may be un-priced until negotiated with the customer. Un-priced change orders are included in estimated contract sales when management believes it is probable they will be recovered through a change in contract price. Amounts representing claims (including change orders unapproved as to both scope and price) and REAs are included in estimated contract sales when management believes it is probable the claim and/or REA will result in additional contract revenue and the amount can be reliably estimated based on the facts and circumstances known to us at the time. As of December 31, 2015, the company has initiated REAs with the U.S. government and an international customer seeking recovery of approximately $300 million under contracts related to two Aerospace Systems programs. A substantial portion of the REAs was initiated during the fourth quarter of 2015. The REAs relate to what we believe is work performed by the company at the direction of our customers that is beyond the scope of the related contracts as well as costs incurred by the company as a result of customer-caused delays and disruption. The total amount of additional contract sales we have assumed as of December 31, 2015 is approximately $225 million.

We are currently negotiating the REAs and the terms of the contracts with our customers. Recognized amounts related to claims and REAs as of December 31, 2014 were not material individually or in aggregate.

The company's U.S. Government contracts generally contain provisions that enable the customer to terminate a contract for default, or for the convenience of the government. If a contract is terminated for default, we may not be entitled to recover any of our costs on partially completed work and may be liable to the government for re-procurement costs of acquiring similar products or services from another contractor, and for certain other damages. Termination of a contract for the convenience of the government may occur when the government concludes it is in the best interests of the government that the contract be terminated. Under a termination for convenience, the contractor is typically entitled to be paid in accordance with the contract's terms for costs incurred prior to the effective date of termination, plus a reasonable profit and settlement expenses. At December 31, 2015, the company did not have any contract terminations in process that we anticipate would have a material effect on our consolidated financial position, annual results of operations and/or cash flows.

Net Estimate-At-Completion (EAC) Adjustments—We recognize changes in estimated contract sales, costs or profits using the cumulative catch-up method of accounting. This method recognizes, in the current period, the cumulative effect of the changes on current and prior periods as net EAC adjustments; sales and profit in future periods of contract performance are recognized as if the revised estimates had been used since contract inception. If it is determined that a loss will result from the performance of a contract, the entire amount of the estimable future loss is charged against income in the period the loss is identified. Loss provisions are first offset against any costs that are included in unbilled accounts receivable or inventoried costs, and any remaining amount is reflected in liabilities.

Significant EAC adjustments on a single contract could have a material effect on the company's consolidated financial position or annual results of operations. Where such adjustments occur, we generally disclose the nature, underlying conditions and financial impact of the adjustments. No discrete event or adjustments to an individual contract were material to the accompanying consolidated statements of earnings and comprehensive income (loss) for each of the three years ended December 31, 2015, 2014, and 2013.

The following table presents the effect of aggregate net EAC adjustments:

	Year Ended December 31		
$ in millions, except per share data	2015	2014	2013
Operating Income	$ 580	$ 664	$ 753
Net Earnings[1]	377	432	489
Diluted earnings per share[1]	1.97	2.04	2.09

[1] Based on statutory tax rates

Sales by Customer Category—The following table presents sales by customer category:

	Year Ended December 31					
	2015		2014		2013	
$ in millions	$	%[1]	$	%[1]	$	%[1]
U.S. Government[2]	$19,458	83%	$20,085	84%	$21,278	86%
International[3]	3,339	14%	3,045	13%	2,493	10%
Other Customers[4]	729	3%	849	3%	890	4%
Total Sales	$23,526		$23,979		$24,661	

[1] Percentage of total sales.

[2] Sales to the U.S. Government include sales from contracts for which Northrop Grumman is the prime contractor, as well as those for which the company is a subcontractor and the ultimate customer is the U.S. Government. Each of the company's segments derives substantial revenue from the U.S. Government.

[3] International sales include foreign military sales contracted through the U.S. Government, direct commercial sales with governments outside the U.S. and commercial sales outside the U.S.

[4] Sales to Other Customers include sales to U.S. state and local governments and U.S. commercial customers.

Accounts Receivable and Inventoried Costs

Accounts receivable include amounts billed and currently due from customers, as well as amounts currently due but unbilled (primarily related to costs incurred on contracts accounted for under the cost-to-cost method of percentage-of- completion accounting). Accounts receivable also include certain estimated contract change amounts, claims or REAs in negotiation that are probable of recovery and amounts retained by the customer pending contract completion.

Inventoried costs primarily relate to work in process on contracts accounted for under the units-of-delivery method of percentage-of-completion accounting. These costs represent accumulated contract costs less the portion of such costs allocated to delivered items. Product inventory primarily consists of raw materials and is stated at the lower of cost or market, generally using the average cost method.

Accumulated contract costs in unbilled accounts receivable and inventoried costs include direct production costs, factory and engineering overhead, production tooling costs, and, for government contracts, allowable general and administrative expenses. According to the provisions of U.S. Government contracts, the customer asserts title to, or a security interest in, inventories related to such contracts as a result of contract advances, performance-based payments, and progress payments. In accordance with industry practice, unbilled accounts receivable and inventoried costs are classified as current assets and include amounts related to contracts having production cycles longer than one year. Payments received in excess of inventoried costs and unbilled accounts receivable amounts on a contract by contract basis are recorded as advance payments and amounts in excess of costs incurred in the consolidated statements of financial position.

3.81 AECOM (SEP)
CONSOLIDATED STATEMENTS OF OPERATIONS (in part)

(in thousands, except per share data)

| | Fiscal Year Ended | | |
	September 30, 2015	September 30, 2014	September 30, 2013
Revenue	$17,989,880	$8,356,783	$8,153,495
Cost of revenue	17,454,692	7,953,607	7,703,507
Gross profit	535,188	403,176	449,988
Equity in earnings of joint ventures	106,245	57,924	24,319
General and administrative expenses	(113,975)	(80,908)	(97,318)
Acquisition and integration expenses	(398,440)	(27,310)	—
Income from operations	129,018	352,882	376,989
Other income	19,139	2,748	3,522
Interest expense	(299,627)	(40,842)	(44,737)
(Loss) income before income tax (benefit) expense	(151,470)	314,788	335,774
Income tax (benefit) expense	(80,237)	82,024	92,578
Net (loss) income	(71,233)	232,764	243,196

NOTES TO CONSOLIDATED FINANCIAL STATEMENTS (in part)

1. Significant Accounting Policies (in part)

Revenue Recognition—The Company generally utilizes a cost-to-cost approach in applying the percentage-of-completion method of revenue recognition. Under this approach, revenue is earned in proportion to total costs incurred, divided by total costs expected to be incurred. Recognition of revenue and profit is dependent upon a number of factors, including the accuracy of a variety of estimates made at the balance sheet date, engineering progress, materials quantities, the achievement of milestones, penalty provisions, labor productivity and cost estimates made at the balance sheet date. Due to uncertainties inherent in the estimation process, actual completion costs may vary from estimates. If estimated total costs on contracts indicate a loss, the Company recognizes that estimated loss in the period the estimated loss first becomes known.

In the course of providing its services, the Company routinely subcontracts for services and incurs other direct costs on behalf of its clients. These costs are passed through to clients and, in accordance with industry practice and GAAP, are included in the Company's revenue and cost of revenue. Because subcontractor services and other direct costs can change significantly from project to project and period to period, changes in revenue may not be indicative of business trends. These other direct costs for the years ended September 30, 2015, 2014 and 2013 were $8.3 billion, $3.5 billion and $3.2 billion, respectively.

Cost-Reimbursable Contracts

Cost-reimbursable contracts consists of two similar contract types: cost-plus and time-and-materials.

Cost-Plus Contracts. The Company enters into two major types of cost-plus contracts:

Cost-Plus Fixed Fee. Under cost-plus fixed fee contracts, the Company charges clients for its costs, including both direct and indirect costs, plus a fixed negotiated fee. The total estimated cost plus the fixed negotiated fee represents the total contract value. The Company recognizes revenue based on the actual labor and other direct costs incurred, plus the portion of the fixed fee it has earned to date.

Cost-Plus Fixed Rate. Under the Company's cost-plus fixed rate contracts, the Company charges clients for its direct and indirect costs based upon a negotiated rate. The Company recognizes revenue based on the actual total costs it has expended and the applicable fixed rate.

Certain cost-plus contracts provide for award fees or a penalty based on performance criteria in lieu of a fixed fee or fixed rate. Other contracts include a base fee component plus a performance-based award fee. In addition, the Company may share award fees with subcontractors. The Company records accruals for fee-sharing as fees are earned. The Company generally recognizes revenue to the extent of costs actually incurred plus a proportionate amount of the fee expected to be earned. The Company takes the award fee or penalty on contracts into consideration when estimating revenue and profit rates, and it records revenue related to the award fees when there is sufficient information to assess anticipated contract performance. On contracts that represent higher than normal risk or technical difficulty, the Company may defer all award fees until an award fee letter is received. Once an award fee letter is received, the estimated or accrued fees are adjusted to the actual award amount.

Certain cost-plus contracts provide for incentive fees based on performance against contractual milestones. The amount of the incentive fees varies, depending on whether the Company achieves above, at, or below target results. The Company originally recognizes revenue on these contracts based upon expected results. These estimates are revised when necessary based upon additional information that becomes available as the contract progresses.

Time-and-Materials Contracts

Time-and-Materials. Under time-and-materials contracts, the Company negotiates hourly billing rates and charges its clients based on the actual time that it expends on a project. In addition, clients reimburse the Company for its actual out-of-pocket costs of materials and other direct incidental expenditures that it incurs in connection with its performance under the contract. Profit margins on time-and-materials contracts fluctuate based on actual labor and overhead costs that it directly charges or allocates to contracts compared to negotiated billing rates. Many of the Company's time-and-materials contracts are subject to maximum contract values and, accordingly, revenue relating to these contracts is recognized as if these contracts were a fixed-price contract.

Guaranteed Maximum Price Contracts

Guaranteed Maximum Price. Guaranteed maximum price contracts (GMP) are common for design-build and commercial and residential projects. GMP contracts share many of the same contract provisions as cost-plus and fixed-price contracts. A contractor performing work pursuant to a cost-plus, GMP or fixed-price contract will all enter into trade contracts directly. Both cost-plus and GMP contracts generally include an agreed lump sum or percentage fee which is called out and separately identified and the contracts are considered 'open' book providing the owner with full disclosure of the project costs. A fixed-price contract provides the owner with a single lump sum amount without specifically identifying the breakdown of fee or costs and is typically 'closed' book thereby providing the owner with little detail as to the project costs. In a GMP contract, unlike the cost-plus contract, we provide the owner with a guaranteed price for the overall construction (adjusted only for change orders issued by the owner) and with a schedule which includes a completion date for the project. In addition, cost overruns in a GMP contract would generally be our responsibility and in the event our actions or inactions result in delays to the project we may be responsible to the owner for costs associated with such delay. For many of our commercial and residential GMP contracts, the final price is generally not established until we have awarded a substantial percentage of the trade contracts and we have negotiated additional contractual limitations, such as mutual waivers of consequential damages as well as aggregate caps on liabilities and liquidated damages.

Fixed-Price Contracts

Fixed-Price. Fixed-price contracting is the predominant contracting method outside of the United States. There are typically two types of fixed-price contracts. The first and more common type, lump-sum, involves performing all of the work under the contract for a specified lump-sum fee. Lump-sum contracts are typically subject to price adjustments if the scope of the project changes or unforeseen conditions arise. The second type, fixed-unit price, involves performing an estimated number of units of work at an agreed price per unit, with the total payment under the contract determined by the actual number of units delivered. The Company recognizes revenue on fixed-price contracts using the percentage-of-completion method described above. Prior to completion, recognized profit margins on any fixed-price contract depend on the accuracy of the Company's estimates and will increase to the extent that its actual costs are below the estimated amounts. Conversely, if the Company's costs exceed these estimates, its profit margins will decrease and the Company may realize a loss on a project. The Company recognizes anticipated losses on contracts in the period in which they become evident.

Service-Related Contracts

Service-Related. Service-related contracts, including operations and maintenance services and a variety of technical assistance services, are accounted for over the period of performance, in proportion to the costs of performance.

Contract Claims—Claims are amounts in excess of the agreed contract price (or amounts not included in the original contract price) that the Company seeks to collect from customers or others for delays, errors in specifications and designs, contract terminations, change orders in dispute or unapproved as to both scope and price or other causes of unanticipated additional costs. The Company records contract revenue related to claims only if it is probable that the claim will result in additional contract revenue and if the amount can be reliably estimated. In such cases, the Company records revenue only to the extent that contract costs relating to the claim have been incurred. As of September 30, 2015 and 2014, the Company had no significant net receivables related to contract claims.

Government Contract Matters—The Company's federal government and certain state and local agency contracts are subject to, among other regulations, regulations issued under the Federal Acquisition Regulations (FAR). These regulations can limit the recovery of certain specified indirect costs on contracts and subjects the Company to ongoing multiple audits by government agencies such as the Defense Contract Audit Agency (DCAA). In addition, most of the Company's federal and state and local contracts are subject to termination at the discretion of the client.

Audits by the DCAA and other agencies consist of reviews of the Company's overhead rates, operating systems and cost proposals to ensure that the Company accounted for such costs in accordance with the Cost Accounting Standards of the FAR (CAS). If the DCAA determines the Company has not accounted for such costs consistent with CAS, the DCAA may disallow these costs. There can be no assurance that audits by the DCAA or other governmental agencies will not result in material cost disallowances in the future.

3.82 HARRIS CORPORATION (JUN)
CONSOLIDATED STATEMENT OF INCOME (in part)

	Fiscal Years Ended		
(In millions, except per share amounts)	2015	2014	2013
Revenue from product sales and services			
Revenue from product sales	$ 3,311	$ 3,189	$ 3,204
Revenue from services	1,772	1,823	1,908
	5,083	5,012	5,112
Cost of product sales and services			
Cost of product sales	(1,969)	(1,857)	(1,919)
Cost of services	(1,393)	(1,453)	(1,466)
	(3,362)	(3,310)	(3,385)
Engineering, selling and administrative expenses	(1,008)	(820)	(914)
Non-operating income (loss)	(108)	4	(41)
Interest income	2	3	2
Interest expense	(130)	(94)	(109)
Income from continuing operations before income taxes	477	795	665

NOTES TO CONSOLIDATED FINANCIAL STATEMENTS (in part)

Note 1: Significant Accounting Policies (in part)

Revenue Recognition—Our segments have the following revenue recognition policies:

Development and Production Contracts: Estimates and assumptions, and changes therein, are important in connection with, among others, our segments' revenue recognition policies related to development and production contracts. Revenue and profits related to development and production contracts are recognized using the percentage-of-completion method, generally based on the ratio of costs incurred to estimated total costs at completion (i.e., the cost-to-cost method) or the ratio of actual units delivered to estimated total units to be delivered under the contract (i.e., the "units-of-delivery" method) with consideration given for risk of performance and estimated profit. Revenue and profits on cost-reimbursable development and production contracts are recognized as allowable costs are incurred on the contract, and become billable to the customer, in an amount equal to the allowable costs plus the profit on those costs.

Development and production contracts are combined when specific aggregation criteria are met. Criteria generally include closely interrelated activities performed for a single customer within the same economic environment. Development and production contracts are generally not segmented. If development and production contracts are segmented, we have determined that they meet specific segmenting criteria. Change orders, claims or other items that may change the scope of a development and production contract are included in contract value only when the value can be reliably estimated and realization is probable. Possible incentives or penalties and award fees applicable to performance on development and production contracts are considered in estimating contract value and profit rates and are recorded when there is sufficient information to assess anticipated contract performance. Incentive provisions that increase earnings based solely on a single significant event are generally not recognized until the event occurs.

Under the percentage-of-completion method of accounting, a single estimated total profit margin is used to recognize profit for each development and production contract over its period of performance. Recognition of profit on development and production fixed-price contracts requires estimates of the total cost at completion and the measurement of progress toward completion. The estimated profit or loss on a development and production contract is equal to the difference between the estimated contract value and the estimated total cost at completion. Due to the long-term nature of many of our programs, developing the estimated total cost at completion often requires judgment. Factors that must be considered in estimating the cost of the work to be completed include the nature and complexity of the work to be performed, subcontractor performance, the risk and impact of delayed performance, availability and timing of funding from the customer and the recoverability of any claims outside the original development and production contract included in the estimate to complete. At the outset of each contract, we gauge its complexity and perceived risks and establish an estimated total cost at completion in line with these expectations. After establishing the estimated total cost at completion, we follow a standard Estimate at Completion ("EAC") process in which management reviews the progress and performance on our ongoing development and production contracts at least quarterly and, in many cases, more frequently. If we successfully retire risks associated with the technical, schedule and cost aspects of a contract, we may lower our estimated total cost at completion commensurate with the retirement of these risks. Conversely, if we are not successful in retiring these risks, we may increase our estimated total cost at completion. Additionally, at the outset of a cost-reimbursable contract (for example, contracts containing award or incentive fees), we establish an estimate of total contract value, or revenue, based on our expectation of performance on the contract. As the cost-reimbursable contract progresses, our estimates of total contract value may increase or decrease if, for example, we receive higher or lower than expected award fees. When adjustments in estimated total costs at completion or in estimates of total contract value are determined, the related impact to operating income is recognized using the cumulative catch-up method, which recognizes in the current period the cumulative effect of such adjustments for all prior periods. Anticipated losses on development and production contracts or programs in progress are charged to operating income when identified. Net EAC adjustments resulting from changes in estimates favorably impacted our operating income by $57 million ($.37 per diluted share) in fiscal 2015, $53 million ($.33 per diluted share) in fiscal 2014 and $47 million ($.29 per diluted share) in fiscal 2013.

Products and Services Other Than Development and Production Contracts: Revenue from product sales other than development and production contracts and revenue from service arrangements are recognized when persuasive evidence of an arrangement exists, the fee is fixed or determinable, collectibility is reasonably assured, and delivery of a product has occurred and title has transferred or services have been rendered. Unearned income on service contracts is amortized by the straight-line method over the term of the contracts. Also, if contractual obligations related to customer acceptance exist, revenue is not recognized for a product or service unless these obligations are satisfied.

Multiple-Element Arrangements: We have entered into arrangements other than development and production contracts that require the delivery or performance of multiple deliverables or elements under a bundled sale. These arrangements are most prevalent in our RF Communications and Integrated Network Solutions segments. For example, in our RF Communications segment, in addition to delivering secure tactical radios and accessories, we may be required to perform or provide installation, design and development solutions for custom communication infrastructures, and extended warranties. In our Integrated Network Solutions segment, the deliverables to our maritime customers may include satellite bandwidth services (voice, data and internet), terrestrial circuits, equipment, installation, and network operations center and other support services.

For arrangements with multiple elements, judgment is required to determine the appropriate accounting, including whether the individual deliverables represent separate units of accounting for revenue recognition purposes, and the timing of revenue recognition for each deliverable. We recognize revenue for contractual deliverables as separate units of accounting when the delivered items have value to the customer on a standalone basis (i.e., if they are sold separately by any vendor or the customer could resell the delivered items on a standalone basis) and, if the arrangement includes a general right of return relative to the delivered items, we consider delivery or performance of the undelivered items as probable and substantially in our control.

Deliverables that are not separable are accounted for as a combined unit of accounting, and revenue generally is recognized when persuasive evidence of an arrangement exists, the fee is fixed or determinable, collectibility is reasonably assured, and delivery of a product has occurred and title has transferred or services have been rendered. If we determine that the deliverables represent separate units of accounting, we recognize the revenue associated with each unit of accounting separately, and contract revenue is allocated among the separate units of accounting at the inception of the arrangement based on relative selling price. If options or change orders materially change the scope of work or price of the contract subsequent to inception, we reevaluate and adjust our prior conclusions regarding units of accounting and allocation of contract revenue as necessary. The allocation of selling price among the separate units of accounting may impact the timing of revenue recognition, but will not change the total revenue recognized on the arrangement. We establish the selling price used for each deliverable based on the vendor-specific objective evidence ("VSOE") of selling price, or third-party evidence ("TPE") of selling price if VSOE of selling price is not available, or best estimate of selling price ("BESP") if neither VSOE of selling price nor TPE of selling price is available. In determining VSOE of selling price, a substantial majority of the recent standalone sales of the deliverable must be priced within a relatively narrow range. In determining TPE of selling price, we evaluate competitor prices for similar deliverables when sold separately. Generally, comparable pricing of our products to those of our competitors with similar functionality cannot be obtained. In determining BESP, we consider both market data and entity-specific factors, including market conditions, the geographies in which our products are sold, our competitive position and strategy, and our profit objectives.

Bill-and-Hold Arrangements: Certain contracts include terms and conditions through which we recognize revenue upon completion of equipment production, which is subsequently stored at our location at the customer's request. Revenue is recognized on such contracts upon the customer's assumption of title and risk of ownership and when collectibility is reasonably assured. At the time of revenue recognition, there is a schedule of delivery of the product consistent with the customer's business practices, the product has been separated from our inventory, and we do not have any remaining performance obligations such that the earnings process is not complete.

Other: Net income or expense related to intellectual property matters is included as a component of the "Non-operating income (loss)" line item in our Consolidated Statement of Income and is recognized on the basis of terms specified in contractual agreements. Shipping and handling fees billed to customers are included in the "Revenue from product sales" line item in our Consolidated Statement of Income and the associated costs are included in the "Cost of product sales" line item in our Consolidated Statement of Income. Also, we record taxes collected from customers and remitted to governmental authorities on a net basis in that they are excluded from revenues.

Note 17: Research and Development

Company-sponsored research and development costs are expensed as incurred. These costs were $277 million, $264 million and $254 million in fiscal 2015, 2014 and 2013, respectively, and are included in the "Engineering, selling and administrative expenses" line item in our Consolidated Statement of Income. These costs in fiscal 2013 included an $18 million write-off of capitalized software in our Integrated Network Solutions segment as a result of a change in accounting estimate. Customer-sponsored research and development costs are incurred pursuant to contractual arrangements, principally U.S. Government-sponsored contracts requiring us to provide a product or service meeting certain defined performance or other specifications (such as designs), and are accounted for principally by the cost-to-cost percentage-of-completion method. Customer-sponsored research and development is included in our revenue and cost of product sales and services.

Discontinued Operations

RECOGNITION AND MEASUREMENT

3.83 FASB ASC 205-20 sets forth the financial accounting and reporting requirements for discontinued operations of a component of an entity. A *component of an entity* comprises operations and cash flows that can be clearly distinguished, operationally and for financial reporting purposes, from the rest of the entity. A component of an entity may be a reportable or an operating segment, a reporting unit, a subsidiary, or an asset group.

3.84 FASB ASC 205-20 uses a single accounting model to account for all long-lived assets to be disposed of (by sale, abandonment, or distribution to owners). This includes asset disposal groups meeting the criteria for presentation as a discontinued operation, as specified in FASB ASC 205-20 . A long-lived asset group classified as held for sale should be measured at the lower of its carrying amount or fair value less cost to sell. Additionally, in accordance with FASB ASC 360, a loss shall be recognized for any write-down to fair value less cost to sell. A gain shall be recognized for any subsequent recovery of cost. Lastly, a gain or loss not previously recognized that results from the sale of the asset disposal group should be recognized at the date of sale.

PRESENTATION

3.85 FASB ASC 205-20-45-3 explains that in a period in which a component of an entity either has been disposed of or is classified as held for sale, the income statement of a business entity or statement of activities of a not-for-profit entity for current and prior periods should report the results of operations of the component, including any gain or loss recognized from the sale or write-down, in discontinued operations. The results of operations of a component classified as held for sale should be reported in discontinued operations in the period(s) in which they occur. The results of discontinued operations, less applicable income taxes (benefit), should be reported as a separate component of income before extraordinary items (if applicable). For example, the results of discontinued operations may be reported in the income statement of a business entity as follows:

Income from continuing operations before income taxes	$XXXX
Income taxes	XXX
Income from continuing operations [a]	$XXXX
Discontinued operations (Note X)	
Loss from operations of discontinued component X (including loss on disposal of $XXX)	XXXX
Income tax benefit	XXXX
Loss on discontinued operations	XXXX
Net income	$XXXX

[a] This caption should be modified appropriately when an entity reports an extraordinary item.

A gain or loss recognized on the disposal should be disclosed either on the face of the income statement or in the notes to the financial statements.

3.86 FASB ASC 205-20-50 explains the disclosures required for all types of discontinued operations. These include the following:
   a. A description of:
      1. The fact and circumstances leading to the disposal or expected disposal
      2. The expected manner and timing of that disposal.
   b. If not separately presented on the face of the statement where net income is reported as part of discontinued operations, the gain or loss recognized in accordance with FASB ASC 205-20-45-3C.
   c. If applicable, the segment(s) in which the discontinued operation is reported under FASB ASC 280, *Segment Reporting*.

3.87 Illustrations of transactions that should and should not be accounted for as business segment disposals are presented in the implementation guidance and illustrations of FASB ASC 205-20-55.

PRESENTATION AND DISCLOSURE EXCERPTS

DISPOSITIONS

3.88 DARDEN RESTAURANTS, INC. (MAY)
CONSOLIDATED STATEMENTS OF EARNINGS

(In millions, except per share data)

	May 31, 2015	May 25, 2014	May 26, 2013
Sales	$6,764.0	$6,285.6	$5,921.0
Costs and expenses:			
Food and beverage	2,085.1	1,892.2	1,743.6
Restaurant labor	2,135.6	2,017.6	1,892.6
Restaurant expenses	1,120.8	1,080.7	980.4
Marketing expenses	243.3	252.3	241.1
General and administrative expenses	430.2	413.1	384.1
Depreciation and amortization	319.3	304.4	278.3
Impairments and disposal of assets, net	62.1	16.4	0.9
Total operating costs and expenses	$6,396.4	$5,976.7	$5,521.0
Operating income	367.6	308.9	400.0
Interest, net	192.3	134.3	126.0
Earnings before income taxes	175.3	174.6	274.0
Income tax (benefit) expense	(21.1)	(8.6)	36.7
Earnings from continuing operations	$ 196.4	$ 183.2	$ 237.3
Earnings from discontinued operations, net of tax expense of $344.8, $32.3 and $72.7, respectively	513.1	103.0	174.6
Net earnings	$ 709.5	$ 286.2	$ 411.9
Basic net earnings per share:			
Earnings from continuing operations	$ 1.54	$ 1.40	$ 1.84
Earnings from discontinued operations	4.02	0.78	1.35
Net earnings	$ 5.56	$ 2.18	$ 3.19

(continued)

	May 31, 2015	May 25, 2014	May 26, 2013
Diluted net earnings per share:			
Earnings from continuing operations	$ 1.51	$ 1.38	$ 1.80
Earnings from discontinued operations	3.96	0.77	1.33
Net earnings	$ 5.47	$ 2.15	$ 3.13
Average number of common shares outstanding:			
Basic	127.7	131.0	129.0
Diluted	129.7	133.2	131.6
Dividends declared per common share	$ 2.20	$ 2.20	$ 2.00

NOTES TO CONSOLIDATED FINANCIAL STATEMENTS (in part)

Note 1—Summary of Significant Accounting Policies (in part)

Basis of Presentation

On May 15, 2014, we entered into an agreement to sell Red Lobster and certain related assets and associated liabilities and closed the sale on July 28, 2014. During fiscal 2007 and 2008, we closed or sold all of our Smokey Bones Barbeque & Grill (Smokey Bones) and Rocky River Grillhouse restaurants and we closed nine Bahama Breeze restaurants. For fiscal 2015, 2014 and 2013 all gains and losses on disposition, impairment charges and disposal costs, along with the sales, costs and expenses and income taxes attributable to the discontinued locations, have been aggregated in a single caption entitled "Earnings from discontinued operations, net of tax expense" in our consolidated statements of earnings for all periods presented. See Note 2—Dispositions for additional information.

Unless otherwise noted, amounts and disclosures throughout these notes to consolidated financial statements relate to our continuing operations.

Note 2—Dispositions

On July 28, 2014, we closed on the sale of 705 Red Lobster restaurants; however, as of May 31, 2015, 9 of the properties remain subject to landlord consents and satisfaction of other contractual requirements. Therefore, the assets of these remaining restaurants continue to be classified as held for sale and recognition of the gain on the related proceeds was deferred. The proceeds of approximately $31.5 million associated with the remaining landlord consents are classified as other current liabilities on our consolidated balance sheet as of May 31, 2015. As the landlord consents and remaining contractual requirements are satisfied, which we expect to occur within the next six months, we will derecognize the related assets and record the commensurate gain on the transaction. All direct cash flows related to operating these businesses were eliminated at the date of sale. Our continuing involvement has been limited to a transition service agreement for up to two years from the date of sale with minimal impact to our cash flows. In conjunction with the sale of Red Lobster, there were 19 locations where Red Lobster shared a land parcel with another Darden brand. The land and related buildings for these 19 Darden locations were included in the sale transaction and simultaneously leased back to Darden. The proceeds associated with the sale of these properties are classified as a financing lease obligation on our consolidated balance sheet as a component of other liabilities and the associated lease payments will amortize the obligation over the life of the properties. Additionally, in the fourth quarter of fiscal 2014, in connection with the expected sale of Red Lobster, we closed two of the six restaurants that housed both a Red Lobster and an Olive Garden in the same building (synergy restaurants). In the first quarter of fiscal 2015, we completed the conversion of the four remaining company-owned synergy restaurants to stand-alone Olive Garden restaurants.

As of May 31, 2015, we received $2.08 billion in cash proceeds, net of transaction-related costs of approximately $29.3 million. During fiscal 2015, we recognized a pre-tax gain on the sale of Red Lobster of $837.0 million, which is included in earnings from discontinued operations in our consolidated statement of earnings.

For fiscal 2015, 2014 and 2013, all gains on disposition, impairment charges and disposal costs, along with the sales, costs and expenses and income taxes attributable to these restaurants, have been aggregated in a single caption entitled "Earnings from discontinued operations, net of tax expense" in our consolidated statements of earnings for all periods presented. No amounts for shared general and administrative operating support expense or interest expense were allocated to discontinued operations. Assets associated with those restaurants not yet disposed of, that are considered held for sale, have been segregated from continuing operations and presented as assets held for sale on our accompanying consolidated balance sheets. In April 2014, the FASB issued ASU 2014-08, Presentation of Financial Statements (Topic 205) and Property, Plant and Equipment (Topic 360), Reporting Discontinued Operations and Disclosures of Disposals of Components of an Entity. This update modifies the requirements for reporting discontinued operations. Under the amendments in ASU 2014-08, the definition of a discontinued operation has been modified to only include those disposals of an entity that represent a strategic shift that has (or will have) a major effect on an entity's operations and financial results. This update also expands the disclosure requirements for disposals that meet the definition of a discontinued operation and requires entities to disclose information about disposals of individually significant components that do not meet the definition of discontinued operations. We elected to early adopt these provisions in the third quarter of fiscal 2015.

Earnings from discontinued operations, net of taxes in our accompanying consolidated statements of earnings are comprised of the following:

| (In millions) | Fiscal Year | | |
	May 31, 2015	May 25, 2014	May 26, 2013
Sales	$ 400.4	$2,472.1	$2,630.9
Restaurant and marketing expenses	353.0	2,134.1	2,212.4
Depreciation and amortization	0.2	124.6	116.4
Other costs and expenses[1]	(810.7)	78.1	54.8
Earnings before income taxes	857.9	135.3	247.3
Income tax expense	344.8	32.3	72.7
Earnings from discontinued operations, net of tax	$ 513.1	$ 103.0	$ 174.6

[1] Amounts for fiscal year ended May 31, 2015 include the gain recognized on the sale of Red Lobster.

The following table presents the carrying amounts of the major classes of assets and liabilities associated with the restaurants reported as discontinued operations and classified as held for sale on our accompanying consolidated balance sheets.

(In millions)	May 31, 2015	May 25, 2014
Current assets	$ —	$ 241.0
Land, buildings and equipment, net	32.9	1,084.8
Other assets	—	64.5
Total assets	$32.9	$1,390.3
Current liabilities	$ —	$ 130.6
Other liabilities	—	84.9
Total liabilities	$ —	$ 215.5

During the third quarter of fiscal 2015, we divested all of our interest in our lobster aquaculture activities and we have no further commitments or obligations with respect to such activities. This divestiture did not represent a strategic shift in our operations, and, accordingly, it did not meet the definition to be reported as a discontinued operation.

SEPARATION OF BUSINESS

3.89 BAXTER INTERNATIONAL INC. (DEC)
CONSOLIDATED STATEMENTS OF INCOME

Years Ended December 31 (In millions, except per share data)	2015	2014	2013
Net sales	$9,968	$10,719	$9,413
Cost of sales	5,822	6,138	5,251
Gross margin	4,146	4,581	4,162
Marketing and administrative expenses	3,094	3,315	3,084
Research and development expenses	603	610	582
Operating income	449	656	496
Net interest expense	126	145	128
Other (income) expense, net	(105)	21	(7)
Income from continuing operations before income taxes	428	490	375
Income tax expense	35	33	60
Income from continuing operations	393	457	315
Income from discontinued operations, net of tax	575	2,040	1,697
Net income	$ 968	$ 2,497	$2,012
Income from continuing operations per common share			
Basic	$ 0.72	$ 0.84	$ 0.58
Diluted	$ 0.72	$ 0.83	$ 0.57
Income from discontinued operations per common share			
Basic	$ 1.06	$ 3.77	$ 3.12
Diluted	$ 1.04	$ 3.73	$ 3.09
Net income per common share			
Basic	$ 1.78	$ 4.61	$ 3.70
Diluted	$ 1.76	$ 4.56	$ 3.66
Weighted-average number of common shares outstanding			
Basic	545	542	543
Diluted	549	547	549

Note 1—Summary of Significant Accounting Policies (in part)

Basis of Presentation

The consolidated financial statements include the accounts of Baxter and its majority-owned subsidiaries that Baxter controls, after elimination of intercompany transactions. Certain reclassifications have been made to conform prior period consolidated financial statements to the current period presentation.

On July 1, 2015, Baxter completed the distribution of approximately 80.5% of the outstanding common stock of its biopharmaceuticals business, Baxalta Incorporated (Baxalta), to Baxter stockholders (the Distribution). The Distribution was made to Baxter's stockholders of record as of the close of business on June 17, 2015, who received one share of Baxalta common stock for each Baxter common share held as of such date. As a result of the Distribution, Baxalta is now an independent public company whose shares trade on the New York Stock Exchange under the symbol "BXLT." Baxter is accounting for its investment in Baxalta common stock as an available-for-sale equity security with a fair value of approximately $5.1 billion as of December 31, 2015 (prior to giving effect to the disposition of 37,573,040 Baxalta shares of common stock on January 27, 2016 in a related debt for equity exchange).

As a result of the separation, the consolidated statements of income, consolidated balance sheets, consolidated statements of cash flow, and related financial information reflect Baxalta's operations, assets and liabilities, and cash flows as discontinued operations for all periods presented. Refer to Note 2 for additional information regarding the separation of Baxalta.

As a result of the separation of Baxalta, Baxter realigned its organizational structure under two reportable segments, Renal and Hospital Products. Refer to Note 17 for additional information regarding the company's segments.

On September 6, 2013, Baxter acquired Indap Holding AB, the holding company for Gambro AB (Gambro), a privately held dialysis product company based in Lund, Sweden, for cash consideration of $3.7 billion. Beginning September 6, 2013, Baxter's financial statements include the assets, liabilities, and operating results of Gambro. Refer to Note 5 for additional information about the Gambro acquisition.

Note 2—Separation of Baxalta Incorporated (in part)

The table following is a summary of the assets and liabilities distributed as part of the separation on July 1, 2015.

(In millions)	
Assets	
Cash and equivalents	$ 2,122
Accounts and other current receivables, net	600
Inventories	2,018
Other current assets	336
Property, plant and equipment, net	4,581
Goodwill	1,026
Other intangible assets, net	614
Other long-term assets	511
Total assets	$11,808
Liabilities	
Accounts payable and accrued liabilities	$ 1,166
Long-term debt and lease obligations	5,253
Other long-term liabilities	1,292
Total liabilities	$ 7,711
Net assets distributed	$ 4,097

In addition, approximately $350 million of accumulated other comprehensive losses, net of tax were distributed to Baxalta. Baxter also retained an investment in Baxalta with a cost basis of $719 million and fair value of $5.1 billion as of December 31, 2015.

The following table is a summary of the operating results of Baxalta, which have been reflected as discontinued operations for the years ended December 31, 2015, 2014 and 2013.

Years ended December 31 (In millions)	2015	2014	2013
Major classes of line items constituting income from discontinued operations before income taxes			
Net sales	$ 2,895	$ 6,523	$ 5,847
Cost of sales	(1,214)	(2,475)	(2,413)
Marketing and administrative expenses	(547)	(769)	(597)
Research and development expenses	(389)	(822)	(664)
Other income and expense items	7	105	2
Total income from discontinued operations before income taxes	752	2,562	2,175
Income tax expense	177	522	478
Total income from discontinued operations	$ 575	$ 2,040	$ 1,697

The assets and liabilities of Baxalta have been classified as held for disposition as of December 31, 2015 and 2014. These amounts consist of the following carrying amounts in each major class.

As of December 31 (In millions)	2015	2014
Carrying amounts of major classes of assets included as part of discontinued operations		
Accounts and other current receivables, net	$228	$ 919
Inventories	8	1,982
Property, plant, and equipment, net	2	4,264
Goodwill	—	947
Other intangible assets, net	—	460
Other	7	791
Total assets of the disposal group	$245	$9,363
Carrying amounts of major classes of liabilities included as part of discontinued operations		
Accounts payable and accrued liabilities	$ 46	$1,325
Other long-term liabilities	—	1,402
Other	—	276
Total liabilities of the disposal group	$ 46	$3,003

For a portion of Baxalta's operations, the legal transfer of Baxalta's assets and liabilities did not occur with the separation of Baxalta on July 1, 2015 due to the time required to transfer marketing authorizations and other regulatory requirements in certain countries. Under the terms of the International Commercial Operations Agreement (ICOA), Baxalta is subject to the risks and entitled to the benefits generated by these operations and assets until legal transfer; therefore, the net economic benefit and any cash collected by these entities are transferred to Baxalta. As of December 31, 2015 Baxter has recorded a liability of $190 million for its obligation to transfer these net assets to Baxalta and net cash outflow of $19 million has been included within the consolidated statement of cash flows as a cash flow from operations—discontinued operations. On February 1, 2016, the legal transfer of approximately $85 million of net assets as of December 31, 2015 was distributed to Baxalta. It is expected that the majority of the remaining operations will be transferred to Baxalta during 2016.

Baxter and Baxalta entered into several additional agreements in connection with the separation, including a transition services agreement (TSA), separation and distribution agreement, manufacturing and supply agreements (MSA), tax matters agreement, an employee matters agreement, a long-term services agreement, and a shareholder's and registration rights agreement.

Pursuant to the TSA, Baxter and Baxalta and their respective subsidiaries are providing to each other, on an interim, transitional basis, various services. Services being provided by Baxter include, among others, finance, information technology, human resources, quality supply chain, and certain other administrative services. The services generally commenced on the Distribution date and are expected to terminate within 24 months (or 36 months in the case of certain information technology services) of the Distribution date. Billings by Baxter under the TSA are recorded as a reduction of the costs to provide the respective service in the applicable expense category, primarily in marketing and administrative expenses, in the consolidated statements of income. In 2015, the company recognized approximately $75 million as a reduction to marketing and administrative expenses related to the TSA.

Pursuant to the MSA, Baxalta or Baxter, as the case may be, manufactures, labels, and packages products for the other party. The terms of the agreements range in initial duration from five to 10 years. In 2015, Baxter recognized approximately $37 million in sales to Baxalta. In addition, Baxter recognized approximately $100 million in cost of sales related to purchases from Baxalta pursuant to the MSA. The cash flows associated with these agreements are included in cash flows from operations—continuing operations.

In December 2015, Baxter sold to Baxalta certain assets for approximately $28 million with no resulting impact to net income.

Note 3—Supplemental Financial Information (in part)

Accounts Payable and Accrued Liabilities

As of December 31 (In millions)	2015	2014
Accounts payable, principally trade	$ 716	$ 677
Common stock dividends payable	137	363
Employee compensation and withholdings	481	485
Property, payroll and certain other taxes	166	184
Infusion pump reserves	52	145
Business optimization reserves	98	89
Accrued rebates	192	174
Separation-related reserves	190	—
All other	634	560
Accounts payable and accrued liabilities	$2,666	$2,677

Note 8—Debt, Credit Facilities and Lease Commitments (in part)

Significant Debt Issuances

In June 2015, the company's then wholly-owned subsidiary Baxalta issued senior notes with a total aggregate principal amount of $5.0 billion. Approximately $4.0 billion of the related net proceeds were distributed to Baxter in connection with the separation. After the separation, Baxter has no obligations as it relates to the Baxalta senior notes or any other Baxalta indebtedness. Refer to the debt tender offer section below in connection with this debt issuance. In June 2013, the company issued $500 million of floating rate senior notes maturing in December 2014, $500 million of senior notes bearing a coupon rate of 0.95% and maturing in June 2016, $750 million of senior notes bearing a coupon rate of 1.85% and maturing in June 2018, $1.25 billion of senior notes bearing a coupon rate of 3.2% and maturing in June 2023, and $500 million of senior notes bearing a coupon rate of 4.5% and maturing in June 2043. Approximately $3.0 billion of the net proceeds from the June 2013 debt issuances were used to finance the acquisition of Gambro in 2013 and the remainder was used for general corporate purposes, including the repayment of commercial paper.

Note 17—Segment Information

As a result of the separation of Baxalta, Baxter has realigned its organizational structure under two reportable segments, Renal and Hospital Products.

Baxter's two segments are strategic businesses that are managed separately as each business develops, manufactures and markets distinct products and services. The segments and a description of their products and services are as follows:

The **Renal** business provides products and services to treat end-stage renal disease, or irreversible kidney failure, along with other renal therapies. The Renal business offers a comprehensive portfolio to meet the needs of patients across the treatment continuum, including technologies and therapies for peritoneal dialysis (PD), in-center hemodialysis (HD), home HD, continuous renal replacement therapy (CRRT) and additional dialysis services.

The **Hospital Products** business manufactures intravenous (IV) solutions and administration sets, premixed drugs and drug-reconstitution systems, pre-filled vials and syringes for injectable drugs, IV nutrition products, infusion pumps, inhalation anesthetics, and biosurgery products. The business also provides products and services related to pharmacy compounding, drug formulation and packaging technologies.

In connection with the segment change, the company uses income from continuing operations before net interest expense, income tax expense, depreciation and amortization expense (Segment EBITDA), on a segment basis to make resource allocation decisions and assess the ongoing performance of the company's business segments.

All prior periods presented have been recast to conform to the new presentation and a change in the company's measure of segment profit or loss to Segment EBITDA as discussed below. Intersegment sales are eliminated in consolidation.

Certain items are maintained at Corporate and are not allocated to a segment. They primarily include most of the company's debt and cash and equivalents and related net interest expense, foreign exchange fluctuations (principally relating to intercompany receivables, payables and loans denominated in a foreign currency) and the majority of the foreign currency hedging activities, corporate headquarters costs, stock compensation expense, nonstrategic investments and related income and expense, certain employee benefit plan costs as well as certain nonrecurring gains, losses, and other charges (such as business optimization, integration and separation-related costs, and asset impairments). Financial information for the company's segments is as follows:

For the Years Ended December 31 (In millions)	2015	2014	2013
Net sales			
Renal	$3,789	$ 4,172	$3,089
Hospital Products	6,179	6,547	6,324
Total net sales	$9,968	$10,719	$9,413
EBITDA			
Renal	$ 566	$ 666	$ 670
Hospital Products	1,998	2,237	2,242
Total segment EBITDA	$2,564	$ 2,903	$2,912
Total Assets			
Renal	$ 4,609	$ 4,928	$ 5,475
Hospital Products	6,632	6,915	7,039
Total segment assets	$11,241	$11,843	$12,514

The following table is a reconciliation of segment EBITDA to income from continuing operations before income taxes per the consolidated statements of income.

For the Years Ended December 31 (In millions)	2015	2014	2013
Total segment EBITDA	$ 2,564	$ 2,903	$ 2,912
Reconciling items			
Depreciation and amortization	(759)	(792)	(635)
Certain foreign exchange fluctuations and hedging activities	197	37	72
Stock compensation	(126)	(126)	(122)
Net interest	(126)	(145)	(128)
Business optimization charges	(130)	6	(161)
Other Corporate items	(1,192)	(1,393)	(1,563)
Income from continuing operations before income taxes	$ 428	$ 490	$ 375

The following table is a reconciliation of segment assets to consolidated total assets per the consolidated balance sheets.

As of December 31 (In millions)	2015	2014	2013
Total segment assets	$11,241	$11,843	$12,514
Cash and equivalents	2,213	2,925	2,733
Deferred income taxes	354	531	298
PP&E, net	932	1,039	1,084
Assets held for disposition	245	9,363	8,280
Other Corporate assets	5,990	437	315
Consolidated total assets	$20,975	$26,138	$25,224

Geographic Information

Net sales are based on product shipment destination and assets are based on physical location.

Years Ended December 31 (In millions)	2015	2014	2013
Net sales			
United States	$ 4,001	$ 3,999	$3,584
Europe	2,774	3,257	2,674
Asia-Pacific	1,972	2,079	1,810
Latin America and Canada	1,221	1,384	1,345
Consolidated net sales	$ 9,968	$10,719	$9,413

As of December 31 (In millions)	2015	2014	2013
PP&E, net			
United States	$1,746	$1,625	$1,633
Europe	1,298	1,466	1,463
Asia-Pacific	757	753	708
Latin America and Canada	585	590	604
Consolidated PP&E, net	$4,386	$4,434	$4,408

Net Sales by Franchise

Effective January 1, 2015, Baxter modified its commercial franchise structure for reporting net sales. Prior period net sales have been recast to reflect the new commercial franchise structure. The following table represents net sales by commercial franchise.

Years Ended December 31	2015	2014	2013
Total Renal[1]	$3,789	$4,172	$3,089
Fluid Systems[2]	2,106	2,129	2,142
Integrated Pharmacy Solutions[3]	2,297	2,535	2,364
Surgical Care[4]	1,323	1,373	1,307
Other[5]	453	510	511
Total Hospital Products	$6,179	$6,547	$6,324

[1] The Renal segment is presented as a separate commercial franchise and includes sales of the company's PD, HD and CRRT.
[2] Principally includes IV therapies, infusion pumps, and administration sets.
[3] Includes sales of the company's premixed and oncology drug platforms, nutrition products and pharmacy compounding services.
[4] Includes sales of the company's inhaled anesthesia products as well as biological products and medical devices used in surgical procedures for hemostasis, tissue sealing and adhesion prevention.
[5] Principally includes sales from the company's pharmaceutical partnering business.

BUSINESS COMPONENT DISPOSALS (UNDER EARLY ADOPTION OF ASU NO. 2014-08)

3.90 GENERAL CABLE CORPORATION (DEC)
CONSOLIDATED STATEMENTS OF OPERATIONS AND COMPREHENSIVE INCOME (LOSS) (in part)

(in millions, except per share data)

	Year Ended		
	Dec 31, 2015	Dec 31, 2014	Dec 31, 2013
Net sales	$4,225.1	$5,389.0	$5,781.3
Cost of sales	3,811.3	5,053.7	5,176.3
Gross profit	413.8	335.3	605.0
Selling, general and administrative expenses	390.8	410.0	429.2
Goodwill impairment charge	0.7	93.5	—
Intangible asset impairment charges	1.7	78.3	—
Operating income (loss)	20.6	(246.5)	175.8
Other income (expense)	(67.0)	(210.8)	(66.6)
Interest income (expense):			
Interest expense	(94.7)	(113.4)	(122.1)
Interest income	1.8	3.3	6.0
	(92.9)	(110.1)	(116.1)
Income (loss) before income taxes	(139.3)	(567.4)	(6.9)
Income tax (provision) benefit	14.7	(6.6)	(30.5)
Equity in net earnings of affiliated companies	0.4	1.2	1.7
Net income (loss) from continuing operations	(124.2)	(572.8)	(35.7)
Net income (loss) from discontinued operations, net of tax	(11.6)	(70.2)	25.6
Net income (loss) including noncontrolling interest	(135.8)	(643.0)	(10.1)
Less: preferred stock dividends	—	—	0.3
Less: net income (loss) attributable to noncontrolling interest	(13.9)	(15.4)	7.7
Net income (loss) attributable to Company common shareholders	$ (121.9)	$ (627.6)	$ (18.1)
Earnings (loss) per share—Net income (loss) from continuing operations attributable to Company common shareholders per common share			
Earnings (loss) per common share-basic	$ (2.32)	$ (11.74)	$ (0.75)
Earnings (loss) per common share-assuming dilution	$ (2.32)	$ (11.74)	$ (0.75)
Earnings (loss) per share—Net income (loss) from discontinued operations attributable to Company common shareholders per common share			
Earnings (loss) per common share-basic	$ (0.17)	$ (1.12)	$ 0.38
Earnings (loss) per common share-assuming dilution	$ (0.17)	$ (1.12)	$ 0.38
Earnings (loss) per share—Net income (loss) attributable to Company common shareholders per common share			
Earnings (loss) per common share-basic	$ (2.49)	$ (12.86)	$ (0.37)
Earnings (loss) per common share-assuming dilution	$ (2.49)	$ (12.86)	$ (0.37)
Dividends per common share	$ 0.72	$ 0.72	$ 0.54

2. Summary of Significant Accounting Policies (in part)

Discontinued Operations

The Company evaluates long-lived assets that have been sold, to be sold or abandoned to determine if the results of the business should classified as discontinued operations in accordance with ASU 2014-08, "Reporting Discontinued Operations and Disclosures of Disposals of Components of an Entity." During the year ended December 31, 2015, the Company determined the disposals of the PDP and PDEP, Fiji, Keystone and Thailand businesses combined with the businesses held for sale (the remaining Asia Pacific Operations) result in the Company's disposal of a major geographical area, Asia Pacific. This disposal is considered a strategic shift that has and will have a major effect on the Company's operations and financial results; therefore, the results of the Asia Pacific Operations have been reclassified as discontinued operations for all periods presented. Previously the results of these businesses included certain allocated corporate costs, which have been reallocated to the remaining continuing operations within the Africa/Asia Pacific segment on a retrospective basis.

As a result of the Company's strategic shift out of the Asia Pacific Operations, the Africa/Asia Pacific segment is now comprised primarily of the Company's Africa businesses. As of December 31, 2015, the Company determined that the remaining businesses in the Africa/Asia Pacific segment, the Africa businesses, did not meet the held for sale criteria set forth in ASC 360 primarily driven by management's belief that the probability of a sale within one year is uncertain. The financial results of the Company's Africa businesses are presented as continuing operations in the Consolidated Financial Statements for all periods presented. Refer to Note 3— Assets and Liabilities Held for Sale and Discontinued Operations for additional details.

New Accounting Pronouncements (in part)

In April 2014, the FASB issued ASU 2014-08, "Reporting Discontinued Operations and Disclosures of Disposals of Components of an Entity", which raises the threshold for determining which disposals are required to be presented as discontinued operations and modifies related disclosure requirements. The revised accounting guidance applies prospectively to all disposals (or classifications as held for sale) of components of an entity and for businesses that, upon acquisition, are classified as held for sale on or after adoption. Early adoption is permitted for disposals (or classifications as held for sale) that have not been previously reported in financial statements. The Company elected to early adopt the guidance and implemented ASU 2014-08 for the year ended December 31, 2014. The effects of applying the revised guidance will vary based upon the nature and size of future disposal transactions. It is expected that fewer disposal transactions will meet the new criteria to be reported as discontinued operations. For the year ended December 31, 2015, the Company reported the results of the Asia Pacific businesses as discontinued operations; refer to Note 3—Assets and Liabilities Held for Sale and Discontinued Operations. The Company will continually evaluate the status of discontinued operations each quarter to ensure compliance with ASU 2014-08 requirements.

3. Assets and Liabilities Held for Sale and Discontinued Operations

In October 2014, the Company announced the intent to divest all of the Company's operations in Africa and Asia Pacific in order to simplify the Company's geographic portfolio and reduce operational complexity. The October divestiture plan is focused on the sale and closure of the Company's non-core assets. The Company expects to incur approximately $14 million in pre-tax charges consisting primarily of legal and transaction fees for the dispositions. Such amounts are reflected in the North America segment. For the year ended December 31, 2015, the Company recognized $3.4 million. The charges were immaterial for the year ended December 31, 2014.

As part of this plan, the Company recognized the following:
- On June 25, 2015, the Company announced it reached a definitive agreement to sell its Asia Pacific operations consisting of Thailand, Alcan (Tianjin) Alloy Products ("China"), General Cable New Zealand Limited ("New Zealand") and General Cable Australia Pty. Ltd ("Australia") in a two-step process, with close on sale of the Thailand operations on August 31, 2015 and expected close on the China, New Zealand and Australia operations (together "the remaining Asia Pacific Operations") on September 30, 2015. On August 31, 2015, the Company completed the sale of its Thailand operations for cash consideration of approximately $88 million. The pre-tax gain recognized in the year ended December 31, 2015 from the disposition of Thailand was $14.5 million, which included post-closing working capital adjustments. On September 29, 2015, the Company received notice from the buyer that certain closing conditions of the definitive agreement to sell were unsatisfied or incapable of satisfaction and terminated the purchase agreement for the remaining Asia Pacific Operations.
- In the first quarter of 2015, the Company completed the sale of its 51% interest in Fiji for cash consideration of $9.3 million. The pre-tax loss recognized in the year ended December 31, 2015 from the disposition of Fiji was $2.6 million.

- In the first quarter of 2015, the Company completed the sale of its 20% interest in Keystone for cash consideration of $11.0 million. The pre-tax gain recognized in the year ended December 31, 2015 from the disposition of Keystone was $3.6 million.
- In the fourth quarter of 2014, the Company completed the sale of its interest in PDP and PDEP for cash consideration of $67.1 million. The pre-tax gain on the sale from the disposition of PDP and PDEP recognized in the year ended December 31, 2014 was $17.6 million

As of December 31, 2015, the Company has initiated actions to respond to the termination of the definitive agreement to sell the remaining Asia Pacific Operations and is actively marketing the assets at a price that is reasonable given the termination of this agreement. During the year ended December 31, 2015, the Company determined that the remaining Asia Pacific Operations met the held for sale criteria set forth in ASC 360—Property, Plant and Equipment to be classified as held for sale. Assets held for sale are measured at the lower of their carrying amount or fair value less cost to sell and depreciation is ceased. Development of estimates of fair values in this circumstance is complex and is dependent upon, among other factors, the nature of the potential sales transaction, composition of assets and/or businesses in the disposal group, the comparability of the disposal group to market transactions, negotiations with third party purchasers, etc. Such factors bear directly on the range of potential fair values and the selection of the best estimates. Key assumptions were developed based on market observable data and, in the absence of such data, internal information that is consistent with what market participants would use in a hypothetical transaction.

As of December 31, 2015, the Company determined that the remaining businesses in the Africa/Asia Pacific segment, the Africa businesses, did not meet the held for sale criteria set forth in ASC 360 primarily driven by management's belief that the probability of a sale within one year is uncertain.

Consistent with the conclusion reached in the second and third quarters of 2015, as of December 31, 2015, the Company determined the disposals of the PDP and PDEP, Fiji, Keystone and Thailand businesses combined with the businesses held for sale (the Asia Pacific Operations) result in the Company's disposal of a major geographical area, Asia Pacific. This disposal is considered a strategic shift that has and will have a major effect on the Company's operations and financial results; therefore, the results of the Asia Pacific Operations have been reclassified as discontinued operations for all periods presented. Previously the results of these businesses included certain allocated corporate costs, which have been reallocated to the remaining continuing operations within the Africa/Asia Pacific segment on a retrospective basis. As a result of the Company's strategic shift out of the Asia Pacific Operations, the Africa/Asia Pacific segment is now comprised primarily of the Company's Africa businesses. The financial results of the Company's Africa businesses are presented as continuing operations in the Consolidated Financial Statements.

The results of operations, financial position and cash flows for the Asia Pacific Operations are separately reported as discontinued operations for all periods presented. Included in Net income (loss) from discontinued operations, net of taxes in the Consolidated Statements of Operations and Comprehensive Income (Loss) were the following (in millions):

	Year Ended		
	December 31, 2015	December 31, 2014	December 31, 2013
Net sales	$289.4	$590.8	$639.9
Cost of sales[1]	270.8	532.9	541.2
Gross profit	18.6	57.9	98.7
Selling, general and administrative expenses	36.0	58.3	62.8
Goodwill impairment charge	3.2	61.6	—
Intangible asset impairment charges	—	20.5	—
Operating income (loss)	(20.6)	(82.5)	35.9
Other income (expense)	(5.3)	(2.1)	(0.1)
Interest expense, net	(1.4)	(1.7)	(1.9)
Pre-tax gain on the disposal of discontinued operations	15.5	17.6	—
Income (loss) before income taxes	(11.8)	(68.7)	33.9
Income tax (provision) benefit	0.1	(1.7)	(8.3)
Equity in net earnings of affiliated companies	0.1	0.2	—
Net income (loss) including noncontrolling interest	$ (11.6)	$ (70.2)	$ 25.6

[1] Based on the estimated expected sales price of the India operations and in accordance with ASC 360, the Company recorded an impairment loss in cost of sales of $13.6 million in the year ended December 31, 2015. As part of the Company's strategic review and asset optimization plans, announced in the second quarter of 2014, the Company recorded an asset impairment charge in cost of sales of $16.5 million in the year ended December 31, 2014, based on the review of its India asset group in accordance with ASC 360.

The pre-tax loss attributable to the parent for the Asia Pacific Operations for the years ended December 31, 2015 and December 31, 2014 was $8.2 million and $53.9 million, respectively. The pre-tax gain attributable to the parent for the Asia Pacific Operations for the year ended December 31, 2013 was $24.9 million.

Financial information for assets and liabilities held for sale were the following (in millions):

	December 31, 2015	December 31, 2014
Assets		
Current assets:		
Cash and cash equivalents	$ 32.7	$ 69.1
Receivables, net of allowances	28.5	111.9
Inventories	38.6	92.2
Deferred income taxes	—	8.4
Prepaid expenses and other	4.1	32.2
Total current assets	103.9	313.8
Property, plant and equipment, net	39.7	87.7
Deferred income taxes	10.3	6.4
Goodwill	—	3.3
Intangible assets, net	—	14.6
Other non-current assets	6.9	7.9
Total assets	$160.8	$433.7
Liabilities		
Current liabilities:		
Accounts payable	$ 17.3	$119.4
Accrued liabilities	21.1	27.3
Current portion of long-term debt	13.2	11.9
Total current liabilities	51.6	158.6
Deferred income taxes	0.2	4.7
Other liabilities	1.5	11.3
Total liabilities	$ 53.3	$174.6

17. Earnings Per Common Share

The Company applies the two-class method of computing basic and diluted earnings per share. Future declarations of dividends and the establishment of future record dates and payment dates are subject to the final determination of our Board of Directors.

A reconciliation of the numerator and denominator of earnings (loss) per common share-basic to earnings (loss) per common share-assuming dilution is as follows (in millions, except per share data):

	Year Ended		
	Dec 31, 2015	Dec 31, 2014	Dec 31, 2013
Amounts attributable to the Company—basic and diluted:			
Net income (loss) from continuing operations	$(124.2)	$(572.8)	$(35.7)
Less: Net income (loss) attributable to continuing operations noncontrolling interest	(10.7)	(0.1)	0.8
Less: preferred stock dividends	—	—	0.3
Net income (loss) from continuing operations attributable to Company common shareholders	$(113.5)	$(572.7)	$(36.8)
Net income (loss) from discontinued operations, net of tax	(11.6)	(70.2)	25.6
Less: Net income attributable to discontinued operations noncontrolling interest	(3.2)	(15.3)	6.9
Net income (loss) from discontinued operations attributable to Company common shareholders	$ (8.4)	$ (54.9)	$ 18.7
Net income (loss) attributable to Company common shareholders	(121.9)	(627.6)	(18.1)
Less: Net income allocated to participating securities[4]	—	—	0.1
Net income (loss) for basic EPS computations[1]	$(121.9)	$(627.6)	$(18.2)
Weighted average shares outstanding for basic EPS computation[2,3]	48.9	48.8	49.4
Earnings (loss) per share calculated—basic:			
Earnings (loss) from continuing operations attributable to Company common shareholders per common share—basic[3]	$ (2.32)	$(11.74)	$(0.75)
Earnings (loss) from discontinued operations attributable to Company common shareholders per common share—basic	$ (0.17)	$ (1.12)	$ 0.38
Earnings (loss) per common share attributable to Company common shareholders—basic[3]	$ (2.49)	$(12.86)	$(0.37)
Weighted average shares outstanding including nonvested shares	48.9	48.8	49.4
Weighted average shares outstanding for diluted EPS computation[2]	48.9	48.8	49.4
Earnings (loss) per share calculation—assuming dilution:			
Earnings (loss) from continuing operations attributable to Company common shareholders per common share—assuming dilution	$ (2.32)	$(11.74)	$(0.75)
Earnings (loss) from discontinued operations attributable to Company common shareholders per common share—assuming dilution	$ (0.17)	$ (1.12)	$ 0.38
Earnings (loss) per common share attributable to Company common shareholders—assuming dilution	$ (2.49)	$(12.86)	$(0.37)

[1] Numerator
[2] Denominator
[3] Under the two class method, Earnings per share—basic reflects undistributed earnings per share for both common stock and unvested share-based payment awards (restricted stock).
[4] Outstanding unvested share-based payment awards that contain rights to non-forfeitable dividends are considered participating securities in undistributed earnings in the calculation above.

As of December 31, 2015, 2014 and 2013, there were approximately 3,646 thousand, 3,057 thousand, and 288 thousand shares excluded from the earnings per common share—assuming dilution computation because their impact was anti-dilutive, respectively.

Under ASC 260—Earnings per Share and ASC 470 and because of the Company's obligation to settle the par value of the Subordinated Convertible Notes in cash, the Company is not required to include any shares underlying the Subordinated Convertible Notes in its weighted average shares outstanding—assuming dilution until the average stock price per share for the quarter exceeds the $36.75 conversion price of the Subordinated Convertible Notes, respectively, and only to the extent of the additional shares that the Company may be required to issue in the event that the Company's conversion obligation exceeds the principal amount of the Subordinated Convertible Notes.

Regarding the Subordinated Convertible Notes, the average stock price threshold conditions had not been met as of December 31, 2015 or December 31, 2014. At any such time in the future the threshold conditions are met, only the number of shares issuable under the "treasury" method of accounting for the share dilution would be included in the Company's earnings per share—assuming dilution calculation, which is based upon the amount by which the average stock price exceeds the conversion price.

The following table provides examples of how changes in the Company's stock price would require the inclusion of additional shares in the denominator of the weighted average shares outstanding—assuming dilution calculation for the Subordinated Convertible Notes.

Share Price	Shares Underlying Subordinated Convertible Notes	Total Treasury Method Incremental Shares[1]
$36.75	—	—
$38.75	603,152	603,152
$40.75	1,147,099	1,147,099
$42.75	1,640,151	1,640,151
$44.75	2,089,131	2,089,131

[1] Represents the number of incremental shares that must be included in the calculation of fully diluted shares under U.S. GAAP.

Extraordinary Items

RECOGNITION AND MEASUREMENT

3.91 FASB ASC 225-20 defines *extraordinary items* as events and transactions that are distinguished by their unusual nature and by the infrequency of their occurrence. Both of the following criteria should be met to classify an event or transaction as an extraordinary item:
- *Unusual nature*. The underlying event or transaction should possess a high degree of abnormality and be of a type clearly unrelated to, or only incidentally related to, the ordinary and typical activities of the entity, taking into account the environment in which the entity operates.
- *Infrequency of occurrence*. The underlying event or transaction should be of a type that would not reasonably be expected to recur in the foreseeable future, taking into account the environment in which the entity operates.

PRESENTATION

3.92 FASB ASC 225-20 also addresses the presentation and disclosure of unusual and infrequently occurring items that do not meet the extraordinary criteria. Such items are reported as a separate component of continuing operations either on the face of the income statement or in the notes. FASB ASC 225-20-55 illustrates events and transactions that should and should not be classified as extraordinary items.

Author's Note
In January 2015, FASB issued ASU No. 2015-01, *Income Statement—Extraordinary and Unusual Items (Subtopic 225-20): Simplifying Income Statement Presentation by Eliminating the Concept of Extraordinary Items*. This ASU eliminates from GAAP the concept of extraordinary items. The amendments in this ASU will eliminate the requirements in Subtopic 225-20 for reporting entities to consider whether an underlying event or transaction is extraordinary, but the presentation and disclosure guidance for items that are unusual in nature or occur infrequently will be retained and expanded to include items that are both unusual in nature and infrequently occurring. The amendments in this ASU are effective for fiscal years, and interim periods within those fiscal years, beginning after December 15, 2015. A reporting entity may apply the amendments prospectively. A reporting entity also may apply the amendments retrospectively to all prior periods presented in the financial statements. Early adoption is permitted provided that the guidance is applied from the beginning of the fiscal year of adoption. The effective date is the same for both public business entities and all other entities. None of the examples that follow contain an example of these disclosures due to the effective date.

3.93 AEROJET ROCKETDYNE HOLDINGS, INC. (NOV)
NOTES TO CONSOLIDATED FINANCIAL STATEMENTS (in part)

Note 14. Unusual Items

Total unusual items expense, a component of other expense, net in the consolidated statements of operations was as follows:

(In millions)	Year Ended		
	2015	**2014**	**2013**
Aerospace and Defense:			
Loss (gain) on legal matters and settlements	$50.0	$ 0.9	$ (1.0)
Rocketdyne Business acquisition related costs	—	—	2.6
Aerospace and defense unusual items	50.0	0.9	1.6
Corporate:			
Rocketdyne Business acquisition related costs	—	—	17.4
Loss on debt repurchased	1.9	60.6	5.0
Loss on legal settlement	—	—	0.5
Loss on bank amendment	—	0.2	—
Corporate unusual items	1.9	60.8	22.9
Total unusual items	$51.9	$61.7	$24.5

Fiscal 2015 Activity:

The Company recorded an expense of $50.0 million associated with a legal settlement. See Note 9(b).

The Company retired $76.0 million principal amount of its delayed draw term loan resulting in $1.9 million of losses associated with the write-off of deferred financing fees.

Fiscal 2014 Activity:

The Company recorded a charge of $0.2 million related to an amendment to the Senior Credit Facility.

The Company recorded $0.9 million for realized losses and interest associated with the failure to register with the SEC the issuance of certain of the Company's common shares under the defined contribution 401(k) employee benefit plan.

A summary of the Company's loss on the $4^1/_{16}$% Debentures repurchased is as follows (in millions):

Principal amount repurchased	$ 59.6
Cash repurchase price	(119.9)
Write-off of deferred financing costs	(0.3)
Loss on $4^1/_{16}$% Debentures repurchased	$ (60.6)

Fiscal 2013 Activity:

The Company recorded a charge of $0.5 million related to a legal settlement.

The Company recorded ($1.0) million for realized gains net of interest associated with the failure to register with the SEC the issuance of certain of the Company's common shares under the defined contribution 401(k) employee benefit plan.

The Company incurred expenses of $20.0 million, including internal labor costs of $1.4 million, related to the Rocketdyne Business acquisition in fiscal 2013.

A summary of the Company's loss on the $4^1/_{16}$% Debentures repurchased is as follows (in millions):

Principal amount repurchased	$ 5.2
Cash repurchase price	(10.1)
Write-off of deferred financing costs	(0.1)
Loss on $4^1/_{16}$% Debentures repurchased	$ (5.0)

3.94 CONSTELLATION BRANDS, INC. (FEB)
NOTES TO CONSOLIDATED FINANCIAL STATEMENTS (in part)

21. Business Segment Information (in part)

Prior to the Beer Business Acquisition, Crown Imports was one of our reportable segments. In connection with the Beer Business Acquisition and the resulting consolidation of the acquired businesses from the date of acquisition, the Crown Imports segment, together with the Brewery Purchase, is now known as the Beer segment. Accordingly, our internal management financial reporting consists of two business divisions: (i) Beer and (ii) Wine and Spirits, and we report our operating results in three segments: (i) Beer, (ii) Wine and Spirits, and (iii) Corporate Operations and Other. In the Beer segment, we have an exclusive perpetual brand license to import, market and sell in the U.S. the Mexican Beer Brands. In the Wine and Spirits segment, we sell a large number of wine brands across all categories—table wine, sparkling wine and dessert wine—and across all price points—popular, premium, super-premium and fine wine, complemented by certain premium spirits brands. Amounts included in the Corporate Operations and Other segment consist of costs of executive management, corporate development, corporate finance, human resources, internal audit, investor relations, legal, public relations and global information technology. The amounts included in the Corporate Operations and Other segment are general costs that are applicable to the consolidated group and are therefore not allocated to the other reportable segments. All costs reported within the Corporate Operations and Other segment are not included in our chief operating decision maker's evaluation of the operating income performance of the other reportable segments. The business segments reflect how our operations are managed, how operating performance within the Company is evaluated by senior management and the structure of our internal financial reporting.

In addition, management excludes items that affect comparability ("Unusual Items") from its evaluation of the results of each operating segment as these Unusual Items are not reflective of continuing operations of the segments. Segment operating performance and segment management compensation are evaluated based upon continuing segment operating income (loss). As such, the performance measures for incentive compensation purposes for segment management do not include the impact of these items.

We evaluate segment operating performance based on operating income (loss) of the respective business units. Unusual Items that impacted comparability in our segment operating income (loss) for each period are as follows:

	For the Years Ended		
(In millions)	February 28, 2015	February 28, 2014	February 28, 2013
Cost of Product Sold			
Net gain (loss) on undesignated commodity derivative contracts	$(32.7)	$ 1.5	$ —
Amortization of favorable interim supply agreement	(28.4)	(6.0)	—
Settlements of undesignated commodity derivative contracts	4.4	(0.5)	—
Flow through of inventory step-up	—	(11.0)	(7.8)
Other losses	(2.8)	—	—
Total cost of product sold	(59.5)	(16.0)	(7.8)
Selling, General and Administrative Expenses			
Transaction, integration and other acquisition-related costs	(30.5)	(51.5)	(27.7)
Other gains (losses)	7.2	(4.2)	1.7
Total selling, general and administrative expenses	(23.3)	(55.7)	(26.0)
Impairment of goodwill and intangible assets	—	(300.9)	—
Gain on remeasurement to fair value of equity method investment	—	1,642.0	—
Unusual Items, Operating income (loss)	$(82.8)	$1,269.4	$(33.8)

The accounting policies of the segments are the same as those described for the Company in the Summary of Significant Accounting Policies in Note 1. Segment information is as follows:

(In millions)	For the Years Ended		
	February 28, 2015	February 28, 2014	February 28, 2013
Beer			
Net sales	$3,188.6	$2,835.6	$2,588.1
Segment operating income	$1,017.8	$ 772.9	$ 448.0
Long-lived tangible assets	$1,485.6	$ 801.3	$ 8.8
Total assets	$8,289.1	$7,420.8	$ 440.5
Capital expenditures	$ 587.3	$ 137.3	$ 1.3
Depreciation and amortization	$ 45.4	$ 29.6	$ 2.5
Wine and Spirits			
Net sales:			
Wine	$2,523.4	$2,554.2	$ 2,495.8
Spirits	316.0	291.3	300.3
Net sales	$2,839.4	$2,845.5	$ 2,796.1
Segment operating income	$ 674.3	$ 637.8	$ 650.2
Equity in earnings of equity method investees	$ 21.5	$ 17.6	$ 13.0
Long-lived tangible assets	$1,071.8	$1,097.4	$ 1,100.5
Investments in equity method investees	$ 73.5	$ 73.3	$ 74.3
Total assets	$6,508.2	$6,515.5	$ 6,921.8
Capital expenditures	$ 96.8	$ 71.7	$ 53.6
Depreciation and amortization	$ 100.0	$ 96.7	$ 91.6
Corporate Operations and Other			
Segment operating loss	$ (109.1)	$ (99.8)	$ (93.5)
Long-lived tangible assets	$ 124.2	$ 115.6	$ 128.5
Total assets	$ 347.2	$ 365.8	$ 547.0
Capital expenditures	$ 35.3	$ 14.8	$ 8.5
Depreciation and amortization	$ 28.2	$ 23.5	$ 23.8
Unusual Items			
Operating income (loss)	$ (82.8)	$1,269.4	$ (33.8)
Equity in losses of equity method investees	$ —	$ (0.1)	$ (1.0)
Depreciation and amortization	$ 28.4	$ 6.0	$ —
Consolidation and Eliminations			
Net sales	$ —	$ (813.4)	$(2,588.1)
Operating income	$ —	$ (142.6)	$ (448.0)
Equity in earnings of Crown Imports	$ —	$ 70.3	$ 221.1
Long-lived tangible assets	$ —	$ —	$ (8.8)
Investments in equity method investees	$ —	$ —	$ 169.3
Total assets	$ —	$ —	$ (271.2)
Capital expenditures	$ —	$ (0.3)	$ (1.3)
Depreciation and amortization	$ —	$ (0.5)	$ (2.5)
Consolidated			
Net sales	$ 6,028.0	$ 4,867.7	$2,796.1
Operating income	$ 1,500.2	$ 2,437.7	$ 522.9
Equity in earnings of equity method investees	$ 21.5	$ 87.8	$ 233.1
Long-lived tangible assets	$ 2,681.6	$ 2,014.3	$1,229.0
Investments in equity method investees	$ 73.5	$ 73.3	$ 243.6
Total assets	$15,144.5	$14,302.1	$7,638.1
Capital expenditures	$ 719.4	$ 223.5	$ 62.1
Depreciation and amortization	$ 202.0	$ 155.3	$ 115.4

Our principal area of operation is in the U.S. Current operations outside the U.S. are in Mexico for the Beer segment and primarily in Canada, New Zealand and Italy for the Wine and Spirits segment. Revenues are attributed to countries based on the location of the customer. Previously, revenues were attributed to countries based on the location of the selling company. Accordingly, the net sales geographic data for the years ended February 28, 2014, and February 28, 2013, has been restated to conform to the new presentation.

Geographic data is as follows:

(In millions)	For the Years Ended		
	February 28, 2015	February 28, 2014	February 28, 2013
Net Sales			
U.S.	$5,360.0	$4,169.8	$2,114.5
Non-U.S. (primarily Canada)	668.0	697.9	681.6
Total	$6,028.0	$4,867.7	$2,796.1

(in millions)	February 28, 2015	February 28, 2014
Long-lived tangible assets		
U.S.	$ 909.7	$ 901.6
Non-U.S. (primarily Mexico)	1,771.9	1,112.7
Total	$2,681.6	$2,014.3

Earnings Per Share

Author's Note

In April 2015, FASB issued ASU No. 2015-06, *Earnings Per Share (Topic 260): Effects on Historical Earnings per Unit of Master Limited Partnership Dropdown Transactions (a consensus of the FASB Emerging Issues Task Force)*. The amendments in this ASU specify that for purposes of calculating historical earnings per unit under the two-class method, the earnings (losses) of a transferred business before the date of a dropdown transaction should be allocated entirely to the general partner. In that circumstance, the previously reported earnings per unit of the limited partners (which are typically the earnings per unit measure presented in the financial statements) would not change as a result of the dropdown transaction. Qualitative disclosures about how the rights to the earnings (losses) differ before and after the dropdown transaction occurs for purposes of computing earnings per unit under the two-class method also are required. The amendments in this ASU are effective for fiscal years, and interim periods within those fiscal years, beginning after December 15, 2015. The amendments in the ASU should be applied retrospectively for all financial statements presented. Early adoption is permitted. None of the examples that follow contain an example of these disclosures due to the effective date.

PRESENTATION

3.95 The computation, presentation, and disclosure requirements for earnings per share (EPS) for entities with publicly held common stock or potential common stock are stated in FASB ASC 260, *Earnings Per Share*. The objective of basic EPS is to measure the performance of an entity over the reporting period. The objective of diluted EPS, which is consistent with that of basic EPS, is to measure the performance of an entity over the reporting period, while giving effect to all dilutive potential common shares that were outstanding during the period. FASB ASC 260 also discusses the application of EPS guidance to master limited partnerships.

PRESENTATION AND DISCLOSURE EXCERPTS

EARNINGS PER SHARE

3.96 PRUDENTIAL FINANCIAL, INC. (DEC)
CONSOLIDATED STATEMENTS OF OPERATIONS (in part)

(in millions, except per share amounts)

	2015	2014	2013
Revenues			
Premiums	$28,521	$29,293	$26,237
Policy charges and fee income	5,972	6,179	5,415
Net investment income	14,829	15,256	14,729
Asset management and service fees	3,772	3,719	3,485

(continued)

	2015	2014	2013
Other income (loss)	0	(1,978)	(3,199)
Realized investment gains (losses), net:			
Other-than-temporary impairments on fixed maturity securities	(180)	(127)	(1,055)
Other-than-temporary impairments on fixed maturity securities transferred to Other comprehensive income	39	71	856
Other realized investment gains (losses), net	4,166	1,692	(5,007)
Total realized investment gains (losses), net	4,025	1,636	(5,206)
Total revenues	57,119	54,105	41,461
Benefits And Expenses			
Policyholders' benefits	30,627	31,587	26,733
Interest credited to policyholders' account balances	3,479	4,263	3,111
Dividends to policyholders	2,212	2,716	2,050
Amortization of deferred policy acquisition costs	2,120	1,973	240
General and administrative expenses	10,912	11,807	11,011
Total benefits and expenses	49,350	52,346	43,145
Income (Loss) From Continuing Operations Before Income Taxes And Equity In Earnings Of Operating Joint Ventures	7,769	1,759	(1,684)
Total income tax expense (benefit)	2,072	349	(1,058)
Income (Loss) From Continuing Operations Before Equity In Earnings Of Operating Joint Ventures	5,697	1,410	(626)
Equity in earnings of operating joint ventures, net of taxes	15	16	59
Income (Loss) From Continuing Operations	5,712	1,426	(567)
Income (loss) from discontinued operations, net of taxes	0	12	7
Net Income (Loss)	5,712	1,438	(560)
Less: Income (loss) attributable to noncontrolling interests	70	57	107
Net Income (Loss) Attributable To Prudential Financial, Inc	$ 5,642	$ 1,381	$ (667)
Earnings Per Share [1]			
Basic earnings per share-Common Stock:			
Income (loss) from continuing operations attributable to Prudential Financial, Inc.	$ 12.37	$ 3.23	$ (1.57)
Income (loss) from discontinued operations, net of taxes	0.00	0.02	0.02
Net income (loss) attributable to Prudential Financial, Inc.	$ 12.37	$ 3.25	$ (1.55)
Diluted earnings per share-Common Stock:			
Income (loss) from continuing operations attributable to Prudential Financial, Inc.	$ 12.17	$ 3.20	$ (1.57)
Income (loss) from discontinued operations, net of taxes	0.00	0.03	0.02
Net income (loss) attributable to Prudential Financial, Inc.	$ 12.17	$ 3.23	$ (1.55)
Dividends declared per share of Common Stock	$ 2.44	$ 2.17	$ 1.73

[1] For 2015, represents consolidated earnings per share of Common Stock. For 2014 and 2013, represents earnings of the Company's former Financial Services Businesses per share of Common Stock. See Note 16 for additional information.

NOTES TO CONSOLIDATED FINANCIAL STATEMENTS (in part)

1. Business and Basis of Presentation (in part)

Prudential Financial, Inc. ("Prudential Financial") and its subsidiaries (collectively, "Prudential" or the "Company" or "PFI") provide a wide range of insurance, investment management, and other financial products and services to both individual and institutional customers throughout the United States and in many other countries. Principal products and services provided include life insurance, annuities, retirement-related services, mutual funds and investment management.

From December 18, 2001, the date of demutualization, through December 31, 2014, the Company organized its principal operations into the Financial Services Businesses and the Closed Block Business, and had two classes of common stock outstanding. The Common Stock, which is publicly-traded (NYSE:PRU), reflected the performance of the Financial Services Businesses, while the Class B Stock, which was issued through a private placement and did not trade on any exchange, reflected the performance of the Closed Block Business.

On January 2, 2015, Prudential Financial repurchased and canceled all of the shares of the Class B Stock (the "Class B Repurchase"). As a result, the Company no longer organizes its principal operations into the Financial Services Businesses and the Closed Block Business. The Company's principal operations are comprised of four divisions: the U.S. Retirement Solutions and Investment Management division, the U.S. Individual Life and Group Insurance division, the International Insurance division and the Closed Block division. The Company's Corporate and Other operations include corporate items and initiatives that are not allocated to business segments and businesses that have been or will be divested, excluding the Closed Block division.

The Closed Block division includes certain in force participating insurance and annuity products and corresponding assets that are used for the payment of benefits and policyholders' dividends on these products (the "Closed Block"), as well as certain related assets and liabilities. See Note 12 for further information on the Closed Block. In connection with demutualization, the Company ceased offering these participating products. The Closed Block division is accounted for as a divested business that is reported separately from the divested businesses that are included in the Company's Corporate and Other operations.

Basis of Presentation

As a result of the Class B Repurchase and resulting elimination of the separation of the Financial Services Businesses and the Closed Block Business, these Consolidated Financial Statements refer to the divisions and segments of the Company that formerly comprised the Financial Services Businesses as "PFI excluding Closed Block division" and refer to the operations that were formerly included in the Closed Block Business as the "Closed Block division," except as otherwise noted. Closed Block Business results were associated with the Company's Class B Stock for periods prior to January 1, 2015.

The Consolidated Financial Statements include the accounts of Prudential Financial, entities over which the Company exercises control, including majority-owned subsidiaries and minority-owned entities such as limited partnerships in which the Company is the general partner, and variable interest entities in which the Company is considered the primary beneficiary. See Note 5 for more information on the Company's consolidated variable interest entities. The Consolidated Financial Statements have been prepared in accordance with accounting principles generally accepted in the United States of America ("U.S. GAAP"). Intercompany balances and transactions have been eliminated.

The Company's Gibraltar Life Insurance Company, Ltd. ("Gibraltar Life") consolidated operations use a November 30 fiscal year end for purposes of inclusion in the Company's Consolidated Financial Statements. Consolidated balance sheet data as of December 31, 2015 and 2014, include the assets and liabilities of Gibraltar Life as of November 30 for each respective year. Consolidated income statement data for the years ended December 31, 2015, 2014 and 2013, include Gibraltar Life's results of operations for the twelve months ended November 30 for each respective year.

2. Significant Accounting Policies and Pronouncements (in part)

Earnings Per Share

As discussed in Note 1, from demutualization through December 31, 2014, the Company had two separate classes of common stock. Basic earnings per share for those periods was computed by dividing available income attributable to each of the two groups of common shareholders by the respective weighted average number of common shares outstanding for the period. Diluted earnings per share included the effect of all dilutive potential common shares that were outstanding during the period.

As a result of the Class B Repurchase, earnings per share of Common Stock for 2015 reflects the consolidated earnings of Prudential Financial. Basic earnings per share is computed by dividing available income attributable to common shareholders by the weighted average number of common shares outstanding for the period. Diluted earnings per share includes the effect of all dilutive potential common shares that were outstanding during the period. See Note 16 for additional information.

As discussed under "Share-Based Payments" above, the Company accounts for excess tax benefits in additional paid-in capital as a single "pool" available to all share-based compensation awards. The Company reflects in assumed proceeds, based on application of the treasury stock method, the excess tax benefits that would be recognized in additional paid-in capital upon exercise or release of the award.

16. Earnings Per Share

From demutualization through December 31, 2014, the Company had two separate classes of common stock. The Common Stock reflected the performance of the Company's former Financial Services Businesses and the Class B Stock reflected the performance of the Company's former Closed Block Business. Earnings per share were calculated separately for each of these two classes of common stock and included a direct equity adjustment to modify the earnings available to each of the classes of common stock for the difference between the allocation of general and administrative expenses to each of the businesses and the cash flows between the businesses related to these expenses. Accordingly, earnings per share of Common Stock presented below for the years ended December 31, 2014 and 2013, reflect earnings attributable to the former Financial Services Businesses.

As discussed in Note 1, on January 2, 2015, Prudential Financial repurchased and canceled all of the 2.0 million shares of the Class B Stock. Accordingly, earnings per share of Common Stock presented below for the year ended December 31, 2015, reflect the consolidated earnings of Prudential Financial. In addition, the Class B Repurchase resulted in the elimination of the separation of the former Financial Services Businesses and Closed Block Business. As a result, there was no direct equity adjustment recorded for the year ended December 31, 2015.

Earnings per share of the Class B Stock for the years ended December 31, 2014 and 2013, is not presented herein as it is not meaningful due to the Class B Repurchase.

A reconciliation of the numerators and denominators of the basic and diluted per share computations of Common Stock based on the consolidated earnings of Prudential Financial for the year ended December 31, 2015, is as follows:

(In millions, except per share amounts)	2015 Income	Weighted Average Shares	Per Share Amount
Basic Earnings Per Share			
Income (loss) from continuing operations	$5,712		
Less: Income (loss) attributable to noncontrolling interests	70		
Less: Dividends and undistributed earnings allocated to participating unvested share-based payment awards	55		
Income (loss) from continuing operations attributable to Prudential Financial available to holders of Common Stock	$5,587	451.7	$12.37
Effect of Dilutive Securities and Compensation Programs			
Add: Dividends and undistributed earnings allocated to participating unvested share-based payment awards—Basic	$55		
Less: Dividends and undistributed earnings allocated to participating unvested share-based payment awards—Diluted	54		
Stock options		2.3	
Deferred and long-term compensation programs		0.9	
Exchangeable Surplus Notes	17	5.5	
Diluted Earnings Per Share			
Income (loss) from continuing operations attributable to Prudential Financial available to holders of Common Stock	$5,605	460.4	$12.17

A reconciliation of the numerators and denominators of the basic and diluted per share computations of Common Stock based on earnings attributable to the former Financial Services Businesses for the years ended December 31, 2014 and 2013, is as follows:

(In millions, except per share amounts)	2014 Income	2014 Weighted Average Shares	2014 Per Share Amount	2013 Income	2013 Weighted Average Shares	2013 Per Share Amount
Basic Earnings Per Share						
Income (loss) from continuing operations attributable to the Financial Services Businesses	$1,579			$(613)		
Direct equity adjustment	(27)			2		
Less: Income (loss) attributable to noncontrolling interests	57			107		
Less: Dividends and undistributed earnings allocated to participating unvested share-based payment awards	14			8		
Income (loss) from continuing operations attributable to the Financial Services Businesses available to holders of Common Stock after direct equity adjustment	$1,481	458.5	$3.23	$(726)	463.1	$(1.57)
Effect of Dilutive Securities and Compensation Programs[1]						
Add: Dividends and undistributed earnings allocated to participating unvested share-based payment awards—Basic	$ 14			$8		
Less: Dividends and undistributed earnings allocated to participating unvested share-based payment awards—Diluted	14			8		
Stock options		3.0			0.0	
Deferred and long-term compensation programs		0.8			0.0	
Exchangeable Surplus Notes	17	5.4		0	0.0	
Diluted Earnings Per Share[1]						
Income (loss) from continuing operations attributable to the Financial Services Businesses available to holders of Common Stock after direct equity adjustment	$1,498	467.7	$3.20	$(726)	463.1	$(1.57)

[1] For the year ended December 31, 2013, weighted average shares for basic earnings per share is also used for calculating diluted earnings per share because dilutive shares and dilutive earnings per share are not applicable when a loss from continuing operations is reported. As a result of the loss from continuing operations available to holders of Common Stock after direct equity adjustment for the year ended December 31, 2013, all potential stock options and compensation programs were considered antidilutive.

Unvested share-based payment awards that contain nonforfeitable rights to dividends are participating securities and included in the computation of earnings per share pursuant to the two-class method. Under this method, earnings attributable to Prudential Financial are allocated between Common Stock and the participating awards, as if the awards were a second class of stock. During periods of income from continuing operations available to holders of Common Stock, after direct equity adjustment as applicable, the calculation of earnings per share excludes the income attributable to participating securities in the numerator and the dilutive impact of these securities from the denominator. In the event of loss from continuing operations available to holders of Common Stock, after direct equity adjustment as applicable, undistributed earnings are not allocated to participating securities and the denominator excludes the dilutive impact of these securities as they do not share in the losses of the Company. For 2013, undistributed earnings were not allocated to participating unvested share-based payment awards as these awards do not participate in losses. Undistributed earnings allocated to participating unvested share-based payment awards for the years ended December 31, 2015 and 2014 were based on 4.4 million and 4.3 million of such awards, respectively, weighted for the period they were outstanding.

Stock options and shares related to deferred and long-term compensation programs that are considered antidilutive are excluded from the computation of dilutive earnings per share. Stock options are considered antidilutive based on application of the treasury stock method or in the event of loss from continuing operations available to holders of Common Stock, after direct equity adjustment as applicable. Shares related to deferred and long-term compensation programs are considered antidilutive in the event of loss from continuing operations available to holders of Common Stock, after direct equity adjustment as applicable. For the years ended December 31, the number of stock options and shares related to deferred and long-term compensation programs that were considered antidilutive and were excluded from the computation of diluted earnings per share, weighted for the portion of the period they were outstanding, are as follows:

(In millions, except per share amounts, based on weighted average)	2015 Shares	2015 Exercise Price Per Share	2014 Shares	2014 Exercise Price Per Share	2013 Shares	2013 Exercise Price Per Share
Antidilutive stock options based on application of the treasury stock method	2.4	$87.97	1.9	$90.30	6.6	$73.51
Antidilutive stock options due to loss from continuing operations available to holders of Common Stock after direct equity adjustment	0.0		0.0		12.2	
Antidilutive shares due to loss from continuing operations available to holders of Common Stock after direct equity adjustment	0.0		0.0		5.2	
Total antidilutive stock options and shares	2.4		1.9		24.0	

In September 2009, the Company issued $500 million of surplus notes with an interest rate of 5.36% per annum which are exchangeable at the option of the note holders for shares of Common Stock. The initial exchange rate for the surplus notes was 10.1235 shares of Common Stock per each $1,000 principal amount of surplus notes, which represents an initial exchange price per share of Common Stock of $98.78; however, the exchange rate is subject to customary anti-dilution adjustments. In calculating diluted earnings per share under the if-converted method, the potential shares that would be issued assuming a hypothetical exchange, weighted for the period the notes are outstanding, are added to the denominator, and interest expense, net of tax, is added to the numerator, if the overall effect is dilutive.

3.97 CALATLANTIC GROUP, INC. (DEC)
CONSOLIDATED STATEMENTS OF OPERATIONS

(Dollars in thousands, except per share amounts)	Year Ended December 31, 2015	2014	2013
Homebuilding:			
Home sale revenues	$ 3,449,047	$ 2,366,754	$ 1,898,989
Land sale revenues	47,364	44,424	15,620
Total revenues	3,496,411	2,411,178	1,914,609
Cost of home sales	(2,676,666)	(1,748,954)	(1,431,797)
Cost of land sales	(43,274)	(43,841)	(13,616)
Total cost of sales	(2,719,940)	(1,792,795)	(1,445,413)
Gross margin	776,471	618,383	469,196
Selling, general and administrative expenses	(390,710)	(275,861)	(230,691)
Income (loss) from unconsolidated joint ventures	1,966	(668)	949
Other income (expense)	(62,177)	(1,733)	6,815
Homebuilding pretax income	325,550	340,121	246,269
Financial Services:			
Revenues	43,702	25,320	25,734
Expenses	(26,763)	(15,477)	(14,305)
Financial services pretax income	16,939	9,843	11,429
Income before taxes	342,489	349,964	257,698
Provision for income taxes	(128,980)	(134,099)	(68,983)
Net income	213,509	215,865	188,715
Less: Net income allocated to preferred shareholder	(32,997)	(51,650)	(57,386)
Less: Net income allocated to unvested restricted stock	(369)	(297)	(265)
Net income available to common stockholders	$ 180,143	$ 163,918	$ 131,064
Income per common share:			
Basic	$ 2.51	$ 2.94	$ 2.59
Diluted	$ 2.26	$ 2.68	$ 2.36
Weighted average common shares outstanding:			
Basic	71,713,747	55,737,548	50,623,649
Diluted	81,512,953	63,257,082	58,234,791
Weighted average additional common shares outstanding if preferred shares converted to common shares	13,135,814	17,562,557	22,165,311
Total weighted average diluted common shares outstanding if preferred shares converted to common shares	94,648,767	80,819,639	80,400,102

2. Summary of Significant Accounting Policies (in part)

i. Earnings Per Common Share

We compute earnings per share in accordance with ASC Topic 260, *Earnings per Share* ("ASC 260"), which requires earnings per share for each class of stock (common stock and participating preferred stock) to be calculated using the two-class method. The two-class method is an allocation of earnings between the holders of common stock and a company's participating security holders. Under the two-class method, earnings for the reporting period are allocated between common shareholders and other security holders based on their respective participation rights in undistributed earnings. Unvested share-based payment awards that contain non-forfeitable rights to dividends or dividend equivalents are participating securities and, therefore, are included in computing earnings per share pursuant to the two-class method.

Basic earnings per common share is computed by dividing income or loss available to common stockholders by the weighted average number of shares of basic common stock outstanding. Our Series B junior participating convertible preferred stock ("Series B Preferred Stock"), which was convertible into shares of our common stock at the holder's option, and our unvested restricted stock, are classified as participating securities in accordance with ASC 260. Net income allocated to the holders of our Series B Preferred Stock and unvested restricted stock is calculated based on the shareholders' proportionate share of weighted average shares of common stock outstanding on an if-converted basis.

For purposes of determining diluted earnings per common share, basic earnings per common share is further adjusted to include the effect of potential dilutive common shares outstanding, including stock options, stock appreciation rights, performance share awards and unvested restricted stock using the more dilutive of either the two-class method or the treasury stock method, and Series B Preferred Stock and convertible debt using the if-converted method. Under the two-class method of calculating diluted earnings per share, net income is reallocated to common stock, the Series B Preferred stock and all dilutive securities based on the contractual participating rights of the security to share in the current earnings as if all of the earnings for the period had been distributed. In the computation of diluted earnings per share, the two-class method and if-converted method for the Series B Preferred Stock resulted in the same earnings per share amounts as the holder of the Series B Preferred Stock had the same economic rights as the holders of the common stock.

In connection with the closing of the merger on October 1, 2015, the Company effected a reverse stock split such that each five shares of common stock of Standard Pacific common stock issued and outstanding immediately prior to the closing of the Merger were combined and converted into one issued and outstanding share of common stock of the Company. As required in accordance with GAAP, all share and earnings per share information noted below have been retroactively adjusted to reflect the reverse stock split. The following table sets forth the components used in the computation of basic and diluted income per share.

	Year Ended December 31,		
(Dollars in thousands, except per share amounts)	2015	2014	2013
Numerator:			
Net income	$ 213,509	$ 215,865	$ 188,715
Less: Net income allocated to preferred shareholder	(32,997)	(51,650)	(57,386)
Less: Net income allocated to unvested restricted stock	(369)	(297)	(265)
Net income available to common stockholders for basic earnings per common share	180,143	163,918	131,064
Effect of dilutive securities:			
Net income allocated to preferred shareholder	32,997	51,650	57,386
Interest on 1.625% convertible senior notes due 2018	47	n/a	n/a
Interest on 0.25% convertible senior notes due 2019	9	n/a	n/a
Interest on 1.25% convertible senior notes due 2032	898	899	899
Net income available to common and preferred stock for diluted earnings per share	$ 214,094	$ 216,467	$ 189,349
Denominator:			
Weighted average basic common shares outstanding	71,713,747	55,737,548	50,623,649
Weighted average additional common shares outstanding if preferred shares converted to common shares (if dilutive)	13,135,814	17,562,557	22,165,311
Total weighted average common shares outstanding if preferred shares converted to common shares	84,849,561	73,300,105	72,788,961
Effect of dilutive securities:			
Share-based awards	816,459	1,256,964	1,348,571
1.625% convertible senior notes due 2018	1,804,192	n/a	n/a
0.25% convertible senior notes due 2019	915,985	n/a	n/a
1.25% convertible senior notes due 2032	6,262,570	6,262,570	6,262,570
Weighted average diluted shares outstanding	94,648,767	80,819,639	80,400,102
Income per share:			
Basic	$ 2.51	$ 2.94	$ 2.59
Diluted	$ 2.26	$ 2.68	$ 2.36

Section 4: Comprehensive Income

Comprehensive Income in Annual Filings

RECOGNITION AND MEASUREMENT

4.01 FASB *Accounting Standards Codification* (ASC) 220, *Comprehensive Income*, requires that items included in other comprehensive income should be classified based on their nature. Other comprehensive income includes the following: foreign currency items, changes in the fair value of certain derivatives, unrealized gains and losses on certain securities, and certain pension or other postretirement benefit items.

PRESENTATION

4.02 FASB ASC 220 requires entities that provide a full set of general-purpose financial statements (that is, financial position, results of operations, and cash flows) to report comprehensive income and its components either in a single continuous financial statement or in two separate but consecutive financial statements. The FASB ASC glossary defines *comprehensive income* as the change in equity (net assets) of a business entity during a period from transactions and other events and circumstances from non-owner sources. It includes all changes in equity during a period except those resulting from investments by owners and distributions to owners. *Other comprehensive income* is defined as revenues, expenses, gains, and losses that under generally accepted accounting principles are included in comprehensive income but excluded from net income. If an entity has only net income, it is not required to report comprehensive income. All items that meet the definition of components of comprehensive income must be reported in a financial statement for the period in which they are recognized. Further, a total amount for comprehensive income should be displayed in the financial statement when the components of other comprehensive income are reported.

4.03 FASB ASC 220-10-45-5 states that if an entity has an outstanding noncontrolling interest, amounts for both net income and comprehensive income attributable to the parent and net income and comprehensive income attributable to the noncontrolling interest in a less-than-wholly-owned subsidiary shall be reported on the face of the financial statement(s) in which net income and comprehensive income are presented in addition to presenting consolidated net income and comprehensive income.

4.04 FASB ASC 220-10-45-12 also states that an entity should disclose the amount of income tax expense or benefit allocated to each component of other comprehensive income, including reclassification adjustments, either on the face of the statement in which those components are displayed or in the notes thereto. Also, FASB ASC 810, *Consolidation*, states that if an entity has an outstanding noncontrolling interest (minority interest), the components of both net income and other comprehensive income attributable to the parent and noncontrolling interest in a less-than-wholly-owned subsidiary are required to be reported on the face of the financial statement in which net income and comprehensive income are presented, in addition to presenting consolidated comprehensive income.

4.05 FASB ASC 220-10-45-15 also requires that adjustments should be made to avoid double counting in comprehensive income items that are displayed as part of net income for a period that also had been displayed as part of other comprehensive income in that period or earlier periods. For example, gains on investment securities that were realized and included in net income of the current period that also had been included in other comprehensive income as unrealized holding gains in the period in which they arose must be deducted through other comprehensive income of the period in which they are included in net income to avoid including them in comprehensive income twice. These adjustments are called *reclassification adjustments*. An entity may display reclassification adjustments on the face of the financial statement in which comprehensive income is reported, or it may disclose them in the notes to the financial statements (that is, either a gross display on the face of the financial statement or a net display on the face of the financial statement and disclosure of the gross change in the notes to the financial statements). FASB ASC 220-10-45-14 A also requires an entity to present the changes in the accumulated balances for each component of other comprehensive income. Both before-tax and net-of-tax presentations are permitted provided the requirements of FASB ASC 220-10-45-12 are met.

PRESENTATION AND DISCLOSURE EXCERPTS

COMBINED STATEMENT OF INCOME AND COMPREHENSIVE INCOME

4.06 INTERNATIONAL FLAVORS & FRAGRANCES INC. (DEC)
CONSOLIDATED STATEMENT OF INCOME AND COMPREHENSIVE INCOME

	Year Ended December 31,		
(Dollars In Thousands Except Per Share Amounts)	2015	2014	2013
Net sales	$3,023,189	$3,088,533	$2,952,896
Cost of goods sold	1,671,590	1,726,383	1,668,691
Gross profit	1,351,599	1,362,150	1,284,205
Research and development expenses	246,101	253,640	259,838
Selling and administrative expenses	509,557	514,891	505,877
Restructuring and other charges, net	7,594	1,298	2,151
Operating profit	588,347	592,321	516,339
Interest expense	46,062	46,067	46,767
Other expense (income), net	3,184	(2,807)	(15,638)
Income before taxes	539,101	549,061	485,210
Taxes on income	119,854	134,518	131,666
Net income	419,247	414,543	353,544
Other comprehensive income (loss):			
Foreign currency translation adjustments	(124,156)	(69,064)	(10,556)
(Losses) gains on derivatives qualifying as hedges	(2,970)	16,383	(3,794)
Pension and postretirement liability adjustment	54,117	(95,038)	25,264
Comprehensive income	$ 346,238	$ 266,824	$ 364,458

	2015	2014	2013
Net income per share — basic	$5.19	$5.09	$4.32
Net income per share — diluted	$5.16	$5.06	$4.29

See Notes to Consolidated Financial Statements

SEPARATE STATEMENT OF COMPREHENSIVE INCOME

4.07 CAMPBELL SOUP COMPANY (JUL)
CONSOLIDATED STATEMENTS OF COMPREHENSIVE INCOME

(millions)

	2015			2014			2013		
	Pre-tax amount	Tax (expense) benefit	After-tax amount	Pre-tax amount	Tax (expense) benefit	After-tax amount	Pre-tax amount	Tax (expense) benefit	After-tax amount
Net earnings			$ 691			$807			$449
Other comprehensive income (loss):									
Foreign currency translation:									
Foreign currency translation adjustments	$(324)	$ 1	(323)	$(12)	$ (1)	(13)	$(95)	$ 3	(92)
Reclassification of currency translation adjustments realized upon disposal of business	—	—	—	(22)	3	(19)	—	—	—
Cash-flow hedges:									
Unrealized gains (losses) arising during period	(5)	3	(2)	(12)	4	(8)	20	(8)	12
Reclassification adjustment for (gains) losses included in net earnings	(1)	1	—	—	—	—	4	(1)	3
Pension and other postretirement benefits:									
Net actuarial gain (loss) arising during the period	(124)	47	(77)	(55)	20	(35)	322	(103)	219
Reclassification of prior service credit included in net earnings	(2)	—	(2)	(2)	—	(2)	(2)	—	(2)
Reclassification of net actuarial loss included in net earnings	98	(35)	63	113	(39)	74	124	(54)	70
Other comprehensive income (loss)	$(358)	$ 17	(341)	$ 10	$(13)	(3)	$373	$(163)	210
Total comprehensive income (loss)			$ 350			$804			$659
Total comprehensive income (loss) attributable to noncontrolling interests			(1)			(10)			(10)
Total comprehensive income (loss) attributable to Campbell Soup Company			$ 351			$814			$669

See accompanying Notes to Consolidated Financial Statements.

4.08 AK STEEL HOLDING CORPORATION (DEC)
CONSOLIDATED STATEMENTS OF COMPREHENSIVE INCOME (LOSS)

(dollars in millions)

	2015	2014	2013
Net income (loss)	$(446.2)	$ (34.1)	$ 17.4
Other comprehensive income (loss), before tax:			
Foreign currency translation gain (loss)	(3.1)	(3.7)	1.2
Cash flow hedges:			
Gains (losses) arising in period	(64.2)	(51.6)	3.5
Reclassification of losses (gains) to net income (loss)	61.4	1.1	(25.2)
Unrealized holding gains on securities:			
Unrealized holding gains (losses) arising in period	—	—	0.2
Pension and OPEB plans:			
Prior service credit (cost) arising in period	(7.7)	10.9	(6.1)
Gains (losses) arising in period	(60.8)	(422.5)	422.3
Reclassification of prior service cost (credits) included in net income (loss)	(60.2)	(68.9)	(76.2)
Reclassification of losses (gains) included in net income (loss)	165.0	6.9	25.3
Other comprehensive income (loss), before tax	30.4	(527.8)	345.0
Income tax expense in other comprehensive income (loss)	13.2	—	22.7
Other comprehensive income (loss)	17.2	(527.8)	322.3
Comprehensive income (loss)	(429.0)	(561.9)	339.7
Less: Comprehensive income attributable to noncontrolling interests	62.8	62.8	64.2
Comprehensive income (loss) attributable to AK Steel Holding Corporation	$(491.8)	$(624.7)	$275.5

See notes to consolidated financial statements.

NOTES TO CONSOLIDATED FINANCIAL STATEMENTS

(dollars in millions, except per share amounts or as otherwise specifically noted)

Note 13—Comprehensive Income (Loss)

Other comprehensive income (loss), net of tax, information is presented below:

	2015	2014	2013
Foreign Currency Translation			
Balance at beginning of period	$ 1.0	$ 4.7	$ 3.5
Other comprehensive income (loss)—foreign currency translation gain (loss)	(3.1)	(3.7)	1.2
Balance at end of period	$ (2.1)	$ 1.0	$ 4.7
Cash Flow Hedges			
Balance at beginning of period	$ (32.2)	$ 18.3	$ 31.7
Other comprehensive income (loss):			
Gains (losses) arising in period	(64.2)	(51.6)	3.5
Income tax expense	24.9	—	1.3
Gains (losses) arising in period, net of tax	(89.1)	(51.6)	2.2
Reclassification of losses (gains) to net income (loss):			
Hot roll carbon steel coil contracts[a]	—	—	(0.4)
Other commodity contracts[b]	61.4	1.1	(24.8)
Subtotal	61.4	1.1	(25.2)
Income tax expense[d]	(25.9)	—	(9.6)
Net amount of reclassification of losses (gains) to net income (loss)	87.3	1.1	(15.6)
Total other comprehensive income (loss), net of tax	(1.8)	(50.5)	(13.4)
Balance at end of period	$ (34.0)	$ (32.2)	$ 18.3

(continued)

	2015	2014	2013
Unrealized Holding Gains on Securities			
Balance at beginning of period	$ 0.4	$ 0.4	$ 0.3
Other comprehensive income (loss):			
Unrealized holding gains (losses) arising in period	—	—	0.2
Income tax expense	—	—	0.1
Unrealized holding gains (losses) arising in period, net of tax	—	—	0.1
Reclassification of gains (losses) to net income (loss)—income tax benefit(d)	0.4	—	—
Total other comprehensive income (loss), net of tax	(0.4)	—	0.1
Balance at end of period	$ —	$ 0.4	$ 0.4
Pension and OPEB Plans			
Balance at beginning of period	$(173.6)	$ 300.0	$ (34.4)
Other comprehensive income (loss):			
Prior service credit (cost) arising in period	(7.7)	10.9	(6.1)
Gains (losses) arising in period	(60.8)	(422.5)	422.3
Subtotal	(68.5)	(411.6)	416.2
Income tax expense (benefit)(d)	(26.0)	—	50.3
Gains (losses) arising in period, net of tax	(42.5)	(411.6)	365.9
Reclassification to net income (loss):			
Prior service costs (credits)(c)	(60.2)	(68.9)	(76.2)
Actuarial (gains) losses(c)	165.0	6.9	25.3
Subtotal	104.8	(62.0)	(50.9)
Income tax (expense) benefit(d)	39.8	—	(19.4)
Amount of reclassification to net income (loss), net of tax	65.0	(62.0)	(31.5)
Total other comprehensive income (loss), net of tax	22.5	(473.6)	334.4
Balance at end of period	$(151.1)	$(173.6)	$300.0

(a) Included in net sales
(b) Included in cost of products sold
(c) Included in pension and OPEB expense (income)
(d) Included in income tax expense (benefit)

TAX EFFECT DISCLOSURE ON THE FACE OF THE FINANCIAL STATEMENTS

4.09 APPLE INC. (SEP)
CONSOLIDATED STATEMENTS OF COMPREHENSIVE INCOME

(In millions)

	Years ended		
	September 26, 2015	September 27, 2014	September 28, 2013
Net income	$53,394	$39,510	$37,037
Other comprehensive income/(loss):			
Change in foreign currency translation, net of tax effects of $201, $50 and $35, respectively	(411)	(137)	(112)
Change in unrealized gains/losses on derivative instruments:			
Change in fair value of derivatives, net of tax benefit/(expense) of $(441), $(297) and $(351), respectively	2,905	1,390	522
Adjustment for net (gains)/losses realized and included in net income, net of tax expense/(benefit) of $630, $(36) and $255, respectively	(3,497)	(149)	(458)
Total change in unrealized gains/losses on derivative instruments, net of tax	(592)	1,539	64
Change in unrealized gains/losses on marketable securities:			
Change in fair value of marketable securities, net of tax benefit/(expense) of $264, $(153) and $458, respectively	(483)	285	(791)
Adjustment for net (gains)/losses realized and included in net income, net of tax expense/(benefit) of $(32), $71 and $82, respectively	59	(134)	(131)
Total change in unrealized gains/losses on marketable securities, net of tax	(424)	151	(922)
Total other comprehensive income/(loss)	(1,427)	1,553	(970)
Total comprehensive income	$51,967	$41,063	$36,067

See accompanying Notes to Consolidated Financial Statements.

4.10 PFIZER INC. (DEC)

CONSOLIDATED STATEMENTS OF COMPREHENSIVE INCOME

(Millions)	Year Ended December 31,		
	2015	**2014**	**2013**
Net income before allocation to noncontrolling interests	$ 6,986	$ 9,168	$22,072
Foreign currency translation adjustments, net	$(3,110)	$(1,992)	$ (535)
Reclassification adjustments[a]	—	(62)	144
	(3,110)	(2,054)	(391)
Unrealized holding gains on derivative financial instruments, net	204	24	488
Reclassification adjustments for realized (gains)/losses[b]	(368)	477	(94)
	(165)	501	394
Unrealized holding gains/(losses) on available-for-sale securities, net	(846)	(640)	151
Reclassification adjustments for realized (gains)/losses[b]	796	222	(237)
	(50)	(418)	(86)
Benefit plans: actuarial gains/(losses), net	(37)	(4,173)	3,714
Reclassification adjustments related to amortization[c]	550	195	581
Reclassification adjustments related to settlements, net[c]	671	101	175
Other	199	188	48
	1,383	(3,690)	4,518
Benefit plans: prior service credits and other, net	432	746	151
Reclassification adjustments related to amortization[c]	(160)	(73)	(58)
Reclassification adjustments related to curtailments, net[c]	(32)	8	1
Other	(3)	(9)	(8)
	237	672	86
Other comprehensive income/(loss), before tax	(1,705)	(4,988)	4,521
Tax provision/(benefit) on other comprehensive income/(loss)[d]	528	(946)	1,928
Other comprehensive income/(loss) before allocation to noncontrolling interests	$(2,232)	$(4,042)	$ 2,593
Comprehensive income before allocation to noncontrolling interests	$ 4,754	$ 5,126	$24,665
Less: Comprehensive income/(loss) attributable to noncontrolling interests	(1)	36	7
Comprehensive income attributable to Pfizer Inc.	$ 4,755	$ 5,090	$24,658

[a] Reclassified into *Gain on disposal of discontinued operations—net of tax* in the consolidated statements of income.

[b] Reclassified into *Other (income)/deductions—net* in the consolidated statements of income.

[c] Generally reclassified, as part of net periodic pension cost, into *Cost of sales, Selling, informational and administrative expenses,* and/or *Research and development expenses,* as appropriate, in the consolidated statements of income. For additional information, see *Note 11. Pension and Postretirement Benefit Plans and Defined Contribution Plans.*

[d] See *Note 5E. Tax Matters: Tax Provision/(Benefit) on Other Comprehensive Income/(Loss).*

Amounts may not add due to rounding.

See Notes to Consolidated Financial Statements, which are an integral part of these statements.

NOTES TO CONSOLIDATED FINANCIAL STATEMENTS (in part)

Note 5. Tax Matters (in part)

E. Tax Provision/(Benefit) on Other Comprehensive Income/(Loss)

The following table provides the components of the tax provision/(benefit) on *Other comprehensive income/(loss)* :

(Millions of Dollars)	Year Ended December 31,		
	2015	**2014**	**2013**
Foreign currency translation adjustments, net[a]	$ 90	$ 42	$ 111
Unrealized holding gains on derivative financial instruments, net	(173)	(199)	217
Reclassification adjustments for realized (gains)/losses	104	262	(63)
	(69)	63	154
Unrealized holding gains/(losses) on available-for-sale securities, net	(104)	(56)	57
Reclassification adjustments for realized (gains)/losses	59	10	(57)
	(45)	(46)	—
Benefit plans: actuarial gains/(losses), net	(23)	(1,416)	1,422
Reclassification adjustments related to amortization	183	61	205

(continued)

(Millions of Dollars)	Year Ended December 31,		
	2015	2014	2013
Reclassification adjustments related to settlements, net	237	35	2
Other	66	61	2
	462	(1,258)	1,631
Benefit plans: prior service credits and other, net	160	281	56
Reclassification adjustments related to amortization	(59)	(28)	(23)
Reclassification adjustments related to curtailments, net	(12)	—	(1)
Other	—	(1)	—
	89	253	32
Tax provision/(benefit) on other comprehensive income/(loss)	$ 528	$ (946)	$1,928

(a) Taxes are not provided for foreign currency translation adjustments relating to investments in international subsidiaries that will be held indefinitely.

FOREIGN CURRENCY TRANSLATION

4.11 THE ESTEE LAUDER COMPANIES INC. (JUN)

CONSOLIDATED STATEMENTS OF COMPREHENSIVE INCOME (LOSS)

(In millions)	Year Ended June 30		
	2015	2014	2013
Net earnings	$1,093.4	$1,209.1	$1,023.8
Other comprehensive income (loss):			
Net unrealized investment gain (loss)	(1.9)	0.9	0.4
Net derivative instrument gain (loss)	69.6	(29.7)	1.2
Amounts included in net periodic benefit cost	(23.8)	(13.0)	125.9
Translation adjustments	(306.0)	87.2	(20.1)
Benefit (provision) for deferred income taxes on components of other comprehensive income	(21.2)	12.5	(51.1)
Total other comprehensive income (loss)	(283.3)	57.9	56.3
Comprehensive income (loss)	810.1	1,267.0	1,080.1
Comprehensive (income) loss attributable to noncontrolling interests:			
Net earnings	(4.5)	(5.0)	(4.0)
Translation adjustments	2.1	(0.7)	(0.9)
	(2.4)	(5.7)	(4.9)
Comprehensive income (loss) attributable to The Estée Lauder Companies Inc.	$ 807.7	$1,261.3	$1,075.2

See notes to consolidated financial statements.

NOTES TO CONSOLIDATED FINANCIAL STATEMENTS (in part)

Note 2 — Summary of Significant Accounting Policies (in part)

Currency Translation and Transactions

All assets and liabilities of foreign subsidiaries and affiliates are translated at year-end rates of exchange, while revenue and expenses are translated at weighted-average rates of exchange for the period. Unrealized translation gains (losses) reported as cumulative translation adjustments through other comprehensive income (loss) ("OCI") attributable to The Estée Lauder Companies Inc. amounted to $(322.5) million, $95.1 million and $(25.6) million, net of tax, in fiscal 2015, 2014 and 2013, respectively.

For the Company's Venezuelan subsidiary operating in a highly inflationary economy, the U.S. dollar is the functional currency. Remeasurement adjustments in financial statements in a highly inflationary economy and other transactional gains and losses are reflected in earnings. During the third quarter of fiscal 2014, the Venezuelan government enacted changes to the foreign exchange controls that expanded the use of its then-existing exchange mechanisms and created another exchange control mechanism ("SICAD II"), which allowed companies to apply for the purchase of foreign currency and foreign currency denominated securities for any legal use or purpose. The Company considered its specific facts and circumstances in determining the appropriate remeasurment rate and determined the SICAD II rate was the most appropriate rate that reflected the economics of its Venezuelan subsidiary's business as of March 24, 2014, when the SICAD II mechanism became operational. As a result, the Company changed the exchange rate used to remeasure the monetary assets and liabilities of its Venezuelan subsidiary from 6.3 to the SICAD II rate, which was 49. 98 as of June 30, 2014. Accordingly, a remeasurement charge of $38.3 million, on a before and after tax basis, was reflected in Selling, general and administrative expenses in the Company's consolidated statement of earnings for the year ended June 30, 2014.

On February 12, 2015, the Venezuelan government introduced a new open market foreign exchange system ("SIMADI"), which effectively replaced the SICAD II mechanism. As the SIMADI is the only mechanism legally available at this time for the Company's highest priority transactions, which are the import of goods, the Company changed the exchange rate used to remeasure the monetary assets and liabilities of its Venezuelan subsidiary to the SIMADI rate during the third quarter of fiscal 2015. Accordingly, a remeasurement charge of $5.3 million, on a before and after tax basis, was reflected in Selling, general and administrative expenses in the Company's consolidated statement of earnings for the year ended June 30, 2015. The net monetary assets of the Company's Venezuelan subsidiary were not material as of June 30, 2015.

The Company enters into foreign currency forward contracts and may enter into option contracts to hedge foreign currency transactions for periods consistent with its identified exposures. Accordingly, the Company categorizes these instruments as entered into for purposes other than trading.

The accompanying consolidated statements of earnings include net exchange (gains) losses on foreign currency transactions, including the effect of the Venezuela remeasurement charges, of $(4.1) million, $46.7 million and $3.5 million in fiscal 2015, 2014 and 2013, respectively.

PENSION AND POSTRETIREMENT PLANS

4.12 PRECISION CASTPARTS CORP. (MAR)
CONSOLIDATED STATEMENTS OF COMPREHENSIVE INCOME

	Fiscal Years Ended		
(In millions)	March 29, 2015	March 30, 2014	March 31, 2013
Net income	$1,533	$1,784	$1,430
Other comprehensive income (loss) ("OCI"), net of tax:			
Foreign currency translation adjustments	(353)	148	(99)
Gain (loss) on available-for-sale securities:			
Unrealized (losses) gains on available-for-sales securities (net of income tax benefit (expense) of $2, $13, and $(8) respectively)	(12)	(22)	15
Less: reclassification adjustment for gains included in net income (net of income tax expense of $0, $1, and $0 respectively)	—	(2)	—
Gain (loss) on derivatives:			
Unrealized (losses) gains due to periodic revaluations (net of income tax benefit (expense) of $6, $(2), and $1 respectively)	(17)	7	1
Less: reclassification adjustment for gains included in net income (net of income tax expense of $0 in all periods)	(1)	(2)	(1)
Pension and post retirement obligations (net of income tax benefit (expense) of $56, $(29), and $23 respectively)	(154)	6	(27)
Other comprehensive (loss) income, net of tax	(537)	135	(111)
Total comprehensive loss (income) attributable to noncontrolling interests	18	(13)	—
Total comprehensive income attributable to PCC	$1,014	$1,906	$1,319

See Notes to Consolidated Financial Statements.

NOTES TO CONSOLIDATED FINANCIAL STATEMENTS (in part)

(In millions, except option share and per share data)

1. Summary of Significant Accounting Policies (in part)

Retirement and Other Postretirement Benefit Plans

We sponsor various defined benefit and defined contribution plans covering substantially all employees. We also sponsor postretirement benefit plans other than pensions, consisting principally of health care coverage to eligible retirees and qualifying dependents, covering approximately 15% of our workforce. The liabilities and net periodic cost of our defined benefit pension and other post-retirement plans are determined using methodologies that involve several actuarial assumptions, the most significant of which are the discount rate, the rate of return on plan assets, and medical trend rate (rate of growth for medical costs). For the United States ("U.S.") plans, the discount rate was determined based on the results of a bond matching model that constructed a portfolio of bonds with credit ratings of AA/Aa or higher that match our expected pension benefit cash flows. The discount rate was determined on the basis of the internal rate of return on the bond portfolio. For the non-U.S. plans, Aon Hewitt, Merrill Lynch and other long-term Corporate bond indices were used as the primary basis for determining discount rates. A portion of net periodic pension cost is included in production costs, which are included in inventories and subsequently recognized in net earnings as inventories are liquidated and charged to cost of sales. We amortize gains and losses, which occur when actual experience differs from actuarial assumptions, over the average future service period of employees. Our funding policy for pension plans is to contribute, at a minimum, the amounts required by applicable laws. During fiscal 2015, 2014 and 2013, we made voluntary contributions to pension plans totaling $8 million, $50 million, and $50 million, respectively.

18. Pension and other Postretirement Benefit Plans (in part)

We sponsor many U.S. and non-U.S. defined benefit pension plans. Benefits provided by these plans are generally based on years of service and compensation. Our general funding policy for qualified pension plans is to contribute amounts at least sufficient to satisfy regulatory funding standards. We also provide postretirement medical benefits for certain eligible employees who have satisfied plan eligibility provisions, which include age and/or service requirements.

Pension and Postretirement Benefit Obligations and Funded Status

Fiscal	Pension Benefits		Other Postretirement Benefits	
	2015	2014	2015	2014
Change in plan assets:				
Beginning fair value of plan assets	$2,267	$2,119	$—	$—
Actual return on plan assets	232	96	—	—
Company contributions	34	78	8	8
Plan participants' contributions	2	2	—	—
Benefits paid	(102)	(112)	(8)	(8)
Exchange rate and other	(108)	84	—	—
Ending fair value of plan assets	$2,325	$2,267	$—	$—
Change in projected benefit obligations:				
Beginning projected benefit obligations	$2,553	$2,466	$ 94	$106
Service cost	45	50	1	1
Interest cost	112	112	4	5
Plan participants' contributions	2	2	—	—
Amendments/curtailments/settlement	(1)	(1)	—	—
Actuarial losses (gains)	353	(51)	6	(10)
Benefits paid	(102)	(112)	(8)	(8)
Exchange rate and other	(119)	87	—	—
Ending projected pension and postretirement benefit obligations	$2,843	$2,553	$ 97	$ 94
Funded Status:				
Fair value of plan assets less than projected pension and postretirement benefit obligations	$ (518)	$ (286)	$(97)	$ (94)
Amounts recognized in the balance sheets:				
Noncurrent asset	$ —	$ 3	$—	$—
Current liabilities	(7)	(6)	(7)	(7)
Noncurrent liabilities	(511)	(283)	(90)	(87)
Net amount recognized	$ (518)	$ (286)	$(97)	$ (94)
Amounts recognized in accumulated other comprehensive loss consist of:				
Net actuarial loss	$ 908	$ 698	$ 14	$ 9
Prior service cost	8	11	—	1
Net amount recognized, before tax effect	$ 916	$ 709	$ 14	$ 10

Of the total amounts included in accumulated other comprehensive loss as of March 29, 2015, we estimate that we will recognize amortization of the following amounts as components of net periodic pension and postretirement benefit cost in fiscal 2016 : net actuarial loss of $58 million and prior service cost of $3 million. Several of our defined benefit pension plans have accumulated benefit obligations in excess of plan assets. As of March 29, 2015, the aggregate projected benefit obligation was $2,133 million, the aggregate accumulated benefit obligation was $1,995 million, and the aggregate fair value of plan assets was $1,682 million associated with these defined benefit pension plans.

Components of Net Periodic Pension Cost

The net periodic pension cost for our pension plans consisted of the following components:

Fiscal	2015	2014	2013
Service cost	$ 47	$ 52	$ 46
Interest cost	112	112	96
Expected return on plan assets	(160)	(171)	(137)
Amortization of prior service cost	3	3	3
Amortization of net actuarial loss	44	51	45
Net periodic pension cost	$ 46	$ 47	$ 53

The net postretirement benefit cost of our postretirement benefit plans consisted of the following components:

Fiscal	2015	2014	2013
Service cost	$1	$1	$1
Interest cost	4	5	4
Amortization of net actuarial loss	1	1	1
Net postretirement benefit cost	$6	$7	$6

Components of Amounts Recognized in Other Comprehensive Income

The changes in plan assets and benefit obligations recognized in other comprehensive income for our pension plans consisted of the following:

Fiscal	2015	2014	2013
Net actuarial loss (gain)	$232	$(23)	$62
Amortization of net actuarial loss	(11)	(7)	(8)
Amortization of prior service cost	(3)	(3)	(3)
Exchange rate (gain) loss	(11)	10	(7)
Total recognized in OCI	$207	$(23)	$44

The changes in plan assets and benefit obligations recognized in other comprehensive income for our postretirement benefit plans consisted of net actuarial loss (gain) of $4 million, $(12) million and $5 million for fiscal 2015, 2014 and 2013, respectively.

Weighted-Average Assumptions

The weighted-average assumptions used in determining the pension and postretirement benefit obligations in our pension and postretirement plans in fiscal 2015 and 2014 were as follows:

U.S. Plans	Pension Benefits		Other Postretirement Benefits	
Fiscal	2015	2014	2015	2014
Discount rate	4.05%	4.70%	4.05%	4.70%
Rate of compensation increase	3.00%	3.00%	3.00%	3.00%

Non-U.S. Plans	Pension Benefits	
Fiscal	2015	2014
Discount rate	3.54%	4.67%
Rate of compensation increase	2.74%	2.98%

As of March 29, 2015, the projected U.S. pension benefit obligation was $1,715 million and the non-U.S. pension benefit obligation was $1,128 million.

The weighted-average assumptions used in determining the net periodic pension and postretirement benefit cost in our pension and postretirement plans in fiscal 2015, 2014 and 2013 were as follows:

U.S. Plans	Pension Benefits			Other Postretirement Benefits		
Fiscal	2015	2014	2013	2015	2014	2013
Discount rate	4.70%	4.25%	4.80%	4.70%	4.25%	4.85%
Expected return on plan assets	7.75%	8.00%	8.00%	—	—	—
Rate of compensation increase	3.00%	3.00%	3.00%	3.00%	3.00%	3.00%

Non-U.S. Plans	Pension Benefits		
Fiscal	2015	2014	2013
Discount rate	4.67%	4.76%	4.98%
Expected return on plan assets	7.25%	7.50%	7.50%
Rate of compensation increase	2.98%	2.98%	2.91%

For the year ended March 29, 2015, our U.S. net periodic pension cost was $44 million and our non-U.S. net periodic pension cost was $2 million.

Health Care Trend Rates

The health care cost trend rates used in fiscal 2015 and 2014 were as follows:

	Other Postretirement Benefits	
Fiscal	2015	2014
Health care cost trend assumed for next year	5.71%	6.62%
Ultimate trend rate	4.30%	4.30%
Year ultimate rate is reached	2094	2092

A one-percentage-point change in assumed health care cost trend rates would have the following effects:

	1 percentage point increase	1 percentage point decrease
Effect on total of service and interest cost components	$—	$—
Effect on postretirement benefit obligation	$ 3	$ (3)

During fiscal 2015, we contributed $34 million to our defined benefit pension plans, of which $8 million was voluntary. In the first quarter of fiscal 2016, we made $31 million of voluntary contributions to our U.S. defined benefit pension plans. We expect to contribute approximately $20 million of required contributions in fiscal 2016, for total contributions to the defined benefit pension plans of approximately $51 million in fiscal 2016. In addition, we contributed $8 million to the other postretirement benefit plans during fiscal 2015. We expect to contribute approximately $7 million to these other postretirement benefit plans during fiscal 2016.

Estimated future benefit payments for our pension and other postretirement benefit plans are expected to be:

Fiscal Year	Pension Benefits	Other Postretirement Benefits
2016	$121	$ 7
2017	113	7
2018	118	7
2019	124	7
2020	129	7
2021–2025	738	31

NET CHANGE IN UNREALIZED GAINS AND LOSSES ON AVAILABLE-FOR-SALE SECURITIES

4.13 TYSON FOODS, INC. (SEP)
CONSOLIDATED STATEMENTS OF COMPREHENSIVE INCOME (in part)

	Three Years Ended October 3, 2015		
In millions	2015	2014	2013
Net Income	$1,224	$856	$778
Other Comprehensive Income (Loss), Net of Taxes:			
Derivatives accounted for as cash flow hedges	2	1	(14)
Investments	(1)	4	(3)
Currency translation	36	(30)	(37)
Postretirement benefits	20	(14)	9
Total Other Comprehensive Income (Loss), Net of Taxes	57	(39)	(45)
Comprehensive Income	1,281	817	733
Less: Comprehensive Income (Loss) Attributable to Noncontrolling Interests	4	(8)	—
Comprehensive Income Attributable to Tyson	$1,277	$825	$733

See accompanying notes.

NOTES TO CONSOLIDATED FINANCIAL STATEMENTS (in part)

Note 1: Business and Summary of Significant Accounting Policies (in part)

Investments: We have investments in joint ventures and other entities. We generally use the cost method of accounting when our voting interests are less than 20 percent. We use the equity method of accounting when our voting interests are in excess of 20 percent and we do not have a controlling interest or a variable interest in which we are the primary beneficiary. Investments in joint ventures and other entities are reported in the Consolidated Balance Sheets in Other Assets.

We also have investments in marketable debt securities. We have determined all of our marketable debt securities are available-for-sale investments. These investments are reported at fair value based on quoted market prices as of the balance sheet date, with unrealized gains and losses, net of tax, recorded in other comprehensive income. The amortized cost of debt securities is adjusted for amortization of premiums and accretion of discounts to maturity. Such amortization is recorded in interest income. The cost of securities sold is based on the specific identification method. Realized gains and losses on the sale of debt securities and declines in value judged to be other than temporary are recorded on a net basis in other income. Interest and dividends on securities classified as available-for-sale are recorded in interest income.

Note 13: Fair Value Measurements (in part)

Available for Sale Securities: Our investments in marketable debt securities are classified as available-for-sale and are reported at fair value based on pricing models and quoted market prices adjusted for credit and non-performance risk. Short-term investments with maturities of less than 12 months are included in Other current assets in the Consolidated Balance Sheets and primarily include certificates of deposit and commercial paper. All other marketable debt securities are included in Other Assets in the Consolidated Balance Sheets and have maturities ranging up to 35 years. We classify our investments in United States government, United States agency, certificates of deposit and commercial paper debt securities as Level 2 as fair value is generally estimated using discounted cash flow models that are primarily industry-standard models that consider various assumptions, including time value and yield curve as well as other readily available relevant economic measures. We classify certain corporate, asset-backed and other debt securities as Level 3 as there is limited activity or less observable inputs into valuation models, including current interest rates and estimated prepayment, default and recovery rates on the underlying portfolio or structured investment vehicle. Significant changes to assumptions or unobservable inputs in the valuation of our Level 3 instruments would not have a significant impact to our consolidated financial statements.

In millions	October 3, 2015			September 27, 2014		
	Amortized Cost Basis	Fair Value	Unrealized Gain/(Loss)	Amortized Cost Basis	Fair Value	Unrealized Gain/(Loss)
Available for Sale Securities:						
Debt Securities:						
United States Treasury and Agency	$ 33	$ 34	$ 1	$25	$25	$—
Corporate and Asset-Backed	60	61	1	65	67	2
Equity Securities:						
Common Stock and Warrants[a]	—	—	—	1	1	—

[a] At October 3, 2015, and September 27, 2014, the amortized cost basis for Equity Securities had been reduced by accumulated other than temporary impairment of approximately nil and $2 million, respectively.

Unrealized holding gains (losses), net of tax, are excluded from earnings and reported in OCI until the security is settled or sold. On a quarterly basis, we evaluate whether losses related to our available-for-sale securities are temporary in nature. Losses on equity securities are recognized in earnings if the decline in value is judged to be other than temporary. If losses related to our debt securities are determined to be other than temporary, the loss would be recognized in earnings if we intend, or more likely than not will be required, to sell the security prior to recovery. For debt securities in which we have the intent and ability to hold until maturity, losses determined to be other than temporary would remain in OCI, other than expected credit losses which are recognized in earnings. We consider many factors in determining whether a loss is temporary, including the length of time and extent to which the fair value has been below cost, the financial condition and near-term prospects of the issuer and our ability and intent to hold the investment for a period of time sufficient to allow for any anticipated recovery. We recognized no other than temporary impairment in earnings for fiscal 2015, and $6 million of other than temporary impairment for fiscal 2014, which was recorded in the Consolidated Statements of Income in Other, net. No other than temporary losses were deferred in OCI as of October 3, 2015, and September 27, 2014.

Note 16: Comprehensive Income (Loss)

The components of accumulated other comprehensive loss are as follows:

In millions	2015	2014
Accumulated other comprehensive income (loss), net of taxes:		
Unrealized net hedging loss	$ (1)	$ (3)
Unrealized net gain on investments	1	2
Currency translation adjustment	(63)	(99)
Postretirement benefits reserve adjustments	(27)	(47)
Total accumulated other comprehensive loss	$(90)	$(147)

The before and after tax changes in the components of other comprehensive income (loss) are as follows:

In millions	2015 Before Tax	Tax	After Tax	2014 Before Tax	Tax	After Tax	2013 Before Tax	Tax	After Tax
Derivatives accounted for as cash flow hedges:									
(Gain) loss reclassified to Cost of Sales	$ 7	$ (3)	$ 4	$ 10	$ (4)	$ 6	$ 5	$ (2)	$ 3
(Gain) loss reclassified to Other Income/Expense	—	—	—	—	—	—	4	(2)	2
Unrealized gain (loss)	(4)	2	(2)	(8)	3	(5)	(31)	12	(19)
Investments:									
(Gain) loss reclassified to Other Income/Expense	(21)	8	(13)	8	(2)	6	(1)	—	(1)
Unrealized gain (loss)	21	(9)	12	(2)	—	(2)	(4)	2	(2)
Currency translation:									
Translation loss reclassified to Cost of Sales[a]	115	(8)	107	—	—	—	(19)	(1)	(20)
Translation adjustment	(86)	15	(71)	(32)	2	(30)	(20)	3	(17)
Postretirement benefits	32	(12)	20	(23)	9	(14)	15	(6)	9
Total Other Comprehensive Income (Loss)	$ 64	$ (7)	$ 57	$(47)	$ 8	$(39)	$(51)	$ 6	$(45)

[a] Translation loss reclassified to Cost of Sales related to disposition of a foreign operation, which is further described in Note 3: Acquisitions and Dispositions.

GAINS AND LOSSES ON DERIVATIVES HELD AS HEDGES

4.14 COCA-COLA ENTERPRISES, INC. (DEC)
CONSOLIDATED STATEMENTS OF COMPREHENSIVE INCOME

(In millions)	Year Ended December 31, 2015	2014	2013
Net income	$ 596	$ 663	$ 667
Components of other comprehensive (loss) income:			
Currency translations			
Pretax activity, net	(337)	(482)	82
Tax effect	—	—	—
Currency translations, net of tax	(337)	(482)	82
Net investment hedges			
Pretax activity, net	163	256	(61)
Tax effect	(57)	(90)	21
Net investment hedges, net of tax	106	166	(40)
Cash flow hedges			
Pretax activity, net	16	(15)	21
Tax effect	(5)	4	(6)
Cash flow hedges, net of tax	11	(11)	15
Pension plan adjustments			
Pretax activity, net	(76)	(79)	57
Tax effect	13	23	(15)
Pension plan adjustments, net of tax	(63)	(56)	42
Other comprehensive (loss) income, net of tax	(283)	(383)	99
Comprehensive income	$ 313	$ 280	$ 766

The accompanying Notes to Consolidated Financial Statements are an integral part of these statements.

Note 1—Business and Summary of Significant Accounting Policies (in part)

Other Comprehensive Income (Loss)

Comprehensive income (loss) is comprised of net income and other adjustments, including foreign currency translation adjustments, hedges of our net investments in our foreign subsidiaries, changes in the fair value of certain derivative financial instruments qualifying as cash flow hedges, and pension plan adjustments. We do not provide income taxes on currency translation adjustments (CTA), as the historical earnings from our foreign subsidiaries are considered to be indefinitely reinvested. If current year earnings are repatriated, the amount to be repatriated is determined in U.S. dollars and converted to the equivalent amount of foreign currency at the time of repatriation; therefore, the repatriation of current year earnings does not have an impact on the CTA component of our accumulated other comprehensive income (AOCI) balance.

The following table summarizes our AOCI as of the dates presented (after tax; in millions):

	Currency Translations	Net Investment Hedges	Cash Flow Hedges[A]	Pension Plan Adjust- ments[B]	Total
Balance at January 1, 2014	$ 41	$ (54)	$ (7)	$(311)	$(331)
Other comprehensive income (loss) before reclassifications	(482)	166	34	20	(262)
Amounts reclassified from AOCI	—	—	(45)	(76)	(121)
Net change in other comprehensive income	(482)	166	(11)	(56)	(383)
Balance at December 31, 2014	(441)	112	(18)	(367)	(714)
Other comprehensive income (loss) before reclassifications	(337)	106	(11)	(85)	(327)
Amounts reclassified from AOCI	—	—	22	22	44
Net change in other comprehensive income (loss)	(337)	106	11	(63)	(283)
Balance at December 31, 2015	$(778)	$218	$ (7)	$(430)	$(997)

[A] For additional information about our cash flow hedges, refer to Note 6.
[B] For additional information about our pension plans, refer to Note 10.

Derivative Financial Instruments

We utilize derivative financial instruments to mitigate our exposure to certain market risks associated with our ongoing operations. The primary risks that we seek to manage through the use of derivative financial instruments include currency exchange risk, commodity price risk, and interest rate risk. All derivative financial instruments are recorded at fair value on our Consolidated Balance Sheets. We do not use derivative financial instruments for trading or speculative purposes. While certain of our derivative instruments are designated as hedging instruments, we also enter into derivative instruments that are designed to hedge a risk, but are not designated as hedging instruments (referred to as an "economic hedge" or "non-designated hedges"). Changes in the fair value of these non-designated hedging instruments are recognized in the expense line item on our Consolidated Statements of Income that is consistent with the nature of the hedged risk. We are exposed to counterparty credit risk on all of our derivative financial instruments. We have established and maintain strict counterparty credit guidelines and enter into hedges only with financial institutions that are investment grade or better. We continuously monitor counterparty credit risk and utilize numerous counterparties to minimize our exposure to potential defaults. We do not require collateral under these agreements. Refer to Note 6.

Note 6—Derivative Financial Instruments (in part)

Cash Flow Hedges

We use cash flow hedges to mitigate our exposure to changes in cash flows attributable to currency fluctuations associated with certain forecasted transactions, including purchases of raw materials and services denominated in non-functional currencies, the receipt of interest and principal on intercompany loans denominated in non-functional currencies, and the payment of interest and principal on debt issuances in a non-functional currency. Effective changes in the fair value of these cash flow hedging instruments are recognized in AOCI on our Consolidated Balance Sheets. The effective changes are then recognized in the period that the forecasted purchases or payments impact earnings in the expense line item on our Consolidated Statements of Income that is consistent with the nature of the underlying hedged item. Any changes in the fair value of these cash flow hedges that are the result of ineffectiveness are recognized immediately in the expense line item on our Consolidated Statements of Income that is consistent with the nature of the underlying hedged item. During the third quarter of 2015, we received $56 million upon maturity of certain of our cross-currency swaps related to intercompany loans.

The following table summarizes our outstanding cash flow hedges as of the dates presented (all contracts denominated in a foreign currency have been converted into U.S. dollars using the period end spot rate):

	December 31, 2015		December 31, 2014	
Type	Notional Amount	Latest Maturity	Notional Amount	Latest Maturity
Foreign currency contracts	USD 700 million	June 2021	USD 1.3 billion	June 2021

The following tables summarize the net of tax effect of our derivative financial instruments designated as cash flow hedges on our AOCI and Consolidated Statements of Income for the periods presented (in millions):

Cash Flow Hedging Instruments	Amount of Gain (Loss) Recognized in AOCI on Derivative Instruments[A]		
	2015	2014	2013
Foreign currency contracts	$(11)	$34	$(6)

Cash Flow Hedging Instruments	Location—Statements of Income	Amount of Gain (Loss) Reclassified from AOCI into Earnings[B]		
		2015	2014	2013
Foreign currency contracts	Cost of sales	$(14)	$ 1	$ 2
Foreign currency contracts	Selling, delivery, and administrative expenses	(1)	—	—
Foreign currency contracts[C]	Other nonoperating expense	(7)	44	(23)
Total		$(22)	$45	$(21)

[A] The amount of ineffectiveness associated with these hedges was not material.

[B] Over the next 12 months, deferred losses totaling $4 million are expected to be reclassified from AOCI as the forecasted transactions occur. The amounts will be recorded on our Consolidated Statements of Income in the expense line item that is consistent with the nature of the underlying hedged item.

[C] The gain (loss) recognized on these currency contracts is offset by the gain (loss) recognized on the remeasurement of the underlying debt instruments; therefore, there is a minimal consolidated net effect in other nonoperating expense on our Consolidated Statements of Income.

Economic (Non-designated) Hedges

We periodically enter into derivative instruments that are designed to hedge various risks but are not designated as hedging instruments. These hedged risks include those related to commodity price fluctuations associated with forecasted purchases of aluminum, sugar, components of PET (plastic), and vehicle fuel. At times, we also enter into other short-term non-designated hedges to mitigate our exposure to changes in cash flows attributable to currency fluctuations associated with short-term intercompany loans and certain cash equivalents denominated in non-functional currencies. Changes in the fair value of outstanding economic hedges are recognized each reporting period in the expense line item on our Consolidated Statements of Income that is consistent with the nature of the hedged risk.

The following table summarizes our outstanding economic hedges as of the dates presented (all contracts denominated in a foreign currency have been converted into U.S. dollars using the period end spot rate):

Type	December 31, 2015		December 31, 2014	
	Notional Amount	Latest Maturity	Notional Amount	Latest Maturity
Foreign currency contracts	USD 210 million	March 2016	USD 222 million	July 2015
Commodity contracts	USD 137 million	December 2020	USD 125 million	December 2017

The following table summarizes the gains (losses) recognized from our non-designated derivative financial instruments on our Consolidated Statements of Income for the periods presented (in millions):

Non-Designated Hedging Instruments	Location—Statements of Income	2015	2014	2013
Commodity contracts	Cost of sales	$(22)	$ 2	$(22)
Commodity contracts	Selling, delivery, and administrative expenses	(16)	(13)	1
Foreign currency contracts	Other nonoperating expense[A]	(5)	11	(1)
	Total	$(43)	$—	$(22)

[A] The gain (loss) recognized on these currency contracts is offset by the (loss) gain recognized on the remeasurement of the underlying hedged items; therefore, there is a minimal consolidated net effect in other nonoperating expense on our Consolidated Statements of Income.

Mark-to-market gains (losses) related to our non-designated commodity hedges are recognized in the earnings of our Corporate segment until such time as the underlying hedged transaction affects the earnings of our Europe operating segment. In the period the underlying hedged transaction occurs, the accumulated mark-to-market gains (losses) related to the hedged transaction are reclassified from the earnings of our Corporate segment into the earnings of our Europe operating segment. This treatment allows our Europe operating segment to reflect the true economic effects of the underlying hedged transaction in the period the hedged transaction occurs without experiencing the mark-to-market volatility associated with these non-designated commodity hedges.

As of December 31, 2015, our Corporate segment included net mark-to-market losses on non-designated commodity hedges totaling $38 million. These amounts will be reclassified into the earnings of our Europe operating segment when the underlying hedged transaction occurs. For additional information about our segment reporting, refer to Note 14.

The following table summarizes the deferred gain (loss) activity in our Corporate segment for the periods presented (in millions):

Gains (Losses) Deferred at Corporate Segment[A]	Cost of Sales	SD&A	Total
Balance at January 1, 2013	$ (5)	$—	$ (5)
Amounts recognized during the period and recorded in our Corporate segment, net	(19)	1	(18)
Amounts transferred from our Corporate segment to our Europe operating segment, net	12	(1)	11
Balance as of December 31, 2013	(12)	—	(12)
Amounts recognized during the period and recorded in our Corporate segment, net	2	(12)	(10)
Amounts transferred from our Corporate segment to our Europe operating segment, net	11	1	12
Balance as of December 31, 2014	1	(11)	(10)
Amounts recognized during the period and recorded in our Corporate segment, net	(21)	(16)	(37)
Amounts transferred from our Corporate segment to our Europe operating segment, net	2	7	9
Balance as of December 31, 2015	$(18)	$(20)	$(38)

[A] Over the next 12 months, deferred losses totaling $24 million are expected to be reclassified from our Corporate segment earnings into the earnings of our Europe operating segment as the underlying hedged transactions occur.

Net Investment Hedges

We have entered into foreign currency forwards, options, and foreign currency denominated borrowings designated as net investment hedges of our foreign subsidiaries. Changes in the fair value of these hedges resulting from currency exchange rate changes are recognized in AOCI on our Consolidated Balance Sheets to offset the change in the carrying value of the net investment being hedged. Any changes in the fair value of these hedges that are the result of ineffectiveness are recognized immediately in other nonoperating expense on our Consolidated Statements of Income. During 2015 we received $32 million upon maturity of our 2015 net investment hedges and during 2014 we settled our net investment hedges prior to their maturity and received $21 million upon settlement.

The following table summarizes our outstanding instruments designated as net investment hedges as of the dates presented:

	December 31, 2015		December 31, 2014	
Type	Notional Amount	Latest Maturity	Notional Amount	Latest Maturity
Foreign currency contracts	USD 1.7 billion	August 2016	USD 250 million	November 2015
Foreign currency denominated debt	USD 2.0 billion	March 2030	USD 1.6 billion	May 2026

The following table summarizes the net of tax effect of our derivative financial instruments designated as net investment hedges on our AOCI for the periods presented (in millions):

	Amount of Gain (Loss) Recognized in AOCI on Derivative Instruments[A]		
Net Investment Hedging Instruments	2015	2014	2013
Foreign currency contracts	$ 12	$ 25	$ (7)
Foreign currency denominated debt	94	141	(33)
Total	$106	$166	$(40)

[A] The amount of ineffectiveness associated with these hedging instruments was not material.

RECLASSIFICATION ADJUSTMENTS

4.15 CISCO SYSTEMS, INC. (JUL)
CONSOLIDATED STATEMENTS OF COMPREHENSIVE INCOME

(In millions)

Years Ended	July 25, 2015	July 26, 2014	July 27, 2013
Net income	$8,981	$7,853	$9,983
Available-for-sale investments:			
Change in net unrealized gains, net of tax benefit (expense) of $14, $(146), and $(2) for fiscal 2015, 2014, and 2013, respectively	(12)	233	(6)
Net gains reclassified into earnings, net of tax expense (benefit) of $57, $111, and $17 for fiscal 2015, 2014, and 2013, respectively	(100)	(189)	(31)
	(112)	44	(37)
Cash flow hedging instruments:			
Change in unrealized gains and losses, net of tax benefit (expense) of $1, $0, and $(1) for fiscal 2015, 2014, and 2013, respectively	(158)	48	73
Net (gains) losses reclassified into earnings	154	(68)	(12)
	(4)	(20)	61
Net change in cumulative translation adjustment and actuarial gains and losses, net of tax benefit (expense) of $63, $(5), and $(1) for fiscal 2015, 2014, and 2013, respectively	(498)	44	(84)
Other comprehensive income (loss)	(614)	68	(60)
Comprehensive income	8,367	7,921	9,923
Comprehensive (income) loss attributable to noncontrolling interests	(2)	1	7
Comprehensive income attributable to Cisco Systems, Inc.	$8,365	$7,922	$9,930

See Notes to Consolidated Financial Statements.

NOTES TO CONSOLIDATED FINANCIAL STATEMENTS (in part)

2. Summary of Significant Accounting Policies (in part)

(I) Derivative Instruments The Company recognizes derivative instruments as either assets or liabilities and measures those instruments at fair value. The accounting for changes in the fair value of a derivative depends on the intended use of the derivative and the resulting designation. For a derivative instrument designated as a fair value hedge, the gain or loss is recognized in earnings in the period of change together with the offsetting loss or gain on the hedged item attributed to the risk being hedged. For a derivative instrument designated as a cash flow hedge, the effective portion of the derivative's gain or loss is initially reported as a component of AOCI and subsequently reclassified into earnings when the hedged exposure affects earnings. The ineffective portion of the gain or loss is reported in earnings immediately. For a derivative instrument designated as a net investment hedge of the Company's foreign operations, the gain or loss is recorded in the cumulative translation adjustment within AOCI together with the offsetting loss or gain of the hedged exposure of the underlying foreign operations. Any ineffective portion of the net investment hedges is reported in earnings during the period of change. For derivative instruments that are not designated as accounting hedges, changes in fair value are recognized in earnings in the period of change. The Company records derivative instruments in the statements of cash flows to operating, investing, or financing activities consistent with the cash flows of the hedged item.

Hedge effectiveness for foreign exchange forward contracts used as cash flow hedges is assessed by comparing the change in the fair value of the hedge contract with the change in the fair value of the forecasted cash flows of the hedged item. Hedge effectiveness for equity forward contracts and foreign exchange net investment hedge forward contracts is assessed by comparing changes in fair value due to changes in spot rates for both the derivative and the hedged item. For foreign exchange option contracts, hedge effectiveness is assessed based on the hedging instrument's entire change in fair value. Hedge effectiveness for interest rate swaps is assessed by comparing the change in fair value of the swap with the change in the fair value of the hedged item due to changes in the benchmark interest rate.

11. Derivative Instruments (in part)

(a) Summary of Derivative Instruments

The Company uses derivative instruments primarily to manage exposures to foreign currency exchange rate, interest rate, and equity price risks. The Company's primary objective in holding derivatives is to reduce the volatility of earnings and cash flows associated with changes in foreign currency exchange rates, interest rates, and equity prices. The Company's derivatives expose it to credit risk to the extent that the counterparties may be unable to meet the terms of the agreement. The Company does, however, seek to mitigate such risks by limiting its counterparties to major financial institutions. In addition, the potential risk of loss with any one counterparty resulting from this type of credit risk is monitored. Management does not expect material losses as a result of defaults by counterparties.

The fair values of the Company's derivative instruments and the line items on the Consolidated Balance Sheets to which they were recorded are summarized as follows (in millions):

	Derivative Assets			Derivative Liabilities		
	Balance Sheet Line Item	July 25, 2015	July 26, 2014	Balance Sheet Line Item	July 25, 2015	July 26, 2014
Derivatives designated as hedging instruments:						
Foreign currency derivatives	Other current assets	$ 10	$ 7	Other current liabilities	$ 11	$ 6
Interest rate derivatives	Other assets	202	148	Other long-term liabilities	—	3
Equity derivatives	Other current assets	—	—	Other current liabilities	—	56
Total		212	155		11	65
Derivatives not designated as hedging instruments:						
Foreign currency derivatives	Other current assets	2	3	Other current liabilities	1	2
Equity derivatives	Other assets	4	2	Other long-term liabilities	—	—
Total		6	5		1	2
Total		$218	$160		$ 12	$67

The effects of the Company's cash flow and net investment hedging instruments on other comprehensive income (OCI) and the Consolidated Statements of Operations are summarized as follows (in millions):

Gains (Losses) Recognized in OCI on Derivatives for the Years Ended (Effective Portion)				Gains (Losses) Reclassified From AOCI Into Income for the Years Ended (Effective Portion)			
	July 25, 2015	July 26, 2014	July 27, 2013	Line Item in Statements of Operations	July 25, 2015	July 26, 2014	July 27, 2013
Derivatives designated as cash flow hedging instruments:							
Foreign currency derivatives	$(159)	$ 48	$73	Operating expenses	$(121)	$ 55	$ 10
				Cost of sales—service	(33)	13	2
Total	$(159)	$ 48	$73	Total	$(154)	$ 68	$ 12
Derivatives designated as net investment hedging instruments:							
Foreign currency derivatives	$ 42	$(15)	$(1)	Other income (loss), net	$ —	$—	$—

As of July 25, 2015, the Company estimates that approximately $5 million of net derivative losses related to its cash flow hedges included in accumulated other comprehensive income (AOCI) will be reclassified into earnings within the next 12 months when the underlying hedged item impacts earnings.

The effect on the Consolidated Statements of Operations of derivative instruments designated as fair value hedges and the underlying hedged items is summarized as follows (in millions):

Derivatives Designated as Fair Value Hedging Instruments	Line Item in Statements of Operations	Gains (Losses) on Derivative Instruments for the Years Ended			Gains (Losses) Related to Hedged Items for the Years Ended		
		July 25, 2015	July 26, 2014	July 27, 2013	July 25, 2015	July 26, 2014	July 27, 2013
Equity derivatives	Other income (loss), net	$ 56	$(72)	$(155)	$ (56)	$ 72	$155
Interest rate derivatives	Interest expense	54	(2)	(78)	(57)	—	78
Total		$110	$(74)	$(233)	$(113)	$ 72	$233

The effect on the Consolidated Statements of Operations of derivative instruments not designated as hedges is summarized as follows (in millions):

Derivatives Not Designated as Hedging Instruments	Line Item in Statements of Operations	Gains (Losses) for the Years Ended		
		July 25, 2015	July 26, 2014	July 27, 2013
Foreign currency derivatives	Other income (loss), net	$(173)	$ 23	$(74)
Total return swaps—deferred compensation	Operating expenses	19	47	61
Equity derivatives	Other income (loss), net	27	34	—
Total		$(127)	$104	$(13)

The notional amounts of the Company's outstanding derivatives are summarized as follows (in millions):

	July 25, 2015	July 26, 2014
Derivatives designated as hedging instruments:		
Foreign currency derivatives—cash flow hedges	$ 1,201	$ 1,618
Interest rate derivatives	11,400	10,400
Net investment hedging instruments	192	345
Equity derivatives	—	238
Derivatives not designated as hedging instruments:		
Foreign currency derivatives	2,023	2,528
Total return swaps—deferred compensation	462	428
Total	$15,278	$15,557

(b) Offsetting of Derivative Instruments

The Company presents its derivative instruments at gross fair values in the Consolidated Balance Sheets. However, the Company's master netting and other similar arrangements with the respective counterparties allow for net settlement under certain conditions, which are designed to reduce credit risk by permitting net settlement with the same counterparty. To further limit credit risk, the Company also enters into collateral security arrangements related to certain derivative instruments whereby cash is posted as collateral between the counterparties based on the fair market value of the derivative instrument. Information related to these offsetting arrangements is summarized as follows (in millions):

	Gross Amounts Offset in the Consolidated Balance Sheet			Gross Amounts Not Offset in the Consolidated Balance Sheet but With Legal Rights to Offset		
July 25, 2015	Gross Amounts Recognized	Gross Amounts Offset	Net Amounts Presented	Gross Derivative Amounts	Cash Collateral	Net Amount
Derivatives assets	$218	$—	$218	$(12)	$(124)	$ 82
Derivatives liabilities	$ 12	$—	$ 12	$(12)	$ —	$—

	Gross Amounts Offset in the Consolidated Balance Sheet			Gross Amounts Not Offset in the Consolidated Balance Sheet but With Legal Rights to Offset		
July 26, 2014	Gross Amounts Recognized	Gross Amounts Offset	Net Amounts Presented	Gross Derivative Amounts	Cash Collateral	Net Amount
Derivatives assets	$160	$—	$160	$(39)	$(60)	$61
Derivatives liabilities	$ 67	$—	$ 67	$(39)	$ (1)	$27

(c) Foreign Currency Exchange Risk

The Company conducts business globally in numerous currencies. Therefore, it is exposed to adverse movements in foreign currency exchange rates. To limit the exposure related to foreign currency changes, the Company enters into foreign currency contracts. The Company does not enter into such contracts for trading purposes.

The Company hedges forecasted foreign currency transactions related to certain operating expenses and service cost of sales with currency options and forward contracts. These currency options and forward contracts, designated as cash flow hedges, generally have maturities of less than 18 months. The Company assesses effectiveness based on changes in total fair value of the derivatives. The effective portion of the derivative instrument's gain or loss is initially reported as a component of AOCI and subsequently reclassified into earnings when the hedged exposure affects earnings. The ineffective portion, if any, of the gain or loss is reported in earnings immediately. During the fiscal years presented, the Company did not discontinue any cash flow hedges for which it was probable that a forecasted transaction would not occur.

The Company enters into foreign exchange forward and option contracts to reduce the short-term effects of foreign currency fluctuations on assets and liabilities such as foreign currency receivables, including long-term customer financings, investments, and payables. These derivatives are not designated as hedging instruments. Gains and losses on the contracts are included in other income (loss), net, and substantially offset foreign exchange gains and losses from the remeasurement of intercompany balances or other current assets, investments, or liabilities denominated in currencies other than the functional currency of the reporting entity.

The Company hedges certain net investments in its foreign operations with forward contracts to reduce the effects of foreign currency fluctuations on the Company's net investment in those foreign subsidiaries. These derivative instruments generally have maturities of up to six months.

15. Comprehensive Income

The components of AOCI, net of tax, and the other comprehensive income (loss), excluding noncontrolling interest, are summarized as follows (in millions):

	Net Unrealized Gains on Available-for-Sale Investments	Net Unrealized Gains (Losses) Cash Flow Hedging Instruments	Cumulative Translation Adjustment and Actuarial Gains and Losses	Accumulated Other Comprehensive Income
Balance at July 28, 2012	$ 409	$ (53)	$ 305	$ 661
Other comprehensive income (loss) before reclassifications attributable to Cisco Systems, Inc.	3	74	(83)	(6)
(Gains) losses reclassified out of AOCI	(48)	(12)	—	(60)
Tax benefit (expense)	15	(1)	(1)	13
Balance at July 27, 2013	379	8	221	608
Other comprehensive income (loss) before reclassifications attributable to Cisco Systems, Inc.	380	48	49	477
(Gains) losses reclassified out of AOCI	(300)	(68)	—	(368)
Tax benefit (expense)	(35)	—	(5)	(40)
Balance at July 26, 2014	424	(12)	265	677
Other comprehensive income (loss) before reclassifications attributable to Cisco Systems, Inc.	(28)	(159)	(563)	(750)
(Gains) losses reclassified out of AOCI	(157)	154	2	(1)
Tax benefit (expense)	71	1	63	135
Balance at July 25, 2015	$ 310	$ (16)	$(233)	$ 61

The net gains (losses) reclassified out of AOCI into the Consolidated Statements of Operations, with line item location, during each period were as follows (in millions):

Comprehensive Income Components	July 25, 2015	July 26, 2014	July 27, 2013	Line Item in Statements of Operations
		Income Before Taxes		
Net unrealized gains on available-for-sale investments				
	$ 157	$300	$48	Other income (loss), net
Net unrealized gains and losses on cash flow hedging instruments				
Foreign currency derivatives	(121)	55	10	Operating expenses
Foreign currency derivatives	(33)	13	2	Cost of sales—service
	(154)	68	12	
Cumulative translation adjustment and actuarial gains and losses				
	(2)	—	—	Operating expenses
Total amounts reclassified out of AOCI	$ 1	$368	$60	

4.16 CONAGRA FOODS, INC. (MAY)

CONSOLIDATED STATEMENTS OF COMPREHENSIVE INCOME (LOSS)

(in millions)

	For the Fiscal Years Ended May								
	2015			2014			2013		
	Pre-Tax Amount	Tax (Expense) Benefit	After-Tax Amount	Pre-Tax Amount	Tax (Expense) Benefit	After-Tax Amount	Pre-Tax Amount	Tax (Expense) Benefit	After-Tax Amount
Net income (loss)	$(725.6)	$484.8	$(240.8)	$617.9	$(302.8)	$315.1	$1,186.3	$(400.2)	$786.1
Other comprehensive income (loss):									
Derivative adjustments:									
Unrealized derivative adjustments	—	—	—	49.6	(18.3)	31.3	51.7	(19.2)	32.5
Reclassification for derivative adjustments included in net income	(0.5)	0.2	(0.3)	55.0	(20.6)	34.4	0.4	(0.1)	0.3
Unrealized gains on available-for-sale securities	0.7	(0.3)	0.4	0.2	(0.1)	0.1	0.3	(0.1)	0.2
Unrealized currency translation gains (losses)	(145.2)	—	(145.2)	(25.7)	—	(25.7)	2.1	—	2.1

(continued)

	For the Fiscal Years Ended May								
	2015			**2014**			**2013**		
	Pre-Tax Amount	**Tax (Expense) Benefit**	**After-Tax Amount**	**Pre-Tax Amount**	**Tax (Expense) Benefit**	**After-Tax Amount**	**Pre-Tax Amount**	**Tax (Expense) Benefit**	**After-Tax Amount**
Pension and post-employment benefit obligations:									
Unrealized pension and post-employment benefit obligations	(94.9)	36.7	(58.2)	23.8	(8.2)	15.6	103.8	(40.0)	63.8
Reclassification for pension and post-employment benefit obligations included in net income	0.8	(0.3)	0.5	3.3	(1.2)	2.1	5.4	(2.0)	3.4
Comprehensive income (loss)	(964.7)	521.1	(443.6)	724.1	(351.2)	372.9	1,350.0	(461.6)	888.4
Comprehensive income attributable to noncontrolling interests	4.6	(0.4)	4.2	8.9	(0.9)	8.0	13.1	(1.6)	11.5
Comprehensive income (loss) attributable to ConAgra Foods, Inc.	$(969.3)	$521.5	$(447.8)	$715.2	$(350.3)	$364.9	$1,336.9	$(460.0)	$876.9

The accompanying Notes are an integral part of the consolidated financial statements.

NOTES TO CONSOLIDATED FINANCIAL STATEMENTS (in part)

(columnar dollars in millions, except per share amounts)

1. Summary of Significant Accounting Policies (in part)

Comprehensive Income —Comprehensive income includes net income, currency translation adjustments, certain derivative-related activity, changes in the value of available-for-sale investments, and changes in prior service cost and net actuarial gains (losses) from pension (for amounts not in excess of the 10% "corridor") and postretirement health care plans.

We generally deem our foreign investments to be essentially permanent in nature and we do not provide for taxes on currency translation adjustments arising from converting the investment denominated in a foreign currency to U.S. dollars. When we determine that a foreign investment, as well as undistributed earnings, are no longer permanent in nature, estimated taxes are provided for the related deferred tax liability (asset), if any, resulting from currency translation adjustments.

The following table details the accumulated balances for each component of other comprehensive income (loss), net of tax (except for currency translation adjustments):

	2015	2014	2013
Unrealized currency translation gains (losses)	$(113.9)	$ 23.7	$ 45.4
Derivative adjustments, net of reclassification adjustments	0.9	1.2	(64.5)
Unrealized losses on available-for-sale securities	(0.7)	(1.1)	(1.2)
Pension and post-employment benefit obligations, net of reclassification adjustments	(215.8)	(158.1)	(175.8)
Accumulated other comprehensive loss	$(329.5)	$(134.3)	$(196.1)

The following table summarizes the reclassifications from accumulated other comprehensive loss into income (loss):

	Fifty-Three Weeks Ended 2015	Fifty-Two Weeks Ended 2014	Affected Line Item in the Consolidated Statement of Operations[1]
Net derivative adjustment, net of tax:			
Cash flow hedges	$(0.5)	$ 0.1	Interest expense, net
Cash flow hedges[2]	—	54.9	Selling, general and administrative expenses
	(0.5)	55.0	Total before tax
	0.2	(20.6)	Income tax expense (benefit)
	$(0.3)	$ 34.4	Net of tax
Amortization of pension and postretirement healthcare liabilities:			
Net prior service benefit	$(4.2)	$ (3.4)	Selling, general and administrative expenses
Net actuarial loss	3.5	6.7	Selling, general and administrative expenses
Curtailment	1.5	—	Cost of goods sold
	0.8	3.3	Total before tax
	(0.3)	(1.2)	Income tax benefit
	$ 0.5	$ 2.1	Net of tax

[1] Amounts in parentheses indicate income recognized in the Consolidated Statements of Operations.
[2] Prior year amount includes $41.8 million less deferred tax benefit of $15.6 million previously reported in accumulated other comprehensive loss.

18. Derivative Financial Instruments

Our operations are exposed to market risks from adverse changes in commodity prices affecting the cost of raw materials and energy, foreign currency exchange rates, and interest rates. In the normal course of business, these risks are managed through a variety of strategies, including the use of derivatives.

Commodity and commodity index futures and option contracts are used from time to time to economically hedge commodity input prices on items such as natural gas, vegetable oils, proteins, packaging materials, dairy, grains, and electricity. Generally, we economically hedge a portion of our anticipated consumption of commodity inputs for periods of up to 36 months. We may enter into longer-term economic hedges on particular commodities, if deemed appropriate. As of May 31, 2015, we had economically hedged certain portions of our anticipated consumption of commodity inputs using derivative instruments with expiration dates through September 2016.

In order to reduce exposures related to changes in foreign currency exchange rates, we enter into forward exchange, option, or swap contracts from time to time for transactions denominated in a currency other than the applicable functional currency. This includes, but is not limited to, hedging against foreign currency risk in purchasing inventory and capital equipment, sales of finished goods, and future settlement of foreign-denominated assets and liabilities. As of May 31, 2015, we had economically hedged certain portions of our foreign currency risk in anticipated transactions using derivative instruments with expiration dates through May 2017.

From time to time, we may use derivative instruments, including interest rate swaps, to reduce risk related to changes in interest rates. This includes, but is not limited to, hedging against increasing interest rates prior to the issuance of long-term debt and hedging the fair value of our senior long-term debt.

Derivatives Designated as Cash Flow Hedges

During 2011, we entered into interest rate swap contracts to hedge the interest rate risk related to our forecasted issuance of long-term debt in April 2014 (based on the anticipated refinancing of the senior long-term debt maturing at that time). We designated these interest rate swaps as cash flow hedges of the forecasted interest payments related to this anticipated debt issuance and recorded the unrealized loss in accumulated other comprehensive loss. In the third quarter of fiscal 2014, we determined that we would not issue long-term debt to refinance the debt maturing in April 2014. Accordingly, we recognized a charge to earnings, within selling, general and administrative expenses, of $54.9 million in fiscal 2014.

During fiscal 2013, we entered into interest rate swap contracts to hedge a portion of the interest rate risk related to our issuance of long-term debt to partially finance the acquisition of Ralcorp. We settled these contracts during the third quarter of fiscal 2013 resulting in a deferred gain of $4.2 million on senior notes maturing in 2043 and a deferred loss of $2.0 million on senior notes maturing in 2023, both recognized in accumulated other comprehensive loss. These amounts are being amortized as a component of net interest expense over the lives of the related debt instruments. The unamortized amounts of the deferred gain and deferred loss at May 31, 2015 were $3.0 million and $1.3 million, respectively.

Derivatives Designated as Fair Value Hedges

During fiscal 2010, we entered into interest rate swap contracts to hedge the fair value of certain of our senior long-term debt instruments maturing in fiscal 2012 and 2014. We designated these interest rate swap contracts as fair value hedges of the debt instruments. During fiscal 2011, we terminated these interest rate swap contracts and received proceeds of $31.5 million. The cumulative adjustment to the fair value of the debt instruments being hedged was included in long-term debt and was amortized as a reduction of interest expense over the remaining lives of the debt instruments through fiscal 2014.

During fiscal 2014, we entered into interest rate swap contracts to hedge the fair value of certain of our senior long-term debt instruments maturing in fiscal 2019 and 2020. These contracts, with a total notional amount of $500 million, effectively converted interest on this debt from fixed rate to floating rate. We designated these interest rate swap contracts as fair value hedges of the debt instruments. During the third quarter of fiscal 2015, we terminated the interest rate swap contracts and received proceeds of $21.9 million. The proceeds include $3.9 million of accrued interest from the interest rate swap contract, gains of $5.4 million representing the change in fair value of the interest rate swap contracts (the ineffective portion of the hedge) recognized within selling, general and administrative expenses and $12.6 million of cumulative adjustment to the fair value of the debt instruments that were hedged (the effective portion of the hedge), that will be amortized as a reduction to interest expense over the remaining life of the debt instruments through fiscal 2020. The unamortized amount of the deferred gain was $11.8 million at May 31, 2015.

Changes in fair value of such derivative instruments were immediately recognized in earnings along with changes in the fair value of the items being hedged (based solely on the change in the benchmark interest rate). In fiscal 2015 and 2014, we recognized gains of $8.9 million and $9.1 million, respectively, representing the fair value of the interest rate swap contracts and losses of $5.8 million and $6.8 million, respectively, representing the change in fair value of the related senior long-term debt. The net gains of $3.1 million and $2.3 million for fiscal 2015 and 2014, respectively, are classified within selling, general and administrative expenses.

The entire change in fair value of the derivative instruments was included in our assessment of hedge effectiveness.

Economic Hedges of Forecasted Cash Flows

Many of our derivatives do not qualify for, and we do not currently designate certain commodity or foreign currency derivatives to achieve, hedge accounting treatment. We reflect realized and unrealized gains and losses from derivatives used to economically hedge anticipated commodity consumption and to mitigate foreign currency cash flow risk in earnings immediately within general corporate expense (within cost of goods sold). The gains and losses are reclassified to segment operating results in the period in which the underlying item being economically hedged is recognized in cost of goods sold. In the event that management determines a particular derivative entered into as an economic hedge of a forecasted commodity purchase has ceased to function as an economic hedge, we cease recognizing further gains and losses on such derivatives in corporate expense and begin recognizing such gains and losses within segment operating results, immediately.

Economic Hedges of Fair Values—Foreign Currency Exchange Rate Risk

We may use options and cross currency swaps to economically hedge the fair value of certain monetary assets and liabilities (including intercompany balances) denominated in a currency other than the functional currency. These derivatives are marked-to-market with gains and losses immediately recognized in selling, general and administrative expenses. These substantially offset the foreign currency transaction gains or losses recognized as values of the monetary assets or liabilities being economically hedged change.

All derivative instruments are recognized on the Consolidated Balance Sheets at fair value (refer to Note 20 for additional information related to fair value measurements). The fair value of derivative assets is recognized within prepaid expenses and other current assets, while the fair value of derivative liabilities is recognized within other accrued liabilities. In accordance with generally accepted accounting principles, we offset certain derivative asset and liability balances, as well as certain amounts representing rights to reclaim cash collateral and obligations to return cash collateral, where master netting agreements provide for legal right of setoff. At May 31, 2015, $5.9 million, representing a right to reclaim cash collateral, was included in prepaid expenses and other current assets, and at May 25, 2014, $6.2 million, representing an obligation to return cash collateral, was included in other accrued liabilities in our Consolidated Balance Sheets.

Derivative assets and liabilities and amounts representing a right to reclaim cash collateral or obligation to return cash collateral were reflected in our Consolidated Balance Sheets as follows:

	May 31, 2015	May 25, 2014
Prepaid expenses and other current assets	$32.2	$38.8
Other accrued liabilities	14.2	10.4

The following table presents our derivative assets and liabilities, at May 31, 2015, on a gross basis, prior to the setoff of $7.3 million to total derivative assets and $13.2 million to total derivative liabilities where legal right of setoff existed:

	Derivative Assets		Derivative Liabilities	
	Balance Sheet Location	Fair Value	Balance Sheet Location	Fair Value
Commodity contracts	Prepaid expenses and other current assets	$20.8	Other accrued liabilities	$26.9
Foreign exchange contracts	Prepaid expenses and other current assets	17.7	Other accrued liabilities	0.4
Other	Prepaid expenses and other current assets	1.0	Other accrued liabilities	0.1
Total derivatives not designated as hedging instruments		$39.5		$27.4
Total derivatives		$39.5		$27.4

The following table presents our derivative assets and liabilities, at May 25, 2014, on a gross basis, prior to the setoff of $13.0 million to total derivative assets and $6.8 million to total derivative liabilities where legal right of setoff existed:

	Derivative Assets		Derivative Liabilities	
	Balance Sheet Location	Fair Value	Balance Sheet Location	Fair Value
Interest rate contracts	Prepaid expenses and other current assets	$ 9.1	Other accrued liabilities	$ —
Total derivatives designated as hedging instruments		$ 9.1		$ —
Commodity contracts	Prepaid expenses and other current assets	$28.6	Other accrued liabilities	$13.9
Foreign exchange contracts	Prepaid expenses and other current assets	13.4	Other accrued liabilities	3.3
Other	Prepaid expenses and other current assets	0.7	Other accrued liabilities	—
Total derivatives not designated as hedging instruments		$42.7		$17.2
Total derivatives		$51.8		$17.2

The location and amount of gains (losses) from derivatives not designated as hedging instruments in our Consolidated Statements of Earnings were as follows:

	For the Fiscal Year Ended May 31, 2015	
Derivatives Not Designated as Hedging Instruments	Location in Consolidated Statement of Operations of Gain (Loss) Recognized on Derivatives	Amount of Gain (Loss) Recognized on Derivatives in Consolidated Statement of Operations
Commodity contracts	Cost of goods sold	$(109.8)
Foreign exchange contracts	Cost of goods sold	1.3
Foreign exchange contracts	Selling, general and administrative expense	10.6
Interest rate contracts	Selling, general and administrative expense	(1.4)
Total gain from derivative instruments not designated as hedging instruments		$ (99.3)

	For the Fiscal Year Ended May 25, 2014	
Derivatives Not Designated as Hedging Instruments	Location in Consolidated Statement of Operations of Gain (Loss) Recognized on Derivatives	Amount of Gain (Loss) Recognized on Derivatives in Consolidated Statement of Operations
Commodity contracts	Cost of goods sold	$ 24.9
Foreign exchange contracts	Cost of goods sold	1.9
Foreign exchange contracts	Selling, general and administrative expense	5.0
Interest rate contracts	Selling, general and administrative expense	(54.9)
Total gain from derivative instruments not designated as hedging instruments		$(23.1)

	For the Fiscal Year Ended May 26, 2013	
Derivatives Not Designated as Hedging Instruments	Location in Consolidated Statement of Operations of Gain (Loss) Recognized on Derivatives	Amount of Gain (Loss) Recognized on Derivatives in Consolidated Statement of Operations
Commodity contracts	Cost of goods sold	$57.6
Foreign exchange contracts	Cost of goods sold	20.3
Commodity contracts	Selling, general and administrative expense	0.1
Foreign exchange contracts	Selling, general and administrative expense	0.1
Total gain from derivative instruments not designated as hedging instruments		$78.1

As of May 31, 2015, our open commodity contracts had a notional value (defined as notional quantity times market value per notional quantity unit) of $554.9 million and $393.1 million for purchase and sales contracts, respectively. As of May 25, 2014, our open commodity contracts had a notional value of $1.4 billion for both purchase and sales contracts. The notional amount of our foreign currency forward and cross currency swap contracts as of May 31, 2015 and May 25, 2014 was $108.6 million and $170.1 million, respectively.

We enter into certain commodity, interest rate, and foreign exchange derivatives with a diversified group of counterparties. We continually monitor our positions and the credit ratings of the counterparties involved and limit the amount of credit exposure to any one party. These transactions may expose us to potential losses due to the risk of nonperformance by these counterparties. We have not incurred a material loss due to nonperformance in any period presented and do not expect to incur any such material loss. We also enter into futures and options transactions through various regulated exchanges.

At May 31, 2015, the maximum amount of loss due to the credit risk of the counterparties, had the counterparties failed to perform according to the terms of the contracts, was $18.6 million.

19. Pension and Postretirement Benefits

We have defined benefit retirement plans ("plans") for eligible salaried and hourly employees. Benefits are based on years of credited service and average compensation or stated amounts for each year of service. We also sponsor postretirement plans which provide certain medical and dental benefits ("other postretirement benefits") to qualifying U.S. employees. Effective August 1, 2013, our defined benefit pension plan for eligible salaried employees was closed to new hire salaried employees. New hire salaried employees will generally be eligible to participate in our defined contribution plan.

We recognize the funded status of our plans and other benefits in the Consolidated Balance Sheets. For our plans, we also recognize as a component of accumulated other comprehensive loss, the net of tax results of the actuarial gains or losses within the corridor and prior service costs or credits that arise during the period but are not recognized in net periodic benefit cost. For our other benefits, we also recognize as a component of accumulated other comprehensive income (loss), the net of tax results of the gains or losses and prior service costs or credits that arise during the period but are not recognized in net periodic benefit cost. These amounts will be adjusted out of accumulated other comprehensive income (loss) as they are subsequently recognized as components of net periodic benefit cost. For our pension plans, we have elected to immediately recognize actuarial gains and losses in our operating results in the year in which they occur, to the extent they exceed the corridor, eliminating amortization. Amounts are included in the components of pension benefit and other postretirement benefit costs, below, as recognized net actuarial loss.

The changes in benefit obligations and plan assets at May 31, 2015 and May 25, 2014 are presented in the following table.

	Pension Benefits		Other Benefits	
	2015	2014	2015	2014
Change in Benefit Obligation				
Benefit obligation at beginning of year	$3,979.0	$3,817.5	$283.5	$302.8
Service cost	88.5	89.0	0.6	0.7
Interest cost	161.3	151.1	9.9	9.7
Plan participants' contributions	—	—	5.9	6.1
Amendments	0.7	2.2	(3.3)	(5.7)
Actuarial loss (gain)	35.7	79.5	(35.9)	(4.6)
Special termination benefits	6.9	0.4	—	—
Benefits paid	(176.7)	(159.5)	(24.3)	(25.1)
Currency	(3.2)	(1.2)	(1.0)	(0.4)
Benefit obligation at end of year	$4,092.2	$3,979.0	$235.4	$283.5
Change in Plan Assets				
Fair value of plan assets at beginning of year	$3,546.0	$3,343.3	$ 0.3	$ 0.1
Actual return on plan assets	178.6	358.8	(0.3)	0.2
Employer contributions	13.5	18.3	18.5	19.0
Plan participants' contributions	—	—	5.9	6.1
Investment and administrative expenses	(18.8)	(13.8)	—	—
Benefits paid	(176.7)	(159.5)	(24.3)	(25.1)
Currency	(3.6)	(1.1)	—	—
Fair value of plan assets at end of year	$3,539.0	$3,546.0	$ 0.1	$ 0.3

The funded status and amounts recognized in our Consolidated Balance Sheets at May 31, 2015 and May 25, 2014 were:

	Pension Benefits		Other Benefits	
	2015	2014	2015	2014
Funded Status	$(553.2)	$(433.0)	$(235.3)	$(283.2)
Amounts Recognized in Consolidated Balance Sheets				
Other assets	$ 20.5	$ 18.8	$ —	$ —
Other accrued liabilities	(10.7)	(10.0)	(23.3)	(25.0)
Other noncurrent liabilities	(563.0)	(441.8)	(212.0)	(258.2)
Net Amount Recognized	$(553.2)	$(433.0)	$(235.3)	$(283.2)
Amounts Recognized in Accumulated Other Comprehensive (Income) Loss (Pre-tax)				
Actuarial net loss	$ 339.6	$ 202.8	$ 16.1	$ 55.3
Net prior service cost (benefit)	14.2	18.7	(25.0)	(29.6)
Total	$ 353.8	$ 221.5	$ (8.9)	$ 25.7
Weighted-Average Actuarial Assumptions Used to Determine Benefit Obligations at May 31, 2015 and May 25, 2014				
Discount rate	4.10%	4.15%	3.50%	3.65%
Long-term rate of compensation increase	3.70%	4.25%	N/A	N/A

The accumulated benefit obligation for all defined benefit pension plans was $3.9 billion at May 31, 2015 and May 25, 2014.

The projected benefit obligation, accumulated benefit obligation, and fair value of plan assets for pension plans with accumulated benefit obligations in excess of plan assets at May 31, 2015 and May 25, 2014 were:

	2015	2014
Projected benefit obligation	$3,805.8	$3,390.9
Accumulated benefit obligation	3,658.3	3,289.3
Fair value of plan assets	3,232.1	2,942.5

Components of pension benefit and other postretirement benefit costs included:

	Pension Benefits			Other Benefits		
	2015	2014	2013	2015	2014	2013
Service cost	$ 88.5	$ 89.0	$ 81.8	$ 0.6	$ 0.7	$ 0.6
Interest cost	161.3	151.1	150.1	9.9	9.7	10.5
Expected return on plan assets	(267.9)	(252.9)	(216.4)	—	—	—
Amortization of prior service cost (benefit)	3.7	3.8	3.6	(7.9)	(7.2)	(8.2)
Special termination benefits	6.9	0.4	—	—	—	—
Recognized net actuarial loss	6.9	2.7	3.6	3.5	6.7	5.9
Curtailment loss	1.5	—	0.8	—	—	—
Benefit cost—Company plans	0.9	(5.9)	23.5	6.1	9.9	8.8
Pension benefit cost—multi-employer plans	12.4	12.6	23.6	—	—	—
Total benefit cost	$ 13.3	$ 6.7	$ 47.1	$ 6.1	$ 9.9	$ 8.8

Special termination benefits granted in connection with the formation of Ardent Mills resulted in the recognition of $6.9 million of expense during fiscal 2015. This expense was included in results of discontinued operations.

Other changes in plan assets and benefit obligations recognized in other comprehensive income (loss) were:

	Pension Benefits		Other Benefits	
	2015	2014	2015	2014
Net actuarial gain (loss)	$(143.8)	$12.7	$35.8	$ 4.9
Amendments	(0.6)	(2.2)	3.3	5.7
Amortization of prior service cost (benefit)	5.2	3.8	(7.9)	(7.2)
Recognized net actuarial loss	6.9	2.7	3.5	6.7
Net amount recognized	$(132.3)	$17.0	$34.7	$10.1

Weighted-Average Actuarial Assumptions Used to Determine Net Expense

	Pension Benefits			Other Benefits		
	2015	2014	2013	2015	2014	2013
Discount rate	4.15%	4.05%	4.50%	3.65%	3.35%	3.90%
Long-term rate of return on plan assets	7.75%	7.75%	7.75%	N/A	N/A	N/A
Long-term rate of compensation increase	4.25%	4.25%	4.25%	N/A	N/A	N/A

We amortize prior service cost for our pension plans and postretirement plans, as well as amortizable gains and losses for our postretirement plans, in equal annual amounts over the average expected future period of vested service. For plans with no active participants, average life expectancy is used instead of average expected useful service.

The amounts in accumulated other comprehensive income (loss) expected to be recognized as components of net expense during the next year are as follows:

	Pension Benefits	Other Benefits
Prior service cost (benefit)	$2.7	$(8.1)
Net actuarial loss	NA	NA

Format of Stockholders' Equity in Annual Filings

PRESENTATION

5.01 *Equity* (sometimes referred to as net assets) is the residual interest in the assets of an entity that remains after deducting its liabilities. As discussed in FASB *Accounting Standards Codification* (ASC) 505-10-50-2, if both financial position and results of operations are presented, disclosure of changes in (*a*) the separate accounts comprising stockholders' equity (in addition to retained earnings) and (*b*) the number of shares of equity securities during at least the most recent annual fiscal period and any subsequent interim period presented is required in order to make the financial statements sufficiently informative. Disclosure of such changes may take the form of separate statements or may be made in the basic financial statements or notes thereto. Most public entities present a statement of stockholders' equity to conform to Rule 3-04 of SEC Regulation S-X.

5.02 FASB ASC 505-10-25-1 explains that additional paid-in capital, however created, should not be used to relieve income of the current or future years of charges that would otherwise be made to the income statement.

5.03 As discussed in FASB ASC 505-20-30-3, in accounting for a stock dividend, a corporation should transfer from retained earnings to the category of capital stock and additional paid-in capital an amount equal to the fair value of the additional shares issued.

5.04 Rule 5-02 of Regulation S-X requires separate captions for additional paid-in capital, other additional capital, and retained earnings. If appropriate, additional paid-in capital and other additional capital may be combined with the stock caption to which it applies.

DISCLOSURE

5.05 FASB ASC 505-10-50-3 states that an entity should explain the pertinent rights and privileges of the various securities outstanding. Examples are dividend and liquidation preferences; contractual rights of security holders to receive dividends or returns from the security issuer's profits, cash flows, or returns on investments; participation rights; call prices and dates; conversion or exercise prices or rates and pertinent dates; sinking-fund requirements; unusual voting rights; and significant terms of contracts to issue additional shares.

5.06 FASB ASC 505-10-50-2 also requires disclosure of changes in the separate accounts comprising shareholders' equity (in addition to retained earnings) and of the changes in the number of shares of equity securities during at least the most recent annual fiscal period. Disclosure of such changes may take the form of separate statements or may be made in the basic financial statements or notes thereto.

PRESENTATION AND DISCLOSURE EXCERPTS

ISSUANCE OF STOCK UNDER EMPLOYEE STOCK PURCHASE PLAN

5.07 GUESS?, INC. (JAN)
CONSOLIDATED STATEMENTS OF STOCKHOLDERS' EQUITY

(in thousands, except share data)

	Guess?, Inc. Stockholders' Equity								
	Common Stock		Paid-in Capital	Retained Earnings	Accumulated Other Comprehensive Income (Loss)	Treasury Stock		Nonredeemable Noncontrolling Interests	Total
	Shares	Amount				Shares	Amount		
Balance at January 28, 2012	89,631,328	$896	$400,178	$1,155,696	$(23,197)	48,457,693	$(357,943)	$18,635	$1,194,265
Net earnings	—	—	—	178,744	—	—	—	2,742	181,486
Foreign currency translation adjustment	—	—	—	—	22,025	—	—	322	22,347
Loss on derivative financial instruments designated as cash flow hedges	—	—	—	—	(6,041)	—	—	—	(6,041)

(continued)

| | Guess?, Inc. Stockholders' Equity | | | | | | | | |
| | Common Stock | | Paid-in Capital | Retained Earnings | Accumulated Other Comprehensive Income (Loss) | Treasury Stock | | Nonredeemable Noncontrolling Interests | Total |
	Shares	Amount				Shares	Amount		
Gain on marketable securities	—	—	—	—	139	—	—	—	139
Prior service cost amortization and actuarial valuation gain (loss) and related amortization on defined benefit plans	—	—	—	—	4,613	—	—	—	4,613
Issuance of common stock under stock compensation plans including tax effect	723,061	7	1,355	—	—	—	—	—	1,362
Issuance of stock under Employee Stock Purchase Plan	50,013	—	750	—	—	(50,013)	436	—	1,186
Share-based compensation	—	—	16,197	88	—	—	—	—	16,285
Dividends	—	—	—	(172,792)	—	—	—	—	(172,792)
Share repurchases	(5,036,418)	(50)	50	—	—	5,036,418	(140,262)	—	(140,262)
Purchase of redeemable noncontrolling interest	—	—	4,857	—	—	—	—	(4,857)	—
Noncontrolling interest capital contribution	—	—	—	—	—	—	—	1,488	1,488
Noncontrolling interest capital distribution	—	—	—	—	—	—	—	(4,237)	(4,237)
Redeemable noncontrolling interest redemption value adjustment	—	—	—	1,246	—	—	—	(217)	1,029
Balance at February 2, 2013	85,367,984	$853	$423,387	$1,162,982	$ (2,461)	53,444,098	$(497,769)	$13,876	$1,100,868
Net earnings	—	—	—	153,434	—	—	—	4,277	157,711
Foreign currency translation adjustment	—	—	—	—	(17,621)	—	—	(804)	(18,425)
Gain on derivative financial instruments designated as cash flow hedges	—	—	—	—	1,669	—	—	—	1,669
Loss on marketable securities	—	—	—	—	(7)	—	—	—	(7)
Plan amendment, prior service cost amortization and actuarial valuation gain (loss) and related amortization on defined benefit plans	—	—	—	—	4,619	—	—	—	4,619
Issuance of common stock under stock compensation plans including tax effect	433,647	6	2,398	—	—	—	—	—	2,404
Issuance of stock under Employee Stock Purchase Plan	43,265	—	569	—	—	(43,265)	411	—	980
Share-based compensation	—	—	13,379	570	—	—	—	—	13,949
Dividends	—	—	—	(68,215)	—	—	—	—	(68,215)
Share repurchases	(882,551)	(9)	9	—	—	882,551	(22,099)	—	(22,099)
Noncontrolling interest capital distribution	—	—	—	—	—	—	—	(1,877)	(1,877)
Redeemable noncontrolling interest redemption value adjustment	—	—	—	(1,591)	—	—	—	—	(1,591)
Balance at February 1, 2014	84,962,345	$850	$439,742	$1,247,180	$ (13,801)	54,283,384	$(519,457)	$15,472	$1,169,986
Net earnings	—	—	—	94,570	—	—	—	2,614	97,184
Foreign currency translation adjustment	—	—	—	—	(114,566)	—	—	(2,141)	(116,707)
Gain on derivative financial instruments designated as cash flow hedges	—	—	—	—	7,270	—	—	—	7,270
Loss on marketable securities	—	—	—	—	(106)	—	—	—	(106)
Prior service credit amortization and actuarial valuation loss and related amortization on defined benefit plans	—	—	—	—	(5,862)	—	—	—	(5,862)
Issuance of common stock under stock compensation plans including tax effect	313,271	3	(1,940)	—	—	—	—	—	(1,937)
Issuance of stock under Employee Stock Purchase Plan	47,538	—	553	—	—	(47,538)	455	—	1,008
Share-based compensation	—	—	15,191	151	—	—	—	—	15,342
Dividends	—	—	—	(76,982)	—	—	—	—	(76,982)
Noncontrolling interest capital distribution	—	—	—	—	—	—	—	(355)	(355)
Redeemable noncontrolling interest redemption value adjustment	—	—	—	605	—	—	—	—	605
Balance at January 31, 2015	85,323,154	$853	$453,546	$1,265,524	$(127,065)	54,235,846	$(519,002)	$15,590	$1,089,446

NOTES TO CONSOLIDATED FINANCIAL STATEMENTS (in part)

(19) Share-Based Compensation (in part)

Share-Based Compensation Plans

The Company has four share-based compensation plans. The Guess?, Inc. 2004 Equity Incentive Plan (the "Plan") provides that the Board of Directors may grant stock options and other equity awards to officers, key employees and certain consultants and advisors to the Company or any of its subsidiaries. Effective May 20, 2014, the Plan was amended to extend the term for an additional ten years and reduce the authorized issuance of shares from 20,000,000 shares of common stock to 15,000,000 shares of common stock. The amendment also extended the ability for the Company to grant certain performance-based awards under the Plan through the beginning of calendar year 2019. All other remaining provisions under the Plan remain in full force and effect. As of January 31, 2015 and February 1, 2014, there were 6,593,723 and 12,151,436 shares available for grant under the Plan, respectively. Stock options granted under the Plan have ten-year terms and typically vest and become fully exercisable in increments of one-fourth of the shares granted on each anniversary from the date of grant. Stock awards/units granted under the Plan typically vest in increments of one-fourth of the shares granted on each anniversary from the date of grant. The three most recent annual grants for stock options and other equity awards had initial vesting periods of nine months followed by three annual vesting periods. The Guess?, Inc. Employee Stock Purchase Plan ("ESPP") allows for qualified employees to participate in the purchase of designated shares of the Company's common stock at a price equal to 85% of the lower of the closing price at the beginning or end of each quarterly stock purchase period. The Guess?, Inc. 2006 Non-Employee Directors' Stock Grant and Stock Option Plan (the "Director Plan") provides for the grant of equity awards to non-employee directors. The Director Plan authorizes the issuance of up to 2,000,000 shares of common stock which consists of 1,000,000 shares that were initially approved for issuance on July 30, 1996 plus an additional 1,000,000 shares that were approved for issuance effective May 9, 2006. As of January 31, 2015 and February 1, 2014, there were 827,463 and 860,432 shares available for grant under this plan, respectively. In addition, the Guess?, Inc. 1996 Equity Incentive Plan, under which equity grants have not been permitted since the approval of the Plan in 2004, continues to govern outstanding awards previously made thereunder.

Share-Based Compensation Expense

Compensation expense for nonvested stock options and stock awards is recognized on a straight-line basis over the vesting period. The Company estimates forfeitures in calculating the expense relating to share-based compensation as opposed to recognizing forfeitures as an expense reduction as they occur.

The following table summarizes the share-based compensation expense recognized under all of the Company's stock plans during fiscal 2015, fiscal 2014 and fiscal 2013 (in thousands):

	Year Ended Jan 31, 2015	Year Ended Feb 1, 2014	Year Ended Feb 2, 2013
Stock options	$ 2,106	$ 2,490	$ 4,633
Nonvested stock awards/units	12,999	11,225	11,337
ESPP	237	234	315
Total share-based compensation expense	$15,342	$13,949	$16,285

ESPP

In January 2002, the Company established an ESPP, the terms of which allow for qualified employees (as defined) to participate in the purchase of designated shares of the Company's common stock at a price equal to 85% of the lower of the closing price at the beginning or end of each quarterly stock purchase period. Prior to March 4, 2009, the ESPP was a straight purchase plan with no holding period requirement. Effective March 4, 2009, the ESPP was amended to require participants to hold any shares purchased under the ESPP after April 1, 2009 for a minimum period of six months after purchase. In addition, all Company employees are subject to the terms of the Company's securities trading policy which generally prohibits the purchase or sale of any Company securities during the two weeks before the end of each fiscal quarter through two days after the public announcement by the Company of its earnings for that period. On January 23, 2002, the Company filed with the Securities and Exchange Commission ("SEC") a Registration Statement on Form S-8 registering 4,000,000 shares of common stock for the ESPP. Effective March 12, 2012, the ESPP was amended and restated to extend the term for an additional ten years.

During fiscal 2015, fiscal 2014 and fiscal 2013, 47,538 shares, 43,265 shares and 50,013 shares of the Company's common stock were issued pursuant to the ESPP at an average price of $21.20, $22.64 and $23.72 per share, respectively.

The fair value of stock compensation expense associated with the Company's ESPP was estimated on the date of grant using the Black-Scholes option-pricing valuation model with the following weighted average assumptions used for grants during fiscal 2015, fiscal 2014 and fiscal 2013.

Valuation Assumptions	Year Ended Jan 31, 2015	Year Ended Feb 1, 2014	Year Ended Feb 2, 2013
Risk-free interest rate	0.0%	0.1%	0.1%
Expected stock price volatility	29.0%	29.7%	46.4%
Expected dividend yield	3.7%	3.1%	2.8%
Expected life of ESPP options (in months)	3	3	3

The weighted average grant date fair value of ESPP options granted during fiscal 2015, fiscal 2014 and fiscal 2013 was $5.02, $5.46 and $6.84, respectively.

COMMON STOCK ISSUED IN AN ACQUISITION

5.08 ABBVIE INC. (DEC)
CONSOLIDATED STATEMENTS OF EQUITY

Years Ended December 31 (in millions)	Common Shares Outstanding	Common Stock	Treasury Stock	Additional Paid-in Capital	Retained Earnings	Accumulated other Comprehensive Loss	Net Parent Company Investment	Total
Balance at December 31, 2012	—	$—	$ —	$ —	$ —	$ (350)	$3,713	$ 3,363
Separation-related adjustments	—	—	—	(1,316)	—	(662)	707	(1,271)
Reclassification of parent company net investment in connection with separation	—	—	—	4,420	—	—	(4,420)	—
Issuance of common shares at separation	1,577	16	—	(16)	—	—	—	—
Net earnings	—	—	—	—	4,128	—	—	4,128
Other comprehensive income, net of tax	—	—	—	—	—	570	—	570
Dividends declared	—	—	—	—	(2,561)	—	—	(2,561)
Share repurchases	(4)	—	(223)	—	—	—	—	(223)
Stock-based compensation plans and other	14	—	(97)	583	—	—	—	486
Balance at December 31, 2013	1,587	16	(320)	3,671	1,567	(442)	—	4,492
Net earnings	—	—	—	—	1,774	—	—	1,774
Other comprehensive loss, net of tax	—	—	—	—	—	(1,589)	—	(1,589)
Dividends declared	—	—	—	—	(2,806)	—	—	(2,806)
Share repurchases	(9)	—	(550)	—	—	—	—	(550)
Stock-based compensation plans and other	13	—	(102)	523	—	—	—	421
Balance at December 31, 2014	1,591	16	(972)	4,194	535	(2,031)	—	1,742
Net earnings	—	—	—	—	5,144	—	—	5,144
Other comprehensive loss, net of tax	—	—	—	—	—	(530)	—	(530)
Dividends declared	—	—	—	—	(3,431)	—	—	(3,431)
Common shares issued to Pharrmacyclics Inc. stockholders	128	1	—	8,404	—	—	—	8,405
Share repurchases	(119)	—	(7,774)	—	—	—	—	(7,774)
Stock-based compensation plans and other	10	—	(93)	482	—	—	—	389
Balance at December 31, 2015	1,610	$ 17	$(8,839)	$13,080	$2,248	$(2,561)	$ —	$ 3,945

NOTES TO CONSOLIDATED FINANCIAL STATEMENTS (in part)

Note 5 Licensing, Acquisitions and Other Arrangements (in part)

Acquisition of Pharmacyclics (in part)

On May 26, 2015, AbbVie acquired Pharmacyclics through a tender offer for approximately $20.8 billion, including cash consideration of $12.4 billion and equity consideration of $8.4 billion. Pharmacyclics is a biopharmaceutical company that develops and commercializes novel therapies for people impacted by cancer. Pharmacyclics markets IMBRUVICA® (ibrutinib), a Bruton's tyrosine kinase (BTK) inhibitor, targeting B-cell malignancies. Each outstanding Pharmacyclics share was exchanged for (i) $152.25 in cash and $109.00 in fair market value of AbbVie common stock, (ii) $261.25 in cash, or (iii) $261.25 in fair market value of AbbVie common stock, at the election of each holder, subject to the election and proration of the consideration at 58 percent cash and 42 percent AbbVie common stock.

The total consideration for the acquisition of Pharmacyclics was approximately $20.8 billion, consisting of cash and approximately 128 million shares of AbbVie common stock, and is summarized as follows:

(In millions)	
Fair value of AbbVie common stock issued to Pharmacyclics stockholders	$ 8,405
Cash consideration paid to Pharmacyclics stockholders	11,749
Cash consideration paid to Pharmacyclics equity award holders	616
Total consideration	$20,770

The acquisition of Pharmacyclics was accounted for as a business combination using the acquisition method of accounting. This method requires, among other things, that assets acquired and liabilities assumed be recognized at fair value as of the acquisition date. The valuation of assets acquired and liabilities assumed in the acquisition has not yet been finalized as of December 31, 2015. As a result, AbbVie recorded preliminary estimates for the fair value of assets acquired and liabilities assumed as of the acquisition date. The completion of the valuation will occur no later than one year from the acquisition date and may result in significant changes to the recognized assets and liabilities.

The following table summarizes preliminary fair values of assets acquired and liabilities assumed as of the May 26, 2015 acquisition date:

(In millions)	
Assets Acquired and Liabilities Assumed	
Cash and equivalents	$ 877
Short-term investments	11
Accounts and other receivables	106
Inventories	492
Other assets	212
Intangible assets	
Definite-lived developed product rights	4,590
Definite-lived license agreements	6,780
Indefinite-lived research and development	7,180
Accounts payable and accrued liabilities	(381)
Deferred income taxes	(6,453)
Other long-term liabilities	(254)
Total identifiable net assets	13,160
Goodwill	7,610
Total assets acquired and liabilities assumed	$20,770

The fair market value step-up adjustment to inventories of $445 million is being amortized to cost of products sold when the inventory is sold to customers, which is expected to be a period of approximately 18 months from the acquisition date.

Intangible assets relate to the IMBRUVICA developed product rights, IPR&D in the United States related to additional indications for IMBRUVICA, and the contractual rights to IMBRUVICA profits and losses outside the United States as a result of the collaboration agreement with Janssen Biotech, Inc. and its affiliates (Janssen), one of the Janssen Pharmaceutical companies of Johnson & Johnson. Refer to Note 6 for additional information regarding the collaboration with Janssen. The acquired definite-lived intangible assets are being amortized over a weighted-average estimated useful life of 12 years using the estimated pattern of economic benefit. The estimated fair value of the IPR&D and identifiable intangible assets was determined using the "income approach," which is a valuation technique that provides an estimate of the fair value of an asset based on market participant expectations of the cash flows an asset would generate over its remaining useful life. Some of the more significant assumptions inherent in the development of those asset valuations include the estimated net cash flows for each year for each asset or product (including net revenues, cost of sales, R&D costs, selling and marketing costs, and working capital/contributory asset charges), the appropriate discount rate to select in order to measure the risk inherent in each future cash flow stream, the assessment of each asset's life cycle, the potential regulatory and commercial success risks, competitive trends impacting the asset and each cash flow stream, as well as other factors.

Goodwill is calculated as the excess of the consideration transferred over the net assets recognized and represents the future economic benefits arising from the other assets acquired that could not be individually identified and separately recognized. Specifically, the goodwill recognized from the acquisition of Pharmacyclics includes expected synergies, including the ability to leverage the respective strengths of each business, expanding the combined company's product portfolio, acceleration of clinical and commercial presence in oncology and establishment of a strong leadership position in hematological oncology. The goodwill is not deductible for tax purposes.

From the acquisition date through December 31, 2015, AbbVie's consolidated statement of earnings for 2015 included net revenues of $774 million and a pre-tax operating loss of $519 million associated with the acquisition. The operating loss included $346 million of acquisition-related compensation expense, $261 million of inventory step-up and intangible asset amortization, and $100 million of transaction and integration costs. Of these costs, $294 million was recorded within SG&A expenses, $152 million within R&D expenses, and $261 million within cost of products sold in the consolidated statement of earnings for 2015.

5.09 STANLEY BLACK & DECKER, INC. (DEC)
CONSOLIDATED STATEMENTS OF CHANGES IN SHAREOWNERS' EQUITY

(Millions of Dollars, Except Per Share Amounts)

	Preferred Stock	Common Stock	Additional Paid In Capital	Retained Earnings	Accumulated Other Comprehensive Loss	ESOP	Treasury Stock	Non-Controlling Interests	Share-owners' Equity
Balance December 29, 2012	$ —	$442.3	$4,473.5	$3,299.5	$ (388.0)	$(62.8)	$(1,097.4)	$60.0	$6,727.1
Net earnings				490.3				(1.0)	489.3
Other comprehensive loss					(111.0)				(111.0)
Cash dividends declared—$1.98 per share				(307.1)					(307.1)
Issuance of common stock			(115.6)				250.1		134.5
Settlement of forward share repurchase contract			350.0				(350.0)		—
Equity units—non-cash stock contract fees			(40.2)						(40.2)
Equity units—offering fees			(9.2)						(9.2
Net premium paid on equity option			(83.2)						(83.2)
Repurchase of common stock (2,225,732 shares)			217.9				(257.1)		(39.2)
Non-controlling interest buyout			(1.1)					(15.2)	(16.3)
Non-controlling interests of acquired businesses								37.5	37.5
Stock-based compensation related			66.4						66.4
Tax benefit related to stock options exercised			20.1						20.1
ESOP and related tax benefit				2.2		9.6			11.8
Balance December 28, 2013	$ —	$442.3	$4,878.6	$3,484.9	$ (499.0)	$(53.2)	$(1,454.4)	$81.3	$6,880.5
Net earnings				760.9				0.5	761.4
Other comprehensive loss					(771.2)				(771.2)
Cash dividends declared—$2.04 per share				(321.3)					(321.3)
Issuance of common stock			(69.4)				129.8		60.4
Forward obligation to purchase treasury shares			(150.0)						(150.0)
Repurchase of common stock (340,576 shares)							(28.2)		(28.2)
Non-controlling interest buyout								(0.6)	(0.6)
Non-controlling interests of acquired businesses								1.6	1.6
Stock-based compensation related			57.1						57.1
Tax benefit related to stock options exercised			10.8						10.8
ESOP and related tax benefit				1.8		9.6			11.4
Balance January 3, 2015	$ —	$442.3	$4,727.1	$3,926.3	$(1,270.2)	$(43.6)	$(1,352.8)	$82.8	$6,511.9
Net earnings				883.7				(1.6)	882.1
Other comprehensive loss					(424.0)				(424.0)
Cash dividends declared—$2.14 per share				(319.9)					(319.9)
Issuance of common stock			(96.1)				231.4		135.3
Forward obligation to purchase treasury shares			(350.0)						(350.0)
Repurchase of common stock (9,227,564 shares)			263.9				(913.7)		(649.8)
Issuance of preferred stock	632.5								632.5
Redemption and conversion of preferred stock	(632.5)		(220.1)				220.1		(632.5)
Non-controlling interest buyout			0.8					(33.6)	(32.8)
Stock-based compensation related			67.9						67.9
Tax benefit related to stock options exercised			28.2						28.2
ESOP and related tax benefit				1.6		8.7			10.3
Balance January 2, 2016	$ —	$442.3	$4,421.7	$4,491.7	$(1,694.2)	$(34.9)	$(1,815.0)	$47.6	$5,859.2

NOTES TO CONSOLIDATED FINANCIAL STATEMENTS *(in part)*

H. Long-Term Debt and Financing Arrangements (in part)

Convertible Preferred Units

In November 2010, the Company issued 6,325,000 Convertible Preferred Units (the "Convertible Preferred Units"), each with a stated amount of $100. The Convertible Preferred Units were comprised of a 1/10, or 10%, undivided beneficial ownership in a $1,000 principal amount junior subordinated note (the "Note") and a Purchase Contract (the "Purchase Contract") obligating holders to purchase one share of the Company's 4.75% Series B Perpetual Cumulative Convertible Preferred Stock (the "Convertible Preferred Stock"). The Company received $613.5 million in cash proceeds from the Convertible Preferred Units offering, net of underwriting fees.

Purchase Contracts

Each Purchase Contract obligated the holder to purchase, on November 17, 2015, for $100, one newly-issued share of Convertible Preferred Stock.

Holders of the Purchase Contracts were paid contract adjustment payments ("contract adjustment payments") at a rate of 0.50% per annum, payable quarterly in arrears on February 17, May 17, August 17 and November 17 of each year. The $14.9 million present value of the contract adjustment payments reduced Shareowners' Equity at inception. As each quarterly contract adjustment payment was made, the related liability was relieved with the difference between the cash payment and the present value of the contract adjustment payment recorded as interest expense.

In accordance with the Purchase Contracts, on November 17, 2015, the Company issued 6,325,000 shares of Convertible Preferred Stock and made the final contract adjustment payment on the Purchase Contracts. The purchase price for the Convertible Preferred Stock was paid using the proceeds of the remarketing described below.

Convertible Preferred Stock

Holders of the Convertible Preferred Stock were entitled to receive cumulative cash dividends at the rate of 4.75% per annum of the $100 liquidation preference per share of the Convertible Preferred Stock. Dividends on the Convertible Preferred Stock were payable, when, as and if declared by the Company's board of directors, quarterly in arrears in conjunction with the contract adjustment payments.

On November 18, 2015, the Company informed holders that it would redeem, on December 24, 2015 (the "Redemption Date"), all outstanding shares of Convertible Preferred Stock that had not previously been converted at a redemption price of $100.49 per share in cash (the "Redemption Price"), which was equal to the liquidation preference per share of Convertible Preferred Stock of $100, plus accrued and unpaid dividends thereon to, but excluding, the Redemption Date.

Substantially all of the holders of Convertible Preferred Stock elected to convert their shares of Convertible Preferred Stock prior to the Redemption Date. The Company elected to settle all conversions of Convertible Preferred Stock through combination settlement, with a specified dollar amount of $100. The amounts due upon conversion were equal to the sum of the Daily Settlement Amounts for each of the 20 consecutive trading days during the observation period, November 23, 2015 through December 21, 2015. Daily Settlement Amount means, for each of the 20 consecutive trading days during the observation period: (1) cash equal to the lesser of (A) $5.00 and (B) 1/20th of the product of the (i) applicable conversion rate on such trading day and (ii) the daily volume-weighted average price of common stock on such trading day (the "Daily Conversion Value"); and (2) to the extent the Daily Conversion Value for such trading day exceeds $5.00, a number of shares of common stock equal to (A) the difference between such Daily Conversion Value and $5.00, divided by (B) the daily volume-weighted average price for such trading day.

The Company settled all conversions on December 24, 2015 by paying $632.5 million in cash for the $100 par value per share of Convertible Preferred Stock and issuing 2.9 million common shares for the excess value of the conversion feature above the $100 face value per share of Convertible Preferred Stock. The conversion rates used in calculating the Daily Conversion Value during the observation period, were 1.3763 (equivalent to a conversion price set at $72.66 per common share) prior to December 2, 2015 and 1.3789 (equivalent to a conversion price set at $72.52 per common share) on and after December 2, 2015.

Notes

The $632.5 million principal amount of the Notes are due November 17, 2018. At maturity, the Company is obligated to repay the principal in cash. The Notes initially bore interest at an initial rate of 4.25% per annum, initially payable quarterly in arrears on the same dates as the contract adjustment payments. The Notes are the Company's direct, unsecured general obligations and are subordinated and junior in right of payment to the Company's existing and future senior indebtedness. The Notes initially ranked equally in right of payment with all of the Company's other junior subordinated debt. The interest rate, payment dates and ranking of the notes were reset in connection with the remarketing, as described below. The Notes were initially pledged as collateral to guarantee the obligations of holders of Purchase Contracts to purchase Convertible Preferred Stock. Upon completion of the remarketing, the Notes were released from that pledge arrangement.

The Company successfully remarketed the Notes on November 5, 2015. In connection with the remarketing, the interest rate on the notes was reset, effective on the November 17, 2015 settlement date of the remarketing, to a rate of 2.45% per annum, payable semi-annually in arrears on May 17 and November 17 of each year, commencing May 17, 2016. Following settlement of the remarketing, the Notes remain the Company's direct, unsecured general obligations subordinated and junior in right of payment to the Company's existing and future senior indebtedness, but the Notes rank senior in right of payment to specified junior indebtedness on the terms and to the extent set forth in the indentures governing such junior indebtedness.

The remarketing resulted in proceeds of $632.5 million. The Company did not directly receive any proceeds from the remarketing. Instead, the proceeds of remarketing were automatically applied to satisfy in full the related unit holders' obligations to purchase Convertible Preferred Stock under their Purchase Contracts.

Interest expense of $1.9 million was recorded for 2015, related to the contractual interest coupon on the 2018 Subordinated Notes based upon the 2.45% annual rate and $23.3 million was recorded in 2015 and $26.9 million each for 2014 and 2013, related to the contractual interest coupon on the Notes based upon the 4.25% annual rate.

The unamortized deferred issuance cost of the Notes was $5.0 million at January 2, 2016, and will be recorded to interest expense over the term of the underlying Notes.

Equity Option

In order to offset the common shares that were deliverable upon conversion of shares of Convertible Preferred Stock, the Company entered into capped call transactions (equity options) with certain major financial institutions (the "capped call counterparties"). The capped call transactions cover, subject to anti-dilution adjustments, the number of shares of common stock equal to the number of shares of common stock underlying the maximum number of shares of Convertible Preferred Stock issuable upon settlement of the Purchase Contracts. Each of the capped call transactions had an original term of approximately five years and initially has a lower strike price of $75.00, which corresponds to the initial conversion price of the Convertible Preferred Stock, and an upper strike price of $97.95, which was approximately 60% higher than the closing price of the common stock on November 1, 2010. The Company paid $50.3 million of cash to fund the cost of the capped call transactions, which was recorded as a reduction of Shareowners' Equity. On August 5, 2015, the Company terminated the capped call options on its common stock and received 1,692,778 shares of common stock.

J. Capital Stock (in part)

Common Stock Activity (in part)

In December 2015, the Company issued 2,869,169 shares of common stock to settle the conversion feature of the Convertible Preferred Stock issued and redeemed through a combination settlement. For further detail on these transactions, see "Other Equity Arrangements" below.

Preferred Stock Purchase Rights

Each outstanding share of common stock has a 1 share purchase right. Each purchase right may be exercised to purchase one two-hundredth of a share of Series A Junior Participating Preferred Stock at an exercise price of $220.00, subject to adjustment. The rights, which do not have voting rights, expire on March 10, 2016, and may be redeemed by the Company at a price of $0.01 per right at any time prior to the tenth day following the public announcement that a person has acquired beneficial ownership of 15% or more of the outstanding shares of common stock. In the event that the Company is acquired in a merger or other business combination transaction, provision shall be made so that each holder of a right (other than a holder who is a 14.9%-or-more shareowner) shall have the right to receive, upon exercise thereof, that number of shares of common stock of the surviving Company having a market value equal to two times the exercise price of the right. Similarly, if anyone becomes the beneficial owner of more than 15% of the then outstanding shares of common stock (except pursuant to an offer for all outstanding shares of common stock which the independent directors have deemed to be fair and in the best interest of the Company), provision will be made so that each holder of a right (other than a holder who is a 14.9%-or-more shareowner) shall thereafter have the right to receive, upon exercise thereof, common stock (or, in certain circumstances, cash, property or other securities of the Company) having a market value equal to two times the exercise price of the right. At January 2, 2016, there were 148,694,959 outstanding rights.

Other Equity Arrangements (in part)

Convertible Preferred Units and Equity Option

As described more fully in *Note H, Long-Term Debt and Financing Arrangements*, in November 2010, the Company issued Convertible Preferred Units comprised of $632.5 million of Notes due November 17, 2018 and Purchase Contracts. The Purchase Contracts obligated the holders to purchase, on November 17, 2015, 6.3 million shares, for $100 per share, of the Company's 4.75% Series B Cumulative Convertible Preferred Stock (the "Convertible Preferred Stock"), resulting in cash proceeds to the Company of $632.5 million.

In accordance with the Purchase Contracts, on November 17, 2015, the Company issued 6.3 million shares of Convertible Preferred Stock. On November 18, 2015, the Company informed holders that it would redeem all outstanding shares of Convertible Preferred Stock on December 24, 2015 (the "Redemption Date") at $100.49 per share in cash (the "Redemption Price"), which is equal to the liquidation preference of $100 per share of Convertible Preferred Stock, plus accrued and unpaid dividends thereon to, but excluding, the Redemption Date.

The Company settled all conversions on December 24, 2015 by paying cash for the $100 par value, or $632.5 million in total, and issuing 2.9 million common shares for the excess value of the conversion feature above the $100 face value per share of Convertible Preferred Stock. The conversion rates used in calculating the Daily Conversion during the observation period, were 1.3763 (equivalent to a conversion price set at $72.66 per common share) prior to December 2, 2015 and 1.3789 (equivalent to a conversion price set at $72.52 per common share) on and after December 2, 2015.

In November 2010, contemporaneously with the issuance of the Convertible Preferred Units described above, the Company paid $50.3 million, or an average of $5.97 per option, to enter into capped call transactions (equity options) on 8.4 million shares of common stock with certain major financial institutions. The purpose of the capped call transactions was to offset the common shares that may be deliverable upon conversion of shares of Convertible Preferred Stock. Refer to *Note H, Long-Term Debt and Financing Arrangements,* for further discussion. In accordance with ASC 815-40, the $50.3 million premium paid was recorded as a reduction to equity.

The capped call transactions cover, subject to customary anti-dilution adjustments, the number of shares of common stock equal to the number of shares of common stock underlying the maximum number of shares of Convertible Preferred Stock issuable upon settlement of the Purchase Contracts. Each of the capped call transactions had a term of approximately five years and initially had a lower strike price of $75.00, which corresponded to the initial conversion price of the Convertible Preferred Stock, and an upper strike price of $97.95, which was approximately 60% higher than the closing price of the common stock on November 1, 2010. On August 5, 2015, the Company net-share settled the capped call options on its common stock and received 1,692,778 shares using an average reference price of $103.97 per common share.

TAX BENEFIT RELATING TO EMPLOYEE STOCK COMPENSATION

5.10 EXPRESS SCRIPTS HOLDING COMPANY (DEC)
CONSOLIDATED STATEMENT OF CHANGES IN STOCKHOLDERS' EQUITY

(In millions)	Number of Shares Common Stock	Common Stock	Additional Paid-in Capital	Accumulated Other Comprehensive (Loss) Income	Retained Earnings	Treasury Stock	Non-controlling Interest	Total
Balance at December 31, 2012	818.1	$8.2	$21,289.7	$ 18.9	$2,068.2	$ —	$10.7	$23,395.7
Net income	—	—	—	—	1,844.6	—	28.1	1,872.7
Other comprehensive loss	—	—	—	(7.2)	—	—	—	(7.2)
Treasury stock acquired	—	—	(149.9)	—	—	(3,905.3)	—	(4,055.2)
Common stock issued under employee plans, net of forfeitures and stock redeemed for taxes	15.9	0.1	(49.7)	—	—	—	—	(49.6)
Amortization of unearned compensation under employee plans	—	—	164.7	—	—	—	—	164.7
Exercise of stock options	—	—	524.0	—	—	—	—	524.0
Tax benefit relating to employee stock compensation	—	—	31.1	—	—	—	—	31.1
Distributions to non-controlling interest	—	—	—	—	—	—	(31.4)	(31.4)
Balance at December 31, 2013	834.0	$8.3	$21,809.9	$ 11.7	$3,912.8	$ (3,905.3)	$ 7.4	$21,844.8
Net income	—	—	—	—	2,007.6	—	27.4	2,035.0
Other comprehensive loss	—	—	—	(9.6)	—	—	—	(9.6)
Treasury stock acquired	—	—	149.9	—	—	(4,642.9)	—	(4,493.0)
Common stock issued under employee plans, net of forfeitures and stock redeemed for taxes	14.6	0.2	(35.4)	—	—	—	—	(35.2)
Amortization of unearned compensation under employee plans	—	—	111.0	—	—	—	—	111.0
Exercise of stock options	—	—	542.4	—	—	—	—	542.4
Tax benefit relating to employee stock compensation	—	—	93.6	—	—	—	—	93.6
Distributions to non-controlling interest	—	—	—	—	—	—	(25.0)	(25.0)
Balance at December 31, 2014	848.6	$8.5	$22,671.4	$ 2.1	$5,920.4	$ (8,548.2)	$ 9.8	$20,064.0
Net income	—	—	—	—	2,476.4	—	23.1	2,499.5
Other comprehensive loss	—	—	—	(16.1)	—	—	—	(16.1)
Treasury stock acquired	—	—	(825.0)	—	—	(4,675.0)	—	(5,500.0)
Common stock issued under employee plans, net of forfeitures and stock redeemed for taxes	5.9	—	(30.0)	—	—	—	—	(30.0)
Amortization of unearned compensation under employee plans	—	—	117.1	—	—	—	—	117.1
Exercise of stock options	—	—	213.2	—	—	—	—	213.2
Tax benefit relating to employee stock compensation	—	—	58.0	—	—	—	—	58.0
Distributions to non-controlling interest	—	—	—	—	—	—	(25.2)	(25.2)
Balance at December 31, 2015	854.5	$8.5	$22,204.7	$(14.0)	$8,396.8	$(13,223.2)	$ 7.7	$17,380.5

1. Summary of Significant Accounting Policies (in part)

Employee stock-based compensation. Grant-date fair values of stock options are estimated using a Black-Scholes valuation model and grant-date fair values of restricted stock units and performance shares are estimated based on the grant-date stock price. Compensation expense is reduced based on estimated forfeitures with adjustments recorded at the time of vesting for actual forfeitures. Forfeitures are estimated based on experience. We use an accelerated method of recognizing compensation cost for awards. Unearned compensation relating to these awards is amortized to non-cash compensation expense over the estimated vesting periods. See Note 9 - Employee benefit plans and stock-based compensation plans for more information regarding stock-based compensation plans.

9. Employee Benefit Plans and Stock-Based Compensation Plans (in part)

Stock-based compensation plans in general. The Board of Directors of ESI previously adopted a long-term incentive plan in 2011 (the "2011 LTIP"), which provides for the grant of stock options, SSRs, restricted stock units, restricted stock awards, performance share awards and other types of awards with various terms to officers, directors and key employees selected by the Compensation Committee of the Board of Directors. The maximum number of shares available for awards under the 2011 LTIP is 30.0 million. As of December 31, 2015, approximately 18.6 million shares of our common stock are available for issuance under the 2011 LTIP.

Subsequent to the effective date of the 2011 LTIP, no additional awards have been or will be granted under the long-term incentive plan (the "2000 LTIP") adopted by ESI in 2000, which provided for the grant of various equity awards with various terms to officers, directors and key employees selected by the Compensation Committee of the Board of Directors. However, this plan is still in existence as there are outstanding grants under the 2000 LTIP.

Effective 2012, we assumed sponsorship of the Medco 2002 stock incentive plan (the "2002 SIP"), allowing us to issue stock options, restricted stock units and other types of awards to officers, employees and directors. As of December 31, 2015, approximately 11.4 million shares are available under the 2002 SIP.

The provisions of the 2000 LTIP, 2011 LTIP and 2002 SIP allow employees to use shares to cover tax withholdings on stock awards. Upon vesting of restricted stock units and performance shares, employees have taxable income subject to statutory withholding requirements. The number of shares issued to employees may be reduced by the number of shares having a market value equal to our minimum statutory withholding for federal, state and local tax purposes. Awards are settled by issuance of new shares. The maximum term of stock options, restricted stock units and performance shares is generally 10 years. The tax benefit related to employee stock compensation recognized during the years ended December 31, 2015, 2014 and 2013 was $41.3 million, $37.3 million and $60.0 million, respectively.

Stock options. We have issued stock options to certain officers, directors and employees to purchase shares of our common stock at fair market value on the date of grant. Stock options generally have three-year graded vesting.

As of December 31, 2015 and 2014, unearned compensation related to stock options was $31.7 million and $28.7 million, respectively. We recorded pre-tax compensation expense related to stock options of $46.0 million, $48.0 million and $77.3 million in the years ended December 31, 2015, 2014 and 2013, respectively. The weighted-average remaining recognition period for stock options is 2.0 years.

A summary of the status of stock options as of December 31, 2015, and changes during the year ended December 31, 2015, is presented below.

	Shares (in millions)	Weighted-Average Exercise Price Per Share	Weighted-Average Remaining Contractual Life (in years)	Aggregate Intrinsic Value (in millions)[1]
Outstanding at beginning of year	20.6	$50.26		
Granted	3.1	84.85		
Exercised	(4.9)	43.64		
Forfeited/cancelled	(0.8)	74.88		
Outstanding at end of period	18.0	57.03	4.9	$548.1
Awards exercisable at period end	12.9	$48.29	3.9	$504.2

[1] Amount by which the market value of the underlying stock exceeds the exercise price of the stock option.

For the years ended December 31, 2015, 2014 and 2013, the windfall tax benefit related to stock options exercised during the year was $58.2 million, $94.0 million and $42.7 million, respectively, and is classified as a financing cash inflow on the consolidated statement of cash flows.

The fair value of stock options granted was estimated on the date of grant using a Black-Scholes multiple option-pricing model with the following weighted-average assumptions:

	Year Ended December 31,		
	2015	2014	2013
Expected life of option	3–5 years	3–5 years	4–5 years
Risk-free interest rate	1.0%–1.7%	0.7%–1.8%	0.6%–1.7%
Expected volatility of stock	19%–26%	21%–29%	27%–37%
Expected dividend yield	None	None	None
Weighted-average volatility of stock	24.0%	27.4%	34.1%

The Black-Scholes model requires subjective assumptions, including future stock price volatility and expected time to exercise, which greatly affect the calculated values. The expected term and forfeiture rate of stock options is derived from historical data on employee exercises and post-vesting employment termination behavior as well as expected behavior on outstanding stock options. The risk-free rate is based on the United States Treasury rates in effect during the corresponding period of grant. The expected volatility is based on the historical volatility of our stock price. These factors could change in the future, which would affect the stock-based compensation expense recognized in future periods.

Cash proceeds and intrinsic value related to total stock options exercised and weighted-average fair value of stock options granted during the years ended December 31, 2015, 2014 and 2013 are provided in the following table:

	Year Ended December 31,		
(In millions, except per share data)	2015	2014	2013
Proceeds from stock options exercised	$213.2	$542.4	$524.0
Intrinsic value of stock options exercised	212.8	476.3	362.0
Weighted-average fair value per share of options granted during the year	$18.03	$17.98	$17.17

SHARE-BASED COMPENSATION

5.11 BROWN SHOE COMPANY, INC. (JAN)

CONSOLIDATED STATEMENTS OF SHAREHOLDERS' EQUITY

($ thousands, except number of shares and per share amounts)	Common Stock Shares	Common Stock Dollars	Additional Paid-In Capital	Accumulated Other Comprehensive Income	Retained Earnings	Total Brown Show Comopany, Inc. Shareholders' Equity	Non-controlling Interests	Total Equity
Balance January 28, 2012	41,970,687	$420	$115,869	$ 9,637	$286,743	$412,669	$1,047	$413,716
Net earnings					27,491	27,491	(287)	27,204
Foreign currency translation adjustment				463		463	12	475
Unrealized loss on derivative financial instruments, net of tax of $33				(155)		(155)		(155)
Pension and other postretirement benefits adjustments, net of tax of $5,777				(9,061)		(9,061)		(9,061)
Comprehensive income						18,738	(275)	18,463
Dividends ($0.28 per share)					(12,011)	(12,011)		(12,011)
Stock issued under employee and director benefit and restricted stock plans	925,676	9	(1,709)			(1,700)		(1,700)
Tax benefit related to share-based plans			944			944		944
Share-based compensation expense			6,489			6,489		6,489
Balance February 2, 2013	42,896,363	$429	$121,593	$ 884	$302,223	$425,129	$ 772	$425,901
Net earnings					38,073	38,073	(177)	37,896
Foreign currency translation adjustment				(4,556)		(4,556)	18	(4,538)
Unrealized gain on derivative financial instruments, net of tax of $289				819		819		819
Pension and other postretirement benefits adjustments, net of tax of $12,319				19,529		19,529		19,529
Comprehensive income						53,865	(159)	53,706
Dividends ($0.28 per share)					(12,105)	(12,105)		(12,105)
Contributions by noncontrolling interests							50	50
Stock issued under employee and director benefit and restricted stock plans	481,916	5	799			804		804
Tax benefit related to share-based plans			3,439			3,439		3,439
Share-based compensation expense			5,567			5,567		5,567
Balance February 1, 2014	43,378,279	$434	$131,398	$ 16,676	$328,191	$476,699	$ 663	$477,362

(continued)

($ thousands, except number of shares and per share amounts)	Common Stock Shares	Common Stock Dollars	Additional Paid-In Capital	Accumulated Other Comprehensive Income	Retained Earnings	Total Brown Show Comopany, Inc. Shareholders' Equity	Non-controlling Interests	Total Equity
Net earnings					82,850	82,850	93	82,943
Foreign currency translation adjustment				(3,101)		(3,101)	(44)	(3,145)
Unrealized loss on derivative financial instruments, net of tax of $408				(514)		(514)		(514)
Pension and other postretirement benefits adjustments, net of tax of $6,494				(10,349)		(10,349)		(10,349)
Comprehensive income						68,886	49	68,935
Dividends ($0.28 per share)					(12,237)	(12,237)		(12,237)
Stock issued under employee and director benefit and restricted stock plans	373,752	3	440			443		443
Tax benefit related to share-based plans			929			929		929
Share-based compensation expense			6,190			6,190		6,190
Balance January 31, 2015	43,752,031	$437	$138,957	$ 2,712	$398,804	$540,910	$ 712	$541,622

NOTES TO CONSOLIDATED FINANCIAL STATEMENTS (in part)

1. Summary of Significant Accounting Policies (in part)

Share-Based Compensation

The Company has share-based incentive compensation plans under which certain officers, employees, and members of the Board of Directors are participants and may be granted stock option, restricted stock, and stock performance awards. Additionally, share-based grants may be made to non-employee members of the Board of Directors in the form of cash-equivalent restricted stock units ("RSUs") at no cost to the non-employee member of the Board of Directors. The Company accounts for share-based compensation in accordance with the fair value recognition provisions of ASC 718, *Compensation—Stock Compensation*, and ASC 505, *Equity*, which require all share-based payments to employees and members of the Board of Directors, including grants of employee stock options, to be recognized as expense in the consolidated financial statements based on their fair values. The fair value of stock options is calculated using the Black-Scholes option pricing formula that requires estimates for expected volatility, expected dividends, the risk-free interest rate, and the expected term of the option. Stock options generally vest over four years, with 25% vesting annually, and expense is recognized on a straight-line basis separately for each vesting portion of the stock option award. Expense for restricted stock is based on the fair value of the restricted stock on the date of grant and is recognized on a straight-line basis generally over a four-year vesting period. Expense for stock performance awards is recognized based upon the fair value of the awards on the date of grant and the anticipated number of shares or units to be awarded on a straight-line basis over the respective term of the award, or individual vesting portion of an award. Expense for the initial grant of RSUs is recognized ratably over the one-year vesting period based upon the fair value of the RSUs, as remeasured at the end of each period. If any of the assumptions used in the Black-Scholes model or the anticipated number of shares to be awarded change significantly, share-based compensation expense may differ materially in the future from that recorded in the current period. See additional information related to share-based compensation in Note 15 to the consolidated financial statements.

15. Share-Based Compensation

The Company has share-based incentive compensation plans under which certain officers, employees and members of the Board of Directors are participants and may be granted stock options, restricted stock and stock performance awards.

ASC 718, *Compensation—Stock Compensation*, and ASC 505, *Equity*, require companies to recognize compensation expense in an amount equal to the fair value of all share-based payments granted to employees over the requisite service period for each award. In certain limited circumstances, the Company's incentive compensation plan provides for accelerated vesting of the awards, such as in the event of a change in control, qualified retirement, death or disability. The Company has a policy of issuing treasury shares in satisfaction of share-based awards.

Share-based compensation expense of $6.2 million, $5.6 million and $6.5 million was recognized in 2014, 2013 and 2012, respectively, as a component of selling and administrative expenses. The following table details the share-based compensation expense by plan and the total related income tax benefit for 2014, 2013 and 2012:

($ thousands)	2014	2013	2012
(Income) expense for share-based compensation plans, net of forfeitures:			
Stock options	$ (46)	$ 248	$ 215
Stock performance awards	—	—	328
Restricted stock grants	6,236	5,319	5,946
Total share-based compensation expense	6,190	5,567	6,489
Less: Income tax benefit	2,397	2,136	2,507
Total share-based compensation expense, net of income tax benefit	$3,793	$3,431	$3,982

In addition to the share-based compensation expense disclosed above, the Company also recognized cash-based expense related to performance share units and cash awards granted under the performance share plans. The Company recognized $6.6 million, $3.7 million and $1.8 million in 2014, 2013 and 2012, respectively, in expense for cash-based awards under the performance share plans.

The Company issued 373,752, 481,916 and 925,676 shares of common stock in 2014, 2013 and 2012, respectively, for restricted stock grants, stock options exercised and stock performance awards issued to employees and common and restricted stock grants issued to directors. There were no significant modifications to any share-based awards in 2014, 2013 or 2012.

Restricted Stock

Under the Company's incentive compensation plans, restricted stock of the Company may be granted at no cost to certain officers, key employees and directors. Plan participants are entitled to cash dividends and voting rights for their respective shares. Restrictions limit the sale or transfer of these shares during the requisite service period, which generally ranges from one to eight years. Expense for restricted stock grants is recognized on a straight-line basis separately for each vesting portion of the stock award based upon fair value of the award on the date of grant. The fair value of the restricted stock grants is the quoted market price for the Company's common stock on the date of grant.

The following table summarizes restricted stock activity for the year ended January 31, 2015:

	Number of Nonvested Restricted Shares	Weighted-Average Grant Date Fair Value
Nonvested at February 1, 2014	1,700,098	$13.25
Granted	281,710	28.17
Vested	(364,238)	14.21
Forfeited	(55,100)	15.89
Nonvested at January 31, 2015	1,562,470	$15.61

For the years ended January 31, 2015, February 1, 2014 and February 2, 2013, restricted shares granted were 281,710, 411,735 and 759,400 respectively. Restricted shares forfeited during 2014, 2013 and 2012 were 55,100, 163,250, and 169,300, respectively. The weighted-average fair value of restricted stock awards granted for the years ended January 31, 2015, February 1, 2014 and February 2, 2013, was $28.17, $17.47 and $9.71, respectively. The total grant date fair value of restricted stock awards vested during the years ended January 31, 2015, February 1, 2014 and February 2, 2013, was $5.2 million, $4.1 million and $4.8 million, respectively. As of January 31, 2015, the total remaining unrecognized compensation cost related to nonvested restricted stock grants amounted to $11.1 million, which will be amortized over the weighted-average remaining requisite service period of 2.5 years.

The Company recognized $0.8 million, $2.9 million and $0.9 million in 2014, 2013 and 2012, respectively, of excess tax benefits related to restricted stock vesting and dividends, which was reflected as an increase to additional paid-in capital.

Performance Share Awards

Under the Company's incentive compensation plans, common stock or cash may be awarded at the end of the performance period at no cost to certain officers and key employees if certain financial goals are met. Under the plan, employees are granted performance share awards at a target number of shares or units, which vest generally over a three-year service period. At the end of the three-year period, the employee will be given an amount of shares between 0% and 200% of the targeted award, depending on the achievement of specified financial goals for the three-year period. If the awards are granted in units, the employee will be given an amount of cash ranging from 0% to 200% of the equivalent market value of the targeted award.

Expense for performance share awards is recognized based upon the fair value of the awards on the date of grant and the anticipated number of shares or cash to be awarded on a straight-line basis for each vesting portion of the stock award. The fair value of the performance share awards is the quoted market price for the Company's common stock on the date of grant. The Company had nonvested outstanding performance share awards for 148,535 units at various target levels as of January 31, 2015, which may result in the payment of up to 297,070 units at the end of the service periods.

The following table summarizes performance share activity for the year ended January 31, 2015:

	Number of Nonvested Stock Performance Awards at Target Level	Number of Nonvested Stock Performance Awards at Maximum Level	Weighted-Average Grant Date Fair Value
Nonvested at February 1, 2014	164,525	329,050	$12.69
Granted	88,185	176,370	28.18
Vested	(84,275)	(168,550)	9.27
Expired	—	—	—
Forfeited	(19,900)	(39,800)	15.96
Nonvested at January 31, 2015	148,535	297,070	$23.39

The weighted-average grant-date fair value of performance share awards granted for 2014, 2013 and 2012 was $28.18, $17.00 and $9.46, respectively. Performance share awards of 84,275, 117,250 and 140,000 vested in 2014, 2013 and 2012, respectively. In addition to the units granted, $2.4 million of performance share awards were granted in cash during 2014. As of January 31, 2015, the remaining unrecognized compensation cost related to nonvested performance share awards was $9.3 million, which will be recognized over the weighted-average remaining service period of 1.4 years.

Stock Options

Stock options are granted to employees at exercise prices equal to the quoted market price of the Company's stock at the date of grant. Stock options generally vest over four years and have a term of 10 years. Compensation cost for all stock options is recognized over the requisite service period for each award. No dividends are paid on unexercised options. Expense for stock options is recognized on a straight-line basis separately for each vesting portion of the stock option award.

The Company granted no stock options in 2014 and 4,000 and 26,000 stock options during 2013 and 2012, respectively. Fair values of options granted in 2013 and 2012 were estimated using the Black-Scholes option-pricing model based on the following assumptions:

	2013	2012
Dividend yield	1.7%	3.1%
Expected volatility	67.7%	66.5%
Risk-free interest rate	1.3%	1.4%
Expected term (in years)	7	7

Dividend yields are based on historical dividend yields. Expected volatilities are based on historical volatilities of the Company's common stock. The risk-free interest rate is based on the U.S. Treasury yield curve in effect at the time of the grant for periods corresponding with the expected term of the options. The expected term of options represents the weighted-average period of time that options granted are expected to be outstanding, giving consideration to vesting schedules and the Company's historical exercise patterns.

Summarized information about stock options outstanding and exercisable at January 31, 2015 is as follows:

	Outstanding			Exercisable	
Exercise Price Range	Number of Options	Weighted-Average Remaining Life (Years)	Weighted-Average Exercise Price	Number of Options	Weighted-Average Exercise Price
$ 3.33–$11.54	82,725	5	$ 6.23	50,350	$ 6.71
$11.55–$14.45	66,000	5	13.95	66,000	13.95
$14.46–$15.35	101,110	1	15.00	96,860	14.99
$15.36–$22.44	91,221	1	20.94	91,221	20.94
$22.45–$35.25	75,747	2	33.50	75,747	33.50
	416,803	3	$17.75	380,178	$18.83

The weighted-average remaining contractual term of stock options outstanding and currently exercisable at January 31, 2015 was 2.9 years and 2.6 years, respectively. The aggregate intrinsic value of stock options outstanding and currently exercisable at January 31, 2015 was $4.9 million and $4.1 million, respectively. Intrinsic value for stock options is calculated based on the exercise price of the underlying awards as compared to the quoted price of the Company's common stock as of the reporting date.

The following table summarizes stock option activity for 2014 under the current and prior plans:

	Number of Options	Weighted-Average Exercise Price
Outstanding at February 1, 2014	751,638	$16.88
Granted	—	—
Exercised	(316,835)	15.21
Forfeited	(18,000)	24.36
Canceled or expired	—	—
Outstanding at January 31, 2015	416,803	$17.75
Exercisable at January 31, 2015	380,178	$18.83

The intrinsic value of stock options exercised was $3.8 million, $4.0 million and $0.5 million for 2014, 2013 and 2012, respectively. The amount of cash received from the exercise of stock options was $3.2 million in 2014, $4.9 million in 2013 and $0.9 million in 2012. In addition, 60,624, 91,157 and 33,033 shares were tendered by employees in satisfaction of the exercise price of stock options during 2014, 2013 and 2012, respectively.

The Company recognized $0.1 million in 2014, $0.5 million in 2013 and less than $0.1 million in 2012 of excess tax benefits related to stock option exercises, which was reflected as an increase to additional paid-in capital.

The following table summarizes nonvested stock option activity for 2014 under the current and prior plans:

	Number of Nonvested Options	Weighted-Average Grant Date Fair Value
Nonvested at February 1, 2014	87,750	$5.08
Granted	—	—
Vested	(46,875)	6.42
Forfeited	(4,250)	7.60
Nonvested at January 31, 2015	36,625	$3.28

The weighted-average grant date fair value of stock options granted for 2013 and 2012 was $9.46 and $5.46, respectively. The total grant date fair value of stock options vested during 2014, 2013 and 2012 was $0.3 million, $0.4 million and $0.5 million, respectively. As of January 31, 2015, the total remaining unrecognized compensation cost related to nonvested stock options amounted to less than $0.1 million, which will be amortized over the weighted-average remaining requisite service period of 1.1 years.

Restricted Stock Units for Non-Employee Directors

Equity-based grants may be made to non-employee directors in the form of cash-equivalent restricted stock units ("RSUs") at no cost to the non-employee director. The RSUs are subject to a vesting requirement (usually one year), earn dividend equivalent units, and are payable in cash on the date the director terminates service or such earlier date as a director may elect, subject to restrictions, based on the then current fair value of the Company's common stock. Dividend equivalents are paid on outstanding RSUs at the same rate as dividends on the Company's common stock, are automatically re-invested in additional RSUs, and vest immediately as of the payment date for the dividend. Expense related to the initial grant of RSUs is recognized ratably over the vesting period based upon the fair value of the RSUs, as remeasured at the end of each period. Expense for the dividend equivalents is recognized at fair value immediately. Gains and losses resulting from changes in the fair value of the RSUs subsequent to the vesting period and through the settlement date are reported in the Company's consolidated statements of earnings. See Note 5 and Note 13 to the consolidated financial statements for information regarding the deferred compensation plan for non-employee directors.

The following table summarizes restricted stock unit activity for the year ended January 31, 2015:

	Outstanding			Accrued[1]	Nonvested RSUs
	Number of Vested RSUs	Number of Nonvested RSUs	Total Number of RSUs	Total Number of RSUs	Weighted-Average Grant Date Fair Value
February 1, 2014	291,855	54,450	346,305	328,155	$21.30
Granted[2]	2,826	39,123	41,949	29,049	28.71
Vested	54,873	(54,873)	—	18,150	21.35
Settled	(57,260)	—	(57,260)	(57,260)	26.23
January 31, 2015	292,294	38,700	330,994	318,094	$28.72

[1] Accrued RSUs include all fully vested awards and a pro-rata portion of nonvested awards based on the elapsed portion of the vesting period.
[2] Granted RSUs include 3,249 RSUs resulting from dividend equivalents paid on outstanding RSUs, of which 2,826 related to outstanding vested RSUs and 423 to outstanding nonvested RSUs.

Information about RSUs granted, vested and settled during 2014, 2013 and 2012 is as follows:

($ thousands, except per unit amounts)	2014	2013	2012
Weighted-average grant date fair value of RSUs granted[1]	$28.69	$21.33	$12.04
Fair value of RSUs vested	1,558	1,600	1,156
RSUs settled	57,260	9,905	6,432

[1] Includes dividend equivalents granted on outstanding RSUs, which vest immediately.

The following table details the RSU compensation expense and the total related income tax benefit for 2014, 2013 and 2012:

($ thousands)	2014	2013	2012
Compensation expense	$ 2,707	$ 3,258	$ 2,769
Income tax benefit	(1,053)	(1,267)	(1,077)
Compensation expense, net of income tax benefit	$ 1,654	$ 1,991	$ 1,692

The aggregate intrinsic value of RSUs outstanding and currently vested at January 31, 2015 is $9.4 million and $8.3 million, respectively. Aggregate intrinsic value for RSUs is calculated based on the average of the high and low prices of the Company's common stock as of the reporting date. As of January 31, 2015 and February 1, 2014, the liabilities associated with the accrued RSUs totaled $8.9 million and $7.8 million, respectively.

Common Stock

DISCLOSURE

5.12 Rule 5-02 of Regulation S-X requires stating on the face of the balance sheet the number of shares issued or outstanding, as appropriate, and the dollar amount. The number of shares authorized should be disclosed on the balance sheet or in the notes.

Preferred Stock

PRESENTATION

5.13 FASB ASC 505-10-50-4 requires that if preferred stock or other senior stock has a preference in involuntary liquidation, the entity should disclose the liquidation preference of the stock (the relationship between the preference in liquidation and the par or stated value of the shares). That disclosure should be made in the Equity section of the balance sheet in the aggregate, either parenthetically or in short.

5.14 FASB ASC 480-10-05-1 requires that an issuer classify certain financial instruments with characteristics of both liabilities and equity as liabilities because those financial instruments embody obligations of the issuer. Some issuances of stock, such as mandatorily redeemable preferred stock, impose unconditional obligations requiring the issuer to transfer assets or issue its equity shares.

DISCLOSURE

5.15 FASB ASC 505-10-50-5 requires disclosure of both of the following either on the face of the statement of financial position or in the notes thereto:
- The aggregate or per-share amounts at which preferred stock may be called or is subject to redemption through sinking-fund operations or otherwise
- The aggregate and per-share amounts of arrearages in cumulative preferred dividends

Rule 5-02 of SEC Regulation S-X also calls for disclosure of the number of shares authorized and the number of shares issued or outstanding, as appropriate.

PRESENTATION AND DISCLOSURE EXCERPT

PREFERRED STOCK

5.16 ALCOA INC. (DEC)
STATEMENT OF CHANGES IN CONSOLIDATED EQUITY

(In millions, except per-share amounts)

	Alcoa Shareholders								
	Preferred Stock	Mandatory Convertible Preferred Stock	Common Stock	Additional Capital	Retained Earnings	Treasury Stock	Accumulated Other Comprehensive Loss	Non-controlling Interests	Total Equity
Balance at December 31, 2012	55	—	1,178	7,560	11,689	(3,881)	(3,402)	3,324	16,523
Net (loss) income	—	—	—	—	(2,285)	—	—	41	(2,244)
Other comprehensive loss (B)	—	—	—	—	—	—	(257)	(338)	(595)
Cash dividends declared:									
Preferred @ $3.75 per share	—	—	—	—	(2)	—	—	—	(2)
Common @ $0.12 per share	—	—	—	—	(130)	—	—	—	(130)
Stock-based compensation (R)	—	—	—	71	—	—	—	—	71
Common stock issued: compensation plans (R)	—	—	—	(122)	—	119	—	—	(3)
Distributions	—	—	—	—	—	—	—	(109)	(109)
Contributions (M)	—	—	—	—	—	—	—	12	12
Other	—	—	—	—	—	—	—	(1)	(1)
Balance at December 31, 2013	55	—	1,178	7,509	9,272	(3,762)	(3,659)	2,929	13,522
Net (loss) income	—	—	—	—	268	—	—	(91)	177
Other comprehensive loss (B)	—	—	—	—	—	—	(1,018)	(254)	(1,272)
Cash dividends declared:									
Preferred–Class A @ $3.75 per share	—	—	—	—	(2)	—	—	—	(2)
Preferred–Class B @ $7.53993 per share	—	—	—	—	(19)	—	—	—	(19)
Common @ $0.12 per share	—	—	—	—	(140)	—	—	—	(140)
Stock-based compensation (R)	—	—	—	87	—	—	—	—	87
Common stock issued: compensation plans (R)	—	—	—	(584)	—	720	—	—	136
Issuance of mandatory convertible preferred stock (R)	—	3	—	1,210	—	—	—	—	1,213
Issuance of common stock (F, K, & R)	—	—	126	1,059	—	—	—	—	1,185
Distributions	—	—	—	—	—	—	—	(120)	(120)
Contributions (M)	—	—	—	—	—	—	—	53	53
Purchase of equity from noncontrolling interest (F)	—	—	—	3	—	—	—	(31)	(28)
Other	—	—	—	—	—	—	—	2	2
Balance at December 31, 2014	$ 55	$ 3	$1,304	$ 9,284	$ 9,379	$(3,042)	$(4,677)	$2,488	$14,794
Net (loss) income	—	—	—	—	(322)	—	—	125	(197)
Other comprehensive loss (B)	—	—	—	—	—	—	(754)	(422)	(1,176)
Cash dividends declared:									
Preferred–Class A @ $3.75 per share	—	—	—	—	(2)	—	—	—	(2)
Preferred–Class B @ $26.8750 per share	—	—	—	—	(67)	—	—	—	(67)
Common @ $0.12 per share	—	—	—	—	(154)	—	—	—	(154)
Equity option on convertible notes (F)	—	—	—	55	—	—	—	—	55
Stock-based compensation (R)	—	—	—	92	—	—	—	—	92
Common stock issued: compensation plans (R)	—	—	—	(195)	—	217	—	—	22
Issuance of common stock (F, K, & R)	—	—	87	783	—	—	—	—	870
Distributions	—	—	—	—	—	—	—	(106)	(106)
Contributions (M)	—	—	—	—	—	—	—	2	2
Other	—	—	—	—	—	—	—	(2)	(2)
Balance at December 31, 2015	$ 55	$ 3	$1,391	$10,019	$ 8,834	$(2,825)	$(5,431)	$2,085	$14,131

(dollars in millions, except per-share amounts)

K. Debt (in part)

Public Debt (in part)

In September 2014, Alcoa completed a public debt offering under its shelf registration statement for $1,250 of 5.125% Notes due 2024 (the "2024 Notes"). Alcoa received $1,238 in net proceeds from the public debt offering reflecting an original issue discount. The net proceeds were used, together with the net proceeds of newly issued mandatory convertible preferred stock (see Note R), to finance the cash portion of the acquisition of Firth Rixson (see Note F). The original issue discount was deferred and is being amortized to interest expense over the term of the 2024 Notes. Interest on the 2024 Notes will be paid semi-annually in April and October, commencing April 2015. Alcoa has the option to redeem the 2024 Notes, as a whole or in part, at any time or from time to time, on at least 30 days, but not more than 60 days, prior notice to the holders of the 2024 Notes at a redemption price specified in the 2024 Notes. The 2024 Notes are subject to repurchase upon the occurrence of a change in control repurchase event (as defined in the 2024 Notes) at a repurchase price in cash equal to 101% of the aggregate principal amount of the 2024 Notes repurchased, plus any accrued and unpaid interest on the 2024 Notes repurchased. The 2024 Notes rank *pari passu* with Alcoa's other unsecured unsubordinated indebtedness.

R. Preferred and Common Stock (in part)

Preferred Stock. Alcoa has two classes of preferred stock: Class A Preferred Stock and Class B Serial Preferred Stock. Class A Preferred Stock has 660,000 shares authorized at a par value of $100 per share with an annual $3.75 cumulative dividend preference per share. There were 546,024 of such shares outstanding at December 31, 2015 and 2014. Class B Serial Preferred Stock has 10 million shares authorized at a par value of $1 per share. There were 2.5 million of such shares outstanding at December 31, 2015 and 2014 (see below).

In September 2014, Alcoa completed a public offering under its shelf registration statement for $1,250 of 25 million depositary shares, each of which represents a 1/10th interest in a share of Alcoa's 5.375% Class B Mandatory Convertible Preferred Stock, Series 1, par value $1 per share, liquidation preference $500 per share (the "Mandatory Convertible Preferred Stock"). The 25 million depositary shares are equivalent to 2.5 million shares of Mandatory Convertible Preferred Stock. Each depositary share entitles the holder, through the depositary, to a proportional fractional interest in the rights and preferences of a share of Mandatory Convertible Preferred Stock, including conversion, dividend, liquidation, and voting rights, subject to terms of the deposit agreement. Alcoa received $1,213 in net proceeds from the public offering reflecting an underwriting discount. The net proceeds were used, together with the net proceeds of issued debt (see Note K), to finance the cash portion of the acquisition of Firth Rixson (see Note F). The underwriting discount was recorded as a decrease to Additional capital on the accompanying Consolidated Balance Sheet.

The Mandatory Convertible Preferred Stock constitutes a series of Alcoa's Class B Serial Preferred Stock, which ranks senior to Alcoa's common stock and junior to Alcoa's Class A Preferred Stock and existing and future indebtedness. Dividends on the Mandatory Convertible Preferred Stock are cumulative in nature and are paid at the rate of $26.8750 per annum per share, which commenced January 1, 2015 (paid on December 30, 2014). Holders of the Mandatory Convertible Preferred Stock generally have no voting rights.

On the mandatory conversion date, October 1, 2017, all outstanding shares of Mandatory Convertible Preferred Stock will automatically convert into shares of Alcoa's common stock. Based on the Applicable Market Value (as defined in the terms of the Mandatory Convertible Preferred Stock) of Alcoa's common stock on the mandatory conversion date, each share of Mandatory Convertible Preferred Stock will be convertible into not more than 30.9406 shares of common stock and not less than 25.7838 shares of common stock, subject to certain anti-dilution and other adjustments as described in the terms of the Mandatory Convertible Preferred Stock. At any time prior to October 1, 2017, a holder may elect to convert shares of Mandatory Convertible Preferred Stock, in whole or in part (but in no event less than one share of Mandatory Convertible Preferred Stock), at the minimum conversion rate of 25.7838 shares of common stock, subject to certain anti-dilution and other adjustments as described in the terms of the Mandatory Convertible Preferred Stock. Alcoa does not have the right to redeem the Mandatory Convertible Preferred Stock.

If Alcoa undergoes a fundamental change, as defined in the terms of the Mandatory Convertible Preferred Stock, holders may elect to convert their Mandatory Convertible Preferred Stock, in whole or in part (but in no event less than one share of Mandatory Convertible Preferred Stock), into shares of Alcoa's common stock. The per share conversion rate under a fundamental change is not less than 25.2994 shares of common stock and not more than 30.9406 shares of common stock. Holders who elect to convert will also receive any accumulated and unpaid dividends and a Fundamental Change Dividend Make-whole Amount (as defined in the terms of the Mandatory Convertible Preferred Stock) equal to the present value of all remaining dividend payments on the Mandatory Convertible Preferred Stock.

Dividends

PRESENTATION

5.17 For public entities with respect to any dividends, Rule 3-04 of Regulation S-X requires the amount per share and in the aggregate for each class of shares to be stated. This may be stated on the financial statements or within the note disclosures. Further, Rule 4-08 of Regulation S-X requires disclosure of any restrictions that limit the payment of dividends.

PRESENTATION AND DISCLOSURE EXCERPTS

CASH AND SPECIAL DIVIDENDS

5.18 KLA-TENCOR CORPORATION (JUN)

CONSOLIDATED STATEMENTS OF STOCKHOLDERS' EQUITY

(In thousands, except per share amounts)	Common Stock and Capital in Excess of Par Value		Retained Earnings (Accumulated Deficit)	Accumulated Other Comprehensive Income (Loss)	Total Stockholders' Equity
	Shares	Amount			
Balances as of June 30, 2012	166,710	$1,089,480	$ 2,247,258	$(21,143)	$ 3,315,595
Net income	—	—	543,149	—	543,149
Other comprehensive loss	—	—	—	(15,503)	(15,503)
Net issuance under employee stock plans	4,099	96,989	—	—	96,989
Repurchase of common stock	(5,374)	(107,973)	(165,281)	—	(273,254)
Cash dividends declared ($1.60 per share)	—	—	(265,893)	—	(265,893)
Stock-based compensation expense	—	70,084	—	—	70,084
Tax benefit for equity awards	—	10,985	—	—	10,985
Balances as of June 30, 2013	165,435	1,159,565	2,359,233	(36,646)	3,482,152
Net income	—	—	582,755	—	582,755
Other comprehensive income	—	—	—	6,375	6,375
Net issuance under employee stock plans	3,848	60,320	—	—	60,320
Repurchase of common stock	(3,835)	(76,839)	(164,004)	—	(240,843)
Cash dividends declared ($1.80 per share)	—	—	(298,871)	—	(298,871)
Stock-based compensation expense	—	60,940	—	—	60,940
Tax benefit for equity awards	—	16,518	—	—	16,518
Balances as of June 30, 2014	165,448	1,220,504	2,479,113	(30,271)	3,669,346
Net income	—	—	366,158	—	366,158
Other comprehensive loss	—	—	—	(10,302)	(10,302)
Net issuance under employee stock plans	1,658	16,186	—	—	16,186
Repurchase of common stock	(9,255)	(26,891)	(581,965)	—	(608,856)
Cash dividends declared ($18.50 per share including a special cash dividend of $16.50 per share declared during the three months ended December 31, 2014)	—	(807,391)	(2,275,668)	—	(3,083,059)
Stock-based compensation expense	—	55,302	—	—	55,302
Tax benefit for equity awards	—	16,664	—	—	16,664
Balances as of June 30, 2015	157,851	$ 474,374	$ (12,362)	$(40,573)	$ 421,439

NOTES TO CONSOLIDATED FINANCIAL STATEMENTS (in part)

Note 7—Debt (in part)

Debt Issuance—Senior Notes: (in part)

In November 2014, the Company issued $2.50 billion aggregate principal amount of senior, unsecured long-term notes (collectively referred to as "Senior Notes"). The Company issued the Senior Notes as part of the leveraged recapitalization plan under which the proceeds from the Senior Notes in conjunction with the proceeds from the term loans (described below) and cash on hand were used (x) to fund a special cash dividend of $16.50 per share, aggregating to approximately $2.76 billion, (y) to redeem $750 million of 2018 Senior Notes, including associated redemption premiums, accrued interest and other fees and expenses and (z) for other general corporate purposes, including repurchases of shares pursuant to the Company's stock repurchase program. The interest rate specified for each series of the Senior Notes will be subject to adjustments from time to time if Moody's Investor Service, Inc. ("Moody's") or Standard & Poor's Ratings Services ("S&P") or, under certain circumstances, a substitute rating agency selected by us as a replacement for Moody's or S&P, as the case may be (a "Substitute Rating Agency"), downgrades (or subsequently upgrades) its rating assigned to the respective series of Senior Notes such that the adjusted rating is below investment grade. If the adjusted rating of any series of Senior Notes from Moody's (or, if applicable, any Substitute Rating Agency) is decreased to Ba1, Ba2, Ba3 or B1 or below, the stated interest rate on such series of Senior Notes as noted above will increase by 25 bps, 50 bps, 75 bps or 100 bps, respectively ("bps" refers to Basis Points and 1% is equal to 100 bps). If the rating of any series of Senior Notes from S&P (or, if applicable, any Substitute Rating Agency) with respect to such series of Senior Notes is decreased to BB +, BB, BB- or B + or below, the stated interest rate on such series of Senior Notes as noted above will increase by 25 bps, 50 bps, 75 bps or 100 bps, respectively. The interest rates on any series of Senior Notes will permanently cease to be subject to any adjustment (notwithstanding any subsequent decrease in the ratings by any of Moody's, S&P and, if applicable, any Substitute Rating Agency) if such series of Senior Notes becomes rated "Baa1" (or its equivalent) or higher by Moody's (or, if applicable, any Substitute Rating Agency) and "BBB +" (or its equivalent) or higher by S&P (or, if applicable, any Substitute Rating Agency), or one of those ratings if rated by only one of Moody's, S&P and, if applicable, any Substitute Rating Agency, in each case with a stable or positive outlook. In October 2014, the Company entered into a series of forward contracts to lock the 10-year treasury rate ("benchmark rate") on a portion of the Senior Notes with a notional amount of $1.00 billion in aggregate.

Note 8—Equity and Long-Term Incentive Compensation Plans (in part)

Equity Incentive Plans—General Information (in part)

The fair value of stock-based awards is measured at the grant date and is recognized as an expense over the employee's requisite service period. For restricted stock units granted without "dividend equivalent" rights, fair value is calculated using the closing price of the Company's common stock on the grant date, adjusted to exclude the present value of dividends which are not accrued on those restricted stock units. In November 2013, the Company's stockholders approved amendments to the 2004 Plan that included, among other things, giving the plan administrator the ability to grant "dividend equivalent" rights in connection with awards of restricted stock units, performance shares, performance units and deferred stock units before they are fully vested as discussed above. The fair value for restricted stock units granted with "dividend equivalent" rights is determined using the closing price of the Company's common stock on the grant date. As of June 30, 2015, the Company accrued $42.0 million of dividends payable, substantially all of which is related to the special cash dividend for the unvested restricted stock units outstanding as of the dividend record date as well as restricted stock units granted with dividend equivalent rights during the fiscal year ended June 30, 2015, which entitle the holders of such equity awards to the same dividend value per share as holders of common stock subject to meeting the vesting requirements of the underlying equity awards. The fair value for purchase rights under the Company's Employee Stock Purchase Plan is determined using a Black-Scholes valuation model.

Quarterly Cash Dividends

On May 7, 2015, the Company's Board of Directors declared a regular quarterly cash dividend of $0.50 per share on the outstanding shares of the Company's common stock, which was paid on June 1, 2015 to the stockholders of record as of the close of business on May 18, 2015. Under the authoritative guidance, a dividend when declared is recognized as a reduction of retained earnings, to the extent available, with any excess recognized as a reduction of additional paid-in-capital. The total amount of regular quarterly cash dividends paid by the Company during the fiscal years ended June 30, 2015 and 2014 was $324.8 million and $298.9 million, respectively. The amount of accrued dividends for quarterly cash dividends for unvested restricted stock units with dividend equivalent rights was $0.9 million as of June 30, 2015. The Company had no accrued dividends for the quarterly cash dividends in the fiscal year ended June 30, 2014.

On July 14, 2015, the Company announced that its Board of Directors had authorized a further increase in the level of the Company's quarterly cash dividend from $0.50 to $0.52 per share. Refer to Note 19, "Subsequent Events" for additional information on dividend increase announced subsequent to June 30, 2015.

Special Cash Dividend

On November 19, 2014, the Company's Board of Directors declared a special cash dividend of $16.50 per share, which was paid on December 9, 2014 to the stockholders of record as of the close of business on December 1, 2014. Additionally, in connection with the special cash dividend, the Company's Board of Directors and the Compensation Committee of the Board of Directors approved a proportionate and equitable adjustment to outstanding equity awards (restricted stock units and stock options), as required under the 2004 Plan, subject to the vesting requirements of the underlying awards. As the adjustment was required by the 2004 Plan, the adjustment to the outstanding awards did not result in any incremental compensation expense due to modification of such awards, under the authoritative guidance. Under the authoritative guidance, the dividend when declared is recognized as a reduction of retained earnings, to the extent available, with any excess recognized as a reduction of additional paid-in-capital. The special cash dividend reduced the retained earnings by $2.1 billion as of the special cash dividend declaration date, reducing the retained earnings amount to zero and the excess amount of the special cash dividend of $646.5 million was charged against additional paid-in capital. The declaration and payment of the special cash dividend are part of the Company's leveraged recapitalization transaction under which the special cash dividend was financed through a combination of existing cash and proceeds from the debt financing disclosed in Note 7, "Debt" that was completed during the three months ended December 31, 2014. The total amount of the special cash dividend accrued by the Company during the three months ended December 31, 2014 was approximately $2.76 billion, substantially all of which was paid out during the three months ended December 31, 2014. As of June 30, 2015, the Company accrued a total of $41.1 million of dividends payable for the special cash dividend with respect to outstanding unvested restricted stock units, which will be paid when such underlying unvested restricted stock units vest. Other than the special cash dividend declared during the three months ended December 31, 2014, the Company historically has not declared any special cash dividends.

Note 19—Subsequent Events

On July 14, 2015, the Company announced that its Board of Directors had authorized a further increase in the level of the Company's quarterly cash dividend from $0.50 to $0.52 per share. On August 6, 2015, the Company announced that its Board of Directors had declared a quarterly cash dividend of $0.52 per share to be paid on September 1, 2015 to stockholders of record as of the close of business on August 17, 2015.

DIVIDENDS ON COMMON AND PREFERRED EQUITY

5.19 THE GOLDMAN SACHS GROUP, INC. (DEC)
CONSOLIDATED STATEMENTS OF CHANGES IN SHAREHOLDERS' EQUITY

	Year Ended December		
$ in millions	2015	2014	2013
Preferred Stock			
Balance, beginning of year	$ 9,200	$ 7,200	$ 6,200
Issued	2,000	2,000	1,000
Balance, end of year	11,200	9,200	7,200
Common Stock			
Balance, beginning of year	9	8	8
Issued	—	1	—
Balance, end of year	9	9	8
Share-based Awards			
Balance, beginning of year	3,766	3,839	3,298
Issuance and amortization of share-based awards	2,308	2,079	2,017
Delivery of common stock underlying share-based awards	(1,742)	(1,725)	(1,378)
Forfeiture of share-based awards	(72)	(92)	(79)
Exercise of share-based awards	(109)	(335)	(19)
Balance, end of year	4,151	3,766	3,839
Additional Paid-in Capital			
Balance, beginning of year	50,049	48,998	48,030
Delivery of common stock underlying share-based awards	2,092	2,206	1,483
Cancellation of share-based awards in satisfaction of withholding tax requirements	(1,198)	(1,922)	(599)
Preferred stock issuance costs	(7)	(20)	(9)
Excess net tax benefit related to share-based awards	406	788	94
Cash settlement of share-based awards	(2)	(1)	(1)
Balance, end of year	51,340	50,049	48,998
Retained Earnings			
Balance, beginning of year	78,984	71,961	65,223
Net earnings	6,083	8,477	8,040
Dividends and dividend equivalents declared on common stock and share-based awards	(1,166)	(1,054)	(988)
Dividends declared on preferred stock	(515)	(400)	(314)
Balance, end of year	83,386	78,984	71,961
Accumulated Other Comprehensive Loss			
Balance, beginning of year	(743)	(524)	(193)
Other comprehensive income/(loss)	25	(219)	(331)
Balance, end of year	(718)	(743)	(524)
Stock Held in Treasury, at Cost			
Balance, beginning of year	(58,468)	(53,015)	(46,850)
Repurchased	(4,195)	(5,469)	(6,175)
Reissued	32	49	40
Other	(9)	(33)	(30)
Balance, end of year	(62,640)	(58,468)	(53,015)
Total shareholders' equity	$ 86,728	$ 82,797	$ 78,467

Note 19. Shareholders' Equity (in part)

Common Equity (in part)

Dividends declared per common share were $2.55 in 2015, $2.25 in 2014 and $2.05 in 2013. On January 19, 2016, Group Inc. declared a dividend of $0.65 per common share to be paid on March 30, 2016 to common shareholders of record on March 2, 2016.

Preferred Equity

The tables below present details about the perpetual preferred stock issued and outstanding as of December 2015.

Series	Shares Authorized	Shares Issued	Shares Outstanding	Depositary Shares Per Share
A	50,000	30,000	29,999	1,000
B	50,000	32,000	32,000	1,000
C	25,000	8,000	8,000	1,000
D	60,000	54,000	53,999	1,000
E	17,500	17,500	17,500	N/A
F	5,000	5,000	5,000	N/A
I	34,500	34,000	34,000	1,000
J	46,000	40,000	40,000	1,000
K	32,200	28,000	28,000	1,000
L	52,000	52,000	52,000	25
M[1]	80,000	80,000	80,000	25
Total	452,200	380,500	380,498	

[1] In April 2015, Group Inc. issued 80,000 shares of Series M perpetual 5.375% Fixed-to-Floating Rate Non-Cumulative Preferred Stock (Series M Preferred Stock).

Series	Liquidation Preference	Redemption Price Per Share	Redemption Value ($ in millions)
A	$ 25,000	$25,000 plus declared and unpaid dividends	$ 750
B	25,000	$25,000 plus declared and unpaid dividends	800
C	25,000	$25,000 plus declared and unpaid dividends	200
D	25,000	$25,000 plus declared and unpaid dividends	1,350
E	100,000	$100,000 plus declared and unpaid dividends	1,750
F	100,000	$100,000 plus declared and unpaid dividends	500
I	25,000	$25,000 plus accrued and unpaid dividends	850
J	25,000	$25,000 plus accrued and unpaid dividends	1,000
K	25,000	$25,000 plus accrued and unpaid dividends	700
L	25,000	$25,000 plus accrued and unpaid dividends	1,300
M	25,000	$25,000 plus accrued and unpaid dividends	2,000
Total			$11,200

In the tables above:
- Each share of non-cumulative Series A, Series B, Series C and Series D Preferred Stock issued and outstanding is redeemable at the firm's option.
- Each share of non-cumulative Series E and Series F Preferred Stock issued and outstanding is redeemable at the firm's option, subject to certain covenant restrictions governing the firm's ability to redeem or purchase the preferred stock without issuing common stock or other instruments with equity-like characteristics. See Note 16 for information about the replacement capital covenants applicable to the Series E and Series F Preferred Stock.
- Each share of non-cumulative Series I Preferred Stock issued and outstanding is redeemable at the firm's option beginning November 10, 2017.
- Each share of non-cumulative Series J Preferred Stock issued and outstanding is redeemable at the firm's option beginning May 10, 2023.
- Each share of non-cumulative Series K Preferred Stock issued and outstanding is redeemable at the firm's option beginning May 10, 2024.
- Each share of non-cumulative Series L Preferred Stock issued and outstanding is redeemable at the firm's option beginning May 10, 2019.
- Each share of non-cumulative Series M Preferred Stock issued and outstanding is redeemable at the firm's option beginning May 10, 2020.

- All shares of preferred stock have a par value of $0.01 per share and, where applicable, each share of preferred stock is represented by the specified number of depositary shares.

Prior to redeeming preferred stock, the firm must receive confirmation that the Federal Reserve Board does not object to such capital actions. All series of preferred stock are pari passu and have a preference over the firm's common stock on liquidation. Dividends on each series of preferred stock, excluding Series L and Series M Preferred Stock, if declared, are payable quarterly in arrears. Dividends on Series L and Series M Preferred Stock, if declared, are payable semi-annually in arrears from the issuance date to, but excluding, May 10, 2019 and May 10, 2020, respectively, and quarterly thereafter. The firm's ability to declare or pay dividends on, or purchase, redeem or otherwise acquire, its common stock is subject to certain restrictions in the event that the firm fails to pay or set aside full dividends on the preferred stock for the latest completed dividend period.

The table below presents the dividend rates of the firm's perpetual preferred stock as of December 2015.

Series	Dividend Rate
A	3 month LIBOR + 0.75%, with floor of 3.75% per annum
B	6.20% per annum
C	3 month LIBOR + 0.75%, with floor of 4.00% per annum
D	3 month LIBOR + 0.67%, with floor of 4.00% per annum
E	3 month LIBOR + 0.77%, with floor of 4.00% per annum
F	3 month LIBOR + 0.77%, with floor of 4.00% per annum
I	5.95% per annum
J	5.50% per annum to, but excluding, May 10, 2023; 3 month LIBOR + 3.64% per annum thereafter
K	6.375% per annum to, but excluding, May 10, 2024; 3 month LIBOR + 3.55% per annum thereafter
L	5.70% per annum to, but excluding, May 10, 2019; 3 month LIBOR + 3.884% per annum thereafter
M	5.375% per annum to, but excluding, May 10, 2020; 3 month LIBOR + 3.922% per annum thereafter

The table below presents preferred dividends declared on the firm's preferred stock.

	Year Ended December					
	2015		2014		2013	
Series	Per Share	$ in Millions	Per Share	$ in Millions	Per Share	$ in Millions
A	$ 950.52	$ 28	$ 945.32	$ 28	$ 947.92	$ 28
B	1,550.00	50	1,550.00	50	1,550.00	50
C	1,013.90	8	1,008.34	8	1,011.11	8
D	1,013.90	54	1,008.34	54	1,011.11	54
E	4,055.55	71	4,044.44	71	4,044.44	71
F	4,055.55	20	4,044.44	20	4,044.44	20
I	1,487.52	51	1,487.52	51	1,553.63	53
J	1,375.00	55	1,375.00	55	744.79	30
K	1,593.76	45	850.00	24	—	—
L	1,425.00	74	760.00	39	—	—
M	735.33	59	—	—	—	—
Total		$515		$400		$314

On January 8, 2016, Group Inc. declared dividends of $239.58, $387.50, $255.56, $255.56, $371.88, $343.75 and $398.44 per share of Series A Preferred Stock, Series B Preferred Stock, Series C Preferred Stock, Series D Preferred Stock, Series I Preferred Stock, Series J Preferred Stock and Series K Preferred Stock, respectively, to be paid on February 10, 2016 to preferred shareholders of record on January 26, 2016. In addition, the firm declared dividends of $1,011.11 per each share of Series E Preferred Stock and Series F Preferred Stock, to be paid on March 1, 2016 to preferred shareholders of record on February 15, 2016.

Stock Splits

RECOGNITION AND MEASUREMENT

5.20 The FASB ASC glossary defines a *stock split* as an issuance by a corporation of its own common shares to its common shareholders without consideration and under conditions indicating that such action is prompted mainly by a desire to increase the number of outstanding shares for the purpose of effecting a reduction in their unit market price and, thereby, of obtaining wider distribution and improved marketability of the shares. It is also sometimes called a stock split-up.

5.21 FASB ASC 505-20 addresses the accounting for stock splits, as well as stock dividends, and provides guidance on determining whether a stock dividend or stock split should be accounted for according to its form or whether it should be accounted for differently.

PRESENTATION AND DISCLOSURE EXCERPTS

STOCK SPLIT

5.22 CF INDUSTRIES HOLDINGS, INC. (DEC)
CONSOLIDATED STATEMENTS OF OPERATIONS

(In millions, except per share amounts)	Year Ended December 31,		
	2015	2014	2013
Net sales	$4,308.3	$4,743.2	$5,474.7
Cost of sales	2,761.2	2,964.7	2,954.5
Gross margin	1,547.1	1,778.5	2,520.2
Selling, general and administrative expenses	169.8	151.9	166.0
Transaction costs	56.9	—	—
Other operating—net	92.3	53.3	(15.8)
Total other operating costs and expenses	319.0	205.2	150.2
Gain on sale of phosphate business	—	750.1	—
Equity in earnings of operating affiliates	(35.0)	43.1	41.7
Operating earnings	1,193.1	2,366.5	2,411.7
Interest expense	133.2	178.2	152.2
Interest income	(1.6)	(0.9)	(4.7)
Other non-operating—net	3.9	1.9	54.5
Earnings before income taxes and equity in earnings of non-operating affiliates	1,057.6	2,187.3	2,209.7
Income tax provision	395.8	773.0	686.5
Equity in earnings of non-operating affiliates—net of taxes	72.3	22.5	9.6
Net earnings	734.1	1,436.8	1,532.8
Less: Net earnings attributable to noncontrolling interest	34.2	46.5	68.2
Net earnings attributable to common stockholders	$ 699.9	$1,390.3	$1,464.6
Net earnings per share attributable to common stockholders[1]:			
Basic	$ 2.97	$ 5.43	$ 4.97
Diluted	$ 2.96	$ 5.42	$ 4.95
Weighted-average common shares outstanding[1]:			
Basic	235.3	255.9	294.4
Diluted	236.1	256.7	296.0

[1] Share and per share amounts have been retroactively restated for all prior periods presented to reflect the five -for-one split of the Company's common stock effected in the form of a stock dividend that was distributed on June 17, 2015.

CONSOLIDATED BALANCE SHEETS

(In millions, except share and per share amounts)	December 31,	
	2015	2014
Assets		
Current assets:		
Cash and cash equivalents	$ 286.0	$ 1,996.6
Restricted cash	22.8	86.1
Accounts receivable—net	267.2	191.5
Inventories	321.2	202.9
Prepaid income taxes	184.6	34.8
Other current assets	45.3	18.6
Total current assets	1,127.1	2,530.5
Property, plant and equipment—net	8,539.0	5,525.8
Investments in and advances to affiliates	297.8	861.5
Goodwill	2,390.1	2,092.8
Other assets	384.9	243.6
Total assets	$12,738.9	$11,254.2
Liabilities and Equity		
Current liabilities:		
Accounts payable and accrued expenses	$ 917.7	$ 589.9
Income taxes payable	5.5	16.0
Customer advances	161.5	325.4
Other current liabilities	130.5	48.4
Total current liabilities	1,215.2	979.7
Long-term debt	5,592.7	4,592.5
Deferred income taxes	916.2	734.6
Other liabilities	627.6	374.9

(continued)

(In millions, except share and per share amounts)	December 31, 2015	December 31, 2014
Equity:		
Stockholders' equity:		
Preferred stock—$0.01 par value, 50,000,000 shares authorized	—	—
Common stock—$0.01 par value, 500,000,000 shares authorized, 2015—235,493,395 shares issued and 2014—245,904,140 shares issued[1]	2.4	2.5
Paid-in capital[1]	1,377.4	1,413.9
Retained earnings	3,057.9	3,175.3
Treasury stock—at cost, 2015—2,411,839 shares and 2014—4,231,090 shares[1]	(152.7)	(222.2)
Accumulated other comprehensive loss	(249.8)	(159.8)
Total stockholders' equity	4,035.2	4,209.7
Noncontrolling interest	352.0	362.8
Total equity	4,387.2	4,572.5
Total liabilities and equity	$12,738.9	$11,254.2

[1] December 31, 2014 amounts have been retroactively restated to reflect the five-for-one split of the Company's common stock effected in the form of a stock dividend that was distributed on June 17, 2015.

CONSOLIDATED STATEMENTS OF EQUITY

(In millions)	$0.01 Par Value Common Stock[1]	Treasury Stock[1]	Paid-In Capital[1]	Retained Earnings	Accumulated Other Comprehensive Income (Loss)	Total Stockholders' Equity	Non-controlling Interest	Total Equity
Balance as of December 31, 2012	$ 3.1	$ (2.3)	$2,489.9	$ 3,461.1	$ (49.6)	$ 5,902.2	$380.0	$ 6,282.2
Net earnings	—	—	—	1,464.6	—	1,464.6	68.2	1,532.8
Other comprehensive income:								
Foreign currency translation adjustment—net of taxes	—	—	—	—	(29.5)	(29.5)	(0.7)	(30.2)
Unrealized net gain on hedging derivatives—net of taxes	—	—	—	—	1.9	1.9	—	1.9
Unrealized net gain on securities—net of taxes	—	—	—	—	1.0	1.0	—	1.0
Defined benefit plans—net of taxes	—	—	—	—	33.6	33.6	—	33.6
Comprehensive income						1,471.6	67.5	1,539.1
Acquisitions of noncontrolling interests in Canadian Fertilizers Limited (CFL)	—	—	(752.5)	—	—	(752.5)	(16.8)	(769.3)
Purchases of treasury stock	—	(1,449.3)	—	—	—	(1,449.3)	—	(1,449.3)
Retirement of treasury stock	(0.3)	1,247.8	(180.1)	(1,067.4)	—	—	—	—
Acquisition of treasury stock under employee stock plans	—	(3.2)	—	—	—	(3.2)	—	(3.2)
Issuance of $0.01 par value common stock under employee stock plans	—	5.2	8.7	(3.6)	—	10.3	—	10.3
Stock-based compensation expense	—	—	12.6	—	—	12.6	—	12.6
Excess tax benefit from stock-based compensation	—	—	13.5	—	—	13.5	—	13.5
Cash dividends ($0.44 per share)[1]	—	—	—	(129.1)	—	(129.1)	—	(129.1)
Distributions declared to noncontrolling interest	—	—	—	—	—	—	(68.5)	(68.5)
Effect of exchange rates changes	—	—	—	—	—	—	0.1	0.1
Balance as of December 31, 2013	$ 2.8	$ (201.8)	$1,592.1	$ 3,725.6	$ (42.6)	$ 5,076.1	$362.3	$ 5,438.4
Net earnings	—	—	—	1,390.3	—	1,390.3	46.5	1,436.8
Other comprehensive income:								
Foreign currency translation adjustment—net of taxes	—	—	—	—	(72.4)	(72.4)	—	(72.4)
Unrealized net loss on hedging derivatives—net of taxes	—	—	—	—	(1.8)	(1.8)	—	(1.8)
Unrealized net gain on securities—net of taxes	—	—	—	—	0.2	0.2	—	0.2
Defined benefit plans—net of taxes	—	—	—	—	(43.2)	(43.2)	—	(43.2)
Comprehensive income						1,273.1	46.5	1,319.6
Purchases of treasury stock	—	(1,923.7)	—	—	—	(1,923.7)	—	(1,923.7)
Retirement of treasury stock	(0.3)	1,905.5	(220.3)	(1,684.9)	—	—	—	—
Acquisition of treasury stock under employee stock plans	—	(3.1)	—	—	—	(3.1)	—	(3.1)
Issuance of $0.01 par value common stock under employee stock plans	—	0.9	16.7	—	—	17.6	—	17.6
Stock-based compensation expense	—	—	16.7	—	—	16.7	—	16.7
Excess tax benefit from stock-based compensation	—	—	8.7	—	—	8.7	—	8.7
Cash dividends ($1.00 per share)[1]	—	—	—	(255.7)	—	(255.7)	—	(255.7)
Distributions declared to noncontrolling interest	—	—	—	—	—	—	(46.0)	(46.0)
Balance as of December 31, 2014	$ 2.5	$ (222.2)	$1,413.9	$ 3,175.3	$(159.8)	$ 4,209.7	$362.8	$ 4,572.5

(continued)

(In millions)	$0.01 Par Value Common Stock[1]	Treasury Stock[1]	Paid-In Capital[1]	Retained Earnings	Accumulated Other Comprehensive Income (Loss)	Total Stockholders' Equity	Non-controlling Interest	Total Equity
					Common Stockholders			
Net earnings	—	—	—	699.9	—	699.9	34.2	734.1
Other comprehensive income:								
Foreign currency translation adjustment—net of taxes	—	—	—	—	(157.3)	(157.3)	—	(157.3)
Unrealized net gain on securities—net of taxes	—	—	—	—	0.2	0.2	—	0.2
Defined benefit plans—net of taxes	—	—	—	—	67.1	67.1	—	67.1
Comprehensive income						609.9	34.2	644.1
Purchases of treasury stock	—	(527.2)	—	—	—	(527.2)	—	(527.2)
Retirement of treasury stock	(0.1)	597.1	(62.0)	(535.0)	—	—	—	—
Acquisition of treasury stock under employee stock plans	—	(1.3)	—	—	—	(1.3)	—	(1.3)
Issuance of $0.01 par value common stock under employee stock plans	—	0.9	7.5	—	—	8.4	—	8.4
Stock-based compensation expense	—	—	16.5	—	—	16.5	—	16.5
Excess tax benefit from stock-based compensation	—	—	1.5	—	—	1.5	—	1.5
Cash dividends ($1.20 per share)	—	—	—	(282.3)	—	(282.3)	—	(282.3)
Distributions declared to noncontrolling interest	—	—	—	—	—	—	(45.0)	(45.0)
Balance as of December 31, 2015	$ 2.4	$ (152.7)	$1,377.4	$ 3,057.9	$(249.8)	$ 4,035.2	$352.0	$ 4,387.2

[1] Amounts have been retroactively restated for all prior periods presented to reflect the five-for-one split of the Company's common stock effected in the form of a stock dividend that was distributed on June 17, 2015.

NOTES TO CONSOLIDATED FINANCIAL STATEMENTS (in part)

1. Background and Basis of Presentation (in part)

Reclassifications and Changes in Presentation (in part)

On May 15, 2015, we announced that our Board of Directors declared a five -for-one split of our common stock to be effected in the form of a stock dividend. On June 17, 2015, stockholders of record as of the close of business on June 1, 2015 (Record Date) received four additional shares of common stock for each share of common stock held on the Record Date. Shares reserved under the Company's equity and incentive plans were adjusted to reflect the stock split. All share and per share data has been retroactively restated to reflect the stock split, except for the number of authorized shares of common stock. Since the par value of the common stock remained at $0.01 per share, the recorded value for common stock has been retroactively restated to reflect the par value of total outstanding shares with a corresponding decrease to paid-in capital.

19. Stock-Based Compensation (in part)

Five-for-One Stock Split

On June 17, 2015, stockholders of record as of the close of business on June 1, 2015 (Record Date) received four additional shares of common stock for each share of common stock held on the Record Date in the form of a stock dividend (five-for-one stock split). Share and per share amounts have been retroactively restated to reflect the five -for-one stock split. Shares reserved under the Company's equity and incentive plans were adjusted to reflect the five-for-one stock split.

REVERSE STOCK SPLIT

5.23 PEABODY ENERGY CORPORATION (DEC)
NOTES TO CONSOLIDATED FINANCIAL STATEMENTS (in part)

(1) Summary of Significant Accounting Policies (in part)

Basis of Presentation (in part)

The consolidated financial statements include the accounts of Peabody Energy Corporation (the Company) and its affiliates. Interests in subsidiaries controlled by the Company are consolidated with any outside shareholder interests reflected as noncontrolling interests, except when the Company has an undivided interest in an unincorporated joint venture. In those cases, the Company includes its proportionate share in the assets, liabilities, revenues and expenses of the jointly controlled entities within each applicable line item of the consolidated financial statements. All intercompany transactions, profits and balances have been eliminated in consolidation. Certain amounts from prior years have been reclassified to conform with the 2015 presentation.

Pursuant to the authorization provided at a special meeting of the Company's stockholders held on September 16, 2015, the Company completed a 1-for-15 reverse stock split of the shares of the Company's common stock on September 30, 2015 (the Reverse Stock Split). As a result of the Reverse Stock Split, every 15 shares of issued and outstanding common stock were combined into one issued and outstanding share of Common Stock, without any change in the par value per share. No fractional shares were issued as a result of the Reverse Stock Split and any fractional shares that would otherwise have resulted from the Reverse Stock Split were paid in cash. The Reverse Stock Split reduced the number of shares of common stock outstanding from approximately 278 million shares to approximately 19 million shares. The number of authorized shares of common stock was also decreased from 800 million shares to 53.3 million shares. The Company's common stock began trading on a reverse stock split-adjusted basis on the New York Stock Exchange on October 1, 2015. All share and per share data included in this report has been retroactively restated to reflect the Reverse Stock Split. Since the par value of the common stock remained at $0.01 per share, the value for "Common stock" recorded to the Company's condensed consolidated balance sheets has been retroactively reduced to reflect the par value of restated outstanding shares, with a corresponding increase to "Additional paid-in capital."

(17) Stockholders' Equity (in part)

Common Stock

Pursuant to the authorization provided at a special meeting of the Company's stockholders held on September 16, 2015, the Company completed a 1-for-15 reverse stock split of the shares of the Company's common stock on September 30, 2015 (the Reverse Stock Split). Refer to Note 1. "Summary of Significant Accounting Policies" for additional details surrounding the Reverse Stock Split. As a result of the Reverse Stock Split, the Company has 53.3 million authorized shares of $0.01 par value common stock. Holders of common stock are entitled to one vote per share on all matters to be voted upon by the stockholders. The holders of common stock do not have cumulative voting rights in the election of directors. Holders of common stock are entitled to receive ratably dividends if, as and when dividends are declared from time to time by the Company's Board of Directors out of funds legally available for that purpose, after payment of dividends required to be paid on outstanding preferred stock or series common stock, as described below. Upon liquidation, dissolution or winding up, any business combination or a sale or disposition of all or substantially all of the assets, the holders of common stock are entitled to receive ratably the assets available for distribution to the stockholders after payment of liabilities and accrued but unpaid dividends and liquidation preferences on any outstanding preferred stock or series common stock. The common stock has no preemptive or conversion rights and is not subject to further calls or assessment by us. There are no redemption or sinking fund provisions applicable to the common stock.

The following table summarizes common stock activity from January 1, 2013 to December 31, 2015:

(In millions)	2015	2014	2013
Shares outstanding at the beginning of the year	18.1	18.0	17.9
Stock grants to employees	0.2	0.1	0.1
Performance share contribution 401 k	0.2	—	—
Shares outstanding at the end of the year	18.5	18.1	18.0

(21) Earnings Per Share (EPS)

Basic and diluted EPS are computed using the two-class method, which is an earnings allocation that determines EPS for each class of common stock and participating securities according to dividends declared and participation rights in undistributed earnings. The Company's restricted stock awards are considered participating securities because holders are entitled to receive non-forfeitable dividends during the vesting term. Diluted EPS includes securities that could potentially dilute basic EPS during a reporting period, for which the Company includes the Debentures and share-based compensation awards. Dilutive securities are not included in the computation of loss per share when a company reports a net loss from continuing operations as the impact would be anti-dilutive.

For all but the performance units, the potentially dilutive impact of the Company's share-based compensation awards is determined using the treasury stock method. Under the treasury stock method, awards are treated as if they had been exercised with any proceeds used to repurchase common stock at the average market price during the period. Any incremental difference between the assumed number of shares issued and purchased is included in the diluted share computation. For the Company's performance units, their contingent features result in an assessment for any potentially dilutive common stock by using the end of the reporting period as if it were the end of the contingency period for all units granted. For further discussion of the Company's share-based compensation awards, see Note 18. "Share-Based Compensation."

A conversion of the Debentures may result in payment for any conversion value in excess of the principal amount of the Debentures in the Company's common stock. For diluted EPS purposes, potential common stock is calculated based on whether the market price of the Company's common stock at the end of each reporting period is in excess of the conversion price of the Debentures. For a full discussion of the conditions under which the Debentures may be converted, the conversion rate to common stock and the conversion price, see Note 12. "Long-term Debt." The effect of the Debentures was excluded from the calculation of diluted EPS for all periods presented herein because to do so would have been anti-dilutive for those periods.

The computation of diluted EPS also excluded aggregate share-based compensation awards of approximately 0.6 million for the year ended December 31, 2015 and 0.2 million for the years ended December 31, 2014 and 2013, respectively, because to do so would have been anti-dilutive for those periods. Because the potential dilutive impact of such share-based compensation awards is calculated under the treasury stock method, anti-dilution generally occurs when the exercise prices or unrecognized compensation cost per share of such awards are higher than the Company's average stock price during the applicable period.

The following illustrates the earnings allocation method utilized in the calculation of basic and diluted EPS. The number of shares and per share amounts for all period presented below have been retroactively restated to reflect the Reverse Stock Split discussed in Note 1. "Summary of Significant Accounting Policies.":

	Year Ended December 31,		
(In millions, except per share amounts)	2015	2014	2013
EPS numerator:			
Loss from continuing operations, net of income taxes	$(1,813.9)	$(749.1)	$(286.0)
Less: Net income attributable to noncontrolling interests	7.1	9.7	12.3
Loss from continuing operations attributable to common stockholders, before allocation of earnings to participating securities	(1,821.0)	(758.8)	(298.3)
Less: Earnings allocated to participating securities	—	1.0	0.8
Loss from continuing operations attributable to common stockholders, after allocation of earnings to participating securities	(1,821.0)	(759.8)	(299.1)
Loss from discontinued operations attributable to common stockholders, after allocation of earnings to participating securities	(175.0)	(28.2)	(226.6)
Net loss attributable to common stockholders, after earnings allocated to participating securities	$(1,996.0)	$(788.0)	$(525.7)
EPS denominator:			
Weighted average shares outstanding — basic and diluted	18.1	17.9	17.8
Basic and diluted EPS attributable to common stockholders:			
Loss from continuing operations	$ (100.34)	$(42.52)	$(16.80)
Loss from discontinued operations	(9.64)	(1.57)	(12.73)
Net loss attributable to common stockholders	$ (109.98)	$(44.09)	$(29.53)

Changes to Retained Earnings

RECOGNITION AND MEASUREMENT

5.24 The retained earnings account is affected by direct charges and credits. Examples of direct charges to retained earnings are net loss for the year, losses on treasury stock transactions, and cash or stock dividends; an example of a direct credit to retained earnings is net income for the year.

PRESENTATION

5.25 In addition to direct charges and credits, the retained earnings account is also affected by opening balance adjustments. Reasons for which the opening balance of retained earnings is properly restated include certain changes in accounting principles, changes in the reporting entity, and corrections of an error in previously issued financial statements.

5.26 FASB ASC 250-10-05-2 requires, unless impracticable or otherwise specified by applicable authoritative guidance, retrospective application to prior periods' financial statements of a change in accounting principle. Retrospective *application* is the application of a different accounting principle to prior accounting periods as if that principle had always been used. More specifically, FASB ASC 250-10-45-5 explains that retrospective application involves the following:

- The cumulative effect of the change on periods prior to those presented should be reflected in the carrying amounts of assets and liabilities as of the beginning of the first period presented.
- An offsetting adjustment, if any, shall be made to the opening balance of retained earnings or other appropriate components of equity or net assets in the statement of financial position for that period.
- Financial statements for each individual prior period presented should be adjusted to reflect the period-specific effects of applying the new accounting principle.

5.27 FASB ASC 250-10-45-23 also requires any accounting error in the financial statements of a prior period discovered after the financial statements are issued or are available to be issued to be reported as an error correction by restating the prior period financial statements. Restatement involves similar requirements as those specified for retrospective application of a change in accounting principle.

5.28 SEC Staff Accounting Bulletin (SAB) No. 108 provides guidance on the consideration of the effects of prior year misstatements in quantifying current year misstatements for the purpose of assessing materiality. SAB No. 108 requires that registrant entities determine the quantitative effect of a financial statement misstatement by using both an income statement ("rollover") and a balance sheet ("iron curtain") approach and evaluate whether, under either approach, the error is material after considering all relevant quantitative and qualitative factors.

PRESENTATION AND DISCLOSURE EXCERPTS

CHANGE IN ACCOUNTING PRINCIPLE

5.29 JOY GLOBAL INC. (OCT)
CONSOLIDATED STATEMENTS OF SHAREHOLDERS' EQUITY

(In thousands, except per share data)

	Common Stock Amount	Capital in Excess of Par Value	Retained Earnings	Treasury Stock	Accumulated Other Comprehensive (Loss) Income	Total
Balance as of October 26, 2012, as adjusted	$129,800	$1,140,680	$ 2,388,440	$(1,116,623)	$ 48,296	$ 2,590,593
Net income, as adjusted	—	—	536,534	—	—	536,534
Change in unrecognized prior service costs on pension and other postretirement obligations, net of taxes, as adjusted	—	—	—	—	793	793
Derivative instrument fair market value adjustment, net of taxes	—	—	—	—	149	149
Foreign currency translation adjustment	—	—	—	—	(19,210)	(19,210)
Treasury stock purchased	—	—	—	(214,106)	—	(214,106)
Share-based compensation expense	—	29,006	—	—	—	29,006
Dividends paid ($0.70 per share)	—	910	(75,235)	—	—	(74,325)
Issuance of restricted stock units and performance shares	178	(3,900)	—	—	—	(3,722)
Exercise of stock options	160	4,110	—	—	—	4,270
Shares issued under employee stock purchase plan	67	3,534	—	—	—	3,601
Excess tax benefit from share-based compensation awards	—	1,728	—	—	—	1,728
Balance as of October 25, 2013, as adjusted	$130,205	$1,176,068	$ 2,849,739	$(1,330,729)	$ 30,028	$ 2,855,311
Net income, as adjusted	—	—	338,118	—	—	338,118
Change in unrecognized prior service costs on pension and other postretirement obligations, net of taxes, as adjusted	—	—	—	—	234	234
Derivative instrument fair market value adjustment, net of taxes	—	—	—	—	(292)	(292)
Foreign currency translation adjustment	—	—	—	—	(36,250)	(36,250)
Treasury stock purchased	—	—	—	(269,336)	—	(269,336)
Share-based compensation expense	—	17,685	—	—	—	17,685
Dividends paid ($0.75 per share)	—	1,024	(75,969)	—	—	(74,945)
Issuance of restricted stock units and performance shares	265	(9,408)	—	—	—	(9,143)
Exercise of stock options	241	8,714	—	—	—	8,955
Shares issued under employee stock purchase plan	83	4,308	—	—	—	4,391
Excess tax benefit from share-based compensation awards	—	1,632	—	—	—	1,632

(continued)

	Common Stock Amount	Capital in Excess of Par Value	Retained Earnings	Treasury Stock	Accumulated Other Comprehensive (Loss) Income	Total
Balance as of October 31, 2014, as adjusted	$130,794	$1,200,023	$ 3,111,888	$(1,600,065)	$ (6,280)	$ 2,836,360
Net loss	—	—	(1,178,004)	—	—	(1,178,004)
Change in unrecognized prior service costs on pension and other postretirement obligations, net of taxes	—	—	—	—	204	204
Derivative instrument fair market value adjustment, net of taxes	—	—	—	—	5,558	5,558
Foreign currency translation adjustment	—	—	—	—	(146,554)	(146,554)
Treasury stock purchased	—	—	—	(50,000)	—	(50,000)
Share-based compensation expense	—	30,634	—	—	—	30,634
Dividends paid ($0.80 per share)	—	1,140	(79,090)	—	—	(77,950)
Issuance of restricted stock units and performance shares	243	(3,635)	—	—	—	(3,392)
Exercise of stock options	27	528	—	—	—	555
Shares issued under employee stock purchase plan	178	3,921	—	—	—	4,099
Tax deficiency from share-based compensation awards	—	(1,501)	—	—	—	(1,501)
Balance as of October 30, 2015	$131,242	$1,231,110	$ 1,854,794	$(1,650,065)	$(147,072)	$ 1,420,009

NOTES TO CONSOLIDATED FINANCIAL STATEMENTS (in part)

2. Significant Accounting Policies (in part)

Basis of Presentation and Principles of Consolidation (in part)

Prior period financial information has been adjusted to reflect the fourth quarter fiscal 2015 change in our method of accounting for actuarial gains and losses and the calculation of expected return on plan assets for all of our pension and other postretirement benefit plans, which is a voluntary change in accounting principle that is required to be adopted retrospectively. Refer to the *Pension and Postretirement Benefits and Costs* section of this footnote for additional information.

Pension and Postretirement Benefits and Costs— In the fourth quarter of 2015, we voluntarily changed our method of accounting for actuarial gains and losses and the calculation of expected return on plan assets for all of our pension and other postretirement benefit plans. We elected to recognize actuarial gains and losses in the statement of operations immediately, as it more clearly depicts the impact of current economic conditions in our consolidated results of operations. This change has been reported through retrospective application of this new policy to all periods presented.

Historically, we deferred actuarial gains and losses from these plans and recognized the financial impact in the statement of operations over future years using a method commonly referred to as the corridor method. Specifically, the net loss (gain) in excess of 10% of the greater of the projected benefit obligation or the market related value of plan assets was amortized on a straight line basis over the average remaining service period of active employees expected to receive benefits under the plan (or over the average life of the participants if all or almost all of the plan participants are inactive). With the immediate recognition of actuarial gains and losses, actuarial gains and losses from these plans are immediately recognized in our results of operations in an annual adjustment that is recorded in the fourth quarter of each year, or more frequently should a re-measurement event occur. The remaining components of net periodic benefit costs, primarily service and interest costs and the expected return on plan assets, will continue to be recorded on a quarterly basis.

In addition, for purposes of calculating the expected return on plan assets, we will no longer use an averaging technique for the market-related value of plan assets, but we are voluntarily changing to the actual fair value of plan assets to adjust for changes in actual versus expected rates of return. The impact of this change will be recorded annually as part of the adjustment described above. Collectively, the immediate recognition of actuarial gains and losses and the immediate recognition of actual versus expected rates of return on plan assets are referred to herein as the "mark to market pension and postretirement plan adjustment."

The mark to market method is preferable to our prior method in that it reflects changes in assumptions and market conditions in the year that they occur versus recognizing them over an extended period of time. The adoption of immediate recognition of actuarial gains and losses and the use of the fair value of plan assets are voluntary changes in accounting principle that are required to be adopted retrospectively. Therefore, all periods presented have been adjusted to reflect these changes adopted by the Company as of the October 30, 2015 annual measurement date. The Company also considered the impact of the revised pension expense on its capitalized inventory balances, and has retrospectively adjusted such balances accordingly.

The cumulative effect of the change on retained earnings as of October 27, 2012, was a pre-tax reduction of $716.3 million, with an offset to accumulated other comprehensive income, and therefore, no net impact to shareholders' equity. The impact of all adjustments made to the financial statements presented is summarized below (amounts in thousands, except per share data):

	2014			2013		
	Previously Reported	Adjusted	Effect of Change	Previously Reported	Adjusted	Effect of Change
Consolidated Statements of Operations:						
Cost of sales	2,667,158	2,654,233	(12,925)	3,389,484	3,399,568	10,084
Product development, selling and administrative expenses	606,347	608,886	2,539	680,001	656,148	(23,853)
Operating income	517,140	527,526	10,386	821,661	835,430	13,769
Income from continuing operations before income taxes	461,792	472,178	10,386	764,157	777,926	13,769
Provision for income taxes	130,755	134,060	3,305	230,219	241,167	10,948
Income from continuing operations	331,037	338,118	7,081	533,938	536,759	2,821
Net income	331,037	338,118	7,081	533,713	536,534	2,821
Basic earnings per share:						
Income from continuing operations	3.31	3.38	0.07	5.03	5.06	0.03
Net income	3.31	3.38	0.07	5.03	5.06	0.03
Diluted earnings per share:						
Income from continuing operations	3.28	3.35	0.07	4.99	5.02	0.03
Net income	3.28	3.35	0.07	4.99	5.02	0.03
Consolidated Statements of Comprehensive Income:						
Net income	331,037	338,118	7,081	533,713	536,534	2,821
Change in unrecognized prior service costs on pension and postretirement benefit obligations, net of tax	10,806	234	(10,572)	19,336	793	(18,543)
Consolidated Balance Sheets:						
Deferred income taxes	70,181	71,897	1,716	41,532	44,399	2,867
Inventories	1,108,308	1,101,955	(6,353)	1,139,744	1,133,820	(5,924)
Retained earnings	3,645,527	3,111,888	(533,639)	3,390,459	2,849,740	(540,719)
Accumulated other comprehensive loss	(535,282)	(6,280)	529,002	(507,634)	30,028	537,662
Consolidated Statements of Cash Flows:						
Operating activities:						
Net income	331,037	338,118	7,081	533,713	536,534	2,821
Changes in deferred income taxes	(6,117)	(2,812)	3,305	12,184	23,134	10,950
Defined benefit employee pension plan expense	14,470	3,309	(11,161)	19,632	(18,494)	(38,126)
Other adjustments to continuing operations, net	(160)	11,008	11,168	6,754	44,905	38,151
Changes in inventories	2,584	3,013	429	199,530	225,305	25,775
Changes in other accrued liabilities	(82,288)	(93,110)	(10,822)	(29,210)	(68,781)	(39,571)

Consistent with prior periods, pension and other postretirement benefit costs and liabilities are still dependent on assumptions used in calculating such amounts. The primary assumptions include discount rates, expected returns on plan assets, mortality rates and rates of compensation increases, as discussed below:

Discount rates: We generally estimate the discount rate for pension and other postretirement benefit obligations using a process based on a hypothetical investment in a portfolio of high-quality bonds that approximates the estimated cash flows of the pension and other postretirement benefit obligations. We believe this approach permits a matching of future cash outflows related to benefit payments with future cash inflows associated with bond coupons and maturities.

Expected returns on plan assets: Our expected return on plan assets is derived from reviews of asset allocation strategies and anticipated future long-term performance of individual asset classes, weighted by the allocation of our plan assets. Our analysis gives appropriate consideration to recent plan performance and historical returns; however, the assumptions are primarily based on long-term, prospective rates of return.

Mortality rates: Fiscal 2014 mortality rates are based on the IRS prescribed annuitant and non-annuitant mortality for 2014 under the Pension Protection Act of 2006. Fiscal 2015 mortality rates are based on the annuitant and non-annuitant mortality tables (RP-2014) released by the Society of Actuaries late in fiscal 2014, adjusted for the mortality improvement scale (MP-2014), as well as for the Company's historical plan experience levels. Adoption of these modified tables had a $35.0 million expense impact to our pension and postretirement plans, which was recognized as part of our fourth quarter fiscal 2015 mark to market adjustment. Further, we considered the recently released updates to the 2014 mortality improvement scale, noting that the modifications would not be significant to our assumptions.

Rates of compensation increases: The rates of compensation increases reflect our long-term actual experience and its outlook, including consideration of expected rates of inflation.

As mentioned above, actual results that differ from these assumptions are immediately recognized in our results of operations in an annual adjustment that is recorded in the fourth quarter of each year, or more frequently should a re-measurement event occur. While we believe that the assumptions used are appropriate, differences in actual experience or changes in assumptions may affect our pension and other postretirement plan obligations and future expense.

15. Retiree Benefits (in part)

Defined Benefit Plans (in part)

We have both U.S. and non-U.S. pension plans. Our funding policy with respect to qualified pension plans is to contribute annually not less than the minimum required by applicable law and regulation nor more than the amount which can be deducted for income tax purposes. We also have an unfunded nonqualified supplemental pension plan that is based on credited years of service and compensation during the last years of employment.

Certain plans outside the United States which supplement or are coordinated with government plans, many of which require funding through mandatory government retirement or insurance company plans, have pension funds or balance sheet accruals which approximate the actuarially computed value of accumulated plan benefits as of October 30, 2015 and October 31, 2014.

Other postretirement benefit plans consist of welfare benefits plans. In 1993, our Board of Directors approved a general approach that culminated in the elimination of all Company contributions towards postretirement healthcare benefits. Increases in costs paid by the Company were capped for certain plans beginning in 1994 and extending through 1998, and Company contributions were eliminated as of January 11, 1999 for most employee groups, excluding certain Underground employees, certain early retirees and specific discontinued operation groups. For certain Underground employees, based on existing plan terms, future eligible retirees will participate in a premium cost-sharing arrangement which is based on age as of March 1, 1993 and position at the time of retirement. Active employees under age 45 as of March 1, 1993 and any new hires after April 1, 1993 will be required to pay 100% of the applicable premium.

As described in Note 2, *Significant Accounting Policies*, during the fourth quarter of 2015, we voluntarily changed our method of accounting for actuarial gains and losses and the calculation of expected return on plan assets for all of our pension and other postretirement benefit plans. All amounts presented have been adjusted to reflect this new policy.

Total pension expense (income) for all defined benefit plans is $38.6 million, $3.3 million and $(18.5) million for fiscal 2015, 2014 and 2013, respectively. Such amounts are prior to any impact of the costs on our recorded inventory balances.

The components of the net periodic benefit cost associated with our U.S. pension plans and pension plans of subsidiaries outside of the U.S. are as follows:

In thousands	U.S. Pension Plans			Non-U.S. Pension Plans		
	October 30, 2015	October 31, 2014 (As adjusted)	October 25, 2013 (As adjusted)	October 30, 2015	October 31, 2014 (As adjusted)	October 25, 2013 (As adjusted)
Components of Net Periodic Benefit Cost (Income):						
Service cost	$ 2,379	$ 2,891	$ 3,794	$ 1,531	$ 3,314	$ 7,492
Interest cost	49,446	52,756	48,453	26,087	30,420	29,216
Expected return on assets	(66,655)	(64,243)	(69,444)	(38,512)	(40,147)	(38,685)
Amortization of prior service cost	—	398	610	66	54	—
Year end mark to market adjustment	61,949	10,356	(42,532)	(324)	(607)	42,602
Curtailment loss	—	7,838	—	—	279	—
Special termination benefits	2,627	—	—	—	—	—
Total net periodic benefit cost	$ 49,746	$ 9,996	$(59,119)	$(11,152)	$ (6,687)	$40,625

In fiscal 2015, the $61.9 million market to market adjustment on U.S. plans includes an approximate $35.0 million impact for the application of updated mortality tables, as discussed further in Note 2, *Significant Accounting Policies*. In addition, $15.2 million of previously reported settlement charges related to our U.K. pension schemes have been accordingly reversed upon the voluntary change in our method of accounting for actuarial gains and losses and the calculation of expected return on plan assets.

In fiscal 2014, we substantially completed negotiations with certain of our U.S. bargaining units to freeze their respective defined benefit plans at the end of the calendar year. These actions resulted in a $7.8 million non-cash pension curtailment charge during the year.

The components of the net periodic benefit cost associated with our other postretirement benefit plans, all of which relate to operations in the U.S., and prior to any related inventory adjustments for the annual mark to market adjustment, are as follows:

In thousands	Other Postretirement Benefit Plans		
	October 30, 2015	October 31, 2014 (As adjusted)	October 25, 2013 (As adjusted)
Components of Net Periodic Benefit Cost:			
Service cost	$ 817	$ 952	$ 1,083
Interest cost	1,162	1,279	1,168
Expected return on assets	(624)	(554)	(427)
Amortization of prior service costs	132	132	69
Year end mark to market adjustment	1,678	30	(1,722)
Total net periodic benefit cost of continuing operations	$3,165	$1,839	$ 171

For other postretirement benefit obligation measurement purposes, the assumed annual rate of increase in the per capita cost of covered health care benefits is 7.00% for pre-65 medical insurance plans in fiscal 2015. The assumed annual rate of increase in per capita cost of covered health care benefits for pre-65 medical insurance plans is then assumed to decrease 0.25% per year to an ultimate rate of 5.0%. The assumed annual rate of increase in the per capita cost of covered health care benefits is 7.50% for post-65 medical insurance plans in fiscal 2015. The assumed annual rate of increase in per capita cost of covered health care benefits for post-65 medical insurance plans is then assumed to decrease 0.25% per year to an ultimate rate of 5.0%. The assumed annual rate of increase in the per capita cost of covered health care benefits is 6.00% for post-65 Medicare supplement plans in fiscal 2015. The assumed annual rate of increase in per capita cost of covered health care benefits for post-65 Medicare Supplement plans is then assumed to decrease 0.25% per year to an ultimate rate of 4.5%. The assumed annual rate of increase in the per capita cost of covered health care benefits is 5.00% for retiree drug subsidies in fiscal 2015 and all subsequent years.

The effect of one percentage point increase in the assumed health care cost trend rates each year would increase the accumulated postretirement benefit obligation as of October 30, 2015 by $0.9 million. The service cost and interest cost components of the net periodic postretirement benefit cost for the year would increase by less than $0.1 million. A one percentage point decrease in the assumed health care cost trend rates each year would decrease the accumulated postretirement benefit obligation as of October 30, 2015 by $0.8 million. The service cost and interest cost components of the net periodic postretirement benefit cost for the year would decrease by less than $0.1 million. Postretirement life insurance benefits have a minimal effect on the total benefit obligation.

The principal assumptions used in determining the funded status and net periodic benefit cost of our pension plans and other postretirement benefit plans are set forth in the following tables. The assumptions for non-U.S. plans were developed on a basis consistent with that for the U.S. plans, adjusted to reflect prevailing economic conditions and interest rate environments.

Significant assumptions used in determining net periodic benefit cost are as follows (in weighted averages):

	U.S. Pension Plans			Non-U.S. Pension Plans			Other Postretirement Benefit Plans		
	2015	2014	2013	2015	2014	2013	2015	2014	2013
Discount rate*	4.40%	4.85%	3.95%	4.09%	4.25%	4.28%	4.00%	4.25%	3.60%
Expected return on plan assets**	6.40%	6.25%	6.50%	6.30%	6.30%	6.64%	7.25%	7.25%	7.40%
Rate of compensation increase	—	—	—	4.21%	4.21%	4.23%	—	—	—

* Due to the mid-year settlement measurements, the fiscal 2015 weighted average discount rate ranged from 3.50%–4.09% throughout the year for the non-U.S. pension plans. Due to the mid-year curtailment measurements, the fiscal 2014 weighted average discount rate ranged from 4.45%–4.85% and 4.25%–4.45% throughout the year for the U.S. pension plans and non-U.S. pension plans, respectively.

** Due to the mid-year settlement measurements, the fiscal 2015 weighted average expected return on plan assets ranged from 5.65%–6.30% for the non-U.S. pension plans. Due to the mid-year curtailment measurements, the fiscal 2014 weighted average expected return on plan assets ranged from 6.25%–6.35% for the U.S. pension plans.

The expected rate of return on pension plan assets for the U.S. pension plans is based on the investment policies adopted by our Pension and Investment Committee. We also use the results from a portfolio simulator as input into our decision. The simulator is based on U.S. capital market conditions as of the valuation date and projects returns based on the U.S. pension plans' current asset allocation. The simulation model calculates an expected rate of return for each asset class by forecasting a range of plausible economic conditions. The model starts with the capital market conditions prevailing at the start of the forecast period and trends the rates of return by asset class to its long-term average. A long-term average return is calculated using a blend of historical capital market data and future expectations.

The expected rate of return on non-U.S. pension plans is based on the plan's current asset allocation policy. An average long-term rate of return is developed for each asset class and the portfolio return represents the weighted average return based on the current asset allocation.

Significant assumptions used in determining benefit obligations are as follows (in weighted averages):

	U.S. Pension Plans		Non-U.S. Pension Plans		Other Postretirement Benefit Plans	
	October 30, 2015	October 31, 2014	October 30, 2015	October 31, 2014	October 30, 2015	October 31, 2014
Discount rate	4.45%	4.40%	3.83%	4.09%	4.10%	4.00%
Rate of compensation increase	—	—	3.72%	4.21%	—	—

Changes in the projected benefit obligations and pension plan assets relating to the Company's defined benefit pension plans and other postretirement benefit plans, together with a summary of the amounts recognized in the Consolidated Balance Sheets, are set forth in the following tables:

	U.S. Pension Plans		Non -U.S. Pension Plans		Other Postretirement Benefit Plans	
In thousands	October 30, 2015	October 31, 2014	October 30, 2015	October 31, 2014	October 30, 2015	October 31, 2014
Change in Benefit Obligations						
Net benefit obligations at beginning of year	$1,157,418	$1,132,274	$725,732	$712,261	$ 31,005	$ 31,358
Service cost	2,379	2,891	1,531	3,314	817	952
Interest cost	49,446	52,756	26,087	30,420	1,162	1,279
Plan participants' contributions	—	—	—	281	—	—
Plan amendments	—	6,256	—	1,733	—	—
Actuarial loss (gain)	20,085	55,793	5,297	32,087	1,088	100
Currency fluctuations	—	—	(33,492)	(8,968)	—	—
Acquisitions	—	—	4,772	—	—	—
Special termination benefits	2,627	—	—	—	—	—
Gross benefits paid	(66,169)	(92,552)	(76,520)	(45,396)	(2,700)	(2,684)
Net benefit obligations at end of year	$1,165,786	$1,157,418	$653,407	$725,732	$ 31,372	$ 31,005
Change in Plan Assets						
Fair value of plan assets at beginning of year	$1,073,023	$1,052,654	$662,141	$638,590	$ 9,293	$ 8,401
Actual return on plan assets	24,791	109,680	44,789	72,807	34	624
Currency fluctuations	—	—	(30,800)	(7,962)	—	—
Employer contributions	2,898	3,241	10,236	3,821	3,128	2,952
Plan participants' contributions	—	—	—	281	—	—
Acquisitions	—	—	1,010	—	—	—
Gross benefits paid	(66,169)	(92,552)	(76,520)	(45,396)	(2,700)	(2,684)
Fair value of plan assets at end of year	$1,034,543	$1,073,023	$610,856	$662,141	$ 9,755	$ 9,293
Funded Status						
Net amount recognized at end of year	$ (131,243)	$ (84,395)	$ (42,551)	$ (63,591)	$(21,617)	$(21,712)
Amounts Recognized in the Consolidated Balance Sheets Consist of:						
Non-current assets	—	—	5,554	—	—	—
Current liabilities	(2,991)	(2,887)	(658)	(720)	(2,078)	(2,103)
Non-current liabilities	(128,252)	(81,508)	(47,447)	(62,871)	(19,539)	(19,609)
Net amount recognized at end of year	$ (131,243)	$ (84,395)	$ (42,551)	$ (63,591)	$(21,617)	$(21,712)
Accumulated benefit obligation	$1,165,786	$1,157,418	$644,486	$702,845	$ —	$ —

The projected benefit obligations, accumulated benefit obligations and fair value of plan assets for underfunded and overfunded plans have been combined for disclosure purposes. The projected benefit obligations, accumulated benefit obligations and fair value of assets for pension plans with an accumulated benefit obligation in excess of plan assets are as follows:

	U.S. Pension Plans		Non U.S. Pension Plans	
In thousands	October 30, 2015	October 31, 2014	October 30, 2015	October 31, 2014
Projected benefit obligation	$1,165,786	$1,157,418	$595,337	$660,144
Accumulated benefit obligation	1,165,786	1,157,418	588,460	641,400
Fair value of plan assets	1,034,543	1,073,023	548,478	595,170

Amounts recognized in accumulated other comprehensive (loss) income as of October 30, 2015 consist of:

	Pension Plans		Other Postretirement Benefit Plans
In thousands	U.S.	Non U.S.	
Prior service cost	—	(1,239)	(471)
Deferred tax	—	248	180
Total accumulated other comprehensive (loss) income	$—	$ (991)	$(291)

The estimated amounts that will be amortized from accumulated other comprehensive (loss) income into net periodic benefit cost during fiscal 2016 are as follows:

| | Pension Plans | | Other Postretirement |
In thousands	U.S.	Non U.S.	Benefit Plans
Prior service cost	—	(67)	(133)

For fiscal 2016, we expect contributions to our employee pension plans to be approximately $10.0 million.

The defined benefit plans have the following target and actual asset allocations in fiscal 2015:

| | U.S. Pension Plan | | Non-U.S. Pension Plans | |
Asset Category	Target Allocation	Actual Allocation	Target Allocation	Actual Allocation
Equity securities	25%	21%	30%	30%
Debt securities	75%	75%	70%	70%
Other	—	4%	—	—%
Total	100%	100%	100%	100%

The U.S. plans' assets are invested to maintain funded ratios over the long-term, while managing the risk that funded ratios fall meaningfully below 100%. The Company has been focused on a plan and an objective to achieve an asset and liability duration match so that interim fluctuations in funded status should be limited by increasing the correlation between assets and liabilities. At this time, the plans' portfolio is significantly invested in duration-matched fixed income securities.

The Company's objectives with respect to its global pension plans are (1) to acquire suitable assets of appropriate liquidity, which will meet the cost of the current and future benefits which the plans provide; (2) to limit the risk of the assets failing to meet the liabilities over the long term; and (3) to minimize the long term costs of the plans by maximizing the correlation with plan liabilities. There is no assurance that these objectives will be met.

The accounting guidance on fair value measurements specifies a fair value hierarchy based on the observability of inputs used in valuation techniques (Level 1, 2 and 3). See Note 18, *Fair Value Measurements,* for a discussion of the fair value hierarchy.

Fair values are determined as follows:
- Equity security values are primarily based on the closing price for identical instruments in active markets or at the bid price for identical instruments in instances in which the security has not traded on the valuation date;
- Fixed income security values are primarily based on models that take into consideration such market-based factors as recent sales, risk-free yield curves and prices of similarly rated bonds; and
- Cash and cash equivalents and other investments are based on the carrying amount, which approximates fair value.

The following tables summarize the fair value of our pension and other postretirement benefit plan assets by category as of October 30, 2015 and October 31, 2014:

| | October 30, 2015 | | | |
In thousands	Level 1	Level 2	Level 3	Total Assets at Fair Value
U.S. Pension Plans				
Equity securities:				
U.S. equities	$ —	$107,733	$ —	$107,733
Non-U.S. equities	—	110,155	—	110,155
Fixed income securities:				
U.S. government bonds	—	324,909	—	324,909
Non-U.S. government bonds	—	12,653	—	12,653
U.S. corporate bonds	—	318,795	—	318,795
Non-U.S. corporate bonds	—	69,737	—	69,737
U.S. commercial mortgage backed securities	—	6,190	—	6,190
U.S. non-government backed collateralized mortgage obligations	—	19,460	887	20,347
U.S. asset backed securities	—	20,631	1,818	22,449
Other plan assets:				
Cash and cash equivalents	52,333	—	—	52,333
Other investments	—	(11,086)	328	(10,758)
Total U.S. Pension Plans assets	$52,333	$979,177	$3,033	$1,034,543

(continued)

In thousands	Level 1	Level 2	Level 3	Total Assets at Fair Value
Non-U.S. Pension Plans				
Equity securities:				
U.S. equities	$ 46,414	$ 2,306	$—	$ 48,720
Non-U.S. equities	114,568	19,350	33	133,951
Fixed income securities:				
Non-U.S. government bonds	—	145,871	—	145,871
U.S. corporate bonds	—	24,293	—	24,293
Non-U.S. corporate bonds	—	181,377	—	181,377
Non-U.S. asset backed securities	—	495	—	495
Non-U.S. annuity insurance products	—	76,480	—	76,480
Other plan assets:				
Cash and cash equivalents	(6,095)	—	—	(6,095)
Other investments	—	5,763	1	5,764
Total Non-U.S. Pension Plans assets	$154,887	$455,935	$ 34	$610,856
Other Postretirement Benefits Plans				
Equity securities:				
U.S. equities	$ 4,772	$ —	$—	$ 4,772
Non-U.S. equities	1,621	—	—	1,621
Fixed income securities:				
U.S. corporate bonds	—	3,284	—	3,284
Other plan assets:				
Cash and cash equivalents	78	—	—	78
Total Other Postretirement Benefit Plans	$ 6,471	$ 3,284	$—	$ 9,755

October 30, 2015 (header for above table)

In thousands	Level 1	Level 2	Level 3	Total Assets at Fair Value
U.S. Pension Plans				
Equity securities:				
U.S. equities	$ —	$ 136,830	$ —	$ 136,830
Non-U.S. equities	—	131,601	—	131,601
Fixed income securities:				
U.S. government bonds	—	318,475	—	318,475
Non-U.S. government bonds	—	17,565	—	17,565
U.S. corporate bonds	—	328,882	—	328,882
Non-U.S. corporate bonds	—	63,306	—	63,306
U.S. commercial mortgage backed securities	—	9,310	457	9,767
U.S. non-government backed collateralized mortgage obligations	—	15,519	1,934	17,453
U.S. asset backed securities	—	25,728	—	25,728
Other plan assets:				
Cash and cash equivalents	25,213	—	—	25,213
Other investments	—	(1,797)	—	(1,797)
Total U.S. Pension Plans assets	$ 25,213	$1,045,419	$2,391	$1,073,023
Non-U.S. Pension Plans				
Equity securities:				
U.S. equities	$ 47,505	$2,644	$ 31	$ 50,180
Non-U.S. equities	119,062	9,084	84	128,230
Fixed income securities:				
Non-U.S. government bonds	—	135,825	—	135,825
U.S. corporate bonds	—	26,131	—	26,131
Non-U.S. corporate bonds	—	218,052	—	218,052
Non-U.S. asset backed securities	—	1,130	—	1,130
Non-U.S. annuity insurance products	—	91,027	—	91,027
Other plan assets:				
Cash and cash equivalents	1,260	—	—	1,260
Other investments	—	10,306	—	10,306
Total Non-U.S. Pension Plans assets	$167,827	$ 494,199	$ 115	$ 662,141
Other Postretirement Benefits Plans				
Equity securities:				
U.S. equities	$ 4,568	$ —	$ —	$ 4,568
Non-U.S. equities	1,351	—	—	1,351
Fixed income securities:				
U.S. corporate bonds	—	3,161	—	3,161
Other plan assets:				
Cash and cash equivalents	213	—	—	213
Total Other Postretirement Benefit Plans	$ 6,132	$ 3,161	$ —	$ 9,293

October 31, 2014 (header for above table)

Below are roll-forwards of assets measured at fair value using Level 3 inputs for the years ended October 30, 2015 and October 31, 2014:

In thousands	Equities	Fixed Income	Other
U.S. Pension Plans			
Balance as of October 25, 2013	$ —	$ —	$ —
Unrealized losses	—	(49)	—
Sales and settlements	—	(108)	—
Purchases	—	2,548	—
Balance as of October 31, 2014	$ —	$ 2,391	$ —
Unrealized losses	—	57	—
Sales and settlements	—	(2,460)	—
Purchases	—	2,741	329
Balance as of October 30, 2015	$ —	$ 2,729	$329
Non-U.S. Pension Plans			
Balance as of October 25, 2013	$ 258	$ —	$ —
Unrealized gains	69	—	—
Realized losses	(47)	—	—
Sales and settlements	(274)	—	—
Purchases	108	—	—
Balance as of October 31, 2014	$ 114	$ —	$ —
Unrealized gains	(29)	—	—
Realized losses	—	—	—
Sales and settlements	(110)	—	—
Purchases	59	—	—
Balance as of October 30, 2015	$ 34	$ —	$ —

The following pension and other postretirement benefit payments (which include expected future service) are expected to be paid in each of the following years:

| | Pension Plan Payments | | Other Postretirement Benefit Plan Payments | | |
| | | | Prior to Medicare | After Medicare | Impact of Medicare |
In thousands	U.S.	Non-U.S.	Part D	Part D	Part D
2016	$ 66,857	$ 25,905	$ 4,930	$ 4,847	$ 83
2017	69,633	26,245	4,666	4,589	77
2018	71,383	27,441	3,925	3,855	70
2019	73,232	28,146	2,966	2,902	64
2020	74,924	29,001	2,576	2,518	58
2021–2025	384,933	158,948	10,412	10,210	202

ADOPTION OF ACCOUNTING STANDARD

5.30 CITIGROUP INC. (DEC)
CONSOLIDATED STATEMENT OF CHANGES IN STOCKHOLDERS' EQUITY

| | Years Ended December 31, | | | | | |
| | Amounts | | | Shares | | |
In millions of dollars, except shares in thousands	2015	2014	2013	2015	2014	2013
Preferred Stock at Aggregate Liquidation Value						
Balance, beginning of year	$ 10,468	$ 6,738	$ 2,562	419	270	102
Issuance of new preferred stock	6,250	3,730	4,270	250	149	171
Redemption of preferred stock	—	—	(94)	—	—	(3)
Balance, end of period	$ 16,718	$ 10,468	$ 6,738	669	419	270
Common Stock and Additional Paid-In Capital						
Balance, beginning of year	$108,010	$107,224	$106,421	3,082,038	3,062,099	3,043,153
Employee benefit plans	357	798	878	17,438	19,928	18,930
Preferred stock issuance expense	(23)	(31)	(78)	—	—	—
Other	(25)	19	3	6	11	16
Balance, end of period	$108,319	$108,010	$107,224	3,099,482	3,082,038	3,062,099
Retained Earnings						
Balance, beginning of year	$117,852	$110,821	$ 97,809			
Adjustment to opening balance, net of taxes[1]	—	—	(332)			
Adjusted balance, beginning of period	$117,852	$110,821	$ 97,477			
Citigroup's net income	17,242	7,310	13,659			
Common dividends[2]	(484)	(122)	(120)			
Preferred dividends	(769)	(511)	(194)			
Tax benefit	—	353	—			
Other	—	1	(1)			
Balance, end of period	$133,841	$117,852	$110,821			

(continued)

In millions of dollars, except shares in thousands	Amounts			Shares		
	2015	**2014**	**2013**	**2015**	**2014**	**2013**
Treasury Stock, at Cost						
Balance, beginning of year	$ (2,929)	$ (1,658)	$ (847)	(58,119)	(32,856)	(14,269)
Employee benefit plans[3]	704	(39)	26	13,318	(483)	(1,629)
Treasury stock acquired[4]	(5,452)	(1,232)	(837)	(101,402)	(24,780)	(16,958)
Balance, end of period	$ (7,677)	$ (2,929)	$ (1,658)	(146,203)	(58,119)	(32,856)
Citigroup's Accumulated Other Comprehensive income (Loss)						
Balance, beginning of year	$ (23,216)	$ (19,133)	$ (16,896)			
Citigroup's total other comprehensive income (loss)	(6,128)	(4,083)	(2,237)			
Balance, end of period	$ (29,344)	$ (23,216)	$ (19,133)			
Total Citigroup common stockholders' equity	$205,139	$199,717	$197,254	2,953,279	3,023,919	3,029,243
Total Citigroup stockholders' equity	$221,857	$210,185	$203,992			
Noncontrolling Interests						
Balance, beginning of year	$ 1,511	$ 1,794	$ 1,948			
Initial origination of a noncontrolling interest	—	—	6			
Transactions between noncontrolling-interest shareholders and the related consolidated subsidiary	—	—	(2)			
Transactions between Citigroup and the noncontrolling-interest shareholders	(164)	(96)	(118)			
Net income attributable to noncontrolling-interest shareholders	90	192	227			
Dividends paid to noncontrolling-interest shareholders	(78)	(91)	(63)			
Other comprehensive income (loss) attributable to noncontrolling-interest shareholders	(83)	(106)	(17)			
Other	(41)	(182)	(187)			
Net change in noncontrolling interests	$ (276)	$ (283)	$ (154)			
Balance, end of period	$ 1,235	$ 1,511	$ 1,794			
Total equity	$223,092	$211,696	$205,786			

(1) Citi adopted ASU 2014-01 *Investments-Equity Method and Joint Ventures (Topic 323): Accounting for Investments in Affordable Housing*, in the first quarter of 2015 on a retrospective basis. This adjustment to opening *Retained earnings* represents the impact to periods prior to January 1, 2013 and is shown as an adjustment to the opening balance since 2013 is the earliest period presented in this statement. See Note 1 to the Consolidated Financial Statements for additional information.

(2) Common dividends declared were $0.01 per share in the first quarter and $0.05 both in the second, third and fourth quarters of 2015 and $0.01 per share in each quarter of 2014.

(3) Includes treasury stock related to (i) certain activity on employee stock option program exercises where the employee delivers existing shares to cover the option exercise, or (ii) under Citi's employee restricted or deferred stock programs where shares are withheld to satisfy tax requirements.

(4) For the twelve months ended December 31, 2015, 2014 and 2013, primarily consists of open market purchases under Citi's Board of Directors-approved common stock repurchase program.

NOTES TO CONSOLIDATED FINANCIAL STATEMENTS (in part)

1. Summary of Significant Accounting Policies (in part)

Accounting Changes (in part)

Accounting for Investments in Tax Credit Partnerships

In January 2014, the FASB issued ASU No. 2014-01, *Investments—Equity Method and Joint Ventures (Topic 323): Accounting for Investments in Qualified Affordable Housing Projects*. Any transition adjustment is reflected as an adjustment to retained earnings in the earliest period presented (retrospective application).

The ASU is applicable to Citi's portfolio of low income housing tax credit (LIHTC) partnership interests. The new standard widens the scope of investments eligible to elect to apply a new alternative method, the proportional amortization method, under which the cost of the investment is amortized to tax expense in proportion to the amount of tax credits and other tax benefits received. Citi qualifies to elect the proportional amortization method under the ASU for its entire LIHTC portfolio. These investments were previously accounted for under the equity method, which resulted in losses (due to amortization of the investment) being recognized in *Other revenue* and tax credits and benefits being recognized in the *Income tax expense* line. In contrast, the proportional amortization method combines the amortization of the investment and receipt of the tax credits/benefits into one line, *Income tax expense*.

Citi adopted ASU 2014-01 in the first quarter of 2015.

The adoption of this ASU was applied retrospectively and cumulatively reduced *Retained earnings* by approximately $349 million, *Other assets* by approximately $178 million, and deferred tax assets by approximately $171 million.

5.31 AMPHENOL CORPORATION (DEC)
CONSOLIDATED STATEMENTS OF CHANGES IN EQUITY

(dollars and shares in millions)

	Common Stock		Additional Paid-in Capital	Retained Earnings	Accumulated Other Comprehensive Loss	Treasury Stock	Noncontrolling Interests	Total Equity
	Shares	Amount						
Balance January 1, 2013	320	$0.3	$336.5	$2,210.2	$(117.0)	$ —	$12.2	$2,442.2
Net income				635.7			3.0	638.7
Other comprehensive income					61.7		0.5	62.2
Purchase of noncontrolling interests			0.7		0.3		(1.0)	—
Acquisitions resulting in noncontrolling interests							10.3	10.3
Distributions to shareholders of noncontrolling interests							(4.4)	(4.4)
Purchase of treasury stock						(324.7)		(324.7)
Retirement of treasury stock	(9)			(324.7)		324.7		—
Stock options exercised, including tax benefit	5		116.5					116.5
Dividends declared ($0.305 per common share)				(96.8)				(96.8)
Stock-based compensation expense			36.1					36.1
Balance December 31, 2013	316	0.3	489.8	2,424.4	(55.0)	—	20.6	2,880.1
Net income				709.1			6.1	715.2
Other comprehensive loss					(150.8)		(0.5)	(151.3)
Acquisitions resulting in noncontrolling interests							7.9	7.9
Distributions to shareholders of noncontrolling interests							(3.6)	(3.6)
Purchase of treasury stock						(539.4)		(539.4)
Retirement of treasury stock	(11)			(539.4)		539.4		—
Stock options exercised, including tax benefit	5		128.2					128.2
Dividends declared ($0.45 per common share)				(140.6)				(140.6)
Stock-based compensation expense			41.4					41.4
Balance December 31, 2014	310	0.3	659.4	2,453.5	(205.8)	—	30.5	2,937.9
Net income				763.5			8.8	772.3
Other comprehensive loss					(143.7)		(1.2)	(144.9)
Acquisitions resulting in noncontrolling interests							7.9	7.9
Distributions to shareholders of noncontrolling interests							(6.1)	(6.1)
Purchase of treasury stock						(248.9)		(248.9)
Retirement of treasury stock	(5)			(248.9)		248.9		—
Stock options exercised, including tax benefit	3		79.7					79.7
Dividends declared ($0.53 per common share)				(163.7)				(163.7)
Stock-based compensation expense			44.2					44.2
Balance December 31, 2015	308	$0.3	$783.3	$2,804.4	$(349.5)	$ —	$39.9	$3,278.4

NOTES TO CONSOLIDATED FINANCIAL STATEMENTS (in part)

(dollars in millions, except per share data)

Note 5—Equity (in part)

Stock Repurchase Program:

In January 2013, the Board of Directors authorized a stock repurchase program under which the Company could repurchase up to 20 million shares of its common stock during the two-year period ending January 31, 2015 (the "2013 Stock Repurchase Program"). During the year ended December 31, 2014, the Company repurchased 11,428,610 shares of its Common Stock for $539.4. These treasury shares have been retired by the Company and common stock and retained earnings were reduced accordingly. At December 31, 2014, the Company had repurchased all shares authorized under the 2013 Stock Repurchase Program.

In January 2015, the Board of Directors authorized a stock repurchase program under which the Company could repurchase up to 10 million shares of Common Stock during the two-year period ending January 20, 2017 (the "2015 Stock Repurchase Program"). During the year ended December 31, 2015, the Company repurchased 4.5 million shares of its Common Stock for $248.9. These treasury shares have been retired by the Company and common stock and retained earnings were reduced accordingly. The price and timing of any future purchases under the 2015 Stock Repurchase Program will depend on factors such as levels of cash generation from operations, the volume of stock option exercises by employees, cash requirements for acquisitions, dividends, economic and market conditions and stock price. The Company did not repurchase any additional shares of Common Stock through January 31, 2016. At January 31, 2016, approximately 5.5 million additional shares of Common Stock may be repurchased under the 2015 Stock Repurchase Program.

5.32 THE E. W. SCRIPPS COMPANY (DEC)

CONSOLIDATED STATEMENTS OF EQUITY

(In thousands, except share data)	Common Stock	Additional Paid-in Capital	Retained Earnings (Accumulated Deficit)	Accumulated Other Comprehensive Loss	Noncontrolling Interests	Total Equity
As of December 31, 2012	$555	$ 517,688	$ 136,293	$(116,840)	$2,214	$ 539,910
Net loss	—	—	(474)	—	(250)	(724)
Changes in defined benefit pension plans	—	—	—	35,811	—	35,811
Change in fair value of derivative	—	—	—	291	—	291
Repurchase 5,065,660 Class A Common Shares	(51)	(55,222)	(18,926)	—	—	(74,199)
Compensation plans: 5,565,932 net shares issued *	56	46,777	—	—	—	46,833
Other	—	—	—	(185)	—	(185)
As of December 31, 2013	560	509,243	116,893	(80,923)	1,964	547,737
Net income (loss)	—	—	10,529	—	(307)	10,222
Changes in defined benefit pension plans	—	—	—	(45,500)	—	(45,500)
Change in fair value of derivative	—	—	—	239	—	239
Repurchase 1,181,560 Class A Common Shares	(12)	(12,496)	(8,729)	—	—	(21,237)
Compensation plans: 2,149,581 net shares issued *	22	20,138	—	—	—	20,160
Excess tax expense of compensation plans	—	8,571	—	—	—	8,571
Other	—	—	—	(259)	—	(259)
As of December 31, 2014	570	525,456	118,693	(126,443)	1,657	519,933
Net loss	—	—	(82,477)	—	—	(82,477)
Changes in defined benefit pension plans	—	—	—	33,825	—	33,825
Change in fair value of derivative	—	—	—	237	—	237
Cash dividends: declared and paid—$1.03 per share	—	—	(59,523)	—	—	(59,523)
Shares issued for acquisition: 26,350,993 shares issued	263	635,737	—	—	—	636,000
Spin-off of Newspapers	—	—	(143,511)	2,326	(1,657)	(142,842)
Repurchase 839,859 Class A Common Shares	(8)	(8,994)	(7,220)	—	—	(16,222)
Compensation plans: 1,313,313 net shares issued *	13	11,786	—	—	—	11,799
Other	—	—	—	253	—	253
As of December 31, 2015	$838	$1,163,985	$(174,038)	$ (89,802)	$ —	$ 900,983

* Net of tax payments related to shares withheld for vested stock and RSUs of $5,237 in 2015, $4,261 in 2014 and $6,270 in 2013.

NOTES TO CONSOLIDATED FINANCIAL STATEMENTS (in part)

1. Summary of Significant Accounting Policies (in part)

Nature of Operations—We are a diverse media enterprise with a portfolio of television, radio and digital media brands. All of our media businesses provide content and advertising services via digital platforms, including the Internet, smartphones and tablets. Our media businesses are organized into the following reportable business segments: television, radio, digital, and syndication and other. Additional information for our business segments is presented in the Notes to Consolidated Financial Statements.

On April 1, 2015, we distributed our newspaper business to our shareholders in a tax-free spin-off. For additional information on the spin-off, see Note 21.

21. Journal Broadcast Merger and Newspaper Spin-off (Discontinued Operations)

On July 30, 2014, Scripps and Journal Communications, Inc. ("Journal") agreed to merge their broadcast operations and spin-off their newspaper businesses and combine them into a separate publicly traded company. On April 1, 2015, Scripps and Journal separated their respective newspaper businesses and merged them, resulting in each becoming a wholly owned subsidiary of Journal Media Group, Inc. Journal Media Group is headquartered in Milwaukee and combines the 13 Scripps newspapers with Journal's *Milwaukee Journal Sentinel*.

Immediately following the spin-off and merger of the newspaper businesses, the Journal broadcast operations, and its related digital businesses, were merged into Scripps. The merged broadcast and digital media company, based in Cincinnati, retains The E. W. Scripps Company name. The company's television operations reach approximately 18% of all U.S. television households, and the Company has approximately 3,800 employees across its television, radio and digital media operations.

As part of the transactions, Scripps' shareholders received a $60 million special cash dividend on April 1, 2015.

Certain agreements between Scripps and Journal Media Group, Inc. became effective in connection with the transactions, including Tax Matters Agreements and a Transition Services Agreement.

Under the Transition Services Agreement, Scripps and Journal Media Group provide certain services to each other for a period that generally does not extend beyond March 31, 2016. The fees for the services are at arms-length amounts. For the year ended December 31, 2015, we received $3.3 million for services provided to Journal Media Group and we paid Journal Media Group $1.2 million for services provided to us. In addition, during the initial transition period, each has paid various invoices for the other party. As of December 31, 2015, Journal Media Group owed Scripps approximately $2.0 million.

The Tax Matters Agreements set forth the allocations and responsibilities of Scripps and Journal Media Group with respect to liabilities for federal, state and local income taxes for periods before and after the spin-off, disputes with taxing authorities and indemnification of income taxes that would become due if the spin-off were taxable. Generally, Scripps is responsible for taxes prior to the separation and Journal Media Group will be responsible for taxes for periods after the separation of their respective businesses.

Until the completion of the spin-off of our newspaper business, generally accepted accounting principles ("GAAP") required us to assess impairment of the newspaper business long-lived assets using the held-and-used model. Under this model, if the expected cash flows over the life of the primary asset of the reporting unit are in excess of the carrying amount there is no impairment. Under this model no impairment charges were recorded at March 31, 2015. At the date of the spin-off of our newspaper business, GAAP required us to assess impairment using the held-for-sale model. This model compares the fair value of the disposal unit to its carrying value and if the fair value is lower, an impairment loss is recorded. Our analysis determined that the carrying value of the newspaper business exceeds its fair value. Discontinued operations includes a $30 million non-cash impairment charge to reduce the carrying value to its estimated fair value. The inputs to the nonrecurring fair value determination of the disposal unit are classified as Level 2 fair value measurements under GAAP.

As a result of the spin-off, Scripps newspapers has been presented as discontinued operations in the financial statements for all periods.

Operating results of our discontinued operations were as follows:

(In thousands)	For the Years Ended December 31,		
	2015	2014	2013
Operating revenues	$ 91,478	$ 370,316	$ 384,514
Total costs and expenses	(79,869)	(349,210)	(353,563)
Depreciation and amortization of intangibles	(3,608)	(16,890)	(17,240)
Other, net	(3,298)	(1,308)	(291)
Loss on disposal of Scripps Newspapers	(30,000)	—	—
(Loss) income on discontinued operations before income taxes	(25,297)	2,908	13,420
Benefit (provision) for income taxes	9,457	(2,143)	(4,059)
Net (loss) income from discontinued operations	(15,840)	765	9,361
Noncontrolling interest	—	(307)	(250)
Net (loss) income from discontinued operations	$(15,840)	$ 1,072	$ 9,611

The Company incurred certain non-recurring costs directly related to the spin-off of our newspapers and acquisition of the Journal broadcast stations of $41 million for the year ended December 31, 2015. Accounting and other professional and consulting fees directly related to the newspaper spin-off of $3 million were allocated to discontinued operations in the Consolidated Statements of Operations. The remaining $38 million was recorded in earnings from continuing operations for the year ended December 31, 2015.

The following table presents a summary of the net assets distributed on April 1, 2015 and the amounts included in discontinued operations as of December 31, 2014.

(In thousands)	As of April 1, 2015	As of December 31, 2014
Assets:		
Total current assets	$ 43,322	$ 44,425
Property, plant and equipment	155,047	185,548
Intangible assets	—	2,001
Other assets	3,829	2,018
Total assets included in the disposal group	202,198	233,992
Liabilities:		
Total current liabilities	47,664	47,642
Deferred income taxes	1,966	14,584
Other liabilities	9,057	13,089
Total liabilities included in the disposal group	58,687	75,315
Net assets included in the disposal group	$143,511	$158,677

5.33 JPMORGAN CHASE & CO. (DEC)

CONSOLIDATED STATEMENTS OF CHANGES IN STOCKHOLDERS' EQUITY

Year Ended December 31, (In millions, except per share data)	2015	2014	2013
Preferred stock			
Balance at January 1	$ 20,063	$ 11,158	$ 9,058
Issuance of preferred stock	6,005	8,905	3,900
Redemption of preferred stock	—	—	(1,800)
Balance at December 31	26,068	20,063	11,158
Common stock			
Balance at January 1 and December 31	4,105	4,105	4,105
Additional paid-in capital			
Balance at January 1	93,270	93,828	94,604
Shares issued and commitments to issue common stock for employee stock-based compensation awards, and related tax effects	(436)	(508)	(752)
Other	(334)	(50)	(24)
Balance at December 31	92,500	93,270	93,828
Retained earnings			
Balance at January 1	129,977	115,435	104,223
Cumulative effect of change in accounting principle	—	—	(284)
Balance at beginning of year, adjusted	129,977	115,435	103,939
Net income	24,442	21,745	17,886
Dividends declared:			
Preferred stock	(1,515)	(1,125)	(805)
Common stock ($1.72, $1.58 and $1.44 per share for 2015, 2014 and 2013, respectively)	(6,484)	(6,078)	(5,585)
Balance at December 31	146,420	129,977	115,435
Accumulated other comprehensive income			
Balance at January 1	2,189	1,199	4,102
Other comprehensive income/(loss)	(1,997)	990	(2,903)
Balance at December 31	192	2,189	1,199
Shares held in RSU Trust, at cost			
Balance at January 1 and December 31	(21)	(21)	(21)
Treasury stock, at cost			
Balance at January 1	(17,856)	(14,847)	(12,002)
Purchase of treasury stock	(5,616)	(4,760)	(4,789)
Reissuance from treasury stock	1,781	1,751	1,944
Balance at December 31	(21,691)	(17,856)	(14,847)
Total stockholders' equity	$247,573	$231,727	$210,857

NOTES TO CONSOLIDATED FINANCIAL STATEMENTS (in part)

Note 1—Basis of Presentation (in part)

Investments in Qualified Affordable Housing Projects

Effective January 1, 2015, the Firm adopted new accounting guidance for investments in affordable housing projects that qualify for the low-income housing tax credit, which impacted the Corporate & Investment Bank ("CIB"). As a result of the adoption of this new guidance, the Firm made an accounting policy election to amortize the initial cost of its qualifying investments in proportion to the tax credits and other benefits received, and to present the amortization as a component of income tax expense; previously such amounts were predominantly presented in other income. The guidance was required to be applied retrospectively, and accordingly, certain prior period amounts have been revised to conform with the current period presentation. The cumulative effect on retained earnings was a reduction of $284 million as of January 1, 2013. The adoption of this accounting guidance resulted in an increase of $907 million and $924 million in other income and income tax expense, respectively, for the year ended December 31, 2014 and $761 million and $798 million, respectively, for the year ended December 2013, which led to an increase of approximately 2% in the effective tax rate for the year ended December 31, 2014 and 2013. The impact on net income and earnings per share in the periods affected was not material. For further information, see Note 26.

Note 26—Income Taxes (in part)

Affordable Housing Tax Credits

The Firm recognized $1.6 billion, $1.6 billion and $1.5 billion of tax credits and other tax benefits associated with investments in affordable housing projects within income tax expense for the years 2015, 2014 and 2013, respectively. The amount of amortization of such investments reported in income tax expense under the current period presentation during these years was $1.1 billion, $1.1 billion and $989 million, respectively. The carrying value of these investments, which are reported in other assets on the Firm's Consolidated balance sheets, was $7.7 billion and $7.3 billion at December 31, 2015 and 2014, respectively. The amount of commitments related to these investments, which are reported in accounts payable and other liabilities on the Firm's Consolidated balance sheets, was $2.0 billion and $1.8 billion at December 31, 2015 and 2014, respectively.

OTHER CHANGES IN RETAINED EARNINGS—DIVIDENDS

5.34 WYNN RESORTS, LIMITED (DEC)
CONSOLIDATED STATEMENTS OF STOCKHOLDERS' EQUITY

(in thousands, except share data)

	Common Stock		Treasury Stock	Additional Paid-in Capital	Accumulated Other Comprehensive Income	Retained Earnings	Total Wynn Resorts, Ltd Stockholders' Deficit	Non-controlling Interest	Total Stockholders' Equity
	Shares Outstanding	Par Value							
Balances, January 1, 2013	100,866,712	$1,137	$(1,127,947)	$818,821	$4,177	$ 44,775	$(259,037)	$362,969	$ 103,932
Stock redemption	—	—	—	—	—	—	—	—	—
Net income	—	—	—	—	—	728,652	728,652	275,505	1,004,157
Currency translation adjustment	—	—	—	—	(1,522)	—	(1,522)	(584)	(2,106)
Net unrealized gain on investment securities	—	—	—	—	258	—	258	61	319
Exercise of stock options	383,151	5	—	20,431	—	—	20,436	—	20,436
Cancellation of restricted stock	(78,500)	(1)	—	1	—	—	—	—	—
Shares repurchased by the company and held as treasury shares	(114,355)	—	(15,472)	—	—	—	(15,472)	—	(15,472)
Issuance of restricted stock	135,400	1	—	(1)	—	—	—	—	—
Cash dividends declared	—	—	—	480	—	(707,297)	(706,817)	(322,305)	(1,029,122)
Excess tax benefits from stock-based compensation	—	—	—	10,474	—	—	10,474	—	10,474
Stock-based compensation	—	—	—	38,521	—	—	38,521	1,212	39,733
Balances, December 31, 2013	101,192,408	1,142	(1,143,419)	888,727	2,913	66,130	(184,507)	316,858	132,351
Net income	—	—	—	—	—	731,554	731,554	231,090	962,644
Currency translation adjustment	—	—	—	—	(203)	—	(203)	(79)	(282)
Net unrealized gain (loss) on investment securities	—	—	—	—	(205)	—	(205)	10	(195)
Exercise of stock options	211,133	2	—	11,643	—	—	11,645	214	11,859
Cancellation of restricted stock	(9,166)	—	—	—	—	—	—	—	—
Shares repurchased by the company and held as treasury shares	(9,578)	—	(2,062)	—	—	—	(2,062)	—	(2,062)
Issuance of restricted stock	54,500	—	—	—	—	—	—	—	—
Shares of subsidiary repurchased for share award plan	—	—	—	—	—	—	—	(2,081)	(2,081)
Cash dividends declared	—	—	—	59	—	(633,197)	(633,138)	(312,287)	(945,425)
Excess tax benefits from stock-based compensation	—	—	—	9,376	—	—	9,376	—	9,376
Stock-based compensation	—	—	—	38,761	—	—	38,761	6,145	44,906
Balances, December 31, 2014	101,439,297	1,144	(1,145,481)	948,566	2,505	164,487	(28,779)	239,870	211,091
Net income	—	—	—	—	—	195,290	195,290	86,234	281,524
Currency translation adjustment	—	—	—	—	(327)	—	(327)	(121)	(448)
Net unrealized loss on investment securities	—	—	—	—	(1,086)	—	(1,086)	—	(1,086)
Exercise of stock options	50,716	1	—	3,025	—	—	3,026	—	3,026
Shares repurchased by the Company and held as treasury shares	(50,869)	—	(7,199)	—	—	—	(7,199)	—	(7,199)
Issuance of restricted stock	132,765	1	—	(1)	—	—	—	—	—
Shares of subsidiary repurchased for share award plan	—	—	—	(3,169)	—	—	(3,169)	(1,222)	(4,391)
Cash dividends declared	—	—	—	—	—	(304,445)	(304,445)	(195,439)	(499,884)
Excess tax benefits from stock-based compensation	—	—	—	387	—	—	387	—	387
Stock-based compensation	—	—	—	34,323	—	—	34,323	4,502	38,825
Balances, December 31, 2015	101,571,909	$1,146	$(1,152,680)	$983,131	$1,092	$ 55,332	$(111,979)	$133,824	$ 21,845

Note 12—Stockholders' Equity (in part)

Common Stock (in part)

The Company is authorized to issue up to 400,000,000 shares of its common stock, $0.01 par value per share (the "Common Stock"). As of December 31, 2015 and 2014, 101,571,909 shares and 101,439,297 shares, respectively, of the Company's Common Stock were outstanding. Except as otherwise provided by the Company's articles of incorporation or Nevada law, each holder of the Common Stock is entitled to one vote for each share held of record on each matter submitted to a vote of stockholders. Holders of the Common Stock have no cumulative voting, conversion, redemption or preemptive rights or other rights to subscribe for additional shares. Subject to any preferences that may be granted to the holders of the Company's preferred stock, each holder of Common Stock is entitled to receive ratably such dividends as may be declared by the Board of Directors out of funds legally available therefore, as well as any distributions to the stockholders and, in the event of liquidation, dissolution or winding up of the Company, is entitled to share ratably in all assets of the Company remaining after payment of liabilities.

In February 2015, the Company paid a cash dividend of $1.50 per share. In each of May 2015, August 2015, and November 2015, the Company paid a cash dividend of $0.50 per share. During the year ended December 31, 2015, the Company recorded $304.4 million as a reduction of retained earnings from cash dividends declared.

In February 2014, May 2014 and August 2014, the Company paid a cash dividend of $1.25 per common share. In November 2014, the Company paid a cash dividend of $1.50 per common share and an additional cash dividend of $1.00 per share. During the year ended December 31, 2014, the Company recorded $633.2 million as a reduction of retained earnings from cash dividends declared.

In February 2013, May 2013, August 2013 and November 2013, the Company paid a dividend of $1.00 per common share. In December 2013, the Company paid a cash dividend of $3.00 per common share. During the year ended December 31, 2013, the Company recorded $707.3 million as a reduction of retained earnings from cash dividends declared.

Note 13—Noncontrolling Interest

In October 2009, WML, an indirect wholly owned subsidiary of the Company and the developer, owner and operator of Wynn Macau and Encore at Wynn Macau, listed its ordinary shares of common stock on The Stock Exchange of Hong Kong Limited. Through an initial public offering, including the over allotment, WML sold 1,437,500,000 shares, 27.7% of this subsidiary's common stock. The shares of WML were not and will not be registered under the Securities Act and may not be offered or sold in the United States absent a registration under the Securities Act, or an applicable exception from such registration requirements. Net income attributable to noncontrolling interest was $86.2 million, $231.1 million and $275.5 million for the years ended December 31, 2015, 2014 and 2013, respectively.

On March 31, 2015, WML paid a dividend of HK $1.05 per share for a total of $702.6 million. The Company's share of this dividend was $507.1 million with a reduction of $195.5 million to noncontrolling interest in the accompanying Consolidated Balance Sheets.

On September 23, 2014, WML paid a dividend of HK $0.70 per share for a total of $469.2 million. The Company's share of this dividend was $338.7 million with a reduction of $130.6 million to noncontrolling interest in the accompanying Consolidated Balance Sheets.

On June 6, 2014, WML paid a dividend of HK $0.98 per share for a total of $655.8 million. The Company's share of this dividend was $474.0 million with a reduction of $181.8 million to noncontrolling interest in the accompanying Consolidated Balance Sheets.

On September 23, 2013, WML paid a dividend of HK $0.50 per share for a total of $334.5 million. The Company's share of this dividend was $241.8 million with a reduction of $92.7 million to noncontrolling interest in the accompanying Consolidated Balance Sheets.

On June 6, 2013, WML paid a dividend of HK $1.24 per share for a total of $828.6 million. The Company's share of this dividend was $599.1 million with a reduction of $229.6 million to noncontrolling interest in the accompanying Consolidated Balance Sheets.

Spinoffs

RECOGNITION AND MEASUREMENT

5.35 The distributions of nonmonetary assets that constitute a business to owners of an entity are commonly referred to as spinoffs. A *business* is defined as an integrated set of activities and assets that is capable of being conducted and managed for the purpose of providing a return in the form of dividends, lower costs, or other economic benefits directly to investors or other owners, members, or participants. Spinoffs are discussed in FASB ASC 505-60.

5.36 FASB ASC 505-60-25-2 requires that the accounting for the distribution of nonmonetary assets to owners of an entity in a spinoff be based on the recorded amount (after reduction, if appropriate, for an indicated impairment of value). An entity's distribution of the shares of a wholly owned or consolidated subsidiary to its shareholders should be recorded based on the carrying value of the subsidiary. Regardless of whether the spun-off operations will be sold immediately after the spinoff, the transaction should not be accounted for as a sale of the accounting spinnee followed by a distribution of the proceeds. In order to determine the required accounting and reporting in a spinoff transaction, an entity needs to determine which party is the accounting spinnor and which is the accounting spinnee. The accounting spinnee should be reported as a discontinued operation by the accounting spinnor if the spinnee is a component of an entity and meets the conditions for such reporting.

PRESENTATION AND DISCLOSURE EXCERPT

SPINOFFS

5.37 AUTOMATIC DATA PROCESSING, INC. (JUN)
STATEMENTS OF CONSOLIDATED STOCKHOLDERS' EQUITY

(In millions, except per share amounts)

	Common Stock		Capital in Excess of Par Value	Retained Earnings	Treasury Stock	Accumulated Other Comprehensive Income
	Shares	Amount				
Balance at June 30, 2012	638.7	$63.9	$ 486.4	$12,438.3	$(7,104.8)	$ 230.2
Net earnings	—	—	—	1,405.8	—	—
Other comprehensive loss	—	—	—	—	—	(214.8)
Stock-based compensation expense	—	—	79.2	—	—	—
Issuances relating to stock compensation plans	—	—	(148.3)	—	384.7	—
Tax benefits from stock compensation plans	—	—	39.6	—	—	—
Treasury stock acquired (10.4 shares)	—	—	—	—	(646.5)	—
Dividends ($1.70 per share)	—	—	—	(823.8)	—	—
Balance at June 30, 2013	638.7	$63.9	$ 456.9	$13,020.3	$(7,366.6)	$ 15.4
Net earnings	—	—	—	1,515.9	—	—
Other comprehensive income	—	—	—	—	—	162.8
Stock-based compensation expense	—	—	110.3	—	—	—
Issuances relating to stock compensation plans	—	—	(78.6)	—	314.5	—
Tax benefits from stock compensation plans	—	—	56.6	—	—	—
Treasury stock acquired (9.0 shares)	—	—	—	—	(697.9)	—
Dividends ($1.88 per share)	—	—	—	(903.3)	—	—
Balance at June 30, 2014	638.7	$63.9	$ 545.2	$13,632.9	$(7,750.0)	$ 178.2
Net earnings	—	—	—	1,452.5	—	—
Other comprehensive income	—	—	—	—	—	(350.6)
Stock-based compensation expense	—	—	112.8	—	—	—
Issuances relating to stock compensation plans	—	—	(67.8)	—	243.0	—
Tax benefits from stock compensation plans	—	—	73.1	—	—	—
Treasury stock acquired (18.2 shares)	—	—	—	—	(1,611.4)	—
Spin-off of CDK Global, Inc.	—	—	—	(1,523.0)	—	(88.2)
Dividend from CDK Global, Inc.	—	—	—	825.0	—	—
Dividends ($1.95 per share)	—	—	—	(927.1)	—	—
Balance at June 30, 2015	638.7	$63.9	$ 663.3	$13,460.3	$(9,118.4)	$(260.6)

NOTES TO CONSOLIDATED FINANCIAL STATEMENTS (in part)

(Tabular dollars in millions, except per share amounts)

Note 2. Divestitures (in part)

On September 30, 2014, the Company completed the tax free spin-off of its former Dealer Services business, which was a separate reportable segment, into an independent publicly traded company called CDK Global, Inc. ("CDK"). As a result of the spin-off, ADP stockholders of record on September 24, 2014 (the "record date") received one share of CDK common stock on September 30, 2014, par value $0.01 per share, for every three shares of ADP common stock held by them on the record date and cash for any fractional shares of CDK common stock. ADP distributed approximately 160.6 million shares of CDK common stock in the distribution. The spin-off was made without the payment of any consideration or the exchange of any shares by ADP stockholders. The spin-off, transitional, and on-going relationships between ADP and CDK are governed by the Separation and Distribution Agreement entered into between ADP and CDK and certain other ancillary agreements.

Incremental costs associated with the spin-off of CDK and divestiture of P2P of $50.1 million for fiscal 2015 are included in discontinued operations on the Statements of Consolidated Earnings.

Note 9. Employee Benefit Plans (in part)

A. Stock-Based Compensation Plans (in part)

As a result of the spin-off of CDK, the number of vested and unvested ADP stock options, their strike price, and the number of unvested performance-based and time-based restricted shares and units were adjusted to preserve the intrinsic value of the awards immediately prior to the spin-off using an adjustment ratio based on the market close price of ADP stock prior to the spin-off and the market open price of ADP stock subsequent to the spin-off. Since these adjustments were considered to be a modification of the awards in accordance to ASC 718, "Stock Compensation," the Company compared the fair value of the awards immediately prior to the spin-off to the fair value immediately after the spin-off to measure potential incremental stock-based compensation expense, if any. The adjustments did not result in an increase in the fair value of the awards and, accordingly, the Company did not record incremental stock-based compensation expense. Unvested ADP stock options, unvested restricted stock, and unvested restricted stock units held by CDK employees were replaced by CDK awards immediately following the spin-off. The stock-based compensation expense associated with the original grant of ADP awards to remaining ADP employees will continue to be recognized within earnings from continuing operations in the Company's Statements of Consolidated Earnings.

In fiscal 2015, the following activity occurred under the Company's existing plans, including the impacts related to the CDK spin-off described above.

Stock Options:

Year Ended June 30, 2015	Number of Options (In thousands)	Weighted Average Price (In dollars)
Options outstanding, beginning of year	7,931	$52
Options granted	949	$86
Options exercised	(2,843)	$40
Options canceled	(175)	$59
Options increased for spin-off adjustment ratio	849	$47
CDK employee options replaced at spin-off with CDK awards	(823)	$54
Options outstanding at June 30, 2015	5,888	$55
Options exercisable at June 30, 2015	3,177	$42
Shares available for future grants, end of year	24,209	
Shares reserved for issuance under stock option plans, end of year	30,097	

Time-Based Restricted Stock and Time-Based Restricted Stock Units:

Year Ended June 30, 2015	Number of Shares (In thousands)	Number of Units (In thousands)
Restricted shares/units outstanding at July 1, 2014	2,341	571
Restricted shares/units granted	949	218
Restricted shares/units vested	(1,083)	(252)
Restricted shares/units forfeited	(148)	(72)
Share/unit increase for spin-off adjustment ratio	267	64
CDK employee restricted shares/units replaced at spin-off with CDK awards	(189)	(43)
Restricted shares/units outstanding at June 30, 2015	2,137	486

Performance-Based Restricted Stock and Performance-Based Restricted Stock Units:

Year Ended June 30, 2015	Number of Shares (In thousands)	Number of Units (In thousands)
Restricted shares/units outstanding at July 1, 2014	803	318
Restricted shares/units granted	339	217
Restricted shares/units vested	(224)	(13)
Restricted shares/units forfeited	(88)	(20)
Share/unit increase for spin-off adjustment ratio	118	67
CDK employee restricted shares/units replaced at spin-off with CDK awards	(45)	(35)
Restricted shares/units outstanding at June 30, 2015	903	534

The aggregate intrinsic value of stock options outstanding and exercisable as of June 30, 2015 was $152.6 million and $120.3 million, respectively, which has a remaining life of 6 years and 4 years, respectively. The aggregate intrinsic value for stock options exercised in fiscal 2015, 2014, and 2013 was $125.3 million, $156.3 million, and $135.1 million, respectively.

The fair value for stock options granted was estimated at the date of grant using the following assumptions:

	2015	2014	2013
Risk-free interest rate	1.5%	1.7%	1.0%
Dividend yield	2.3%	2.4%	2.9%
Weighted average volatility factor	23.4%	23.8%	23.5%
Weighted average expected life (in years)	5.4	5.4	5.4
Weighted average fair value (in dollars)[(A)]	$14.29	$11.89	$7.59

The weighted average fair values of shares granted were as follows:

Year Ended June 30,	2015	2014	2013
Performance-based restricted stock[(A)]	$64.91	$53.08	$48.46
Time-based restricted stock[(A)]	$73.83	$62.85	$51.62

[(A)] The weighted average fair values of grants before September 30, 2014 were adjusted to reflect the impact of the spin-off of CDK.

B. Pension Plans (in part)

The Company's pension plans with accumulated benefit obligations in excess of plan assets as of June 30, 2015 and 2014 had the following projected benefit obligation, accumulated benefit obligation and fair value of plan assets:

June 30,	2015	2014
Projected benefit obligation	$131.5	$142.6
Accumulated benefit obligation	$117.4	$127.8
Fair value of plan assets	$ 4.5	$ 16.7

The components of net pension expense were as follows:

	2015	2014	2013
Service cost—benefits earned during the period	$ 68.4	$ 66.4	$ 67.2
Interest cost on projected benefits	62.8	62.6	55.1
Expected return on plan assets	(129.7)	(119.4)	(109.5)
Net amortization and deferral	17.2	20.1	30.9
Special termination benefits and plan curtailments	3.2	—	—
Net pension expense	$ 21.9	$ 29.7	$ 43.7

Net pension expense for fiscal 2015, 2014, and 2013 includes $4.3 million, $5.4 million, and $6.1 million, respectively, reported within earnings from discontinued operations on the Statements of Consolidated Earnings. Included within pension expense related to discontinued operations for fiscal 2015 were total one-time charges of $3.2 million for curtailment charges and special termination benefits directly attributable to the spin-off of CDK.

Note 12. Reclassification Out of Accumulated Other Comprehensive Income

Comprehensive income is a measure of income that includes both net earnings and other comprehensive income (loss). Other comprehensive income (loss) results from items deferred on the Consolidated Balance Sheets in stockholders' equity. Other comprehensive income (loss) was $(350.6) million, $162.8 million, and $(214.8) million in fiscal 2015, 2014, and 2013, respectively. Changes in Accumulated Other Comprehensive Income ("AOCI") by component are as follows:

	Currency Translation Adjustment	Net Gains on Available-for-Sale Securities	Pension Liability	Accumulated Other Comprehensive Income
Balance at June 30, 2012	$ 42.0	$ 461.3	$(273.1)	$ 230.2
Other comprehensive (loss) income before reclassification adjustments	(2.4)	(394.6)	68.2	(328.8)
Tax effect	—	138.5	(25.7)	112.8
Reclassification adjustments to net earnings	—	(28.6)(A)	31.7(B)	3.1
Tax effect	—	10.1	(12.0)	(1.9)
Balance at June 30, 2013	$ 39.6	$ 186.7	$(210.9)	$ 15.4
Other comprehensive income before reclassification adjustments	58.4	53.5	102.8	214.7
Tax effect		(18.2)	(39.7)	(57.9)
Reclassification adjustments to net earnings	1.5(C)	(16.5)(A)	20.7(B)	5.7
Tax effect		6.1	(5.8)	0.3
Balance at June 30, 2014	$ 99.5	$ 211.6	$(132.9)	$ 178.2
Other comprehensive loss before reclassification adjustments	(240.8)	(103.0)	(87.4)	(431.2)
Tax effect		38.6	32.7	71.3
Reclassification adjustments to net earnings	1.2(C)	(4.9)(A)	17.9(B)	14.2
Tax effect		1.6	(6.5)	(4.9)
Reclassification adjustments to retained earnings	(88.2)(D)	—	—	(88.2)
Balance at June 30, 2015	$ (228.3)	$ 143.9	$(176.2)	$(260.6)

(A) Reclassification adjustments out of AOCI are included within Other income, net, on the Statements of Consolidated Earnings.
(B) Reclassification adjustments out of AOCI are included in net pension expense (see Note 9).
(C) Reclassification adjustments out of AOCI are included within net earnings from discontinued operations, on the Statements of Consolidated Earnings.
(D) Reclassification adjustment out of AOCI is related to the CDK spin-off and included in retained earnings on the Consolidated Balance Sheets.

Treasury Stock

PRESENTATION

5.38 Repurchased common stock is often referred to as treasury stock or treasury shares. FASB ASC 505-30-45-1 discusses the balance sheet presentation of treasury stock and states that if a corporation's stock is acquired for purposes other than retirement (formal or constructive), or if ultimate disposition has not yet been decided, the cost of acquired stock may be shown separately as a deduction from the total of capital stock, additional paid-in capital, and retained earnings or may be accorded the accounting treatment appropriate for retired stock.

5.39 A repurchase of shares at a price significantly in excess of the current market price creates a presumption that the repurchase price includes amounts attributable to items other than the shares repurchased. FASB ASC 505-30-30-2 explains that a repurchase of shares at a price significantly in excess of the current market price may require an entity to allocate amounts to other elements of the transaction.

PRESENTATION AND DISCLOSURE EXCERPT

TREASURY STOCK

5.40 AUTONATION, INC. (DEC)
CONSOLIDATED BALANCE SHEETS

(In millions, except share and per share data)

	2015	2014
Assets		
Current Assets:		
Cash and cash equivalents	$ 74.1	$ 75.4
Receivables, net	908.2	817.8
Inventory	3,612.0	2,899.0
Other current assets	117.1	207.0
Total Current Assets	4,711.4	3,999.2
Property and Equipment, Net	2,667.4	2,422.0

(continued)

	2015	2014
Goodwill, Net	1,394.5	1,314.7
Other Intangible Assets, Net	439.9	354.7
Other Assets	345.1	309.1
Total Assets	$9,558.3	$8,399.7
Liabilities and Shareholders' Equity		
Current Liabilities:		
Vehicle floorplan payable—trade	$2,565.8	$2,090.7
Vehicle floorplan payable—non-trade	1,161.3	1,006.5
Accounts payable	299.9	264.7
Commercial paper	599.5	—
Current maturities of long-term debt	13.4	25.0
Other current liabilities	529.2	495.1
Total Current Liabilities	5,169.1	3,882.0
Long-Term Debt, Net of Current Maturities	1,753.7	2,103.4
Deferred Income Taxes	78.6	137.9
Other Liabilities	207.6	204.3
Commitments and Contingencies (Note 8)		
Shareholders' Equity:		
Preferred stock, par value $0.01 per share; 5,000,000 shares authorized; none issued	—	—
Common stock, par value $0.01 per share; 1,500,000,000 shares authorized; 120,562,149 shares issued at December 31, 2015, and 163,562,149 shares issued at December 31, 2014, including shares held in treasury	1.2	1.6
Additional paid-in capital	5.2	61.8
Retained earnings	2,702.8	3,756.6
Treasury stock, at cost; 9,758,091 and 50,248,909 shares held, respectively	(359.9)	(1,747.9)
Total Shareholders' Equity	2,349.3	2,072.1
Total Liabilities and Shareholders' Equity	$9,558.3	$8,399.7

CONSOLIDATED STATEMENTS OF SHAREHOLDERS' EQUITY

(In millions, except share data)

	Common Stock		Additional Paid-In Capital	Retained Earnings	Treasury Stock	Total
	Shares	Amount				
Balance At December 31, 2012	163,562,149	$ 1.6	$ 26.6	$ 2,963.0	$(1,302.7)	$1,688.5
Net income	—	—	—	374.9	—	374.9
Repurchases of common stock	—	—	—	—	(55.7)	(55.7)
Stock-based compensation expense	—	—	21.3	—	—	21.3
Shares awarded under stock-based compensation plans, including excess income tax benefit of $10.0	—	—	(5.1)	—	37.8	32.7
Balance At December 31, 2013	163,562,149	$ 1.6	$ 42.8	$ 3,337.9	$(1,320.6)	$2,061.7
Net income	—	—	—	418.7	—	418.7
Repurchases of common stock	—	—	—	—	(487.7)	(487.7)
Stock-based compensation expense	—	—	26.3	—	—	26.3
Shares awarded under stock-based compensation plans, including excess income tax benefit of $18.0	—	—	(7.3)	—	60.4	53.1
Balance At December 31, 2014	163,562,149	$ 1.6	$ 61.8	$ 3,756.6	$(1,747.9)	$2,072.1
Net income	—	—	—	442.6	—	442.6
Repurchases of common stock	—	—	—	—	(237.3)	(237.3)
Treasury stock cancellation	(43,000,000)	(0.4)	(78.7)	(1,496.4)	1,575.5	—
Stock-based compensation expense	—	—	24.0	—	—	24.0
Shares awarded under stock-based compensation plans, including excess income tax benefit of $17.9	—	—	(1.9)	—	49.8	47.9
Balance At December 31, 2015	120,562,149	$ 1.2	$ 5.2	$ 2,702.8	$ (359.9)	$2,349.3

NOTES TO CONSOLIDATED FINANCIAL STATEMENTS (in part)

(All tables in millions, except per share data)

1. Description of Business and Summary of Significant Accounting Policies (in part)

Stock-Based Compensation

We grant stock-based awards in the form of stock options, restricted stock, and restricted stock units ("RSUs"). Stock options granted under all plans are non-qualified. Upon exercise, shares of common stock are issued from our treasury stock. We use the Black-Scholes valuation model to determine compensation expense associated with our stock options. Restricted stock awards, which are considered nonvested share awards as defined under generally accepted accounting principles, and RSUs are issued from our treasury stock. Compensation cost for restricted stock awards and RSUs is based on the closing price of our common stock on the date of grant. Certain of our equity-based compensation plans contain provisions that provide for vesting of awards upon retirement. Accordingly, compensation cost for stock-based awards is recognized on a straight-line basis, net of estimated forfeitures, over the shorter of the stated vesting period or the period until employees become retirement-eligible. See Note 10 of the Notes to Consolidated Financial Statements for more information about our stock-based compensation arrangements.

9. Shareholders' Equity

A summary of shares repurchased under our share repurchase program authorized by our Board of Directors follows:

	2015	2014	2013
Shares repurchased	3.9	9.4	1.1
Aggregate purchase price	$235.1	$485.1	$ 53.5
Average purchase price per share	$60.49	$51.59	$47.37

From January 1, 2016 through February 8, 2016, we repurchased 3.6 million shares for an aggregate purchase price of $160.3 million (average purchase price per share of $44.79). As of February 8, 2016, $135.3 million remained available for share repurchases under our stock repurchase limit most recently authorized by our Board of Directors.

Our Board of Directors authorized the retirement of 43.0 million shares of our treasury stock in October 2015, which assumed the status of authorized but unissued shares. Upon the retirement of treasury stock, it is our policy to charge the excess of the cost of the treasury stock over its par value entirely to additional paid-in capital. Any amounts exceeding additional paid-in capital are charged to retained earnings. This retirement had the effect of reducing treasury stock and issued common stock, which includes treasury stock. Our common stock, additional paid-in capital, retained earnings, and treasury stock accounts were adjusted accordingly. There was no impact to shareholders' equity or outstanding common stock.

We have 5.0 million authorized shares of preferred stock, par value $0.01 per share, none of which are issued or outstanding. The Board of Directors has the authority to issue the preferred stock in one or more series and to establish the rights, preferences, and dividends.

A summary of shares of common stock issued in connection with the exercise of stock options follows:

	2015	2014	2013
Shares issued	1.3	1.7	1.1
Proceeds from the exercise of stock options	$ 30.0	$ 35.1	$ 22.7
Average exercise price per share	$23.33	$20.50	$20.31

The following table presents a summary of shares of common stock issued in connection with grants of restricted stock and shares surrendered to AutoNation to satisfy tax withholding obligations in connection with the vesting of restricted stock (in actual number of shares):

	2015	2014	2013
Shares issued	159,442	154,540	137,144
Shares surrendered to AutoNation to satisfy tax withholding obligations in connection with the vesting of restricted stock	36,712	46,752	44,738

Other Components of Stockholders' Equity

PRESENTATION

5.41 For public entities, Rule 3-04 of Regulation S-X requires that an analysis of the changes in each caption of stockholders' equity and noncontrolling interests presented in the balance sheets be given in a note or separate statement. This analysis should be presented in the form of a reconciliation of the beginning balance to the ending balance for each period for which an income statement is required to be filed, with all significant reconciling items described by appropriate captions.

5.42 Many of the survey entities present accounts other than capital stock, additional paid-in capital, retained earnings, accumulated other comprehensive income, and treasury stock in the "Stockholders' Equity" section of the balance sheet. Other stockholders' equity accounts appearing on the balance sheets of the survey entities include, but are not limited to, deferred compensation, noncontrolling interest, and employee benefit stock, in each instance pursuant to relevant FASB ASC requirements. Other items, such as foreign currency translation adjustments, unrealized gains and losses on certain investments in debt and equity securities, and defined benefit postretirement plan adjustments, are considered components of other comprehensive income. FASB ASC 220-10-45-14 provides guidance for reporting other comprehensive income in the Equity section of a statement of financial position.

DISCLOSURE

5.43 Rule 3-04 of SEC Regulation S-X requires an SEC registrant to disclose an analysis of the changes in each caption of other stockholders' equity and noncontrolling interests presented in the balance sheets in a note or separate statement (see also FASB ASC 505-10-S99-1).

5.44 FASB ASC 810, *Consolidation*, establishes accounting and reporting standards for the noncontrolling interest in a subsidiary. It clarifies that a noncontrolling interest in a subsidiary is an ownership interest in the consolidated entity that should be reported as equity in the consolidated financial statements but separate from the parent's equity, and clearly identified and labeled. In addition, FASB ASC 810 requires expanded disclosures in the consolidated financial statements that clearly identify and distinguish between the interests of the parent's owners and the interests of the noncontrolling owners of a subsidiary. Those expanded disclosures include a reconciliation of the beginning and ending balances of the equity attributable to the parent and noncontrolling owners and a schedule showing the effects of changes in a parent's ownership interest in a subsidiary on the equity attributable to the parent.

PRESENTATION AND DISCLOSURE EXCERPTS

DEFERRED COMPENSATION

5.45 UNITED PARCEL SERVICE, INC. (DEC)
CONSOLIDATED BALANCE SHEETS

(In millions)

	December 31,	
	2015	2014
Assets		
Current Assets:		
Cash and cash equivalents	$ 2,730	$ 2,291
Marketable securities	1,996	992
Accounts receivable, net	7,134	6,661
Other current assets	1,348	1,274
Total Current Assets	13,208	11,218
Property, Plant and Equipment, Net	18,352	18,281
Goodwill	3,419	2,184
Intangible Assets, Net	1,549	847
Investments and Restricted Cash	473	489
Deferred Income Tax Assets	255	1,219
Other Non-Current Assets	1,055	1,202
Total Assets	$38,311	$35,440
Liabilities And Shareowners' Equity		
Current Liabilities:		
Current maturities of long-term debt and commercial paper	$ 3,018	$ 923
Accounts payable	2,587	2,754
Accrued wages and withholdings	2,253	2,373
Hedge margin liabilities	717	548
Self-insurance reserves	657	656
Other current liabilities	1,464	1,367
Total Current Liabilities	10,696	8,621
Long-Term Debt	11,316	9,856
Pension and Postretirement Benefit Obligations	10,638	11,452
Deferred Income Tax Liabilities	115	78
Self-Insurance Reserves	1,831	1,916

(continued)

	December 31,	
	2015	2014
Other Non-Current Liabilities	1,224	1,359
Shareowners' Equity:		
Class A common stock (194 and 201 shares issued in 2015 and 2014)	2	2
Class B common stock (693 and 705 shares issued in 2015 and 2014)	7	7
Additional paid-in capital	—	—
Retained earnings	6,001	5,726
Accumulated other comprehensive loss	(3,540)	(3,594)
Deferred compensation obligations	51	59
Less: Treasury stock (1 share in 2015 and 2014)	(51)	(59)
Total Equity for Controlling Interests	2,470	2,141
Noncontrolling Interests	21	17
Total Shareowners' Equity	2,491	2,158
Total Liabilities and Shareowners' Equity	$38,311	$35,440

NOTES TO CONSOLIDATED FINANCIAL STATEMENTS (in part)

Note 10. Shareowners' Equity (in part)

Deferred Compensation Obligations and Treasury Stock

We maintain a deferred compensation plan whereby certain employees were previously able to elect to defer the gains on stock option exercises by deferring the shares received upon exercise into a rabbi trust. The shares held in this trust are classified as treasury stock, and the liability to participating employees is classified as "deferred compensation obligations" in the shareowners' equity section of the consolidated balance sheets. The number of shares needed to settle the liability for deferred compensation obligations is included in the denominator in both the basic and diluted earnings per share calculations. Employees are generally no longer able to defer the gains from stock options exercised subsequent to December 31, 2004. Activity in the deferred compensation program for the years ended December 31, 2015, 2014 and 2013 is as follows (in millions):

	2015		2014		2013	
	Shares	Dollars	Shares	Dollars	Shares	Dollars
Deferred Compensation Obligations:						
Balance at beginning of year		$ 59		$ 69		$ 78
Reinvested dividends		3		2		4
Options exercise deferrals		—		—		—
Benefit payments		(11)		(12)		(13)
Balance at end of year		$ 51		$ 59		$ 69
Treasury Stock:						
Balance at beginning of year	(1)	$(59)	(1)	$(69)	(1)	$(78)
Reinvested dividends	—	(3)	—	(2)	—	(4)
Options exercise deferrals	—	—	—	—	—	—
Benefit payments	—	11	—	12	—	13
Balance at end of year	(1)	$(51)	(1)	$(59)	(1)	$(69)

WARRANTS

5.46 THE KRAFT HEINZ COMPANY (DEC)
CONSOLIDATED STATEMENTS OF EQUITY

(in millions)

	Common Stock	Warrants	Additional Paid-in Capital	Retained Earnings/ (Deficit)	Accumulated Other Comprehensive In- come/(Losses)	Treasury Stock	Noncontrolling Interest	Total Equity
Successor								
Balance at February 8, 2013	$—	$—	$ —	$ —	$ —	$—	$—	$ —
Fair value of noncontrolling interest as of June 8, 2013	—	—	—	—	—	—	230	230
Net (loss)/income excluding redeemable noncontrolling interest	—	—	—	(77)	—	—	5	(72)
Other comprehensive income/(loss) excluding redeemable noncontrolling interest	—	—	—	—	232	—	(13)	219

(continued)

	Common Stock	Warrants	Additional Paid-in Capital	Retained Earnings/ (Deficit)	Accumulated Other Comprehensive Income/(Losses)	Treasury Stock	Noncontrolling Interest	Total Equity
Dividends declared-Series A Preferred Stock	—	—	(360)	—	—	—	—	(360)
Dividends declared-noncontrolling interest	—	—	—	—	—	—	(6)	(6)
Accretion of Series A Preferred Stock to redemption value	—	—	(687)	—	—	—	—	(687)
Warrants issued	—	367	—	—	—	—	—	367
Issuance of common stock to Sponsors	4	—	8,496	—	—	—	—	8,500
Exercise of stock options, issuance of other stock awards, and other	—	—	1	—	—	—	—	1
Balance at December 29, 2013	$4	$367	$ 7,450	$ (77)	$ 232	$—	$216	$ 8,192
Net income excluding redeemable noncontrolling interest	—	—	—	657	—	—	14	671
Other comprehensive loss excluding redeemable noncontrolling interest	—	—	—	—	(806)	—	(4)	(810)
Dividends declared-Series A Preferred Stock	—	—	(142)	(578)	—	—	—	(720)
Dividends declared-noncontrolling interest	—	—	—	—	—	—	(7)	(7)
Exercise of stock options, issuance of other stock awards, and other	—	—	12	(2)	—	—	—	10
Balance at December 28, 2014	$ 4	$367	$ 7,320	$ —	$(574)	$—	$219	$ 7,336
Net income excluding redeemable noncontrolling interest	—	—	—	634	—	—	13	647
Other comprehensive loss excluding redeemable noncontrolling interest	—	—	—	—	(97)	—	(18)	(115)
Dividends declared-Series A Preferred Stock	—	—	(360)	(540)	—	—	—	(900)
Dividends declared-common stock	—	—	(1,972)	(92)	—	—	—	(2,064)
Dividends declared-noncontrolling interest	—	—	—	—	—	—	(6)	(6)
Exercise of warrants	—	(367)	367	—	—	—	—	—
Issuance of common stock to Sponsors	2	—	9,998	—	—	—	—	10,000
Acquisition of Kraft Foods Group, Inc.	6	—	42,849	—	—	—	—	42,855
Exercise of stock options, issuance of other stock awards, and other	—	—	173	(2)	—	(31)	—	140
Balance at January 3, 2016	$ 12	$—	$58,375	$ —	$(671)	$(31)	$208	$57,893

NOTES TO CONSOLIDATED FINANCIAL STATEMENTS (in part)

Note 1. Background and Basis of Presentation (in part)

Organization

On July 2, 2015 (the "2015 Merger Date"), through a series of transactions, we consummated the merger of Kraft Foods Group, Inc. ("Kraft") with and into a wholly-owned subsidiary of H.J. Heinz Holding Corporation ("Heinz") (the "2015 Merger"). At the closing of the 2015 Merger, Heinz was renamed The Kraft Heinz Company ("Kraft Heinz").

Before the consummation of the 2015 Merger, Heinz was controlled by Berkshire Hathaway Inc. ("Berkshire Hathaway") and 3G Global Food Holdings, L.P. ("3G Capital," and together with Berkshire Hathaway, the "Sponsors") following their acquisition of H. J. Heinz Company (the "2013 Merger") on June 7, 2013 (the "2013 Merger Date"). The Sponsors initially owned 850 million shares of common stock in Heinz; Berkshire Hathaway also held a warrant to purchase 46 million additional shares of common stock, which it exercised in June 2015. Additionally, in connection with the 2013 Merger, we issued an $8.0 billion preferred stock investment in Heinz which entitles Berkshire Hathaway to a 9.00% annual dividend. Prior to, but in connection with, the 2015 Merger, the Sponsors made equity investments whereby they purchased an additional 500 million newly issued shares of Heinz common stock for an aggregate purchase price of $10.0 billion.

Immediately prior to the consummation of the 2015 Merger, each share of Heinz issued and outstanding common stock was reclassified and changed into 0.443332 of a share of Kraft Heinz common stock. All share and per share amounts in the consolidated financial statements and related notes have been retroactively adjusted for all historical Successor periods presented to give effect to this conversion, including reclassifying an amount equal to the change in value of common stock to additional paid-in capital. In the 2015 Merger, all outstanding shares of Kraft common stock were converted into the right to receive, on a one-for-one basis, shares of Kraft Heinz common stock. Deferred shares and restricted shares of Kraft were converted to deferred shares and restricted shares of Kraft Heinz, as applicable. Upon the completion of the 2015 Merger, the Kraft shareholders of record immediately prior to the closing of the 2015 Merger received a special cash dividend of $16.50 per share.

On June 7, 2013, H. J. Heinz Company was acquired by Heinz (formerly known as Hawk Acquisition Holding Corporation), a Delaware corporation controlled by the Sponsors, pursuant to the Agreement and Plan of Merger, dated February 13, 2013 (the "2013 Merger Agreement"), as amended by the Amendment to Agreement and Plan of Merger, dated March 4, 2013 (the "Amendment"), by and among H. J. Heinz Company, Heinz, and Hawk Acquisition Sub, Inc. ("Hawk").

See Note 2, *Merger and Acquisition*, for additional information on the 2015 Merger and the 2013 Merger.

Periods Presented

The 2013 Merger established a new accounting basis for Heinz. Accordingly, the consolidated financial statements present both Predecessor and Successor periods, which relate to the accounting periods preceding and succeeding the completion of the 2013 Merger. The Predecessor and Successor periods are separated by a vertical line on the face of the consolidated financial statements to highlight the fact that the financial information for such periods has been prepared under two different historical-cost bases of accounting.

Additionally, on October 21, 2013, our Board of Directors approved a change in our fiscal year-end from the Sunday closest to April 30 to the Sunday closest to December 31. In 2013, as a result of the change in fiscal year-end, the 2013 Merger, and the creation of Hawk, there are three 2013 reporting periods as described below.

The "Successor (Heinz, renamed to The Kraft Heinz Company at the closing of the 2015 Merger) Period" includes:
- The consolidated financial statements for the year ended January 3, 2016 (a 53 week period, including a full year of Heinz results and post-2015 Merger results of Kraft);
- The consolidated financial statements for the year ended December 28, 2014 (a 52 week period, including a full year of Heinz results); and
- The period from February 8, 2013 through December 29, 2013 (the "2013 Successor Period"), reflecting:
  — The creation of Hawk on February 8, 2013 and the activity from February 8, 2013 to June 7, 2013, which related primarily to the issuance of debt and recognition of associated issuance costs and interest expense; and
  — All activity subsequent to the 2013 Merger. Therefore, the 2013 Successor Period includes 29 weeks of operating activity (June 8, 2013 to December 29, 2013). We indicate on our financial statements the weeks of operating activities in this period.

The "Predecessor (H. J. Heinz Company) Period" includes, but is not limited to:
- The consolidated financial statements of H. J. Heinz Company prior to the 2013 Merger on June 7, 2013, which includes the period from April 29, 2013 through June 7, 2013 (the "2013 Predecessor Period"); this represents six weeks of activity from April 29, 2013 through the 2013 Merger; and
- The consolidated financial statements of H. J. Heinz Company for the fiscal year from April 30, 2012 to April 28, 2013 ("Fiscal 2013").

Note 2. Merger and Acquisition (in part)

2013 Merger

Transaction Overview:

As discussed in Note 1, *Background and Basis of Presentation*, the 2013 Merger occurred on June 7, 2013. Under the Merger Agreement between H. J. Heinz Company, Heinz, and Hawk, Hawk merged with and into H. J. Heinz Company, with H. J. Heinz Company surviving as a wholly-owned subsidiary of H.J. Heinz Corporation II. H.J. Heinz Corporation II was an indirect wholly-owned subsidiary of Heinz, which was controlled by the Sponsors. Upon completion of the 2013 Merger, H. J. Heinz Company's shareholders received $72.50 in cash, without interest and less applicable taxes, for each share of common stock held prior to the effective time of the 2013 Merger. Additionally, all outstanding stock option awards, restricted stock units ("RSUs") (except for certain retention RSUs which continued on their original terms), and restricted stock awards were automatically canceled and converted into the right to receive cash consideration of $72.50.

The total consideration paid in connection with the 2013 Merger was $28.8 billion, including the assumption of H. J. Heinz Company's outstanding debt, which was funded by equity contributions from the Sponsors totaling $16.5 billion, comprised of $8.5 billion of common stock, $7.6 billion of preferred stock and $0.4 billion of warrants, as well as proceeds received by Hawk of approximately $11.5 billion (of which $9.5 billion was drawn at the close of the transaction), and $3.1 billion upon issuance of the 4.250% Second Lien Senior Secured Notes, less applicable debt issuance costs of $316 million. As a result of the 2013 Merger, we assumed the liabilities and obligations of Hawk.

Note 13. Preferred Stock and Warrants (in part)

In connection with the 2013 Merger, we issued 80,000 shares of 9.00% Series A Cumulative Redeemable Preferred Stock ("Series A Preferred Stock") and warrants to purchase 46 million Heinz common shares, at an exercise price of $0.01 per common share (the "Warrants"), for an aggregate purchase price of $8.0 billion. We allocated the proceeds to the Series A Preferred Stock ($7.6 billion) and the Warrants ($367 million) on a relative fair value basis. In June 2015, Berkshire Hathaway exercised the Warrants to purchase the additional 46 million Heinz common shares, which were subsequently reclassified and changed into approximately 20 million shares of Kraft Heinz common stock.

Note 14. Common Stock

Our Amended and Restated Certificate of Incorporation authorizes the issuance of up to 5.0 billion shares of common stock.

Immediately prior to the consummation of the 2015 Merger, each share of Heinz issued and outstanding common stock was reclassified and changed into 0.443332 of a share of Kraft Heinz common stock. All successor share and per share amounts have been retroactively adjusted for all historical Successor periods presented to give effect to this conversion. In the 2015 Merger, all outstanding shares of Kraft common stock were converted into the right to receive, on a one-for-one basis, shares of Kraft Heinz common stock.

Shares of common stock issued, in treasury and outstanding were (in thousands of shares):

	Shares Issued	Treasury Shares	Shares Outstanding
Predecessor (H. J. Heinz Company)			
Balance at April 29, 2012	431,096	(110,871)	320,225
Exercise of stock options, issuance of other stock awards, and other	—	1,041	1,041
Balance at April 28, 2013	431,096	(109,830)	321,266
Exercise of stock options, issuance of other stock awards, and other	—	33	33
Balance at June 7, 2013	431,096	(109,797)	321,299
Successor			
Balance at February 8, 2013	—	—	—
Issuance of common stock to Sponsors	376,832	—	376,832
Balance at December 29, 2013	376,832	—	376,832
Exercise of stock options, issuance of other stock awards, and other	178	—	178
Balance at December 28, 2014	377,010	—	377,010
Exercise of warrants	20,480	—	20,480
Issuance of common stock to Sponsors	221,666	—	221,666
Acquisition of Kraft Foods Group, Inc.	592,898	—	592,898
Exercise of stock options, issuance of other stock awards, and other	2,338	(413)	1,925
Balance at January 3, 2016	1,214,392	(413)	1,213,979

Upon completion of the 2013 Merger, all outstanding shares of H. J. Heinz Company were canceled and automatically converted into the right to receive $72.50.

NONCONTROLLING INTEREST

5.47 CHESAPEAKE ENERGY CORPORATION (DEC)
CONSOLIDATED STATEMENTS OF STOCKHOLDERS' EQUITY

($ in millions)	Years Ended December 31,		
	2015	**2014**	**2013**
Preferred Stock:			
Balance, beginning and end of period	$ 3,062	$ 3,062	$ 3,062
Common Stock:			
Balance, beginning and end of period	7	7	7
Paid-In Capital:			
Balance, beginning of period	12,531	12,446	12,293
Stock-based compensation	71	47	162
Exercise of stock options	—	23	4
Dividends on common stock	(59)	—	—
Dividends on preferred stock	(128)	—	—
Increase (decrease) in tax benefit from stock-based compensation	(12)	15	(13)
Balance, end of period	12,403	12,531	12,446

(continued)

($ in millions)	Years Ended December 31,		
	2015	2014	2013
Retained Earnings (Accumulated Deficit):			
Balance, beginning of period	1,483	688	437
Net income (loss) attributable to Chesapeake	(14,685)	1,917	724
Dividends on common stock	—	(234)	(233)
Dividends on preferred stock	—	(171)	(171)
Spin-off of oilfield services business	—	(270)	—
Repurchase of preferred shares of CHK Utica	—	(447)	(69)
Balance, end of period	(13,202)	1,483	688
Accumulated Other Comprehensive Income (Loss):			
Balance, beginning of period	(143)	(162)	(182)
Hedging activity	44	24	22
Investment activity	—	(5)	(2)
Balance, end of period	(99)	(143)	(162)
Treasury Stock—Common:			
Balance, beginning of period	(37)	(46)	(48)
Purchase of 54,493, 34,678 and 251,403 shares for company benefit plans	(1)	(1)	(6)
Release of 231,081, 422,395 and 397,098 shares from company benefit plans	5	10	8
Balance, end of period	(33)	(37)	(46)
Total Chesapeake Stockholders' Equity	2,138	16,903	15,995
Noncontrolling Interests:			
Balance, beginning of period	1,302	2,145	2,327
Net income attributable to noncontrolling interests	50	139	170
Distributions to noncontrolling interest owners	(78)	(169)	(215)
Repurchase of noncontrolling interest of CHK C-T	(1,015)	—	—
Repurchase of preferred shares of CHK Utica	—	(807)	(143)
Sales of noncontrolling interests	—	—	6
Deconsolidation of investments, net	—	(6)	—
Balance, end of period	259	1,302	2,145
Total Equity	$ 2,397	$18,205	$18,140

NOTES TO CONSOLIDATED FINANCIAL STATEMENTS (in part)

1. Basis of Presentation and Summary of Significant Accounting Policies (in part)

Noncontrolling Interests

Noncontrolling interests represent third-party equity ownership in certain of our consolidated subsidiaries and are presented as a component of equity. See Note 8 for further discussion of noncontrolling interests.

8. Equity (in part)

Noncontrolling Interests

Cleveland Tonkawa Financial Transaction. We formed CHK C-T in March 2012 to continue development of a portion of our oil and natural gas assets in our Cleveland and Tonkawa plays. In exchange for all of the common shares of CHK C-T, we contributed to CHK C-T approximately 245,000 net acres of leasehold and the existing wells within an area of mutual interest in the plays between the top of the Tonkawa and the top of the Big Lime formations covering Ellis and Roger Mills counties in western Oklahoma. In March 2012, in a private placement, third-party investors contributed $1.25 billion in cash to CHK C-T in exchange for (i) 1.25 million preferred shares, and (ii) our obligation to deliver a 3.75% overriding royalty interest (ORRI) in the existing wells and up to 1,000 future net wells to be drilled on the contributed play leasehold. We initially committed to drill and complete, for the benefit of CHK C-T in the area of mutual interest, a minimum cumulative total of 300 net wells. We ultimately drilled and completed 190 net wells, and the drilling commitment was suspended in January 2015.

During 2015, CHK C-T sold all of its oil and natural gas properties to FourPoint Energy, LLC (FourPoint) and immediately used the consideration received, plus other cash it had on hand, to repurchase and cancel all of the outstanding preferred shares in CHK C-T. Chesapeake is responsible for post-closing adjustments to the purchase price and has certain indemnity obligations in connection with the sale to FourPoint. In connection with the repurchase and cancellation of the CHK C-T preferred stock and related agreements with the CHK C-T investors, we eliminated quarterly preferred dividend payments and all related future drilling and ORRI commitments attributable to CHK C-T. The sale of the oil and natural gas properties was accounted for as a reduction of capitalized costs with no gain or loss recognized.

As of December 31, 2014, $1.015 billion of noncontrolling interests on our consolidated balance sheets was attributable to CHK C-T. For 2015, 2014 and 2013, income of $50 million, $75 million and $75 million, respectively, was attributable to the noncontrolling interests of CHK C-T.

Utica Financial Transaction. We formed CHK Utica, L.L.C. (CHK Utica) in October 2011 to develop a portion of our Utica Shale oil and natural gas assets. In exchange for all of the common shares of CHK Utica, we contributed to CHK Utica approximately 700,000 net acres of leasehold and the existing wells within an area of mutual interest in the Utica Shale play covering 13 counties located primarily in eastern Ohio. During November and December 2011, in private placements, third-party investors contributed $1.25 billion in cash to CHK Utica in exchange for (i) 1.25 million preferred shares, and (ii) our obligation to deliver a 3% ORRI in 1,500 net wells to be drilled on certain of our Utica Shale leasehold.

In July 2014, we repurchased all of the outstanding preferred shares of CHK Utica from third-party preferred shareholders for approximately $1.254 billion, or approximately $1,189 per share including accrued dividends. The $447 million difference between the cash paid for the preferred shares and the carrying value of the noncontrolling interest acquired was reflected in retained earnings and as a reduction to net income available to common stockholders for purposes of our EPS computations. Pursuant to the transaction, our obligation to pay quarterly dividends to third-party preferred shareholders was eliminated. In addition, the development agreement was terminated pursuant to the transaction, which eliminated our obligation to drill and complete a minimum number of wells within a specified period for the benefit of CHK Utica. Our repurchase of the outstanding preferred shares in CHK Utica did not affect our obligation to deliver a 3% ORRI in 1,500 net wells on certain Utica Shale leasehold.

The CHK Utica investors' right to receive, proportionately, a 3% ORRI in the first 1,500 net wells drilled on our Utica Shale leasehold is subject to an increase to 4% on net wells earned in any year following a year in which we do not meet our net well commitment under the ORRI obligation, which runs through 2023. However, in no event are we required to deliver to investors more than a total ORRI of 3% in 1,500 net wells. If at any time we hold fewer net acres than would enable us to drill all then-remaining net wells on 150-acre spacing, the investors have the right to require us to repurchase their right to receive ORRIs in the remaining net wells at the then-current fair market value of the remaining ORRIs. We retain the right to repurchase the investors' right to receive ORRIs in the remaining net wells at the then-current fair market value of the remaining ORRIs once we have drilled a minimum of 1,300 net wells. As of December 31, 2015, we had drilled 499 net wells. The obligation to deliver future ORRIs has been recorded as a liability which will be settled through the future conveyance of the underlying ORRIs to the investors on a net-well basis, at which time the associated liability will be reversed and the sale of the ORRIs reflected as an adjustment to the capitalized cost of our oil and natural gas properties. Because we did not meet our ORRI commitment in 2012, the ORRI increased to 4% for wells earned in 2013, and the ultimate number of wells in which we must assign an interest was reduced accordingly. We met our ORRI conveyance commitments as of December 31, 2013, 2014 and 2015.

In 2014 and 2013, income of approximately $43 million and $79 million, respectively, was attributable to the noncontrolling interests of CHK Utica.

Chesapeake Granite Wash Trust. In November 2011, Chesapeake Granite Wash Trust (the Trust) sold 23,000,000 common units representing beneficial interests in the Trust at a price of $19.00 per common unit in its initial public offering. The common units are listed on the New York Stock Exchange and trade under the symbol "CHKR". We own 12,062,500 common units and 11,687,500 subordinated units, which in the aggregate represent an approximate 51% beneficial interest in the Trust. The Trust has a total of 46,750,000 units outstanding.

In connection with the Trust's initial public offering, we conveyed royalty interests to the Trust that entitle the Trust to receive (i) 90% of the proceeds (after deducting certain post-production expenses and any applicable taxes) that we receive from the production of hydrocarbons from 69 then-producing wells, and (ii) 50% of the proceeds (after deducting certain post-production expenses and any applicable taxes) in 118 development wells that have been or will be drilled on approximately 45,400 gross acres (29,000 net acres) in the Colony Granite Wash play in Washita County in the Anadarko Basin of western Oklahoma. Pursuant to the terms of a development agreement with the Trust, we are obligated to drill and complete, or cause to be drilled and completed, the development wells at our own expense prior to June 30, 2016, and the Trust is not responsible for any costs related to the drilling and completion of the development wells or any other operating or capital costs of the Trust properties. In addition, we granted to the Trust a lien on our remaining interests in the undeveloped properties that are subject to the development agreement in order to secure our drilling obligation to the Trust, although the maximum amount recoverable by the Trust under the lien was limited to $263 million initially and is proportionately reduced as we fulfill our drilling obligation over time. As of December 31, 2015, we had drilled and completed or caused to be drilled and completed approximately 106 development wells, as calculated under the development agreement, and the maximum amount recoverable under the drilling support lien was approximately $27 million.

The subordinated units we hold in the Trust are entitled to receive pro rata distributions from the Trust each quarter if and to the extent there is sufficient cash to provide a cash distribution on the common units that is not less than the applicable subordination threshold for the quarter. If there is not sufficient cash to fund a distribution on all of the Trust units, the distribution to be made with respect to the subordinated units is reduced or eliminated for the quarter in order to make a distribution, to the extent possible, of up to the subordination threshold amount on the common units. The distribution made with respect to the subordinated units to Chesapeake was either reduced or eliminated for each of the most recent 14 quarters. In exchange for agreeing to subordinate a portion of our Trust units, and in order to provide additional financial incentive to us to satisfy our drilling obligation and perform operations on the underlying properties in an efficient and cost-effective manner, Chesapeake is entitled to receive incentive distributions equal to 50% of the amount by which the cash available for distribution on the Trust units in any quarter exceeds the applicable incentive threshold for the quarter. The remaining 50% of cash available for distribution in excess of the applicable incentive threshold is to be paid to Trust unitholders, including Chesapeake, on a pro rata basis. Through December 31, 2015, no incentive distributions had been made. At the end of the fourth full calendar quarter following our satisfaction of our drilling obligation with respect to the development wells, the subordinated units will automatically convert into common units on a one-for-one basis and our right to receive incentive distributions will terminate. After this time, the common units will no longer have the protection of the subordination threshold, and all Trust unitholders will share in the Trust's distributions on a pro rata basis.

For the years ended December 31, 2015, 2014 and 2013, the Trust declared and paid the following distributions:

Production Period	Distribution Date	Cash Distribution per Common Unit	Cash Distribution per Subordinated Unit
June 2015—August 2015	November 30, 2015	$0.3232	$ —
March 2015—May 2015	August 31, 2015	$0.3579	$ —
December 2014—February 2015	June 1, 2015	$0.3899	$ —
September 2014—November 2014	March 2, 2015	$0.4496	$ —
June 2014—August 2014	December 1, 2014	$0.5079	$ —
March 2014—May 2014	August 29, 2014	$0.5796	$ —
December 2013—February 2014	May 30, 2014	$0.6454	$ —
September 2013—November 2013	March 3, 2014	$0.6624	$ —
June 2013—August 2013	November 29, 2013	$0.6671	$ —
March 2013—May 2013	August 29, 2013	$0.6900	$0.1432
December 2012—February 2013	May 31, 2013	$0.6900	$0.3010
September 2012—November 2012	March 1, 2013	$0.6700	$0.3772

We have determined that the Trust is a variable interest entity (VIE) and that Chesapeake is the primary beneficiary. As a result, the Trust is included in our consolidated financial statements. As of December 31, 2015 and 2014, approximately $259 million and $287 million, respectively, of noncontrolling interests on our consolidated balance sheets were attributable to the Trust. In 2015 we had net income of a nominal amount and in 2014 and 2013 we had net income of $24 million and $20 million, respectively, attributable to the Trust's noncontrolling interests in our consolidated statements of operations as income. See Note 15 for further discussion of VIEs.

15. Variable Interest Entities (in part)

We consolidate the activities of VIEs for which we are the primary beneficiary. In order to determine whether we own a variable interest in a VIE, we perform a qualitative analysis of the entity's design, organizational structure, primary decision makers and relevant agreements.

Consolidated VIE

Chesapeake Granite Wash Trust. For a discussion of the formation, operations and presentation of the Trust, see *Noncontrolling Interests* in Note 8. The Trust is considered a VIE due to the lack of voting or similar decision-making rights by its equity holders regarding activities that have a significant effect on the economic success of the Trust. Our ownership in the Trust and our obligations under the development agreement and related drilling support lien constitute variable interests. We have determined that we are the primary beneficiary of the Trust because (i) we have the power to direct the activities that most significantly impact the economic performance of the Trust via our obligations to perform under the development agreement, and (ii) as a result of the subordination and incentive thresholds applicable to the subordinated units we hold in the Trust, we have the obligation to absorb losses and the right to receive residual returns that potentially could be significant to the Trust. As a result, we consolidate the Trust in our financial statements, and the common units of the Trust owned by third parties are reflected as a noncontrolling interest.

The Trust is a consolidated entity whose legal existence is separate from Chesapeake and our other consolidated subsidiaries, and the Trust is not a guarantor of any of Chesapeake's debt. The creditors or beneficial holders of the Trust have no recourse to the general credit of Chesapeake; however, we have certain obligations to the Trust through the development agreement that are secured by a drilling support lien on our retained interest in the development wells up to a specified maximum amount recoverable by the Trust, which could result in the

Trust acquiring all or a portion of our retained interest in the undeveloped portion of an area of mutual interest, if we do not meet our drilling commitment. In consolidation, as of December 31, 2015, $1 million of cash and cash equivalents, $488 million of proved oil and natural gas properties, $428 million of accumulated depreciation, depletion and amortization and $8 million of other current liabilities were attributable to the Trust. We have presented parenthetically on the face of the consolidated balance sheets the assets of the Trust that can be used only to settle obligations of the Trust and the liabilities of the Trust for which creditors do not have recourse to the general credit of Chesapeake.

Section 6: **Statement of Cash Flows**

General

PRESENTATION

6.01 FASB *Accounting Standards Codification* (ASC) 230, *Statement of Cash Flows*, requires entities to present a statement of cash flows that classifies cash receipts and payments by operating, investing, and financing activities. The information provided in a statement of cash flows, if used with related disclosures and information in the other financial statements, should help investors, creditors, and others assess the following:
- The entity's ability to generate positive future net cash flows
- The entity's ability to meet its obligations, its ability to pay dividends, and its needs for external financing
- The reasons for differences between net income and associated cash receipts and payments
- The effects on an entity's financial position of both its cash and noncash investing and financing transactions during the period

6.02 Paragraphs 4–6 of FASB ASC 230-10-45 provide that the statement of cash flows explains the change in cash and cash equivalents during a period. *Cash equivalents* are defined by the FASB ASC glossary to be short-term, highly liquid investments that have both of the following characteristics:
- Readily convertible to known amounts of cash
- So near their maturity that they present an insignificant risk of changes in value because of changes in interest rates

Generally, only investments with original maturities of three months or less qualify under that definition. *Original maturity* means original maturity to the entity holding the investment.

6.03 FASB ASC 230-10-45-4 states that the amount of cash and cash equivalents at the beginning and end of the period reported on a statement of cash flows should agree with the amount of cash and cash equivalents reported on a statement of financial position. Because not all investments that qualify are required to be treated as cash equivalents, an entity should establish a policy concerning which short-term, highly liquid investments that satisfy the definition of *cash equivalents* are treated as such.

6.04 Paragraphs 7–9 of FASB ASC 230-10-45 explain that generally, cash receipts and payments should be reported separately and not netted. For certain items, the turnover is quick, the amounts are large, and the maturities are short. For certain other items, such as demand deposits of a bank and customer accounts payable of a broker-dealer, the entity is substantively holding or disbursing cash on behalf of its customers. Only the net changes during the period in assets and liabilities with those characteristics need be reported because knowledge of the gross cash receipts and payments related to them may not be necessary to understand the entity's operating, investing, and financing activities. Specifically, provided that the original maturity of the asset or liability is three months or less, cash receipts and payments pertaining to investments (other than cash equivalents), loans receivable, and debt qualify for net reporting based on this rationale.

6.05 FASB ASC 830-230-45-1 specifies that the effect of exchange rate changes on cash balances held in foreign currencies be reported as a separate part of the reconciliation of the change in cash and cash equivalents during the period in the statement of cash flows. Further, a statement of cash flows of an entity with foreign exchange transactions or foreign operations should report the reporting currency equivalent of foreign currency cash flows using the exchange rates in effect at the time of the cash flows. An appropriately weighted average exchange rate for the period may be used for translation if the result is substantially the same as if the rates at the dates of the cash flows were used.

DISCLOSURE

6.06 FASB ASC 230-10-50-1 explains that an entity should disclose its policy regarding cash equivalent classification, and any change to that policy is a change in accounting principle that should be affected by restating financial statements for earlier years presented for comparative purposes. FASB ASC 230-10-50-2 specifies that if the indirect method is used, amounts of interest (net of capitalized amounts) and income tax payments during the period are required to be disclosed.

6.07 Paragraphs 3–6 of FASB ASC 230-10-50 require the disclosure of information about noncash investing and financing activities. Examples of noncash investing and financing transactions include converting debt to equity; acquiring assets by assuming directly related liabilities, such as purchasing a building by incurring a mortgage to the seller; obtaining an asset by entering into a capital lease; obtaining a building or investment asset by receiving a gift; and exchanging noncash assets or liabilities for other noncash assets or liabilities. If only a few noncash transactions exist, it may be convenient to include them on the same page as the statement of cash flows. Otherwise, the transactions may be reported elsewhere in the financial statements and clearly referenced to the statement of cash flows.

PRESENTATION AND DISCLOSURE EXCERPTS

CASH AND CASH EQUIVALENTS

6.08 OFFICE DEPOT, INC. (DEC)
MANAGEMENT'S DISCUSSION AND ANALYSIS OF FINANCIAL CONDITION AND RESULTS OF OPERATIONS (in part)

Liquidity and Capital Resources

Liquidity

At December 26, 2015, we had $1.1 billion in cash and equivalents and another $1.2 billion available under the Amended Credit Agreement (as defined in Note 8, "Debt," of the Consolidated Financial Statements) based on the December 2015 borrowing base certificate, for a total liquidity of $2.2 billion. The Amended Credit Agreement provides for an asset based, multi-currency revolving credit facility of up to $1.25 billion and expires May 25, 2017. We consider our resources adequate to satisfy our cash needs for at least the next twelve months.

Cash and cash equivalents held outside the United States, at December 26, 2015, amounted to $253 million and could result in additional tax expense if repatriated. Refer to Note 9, "Income Taxes" of the Consolidated Financial Statements for additional information.

No amounts were drawn under the Amended Credit Agreement during 2015 and no amounts were outstanding at December 26, 2015. There were letters of credit outstanding under the Amended Credit Agreement at the end of the year totaling $84 million.

The Company had short-term borrowings of $4 million at December 26, 2015 under various local currency credit facilities for international subsidiaries that had an effective interest rate at the end of the year of approximately 4%. The maximum month end balance occurred in June 2015 at $6 million and the maximum monthly average amount occurred in July 2015 at $5 million. The majority of these short-term borrowings represent outstanding balances on uncommitted lines of credit, which do not contain financial covenants.

The Company was in compliance with all applicable financial covenants at December 26, 2015.

Since the Merger date, we have incurred significant expenses associated with the Merger and integration actions, including costs associated with the Real Estate Strategy, and we have incurred significant expenses from restructuring activities in Europe. Approximately $100 million of net cash Merger integration costs are anticipated through the remaining integration period.

In 2016, the Company expects capital expenditures to be approximately $250 million, including approximately $50 million related to Merger integration.

We have entered into the Staples Merger Agreement with Staples and have agreed to pay a fee of $185 million to Staples if each of the following conditions are met: (i) the Staples Merger Agreement is terminated by the Company before the date permitted by the Staples Merger Agreement, as amended, (ii) a third party has made an acquisition proposal before the termination of the Staples Merger Agreement, and (iii) within 12 months of the termination of the Staples Merger Agreement, the Company enters into an alternative transaction. Staples is required to pay Office Depot a termination fee of $250 million if the Staples Merger Agreement is terminated in certain circumstances relating to the antitrust regulatory review process. On February 2, 2016, the Company and Staples entered into a letter agreement to waive, until May 16, 2016, certain of their respective rights to terminate the Staples Merger Agreement.

In addition, whether or not the Staples Acquisition is completed, the uncertainty related to the proposed Staples Acquisition could continue to adversely impact our business through several factors, including, but not limited to: (i) our current customers may experience uncertainty associated with the Staples Acquisition and may attempt to negotiate changes in existing business relationships or consider entering into business relationships with parties other than us; (ii) we may face additional challenges in competing for new and renewal business; (iii) vendors or suppliers may seek to modify or terminate their business relationships with us; and (iv) our ability to retain and hire associates.

In 2016, the Company expects to incur $30 million of additional expenses related to the extended regulator reviews of the pending acquisition by Staples. The $72 million accrued retention will be paid in the first quarter of 2016, regardless of review decisions.

Cash Flows

Cash provided by (used in) operating, investing and financing activities is summarized as follows:

(In millions)	2015	2014	2013
Operating activities	$126	$156	$ (107)
Investing activities	(74)	(28)	1,028
Financing activities	(25)	15	(640)

Operating Activities

The 2015 and 2014 operating cash flows reflect a full year of operations as a combined company compared to the 2013 impact of the OfficeMax business only following the Merger date of November 5, 2013. Operating activities reflect outflows related to Merger and integration activities in all three years. Cash used in operating activities in 2013 was negatively impacted by the payment of $147 million of income taxes related to the Company's gain on the disposition of the investment in Office Depot de Mexico. The source of cash from this gain is shown in Investing activities.

Changes in net working capital for 2015 resulted in a $276 million use of cash compared to $10 million in 2014 and $77 million in 2013. The working capital factors in 2015 includes $77 million settlement payment of the Legal Accrual, the payment of the 2014 accrued incentive pay, and a net use of cash in integration related activities. Additionally, inventory levels are higher at year-end 2015 when compared to the 2014 period, impacted by the supply chain integration. The working capital factors in 2014 are largely attributable to timing, including the impact on certain payables of a one day shift in the retail calendar. The change in accounts receivable in 2013 was influenced by the timing of certain vendor arrangements, largely offset by proceeds from an account receivable factoring agreement in France. The increase in inventories in 2013 reflects building above prior year levels for the back to business selling cycle. Inventory balances were lower at the end of 2012 as a result of initiatives to better manage working capital. The working capital changes in 2013 were also impacted by the timing of the Merger, which caused the consolidated cash flows to reflect the changes in the OfficeMax working capital accounts from the Merger date through year-end 2013.

The timing of changes in working capital is subject to variability during the year and across years depending on a variety of factors, including period end sales, the flow of goods, credit terms, timing of promotions, vendor production planning, new product introductions and working capital management. For our accounting policy on cash management, refer to Note 1, "Summary of Significant Accounting Policies," of the Consolidated Financial Statements.

The Company expects total Company sales in 2016 to be lower than 2015, primarily due to its decision to close certain stores, continued business disruption from the pending Staples Acquisition, challenging market trends in our industry, and the negative impact of currency translation.

Investing Activities

During 2015, $163 million was used for capital expenditures and $9 million was used for acquisition of an interior furniture business. These outflows were partially offset by $97 million of proceeds from the disposition of assets and other, primarily, the sale of warehouse facilities that previously were classified as held for sale. Additional facility sales are anticipated as the Real Estate Strategy is implemented. The use of cash in 2014 reflects $123 million of capital expenditures, partially offset by $43 million proceeds from the disposition of Grupo OfficeMax, $43 million proceeds from the sale of Boise Cascade Company common stock, and $12 million proceeds from the disposition of assets and other.

The source of cash in 2013 results primarily from $675 million in net proceeds from the disposition of the joint venture Office Depot de Mexico and $460 million in cash acquired from OfficeMax at the Merger date. The cash proceeds from the sale of Office Depot de Mexico provided additional liquidity for the preferred stock retirement, debt maturity and for the needs of the combined Company for Merger-related expenses. A $35 million return of investment in Boise Cascade Holdings also contributed to the source of cash in 2013. Capital expenditures in 2013 were $137 million.

Financing Activities

During 2015, payments on short- and long-term borrowings were $51 million, partially offset by proceeds from short- and long-term borrowings of $20 million and employee share-based transactions of $7 million. The 2014 source of cash resulted from net proceeds from exercise of employee share-based transactions of $39 million and proceeds from borrowings of $21 million. Payments on long and short-term borrowings were $45 million during 2014.

In 2013, the Company redeemed 50% of its preferred stock in July and the remaining 50% in November with total cash payments of $431 million. The redemption payment of $431 million includes the liquidation preference of $407 million and redemption premium of $24 million, measured at 6% of the liquidation preference. The premium of $24 million is included in the $63 million dividend of preferred stock. Contractual dividends on preferred stock were paid in cash in 2013. Also in 2013, the Company repaid the $150 million of 6.25% senior notes at maturity. Net repayments on long and short-term borrowings were $21 million in 2013.

FOREIGN CURRENCY CASH FLOWS

6.09 ORACLE CORPORATION (MAY)
QUANTITATIVE AND QUALITATIVE DISCLOSURES ABOUT MARKET RISK (in part)

Currency Risk

Foreign Currency Transaction and Translation Risks—Foreign Currency Borrowings and Related Hedges

In July 2013, we issued €1.25 billion of 2.25% notes due January 2021 (January 2021 Notes) and we entered into certain cross-currency swap agreements to manage the related foreign exchange risk by effectively converting the fixed-rate Euro denominated debt, including the annual interest payments and the payment of principal at maturity, to a fixed-rate, U.S. Dollar denominated debt. The economic effect of the swap agreements was to eliminate the uncertainty of the cash flows in U.S. Dollars associated with the January 2021 Notes by fixing the principal amount of the January 2021 Notes at $1.6 billion with an annual interest rate of 3.53%. The critical terms of the cross-currency swap agreements match the critical terms of January 2021 Notes, including the notional amounts and maturity dates. We do not use these cross-currency swap arrangements for trading purposes. We are accounting for these interest rate swap agreements as cash flow hedges pursuant to ASC 815. The fair values of these cross-currency swap agreements as of May 31, 2015 and 2014 were a $(244) million loss and a $74 million gain, respectively. The changes in the fair values of the cross-currency swap agreements during fiscal 2015 were primarily attributable to the decline in the value of the Euro relative to the U.S. Dollar. If the Euro weakened by 10% as of May 31, 2015, we estimate the change would decrease the fair values of the cross-currency swap agreements by $174 million. If interest rates that correspond to the remaining term of the January 2021 Notes decreased by 100 basis points as of May 31, 2015, we estimate the change would decrease the fair values of the cross-currency swap agreements by $91 million. Additional details regarding our senior notes and related cross-currency swap agreements are included in Notes 8 and 11 of Notes to Consolidated Financial Statements included elsewhere in this Annual Report.

In July 2013, we also issued €750 million of 3.125% notes due July 2025 (2025 Notes). We designated the 2025 Notes as a net investment hedge of our investments in certain of our international subsidiaries that use the Euro as their functional currency in order to reduce the volatility in stockholders' equity caused by the changes in foreign currency exchange rates of the Euro with respect to the U.S. Dollar. As a result, the change in the carrying value of the Euro denominated 2025 Notes due to fluctuations in foreign currency exchange rates on the effective portion is recorded in accumulated other comprehensive loss on our consolidated balance sheet and is also presented as a line item in our consolidated statements of comprehensive income included elsewhere in this Annual Report and totaled $208 million of net other comprehensive gains for fiscal 2015. Any remaining change in the carrying value of the 2025 Notes representing the ineffective portion of the net investment hedge is recognized in non-operating income (expense), net. We did not record any ineffectiveness during fiscal 2015.

Fluctuations in the exchange rates between the Euro and the U.S. Dollar will impact the amount of U.S. Dollars that we will require to settle the 2025 Notes at maturity. If the U.S. Dollar weakened by 10% in comparison to the Euro as of May 31, 2015, we estimate our obligation to cash settle the principal portion of the 2025 Notes in U.S. Dollars would increase by approximately $81 million.

Foreign Currency Transaction Risk—Foreign Currency Forward Contracts

We transact business in various foreign currencies and have established a program that primarily utilizes foreign currency forward contracts to offset the risks associated with the effects of certain foreign currency exposures. Under this program, our strategy is to enter into foreign currency forward contracts so that increases or decreases in our foreign currency exposures are offset by gains or losses on the foreign currency forward contracts in order to mitigate the risks and volatility associated with our foreign currency transactions. We may suspend this program from time to time. Our foreign currency exposures typically arise from intercompany sublicense fees, intercompany loans and other intercompany transactions. Our foreign currency forward contracts are generally short-term in duration.

We neither use these foreign currency forward contracts for trading purposes nor do we designate these forward contracts as hedging instruments pursuant to ASC 815. Accordingly, we record the fair values of these contracts as of the end of our reporting period to our consolidated balance sheet with changes in fair values recorded to our consolidated statement of operations. Given the short duration of the forward contracts, the amount recorded is not significant. The balance sheet classification for the fair values of these forward contracts is prepaid expenses and other current assets for a net unrealized gain position and other current liabilities for a net unrealized loss position. The statement of operations classification for changes in fair values of these forward contracts is non-operating income (expense), net for both realized and unrealized gains and losses.

We expect that we will continue to realize gains or losses with respect to our foreign currency exposures, net of gains or losses from our foreign currency forward contracts. Our ultimate realized gain or loss with respect to foreign currency exposures will generally depend on the size and type of cross-currency transactions that we enter into, the currency exchange rates associated with these exposures and changes in those rates, the net realized gain or loss on our foreign currency forward contracts and other factors. As of May 31, 2015 and 2014, the notional amounts of the forward contracts we held to purchase U.S. Dollars in exchange for other major international currencies were $2.2 billion and $3.6 billion, respectively. As of May 31, 2015 and 2014, the notional amounts of forward contracts we held to sell U.S. Dollars in exchange for other major international currencies were $1.2 billion and $2.0 billion, respectively. The fair values of our outstanding foreign currency forward contracts were nominal at May 31, 2015 and 2014. Net foreign exchange transaction losses included in non-operating income (expense), net in the accompanying consolidated statements of operations were $157 million, $375 million and $162 million in fiscal 2015, 2014 and 2013, respectively. Included in the net foreign exchange transaction losses for fiscal 2015, fiscal 2014 and fiscal 2013 were foreign currency remeasurement losses relating to our Venezuelan subsidiary's operations of $23 million, $213 million and $64 million, respectively (see Note 1 of Notes to Consolidated Financial Statements included elsewhere in this Annual Report for additional information). As a large portion of our consolidated operations are international, we could experience additional foreign currency volatility in the future, the amounts and timing of which are unknown.

Foreign Currency Translation Risk—Impact on Cash, Cash Equivalents and Marketable Securities

Fluctuations in foreign currencies impact the amount of total assets and liabilities that we report for our foreign subsidiaries upon the translation of these amounts into U.S. Dollars. In particular, the amount of cash, cash equivalents and marketable securities that we report in U.S. Dollars for a significant portion of the cash held by these subsidiaries is subject to translation variance caused by changes in foreign currency exchange rates as of the end of each respective reporting period (the offset to which is substantially recorded to accumulated other comprehensive loss on our consolidated balance sheet and is also presented as a line item in our consolidated statements of comprehensive income included elsewhere in this Annual Report).

As the U.S. Dollar fluctuated against certain international currencies as of the end of fiscal 2015, the amount of cash, cash equivalents and marketable securities that we reported in U.S. Dollars for foreign subsidiaries that hold international currencies as of May 31, 2015 decreased relative to what we would have reported using a constant currency rate as of May 31, 2014. As reported in our consolidated statements of cash flows, the estimated effects of exchange rate changes on our reported cash and cash equivalents balances in U.S. Dollars for fiscal 2015, 2014 and 2013 were decreases of $1.2 billion, $158 million and $110 million, respectively. The following table includes estimates of the U.S. Dollar equivalent of cash, cash equivalents and marketable securities denominated in certain major foreign currencies that we held as of May 31, 2015:

(In millions)	U.S. Dollar Equivalent at May 31, 2015
Euro	$2,190
Japanese Yen	1,143
Indian Rupee	674
Saudi Arabian Riyal	445
Chinese Renminbi	427
Australian Dollar	397
South African Rand	344
Canadian Dollar	231
Other foreign currencies	1,802
Total cash, cash equivalents and marketable securities denominated in foreign currencies	$7,653

If overall foreign currency exchange rates in comparison to the U.S. Dollar uniformly weakened by 10%, the amount of cash, cash equivalents and marketable securities we would report in U.S. Dollars would decrease by approximately $765 million, assuming constant foreign currency cash, cash equivalents and marketable securities balances.

1. Organization and Significant Accounting Policies (in part)

Derivative Financial Instruments (in part)

During fiscal 2015, 2014 and 2013, we used derivative and non-derivative financial instruments to manage foreign currency and interest rate risks (see Note 11 below for additional information). We account for these instruments in accordance with ASC 815, *Derivatives and Hedging* (ASC 815), which requires that every derivative instrument be recorded on the balance sheet as either an asset or liability measured at its fair value as of the reporting date. ASC 815 also requires that changes in our derivatives' fair values be recognized in earnings, unless specific hedge accounting and documentation criteria are met (i.e., the instruments are accounted for as hedges).

Foreign Currency

We transact business in various foreign currencies. In general, the functional currency of a foreign operation is the local country's currency. Consequently, revenues and expenses of operations outside the United States are translated into U.S. Dollars using weighted average exchange rates while assets and liabilities of operations outside the United States are translated into U.S. Dollars using exchange rates at the balance sheet date. The effects of foreign currency translation adjustments are included in stockholders' equity as a component of accumulated other comprehensive loss in the accompanying consolidated balance sheets and related periodic movements are summarized as a line item in our consolidated statements of comprehensive income. Net foreign exchange transaction losses included in non-operating income (expense), net in the accompanying consolidated statements of operations were $157 million, $375 million and $162 million in fiscal 2015, 2014 and 2013, respectively.

Non-Operating Income (Expense), net

Non-operating income (expense), net consists primarily of interest income, net foreign currency exchange gains (losses), the noncontrolling interests in the net profits of our majority-owned subsidiaries (primarily Oracle Financial Services Software Limited and Oracle Japan) and net other income (losses), including net realized gains and losses related to all of our investments and net unrealized gains and losses related to the small portion of our investment portfolio that we classify as trading.

(In millions)	Year Ended May 31,		
	2015	2014	2013
Interest income	$ 349	$ 263	$ 237
Foreign currency losses, net	(157)	(375)	(162)
Noncontrolling interests in income	(113)	(98)	(112)
Other income, net	27	69	48
Total non-operating income (expense), net	$ 106	$(141)	$ 11

Included in foreign currency losses, net for fiscal 2015 were foreign currency remeasurement losses of $23 million, related to our Venezuelan subsidiary due to the continued "highly inflationary" designation of the Venezuelan economy in accordance with ASC 830, *Foreign Currency Matters*; the introduction of currency exchange legislation in Venezuela in February 2015 to create a new foreign exchange mechanism known as SIMADI; and the remeasurement of certain assets and liabilities of our Venezuelan subsidiary pursuant to the SIMADI rate, which we determined, based upon our specific facts and circumstances, was the most appropriate for the reporting of our Venezuelan subsidiary's Bolivar based transactions and net monetary assets in U.S. Dollars. We incurred losses related to our Venezuelan subsidiary of $213 million and $64 million during fiscal 2014 and 2013, respectively, for generally similar reasons.

11. Derivative Financial Instruments (in part)

Cash Flow Hedges—Cross Currency Swap Agreements

In connection with the issuance of our January 2021 Notes, we entered into certain cross-currency swap agreements to manage the related foreign currency exchange risk by effectively converting the fixed-rate, Euro denominated January 2021 Notes, including the annual interest payments and the payment of principal at maturity, to fixed-rate, U.S. Dollar denominated debt. The economic effect of the swap agreements was to eliminate the uncertainty of the cash flows in U.S. Dollars associated with the January 2021 Notes by fixing the principal amount of the January 2021 Notes at $1.6 billion with a fixed annual interest rate of 3.53%. We have designated these cross-currency swap agreements as qualifying hedging instruments and are accounting for these as cash flow hedges pursuant to ASC 815. The critical terms of the cross-currency swap agreements correspond to the January 2021 Notes, including the annual interest payments being hedged, and the cross-currency swap agreements mature at the same time as the January 2021 Notes.

We used the hypothetical derivative method to measure the effectiveness of our cross-currency swap agreements. The fair values of these cross-currency swap agreements are recognized as other assets or other non-current liabilities in our consolidated balance sheets. The effective portions of the changes in fair values of these cross-currency swap agreements are reported in accumulated other comprehensive loss in our consolidated balance sheets and an amount is reclassified out of accumulated other comprehensive loss into non-operating income (expense), net in the same period that the carrying value of the Euro denominated January 2021 Notes is remeasured and the interest expense is recognized. The ineffective portion of the unrealized gains and losses on these cross-currency swaps, if any, is recorded immediately to non-operating income (expense), net. We evaluate the effectiveness of our cross-currency swap agreements on a quarterly basis. We did not record any ineffectiveness for fiscal 2015 or 2014. The cash flows related to the cross-currency swap agreements that pertain to the periodic interest settlements are classified as operating activities and the cash flows that pertain to the principal balance are classified as financing activities.

We do not use any cross-currency swap agreements for trading purposes.

Net Investment Hedge—Foreign Currency Borrowings

In July 2013, we designated our July 2025 Notes as a net investment hedge of our investments in certain of our international subsidiaries that use the Euro as their functional currency in order to reduce the volatility in stockholders' equity caused by the changes in foreign currency exchange rates of the Euro with respect to the U.S. Dollar.

We used the spot method to measure the effectiveness of our net investment hedge. Under this method, for each reporting period, the change in the carrying value of the Euro denominated July 2025 Notes due to remeasurement of the effective portion is reported in accumulated other comprehensive loss on our consolidated balance sheet and the remaining change in the carrying value of the ineffective portion, if any, is recognized in non-operating income (expense), net in our consolidated statements of operations. We evaluate the effectiveness of our net investment hedge at the beginning of every quarter. We did not record any ineffectiveness for fiscal 2015 or 2014.

Foreign Currency Forward Contracts Not Designated as Hedges

We transact business in various foreign currencies and have established a program that primarily utilizes foreign currency forward contracts to offset the risks associated with the effects of certain foreign currency exposures. Under this program, our strategy is to enter into foreign currency forward contracts so that increases or decreases in our foreign currency exposures are offset by gains or losses on the foreign currency forward contracts in order to mitigate the risks and volatility associated with our foreign currency transactions. We may suspend this program from time to time. Our foreign currency exposures typically arise from intercompany sublicense fees, intercompany loans and other intercompany transactions that are generally expected to be cash settled in the near term. Our foreign currency forward contracts are generally short-term in duration. Our ultimate realized gain or loss with respect to currency fluctuations will generally depend on the size and type of cross-currency exposures that we enter into, the currency exchange rates associated with these exposures and changes in those rates, the net realized and unrealized gains or losses on foreign currency forward contracts to offset these exposures and other factors.

We neither use these foreign currency forward contracts for trading purposes nor do we designate these forward contracts as hedging instruments pursuant to ASC 815. Accordingly, we recorded the fair values of these contracts as of the end of our reporting period to our consolidated balance sheet with changes in fair values recorded to our consolidated statement of operations. The balance sheet classification for the fair values of these forward contracts is prepaid expenses and other current assets for a net unrealized gain position and other current liabilities for a net unrealized loss position. The statement of operations classification for changes in fair values of these forward contracts is non-operating income (expense), net, for both realized and unrealized gains and losses.

As of May 31, 2015 and 2014, respectively, the notional amounts of the forward contracts we held to purchase U.S. Dollars in exchange for other major international currencies were $2.2 billion and $3.6 billion, respectively, and the notional amounts of forward contracts we held to sell U.S. Dollars in exchange for other major international currencies were $1.2 billion and $2.0 billion, respectively. The fair values of our outstanding foreign currency forward contracts were nominal at May 31, 2015 and 2014.

Included in our non-operating income (expense), net were $60 million, $(69) million and $(64) million of net gains (losses) related to these forward contracts for the years ended May 31, 2015, 2014 and 2013, respectively. The cash flows related to these foreign currency contracts are classified as operating activities.

The effects of derivative and non-derivative instruments designated as hedges on certain of our consolidated financial statements were as follows as of or for each of the respective periods presented below (amounts presented exclude any income tax effects):

Fair Values of Derivative and Non-Derivative Instruments Designated as Hedges in Consolidated Balance Sheets

(In millions)	May 31, 2015		May 31, 2014	
	Balance Sheet Location	Fair Value	Balance Sheet Location	Fair Value
Interest rate swap agreements designated as fair value hedges	Other assets	$ 74	Other assets	$ 15
Interest rate swap agreements designated as fair value hedges	Not applicable	$ —	Prepaid expenses and other current assets	$ 8
Cross-currency swap agreements designated as cash flow hedges	Other non-current liabilities	$(244)	Other assets	$ 74
Foreign currency borrowings designated as net investment hedge	Notes payable, non-current	$(981)	Notes payable, non-current	$(1,116)

Effects of Derivative and Non-Derivative Instruments Designated as Hedges on Income and Other Comprehensive Income (OCI) or Loss (OCL)

(In millions)	Amount of (Loss) Gain Recognized in Accumulated OCI or OCL (Effective Portion)			Location and Amount of (Loss) Gain Reclassified from Accumulated OCI or OCL into Income (Effective Portion)		
	Year Ended May 31,				Year Ended May 31,	
	2015	2014			2015	2014
Cross-currency swap agreements designated as cash flow hedges	$(318)	$ 74		Non-operating income (expense), net	$(348)	$69
Foreign currency borrowings designated as net investment hedge	$ 208	$(34)		Not applicable	$ —	$ —

(In millions)	Location and Amount of Gain (Loss) Recognized in Income on Derivative			Location and Amount of (Loss) Gain on Hedged Item Recognized in Income Attributable to Risk Being Hedged		
		Year Ended May 31,			Year Ended May 31,	
		2015	2014		2015	2014
Interest rate swap agreements designated as fair value hedges	Interest expense	$51	$(18)	Interest expense	$(51)	$18

INTEREST AND INCOME TAX PAYMENTS

6.10 THE NEW YORK TIMES COMPANY (DEC)

CONSOLIDATED STATEMENTS OF CASH FLOWS (in part)

(In thousands)	Years Ended		
	December 27, 2015	December 28, 2014	December 29, 2013
Net cash provided by operating activities	175,326	80,491	34,855
Net cash (used in)/provided by investing activities	(30,703)	(324,717)	(353,657)
Net cash used in financing activities	(214,211)	(61,386)	(19,259)
Net (decrease)/increase in cash and cash equivalents	(69,588)	(305,612)	(338,061)
Effect of exchange rate changes on cash and cash equivalents	(1,243)	(526)	316
Cash and cash equivalents at the beginning of the year	176,607	482,745	820,490
Cash and cash equivalents at the end of the year	$ 105,776	$ 176,607	$ 482,745

See Notes to the Consolidated Financial Statements.

SUPPLEMENTAL DISCLOSURES TO CONSOLIDATED STATEMENTS OF CASH FLOWS

Cash Flow Information

(In thousands)	Years Ended		
	December 27, 2015	December 28, 2014	December 29, 2013
Cash Payments			
Interest, net of capitalized interest	$41,449	$54,252	$54,821
Income tax payment/(refunds) – net	$21,078	$21,325	$42,792

See Notes to the Consolidated Financial Statements.

Non-Cash Investing Activities

In each of 2014 and 2013, we received approximately $7 million of the total amount held in escrow to satisfy certain indemnification provisions related to the sale of our remaining ownership interest in Indeed.com in 2012.

6.11 AK STEEL HOLDING CORPORATION (DEC)

NOTES TO CONSOLIDATED FINANCIAL STATEMENTS (in part)

(dollars in millions, except per share amounts or as otherwise specifically noted)

Note 18—Supplementary Cash Flow Information

Net cash paid (received) during the period for interest, net of capitalized interest, and income taxes are presented below:

	2015	2014	2013
Net cash paid (received) during the period for:			
Interest, net of capitalized interest	$161.3	$121.9	$116.2
Income taxes	0.7	(0.3)	1.2

Included in net cash flows from operations was cash provided by SunCoke Middletown of $87.4, $66.4 and $82.6 for the years ended December 31, 2015, 2014 and 2013. Consolidated cash and cash equivalents at December 31, 2015, and 2014, include SunCoke Middletown's cash and cash equivalents of $7.6 and $18.2. SunCoke Middletown's cash and cash equivalents have no compensating balance arrangements or legal restrictions, but is not available for our use.

We had capital investments during the years ended December 31, 2015, 2014 and 2013, that had not been paid as of the end of the respective period. These amounts are included in accounts payable and accrued liabilities and have been excluded from the consolidated statements of cash flows until paid. We also granted restricted stock to certain employees and restricted stock units to directors under the SIP. Non-cash investing and financing activities for the years ended December 31, 2015, 2014 and 2013, are presented below:

	2015	2014	2013
Capital investments	$37.4	$29.5	$10.2
Issuance of restricted stock and restricted stock units	4.1	4.5	3.0

NONCASH ACTIVITIES

6.12 FLOWERS FOODS, INC. (DEC)

CONSOLIDATED STATEMENTS OF CASH FLOWS (in part)

(Amounts in thousands)	Fiscal 2015 52 Weeks	Fiscal 2014 53 Weeks	Fiscal 2013 52 Weeks
Net cash provided by operating activities	324,233	313,970	270,484
Net cash disbursed for investing activities	(467,508)	(33,313)	(502,885)
Net cash provided by (disbursed for) financing activities	150,130	(281,664)	227,656
Net increase (decrease) in cash and cash equivalents	6,855	(1,007)	(4,745)
Cash and cash equivalents at beginning of period	7,523	8,530	13,275
Cash and cash equivalents at end of period	$ 14,378	$ 7,523	$ 8,530
Schedule of non cash investing and financing activities:			
Issuance of executive deferred compensation plan common stock	$ 206	$ 264	$ —
Capital and right-to-use lease obligations	$ 2,298	$ 12,399	$ 8,971
Issuance of notes receivable on new distribution territories	$ 18,744	$ 44,346	$ 22,611
Shares issued for the Alpine acquisition	$ 12,602	$ —	$ —
Purchase of property, plant and equipment included in accounts payable	$ 3,637	$ 1,094	$ 435
Supplemental disclosures of cash flow information:			
Cash paid during the period for:			
Interest	$ 24,112	$ 26,065	$ 25,996
Income taxes paid, net of refunds of $7,587, $4,240 and $323, respectively	$ 80,062	$ 78,587	$ 83,525

NOTES TO CONSOLIDATED FINANCIAL STATEMENTS (in part)

Note 5. Notes Receivable

The company provides direct financing to certain independent distributors for the purchase of the independent distributors' distribution rights and records the notes receivable on the Consolidated Balance Sheets. The distribution rights are financed for up to ten years. During fiscal years 2015, 2014, and 2013, $22.0 million, $20.9 million, and $16.0 million, respectively, was recorded as interest income relating to these notes receivable. The notes receivable are collateralized by the independent distributors' distribution rights. Additional details are included in Note 14, *Fair Value of Financial Instruments*.

Note 8. Acquisitions (in part)

Alpine Valley Bread Company

On October 13, 2015, the company completed the acquisition of 100% of the outstanding common stock of Alpine, a leading organic bread baker, from its shareholders for total consideration of approximately $121.9 million inclusive of payments for certain tax benefits. We paid cash of $109.3 million and issued 481,540 shares of our common stock to the sellers in a private placement. We believe the acquisition of Alpine strengthens our position as the second-largest baker in the U.S. by giving us access to the fast growing organic bread category. The Alpine acquisition has been accounted for as a business combination and is included in our Warehouse Segment. The results of Alpine's operations are included in the company's Consolidated Financial Statements beginning on October 14, 2015. The total preliminary goodwill recorded for this acquisition was $36.0 million and it is deductible for tax purposes.

During fiscal 2015, the company incurred $1.6 million of acquisition-related costs for Alpine. The acquisition-related costs for Alpine are recorded in the selling, distribution and administrative expense line item in our Consolidated Statements of Income. Alpine contributed $11.9 million in sales during fiscal 2015. Alpine's operating income since the acquisition was immaterial to our fiscal 2015 results of operations.

The following table summarizes the consideration paid for Alpine based on the fair value at the acquisition date. This table is based on preliminary valuations for the assets acquired and liabilities assumed. The identifiable intangible assets, property, plant and equipment, and certain financial assets are still under review. We will continue reviewing the final recognized amounts of identifiable assets acquired and liabilities assumed (amounts in thousands):

Fair Value of Consideration Transferred:	
Cash consideration paid	$109,340
Stock consideration paid	12,602
Total consideration paid	121,942
Recognized Amounts of Identifiable Assets Acquired and Liabilities Assumed:	
Property, plant, and equipment	15,614
Identifiable intangible assets	64,600
Financial assets	5,687
Net recognized amounts of identifiable assets acquired	85,901
Goodwill	$ 36,041

The following table presents the acquired intangible assets subject to amortization (amounts in thousands, except amortization periods):

	Total	Weighted average Amortization Years	Attribution Method
Trademarks	$20,900	40.0	Straight-line
Customer relationships	43,700	25.0	Sum of year digits
	$64,600	29.9	

Alpine operates two production facilities in Mesa, Arizona and has widespread distribution across the U.S. The primary reason for the acquisition was to purchase a brand of organic bakery products in the U.S. and to add organic production capacity.

The fair value of trade receivables is $4.8 million. The gross amount of the receivable is $4.8 million with an immaterial amount determined to be uncollectible. We did not acquire any other class of receivables as a result of the acquisition.

Note 12. Debt, Lease and Other Commitments (in part)

Long-term debt, including capital lease obligations, consisted of the following at January 2, 2016 and January 3, 2015:

(Amounts in thousands)	Interest Rate at January 2, 2016	Final Maturity	January 2, 2016	January 3, 2015
Unsecured credit facility	2.68%	2020	$ 160,000	$ 53,000
Unsecured new term loan	1.92%	2018	240,000	270,000
4.375% senior notes due April 1, 2022	4.38%	2022	399,400	399,304
Accounts receivable securitization	1.15%	2018	170,000	—
Capital lease obligations	3.82%	2020	20,228	22,526
Other notes payable	2.10%	2020	18,989	18,606
			1,008,617	763,436
Current maturities of long-term debt and capital lease obligations			74,685	34,496
Long-term debt and capital lease obligations			$ 933,932	$728,940

Leases

The company leases certain property and equipment under various operating and capital lease arrangements that expire over the next 21 years. The property leases include distribution facilities, thrift store locations, and three manufacturing facilities. The equipment leases include production, sales, distribution, and office equipment. Initial lease terms range from two to 26 years. Many of the operating leases provide the company with the option, after the initial lease term, either to purchase the property at the then fair value or renew its lease at fair value rents for periods from one month to ten years. Rent escalations vary in these leases, from no escalation over the initial lease term, to escalations linked to changes in economic variables such as the Consumer Price Index. Rental expense is recognized on a straight-line basis. The capital leases are primarily used for distribution vehicle financing and are discussed in Note 13, *Variable Interest Entities*, below. Future minimum lease payments under scheduled capital leases that have initial or remaining non-cancelable terms in excess of one year are as follows:

(Amounts in thousands)	Capital Leases
2016	$ 5,222
2017	5,091
2018	5,223
2019	3,591
2020	710
2021 and thereafter	1,959
Total minimum payments	21,796
Amount representing interest	1,568
Obligations under capital leases	20,228
Obligations due within one year	4,685
Long-term obligations under capital leases	$15,543

The table below presents the total future minimum lease payments under scheduled operating leases that have initial or remaining non-cancelable terms in excess of one year (amounts in thousands):

(Amounts in thousands)	Operating Leases
2016	$ 60,550
2017	59,103
2018	45,232
2019	39,849
2020	38,117
2021 and thereafter	287,995
Total minimum payments	$530,846

Rent expense for all operating leases amounted to $87.9 million, $88.7 million, and $90.3 million for fiscal years 2015, 2014, and 2013.

Deferred Compensation

The Executive Deferred Compensation Plan ("EDCP") consists of unsecured general obligations of the company to pay the deferred compensation of, and our contributions to, participants in the EDCP. The obligations will rank equally with our other unsecured and unsubordinated indebtedness payable from the company's general assets.

The company's directors and certain key members of management are eligible to participate in the EDCP. Directors may elect to defer all or any portion of their annual retainer fee and meeting fees. Deferral elections by directors must be made prior to the beginning of each year and are thereafter irrevocable. Eligible employees may elect to defer up to 75% of their base salaries, and up to 100% of any cash bonuses and other compensation through December 31, 2015. Effective January 1, 2016, employees may elect to defer up to 75% of their base salaries, any cash bonuses, and other compensation. Deferral elections by eligible executives must be made prior to the beginning of each year and are thereafter irrevocable during that year. The portion of the participant's compensation that is deferred depends on the participant's election in effect with respect to his or her elective contributions under the EDCP. The amount outstanding at January 2, 2016 and January 3, 2015 was $14.8 million and $14.5 million of which $2.2 million and $1.9 million, respectively, are recorded as current liabilities.

Note 14. Fair Value of Financial Instruments (in part)

The carrying value of cash and cash equivalents, accounts receivable, and short-term debt approximates fair value because of the short-term maturity of the instruments. Notes receivable are entered into in connection with the purchase of independent distributors' distribution rights by independent distributors. These notes receivable are recorded in the Consolidated Balance Sheet at carrying value, which represents the closest approximation of fair value. Fair value is defined as the price that would be received to sell an asset or paid to transfer a liability in an orderly transaction between market participants at the measurement date. As a result, the appropriate interest rate that should be used to estimate the fair value of the distribution rights notes is the prevailing market rate at which similar loans would be made to independent distributors with similar credit ratings and for the same maturities. However, the company financed approximately 3,400 and 3,700 independent distributors' distribution rights as of January 2, 2016 and January 3, 2015, respectively, all with varied financial histories and credit risks. Considering the diversity of credit risks among the independent distributors, the company has no method to accurately determine a market interest rate to apply to the notes. The distribution rights are generally financed for up to ten years and the distribution rights notes are collateralized by the independent distributors' distribution rights. The company maintains a wholly-owned subsidiary to assist in financing the distribution rights purchase activities if requested by new independent distributors, using the distribution rights and certain associated assets as collateral. These notes receivable earn interest at a fixed rate.

At January 2, 2016 and January 3, 2015, respectively, the carrying value of the distribution rights notes receivable was as follows (amounts in thousands):

	January 2, 2016	January 3, 2015
Distribution rights notes receivable	$174,904	$182,188
Current portion of distribution rights notes receivable recorded in accounts and notes receivable, net	20,593	20,283
Long-term portion of distribution rights notes receivable	$154,311	$161,905

Interest income for the distribution rights notes receivable was as follows (amounts in thousands):

	Interest Income
Fiscal 2015	$21,967
Fiscal 2014	$20,947
Fiscal 2013	$16,015

At January 2, 2016 and January 3, 2015, the company has evaluated the collectability of the distribution rights notes receivable and determined that a reserve is not necessary. Payments on these notes are collected by the company weekly in conjunction with the settlement process.

Cash Flows From Operating Activities

PRESENTATION

6.13 FASB ASC 230-10-45 defines those transactions and events that constitute operating cash receipts and payments. Cash inflows from operating activities include the following:
- Cash receipts from sales of goods or services, including receipts from the collection or sale of accounts and both short- and long-term notes receivable from customers arising from those sales. Goods include certain loans and other debt and equity instruments of other entities that are acquired specifically for resale.
- Cash receipts from returns on loans, other debt instruments of other entities, and equity securities—interest and dividends.
- All other cash receipts that do not stem from transactions defined as investing or financing activities, such as amounts received to settle lawsuits; proceeds of insurance settlements, except for those that are directly related to investing or financing activities, such as from destruction of a building; and refunds from suppliers.

Cash outflows from operating activities include the following:
- Cash payments to acquire materials for manufacture or goods for resale, including principal payments on accounts and both short- and long-term notes payable to suppliers for those materials or goods. Goods include certain loans and other debt and equity instruments of other entities that are acquired specifically for resale.
- Cash payments to other suppliers and employees for other goods or services.
- Cash payments to governments for taxes, duties, fines, and other fees or penalties and the cash that would have been paid for income taxes if increases in the value of equity instruments issued under share-based payment arrangements that are not included in the cost of goods or services recognizable for financial reporting purposes also had not been deductible in determining taxable income.
- Cash payments to lenders and other creditors for interest.
- Cash payments made to settle an asset retirement obligation.
- All other cash payments that do not stem from transactions defined as investing or financing activities, such as payments to settle lawsuits, cash contributions to charities, and cash refunds to customers.

6.14 Entities can present operating activities using either the direct or indirect method. However, FASB ASC 230-10-45-30 also requires entities using the direct method to provide a reconciliation of net income to net cash flow from operating activities in a separate schedule.

6.15 FASB ASC 230-10-45-28 also notes that when reconciling net income to net cash flow from operating activities, a business entity should adjust net income to remove past operating cash receipts and payments and accruals of expected future operating cash receipts and payments, including changes during the period in inventory and receivables and payables pertaining to operating activities. Additionally, all items that are included in net income, such as depreciation and amortization expense, that do not affect net cash provided from, or used for, operating activities should be adjusted for.

PRESENTATION AND DISCLOSURE EXCERPTS

DIRECT METHOD

6.16 CVS HEALTH CORPORATION (DEC)
CONSOLIDATED STATEMENTS OF CASH FLOWS

| | Year Ended December 31, | | |
In millions	2015	2014	2013
Cash flows from operating activities:			
Cash receipts from customers	$ 148,954	$ 132,406	$114,993
Cash paid for inventory and prescriptions dispensed by retail network pharmacies	(122,498)	(105,362)	(91,178)
Cash paid to other suppliers and employees	(14,162)	(15,344)	(14,295)
Interest received	21	15	8
Interest paid	(629)	(647)	(534)
Income taxes paid	(3,274)	(2,931)	(3,211)
Net cash provided by operating activities	8,412	8,137	5,783
Cash flows from investing activities:			
Purchases of property and equipment	(2,367)	(2,136)	(1,984)
Proceeds from sale-leaseback transactions	411	515	600
Proceeds from sale of property and equipment and other assets	35	11	54
Acquisitions (net of cash acquired) and other investments	(11,475)	(2,439)	(415)
Purchase of available-for-sale investments	(267)	(157)	(226)
Maturity of available-for-sale investments	243	161	136
Net cash used in investing activities	(13,420)	(4,045)	(1,835)
Cash flows from financing activities:			
Increase (decrease) in short-term debt	(685)	685	(690)
Proceeds from issuance of long-term debt	14,805	1,483	3,964
Repayments of long-term debt	(2,902)	(3,100)	—
Payment of contingent consideration	(58)	—	—
Dividends paid	(1,576)	(1,288)	(1,097)
Proceeds from exercise of stock options	299	421	500
Excess tax benefits from stock-based compensation	127	106	62
Repurchase of common stock	(5,001)	(4,001)	(3,976)
Other	(3)	—	—
Net cash provided by (used in) financing activities	5,006	(5,694)	(1,237)
Effect of exchange rate changes on cash and cash equivalents	(20)	(6)	3
Net increase (decrease) in cash and cash equivalents	(22)	(1,608)	2,714
Cash and cash equivalents at the beginning of the year	2,481	4,089	1,375
Cash and cash equivalents at the end of the year	$ 2,459	$ 2,481	$ 4,089
Reconciliation of net income to net cash provided by operating activities:			
Net income	$ 5,239	$ 4,644	$ 4,592
Adjustments required to reconcile net income to net cash provided by operating activities:			
Depreciation and amortization	2,092	1,931	1,870
Stock-based compensation	230	165	141
Loss on early extinguishment of debt	—	521	—
Deferred income taxes and other noncash items	(266)	(58)	(86)
Change in operating assets and liabilities, net of effects from acquisitions:			
Accounts receivable, net	(1,594)	(737)	(2,210)
Inventories	(1,141)	(770)	12
Other current assets	355	(383)	105
Other assets	2	9	(135)
Accounts payable and claims and discounts payable	2,834	1,742	1,024
Accrued expenses	765	1,060	471
Other long-term liabilities	(104)	13	(1)
Net cash provided by operating activities	$ 8,412	$ 8,137	$ 5,783

INDIRECT/RECONCILIATION METHOD

6.17 VISTEON CORPORATION (DEC)
CONSOLIDATED STATEMENTS OF CASH FLOWS [1]

(Dollars in Millions)	Year Ended December 31		
	2015	**2014**	**2013**
Operating Activities			
Net income (loss)	$ 2,328	$ (206)	$ 775
Adjustments to reconcile net income (loss) to net cash provided from operating activities:			
Gain on Climate Transaction	(2,324)	—	—
Gain on non-consolidated affiliate transactions	(62)	(2)	(470)
Depreciation and amortization	169	270	262
Losses on divestitures and impairments	121	326	—
Pension settlement gain	—	(23)	—
Equity in net income of non-consolidated affiliates, net of dividends remitted	1	10	(26)
Non-cash stock-based compensation	8	8	15
Loss on debt extinguishment	5	23	2
Other non-cash items	6	11	4
Changes in assets and liabilities:			
Accounts receivable	1	(121)	(21)
Inventories	(20)	(27)	(49)
Accounts payable	33	22	103
Accrued income taxes	6	14	(54)
Other assets and other liabilities	66	(21)	(229)
Net cash provided from operating activities	338	284	312
Investing Activities			
Capital expenditures	(187)	(340)	(269)
Short-term investments, net	(47)	—	—
Loan to non-consolidated affiliate	(10)	—	—
Net proceeds from Climate Transaction	2,664	—	—
Proceeds from asset sales and business divestitures	91	66	977
Acquisition of businesses, net of cash acquired	(4)	(311)	(10)
Payments associated with business divestitures, net	(156)	(147)	—
Other	7	(8)	—
Net cash provided from (used by) investing activities	2,358	(740)	698
Financing Activities			
Short-term debt, net	2	39	(20)
Proceeds from issuance of debt, net of issuance costs	—	619	204
Principal payments on debt	(250)	(18)	(6)
Repurchase of common stock	(500)	(500)	(250)
Repurchase of long-term notes	—	(419)	(52)
Dividends paid to non-controlling interests	(55)	(97)	(22)
Exercised warrants and stock options	40	17	5
Stock based compensation tax withholding payments	(10)	—	—
Other	(1)	—	—
Net cash used by financing activities	(774)	(359)	(141)
Effect of exchange rate changes on cash and equivalents	(20)	(35)	(17)
Net increase (decrease) in cash and equivalents	1,902	(850)	852
Cash and equivalents at beginning of the year	827	1,677	825
Cash and equivalents at end of the year	$ 2,729	$ 827	$1,677
Supplemental Disclosures:			
Cash paid for interest	$ 24	$ 39	$ 43
Cash paid for income taxes, net of refunds	$ 67	$ 130	$ 291

[1] The Company has combined cash flows from discontinued operations with cash flows from continuing operations within the operating, investing and financing categories. As such, cash and equivalents above include $1 million and $351 million of assets held for sale reflected in Current assets held for sale on the Consolidated Balance Sheets as of December 31, 2015 and 2014, respectively.

6.18 BAKER HUGHES INCORPORATED (DEC)
CONSOLIDATED STATEMENTS OF CASH FLOWS (in part)

	Year Ended December 31,		
(In millions)	2015	2014	2013
Cash flows from operating activities:			
Net (loss) income	$(1,974)	$1,731	$1,103
Adjustments to reconcile net (loss) income to net cash flows from operating activities:			
Depreciation and amortization	1,742	1,814	1,698
(Benefit) provision for deferred income taxes	(809)	(70)	1
Gain on disposal or deconsolidation of assets	(157)	(297)	(275)
Stock-based compensation cost	120	122	115
Provision for doubtful accounts	193	102	75
Loss on impairment of assets	1,436	—	—
Changes in operating assets and liabilities:			
Accounts receivable	1,943	(524)	(453)
Inventories	1,092	(259)	(120)
Accounts payable	(1,349)	291	845
Income taxes payable	(305)	90	(31)
Other operating items, net	(136)	(47)	203
Net cash flows provided by operating activities	1,796	2,953	3,161

NOTES TO CONSOLIDATED FINANCIAL STATEMENTS (in part)

Note 1. Summary of Significant Accounting Policies (in part)

Impairment of PP&E, Intangibles, Other Long-lived Assets and Goodwill (in part)

We review PP&E, intangible assets and certain other long-lived assets for impairment whenever events or changes in circumstances indicate that the carrying amount may not be recoverable and at least annually for certain intangible assets. The determination of recoverability is made based upon the estimated undiscounted future net cash flows. The amount of impairment loss, if any, is determined by comparing the fair value, as determined by a discounted cash flow analysis, with the carrying value of the related assets.

We perform an annual impairment test of goodwill for each of our reporting units as of October 1, or more frequently if an event occurs or circumstances change to indicate that it is more likely than not that an impairment may exist. Our reporting units are based on our organizational and reporting structure and are the same as our five reportable segments. Corporate and other assets and liabilities are allocated to the reporting units to the extent that they relate to the operations of those reporting units in determining their carrying amount. When performing the annual impairment test we have the option of first performing a qualitative assessment to determine the existence of events and circumstances that would lead to a determination that it is more likely than not that the fair value of a reporting unit is less than its carrying amount. If such a conclusion is reached, we would then be required to perform a quantitative impairment assessment of goodwill. However, if the assessment leads to a determination that it is more likely than not that the fair value of a reporting unit is greater than its carrying amount, then no further assessments are required. In 2015 and 2014, we performed a qualitative assessment for our annual goodwill impairment test. In 2013, a quantitative assessment for the determination of impairment was made by comparing the carrying amount of each reporting unit with its fair value, which is generally calculated using a combination of market, comparable transaction and discounted cash flow approaches.

Note 3. Impairment and Restructuring Charges (in part)

Impairment Charges

We conduct impairment tests on long-lived assets whenever events or changes in circumstances indicate that the carrying value may not be recoverable based on estimated future cash flows. In the fourth quarter of 2015, negative market sentiment increased and oil prices fell to a seven year low. Additionally, the current market outlook is for a prolonged recovery. We considered these events to be possible impairment indicators and performed testing of long-lived assets for impairment.

As a result of our testing, certain machinery and equipment, with a total carrying value of $1.64 billion, was written down to its estimated fair value, resulting in an impairment charge of $1.05 billion. Additionally, certain intangible assets, comprised of customer relationships and trade names, with a total carrying value of $178 million, were written down to their estimated fair values, resulting in an impairment charge of $116 million. Total impairment charges for 2015 were $1.16 billion. The majority of the machinery and equipment and intangible assets impaired related to our pressure pumping business in North America. The estimated fair values for these assets were determined using discounted future cash flows. The significant level 3 unobservable inputs used in the determination of the fair value of these assets were the estimated future cash flows and the weighted average cost of capital of 9.8%.

Restructuring Charges

Beginning in the second half of 2014 and throughout 2015, the oil and natural gas market experienced a significant over supply of capacity leading to a substantial and rapid decline in oil prices resulting in significantly lower activity and customer spending. Accordingly, to adjust to the lower level of activity, beginning in the first quarter of 2015, we initiated actions to restructure and adjust our operations and cost structure to reflect current and expected near-term activity levels. These restructuring activities included workforce reductions, contract terminations, facility closures and the removal of excess machinery and equipment that resulted in asset impairments. As a result of these restructuring activities, we recorded restructuring charges of $830 million in 2015. Depending on future market conditions and activity levels, further actions may be necessary to adjust our operations which may result in additional charges.

Our restructuring charges as summarized below:

Restructuring Charges	Year Ended December 31, 2015
Workforce reductions	$436
Contract terminations	121
Impairment of buildings and improvements	82
Impairment of machinery and equipment	191
Total restructuring charges	$830

Workforce reduction costs: During 2015, we initiated workforce reductions that will result in the elimination of approximately 18,000 positions worldwide. As of December 31, 2015, we have eliminated approximately 17,000 positions. As a result of these workforce reductions, we recorded a charge for severance expense of $436 million during 2015, net of related employee benefit plan gains of $10 million. As of December 31, 2015, we have made payments totaling $365 million relating to workforce reductions. We expect that substantially all of the accrued severance remaining will be paid by the middle of 2016.

Contract termination costs: During 2015, we incurred costs of $121 million to terminate or restructure various contracts, primarily in North America. This includes the accrual for costs to settle leases on closed facilities and certain equipment, and other estimated exit costs, and is net of expected sublease income. This also includes costs to terminate or restructure certain take-or-pay supply contracts related to the purchase of materials used in our pressure pumping operations in North America, including the write-off of $14 million of prepayments made in 2014. As of December 31, 2015, we have made payments totaling $81 million relating to contract termination costs.

Impairment of buildings and improvements: We are consolidating facilities and shutting down certain operations and as a result are closing and abandoning or selling certain facilities, both owned and leased. During 2015, we recognized $82 million of impairment charges related to facilities primarily in North America and Latin America. For leased facilities, this charge includes the impairment of the leasehold improvements made to those facilities.

Impairment of machinery and equipment: We are exiting or substantially downsizing our presence in select markets primarily in our pressure pumping product line in North America and Latin America. During 2015, we recognized $191 million of impairment losses to adjust the carrying value of certain machinery and equipment to its fair value, net of costs to dispose. We are currently in the process of disposing of this machinery and equipment through sale or scrap.

ADJUSTMENTS TO RECONCILE NET INCOME—INVESTMENT GAINS

6.19 BERKSHIRE HATHAWAY INC. (DEC)
CONSOLIDATED STATEMENTS OF CASH FLOWS (in part)

(dollars in millions)

	Year Ended December 31,		
	2015	2014	2013
Cash Flows From Operating Activities:			
Net earnings	$24,414	$20,170	$19,845
Adjustments to reconcile net earnings to operating cash flows:			
Investment gains/losses	(9,373)	(3,575)	(4,065)
Depreciation and amortization	7,779	7,370	6,508
Other	751	(341)	373
Changes in operating assests and liabilities:			
Losses and loss adjustment expenses	2,262	7,404	578
Deferred charges reinsurance assumed	84	(3,413)	(340)
Unearned premiums	1,392	1,159	519
Receivables and originated loans	(1,650)	(1,890)	1,035
Derivative contract assets and liabilities	(974)	(520)	(2,430)
Income taxes	5,718	4,905	3,514
Other	1,088	741	2,167
Net cash flows from operating activities	31,491	32,010	27,704

NOTES TO CONSOLIDATED FINANCIAL STATEMENTS (in part)

(1) Significant Accounting Policies and Practices (in part)

(d) Investments

We determine the appropriate classification of investments in fixed maturity and equity securities at the acquisition date and re-evaluate the classification at each balance sheet date. Held-to-maturity investments are carried at amortized cost, reflecting the ability and intent to hold the securities to maturity. Trading investments are securities acquired with the intent to sell in the near term and are carried at fair value. All other securities are classified as available-for-sale and are carried at fair value with net unrealized gains or losses reported as a component of accumulated other comprehensive income. Substantially all of our investments in equity and fixed maturity securities are classified as available-for-sale.

We utilize the equity method to account for investments when we possess the ability to exercise significant influence, but not control, over the operating and financial policies of the investee. The ability to exercise significant influence is presumed when an investor possesses more than 20% of the voting interests of the investee. This presumption may be overcome based on specific facts and circumstances that demonstrate that the ability to exercise significant influence is restricted. We apply the equity method to investments in common stock and to other investments when such other investments possess substantially identical subordinated interests to common stock.

In applying the equity method, we record the investment at cost and subsequently increase or decrease the carrying amount of the investment by our proportionate share of the net earnings or losses and other comprehensive income of the investee. We record dividends or other equity distributions as reductions in the carrying value of the investment. In the event that net losses of the investee reduce the carrying amount to zero, additional net losses may be recorded if other investments in the investee are at-risk, even if we have not committed to provide financial support to the investee. Such additional equity method losses, if any, are based upon the change in our claim on the investee's book value.

Investment gains and losses arise when investments are sold (as determined on a specific identification basis) or are other-than-temporarily impaired. If a decline in the value of an investment below cost is deemed other than temporary, the cost of the investment is written down to fair value, with a corresponding charge to earnings. Factors considered in determining whether an impairment is other than temporary include: the financial condition, business prospects and creditworthiness of the issuer, the relative amount of the decline, our ability and intent to hold the investment until the fair value recovers and the length of time that fair value has been less than cost. With respect to an investment in a fixed maturity security, we recognize an other-than-temporary impairment if we (a) intend to sell or expect to be required to sell the security before its amortized cost is recovered or (b) do not expect to ultimately recover the amortized cost basis even if we do not intend to sell the security. Under scenario (a), we recognize losses in earnings and under scenario (b), we recognize the credit loss component in earnings and the difference between fair value and the amortized cost basis net of the credit loss in other comprehensive income.

(6) Investments in The Kraft Heinz Company

On June 7, 2013, Berkshire and an affiliate of the global investment firm 3G Capital (such affiliate, "3G"), through a newly formed holding company, H.J. Heinz Holding Corporation ("Heinz Holding"), acquired H.J. Heinz Company ("Heinz"). Berkshire and 3G each made equity investments in Heinz Holding, which, together with debt financing obtained by Heinz Holding, was used to acquire Heinz. Heinz is one of the world's leading marketers and producers of healthy, convenient and affordable foods specializing in ketchup, sauces, meals, soups, snacks and infant nutrition. Heinz is comprised of a global family of leading branded products, including Heinz ® Ketchup, sauces, soups, beans, pasta, infant foods, Ore-Ida ® potato products, Weight Watchers ® Smart Ones ® entrées and T.G.I. Friday's ® snacks.

Berkshire's initial investments consisted of 425 million shares of Heinz Holding common stock, warrants, which were exercised in June 2015, to acquire approximately 46 million additional shares of common stock at one cent per share, and cumulative compounding preferred stock ("Preferred Stock") with a liquidation preference of $8 billion. The aggregate cost of these investments was $12.25 billion. 3G also acquired 425 million shares of Heinz Holding common stock for $4.25 billion. In addition, Heinz Holding reserved 39.6 million shares of common stock for issuance to its management and directors under equity grants, including stock options.

In March 2015, Heinz Holding and Kraft Foods Group, Inc. ("Kraft") entered into a merger agreement under which Kraft shareholders were entitled to receive one share of newly issued Heinz Holding common stock for each share of Kraft common stock and a special cash dividend of $16.50 per share. Kraft is one of North America's largest consumer packaged food and beverage companies, with annual revenues of more than $18 billion. The company's iconic brands include *Kraft, Capri Sun, Jell-O, Kool-Aid, Lunchables, Maxwell House, Oscar Mayer, Philadelphia, Planters* and *Velveeta*.

On July 1, 2015, Berkshire acquired 262.9 million shares of newly issued common stock of Heinz Holding for $5.26 billion and 3G acquired 237.1 million shares of newly issued common stock for $4.74 billion. Immediately thereafter, Heinz Holding executed a reverse stock split at a rate of 0.443332 of a share for each share. Upon completion of these transactions, Berkshire owned approximately 325.4 million shares of Heinz Holding common stock, or 52.5% of the then outstanding shares. The merger transaction closed on July 2, 2015, at which time Heinz Holding was renamed The Kraft Heinz Company ("Kraft Heinz") and Kraft Heinz issued approximately 593 million new shares of its common stock to the former Kraft shareholders. Following the issuance of these additional shares, Berkshire and 3G together owned approximately 51% of the outstanding Kraft Heinz common stock, with Berkshire owning approximately 26.8% and 3G owning 24.2%. Our investments in Kraft Heinz are summarized as follows (in millions).

	Carrying Value	
	December 31, 2015	December 31, 2014
Common stock	$15,714	$ 3,950
Preferred Stock	7,710	7,710
	$23,424	$11,660

We account for our investment in Kraft Heinz common stock on the equity method. Dividends earned on the Preferred Stock and our equity method earnings or loss on the common stock were $730 million in 2015, $694 million in 2014 and $146 million in 2013 and are included in interest, dividend and other investment income in our Consolidated Statements of Earnings.

As previously discussed, the issuance of new common stock by Kraft Heinz for Kraft common stock reduced our ownership of Kraft Heinz from approximately 52.5% to 26.8%. Under the equity method, the issuance of shares by an investee is accounted for by the investor as if the investor had sold a proportionate share of its investment. As a result, we recorded a non-cash pre-tax holding gain of approximately $6.8 billion in the third quarter of 2015, representing the excess of the fair value of Kraft Heinz common stock at the date of the merger over our carrying value associated with the reduction in our ownership.

The Preferred Stock possesses no voting rights except as are required by law or for certain matters. The Preferred Stock is entitled to dividends at 9% per annum whether or not declared, is senior in priority to the common stock and is callable after June 7, 2016 at the liquidation value plus an applicable premium and any accrued and unpaid dividends. Kraft Heinz has announced its intention to call the Preferred Stock after June 7, 2016 and prior to June 7, 2017, although it is not obligated to do so. The redemption value of the Preferred Stock as of June 7, 2016 is approximately $8.3 billion. After June 7, 2021, Berkshire can cause Kraft Heinz to attempt to sell shares of common stock through public offerings or other issuances, the proceeds of which would be required to be used to redeem any outstanding shares of the Preferred Stock. We account for our investment in the Preferred Stock as an equity investment and it is carried at cost.

Summarized consolidated financial information of Kraft Heinz follows (in millions).

	January 3, 2016	December 28, 2014
Assets	$122,973	$36,571
Liabilities	56,737	20,886

	Year ending January 3, 2016	Year ending December 28, 2014	June 7, 2013 through December 29, 2013
Sales	$18,338	$10,922	$6,240
Net earnings (loss)	$ 634	$ 657	$ (77)

(7) Investment Gains/Losses

Investment gains/losses, including other-than-temporary impairment ("OTTI") losses, for each of the three years ending December 31, 2015 are summarized below (in millions).

	2015	2014	2013
Fixed maturity securities—			
Gross gains from sales and other disposals	$ 104	$ 360	$1,783
Gross losses from sales and other disposals	(171)	(89)	(139)
Equity securities—			
Gross gains from sales and redemptions	9,526	4,016	1,253
Gross losses from sales and redemptions	(103)	(125)	(62)
OTTI losses	(26)	(697)	(228)
Other	43	110	1,458
	$9,373	$3,575	$4,065

Investment gains from equity securities in 2015 included a non-cash holding gain of approximately $6.8 billion in connection with our investment in Kraft Heinz common stock (see Note 6). Gains from equity securities during 2014 included non-cash holding gains of approximately $2.1 billion from the exchange of Phillips 66 ("PSX") common stock in connection with the acquisition of Phillips Specialty Products Inc. (subsequently renamed Lubrizol Specialty Products Inc. ("LSPI")) and the exchange of Graham Holding Company ("GHC") common stock for WPLG, Inc. ("WPLG"). The PSX/LSPI exchange was completed on February 25, 2014 and the GHC/WPLG exchange was completed on June 30, 2014. These holding gains represented the excess of the respective fair value of the net assets of LSPI and WPLG received over the respective cost basis of the PSX and GHC shares exchanged.

In October 2013, we realized a gain of $680 million with respect to the repurchase of $4.4 billion par amount of 11.45% Wrigley subordinated notes, which we acquired in 2008 for $4.4 billion in connection with the Mars acquisition of Wrigley. We also realized additional gains in 2013 from the dispositions and conversions of corporate bonds. Other investment gains/losses in 2013 included $1.4 billion related to the changes in the valuations of warrants of General Electric Company ("GE") and The Goldman Sachs Group ("GS"), which we acquired in 2008 and exercised in October 2013.

We record investments in equity and fixed maturity securities classified as available-for-sale at fair value and record the difference between fair value and cost in other comprehensive income. OTTI losses recognized in earnings represent reductions in the cost basis of the investment, but not the fair value. Accordingly, such losses that are included in earnings are generally offset by a credit to other comprehensive income, producing no net effect on shareholders' equity as of the balance sheet date. In 2014, we recorded an OTTI charge of $678 million related to our investment in equity securities of Tesco PLC. We recorded OTTI losses on bonds issued by Texas Competitive Electric Holdings of $228 million in 2013.

ADJUSTMENTS TO RECONCILE NET INCOME—PENSION TERMINATION EXPENSE

6.20 BOSTON SCIENTIFIC CORPORATION (DEC)
CONSOLIDATED STATEMENTS OF CASH FLOWS (in part)

	Year Ended December 31,		
In millions	2015	2014	2013
Operating Activities			
Net income (loss)	$(239)	$(119)	$(121)
Adjustments to reconcile net income (loss) to cash provided by operating activities			
Gain on sale of businesses	—	(12)	(38)
Depreciation and amortization	769	725	689
Deferred and prepaid income taxes	(532)	(397)	(223)
Stock-based compensation expense	107	103	105
Goodwill impairment charges	—	—	423
Intangible asset impairment charges	19	195	53
Net losses (gains) on investments and notes receivable	9	(27)	9
Contingent consideration expense (benefit)	123	(85)	4
Payment of contingent consideration in excess of amounts established in purchase accounting	(57)	(103)	(5)

(continued)

In millions	Year Ended December 31,		
	2015	2014	2013
Pension termination charges	44	—	—
Inventory step-up amortization	36	9	—
Other, net	41	18	31
Increase (decrease) in cash flows from operating assets and liabilities:			
Trade accounts receivable	(17)	53	(101)
Inventories	3	(81)	(7)
Other assets	(23)	(33)	91
Accounts payable and accrued expenses	(20)	620	(9)
Other liabilities	337	403	209
Cash provided by operating activities	600	1,269	1,110

NOTES TO THE CONSOLIDATED FINANCIAL STATEMENTS (in part)

Note A – Significant Accounting Policies (in part)

Costs Associated with Exit Activities (in part)

We record employee termination costs in accordance with ASC Topic 712, *Compensation—Nonretirement and Postemployment Benefits*, if we pay the benefits as part of an on-going benefit arrangement, which includes benefits provided as part of our established severance policies or that we provide in accordance with international statutory requirements. We accrue employee termination costs associated with an on-going benefit arrangement if the obligation is attributable to prior services rendered, the rights to the benefits have vested, the payment is probable and we can reasonably estimate the liability. We account for employee termination benefits that represent a one-time benefit in accordance with ASC Topic 420, *Exit or Disposal Cost Obligations*. We record such costs into expense over the employee's future service period, if any.

Employee Retirement Plans

Following our 2006 acquisition of Guidant Corporation, we sponsored the Guidant Retirement Plan, a frozen noncontributory defined benefit plan covering a select group of current and former employees. The plan was partially frozen as of September 25, 1995 and completely frozen as of May 31, 2007, and was terminated effective December 1, 2014. During 2015, we finalized the termination process and settled the plan's obligations. As a result, we recorded pension termination charges of $44 million for the year ended December 31, 2015.

We continue to sponsor the Guidant Supplemental Retirement Plan, a frozen, nonqualified defined benefit plan for certain former officers and employees of Guidant. The Guidant Supplemental Retirement Plan was partially funded through a Rabbi Trust that contains segregated company assets used to pay the benefit obligations related to the plan. We also maintain an Executive Retirement Plan, a defined benefit plan covering executive officers and division presidents and certain persons that may have served in these roles. Participants may retire with unreduced benefits once retirement conditions have been satisfied. In addition, we maintain retirement plans covering certain international employees.

We use a December 31 measurement date for these plans and record the underfunded portion as a liability, recognizing changes in the funded status through other comprehensive income (OCI). The outstanding obligation as of December 31, 2015 and 2014 is as follows:

(In millions)	As of December 31, 2015			As of December 31, 2014		
	Projected Benefit Obligation (PBO)	Fair value of Plan Assets	Underfunded PBO Recognized	Projected Benefit Obligation (PBO)	Fair value of Plan Assets	Underfunded PBO Recognized
Executive Retirement Plan	$ 14	$—	$14	$ 13	$—	$13
Guidant Retirement Plan (frozen)	—	—	—	148	140	8
Guidant Supplemental Retirement Plan (frozen)	33	—	33	34	—	34
International Retirement Plans	84	52	32	90	51	39
	$131	$ 52	$79	$285	$191	$94

The value of the Rabbi Trust assets used to pay the Guidant Supplemental Retirement Plan benefits included in our accompanying consolidated financial statements was approximately $11 million as of December 31, 2015 and $14 million as of December 31, 2014.

The critical assumptions associated with our employee retirement plans as of December 31, 2015 are as follows:

	Discount Rate	Expected Return on Plan Assets	Rate of Compensation Increase
Executive Retirement Plan	3.75%		3.00%
Guidant Supplemental Retirement Plan (frozen)	4.25%		
International Retirement Plans	1.00%–2.20%	3.00%–4.10%	3.00%–6.78%

We base our discount rate on the rates of return available on high-quality bonds with maturities approximating the expected period over which benefits will be paid. The rate of compensation increase is based on historical and expected rate increases. We base our rate of expected return on plan assets on historical experience, our investment guidelines and expectations for long-term rates of return.

A rollforward of the changes in the fair value of plan assets for our funded retirement plans during 2015 and 2014 is as follows:

	Year Ended December 31,	
(In millions)	2015	2014
Beginning fair value	$ 191	$166
Actual return on plan assets	1	26
Employer contributions	6	16
Benefits paid	(145)	(11)
Net transfers in (out)	—	—
Foreign currency exchange	(1)	(6)
Ending fair value	$ 52	$191

We also sponsor a voluntary 401(k) Retirement Savings Plan for eligible employees. We match 200 percent of employee elective deferrals for the first two percent of employee eligible compensation, and 50 percent of employee elective deferrals greater than two percent, but not exceeding six percent, of employee eligible compensation. Total expense for our matching contributions to the plan was $69 million in 2015, $63 million in 2014, and $59 million in 2013 .

ADJUSTMENTS TO RECONCILE NET INCOME—ACQUIRED IN-PROCESS RESEARCH & DEVELOPMENT (IPR&D)

6.21 ELI LILLY AND COMPANY (DEC)

CONSOLIDATED STATEMENTS OF CASH FLOWS (in part)

	Year Ended December 31		
(Dollars in millions)	2015	2014	2013
Cash Flows from Operating Activities			
Net income	$2,408.4	$2,390.5	$4,684.8
Adjustments to Reconcile Net Income to Cash Flows from Operating Activities:			
Depreciation and amortization	1,427.7	1,379.0	1,445.6
Change in deferred income taxes	(748.4)	36.8	265.9
Stock-based compensation expense	217.8	156.0	144.9
Acquired in-process research and development	535.0	200.2	57.1
Income related to termination of the exenatide collaboration with Amylin Pharmaceuticals, Inc. (Note 4)	—	—	(495.4)
Net proceeds from (payments for) terminations of interest rate swaps	(186.1)	340.7	—
Other non-cash operating activities, net	36.4	13.8	25.1
Other changes in operating assets and liabilities, net of acquisitions and divestitures:			
Receivables—(increase) decrease	(304.5)	117.4	(152.7)
Inventories—(increase) decrease	(736.3)	(307.1)	(286.5)
Other assets—(increase) decrease	(338.8)	411.5	116.5
Accounts payable and other liabilities—increase (decrease)	461.6	(371.7)	(70.3)
Net Cash Provided by Operating Activities	2,772.8	4,367.1	5,735.0

NOTES TO CONSOLIDATED FINANCIAL STATEMENTS (in part)

(Tables present dollars in millions, except per-share data)

Note 1: Summary of Significant Accounting Policies (in part)

Research and Development Expenses and Acquired In-Process Research and Development

Research and development expenses include the following:
- Research and development costs, which are expensed as incurred.
- Milestone payment obligations incurred prior to regulatory approval of the product, which are accrued when the event requiring payment of the milestone occurs.

Acquired in-process research and development (IPR&D) expense includes the initial costs of IPR&D projects, acquired directly in a transaction other than a business combination, that do not have an alternative future use.

Note 3: Acquisitions

During 2015 and 2014, we completed the acquisitions of Novartis Animal Health (Novartis AH) and Lohmann SE (Lohmann AH), respectively. Additionally, on October 1, 2015, Bristol-Myers Squibb Company and E.R. Squibb (collectively, BMS) transferred to us their commercialization rights with respect to Erbitux ® in the U.S. and Canada (collectively, North America) through a modification of our existing arrangement. These transactions were accounted for as business combinations under the acquisition method of accounting. See Note 4 for additional information related to the Erbitux arrangement. The assets acquired and liabilities assumed were recorded at their respective fair values as of the acquisition date in our consolidated financial statements. The determination of estimated fair value required management to make significant estimates and assumptions. The excess of the purchase price over the fair value of the acquired net assets, where applicable, has been recorded as goodwill. The results of operations of these acquisitions are included in our consolidated financial statements from the date of acquisition.

In addition to the acquisitions of businesses, we also acquired assets in development in 2015, 2014, and 2013 which are further discussed below in Product and Other Acquisitions and in Note 4. Upon acquisition, the acquired IPR&D related to these products was immediately written off as an expense because the products had no alternative future use. For the years ended December 31, 2015, 2014, and 2013, we recorded acquired IPR&D charges of $535.0 million, $200.2 million, and $57.1 million, respectively. The charges were associated with the transactions discussed below in Product and Other Acquisitions, the 2015 upfront fee of $200.0 million related to tanezumab, and the 2014 charge of $55.2 million related to the transfer to us of Boehringer Ingelheim's rights to co-promote our new insulin glargine product in countries where it was not yet approved. See Note 4 for additional information related to the tanezumab and Boehringer Ingelheim arrangements.

Acquisitions of Businesses

Novartis AH Acquisition

Overview of Transaction

On January 1, 2015, we acquired from Novartis AG all of the shares of certain Novartis subsidiaries and all of the assets and liabilities of other Novartis subsidiaries that are exclusively related to the Novartis AH business in an all-cash transaction for a total purchase price of $5.28 billion. As of December 31, 2014, there was $5.41 billion of cash held in escrow for the pending acquisition of Novartis AH. This cash was classified as restricted cash, a noncurrent asset, on our consolidated balance sheet.

As a condition to the clearance of the transaction under the Hart-Scott-Rodino Antitrust Improvements Act, following the closing of the acquisition of Novartis AH, we divested certain animal health assets in the U.S. related to the Sentinel ® canine parasiticide franchise to Virbac Corporation for approximately $410 million.

The acquired Novartis AH business consists of the research and development, manufacture, marketing, sale and distribution of veterinary products to prevent and treat diseases in pets, farm animals, and farmed fish. Under the terms of the agreement, we acquired manufacturing sites, research and development facilities, a global commercial infrastructure and portfolio of products, a pipeline of projects in development, and employees.

Assets Acquired and Liabilities Assumed

The following table summarizes the amounts recognized for assets acquired and liabilities assumed as of the acquisition date:

Estimated Fair Value at January 1, 2015	
Inventories	$ 380.2
Acquired in-process research and development	298.0
Marketed products[(1)]	1,953.0
Property and equipment	199.9
Assets held for sale (primarily the U.S. Sentinel rights)	422.7
Accrued retirement benefits	(108.7)
Deferred income taxes	(60.1)

(continued)

Estimated Fair Value at January 1, 2015	
Other assets and liabilities—net	(73.0)
Total identifiable net assets	3,012.0
Goodwill[2]	2,271.1
Total consideration transferred—net of cash acquired	$5,283.1

[1] These intangible assets, which will be amortized to cost of sales on a straight-line basis over their estimated useful lives, are expected to have a weighted average useful life of 19 years.

[2] The goodwill recognized from this acquisition is attributable primarily to expected synergies that we believe will result from combining the operations of Novartis AH with our legacy animal health business, future unidentified projects and products, and the assembled workforce of Novartis AH. Approximately $950 million of the goodwill associated with this acquisition is estimated to be deductible for tax purposes.

Actual and Supplemental Pro Forma Information

Our consolidated statement of operations for the year ended December 31, 2015 includes Novartis AH revenue of $1.02 billion. Novartis AH has been partially integrated into our animal health segment and as a result of these integration efforts, certain parts of the animal health business are operating on a combined basis, and we cannot distinguish the operations between Novartis AH and our legacy animal health business.

The following unaudited pro forma financial information presents the combined consolidated results of our operations with Novartis AH as if the portion of Novartis AH that we retained after the sale to Virbac had been acquired as of January 1, 2014. We have adjusted the historical consolidated financial information to give effect to pro forma events that are directly attributable to the acquisition. The unaudited pro forma financial information is not necessarily indicative of what our consolidated results of operations would have been had we completed the acquisition at the beginning of 2014. In addition, the unaudited pro forma financial information does not attempt to project the future results of operations of our combined company.

	Unaudited Pro Forma Consolidated Results	
	2015	2014
Revenue	$19,958.7	$20,696.7
Net income	2,518.1	2,127.9
Diluted earnings per share	2.36	1.98

The unaudited pro forma financial information above reflects primarily the following pro forma pretax adjustments:
- Additional amortization expense of approximately $104 million for the year ended December 31, 2014, related to the fair value of identifiable intangible assets acquired.
- Additional cost of sales in 2014, and a corresponding reduction in cost of sales in 2015, of approximately $153 million related to the fair value adjustments to acquisition date inventory that has been sold in the year ended December 31, 2015.
- A decrease to pro forma net income of approximately $112 million in the year ended December 31, 2014, associated with an increase to interest expense related to the incremental debt that we issued to partially finance the acquisition and a reduction of interest income associated with investments which would have been used to partially fund the acquisition.

In addition, all of the above adjustments were adjusted for the applicable tax impact. The taxes associated with the adjustments above reflect the statutory tax rates in the various jurisdictions where the fair value adjustments occurred.

Lohmann AH Acquisition

On April 30, 2014, we acquired Lohmann AH, a privately-held company headquartered in Cuxhaven, Germany, through a stock purchase for a total purchase price of $591.2 million, comprised of $551.4 million of net cash plus $39.8 million of assumed debt. Lohmann AH was a global leader in poultry vaccines. As part of this transaction, we acquired the rights to a range of vaccines, commercial capabilities, and manufacturing sites in Germany and the U.S. The acquisition was not material to our consolidated financial statements.

The following table summarizes the amounts recognized for assets acquired and liabilities assumed as of the acquisition date:

Estimated Fair Value at April 30, 2014	
Marketed products	$275.4
Other intangible assets	23.9
Property and equipment	81.9
Deferred income taxes	(92.7)
Other assets and liabilities—net	51.1
Total identifiable net assets	339.6
Goodwill[1]	251.6
Total consideration transferred—net of cash acquired	$591.2

[1] Goodwill associated with this acquisition is not deductible for tax purposes.

Product and Other Acquisitions

The following table summarizes our product and other acquisitions which are discussed in detail below:

Counterparty	Compound(s) or Therapy	Acquisition Month	Phase of Development[1]	Acquired IPR&D Expense
Innovent Biologics, Inc. (Innovent)	Monoclonal antibody targeting protein CD-20 Immuno-oncology molecule cMet monoclonal antibody	March 2015	Pre-clinical[2]	$56.0
Hanmi Pharmaceutical Co., Ltd. (Hanmi)	BTK Inhibitor—HM71224	April 2015	Phase I	50.0
BioNTech AG (BioNTech)	Cancer immunotherapies	May 2015	Pre-clinical	30.0
Locemia Solutions	Intranasal glucagon	October 2015	Phase III	149.0
Undisclosed	Technology collaboration	December 2015	N/A	25.0
Halozyme Therapeutics, Inc. (Halozyme)	Recombinant human hyaluronidase enzyme—rHuPH20	December 2015	N/A	25.0
Immunocore Limited (Immunocore)	T cell-based cancer therapies	July 2014	Pre-clinical	45.0
AstraZeneca UK Limited (AstraZeneca)	Oral beta-secretase cleaving enzyme inhibitor—AZD3293	September 2014	Phase I	50.0
Adocia	BioChaperone Lispro	December 2014	Phase I	50.0
Arteaus Therapeutics	Calcitonin gene-related peptide (CGRP) monoclonal antibody	December 2013	Phase II	57.1

[1] The phase of development presented is as of the date of the arrangement.

[2] Prior to acquisition, Innovent's monoclonal antibody targeting protein CD-20 had received investigational new drug approval in China to begin Phase I development.

In connection with the arrangements described herein, our partners may be entitled to future royalties based on sales should these products be approved for commercialization and/or milestones based on the successful progress of the drug candidate through the development process.

Our collaboration agreement with Innovent is to develop and commercialize a portfolio of cancer treatments. In China, we will be responsible for the commercialization efforts, while Innovent will lead the development and manufacturing efforts. Innovent also has co-promotion rights in China. We will be responsible for development, manufacturing, and commercialization efforts of Innovent's pre-clinical immuno-oncology molecules outside of China. Separate from the collaboration, we will continue the development of our cMet monoclonal antibody gene outside of China.

Our collaboration agreement with Hanmi is to develop and commercialize Hanmi's compound being investigated for the treatment of autoimmune and other diseases. We received rights to the molecule for all indications on a worldwide basis excluding China, Hong Kong, Taiwan, and Korea. We will be responsible for leading development, regulatory, manufacturing, and commercial efforts in our territories.

Our research collaboration with BioNTech is to discover novel cancer immunotherapies.

Our global collaboration and license agreement with Halozyme is to develop and commercialize products combining our proprietary compounds with Halozyme's ENHANZE ™ platform to aid in the dispersion and absorption of other injected therapeutic drugs.

Our co-discovery and co-development collaboration with Immunocore is to research and potentially develop pre-clinical novel T cell-based cancer therapies.

Our collaboration agreement with AstraZeneca is for the worldwide co-development and co-commercialization of AstraZeneca's molecule being investigated for the potential treatment of Alzheimer's disease. We are responsible for leading development efforts, while AstraZeneca will be responsible for manufacturing efforts. If successful, both parties will take joint responsibility for commercialization of AZD3293. Under the agreement, both parties will share equally in the ongoing development costs, gross margins, and certain other costs associated with commercialization of the molecule.

Our collaboration agreement with Adocia is for the worldwide development and commercialization of Adocia's ultra-rapid insulin, a molecule being developed for the treatment of patients with type 1 and type 2 diabetes. We will be responsible for leading development, manufacturing, and commercialization efforts.

We acquired all development and commercial rights from Arteaus Therapeutics for a CGRP antibody being studied as a potential treatment for the treatment of cluster headache and migraine prevention.

6.22 RITE AID CORPORATION (FEB)

CONSOLIDATED STATEMENTS OF CASH FLOWS (in part)

(In thousands)

	Year Ended		
	February 28, 2015 (52 Weeks)	**March 1, 2014 (52 Weeks)**	**March 2, 2013 (52 Weeks)**
Operating Activities:			
Net income	$ 2,109,173	$249,414	$ 118,105
Adjustments to reconcile to net cash provided by operating activities:			
Depreciation and amortization	416,628	403,741	414,111
Lease termination and impairment charges	41,945	41,304	70,859
Gain from lease termination	—	(8,750)	—
LIFO (credit) charge	(18,857)	104,142	(147,882)
Gain on sale of assets, net	(3,799)	(15,984)	(16,776)
Stock-based compensation expense	23,390	16,194	17,717
Loss on debt retirements, net	18,512	62,443	140,502
Changes in deferred taxes	(1,726,487)	—	—
Excess tax benefit on stock options and restricted stock	(41,563)	(26,665)	—
Changes in operating assets and liabilities:			
Accounts receivable	(25,902)	(28,051)	82,721
Inventories	129,985	56,557	130,100
Accounts payable	(169,952)	(100,774)	(68)
Other assets and liabilities, net	(104,114)	(51,525)	10,199
Net cash provided by operating activities	648,959	702,046	819,588

NOTES TO CONSOLIDATED FINANCIAL STATEMENTS (in part)

(In thousands, except per share amounts)

1. Summary of Significant Accounting Policies (in part)

Impairment of Long-Lived Assets

Asset impairments are recorded when the carrying value of assets are not recoverable. For purposes of recognizing and measuring impairment of long-lived assets, the Company categorizes assets of operating stores as "Assets to Be Held and Used" and "Assets to Be Disposed Of." The Company evaluates assets at the store level because this is the lowest level of identifiable cash flows ascertainable to evaluate impairment. Assets being tested for recoverability at the store level include tangible long-lived assets and identifiable, finite-lived intangibles that arose in purchase business combinations. Corporate assets to be held and used are evaluated for impairment based on excess cash flows from the stores that support those assets.

The Company reviews long-lived assets to be held and used for impairment annually or whenever events or changes in circumstances indicate that the carrying amount of an asset may not be recoverable. If the sum of the undiscounted expected future cash flows is less than the carrying amount of the asset, the Company recognizes an impairment loss. Impairment losses are measured as the amount by which the carrying amount of the asset exceeds the fair value of the asset. When fair values are not available, the Company estimates fair value using the expected future cash flows discounted at a rate commensurate with the risks associated with the recovery of the asset.

5. Lease Termination and Impairment Charges

Impairment Charges

The Company evaluates long-lived assets for impairment whenever events or changes in circumstances indicate that an asset group has a carrying value that may not be recoverable. The individual operating store is the lowest level for which cash flows are identifiable. As such, the Company evaluates individual stores for recoverability of assets. To determine if a store needs to be tested for recoverability, the Company considers items such as decreases in market prices, changes in the manner in which the store is being used or physical condition, changes in legal factors or business climate, an accumulation of losses significantly in excess of budget, a current period operating or cash flow loss combined with a history of operating or cash flow losses or a projection of continuing losses, or an expectation that the store will be closed or sold.

The Company monitors new and recently relocated stores against operational projections and other strategic factors such as regional economics, new competitive entries and other local market considerations to determine if an impairment evaluation is required. For other stores, it performs a recoverability analysis if it has experienced current-period and historical cash flow losses.

In performing the recoverability test, the Company compares the expected future cash flows of a store to the carrying amount of its assets. Significant judgment is used to estimate future cash flows. Major assumptions that contribute to its future cash flow projections include expected sales, gross profit, and distribution expenses; expected costs such as payroll, occupancy costs and advertising expenses; and estimates for other significant selling, and general and administrative expenses. Many long-term macro-economic and industry factors are considered, both quantitatively and qualitatively, in the future cash flow assumptions. In addition to current and expected economic conditions such as inflation, interest and unemployment rates that affect customer shopping patterns, the Company considers that it operates in a highly competitive industry which includes the actions of other national and regional drugstore chains, independently owned drugstores, supermarkets, mass merchandisers, dollar stores and internet pharmacies. Additionally, the Company takes into consideration that certain operating stores are executing specific improvement plans which are monitored quarterly to recoup recent capital investments, such as an acquisition of an independent pharmacy, which it has made to respond to specific competitive or local market conditions, or have specific programs tailored towards a specific geography or market.

The Company recorded impairment charges of $14,438 in fiscal 2015, $13,077 in fiscal 2014 and $24,892 in fiscal 2013. The Company's methodology for recording impairment charges has been consistently applied in the periods presented.

At February 28, 2015, $1.978 billion of the Company's long-lived assets, including intangible assets, were associated with 4,570 active operating stores.

If an operating store's estimated future undiscounted cash flows are not sufficient to cover its carrying value, its carrying value is reduced to fair value which is its estimated future discounted cash flows. The discount rate is commensurate with the risks associated with the recovery of a similar asset.

An impairment charge is recorded in the period that the store does not meet its original return on investment and/or has an operating loss for the last 2 years and its projected cash flows do not exceed its current asset carrying value. The amount of the impairment charge is the entire difference between the current asset carrying value and the estimated fair value of the assets using discounted future cash flows. Most stores are fully impaired in the period that the impairment charge is originally recorded.

The Company recorded impairment charges for active stores of $12,126 in fiscal 2015, $11,748 in fiscal 2014 and $23,973 in fiscal 2013.

The Company reviews key performance results for active stores on a quarterly basis and approves certain stores for closure. Impairment for closed stores, if any (many stores are closed on lease expiration), are recorded in the quarter the closure decision is approved. Closure decisions are made on an individual store or regional basis considering all of the macro-economic, industry and other factors, in addition to, the active store's individual operating results. The Company recorded impairment charges for closed facilities of $2,312 in fiscal 2015, $1,329 in fiscal 2014 and $919 in fiscal 2013.

The following table summarizes the impairment charges and number of locations, segregated by closed facilities and active stores that have been recorded in fiscal 2015, 2014 and 2013:

| | Year Ended | | | | | |
| | February 28, 2015 | | March 1, 2014 | | March 2, 2013 | |
(In thousands, except number of stores)	Number	Charge	Number	Charge	Number	Charge
Closed facilities:						
Actual and approved store closings	24	$ 372	31	$ 531	29	$ 325
Actual and approved relocations	2	50	—	—	—	—
Existing surplus properties	9	1,890	7	798	5	594
Total impairment charges-closed facilities	35	2,312	38	1,329	34	919
Active stores:						
Stores previously impaired[1]	376	6,949	378	4,162	469	5,835
New, relocated and remodeled stores[2]	2	1,108	1	4,028	14	9,190
Remaining stores not meeting the recoverability test[3]	16	4,069	17	3,558	47	8,948
Total impairment charges—active stores	394	12,126	396	11,748	530	23,973
Total impairment charges—all locations	429	$14,438	434	$13,077	564	$24,892

[1] These charges are related to stores that were impaired for the first time in prior periods. Most active stores, requiring an impairment charge, are fully impaired in the first period that they do not meet their asset recoverability test. However, we do often make capital additions to certain stores to improve their operating results or to meet geographical competition, which if later are deemed to be unrecoverable, will be impaired in future periods. Of this total, 369, 375 and 464 stores for fiscal years 2015, 2014 and 2013 respectively have been fully impaired. Also included in these charges are an insignificant number of stores, which were only partially impaired in prior years based on our analysis that supported a reduced net book value greater than zero, but now require additional charges.

[2] These charges are related to new stores (open at least 3 years) and relocated stores (relocated in the last 2 years) and significant strategic remodels (remodeled in the last year) that did not meet their recoverability test during the current period. These stores have not met their original return on investment projections and have a historical loss of at least 2 years. Their future cash flow projections do not recover their current carrying value. Of this total, 1, 1 and 14 stores for fiscal years 2015, 2014 and 2013 respectively have been fully impaired.

[3] These charges are related to the remaining active stores that did not meet the recoverability test during the current period. These stores have a historical loss of at least 2 years. Their future cash flow projections do not recover their current carrying value. Of this total, 14, 14 and 43 stores for fiscal years 2015, 2014 and 2013 respectively have been fully impaired.

The primary drivers of its impairment charges are each store's current and historical operating performance and the assumptions that the Company makes about each store's operating performance in future periods. Projected cash flows are updated based on the next year's operating budget which includes the qualitative factors noted above. The Company utilizes the three-level valuation hierarchy for the recognition and disclosure of fair value measurements. The categorization of assets and liabilities within this hierarchy is based upon the lowest level of input that is significant to the measurement of fair value. The three levels of the hierarchy consist of the following:

- Level 1—Inputs to the valuation methodology are unadjusted quoted prices in active markets for identical assets or liabilities that the Company has the ability to access at the measurement date.
- Level 2—Inputs to the valuation methodology are quoted prices for similar assets and liabilities in active markets, quoted prices in markets that are not active or inputs that are observable for the asset or liability, either directly or indirectly, for substantially the full term of the instrument.
- Level 3—Inputs to the valuation methodology are unobservable inputs based upon management's best estimate of inputs market participants could use in pricing the asset or liability at the measurement date, including assumptions about risk.

Long-lived non-financial assets are measured at fair value on a nonrecurring basis for purposes of calculating impairment using Level 2 and Level 3 inputs as defined in the fair value hierarchy. The fair value of long-lived assets using Level 2 inputs is determined by evaluating the current economic conditions in the geographic area for similar use assets. The fair value of long-lived assets using Level 3 inputs is determined by estimating the amount and timing of net future cash flows (which are unobservable inputs) and discounting them using a risk-adjusted rate of interest (which is Level 1). The Company estimates future cash flows based on its experience and knowledge of the market in which the store is located. Significant increases or decreases in actual cash flows may result in valuation changes.

The table below sets forth by level within the fair value hierarchy the long-lived assets as of the impairment measurement date for which an impairment assessment was performed and total losses as of February 28, 2015 and March 1, 2014:

	Quoted Prices in Active Markets for Identical Assets (Level 1)	Significant Other Observable Inputs (Level 2)	Significant Unobservable Inputs (Level 3)	Fair Values as of Impairment Date	Total Charges February 28, 2015
Long-lived assets held and used	$—	$3,692	$16,992	$20,684	$(12,503)
Long-lived assets held for sale	—	6,024	—	6,024	(1,935)
Total	$—	$9,716	$16,992	$26,708	$(14,438)

	Quoted Prices in Active Markets for Identical Assets (Level 1)	Significant Other Observable Inputs (Level 2)	Significant Unobservable Inputs (Level 3)	Fair Values as of Impairment Date	Total Charges March 1, 2014
Long-lived assets held and used	$—	$ 42	$15,051	$15,093	$(12,279)
Long-lived assets held for sale	—	14,656	—	14,656	(798)
Total	$—	$14,698	$15,051	$29,749	$(13,077)

Lease Termination Charges

Charges to close a store, which principally consist of continuing lease obligations, are recorded at the time the store is closed and all inventory is liquidated, pursuant to the guidance set forth in ASC 420, "Exit or Disposal Cost Obligations." The Company calculates the liability for closed stores on a store-by-store basis. The calculation includes the discounted effect of future minimum lease payments and related ancillary costs, from the date of closure to the end of the remaining lease term, net of estimated cost recoveries that may be achieved through subletting or favorable lease terminations. The Company evaluates these assumptions each quarter and adjusts the liability accordingly.

In fiscal 2015, 2014 and 2013, the Company recorded lease termination charges of $27,507, $28,227 and $45,967, respectively. These charges related to changes in future assumptions, interest accretion and provisions for 10 stores in fiscal 2015, 15 stores in fiscal 2014, and 14 stores in fiscal 2013.

As part of its ongoing business activities, the Company assesses stores and distribution centers for potential closure. Decisions to close or relocate stores or distribution centers in future periods would result in lease termination charges for lease exit costs and liquidation of inventory, as well as impairment of assets at these locations. The following table reflects the closed store and distribution center charges that relate to new closures, changes in assumptions and interest accretion:

| | Year Ended | | |
	February 28, 2015 (52 Weeks)	March 1, 2014 (52 Weeks)	March 2, 2013 (52 Weeks)
Balance—beginning of year	$284,270	$323,757	$367,864
Provision for present value of noncancellable lease payments of closed stores	1,661	11,646	14,440
Changes in assumptions about future sublease income, terminations and change in interest rates	7,560	(4,343)	9,023
Interest accretion	18,988	21,250	23,246
Cash payments, net of sublease income	(71,432)	(68,040)	(90,816)
Balance—end of year	$241,047	$284,270	$323,757

The Company's revenues and income before income taxes for fiscal 2015, 2014, and 2013 included results from stores that have been closed or are approved for closure as of February 28, 2015. The revenue, operating expenses and income before income taxes of these stores for the periods are presented as follows:

| | Year Ended | | |
	February 28, 2015	March 1, 2014	March 2, 2013
Revenues	$59,520	$175,868	$306,501
Operating expenses	68,425	192,416	332,146
Gain from sale of assets	(5,516)	(13,075)	(19,877)
Other expenses (income)	571	(8,197)	1,647
(Loss) income before income taxes	(3,960)	4,724	(7,415)
Included in these stores' (loss) income before income taxes are:			
Depreciation and amortization	300	1,126	2,817
Inventory liquidation charges	588	621	1,039

The above results are not necessarily indicative of the impact that these closures will have on revenues and operating results of the Company in the future, as the Company often transfers the business of a closed store to another Company store, thereby retaining a portion of these revenues and operating expenses.

Cash Flows From Investing Activities

PRESENTATION

6.23 FASB ASC 230 defines those transactions and events that constitute investing cash receipts and payments. Investing activities include making and collecting loans and acquiring and disposing of debt or equity instruments and property, plant, and equipment (PPE) and other productive assets. Paragraphs 20–21 of FASB ASC 230-10-45 explain that investing activities exclude acquiring and disposing of certain loans or other debt or equity instruments that are acquired specifically for resale. Cash flows from purchases, sales, and maturities of available-for-sale securities should be classified as cash flows from investing activities and reported gross in the statement of cash flows. Cash inflows from investing activities include the following:

- Receipts from collections or sales of loans made by the entity and of other entities' debt instruments, other than cash equivalents and certain debt instruments that are acquired specifically for resale, that were purchased by the entity.
- Receipts from sales of equity instruments of other entities, other than certain equity instruments carried in a trading account, and from returns of investment in those instruments.
- Receipts from sales of PPE and other productive assets.
- Receipts from sales of loans that were not specifically acquired for resale. If loans were acquired as investments, cash receipts from sales of those loans shall be classified as investing cash inflows, regardless of a change in the purpose for holding those loans.

Cash outflows from investing activities include the following:

- Disbursements for loans made by the entity and payments to acquire debt instruments of other entities, other than cash equivalents and certain debt instruments that are acquired specifically for resale.
- Payments to acquire equity instruments of other entities, other than certain equity instruments carried in a trading account.
- Payments at the time of purchase or soon before or after purchase to acquire PPE and other productive assets, including interest capitalized as part of the cost of those assets. Generally, only advance payments, the down payment, or other amounts paid at the time of purchase or soon before or after the purchase of PPE and other productive assets are investing cash outflows. However, incurring directly related debt to the seller is a financing transaction; thus, subsequent payments of principal on that debt are financing cash outflows.

PRESENTATION AND DISCLOSURE EXCERPTS

ACQUISITIONS

6.24 THE DUN & BRADSTREET CORPORATION (DEC)

CONSOLIDATED STATEMENTS OF CASH FLOWS (in part)

	For the Years Ended December 31,		
(Amounts in millions)	2015	2014	2013
Cash Flows from Investing Activities:			
Proceeds from Sales of Businesses and Property, Net of Cash Divested	159.8	—	0.8
Payments for Acquisitions of Businesses, Net of Cash Acquired	(444.2)	(8.3)	—
Investment in Debt Security	(6.3)	—	—
Cash Settlements of Foreign Currency Contracts	(15.6)	(7.7)	(7.2)
Capital Expenditures	(12.8)	(9.8)	(7.1)
Additions to Computer Software and Other Intangibles	(52.0)	(37.4)	(42.2)
Net, Other	—	(0.1)	(0.2)
Net Cash Used in Investing Activities from Continuing Operations	(371.1)	(63.3)	(55.9)
Net Cash Used in Investing Activities from Discontinued Operations	(5.4)	(6.7)	(5.7)
Net Cash Used in Investing Activities	(376.5)	(70.0)	(61.6)

NOTES TO CONSOLIDATED FINANCIAL STATEMENTS (in part)

(Tabular dollar amounts in millions, except per share data)

Note 2. Recent Accounting Pronouncements (in part)

In September 2015, the FASB issued ASU 2015-16 "Business Combinations (Topic 805): Simplifying the Accounting for Measurement-Period Adjustments." This standard eliminates the requirement for an acquirer in a business combination to account for measurement-period adjustments retrospectively. The new standard requires an acquirer to recognize a measurement-period adjustment during the period in which it determines the amount of the adjustment. In addition, it requires the acquirer to record in the same period's financial statements, the effect on earnings of changes in depreciation, amortization, or other income effects, if any, as a result of the change to the provisional amounts as if the accounting had been completed at the acquisition date. This standard was effective prospectively for fiscal years beginning after December 15, 2015, and interim periods within those fiscal years. Early application is permitted. We have adopted the guidance of this standard prospectively during the quarter ended September 30, 2015 in connection with the accounting for measurement-period adjustments related to our acquisitions of Dun & Bradstreet Credibility Corp. ("DBCC") and NetProspex. The adoption of this authoritative guidance did not have a material impact on our consolidated financial statements. See Note 18 to the consolidated financial statements included in this Annual Report for further details on the acquisitions.

Note 18. Acquisitions

Dun & Bradstreet Credibility Corp.

On May 12, 2015, we acquired a 100% equity interest in DBCC. DBCC provides business credit building and credibility solutions. The company's headquarters is in Los Angeles, CA, with offices throughout the United States. As a result of this acquisition, we formed a new business, Dun & Bradstreet Emerging Businesses, a combination of DBCC's technology and data solutions with Dun & Bradstreet's small and mid-sized operations. The new business has been established to expand our capabilities to deliver more sophisticated solutions to the diverse needs of emerging business customers. The results of DBCC have been included in our consolidated financial statements since the date of acquisition.

The acquisition was accounted for in accordance with ASC 805, "Business Combinations." Total consideration included an initial cash payment of $320.0 million, at the closing of the transaction, and an earnout of up to $30.0 million based on the achievement of sales, EBITDA, operating expense and operating income targets through December 31, 2018. In connection with this potential earnout payment, we recorded total contingent consideration liability of $11.2 million initially, representing the estimated fair value of the contingent consideration we expected to pay (see further discussion within this Note). Of the $320.0 million initial cash payment, a part of the merger consideration was placed in escrow to indemnify the Company against a portion of the losses, if any, arising out of certain class action litigation matters and for other customary matters, subject to caps and other conditions. As of the acquisition date, discovery in the cases was ongoing, and the Company was investigating the allegations. We therefore did not have sufficient information upon which to determine that a loss in connection with these litigations was probable, reasonably possible or estimable, and thus no reserve was established nor was a range of loss disclosed. Hence no associated indemnification asset was recognized on the acquisition date. For further detail, see Note 13 to our consolidated financial statements included in this Annual Report on Form 10-K.

As a result of the acquisition, DBCC's previous claim under its pending legal action against us was discontinued with prejudice. We also effectively terminated other preexisting contractual arrangements with DBCC. We have initially determined these preexisting relationships were settled at market value on the acquisition date and therefore no settlement gain or loss was recognized. Transaction costs of $6.9 million were included in operating expenses in the consolidated statement of operations and comprehensive income (loss). The acquisition was accounted for as a purchase transaction, and accordingly, the assets and liabilities of the acquired entity were recorded at their estimated fair values at the date of the acquisition.

The preliminary fair values of the acquired assets and liabilities are subject to change within the one-year measurement period. We expect to continue to obtain information to determine the fair values of the net assets acquired at the acquisition date during the measurement period. Since the initial valuation reflected in our financial results as of June 30, 2015, we have recorded adjustments to the preliminary valuation of assets and liabilities, resulting in a net decrease of goodwill of $2.7 million in the third quarter of 2015. The reduction of $2.7 million in goodwill reflected an adjustment to the fair value of the contingent consideration liability as a result of applying a higher risk premium based upon further analysis. As of September 30, 2015, the fair value of the contingent liability was $8.5 million. We have also early adopted ASU 2015-16 "Business Combinations (Topic 805)" in the third quarter of 2015. Accordingly, adjustments to the initial purchase price allocation identified during the measurement period were recognized in the reporting period in which the adjustment amounts are determined.

The table below reflects the purchase price related to the acquisition and the resulting preliminary purchase price allocation as of December 31, 2015:

	Amortization Life (years)	Initial Purchase Price Allocation at June 30, 2015	Measurement Period Adjustments	Preliminary Purchase Price Allocation at December 31, 2015
Current Assets		$ 2.0	$ —	$ 2.0
Intangible Assets:				
Reacquired Right	Indefinite	153.2	—	153.2
Customer Relationships	8.0	82.5	—	82.5
Technology	6.5	45.6	—	45.6
Goodwill	Indefinite	210.1	(2.7)	207.4
Other		3.5	—	3.5
Total Assets Acquired		$496.9	$(2.7)	$494.2
Deferred Revenue		$ 45.6	$ —	$ 45.6
Deferred Tax Liability		107.0	—	107.0
Other Liabilities		13.1	—	13.1
Total Liabilities Assumed		$165.7	—	$165.7
Total Upfront Purchase Price		$320.0	$ —	$320.0
Fair Value of Contingent Consideration		11.2	(2.7)	8.5
Total Consideration		$331.2	$(2.7)	$328.5

The fair value of the reacquired right intangible asset was determined by applying the income approach; specifically, a multi-period excess earnings method. The valuation was based on the present value of the net earnings, or after-tax cash flows attributable to the measured asset.

The technology intangible asset represents DBCC's innovative technology platform that enables product launching and fulfillment, customer relationship management, telephony, finance, data warehousing and business intelligence. The fair value of this intangible asset was determined by applying the income approach; specifically, a relief-from-royalty method.

The fair value of the customer relationships intangible asset was determined by applying the replacement cost approach.

The fair value of the contingent consideration was estimated based on an option-pricing model. The model estimated the possible outcome of each of the performance targets (e.g. Revenue) during the earn out period and the associated estimated expected earn out payments. The expected earn out payments were then discounted to present value on the acquisition date.

The fair value of deferred revenue was determined based on estimated direct costs to fulfill the related obligations, plus a reasonable profit margin.

We believe that the information gathered to date provides a reasonable basis for estimating the fair values of assets acquired and liabilities assumed, but if facts and circumstances arise that necessitate change, we will adjust the associated fair values. Thus, the provisional measurements of fair value set forth above may be subject to further change. We expect to complete the purchase accounting process as soon as practicable but no later than one year from the acquisition date.

Subsequent to the acquisition date, an amendment was negotiated related to the Earnout Agreement reflecting revised targets through December 31, 2018. As a result, we have increased the fair value of the contingent consideration liability from $8.5 million to $15.1 million as of December 31, 2015. For financial reporting purposes, since this adjustment does not reflect facts and circumstances existing on the acquisition date, it is not considered a measurement period adjustment in accordance with ASC 805. The adjustment of $6.6 million to the fair value of the contingent consideration liability was included in "Operating Costs" in our Americas segment in the fourth quarter of 2015. The payment of earnout for the year ended December 31, 2015 will be $6.0 million.

The goodwill was assigned to our North America reporting unit, which is part of the Americas reportable segment. The value of the goodwill is associated with the strength of DBCC's management team and its business model. The combined expertise will enhance our ability to develop products and provide us growth opportunity with small and mid-size businesses. The intangible assets, with useful lives from 6.5 to 8 years, are being amortized over a weighted-average useful life of 7.5 years. The intangibles have been recorded within Other Intangibles in our consolidated balance sheet since the date of acquisition.

Income Taxes

We established deferred tax liabilities on certain intangibles acquired as part of the acquisition for which there is no tax basis. In addition, the goodwill acquired is not deductible for tax purposes.

NetProspex

On January 5, 2015, we acquired a 100% equity interest in NetProspex. NetProspex is based out of Waltham, Massachusetts and provides business-to-business professional contact data and data management services. The acquisition combines NetProspex's comprehensive professional contact database with our global data and analytics. This will further enable our customers to better understand their ideal customers, identify and prioritize opportunities, and grow their business. The results of NetProspex have been included in our consolidated financial statements since the date of acquisition.

The acquisition was accounted for in accordance with ASC 805. The acquisition was valued at $124.5 million, net of cash assumed. Transaction costs of $2.3 million were included in operating expenses in the unaudited consolidated statement of operations and comprehensive income (loss). The acquisition was accounted for as a purchase transaction, and accordingly, the assets and liabilities of the acquired entity were recorded at their estimated fair values at the date of the acquisition.

The table below reflects the purchase price related to the acquisition and the resulting purchase price allocation as of December 31, 2015:

	Amortization Life (years)	Initial Purchase Price Allocation at March 31, 2015	Measurement Period Adjustments	Final Purchase Price Allocation at December 31, 2015
Current Assets		$ 10.8	$ —	$ 10.8
Intangible Assets:				
Data Supply Agreement	5.5	1.1	—	1.1
Customer Relationships	5.5	6.5	—	6.5
Database	2.0	3.2	—	3.2
Technology	6.5	18.8	—	18.8
Database Screening Tool	9.0	9.5	—	9.5
Goodwill	Indefinite	87.0	(1.9)	85.1
Other		1.0	—	1.0
Total Assets Acquired		$137.9	$(1.9)	$136.0
Total Liabilities Assumed		9.5	(1.9)	7.6
Total Purchase Price		$128.4	—	$128.4
Less:				
Cash Assumed		(4.2)	—	(4.2)
Acceleration of Vesting for NetProspex Options		0.3	—	0.3
Net Cash Consideration		$124.5	$ —	$124.5

On the acquisition date, certain of NetProspex's outstanding options were accelerated for vesting. In accordance with ASC 805, the amounts paid for the acceleration of the vesting for the options that are without existing change in control clauses are treated as post-acquisition expense. As a result, $0.3 million was included in "Operating Costs" in our Americas segment for the three months ended March 31, 2015.

As with our DBCC acquisition discussed above, we continued to obtain information to determine the fair values of the net assets acquired at the acquisition date during the measurement period. The measurement-period adjustment recorded in the third and fourth quarter of 2015 for NetProspex was related to the deferred tax liability based on additional tax credit and net operating loss carryforwards identified during the period. The adjustment has resulted in a net decrease of goodwill of $1.9 million.

The technology intangible asset represents NetProspex's data service platform and method to deliver customer services and solutions. The fair value of this intangible asset was determined by applying the income approach; specifically, a relief-from-royalty method.

The database screening tool intangible asset is a key component in NetProspex's data management process. It facilitates efficient identification and classification of data during collection as well as customer engagement. The fair value of this intangible asset was determined by applying the income approach through a discounted cash flow analysis.

The fair value of the customer relationships and data supply agreement intangible assets was determined by applying the income approach through a discounted cash flow analysis.

The fair value of the database intangible asset was determined by applying the replacement cost approach.

The fair value of deferred revenue was determined based on estimated direct costs to fulfill the related obligations, plus a reasonable profit margin.

The goodwill was assigned to our North America reporting unit, which is part of the Americas reportable segment. The primary item that generated the goodwill is the value of NetProspex's workforce and its process associated with product development which provides potential growth opportunity in Sales and Marketing Solutions. The intangible assets, with useful lives from 2 to 9 years, are being amortized over a weighted-average useful life of 6.5 years. The intangibles have been recorded as "Trademarks, Patents and Other" within Other Intangibles in our consolidated balance sheet since the date of acquisition.

Tax Treatment of Goodwill

The goodwill acquired is not deductible for tax purposes.

Unaudited Pro Forma Financial Information

The following unaudited pro forma statements of operations data presents the combined results of the Company and its business acquisitions (DBCC and NetProspex) completed during the year ended December 31, 2015, assuming that the business acquisitions completed during 2015 had occurred on January 1, 2014.

	For the Year Ended December 31,	
	2015	2014
Reported GAAP Revenue[1]	$1,637.1	$1,584.5
Add: DBCC and NetProspex Pre-acquisition Revenue	42.4	128.4
Pro Forma Revenue	$1,679.5	$1,712.9
Reported GAAP Net Income (Loss) Attributable to Dun & Bradstreet Common Shareholders[2]	$ 168.8	$ 294.4
Pro Forma Adjustments—Net of Income Tax:		
Pre-acquisition Net Income (Losses)	0.3	10.8
Amortization for Intangible Assets	(4.0)	(15.2)
Acquisition-Related Costs[3]	13.5	(13.5)
Pro Forma Net Income (Loss) Attributable to Dun & Bradstreet Common Shareholders	$ 178.6	$ 276.5

[1] Reported GAAP revenue includes revenue from DBCC and NetProspex since their respective acquisition dates of $71.2 million and $17.6 million, respectively, for the year ended December 31, 2015, net of the impact of the deferred revenue fair value adjustment of $18.2 million and $1.7 million, respectively.

[2] Reported GAAP Net Income (Loss) Attributable to Dun & Bradstreet Common Shareholders includes net loss from DBCC and NetProspex since their respective acquisition dates of $0.3 million and $12.2 million, respectively, for the year ended December 31, 2015.

(3) Acquisition-related costs include transaction costs, retention costs and other one-time costs.

DIVESTITURES

6.25 VISTEON CORPORATION (DEC)
CONSOLIDATED STATEMENTS OF CASH FLOWS 1 (in part)

	Year Ended December 31		
(Dollars in Millions)	2015	2014	2013
Investing Activities			
Capital expenditures	(187)	(340)	(269)
Short-term investments, net	(47)	—	—
Loan to non-consolidated affiliate	(10)	—	—
Net proceeds from Climate Transaction	2,664	—	—
Proceeds from asset sales and business divestitures	91	66	977
Acquisition of businesses, net of cash acquired	(4)	(311)	(10)
Payments associated with business divestitures, net	(156)	(147)	—
Other	7	(8)	—
Net cash provided from (used by) investing activities	2,358	(740)	698

(1) The Company has combined cash flows from discontinued operations with cash flows from continuing operations within the operating, investing and financing categories. As such, cash and equivalents above include $1 million and $351 million of assets held for sale reflected in Current assets held for sale on the Consolidated Balance Sheets as of December 31, 2015 and 2014, respectively.

NOTES TO CONSOLIDATED FINANCIAL STATEMENTS (in part)

Note 1. Description of Business (in part)

Visteon Corporation (the "Company" or "Visteon") is a global automotive supplier that designs, engineers and manufactures innovative electronics products for nearly every original equipment vehicle manufacturer ("OEM") worldwide including Ford, Nissan, Renault, Mazda, BMW, General Motors and Honda. Visteon is headquartered in Van Buren Township, Michigan and has an international network of manufacturing operations, technical centers and joint venture operations, supported by approximately 11,000 employees, dedicated to the design, development, manufacture and support of its product offerings and its global customers. The Company's manufacturing and engineering footprint is principally located outside of the U.S., with a heavy concentration in low-cost geographic regions. Visteon delivers value for its customers and stockholders through its technology-focused core vehicle cockpit electronics business. The Company's cockpit electronics product portfolio includes audio systems, information displays, instrument clusters, head up displays, infotainment systems, and telematics solutions. The Company's vehicle cockpit electronics business is comprised of and reported under the Electronics segment. In addition to the Electronics segment, the Company has residual operations in South America and Europe previously associated with the former Interiors and Climate businesses, not subject to discontinued operations classification, that comprise Other.

Exit of Climate Business

On June 9, 2015, Visteon completed the sale to Hahn & Co. Auto Holdings Co., Ltd. ("Hahn") and Hankook Tire Co., Ltd. ("Hankook" and, together with Hahn, the "Purchasers") of all of its shares of Halla Visteon Climate Control Corporation, a Korean corporation ("HVCC"), for approximately $3.4 billion, or KRW 52,000 per share after adjusting for the 2014 dividend paid by HVCC to Visteon, pursuant to and in accordance with the Share Purchase Agreement, dated as of December 17, 2014 (the "HVCC Purchase Agreement"), among Visteon and the Purchasers (the "Climate Transaction"). Visteon recorded a pre-tax gain of $2.3 billion in connection with the sale. See Note 4 "Divestitures" and Note 5 "Discontinued Operations" for additional disclosures.

Note 2. Summary of Significant Accounting Policies (in part)

Discontinued Operations: The Company reports operating results for discontinued operations separately from continuing operations to distinguish the financial impact of disposal transactions from ongoing operations. Through December 31, 2014, the Company reported discontinued operations when the operations and cash flows of a component of the Company had been eliminated from ongoing operations. For a component to be disposed of by sale, financial results were classified as discontinued only when held for sale criteria were met. For a component to be disposed of other than by sale, financial results were not classified as discontinued until abandonment, distribution, or exchange occurred, depending on the manner of disposal. The operating results of the operations associated with the 2014 Interiors Divestiture are presented as discontinued operations.

In April 2014, the Financial Accounting Standards Board ("FASB") issued Accounting Standards Update ("ASU") No. 2014-8, "Reporting Discontinued Operations and Disclosures of Disposals of Components of an Entity". This ASU changes the requirements for reporting discontinued operations to disposals of components of an entity that represent strategic shifts that have a major effect on an entity's operations and financial results and does not prohibit continuing involvement. The standard also expands the disclosures for discontinued operations and requires new disclosures related to individually material disposals that do not qualify for discontinued operations reporting. The guidance was effective for interim and annual periods beginning after December 15, 2014, and should be applied prospectively. The Company adopted this standard effective January 1, 2015. In June 2015, the Company completed the sale of all of its shares of HVCC to the Purchasers for approximately $3.4 billion, or KRW 52,000 per share after adjusting for the 2014 dividend paid by HVCC to Visteon as further described in Note 4 "Divestitures" and Note 5 "Discontinued Operations". Accordingly, the vast majority of assets and liabilities and operating results for the previously reported Climate Segment are presented as discontinued operations. Previously reported assets and liabilities associated with the Interiors Divestiture are presented as held for sale to conform with the Climate Transaction presentation.

Note 4. Divestitures (in part)

Climate Transaction

On June 9, 2015, Visteon completed the sale of all its shares in HVCC to the Purchasers. The Climate Transaction closed for approximately $3.4 billion, or KRW 52,000 per share after adjusting for the 2014 dividend paid by HVCC to Visteon. The Company received net cash proceeds of approximately $2.7 billion and recognized a pre-tax gain of approximately $2.3 billion in June, 2015.

In connection with the closing of the Climate Transaction, Visteon, HVCC and/or the Purchasers have entered into certain other agreements, including a transition agreement (pursuant to which the parties will provide certain transition services for a specified period following the closing), a remediation agreement (pursuant to which Visteon will provide certain IT services for a period of time), engineering and support agreements (pursuant to which the parties will support certain operations of the other following the closing), and a letter agreement (pursuant to which Visteon has agreed to purchase from HVCC certain electronics operations located in India). Assets and liabilities associated with the Climate Transaction met the "held for sale" criteria during the second quarter ended June 30, 2015 and were reclassified as such in the December 31, 2014, Consolidated Balance Sheet.

The gain is summarized below (dollars in millions):

Gross proceeds[1]	$3,423
Korea withholding tax[2]	(377)
Professional fees[3]	(20)
Korea security transaction tax[4]	(17)
Divested cash balances[5]	(345)
Net cash provided from investing activities	2,664
Net assets divested, excluding cash balances[5]	(565)
Information technology separation and service obligations[6]	(53)
Employee related charges[7]	(45)
Electronics business repurchase obligation[8]	(50)
Professional fees[3]	(4)
Korea withholding tax recoverable[2]	377
Net gain on Climate Transaction	$2,324

[1] Gross proceeds of $3.423 billion were received in connection with the Climate Transaction, translated at a spot rate of 1121.5 KRW to USD on June 9, 2015. Impacts of related hedging activities and exchange on proceeds conversion into USD are included in the Company's consolidated statements of comprehensive income as "Other expense, net" for the years ended December 31, 2015 and 2014.

[2] In connection with the transaction, the Company recorded a tax recoverable of $377 million for Korean capital gains tax withheld by the Purchasers and paid to the Korean government. This amount reduced proceeds classified as net cash provided from investing activities within the Company's consolidated statements of cash flows for the year ended December 31, 2015. The Company received the entire amount of the expected capital gains withholding tax in January 2016, amounting to $355 million as adjusted for interest and exchange as the refund was denominated in Korean won. Net exchange and interest impacts are recorded as provision for income taxes within discontinued operations.

[3] Professional fees of $24 million, representing fees paid to financial advisors, were based on a percentage of the gross proceeds, partially offset by previously paid retainer fees of $4 million, for a net payment of $20 million reducing proceeds classified as net cash provided from investing activities within the Company's consolidated statements of cash flows for the year ended December 31, 2015.

[4] Security transaction taxes of $17 million were remitted to the Korean government as of the transaction close, reducing proceeds classified as net cash provided from investing activities within the Company's consolidated statements of cash flows for the year ended December 31, 2015.

[5] Net assets of $910 million, including assets, liabilities, accumulated other comprehensive income and non-controlling interests, were divested in connection with the Climate Transaction. Divested assets included $345 million of cash balances, reflected as a reduction of transaction proceeds classified as net cash provided from investing activities within the Company's consolidated statements of cash flows for the year ended December 31, 2015.

[6] In connection with the Climate Transaction, the Company has entered an agreement pursuant to which Visteon will provide information technology ongoing and separation services for HVCC to fully operate as an independent entity with estimated costs of approximately $53 million. The remaining information technology liability is included in the Company's consolidated balance sheets as "Other current liabilities" as of December 31, 2015.

[7] Employee related charges of $45 million include bonus payments, the Company's assumption of incentive plan liabilities, and impacts of employment change in control provisions. Bonus payments of $30 million are classified in the Company's net cash provided from operating activities within the Company's consolidated statements of cash flows for the year ended December 31, 2015. Amounts remaining to be paid are included in the Company's consolidated balance sheets as "Accrued employee liabilities" as of December 31, 2015.

[8] In connection with the Climate Transaction, the Company has entered an agreement to purchase certain electronics operations located in India, expected to close in 2016 after legal separation and regulatory approvals are met. The Company has recorded a repurchase obligation of $50 million, representing the estimated purchase price of the subject business. The Company continues to consolidate the business, with net assets of approximately $22 million, based on the Company's continued controlling financial interest. The Company's controlling financial interest was evaluated based on continued operating control and obligation to fund losses or benefit from earnings. The business is included in a legal entity currently owned by HVCC and therefore the Electronics business assets are not available for general corporate purposes. The repurchase commitment is included in the Company's consolidated balance sheets as "Other current liabilities" as of December 31, 2015.

BUSINESS COMBINATIONS

6.26 ST. JUDE MEDICAL, INC. (DEC)

CONSOLIDATED STATEMENTS OF CASH FLOWS (in part)

(in millions)

Fiscal Year Ended	January 2, 2016	January 3, 2015	December 28, 2013
Investing Activities			
Purchases of property, plant and equipment	(186)	(190)	(222)
Business combination payments, net of cash acquired	(3,252)	(147)	(292)
Proceeds from sale of investments	30	7	10
Other investing activities, net	(37)	(9)	(18)
Net cash used in investing activities	(3,445)	(339)	(522)

NOTES TO THE CONSOLIDATED FINANCIAL STATEMENTS (in part)

Note 2—Business Combinations

Fiscal Year 2015

Thoratec: In October 2015, the Company acquired all the outstanding shares of Thoratec Corporation (Thoratec). Under the terms of the agreement, each outstanding Thoratec share was converted into the right to receive $63.50 per share in cash. Thoratec, headquartered in Pleasanton, California, develops, manufactures and markets proprietary medical devices used for mechanical circulatory support for the treatment of heart failure patients. Certain "in-the-money" unvested options to purchase Thoratec shares that were outstanding and unexercised immediately prior to completion of the acquisition were exchanged for St. Jude Medical restricted stock awards; each unvested Thoratec restricted stock unit and performance share unit that was outstanding immediately prior to completion of the acquisition was converted into St. Jude Medical restricted stock units; and certain "in-the-money" unvested options to purchase Thoratec shares, unvested restricted stock units, and unvested Thoratec performance share units previously awarded to certain employees were accelerated upon the acquisition (collectively "accelerated and replacement equity awards"). The aggregate fair value of the accelerated and replacement equity awards of $166 million was based on St. Jude Medical, Inc.'s stock price at the date of acquisition. The value of the replacement equity awards not earned was $57 million as of the date of acquisition and will be expensed over the remaining requisite service periods ranging up to four years (see Note 7). Additionally, during 2015, the Company recognized direct transaction costs of $22 million in *selling, general and administrative expense* in the Company's *Consolidated Statements of Earnings*.

The purchase price allocation is considered preliminary, largely with respect to certain tax-related assets and liabilities and legal contingencies. Significant judgment is required in determining the estimated fair values of identifiable intangible assets, including IPR&D assets, and certain other assets and liabilities. Such valuation requires significant estimates and assumptions inherent in the initial measurements including, but not limited to:

- Timing and amount of revenue and future cash flows, which often depend on estimates of relevant market sizes, expected market growth rates, trends in technology (including the impacts of anticipated product introductions by competitors, legal agreements and patent litigation), the expected useful lives of acquired technologies and the expected completion date of IPR&D projects;
- Expected costs to develop the IPR&D projects into commercially viable products, which include the stage of completion, the complexity of the work to complete, the contribution of core technologies and other acquired assets and the required clinical investment to obtain regulatory approval;
- The discount rate reflecting the risk inherent in future cash flows; and
- Perpetual growth rate used to calculate the terminal value, where applicable.

The following table summarizes the preliminary purchase price allocation of the values of net assets as a result of the Company's acquisition of Thoratec in October 2015 (in millions):

	Thoratec
Accounts receivable	$ 76
Inventories	150
Other current and noncurrent assets	44
Property, plant and equipment	57
Goodwill	2,142
Intangible assets	1,490
Accounts payable	(22)
Other current and noncurrent liabilities	(69)
Contingent consideration liabilities	(33)
Deferred income tax assets/(liabilities)	(548)
Net assets	$3,287
Cash consideration paid to Thoratec shareholders	$3,484
Cash consideration paid for vested Thoratec share awards	30
Total cash paid	$3,514
Less: cash acquired	(262)
Net cash consideration	$3,252
Fair value of equity awards exchanged in business combination	35
Total purchase consideration	$3,287

The goodwill recorded as a result of the Thoratec acquisition is not deductible for income tax purposes. The goodwill is largely attributable to strategic opportunities for growing the Company's portfolio of products treating heart failure by offering more comprehensive therapy options across the care continuum. Synergies are also expected to arise upon the integration of Thoratec, the benefits of utilizing the existing workforce, technology innovation and cross-selling opportunities. Additionally, IPR&D projects that did not have substance at the acquisition date are not separately identified. IPR&D intangible assets include Thoratec projects for its next generation left ventricular assist device and percutaneous heart pumps, which have not been approved for commercialization in the U.S. We currently expect approvals for U.S. commercialization to occur at various times in 2018 and 2019. In connection with the acquisition of Thoratec, the Company recognized $714 million of indefinite-lived IPR&D intangible assets, $683 million of purchased technology and patent definite-lived intangible assets that have an estimated weighted average useful life of 9.8 years and a $93 million trademark definite-lived intangible asset that has an estimated useful life of 16.0 years.

The consolidated results of the Company for the fiscal year ended January 2, 2016, include Thoratec's results of operations from the acquisition date through January 2, 2016. Net sales and net losses of Thoratec during this period and included in the Company's *Consolidated Financial Statements* for the fiscal year ended January 2, 2016 totaled $136 million and $94 million, respectively.

The following unaudited pro forma information provides the effect of the Company's acquisition of Thoratec as if the acquisition had occurred on December 29, 2013 (in millions):

(Unaudited)	2015	2014
Pro forma net sales	$5,919	$6,099
Pro forma net earnings attributable to St. Jude Medical, Inc.	$ 970	$ 767

The historical consolidated financial information of the Company and Thoratec has been adjusted in the pro forma information to give effect to pro forma events that are (a) directly attributable to the acquisition and related financing, (b) expected to have a continuing impact on St. Jude Medical, Inc., and (c) factually supportable. In order to reflect the occurrence of the acquisition on December 29, 2013, as required, the unaudited pro forma results include adjustments to reflect, among other things, the incremental intangible asset amortization to be incurred based on the preliminary values of each identifiable intangible asset and the interest expense from debt financing obtained to fund the cash consideration transferred. Pro forma adjustments were tax effected at the Company's historical statutory rates in effect for the respective periods. The unaudited pro forma amounts are not necessarily indicative of the combined results of operations that would have been realized had the acquisition and related financing occurred on December 29, 2013, nor are they meant to be indicative of any anticipated combined results of operations that St. Jude Medical, Inc. will experience after the transaction. In addition, the amounts do not include any adjustments for actions that may be taken following the completion of the transaction, such as expected cost savings, operating synergies or revenue enhancements that may be realized subsequent to the transaction. Pro forma 2015 net earnings attributable to St. Jude Medical, Inc. were adjusted to exclude the following in fiscal year 2015: $16 million of direct transaction costs, $19 million of nonrecurring expense related to the fair value adjustment to acquisition-date inventory, $64 million of nonrecurring stock-based compensation expenses for Thoratec equity awards accelerated at closing, $46 million of severance and other termination payments and $15 million of retention bonuses, consulting expenses and other bonus payments. These items were included in the proforma 2014 net earnings attributable to St. Jude Medical, Inc.

Fiscal Year 2014

NeuroTherm: In August 2014, the Company acquired all the outstanding shares of NT Holding Company (NeuroTherm) for $147 million in net cash consideration and assumed $50 million of debt, which has been repaid. Additionally, the Company recognized direct transaction costs of $1 million in *selling, general and administrative expense* in the Company's *Consolidated Statements of Earnings*. NeuroTherm, headquartered in Wilmington, Massachusetts, is involved in the business of marketing, designing, manufacturing and distributing radio frequency ablation medical devices and the related consumable items for pain management and interventional radiology markets.

The goodwill recorded as a result of the NeuroTherm acquisition is not deductible for income tax purposes. The goodwill is largely attributable to strategic opportunities for growing the Company's neuromodulation product portfolio to provide additional product offerings and therapy options, synergies expected to arise after the acquisition and the benefits of the existing workforce related to the acquired business. In connection with the acquisition of NeuroTherm, the Company recognized $87 million of developed technology intangible assets that have estimated useful lives ranging from 11 to 12 years and a $2 million other intangible asset that has an estimated useful life of 5 years.

During the fourth quarter of 2014, the Company reflected a fair value adjustment and recorded a $7 million decrease to goodwill and deferred income tax assets/(liabilities). All other adjustments to the preliminary purchase price allocation within the allocation period were not material. The following table summarizes the final purchase price allocation of the fair values of net assets as a result of the Company's acquisition of NeuroTherm in August 2014 (in millions):

	NeuroTherm
Current assets	$ 22
Property, plant and equipment	2
Goodwill	125
Intangible assets	89
Current liabilities	(13)
Deferred income tax assets/(liabilities)	(28)
Long-term debt	(50)
Net assets	$147
Cash paid	$148
Less: Cash acquired	(1)
Net cash consideration	$147

The results of NeuroTherm since the date of acquisition and pro forma disclosures of the consolidated results of the Company with the full year effects of NeuroTherm have not been separately presented since the impact to the Company's results of operations was not material.

Fiscal Year 2013

Endosense: In August 2013, the Company acquired all the outstanding shares of Endosense S.A. (Endosense) for the equivalent of $171 million (160 million Swiss Francs) in net cash consideration using available cash from outside the United States. Endosense is based in Geneva, Switzerland and develops, manufactures and markets the TactiCath® irrigated ablation catheter to provide physicians a real-time, objective measure of the force to apply to the heart wall during a catheter ablation procedure. At the time of acquisition, the Endosense force-sensing technology was CE Mark-approved for atrial fibrillation and supra ventricular tachycardia ablation. Under the terms of the acquisition agreement, the Company was obligated to make an additional cash payment of up to 150 million Swiss Francs, contingent upon both the achievement and timing of U.S. Food and Drug Administration (FDA) approval. Consistent with the provisions of Accounting Standards Codification (ASC) Topic 805, *Business Combinations* (ASC Topic 805) the Company accrued the contingent payment on the date of acquisition after determining its fair value of $132 million in arriving at $303 million of total consideration, net of cash acquired. The contingent consideration liability has been remeasured to fair value at each reporting period with changes in fair value reflected in the *Consolidated Statements of Earnings*. In October 2014, the Company received FDA approval of the TactiCath® irrigated ablation catheter and paid $155 million to settle the contingent consideration liability (see Note 11).

The goodwill recorded as a result of the Endosense acquisition is not deductible for income tax purposes. The goodwill represents the strategic opportunities for growing the Company's atrial fibrillation product portfolio and the expected revenue growth from increased market penetration from future products and customers. The Company now has the potential to integrate the force-sensing technology to offer a MediGuide™-enabled force-sensing ablation catheter and incorporate force-sensing data into its EnSite Velocity™ Mapping System. In connection with the acquisition of Endosense, the Company recognized $20 million of developed technology intangible assets that have an estimated useful life of 7 years and $33 million of IPR&D that was capitalized as an indefinite-lived intangible asset. During 2014, the IPR&D was reclassified to a purchased technology definite-lived intangible asset upon receiving FDA approval.

The results of Endosense since the date of acquisition and pro forma disclosures of the consolidated results of the Company with the full year effects of Endosense have not been separately presented since the impact to the Company's results of operations was not material.

Nanostim: In October 2013, the Company exercised its exclusive fixed price purchase option and acquired all the outstanding shares of Nanostim, Inc. (Nanostim) for $121 million in net cash consideration. The Company previously held an investment in Nanostim, which provided the Company with an 18% voting equity interest. Nanostim is based in Sunnyvale, California and has developed the first leadless, miniaturized cardiac pacemaker system, which received CE Mark approval in August 2013. The Nanostim™ leadless pacemaker also received FDA conditional approval in September 2013 for its Investigational Device Exemption application and pivotal clinical trial protocol to begin evaluating the technology in the U.S. The Company previously concluded that Nanostim was a VIE, but that St. Jude Medical was not the primary beneficiary as it did not retain power to direct the activities of Nanostim that most significantly impacted its economic performance. The Company previously reflected its investment in Nanostim as a cost method investment in *other assets*.

At the time of acquisition, the Company's 18% voting equity interest in Nanostim was remeasured to fair value of $33 million, which approximated its carrying value, and the related remeasurement gain was not material. Under the terms of the acquisition agreement, the Company was obligated to make additional cash payments of up to $65 million, contingent upon the achievement and timing of certain revenue-based milestones. The Company accrued the contingent payment after determining its fair value of $56 million as of the date of acquisition in arriving at $210 million of total consideration, net of cash acquired (see Note 11).

The goodwill recorded as a result of the Nanostim acquisition is not deductible for income tax purposes. The goodwill represents the strategic opportunities for growing the Company's Cardiac Rhythm Management business through expected revenue growth from increased market penetration and consumer preference for a miniaturized, leadless pacemaker as well as the potential for future product indications. In connection with the acquisition of Nanostim, the Company recognized $34 million of developed technology intangible assets that have an estimated useful life of 10 years and $27 million of IPR&D that was capitalized as an indefinite-lived intangible asset.

The results of Nanostim since the date of acquisition and pro forma disclosures of the consolidated results of the Company with the full year effects of Nanostim have not been separately presented since the impact to the Company's results of operations was not material.

Spinal Modulation: In June 2013, the Company made an equity investment of $40 million in Spinal Modulation, a privately-held company that is focused on the development of an intraspinal neuromodulation therapy that delivers spinal cord stimulation targeting the dorsal root ganglion to manage chronic pain. The investment agreement resulted in a 19% voting equity interest and provided the Company with the exclusive right, but not the obligation, to acquire Spinal Modulation. Additionally, in connection with the investment and contingent acquisition agreement, the Company also entered into an exclusive international distribution agreement, and obtained significant decision-making rights over Spinal Modulation's operations and economic performance. Accordingly, effective June 7, 2013, the Company determined that Spinal Modulation was a VIE for which St. Jude Medical was the primary beneficiary with the financial condition and results of operations of Spinal Modulation included in St. Jude Medical's *Consolidated Financial Statements*. During 2015, the Company exercised its exclusive option to acquire the remaining ownership interest in Spinal Modulation (see Note 6).

The goodwill recognized in connection with the Spinal Modulation transaction was not deductible for income tax purposes. The goodwill represents the strategic opportunities for growing the Company's neuromodulation chronic pain portfolio as well as the expected revenue growth from increased market penetration. The Company recognized $45 million of indefinite-lived IPR&D intangible assets. The Company also recognized $7 million of purchased technology intangible assets with an estimated useful life of 12 years.

CardioMEMS: During 2010, the Company made an equity investment of $60 million in CardioMEMS, a privately-held company based in Atlanta, Georgia that is focused on the development of a wireless monitoring technology that can be placed directly into the pulmonary artery to assess cardiac performance via measurement of pulmonary artery pressure. The investment agreement resulted in the Company obtaining a 19% voting equity interest and provided the Company with the exclusive right, but not the obligation, to acquire CardioMEMS for an additional payment of $375 million less any net debt payable to St. Jude Medical under a separate loan agreement entered into between CardioMEMS and the Company.

In the first quarter of 2013, the Company obtained significant decision-making rights over CardioMEMS' operations and provided debt financing of $28 million to CardioMEMS which was collateralized by substantially all the assets of CardioMEMS including its intellectual property. In July 2013, the Company provided $9 million of additional debt financing to CardioMEMS. In accordance with U.S. GAAP, the Company reconsidered its arrangements with CardioMEMS and determined that effective February 27, 2013, CardioMEMS was a VIE for which St. Jude Medical was the primary beneficiary with the financial condition and results of operations of CardioMEMS included in St. Jude Medical's *Consolidated Financial Statements*. The Company recognized a $29 million charge to *other (income) expense* in the Company's *Consolidated Statements of Earnings* during the first quarter of 2013 to adjust the carrying value of its equity investment and fixed price purchase option to fair value. During 2014, the Company exercised its exclusive option to acquire the remaining ownership interest in CardioMEMS (see Note 6).

The goodwill recognized in connection with the initial consolidation of CardioMEMS as a VIE was not deductible for income tax purposes. The goodwill represents the strategic opportunities for growing the Company's cardiac rhythm management and heart failure therapy product portfolio as well as the expected revenue growth from increased market penetration. The Company recognized $63 million of indefinite-lived IPR&D intangible assets. During 2014, the IPR&D was reclassified to a purchased technology definite-lived intangible asset upon receiving FDA approval.

Adjustments in 2014 to the preliminary purchase price allocations within the respective allocation periods were not material. The following table summarizes the final purchase price allocation of the fair values of the net assets as a result of the Company's acquisitions of Endosense and Nanostim and the initial consolidations of Spinal Modulation and CardioMEMS as variable interest entities for which St. Jude Medical, Inc. was the primary beneficiary (in millions):

	Endosense	Nanostim	Spinal Modulation	CardioMEMS
Cash and cash equivalents	$—	$—	$ 41	$ 33
Current assets	2	1	9	3
Goodwill	258	149	46	83
In-process research and development (IPR&D)	33	27	45	63
Other intangible assets	20	34	7	—
Other assets	1	1	1	2
Current liabilities	(11)	(2)	(6)	(13)
Deferred income tax assets/(liabilities)	—	—	(19)	(23)
Other liabilities	—	—	—	(5)
Net assets	$303	$210	$124	$143
Cash paid	$180	$124	$—	$—
Less: Cash acquired	(9)	(3)	—	—
Net cash consideration	$171	$121	$—	$—
Contingent consideration	132	56	—	—
Fair value of St. Jude Medical, Inc.'s previously held interest	—	33	—	31
Acquisition of controlling ownership interest	—	—	40	—
Debt financing	—	—	—	28
Additions in noncontrolling ownership interest	—	—	84	84
Total purchase consideration	$303	$210	$124	$143

The cash and cash equivalent balances of Spinal Modulation and CardioMEMS are inclusive of the equity investment and debt financing, respectively.

MERGER

6.27 ORBITAL ATK, INC. (MAR)
CONSOLIDATED STATEMENTS OF CASH FLOWS (in part)

	Years Ended March 31		
(Amounts in thousands)	2015	2014	2013
Investing Activities			
Continuing operations:			
Capital expenditures	(112,704)	(105,730)	(73,494)
Cash acquired in Merger with Orbital	253,734	—	—
Cash dividend received from Vista Outdoor, net of cash transferred to Vista Outdoor in conjunction with the Distribution of Sporting Group	188,878	—	—
Proceeds from the disposition of property plant and equipment	2,290	5,488	172
Cash provided by (used for) investing activities of continuing operations	332,198	(100,242)	(73,322)
Cash used for investing activities of discontinued operations	(30,585)	(1,341,747)	(23,395)
Cash provided by (used for) investing activities	301,613	(1,441,989)	(96,717)

NOTES TO THE CONSOLIDATED FINANCIAL STATEMENTS (in part)

(Amounts in thousands except share and per share data and unless otherwise indicated)

1. Summary of Significant Accounting Policies (in part)

Nature of Operations. Orbital ATK, Inc. (the "Company") is an aerospace and defense company that operates in the United States and internationally. The Company designs, builds and delivers space, defense and aviation systems for customers around the world, both as a prime contractor and merchant supplier. The Company was incorporated in Delaware in 1990 and is headquartered in Dulles, Virginia.

On February 9, 2015, the Company completed a tax-free spin-off of and distribution of its Sporting Group to its stockholders (the "Distribution") as a new public company called Vista Outdoor Inc. ("Vista Outdoor"). Immediately following the Distribution, the Company combined with Orbital Sciences Corporation ("Orbital") through the merger of a Company subsidiary with Orbital (the "Merger"). These transactions are discussed in greater detail in Note 4. Following the Distribution and Merger, the Company changed its name from Alliant Techsystems Inc. to Orbital ATK, Inc.

As a result of the Distribution, the Sporting Group is no longer reported within the Company's results from continuing operations but is reported as a discontinued operation for all periods presented. The Company used the acquisition method to account for the Merger; accordingly, the results of Orbital have been included in the Company's consolidated financial statements since the date of the Merger.

Following the Distribution and Merger, the Company reorganized its business groups and realigned its reporting segments. The Company's remaining businesses, combined with the businesses of Orbital, are now reported in three segments: Flight Systems Group, Defense Systems Group and Space Systems Group, as discussed in Note 16.

4. Mergers, Acquisitions and Divestiture (in part)

Fiscal 2015

On February 9, 2015, the Company completed the spin-off and Distribution of Sporting Group to its stockholders and Merged with Orbital pursuant to a transaction agreement, dated April 28, 2014 (the "Transaction Agreement"). The Company completed the Merger with Orbital in order to create a global aerospace and defense Company with greater technical and industrial capabilities and increased financial resources. Both the Distribution and Merger were structured to be tax-free to U.S. stockholders for U.S. federal income tax purposes. Under the Transaction Agreement, a subsidiary of the Company merged with and into Orbital, with Orbital continuing as a wholly-owned subsidiary of the Company.

Pursuant to the Distribution, Company stockholders received 2 shares of Vista Outdoor for each share of Company common stock held. The Company distributed a total of approximately 63.9 million shares of Vista Outdoor common stock to its stockholders of record as of the close of business on February 2, 2015 the record date for the Distribution. As a result of the Distribution, the Sporting Group is no longer reported within the Company's results from continuing operations but is reported as a discontinued operation for all periods presented in accordance with ASC Topic 205, "Presentation of Financial Statements."

In connection with the Merger, each outstanding share of Orbital common stock was converted into the right to receive 0.449 shares of Company common stock. The Company issued approximately 27.4 million shares of common stock to Orbital stockholders. Immediately following the Merger, Orbital stockholders owned 46.2% of the common stock of the Company and existing stockholders owned 53.8%. Based on the closing price of the Company common stock following the Distribution on February 9, 2015 as reported on the New York Stock Exchange, the aggregate value of the consideration paid or payable to former holders of Orbital common stock was approximately $1.8 billion. The Company used the acquisition method to account for the Merger; accordingly, the results of Orbital have been included in the Company's consolidated financial statements since the date of the Merger.

In connection with the closing of the Merger and the Distribution, the Company redeemed its 6.875% Senior Subordinated Notes due 2020. See Note 9 for further details.

Orbital's sales and pre-tax income included in the Company's financial statements for the post-Merger period of February 9, 2015 through March 31, 2015 were approximately $191 million and $16 million, respectively.

Transaction costs of $34,900 related to the Distribution and Merger were recorded as incurred in general and administrative expenses during fiscal 2015.

Preliminary Valuation of Net Assets Acquired

Certain estimated values, including: goodwill, intangibles, property, plant and equipment, and deferred taxes, are not final and the preliminary purchase price allocations are subject to change as the Company completes the analysis of the fair value at the date of the Merger. The final determination of the fair value of assets and liabilities will be completed within the 12-month measurement period from the date of the Merger as required. The size of the Merger will necessitate the use of this measurement period to adequately analyze and assess a number of the factors used in establishing the asset and liability fair values as of the Merger date including the significant contractual and operational factors and assumptions underlying contract related intangibles and property, plant and equipment fair values, and the related tax impacts of any changes made.

The consideration paid for Orbital's assets and liabilities was determined using the fair market value of the Company stock issued at the date of the Merger along with restricted stock awards granted to certain employees of Orbital.

The following table summarizes the preliminary fair value of the assets acquired and liabilities assumed at the Merger date and the preliminary goodwill generated from the transaction:

Purchase Price:	
Value of common shares issued to Orbital shareholders[1]	$1,749,323
Value of replacement equity-based awards to holders of Orbital equity-based awards[2]	8,654
Total purchase price	$1,757,977
Preliminary value of assets acquired and liabilities assumed:	
Cash	$ 253,734
Net receivables	562,639
Net inventories	75,294
Intangibles	164,000
Property, plant and equipment	281,654
Other assets	36,878
Goodwill	866,106
Accounts payable	(52,028)
Deferred tax liabilities, net	(51,537)
Other liabilities	(378,763)
Total purchase price	$1,757,977

[1] Equals 27.4 million Orbital ATK shares issued to Orbital shareholders multiplied by the Company's Merger-date share price of $63.94.
[2] The fair value of replacement equity-based awards attributable to pre-Merger service was recorded as part of the consideration transferred in the Merger.

Goodwill recognized from the Merger primarily relates to the expanded market opportunities, expected synergies and benefits of increased scale and scope of combined human, physical and financial resources attributable to merging the operations of the two companies. As stated above, the Merger was a tax-free transaction and as such, there is no goodwill that is deductible for tax purposes.

In determining the fair value of identifiable assets acquired and liabilities assumed, a review was conducted for any significant contingent assets or liabilities existing as of the Merger date. The preliminary assessment did not note any significant contingencies related to any legal or government action.

MARKETING AND LICENSE AGREEMENT

6.28 THE SCOTTS MIRACLE-GRO COMPANY (SEP)
CONSOLIDATED STATEMENTS OF CASH FLOWS (in part)

(In millions)

	Year Ended September 30,		
	2015	**2014**	**2013**
Investing Activities			
Proceeds from sale of long-lived assets	5.5	3.7	3.6
Proceeds from sale of business, net of transaction costs	—	7.2	—
Investments in property, plant and equipment	(61.7)	(87.6)	(60.1)
Proceeds from sale and leaseback transaction	—	35.1	—
Investment in unconsolidated affiliate	—	—	(4.5)
Investment in marketing and license agreement	(300.0)	—	—
Investments in acquired businesses, net of cash acquired	(180.2)	(114.0)	(3.2)
Net cash used in investing activities	(536.4)	(155.6)	(64.2)

NOTES TO CONSOLIDATED FINANCIAL STATEMENTS (in part)

Note 6. Marketing Agreement

The Scotts Company LLC and Monsanto are parties to an Amended and Restated Exclusive Agency and Marketing Agreement (the "Marketing Agreement"), pursuant to which the Company has served since its 1998 fiscal year as Monsanto's exclusive agent for the marketing and distribution of consumer Roundup® herbicide products (with additional rights to new products containing glyphosate or other similar non-selective herbicides) in the consumer lawn and garden market. Under the terms of the Marketing Agreement, the Company is entitled to receive an annual commission from Monsanto as consideration for the performance of the Company's duties as agent. The annual gross commission under the Marketing Agreement is calculated as a percentage of the actual earnings before interest and income taxes of the consumer Roundup® business in the markets covered by the Marketing Agreement subject to the achievement of annual earnings thresholds. The Marketing Agreement also requires the Company to make annual payments of $20 million to Monsanto as a contribution against the overall expenses of the consumer Roundup® business. From 1998 until May 15, 2015, the Marketing Agreement covered the United States and other specified countries, including Australia, Austria, Belgium, Canada, France, Germany, the Netherlands and the United Kingdom. On May 15, 2015, the territories were expanded to cover additional countries as outlined below.

In consideration for the rights granted to the Company under the Marketing Agreement in 1998, the Company paid a marketing fee of $32 million to Monsanto. The Company deferred this amount on the basis that the payment will provide a future benefit through commissions that will be earned under the Marketing Agreement. The economic useful life over which the marketing fee is being amortized is 20 years, with a remaining unamortized amount of $2.6 million and remaining amortization period of less than 3 years as of September 30, 2015.

On May 15, 2015, the Company and Monsanto entered into an Amendment to the Marketing Agreement (the "Marketing Agreement Amendment"), a Lawn and Garden Brand Extension Agreement (the "Brand Extension Agreement") and a Commercialization and Technology Agreement (the "Commercialization and Technology Agreement"). In consideration for these agreements, the Company paid $300.0 million to Monsanto on August 14, 2015 using borrowings under its credit facility.

Among other things, the Marketing Agreement Amendment amends the Marketing Agreement in the following significant respects:
- Expands the territories in which the Company may serve as Monsanto's exclusive agent in the consumer lawn and garden market to include all countries other than Japan and countries subject to a comprehensive U.S. trade embargo or certain other embargoes and trade restrictions.
- Eliminates the initial and renewal terms that the original Marketing Agreement applied to European Union ("EU") countries. As amended, the term of the Marketing Agreement will now continue indefinitely for all included markets, including EU countries within the included markets, unless and until otherwise terminated in accordance with the Marketing Agreement.
- Revises the procedures of the Marketing Agreement relating to a potential sale of the consumer Roundup® business to (1) require Monsanto to negotiate exclusively with the Company with respect to any potential Roundup® sale for 60 days after the Company receives notice from Monsanto regarding a potential Roundup® sale and (2) provide the Company with a right of first offer and a right of last look in connection with a potential Roundup® sale to a third party. In addition, if the Company makes a bid in connection with a Roundup® sale, the then-applicable termination fee would serve as a credit against the purchase price and the Monsanto board of directors would not be permitted to discount the value of the Company's bid compared to a competing bid as a result of the termination fee discount.
- Requires the Company to (1) provide notice to Monsanto of certain proposals and processes that may result in a sale of the Company and (2) conduct non-exclusive negotiations with Monsanto with respect to such a sale.
- Increases the minimum termination fee payable under the Marketing Agreement to the greater of (1) $200 million or (2) four times (A) the average of the program earnings before interest or income taxes for the three trailing program years prior to the year of termination, minus (B) the 2015 program earnings before interest or income taxes.
- Amends Monsanto's termination rights and provides additional rights to the Company in the event of a termination, as follows:
  — delays the effectiveness of a notice of termination given by Monsanto as a result of a change of control with respect to Monsanto or a sale of the consumer Roundup® business to a third party from (1) the end of the later of 12 months or the next program year to (2) the end of the fifth full program year after Monsanto gives such notice;
  — eliminates Monsanto's termination rights for a regional performance default, a change of significant ownership of the Company or an uncured or incurable egregious injury (as each are defined in the Marketing Agreement); and
  — eliminates Monsanto's termination rights in connection with a change in control of the Company or Scotts Miracle-Gro as long as the Company has determined, in its reasonable commercial opinion, that the acquirer can and will fully perform the duties and obligations of the Company under the Marketing Agreement.
- Expands the Company's termination rights to include termination for a brand decline event (as defined in the Marketing Agreement Amendment) occurring before program year 2023.
- Expands the Company's assignment rights to allow the Company to transfer its rights, interests and obligations under the Marketing Agreement with respect to (1) the North America territories and (2) one or more other included markets for up to three other assignments.
- Amends the commission structure by (1) eliminating the commission threshold for program years 2016, 2017 and 2018 (2) setting the commission threshold for the subsequent program years at $40 million and (3) establishing the commission payable by Monsanto to the Company for each program year at an amount equal to 50% of the program earnings before interest and income taxes for such program year.

The Brand Extension Agreement provides the Company a worldwide, exclusive license to use the Roundup® brand on additional products offered by the Company outside of the non-selective weed category within the residential lawn and garden market. The application of the Roundup® brand to these additional products is subject to a product review and approval process developed between the Company and Monsanto. Monsanto will maintain oversight of its brand, the handling of brand registrations covering these new products and new territories, as well as primary responsibility for brand enforcement. The Brand Extension Agreement has an initial term of 20 years, which will automatically renew for additional successive 20 year terms, at the Company's sole option, for no additional monetary consideration.

The Commercialization and Technology Agreement provides for the Company and Monsanto to further develop and commercialize new products and technology developed at Monsanto and intended for introduction into the residential lawn and garden market. Under the Commercialization and Technology Agreement, the Company receives an exclusive first look at new Monsanto technology and products and an annual review of Monsanto's developing products and technologies. The Commercialization and Technology Agreement has a term of 30 years (subject to early termination upon a termination event under the Marketing Agreement or the Brand Extension Agreement).

The Company recorded the $300 million consideration paid by the Company to Monsanto in connection with the entry into the Marketing Agreement Amendment, the Brand Extension Agreement and the Commercialization and Technology Agreement as intangible assets and the related economic useful life of such assets is indefinite. The identifiable intangible assets include the Marketing Agreement Amendment and the Brand Extension Agreement with allocated fair value of $188.3 million and $111.7 million, respectively. The estimated fair values of the identifiable intangible assets were determined using an income-based approach, which includes market participant expectations of cash flows that an asset will generate over the remaining useful life discounted to present value using an appropriate rate of return.

Under the terms of the Marketing Agreement, the Company performs certain functions, primarily manufacturing conversion services (in North America), distribution and logistics, and selling and marketing support, on behalf of Monsanto in the conduct of the consumer Roundup® business. The actual costs incurred for these activities are charged to and reimbursed by Monsanto. The Company records costs incurred under the Marketing Agreement for which the Company is the primary obligor on a gross basis, recognizing such costs in "Cost of sales" and the reimbursement of these costs in "Net sales," with no effect on gross profit dollars or net income.

The gross commission earned under the Marketing Agreement, the contribution payments to Monsanto and the amortization of the initial marketing fee paid to Monsanto in 1998 are included in the calculation of net sales in the Company's Consolidated Statements of Operations. The elements of the net commission and reimbursements earned under the Marketing Agreement and included in "Net sales" are as follows:

(In millions)	Year Ended September 30		
	2015	2014	2013
Gross commission	$ 88.7	$ 85.2	$ 81.8
Contribution expenses	(20.0)	(20.0)	(20.0)
Amortization of marketing fee	(0.8)	(0.8)	(0.8)
Net commission income	67.9	64.4	61.0
Reimbursements associated with Marketing Agreement	63.3	63.0	62.0
Total net sales associated with Marketing Agreement	$131.2	$127.4	$123.0

Cash Flows From Financing Activities

PRESENTATION

6.29 FASB ASC 230-10-45 defines those transactions and events that constitute financing cash receipts and payments. Cash inflows from financing activities include the following:
- Proceeds from issuing equity instruments.
- Proceeds from issuing bonds, mortgages, and notes and from other short- or long-term borrowing.
- Receipts from contributions and investment income that, by donor stipulation, are restricted for the purposes of acquiring, constructing, or improving PPE or other long-lived assets or establishing or increasing a permanent or term endowment.
- Proceeds received from derivative instruments that include financing elements at inception, regardless of whether the proceeds were received at inception or over the term of the derivative instrument, other than a financing element inherently included in an at-the-market derivative instrument with no prepayments.
- Cash that is recognizable for financial reporting purposes because it is retained as a result of the tax deductibility of increases in the value of equity instruments issued under share-based payment arrangements that are not included in the cost of goods or services. For this purpose, excess tax benefits should be determined on an individual award (or portion thereof) basis.

Cash outflows from financing activities include the following:

- Payments of dividends or other distributions to owners, including outlays to reacquire the entity's equity instruments.
- Repayments of borrowed amounts.
- Other principal payments to creditors who have extended long-term credit.
- Distributions to counterparties of derivative instruments that include financing elements at inception, other than a financing element inherently included in an at-the-market derivative instrument with no prepayments. The distributions may be either at inception or over the term of the derivative instrument.
- Payments for debt issue costs.

PRESENTATION AND DISCLOSURE EXCERPTS

DEBT PROCEEDS AND REPAYMENTS

6.30 KB HOME (NOV)
CONSOLIDATED STATEMENTS OF CASH FLOWS (in part)

(In Thousands)

	Years Ended November 30,		
	2015	2014	2013
Cash flows from financing activities:			
Change in restricted cash	17,891	14,671	456
Proceeds from issuance of debt	250,000	400,000	680,000
Payment of debt issuance costs	(4,561)	(5,448)	(16,525)
Repayment of senior notes	(199,906)	—	(225,394)
Payments on mortgages and land contracts due to land sellers and other loans	(22,877)	(36,918)	(66,296)
Proceeds from issuance of common stock, net	—	137,045	109,503
Issuance of common stock under employee stock plans	740	1,896	2,181
Excess tax benefits from stock-based compensation	157	—	—
Payments of cash dividends	(9,186)	(8,982)	(8,366)
Stock repurchases	(567)	(546)	(8,488)
Net cash provided by financing activities	31,691	501,718	467,071

NOTES TO CONSOLIDATED FINANCIAL STATEMENTS (in part)

Note 13. Notes Payable (in part)

Notes payable consisted of the following (in thousands):

	November 30,	
	2015	2014
Mortgages and land contracts due to land sellers and other loans (at interest rates of 4% to 7% at November 30, 2015 and 5% to 7% at November 30, 2014)	$ 35,664	$ 38,250
6 1/4% Senior notes due June 15, 2015	—	199,891
9.10% Senior notes due September 15, 2017	263,475	262,729
7 1/4% Senior notes due June 15, 2018	299,554	299,402
4.75% Senior notes due May 15, 2019	400,000	400,000
8.00% Senior notes due March 15, 2020	346,843	346,253
7.00% Senior notes due December 15, 2021	450,000	450,000
7.50% Senior notes due September 15, 2022	350,000	350,000
7.625% Senior notes due May 15, 2023	250,000	—
1.375% Convertible senior notes due February 1, 2019	230,000	230,000
Total	$2,625,536	$2,576,525

Senior Notes. All of our senior notes outstanding at November 30, 2015 and 2014 represent senior unsecured obligations and rank equally in right of payment with all of our existing and future indebtedness. All of our outstanding senior notes were issued in underwritten public offerings.

The key terms of each of our senior notes outstanding as of November 30, 2015 were as follows (dollars in thousands):

Notes Payable	Principal	Issuance Date	Maturity Date	Redeemable Prior to Maturity	Effective Interest Rate
9.10% Senior notes	$265,000	July 30, 2009	September 15, 2017	Yes[a]	9.5%
7 1/4% Senior notes	300,000	April 3, 2006	June 15, 2018	Yes[a]	7.3
4.75% Senior notes	400,000	March 25, 2014	May 15, 2019	Yes[b]	4.8
8.00% Senior notes	350,000	February 7, 2012	March 15, 2020	Yes[a]	8.3
7.00% Senior notes	450,000	October 29, 2013	December 15, 2021	Yes[b]	7.0
7.50% Senior notes	350,000	July 31, 2012	September 15, 2022	Yes[a]	7.5
7.625% Senior notes	250,000	February 17, 2015	May 15, 2023	Yes[b]	7.6
1.375% Convertible senior notes	230,000	January 29, 2013	February 1, 2019	Yes[c]	1.4

[a] At our option, these notes may be redeemed, in whole at any time or from time to time in part, at a redemption price equal to the greater of (i) 100% of the principal amount of the notes being redeemed and (ii) the sum of the present values of the remaining scheduled payments of principal and interest on the notes being redeemed (exclusive of interest accrued to the applicable redemption date), discounted to the redemption date at a defined rate, plus, in each case, accrued and unpaid interest on the notes being redeemed to the applicable redemption date.

[b] At our option, these notes may be redeemed, in whole at any time or from time to time in part, at a redemption price equal to the greater of (i) 100% of the principal amount of the notes being redeemed and (ii) the sum of the present values of the remaining scheduled payments of principal and interest on the notes being redeemed (exclusive of interest accrued to the applicable redemption date), discounted to the redemption date at a defined rate, plus, in each case, accrued and unpaid interest on the notes being redeemed to, but excluding, the applicable redemption date, except that three months prior to the stated maturity dates for the 4.75% Senior Notes due 2019 and the 7.00% Senior Notes due 2021 and until their respective maturity, and six months prior to the stated maturity date for the 7.625% Senior Notes due 2023 and until their maturity, the redemption price will be equal to 100% of the principal amount of the notes being redeemed, plus, in each case, accrued and unpaid interest on the notes being redeemed to, but excluding, the applicable redemption date.

[c] We may not redeem the notes prior to November 6, 2018. On or after November 6, 2018, and prior to the stated maturity date, we may, at our option, redeem all or part of the notes at a redemption price equal to 100% of the principal amount of the notes being redeemed plus accrued and unpaid interest to, but excluding the redemption date.

If a change in control occurs as defined in the instruments governing our senior notes, we would be required to offer to purchase all of our outstanding senior notes (with the exception of the amount outstanding related to our 7 1/4% Senior Notes due 2018) at 101% of their principal amount, together with all accrued and unpaid interest, if any. If a fundamental change, as defined in the instruments governing the 1.375% Convertible Senior Notes due 2019, occurs prior to the stated maturity date, the holders may require us to purchase for cash all or any portion of their 1.375% Convertible Senior Notes due 2019 at 100% of the principal amount of the notes, plus accrued and unpaid interest to, but not including, the fundamental change purchase date.

In 2015, we used a portion of the total net proceeds of $245.4 million from the issuance of the 7.625% Senior Notes due 2023 to retire the remaining $199.9 million in aggregate principal amount of our 6 1/4% Senior Notes due 2015 at their maturity on June 15, 2015. The remainder of the net proceeds was used for general corporate purposes, including working capital, land acquisition and land development.

DEBT ISSUANCE COSTS

6.31 THE PRICELINE GROUP INC. (DEC)
CONSOLIDATED STATEMENTS OF CASH FLOWS (in part)

(In thousands)

	Year Ended December 31,		
	2015	2014 See Note 2	2013 See Note 2
Financing Activities:			
Proceeds from revolving credit facility	225,000	995,000	—
Payments related to revolving credit facility	(225,000)	(995,000)	—
Proceeds from the issuance of long-term debt	2,399,034	2,264,753	978,982
Payment of debt issuance costs—revolving credit facility	(4,005)	—	—
Payments related to conversion of senior notes	(147,629)	(125,136)	(414,569)
Repurchase of common stock	(3,089,055)	(750,378)	(883,515)
Payments of contingent consideration	(10,700)	—	—
Payments to purchase subsidiary shares from noncontrolling interests	—	—	(192,530)
Payments of stock issuance costs	—	—	(1,191)
Proceeds from exercise of stock options	20,851	16,389	91,607
Proceeds from the termination of conversion spread hedges	—	—	19
Excess tax benefits on stock-based awards	101,508	23,366	17,686
Net cash (used in) provided by financing activities	(729,996)	1,428,994	(403,511)

10. Debt (in part)

Revolving Credit Facility

In June 2015, the Company entered into a $2.0 billion five-year unsecured revolving credit facility with a group of lenders. Borrowings under the revolving credit facility will bear interest, at the Company's option, at a rate per annum equal to either (i) the adjusted LIBOR for the interest period in effect for such borrowing plus an applicable margin ranging from 0.875% to 1.50%; or (ii) the greatest of (a) Bank of America, N.A.'s prime lending rate, (b) the federal funds rate plus 0.5%, and (c) an adjusted LIBOR for an interest period of one month plus 1.00%, plus an applicable margin ranging from 0.00% to 0.50%. Undrawn balances available under the revolving credit facility are subject to commitment fees at the applicable rate ranging from 0.085% to 0.20%.

The revolving credit facility provides for the issuance of up to $70.0 million of letters of credit as well as borrowings of up to $50.0 million on same-day notice, referred to as swingline loans. Borrowings under the revolving credit facility may be made in U.S. Dollars, Euros, British Pounds Sterling and any other foreign currency agreed to by the lenders. The proceeds of loans made under the facility will be used for working capital and general corporate purposes, which could include acquisitions or share repurchases. As of December 31, 2015, there were no borrowings outstanding and approximately $2.5 million of letters of credit issued under this new facility. The Company paid $4.0 million in debt issuance costs related to the revolving credit facility during the year ended December 31, 2015.

Upon entering into this new revolving credit facility, the Company terminated its $1.0 billion five-year revolving credit facility entered into in October 2011 and recognized interest expense of $1.0 million related to the write-off of the remaining unamortized debt issuance costs. As of December 31, 2014, there were no borrowings outstanding and approximately $4.0 million of letters of credit issued under this revolving credit facility.

ISSUANCE OF TANGIBLE EQUITY UNITS

6.32 ANADARKO PETROLEUM CORPORATION (DEC)
CONSOLIDATED STATEMENTS OF CASH FLOWS (in part)

	Years Ended December 31,		
Millions	2015	2014	2013
Cash Flows from Financing Activities			
Borrowings, net of issuance costs	4,632	2,879	958
Repayments of debt	(4,033)	(1,425)	(710)
Financing portion of net cash paid in settlement of derivative instruments	(35)	(222)	—
Increase (decrease) in outstanding checks	(23)	62	(13)
Dividends paid	(553)	(505)	(274)
Repurchase of common stock	(55)	(45)	(54)
Issuance of common stock, including tax benefit on share-based compensation awards	34	121	146
Sale of subsidiary units	187	1,026	724
Issuance of tangible equity units — equity component	348	—	—
Distributions to noncontrolling interest owners	(282)	(216)	(156)
Contributions from noncontrolling interest owners	—	—	2
Net cash provided by (used in) financing activities	220	1,675	623

NOTES TO CONSOLIDATED FINANCIAL STATEMENTS (in part)

10. Tangible Equity Units

In June 2015, the Company issued 9.2 million 7.50% tangible equity units (TEUs) at a stated amount of $50.00 per TEU and raised net proceeds of $445 million. Each TEU is comprised of a prepaid equity purchase contract for common units of WGP and a senior amortizing note. Subsequent to issuance, each TEU may be legally separated into the two components. The prepaid equity purchase contract is considered a freestanding financial instrument, indexed to WGP common units, and meets the conditions for equity classification.

Anadarko allocated the proceeds from the issuance of the TEUs to equity and debt based on the relative fair values of their respective components as follows:

Millions, except price per TEU	Equity Component	Debt Component	Total
Price per TEU	$39.05	$10.95	$50.00
Gross proceeds	359	101	460
Less issuance costs	11	4	15
Net proceeds	$ 348	$ 97	$ 445

The prepaid equity purchase contracts were recorded in noncontrolling interests, net of issuance costs, and the senior amortizing notes were recorded in short-term debt and long-term debt on the Company's Consolidated Balance Sheet.

Equity Component Unless settled earlier at the holder's option, each purchase contract has a mandatory settlement date of June 7, 2018. Anadarko has a right to elect to issue and deliver shares of Anadarko Petroleum Corporation common stock (APC shares) in lieu of delivering WGP common units at settlement. The Company will deliver WGP common units (or APC shares) on the settlement date at the settlement rate based upon the applicable market value of WGP common units (or APC shares) as follows:

Applicable Market Value of WGP Common Units[1]	Settlement Rate per Purchase Contract	
	WGP Common Units	APC Shares (if elected)[1]
Exceeds $69.8422 (Threshold Appreciation Price)	0.7159 units (Minimum Settlement Rate)	a number of shares equal to (a) the Minimum Settlement Rate, multiplied by the applicable market value of WGP common units, divided by (b) 98% of the applicable market value of APC shares
Less than or equal to the Threshold Appreciation Price, but greater than or equal to $58.20 (Reference Price)	a number of units equal to $50.00, divided by the applicable market value of WGP common units	a number of shares equal to $50.00, divided by 98% of the applicable market value of APC shares
Less than the Reference Price	0.8591 units (Maximum Settlement Rate)	a number of shares equal to (a) the Maximum Settlement Rate, multiplied by the applicable market value of WGP common units, divided by (b) 98% of the applicable market value of APC shares

[1] The applicable market value is the average of the daily volume-weighted average prices of WGP common units (or APC shares) for the 20 consecutive trading days beginning on, and including, the 23rd scheduled trading day immediately preceding June 7, 2018.

The WGP common units underlying the purchase contract are currently issued and outstanding, and are owned by a wholly owned subsidiary of Anadarko. In the event Anadarko elects to settle in APC shares, the number of such shares issued and delivered upon settlement of each purchase contract is subject to adjustment and cannot exceed four shares under any circumstance (APC share cap). The above fixed settlement rates for WGP common units and the APC share cap are subject to adjustment upon the occurrence of certain specified dilutive events such as certain increases in the WGP distribution rate.

Debt Component Each senior amortizing note has an initial principal amount of $10.95 and bears interest at 1.50% per year. Beginning September 7, 2015, Anadarko will pay equal quarterly cash installments of $0.9375 per amortizing note (except for the September 7, 2015 installment payment, which was $0.9063 per amortizing note). The payments constitute a payment of interest and partial repayment of principal, with the aggregate per-year payments of principal and interest equating to a 7.50% cash payment with respect to each TEU. The senior amortizing notes have a final installment payment date of June 7, 2018, and are senior unsecured obligations of the Company.

20. Noncontrolling Interests

WGP, a publicly traded consolidated subsidiary, is a limited partnership that owns interests in WES. In 2015, Anadarko sold 2.3 million WGP common units to the public and raised net proceeds of $130 million and in 2014 sold approximately 6 million WGP common units to the public and raised net proceeds of $335 million. In June 2015, Anadarko issued 9.2 million TEUs, which include an equity component that may be settled in WGP common units. For additional disclosure of the TEU effect on noncontrolling interests, see *Note 10—Tangible Equity Units*. At December 31, 2015, Anadarko's ownership interest in WGP consisted of an 87.3% limited partner interest and the entire non-economic general partner interest. The remaining 12.7% limited partner interest in WGP was owned by the public.

WES, a publicly traded consolidated subsidiary, is a limited partnership that acquires, owns, develops, and operates midstream assets. WES issued approximately 874 thousand common units to the public and raised net proceeds of $57 million in 2015, issued approximately 10 million common units to the public and raised net proceeds of $691 million in 2014, and issued approximately 12 million common units to the public and raised net proceeds of $725 million in 2013. In addition, WES issued 11 million Class C units to Anadarko in 2014 to partially fund the DBM acquisition. These units will receive quarterly distributions in the form of additional Class C units until the end of 2017, unless WES elects to convert the units to common units earlier or Anadarko elects to extend the conversion date. During 2015, WES distributed 498 thousand Class C units to Anadarko. At December 31, 2015, WGP's ownership interest in WES consisted of a 34.6% limited partner interest, the entire 1.8% general partner interest, and all of the WES incentive distribution rights. At December 31, 2015, Anadarko also owned an

8.5% limited partner interest in WES through other subsidiaries' ownership of common and Class C units. The remaining 55.1% limited partner interest in WES was owned by the public.

PURCHASE OF REDEEMABLE NONCONTROLLING INTERESTS

6.33 DISCOVERY COMMUNICATIONS, INC. (DEC)
CONSOLIDATED STATEMENTS OF CASH FLOWS (in part)

(in millions)

	Year Ended December 31,		
	2015	2014	2013
Financing Activities			
Commercial paper (repayments) borrowings, net	(136)	229	—
Borrowings under revolving credit facility	1,016	698	—
Principal repayments of revolving credit facility	(265)	(660)	—
Borrowings from debt, net of discount	936	415	1,198
Principal repayments of debt	(849)	—	—
Principal repayments of capital lease obligations	(27)	(19)	(32)
Repurchases of stock	(951)	(1,422)	(1,305)
Purchase of redeemable noncontrolling interests	(548)	(1)	—
Payments to redeemable noncontrolling interests	(42)	(2)	—
Equity-based plan proceeds, net	6	44	73
Hedge of borrowings from debt instruments	(29)	—	—
Other financing activities, net	(13)	(16)	(19)
Cash used in financing activities	(902)	(734)	(85)

NOTES TO CONSOLIDATED FINANCIAL STATEMENTS (in part)

Note 3. Acquisitions and Dispositions (in part)

Acquisitions (in part)

Eurosport (in part)

On December 21, 2012, the Company acquired a 20% equity method investment in Eurosport, which includes both Eurosport International and Eurosport France. On May 30, 2014, the Company acquired an additional 31% equity in Eurosport International to obtain a controlling interest in Eurosport International for €259 million ($351 million) and committed to acquire a similar controlling interest in Eurosport France upon resolution of certain regulatory matters. The outstanding regulatory matters in France were subsequently resolved, and on March 31, 2015 the Company completed its acquisition of an additional 31% interest in Eurosport France for total consideration of €36 million ($38 million). These transactions gave the Company a 51% controlling stake in Eurosport. The Company recognized gains of $2 million and $29 million for the years ended December 31, 2015 and 2014, respectively, to account for the difference between the carrying value and the fair value of the previously held 20% equity method investments in Eurosport France and Eurosport International, respectively. The gains were included in other (expense) income, net in the Company's consolidated statements of operations. (See Note 18.) On October 1, 2015, TF1 put its remaining 49% interest in Eurosport to the Company for €491 million ($548 million). (See Note 11.)

Note 11. Redeemable Noncontrolling Interests

Redeemable noncontrolling interests reflected as of the balance sheet date are the greater of the noncontrolling interest balances adjusted for comprehensive income items and distributions or the redemption values remeasured at the period end foreign exchange rates (i.e., the "floor"). Adjustments to the carrying amount of redeemable noncontrolling interests to redemption value as a result of changes in exchange rates are reflected in currency translation adjustments, a component of other comprehensive (loss) income; however, such currency translation adjustments to redemption value are allocated to Discovery stockholders only. Redeemable noncontrolling interest adjustments of redemption value to the floor are reflected in retained earnings. Any adjustment of redemption value to the floor that reflects a redemption in excess of fair value is included as an adjustment to net income available to Discovery Communications, Inc. stockholders in the calculation of earnings per share. There were no current period adjustments to reflect a redemption in excess of fair value. (See Note 17.)

The table below presents the reconciliation of changes in redeemable noncontrolling interests (in millions).

	December 31,		
	2015	2014	2013
Beginning balance	$ 747	$ 36	$—
Initial fair value of redeemable noncontrolling interests of acquired businesses	60	796	41
Purchase of subsidiary shares at fair value	(551)	(6)	—
Cash distributions to redeemable noncontrolling interests	(42)	(2)	—
Comprehensive (loss) income adjustments:			
Net income (loss) attributable to redeemable noncontrolling interests	13	(4)	1
Other comprehensive loss attributable to redeemable noncontrolling interests	(23)	(40)	(3)
Currency translation on redemption values	(36)	(64)	(5)
Retained earnings adjustments:			
Adjustments to redemption value	73	31	2
Ending balance	$ 241	$747	$ 36

Redeemable noncontrolling interests consist of the arrangements described below:

In connection with the acquisition of a controlling interest in Eurosport France on March 31, 2015 and Eurosport International on May 30, 2014, the Company recognized $60 million and $558 million, respectively, for TF1's 49% redeemable noncontrolling interest. On July 22, 2015, TF1 exercised its right to put the entirety of its remaining 49% noncontrolling interest in Eurosport to the Company for €491 million ($551 million as of the date redemption became mandatory, and $548 million on October 1, 2015 when the transaction closed). The difference between the carrying amount of the redeemable noncontrolling interest and its fair value at the date of exercise resulted in a €25 million ($28 million) adjustment to retained earnings, recognized as a component of redeemable noncontrolling interest adjustments to redemption value on the consolidated statements of equity. Upon acquisition of TF1's noncontrolling interest, the Company adjusted the accumulated other comprehensive income balance of $61 million attributable to TF1 and allocated it to Discovery stockholders.

In connection with the acquisition of a controlling interest in Discovery Family on September 23, 2014, the Company recognized $238 million for Hasbro's redeemable noncontrolling interest in Discovery Family. Hasbro has the right to put the entirety of its remaining 40% non-controlling interest to the Company for one year after December 31, 2021, or in the event a Discovery performance obligation related to Discovery Family is not met. Embedded in the redeemable noncontrolling interest is also a Discovery call right that is exercisable for one year after December 31, 2021. Upon the exercise of the put or call options, the price to be paid for the redeemable noncontrolling interest is a function of the then-current fair market value of the redeemable noncontrolling interest, to which certain discounts and floor values may apply in specified situations depending upon the party exercising the put or call and the basis for the exercise of the put or call. As Hasbro's put right is outside the control of the Company, Hasbro's 40% noncontrolling interest is presented as redeemable noncontrolling interest outside of permanent equity on the Company's consolidated balance sheet.

In connection with the acquisition of SBS Nordic on April 9, 2013, the Company recognized $6 million redeemable noncontrolling interest for the fair value of a noncontrolling interest in one of its Danish subsidiaries. On November 19, 2014, the Company purchased the noncontrolling interest for $1 million. The difference between the consideration transferred and the recorded value of the previous redeemable noncontrolling interest was recorded to additional paid-in capital.

In connection with the acquisition of a controlling interest in Discovery Japan on January 10, 2013, J:COM obtained the right to put all, but not less than all, of its 20% noncontrolling interest to Discovery at any time for cash. Through January 10, 2017, the redemption value is the January 10, 2013 fair value denominated in Japanese yen; thereafter, the redemption value is the greater of the then-current fair value or the January 10, 2013 fair value denominated in Japanese yen.

BORROWINGS UNDER ACCOUNTS RECEIVABLE SECURITIZATION PROGRAM

6.34 ARCBEST CORPORATION (DEC)
CONSOLIDATED STATEMENTS OF CASH FLOWS (in part)

	Year Ended December 31		
(In thousands)	2015	2014	2013
Financing Activities			
Borrowings under credit facilities	70,000	—	—
Borrowings under accounts receivable securitization program	35,000	—	—
Payments on long-term debt	(100,813)	(40,440)	(43,176)
Net change in book overdrafts	3,843	2,486	(37)
Net change in restricted cash	2	516	7,756
Deferred financing costs	(875)	(76)	(71)
Payment of common stock dividends	(6,837)	(4,102)	(3,233)
Purchases of treasury stock	(12,765)	—	—
Proceeds from the exercise of stock options	—	1,136	2,785
Net Cash Used In Financing Activities	(12,445)	(40,480)	(35,976)

Note C—Financial Instruments and Fair Value Measurements (in part)

Fair Value Disclosure of Financial Instruments

Fair value and carrying value disclosures of financial instruments as of December 31 are presented in the following table:

	2015		2014	
(In thousands)	Carrying Value	Fair Value	Carrying Value	Fair Value
Credit Facility[1]	$ 70,000	$ 70,000	$ —	$ —
Term Loan[2]	—	—	70,000	70,000
Accounts receivable securitization borrowings[3]	35,000	35,000	—	—
Notes payable[4]	106,703	106,495	56,759	56,743
	$211,703	$211,495	$126,759	$126,743

[1] The revolving credit facility (the "Credit Facility") under the Company's Amended and Restated Credit Agreement, which was entered into in January 2015, carries a variable interest rate based on LIBOR, plus a margin, that is considered to be priced at market for debt instruments having similar terms and collateral requirements (Level 2 of the fair value hierarchy).

[2] The Term Loan, which was entered into on June 15, 2012 and converted to borrowings under the Credit Facility on January 2, 2015, carried a variable interest rate based on LIBOR, plus a margin, that was considered to be priced at market for debt instruments having similar terms and collateral requirements (Level 2 of the fair value hierarchy).

[3] Borrowings under the Company's accounts receivable securitization program carry a variable interest rate based on LIBOR, plus a margin, that is considered to be priced at market for debt instruments having similar terms and collateral requirements (Level 2 of the fair value hierarchy).

[4] Fair value of the notes payable was determined using a present value income approach based on quoted interest rates from lending institutions with which the Company would enter into similar transactions (Level 2 of the fair value hierarchy).

Note G—Long-Term Debt and Financing Arrangements (in part)

Long-Term Debt Obligations (in part)

Long-term debt consisted of borrowings outstanding under the Company's revolving credit facility and accounts receivable securitization program, both of which are further described in Financing Arrangements within this Note, and notes payable and capital lease obligations related to the financing of revenue equipment (tractors and trailers used primarily in ABF Freight's operations), real estate, and certain other equipment as follows:

	December 31	
(In thousands)	2015	2014
Credit Facility (interest rate of 1.7% at December 31, 2015)	$ 70,000	$ —
Term Loan[1]	—	70,000
Accounts receivable securitization borrowings (interest rate of 1.1% at December 31, 2015)	35,000	—
Notes payable (weighted-average interest rate of 1.9% at December 31, 2015)	106,703	56,759
Capital lease obligations (weighted-average interest rate of 5.8% at December 31, 2015)	806	971
	212,509	127,730
Less current portion	44,910	25,256
Long-term debt, less current portion	$167,599	$102,474

[1] The Term Loan was converted to the Credit Facility on January 2, 2015.

Scheduled maturities of long-term debt obligations as of December 31, 2015 were as follows:

			Accounts Receivable	Notes Payable Capital Lease Obligations[2]	
(In thousands)	Total	Credit Facility[1]	Securitization Program[1]	Revenue Equipment	Land and Structures
2016	$ 48,512	$ 1,375	$ 536	$ 46,388	$213
2017	43,698	1,802	750	40,927	219
2018	59,130	2,101	35,002	21,801	226
2019	2,732	2,259	—	241	232
2020	70,025	70,006	—	—	19
Thereafter	—	—	—	—	—
Total payments	224,097	77,543	36,288	109,357	909
Less amounts representing interest	11,588	7,543	1,288	2,654	103
Long-term debt	$212,509	$70,000	$35,000	$106,703	$806

[1] The future interest payments included in the scheduled maturities due are calculated using variable interest rates based on the LIBOR swap curve, plus the anticipated applicable margin.

[2] Minimum payments of capital lease obligations include maximum amounts due under rental adjustment clauses contained in the capital lease agreements.

On January 2, 2015, the Company entered into an amendment to extend the maturity date of its accounts receivable securitization program until January 2, 2018. On February 1, 2015, the Company amended and restated the accounts receivable securitization program to increase the amount of cash proceeds provided under the facility from $75.0 million to $100.0 million, with an accordion feature allowing the Company to request additional borrowings up to $25.0 million, subject to certain conditions. Under this program, certain subsidiaries of the Company continuously sell a designated pool of trade accounts receivables to a wholly owned subsidiary which, in turn, may borrow funds on a revolving basis. This wholly owned consolidated subsidiary is a separate bankruptcy-remote entity, and its assets would be available only to satisfy the claims related to the lender's interest in the trade accounts receivables. Borrowings under the accounts receivable securitization program bear interest based upon LIBOR, plus a margin, and an annual facility fee. The securitization agreement contains representations and warranties, affirmative and negative covenants, and events of default that are customary for financings of this type, including a maximum adjusted leverage ratio covenant. As of December 31, 2015, $35.0 million was borrowed under the accounts receivable securitization program. The Company was in compliance with the covenants under the accounts receivable securitization program as of December 31, 2015.

The accounts receivable securitization program includes a provision under which the Company may request and the letter of credit issuer may issue standby letters of credit, primarily in support of workers' compensation and third-party casualty claims liabilities in various states in which the Company is self-insured. The outstanding standby letters of credit reduce the availability of borrowings under the program. As of December 31, 2015, standby letters of credit of $20.1 million have been issued under the program, which reduced the available borrowing capacity to $44.9 million.

PAYMENT OF CONTINGENT CONSIDERATION

6.35 CVS HEALTH CORPORATION (DEC)
CONSOLIDATED STATEMENTS OF CASH FLOWS (in part)

	Year Ended December 31,		
In millions	2015	2014	2013
Cash flows from financing activities:			
Increase (decrease) in short-term debt	(685)	685	(690)
Proceeds from issuance of long-term debt	14,805	1,483	3,964
Repayments of long-term debt	(2,902)	(3,100)	—
Payment of contingent consideration	(58)	—	—
Dividends paid	(1,576)	(1,288)	(1,097)
Proceeds from exercise of stock options	299	421	500
Excess tax benefits from stock-based compensation	127	106	62
Repurchase of common stock	(5,001)	(4,001)	(3,976)
Other	(3)	—	—
Net cash provided by (used in) financing activities	5,006	(5,694)	(1,237)

NOTES TO CONSOLIDATED FINANCIAL STATEMENTS (in part)

3 Acquisitions (in part)

Coram Acquisition (in part)

On January 16, 2014, the Company acquired 100% of the voting interests of Coram LLC and its subsidiaries (collectively, "Coram"), the specialty infusion services and enteral nutrition business unit of Apria Healthcare Group Inc. ("Apria"), for cash consideration of approximately $2.1 billion, plus contingent consideration of approximately $0.1 billion. The purchase price was also subject to a working capital adjustment, which resulted in the Company receiving $9 million from Apria. Coram is one of the nation's largest providers of comprehensive infusion services, caring for approximately 240,000 patients annually. Coram has approximately 4,600 employees, including approximately 600 nurses and 250 dietitians, operating primarily through 83 branch locations and six centers of excellence for patient intake.

The contingent consideration is based on the Company's future realization of Coram's tax net operating loss carryforwards ("NOLs") as of the date of the acquisition. The Company will pay the seller the first $60 million in tax savings realized from the future utilization of the Coram NOLs, plus 50% of any additional future tax savings from the remaining NOLs. The fair value of the contingent consideration liability associated with the future realization of the Coram NOLs was determined using Level 3 inputs based on the present value of contingent payments expected to be made based on the Company's estimate of the amount and timing of Coram NOLs that will ultimately be realized. The change in fair value of the contingent consideration liability recognized in earnings for the year ended December 31, 2014 was immaterial and for the year ended December 31, 2015 was approximately $4 million. During the year ended December 31, 2015, the Company made contingent consideration payments to Apria of approximately $58 million.

Presentation in Annual Report

PRESENTATION

7.01 This section reviews the format and content of independent auditors' reports appearing in the annual reports of the 350 survey entities. Auditing Standard (AS) 3101, *Reporting on Audits of Financial Statements* (AICPA, *PCAOB Standards and Related Rules*) (formerly AU section 508), applies to auditors' reports of issuers issued in connection with audits of historical financial statements that are intended to present financial position, results of operations, and cash flows in conformity with generally accepted accounting principles (GAAP).

7.02 With the adoption of the clarified auditing standards, the following AU-C sections (AICPA, *Professional Standards*), are applicable to the auditor's report:

- AU-C section 560, *Subsequent Events and Subsequently Discovered Facts*
- AU-C section 600, *Special Considerations—Audits of Group Financial Statements (Including the Work of Component Auditors)*
- AU-C section 700, *Forming an Opinion and Reporting on Financial Statements*
- AU-C section 705, *Modifications to the Opinion in the Independent Auditor's Report*
- AU-C section 706, *Emphasis-of-Matter Paragraphs and Other-Matter Paragraphs in the Independent Auditor's Report*
- AU-C section 708, *Consistency of Financial Statements*
- AU-C section 800, *Special Considerations—Audits of Financial Statements Prepared in Accordance With Special Purpose Frameworks*
- AU-C section 805, *Special Considerations—Audits of Single Financial Statements and Specific Elements, Accounts, or Items of a Financial Statement*
- AU-C section 810, *Engagements to Report on Summary Financial Statements*
- AU-C section 905, *Alert That Restricts the Use of the Auditor's Written Communication*
- AU-C section 910, *Financial Statements Prepared in Accordance With a Financial Reporting Framework Generally Accepted in Another Country*

As stated, AICPA clarified auditing standards apply to audits of nonissuers. PCAOB Auditing Standards apply to audits of issuers.

7.03 Section 103(a) of the Sarbanes-Oxley Act of 2002 authorized the PCAOB to establish auditing and related professional practice standards to be used by public accounting firms registered with the PCAOB. PCAOB Rule 3100, *Compliance With Auditing and Related Professional Practice Standards* (AICPA, *PCAOB Standards and Related Rules*, Select Rules of the Board), requires auditors to comply with all applicable auditing and related professional practice standards of the PCAOB.

Auditors' Reports

PRESENTATION

NONISSUERS

7.04 AU-C section 700 explains and provides examples of the unmodified auditor's report. The report should be written and include
- title,
- addressee,
- introductory paragraph,
- paragraph explaining management's responsibilities for the financial statements,
- auditor's responsibility,
- auditor's opinion,
- other reporting responsibilities (if applicable),
- signature of the auditor,
- auditor's address, and
- date of the auditor's report.

7.05 Paragraph .23 of AU-C section 700 states that the auditor's report should have a title that includes the word *independent* to clearly indicate that it is the report of an independent auditor.

7.06 Paragraph .24 of AU-C section 700 states that the auditor's report should be addressed as required by the circumstances of the engagement.

7.07 The introductory paragraph, as described by paragraph .25 of AU-C section 700, should
- identify the entity whose financial statements have been audited,
- state that the financial statements have been audited,
- identify the title of each statement that the financial statements comprise, and
- specify the date or period covered by each financial statement that the financial statements comprise.

7.08 Paragraphs .26–.28 of AU-C section 700 describe what should be included in the paragraph explaining management's responsibilities for the financial statements. These responsibilities include management's responsibility for the preparation and fair presentation of the financial statements in accordance with the applicable financial reporting framework. The description of management's responsibilities should not reference a separate statement by management if such a statement is included in a document containing the auditor's report.

7.09 Paragraphs .29–.33 of AU-C section 700 explain what should be included in the auditor's responsibility portion of the auditor's report. Included in these responsibilities is that the audit was conducted in accordance with GAAS and determining whether the audit evidence obtained is sufficient and appropriate to provide a basis for the auditor's opinion.

7.10 Paragraphs .34–.36 of AU-C section 700 describe the opinion paragraph of the auditor's report. This paragraph should state that the financial statements present fairly, in all material respects, the financial position of the entity as of the balance sheet date and the results of its operations and its cash flows for the period then ended, in accordance with the applicable financial reporting framework. The auditor's opinion should also identity the applicable financial reporting framework and its origin.

7.11 Paragraphs .42–.44 of AU-C section 700 describe the requirements for an auditor's report for audits conducted in accordance with both GAAS and another set of auditing standards, including PCAOB standards.

7.12 Paragraph .A63 of AU-C section 700 presents examples of the auditor's standard reports for single year financial statements and comparative two year financial statements. Two of these examples follow.

An Auditor's Report on a Single Year Prepared in Accordance With Accounting Principles Generally Accepted in the United States of America

Circumstances include the following:
- Audit of a complete set of general purpose financial statements (single year).
- The financial statements are prepared in accordance with accounting principles generally accepted in the United States of America.

INDEPENDENT AUDITOR'S REPORT

[Appropriate Addressee]

Report on the Financial Statements[1]

We have audited the accompanying financial statements of ABC Company, which comprise the balance sheet as of December 31, 20X1, and the related statements of income, changes in stockholders' equity, and cash flows for the year then ended, and the related notes to the financial statements.

Management's Responsibility for the Financial Statements

Management is responsible for the preparation and fair presentation of these financial statements in accordance with accounting principles generally accepted in the United States of America; this includes the design, implementation, and maintenance of internal control relevant to the preparation and fair presentation of financial statements that are free from material misstatement, whether due to fraud or error.

Auditor's Responsibility

Our responsibility is to express an opinion on these financial statements based on our audit. We conducted our audit in accordance with auditing standards generally accepted in the United States of America. Those standards require that we plan and perform the audit to obtain reasonable assurance about whether the financial statements are free from material misstatement.

An audit involves performing procedures to obtain audit evidence about the amounts and disclosures in the financial statements. The procedures selected depend on the auditor's judgment, including the assessment of the risks of material misstatement of the financial statements, whether due to fraud or error. In making those risk assessments, the auditor considers internal control relevant to the entity's preparation and fair presentation of the financial statements in order to design audit procedures that are appropriate in the circumstances, but not for the purpose of expressing an opinion on the effectiveness of the entity's internal control.[2] Accordingly, we express no such opinion. An audit also includes evaluating the appropriateness of accounting policies used and the reasonableness of significant accounting estimates made by management, as well as evaluating the overall presentation of the financial statements.

We believe that the audit evidence we have obtained is sufficient and appropriate to provide a basis for our audit opinion.

Opinion

In our opinion, the financial statements referred to above present fairly, in all material respects, the financial position of ABC Company as of December 31, 20X1, and the results of its operations and its cash flows for the year then ended in accordance with accounting principles generally accepted in the United States of America.

Report on Other Legal and Regulatory Requirements

[Form and content of this section of the auditor's report will vary depending on the nature of the auditor's other reporting responsibilities.]

[Auditor's signature]
[Auditor's city and state]
[Date of the auditor's report]

---

[1] The subtitle "Report on the Financial Statements" is unnecessary in circumstances when the second subtitle, "Report on Other Legal and Regulatory Requirements," is not applicable.

[2] In circumstances when the auditor also has responsibility to express an opinion on the effectiveness of internal control in conjunction with the audit of the financial statements, this sentence would be worded as follows: "In making those risk assessments, the auditor considers internal con-trol relevant to the entity's preparation and fair presentation of the financial statements in order to design audit procedures that are appropriate in the circumstances." In addition, the next sentence, "Accordingly, we express no such opinion." would not be included.

An Auditor's Report on Consolidated Comparative Financial Statements Prepared in Accordance With Accounting Principles Generally Accepted in the United States of America

Circumstances include the following:
- Audit of a complete set of general purpose consolidated financial statements (comparative).
- The financial statements are prepared in accordance with accounting principles generally accepted in the United States of America.

INDEPENDENT AUDITOR'S REPORT

[Appropriate Addressee]

Report on the Financial Statements[3]

We have audited the accompanying consolidated financial statements of ABC Company and its subsidiaries, which comprise the consolidated balance sheets as of December 31, 20X1 and 20X0, and the related consolidated statements of income, changes in stockholders' equity, and cash flows for the years then ended, and the related notes to the financial statements.

Management's Responsibility for the Financial Statements

Management is responsible for the preparation and fair presentation of these consolidated financial statements in accordance with accounting principles generally accepted in the United States of America; this includes the design, implementation, and maintenance of internal control relevant to the preparation and fair presentation of consolidated financial statements that are free from material misstatement, whether due to fraud or error.

Auditor's Responsibility

Our responsibility is to express an opinion on these consolidated financial statements based on our audits. We conducted our audits in accordance with auditing standards generally accepted in the United States of America. Those standards require that we plan and perform the audit to obtain reasonable assurance about whether the consolidated financial statements are free from material misstatement.

An audit involves performing procedures to obtain audit evidence about the amounts and disclosures in the consolidated financial statements. The procedures selected depend on the auditor's judgment, including the assessment of the risks of material misstatement of the consolidated financial statements, whether due to fraud or error. In making those risk assessments, the auditor considers internal control relevant to the entity's preparation and fair presentation of the consolidated financial statements in order to design audit procedures that are appropriate in the circumstances, but not for the purpose of expressing an opinion on the effectiveness of the entity's internal control.[4] Accordingly, we express no such opinion. An audit also includes evaluating the appropriateness of accounting policies used and the reasonableness of significant accounting estimates made by management, as well as evaluating the overall presentation of the consolidated financial statements.

We believe that the audit evidence we have obtained is sufficient and appropriate to provide a basis for our audit opinion.

Opinion

In our opinion, the consolidated financial statements referred to above present fairly, in all material respects, the financial position of ABC Company and its subsidiaries as of December 31, 20X1 and 20X0, and the results of their operations and their cash flows for the years then ended in accordance with accounting principles generally accepted in the United States of America.

Report on Other Legal and Regulatory Requirements

[Form and content of this section of the auditor's report will vary depending on the nature of the auditor's other reporting responsibilities.]

[Auditor's signature]
[Auditor's city and state]
[Date of the auditor's report]

---

[3] The subtitle "Report on the Financial Statements" is unnecessary in circumstances when the second subtitle, "Report on Other Legal and Regulatory Requirements," is not applicable.

[4] In circumstances when the auditor also has responsibility to express an opinion on the effectiveness of internal control in conjunction with the audit of the consolidated financial statements, this sentence would be worded as follows: "In making those risk assessments, the auditor considers internal control relevant to the entity's preparation and fair presentation of the consolidated financial statements in order to design audit procedures that are appropriate in the circumstances." In addition, the next sentence, "Accordingly, we express no such opinion." would not be included.

7.13 If the statements of income, retained earnings, and cash flows are presented on a comparative basis for one or more periods, but the balance sheet(s) as of the end of one or more of the prior period(s) is not presented, the phrase "for the years then ended" should be changed to indicate that the auditor's opinion applies to each period for which statements of income, retained earnings, and cash flows are presented, such as "for each of the three years in the period ended [date of latest balance sheet]."

7.14 FASB *Accounting Standards Codification* (ASC) 220, *Comprehensive Income*, requires entities that provide a full set of general-purpose financial statements (that is, financial position, results of operations, and cash flows) to report comprehensive income and its components either in a single continuous financial statement or in two separate but consecutive financial statements.

7.15 FASB ASC 505-10-50-2 allows for changes in the separate accounts comprising stockholders' equity to be presented either on the face of the basic financial statements or in the form of a separate statement, such as a statement of changes in stockholders' equity.

ISSUERS

7.16 Paragraph .08(a) of AS 3101 states that the title of an auditor's report should include the word *independent*.

7.17 Paragraph .09 of AS 3101 states the following:

The report may be addressed to the company whose financial statements are being audited or to its board of directors or stockholders. A report on the financial statements of an unincorporated entity should be addressed as circumstances dictate, for example, to the partners, to the general partner, or to the proprietor. Occasionally, an auditor is retained to audit the financial statements of a company that is not a client; in such a case, the report is customarily addressed to the client and not to the directors or stockholders of the company whose financial statements are being audited.

7.18 For audits of public entities (that is, *issuers*, as defined by the Sarbanes-Oxley Act of 2002, and other entities, when prescribed by the rules of the SEC), paragraph .08 of AS 3101 directs auditors to state that the engagement was conducted in accordance with "the standards of the Public Company Accounting Oversight Board (United States)" whenever the auditor has performed the engagement in accordance with the PCAOB's standards. An example of a standard independent registered auditor's report presented in AS 3101 follows:

REPORT OF INDEPENDENT REGISTERED PUBLIC ACCOUNTING FIRM

We have audited the accompanying balance sheets of X Company as of December 31, 20X2 and 20X1, and the related statements of income, retained earnings, and cash flows for the years then ended. These financial statements are the responsibility of the Company's management. Our responsibility is to express an opinion on these financial statements based on our audits.

We conducted our audits in accordance with auditing standards generally accepted in the United States of America. Those standards require that we plan and perform the audit to obtain reasonable assurance about whether the financial statements are free of material misstatement. An audit includes examining, on a test basis, evidence supporting the amounts and disclosures in the financial statements. An audit also includes assessing the accounting principles used and significant estimates made by management, as well as evaluating the overall financial statement presentation. We believe that our audits provide a reasonable basis for our opinion.

In our opinion, the financial statements referred to above present fairly, in all material respects, the financial position of X company as of (at) December 31, 20X2 and 20X1, and the results of its operations and its cash flows for the years then ended in conformity with accounting principles generally accepted in the United States of America.

[*Signature*]
[*City and State or Country*]
[*Date*]

7.19 For audit requirements on reporting on internal controls over financial reporting, refer to paragraph 7.62.

PRESENTATION AND DISCLOSURE EXCERPTS

PRICEWATERHOUSECOOPERS LLP AUDITOR'S REPORT

7.20 PRAXAIR, INC. (DEC)
REPORT OF INDEPENDENT REGISTERED PUBLIC ACCOUNTING FIRM

To The Board of Directors and Shareholders of Praxair, Inc.:

In our opinion, the accompanying consolidated balance sheets and the related consolidated statements of income, comprehensive income, equity and cash flows present fairly, in all material respects, the financial position of Praxair and its subsidiaries at December 31, 2015 and 2014, and the results of their operations and their cash flows for each of the three years in the period ended December 31, 2015 in conformity with accounting principles generally accepted in the United States of America. Also in our opinion, the Company maintained, in all material respects, effective internal control over financial reporting as of December 31, 2015, based on criteria established in *Internal Control—Integrated Framework (2013)* issued by the Committee of Sponsoring Organizations of the Treadway Commission (COSO). The Company's management is responsible for these financial statements, for maintaining effective internal control over financial reporting and for its assessment of the effectiveness of internal control over financial reporting, included in the accompanying Management's Report on Internal Control over Financial Reporting. Our responsibility is to express opinions on these financial statements and on the Company's internal control over financial reporting based on our integrated audits. We conducted our audits in accordance with the standards of the Public Company Accounting Oversight Board (United States). Those standards require that we plan and perform the audits to obtain reasonable assurance about whether the financial statements are free of material misstatement and whether effective internal control over financial reporting was maintained in all material respects. Our audits of the financial statements included examining, on a test basis, evidence supporting the amounts and disclosures in the financial statements, assessing the accounting principles used and significant estimates made by management, and evaluating the overall financial statement presentation. Our audit of internal control over financial reporting included obtaining an understanding of internal control over financial reporting, assessing the risk that a material weakness exists, and testing and evaluating the design and operating effectiveness of internal control based on the assessed risk. Our audits also included performing such other procedures as we considered necessary in the circumstances. We believe that our audits provide a reasonable basis for our opinions.

A company's internal control over financial reporting is a process designed to provide reasonable assurance regarding the reliability of financial reporting and the preparation of financial statements for external purposes in accordance with generally accepted accounting principles. A company's internal control over financial reporting includes those policies and procedures that (i) pertain to the maintenance of records that, in reasonable detail, accurately and fairly reflect the transactions and dispositions of the assets of the company; (ii) provide reasonable assurance that transactions are recorded as necessary to permit preparation of financial statements in accordance with generally accepted accounting principles, and that receipts and expenditures of the company are being made only in accordance with authorizations of management and directors of the company; and (iii) provide reasonable assurance regarding prevention or timely detection of unauthorized acquisition, use, or disposition of the company's assets that could have a material effect on the financial statements.

Because of its inherent limitations, internal control over financial reporting may not prevent or detect misstatements. Also, projections of any evaluation of effectiveness to future periods are subject to the risk that controls may become inadequate because of changes in conditions, or that the degree of compliance with the policies or procedures may deteriorate.

/s/ PricewaterhouseCoopers LLP
Stamford, Connecticut
February 24, 2016

STATEMENTS OF EARNINGS AND COMPREHENSIVE INCOME

7.21 THE PROCTER & GAMBLE COMPANY (JUN)
REPORT OF INDEPENDENT REGISTERED PUBLIC ACCOUNTING FIRM

To the Board of Directors and Stockholders of
The Procter & Gamble Company

We have audited the accompanying Consolidated Balance Sheets of The Procter & Gamble Company and subsidiaries (the "Company") as of June 30, 2015 and 2014, and the related Consolidated Statements of Earnings, Comprehensive Income, Shareholders' Equity, and Cash Flows for each of the three years in the period ended June 30, 2015. These financial statements are the responsibility of the Company's management. Our responsibility is to express an opinion on these financial statements based on our audits.

We conducted our audits in accordance with the standards of the Public Company Accounting Oversight Board (United States). Those standards require that we plan and perform the audit to obtain reasonable assurance about whether the financial statements are free of material misstatement. An audit includes examining, on a test basis, evidence supporting the amounts and disclosures in the financial statements. An audit also includes assessing the accounting principles used and significant estimates made by management, as well as evaluating the overall financial statement presentation. We believe that our audits provide a reasonable basis for our opinion.

In our opinion, such Consolidated Financial Statements present fairly, in all material respects, the financial position of The Procter & Gamble Company and subsidiaries at June 30, 2015 and 2014, and the results of their operations and their cash flows for each of the three years in the period ended June 30, 2015, in conformity with accounting principles generally accepted in the United States of America.

We have also audited, in accordance with the standards of the Public Company Accounting Oversight Board (United States), the Company's internal control over financial reporting as of June 30, 2015, based on the criteria established in *Internal Control—Integrated Framework (2013)* issued by the Committee of Sponsoring Organizations of the Treadway Commission and our report dated August 7, 2015 expressed an unqualified opinion on the Company's internal control over financial reporting.

/s/ Deloitte & Touche LLP
Cincinnati, Ohio
August 7, 2015

STATEMENT OF CHANGES IN STOCKHOLDERS' EQUITY

7.22 SYSCO CORPORATION (JUN)
REPORT OF INDEPENDENT REGISTERED PUBLIC ACCOUNTING FIRM ON CONSOLIDATED FINANCIAL STATEMENTS

The Board of Directors and Shareholders of Sysco Corporation

We have audited the accompanying consolidated balance sheets of Sysco Corporation (a Delaware Corporation) and subsidiaries (the "Company") as of June 27, 2015 and June 28, 2014, and the related consolidated results of operations, and statements of comprehensive income, changes in shareholders' equity and cash flows for each of the three years in the period ended June 27, 2015. These financial statements are the responsibility of the Company's management. Our responsibility is to express an opinion on these financial statements based on our audits.

We conducted our audits in accordance with the standards of the Public Company Accounting Oversight Board (United States). Those standards require that we plan and perform the audit to obtain reasonable assurance about whether the financial statements are free of material misstatement. An audit includes examining, on a test basis, evidence supporting the amounts and disclosures in the financial statements. An audit also includes assessing the accounting principles used and significant estimates made by management, as well as evaluating the overall financial statement presentation. We believe that our audits provide a reasonable basis for our opinion.

In our opinion, the financial statements referred to above present fairly, in all material respects, the consolidated financial position of the Company as of June 27, 2015 and June 28, 2014, and the consolidated results of its operations and its cash flows for each of the three years in the period ended June 27, 2015, in conformity with U.S. generally accepted accounting principles.

We also have audited, in accordance with the standards of the Public Company Accounting Oversight Board (United States), the Company's internal control over financial reporting as of June 27, 2015, based on criteria established in Internal Control-Integrated Framework issued by the Committee of Sponsoring Organizations of the Treadway Commission (2013 framework) and our report dated August 24, 2015 expressed an unqualified opinion thereon.

/s/ Ernst & Young LLP
Houston, Texas
August 24, 2015

Reference to the Report of Other Auditors

PRESENTATION

NONISSUERS

7.23 AU-C section 600 establishes requirements and provides guidance for the independent auditor in deciding (*a*) whether he or she may use the work and reports of component auditors who have audited the financial statements of one or more subsidiaries, divisions, branches, components, or investments included in the financial statements presented and (*b*) the form and content of the principal auditor's report in these circumstances.

7.24 Paragraph .25 of AU-C section 600 explains that when the group engagement partner decides to make reference to the component auditor, the following should be true:
- The component's financial statements are prepared using the same financial reporting framework as the group financial statements.
- The component auditor has performed an audit of the financial statements of the component in accordance with generally accepted auditing standards.
- The component auditor has issued an auditor's report that is not restricted as to use.

7.25 As described in paragraph .28 of AU-C section 600, the group financial statements should clearly indicate that the component was not audited by the auditor of the group financial statements but was audited by the component auditor and should include the magnitude of the portion of the financial statements audited by the component auditor. As described in paragraph .A58 of AU-C section 600, the disclosure of the magnitude of the portion of the financial statements audited by a component auditor may be achieved by stating either the dollar amounts or percentages (whichever most clearly describes the portion of the financial statements audited by a component auditor) of one or more of the following: total assets, total revenues, or other appropriate criteria. When two or more component auditors participate in the audit, the dollar amounts or the percentages covered by the component auditors may be stated in the aggregate.

7.26 Paragraph .29 of AU-C section 600 explains that if the group engagement partner decides to name a component auditor in the auditor's report on the group financial statements, then the component auditor's express permission should be obtained and the component's auditor's report should be presented together with that of the auditor's report on the group financial statements.

7.27 Exhibit A of AU-C section 600 contains an example of appropriate reporting in the auditor's report on the group financial statements when reference is made to the audit of a component auditor.

ISSUERS

7.28 AS 1205, *Part of the Audit Performed by Other Independent Auditors* (AICPA, *PCAOB Standards and Related Rules*) (formerly PCAOB AS No. 5) provides guidance to help a principal auditor decide whether to make reference in his or her report to the audit performed by another auditor. Regardless of whether the principal auditor decides to make reference to the audit of the other auditor, there are certain procedures he or she should perform.
- Make inquiries regarding the professional reputation and standing of the other auditor
- Obtain a representation from the other auditor that he or she is independent under the requirements of the PCAOB and the requirements of the SEC
- Ascertain through communication with the other auditor
  - that he or she is aware that the financial statements of the component, which he or she is to audit are to be included in the financial statements on which the principal auditor will report and that the other auditor's report thereon will be relied upon (and, where applicable, referred to) by the principal auditor.
  - that he or she is familiar with accounting principles generally accepted in the United States of America and with the standards of the PCAOB and will conduct his or her audit and report in accordance therewith.

- that he has knowledge of the relevant financial reporting requirements for statements and schedules to be filed with regulatory agencies such as the SEC, if appropriate.
- that a review will be made of matters affecting elimination of intercompany transactions and accounts and, if appropriate in the circumstances, the uniformity of accounting practices among the components included in the financial statements.

7.29 When the principal auditor decides not to make reference to the audit of the other auditor, he or she must obtain and review and retain the following information from the other auditor, as prescribed in AS 3101:

- An engagement completion document consistent with paragraphs .12–.13 of AS 1215, *Audit Documentation* (AICPA, *PCAOB Standards and Related Rules*) (formerly PCAOB AS No. 3). This engagement completion document should include all cross-referenced, supporting audit documentation.
- A list of significant risks, the auditor's responses, and the results of the auditor's related procedures.
- Sufficient information relating to any significant findings or issues that are inconsistent with or contradict the auditor's final conclusions, as described in paragraph .08 of AS 1215.
- Any findings affecting the consolidating or combining of accounts in the consolidated financial statements.
- Sufficient information to enable the office issuing the auditor's report to agree or to reconcile the financial statement amounts audited by the other auditor to the information underlying the consolidated financial statements.
- A schedule of accumulated misstatements, including a description of the nature and cause of each accumulated misstatement, and an evaluation of uncorrected misstatements, including the quantitative and qualitative factors the auditor considered to be relevant to the evaluation.
- All significant deficiencies and material weaknesses in internal control over financial reporting, including a clear distinction between those two categories.
- Letters of representations from management.
- All matters to be communicated to the audit committee.

PRESENTATION AND DISCLOSURE EXCERPT

REFERENCE TO OTHER AUDITORS

7.30 PENSKE AUTOMOTIVE GROUP, INC. (DEC)
REPORT OF INDEPENDENT REGISTERED PUBLIC ACCOUNTING FIRM

To the Board of Directors and Stockholders of Penske Automotive Group, Inc.
Bloomfield Hills, Michigan

We have audited the accompanying consolidated balance sheets of Penske Automotive Group, Inc. and subsidiaries (the "Company") as of December 31, 2015 and 2014, and the related consolidated statements of income, comprehensive income, equity, and cash flows for each of the three years in the period ended December 31, 2015. Our audits also included the financial statement schedule listed in the Index at Item 15. We also have audited the Company's internal control over financial reporting as of December 31, 2015, based on criteria established in Internal Control—Integrated Framework (2013) issued by the Committee of Sponsoring Organizations of the Treadway Commission. The Company's management is responsible for these financial statements and financial statement schedule, for maintaining effective internal control over financial reporting, and for its assessment of the effectiveness of internal control over financial reporting, included in the accompanying Management Report on Internal Control Over Financial Reporting. Our responsibility is to express an opinion on these financial statements and financial statement schedule and an opinion on the Company's internal control over financial reporting based on our audits. We did not audit the financial statements or the effectiveness of internal control over financial reporting of UAG UK Holdings Limited and subsidiaries (a consolidated subsidiary), which statements reflect total assets constituting 41% and 40% of consolidated total assets as of December 31, 2015 and 2014, respectively, and tot al revenues constituting 39%, 40%, and 37% of consolidated total revenues for the years ended December 31, 2015, 2014, and 2013, respectively. Those financial statements and the effectiveness of UAG UK Holdings Limited and subsidiaries' internal control over financial reporting were audited by other auditors whose reports have been furnished to us, and our opinion, insofar as it relates to the amounts included for UAG UK Holdings Limited and subsidiaries and to the effectiveness of UAG UK Holdings Limited and subsidiaries' internal control over financial reporting, is based solely on the reports of the other auditors.

As described in the accompanying Management Report on Internal Control Over Financial Reporting, management excluded from its assessment the internal control over financial reporting at Jacobs Holding GmbH (a subsidiary of UAG UK Holdings Limited) which was acquired in September 2015 and which represent total assets constituting 2% of the Company's total assets and 1% of the Company's total revenues as of December 31, 2015 and for the year ended December 31, 2015. Accordingly, our audit and that of the other auditors did not include the internal control over financial reporting at Jacobs Holding GmbH.

We conducted our audits in accordance with the standards of the Public Company Accounting Oversight Board (United States). Those standards require that we plan and perform the audit to obtain reasonable assurance about whether the financial statements are free of material misstatement and whether effective internal control over financial reporting was maintained in all material respects. Our audits of the financial statements included examining, on a test basis, evidence supporting the amounts and disclosures in the financial statements, assessing the accounting principles used and significant estimates made by management, and evaluating the overall financial statement presentation. Our audit of internal control over financial reporting included obtaining an understanding of internal control over financial reporting, assessing the risk that a material weakness exists, and testing and evaluating the design and operating effectiveness of internal control based on the assessed risk. Our audits also included performing such other procedures as we considered necessary in the circumstances. We believe that our audits and the reports of the other auditors provide a reasonable basis for our opinions.

A company's internal control over financial reporting is a process designed by, or under the supervision of, the company's principal executive and principal financial officers, or persons performing similar functions, and effected by the company's board of directors, management, and other personnel to provide reasonable assurance regarding the reliability of financial reporting and the preparation of financial statements for external purposes in accordance with generally accepted accounting principles. A company's internal control over financial reporting includes those policies and procedures that (1) pertain to the maintenance of records that, in reasonable detail, accurately and fairly reflect the transactions and dispositions of the assets of the company; (2) provide reasonable assurance that transactions are recorded as necessary to permit preparation of financial statements in accordance with generally accepted accounting principles, and that receipts and expenditures of the company are being made only in accordance with authorizations of management and directors of the company; and (3) provide reasonable assurance regarding prevention or timely detection of unauthorized acquisition, use, or disposition of the company's assets that could have a material effect on the financial statements.

Because of the inherent limitations of internal control over financial reporting, including the possibility of collusion or improper management override of controls, material misstatements due to error or fraud may not be prevented or detected on a timely basis. Also, projections of any evaluation of the effectiveness of the internal control over financial reporting to future periods are subject to the risk that the controls may become inadequate because of changes in conditions, or that the degree of compliance with the policies or procedures may deteriorate.

In our opinion, based on our audits and the reports of the other auditors, the consolidated financial statements referred to above present fairly, in all material respects, the financial position of Penske Automotive Group, Inc. and subsidiaries as of December 31, 2015 and 2014, and the results of their operations and their cash flows for each of the three years in the period ended December 31, 2015, in conformity with accounting principles generally accepted in the United States of America. Also, in our opinion, based on our audits and (as to the amounts included for UAG UK Holdings Limited and subsidiaries) the reports of the other auditors, such financial statement schedule, when considered in relation to the basic consolidated financial statements taken as a whole, presents fairly, in all material respects, the information set forth therein. Also, in our opinion based on our audit and the reports of other auditors, the Company maintained, in all material respects, effective internal control over financial reporting as of December 31, 2015, based on the criteria established in Internal Control—Integrated Framework (2013) issued by the Committee of Sponsoring Organizations of the Treadway Commission.

/s/ Deloitte & Touche LLP
Detroit, Michigan
February 25, 2016

REPORT OF INDEPENDENT REGISTERED PUBLIC ACCOUNTING FIRM

The Board of Directors and Stockholders
UAG UK Holdings Limited:

We have audited the consolidated balance sheet of UAG UK Holdings Limited ("UAG") and subsidiaries (together the "Company") as of December 31, 2015, and the related consolidated statements of income, comprehensive income, equity and cash flows for the year then ended. In connection with our audits of the consolidated financial statements, we also have audited the related financial statement schedule. We also have audited UAG's internal control over financial reporting as of December 31, 2015, based on criteria established in Internal Control—Integrated Framework (2013) issued by the Committee of Sponsoring Organizations of the Treadway Commission (COSO). UAG's management is responsible for these consolidated financial statements and the financial statement schedule, for maintaining effective internal control over financial reporting, and for its assessment of the effectiveness of internal control over financial reporting, included in the accompanying Management Report on Internal Control over Financial Reporting. Our responsibility is to express an opinion on these consolidated financial statements and the financial statement schedule and an opinion on UAG's internal control over financial reporting based on our audits.

We conducted our audits in accordance with the standards of the Public Company Accounting Oversight Board (United States). Those standards require that we plan and perform the audits to obtain reasonable assurance about whether the financial statements are free of material misstatement and whether effective internal control over financial reporting was maintained in all material respects. Our audit s of the consolidated financial statements included examining, on a test basis, evidence supporting the amounts and disclosures in the financial statements, assessing the accounting principles used and significant estimates made by management, and evaluating the overall financial statement presentation. Our audit of internal control over financial reporting included obtaining an understanding of internal control over financial reporting, assessing the risk that a material weakness exists, and testing and evaluating the design and operating effectiveness of internal control based on the assessed risk. Our audits also included performing such other procedures as we considered necessary in the circumstances. We believe that our audits provide a reasonable basis for our opinions.

A company's internal control over financial reporting is a process designed to provide reasonable assurance regarding the reliability of financial reporting and the preparation of financial statements for external purposes in accordance with generally accepted accounting principles. A company's internal control over financial reporting includes those policies and procedures that (1) pertain to the maintenance of records that, in reasonable detail, accurately and fairly reflect the transactions and dispositions of the assets of the company; (2) provide reasonable assurance that transactions are recorded as necessary to permit preparation of financial statements in accordance with generally accepted accounting principles, and that receipts and expenditures of the company are being made only in accordance with authorizations of management and directors of the company; and (3) provide reasonable assurance regarding prevention or timely detection of unauthorized acquisition, use, or disposition of the company's assets that could have a material effect on the financial statements.

Because of its inherent limitations, internal control over financial reporting may not prevent or detect misstatements. Also, projections of any evaluation of effectiveness to future periods are subject to the risk that controls may become inadequate because of changes in conditions, or that the degree of compliance with the policies or procedures may deteriorate.

In our opinion, the consolidated financial statements referred to above present fairly, in all material respects, the financial position of the Company as of December 31, 2015, and the results of its operations and its cash flows for the year then ended, in conformity with U.S. generally accepted accounting principles. In addition, in our opinion, the related financial statement schedule, when considered in relation to the basic consolidated financial statements taken as a whole, presents fairly, in all material respects, the information set forth therein. Also in our opinion, UAG maintained, in all material respects, effective internal control over financial reporting as of December 31, 2015, based on criteria established in Internal Control—Integrated Framework (2013) issued by the Committee of Sponsoring Organizations of the Treadway Commission.

UAG acquired a controlling interest in Jacobs Holding GmbH ("Jacobs"), a German automotive retailer, in September 2015. Management has excluded Jacobs from its assessment of effectiveness of the Company's internal control over financial reporting as of December 31, 2015. Jacobs represents 6% of the Company's total assets and 3% of the Company's total revenues as of and for the year ended December 31, 2015. Our audit of internal control over financial reporting of UAG also excluded an evaluation of the internal control over financial reporting of Jacobs.

/s/ KPMG LLP
Milton Keynes, United Kingdom
February 25, 2016

REPORT OF INDEPENDENT REGISTERED PUBLIC ACCOUNTING FIRM

The Board of Directors and Stockholders
UAG UK Holdings Limited:

We have audited the consolidated balance sheet of UAG UK Holdings Limited ("UAG") and subsidiaries (together the "Company") as of December 31, 2014, and the related consolidated statements of income, comprehensive income, equity and cash flows for each of the years in the two-year period then ended. In connection with our audits of the consolidated financial statements, we also have audited the related financial statement schedule. These consolidated financial statements and financial statement schedule are the responsibility of UAG's management. Our responsibility is to express an opinion on these consolidated financial statements and financial statement schedule based on our audits.

We conducted our audits in accordance with the standards of the Public Company Accounting Oversight Board (United States). Those standards require that we plan and perform the audits to obtain reasonable assurance about whether the financial statements are free of material misstatement. An audit includes examining, on a test basis, evidence supporting the amounts and disclosures in the financial statements. An audit also includes assessing the accounting principles used and significant estimates made by management, as well as evaluating the overall financial statement presentation. We believe that our audits provide a reasonable basis for our opinion.

In our opinion, the consolidated financial statements referred to above present fairly, in all material respects, the financial position of the Company as of December 31, 2014, and the results of its operations and its cash flows for each of the years in the two-year period then ended, in conformity with U.S. generally accepted accounting principles. Also, in our opinion, the related financial statement schedule, when considered in relation to the basic consolidated financial statements taken as a whole, presents fairly, in all material respects, the information set forth therein.

/s/ KPMG Audit Plc
Birmingham, United Kingdom
February 26, 2015

Uncertainties

Author's Note

In August 2014, FASB issued Accounting Standards Update (ASU) No. 2014-15, *Presentation of Financial Statements—Going Concern (Subtopic 205-40): Disclosure of Uncertainties about an Entity's Ability to Continue as a Going Concern.* Previously, there was no guidance in GAAP about management's responsibility to evaluate whether there is substantial doubt about an entity's ability to continue as a going concern or to provide related footnote disclosures. The amendments in this ASU require management to assess an entity's ability to continue as a going concern by incorporating and expanding upon certain principles that are currently in U.S. auditing standards. Specifically, the amendments (1) provide a definition of the term *substantial doubt*, (2) require an evaluation every reporting period, including interim periods, (3) provide principles for considering the mitigating effect of management's plans, (4) require certain disclosures when substantial doubt is alleviated as a result of consideration of management's plans, (5) require an express statement and other disclosures when substantial doubt is not alleviated, and (6) require an assessment for a period of one year after the date that the financial statements are issued (or available to be issued). The amendments in this ASU are effective for the annual period ending after December 15, 2016, and for annual periods and interim periods thereafter. Early application is permitted.

PRESENTATION

NONISSUERS

7.31 Paragraph .A13 of AU-C section 705 explains that an audit includes an assessment of whether the audit evidence related to uncertainties supports management's analysis. Absence of the existence of information related to the outcome of an uncertainty does not necessarily lead to a conclusion that the audit evidence supporting management's assertion is not sufficient. Rather, the auditor's professional judgment regarding the sufficiency of the audit evidence is based on the audit evidence that is, or should be, available. This does not apply to uncertainties related to going concern situations, for which AU-C section 570, *The Auditor's Consideration of an Entity's Ability to Continue as a Going Concern* (AICPA, *Professional Standards*), provides guidance.

ISSUERS

7.32 Paragraph .11 of AS 3101 indicates that certain circumstances, although not affecting the auditor's unqualified opinion, may require that the auditor add an explanatory paragraph (or other explanatory language) to the standard report. These circumstances include substantial doubt about the entity's ability to continue as a going concern. AS 2415, *Consideration of an Entity's Ability to Continue as a Going Concern* (AICPA, *PCAOB Standards and Related Rules*) (formerly AU section 341) also describes the auditor's responsibility to evaluate whether there is substantial doubt about the entity's ability to continue as a going concern for a reasonable period of time and, when applicable, to consider the adequacy of financial statement disclosure and include an explanatory paragraph in the report to reflect his or her conclusions.

PRESENTATION AND DISCLOSURE EXCERPT

GOING CONCERN

7.33 PEABODY ENERGY CORPORATION (DEC)
REPORT OF INDEPENDENT REGISTERED PUBLIC ACCOUNTING FIRM

The Board of Directors and Stockholders of Peabody Energy Corporation

We have audited the accompanying consolidated balance sheets of Peabody Energy Corporation (the Company) as of December 31, 2015 and 2014, and the related consolidated statements of operations, comprehensive income, changes in stockholders' equity, and cash flows for each of the three years in the period ended December 31, 2015. Our audits also included the financial statement schedule listed in the Index at Item 15(a). These financial statements and schedule are the responsibility of the Company's management. Our responsibility is to express an opinion on these financial statements and schedule based on our audits.

We conducted our audits in accordance with the standards of the Public Company Accounting Oversight Board (United States). Those standards require that we plan and perform the audit to obtain reasonable assurance about whether the financial statements are free of material misstatement. An audit includes examining, on a test basis, evidence supporting the amounts and disclosures in the financial statements. An audit also includes assessing the accounting principles used and significant estimates made by management, as well as evaluating the overall financial statement presentation. We believe that our audits provide a reasonable basis for our opinion.

In our opinion, the financial statements referred to above present fairly, in all material respects, the consolidated financial position of Peabody Energy Corporation at December 31, 2015 and 2014, and the consolidated results of its operations and its cash flows for each of the three years in the period ended December 31, 2015, in conformity with U.S. generally accepted accounting principles. Also, in our opinion, the related financial statement schedule, when considered in relation to the basic financial statements taken as a whole, presents fairly, in all material respects the information set forth therein.

The accompanying consolidated financial statements have been prepared assuming the Company will continue as a going concern. As discussed in Note 1 to the financial statements, the Company incurred a substantial loss from operations and had negative cash flows from operating activities for the year ended December 31, 2015. The Company's operating plan indicates that it will continue to incur losses from operations, generate negative cash flows from operating activities and violate certain debt covenants during the year ended December 31, 2016. These projections and certain liquidity risks raise substantial doubt about the Company's ability to meet its obligations as they become due within one year after the date of this report and continue as a going concern. Management's plans in regards to these matters are also described in Note 1. The consolidated financial statements do not include any adjustments that might result from the outcome of this uncertainty, other than the reclassification of long-term debt and the related debt issuance costs to current liabilities and current assets, respectively.

We also have audited, in accordance with the standards of the Public Company Accounting Oversight Board (United States), Peabody Energy Corporation's internal control over financial reporting as of December 31, 2015, based on criteria established in Internal Control-Integrated Framework issued by the Committee of Sponsoring Organizations of the Treadway Commission (2013 framework), and our report dated March 15, 2016 expressed an unqualified opinion thereon.

/s/ Ernst & Young LLP
St. Louis, Missouri
March 15, 2016

NOTES TO CONSOLIDATED FINANCIAL STATEMENTS (in part)

(1) Summary of Significant Accounting Policies (in part)

Going Concern, Liquidity and Management's Plan

As of December 31, 2015, the Company's available liquidity was $1.2 billion, which was substantially comprised of $940.0 million available for borrowing under a $1.65 billion revolving credit facility (the 2013 Revolver, as more fully described in Note 12. "Long-term Debt") and $261.3 million of cash and cash equivalents. During February 2016, the Company borrowed the maximum amount available under the 2013 Revolver for general corporate purposes. As of March 11, 2016, our available liquidity declined to $0.9 billion, which consisted primarily of cash and cash equivalents.

The Company incurred a substantial loss from operations and had negative cash flows from operating activities for the year ended December 31, 2015. The Company's current operating plan indicates that it will continue to incur losses from operations and generate negative cash flows from operating activities. These projections and certain liquidity risks raise substantial doubt about whether the Company will meet its obligations as they become due within one year after the date of this report. The Company also elected to exercise the 30-day grace period with respect to a $21.1 million semi-annual interest payment due March 15, 2016 on its 6.50% Senior Notes due September 2020 and a $50.0 million semi-annual interest payment due March 15, 2016 on its 10.00% Senior Secured Second Lien Notes due March 2022, as provided for in the indentures governing these notes. Failure to pay these interest amounts on March 15, 2016 is not immediately an event of default under the indentures governing the Notes, but would become an event of default if the payment is not made within 30 days of such date. As a result of these factors, as well as the continued uncertainty around global coal fundamentals, the stagnated economic growth of certain major coal-importing nations, and the potential for significant additional regulatory requirements imposed on coal producers, among other matters, there exists substantial doubt whether the Company will be able to continue as a going concern.

The accompanying consolidated financial statements are prepared on a going concern basis and do not include any adjustments that might result from uncertainty about our ability to continue as a going concern, other than the reclassification of certain long-term debt and the related debt issuance costs to current liabilities and current assets, respectively. The report from the Company's independent registered public accounting firm on its consolidated financial statements included herein includes an uncertainty paragraph that summarizes the salient facts or conditions that raise substantial doubt about the Company's ability to continue as a going concern.

The Company is currently exploring alternatives for other sources of capital for ongoing liquidity needs and transactions to enhance its ability to comply with the financial covenants under its 2013 Credit Facility. The Company is working to improve its operating performance and its cash, liquidity and financial position. This includes: pursuing the sale of non-strategic surplus land and coal reserves as well as existing mines, particularly the sale of the Company's El Segundo and Lee Ranch coal mines and related assets located in New Mexico and its Twentymile Mine in Colorado; continuing to drive cost improvements across the company, attempting to negotiate alternative payment terms with creditors; maintaining its current level of self-bonding and/or replacing self-bonding with other financial instruments on reasonable terms; evaluating potential debt buybacks, debt exchanges and new financing to improve its liquidity and reduce its financial obligations; and obtaining waivers of going concern and financial covenant violations under the 2013 Credit Facility. The Company has engaged financial and other advisors to assist in those efforts.

However, there can be no assurance that management's plan to improve the Company's operating performance and financial position will be successful or that the Company will be able to obtain additional financing on commercially reasonable terms or at all. As a result, the Company's liquidity and ability to timely pay its obligations when due could be adversely affected. Furthermore, the Company's creditors may resist renegotiation or lengthening of payment and other terms, or could seek shorter payment terms, through legal action or otherwise. If the Company is not able to timely, successfully or efficiently implement the strategies that it is pursuing to improve its operating performance and financial position, obtain alternative sources of capital or otherwise meet its liquidity needs, the Company may need to voluntarily seek protection under Chapter 11 of the U.S. Bankruptcy Code.

The 2013 Credit Facility and the indentures governing our 6.00%, 6.25%, 6.50% and 7.875% Senior Notes and our Senior Secured Second Lien Notes and the instruments governing our capital leases include cross-acceleration provisions, whereby the debt owing under such agreements would be accelerated upon certain events, include a failure by us to service the debt in accordance with the relevant agreement. The 2013 Credit Facility and its governing documents contain covenants that, among other things, require the Company to furnish audited financial statements as soon as available, but in any event within 90 days after the fiscal year end without a "going concern" uncertainty paragraph in the auditor's opinion. The consolidated financial statements for the year ended December 31, 2015 included herein contain such a paragraph. In addition, the Company currently anticipates that its reported Adjusted EBITDA and other sources of earnings or adjustments used to calculate Consolidated EBITDA (if such other sources of earnings or adjustments do not include the proceeds of certain targeted asset sales) will fall below its Consolidated Net Cash Interest Charges during 2016, and it anticipates it will not comply with its financial covenants as of March 31, 2016. Absent waivers or cures, non-compliance with such covenants would constitute a default under the 2013 Credit Facility. It is possible the Company could obtain waivers from its lenders; however, since there is substantial doubt about whether the Company will meet its obligations as they become due within one year after the date of issuance of this report, the Company has classified debt that could become accelerated as current in the consolidated financial statements as of December 31, 2015. To the extent that the lenders demand payment, the Company will then write-off any remaining original issue discounts and any unamortized debt issuance costs related to the debt, which totaled $75.9 million at December 31, 2015.

Going Concern. In August 2014, the FASB issued disclosure guidance that requires management to evaluate, at each annual and interim reporting period, whether substantial doubt exists about an entity's ability to continue as a going concern and, if applicable, to provide related disclosures. As outlined by that guidance, substantial doubt about an entity's ability to continue as a going concern exists when relevant conditions and events, considered in the aggregate, indicate that it is probable that an entity will be unable to meet its obligations as they become due within one year after the date that the financial statements are issued (or are available to be issued). The new guidance will be effective for annual reporting periods ending after December 15, 2016 (the year ending December 31, 2016 for the Company) and interim periods thereafter, with early adoption permitted.

Lack of Consistency

PRESENTATION

NONISSUERS

7.34 As required by paragraph .08 of AU-C section 708, if there has been a change in accounting principles and the method of their application has a material effect on the financial statements, the auditor should include an emphasis-of-matter paragraph in the report. Such paragraph should follow the opinion paragraph and identify the nature of the change and refer the reader to the note in the financial statements that discusses the change in detail.

7.35 Paragraph .09 of AU-C section 708 states that the auditor should include an emphasis-of-matter paragraph relating to a change in accounting principle in reports on financial statements in the period of the change, and in subsequent periods, until the new accounting principle is applied in all periods presented. If the change in accounting principle is accounted for by retrospective application to the financial statements of all prior periods presented, the emphasis-of-matter paragraph is needed only in the period of such change.

ISSUERS

7.36 Although the information in paragraphs 7.34–.35 apply to issuers as well, AS 2820, *Evaluating Consistency of Financial Statements* (AICPA, *PCAOB Standards and Related Rules*), further states that the auditor should evaluate a change in accounting principle to determine whether the
- newly adopted accounting principle is a generally accepted accounting principle.
- method of accounting for the effect of the change is in conformity with GAAP.
- disclosures related to the accounting change are adequate.
- company has justified that the alternative accounting principle is preferable.

7.37 AS 2820 further states that if the auditor concludes that the criteria in paragraph 7.36 for a change in accounting principle are not met, the auditor should consider the matter to be a departure from GAAP and, if the effect of the change in accounting principle is material, should issue a qualified or an adverse opinion, as described in AS 3101.

7.38 In addition to a change in accounting principle, a lack of consistency can also be the result of a correction of a material misstatement in previously issued financial statements. Paragraphs .18A–C of AS 3101 state that the correction of a material misstatement in previously issued financial statements should be recognized in the auditor's report on the audited financial statements through the addition of an explanatory paragraph following the opinion paragraph.

7.39 The explanatory paragraph should include a
- statement that the previously issued financial statements have been restated for the correction of a misstatement in the respective period.
- reference to the company's disclosure of the correction of the misstatement.

7.40 This type of explanatory paragraph in the auditor's report should be included in reports on financial statements when the related financial statements are restated to correct the prior material misstatement. The paragraph need not be repeated in subsequent years.

PRESENTATION AND DISCLOSURE EXCERPTS

EMPLOYEE BENEFITS

7.41 FORD MOTOR COMPANY (DEC)
REPORT OF INDEPENDENT REGISTERED PUBLIC ACCOUNTING FIRM (in part)

To the Board of Directors and Stockholders of
Ford Motor Company

In our opinion, the accompanying consolidated balance sheets and the related consolidated statements of income, comprehensive income, equity and cash flows present fairly, in all material respects, the financial position of Ford Motor Company and its subsidiaries at December 31, 2015 and December 31, 2014, and the results of their operations and their cash flows for each of the three years in the period ended December 31, 2015 in conformity with accounting principles generally accepted in the United States of America. In addition, in our opinion, the financial statement schedule listed in the index appearing under Item 15(a)(2) presents fairly, in all material respects, the information set forth therein when read in conjunction with the related consolidated financial statements. Also in our opinion, the Company maintained, in all material respects, effective internal control over financial reporting as of December 31, 2015, based on criteria established in *Internal Control—Integrated Framework (2013)* issued by the Committee of Sponsoring Organizations of the Treadway Commission (COSO). The Company's management is responsible for these financial statements and the financial statement schedule, for maintaining effective internal control over financial reporting and for its assessment of the effectiveness of internal control over financial reporting, included in Management's Report on Internal Control over Financial Reporting appearing under Item 9A. Our responsibility is to express opinions on these financial statements, on the financial statement schedule, and on the Company's internal control over financial reporting based on our integrated audits. We conducted our audits in accordance with the standards of the Public Company Accounting Oversight Board (United States). Those standards require that we plan and perform the audits to obtain reasonable assurance about whether the financial statements are free of material misstatement and whether effective internal control over financial reporting was maintained in all material respects. Our audits of the financial statements included examining, on a test basis, evidence supporting the amounts and disclosures in the financial statements, assessing the accounting principles used and significant estimates made by management, and evaluating the overall financial statement presentation. Our audit of internal control over financial reporting included obtaining an understanding of internal control over financial reporting, assessing the risk that a material weakness exists, and testing and evaluating the design and operating effectiveness of internal control based on the assessed risk. Our audits also included performing such other procedures as we considered necessary in the circumstances. We believe that our audits provide a reasonable basis for our opinions.

As discussed in Note 1 to the consolidated financial statements, the Company changed the manner in which it accounts for defined benefit pension and other postretirement employee benefit plans in 2015.

The accompanying sector balance sheets and the related sector statements of income and of cash flows, included as supplemental information, have been subjected to audit procedures performed in conjunction with the audit of the Company's consolidated financial statements. The supplemental information is the responsibility of the Company's management. Our audit procedures included determining whether the supplemental information reconciles to the financial statements or the underlying accounting and other records, as applicable, and performing procedures to test the completeness and accuracy of the information presented in the supplemental information. In our opinion, the sector balance sheets and the related sector statements of income and of cash flows are fairly stated, in all material respects, in relation to the consolidated financial statements as a whole.

A company's internal control over financial reporting is a process designed to provide reasonable assurance regarding the reliability of financial reporting and the preparation of financial statements for external purposes in accordance with generally accepted accounting principles. A company's internal control over financial reporting includes those policies and procedures that (i) pertain to the maintenance of records that, in reasonable detail, accurately and fairly reflect the transactions and dispositions of the assets of the company; (ii) provide reasonable assurance that transactions are recorded as necessary to permit preparation of financial statements in accordance with generally accepted accounting principles, and that receipts and expenditures of the company are being made only in accordance with authorizations of management and directors of the company; and (iii) provide reasonable assurance regarding prevention or timely detection of unauthorized acquisition, use, or disposition of the company's assets that could have a material effect on the financial statements.

Because of its inherent limitations, internal control over financial reporting may not prevent or detect misstatements. Also, projections of any evaluation of effectiveness to future periods are subject to the risk that controls may become inadequate because of changes in conditions, or that the degree of compliance with the policies or procedures may deteriorate.

/s/ PricewaterhouseCoopers LLP
PricewaterhouseCoopers LLP
Detroit, Michigan
February 11, 2016

NOTES TO THE FINANCIAL STATEMENTS (in part)

Note 1. Presentation (in part)

Change in Accounting

Pension and Other Postretirement Employee Benefits ("OPEB"). On December 31, 2015, we adopted a change in accounting method for certain components of expense related to our defined benefit pension and OPEB plans. Under the new method, we recognize remeasurement gains and losses immediately in net income and use fair value to calculate the expected return on plan assets. Historically, we recognized remeasurement gains and losses as a component of *Accumulated other comprehensive income/(loss)* and amortized them as a component of net periodic benefit cost, subject to a corridor, over the remaining service period of our active employees. In addition, we previously used a market-related value of plan assets that recognized changes in fair value over time to calculate the expected return on plan assets.

We believe this change in accounting method is preferable as it better recognizes the current performance of our pension and OPEB plans in our net income in the year incurred. Additionally, our segment reporting shown in Note 24 now provides better transparency into the underlying operating results of Ford's Automotive business units. We have retrospectively applied this change in accounting method to all prior periods. As of January 1, 2013, the cumulative effect of the change resulted in a decrease of $18 billion in *Retained earnings* and an increase of $18 billion in *Accumulated other comprehensive income/(loss)*, both components of total equity in our consolidated and sector balance sheets.

The effect of the change related to our defined benefit pension and OPEB plans on our consolidated financial statements at December 31 was as follows (in millions, except per share amounts):

	2015	2014			2013		
	Effect of Change Higher/(Lower)	As Revised	Previously Reported	Effect of Change Higher/(Lower)	As Revised	Previously Reported	Effect of Change Higher/(Lower)
Income statement							
Automotive cost of sales	$(581)	$125,025	$123,516	$1,509	$120,190	$125,195	$(5,005)
Selling, administrative, and other expenses	(337)	15,716	14,117	1,599	10,850	13,176	(2,326)
Income before income taxes	918	1,234	4,342	(3,108)	14,371	7,040	7,331
Provision for/(Benefit from) income taxes	293	4	1,156	(1,152)	2,425	(135)	2,560
Net income	625	1,230	3,186	(1,956)	11,946	7,175	4,771
Net income attributable to Ford Motor Company	625	1,231	3,187	(1,956)	11,953	7,182	4,771
Basic earnings per share attributable to Ford Motor Company	0.16	0.31	0.81	(0.50)	3.04	1.83	1.21
Diluted earnings per share attributable to Ford Motor Company	0.15	0.31	0.80	(0.49)	2.94	1.77	1.17

	2015	2014		
	Effect of Change Higher/(Lower)	As Revised	Previously Reported	Effect of Change Higher/(Lower)
Balance sheet				
Inventories	$ (61)	$ 7,870	$ 7,866	$ 4
Deferred income taxes, net	79	13,454	13,069	385
Other assets	—	6,052	6,353	(301)
Other liabilities and deferred revenue	2	44,032	43,577	455
Retained earnings/(Accumulated deficit)	(14,509)	9,422	24,556	(15,134)
Accumulated other comprehensive income/(loss)	14,525	(5,265)	(20,032)	14,767

	2015	2014			2013		
	Effect of Change Higher/(Lower)	As Revised	Previously Reported	Effect of Change Higher/(Lower)	As Revised	Previously Reported	Effect of Change Higher/(Lower)
Cash Flows from Operating Activities							
Net income	$ 625	$ 1,230	$ 3,186	$(1,956)	$11,946	$ 7,175	$ 4,771
Pension and OPEB expense	(997)	4,429	1,249	3,180	(4,930)	2,543	(7,473)
Provision for deferred income taxes	293	(94)	1,063	(1,157)	1,585	(848)	2,433
Decrease/(Increase) in accounts receivable and other assets	—	(2,896)	(2,897)	1	(1,913)	(2,040)	127
Decrease/(Increase) in inventory	65	(936)	(875)	(61)	(437)	(572)	135
Increase/(Decrease) in accounts payable and accrued and other liabilities	14	5,729	5,734	(5)	1,232	1,231	1
Other	—	(467)	(465)	(2)	(706)	(712)	6

Total cash flows from operating activities was unchanged.

In the first quarter of 2015, we recorded a $782 million adjustment to correct for an understatement in the year-end 2014 valuation of our U.S. pension benefit obligation. The adjustment reduced *Other assets* by $301 million and increased *Other liabilities and deferred revenue* by $481 million. The resulting after-tax adjustment to *Other comprehensive income* was a loss of $508 million. We originally determined this adjustment to be immaterial to our current or prior period financial statements. As a result of the change in accounting described above and the retrospective application to 2014, this after-tax loss is now reported in the revised 2014 *Net income* and also reflected in the related balance sheet amounts as of December 31, 2014.

MARKETABLE SECURITIES

7.42 3M COMPANY (DEC)
REPORT OF INDEPENDENT REGISTERED PUBLIC ACCOUNTING FIRM

To the Stockholders and Board of Directors of 3M Company

In our opinion, the consolidated financial statements listed in the accompanying index present fairly, in all material respects, the financial position of 3M Company and its subsidiaries (the "Company") at December 31, 2015 and 2014, and the results of their operations and their cash flows for each of the three years in the period ended December 31, 2015 in conformity with accounting principles generally accepted in the United States of America. Also in our opinion, the Company maintained, in all material respects, effective internal control over financial reporting as of December 31, 2015, based on criteria established in *Internal Control—Integrated Framework (2013)* issued by the Committee of Sponsoring Organizations of the Treadway Commission (COSO). The Company's management is responsible for these financial statements, for maintaining effective internal control over financial reporting and for its assessment of the effectiveness of internal control over financial reporting, included in the accompanying Management's Report on Internal Control over Financial Reporting. Our responsibility is to express opinions on these financial statements and on the Company's internal control over financial reporting based on our integrated audits. We conducted our audits in accordance with the standards of the Public Company Accounting Oversight Board (United States). Those standards require that we plan and perform the audits to obtain reasonable assurance about whether the financial statements are free of material misstatement and whether effective internal control over financial reporting was maintained in all material respects. Our audits of the financial statements included examining, on a test basis, evidence supporting the amounts and disclosures in the financial statements, assessing the accounting principles used and significant estimates made by management, and evaluating the overall financial statement presentation. Our audit of internal control over financial reporting included obtaining an understanding of internal control over financial reporting, assessing the risk that a material weakness exists, and testing and evaluating the design and operating effectiveness of internal control based on the assessed risk. Our audits also included performing such other procedures as we considered necessary in the circumstances. We believe that our audits provide a reasonable basis for our opinions.

As discussed in Note 1 to the consolidated financial statements, the Company changed the manner in which it accounts for marketable securities and deferred tax assets and liabilities in 2015.

A company's internal control over financial reporting is a process designed to provide reasonable assurance regarding the reliability of financial reporting and the preparation of financial statements for external purposes in accordance with generally accepted accounting principles. A company's internal control over financial reporting includes those policies and procedures that (i) pertain to the maintenance of records that, in reasonable detail, accurately and fairly reflect the transactions and dispositions of the assets of the company; (ii) provide reasonable assurance that transactions are recorded as necessary to permit preparation of financial statements in accordance with generally accepted accounting principles, and that receipts and expenditures of the company are being made only in accordance with authorizations of management and directors of the company; and (iii) provide reasonable assurance regarding prevention or timely detection of unauthorized acquisition, use, or disposition of the company's assets that could have a material effect on the financial statements.

Because of its inherent limitations, internal control over financial reporting may not prevent or detect misstatements. Also, projections of any evaluation of effectiveness to future periods are subject to the risk that controls may become inadequate because of changes in conditions, or that the degree of compliance with the policies or procedures may deteriorate.

As described in Management's Report on Internal Control over Financial Reporting, management has excluded Capital Safety Group S.A.R.L. ("Capital Safety") and Polypore International, Inc.'s Separations Media Business ("Polypore Separations Media") from its assessment of internal control over financial reporting as of December 31, 2015 because these businesses were acquired by the Company in purchase business combinations during 2015. We have also excluded Capital Safety and Polypore Separations Media from our audit of internal control over financial reporting. Capital Safety is a wholly-owned subsidiary of the Company and the Company acquired the assets and liabilities of Polypore Separations Media whose total assets and total net sales, in the aggregate, represent less than 2 percent and less than 1 percent, respectively, of the related consolidated financial statement amounts as of and for the year ended December 31, 2015.

/s/ PricewaterhouseCoopers LLP
PricewaterhouseCoopers LLP
Minneapolis, Minnesota
February 11, 2016

NOTES TO CONSOLIDATED FINANCIAL STATEMENTS (in part)

Note 1. Significant Accounting Policies (in part)

Basis of presentation: Certain balances relative to prior periods have been reclassified to conform to December 31, 2015 presentation in connection with the following, each of which is further discussed in the indicated section of Note 1:
- Change in method of classification of certain marketable securities previously classified as non-current to current as further discussed in the Marketable securities section; and
- Adoption of Accounting Standards Update (ASU) No. 2015-03, *Simplifying the Presentation of Debt Issuance Costs*, and ASU No. 2015-17, *Balance Sheet Classification of Deferred Taxes*, in the fourth quarter of 2015 on a retrospective basis as further discussed in the New Accounting Pronouncements section.

Marketable securities: Effective December 31, 2015, the Company changed the method of classification of certain securities previously classified as non-current to current. This new method classifies these securities as current or non-current based on the nature of the securities and availability for use in current operations while the prior classification was based on management's intended holding period, the security's maturity date and liquidity considerations based on market conditions. The Company believes this method is preferable because it is consistent with how the Company manages its capital structure and liquidity. The prior period balance has been reclassified to conform to the current year presentation:

(Millions)	December 31, 2014		
	Previously Reported	Impact	As Adjusted
Marketable securities—current	$ 626	$ 813	$1,439
Marketable securities—non-current	828	(813)	15
Total marketable securities	$1,454	$ —	$1,454

3M reviews impairments associated with its marketable securities in accordance with the measurement guidance provided by ASC 320, *Investments-Debt and Equity Securities*, when determining the classification of the impairment as "temporary" or "other-than-temporary". A temporary impairment charge results in an unrealized loss being recorded in the other comprehensive income component of shareholders' equity. Such an unrealized loss does not reduce net income for the applicable accounting period because the loss is not viewed as other-than-temporary. The factors evaluated to differentiate between temporary and other-than-temporary include the projected future cash flows, credit ratings actions, and assessment of the credit quality of the underlying collateral, as well as other factors.

Note 9. Marketable Securities

The Company invests in agency securities, corporate securities, asset-backed securities and other securities. The following is a summary of amounts recorded on the Consolidated Balance Sheet for marketable securities (current and non-current).

(Millions)	December 31, 2015	December 31, 2014
U.S. government agency securities	$ —	$ 108
Foreign government agency securities	10	95
Corporate debt securities	10	619
Commercial paper	12	—
Certificates of deposit/time deposits	26	41
U.S. treasury securities	—	38
U.S. municipal securities	3	—
Asset-backed securities:		
Automobile loan related:	26	282
Credit card related	10	162
Equipment lease related	2	48
Other	19	46
Asset-backed securities total	57	538
Current marketable securities	$118	$1,439
U.S. municipal securities	$9	$15
Non-current marketable securities	$9	$15
Total marketable securities	$127	$1,454

Classification of marketable securities as current or non-current is based on the nature of the securities and availability for use in current operations. At December 31, 2015 and 2014, gross unrealized gains and/or losses (pre-tax) were not material. Refer to Note 6 for a table that provides the net realized gains (losses) related to sales or impairments of debt and equity securities, which includes marketable securities. The gross amounts of the realized gains or losses were not material. Cost of securities sold use the first in, first out (FIFO) method. Since these marketable securities are classified as available-for-sale securities, changes in fair value will flow through other comprehensive income, with amounts reclassified out of other comprehensive income into earnings upon sale or "other-than-temporary" impairment.

3M reviews impairments associated with its marketable securities in accordance with the measurement guidance provided by ASC 320, *Investments-Debt and Equity Securities*, when determining the classification of the impairment as "temporary" or "other-than-temporary". A temporary impairment charge results in an unrealized loss being recorded in the other comprehensive income component of shareholders' equity. Such an unrealized loss does not reduce net income attributable to 3M for the applicable accounting period because the loss is not viewed as other-than-temporary. The factors evaluated to differentiate between temporary and other-than-temporary include the projected future cash flows, credit ratings actions, and assessment of the credit quality of the underlying collateral, as well as other factors.

The balance at December 31, 2015, for marketable securities by contractual maturity are shown below. Actual maturities may differ from contractual maturities because the issuers of the securities may have the right to prepay obligations without prepayment penalties.

(Millions)	December 31, 2015
Due in one year or less	$ 52
Due after one year through five years	74
Due after five years through ten years	1
Due after ten years	—
Total marketable securities	$127

3M has a diversified marketable securities portfolio of $127 million as of December 31, 2015. Within this portfolio, current asset-backed securities (estimated fair value of $57 million) primarily include interests in automobile loans, credit cards and equipment leases. 3M's investment policy allows investments in asset-backed securities with minimum credit ratings of Aa2 by Moody's Investors Service or AA by Standard & Poor's or Fitch Ratings or DBRS. Asset-backed securities must be rated by at least two of the aforementioned rating agencies, one of which must be Moody's Investors Service or Standard & Poor's. At December 31, 2015, all asset-backed security investments were in compliance with this policy. Approximately 75.8 percent of all asset-backed security investments were rated AAA or A-1 + by Standard & Poor's and/or Aaa or P-1 by Moody's Investors Service and/or AAA or F1 + by Fitch Ratings. Interest rate risk and credit risk related to the underlying collateral may impact the value of investments in asset-backed securities, while factors such as general conditions in the overall credit market and the nature of the underlying collateral may affect the liquidity of investments in asset-backed securities. 3M does not currently expect risk related to its holding in asset-backed securities to materially impact its financial condition or liquidity.

DEFERRED TAX LIABILITIES AND ASSETS

7.43 ABBOTT LABORATORIES (DEC)
REPORT OF INDEPENDENT REGISTERED PUBLIC ACCOUNTING FIRM

The Board of Directors and Shareholders of Abbott Laboratories:

We have audited the accompanying consolidated balance sheets of Abbott Laboratories and subsidiaries as of December 31, 2015 and 2014, and the related consolidated statements of earnings, comprehensive income, shareholders' investment and cash flows for each of the two years in the period ended December 31, 2015. These financial statements are the responsibility of the Company's management. Our responsibility is to express an opinion on these financial statements based on our audits.

We conducted our audits in accordance with the standards of the Public Company Accounting Oversight Board (United States). Those standards require that we plan and perform the audit to obtain reasonable assurance about whether the financial statements are free of material misstatement. An audit includes examining, on a test basis, evidence supporting the amounts and disclosures in the financial statements. An audit also includes assessing the accounting principles used and significant estimates made by management, as well as evaluating the overall financial statement presentation. We believe that our audits provide a reasonable basis for our opinion.

In our opinion, the financial statements referred to above present fairly, in all material respects, the consolidated financial position of Abbott Laboratories and subsidiaries at December 31, 2015 and 2014, and the consolidated results of their operations and their cash flows for each of the two years in the period ended December 31, 2015, in conformity with U.S. generally accepted accounting principles.

As discussed in Note 1 to the consolidated financial statements, the Company changed its method for classifying deferred tax liabilities and assets as a result of the adoption of the amendments to the FASB Accounting Standards Codification resulting from Accounting Standards Update No. 2015-17, "Income Taxes (Topic 740)," effective December 31, 2015.

We also have audited, in accordance with the standards of the Public Company Accounting Oversight Board (United States), Abbott Laboratories and subsidiaries' internal control over financial reporting as of December 31, 2015, based on criteria established in Internal Control—Integrated Framework issued by the Committee of Sponsoring Organizations of the Treadway Commission (2013 framework), and our report dated February 19, 2016 expressed an unqualified opinion thereon.

/s/ Ernst & Young LLP
Chicago, Illinois
February 19, 2016

CONSOLIDATED BALANCE SHEET (in part)

(dollars in millions)

	December 31	
	2015	**2014**
Assets		
Current Assets:		
Cash and cash equivalents	$ 5,001	$ 4,063
Investments, primarily bank time deposits and U.S. treasury bills	1,124	397
Trade receivables, less allowances of — 2015: $337; 2014: $310	3,418	3,586
Inventories:		
Finished products	1,744	1,807
Work in process	316	278
Materials	539	558
Total inventories	2,599	2,643
Other prepaid expenses and receivables	1,908	1,975
Current assets held for disposition	105	892
Total Current Assets	14,155	13,556
Investments	4,041	229
Property and Equipment, at Cost:		
Land	432	457
Buildings	2,769	2,968
Equipment	8,254	8,480
Construction in progress	928	727
	12,383	12,632

(continued)

	December 31	
	2015	**2014**
Less: accumulated depreciation and amortization	6,653	6,697
Net Property and Equipment	5,730	5,935
Intangible Assets, net of amortization	5,562	6,198
Goodwill	9,638	10,067
Deferred Income Taxes and Other Assets	2,119	3,288
Non-current Assets Held for Disposition	2	1,934
	$41,247	$41,207
Liabilities and Shareholders' Investment (in part)		
Current Liabilities:		
Short-term borrowings	$3,127	$ 4,382
Trade accounts payable	1,081	1,064
Salaries, wages and commissions	746	776
Other accrued liabilities	3,043	2,878
Dividends payable	383	362
Income taxes payable	430	270
Current portion of long-term debt	3	55
Current liabilities held for disposition	373	680
Total Current Liabilities	9,186	10,467
Long-term Debt	5,871	3,393
Post-employment Obligations and other long-term liabilities	4,864	5,600
Non-current liabilities held for disposition	—	108
Commitments and Contingencies		

NOTES TO CONSOLIDATED FINANCIAL STATEMENTS (in part)

Note 1—Summary of Significant Accounting Policies (in part)

INCOME TAXES—Deferred income taxes are provided for the tax effect of differences between the tax bases of assets and liabilities and their reported amounts in the financial statements at the enacted statutory rate to be in effect when the taxes are paid. U.S. income taxes are provided on those earnings of foreign subsidiaries which are intended to be remitted to the parent company. Deferred income taxes are not provided on undistributed earnings reinvested indefinitely in foreign subsidiaries as working capital and plant and equipment. Interest and penalties on income tax obligations are included in taxes on income.

In November 2015, the FASB issued ASU 2015-17, *Balance Sheet Classification of Deferred Taxes*, which requires entities to classify all deferred tax assets and liabilities as non-current on the balance sheet. The standard may be adopted on either a prospective or retrospective basis. The standard is effective for fiscal years beginning after December 15, 2016, and early adoption is permitted. Effective December 31, 2015, Abbott adopted ASU 2015-17 and applied the new standard retrospectively. As a result of applying ASU 2015-17 to the previously reported Consolidated Balance Sheet as of December 31, 2014, Deferred income taxes within the Total Current Assets line decreased and the Deferred income taxes and other assets line increased by approximately $1.7 billion, respectively; Other accrued liabilities within the Total Current Liabilities line decreased by $65 million and the Post-employment obligations and other long-term liabilities line increased by $12 million. Reclassification of the deferred tax balances from current to noncurrent affected the netting of these balances as a deferred tax asset or liability in various jurisdictions.

DEBT ISSUANCE COSTS

7.44 DOMINO'S PIZZA, INC. (DEC)
REPORT OF INDEPENDENT REGISTERED PUBLIC ACCOUNTING FIRM

To the Stockholders and Board of Directors of Domino's Pizza, Inc.:

In our opinion, the consolidated financial statements listed in the index appearing under Item 15(a)(1) present fairly, in all material respects, the financial position of Domino's Pizza, Inc. and its subsidiaries at January 3, 2016 and December 28, 2014, and the results of their operations and their cash flows for each of the three years in the period ended January 3, 2016 in conformity with accounting principles generally accepted in the United States of America. In addition, in our opinion, the financial statement schedules listed in the index appearing under Item 15(a)(2) present fairly, in all material respects, the information set forth therein when read in conjunction with the related consolidated financial statements. Also in our opinion, the Company maintained, in all material respects, effective internal control over financial reporting as of January 3, 2016, based on criteria established in Internal Control – Integrated Framework (2013) issued by the

Committee of Sponsoring Organizations of the Treadway Commission (COSO). The Company's management is responsible for these financial statements and financial statement schedules, for maintaining effective internal control over financial reporting and for its assessment of the effectiveness of internal control over financial reporting, included in Management's Annual Report on Internal Control over Financial Reporting, appearing under Item 9(A). Our responsibility is to express opinions on these financial statements, on the financial statement schedules, and on the Company's internal control over financial reporting based on our integrated audits. We conducted our audits in accordance with the standards of the Public Company Accounting Oversight Board (United States). Those standards require that we plan and perform the audits to obtain reasonable assurance about whether the financial statements are free of material misstatement and whether effective internal control over financial reporting was maintained in all material respects. Our audits of the financial statements included examining, on a test basis, evidence supporting the amounts and disclosures in the financial statements, assessing the accounting principles used and significant estimates made by management, and evaluating the overall financial statement presentation. Our audit of internal control over financial reporting included obtaining an understanding of internal control over financial reporting, assessing the risk that a material weakness exists, and testing and evaluating the design and operating effectiveness of internal control based on the assessed risk. Our audits also included performing such other procedures as we considered necessary in the circumstances. We believe that our audits provide a reasonable basis for our opinions.

As discussed in Note 1 to the consolidated financial statements, the Company changed the manner in which it accounts for the classification of debt issuance costs and deferred tax assets and liabilities.

A company's internal control over financial reporting is a process designed to provide reasonable assurance regarding the reliability of financial reporting and the preparation of financial statements for external purposes in accordance with generally accepted accounting principles. A company's internal control over financial reporting includes those policies and procedures that (i) pertain to the maintenance of records that, in reasonable detail, accurately and fairly reflect the transactions and dispositions of the assets of the company; (ii) provide reasonable assurance that transactions are recorded as necessary to permit preparation of financial statements in accordance with generally accepted accounting principles, and that receipts and expenditures of the company are being made only in accordance with authorizations of management and directors of the company; and (iii) provide reasonable assurance regarding prevention or timely detection of unauthorized acquisition, use, or disposition of the company's assets that could have a material effect on the financial statements.

Because of its inherent limitations, internal control over financial reporting may not prevent or detect misstatements. Also, projections of any evaluation of effectiveness to future periods are subject to the risk that controls may become inadequate because of changes in conditions, or that the degree of compliance with the policies or procedures may deteriorate.

/s/ PricewaterhouseCoopers LLP
Detroit, Michigan
February 25, 2016

CONSOLIDATED BALANCE SHEETS (in part)

(In thousands, except share and per share amounts)

	January 3, 2016	December 28, 2014
Liabilities and Stockholders' Deficit (in part)		
Current Liabilities:		
Current portion of long-term debt	$ 59,333	$ 565
Accounts payable	106,927	86,552
Accrued compensation	32,999	23,618
Accrued interest	20,459	14,008
Insurance reserves	17,597	14,465
Dividends payable	557	14,351
Advertising fund liabilities	99,159	72,055
Other accrued liabilities	38,952	39,994
Total current liabilities	375,983	265,608
Long-Term Liabilities:		
Long-term debt, less current portion	2,181,460	1,500,599
Insurance reserves	23,314	26,951
Deferred income taxes	—	5,588
Other accrued liabilities	19,339	17,052
Total long-term liabilities	2,224,113	1,550,190
Total liabilities	2,600,096	1,815,798

(1) Description of Business and Summary of Significant Accounting Policies (in part)

Debt Issuance Costs

Debt issuance costs primarily include the expenses incurred by the Company as part of the 2012 and 2015 Recapitalizations (Note 4). Amortization is provided on a straight-line basis (which is materially consistent with the effective interest method) over the expected term of the respective debt instrument to which the costs relate and is included in interest expense.

In connection with the 2012 Recapitalization, the Company recorded $39.9 million of debt issuance costs. In connection with the 2015 Recapitalization, the Company wrote-off approximately $6.9 million of these costs in connection with the extinguishment of $551 million of the 2012 Fixed Rate Notes. The remaining debt issuance costs related to the 2012 Recapitalization are being amortized into interest expense over the seven-year expected term of the 2012 Fixed Rate Notes. Additionally, in connection with the 2015 Recapitalization, the Company recorded $17.4 million of debt issuance costs, which are being amortized into interest expense over the five and ten-year expected terms of the 2015 Fixed Rate Notes.

In connection with the aforementioned write-off of debt issuance costs and scheduled principal payments of its Fixed Rate Notes (Note 4), the Company expensed debt issuance costs of approximately $6.9 million, $0.2 million and $0.5 million in 2015, 2014 and 2013, respectively. Debt issuance cost expense, including the aforementioned amounts, was approximately $12.4 million, $5.7 million and $6.1 million in 2015, 2014 and 2013, respectively.

New Accounting Pronouncements (in part)

In April 2015, the FASB issued ASU 2015-03, *Simplifying the Presentation of Debt Issuance Costs*, ("ASU 2015-03"). ASU 2015-03 requires that debt issuance costs be presented as a direct deduction from the carrying amount of the related debt liability, consistent with the presentation of debt discounts. Prior to the issuance of ASU 2015-03, debt issuance costs were required to be presented as deferred charge assets, separate from the related debt liability. ASU 2015-03 does not change the recognition and measurement requirements for debt issuance costs. The Company early-adopted ASU 2015-03 as of the end of fiscal 2015, and applied its provisions retrospectively. The adoption of ASU 2015-03 resulted in the reclassification of $27.9 million and $22.9 million of unamortized debt issuance costs related to the Company's Fixed Rate Notes from other non-current assets to long-term debt within its consolidated balance sheets as of both January 3, 2016 and December 28, 2014, respectively (refer to Note 4 of the financial statements for additional detail). Other than this reclassification, the adoption of ASU 2015-03 did not have an impact on the Company's consolidated financial statements.

(4) Recapitalizations and Financing Arrangements (in part)

Debt Issuance Costs and Transaction-Related Expenses

In connection with the 2012 Recapitalization, the Company recorded $39.9 million of debt issuance costs. In connection with the 2015 Recapitalization, the Company wrote-off approximately $6.9 million of these costs in connection with the extinguishment of $551 million of the 2012 Fixed Rate Notes. The remaining debt issuance costs related to the 2012 Recapitalization are being amortized into interest expense over the seven-year expected term of the 2012 Fixed Rate Notes. Additionally, in connection with the 2015 Recapitalization, the Company recorded $17.4 million of debt issuance costs, which are being amortized into interest expense over the five and ten-year expected terms of the 2015 Fixed Rate Notes.

During fiscal 2015 and in connection with the 2015 Recapitalization, the Company incurred approximately $8.1 million of net expenses. This consisted primarily of the aforementioned $6.9 million net write-off of deferred financing fees. The Company also incurred approximately $0.4 million of interest expense on the 2012 Fixed Rate Notes subsequent to the closing of the 2015 Recapitalization but prior to the repayment of the 2012 Fixed Rate Notes, resulting in the payment of interest on both the full amount of the 2012 and 2015 Fixed Rate Notes for a short period of time. Further, the Company incurred $0.9 million of other net 2015 Recapitalization-related general and administrative expenses, including legal and professional fees.

Consolidated Long-Term Debt

At January 3, 2016 and December 28, 2014, consolidated long-term debt consisted of the following (in thousands):

	2015	2014
5.216% Class A-2 Notes; expected repayment date January 2019; legal final maturity January 2042	$ 962,719	$1,521,844
3.484% Class A-2-I Notes; expected repayment date October 2020; legal final maturity October 2045	500,000	—
4.474% Class A-2-II Notes; expected repayment date October 2025; legal final maturity October 2045	800,000	—
2012 Variable Funding Notes	—	—
2015 Variable Funding Notes	—	—
Capital lease obligations	5,996	2,267
Debt issuance costs, net of accumulated amortization of $14.7 million in 2015 and $17.0 million in 2014	(27,922)	(22,947)
Total debt	2,240,793	1,501,164
Less—current portion	59,333	565
Consolidated long-term debt, net of debt issuance costs	$2,181,460	$1,500,599

Emphasis of a Matter

PRESENTATION

NONISSUERS

7.45 Paragraph .06 of AU-C section 706 explains that if the auditor considers it necessary to draw users' attention to a matter appropriately presented or disclosed in the financial statements, the auditor should include an emphasis-of-matter paragraph. Paragraph .07 of AU-C section 706 states that the emphasis-of-matter paragraph should

- be included immediately after the opinion paragraph in the auditor's report,
- use the heading "Emphasis of Matter" or other appropriate heading,
- include in the paragraph a clear reference to the matter being emphasized and to where relevant disclosures that fully describe the matter can be found in the financial statements, and
- indicate that the auditor's opinion is not modified with respect to the matter emphasized.

7.46 Other-matter paragraphs should be included in the auditor's report when the auditor considers it necessary to communicate matters other than those that are presented or disclosed in the financial statements, as described in paragraph .08 of AU-C section 706. The paragraph should be included immediately after the opinion paragraph and any emphasis-of-matter paragraph or elsewhere in the auditor's report if the content of the other-matter paragraph is relevant to the "Other Reporting Responsibilities" section.

ISSUERS

7.47 Paragraph .19 of AS 3101 states the following:

In any report on financial statements, the auditor may emphasize a matter regarding the financial statements. Such explanatory information should be presented in a separate paragraph of the auditor's report. Phrases such as "with the foregoing [following] explanation" should not be used in the opinion paragraph if an emphasis paragraph is included in the auditor's report. Emphasis paragraphs are never required; they may be added solely at the auditor's discretion. Examples of matters the auditor may wish to emphasize are—

- That the entity is a component of a larger business enterprise.
- That the entity has had significant transactions with related parties.
- Unusually important subsequent events.
- Accounting matters, other than those involving a change or changes in accounting principles, affecting the comparability of the financial statements with those of the preceding period.

PRESENTATION AND DISCLOSURE EXCERPT

EMPHASIS OF A MATTER

7.48 FIDELITY NATIONAL INFORMATION SERVICES, INC. (DEC)
REPORT OF INDEPENDENT REGISTERED PUBLIC ACCOUNTING FIRM

The Board of Directors and Stockholders
Fidelity National Information Services, Inc.:

We have audited the accompanying consolidated balance sheets of Fidelity National Information Services, Inc. and subsidiaries (the Company) as of December 31, 2015 and 2014, and the related consolidated statements of earnings, comprehensive earnings, equity, and cash flows for each of the years in the three-year period ended December 31, 2015. These consolidated financial statements are the responsibility of the Company's management. Our responsibility is to express an opinion on these consolidated financial statements based on our audits.

We conducted our audits in accordance with the standards of the Public Company Accounting Oversight Board (United States). Those standards require that we plan and perform the audit to obtain reasonable assurance about whether the financial statements are free of material misstatement. An audit includes examining, on a test basis, evidence supporting the amounts and disclosures in the financial statements. An audit also includes assessing the accounting principles used and significant estimates made by management, as well as evaluating the overall financial statement presentation. We believe that our audits provide a reasonable basis for our opinion.

In our opinion, the consolidated financial statements referred to above present fairly, in all material respects, the financial position of Fidelity National Information Services, Inc. and subsidiaries as of December 31, 2015 and 2014, and the results of their operations and their cash flows for each of the years in the three-year period ended December 31, 2015, in conformity with U.S. generally accepted accounting principles.

We also have audited, in accordance with the standards of the Public Company Accounting Oversight Board (United States), Fidelity National Information Services, Inc.'s and subsidiaries' internal control over financial reporting as of December 31, 2015, based on criteria established in *Internal Control—Integrated Framework (2013)* issued by the Committee of Sponsoring Organizations of the Treadway Commission (COSO), and our report dated February 26, 2016, expressed an unqualified opinion on the effectiveness of the Company's internal control over financial reporting.

As discussed in note 6 to the consolidated financial statements, the Company acquired SunGard on November 30, 2015.

/s/ KPMG LLP
February 26, 2016
Jacksonville, Florida
Certified Public Accountants

NOTES TO CONSOLIDATED FINANCIAL STATEMENTS (in part)

(1) Basis of Presentation (in part)

On August 12, 2015, FIS and certain of its wholly owned subsidiaries entered into an Agreement and Plan of Merger with SunGard and SunGard Capital Corp. II (collectively "SunGard") pursuant to which, through a series of mergers, FIS acquired SunGard (collectively the "SunGard acquisition" or the "Acquisition"). FIS completed the SunGard acquisition on November 30, 2015, and SunGard's results of operations and financial position are included in the Consolidated Financial Statements and within the GFS segment from and after the date of acquisition.

(6) Acquisitions (in part)

SunGard

FIS completed the SunGard acquisition on November 30, 2015, and SunGard's results of operations and financial position are included in the Consolidated Financial Statements from and after the date of acquisition. The SunGard acquisition increased our existing portfolio of solutions to automate a wide range of complex business processes for financial services institutions and corporate and government treasury departments, adding trading, securities operations, administering investment portfolios, accounting for investment assets, and managing risk and compliance requirements. In addition, the Acquisition now enables us to provide software and technology services to domestic governments at all levels, nonprofits and utilities and to kindergarten through 12th grade ("K-12") educational institutions.

Through a series of mergers, FIS acquired 100 percent of the equity of SunGard, for a total purchase price as follows (in millions):

Cash consideration, including SunGard transaction fees paid at closing	$2,334.8
Value of stock and vested equity awards exchanged for FIS shares	2,696.8
Value of vested portion of SunGard stock awards exchanged for FIS awards	47.5
	$5,079.1

We recorded a preliminary allocation of the purchase price to SunGard tangible and identifiable intangible assets acquired and liabilities assumed based on their estimated fair values as of November 30, 2015. The provisional amounts for intangible assets are based on independent third-party valuations performed. Goodwill was recorded as the residual amount by which the purchase price exceeded the provisional fair value of the net assets acquired. Land and building valuations based on appraisals performed by certified property appraisers were underway as of December 31, 2015. Our evaluations of the facts and circumstances available as of November 30, 2015 to assign fair values to other assets acquired and liabilities assumed are ongoing, as are our assessments of the economic characteristics of the acquired software and other intangibles. These evaluations may result in changes to the provisional amounts recorded.

In accordance with ASU 2015-16, *Business Combinations (Topic 805): Simplifying the Accounting for Measurement-Period Adjustments*, the financial statements will not be retrospectively adjusted for any measurement-period adjustments that occur in subsequent periods. Rather, we will recognize any adjustments to provisional amounts that are identified during the measurement period in the reporting period in which the adjustment is determined. We will also be required to record, in the same period's financial statements, the effect on earnings of changes in depreciation, amortization, or other income effects, if any, as a result of any change to the provisional amounts, calculated as if the accounting had been completed at the acquisition date.

The preliminary purchase price allocation is as follows (in millions):

Cash	$ 631.1
Trade and other receivables	559.4
Property and equipment	135.5
Computer software	674.3
Intangible assets	4,190.0
Other assets	73.7
Goodwill	5,993.8
Liabilities assumed and noncontrolling interest	(7,178.7)
	$ 5,079.1

The following table summarizes the liabilities assumed in the SunGard acquisition (in millions):

Long-term debt, subsequently retired	$4,737.9
Deferred income taxes	1,650.2
Deferred revenue	278.3
Other liabilities and noncontrolling interest	512.3
	$7,178.7

The gross contractual amount of trade and other receivables acquired was approximately $583.3 million. The difference between that total and the provisional amount reflected above represents our best estimate at the acquisition date of the contractual cash flows not expected to be collected. This difference was derived using SunGard's historical bad debts, sales allowances and collection trends.

In connection with the Acquisition, we also granted approximately 2.4 million restricted stock units in replacement of similar outstanding unvested awards held by SunGard employees. The amounts attributable to services already rendered were included as an adjustment to the purchase price and the amounts attributable to future services will be expensed over the remaining vesting period based on a valuation as of the date of closing.

Pro Forma Results

SunGard's revenues and pre-tax loss from continuing operations of $253.9 million and $11.7 million, respectively, from November 30, 2015 through December 31, 2015, are included in the Consolidated Statements of Earnings. Selected unaudited pro forma results of operations for the years ended December 31, 2015 and 2014, assuming the Acquisition had occurred as of January 1, 2014, are presented for comparative purposes below (in millions, except per share amounts):

	2015	2014
Total processing and services revenues	$9,139.1	$8,985.8
Net earnings (loss) from continuing operations attributable to FIS common stockholders	$ 388.8	$ (35.4)
Pro forma earnings (loss) per share—basic from continuing operations attributable to FIS common stockholders	$ 1.19	$ (0.11)
Pro forma earnings (loss) per share—diluted from continuing operations attributable to FIS common stockholders	$ 1.17	$ (0.11)

Pro forma results include impairment charges of $339.0 million and merger and integration related costs of $200.0 million on a pre-tax basis for 2014. The pro forma results do not include any anticipated synergies, but do include the impacts of purchase accounting adjustments and conforming commission policies. SunGard elected to expense commission payments as incurred whereas FIS recognizes commission expense over the period that the related revenue is recognized. The pro forma earnings (pre-tax) have been increased by $11.9 million and $15.1 million for 2015 and 2014, respectively, to conform SunGard's expense recognition to FIS' policy. SunGard's policies and practices surrounding software development and capitalization of related costs differed from those used by FIS and will be conformed to those of FIS prospectively. As a result, FIS expects that more development costs will qualify to be capitalized than SunGard has recorded historically. It is not practicable to determine what the impact of the changes in application of the capitalization principles would have been for purposes of these pro forma results.

Excluding the impact of deferred revenue adjustments, total pro forma revenues would be $9,148.9 million and $9,222.8 million for 2015 and 2014, respectively.

Departures From Unmodified (Unqualified) Opinions

PRESENTATION

> *Author's Note*
> The clarified auditing standards use the term *unmodified opinions*, and the extant standards as adopted by the PCAOB use the term *unqualified opinions*.

NONISSUERS

7.49 Paragraph .07 of AU-C section 705 states that the auditor should modify the opinion in the auditor's report when the auditor concludes that the financial statements as a whole are materially misstated or when the auditor is unable to obtain sufficient appropriate audit evidence to conclude that the financial statements as a whole are free from material misstatement.

ISSUERS

7.50 AS 3101 does not require auditors to express qualified opinions about the effects of uncertainties or lack of consistency.

7.51 Under AS 3101, departures from unqualified opinions include opinions qualified because of a scope limitation or departure from GAAP, including inadequate disclosures; adverse opinions; and disclaimers of opinion. Paragraphs .20–.63 of AS 3101 discuss these departures. None of the auditors' reports issued in connection with the financial statements of the survey entities contained a *departure*, as defined by AS 3101.

Reports on Comparative Financial Statements

PRESENTATION

NONISSUERS

7.52 AU-C section 700 discusses reports on comparative statements. Paragraph .53 of AU-C section 700 states that when reporting on prior period financial statements in connection with the current period's audit, if the auditor's opinion on such prior period financial statements

PRESENTATION AND DISCLOSURE EXCERPT

CHANGE IN AUDITORS

7.54 BRUNSWICK CORPORATION (DEC)
REPORT OF INDEPENDENT REGISTERED PUBLIC ACCOUNTING FIRM

To the Board of Directors and Shareholders of Brunswick Corporation
Lake Forest, Illinois

We have audited the accompanying consolidated balance sheets of Brunswick Corporation and subsidiaries (the "Company") as of December 31, 2015 and 2014, and the related consolidated statements of operations, comprehensive income, shareholders' equity, and cash flows for the years ended December 31, 2015 and 2014. Our audits also included the financial statement schedule listed in the Index at Item 15. These financial statements and financial statement schedule are the responsibility of the Company's management. Our responsibility is to express an opinion on the financial statements and financial statement schedule based on our audits.

We conducted our audits in accordance with the standards of the Public Company Accounting Oversight Board (United States). Those standards require that we plan and perform the audit to obtain reasonable assurance about whether the financial statements are free of material misstatement. An audit includes examining, on a test basis, evidence supporting the amounts and disclosures in the financial statements. An audit also includes assessing the accounting principles used and significant estimates made by management, as well as evaluating the overall financial statement presentation. We believe that our audits provide a reasonable basis for our opinion.

In our opinion, such consolidated financial statements present fairly, in all material respects, the financial position of Brunswick Corporation and subsidiaries at December 31, 2015 and 2014, and the results of their operations and their cash flows for the years ended December 31, 2015 and 2014, in conformity with accounting principles generally accepted in the United States of America. Also, in our opinion, such financial statement schedule, when considered in relation to the basic consolidated financial statements taken as a whole, presents fairly, in all material respects, the information set forth therein.

We have also audited, in accordance with the standards of the Public Company Accounting Oversight Board (United States), the Company's internal control over financial reporting as of December 31, 2015, based on the criteria established in *Internal Control—Integrated Framework (2013)* issued by the Committee of Sponsoring Organizations of the Treadway Commission and our report dated February 17, 2016 expressed an unqualified opinion on the Company's internal control over financial reporting.

/s/ DELOITTE AND TOUCHE LLP
Chicago, Illinois
February 17, 2016

REPORT OF INDEPENDENT REGISTERED PUBLIC ACCOUNTING FIRM

Board of Directors and Shareholders
Brunswick Corporation

We have audited the accompanying consolidated statements of operations and comprehensive income, shareholders' equity, and cash flows of Brunswick Corporation for each year ended December 31, 2013. Our audits also included the financial statement schedule listed in the

Index at Item 15. These financial statements and schedule are the responsibility of the Company's management. Our responsibility is to express an opinion on these financial statements and schedule based on our audit.

We conducted our audit in accordance with the standards of the Public Company Accounting Oversight Board (United States). Those standards require that we plan and perform the audit to obtain reasonable assurance about whether the financial statements are free of material misstatement. An audit includes examining, on a test basis, evidence supporting the amounts and disclosures in the financial statements. An audit also includes assessing the accounting principles used and significant estimates made by management as well as evaluating the overall financial statement presentation. We believe that our audit provides a reasonable basis for our opinion.

In our opinion, the financial statements referred to above present fairly, in all material respects, the consolidated results of operations and cash flows of Brunswick Corporation for the year ended December 31, 2013, in conformity with U.S. generally accepted accounting principles. Also, in our opinion, the related financial statement schedule, when considered in relation to the basic financial statements taken as a whole, presents fairly in all material respects the information set forth therein.

/s/ ERNST & YOUNG LLP
Chicago, Illinois
February 14, 2014, except for Note 2, as to which the date is February 20, 2015

Opinion Expressed on Supplementary Financial Information

PRESENTATION

Author's Note
Because the report on supplementary financial information is applicable only for issuers, the following guidance is not intended for nonissuers.

7.55 Annual reports to security holders may be combined with the required information of SEC Form 10-K and are suitable for filing with the SEC if certain conditions are satisfied. Accordingly, many survey entities prepare an integrated annual report or simply provide to stockholders a copy of Form 10-K in lieu of the annual report. Form 10-K requires inclusion of certain supplementary financial information, including schedules (Article 12 of Regulation S-X) that must be audited. The report on the audit of schedules may be a separate report or combined with the report on the audit of the basic financial statements.

PRESENTATION AND DISCLOSURE EXCERPTS

SUPPLEMENTARY FINANCIAL INFORMATION

7.56 THE NEW YORK TIMES COMPANY (DEC)
REPORT OF INDEPENDENT REGISTERED PUBLIC ACCOUNTING FIRM ON CONSOLIDATED FINANCIAL STATEMENTS

To the Board of Directors and Stockholders of The New York Times Company
New York, New York

We have audited the accompanying consolidated balance sheets of The New York Times Company as of December 27, 2015 and December 28, 2014, and the related consolidated statements of operations, comprehensive income/(loss), changes in stockholders' equity, and cash flows for each of the three fiscal years in the period ended December 27, 2015. Our audits also included the financial statement schedule listed at Item 15(A)(2) of The New York Times Company's 2015 Annual Report on Form 10-K. These financial statements and schedule are the responsibility of The New York Times Company's management. Our responsibility is to express an opinion on these financial statements and schedule based on our audits.

We conducted our audits in accordance with the standards of the Public Company Accounting Oversight Board (United States). Those standards require that we plan and perform the audit to obtain reasonable assurance about whether the financial statements are free of material misstatement. An audit includes examining, on a test basis, evidence supporting the amounts and disclosures in the financial statements. An audit also includes assessing the accounting principles used and significant estimates made by management, as well as evaluating the overall financial statement presentation. We believe that our audits provide a reasonable basis for our opinion.

In our opinion, the financial statements referred to above present fairly, in all material respects, the consolidated financial position of The New York Times Company at December 27, 2015 and December 28, 2014, and the consolidated results of its operations and its cash flows for each of the three fiscal years in the period ended December 27, 2015, in conformity with U.S. generally accepted accounting principles. Also, in our opinion, the related financial statement schedule, when considered in relation to the basic financial statements taken as a whole, presents fairly in all material respects, the information set forth therein.

We also have audited, in accordance with the standards of the Public Company Accounting Oversight Board (United States), The New York Times Company's internal control over financial reporting as of December 27, 2015, based on criteria established in Internal Control—Integrated Framework issued by the Committee of Sponsoring Organizations of the Treadway Commission (2013 framework), and our report dated February 24, 2016 expressed an unqualified opinion thereon.

/s/ Ernst & Young LLP
New York, New York
February 24, 2016

SCHEDULE II—VALUATION AND QUALIFYING ACCOUNTS

For the Three Years Ended December 27, 2015:

(In thousands)	Balance at Beginning of Period	Additions Charged to Operating Costs and Other	Deductions[1]	Balance at End of Period
Accounts Receivable Allowances:				
Year ended December 27, 2015	$12,860	$13,999	$13,374	$13,485
Year ended December 28, 2014	$14,252	$11,384	$12,776	$12,860
Year ended December 29, 2013	$15,452	$ 9,377	$10,577	$14,252
Valuation Allowance for Deferred Tax Assets:				
Year ended December 27, 2015	$41,136	$ —	$ 4,932	$36,204
Year ended December 28, 2014	$42,295	$ —	$ 1,159	$41,136
Year ended December 29, 2013	$42,138	$ 2,432	$ 2,275	$42,295

[1] Includes write-offs, net of recoveries.

ITEM 15. EXHIBITS AND FINANCIAL STATEMENT SCHEDULES (in part)

(A) Documents Filed as Part of This Report

(1) Financial Statements

As listed in the index to financial information in "Item 8—Financial Statements and Supplementary Data."

(2) Supplemental Schedules

The following additional consolidated financial information is filed as part of this Annual Report on Form 10-K and should be read in conjunction with the Consolidated Financial Statements set forth in "Item 8—Financial Statements and Supplementary Data." Schedules not included with this additional consolidated financial information have been omitted either because they are not applicable or because the required information is shown in the Consolidated Financial Statements.

	Page
Consolidated Schedule for the Three Years Ended December 27, 2015	
II—Valuation and Qualifying Accounts	91

Separate financial statements and supplemental schedules of associated companies accounted for by the equity method are omitted in accordance with the provisions of Rule 3-09 of Regulation S-X.

7.57 LA-Z-BOY INCORPORATED (APR)
ITEM 15. EXHIBITS, FINANCIAL STATEMENT SCHEDULES (in part)

(a) The Following Documents are Filed as Part of This Report:

(1) Financial Statements:

Management's Report to Our Shareholders
Report of Independent Registered Public Accounting Firm
Consolidated Statement of Income for each of the three fiscal years ended April 25, 2015, April 26, 2014, and April 27, 2013
Consolidated Statement of Comprehensive Income for each of the three fiscal years ended April 25, 2015, April 26, 2014, and April 27, 2013
Consolidated Balance Sheet at April 25, 2015, and April 26, 2014
Consolidated Statement of Cash Flows for the fiscal years ended April 25, 2015, April 26, 2014, and April 27, 2013
Consolidated Statement of Changes in Equity for the fiscal years ended April 25, 2015, April 26, 2014, and April 27, 2013
Notes to Consolidated Financial Statements

(2) Financial Statement Schedules:

Report of Independent Registered Public Accounting Firm on Financial Statement Schedule
Schedule II—Valuation and Qualifying Accounts for the fiscal years ended April 25, 2015, April 26, 2014, and April 27, 2013
The Report of Independent Registered Public Accounting Firm and Schedule II immediately follow this item.
All other schedules are omitted because they are not applicable or not required because the required information is included in the financial statements or notes thereto.

REPORT OF INDEPENDENT REGISTERED PUBLIC ACCOUNTING FIRM ON FINANCIAL STATEMENT SCHEDULE

To the Board of Directors and Shareholders of La-Z-Boy Incorporated:

Our audits of the consolidated financial statements and of the effectiveness of internal control over financial reporting referred to in our report dated June 16, 2015 appearing in this Form 10-K also included an audit of the financial statement schedule listed in Item 15(a)(2) of this Form 10-K. In our opinion, this financial statement schedule presents fairly, in all material respects, the information set forth therein when read in conjunction with the related consolidated financial statements.

/s/ PricewaterhouseCoopers LLP
Detroit, Michigan
June 16, 2015

SCHEDULE II VALUATION AND QUALIFYING ACCOUNTS

(Dollars in thousands)

		Additions			
Description	Balance at Beginning of Year	Charged to Costs and Expenses	Charged to Other Accounts	Deductions	Balance at End of Year
Allowance for doubtful accounts, deducted from accounts receivable:					
April 25, 2015	$12,368	$(2,206)	$ —	$(5,540)[a]	$ 4,622
April 26, 2014	21,607	(2,926)	—	(6,313)[a]	12,368
April 27, 2013	22,254	495	—	(1,142)[a]	21,607
Allowance for deferred tax assets:					
April 25, 2015	$ 4,700	$ —	$ 39[c]	$ (417)[b]	$ 4,322
April 26, 2014	6,619	(135)	—	(1,784)[b]	4,700
April 27, 2013	8,258	131	(1,572)[c]	(198)[b]	6,619

[a] Deductions represented uncollectible accounts written off less recoveries of accounts receivable written off in prior years.
[b] Valuation allowance release.
[c] Represents impact of adjusting gross deferred tax assets.

Dating of Report

PRESENTATION

NONISSUERS

7.58 Dating of the auditor's report is discussed in both AU-C section 700 and AU-C section 560. Paragraph .41 of AU-C section 700 states that the auditor's report should be dated no earlier than the date on which the auditors has obtained sufficient appropriate audit evidence on which to base the auditor's opinion, including evidence that
- the audit documentation has been reviewed;
- all the statements that the financial statements comprise, including the related notes, have been prepared; and
- management has asserted that they have taken responsibility for those financial statements.

7.59 Paragraph .13 of AU-C section 560 states that if management revises the financial statements, the auditor should perform the audit procedures necessary in the circumstances on the revision. The auditor also should either
- date the auditor's report as of a later date; extend the audit procedures referred to in paragraphs .09–.10 to the new date of the auditor's report on the revised financial statements; and request written representations from management as of the new date of the auditor's report, or
- include an additional date in the auditor's report on the revised financial statements that is limited to the revision (that is, dual-date the auditor's report for that revision), thereby indicating that the auditor's procedures subsequent to the original date of the auditor's report are limited solely to the revision of the financial statements described in the relevant note to the financial statements.

ISSUERS

7.60 Paragraphs .01 and .05 of AS 3110, *Dating of the Independent Auditor's Report* (AICPA, *PCAOB Standards and Related Rules*) (formerly AU section 530), state the following:

.01 The auditor should date the audit report no earlier than the date on which the auditor has obtained sufficient appropriate evidence to support the auditor's opinion. Paragraph .05 describes the procedure to be followed when a subsequent event occurring after the report date is disclosed in the financial statements.

Note: When performing an integrated audit of financial statements and internal control over financial reporting, the auditor's reports on the company's financial statements and on internal control over financial reporting should be dated the same date.

Note: If the auditor concludes that a scope limitation will prevent the auditor from obtaining the reasonable assurance necessary to express an opinion on the financial statements, then the auditor's report date is the date that the auditor has obtained sufficient appropriate evidence to support the representations in the auditor's report.

.05 The independent auditor has two methods for dating the report when a subsequent event disclosed in the financial statements occurs after the auditor has obtained sufficient appropriate evidence on which to base his or her opinion, but before the issuance of the related financial statements. The auditor may use "dual dating," for example, "February 16, 20____, except for Note____, as to which the date is March 1, 20____," or may date the report as of the later date. In the former instance, the responsibility for events occurring subsequent to the original report date is limited to the specific event referred to in the note (or otherwise disclosed). In the latter instance, the independent auditor's responsibility for subsequent events extends to the later report date and, accordingly, the procedures outlined in paragraph .12 of AS 2801, *Subsequent Events* (AICPA, *PCAOB Standards and Related Rules*) (formerly AU section 560) generally should be extended to that date.

PRESENTATION AND DISCLOSURE EXCERPT

DATING OF REPORT

7.61 THE KRAFT HEINZ COMPANY (DEC)
REPORT OF INDEPENDENT REGISTERED PUBLIC ACCOUNTING FIRM

To the Shareholders and Board of Directors of The Kraft Heinz Company

In our opinion, the accompanying consolidated balance sheets as of January 3, 2016 and December 28, 2014, and the related consolidated statements of income, of comprehensive income, of equity and of cash flows for the fiscal years ended January 3, 2016 and December 28, 2014 and for the period from February 8, 2013 through December 29, 2013, present fairly, in all material respects, the financial position of The Kraft Heinz Company and its subsidiaries (Successor) at January 3, 2016 and December 28, 2014, and the results of their operations and their cash flows for the fiscal years ended January 3, 2016 and December 28, 2014 and for the period from February 8, 2013 through December 29, 2013 in conformity with accounting principles generally accepted in the United States of America. In addition, in our opinion, the financial statement schedule of valuation and qualifying accounts for the fiscal years ended January 3, 2016 and December 28, 2014 and for the period from February 8, 2013 through December 29, 2013 appearing under item 15 presents fairly, in all material respects, the information set forth therein when read in conjunction with the related consolidated financial statements. These financial statements and financial statement schedule are the responsibility of the Company's management. Our responsibility is to express an opinion on these financial statements and the financial statement schedule based on our audits. We conducted our audits of these statements in accordance with the standards of the Public Company Accounting Oversight Board (United States). Those standards require that we plan and perform the audit to obtain reasonable assurance about whether the financial statements are free of material misstatement. An audit includes examining, on a test basis, evidence supporting the amounts and disclosures in the financial statements, assessing the accounting principles used and significant estimates made by management, and evaluating the overall financial statement presentation. We believe that our audits provide a reasonable basis for our opinion.

As discussed in Note 1 to the consolidated financial statements, during 2015 the Company changed the manner in which it accounts for certain warehouse and distribution costs associated with the distribution of finished products to customers, the manner in which it accounts for trademark and license intangible asset impairments and amortization and the manner in which it accounts for debt issuance costs.

/s/ PRICEWATERHOUSECOOPERS LLP
Chicago, Illinois
March 3, 2016

REPORT OF INDEPENDENT REGISTERED PUBLIC ACCOUNTING FIRM

To the Shareholders and Board of Directors of H. J. Heinz Company

In our opinion, the accompanying consolidated statements of income, of comprehensive income, of equity and of cash flows for the period from April 29, 2013 to June 7, 2013 and for the fiscal year ended April 28, 2013 present fairly, in all material respects, the results of operations and cash flows of H. J. Heinz Company and its subsidiaries (Predecessor) for the period from April 29, 2013 to June 7, 2013 and for the fiscal year ended April 28, 2013 in conformity with accounting principles generally accepted in the United States of America. In addition, in our opinion, the financial statement schedule of valuation and qualifying accounts for the period from April 29, 2013 to June 7, 2013 and for the fiscal year ended April 28, 2013 appearing under item 15 presents fairly, in all material respects, the information set forth therein when read in conjunction with the related consolidated financial statements. These financial statements and financial statement schedule are the responsibility of the Company's management. Our responsibility is to express an opinion on these financial statements and the financial statement schedule based on our audits. We conducted our audits of these statements in accordance with the standards of the Public Company Accounting Oversight Board (United States). Those standards require that we plan and perform the audit to obtain reasonable assurance about whether the financial statements are free of material misstatement. An audit includes examining, on a test basis, evidence supporting the amounts and disclosures in the financial statements, assessing the accounting principles used and significant estimates made by management, and evaluating the overall financial statement presentation. We believe that our audits provide a reasonable basis for our opinion.

As discussed in Note 1 to the consolidated financial statements, during 2015 the Company changed the manner in which it accounts for certain warehouse and distribution costs associated with the distribution of finished products to customers and the manner in which it accounts for trademark and license intangible asset impairments and amortization.

/s/ PRICEWATERHOUSECOOPERS LLP
Chicago, Illinois
March 7, 2014, except for the changes in the manner of accounting for certain warehouse and distribution costs and trademark and license intangible asset impairments and amortization as discussed in Note 1 and the effects of the change in the composition of reportable segments discussed in Note 20, as to which the date is March 3, 2016

NOTES TO CONSOLIDATED FINANCIAL STATEMENTS (in part)

Note 1. Background and Basis of Presentation (in part)

Changes in Accounting and Reporting: (in part)

In 2015, we made the following changes in accounting and reporting to harmonize our accounting and reporting as Kraft Heinz:

- We made a voluntary change in accounting policy to classify certain warehouse and distribution costs (including shipping and handling costs) associated with the distribution of finished product to our customers as cost of products sold, which were previously recorded in selling, general and administrative expenses ("SG&A"). We made this voluntary change in accounting policy because we believe this presentation is preferable, as the classification in cost of products sold better reflects the cost of producing and distributing products. Additionally, this presentation enhances the comparability of our financial statements with industry peers and aligns with how we now internally manage and review costs. As required by accounting principles generally accepted in the United States of America ("U.S. GAAP"), the change has been reflected in the consolidated statements of income through retrospective application of the change in accounting policy. The impact of this change was to increase cost of products sold and decrease SG&A by $666 million for the year ended December 28, 2014, $367 million in the 2013 Successor Period, $66 million in the 2013 Predecessor Period, and $656 million in Fiscal 2013.
- We made a voluntary change in accounting policy to classify our trademark and license intangible asset impairments and amortization in SG&A, which were previously recorded in cost of products sold. We made this voluntary change in accounting policy because we believe this presentation is preferable, as removing these expenses from cost of products sold better aligns cost of products sold with costs directly associated with generating revenue. Additionally, this presentation enhances the comparability of our financial statements with industry peers and aligns with how we now internally manage and review costs. As required by U.S. GAAP, the change has been reflected in the consolidated statements of income through retrospective application of the change in accounting policy. The impact of this change was to increase SG&A and decrease cost of products sold by $244 million for the year ended December 28, 2014, $11 million in the 2013 Successor Period, $2 million in the 2013 Predecessor Period, and $13 million in Fiscal 2013.
- In 2015, we determined that we had previously misclassified customer related intangible asset amortization. Such costs were previously included in cost of products sold but should have been included in SG&A. We have revised the classification to report these expenses in SG&A in the consolidated statements of income for all prior periods presented. The impact of this revision was to increase SG&A and decrease cost of products sold by $68 million for the year ended December 28, 2014, $36 million in the 2013 Successor Period, $1 million in the 2013 Predecessor Period, and $18 million in Fiscal 2013. These misstatements were not material to our current or any prior period financial statements.
- We separately presented sold receivables on our consolidated balance sheets and consolidated statements of cash flows to align with current period presentation.

Note 20. Segment Reporting

We manufacture and market food and beverage products, including condiments and sauces, cheese and dairy, meals, meats, refreshment beverages, coffee, and other grocery products, throughout the world.

Following the 2015 Merger, we revised our segment structure and began to manage and report our operating results through four segments. We have three reportable segments defined by geographic region: United States, Canada, and Europe. Our remaining businesses are combined and disclosed as "Rest of World". Rest of World is comprised of three operating segments: Asia Pacific, Latin America, and Russia, India, the Middle East and Africa ("RIMEA"). We began to report on our reorganized segment structure during the third quarter of 2015 and have reflected this structure for all historical periods presented.

Management evaluates segment performance based on several factors including net sales and segment adjusted earnings before interest, tax, depreciation and amortization ("Segment Adjusted EBITDA"). Management uses Segment Adjusted EBITDA to evaluate segment performance and allocate resources. Segment Adjusted EBITDA assists management in comparing our performance on a consistent basis for purposes of business decision-making by removing the impact of certain items that management believes do not directly reflect our core operations. These items include depreciation and amortization (including amortization of postretirement benefit plans prior service credits), equity award compensation expense, integration and restructuring expenses, merger costs, unrealized gains and losses on commodity hedges (the unrealized gains and losses are recorded in general corporate expenses until realized; once realized, the gains and losses are recorded in the applicable segment operating results), impairment losses, gain/loss associated with the sale of a business, nonmonetary currency devaluation, and certain general corporate expenses. In addition, consistent with the manner in which management evaluates segment performance and allocates resources, Segment Adjusted EBITDA includes the operating results of Kraft on a pro forma basis, as if Kraft had been acquired as of December 30, 2013. There are no pro forma adjustments to any of the numbers disclosed in this note to the consolidated financial statements except for the Segment Adjusted EBITDA reconciliation.

Consistent with internal management reporting, there are no pro forma adjustments in any of the 2013 periods presented as it would be impracticable to develop adjustments that would be meaningful. The information would not be meaningful due to the difficulty of interpreting these pro forma impacts on the various durations of the multiple 2013 periods presented, as well as, the length of time that has passed since 2013 makes it difficult to assess how the company would have performed if Kraft and Heinz had been a combined company at that time.

Management does not use assets by segment to evaluate performance or allocate resources and therefore, we do not disclose assets by segment.

Our net sales by segment and Segment Adjusted EBITDA were:

	Successor			Predecessor (H. J. Heinz Company)	
(In millions)	January 3, 2016 (53 weeks)	December 28, 2014 (52 weeks)	February 8– December 29, 2013 (29 weeks)	April 29– June 7, 2013 (6 weeks)	April 28, 2013 (52 weeks)
Net sales:					
United States	$11,124	$ 3,615	$2,072	$ 371	$ 3,857
Canada	1,437	631	371	73	709
Europe	2,485	2,973	1,659	269	3,049
Rest of World	3,292	3,703	2,138	400	3,914
Total net sales	$18,338	$10,922	$6,240	$1,113	$11,529

	Successor			Predecessor (H. J. Heinz Company)	
(In millions)	January 3, 2016 (53 weeks)	December 28, 2014 (52 weeks)	February 8– December 29, 2013 (29 weeks)	April 29– June 7, 2013 (6 weeks)	April 28, 2013 (52 weeks)
Segment Adjusted EBITDA:					
United States	$ 4,783	$ 4,499	$ 519	$ 81	$ 932
Canada	541	615	99	16	175
Europe	909	898	349	42	671
Rest of World	670	689	256	58	485
General corporate expenses	(164)	(175)	(58)	(25)	(164)
Depreciation and amortization (excluding integration and restructuring expenses)	(779)	(924)	(216)	(34)	(340)
Integration and restructuring expenses	(1,117)	(743)	(411)	6	(1)
Merger costs	(194)	(68)	(158)	(112)	(45)
Amortization of inventory step-up	(347)	—	(383)	—	—
Unrealized gains/(losses) on commodity hedges	41	(79)	—	—	—
Impairment losses	(58)	(221)	—	—	—
Gain on sale of business	21	—	—	—	—
Nonmonetary currency devaluation	(57)	—	—	—	—
Equity award compensation expense (excluding integration and restructuring expenses)	(61)	(108)	(5)	(4)	(51)
Other pro forma adjustments	(1,549)	(2,815)	—	—	—
Operating income/(loss)	2,639	1,568	(8)	28	1,662
Interest expense	1,321	686	409	35	284
Other expense/(income), net	305	79	(119)	123	34
Income/(loss) from continuing operations before income taxes	$ 1,013	$ 803	$(298)	$(130)	$1,344

Total depreciation and amortization expense and capital expenditures by segment were:

(In millions)	Successor January 3, 2016 (53 weeks)	Successor December 28, 2014 (52 weeks)	Successor February 8– December 29, 2013 (29 weeks)	Predecessor (H. J. Heinz Company) April 29– June 7, 2013 (6 weeks)	Predecessor (H. J. Heinz Company) April 28, 2013 (52 weeks)
Depreciation and Amortization Expense:					
United States	$484	$191	$125	$12	$104
Canada	36	83	28	4	23
Europe	83	121	60	9	90
Rest of World	88	103	55	10	96
Non-Operating[a]	49	32	12	5	31
Total depreciation and amortization expense	$740	$530	$280	$40	$344

[a] Includes corporate overhead and general corporate expenses.

(In millions)	Successor January 3, 2016 (53 weeks)	Successor December 28, 2014 (52 weeks)	Successor February 8– December 29, 2013 (29 weeks)	Predecessor (H. J. Heinz Company) April 29– June 7, 2013 (6 weeks)	Predecessor (H. J. Heinz Company) April 28, 2013 (52 weeks)
Capital Expenditures:					
United States	$377	$146	$ 42	$ 9	$ 68
Canada	19	2	5	1	39
Europe	102	95	40	5	92
Rest of World	103	93	67	6	144
Non-Operating[a]	47	63	48	99	56
Total capital expenditures	$648	$399	$202	$120	$399

[a] Includes corporate overhead and general corporate expenses.

Concentration of Risk:

For the year ended January 3, 2016 Wal-Mart Stores Inc., our largest customer, represented approximately 20% of our net sales. For the year ended December 28, 2014, the 2013 Successor Period, the 2013 Predecessor Period, and Fiscal 2013 Wal-Mart Stores Inc., represented approximately 10% of our net sales. All of our segments have sales to Wal-Mart Stores Inc.

Our net sales by product category were:

(In millions)	Successor January 3, 2016 (53 weeks)	Successor December 28, 2014 (52 weeks)	Successor February 8– December 29, 2013 (29 weeks)	Predecessor (H. J. Heinz Company) April 29– June 7, 2013 (6 weeks)	Predecessor (H. J. Heinz Company) April 28, 2013 (52 weeks)
Condiments and sauces	$ 5,846	$ 5,489	$3,081	$ 534	$ 5,376
Cheese and dairy	2,795	—	—	—	—
Ambient meals	1,858	1,544	865	140	1,646
Frozen and chilled meals	2,210	2,000	1,199	199	2,318
Meats	1,480	199	122	20	277
Refreshment beverages	665	—	—	—	—
Coffee	710	—	—	—	—
Infant/nutrition	902	1,116	624	119	1,189
Desserts, toppings and baking	521	—	—	—	—
Nuts and salted snacks	562	—	—	—	—
Other	789	574	349	101	723
Total net sales	$18,338	$10,922	$6,240	$1,113	$11,529

We had significant net sales in the United States, Canada, and the United Kingdom. Sales are based on the location in which the sale originated. Our net sales by country were:

(In millions)	Successor January 3, 2016 (53 weeks)	Successor December 28, 2014 (52 weeks)	Successor February 8– December 29, 2013 (29 weeks)	Predecessor (H. J. Heinz Company) April 29– June 7, 2013 (6 weeks)	Predecessor (H. J. Heinz Company) April 28, 2013 (52 weeks)
Net sales:					
United States	$11,124	$ 3,615	$2,072	$ 371	$ 3,857
Canada	1,437	631	371	73	709
United Kingdom	1,334	1,549	860	131	1,598
Other	4,443	5,127	2,937	538	5,365
Total net sales	$18,338	$10,922	$6,240	$1,113	$11,529

We had significant long-lived assets in the United States and the United Kingdom. Long-lived assets include property, plant and equipment, goodwill, trademarks, and other intangibles, net of related depreciation and amortization. Our long-lived assets by country were:

(In millions)	January 3, 2016	December 28, 2014
Long-lived assets:		
United States	$ 94,504	$15,957
United Kingdom	6,742	6,777
Canada	5,871	2,378
Other	4,578	5,400
Total long-lived assets	$111,695	$30,512

Auditors' Reports on Internal Control Over Financial Reporting

PRESENTATION

> **Author's Note**
> Because the report on internal control over financial reporting is required only for issuers, the following guidance is not applicable for nonissuers.

7.62 Section 404(a) of the Sarbanes-Oxley Act of 2002 requires that management of a public entity assess the effectiveness of the entity's internal control over financial reporting as of the end of the entity's most recent *fiscal* year and include in the entity's annual report management's conclusions about the effectiveness of the entity's internal control structure and procedures. Management is required to state a direct conclusion about whether the entity's internal control over financial reporting is effective. Management's report on internal control over financial reporting is required to include the following:

- A statement of management's responsibility for establishing and maintaining adequate internal control over financial reporting for the entity
- A statement identifying the framework used by management to conduct the required assessment of the effectiveness of the entity's internal control over financial reporting
- An assessment of the effectiveness of the entity's internal control over financial reporting as of the end of the entity's most recent fiscal year, including an explicit statement about whether that internal control over financial reporting is effective
- A statement that the registered public accounting firm that audited the financial statements included in the annual report has issued an attestation report on management's assessment of the entity's internal control over financial reporting

7.63 Under Section 404(b) of the Sarbanes-Oxley Act of 2002, the auditor who audits the public entity's financial statements included in the annual report is required to audit the entity's internal control over financial reporting. In addition, the auditor is required to audit and report on management's assessment of the effectiveness of internal control over financial reporting. Under AS 2201, *An Audit of Internal Control Over Financial Reporting That is Integrated with an Audit of Financial Statements* (AICPA, *PCAOB Standards and Related Rules*) (formerly PCAOB AS No. 5), the auditor's objective in an audit of internal control over financial reporting is to express an opinion on the effectiveness of the entity's internal control over financial reporting. The audit of internal control over financial reporting should be integrated with the audit of the financial statements. Accordingly, independent auditors engaged to audit the financial statements of such entities also are required to audit and report on the entity's internal control over financial reporting as of the end of such fiscal year. Further, if the auditor determines that elements of management's annual report on internal control over financial reporting are incomplete or improperly presented, the auditor should modify the report to include an explanatory paragraph describing the reasons for this determination and identify and fairly describe any material weakness. Paragraph .86 of AS 2201 allows the auditor to issue a combined report (that is, one report containing both an opinion on the financial statements and an opinion on internal control over financial reporting) or separate reports on the entity's financial statements and on internal control over financial reporting.

7.64 In September 2010, the SEC approved a final rule related to the Dodd-Frank Wall Street Reform and Consumer Protection Act (Dodd-Frank Act). The Dodd-Frank Act provides that Section 404(b) of the Sarbanes-Oxley Act of 2002 shall not apply with respect to any audit report prepared for an issuer that is neither an accelerated filer nor a large accelerated filer. Prior to the Dodd-Frank Act, a nonaccelerated filer would have been required, under existing SEC rules, to include an attestation report of its registered public accounting firm on internal control over financial reporting in the filer's annual report filed with the SEC for fiscal years ending on or after June 15, 2010.

PRESENTATION AND DISCLOSURE EXCERPTS

SEPARATE REPORT ON INTERNAL CONTROL

7.65 APPLE INC. (SEP)
REPORT OF INDEPENDENT REGISTERED PUBLIC ACCOUNTING FIRM

The Board of Directors and Shareholders of Apple Inc.

We have audited the accompanying consolidated balance sheets of Apple Inc. as of September 26, 2015 and September 27, 2014, and the related consolidated statements of operations, comprehensive income, shareholders' equity and cash flows for each of the three years in the period ended September 26, 2015. These financial statements are the responsibility of the Company's management. Our responsibility is to express an opinion on these financial statements based on our audits.

We conducted our audits in accordance with the standards of the Public Company Accounting Oversight Board (United States). Those standards require that we plan and perform the audit to obtain reasonable assurance about whether the financial statements are free of material misstatement. An audit includes examining, on a test basis, evidence supporting the amounts and disclosures in the financial statements. An audit also includes assessing the accounting principles used and significant estimates made by management, as well as evaluating the overall financial statement presentation. We believe that our audits provide a reasonable basis for our opinion.

In our opinion, the financial statements referred to above present fairly, in all material respects, the consolidated financial position of Apple Inc. at September 26, 2015 and September 27, 2014, and the consolidated results of its operations and its cash flows for each of the three years in the period ended September 26, 2015, in conformity with U.S. generally accepted accounting principles.

We also have audited, in accordance with the standards of the Public Company Accounting Oversight Board (United States), Apple Inc.'s internal control over financial reporting as of September 26, 2015, based on criteria established in *Internal Control—Integrated Framework* issued by the Committee of Sponsoring Organizations of the Treadway Commission (2013 framework) and our report dated October 28, 2015 expressed an unqualified opinion thereon.

/s/ Ernst & Young LLP

San Jose, California
October 28, 2015

REPORT OF INDEPENDENT REGISTERED PUBLIC ACCOUNTING FIRM

The Board of Directors and Shareholders of Apple Inc.

We have audited Apple Inc.'s internal control over financial reporting as of September 26, 2015, based on criteria established in *Internal Control—Integrated Framework* issued by the Committee of Sponsoring Organizations of the Treadway Commission (2013 framework) ("the COSO criteria"). Apple Inc.'s management is responsible for maintaining effective internal control over financial reporting, and for its assessment of the effectiveness of internal control over financial reporting included in the accompanying Management's Annual Report on Internal Control Over Financial Reporting. Our responsibility is to express an opinion on the Company's internal control over financial reporting based on our audit.

We conducted our audit in accordance with the standards of the Public Company Accounting Oversight Board (United States). Those standards require that we plan and perform the audit to obtain reasonable assurance about whether effective internal control over financial reporting was maintained in all material respects. Our audit included obtaining an understanding of internal control over financial reporting, assessing the risk that a material weakness exists, testing and evaluating the design and operating effectiveness of internal control based on the assessed risk, and performing such other procedures as we considered necessary in the circumstances. We believe that our audit provides a reasonable basis for our opinion.

A company's internal control over financial reporting is a process designed to provide reasonable assurance regarding the reliability of financial reporting and the preparation of financial statements for external purposes in accordance with generally accepted accounting principles. A company's internal control over financial reporting includes those policies and procedures that (1) pertain to the maintenance of records that, in reasonable detail, accurately and fairly reflect the transactions and dispositions of the assets of the company; (2) provide reasonable assurance that transactions are recorded as necessary to permit preparation of financial statements in accordance with generally accepted accounting principles, and that receipts and expenditures of the company are being made only in accordance with authorizations of management and directors of the company; and (3) provide reasonable assurance regarding prevention or timely detection of unauthorized acquisition, use, or disposition of the company's assets that could have a material effect on the financial statements.

Because of its inherent limitations, internal control over financial reporting may not prevent or detect misstatements. Also, projections of any evaluation of effectiveness to future periods are subject to the risk that controls may become inadequate because of changes in conditions, or that the degree of compliance with the policies or procedures may deteriorate.

In our opinion, Apple Inc. maintained, in all material respects, effective internal control over financial reporting as of September 26, 2015, based on the COSO criteria.

We also have audited, in accordance with the standards of the Public Company Accounting Oversight Board (United States), the 2015 consolidated financial statements of Apple Inc. and our report dated October 28, 2015 expressed an unqualified opinion thereon.

/s/ Ernst & Young LLP

San Jose, California
October 28, 2015

COMBINED REPORT ON FINANCIAL STATEMENTS AND INTERNAL CONTROL

7.66 THE MCCLATCHY COMPANY (DEC)
REPORT OF INDEPENDENT REGISTERED PUBLIC ACCOUNTING FIRM

To the Board of Directors and Stockholders of The McClatchy Company:

We have audited the accompanying consolidated balance sheets of The McClatchy Company and its subsidiaries (the "Company") as of December 27, 2015 and December 28, 2014, and the related consolidated statements operations, comprehensive income (loss), stockholders' equity, and cash flows for each of the three years in the period ended December 27, 2015. We also have audited the Company's internal control over financial reporting as of December 27, 2015, based on criteria established in Internal Control—Integrated Framework (2013) issued by the Committee of Sponsoring Organizations of the Treadway Commission. The Company's management is responsible for these financial statements, for maintaining effective internal control over financial reporting, and for its assessment of the effectiveness of internal control over financial reporting, included in the accompanying "Management Report on Internal Control over Financial Reporting." Our responsibility is to express an opinion on these financial statements and an opinion on the Company's internal control over financial reporting based on our audits.

We conducted our audits in accordance with the standards of the Public Company Accounting Oversight Board (United States). Those standards require that we plan and perform the audits to obtain reasonable assurance about whether the financial statements are free of material misstatement and whether effective internal control over financial reporting was maintained in all material respects. Our audits of the financial statements included examining, on a test basis, evidence supporting the amounts and disclosures in the financial statements, assessing the accounting principles used and significant estimates made by management, and evaluating the overall financial statement presentation. Our audit of internal control over financial reporting included obtaining an understanding of internal control over financial reporting, assessing the risk that a material weakness exists, and testing and evaluating the design and operating effectiveness of internal control based on the assessed risk. Our audits also included performing such other procedures as we considered necessary in the circumstances. We believe that our audits provide a reasonable basis for our opinions.

A company's internal control over financial reporting is a process designed by, or under the supervision of, the company's principal executive and principal financial officers, or persons performing similar functions, and effected by the company's board of directors, management, and other personnel to provide reasonable assurance regarding the reliability of financial reporting and the preparation of financial statements for external purposes in accordance with generally accepted accounting principles. A company's internal control over financial reporting includes those policies and procedures that (1) pertain to the maintenance of records that, in reasonable detail, accurately and fairly reflect the transactions and dispositions of the assets of the company; (2) provide reasonable assurance that transactions are recorded as necessary to permit preparation of financial statements in accordance with generally accepted accounting principles, and that receipts and expenditures of the company are being made only in accordance with authorizations of management and directors of the company; and (3) provide reasonable assurance regarding prevention or timely detection of unauthorized acquisition, use, or disposition of the company's assets that could have a material effect on the financial statements.

Because of the inherent limitations of internal control over financial reporting, including the possibility of collusion or improper management override of controls, material misstatements due to error or fraud may not be prevented or detected on a timely basis. Also, projections of any evaluation of the effectiveness of the internal control over financial reporting to future periods are subject to the risk that the controls may become inadequate because of changes in conditions, or that the degree of compliance with the policies or procedures may deteriorate.

In our opinion, the consolidated financial statements referred to above present fairly, in all material respects, the financial position of the Company and its subsidiaries as of December 27, 2015 and December 28, 2014, and the results of their operations and their cash flows for each of the three years in the period ended December 27, 2015, in conformity with accounting principles generally accepted in the United States of America. Also in our opinion, the Company maintained, in all material respects, effective internal control over financial reporting as of December 27, 2015, based on criteria established in Internal Control—Integrated Framework (2013) issued by the Committee of Sponsoring Organizations of the Treadway Commission.

/S/ DELOITTE & TOUCHE LLP
Sacramento, California
March 7, 2016

REPORT ON INTERNAL CONTROL WITH SPECIFIC ITEMS EXCLUDED

7.67 AUTODESK, INC. (JAN)
REPORT OF INDEPENDENT REGISTERED PUBLIC ACCOUNTING FIRM

The Board of Directors and Stockholders of Autodesk, Inc.

We have audited Autodesk, Inc.'s internal control over financial reporting as of January 31, 2015, based on criteria established in Internal Control—Integrated Framework issued by the Committee of Sponsoring Organizations of the Treadway Commission (2013 framework) (the COSO criteria). Autodesk, Inc.'s management is responsible for maintaining effective internal control over financial reporting, and for its assessment of the effectiveness of internal control over financial reporting included in the accompanying Management's Report on Internal Control Over Financial Reporting. Our responsibility is to express an opinion on the company's internal control over financial reporting based on our audit.

We conducted our audit in accordance with the standards of the Public Company Accounting Oversight Board (United States). Those standards require that we plan and perform the audit to obtain reasonable assurance about whether effective internal control over financial reporting was maintained in all material respects. Our audit included obtaining an understanding of internal control over financial reporting, assessing the risk that a material weakness exists, testing and evaluating the design and operating effectiveness of internal control based on the assessed risk, and performing such other procedures as we considered necessary in the circumstances. We believe that our audit provides a reasonable basis for our opinion.

A company's internal control over financial reporting is a process designed to provide reasonable assurance regarding the reliability of financial reporting and the preparation of financial statements for external purposes in accordance with generally accepted accounting principles. A company's internal control over financial reporting includes those policies and procedures that (1) pertain to the maintenance of records that, in reasonable detail, accurately and fairly reflect the transactions and dispositions of the assets of the company; (2) provide reasonable assurance that transactions are recorded as necessary to permit preparation of financial statements in accordance with generally accepted accounting principles, and that receipts and expenditures of the company are being made only in accordance with authorizations of management and directors of the company; and (3) provide reasonable assurance regarding prevention or timely detection of unauthorized acquisition, use, or disposition of the company's assets that could have a material effect on the financial statements.

Because of its inherent limitations, internal control over financial reporting may not prevent or detect misstatements. Also, projections of any evaluation of effectiveness to future periods are subject to the risk that controls may become inadequate because of changes in conditions, or that the degree of compliance with the policies or procedures may deteriorate.

As indicated in the accompanying Management's Report on Internal Control Over Financial Reporting, management's assessment of and conclusion on the effectiveness of internal control over financial reporting did not include the internal controls of Delcam, plc, which is included in the 2015 consolidated financial statements of Autodesk, Inc. and constituted 6 percent of total assets as of January 31, 2015 and 2 percent of revenues, for the year then ended. Our audit of internal control over financial reporting of Autodesk, Inc. also did not include an evaluation of the internal control over financial reporting of Delcam plc.

In our opinion, Autodesk, Inc. maintained, in all material respects, effective internal control over financial reporting as of January 31, 2015, based on the COSO criteria.

We also have audited, in accordance with the standards of the Public Company Accounting Oversight Board (United States), the consolidated balance sheets of Autodesk, Inc. as of January 31, 2015 and 2014, and the related consolidated statements of operations, comprehensive income, stockholders' equity, and cash flows for each of the three years in the period ended January 31, 2015 of Autodesk, Inc. and our report dated March 18, 2015 expressed an unqualified opinion thereon.

/s/ ERNST & YOUNG LLP
San Francisco, California
March 18, 2015

REPORT ON INTERNAL CONTROL WITH INEFFECTIVE INTERNAL CONTROLS

7.68 DONALDSON COMPANY, INC. (JUL)
REPORT OF INDEPENDENT REGISTERED PUBLIC ACCOUNTING FIRM

To the Shareholders and Board of Directors of Donaldson Company, Inc.

In our opinion, the accompanying consolidated balance sheets and the related consolidated statements of earnings, comprehensive income, changes in shareholders' equity and cash flows present fairly, in all material respects, the financial position of Donaldson Company, Inc. and its subsidiaries at July 31, 2015 and July 31, 2014, and the results of their operations and their cash flows for each of the three years in the period ended July 31, 2015 in conformity with accounting principles generally accepted in the United States of America. In addition, in our opinion, the financial statement schedule listed in the index appearing under Item 15(2) presents fairly, in all material respects, the information set forth therein when read in conjunction with the related consolidated financial statements. Also in our opinion, the Company did not maintain, in all material respects, effective internal control over financial reporting as of July 31, 2015, based on criteria established in *Internal Control—Integrated Framework* (2013) issued by the Committee of Sponsoring Organizations of the Treadway Commission (COSO) because a material weakness in internal control over financial reporting related to recognition of revenue in its European Gas Turbine Products business existed as of that date. Specifically, transactions were not recorded in the proper period because the design of the controls did not contemplate effective review of delivery terms associated with Gas Turbine Products business projects revenue and the fulfillment of certain contractual terms by the Company was not sufficiently verified by reference to independent third party documentation. A material weakness is a deficiency, or a combination of deficiencies, in internal control over financial reporting, such that there is a reasonable possibility that a material misstatement of the annual or interim financial statements will not be prevented or detected on a timely basis. The material weakness referred to above is described in the accompanying Management's Report on Internal Control over Financial Reporting. We considered this material weakness in determining the nature, timing, and extent of audit tests applied in our audit of the July 31, 2015 consolidated financial statements and our opinion regarding the effectiveness of the Company's internal control over financial reporting does not affect our opinion on those consolidated financial statements. The Company's management is responsible for these financial statements and financial statement schedule, for maintaining effective internal control over financial reporting and for its assessment of the effectiveness of internal control over financial reporting included in management's report referred to above. Our responsibility is to express opinions on these financial statements, on the financial statement schedule, and on the Company's internal control over financial reporting based on our integrated audits. We conducted our audits in accordance with the standards of the Public Company Accounting Oversight Board (United States). Those standards require that we plan and perform the audits to obtain reasonable assurance about whether the financial statements are free of material misstatement and whether effective internal control over financial reporting was maintained in all material respects. Our audits of the financial statements included examining, on a test basis, evidence supporting the amounts and disclosures in the financial statements, assessing the accounting principles used and significant estimates made by management, and evaluating the overall financial statement presentation. Our audit of internal control over financial reporting included obtaining an understanding of internal control over financial reporting, assessing the risk that a material weakness exists, and testing and evaluating the design and operating effectiveness of internal control based on the assessed risk. Our audits also included performing such other procedures as we considered necessary in the circumstances. We believe that our audits provide a reasonable basis for our opinions.

A company's internal control over financial reporting is a process designed to provide reasonable assurance regarding the reliability of financial reporting and the preparation of financial statements for external purposes in accordance with generally accepted accounting principles. A company's internal control over financial reporting includes those policies and procedures that (i) pertain to the maintenance of records that, in reasonable detail, accurately and fairly reflect the transactions and dispositions of the assets of the company; (ii) provide reasonable assurance that transactions are recorded as necessary to permit preparation of financial statements in accordance with generally accepted accounting principles, and that receipts and expenditures of the company are being made only in accordance with authorizations of management and directors of the company; and (iii) provide reasonable assurance regarding prevention or timely detection of unauthorized acquisition, use, or disposition of the company's assets that could have a material effect on the financial statements.

Because of its inherent limitations, internal control over financial reporting may not prevent or detect misstatements. Also, projections of any evaluation of effectiveness to future periods are subject to the risk that controls may become inadequate because of changes in conditions, or that the degree of compliance with the policies or procedures may deteriorate.

/s/ PricewaterhouseCoopers LLP
PricewaterhouseCoopers LLP
Minneapolis, Minnesota
November 09, 2015

7.69 THE HERSHEY COMPANY (DEC)
REPORT OF INDEPENDENT REGISTERED PUBLIC ACCOUNTING FIRM

The Board of Directors and Stockholders
The Hershey Company:

We have audited the accompanying consolidated balance sheets of The Hershey Company and subsidiaries (the "Company") as of December 31, 2015 and 2014, and the related consolidated statements of income, comprehensive income, cash flows and stockholders' equity for each of the years in the three-year period ended December 31, 2015. In connection with our audits of the consolidated financial statements, we also have audited the related consolidated financial statement schedule. We also have audited the Company's internal control over financial reporting as of December 31, 2015, based on criteria established in *Internal Control—Integrated Framework (2013)* issued by the Committee of Sponsoring Organizations of the Treadway Commission (COSO)"). The Company's management is responsible for these consolidated financial statements and financial statement schedule, for maintaining effective internal control over financial reporting, and for its assessment of the effectiveness of internal control over financial reporting, included in the accompanying Management Report on Internal Control over Financial Reporting. Our responsibility is to express an opinion on these consolidated financial statements and financial statement schedule, and an opinion on the Company's internal control over financial reporting based on our audits.

We conducted our audits in accordance with the standards of the Public Company Accounting Oversight Board (United States). Those standards require that we plan and perform the audits to obtain reasonable assurance about whether the financial statements are free of material misstatement and whether effective internal control over financial reporting was maintained in all material respects. Our audits of the consolidated financial statements included examining, on a test basis, evidence supporting the amounts and disclosures in the financial statements, assessing the accounting principles used and significant estimates made by management, and evaluating the overall financial statement presentation. Our audit of internal control over financial reporting included obtaining an understanding of internal control over financial reporting, assessing the risk that a material weakness exists, and testing and evaluating the design and operating effectiveness of internal control based on the assessed risk. Our audits also included performing such other procedures as we considered necessary in the circumstances. We believe that our audits provide a reasonable basis for our opinions.

A company's internal control over financial reporting is a process designed to provide reasonable assurance regarding the reliability of financial reporting and the preparation of financial statements for external purposes in accordance with generally accepted accounting principles. A company's internal control over financial reporting includes those policies and procedures that (1) pertain to the maintenance of records that, in reasonable detail, accurately and fairly reflect the transactions and dispositions of the assets of the company; (2) provide reasonable assurance that transactions are recorded as necessary to permit preparation of financial statements in accordance with generally accepted accounting principles, and that receipts and expenditures of the company are being made only in accordance with authorizations of management and directors of the company; and (3) provide reasonable assurance regarding prevention or timely detection of unauthorized acquisition, use, or disposition of the company's assets that could have a material effect on the financial statements.

Because of its inherent limitations, internal control over financial reporting may not prevent or detect misstatements. Also, projections of any evaluation of effectiveness to future periods are subject to the risk that controls may become inadequate because of changes in conditions, or that the degree of compliance with the policies or procedures may deteriorate.

A material weakness is a deficiency, or a combination of deficiencies, in internal control over financial reporting, such that there is a reasonable possibility that a material misstatement of the company's annual or interim financial statements will not be prevented or detected on a timely basis. A material weakness existed as of December 31, 2015 related to the Company's accounting for cocoa derivative financial instruments. This material weakness was considered in determining the nature, timing, and extent of audit tests applied in our audit of the 2015 consolidated financial statements, and this material weakness does not affect our opinion included below on those financial statements.

In our opinion, the consolidated financial statements referred to above present fairly, in all material respects, the financial position of The Hershey Company and subsidiaries as of December 31, 2015 and 2014, and the results of their operations and their cash flows for each of the years in the three-year period ended December 31, 2015, in conformity with U.S. generally accepted accounting principles. Also in our opinion, the related consolidated financial statement schedule, when considered in relation to the basic consolidated financial statements taken as a whole, presents fairly, in all material respects, the information set forth therein.

Also in our opinion, because of the effect of the aforementioned material weakness on the achievement of the objectives of the control criteria, The Hershey Company and subsidiaries has not maintained effective internal control over financial reporting as of December 31, 2015, based on criteria established in *Internal Control-Integrated Framework (2013)* issued by the Committee of Sponsoring Organizations of the Treadway Commission.

We do not express an opinion or any other form of assurance on management's statements referring to actions taken after December 31, 2015, relative to the aforementioned material weakness in internal control over financial reporting.

/s/ KPMG LLP
New York, New York
February 26, 2016

General Management and Special-Purpose Committee Reports

PRESENTATION

7.70 Some survey entities presented a report of management on financial statements. These reports may include the following:
- Description of management's responsibility for preparing the financial statements
- Description of Audit Committee activities
- Identification of independent auditors
- General description of the entity's system of internal control

Occasionally, survey entities presented a report of a special-purpose committee, such as the audit committee or compensation committee.

PRESENTATION AND DISCLOSURE EXCERPTS

REPORT OF MANAGEMENT

7.71 WAL-MART STORES, INC. (JAN)
MANAGEMENT'S REPORT TO OUR SHAREHOLDERS

Wal-Mart Stores, Inc.

Management of Wal-Mart Stores, Inc. ("Walmart," the "company" or "we") is responsible for the preparation, integrity and objectivity of Walmart's Consolidated Financial Statements and other financial information contained in this Annual Report to Shareholders. Those Consolidated Financial Statements were prepared in conformity with accounting principles generally accepted in the United States. In preparing those Consolidated Financial Statements, management is required to make certain estimates and judgments, which are based upon currently available information and management's view of current conditions and circumstances.

The Audit Committee of the Board of Directors, which consists solely of independent directors, oversees our process of reporting financial information and the audit of our Consolidated Financial Statements. The Audit Committee stays informed of the financial condition of Walmart and regularly reviews management's financial policies and procedures, the independence of our independent auditors, our internal control over financial reporting and the objectivity of our financial reporting. Both the independent auditors and the internal auditors have free access to the Audit Committee and meet with the Audit Committee periodically, both with and without management present.

Acting through our Audit Committee, we have retained Ernst & Young LLP, an independent registered public accounting firm, to audit our Consolidated Financial Statements found in this Annual Report to Shareholders. We have made available to Ernst & Young LLP all of our financial records and related data in connection with their audit of our Consolidated Financial Statements. We have filed with the Securities and Exchange Commission ("SEC") the required certifications related to our Consolidated Financial Statements as of and for the year ended January 31, 2015. These certifications are attached as exhibits to our Annual Report on Form 10-K for the year ended January 31, 2015. Additionally, we have also provided to the New York Stock Exchange the required annual certification of our Chief Executive Officer regarding our compliance with the New York Stock Exchange's corporate governance listing standards.

MANAGEMENT'S REPORT ON INTERNAL CONTROL OVER FINANCIAL REPORTING

7.72 POLARIS INDUSTRIES INC. (DEC)
MANAGEMENT'S REPORT ON INTERNAL CONTROL OVER FINANCIAL REPORTING

Management is responsible for establishing and maintaining an adequate system of internal control over financial reporting of the Company. This system is designed to provide reasonable assurance regarding the reliability of financial reporting and the preparation of financial statements for external purposes in accordance with United States generally accepted accounting principles.

Our internal control over financial reporting includes those policies and procedures that (1) pertain to the maintenance of records that, in reasonable detail, accurately and fairly reflect the transactions and dispositions of the assets of the Company; (2) provide reasonable assurance that transactions are recorded as necessary to permit preparation of financial statements in accordance with generally accepted accounting principles, and that receipts and expenditures of the Company are being made only in accordance with authorizations of management and directors of the Company; and (3) provide reasonable assurance regarding prevention or timely detection of unauthorized acquisition, use, or disposition of the Company's assets that could have a material effect on the financial statements.

Because of its inherent limitations, internal control over financial reporting may not prevent or detect misstatements. Also, projections of any evaluation of effectiveness to future periods are subject to the risk that controls may become inadequate because of changes in conditions, or that the degree of compliance with the policies or procedures may deteriorate.

Management conducted an evaluation of the effectiveness of the system of internal control over financial reporting as of December 31, 2015. In making this evaluation, management used the criteria set forth by the Committee of Sponsoring Organizations of the Treadway Commission (COSO) in Internal Control—2013 Integrated Framework. Based on management's evaluation and those criteria, management concluded that the Company's system of internal control over financial reporting was effective as of December 31, 2015.

Management's internal control over financial reporting as of December 31, 2015 has been audited by Ernst & Young LLP, an independent registered public accounting firm, as stated in their report appearing on the following page, in which they expressed an unqualified opinion thereon.

/ S / S COTT W. W INE
Scott W. Wine
Chairman and Chief Executive Officer

/ S / M ICHAEL T. S PEETZEN
Michael T. Speetzen
Executive Vice President—Finance and Chief Financial Officer

February 19, 2016

Further discussion of our internal controls and procedures is included in Item 9A of this report, under the caption "Controls and Procedures."

7.73 AEROJET ROCKETDYNE HOLDINGS, INC. (NOV)
CONTROLS AND PROCEDURES (in part)

Disclosure Controls and Procedures

As of November 30, 2015, we conducted an evaluation under the supervision and with the participation of our management, including our Chief Executive Officer and Chief Financial Officer, of the effectiveness of the design and operation of our disclosure controls and procedures. The term "disclosure controls and procedures," as defined in Rules 13a-15(e) and 15d-15(e) under the Securities Exchange Act of 1934, as amended ("Exchange Act"), means controls and other procedures of a company that are designed to provide reasonable assurance that information required to be disclosed by the Company in the reports it files or submits under the Exchange Act is recorded, processed, summarized and reported, within the time periods specified in the SEC's rules and forms. Disclosure controls and procedures are also designed to provide reasonable assurance that such information is accumulated and communicated to the Company's management, including its Chief Executive Officer and Chief Financial Officer, to allow timely decisions regarding required disclosure. Based on this evaluation, our Chief Executive Officer and Chief Financial Officer have concluded that the Company's disclosure controls and procedures were not effective as of November 30, 2015 because of the material weaknesses in our internal control over financial reporting described below. In light of the material weaknesses described below, management performed additional analysis and other post-closing procedures, including substantial work performed during the restatement process that identified adjustments resulting in the restatement to our previously issued financial statements to ensure our consolidated financial statements are prepared in accordance with generally accepted accounting principles. Accordingly, management has concluded that the Company's consolidated financial statements included in this Annual Report on Form 10-K fairly present, in all material respects, our financial condition, results of operations and cash flows for the periods presented therein.

Management's Report on Internal Control Over Financial Reporting

Our management is responsible for establishing and maintaining adequate "internal control over financial reporting," as defined in Rules 13a-15(f) and 15 d-15(f) under the Exchange Act. The rules define internal control over financial reporting as a process designed by, or under the supervision of, the Company's Chief Executive Officer and Chief Financial Officer, to provide reasonable assurance regarding the reliability of financial reporting and the preparation of financial statements for external purposes in accordance with generally accepted accounting principles. Our internal control over financial reporting includes those policies and procedures that:
  - Pertain to the maintenance of records that, in reasonable detail, accurately and fairly reflect the transactions and dispositions of the assets of the Company;
  - Provide reasonable assurance that transactions are recorded as necessary to permit preparation of financial statements in accordance with generally accepted accounting principles, and that receipts and expenditures of the Company are being made only in accordance with authorizations of management and directors of the Company; and
  - Provide reasonable assurance regarding prevention or timely detection of unauthorized acquisition, use or disposition of the Company's assets that could have a material effect on the financial statements.

Because of its inherent limitations, internal control over financial reporting may not prevent or detect misstatements. In addition, projections of any evaluation of effectiveness to future periods are subject to the risk that controls may become inadequate because of changes in conditions, or that the degree of compliance with the policies or procedures may deteriorate.

With the participation of the Chief Executive Officer and the Chief Financial Officer, our management conducted an evaluation of the effectiveness of our internal control over financial reporting based on the criteria established in *Internal Control—Integrated Framework* (2013) issued by the Committee of Sponsoring Organizations of the Treadway Commission ("COSO").

A material weakness is a deficiency, or a combination of deficiencies, in internal control over financial reporting, such that there is a reasonable possibility that a material misstatement of the company's annual or interim financial statements will not be prevented or detected on a timely basis. In connection with management's evaluation of the effectiveness of our internal control over financial reporting described above, management has identified control deficiencies that constituted material weaknesses in our internal control over financial reporting as of November 30, 2015, as described below:
  - We did not adequately design controls related to purchase accounting considerations for long-term customer contracts acquired as part of a business combination. Specifically, we did not have appropriate controls in place to (i) ensure that the estimate of the acquired contracts' percentage of completion used to recognize revenue was based on our estimate of remaining effort on such contracts at the acquisition date instead of the inception date of the contract; (ii) identify changes to the results of the fair value assessment of acquired customer contracts performed by the Company's third party valuation expert during the measurement period following the close of the transaction; and (iii) evaluate the long-term contract accounting policies of the acquired business to determine the impact on the fair value of acquired contracts.

The above material weakness resulted in errors in net sales, accounts receivable and goodwill in the consolidated financial statements for the year ended November 30, 2013, and errors in net sales and accounts receivable in the consolidated financial statements for the year ended November 30, 2014, and the unaudited quarterly financial information for the first three quarters in fiscal 2015 and each of the quarters in fiscal 2014. These errors were corrected through restatement of those periods.
  - We did not maintain effective controls over the integration of the Company's accounting policies, practices and controls applicable to the acquired Rocketdyne Business, including those over the segmentation criteria applicable to long-term contracts. Specifically, we did not provide oversight to, or fully evaluate the results of an accounting conclusion reached by Rocketdyne management regarding significant customer contract amendments.

This material weakness resulted in errors in net sales and accounts receivable in the consolidated financial statements for the years ended November 30, 2013 and 2014, and the unaudited quarterly financial information for the first three quarters in fiscal 2015 and each of the quarters in fiscal 2014. These errors were corrected through restatement of those periods.

Additionally, these material weaknesses could result in a material misstatement of the aforementioned account balances or disclosures that would result in a misstatement to the annual or interim consolidated financial statements that would not be prevented or detected.

Because of the material weaknesses, management concluded that the Company did not maintain effective internal control over financial reporting as of November 30, 2015, based on criteria in *Internal Control—Integrated Framework* (2013) issued by the COSO.

The effectiveness of our internal control over financial reporting as of November 30, 2015 has been audited by PricewaterhouseCoopers LLP, our independent registered public accounting firm. Their report appears in Item 8 of this Form 10-K.

Remediation Efforts to Address Material Weaknesses

We are currently evaluating the internal controls related to business combinations, and intend to incorporate the following changes into the processes, procedures and internal controls currently in place to:
- Ensure the percent complete on all acquired long-term customer contracts is reset to zero upon acquisition;
- Verify that all acquired long-term customer contracts are appropriately evaluated for necessary fair value adjustments during the measurement period following the close of the transaction; and
- Assess acquiree accounting policies and evaluate the impact of those policies on the fair value of acquired long-term customer contracts upon acquisition.

In addition, with the transition of our Rocketdyne Business from a third party hosted enterprise resource planning ("ERP") system to the Company's Oracle ERP system and business processes in 2015, we have also aligned our contract accounting structure under common leadership. In doing so, this resulted in common controls over the application of contract accounting on all of our long-term contracts. Although this change was not applied retrospectively, our management believes the controls over our contract accounting efforts now in place will be sufficient to address the material weakness in future periods.

As part of our ongoing monitoring effort of the Company's internal control over financial reporting, we will report progress and status of the above remediation efforts to the Audit Committee on a periodic basis throughout the year.

Remediation of Prior Year Material Weaknesses

We previously identified and disclosed in our Form 10-K for the year ended November 30, 2014, as well as in our Forms 10-Q for each interim period in fiscal 2015, material weaknesses in our internal control over financial reporting regarding the following:
- We did not maintain effective controls over information and communications between the Aerojet Rocketdyne parent, the Rocketdyne Business and other third parties performing services for the Company under Transition Service Agreements ("TSA") associated with the acquisition of the Rocketdyne Business; and
- We did not maintain effective controls over the timely capitalization and depreciation of assets placed into service at the acquired Rocketdyne Business.

Throughout fiscal 2015, we implemented changes to our processes to improve our internal control over financial reporting. The following steps have been taken to remediate the conditions leading to the above stated material weaknesses:
- Effective January 1, 2015, we transitioned our Rocketdyne Business from a third party hosted ERP system and third party TSAs to our Oracle ERP system and internal shared services business processes and controls.
- Assessed the organizational structure of our accounting and finance function and reassigned certain personnel to ensure appropriate oversight maintained across the organization.

REPORT OF THE AUDIT AND COMPLIANCE COMMITTEE

7.74 COMMUNITY HEALTH SYSTEMS, INC. (DEC)
AUDIT AND COMPLIANCE COMMITTEE REPORT

The Audit and Compliance Committee of the Board of Directors of the Company is composed of three directors, each of whom is "independent" as defined by the listing standards of the NYSE and Section 10 A-3 of the Exchange Act. All of our Audit and Compliance Committee members meet the Securities and Exchange Commission definition of "audit committee financial expert." The Audit and

Compliance Committee operates under a written charter adopted by the Board of Directors, which is posted on our corporate website (http://www.chs.net) and which is reviewed by the Committee annually, in conjunction with the Committee's annual self-evaluation. The Company's management is responsible for its internal controls and the financial reporting process. Our independent registered public accounting firm, Deloitte & Touche LLP, is responsible for performing an independent audit of our consolidated financial statements in accordance with the standards of the Public Company Accounting Oversight Board (United States) and to issue its reports thereon. The Audit and Compliance Committee is responsible for, among other things, monitoring and overseeing these processes, and recommending to the Board of Directors: (i) that the audited consolidated financial statements be included in the Company's Annual Report on Form 10-K; and (ii) the selection of the independent registered public accounting firm to audit the consolidated financial statements of the Company.

In keeping with that responsibility, the Audit and Compliance Committee has reviewed and discussed the Company's audited consolidated financial statements with management and with the independent registered public accounting firm, reviewed internal controls and accounting procedures and provided oversight review of the Company's corporate compliance program. In addition, the Audit and Compliance Committee has discussed with the Company's independent registered public accounting firm the matters required to be discussed by the applicable requirements of the Public Company Accounting Oversight Board.

The Audit and Compliance Committee discussed with the Company's internal auditors and independent registered public accounting firm the overall scope and plans for their respective audits. The Audit and Compliance Committee met with the internal auditors and the independent registered public accounting firm with and without management present to discuss the results of their examinations, their evaluations of the Company's internal controls and the overall quality of the Company's financial reporting.

The Audit and Compliance Committee has received the written disclosures and the letter from the independent registered public accounting firm required by applicable requirements of the Public Company Accounting Oversight Board regarding the independent accountant's communications with the audit committee concerning independence. The Audit and Compliance Committee has discussed with the independent registered public accounting firm its independence and also has reviewed the amount of fees paid to the independent registered accounting firm for audit and non-audit services.

Based on the Audit and Compliance Committee's discussions with management and the independent registered public accounting firm and the Audit and Compliance Committee's review of the representations of management and the materials it received from the independent registered public accounting firm as described above, the Audit and Compliance Committee recommended to the Board of Directors that the audited consolidated financial statements be included in the Company's Annual Report on Form 10-K for the year ended December 31, 2015 for filing with the SEC.

This report is respectfully submitted by the Audit and Compliance Committee of the Board of Directors.

THE AUDIT AND COMPLIANCE COMMITTEE
John A. Clerico, Chair
James S. Ely III
John A. Fry

List of 350 Survey Entities and Where in the Text Excerpts From Their Annual Reports Can Be Found

The following table lists the 350 entities surveyed in alphabetical order, as well as where in the text their annual reports are excerpted.

Company Name	Month of Fiscal Year End	Accounting Technique Illustration
3M Company	December	7.42
A. O. Smith Corporation	December	
Abbott Laboratories	December	7.43
AbbVie Inc.	December	5.08
ABM Industries Incorporated	October	
Acuity Brands, Inc.	August	
AECOM	September	3.11, 3.81
Aerojet Rocketdyne Holdings, Inc.	November	3.93, 7.73
AGCO Corporation	December	2.80
Air Products and Chemicals, Inc.	September	2.156
Airgas, Inc.	March	3.59
AK Steel Holding Corporation	December	4.08, 6.11
Alcoa Inc.	December	2.148, 5.16
Allegheny Technologies Incorporated	December	2.103
Alliance One International, Inc.	March	1.76, 2.42, 3.38
Alphabet Inc.	December	
Altria Group, Inc.	December	
Amazon.com, Inc.	December	1.84
American International Group, Inc.	December	
AmerisourceBergen Corporation	September	
AMETEK, Inc.	December	
Amkor Technology, Inc.	December	
Amphenol Corporation	December	5.31
Anadarko Petroleum Corporation	December	1.100, 2.122, 3.22, 6.32
Analog Devices, Inc.	October	
Ann Inc.	January	2.88, 3.07
Anthem, Inc.	December	3.16
Apache Corporation	December	3.29
Apple Inc.	September	2.152, 4.09, 7.65
Applied Materials, Inc.	October	
ArcBest Corporation	December	3.32, 6.34
Archer-Daniels-Midland Company	December	2.30
Armstrong World Industries, Inc.	December	1.28
Arrow Electronics, Inc.	December	
Ashland Inc.	September	1.52, 3.17
AT&T Inc.	December	
Atmel Corporation	December	1.116
Autodesk, Inc.	January	2.77, 7.67
Automatic Data Processing, Inc.	June	5.37
AutoNation, Inc.	December	5.40
AutoZone, Inc.	August	
Avis Budget Group, Inc.	December	
Avnet, Inc.	June	
Avon Products, Inc.	December	2.114

Company Name	Month of Fiscal Year End	Accounting Technique Illustration
Axiall Corporation	December	1.85, 3.48
B/E Aerospace, Inc.	December	
Badger Meter, Inc.	December	
Baker Hughes Incorporated	December	3.39, 6.18
Ball Corporation	December	2.85
Barnes & Noble, Inc.	April	1.27
Bassett Furniture Industries, Incorporated	November	1.74
Baxter International Inc.	December	3.89
BB&T Corporation	December	2.19
Becton, Dickinson and Company	September	
Berkshire Hathaway Inc.	December	2.57, 6.19
Best Buy Co., Inc.	January	
Boeing Company, The	December	
Bon-Ton Stores, Inc., The	January	
Boston Scientific Corporation	December	2.118, 6.20
Briggs & Stratton Corporation	June	
Brink's Company, The	December	1.51, 2.154
Brown Shoe Company, Inc.	January	5.11
Brown-Forman Corporation	April	
Brunswick Corporation	December	7.54
CA, Inc.	March	1.26
Cablevision Systems Corporation	December	
Cabot Corporation	September	3.42
CACI International Inc	June	
CalAtlantic Group, Inc.	December	3.97
Campbell Soup Company	July	4.07
Cardinal Health, Inc.	June	
Career Education Corporation	December	
Carlisle Companies Incorporated	December	
Carpenter Technology Corporation	June	
Caterpillar Inc.	December	2.18, 3.54
CBS Corporation	December	
CenturyLink, Inc.	December	2.56
Cenveo, Inc.	December	2.146, 3.43
CF Industries Holdings, Inc.	December	5.22
Charter Communications, Inc.	December	1.119, 2.76
Chesapeake Energy Corporation	December	2.151, 5.47
Chevron Corporation	December	
Children's Place Retail Stores, Inc., The	January	
Cisco Systems, Inc.	July	1.23, 2.94, 4.15
Citigroup Inc.	December	2.20, 5.30
Cliffs Natural Resources Inc.	December	1.50, 3.18
Clorox Company, The	June	
Coach, Inc.	June	
Coca-Cola Company, The	December	1.123, 2.61
Coca-Cola Enterprises, Inc.	December	4.14
Coherent, Inc.	September	3.13
Colgate-Palmolive Company	December	
Comcast Corporation	December	2.62, 2.79
Commercial Metals Company	August	2.29, 3.41
Community Health Systems, Inc.	December	1.86, 7.74
Computer Sciences Corporation	March	1.47, 3.35
ConAgra Foods, Inc.	May	1.69, 4.16
ConocoPhillips	December	3.37
Constellation Brands, Inc.	February	3.94
Convergys Corporation	December	
Cooper Tire & Rubber Company	December	
Corning Incorporated	December	3.14
Costco Wholesale Corporation	August	
Crane Co.	December	
CSX Corporation	December	
Cummins Inc.	December	2.147, 3.10
CVS Health Corporation	December	1.46, 2.121, 3.61, 6.16, 6.35
Dana Holding Corporation	December	
Danaher Corporation	December	1.54

Company Name	Month of Fiscal Year End	Accounting Technique Illustration
Darden Restaurants, Inc.	May	3.88
Dean Foods Company	December	
Deere & Company	October	
Discovery Communications, Inc.	December	3.88, 6.33
Dollar General Corporation	January	2.137
Domino's Pizza, Inc.	December	7.44
Donaldson Company, Inc.	July	7.68
Dover Corporation	December	
Dow Chemical Company, The	December	1.68, 3.31
Dun & Bradstreet Corporation, The	December	1.24, 6.24
E. I. du Pont de Nemours and Company	December	
E. W. Scripps Company, The	December	5.10, 5.32
Eastman Chemical Company	December	
eBay Inc.	December	1.49
Ecolab Inc.	December	
Electronic Arts Inc.	March	1.48
Eli Lilly and Company	December	6.21
EMC Corporation	December	
EMCOR Group, Inc.	December	
Emerson Electric Co.	September	
Energizer Holdings, Inc.	September	
Equifax Inc.	December	2.116, 3.30
Estee Lauder Companies Inc., The	June	4.11
Express Scripts Holding Company	December	5.10
Exxon Mobil Corporation	December	3.24
FedEx Corporation	May	
Fidelity National Information Services, Inc.	December	2.78, 2.143, 7.48
First Solar, Inc.	December	1.56, 2.112
Flowers Foods, Inc.	December	2.83, 6.12
Fluor Corporation	December	3.52
FMC Corporation	December	
Foot Locker, Inc.	January	
Ford Motor Company	December	7.41
Fred's, Inc.	January	
Freeport-McMoRan Inc.	December	1.77, 3.69
GameStop Corp.	January	
General Cable Corporation	December	3.90
General Dynamics Corporation	December	
General Electric Company	December	
General Mills, Inc.	May	
Genuine Parts Company	December	
Gilead Sciences, Inc.	December	
Goldman Sachs Group, Inc., The	December	2.111, 5.19
Goodyear Tire & Rubber Company, The	December	
Graham Holdings Company	December	
Greif, Inc.	October	
Griffon Corporation	September	
Guess?, Inc.	January	3.50, 5.07
Halliburton Company	December	
Hanesbrands Inc.	December	1.102, 3.78
Harley-Davidson, Inc.	December	3.25
Harman International Industries, Incorporated	June	2.130
Harris Corporation	June	3.40, 3.82
Hasbro, Inc.	December	
Health Net, Inc.	December	
Hershey Company, The	December	7.69
Hess Corporation	December	
Hill-Rom Holdings, Inc.	September	
Home Depot, Inc., The	January	
Honeywell International Inc.	December	2.89
Hormel Foods Corporation	October	
Hovnanian Enterprises, Inc.	October	3.26
HP Inc.	October	1.36

Company Name	Month of Fiscal Year End	Accounting Technique Illustration
Humana Inc.	December	
Huntsman Corporation	December	
IAC/InterActiveCorp	December	
IDT Corporation	July	1.120
Illinois Tool Works Inc.	December	
Ingram Micro Inc.	December	
Ingredion Incorporated	December	
Insperity, Inc.	December	2.102
Intel Corporation	December	2.46
International Business Machines Corporation	December	2.87
International Flavors & Fragrances Inc.	December	4.06
International Paper Company	December	
Interpublic Group of Companies, Inc., The	December	
Iron Mountain Incorporated	December	
ITT Corporation	December	2.150
J. C. Penney Company, Inc.	January	
J. M. Smucker Company, The	April	
Jabil Circuit, Inc.	August	
Jack in the Box Inc.	September	
Jarden Corporation	December	
Johnson & Johnson	December	1.87, 3.21
Johnson Controls, Inc.	September	
Joy Global Inc.	October	5.29
JPMorgan Chase & Co.	December	5.33
Juniper Networks, Inc.	December	
KB Home	November	1.22, 1.88, 6.30
Kellogg Company	December	
Kimberly-Clark Corporation	December	
Kinder Morgan, Inc.	December	2.74
KLA-Tencor Corporation	June	5.18
Kohl's Corporation	January	3.20
Kraft Heinz Company, The	December	5.46, 7.61
Kroger Co., The	January	
L.S. Starrett Company, The	June	
L-3 Communications Holdings, Inc.	December	2.48
Lam Research Corporation	June	2.128
Las Vegas Sands Corp.	December	
La-Z-Boy Incorporated	April	
Lear Corporation	December	2.126
Lee Enterprises, Incorporated	September	
Leggett & Platt, Incorporated	December	
Lennar Corporation	November	
Lockheed Martin Corporation	December	
Louisiana-Pacific Corporation	December	3.57
Lowe's Companies, Inc.	January	
Macy's Inc	January	
Manitowoc Company, Inc., The	December	1.114
Marriott International, Inc.	December	
MasterCard Incorporated	December	2.119
McClatchy Company, The	December	7.66
McKesson Corporation	March	
Merck & Co., Inc.	December	
Meritor, Inc.	September	2.31
MetLife, Inc.	December	3.09, 3.15
MGM Resorts International	December	
Micron Technology, Inc.	August	
Microsoft Corporation	June	
Molson Coors Brewing Company	December	2.144
Monsanto Company	August	
Morgan Stanley	December	3.60
Mosaic Company, The	December	
Motorola Solutions, Inc.	December	
Mueller Industries, Inc.	December	
Murphy Oil Corporation	December	
NACCO Industries, Inc.	December	2.109, 2.149

Company Name	Month of Fiscal Year End	Accounting Technique Illustration
National Oilwell Varco, Inc.	December	1.101, 2.113, 3.33, 3.56
NetApp, Inc.	April	
New York Times Company, The	December	6.10, 7.56
Newell Rubbermaid Inc.	December	2.44
NewMarket Corporation	December	
Nike, Inc.	May	1.57, 3.23
Noble Energy, Inc.	December	1.73
Northrop Grumman Corporation	December	3.80
NVR, Inc.	December	
Office Depot, Inc.	December	6.08
Oracle Corporation	May	6.09
Orbital ATK, Inc.	March	3.49, 3.68, 6.27
Owens-Illinois, Inc.	December	1.83
PACCAR Inc	December	
Parker-Hannifin Corporation	June	
Peabody Energy Corporation	December	2.136, 3.36, 3.75, 5.23, 7.33
Penske Automotive Group, Inc.	December	7.30
PepsiCo, Inc.	December	
PerkinElmer, Inc.	December	
Pfizer Inc.	December	4.10
Pilgrim's Pride Corporation	December	
Pitney Bowes Inc.	December	
Plum Creek Timber Company, Inc.	December	
PNC Financial Services Group, Inc., The	December	
Polaris Industries Inc.	December	2.106, 3.58, 7.72
PolyOne Corporation	December	2.117
PPG Industries, Inc.	December	
Praxair, Inc.	December	7.20
Precision Castparts Corp.	March	2.38, 4.12
Priceline Group Inc., The	December	1.107, 2.155, 6.31
Procter & Gamble Company, The	June	7.21
Prudential Financial, Inc.	December	1.25, 3.96
PulteGroup, Inc.	December	
PVH Corp.	January	
QUALCOMM Incorporated	September	
Ralph Lauren Corporation	March	2.39, 3.74
Raytheon Company	December	
Regal Beloit Corporation	December	2.120
Regal Entertainment Group	December	1.79
Republic Services, Inc.	December	2.145
Reynolds American Inc.	December	
Rite Aid Corporation	February	1.78, 3.28, 6.22
Rockwell Automation, Inc.	September	
Rockwell Collins, Inc.	September	
Schnitzer Steel Industries, Inc.	August	
Scotts Miracle-Gro Company, The	September	1.21, 1.30, 6.28
Seaboard Corporation	December	
Sealed Air Corporation	December	
Service Corporation International	December	
Sherwin-Williams Company, The	December	
Snap-on Incorporated	December	2.66
Spectrum Brands Holdings, Inc.	September	
SPX Corporation	December	1.20, 1.29, 2.131
St. Jude Medical, Inc.	December	6.26
Stanley Black & Decker, Inc.	December	2.37, 3.62, 3.67, 5.09
Steel Dynamics, Inc.	December	
Steelcase Inc.	February	
Stryker Corporation	December	
SYNNEX Corporation	November	
Sysco Corporation	June	7.22
Target Corporation	January	2.40
Teleflex Incorporated	December	
Tempur Sealy International, Inc.	December	
Tenet Healthcare Corporation	December	2.127, 3.76
Tenneco Inc.	December	

Company Name	Month of Fiscal Year End	Accounting Technique Illustration
Terex Corporation	December	3.08
Texas Instruments Incorporated	December	1.53, 2.63
Textron Inc.	December	
Thermo Fisher Scientific Inc.	December	
Tiffany & Co.	January	3.63
Time Warner Inc.	December	
Toll Brothers, Inc.	October	
Tupperware Brands Corporation	December	2.75
Tutor Perini Corporation	December	2.45
Tyson Foods, Inc.	September	4.13
Unifi, Inc.	June	1.118, 3.27
Unisys Corporation	December	
United Continental Holdings, Inc.	December	
United Parcel Service, Inc.	December	3.51, 5.45
United States Steel Corporation	December	
UnitedHealth Group Incorporated	December	
Universal Corporation	March	1.37, 1.89, 2.43
Universal Forest Products, Inc.	December	
Universal Health Services, Inc.	December	2.115
Valero Energy Corporation	December	3.70, 3.77
Varian Medical Systems, Inc.	September	
Verizon Communications Inc.	December	2.138
Viacom Inc.	September	
Viavi Solutions Inc.	June	
Visa Inc.	September	
Vishay Intertechnology, Inc.	December	1.31
Visteon Corporation	December	1.55, 6.17, 6.25
Vulcan Materials Company	December	1.99
W. R. Grace & Co.	December	1.115, 2.84
Wal-Mart Stores, Inc.	January	7.71
Walt Disney Company, The	September	
Waste Management, Inc.	December	
Wendy's Company, The	December	3.03, 3.12
Werner Enterprises, Inc.	December	
Western Union Company, The	December	
Weyerhaeuser Company	December	
Whirlpool Corporation	December	
Whole Foods Market, Inc.	September	
Williams-Sonoma, Inc.	January	2.47
Winnebago Industries, Inc.	August	2.86
Worthington Industries, Inc.	May	
Wyndham Worldwide Corporation	December	
Wynn Resorts, Limited	December	5.34
Xerox Corporation	December	3.34
Xilinx, Inc.	March	
Yahoo! Inc.	December	2.95
YUM! Brands, Inc.	December	
Zimmer Biomet Holdings, Inc.	December	

Appendix of Survey Entity Industries ....

List of Industries Represented by the 350 Survey Entities

The following table lists the industries represented by the 350 survey entities and lists the entities within each industry classification. All industry classifications were obtained from Morningstar, Inc.

Industry Classification	Company Name
Basic Materials/Agricultural Inputs	CF Industries Holdings, Inc.
	E. I. du Pont de Nemours and Company
	Monsanto Company
	Scotts Miracle-Gro Company, The
Basic Materials/Aluminum	Alcoa Inc.
Basic Materials/Building Materials	Armstrong World Industries, Inc.
	Griffon Corporation
	Vulcan Materials Company
Basic Materials/Chemicals	Air Products and Chemicals, Inc.
	Ashland Inc.
	Axiall Corporation
	Dow Chemical Company, The
	Eastman Chemical Company
	FMC Corporation
	Huntsman Corporation
	International Flavors & Fragrances Inc.
	PolyOne Corporation
Basic Materials/Coal	Peabody Energy Corporation
Basic Materials/Copper	Freeport-McMoRan Inc.
Basic Materials/Industrial Metals & Minerals	Cliffs Natural Resources Inc.
Basic Materials/Lumber & Wood Production	Louisiana-Pacific Corporation
	Universal Forest Products, Inc.
Basic Materials/Paper & Paper Products	Cenveo, Inc.
	International Paper Company
Basic Materials/Specialty Chemicals	Cabot Corporation
	Mosaic Company, The
	NewMarket Corporation
	PPG Industries, Inc.
	Praxair, Inc.
	W. R. Grace & Co.
Basic Materials/Steel	AK Steel Holding Corporation
	Carpenter Technology Corporation
	Commercial Metals Company
	Schnitzer Steel Industries, Inc.
	Steel Dynamics, Inc.
	Worthington Industries, Inc.
Communication Services/Pay TV	Cablevision Systems Corporation
	Charter Communications, Inc.
	Comcast Corporation
Communication Services/Telecom Services	AT&T Inc.
	CenturyLink, Inc.
	IDT Corporation
	Verizon Communications Inc.
Consumer Cyclical/Advertising Agencies	Interpublic Group of Companies, Inc., The

Industry Classification	Company Name
Consumer Cyclical/Apparel Manufacturing	Guess?, Inc.
	Hanesbrands Inc.
	PVH Corp.
	Ralph Lauren Corporation
Consumer Cyclical/Apparel Stores	Ann Inc.
	Children's Place Retail Stores, Inc., The
Consumer Cyclical/Auto & Truck Dealerships	AutoNation, Inc.
	Penske Automotive Group, Inc.
Consumer Cyclical/Auto Manufacturers	Ford Motor Company
Consumer Cyclical/Auto Parts	AutoZone, Inc.
	Dana Holding Corporation
	Johnson Controls, Inc.
	Lear Corporation
	Tenneco Inc.
	Visteon Corporation
Consumer Cyclical/Broadcasting—TV	CBS Corporation
Consumer Cyclical/Department Stores	Bon-Ton Stores, Inc., The
	J. C. Penney Company, Inc.
	Kohl's Corporation
	Macy's Inc
Consumer Cyclical/Footwear & Accessories	Brown Shoe Company, Inc.
	Foot Locker, Inc.
	Nike, Inc.
Consumer Cyclical/Home Furnishings & Fixtures	Bassett Furniture Industries, Incorporated
	Jarden Corporation
	La-Z-Boy Incorporated
	Leggett & Platt, Incorporated
	Tempur Sealy International, Inc.
Consumer Cyclical/Home Improvement Stores	Home Depot, Inc., The
	Lowe's Companies, Inc.
Consumer Cyclical/Leisure	Brunswick Corporation
	Hasbro, Inc.
	Priceline Group Inc., The
	Regal Entertainment Group
Consumer Cyclical/Lodging	Marriott International, Inc.
	Wyndham Worldwide Corporation
Consumer Cyclical/Luxury Goods	Coach, Inc.
	Tiffany & Co.
Consumer Cyclical/Media—Diversified	Discovery Communications, Inc.
	Time Warner Inc.
	Viacom Inc.
	Walt Disney Company, The
Consumer Cyclical/Packaging & Containers	Ball Corporation
	Greif, Inc.
	Owens-Illinois, Inc.
	Sealed Air Corporation
Consumer Cyclical/Personal Services	Service Corporation International
	Western Union Company, The
Consumer Cyclical/Publishing	E. W. Scripps Company, The
	Lee Enterprises, Incorporated
	McClatchy Company, The
	New York Times Company, The
Consumer Cyclical/Recreational Vehicles	Harley-Davidson, Inc.
	Polaris Industries Inc.
	Winnebago Industries, Inc.
Consumer Cyclical/Residential Construction	CalAtlantic Group, Inc.
	Hovnanian Enterprises, Inc.
	KB Home
	Lennar Corporation
	NVR, Inc.
	PulteGroup, Inc.
	Toll Brothers, Inc.
Consumer Cyclical/Resorts & Casinos	Las Vegas Sands Corp.
	MGM Resorts International
	Wynn Resorts, Limited

Industry Classification	Company Name
Consumer Cyclical/Restaurants	Darden Restaurants, Inc.
	Domino's Pizza, Inc.
	Jack in the Box Inc.
	Wendy's Company, The
	YUM! Brands, Inc.
Consumer Cyclical/Rubber & Plastics	Carlisle Companies Incorporated
	Cooper Tire & Rubber Company
	Goodyear Tire & Rubber Company, The
Consumer Cyclical/Specialty Retail	Amazon.com, Inc.
	Barnes & Noble, Inc.
	Best Buy Co., Inc.
	eBay Inc.
	GameStop Corp.
	Office Depot, Inc.
	Sherwin-Williams Company, The
	Williams-Sonoma, Inc.
Consumer Cyclical/Textile Manufacturing	Unifi, Inc.
Consumer Defensive/Beverages—Brewers	Molson Coors Brewing Company
Consumer Defensive/Beverages—Soft Drinks	Coca-Cola Company, The
	Coca-Cola Enterprises, Inc.
	PepsiCo, Inc.
Consumer Defensive/Beverages—Wineries & Distilleries	Brown-Forman Corporation
	Constellation Brands, Inc.
Consumer Defensive/Confectioners	Hershey Company, The
Consumer Defensive/Discount Stores	Costco Wholesale Corporation
	Dollar General Corporation
	Fred's, Inc.
	Target Corporation
	Wal-Mart Stores, Inc.
Consumer Defensive/Education & Training Services	Career Education Corporation
	Graham Holdings Company
Consumer Defensive/Farm Products	Archer-Daniels-Midland Company
	Hormel Foods Corporation
	Pilgrim's Pride Corporation
	Seaboard Corporation
	Tyson Foods, Inc.
Consumer Defensive/Food Distribution	Sysco Corporation
Consumer Defensive/Grocery Stores	Kroger Co., The
	Whole Foods Market, Inc.
Consumer Defensive/Household & Personal Products	Avon Products, Inc.
	Clorox Company, The
	Colgate-Palmolive Company
	Energizer Holdings, Inc.
	Estee Lauder Companies Inc., The
	Kimberly-Clark Corporation
	Newell Rubbermaid Inc.
	Procter & Gamble Company, The
	Tupperware Brands Corporation
Consumer Defensive/Packaged Foods	Campbell Soup Company
	ConAgra Foods, Inc.
	Dean Foods Company
	Flowers Foods, Inc.
	General Mills, Inc.
	Ingredion Incorporated
	J. M. Smucker Company, The
	Kellogg Company
	Kraft Heinz Company, The
Consumer Defensive/Pharmaceutical Retailers	CVS Health Corporation
	Rite Aid Corporation
Consumer Defensive/Tobacco	Alliance One International, Inc.
	Altria Group, Inc.
	Reynolds American Inc.
	Universal Corporation

Industry Classification	Company Name
Energy/Oil & Gas E&P	Apache Corporation
	Chesapeake Energy Corporation
	Murphy Oil Corporation
	Noble Energy, Inc.
Energy/Oil & Gas Equipment & Services	Baker Hughes Incorporated
	Halliburton Company
	National Oilwell Varco, Inc.
Energy/Oil & Gas Integrated	Chevron Corporation
	ConocoPhillips
	Exxon Mobil Corporation
	Hess Corporation
Energy/Oil & Gas Midstream	Kinder Morgan, Inc.
Energy/Oil & Gas Refining & Marketing	Valero Energy Corporation
Financial Services/Banks—Global	Citigroup Inc.
	JPMorgan Chase & Co.
Financial Services/Banks—Regional—US	BB&T Corporation
	PNC Financial Services Group, Inc., The
Financial Services/Capital Markets	Goldman Sachs Group, Inc., The
	Morgan Stanley
Financial Services/Credit Services	MasterCard Incorporated
	Visa Inc.
Financial Services/Insurance—Diversified	American International Group, Inc.
	Berkshire Hathaway Inc.
Financial Services/Insurance—Life	MetLife, Inc.
	Prudential Financial, Inc.
Healthcare/Biotechnology	Gilead Sciences, Inc.
Healthcare/Drug Manufacturers—Major	Abbott Laboratories
	AbbVie Inc.
	Eli Lilly and Company
	Johnson & Johnson
	Merck & Co., Inc.
	Pfizer Inc.
Healthcare/Health Care Plans	Anthem, Inc.
	Express Scripts Holding Company
	Health Net, Inc.
	UnitedHealth Group Incorporated
Healthcare/Medical Care	Community Health Systems, Inc.
	Tenet Healthcare Corporation
	Universal Health Services, Inc.
Healthcare/Medical Devices	St. Jude Medical, Inc.
	Stryker Corporation
	Teleflex Incorporated
	Zimmer Biomet Holdings, Inc.
Healthcare/Medical Distribution	AmerisourceBergen Corporation
	Cardinal Health, Inc.
	McKesson Corporation
Healthcare/Medical Instruments & Supplies	Baxter International Inc.
	Becton, Dickinson and Company
	Boston Scientific Corporation
	Hill-Rom Holdings, Inc.
	PerkinElmer, Inc.
	Thermo Fisher Scientific Inc.
	Varian Medical Systems, Inc.
Industrials/Aerospace & Defense	Aerojet Rocketdyne Holdings, Inc.
	B/E Aerospace, Inc.
	Boeing Company, The
	General Dynamics Corporation
	L-3 Communications Holdings, Inc.
	Lockheed Martin Corporation
	Orbital ATK, Inc.
	Raytheon Company
	Rockwell Collins, Inc.
Industrials/Airlines	United Continental Holdings, Inc.

Industry Classification	Company Name
Industrials/Business Equipment	Pitney Bowes Inc.
	Steelcase Inc.
	Xerox Corporation
Industrials/Business Services	ABM Industries Incorporated
	Automatic Data Processing, Inc.
	Dun & Bradstreet Corporation, The
	Ecolab Inc.
	Equifax Inc.
	Fidelity National Information Services, Inc.
	Humana Inc.
	Iron Mountain Incorporated
	SYNNEX Corporation
Industrials/Conglomerates	Northrop Grumman Corporation
	Spectrum Brands Holdings, Inc.
Industrials/Diversified Industrials	3M Company
	A. O. Smith Corporation
	Airgas, Inc.
	AMETEK, Inc.
	Anadarko Petroleum Corporation
	Briggs & Stratton Corporation
	Crane Co.
	Danaher Corporation
	Donaldson Company, Inc.
	Dover Corporation
	Emerson Electric Co.
	General Cable Corporation
	General Electric Company
	Honeywell International Inc.
	Illinois Tool Works Inc.
	ITT Corporation
	Parker-Hannifin Corporation
	Regal Beloit Corporation
	Rockwell Automation, Inc.
	SPX Corporation
	Textron Inc.
Industrials/Engineering & Construction	AECOM
	EMCOR Group, Inc.
	Fluor Corporation
	Tutor Perini Corporation
Industrials/Farm & Construction Equipment	AGCO Corporation
	Caterpillar Inc.
	Deere & Company
	Joy Global Inc.
	Manitowoc Company, Inc., The
	NACCO Industries, Inc.
	Terex Corporation
Industrials/Industrial Distribution	Genuine Parts Company
Industrials/Integrated Shipping & Logistics	FedEx Corporation
	United Parcel Service, Inc.
Industrials/Metal Fabrication	Allegheny Technologies Incorporated
	Mueller Industries, Inc.
	Precision Castparts Corp.
	United States Steel Corporation
Industrials/Railroads	CSX Corporation
Industrials/Rental & Leasing Services	Avis Budget Group, Inc.
Industrials/Security & Protection Services	Brink's Company, The
Industrials/Staffing & Outsourcing Services	Insperity, Inc.
Industrials/Tools & Accessories	L.S. Starrett Company, The
	Snap-on Incorporated
	Stanley Black & Decker, Inc.
Industrials/Truck Manufacturing	Cummins Inc.
	PACCAR Inc

Industry Classification	Company Name
Industrials/Trucking	ArcBest Corporation
	Werner Enterprises, Inc.
Industrials/Waste Management	Republic Services, Inc.
	Waste Management, Inc.
Real Estate/REIT—Industrial	Plum Creek Timber Company, Inc.
	Weyerhaeuser Company
Technology/Communications Equipment	Cisco Systems, Inc.
	Harris Corporation
	Juniper Networks, Inc.
	Motorola Solutions, Inc.
	QUALCOMM Incorporated
	Viavi Solutions Inc.
Technology/Computer Distribution	Ingram Micro Inc.
Technology/Computer Systems	Apple Inc.
	HP Inc.
	International Business Machines Corporation
Technology/Consumer Electronics	Harman International Industries, Incorporated
	Whirlpool Corporation
Technology/Contract Manufacturers	Jabil Circuit, Inc.
Technology/Data Storage	EMC Corporation
	NetApp, Inc.
Technology/Electronic Components	Acuity Brands, Inc.
	Amphenol Corporation
	Corning Incorporated
	Vishay Intertechnology, Inc.
Technology/Electronic Gaming & Multimedia	Electronic Arts Inc.
Technology/Electronics Distribution	Arrow Electronics, Inc.
	Avnet, Inc.
Technology/Information Technology Services	CACI International Inc
	Computer Sciences Corporation
	Unisys Corporation
Technology/Internet Content & Information	Alphabet Inc.
	IAC/InterActiveCorp
	Yahoo! Inc.
Technology/Scientific & Technical Instruments	Badger Meter, Inc.
	Coherent, Inc.
Technology/Semiconductor Equipment & Materials	Applied Materials, Inc.
	KLA-Tencor Corporation
	Lam Research Corporation
Technology/Semiconductor Memory	Micron Technology, Inc.
Technology/Semiconductors	Amkor Technology, Inc.
	Analog Devices, Inc.
	Atmel Corporation
	Intel Corporation
	Meritor, Inc.
	Texas Instruments Incorporated
	Xilinx, Inc.
Technology/Software—Application	Autodesk, Inc.
	Convergys Corporation
Technology/Software—Infrastructure	CA, Inc.
	Microsoft Corporation
	Oracle Corporation
Technology/Solar	First Solar, Inc.

Index of Authoritative Accounting & Auditing Guidance

Subject Index

A

net realizable value, 2.32
presentation, 2.34
presentation and disclosure excerpts, 2.37–2.40
recognition and measurement, 2.32–2.33
retail method, 2.40

Investees, income from, 3.10

Investments
cash flows from. *See* Cash flows from investing activities
cash inflows from financing activities, 6.29
change in value of, revenues and gains, 3.16
equity losses of affiliates, 3.36
fair value estimates, 1.105
gains, 3.16, 6.19
impairment, 2.10, 3.30
joint ventures, accounting method. *See* Joint ventures
other noncurrent assets, 2.81
pension plan strategies disclosure, 3.45

Involuntary liquidation, 5.13

Issuers
comparative financial statements, 7.53
dating of auditors' report, 7.60
departures from unmodified opinions, 7.50–7.51
emphasis of a matter in auditors' report, 7.47
independent auditors' report, 7.16–7.19
lack of consistency in independent auditors' report, 7.36–7.40
reference to report of other auditors, 7.28–7.29
reports on comparative financial statements, 7.53
uncertainties, 7.32

J

Joint and several liability arrangements, short-term debt, 2.90

Joint ventures
balance sheets, 2.58–2.66
disclosure, 2.60
equity in earnings of joint ventures, 3.11
presentation, 2.59
presentation and disclosure excerpts, 2.61–2.63
recognition and measurement, 2.58

L

Lack of consistency in independent auditors' report
correction of errors and restatement, 7.34–7.40
debt issuance costs, 7.44
deferred taxes, 7.43
employee benefits, 7.41
issuers, 7.36–7.40
marketable securities, 7.42
nonissuers, 7.34–7.35
presentation, 7.34–7.40
presentation and disclosure excerpts, 7.41–7.44

Land, 2.81. *See also* Property, plant, and equipment

Last-in, first-out (LIFO) inventory, 2.32, 2.35–2.36, 2.38

Lawsuits. *See* Litigation

Leases
agreements as commitments, 1.79
lessee, 2.136–2.137
lessor, 2.138

long-term. *See* Long-term leases
operating, 2.132, 2.134, 2.135

Legal matters, contingencies, 1.83

Lessee leases, 2.136–2.137

Lessor leases, 2.138

Letters of credit, 1.75

Liabilities
contingent liabilities, 2.142
current liabilities, 2.99, 2.123
deferred taxes, 7.43
employee compensatory plans, 3.55
fair value measurement, 1.58, 1.105, 1.106
income taxes, disclosure, 3.73
noncurrent liabilities, 2.99
offsetting with assets, 1.12
other current. *See* Other current liabilities
other noncurrent. *See* Other noncurrent liabilities
pension plan disclosures, 3.45
preferred stock classified as, 5.14
professional liability claims, 1.86
servicing liabilities, fair value, 2.25

License agreement, 6.27

Life insurance cash surrender value, 2.81, 2.86

LIFO. *See* Last-in, first-out (LIFO) inventory

Limited partnership dropdown transactions, 3.95

Line of credit, 1.99

Liquidation, involuntary, 5.13

Liquidation basis of accounting, 1.19

Liquidity, 1.23

Litigation
expenses and losses, 3.35
other current liabilities, 2.119
other noncurrent liabilities, 2.150
revenues and gains, 3.14

Loans. *See also* Credit agreements; Debt
due-on-demand arrangements, 2.90
loans payable, 2.92

Long-lived assets, property, plant, and equipment, 2.54

Long-term assets held for sale. *See* Held for sale

Long-term debt
balance sheet, 2.123–2.128
collateralized, 2.127
convertible, 2.128
current amount, 2.109
disclosure, 2.124–2.125
presentation, 2.123
presentation and disclosure excerpts, 2.126–2.128
unsecured, 2.126

Long-term leases
balance sheet, 2.132–2.138
commitments, 1.75
disclosure, 2.135
lessee leases, 2.136–2.137
lessor leases, 2.138
presentation, 2.133–2.134
presentation and disclosure excerpts, 2.136–2.138
recognition and measurement, 2.132

Long-term prepayments, 2.81

O

Obligations. *See* Liabilities

Operating activities. *See* Cash flows from operating activities

Operating leases on balance sheet, 2.132, 2.134, 2.135

Operating losses
 as carryforward, 3.75–3.76
 disclosure of, 3.73

Operating segments of public entities, 1.32–1.34

Operations
 discontinued. *See* Discontinued operations
 discontinued, as other noncurrent liabilities, 2.146
 results of, management's discussion and analysis (MD&A), 1.09

Operations, nature of, 1.28

Opinions. *See also* Independent auditors' report
 departures from unmodified opinions, 7.49–7.51
 expressed on supplementary financial information, 7.55–7.56
 opinion paragraph, auditors' report, 7.04, 7.10, 7.12, 7.13

Options. *See* Stock options

Original maturity, 6.02

Other additional capital, 5.04

Other changes in retained earnings, 5.31–5.34

Other components of stockholders' equity
 deferred compensation, 5.45
 disclosure, 5.43–5.44
 noncontrolling interest, 5.47
 presentation, 5.41–5.42
 presentation and disclosure excerpts, 5.45–5.47
 warrants, 5.46

Other comprehensive income
 accumulated. *See* Accumulated other comprehensive income
 comprehensive. *See* Comprehensive income
 defined, 4.02
 items included in, 4.01, 5.42

Other current assets
 advances, 2.43
 assets held for sale, 2.44
 balance sheet, 2.41–2.48
 contracts, 2.48
 costs and estimated earnings in excess of billings, 2.45
 deferred taxes, 2.42
 derivatives, 2.46
 prepaid expenses, 2.47
 presentation, 2.41
 presentation and disclosure excerpts, 2.42–2.48

Other current liabilities
 asset retirement obligation, 2.122
 balance sheet, 2.110–2.122
 claims and discounts, 2.121
 contingent consideration, 2.118
 costs and estimated earnings in excess of billings, 2.113
 deferred revenue, 2.116, 2.152
 deposits, 2.111
 derivatives, 2.120
 discontinued operations, 2.114
 environment, 2.117
 insurance, 2.115
 litigation, 2.119
 presentation, 2.110

presentation and disclosure excerpts, 2.111–2.122
 product warranties, 2.112

Other income, disclosure of, 3.06

Other noncurrent assets
 assets held for sale, 2.83
 balance sheet, 2.81–2.89
 cash surrender value of life insurance, 2.86
 derivatives, 2.87
 disclosure, 2.82
 insurance claims, 2.89
 pension assets, 2.84
 presentation and disclosure excerpts, 2.83–2.89
 recognition and measurement, 2.81
 restricted cash, 2.81, 2.85
 software, 2.88

Other noncurrent liabilities
 asset retirement obligations, 2.149
 balance sheet, 2.139–2.152
 deferred income taxes, 2.143
 derivatives, 2.151
 discontinued operations, 2.146
 environmental, 2.148
 insurance, 2.145
 litigation, 2.150
 presentation, 2.139–2.142
 presentation and disclosure excerpts, 2.143–2.152
 unrecognized tax benefits, 2.144
 warranties, 2.147

Other-than-temporary impairments, 2.10

P

Parent companies
 changes in ownership interest, 1.63
 deconsolidation of subsidiaries, 1.64
 derecognition of asset group, 1.64
 disclosures, 1.66

Parent-entity (separate) financial statements, 1.62, 7.14–7.15

Partnership dropdown transactions, 3.95

Payables
 income taxes payable, 2.106
 loans payable, 2.92
 short-term notes payable, 2.92
 trade accounts, 2.96–2.98

Penalties, 3.28

Pensions and other postretirement benefits. *See also* Employee-related
 liabilities
 adjustments, comprehensive income, 3.44, 4.12
 changes in accounting principles, 1.47
 commitments, 1.75
 defined benefit plans, 3.45
 defined contribution plans, 3.49
 disclosure, 3.45–3.47
 income statement, 3.44–3.52
 multi-employer pension plans, 3.45, 3.47, 3.51
 as noncurrent asset, 2.84
 pension termination expense, 6.20
 plan amendment, 3.52
 presentation and disclosure excerpts, 3.48–3.52
 recognition and measurement, 3.44
 supplemental retirement plans, 3.50